THE OXFORD HANDBOOK OF

FINANCIAL REGULATION

THE OXFORD HANDBOOK OF

FINANCIAL REGULATION

Edited by

NIAMH MOLONEY, EILÍS FERRAN,

and

JENNIFER PAYNE

OXFORD
UNIVERSITY PRESS

OXFORD
UNIVERSITY PRESS

Great Clarendon Street, Oxford, OX2 6DP,
United Kingdom

Oxford University Press is a department of the University of Oxford.
It furthers the University's objective of excellence in research, scholarship,
and education by publishing worldwide. Oxford is a registered trade mark of
Oxford University Press in the UK and in certain other countries

First Edition published in 2015

Impression: 1

Published in the United States of America by Oxford University Press
198 Madison Avenue, New York, NY 10016, United States of America

British Library Cataloguing in Publication Data
Data available

Library of Congress Control Number: 2015934487

ISBN 978–0–19–968720–6

Printed and bound by
CPI Group (UK) Ltd, Croydon, CR0 4YY

Table of Contents

PART III DELIVERING OUTCOMES AND REGULATORY TECHNIQUES

PART IV FINANCIAL STABILITY

PART V MARKET EFFICIENCY, TRANSPARENCY, AND INTEGRITY

PART VI CONSUMER PROTECTION

List of Abbreviations

ABI	Association of British Insurers
ABSs	asset-backed securities
AIG	American International Group
APRA	Australian Prudential Regulation Authority
ASIC	Australian Securities and Investments Commission
ATSs	alternative trading systems
BaFin	*Bundesaufsichtsamt für das Finanzwesen*
BAV	*Bundesaufsichtsamt für das Versicherungswesen*
BCBS	Basel Committee on Banking Supervision
BEM	book-entry money
BHCA	Bank Holding Company Act
BIS	Bank for International Settlements
BoE	Bank of England
BRRD	Bank Recovery and Resolution Directive
BTSs	Binding Technical Standards
CAs	clearing agencies
CBRA	Conduct of Business Regulatory Agency
CCAR	Comprehensive Capital Analysis and Review
CCB	countercyclical capital buffer
CCP	central counterparty
CDOs	collateralized debt obligations
CDSs	credit default swaps
CEA	Commodity Exchange Act
CEBS	Committee of European Banking Supervisors
CEIOPS	Committee of European Insurance and Occupational Pensions Supervisors
CEPR	Centre for Economic Policy Research
CESR	Committee of European Securities Regulators
CFPB	Consumer Financial Protection Bureau
CFR	Code of Federal Regulations
CFTC	Commodity Futures Trading Commission
CJEU	Court of Justice of the European Union
COB	conduct of business
CoCos	contingent convertible instruments
CoPoD	conditional probabilities of distress
CPSS	Committee on Payment and Settlement Systems
CRAs	credit rating agencies
CRD	Capital Requirements Directive

CROs	chief risk officers
CRR	Capital Requirements Regulation
CRT	credit risk transfer
CSDs	central securities depositories
CVAR	cointegrated vector autoregression
DCM	Designated Contract Market
DCOs	Derivatives Clearing Organizations
DGI	data gap initiative
DoJ	Department of Justice
DSB	Dispute Settlement Body
DSIBs	domestic systemically important banks
DSM	Dispute Settlement Mechanism
EACH	European Association of CCP Clearing Houses
EBA	European Banking Authority
EBC	European Banking Committee
EBU	European Banking Union
ECB	European Central Bank
ECMH	efficient capital market hypothesis
ECtHR	European Court of Human Rights
EIOPA	European Insurance and Occupational Pensions Authority
EIOPC	European Insurance and Occupational Pensions Committee
EMIR	European Market Infrastructure Regulation
ESAs	European Supervisory Authorities
ESC	European Securities Committee
ESFS	European System of Financial Supervision
ESM	European Stability Mechanism
ESMA	European Securities and Markets Authority
ESRB	European Systemic Risk Board
ETFs	exchange-traded funds
EU	European Union
FAT	Financial Activities Tax
FATF	Financial Action Task Force
FCA	Financial Conduct Authority
FDIC	Federal Deposit Insurance Corporation
FFIEC	Federal Financial Institutions Examination Council
FINRA	Financial Industry Regulatory Authority
FMIs	financial market infrastructures
FPC	Financial Policy Committee
FSA	Financial Services Authority
FSAP	Financial Sector Assessment Program/Financial Services Action Plan
FSB	Financial Stability Board
FSC	Financial Stability Contribution
FSCS	Financial Services Compensation Scheme
FSF	Financial Stability Forum
FSMA 2000	Financial Services and Markets Act 2000
FSOC	Financial Stability Oversight Council
G20	Group of 20

GATS	General Agreement on Trade in Services
GATT	General Agreement on Tariffs and Trade
GFC	Global Financial Crisis
GFSR	Global Financial Stability Report
GSIBs	global systemically important banks
GSIFIs	global systemically important financial institutions
GSIIs	global systemically important insurers
HFT	high-frequency trading
HKMA	Hong Kong Markets Authority
IAIS	International Association of Insurance Supervisors
IASB	International Accounting Standards Board
ICAAP	internal capital adequacy assessment process
ICB	Independent Commission on Banking
ICG	individual capital guidance
IFRS	International Financial Reporting Standards
IMF	International Monetary Fund
IOSCO	International Organization of Securities Commissions
ISD	Investment Services Directive
ISDA	International Swaps and Derivatives Association
ITO	International Trade Organization
ITSs	Implementing Technical Standards
JPoD	joint probability of distress
KIID	Key Investor Information Document
LEI	legal entity identifier
LIBOR	London interbank offered rate
LSE	London Stock Exchange
LTV	loan-to-value requirements
MAD	Market Abuse Directive
MAR	Market Abuse Regulation
MBSs	mortgage-backed securities
MCR	Minimum Capital Requirement
MD	mandatory disclosure
MiFID	Market in Financial Instruments Directive
MiFIR	Market in Financial Instruments Regulation
MLG	multilevel governance
MMFs	Money Market Funds
MMOU	Multilateral Memorandum of Understanding
MOU	Memorandum of Understanding
MPE	multiple point of entry
MTFs	multilateral trading facilities
NAV	net asset value
NBBO	National Best Bid and Offer
NCBs	national central banks
NCUA	National Credit Union Administration
NFA	National Futures Association
NSAs	national supervisory authorities
NYSE	New York Stock Exchange

OCC	Office of the Comptroller of Currency
OECD	Organization for Economic Cooperation and Development
OFR	Office of Financial Research
OIO	Office of Insurance Oversight
OLA	Orderly Liquidation Authority
ONI	Office of National Insurance
ORSA	Own Risk Solvency Assessment
OSFI	Office of the Superintendent of Financial Institutions
OTC	over-the-counter
OTF	organized trading facility
OTS	Office of Thrift Supervision
PAIRS	probability and impact rating system
PFRA	Prudential Financial Regulatory Agency
PIF	Proactive Intervention Framework
PPI	personal protection insurance
PRA	Prudential Regulation Authority
PRIIPs	packaged retail and insurance-based investment products
PWG	President's Working Group on Financial Markets
RDR	retail distribution review
RMs	regulated markets
ROSCs	Reports on the Observance of Standards and Codes
RRPs	resolution and recovery plans
RTSs	Regulatory Technical Standards
SBSEF	security-based swap execution facility
SCDOs	synthesized collateralized debt obligations
SCR	Solvency Capital Requirement
SEC	Securities and Exchange Commission
SEF	Swap Execution Facility
SEP	Supervisory Enhancement Programme
SIB	Securities and Investments Board
SIFs	significant influence functions
SIFIs	systemically important financial institutions
SOARS	supervisory oversight and response system
SPE	single point of entry
SPV	special purpose vehicle
SRB	Single Resolution Board
SREP	supervisory review and evaluation process
SRF	Single Resolution Fund
SRM	Single Resolution Mechanism
SROs	self-regulatory organizations
SRR	Special Resolution Regime
SSM	Single Supervisory Mechanism
TBT	'too-big-to'
TCF	Treating Customers Fairly
TEU	Treaty on European Union
TFEU	Treaty on the Functioning of the European Union
TRs	trade repositories

UCITSs	Undertakings for Collective Investment in Transferable Securities
UK	United Kingdom
US	United States
VaR	value-at-risk
WTO	World Trade Organization

List of Contributors

Kern Alexander is the Chair of Law and Finance at the University of Zurich and Senior Research Fellow at the Centre for Financial Analysis & Policy, University of Cambridge.

John Armour is Hogan Lovells Professor of Law and Finance at Oxford University and a Fellow of the European Corporate Governance Institute. He has published widely in the fields of company law, corporate finance, and corporate insolvency. He has been involved in policy-related projects commissioned by the UK's Department of Trade and Industry, Financial Services Authority and Insolvency Service, the Commonwealth Secretariat, the Jersey Economic Development Department, and the World Bank. He currently serves as a member of the European Commission's Informal Company Law Expert Group.

Douglas W Arner is a Professor in the Faculty of Law of the University of Hong Kong and Project Coordinator of a major five-year project on 'Enhancing Hong Kong's Future as a Leading International Financial Centre'. He is Co-Director of the Duke University-HKU Asia-America Institute in Transnational Law, a Senior Visiting Fellow of Melbourne Law School, and a member of the Hong Kong Financial Services Development Council. His latest book is *Rethinking Global Finance and its Regulation* (CUP, 2015, ed. with Ross Buckley and Emilios Avgouleas).

Emilios Avgouleas is the holder of the International Banking Law and Finance Chair at the University of Edinburgh, the Head of the Commercial Law Subject Area in the Law School, and the director of the Edinburgh LLM in International Banking Law and Finance. He has published extensively in the wider field of International and European finance law and economics and behavioural finance. He is the author of a large number of scholarly articles and two monographs: *Governance of Global Financial Markets: The Law, the Economics, the Politics* (CUP, 2012); and *The Mechanics and Regulation of Market Abuse: A Legal and Economic Analysis* (OUP, 2005).

Julia Black is Professor of Law and Pro Director for Research at the London School of Economics and Political Science. She has written extensively on issues relating to regulation in financial markets and more widely. She has advised regulators in the UK and elsewhere on issues of regulatory strategy and acted as an academic advisor to the Bank of England's Fair and Effective Markets Review (2014–15).

Chris Brummer is a Professor of Law at Georgetown University Law Center where he specializes in international financial regulation. He is also the C. Boyden Gray Fellow and Project Director for the Transatlantic Finance Initiative at the Atlantic Council and senior fellow at the Milken Institute. His latest book is *Minilateralism: How Trade Alliances, Soft Law and Financial Engineering Are Redefining Economic Statecraft* (CUP, 2014).

Simon Deakin is Professor of Law and Director of the Centre for Business Research at the University of Cambridge and a Fellow of Peterhouse.

Olivia Dixon is a Lecturer in the Regulation of Investment and Financial Markets at the University of Sydney Law School.

Luca Enriques is the Allen & Overy Professor of Corporate Law at the Faculty of Law of Oxford University, where he is also a Fellow at Jesus College. He has published widely in the fields of corporate law and financial regulation. He is the Editor of the ECGI Working Paper Series in Law and an ECGI Research Fellow and advises the Italian Ministry of the Economy and Finance on corporate law and financial regulation matters.

Michelle Everson is Professor of Law in the School of Law at Birkbeck, University of London.

Eilís Ferran is Professor of Company & Securities Law at the University of Cambridge, a University JM Keynes Fellow in Financial Economics, and a Fellow of the British Academy. She has written extensively on UK, EU, and international financial regulation. A new edition of her textbook *Principles of Corporate Finance Law* (OUP) was published in 2014. She served as the Specialist Adviser to the UK Parliament House of Lords European Union Committee in its inquiry into Banking Union (September–December 2012) and was a member of the Stakeholder Group of the European Banking Authority.

Guido Ferrarini is Professor of Business Law and Capital Markets Law at the University of Genoa.

Andreas Martin Fleckner is a Senior Research Fellow at the Max Planck Institute for Comparative and International Private Law, Hamburg.

Sergio Gilotta is Assistant Professor of Business Law at the University of Bologna, Faculty of Law, where he teaches Financial Regulation and Business Law. He has written in the fields of Italian and EU Corporate Law and Financial Regulation. He holds a PhD from the University of Bologna and an LLM from Harvard.

Brigitte Haar is Professor of Law, House of Finance, Goethe-University Frankfurt, Member of the Executive Committee of the House of Finance, Director of the Doctorate/PhD Programme Law and Economics of Money and Finance, and principal investigator of the research centre 'Sustainable Architecture for Finance in Europe' (SAFE) at Goethe-University. She has written extensively on financial regulation and comparative corporate governance with a special focus on the EU, the US, and Germany and is one of the founder editors of the *European Business Organization Law Review*. Her external appointments include membership of the Administrative and Consumer Advisory Councils of the German Federal Financial Supervisory Authority (BaFin).

Rosa M Lastra is Professor in International Financial and Monetary Law at the Centre for Commercial Law Studies, Queen Mary University of London. She is a member of the Monetary Committee of the International Law Association, of the European Shadow Financial Regulatory Committee, and of the International Insolvency Institute. She is an observer at the ILA Sovereign Bankruptcy Group and a senior research associate of the Financial Markets Group of the London School of Economics and Political Science. She has consulted with various governmental and intergovernmental institutions, including the International Monetary Fund, the European Central Bank, the World Bank, the Asian Development Bank, the Federal Reserve Bank of New York, and the House of Lords.

Iain MacNeil is the Alexander Stone Chair of Commercial Law at the University of Glasgow. His main interests are corporate governance, investment, and financial regulation. He is the author of *An Introduction to the Law on Financial Investment* (2nd edn, Hart, 2012) and a member of the securities regulation committee of the International Law Association (ILA).

Colin Mayer is the Peter Moores Professor of Management Studies at the Saïd Business School, University of Oxford and the former Dean of the Saïd Business School. He is a Fellow of the British Academy, a Fellow of the European Corporate Governance Institute, a Professorial Fellow of Wadham College, Oxford, and an Honorary Fellow of Oriel College, Oxford, and of St Anne's College, Oxford.

Harry McVea is a Professor of Law at the University of Bristol, where he has taught since 1989, and a Senior Associate Research Fellow at the Institute of Advanced Legal Studies, London. He has previously been a Visiting Fulbright Scholar at the University of California, Berkeley, Boalt Hall School of Law (1994–95), and a Visiting Parsons Scholar at the Faculty of Law, University of Sydney (2003). He has published widely in the area of financial regulation and is the author of *Financial Conglomerates and the Chinese Wall* (OUP).

Niamh Moloney is Professor of Financial Markets Law at the London School of Economics and Political Science where she specializes in EU financial regulation.

Her external appointments include membership of the advisory Stakeholder Group of the European Securities and Markets Authority and Special Adviser to the UK Parliament House of Lords inquiry into the EU's regulatory response to the financial crisis (July 2014–January 2015). Her recent publications include *EU Securities and Financial Markets Regulation* (OUP, 2014).

Peter O Mülbert is Professor of Law at the Faculty of Law and Economics and Director of the Center for German and International Law of Financial Services, University of Mainz. He has written extensively on German and EU company law, corporate governance, capital markets law, and financial regulation.

Eric J Pan is Associate Director of the Office of International Affairs at the U.S. Securities and Exchange Commission where he oversees international regulatory policy. He represents the SEC in the Financial Stability Board, International Organization of Securities Commissions, OTC Derivatives Regulators Group, US-EU Financial Markets Regulatory Dialogue, and various other multilateral and bilateral fora. Before joining the SEC, he was a professor at the Benjamin N. Cardozo School of Law in New York and Director of The Heyman Center on Corporate Governance. He was also an Associate Fellow in International Economics and International Law at the Royal Institute of International Affairs in London. Pan is a member of The American Law Institute and serves on the editorial board of several academic journals.

Frank Partnoy is the George E. Barrett Professor of Law and Finance and the founding director of the Center for Corporate and Securities Law at the University of San Diego. His books include *Corporations: A Contemporary Approach* (West, 2014), *F.I.A.S.C.O.: Blood in the Water on Wall Street* (Norton, 2010), *Infectious Greed: How Deceit and Risk Corrupted the Financial Markets* (PublicAffairs, 2009), and *The Match King: Ivar Kreuger, the Financial Genius behind a Century of Wall Street Scandals* (PublicAffairs, 2008), which was a finalist for the *Financial Times*/Goldman Sachs Business Book of the Year.

Jennifer Payne is Professor of Corporate Finance Law at the University of Oxford where she specializes in corporate finance law and financial regulation. She has written widely in this field. Her recent books include *Corporate Finance Law: Principles and Policy* (Hart, 2011, with Louise Gullifer; 2nd edn, 2015).

Paolo Saguato is LSE Fellow in Financial Regulation at the London School of Economics and Political Science where he specializes in US and EU financial regulation.

Matt Smallcomb is an associate at Cleary Gottlieb Steen & Hamilton LLP in New York where his practice focuses on corporate and financial transactions.

Dimity Kingsford Smith is Professor of Law at the University of New South Wales.

Andrew F Tuch is Associate Professor of Law at Washington University Law School, where he specializes in financial regulation and corporations law. He has published widely in the US, the UK, and Australia. He was an Olin Fellow in Law and Economics and a Fellow of the Program of Corporate Governance at Harvard Law School from 2008 to 2012.

INTRODUCTION

I. Financial Regulation in Perspective

Seven years on from the catastrophic events of autumn 2008, the Global Financial Crisis (GFC) still strongly influences policy, politics, and popular opinion. The arcane language of 'bank bailouts', 'systemic risk', and 'too big to fail' has entered the mainstream. International summits regularly see heads of government grappling with complex regulatory decisions which were previously the concern of specialist regulators, and international wrangles on the cross-border application of financial regulation can destabilize geopolitics. The minutiae of financial regulation are regularly debated in parliaments globally. The stark implications of weak financial regulation have become clear. Political disruption has followed from crisis-era austerity programmes. Financial regulation matters now as it has never before.

The recent seismic changes to financial regulation and to related theory and method cry out for careful consideration and contextualization. A burgeoning scholarly (as well as popular) literature has duly followed. But financial regulation has a long and complex history. While the GFC casts a very long shadow on the shape of current financial regulation, the present regime has had a longer gestation and has emerged from multiple turbulent periods of financial system disruption, reform, and new thinking. Financial regulation still has, nonetheless, something of a frontier quality. Scholars continue to debate fundamental questions as to the role of the state in the construction and regulation of the financial system, while policy-makers continue to grapple with persistent and troubling regulatory conundrums, including with respect to the nature of complexity and uncertainty in the financial system and how they might best be addressed.

Since the 1980s, the intellectual debate has moved beyond its traditional framing within neoclassical economics theory and now engages with myriad modes of analysis, ranging from systems theory, to behavioural finance, to governance theory and beyond. Although the economic dimension of the financial system has long shaped the regulatory debate, its social and political dimensions are increasingly coming to the fore. In particular, since the GFC financial regulation has come to be probed by social scientists of many hues, including political scientists, political economists, financial economists, regulatory theorists, and international relations specialists. Changes in policy thinking and in regulatory design have seen the scope of financial regulation grow exponentially in depth and breadth, the traditional regulatory toolkit vastly expanded, and the field of operation of financial regulation extend beyond domestic financial systems to regional and international systems. Change and innovation have encompassed regulation in action (in particular supervision and enforcement) as well as rule design. The institutional structures which support rulemaking and the supervision of financial system participants have experienced radical reform. The time is ripe for synthesis, consideration, and speculation as to future directions and, accordingly, for this Oxford Handbook of Financial Regulation.

The Handbook was put together over an extraordinary and challenging period in financial regulation policy and scholarship as the global financial system was repaired and radical changes were made to financial regulation. But it does not seek only to consider the ramifications of the GFC for scholarly engagement and for regulatory design, although such an assessment does form part of the Handbook's inquiry. It has a wider purpose. The Handbook seeks to consider the forces which have shaped financial regulation, to probe the purpose and nature of financial regulation, to capture and organize the multiplicity of rules and governance devices which can be regarded as financial regulation, to do so in a wide historical context, and to engage with the array of policy design innovations and scholarly perspectives which have influenced its design.

II. The Financial System and Financial Regulation

The financial system, which is the concern of financial regulation, can be surprisingly difficult to capture. As is discussed throughout this Handbook, fundamental questions as to the purpose of the financial system and as to the role of the state in the financial system continue to bedevil scholars and policymakers. Financial regulation is not unique in the wider field of regulation in grappling with a constantly shifting regulated community. But it faces particular challenges as the financial system is highly dynamic. Stripped back to its essentials, the financial system is concerned with financial intermediation, or the process through which funds are transferred from those in surplus to those in deficit and returns are achieved relative to the risk undertaken. Bank-based intermediation manages this process by means of maturity transformation: the provision by banks of long-term loan assets to capital seekers, based on the short-term bank deposit liabilities which provide returns for capital suppliers. Market-based intermediation is based on the raising of funds by capital seekers through marketable instruments (such as shares and bonds) which provide capital suppliers with a return. It engages an array of related market intermediaries and infrastructures in support of this process. Overall, the financial system supports the raising of capital and the acquisition of returns through multiple interrelated mechanisms which manage the costs of intermediation. The financial system, for example, allows capital suppliers to hedge their risks and capital seekers to reduce their cost of capital. Similarly, it supports liquidity in loan and securities assets and, accordingly, facilitates capital suppliers in realizing the assets through which they fund capital seekers. A raft of studies—many of which long predate the GFC—underscores the importance of the financial system and of financial intermediation to economic development. But, as is discussed throughout this Handbook, although empiricism has become strongly associated with theory and method on financial regulation (a recent example being the law and finance method of classifying rules and their origins and of charting their impact on financial system development), empirical studies in the financial regulation sphere are rarely conclusive and methodological approaches continue to develop. This is reflected in the long-standing debate on the direction of causality between strong financial intermediation and strong economic development, and on the relative benefits and risks of particular types of financial intermediation. Nonetheless, the scholarly and policy association between financial intermediation and economic development is a strong one.

But the financial system is, as is considered across the Handbook, continually evolving. The intermediation process is strongly associated with innovation and with a tendency to ever more intense intermediation. To take one example, the related process of financialization (or the embedding of the financial system within the economy) has led to households becoming dependent on financial system returns and exposed to financial system risk through an array of increasingly complex financial products and evolving distribution systems. The orthodox understanding of banking business as being primarily oriented towards financing new business investment has become increasingly at odds with the reality of most credit being advanced to finance the purchase of existing assets, in particular land, and to satisfy consumer consumption preferences. To take another example, innovation within the financial system tends to lead to ever more sophisticated means for the management of risk and to the dispersal of risk through complex layers of intermediation. But the intensification of intermediation can have profound consequences for the role of the state in the financial system. As the financial system has become more sophisticated, and as financial system infrastructures and intermediaries have developed, the process of intermediation has become somewhat disconnected from the core capital supply function and increasingly concerned with the generation of fees and returns through various forms of financial alchemy. This can lead to a severing of the relationship between risk and return and can distort the financial system's ability to manage risks. The social purpose of the financial system has accordingly come under scrutiny—particularly since the GFC.

While the causes of the GFC are many and are still contested, the conventional narrative ties the crisis to a destabilizing build up of cheap debt (leverage) in the financial system and to a related and destructive search for yield which, coupled to burgeoning financial innovation by intermediating actors, led to the development of products (including securitization products) which transferred leverage into financial markets. Financial markets, undermined by an array of weaknesses—regulatory and otherwise, and including the extent to which counterparties across the financial system were interconnected—proved unable to manage the build-up of risk effectively. Financial stability was catastrophically undermined as banks, in particular, suffered initially liquidity and subsequently solvency crises as they struggled to meet their funding requirements. The oft-quoted assertion by then UK Financial Services Authority Chairman Lord Turner that financial system innovation was not always 'socially useful'[1] reflects the widespread crisis-era unease as to levels of financial intermediation as well as uncertainty as to the purpose of the financial system, particularly in light of the welfare costs which the GFC generated. But this unease contrasts with the strong pre-crisis support of intense levels of financial intermediation.

Shifting perspectives on the social purpose and welfare costs associated with the financial system have long made identification of the role of the state in the financial system and the purpose of financial regulation challenging. The traditional neoclassical economics analysis of financial regulation posits that it should seek to address market failures which disrupt the efficient allocation of resources by the financial system. Information asymmetries have long been identified as a classic market failure in this area. So too have externalities, given the extent to which counterparties in the financial system are interrelated and the scale on which, as a result, risks can be transmitted. These market failures can lead to disruption to the efficient operation of the financial system, particularly where risks and costs are not efficiently internalized within financial system participants but are externalized

[1] This comment was originally made during a roundtable discussion between Lord Turner and a panel of financial experts on 27 August 2009, and published in the September 2009 issue of *Prospect Magazine*.

into the wider financial system and generate stability risks. Large-scale damage to the real economy can follow. As is discussed across this Handbook, the cycle of financial system expansion, crisis, and regulatory reaction is a familiar one.

But this conventional account of the rationale for regulation masks the multitude of financial system complexities, institutional incentives (whether financial system or regulatory), shifting political priorities, and nuanced policy choices which shape financial regulation. In particular, the purpose and related reach of financial regulation remains highly contested. For example, what type of financial system should (or can) regulation seek? The EU has long been struggling to embed market finance in the single market by deploying a range of mechanisms, including regulatory tools. This project (recently repackaged as the EU's 'Capital Markets Union' agenda) has received considerable impetus from the crisis. But the EU's regulatory ambitions in this regard are not without critics, and it is far from clear that regulation can drive particular models of intermediation, even if optimum models could be identified. In the US, current scholarship queries the ongoing institutionalization of the financial market and the implications for the treatment of the long-standing cohort of household investors as the 'public market' within which the highest levels of regulation applies shrinks, in part because of regulatory fiat, in part because of market developments. Similarly, is there an optimum level of financial intermediation (whether market- or bank-based) and can its achievement be supported through regulation—at what point do financial system activities become 'socially useless' and what is the role of the state in this regard? The questions become no less complex on drilling into the workings of the financial system. Who should be the lender of last resort to the financial system? How should losses be allocated, given the public interest in financial stability? How much risk can financial consumers be expected to absorb? The answers are not, as the discussions in the Handbook attest, straightforward.

The location of regulation is similarly contested, as is discussed in this Handbook. It is axiomatic that markets are global and interconnected but how then should regulation be organized and is there (or should there be) such a creature as international financial regulation? How can cross-border risk transmission be addressed on a global basis? Regulation aside, supervision and rescue/resolution pose multiple conundrums. These become acute where questions as to the allocation of losses, whether to the taxpayer or otherwise, arise in the context of cross-border financial system participants. By providing for the mutualization across EU Member States of the costs and risks of bank supervision and resolution, Banking Union is an epochal achievement. But, and underscoring the difficulties which international institutional organization poses to financial regulation, its existence is owed to the massive turbulence which beset euro area sovereign debt markets over 2010–12. The chaos unleashed threatened the existence of the euro and wrought the political conditions needed such that the political and constitutional risks which a project of this scale engaged could be taken.

Turning to the means through which grander political decisions and compromises as to the purpose and organization of regulation of the financial system take form, financial regulation is traditionally associated with three main objectives and their related regulatory tools. These objectives are the support of financial stability; market efficiency, transparency, and integrity; and consumer protection. Underpinning all of these is the concern to ensure the financial system supports economic growth and, particularly since the GFC, does not put taxpayers' funds at risk. The regulatory tools deployed to deliver these objectives can, very broadly, be classified into conduct-related tools and prudential-related tools. Conduct regulation can be associated with client- and market-facing conduct, addressing, for example, the protection of financial consumers when receiving investment advice, the risk that particular conduct amounts to market abuse, and the promotion of market efficiency by seeking to ensure that firms seeking capital do not defraud the market. Prudential regulation is directed towards financial stability and has two dimensions. Micro-prudential regulation is directed to the stability of individual financial system participants; macro-prudential regulation is directed to the stability of the system as a whole. Within (and across) these two very broad and blunt classifications sit a multitude of regulatory tools. The micro-prudential toolbox, for example, might include licensing rules; capital, solvency, liquidity, and leverage requirements; corporate governance, remuneration, and risk-management rules; deposit guarantees; and rescue and resolution procedures which activate when a financial system participant is at risk of failure. Macro-prudential tools might include capital buffers which dampen bank-lending activity to reflect the risks of the economic cycle.

The nature and intensity of regulation vary according to the financial system participant. The optimal fixing of the regulatory perimeter remains a major preoccupation of financial regulation, notwithstanding the crisis-era G20 commitment to close regulatory gaps. The related debates as to where and how to fix the perimeter of financial regulation reflect one of the field's most enduring questions: how to set the balance between financial system self-discipline and state intervention, given their respective risks and benefits. But it is clear that the regulatory trajectory is towards intensification of intervention. The crisis-era imposition of infrastructures on much of the over-the-counter (OTC) derivatives market through trading venue and central clearing requirements, for example, has led to an exponential increase in the intensity of the conduct and prudential regulation of this market.

The regulatory toolbox deployed at any point in time, and the reach of regulatory tools, reflect an array of determinative factors, including political and economic conditions, financial system features, and the received regulatory wisdom of the period. All of these factors are almost continually in flux, as the Handbook's discussion of the different elements of financial regulation underlines.

Different social science perspectives illuminate how and why financial regulation has developed in its current form and these insights enrich discussions across the Handbook. Governance theory, for example, provides insights on issues such as how institutional design choices shape regulation, while international relations theory casts light on, among other things, how the international financial system can and should be governed and how it can have an impact on domestic regulation. Financial economics illustrates how finance theory and, in particular, the influential but contested Efficient Capital Market Hypothesis (ECMH), can drive regulatory policy and market practice, while political economy provides an understanding of the institutional dynamics which shape financial systems and their regulation. Behavioural psychology and finance also play an important role, particularly in deepening understanding of the process of financial innovation. Political science, to take a final example, deepens understanding of financial regulation by conceptualizing the social and financial citizen and exposing how notions of citizenship can influence consumer financial regulation and policy. But this Handbook of Financial Regulation is, at bedrock, concerned with the role of law in the financial system. Despite the richness of its intellectual hinterland and also many years of state intervention, the extent to which law should have a role in, and the nature of its impact on, the financial system remains contested. The response to the GFC provides rich evidence of the ease with which rules can be bent or disregarded when chaos strikes.

An explanation of how the organization of the Handbook reflects the major questions and challenges associated with financial regulation is warranted. Part I considers the relationship between the financial system and regulation. The Chapters in this Part explore the complexities and tensions that underlie financial regulation, and examine many of the horizontal themes which underpin this area of regulation and which frame the debates as to how financial regulation should be designed. Chapter 1 (Deakin) addresses the evolution of theory and method in law and finance and, with particular reference to how new theories and methods in law and finance have developed post-crisis, considers how finance theory has developed and informed legal understanding of financial regulation. Chapter 2 (Mayer) examines the relationship between economic development, financial systems, and law and the complexity of this relationship, as reflected in the institutional structures which can substitute for regulation and, for example, in the development of new forms of finance, such as mobile money. The crisis-prone nature of the financial system and the pivotal relationship between financial systems, crises, and regulation, which has had and continues to have a defining influence on the shape of financial regulation, is considered in broad historical perspective in Chapter 3 (Partnoy).

Part II examines the organization of financial regulation from institutional and system-based perspectives. Chapter 4 (Ferran) considers the debate on the key issues that are relevant to the task of designing domestic supervisory institutions to contribute to the achievement of the goals of financial regulation. Chapter 5 (Brummer and Smallcomb) examines organizational questions from the international perspective and assesses the international architecture which supports the international financial system and, in particular, how the international financial system engages with dispute resolution. Part II also addresses the distinct organizational and related institutional issues raised by regional financial systems. Chapter 6 (Haar) examines how the EU addresses the regulation of its single financial market, including with reference to Banking Union, while Chapter 7 (Pan) considers the distinct issues raised by the US financial system and its federal organization.

Part III considers how financial regulation seeks to achieve particular outcomes and the particular regulatory and supervisory strategies and market-based institutions and mechanisms which can be deployed. Chapter 8 (Black) addresses the nature and evolution of key regulatory styles and supervisory strategies, notably risk-based regulation, management-based regulation, and principles-based, outcomes-focused, and judgment-based regulation. Chapter 9 (Payne) examines the role of gatekeepers, such as rating agencies and investment analysts, and whether the regulatory regime which now applies to gatekeepers is effective. Chapter 10 (MacNeil) considers the role of enforcement and sanctioning in the regulatory governance of the financial system, including with respect to the empirical evidence on enforcement strategies and the cross-border dimension.

The remaining three Parts (IV–VI) address the three major recurring objectives of financial regulation over the last 30–40 years or so and which remain widely used as the primary organizational tools of financial regulation scholarship and policy, even as regulatory tools and policy, the scholarly debate, and the financial system have evolved. They are: financial stability (Part IV); market efficiency, transparency, and integrity (Part V); and consumer protection (Part VI). While these three objectives have experienced varying degrees of prominence in different periods (financial stability, for example, being the current major preoccupation of financial regulation), they have been persistent features of the scholarly discussion and policy debate on financial regulation and are now regarded as the anchors of financial regulation internationally.

Part IV on financial stability addresses the major policy and political concern of the crisis-era period, as reflected in the G20 reform agenda's concern to secure financial stability and protect taxpayers from the costs of financial system rescue. But financial stability has long been a concern of financial regulation even if, until the GFC, it was primarily associated with the banking sector and with related prudential regulation. The achievement of financial stability and, in particular, the management of system interconnectedness, has since come to shape regulation of the financial markets, while the traditional stability-orientated regulation of the banking sector has come to embrace recovery, resolution, and rescue, as well as a considerably more sophisticated approach to the monitoring and containment of institution and system-wide risk. Financial stability has also emerged as a priority concern of international engagement, leading to considerable innovation in the design of governance structures for the international financial system. Chapter 11 (Lastra) examines the regulatory and institutional issues associated with the management of systemic risk—the identification and containment of which has emerged as one of the major policy innovations of the crisis-era—and macro-prudential supervision, and from domestic, regional, and international dimensions. Chapter 12 (Alexander) considers a cornerstone of financial stability regulation—capital regulation—and examines the transformation of bank capital from a balance-sheet item for risk management to a mainstay of banking soundness under the Basel Accords, most recently the Basel III agreement. Chapter 13 (Mülbert) addresses the interplay between micro-prudential and macro-prudential regulation, and the alternative and complementary techniques for securing micro-prudential and macro-prudential stability beyond capital, including deposit protection, disclosure, and central clearing. Chapter 14 (Everson) considers the distinct financial stability risks and related regulatory tools in the insurance market, examining the particular social and economic purposes of insurance, its role in risk redistribution, how its regulation has evolved, and the undercutting tensions in the regulatory project. Chapter 15 (Armour) examines financial stability from the crisis management and resolution perspective which came to centre stage over the crisis-era and examines the 'first-generation' special resolution regimes for financial institutions and the 'second-generation' reforms, including rescue and resolution planning regimes and international coordination arrangements. Chapter 16 (Arner) considers how financial stability can be secured on a cross-border basis, the distinct set of institutional and coordination risks to financial stability arising from the cross-border activities of financial institutions, the tools which can be deployed in response, and the prospects for globalization.

Part V on market efficiency, transparency, and integrity examines the three long-standing objectives of financial regulation which are strongly associated with market-based intermediation and their policy articulation and contextual and scholarly framework. Chapter 17 (Enriques and Gilotta) considers mandatory disclosure—a foundational tool of market regulation which is directed to the remedying of information asymmetries and which continues to shape regulatory design despite its effectiveness being highly contested. Chapter 18 (Tuch) considers conduct regulation, a central element of intermediary regulation which governs intermediary conduct and which is composed of a dense matrix of interlocking rules, many of which have experienced significant change over recent years and which, by contrast with much of financial regulation, have been subject to private litigation which has shaped the nature of regulation in this area. Chapter 19 (Ferrarini and Saguato) examines financial market infrastructures, including trading venues and central clearing counterparties, and the distinct forms of market regulation which apply to these intermediaries which are increasingly becoming the location of more intense risk and of related regulation. Chapter 20 (Fleckner) addresses the particular risks and regulatory design issues which are generated by trading practices and considers how one of the oldest elements of market regulation has come to grapple with the most innovative of market activities—whether high frequency trading or the operation of dark pools—and the regulatory challenges and policy conflicts which can arise. Chapter 21 (McVea) examines market integrity and considers how the risks which market abuse (in particular, insider dealing and market manipulation) poses to the financial system can be addressed and the related regulatory choices which arise, charting the major shifts in the debate on how market integrity can be supported. The challenges which financial innovation poses to regulatory design and regulatory thinking are considered in Chapter 22 (Avgouleas), which probes the notion of financial innovation and the process from which it emerges and considers contemporary regulation of financial innovation, including with respect to shadow banking.

The final Part VI of the Handbook considers the consumer financial system, the regulation of which frequently challenges the traditional conception of financial regulation as supporting economic efficiency goals and which engages, in particular, the social and political dimensions of the financial system. Chapter 23 (Kingsford Smith and Dixon) examines the experience of regulating in the financial consumer interest, the impact of financialization, and the importance of the conceptualization of the consumer as a financial citizen and the implications of financial citizenship for regulatory design. The distinct regulatory tools deployed in the consumer financial markets (disclosure, distribution, and product intervention) are examined in Chapter 24 (Moloney), which considers the evolution of these tools and how they expose underlying tensions in consumer financial policy and regulation.

This Handbook accordingly seeks to provide a comprehensive, wide-ranging, and authoritative discussion of the major themes that have arisen in financial regulation. The aim is not to provide neat answers to the debates, but rather to frame the issues, to illuminate the tensions and difficulties which bedevil these areas, and to prompt further discussion about these issues, between scholars, practitioners, central bankers, regulators, policymakers, and consumer bodies. Underpinning the inquiries across the Handbook is the recognition of the vital contribution that financial regulatory policy can make to helping economies achieve sustainable growth. Our distinguished contributors elucidate the complexities and challenges involved in the search for suitable policy pathways and offer valuable insights on the shaping of regulatory policy to improve economic development and the well-being of society.

Niamh Moloney
Eilís Ferran
Jennifer Payne
London, Cambridge, and Oxford, 1 April 2015

PART I

FINANCIAL SYSTEMS AND REGULATION

CHAPTER 1

THE EVOLUTION OF THEORY AND METHOD IN LAW AND FINANCE

SIMON DEAKIN

I. Introduction

The idea of the self-regulating financial market experienced an abrupt empirical refutation in the course of a few weeks in New York and London in September 2008. Yet, the theory of finance seemed to carry on as if nothing had happened. Adherents of the efficient capital market hypothesis (ECMH) maintained that the financial crisis validated their position: stock market prices accurately predicted an impending recession caused by misguided government regulation.[1] The ECMH remains today the default view of financial economics[2] and continues to inform mainstream legal understandings of the operation of capital markets.[3] A minority position in economic theory points to the presence of various kinds of 'irrational' or sub-optimal outcomes in financial markets, resulting from asymmetric information, herd effects, and similar market distortions.[4] This line of thought predates the crisis, but has had limited influence over policymakers.[5]

It is arguable that data, no matter how compelling, are insufficient to undermine a theory which remains coherent in its own terms.[6] This may, however, be to understate the impact of events on the conventional wisdom which at any given time shapes a disciplinary field and its application in spheres of business and policy. Imperceptibly, at first, and then with seeming irreversibility, paradigms can shift.[7] The process normally begins at the fringes of a discipline, at the point where the

[1] Cassidy, J, 'Interview with Eugene Fama', *The New Yorker*, 13 January 2010, cites Fama as saying: 'I think [the ECMH] did quite well in this episode. Stock prices typically decline prior to and in a state of recession. This was a particularly severe recession. Prices started to decline in advance of when people recognized that it was a recession and then continued to decline. There was nothing unusual about that. That was exactly what you would expect if markets were efficient.' Asked whether the responsibility for the crisis lay with the stock market, he is reported to have said: 'That was government policy; that was not a failure of the market'.

[2] 'The impact of the theory of efficient markets has proven to be durable, and seems likely to continue to be so, despite its inevitable and painfully obvious limitations': Ball, R, 'The Global Financial Crisis and the Efficient Capital Market Hypothesis: What Have we Learned?' (2009) 16 *Journal of Applied Corporate Finance* 8, 16.

[3] The US Supreme Court's decision in *Basic Inc. v Levinson* 485 US 224 (1988) elevated the ECMH to the level of a legal presumption underpinning the 'fraud on the market' theory of corporate liability to investors for false or misleading disclosures. In *Erica P. John Fund Inc. v Halliburton Co.* 573 US __ (2014) (not yet reported), the Supreme Court essentially upheld the presumption that market prices reflect available information while qualifying some of its effects.

[4] See Shiller, R, *Irrational Exuberance* (2000).

[5] This may be because economists from the 'inefficient markets' school do not go so far as to argue that market instability renders finance unsuitable as a mechanism of resource allocation in society. See Shiller, R, *Finance and the Good Society* (2012).

[6] Stigler, G, 'The Process and Progress of Economics' (1983) 91 *Journal of Political Economy* 529, 534–5, referring to the 'base of persistent theory' which lends order to a science or discipline.

[7] Galbraith, JK, *The Affluent Society* (1998) 11: 'the enemy of the conventional wisdom is not ideas but the march of events'.

theoretical core is most exposed to contact with events and interests. Thus it is not surprising that the ECMH should have recently come under pressure not at the level of high theory but in the very concrete context of securities litigation. Whether it was right for the US courts, in the 1980s, to borrow an economic concept such as the ECMH for the purpose of quantifying shareholders' claims for losses arising from misleading disclosures by listed companies, is open to question. The ECMH is, in principle, a claim which is susceptible to empirical testing, and which awaits falsification if economic science is to progress. To treat it as a natural feature of securities markets involves some methodological slippage. Of course, the translation of the idea from finance to law in the *Basic* case was not a neutral act of observation: it was a normative move, which sought to validate the idea of spontaneous order as a fundamental organizing principle of economic life. That process is now going into reverse, and just as the recent legal challenge to the use of ECMH in US securities law[8] may signal the diminishing political value of the model of the self-regulating market, so a more fundamental rethinking of theoretical paradigms in the field of law and finance cannot be much longer delayed.

This Chapter is concerned less with the origins and nature of the financial crisis, a subject which has been extensively explored elsewhere, as with the emergence of new theories and methods in post-crisis law and finance. It will be suggested that a common thread linking these paradigms is their use of evolutionary concepts and reasoning.[9] The efficient market hypothesis assumes a world of rational agents whose interests are aligned, in a perfect equilibrium, through the impersonal operation of the price mechanism. The state's role is the minimal one of ensuring the basic conditions for exchange and overcoming information asymmetries. Otherwise, it keeps out of the way so as not to interfere with the workings of the market. In an evolutionary perspective, by contrast, agents with bounded rationality use heuristics to coordinate their actions and build institutions to overcome obstacles to cooperation. Institutions are evolved and, hence, imperfect solutions to collective action problems. Spontaneous orders exist but suffer from design flaws which can be addressed through policy interventions, which are themselves contingent and incomplete. The state and the market, law and finance, are institutions of a particular kind, that is, complex systems with adaptive properties. They relate to each other not through a process of linear adjustment, but through a co-evolutionary

[8] In *Erica P. John Fund Inc. v Halliburton Co.* 573 US __ (2014) (not yet reported).

[9] The term 'evolutionary', in this context, does not refer to 'biological' or 'genetic' theories of social structure ('sociobiology' or 'evolutionary psychology'), but instead to a class of models and methods which focuses on the dynamic properties of systems, which adapt to their environment over time. These models and methods share common elements with biological ones but are not reducible to them. They include 'complex' representations of market structure (Section II), learning models of individual behaviour (Section III), accounts of legal and financial coevolution (Section IV), regression models for analysing longitudinal data (Section V), and theories of endogenous policymaking (Section VI). See further below.

dynamic, which alternates between stasis and crisis. There can be no market without the state, and no finance without law,[10] since the two are intertwined, but since the reverse is also true, there is a limit to how far the legal system can be used as instrument of policy. The law is an 'embedded technology' which depends on linking to its environment or context if it is to function effectively. Thus, the new paradigm does necessarily not lead to the conclusion that 'more regulation is better'. It does, however, imply that a more nuanced and, hence, policy-useful, understanding can be obtained of how financial market regulation works.

To develop these themes, Section II examines the idea of financial (and other) markets as complex, adaptive systems, and explores the significance of studying the emergence of prices as a learning process, in which agents' expectations and actions adjust to a changing environment. Section III looks at the implications of behavioural economics for law and finance, and Section IV considers the theme of the coevolution of the legal and financial systems. Section V discusses methodological issues arising in the context of the empirical study of law and finance. Reference here is made to data-coding techniques ('leximetrics') and statistical methods (time-series econometrics), which are being used to study the temporal dimension of legal and financial systems. Section VI discusses how a learning model of the policymaking process can aid understanding of financial crises. Section VII concludes.

II. Theorizing Financial Markets: From Equilibria to Complex Systems

The ECMH is a special case of a wider set of models which purport to show how competition results in stable states and market equilibria, in which prices clear and resources are allocated to their most efficient use. The mathematical formulation of a competitive economy first presented by Léon Walras in *Éléments de l'économie politique pure* (originally published in 1874)[11] predicts that prices will adjust to fluctuations in supply and demand, but fails to explain how they do so. Walras assumed that, out of equilibrium, adjustment of prices (*tâtonnement*) would occur through the operation of a mechanism, which he termed

[10] Pistor, K, 'A Legal Theory of Finance' (2013) 41 *Journal of Comparative Economics* 315.

[11] Walras, L, *Elements of Pure Economics* (1954).

the auctioneer (*crieur*), for making prices public. The *crieur* was a real-life institution—an official of the Paris Bourse—who called out the prices of traded securities and adjusted them up and down to reflect the different bids made by buyers and sellers.[12]

Walras adapted the institution of the *crieur* to his model of a national economy in which firms combine labour, materials, and capital to produce outputs which they sell to individuals and households at market prices. Prices enable markets to clear because, assuming rational behaviour on the part of agents, sellers will adjust their offers down to match a shortage of demand while buyers, correspondingly, will raise theirs in response to a shortage of supply. Thus, when the economy is out of equilibrium, any individual buyer or seller always has an incentive to adjust their prices to reflect a mismatch of supply and demand. In this way, the decentralized decisions of market actors lead to a convergence of prices and to an equilibrium point at which supply and demand are equalized. However, Walras did not model *this* process.[13] Using a series of interlocking differential equations, he presented a formal mathematical proof for the existence of a general market equilibrium, but the convergence process could not be modelled in the same way. Walras appears to have thought that the process whereby information from individual trading decisions became common knowledge among market agents was analytically, that is, mathematically, intractable. Thus, he presupposed that price information would be regularly updated and publicized through a society-wide equivalent of the *crieur*: 'the markets that are best organised from the competitive standpoint are those in which purchases and sales are made by auction, through the instrumentality of stockbrokers, commercial brokers or criers acting as agents who centralise transactions in such a way that the terms of every exchange are openly announced'.[14]

Thus, Walras' models demonstrated that prices and quantities would be aligned in a series of equilibria across all markets, which would clear simultaneously, *if* information concerning prices was publicly available. However, later studies showed that the knowledge need by the 'auctioneer' to carry out this task is not trivial.[15] The auctioneer is generally modelled as adjusting prices up and down on the basis of information concerning excess demand. To do this requires knowledge of all relevant cross-elasticities of demand; that is to say, the extent to which trading decisions are sensitive to movements in prices for different products. This is

[12] The *crieur* was a legal office originating in commercial legislation of the immediate post-revolutionary period: 'Il y a pour le service de la Bourse un crieur public … Il annoncera les cotes des effets publics négociés sur le parquet.' Ordonnance de 29 germinal, an 4 (1801).

[13] On this point, see Gintis, H, 'The Dynamics of Pure Market Exchange' in Aoki, M, Binmore, K, Deakin, S, and Gintis, H (eds), *Complexity and Institutions: Markets, Norms and Corporations* (2012).

[14] Walras, n 11 above, 169.

[15] These are reviewed in Fisher, F, *Disequilibrium Foundations of Equilibrium Economics* (1983).

a very strict condition, and is not self-generating, in the sense of being derivable from the behaviour of market actors alone.[16]

From the middle of the twentieth century, following Walras' lead, research into competitive markets focused on refining the mathematical form of a general, economy-wide equilibrium. Examining the institutional conditions for price adjustment in capital (or other) markets, such as, for example, the provisions of the *Code commercial* underpinning the office of the *crieur*, did not form part of this research project. Writing in 1988, Ronald Coase observed that financial markets, 'often used by economists as example of a perfect market and perfect competition', were also a good case of 'markets in which transactions are highly regulated (and this quite apart from any governmental regulation that there might be)', from which he drew the lesson that 'for anything approaching perfect competition to exist an intricate system of rules and regulations would normally be needed'.[17] His perception went apparently unnoticed and certainly unremarked on in mainstream financial research.

The theory of the efficient capital market was set out by Eugene Fama in a series of papers from the mid-1960s.[18] Fama began from the premise that the capital market could be described as efficient if prices fully reflected all available information about securities. Prices would then 'provide accurate signals for resource allocation'.[19] Fama did not seek to identify the source of market efficiency, any more than Walras did. His main concern was to review the empirical evidence on the 'adjustment of security prices to three relevant information subsets'.[20] These were, respectively, information embodied in historic prices (corresponding to the 'weak form' of the ECMH); all information in the public domain, such as company reports and market disclosures (the 'semi-strong form'); and all information relevant to price formation, including that available only to private actors (the 'strong form').[21] The principal criterion for judging the efficiency of prices was expected returns from investments as reflected in price changes. Evidence that share prices followed a 'random walk' was viewed as confirmation that information about companies and the securities they issued, which was assumed to be stochastic, was being rapidly assimilated into prices. Fama built on the model of Bachelier's *Théorie de la speculation*,[22] which had proposed as early as 1900 that prices of securities moved independently of one another in a random pattern. Fama interpreted the random walk as implying a finite variance to prices which would produce a 'normal' (or 'Gaussian') distribution. The empirical literature he reviewed suggested that there was evidence of non-normal distributions in capital markets, but that the effects

[16] Gintis, n 13 above. [17] Coase, RH, *The Firm, the Market and the Law* (1988) 9.

[18] In particular, Fama, E, 'The Behaviour of Stock Market Prices' (1965) 38 *Journal of Business* 34 and 'Efficient Capital Markets: A Review of Theory and Empirical Work' (1970) 25 *Journal of Finance* 383.

[19] ibid, 383. [20] ibid. [21] ibid.

[22] Bachelier, L, *Théorie de la speculation* (1900).

were too small to undermine the proposition that the market was mostly operating in an efficient way. Even the strong form of the hypothesis held up, so that he was able to conclude that insiders with monopolistic information were not systematically distorting the market to the disadvantage of other investors. He also arrived at the conclusion that while interdependencies across share prices did exist, they were not large enough to allow specialist investment strategies, involving targeted selection of stocks, to be profitable.

Since Fama's first papers appeared there has been a large literature on various aspects of the ECMH. Defenders of the hypothesis maintain that its empirical validity has been largely confirmed.[23] However, the empirical validation of the ECMH, such as it is, needs to be put in the context of what exactly the hypothesis claims to show. In Fama's approach, the efficiency of the capital market does not equate to stability of stock prices. On the contrary, the capital market is likely to be unstable precisely when the external environment itself is in flux. Turbulence in the world beyond the financial domain will be more or less instantaneously translated into volatile stock prices. This is why the events of September 2008 could be read as confirming the ECMH. Nor does the hypothesis, in either its strong or weaker forms, have anything very much to say about the relationship between finance and the wider economy. Whether the market allocates ownership of the economy's capital stock in an efficient way does not predetermine whether the relationship between capital, labour, and production is an efficient one in the sense of providing for the optimal use of a given society's scarce resources, let alone ensuring the well-being of the members of that society.

The economic literature on the ECMH, like that on competitive markets more generally, claims to show that the market is efficient, but not how it comes to be so. Institutionally informed attempts to identify particular mechanisms of market efficiency are more specific in pointing to 'trading processes that, with more or less promptness (or "relative efficiency"), force prices to a new, fully informed equilibrium'.[24] Ron Gilson and Reinier Kraakman's analysis, which appeared in 1984, identified the role played by market intermediaries, including investment banks, arbitrageurs, researchers, and brokers, on the one hand, and disclosure rules and other features of securities market regulation, on the other, in assisting the process of information diffusion. They argued that 'as information costs decline, more—and better—information is available to more traders, and the market becomes more efficient, both because the information is better and because its wider distribution triggers a more effective capital market mechanism'.[25] Gilson

[23] See, for recent overviews, Malkiel, B, 'The Efficient Market Hypothesis and its Critics' (2003) 17 *Journal of Economic Perspectives* 59 and 'Reflections on the Efficient Market Hypothesis: 30 Years Later' (2005) 40 *Financial Review* 1.

[24] Gilson, R and Kraakman, R, 'The Mechanisms of Market Efficiency' (1984) 70 *Virginia Law Review* 549, 565.

[25] ibid, 561.

and Kraakman's approach implies that a mixture of strategically orientated behaviour on the part of different categories of market actors and a benign regulatory environment can induce greater efficiency in the pricing of securities, although this effect is not universally present in capital markets, the efficiency of which is, they have consistently emphasized, a matter of degree.[26] Their position can be interpreted as offering qualified support for an ECMH which is underpinned, in part, by legal and regulatory mechanisms for generating transparency and accuracy in the pricing of securities.

Evolutionary models take the argument to the next stage by seeking to show how market efficiency can arise endogenously from strategic interactions of 'heterogeneous' agents; that is to say, market actors with divergent expectations, based on their own prior experiences and differential degrees of access to information. These models are 'evolutionary' in the sense of describing strategies of actors that adapt to a changing environment and embody the effects of social learning. In contrast to the Walrasian model, no assumption is made about the existence of public prices, nor is there any positing of an auctioneer, institutional or otherwise. Instead, the starting assumption is that agents have private information concerning prices which they treat as 'strategic' variables; that is, as data points containing information about other actors' likely strategic choices. In a competitive economy with many agents, no single agent has the information or computational capacity to choose the best response to the full profile of market prices. In these circumstances, agents will base their strategies on their experience of previous trades and on their observation and imitation of the strategies of others. Imitation operates through a 'replicator dynamic' according to which the number of agents using a given strategy grows in proportion to the utility it is expected to generate. Herbert Gintis has analysed this type of endogenous price formation using a Markov process, a mathematical modelling technique which can be used to simulate temporal transitions across distinct game theoretical domains or states of play.[27] His model predicts that from an initial random distribution of private prices, a set of stable 'quasi-public' prices emerges across a finite number of transitions, and that over the longer term, an equilibrium with approximate market-clearing properties is endogenously generated.

When prices are modelled in this way as emergent variables arising from interdependent strategies of a large number of agents, the resulting market structure

[26] See Gilson, R and Kraakman, R, Market Efficiency after the Financial Crisis: It's Still a Matter of Information Costs (2014), Stanford Law and Economics Olin Working Paper 458; European Corporate Governance Institute (ECGI) Law Working Paper 242/2014; Columbia Law and Economics Working Paper 470, available at SSRN: <http://ssrn.com/abstract=2396608> or <http://dx.doi.org/10.2139/ssrn.2396608>.

[27] Gintis, H, 'Markov Processes and Social Exchange: Theory and Applications' (2013) 4 *ACM Transactions on Intelligent Systems and Technology* Article 53, 19 pages, DOI: <http://dx.doi.org/101145/2483669.2483686>.

has the properties of a *complex adaptive system*. Whereas neoclassical theory models the market as an equilibrium solution to the problem of allocating scarce means to alternate uses at least overall cost, a 'complex' economy is in a non-equilibrium state which falls short of an ideal resource allocation. It is a *non-ergodic* system consisting of distinct temporal states and time-irreversible transitions, operating under the influence of initial conditions and contingent events in the form of exogenous shocks which can alter the economy's equilibrium path.[28] Bachelier's random walk model[29] can be interpreted this way, and early mathematical formulations which predated the ECMH, including those formulated by MFM Osborne[30] and Benoît Mandelbrot,[31] also suggest that financial markets have dynamic and non-ergodic properties.

Where a financial market is in a non-equilibrium state, gains from trade are possible, so that there are opportunities for profit from arbitrage and targeted stock selection. Prices of securities will commonly display the 'fat tails' characteristic of non-Gaussian distributions. Traders' imitative and experiential strategies can give rise to endogenous 'bubbles'. Price changes will be cumulative and path dependent: 'agents may change their expectations as they learn and, given the self-reinforcing aspect of their expectations, prices will move with the expectations'.[32] This model goes some way towards recognizing the significant presence of arbitrage and of specialist investment vehicles, such as private equity and activist hedge funds, in contemporary securities markets, beyond the point predicted by the ECMH.

Evolutionary models may also throw light on the role of disclosure rules in securities markets. Some models suggest that endogenous prices may display resistance to extreme fluctuations of the kind experienced by publicly organized securities markets at times of crisis, such as the aftermath of the dotcom boom in 2000, or the crisis of autumn 2008. The insight here is that in a context where prices are public knowledge, agents may respond to new information by shifting their strategies in a more synchronized way (an extreme form of 'herding'). Thus, public prices based on full information may make capital (and other) markets *more prone* to the destabilizing effects of external shocks.[33] If this is correct, there is a limit to how far information flows, whether down to market intermediaries or disclosure rules, can be expected to induce more efficient outcomes. It is possible that disclosure rules underpinning public prices are responsible for price movements which are *both*

[28] See Peters, O, 'Optimal Leverage from Non-ergodicity' (2011) 11 *Quantitative Finance* 1593.

[29] Bachelier, n 22 above.

[30] Osborne, MFM, 'Brownian Motion in the Stock Market' (1959) 7 *Operations Research* 145.

[31] Mandelbrot, B, 'Forecasts of Future Prices, Unbiased Markets and Martingale Models' (1966) 39 *Journal of Business* 242.

[32] Kirman, A, Foellmer, H, and Horst, U, 'Equilibrium in Financial Markets with Heterogeneous Agents: A New Perspective' (2005) 41 *Journal of Mathematical Economics* 123, 125.

[33] Gintis, n 13 above.

unstable and inefficient, the opposite result to that predicted by the legal literature on the efficient market hypothesis.

III. Behavioural Law and Finance

A further development with implications for the understanding of financial markets is the behavioural turn which, since the 1990s, has led many social scientists to question the rational actor model. Because the assumption of rationality is at the core of the neoclassical model, behavioural analyses would seem to cast further doubt over the model of the self-regulating market. However, there are several strands to behaviouralism, which need to be disentangled when assessing its significance for legal design and policy.[34]

One line of behavioural research, identified with the work of Daniel Kahneman and Amos Tversky,[35] argues that individuals make systematic errors in decision-making, the roots of which are biological. This 'hard-wiring' of the brain can be understood in genetic terms as the consequence of path dependence in human evolution: human psychology is shaped by past natural and social environments, which continue to exercise their influence through genetic transmission because of the relatively short time that human beings have had to adapt to modern societal conditions. One version of this hypothesis, associated with the field of evolutionary psychology, argues that genetic factors directly influence human institutions, including markets and legal systems.[36] Another, dual inheritance theory or gene-culture coevolution,[37] posits that while there may be a biological 'substrate' to human society, genetic influences have become intertwined with social or 'cultural' practices, and that the latter have an evolutionary dynamic of their own, which is not reducible to genetic factors. While this debate remains unresolved thanks in part to a lack of data on the conditions under which the human genome can be assumed to have developed, there is sufficient evidence of cognitive biases in decision-making to suggest that there is a distinct human psychological profile, which may be hard-wired to a lesser or greater extent, and which is at odds with the

[34] See Altmann, M, 'Implications of Behavioural Economics for Financial Literacy and Public Policy' (2005) 41 *Journal of Socio-Economics* 677.

[35] Kahneman, D and Tversky, A (eds), *Choices, Values and Frames* (2000); Kahneman, D, *Thinking, Fast and Slow* (2011).

[36] Tooby, J and Cosmides, L, 'Evolutionary Psychology: Conceptual Foundations' in Buss, D (ed.), *Evolutionary Psychology Handbook* (2005).

[37] Richerson, P, Boyd, R, and Henrich, J, 'Gene-culture Coevolution in the Age of Genomics' (2010) 107 *Proceedings of the National Academy of Sciences (USA)* 8985.

rational actor model. Cognitive biases identified through experimental and other empirical research include overconfidence (which has been found to be particularly common in investment decisions), herding or mimicking, loss aversion (as reflected in the 'endowment effect'), status quo biases, framing effects (according to which the context in which information is presented affects actors' perceptions), and anchoring (the tendency to rely on initial information).

A second strand in the behavioural literature accepts that human beings are physiologically and psychologically incapable of acting according to the predictions of the rational actor model, but that decision-making is often not 'irrational' once the presence of uncertainty is taken into account. Human beings have developed 'heuristics', experience-based shortcuts to decision-making, which are evolved responses to choice environments characterized by incomplete information. For example, the endowment effect, according to which agents place an unduly high value on an asset they already possess as opposed to one they may at some future point acquire, may be a good response to asymmetric information concerning the quality of the item in question, or simply uncertainty over valuation. Heuristics like this may have a genetic origin, but could also be acquired through observation and, more generally, stored and transmitted via 'cultural' mechanisms such as social norms and institutions. This approach is characteristic of the work of the psychologist Gerd Gigerenzer,[38] whose analyses of decision-making under conditions of uncertainty are arguably more clearly aligned with the foundational work of Herbert Simon on bounded rationality[39] than is the case with the cognitive biases approach of Kahneman.

'Nudge' theory, developed by Cass Sunstein and Richard Thaler from the insights of Kahneman and Tversky, argues that behavioural analyses can be put to use in devising regulatory strategies which correct for the effects of 'irrational' behaviour.[40] Their approach is 'paternalistic' in the sense of correcting sub-optimal choices by individuals, but 'libertarian' in the emphasis placed on enhancing the quality of the choice environment by indirect means, so leaving scope for individuals' preferences to be fully (and 'correctly') expressed through exchange. From an evolutionary perspective, this strategy is open to question on a number of grounds.[41] First, if trading takes place in 'complex' markets characterized by out-of-equilibrium states, the restoration of 'rational' contracting will not, in itself, lead to optimal resource allocations. Second, what appears as 'irrational' behaviour

[38] Gigerenza, G, *Rationality for Mortals: How People Cope with Uncertainty* (2008).

[39] Simon, H, 'A Behavioural Model of Rational Choice' (1955) 69 *Quarterly Journal of Economics* 99 and 'Rationality as Process and as Product of Thought' (1978) 68 *American Economic Review* 1.

[40] Sunstein, C and Thaler, R, *Nudge: Improving Decisions about Health, Wealth, and Happiness* (2008).

[41] See Oliver, A, 'From Nudging to Budging: Using Behavioural Economics to Inform Public Sector Policy' (2013) 42 *Journal of Social Policy* 685.

from the benchmark of the rational actor model may simply reflect responses to an uncertain market settings which are the best available in the circumstances. Third, evolved heuristics based on social learning may be a more effective way of dealing with complex choice environments than solutions devised by regulators with limited information on the contexts in question.

In practice, there may not be much difference between 'nudge' theory and the 'heuristics' approach on the detail of legal and regulatory policy. There is consensus on the difficulty of crafting regulatory responses to cognitive biases which are hard to model in complex social and economic contexts. In particular, it would seem to be beyond the scope of current models to provide a fine-grained understanding of behaviour in non-ergodic markets.[42] Targeted regulatory interventions run the risk of undermining evolved heuristics which may be working sufficiently well as qualifiedly efficient responses to market imperfections.

There is, nevertheless, a growing literature which applies behavioural analysis to financial markets.[43] On one view, behavioural economics supports a range of regulatory interventions which are designed to induce self-regulation on the part of market actors, or otherwise to stimulate problem solving through private ordering. These include proposals for default rules, targeted information disclosure, and cooling-off periods for the protection of consumers who are generally considered to be less well informed and more prone to error than market professionals and other repeat players. Default rules can be drafted in such a way as to take into account the endowment effect and status-quo bias (overvaluing existing assets) and anchoring effects. This approach has led to specific policy recommendations in relation to residential mortgages and consumer credit. So-called sticky defaults for the protection of consumers, which are hard to opt out of, are one such mechanism. Cooling-off, through the use of waiting periods or withdrawal periods, can be used to address 'self-control' bias.

Another theme to emerge from this literature is more that information is not necessarily beneficial to decision-making.[44] Individuals do not always use all the information that is provided, and may act on certain categories of information which they believe to be important. Framing and anchoring effects are relevant here. Forced disclosure may be counterproductive in circumstances where it leads to greater complexity and detail in contractual documentation. Information presentation (addressing the framing bias) may be more useful than requiring additional disclosure. Warnings need to be tailored and specific.

[42] Raines, J and Leathers, C, 'Behavioural Finance and Post-Keynesian Institutionalist Theories of Financial Markets' (2011) 33 *Journal of Post-Keynesian Economics* 535; Juurikkala, O, 'Behavioural Paradox: Why Investor Irrationality Calls for Lighter and Simpler Financial Regulation' (2012) 18 *Fordham Journal of Corporate and Financial Law* 33.

[43] See generally Juurikkala, n 42 above, for an overview of the field.

[44] Lusardi, A, Financial Literacy: An Essential Tool for Informed Consumer Choice? (2008), National Bureau of Economic Research Working Paper No 14084.

A third issue relates to the complexity of legal rules. Some accounts argue for simple and stable rules on the grounds that they are most likely to give rise to positive learning effects on the part of consumers with limited information and resources. This is sometimes coupled with the argument that excessive protection of consumers will exacerbate the effects of 'overconfidence bias', and reduce the scope for learning from error through which heuristics can form.[45]

It is perhaps not surprising that accounts which focus on the 'irrationality' of consumers and investors, rather than the informational advantages enjoyed by repeat players in financial markets, often end up validating 'light touch' regulation as an appropriate response to cognitive failures. The idea that markets cannot be perfected, even with sophisticated rulemaking, also plays to a deregulatory agenda. If biases are regarded as hard-wired, there is a further reason for caution over the prospects for regulation. Whether behavioural analyses can bear the weight of directing policy in this way is an open question in the light of current knowledge.

A small but developing empirical literature is exploring the effects of behaviourally inspired regulations in financial markets. These studies suggest that simplifying the decision-making process can be beneficial to consumers, as it reduces barriers to information processing. [46] Financial training and education is, it seems, less successful in overcoming psychological barriers to effective decision-making, such as procrastination, loss aversion and the status quo bias.[47] Individually tailored programmes are more effective than generic training schemes, and the most successful are those which give participants the opportunity to put decisions into practice and learn from the experience.[48]

IV. Coevolution of Legal and Financial Systems

The implications of viewing the state and its component parts, including the law, as a complex system, are as far reaching as they are in the case of the market. The state is now presented not as a sovereign power but as a semi-endogenous normative order, which to some degree reflects conditions in the economy. The state–market

[45] Juurikkala, n 42 above. [46] Lusardi, n 44 above.

[47] De Meza, D, Irlenbusch, B, and Reyniers, D, *Financial Capability: A Behavioural Economics Perspective* (2008).

[48] Lyons, A, 'Consideraciones clave para una evaluación eficaz de los programas de educación económica y financiera', paper presented at the 4th Simposio *La educación económica y financiera en México*, México DF: Museo Interactivo de Economía, 10 September 2010.

relation is one of mutually reinforcing behavioural equilibria, which 'coevolve' via a process of approximate mutual alignment. Legal rules are 'summary representations' of state of play among social actors and so the law is a 'cognitive resource' which stores and transmits the knowledge required for societal coordination.[49] This approach is consistent with the view, widely developed in legal and regulatory studies since the mid-1990s, that the state can influence behaviour in many ways other through than a 'command and control' approach to regulation.[50] Even where its role is residual or indirect, it remains an integral feature of the market, not an impediment to it. The issue for research in law and finance is how to model the feedback loops, which allow the legal system to both reflect and shape market behaviour.

Recognizing the domain-specific nature of legal rules is an essential first step to building such models. Laws may be understood as responding to and reflect agents' preferences and strategies, but the legal system is not just private ordering writ large. Legal systems endow social norms with a *public* and *systemic* character.[51] Legal rules are public in the sense of being publicly stated and recorded, and so, in principle, generally accessible and ascertainable; they are systemic in the sense of being linked to each other and to higher-level abstractions ('concepts' or 'principles') which serve as tools of interpretation.[52] Both these features serve to stabilize the meaning of legal rules and so enhance their functional value as mechanisms of coordination by comparison to social norms which, their customary character notwithstanding, operate at the level of private knowledge only.

The stability of legal rules does not imply the absence of mutability or variability; legal systems are capable of adaptation and hence of evolution in the context of a changing external environment.[53] At the same time, the 'closure' which the legal system achieves with regard to its environment ensures that the fit between legal rules and social practices is rarely exact,[54] and that the law, for the most part, lags behind changes in behaviour and in the content of social norms.[55] Thus, it is possible to view legal rules as *endogenous over the long run*, in the sense of adjusting over time to social practices, while accepting that they appear as *exogenous in the short run* to actors who have to take them as they are.[56] Courts are reactive in the sense that they can only advance the law on the basis of the cases that come before them. Legislatures can

[49] Aoki, M, *Corporations in Evolving Diversity* (2010) ch 4.

[50] See in particular Ayres, I and Braithwaite, J, *Responsive Regulation: Transcending the Deregulation Debate* (1992); Black, J, *Rules and Regulators* (1997).

[51] Deakin, S, Gindis, D, Hodgson, G, Huang, K, and Pistor, K, 'Legal Institutionalism: Capitalism and the Constitutive Role of Law' (2015) *Journal of Comparative Economics*, forthcoming.

[52] Luhmann, N, *Law as a Social System*, Ziegert, K (trans) and Kastner, F, Nobles, R, Schiff, D, and Ziegert, R (eds), (2004), in particular 148–9 and 340–6.

[53] Deakin, S, 'Evolution for our Time: A Theory of Legal Memetics' (2003) 55 *Current Legal Problems* 1.

[54] Luhmann, n 52 above, 476.

[55] Deakin, n 53 above.

[56] See Buchanan, J, Chai, D, and Deakin, S, *Hedge Fund Activism in Japan: The Limits of Shareholder Primacy* (2012) ch 2.

respond more immediately to perceived shortcomings in the content of rules and can address legal reform in a more systematic and detailed way than courts can. Mainly for this reason, even in legal systems with a common law origin, the vast majority of the rules of company law are not judge-made, but are statutory in form.[57]

In this context the possibility of public sanctions being imposed for the breach of legal rules is often is a double-edged sword; strict enforcement is not just expensive but may also be counterproductive in contexts where the legitimacy of legal rules is in question, giving rise to avoidance strategies.[58] The binding force of legal rules would seem to depend only partly on the likelihood of public sanctioning, and more on the extent of acceptance, across a given population of actors, of a meta-norm of respect for prescriptions of a public-legal character.[59] As a meta-norm of this kind is a function of the perceived legitimacy of laws in general, it is likely to be dependent in practice on the effectiveness of procedures for ensuring participation in and validation of the lawmaking process by those to whom the rules are addressed; in line with this view, empirical studies suggest that trust in public institutions and respect for legal norms is higher in democracies.[60] It would seem that participation in rulemaking and respect for the meta-norm of the rule of law together stabilize the conditions for societal coordination. However, the fit between legal evolution and societal change is not exact, and it is possible that the law responds to developments in the economy in certain periods and shapes it in others.

A growing body of historical research points to complex interactions between legal rules establishing property rights and other preconditions of economic exchange, on the one hand, and the emergence of modern financial markets, on the other. In the British industrial revolution of the eighteenth to the mid-nineteenth centuries, most manufacturing enterprises were legally constituted as 'unincorporated partnerships' with incomplete asset partitioning, and limited liability for shareholders was the exception. Entity shielding and protection for shareholders from liability for the firm's trading debts were achieved through other means. The trust form was used as a functional substitute for the separate corporate personality which was available for state-backed trading companies and utilities at this point, although this route involved high transaction costs and did not always secure investors against third-party claims.[61] The introduction of general access to incorporation coupled with limited liability through a series of legislative reforms in the 1840s and 1850s cannot have been essential to industrialization in Britain, since it was already substantially advanced by this point. Moreover, incorporation appears

[57] Deakin, S and Carvalho, F, 'System and Evolution in Corporate Governance' in Zumbansen, P and Calliess, G-P (eds), *Law, Economics and Evolutionary Theory* (2011).

[58] Ayres and Braithwaite, n 50 above.

[59] Deakin et al., n 51 above.

[60] Gintis, H, *The Bounds of Reason: Game Theory and the Unification of the Behavioural Sciences* (2009) 78–82.

[61] Harris, R, *Industrializing English Law: Entrepreneurship and Business Organization 1720–1844* (2000).

to have had a limited impact on firms' capital structures in the succeeding decades, suggesting the presence of path dependencies.[62] A relevant counter-example is that of the US state of California which adopted limited liability as late as the 1930s. There is evidence that California-incorporated firms had lower share turnover, made greater use of debt and had a higher return on equity (reflecting a risk premium for holding stock) than comparable firms in other US jurisdictions prior to this point. However, the absence of limited liability does not appear to have translated into lower profitability or growth on the part of Californian firms.[63]

Legal rules appear to have played a more than nominal or symbolic role in the emergence of financial markets, in particular by reducing transaction costs associated with corporate finance. However, there is not a one-to-one relation between legal forms and financial outcomes. The near universal adoption of the legal model of the company limited by share capital and the associated rise of markets for corporate securities of particular kinds may owe something to the crowding out of alternatives. Thus, it is not obvious, for example, that the progressive elimination, in a number of countries over the course of the last century, of exceptions to shareholders' limited liability in the case of banks and other financial firms, can be equated with the 'deselection' of inefficient rules.[64]

V. Testing the Legal Origin Hypothesis: Leximetrics and Time-Series Econometrics

The empirical study of law and finance has been revolutionized by methodological advances in the quantification of legal rules ('leximetrics'), which began in the mid-1990s.[65] However, the methods used are still in an early stage of development, and the implications of this line of work for policy are contested.

[62] Hickson, C and Turner, J, 'The Trading of Unlimited Liability Bank Shares in Nineteenth Century Ireland: The Bagehot Hypothesis' (2003) 63 *Journal of Economic History* 931; Acheson, G, Hickson, C, and Turner, J, 'Does Limited Liability Matter? Evidence from Nineteenth-century British Banking' (2010) 6 *Review of Law and Economics* 247.

[63] Bargeron, L and Lehn, K, Does Limited Liability Matter: An Analysis of California Firms, 1920–1940 (2012), available at SSRN: <http://ssrn.com/abstract=2105718>.

[64] Bruner, C, 'Conceptions of Corporate Purpose in Post-crisis Financial Firms' (2012) 36 *Seattle University Law Review* 527.

[65] Siems, M and Deakin, S, 'Comparative Law and Finance: Past, Present and Future Research' (2010) 166 *Journal of Institutional and Theoretical Economics* 120.

The impetus for the quantification of legal rules came from attempts to identify correlations between the legal environment for shareholders' and creditors' rights, on the one hand, and financial outcomes, on the other. The first results suggested that legal protection of investors and creditors did affect flows of equity finance and bank lending, respectively.[66] Coupled with the finding that common law (or English legal origin) systems placed greater weight on the protection of shareholder and creditor interests than countries with a civil law (French, German, or Scandinavian) base,[67] this led to the claim of a causal link running from legal origin (or the 'infrastructure' of legal systems) through the content of country-level legal rules to national financial structures.[68]

In econometric studies of the role of institutions in shaping economic behaviour and performance, a major problem is posed by the endogeneity of rules and policies to their context: correlation does not imply causation if it is just as likely that institutions are a response to economic conditions as an external force shaping outcomes. Legal origin theory offered a way round this problem, by identifying a variable—the common law or civil law origin of a country's legal system—which was, in all but a few cases, genuinely exogenous, in the sense of being unrelated to the industrial and financial structures of the country concerned. Leaving aside parent systems—those in which the infrastructure of lawmaking emerged alongside related social and economic structures—it is largely a matter of chance that a given country inherited its legal institutions from the common law or civil law tradition. Military conquest and colonization were the main drivers of legal origin, with few countries consciously choosing one legal approach over the other for reasons related to the course of indigenous social and economic development.[69] The legal origin variable initially appeared as an 'instrument' which was used to clarify the direction of causation from law to the economy,[70] but was later adopted as an exogenous variable in its own right,[71] around the time that researchers and policymakers alike were beginning to recognize the limits of globalization. The persistence of diverse national conditions could now be ascribed to institutional path dependencies which could, nevertheless, be overcome though reforms which generally took as their premise the superiority of common law modes of law and governance.

The legal origin approach has proved hugely influential on policymakers at global and national level and has engendered a large literature, much of it critical of the methods used in the first studies. These criticisms have led to

[66] La Porta, R, Lopez-de-Silanes, F, Shleifer, A, and Vishny, R, 'Law and Finance' (1998) 106 *Journal of Political Economy* 1113.

[67] ibid.

[68] La Porta, R, Lopez-de-Silanes, F, and Shleifer, A, 'The Economic Consequences of Legal Origins' (2008) 46 *Journal of Economic Literature* 285.

[69] Glaeser, E and Shleifer, R, 'Legal Origins' (2002) 117 *Quarterly Journal of Economics* 1193.

[70] La Porta et al., n 66 above.

[71] La Porta et al., n 68 above.

Table 1.1 Coding protocols for board independence and shareholder protection during takeover bids, CBR Shareholder Protection Index

Independent board members	Equals 1 if at least half of the board members must be independent; equals 0.5 if 25 per cent of them must be independent; equals 0 otherwise.
Mandatory bid	Equals 1 if there is a mandatory public bid for the entirety of shares in case of purchase of 30 per cent or one-third of the shares; equals 0.5 if the mandatory bid is triggered at a higher percentage (such as 40 or 50 per cent); further, it equals 0.5 if there is a mandatory bid but the bidder is only required to buy part of the shares; equals 0 if there is no mandatory bid at all.

Source: CBR Leximetric Database (<http://www.cbr.cam.ac.uk/>)

refinements of the methods used in data collection. Research has over time become more attuned to the difficulties involved in seeking to quantify legal and other institutional phenomena, and to the need for transparency in the coding process. 'Leximetric' data-coding entails a particular methodology which breaks down the process of index construction into a series of stages.[72] The first is the identification of a phenomenon of interest ('company law'), which can then be expressed as a conceptual construct ('protection' of the shareholder). The next stage is to express the construct in numerical terms, as an 'indicator' or 'variable', and then to use a coding algorithm or protocol which sets out a series of steps for assigning a value to the law or rule in question (see Table 1.1 for an example). Values are arrived at using a measurement scale (for example, 1–100 or 0–1). Once the law has been researched and initial values assigned, it is necessary to consider how far to apply differential weights to individual indicators or groups of indicators, and how far to aggregate or average scores to produce an overall index of legal change. The application of these methods has made it possible to construct historical datasets, tracking legal changes over periods of several decades.

The availability of data on legal systems in the form of multi-year time series poses new opportunities for research, but also additional methodological problems. It now becomes possible to test for the delayed or lagged effect of legal reforms, and to take into account the possibility of two-way causal flows between law and the economy, as the two systems 'coevolve'. Time series data, however, often display the property of 'non-stationarity', which indicates the persistent effect of exogenous

[72] Siems and Deakin, n 65 above.

shocks on relationships between variables. Non-stationarity, which is characteristic of both of historical financial data and of the longitudinal data generated by 'leximetric' coding of legal systems data, complicates the statistical analysis of time series, giving rise to the risk of false results through 'autocorrelation'. The problem of autocorrelation was identified in the 1920s[73] and solutions were first proposed in the 1980s,[74] but they have only slowly come to have a significant influence on research in finance and other sub-fields of economics.

Among the solutions to the problem of non-stationarity developed in the field of time series econometrics, cointegrated vector autoregression (CVAR) models are potentially relevant for the study of coevolutionary dynamics in the relation between the legal and financial systems.[75] These are models which build in the possibility of two-way causal flows and lagged (or delayed) effects in relationships between non-stationary variables. The CVAR regression model 'sees the world as a highly complex dynamic system, the properties of which must be inferred from data reflecting a single (nonreplicable) realisation of a multivariate, path-dependent process'.[76] Its design is intended to capture both short-run variations around an essentially stable equilibrium, and long-run deviations from the equilibrium path. It can, therefore, be used to test both for the immediate consequences, upon the economic system, of legal reforms aimed, for example, at stimulating financial development, and for long-run effects which may outlast an initial return to equilibrium as market actors adjust to a new legal environment. The CVAR implies the use of a 'post-Walrasian' approach to statistical analysis, to go with a non-ergodic, evolutionary conception of the economy and of the place of law within it.

As the legal origin field has developed and deepened in the light of these and other methodological refinements, some of the initial claims have been reassessed. It has become clear that the legal origin variable is a proxy for a complex and interrelated set of legal and institutional factors which cannot be adequately captured by the binary divide between the common law and civil law, even allowing for further subdivision within the civil law groups of systems. Arguments that common law modes of legal reasoning are inherently more 'market friendly' than civil law ones lack a clear theoretical foundation[77] as well as empirical support. The claim that common law institutions generate faster growth than civil law,

[73] Yule, GU, 'Why Do we Sometimes Get Nonsense Correlations between Time-series? A Study in Sampling and the Nature of Time-series' (1926) 89 *Journal of the Royal Statistical Society* 1.

[74] Engle, R and Granger, C, 'Cointegration and Error Correction: Representation, Estimation, and Testing' (1987) 55 *Econometrica* 251.

[75] Juselius, K, 'Time to Reject the Privileging of Economic Theory over Empirical Evidence? A Reply to Lawson' (2011) 35 *Cambridge Journal of Economics* 423.

[76] Hoover, K, Johansen, S, and Juselius, K, 'Allowing the Data to Speak Freely: The Macroeconometrics of the Cointegrated Vector Autoregression' (2008) 98 *American Economic Review* 251, 253.

[77] Ahlering, B and Deakin, S, 'Labor Regulation, Corporate Governance, and Legal Origin: A Case of Institutional Complementarity?' (2007) 41 *Law & Society Review* 865.

had to be abandoned in the light of analyses incorporating a wider range of control variables.[78]

Some of the other stylized facts associated with the legal origin claim have stood up better to later analyses. For example, the claim that common law systems are generally more shareholder-friendly than civil law ones, at least in the sense of protecting minority shareholders against predation or opportunism by management,[79] is supported by longitudinal data on legal change.[80] However, the same studies cast doubt on the idea that legal origin is a significant impediment to convergence, at least as far as the formal law is concerned, as they show civil law systems 'catching up' with common law ones over the course of the 1990s and 2000s. Among the more significant changes here were the widespread adoption of takeover regulations modelled on the UK's Takeover Code and of corporate governance standards requiring (or at least strongly encouraging) independent boards. Pro-shareholder corporate law reform has been shown to be a near-global phenomenon, with developing countries and emerging markets among those experiencing the most rapid adjustment of their corporate governance systems (see Figures 1.1 and 1.2).

Econometric analysis using the CVAR approach has explored the wider economic effects of these changes. First results suggest that the adoption of pro-shareholder laws and corporate governance standards has had a discernible impact on financial development at country level, as measured by the extent of stock market capitalization as a proportion of national GDP, numbers of listed companies, and volumes of shares traded. This effect is not, however, uniform across different countries. It is more marked in common law systems than in those of the civil law, and affects developing countries and emerging markets to a greater extent than already developed ones.[81] A number of effects appear to be present in this finding. First, the results appear to show that laws for shareholder protection originating in common law systems, in particular Britain and the US, will have an impact on the economies of other common law systems, but equally that they will not bed down as effectively in civil law countries with different legal cultures and institutions. Second, it appears that legal reforms can be used to stimulate financial development in emerging markets and transition countries whose capital markets are at an early stage of their evolution, but will have less of an effect on financial markets in already industrialized countries.[82]

[78] La Porta et al., n 68 above. [79] La Porta et al., n 66 above.

[80] Armour, J, Deakin, S, Sarkar, P, Siems, M, and Singh, A, 'Shareholder Protection and Stock Market Development: An Empirical Test of the Legal Origins Hypothesis' (2009) 6 *Journal of Empirical Legal Studies* 343; Deakin, S, Sarkar, P, and Singh, A, 'An End to Consensus? The Selective Impact of Corporate Law Reform on Financial Development' in Aoki, M, Binmore, K, Deakin, S, and Gintis, H. (eds), *Complexity and Institutions: Markets, Norms and Corporations* (2012).

[81] Deakin et al., n 80 above.

[82] ibid.

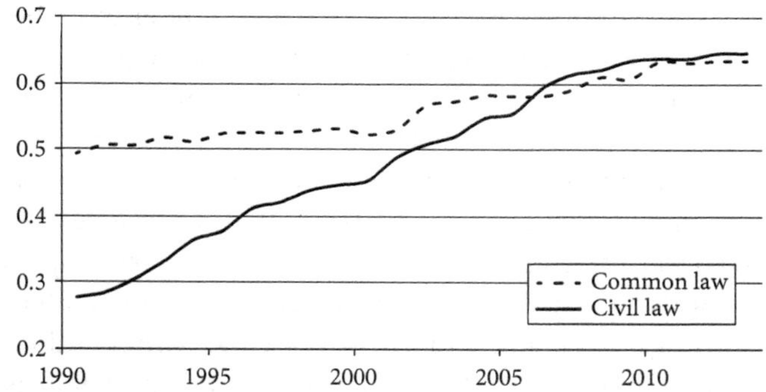

Figure 1.1 Shareholder protection in 30 countries, 1990–2014, comparing common law and civil law origin countries

Note: The countries in the data set are Argentina, Austria, Belgium, Brazil, Canada, Chile, China, the Czech Republic, Cyprus, Estonia, France, Germany, India, Italy, Japan, Latvia, Lithuania, Malaysia, Mexico, the Netherlands, Pakistan, Poland, Russia, Slovenia, Sweden, South Africa, Spain, Switzerland, Turkey, the UK, and the USA

Source: CBR Leximetric Database (<http://www.cbr.cam.ac.uk/>)

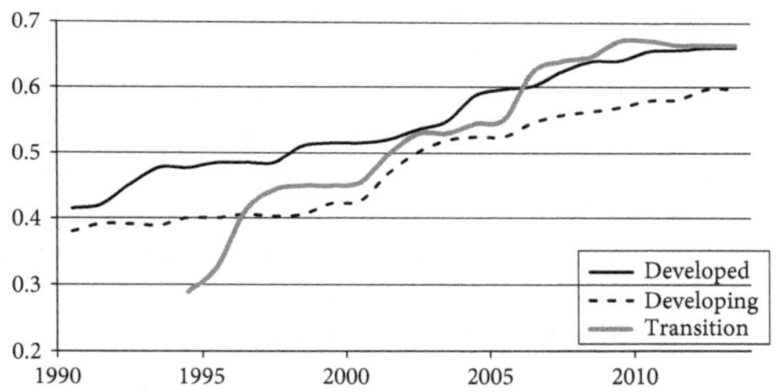

Figure 1.2 Shareholder protection in 30 countries, 1990–2014, comparing developed, developing, and transition countries

Source: CBR Leximetric Database (<http://www.cbr.cam.ac.uk/>)

VI. Financial Crises and the Policy Cycle

Behavioural economics has highlighted the importance of learning from past mistakes in the emergence of heuristics which aid contracting in complex environments. In the field of financial policy, however, there is evidence that the lessons of the past can easily be forgotten. Financial policy moves in cycles, as institutional solutions developed in times of crisis are eroded away under more benign market conditions, before a new crisis is triggered and the cycle begins again. This is the implication of Hyman Minsky's theory of financial instability and, it would seem, of the 2008 crisis, which Minsky predicted.[83]

Minsky offers an evolutionary account of firms' reliance on external finance for growth. In a first phase, characterized by what Minsky termed 'hedge finance', firms are able to cover both principal and interest on loans from operating profits. In the second phase, 'speculative finance', firms are able to meet interest payments from retained earnings, but cannot repay the principal without taking on further debt. In the third and final phase, 'Ponzi finance', operating revenue is insufficient to meet both principal and interest, and firms take on debt simply to cover interest payments as they fall due. The greater the extent of 'speculative' and 'Ponzi' finance in a given economy, the more unstable it is, because of the exposure of firms to movements in interest rates.[84]

Minsky critically argued that financial instability was endogenously generated, by virtue of the relationship between short-term and long-term interest rates, on the one hand, and firm behaviour, on the other. In the 'hedge' phase of the cycle, short-term interest rates are lower than long-term ones, encouraging firms to use short-term debt to finance longer-term investments. The differential between short-term and long-term interest rates triggers an investment boom, which drives up the price of assets and encourages further speculation on the part of both lenders and borrowers. The effect of such a 'bubble' is to increase not just prices but also short-term interest rates, putting firms under pressure to borrow in order to pay down their debts. As the extent of 'Ponzi' finance grows, the pressures on firms intensify, to the point where they have to start liquidating assets in order to survive. Asset sales lead to a drop in prices and a period of deflation and reduced growth during which debt is gradually 'purged' and the cycle begins again.[85]

Policy is also endogenous to the financial cycle. In response to a crisis, policymakers curtail the powers of banks and other lenders in order to minimize the possibility of speculative lending. Financial institutions are a source of instability in the economy since they are in a position to profit from speculative lending although, in common with the firms they lend to, they are also at risk once the financial market reaches the 'Ponzi' stage of the cycle. Governmental bodies, including central banks, which act as lenders of last resort to private banks, have an incentive to restrict lending, and may use various regulatory devices to that end, such as the imposition of quotas and controls, or the separation of retail and investment banking functions. Once stability is restored, however, regulators come under pressure to remove these constraints, which, under benign conditions,

[83] Minsky, H, *Stabilising an Unstable Economy* (2008) (originally published in 1986).

[84] ibid, 230–3. [85] ibid, 239.

are seen as having outlived their purpose.[86] This is also the point in the cycle at which theories of self-regulation and spontaneous order in markets tend to enjoy a renewed credibility.

Writing in the 1980s when the process of dismantling the framework of financial market regulation put in place in the New Deal era was well underway, Minsky was critical of the application to banks and financial market institutions of the logic of shareholder value.[87] Aligning the interests of financial executives with shareholders would, he argued, exacerbate the tendency towards instability, since pressure from investors for higher returns would encourage banks to take on debt themselves in order to finance asset purchases and to support takeover activity. Minsky could not have anticipated the historically unprecedented levels of leverage which became normal for private sector banks in the years and months leading up to the 'credit crunch' which began in August 2007, but he would not have been surprised by the use of special purpose vehicles and 'repo' transactions to flatter bank earnings in the case of financial firms whose strategies centred on the goal of share price maximization in this period.

In the wake of the 2008 crisis, a number of studies reported correlations between the vulnerability of British and US banks and other financial sector firms, and the degree to which they had put in place pro-shareholder governance mechanisms, such as independent boards and stock options for senior managers.[88] In Britain, the financial institutions most exposed to the risk of failure during the crisis were either former mutuals or banks themselves formed from hostile takeovers.[89] High leverage and 'Ponzi' lending (in Minsky's sense) were the immediate causes of the failure of these institutions, which were saved from insolvency only by direct financial support from government.

Minsky's theory predicts endogenous instability and periodic crises in the financial market, which can be contained by regulatory means, but only temporarily. We currently lack a good account of how, if at all, the cycle of instability can be broken, and a more enduring form of financial stability established. One lesson to take from Minsky, however, is to be sceptical of theories which see spontaneous order as a natural property of markets, since these ideas operate as a constraint on the development of effective policy responses to financial market instability.

[86] ibid, 280. [87] ibid, 266.

[88] See Beltratti, A and Stulz, R, Why Did Some Banks Perform Better during the Credit Crisis? A Cross-country Study of the Impact of Governance and Regulation, Fisher College of Business Working Paper No 2009-03-012; Erkens, D, Hung, M, and Matos, P, Corporate Governance in the 2007–8 Financial Crisis: Evidence from Financial Institutions Worldwide, ECGI Finance Working Paper No 249/2009; Fahlenbrach, R and Stulz, R, Bank CEO Incentives and the Credit Crisis, ECGI Finance Working Paper No 256/2009; Mülbert, P, Corporate Governance of Banks after the Financial Crisis—Theory, Evidence, Reforms, ECGI Law Working Paper No 130/2009; Ferreira, D, Kershaw, D, Kirchmaier, T, and Schuster, EP, Shareholder Empowerment and Bank Bailouts, ECGI Finance Working Paper No 345/2013.

[89] Financial Services Authority Board, *The Failure of the Royal Bank of Scotland* (2011).

VII. Conclusion

The roots of the financial crisis of 2008 lie at least partly in theories which shaped practices and influenced policy in preceding decades. Principal among these was the idea that self-organizing financial markets were efficient in the sense of aligning prices with the underlying values of securities. During the course of the twentieth century, economic theory developed increasingly sophisticated mathematical models of market structure, which described the competitive economy as a series of interlocking equilibria. The Efficient Capital Market Hypothesis emerged from this wider research project. At its core was the idea that securities prices reflected all available information, and hence operated as an efficient signal to market actors. The ECMH did not necessarily predict stability: in a turbulent trading environment, prices would accurately reflect any volatility in the wider economy. But this important qualification was mostly put to one side by policymakers who saw in the ECMH a validation of the idea of the self-regulating market. Nor was this an illegitimate inference to draw from a body of work which maintained that, if there were inefficiencies in the allocation of capital, this was not the responsibility of market mechanisms, which could be expected to operate efficiently with limited intervention from government or regulation.

The events of autumn 2008 do not in themselves invalidate the ECMH, which can be read as predicting market volatility in response to adverse conditions in the wider economy. But since this is tantamount to saying that whatever result the market achieves must, by definition, be efficient, it effectively renders the ECMH non-falsifiable. Perhaps all along the ECMH has been an article of faith more than anything else, but if this is so, it is not surprising that the search is on for alternative ways of thinking about financial markets.

In this Chapter a number of theories have been examined which have in common an 'evolutionary' perspective, according to which the components of the economy are modelled as systems which interact with and adapt to their external environment. Evolutionary models of market structure treat prices as strategic variables which emerge on the basis of learning and experience acquired by agents engaging in decentralized exchange. In uncertain choice environment, human agency is shaped by heuristics which aid coordination, and institutions which encode the results of social learning. The law is one such institution, which operates as a cognitive resource to stabilize expectations and align actors' strategies. The idea that the law and the market are both adaptive systems, which coevolve or adjust to each other's equilibrium path, suggests that they are interrelated at a deep level, but it also points to limits to regulatory strategies based on a 'command and control' approach: there are limits to how far law can be used in an instrumental way to reshape market outcomes.

Thinking about financial markets in systemic terms does not, then, translate into an argument for more regulation over less. However, the idea that systemic and behavioural insights favour a 'light touch' approach to regulation does not help to advance the debate in a post-crisis context. The behavioural literature is diverse. Parts of it can be read as supporting sophisticated regulatory interventions based on the idea of 'nudging' market actors to more efficient outcomes. Nudge theory wants to have the best of both worlds: transactions are shaped by actors' decisions, but inefficient outcomes are avoided through alterations to the 'architecture' of choice. For the results of market exchange to be precisely calibrated in this way requires more information than regulators can be expected to have. It is more plausible to see a role for the legal system in supporting the evolved heuristics which actors use to overcome uncertainty in complex environments. The legal system can do this in various ways which may involve support for self-regulation in certain contexts and applying public sanctions in others. Case-by-case analysis of the role of legal regulation in specific market contexts may be more productive than a one-size-fits-all approach. As an adaptive system in its own right, the law is in a position to adjust to economic perturbations, and to embed the results of policy learning in enduring institutions.

The debate over the appropriate form of financial market regulation will not be settled any time soon. However, we would be making progress if we moved beyond the efficient market hypothesis, in favour of an explicitly evolutionary conception of the law–finance relation. In the not-too-distant future, we can expect the field of law and finance to look very different.

Bibliography

Acheson, G, Hickson, C, and Turner, J, 'Does Limited Liability Matter? Evidence from Nineteenth-century British Banking' (2010) 6 *Review of Law and Economics* 247.

Ahlering, B and Deakin, S, 'Labor Regulation, Corporate Governance, and Legal Origin: A Case of Institutional Complementarity?' (2007) 41 *Law & Society Review* 865.

Altmann, M, 'Implications of Behavioural Economics for Financial Literacy and Public Policy' (2005) 41 *Journal of Socio-Economics* 677.

Aoki, M, *Corporations in Evolving Diversity* (2010).

Armour, J, Deakin, S, Sarkar, P, Siems, M, and Singh, A, 'Shareholder Protection and Stock Market Development: An Empirical Test of the Legal Origins Hypothesis' (2009) 6 *Journal of Empirical Legal Studies* 343.

Ayres, I and Braithwaite, J, *Responsive Regulation: Transcending the Deregulation Debate* (1992).

Bachelier, L, *Théorie de la speculation* (1900).

Ball, R, 'The Global Financial Crisis and the Efficient Capital Market Hypothesis: What Have we Learned?' (2009) 16 *Journal of Applied Corporate Finance* 8.

Bargeron, L and Lehn, K, Does Limited Liability Matter: An Analysis of California Firms, 1920–1940 (2012), available at SSRN: <http://ssrn.com/abstract=2105718>.

Beltratti, A and Stulz, R, Why Did Some Banks Perform Better during the Credit Crisis? A Cross-country Study of the Impact of Governance and Regulation, Fisher College of Business Working Paper No 2009-03-012.

Black, J, *Rules and Regulators* (1997).

Bruner, C, 'Conceptions of Corporate Purpose in Post-crisis Financial Firms' (2012) 36 *Seattle University Law Review* 527.

Buchanan, J, Chai, D, and Deakin, S, *Hedge Fund Activism in Japan: The Limits of Shareholder Primacy* (2012).

Coase, RH, *The Firm, the Market and the Law* (1988).

De Meza, D, Irlenbusch, B, and Reyniers, D, *Financial Capability: A Behavioural Economics Perspective* (2008).

Deakin, S, 'Evolution for our Time: A Theory of Legal Memetics' (2003) 55 *Current Legal Problems* 1.

Deakin, S and Carvalho, F, 'System and Evolution in Corporate Governance' in Zumbansen, P and Calliess, G-P (eds), *Law, Economics and Evolutionary Theory* (2011).

Deakin, S, Sarkar, P, and Singh, A, 'An End to Consensus? The Selective Impact of Corporate Law Reform on Financial Development' in Aoki, M, Binmore, K, Deakin, S, and Gintis, H (eds), *Complexity and Institutions: Markets, Norms and Corporations* (2012).

Engle, R and Granger, C, 'Cointegration and Error Correction: Representation, Estimation, and Testing' (1987) 55 *Econometrica* 251.

Erkens, D, Hung, M, and Matos, P, Corporate Governance in the 2007–8 Financial Crisis: Evidence from Financial Institutions Worldwide, ECGI Finance Working Paper No 249/2009.

Fahlenbrach, R and Stulz, R, Bank CEO Incentives and the Credit Crisis, ECGI Finance Working Paper No 256/2009.

Fama, E, 'The Behaviour of Stock Market Prices' (1965) 38 *Journal of Business* 34.

Fama, E, 'Efficient Capital Markets: A Review of Theory and Empirical Work' (1970) 25 *Journal of Finance* 383.

Ferreira, D, Kershaw, D, Kirchmaier, T, and Schuster, EP, Shareholder empowerment and bank bailouts, ECGI Finance Working Paper No 345/2013.

Financial Services Authority Board, *The Failure of the Royal Bank of Scotland* (2011).

Fisher, F, *Disequilibrium Foundations of Equilibrium Economics* (1983).

Galbraith, JK, *The Affluent Society* (1998).

Gilson, R and Kraakman, R, Market Efficiency after the Financial Crisis: It's Still a Matter of Information Costs (2014), Stanford Law and Economics Olin Working Paper No 458; European Corporate Governance Institute (ECGI) Law Working Paper No 242/2014; Columbia Law and Economics Working Paper No 470, available at SSRN: <http://ssrn.com/abstract=2396608> or <http://dx.doi.org/10.2139/ssrn.2396608>.

Gilson, R and Kraakman, R, 'The Mechanisms of Market Efficiency' (1984) 70 *Virginia Law Review* 549.

Gintis, H, *The Bounds of Reason: Game Theory and the Unification of the Behavioural Sciences* (2009).

Gintis, H, 'The Dynamics of Pure Market Exchange' in Aoki, M, Binmore, K, Deakin, S, and Gintis, H (eds), *Complexity and Institutions: Markets, Norms and Corporations* (2012).

Gintis, H, 'Markov Processes and Social Exchange: Theory and Applications' (2013) 4 *ACM Transactions on Intelligent Systems and Technology* Article 53, 19 pages, DOI: <http://dx.doi.org/101145/2483669.2483686>.

Glaeser, E and Shleifer, R, 'Legal Origins' (2002) 117 *Quarterly Journal of Economics* 1193.

Harris, R, *Industrializing English Law: Entrepreneurship and Business Organization 1720–1844* (2000).

Hickson, C and Turner, J, 'The Trading of Unlimited Liability Bank Shares in Nineteenth Century Ireland: The Bagehot Hypothesis' (2003) 63 *Journal of Economic History* 931.

Hoover, K, Johansen, S, and Juselius, K, 'Allowing the Data to Speak Freely: The Macroeconometrics of the Cointegrated Vector Autoregression' (2008) 98 *American Economic Review* 251.

Juselius, K, 'Time to Reject the Privileging of Economic Theory over Empirical Evidence? A Reply to Lawson' (2011) 35 *Cambridge Journal of Economics* 423.

Juurikkala, O, 'Behavioural Paradox: Why Investor Irrationality Calls for Lighter and Simpler Financial Regulation' (2012) 18 *Fordham Journal of Corporate and Financial Law* 33.

Kahneman, D, *Thinking, Fast and Slow* (2011).

Kahneman, D and Tversky, A (eds), *Choices, Values and Frames* (2000).

Kirman, A, Foellmer, H, and Horst, U, 'Equilibrium in Financial Markets with Heterogeneous Agents: A New Perspective' (2005) 41 *Journal of Mathematical Economics* 123.

La Porta, R, Lopez-de-Silanes, F, and Shleifer, A, 'The Economic Consequences of Legal Origins' (2008) 46 *Journal of Economic Literature* 285.

La Porta, R, Lopez-de-Silanes, F, Shleifer, A, and Vishny, R, 'Law and Finance' (1998) 106 *Journal of Political Economy* 1113.

Luhmann, N, *Law as a Social System*, Ziegert, K (trans) and Kastner, F, Nobles, R, Schiff, D, and Ziegert, R (eds), (2004).

Lusardi, A, Financial Literacy: An Essential Tool for Informed Consumer Choice? (2008) National Bureau of Economic Research Working Paper No 14084.

Malkiel, B, 'The Efficient Market Hypothesis and Its Critics' (2003) 17 *Journal of Economic Perspectives* 59.

Malkiel, B, 'Reflections on the Efficient Market Hypothesis: 30 Years Later' (2005) 40 *Financial Review* 1.

Mandelbrot, B, 'Forecasts of Future Prices, Unbiased Markets and Martingale Models' (1966) 39 *Journal of Business* 242.

Minsky, H, *Stabilising an Unstable Economy* (2008).

Mülbert, P, Corporate Governance of Banks after the Financial Crisis—Theory, Evidence, Reforms, ECGI Law Working Paper No 130/2009.

Oliver, A, 'From Nudging to Budging: Using Behavioural Economics to Inform Public Sector Policy' (2013) 42 *Journal of Social Policy* 685.

Osborne, MFM, 'Brownian Motion in the Stock Market' (1959) 7 *Operations Research* 145.

Peters, O, 'Optimal Leverage from Non-ergodicity' (2011) 11 *Quantitative Finance* 1593.

Pistor, P, 'A Legal Theory of Finance' (2013) 41 *Journal of Comparative Economics* 315.

Raines, J and Leathers, C, 'Behavioural Finance and Post-Keynesian Institutionalist Theories of Financial Markets' (2011) 33 *Journal of Post-Keynesian Economics* 535.

Richerson, P, Boyd, R, and Henrich, J, 'Gene-culture Coevolution in the Age of Genomics' (2010) 107 *Proceedings of the National Academy of Sciences (USA)* 8985.

Shiller, R, *Finance and the Good Society* (2012).

Shiller, R, *Irrational Exuberance* (2000).

Siems, M and Deakin, S, 'Comparative Law and Finance: Past, Present and Future Research' (2010) 166 *Journal of Institutional and Theoretical Economics* 120.

Simon, H, 'A Behavioural Model of Rational Choice' (1955) 69 *Quarterly Journal of Economics* 99.

Simon, H, 'Rationality as Process and as Product of Thought' (1978) 68 *American Economic Review* 1.

Stigler, G 'The Process and Progress of Economics' (1983) 91 *Journal of Political Economy* 529.

Sunstein, C and Thaler, R, *Nudge: Improving Decisions about Health, Wealth, and Happiness* (2008).

Tooby, J and Cosmides, L, 'Evolutionary Psychology: Conceptual Foundations' in Buss, D (ed.), *Evolutionary Psychology Handbook* (2005).

Walras, L, *Elements of Pure Economics* (1954).

Yule, GU, 'Why Do we Sometimes Get Nonsense Correlations between Time-series? A Study in Sampling and the Nature of Time-series' (1926) 89 *Journal of the Royal Statistical Society* 1.

CHAPTER 2

ECONOMIC DEVELOPMENT, FINANCIAL SYSTEMS, AND THE LAW

COLIN MAYER

I. Introduction

WHAT are the preconditions for the development of financial systems? The traditional answer given is that the creation of banking systems and equity markets is critical to financial development and the way of achieving these is through detailed regulation of banks and strong protection of minority investors. This Chapter* will argue that virtually every element of that traditional view is wrong—the key components of a financial system are not those which have been suggested to date and the way of achieving them is very different from the conventional prescription.

There is now a considerable body of evidence of a relationship between financial development and economic growth. Several studies report a relation between the size of financial systems at the start of a period and subsequent economic growth. Controlling for other considerations, financial development appears to contribute to growth. A variety of measures of financial development are relevant—the volume of monetary assets, the size of banking systems, and the size of stock markets, to name a few.[1]

To the extent that it is possible to establish the channel by which financial development contributes to growth, it appears to be through the external financing of firms. Comparing the growth of different industries across countries or companies suggests that there is an interrelationship between their growth rates, the degree to which they are dependent on external finance and the development of financial systems in which they are operating.[2] In other words, financial development confers particular advantages on industries and companies that are especially dependent on external finance.

These results are consistent with the view that a primary function of financial institutions is to improve allocation of funds within an economy. Institutions that direct financing to activities that are most dependent on external finance assist corporate, industrial, and economic growth. The studies therefore provide empirical confirmation at an aggregate or industry level for the theoretical underpinning of financial institutions.

The question that these studies leave unanswered is which institutions are particularly well suited to performing these functions. Do all institutions serve

* I am very grateful to Eilís Ferran for very helpful comments on a previous draft of the Chapter. Section II of the Chapter is based on papers published with Julian Franks, Hideaki Miyajima, Stefano Rossi, and Hannes Wagner. Section III draws on papers written with Xavier Freixas and Jeffrey Gordon. Section IV draws on papers written with Michael Klein and Ignacio Mas.

[1] See, eg, Levine, R, 'Financial Development and Economic Growth: View and Agenda' (1997) 35 *Journal of Economic Literature*; Levine, R, 'Finance and Growth: Theory and Evidence' in Aghion, P and Durlauf, S (eds), *Handbook of Economic Growth* (2005).

[2] Rajan, R and Zingales, L, 'Financial Dependence and Growth' (1998) 88 *American Economic Review*.

companies equally or are some institutions especially well adapted to the financing of particular; for example, high-tech industries?

A second set of issues concerns the policies that can be used to influence the development of institutions. Over the last few years a literature has emerged emphasizing the important role which legal and regulatory structures and, in particular, protection of investors play in promoting institutional development. This literature has suggested that protection of investors is a crucial determinant. Since the development of financial systems is, in turn, related to the external financing of firms, this points to a key role for investor protection in promoting the external financing and growth of firms. The policy message that emerges from these studies is clear: improve investor protection, in particular minority investor protection, and financial development, investment, and growth will follow.

Recent evidence from examining the evolution of financial systems and corporate sectors over long periods of time has cast serious doubt on this view. Studies of the evolution of financial markets in Germany, Japan, and the UK over the last century point to the importance of equity finance in the early evolution of capital markets. However, they suggest a limited role for formal systems of regulation in its development and, instead, emphasize the significance of informal relations of trust in promoting the participation of outside investors in corporate equity. The experience of Japan described below should be a particularly salutary reminder not only of the possible limited relevance of investor protection to equity market development, but also of its potential unintended and perverse consequences.

While regulation may only have a limited role to play in the development of equity markets, it is critical to the protection of banks. The financial crisis has been the single greatest economic shock of the twenty-first century to date. What has traditionally been regarded as a conservative, safe sector of the economy has brought several economies to their knees and inflicted serious wounds on others. This has raised questions about the role of bankers, credit rating agencies, and regulators, among others, in the failure.

The traditional focus of bank regulation has been on their detailed governance, conduct, and competence: what might be termed the micro-regulation of individual banks. Evidence of performance of banks during the financial crisis casts doubt on this approach and suggests that far from enhancing the safety of banks it might actually have been associated with greater risk-taking. Recently, there has been greater emphasis placed on macro-prudential regulation and, in particular, on the imposition of tougher capital and liquidity requirements to protect the financial system as a whole. This includes the provision of public insurance to investors in failing institutions, especially in the form of deposit insurance, and the restructuring and rescuing of failing institutions.

This Chapter suggests that the macro-prudential approach to regulation is appropriate in a way in which micro-regulation through corporate governance and conduct of business rules may not be. But it goes on to argue that this provision of macro-prudential regulation should be thought of in the context of a partnership between the state and the banking system in which the state provides banks with protection against systemic risks in exchange for the banking sector performing certain essential economic and public functions. In essence, it is this public function that justifies state provision of systemic insurance to these institutions in a form not available elsewhere.

All of this presumes that the starting assumption that equity markets and banks are critical to economic development is correct. The Chapter will conclude by suggesting that even this assertion is open to question. The first illustration of this is mobile money in which the role of banks in a country's payment system is bypassed. It suggests that banks may not be as central to the provision of payments as they are sometimes thought to be and that regulation, which presumes that they are, might deter innovation of potentially superior forms. The second example is the emergence of China and Korea as major economic powers over the past 50 years. Both of these economies have developed their corporate sectors on the basis of equity markets that are very different from traditional dispersed-ownership systems and they raise questions about the types of finance that are most conducive to economic development.

The Chapter begins in Section II by exploring the role of formal and informal relations in the development of financial systems. It looks back at the long-run evolution of capital markets in Germany, Japan, and the UK during the twentieth century and describes the role of informal institutional arrangements that promoted trust between investors and firms. It contrasts ownership and control across countries and considers the influence of law and regulation on these differences. It argues that informal relations of trust are at least as important in financial development as more formal legal and regulatory arrangements.

The second part of the Chapter in Section III turns from equity institutions to banks. It considers policy responses to the recent financial crisis and the switch that occurred from the micro-regulation of individual institutions to macro-prudential regulation of the banking system as a whole. It argues that in return for providing this systemic risk protection, there should be corresponding obligations on banks to deliver the public and social functions that justify the provision of insurance.

Finally, the last part of the Chapter in Section IV returns to the underlying question of what type of financial institution is necessary for economic development. It questions many of the familiar answers by discussing, first, the explosion of mobile money as a payments mechanism in several developing economies and, second, the emergence of China and Korea as major economic powers and current proposals for reform in these two countries.

II. Equity Markets

In an influential set of articles, La Porta, Lopez-de-Silanes, Shleifer, and Vishny[3] argued that the successful development of financial systems in different countries depends on legal origins and regulation to protect investors. The argument ran as follows. Where the law provides strong protection then minorities can invest with confidence. Where the law offers little protection then investors do not invest or seek protection through other means; for example, by taking large stakes in companies. The structure of financial systems is, therefore, a product of the legal systems within which they operate.

La Porta et al.'s analysis begins by classifying legal systems into four different 'origins': Anglo-Saxon, French, German, and Scandinavian. By and large, countries of Anglo-Saxon legal origin tend to give external investors the best protection, while countries of French legal origin give them the worst; countries of German or Scandinavian legal origin are somewhere in-between. La Porta et al. go on to demonstrate that financial systems are better developed in countries of Anglo-Saxon legal origin than in those of, in particular, French legal origin. The message that emerges from these articles is clear. Strong minority-investor protection is a prerequisite for the successful development of financial systems. Combined with the observation that financial development is associated with subsequent economic growth, the policy prescription is even more powerful. Countries should strengthen minority-investor protection to promote economic growth.

Using several different measures, Beck et al.[4] report that financial development is further advanced in common-law than French civil-law systems. Controlling for differences in government and environmental endowments, they find that legal traditions remain an important explanation of cross-country differences in financial development. The difference in financial development between common-law and French civil-law countries is more pronounced than that between common-law and German civil-law countries. This is consistent with the view that it is the adaptability of, rather than the static differences in, legal systems that influences financial development.

In an attempt to provide a clearer analysis of the role of investor protection in financial development, attention has recently turned to longer-run historical

[3] La Porta, R, Lopez-de-Silanes, F, Shleifer, A, and Vishny, R, 'Legal Determinants of External Finance' (1997) 52 *Journal of Finance*; 'Law and Finance' (1998) 106 *Journal of Political Economy*; 'The Quality of Government' (1999) 15 *Journal of Law, Economics, and Organization*; 'Investor Protection and Corporate Governance' (2000) 58 *Journal of Financial Economics*.

[4] Beck, T, Demirgüç-Kunt, A, and Levine, R, 'Legal Theories of Financial Development' (2001) 17 *Oxford Review of Economic Policy*.

analyses of the emergence of financial systems in different countries and these shed a very different light on the relation between regulation and financial development.

1. The UK

By some criteria, the UK[5] had even more flourishing stock markets at the start of the century than at the end. It certainly had more of them. In the first half of the century from 1900 to 1950, not only was there a flourishing London Stock Exchange but there were also more than 19 provincial exchanges, which specialized in particular industries. For example, the Birmingham exchange was important for cycle and rubber tube stocks; Sheffield for iron, coal, and steel; and Bradford for wool. Thomas[6] describes how 'the number of commercial and industrial companies quoted in the Manchester stock exchange list increased from 70 in 1885 to nearly 220 in 1906. Most of these were small companies with capitals ranging from £50,000 to £200,000' and 'by the mid 1880s Sheffield, along with Oldham, was one of the two most important centres of joint stock in the country, with 44 companies, with a paid up capital of £12 million'.[7]

One of the features of stock markets around the world today is the modest amount of finance that in aggregate they raise for their corporate sectors, even in countries with large stock markets such as the UK and the US. However, stock markets are important sources of finance for two purposes: first, for financing small, rapidly expanding firms and, second, for funding acquisitions by large firms. Equity issues for internal investment are commonplace in recently listed companies and by larger firms taking over others. To establish the financing patterns of companies early in the twentieth century, Franks, Mayer, and Rossi[8] collected data on companies that were incorporated in Britain at the start of the twentieth century and are still in existence today. They looked at how much equity they issued and in what form. The answer was that much was issued in the form of ordinary equity and some as preference shares that receive dividends ahead of ordinary shareholders. Even at the beginning of the twentieth century, there was no evidence of the feature of many countries today, namely the issue of more than one class of ordinary shares (dual class shares) but firms did issue a great deal of ordinary shares.

Strikingly, the main purpose to which equity issues were put at the beginning of the twentieth century is the same as it is today—acquisitions. Firms grew rapidly through acquiring others and issued equity to do this. So, acquisitions have been an important component of the growth of UK firms for more than a century and the existence of a large and vibrant stock market has contributed to this.

[5] This section is based on Franks, J, Mayer, C, and Rossi, S, 'Ownership: Evolution and Regulation' (2009) 22, *Review of Financial Studies*.

[6] Thomas, W, *The Provincial Stock Exchanges* (1973).

[7] Ibid, 133 and 124.

[8] Franks et al., n 5 above.

What about ownership? When did this become dispersed? Franks, Mayer, and Rossi[9] took the companies incorporated at the start of the twentieth century and examined the rate at which their ownership became dispersed, in the sense that the minimum number of shareholders required to control a certain percentage (for example, 25 per cent) of their equity increased. What they found was striking. The rate at which ownership of firms at the beginning of the twentieth century became dispersed was rapid and very similar to that in the second half of the century. The main reason for the rapid dispersion was not so much that directors and founding families sold their initial shareholdings but that their shares were diluted through takeovers. What happened and continued to happen throughout the twentieth century was that firms issued shares to acquire others and in the process they diluted the shareholding of their directors and founders. For example, if a family initially owned all 1 million shares in a company and issued another 1 million to purchase another firm, then the family's shareholding declined from 100 per cent to 50 per cent. So the dispersed ownership of the UK is not a recent phenomenon. It set in early in the twentieth century and persisted throughout, and it has consistently been associated with rapid growth through acquisitions. There is no evidence of the UK stock market having undergone a fundamental shift during the twentieth century.

The stability of the UK financial system during the twentieth century stands in marked contrast to its regulation. At the beginning of the century, investor protection in the UK was weak and UK stock markets were largely unregulated. According to an index of anti-director rights, compiled by La Porta et al.,[10] the UK scored very low—one out of a possible six—about the same score as Germany in 1990. In contrast to the view that common law is associated with strong investor protection, the common law in England contributed directly to the lack of protection of minorities. In a famous case in 1843—*Foss v Harbottle*—a shareholder sued directors of a company for misuse of company funds.[11] The court found in favour of the directors because their actions had been approved by a majority of shareholders. The dominance of the strict majority was enshrined in English law and remained so for 100 years until landmark legislation was passed in 1948 requiring substantially increased disclosure from listed companies and empowering 10 per cent or more of shareholders to call extraordinary meetings if dissatisfied with directors' actions. These provisions marked a step change in La Porta et al.'s measure of shareholder rights raising it from one at the beginning of the century to three in 1948. With the passage of legislation in 1980–5, it rose further to a score of five, where it remains today.

[9] Thomas, n 6 above.

[10] La Porta, R, Lopez-de-Silanes, F, Shleifer, A, and Vishny, R, 'Law and Finance' (1998) 106 *Journal of Political Economy*.

[11] 67 ER 189, (1843) 2 Hare 46.

Thus, during the twentieth century there was a substantial increase in investor protection from a virtual absence in the first half to a high degree of protection by the 1980s. But despite this pronounced shift there was no change in the importance of stock markets in terms of their size or usage by the corporate sector. This runs quite counter to the law and finance theories that associate strong investor protection with financial market activity. The UK operated a large and vibrant stock market for the first half of the twentieth century without investor protection. For those who regard regulation as a prerequisite for market development, this is surprising. How could stock markets have flourished in the UK in the absence of investor protection?

One bit of evidence on this puzzle is the orderly way in which some aspects of stock markets operated. The takeover market in the UK is now conducted according to a set of self-regulatory rules known as the Takeover Code overseen by the Takeover Panel.[12] These stipulate how takeovers should be conducted and, in particular, lay down the basis on which the shareholders of the target firm should be treated. One of these rules states that all shareholders in the target firm should be offered the same price for each of their shares. This is designed to avoid a practice that is common in many countries by which some, namely large shareholders that own controlling blocks, are offered one price and small minority shareholders are offered another, lower one.

These rules were introduced at the end of the 1960s. Before that the takeover market was essentially unregulated. Directors of acquiring firms therefore could, in principle, have followed the practice of gaining control of firms by purchasing blocks of shares at one price and offering other shareholders a lower price. This is clearly cheaper than paying everyone the same price. They could have done this but they did not. Repeatedly, they offered all shareholders the same price and also sold their own shares at the same price as was offered to other shareholders. Franks, Mayer, and Rossi[13] report that out of 33 acquisitions that occurred between 1919 and 1939, there was not a single case of price discrimination and, in virtually every case, almost all of the shares in the acquired company were purchased. In other words, a law of one price prevailed without a law of one price being enacted. It occurred by convention rather than regulation.

Why? One clue comes from the observation above on the importance of local stock markets. At the beginning of the century, companies were very dependent on local shareholders to raise finance; in particular, for acquisitions. Their

[12] The Takeover Panel is designated as the supervisory authority responsible for performing certain regulatory functions in relation to takeovers pursuant to the Directive on Takeover Bids (2004/25/EC). Its statutory functions are set out in Chapter 1 of Part 28 of the Companies Act 2006.

[13] Franks, J, Mayer, C, and Rossi, S, 'Spending Less Time with the Family: The Decline of Family Ownership in the UK' in Morck, R (ed.), *A History of Corporate Governance Around the World* (2005).

reputation among local investors was critically important to allow access to external sources of finance. Directors were keen to uphold the interests of their shareholders to allow them to access finance for future expansion. In other words, their dependence on local investors for future expansion acted as a commitment device.

As firms expanded through acquisition, their activities developed beyond their hometowns. Their shareholder base also expanded and was no longer geographically concentrated. The need for more formal systems of information disclosure through company accounts and listing rules became more acute. The result was the 1948 Companies Act and the London Stock Exchange Listing Rules that together substantially strengthened information disclosure.

Regulation not only responded to changing patterns of ownership and financing of firms but also, in turn, influenced subsequent developments. In the first half of the nineteenth century, there were a large number of small local banks in Britain that were closely involved in the financing of firms. However, the existence of small banks empowered to engage in note issuance caused serious stability problems. Between 1809 and 1830, there were 311 bankruptcies of local banks. Large banks are less exposed to local market conditions and have more resources available to them than small banks. Encouraged by the Bank of England, banks withdrew from the illiquid investments in which they were engaged and began to spread their activities geographically frequently through mergers. A convenient relation emerged by which the clearing banks faced little competition and the Bank of England little financial failure. As a consequence, today there is a high level of concentration of corporate lending in Britain and a noticeable absence of local banking.

Similarly, changes in corporate law in Britain in the middle of the twentieth century prompted a wave of hostile takeovers during the 1950s and 1960s, particularly in response to the greater disclosure of accounting information on the book value of companies. For a brief period of time, the unregulated takeover market encouraged Continental European-style ownership patterns with dual classes of shares and pyramid-ownership structures. However, these prompted calls for the hostile takeover market to be regulated and, in response, the Takeover Panel was established and the Takeover Code introduced at the end of the 1960s. This, in turn, discouraged the persistence of dual-class share ownership and pyramids.

It is, therefore, important to view regulatory changes as at least in part a response to emerging crises and, in turn, a determinant of the subsequent patterns of ownership and financing of corporations. Sarbanes–Oxley in the US is a more recent example of this: corporate governance scandals prompted the introduction of significant legislative changes that have, in turn, affected the structure of ownership and control of US corporations.

2. Germany

Ownership of corporations in Germany[14] is today highly concentrated in the hands of families and other companies. Franks, Mayer, and Wagner[15] provide the first long-run study of ownership and control of German corporations by assembling data on the ownership and financing of firms from samples spanning almost a century from 1860 to 1950. At first sight, German financial markets at the beginning of the twentieth century looked remarkably similar to their UK counterparts. There were a large number of firms listed on German stock markets and firms raised large amounts of equity finance. This runs counter to the conventional view of Germany as a bank-oriented financial system. Firms raised little finance from banks and surprisingly large amounts from stock markets.

As in the UK, issuance of equity caused the ownership of founding families and insider directors to be rapidly diluted. Even by the start of the twentieth century, founding family ownership was modest and ownership by members of firms' supervisory boards, which was large at the beginning of the century, declined rapidly thereafter. But there was one important difference between Germany and the UK. In the UK, much of the new equity issuance went to fund acquisitions and mergers. In Germany it did not. To the extent that companies invested in other firms it was in the form of partial share stakes rather than full acquisitions. As a consequence, new equity was frequently purchased by other companies in blocks rather than by dispersed shareholders.

Furthermore, where equity was widely held by individual investors it was generally held on their behalf by custodian banks. Banks were able to cast a large number of votes at shareholder meetings, not only in respect of their own shareholdings which were in general modest, but also as proxies for other shareholders. As a result, concentration of ownership did not decline at anything like the rate observed in the UK over the same period. This is the case, even if one assumes that all bank proxies were voted on behalf of dispersed shareholders. Thus, a central conclusion of Franks, Mayer, and Wagner[16] is that concentration of ownership declined much less than in the UK.

Regulation, or rather existing measures of investor protection, do not explain these differences. Indices of both shareholder anti-director rights and levels of private enforcement are identical and equally low in Germany and the UK in the first three decades of the twentieth century. In this regard, the high level of stock market activity at the beginning of the twentieth century is surprising in both

[14] This section is based on Franks, J, Mayer, C, and Wagner, H, 'The Origins of the German Corporation: Finance, Ownership and Control' (2006) 10, *Review of Finance*.

[15] Ibid. [16] Ibid, n 14 above.

countries. Small investors would not have been expected to subscribe to new equity issues in the absence of either strong anti-director or private enforcement provisions. Something else must have encouraged them to participate.

Trust mechanisms were different in Germany from those in the UK. Franks, Mayer, and Wagner[17] argue that they were associated with the role of banks as promoters of new equity issues, custodians of individual shareholdings, and voters of proxies on behalf of individual investors. An English economic historian, Lavington,[18] argued that banks provided a more secure basis for the issuance of IPOs in Germany than promoters in the UK whose interests were primarily confined to selling issues rather than ongoing relationships with companies. Regulation at the end of the nineteenth century contributed to this by conferring rights not on minority investors but on the banks, which as the promoters of corporate equity were able to control firms' access to the German stock markets. In the same way as firms in Britain upheld their reputation among local investors to gain access to equity markets, so German firms depended on banks as the gatekeepers to securities markets. How the two arrangements compared in protecting the interests of investors is an unresolved issue.

The overall picture that emerges in Germany is of firms issuing equity to fund their growth to other companies and individual investors. They were not growing through full acquisitions but through companies taking partial stakes in each other and individuals holding shares via banks. Equity finance was, therefore, intermediated by companies and banks. In contrast, in Britain, there was little intermediation by financial institutions until the second half of the twentieth century and then it came from pension funds and life assurance companies rather than credit institutions. There has never been significant intermediation by inter-corporate pyramids in Britain.

In essence, Franks, Mayer, and Wagner[19] document the creation of the 'insider system' of ownership that Franks and Mayer[20] describe in modern-day corporate Germany. This is characterized by inter-corporate holdings in the form of pyramids and complex webs of shareholdings, extensive bank proxy voting, and family ownership. What distinguished its emergence from the dispersed ownership of the UK were two things: first, the partial rather than full acquisition of shares by one company in another, thereby creating corporate pyramids and inter-corporate holdings and, second, the intermediation of equity shareholdings by banks. It is, therefore, insider not in the sense of ownership by directors but in terms of voting control remaining within the corporate and banking

[17] Ibid, n 14 above. [18] Lavington, F, *The English Capital Market* (1921).

[19] Franks et al., n 14 above.

[20] Franks, J and Mayer, C, 'Ownership and Control' in Siebert, H (ed.), *Trends in Business Organization: Do Participation and Cooperation Increase Competitiveness?*, (1995) reprinted in (1997) 9 *Journal of Applied Corporate Finance*; 'Ownership and Control of German Corporations' (2001) 14 *Review of Financial Studies.*

sector, rather than being transferred to outside individual shareholders as in the UK and the US.

Can regulation explain these developments? At one level, the clear answer to emerge from this Chapter is no. Investor protection was equally weak in Germany and the UK in the first three decades of the century when most of the developments documented in this Chapter occurred. But that response is probably more a reflection of the inadequacies of existing measures of investor protection than of the irrelevance of law and regulation. By the beginning of the twentieth century, Germany had enacted a corporate code that provided more extensive corporate governance than existed in virtually any other country at the time. This may have been critical to the rapid development of the German stock market at the end of the nineteenth and the beginning of the twentieth century. Furthermore, the Exchange Act of 1896 reinforced the control of the banks over German securities markets. Companies became dependent on banks for access to securities markets in the way in which firms in Britain were dependent on local investors for sources of equity. And since banks acted as custodians of minority-investor shares, they could also, in principle, encourage firms to uphold minority shareholder as well as their own interests. Whether they did or whether their dual role as investors and custodians was a source of conflict is a critical issue.

3. Japan

In many respects, the most striking country of the three reviewed here is Japan.[21] As Franks et al. describe,[22] it is striking because today we regard Japan as the archetypal banking system with companies closely interwoven and largely owned by banks and stock markets playing little role in the financing and ownership of firms. Whether or not that is true today, it certainly was not earlier in the twentieth century. On the contrary, in many respects Japan displays the highest dispersion of ownership of the three countries at the beginning of the twentieth century. There were not many firms listed on the Japanese stock markets but ownership of the newly industrialized companies, such as the cotton-spinning firms, which were listed at the beginning of the century became dispersed at a remarkably rapid pace. This was so pronounced that measures of concentration are in general lower for Japan than they are even in the stock market economy of the UK at the same time.

A second feature of Japan that is particularly interesting is the rapid change in investor protection that occurred just after the Second World War. The US occupation dismantled the *zaibatsu* family firms that dominated pre-war Japan and introduced legislation that transformed weak investor protection in the first half

[21] This section is based on Franks, J, Mayer, C, and Miyajima, H, 'The Ownership of Japanese Corporations in the 20th Century' (2014) 27, *Review of Financial Studies*.

[22] Ibid.

of the century into some of the strongest in the world in the second half of the century. Dispersion of ownership, therefore, occurred in Japan in the first half of the century in the absence of strong investor protection and the emergence of the insider system of ownership in the second half of the century by which banks and companies had cross-shareholdings in each other occurred against the backdrop of strong investor protection. The move from outsider, dispersed ownership to insider cross-shareholdings, therefore, coincides with a marked strengthening of investor protection, quite contrary to what was expected at the time and would be predicted by the law and finance literature today.

As in Germany and the UK, Japan raises the question of how ownership dispersion occurred in the absence of strong investor protection. Franks, Mayer, and Miyajima point again to informal arrangements of trust as being critical to the dispersion of ownership. But unlike in the UK, these were not attributable to the prevalence of local stock exchanges. Most companies were listed on one of two stock exchanges—Osaka and Tokyo. Nor, unlike in Germany, did banks play an important role in the relations between investors and firms in the first half of the century. Instead, in the first two decades of the twentieth century particular individuals rather than institutions were critical to the ability of companies to be able to access stock markets. These individuals were known as business coordinators and had some of the characteristics of today's private equity investors, particularly business angels. They were prominent members of the business community, sometimes senior figures in the local chambers of commerce, who sat on the boards of several firms. Their reputation acted as a validation of the soundness of the companies with which they were associated.

The role of business coordinators diminished from the 1920s onwards and their place was taken by the family firms, the *zaibatsu*, which were incorporated during and after the First World War and in the 1930s sold their subsidiaries on stock markets. In this case, the reputation of the *zaibatsu* families appears to have been important in facilitating access to stock markets. The dismantling of the *zaibatsu* in the aftermath of the Second World War left a vacuum that individual investors failed to fill despite the existence of strong investor protection and, instead, an insider system of corporate control by a combination of banks and corporations emerged.

In sum, all three countries (ie, the UK, Germany, and Japan) illustrate that it was not investor protection that allowed stock markets to develop at the beginning of the twentieth century. In all three cases, stock markets flourished and ownership was dispersed in the absence of strong investor protection. Instead, other institutions and individuals were important in upholding relations of trust between investors and firms. In the case of the UK, it was local stock markets; in Germany, the banks; and in Japan, business coordinators and *zaibatsu* families. Where regulatory reform attempted to prescribe a particular type of financial system in post-Second World War Japan, it had the entirely unintended consequence of promoting the emergence of an insider rather than an outsider system of corporate control. Strong investor protection is, therefore, neither a necessary condition for the development of outsider systems of corporate ownership as illustrated by each of Germany, Japan, and the UK in the first half of the twentieth century, nor a sufficient condition as demonstrated by Japan in the second half of the twentieth century.

The absence of a clear relation between regulation and the development of equity markets stands in marked contrast to bank regulation.

III. Regulating the Banking System

Banks play a key role in the transfer of property rights through the payment system,[23] the network of interbank flows, and the management of liquidity.[24] These functions are essential to the economy and their protection is, therefore, the appropriate concern of the state, as well as individual investors. The main threat to these functions comes from the risk of the bankruptcy of banks and the state exercises its authority through the delegated responsibility of regulators to engage in prudential supervision to prevent excessive risk-taking by banks—the 'representation hypothesis' in which regulatory authorities represent small uninformed dispersed depositors.[25]

There are two forms in which banks are regulated—the micro-regulation of the governance, capital, and conduct of individual banks, and the macro-prudential regulation of the banking system as a whole.

1. Micro-regulation of banks

The financial crisis provoked a rash of reports and recommendations concerning the governance and conduct of financial institutions. In the UK, the Walker Report,[26] the Financial Reporting Council,[27] and the then Financial Services Authority all considered ways to improve corporate governance of financial institutions. In Europe, the European Commission produced a Green Paper on the Corporate Governance of Financial Institutions[28] and Non-Financial Corporations.[29] In the

[23] This section draws on Freixas, X and Mayer, C, 'Banking, Finance and the Role of the State' (2011) 27 *Oxford Review of Economic Policy* and Mayer, C and Gordon, J, The Micro, Macro and International Design of Financial Regulation (2012), Columbia Law and Economics Working Paper No. 422.

[24] For an overview of the role of banks see Freixas, X and Rochet, C, *Microeconomics of Banking* (2nd edn, 2008) ch 2.

[25] Dewatripont, M and Tirole, J, *The Prudential Regulation of Banks* (1994).

[26] Walker, D, A Review of Corporate Governance in UK Banks and Other Financial Industry Entities (2009).

[27] Financial Reporting Council, The UK Corporate Governance Code (2010).

[28] European Commission, Corporate Governance in Financial Institutions and Remuneration Policies, COM (2010) 284.

[29] European Commission, The EU Corporate Governance Framework, COM (2011) 164.

US, the Dodd–Frank Act was concerned with, among other things, bank corporate governance.

Behind all of these reports lay a belief that the collapse of financial institutions is at least in part attributable to poor corporate governance. A failure to measure, monitor, and manage risks was thought to have been widespread in the financial sector before the crisis. The required response was to improve the competence, training, and engagement of management. Rules on the appointment, training, induction, commitment, and independence of directors of financial institutions needed to be strengthened. There should have been greater authority in the hands of chief risk officers, and more oversight by auditors and risk committees prior to the financial crisis. There should have been better alignment of managerial incentives with the interests of stakeholders, better communication between shareholders and management, more shareholder engagement, and better stewardship by investing institutions.

A very prescriptive set of proposals regarding the corporate governance and conduct of banks, therefore, emerged from the crisis. Unfortunately, there is little evidence to support the view that these responses would have mitigated the problem and, indeed, there are reasons for believing that they could have exacerbated it. This apparently perverse conclusion derives from empirical observations and theoretical objections to the proposed policy prescriptions.

First, studies of the performance of financial institutions suggest that those with better corporate governance standards as conventionally defined may have performed worse during the financial crisis and higher-powered incentives were associated with more risk-taking by financial institutions.[30] The theoretical basis for these concerns is that there is a potential divergence of interest between different classes of investors related to the failure of the conditions associated with the Modigliani and Miller theorem to hold. With limited liability and imperfect pricing of debt contracts, in particular of deposits that may be explicitly or implicitly insured, shareholders have a call option on the firm, which means that they benefit from the upside benefits of favourable outcomes but do not bear all of the consequences of downside losses; instead, these are borne by the creditors. As a result, while debtors seek conservative low-risk conduct by the institutions in which they invest, shareholders benefit from higher-risk strategies. Increasing corporate governance standards in the conventional sense of making managers

[30] See Adams, R, 'Governance and the Financial Crisis' (2012) 12 *International Review of Finance*; Beltratti, A and Stulz, R, 'The Credit Crisis Around the Globe: Why Did Some Banks Perform Better?' (2012) 105 *Journal of Financial Economics*; Erkens, D, Hung, M, and Matos, P, 'Corporate Governance in the 2007–2008 Financial Crisis: Evidence from Financial Institutions Worldwide' (2012) *Journal of Corporate Finance*; Ferreira, D, Kirchmaier, T, and Metzger, D, Boards of Banks (2010), ECGI Finance Working Paper No 289/2010; and Minton, B, Taillard, J, and Williamson, R, 'Financial Expertise of the Board, Risk Taking and Performance: Evidence from Bank Holding Companies' (2014) 49(2) *Journal of Financial and Quantitative Analysis* 351.

more accountable to their shareholders, thereby diminishing the agency problem between managers and shareholders, may benefit shareholders at the expense of creditors. The failure of financial institutions was not, therefore, due to weak but strong corporate governance.

This problem of a divergence of interest between creditors and shareholders is even more serious in banks that enjoy explicit insurance from the state, where industry schemes are insufficient, in the form of deposit insurance or implicit insurance in the form of bailouts to prevent those that are 'too big to fail' from going under. In that case, not even creditors bear all of the downside risks; some are absorbed by taxpayers who ultimately bear the costs of bank bailouts.

Enhancing corporate governance standards is, therefore, not beneficial unless in the process it aligns the interests of those managing institutions with those who ultimately bear the risks as well as the returns from their decisions and actions. In fact, in the absence of such an alignment, strengthening the relation of managerial interests with one party at the expense of another may diminish not enhance social welfare, as the experience of the banks during the financial crisis suggests.

This problem would at least, in principle, appear to be avoided by conferring authority on regulators, whose job it is to protect customers rather than shareholders. In addition to corporate governance standards, regulators have strengthened rules regarding the certification of employees of financial institutions and the rules of conduct by which they should transact their business. Prior to the financial crisis, there was widespread support for the principle-based approach of the UK financial regulatory authorities as against the more detailed and prescriptive rule-based approach of the US regulatory authorities. However, with the failure of UK as well as US financial institutions, there has been a move to more prescriptive regulatory rules in both regimes. Principle-based regulation relies on a degree of trust on the part of regulators that financial institutions will implement internal practices that are consistent with the spirit as well as the letter of the principles. Such trust was eroded by the widespread abuse that was revealed by the financial crisis.

There are, however, two fundamental problems with the application of detailed rules by regulators. First, they assume that the regulator knows and can observe best practice. This is particularly implausible in the context of financial investments that by their very nature are subjective. Second, the implementation of rules of good conduct presumes that they are universally applied. If, instead, different regulatory authorities adopt different rules, then financial institutions will simply seek those that are best suited to their particular way of doing business. This gives rise to regulatory arbitrage and runs to the bottom by which the lowest common denominator of regulatory standards prevails.

2. Macro-prudential regulation of banking systems

The type of highly prescriptive micro-prudential regulation of the past, therefore, had significant deficiencies associated with it. The crisis triggered a complete rethinking of the structure of bank regulation and a wave of new proposals designed to avoid a recurrence of previous problems.[31] There was a widely held view that there has been too much emphasis placed on micro-regulation of individual institutions and too little on the macro-prudential regulation of the financial system as a whole.[32] New institutions were created to manage macro-prudential regulation; for example, the European Systemic Risk Board in Europe and the Financial Stability Oversight Council in the US. A number of techniques, collectively known as the 'safety net', were developed to prevent bank crises and limit their impact. These included capital regulation, structural remedies, intervention procedures, and deposit insurance.[33]

On risk-based capital regulation, capital requirements were increased significantly to discourage incentives to shift risks from shareholders to creditors which existed prior to the financial crisis and were thought to have contributed to excessive risk-taking by banks.[34] Basel III requires that all banks and systemically important financial institutions (SIFIs) hold additional and higher-quality capital, and the measurement of risk has been extended to include risks associated with securitization and counterparty failure; in particular, in credit default swaps.

On structural remedies, in the UK, the Independent Commission on Banking (the ICB) proposed that retail banking be ring-fenced from other banking activities in 2011 and these proposals were subsequently adopted by the UK Government.[35] This is in line with the view that a primary objective of banking regulation should be the preservation of the payments system as well as other retail services. By ring-fencing retail-banking activities, the UK authorities will be able to protect the

[31] See, eg, Brunnermeier, M, Crockett, A, Goodhart, C, Persaud, A, and Shin, H, *The Fundamental Principles of Financial Regulation* (2009) 11 Geneva Reports on the World Economy and French, K, Baily, M, Campbell, J, Cochrane, J, Diamond, D, Duffie, D, Kashyap, A, Mishkin, F, Rajan, R, Scharfstein, D, Shiller, R, Shin, H, Slaughter, M, Stein, J, and Stulz, R, *The Squam Lake Report: Fixing the Financial System* (2010).

[32] See, eg, Borio, C, 'Towards a Macro-prudential Framework for Financial Supervision and Regulation?' (2003) 49 *CESifo Economic Studies*; Crockett, A, Marrying the Micro- and Macro-prudential Dimensions of Financial Stability (2000), BIS Speeches 21; Hanson, S, Kashyap, A, and Stein, J, 'A Macroprudential Approach to Financial Regulation' (2011) 25 *Journal of Economic Perspectives*; and Shin, H, Macroprudential Policies Beyond Basel III (2011), Bank for International Settlement Papers 60.

[33] See, eg, Schich, S, 'Financial Crisis: Deposit Insurance and Related Financial Safety Net Aspects' (2008) *Financial Market Trends*.

[34] See Admati, A and Hellwig, M, *The Bankers' New Clothes: What's Wrong with Banking and What to Do About It* (2013); and Miles, D, Yang, J, and Marcheggiano, G, 'Optimal Bank Capital' (2012) 123 *Economic Journal*.

[35] Independent Commission on Banking, Final Report (2011).

payments system without having to insure the high-risk products that wholesale banking provides. Had it been in place in 2007, the ring-fence would have allowed the regulatory authorities to declare Northern Rock bankrupt at little or no cost to taxpayers and would have avoided the costs imposed on taxpayers from incomplete securitization. The Volcker Rule, which prohibits proprietary trading, is an alternative separation of safe and risky investments.[36] While the ICB segments different activities within a particular institution, the Volcker Rule only permits certain types of investments.[37]

Bank resolutions comprise a three-stage process. The first occurs when the bank is in distress and either cannot obtain funds from the market or, if it can, only at such a high cost as to impose further losses on its investments. The second stage is a bargaining process between the bank's shareholders and the regulatory agency, where the regulatory agency is interested in a swift resolution while the shareholders' and managers' objectives are to maximize the value of their shares. In the third stage, either a solution is found that restores the bank as a viable entity or it is put into bankruptcy.

Deposit insurance has been a critical part of the protection afforded to the banking system. It is justified by the risks of runs that can otherwise occur in banking as a consequence of the liquidity and maturity transformation functions that banks perform. Holding long-term and illiquid assets means that banks are vulnerable to withdrawals of their short-term liquid deposits. Deposit insurance makes investors less concerned about the effects of bank runs on the value of their deposits.

The effectiveness of deposit insurance relies on it being complete. The partial deposit insurance that was present in many countries before the financial crisis was not adequate. The possibility of even a small loss meant that, faced with bank failures, it was optimal for depositors to withdraw their funds. To avoid this from occurring, many countries were forced to raise deposit insurance during the crisis to a point that it provided complete coverage for all but the largest retail holdings.

In principle, complete deposit insurance should make deposits risk-free. Knowing that it is in place, depositors will appreciate that their investments are fully protected and have no need to withdraw their monies during the crisis. As a consequence, the deposit insurance will never be required to make a payment and there will be no call on the deposit insurance fund or the government to compensate investors. However, that presumes that the banking industry and the government are always capable of compensating investors in the event of failures. As the

[36] See Whitehead, C, 'The Volcker Rule and Evolving Financial Markets' (2011) 1 *Harvard Business Law Review*.

[37] Research on the issue of separation has focused on the US evidence before and after the Glass–Steagall Act. See Kroszner, R and Rajan, R, 'Is the Glass–Steagall Act Justified? A Study of the U.S. Experience with Universal Banking before 1933' (1994) 84 *American Economic Review*.

cases of Ireland and Iceland have illustrated, where banking systems are large in relation to the overall size of economies and, therefore, the possible losses associated with bank failures are high in relation to the tax capacity of a country, then bank failures may threaten the solvency of countries.[38] In those cases, depositors will appreciate that even 100 per cent deposit insurance does not guarantee the security of their investments and a financial crisis will still pose a risk of runs.

The threat to governments is exacerbated by 'too big to fail' considerations. The significance of some financial institutions to the economy is so great that governments cannot allow them to fail. Even in the absence of deposit insurance, there are implicit if not explicit guarantees that impose large and sometimes unsustainable obligations on the public sector. As recent experience in Europe illustrates, this makes the consequences of financial failure not just of national but also of international significance. International coordination is required to rescue countries that are unable to bail out their financial sectors on their own.

Increasingly, the focus of bank regulation has been appropriately on protection against risks of failure of the banking system as a whole as against failure of individual institutions. In return for this provision of government insurance against systemic failures, banks should in return commit to provide certain economic and public functions.

3. The government-banking sector partnership

The starting point for defining the partnership between the state and the banking sector is to determine its scope. What really are the commanding heights of the financial system? What is essential to the operation of an economy? What will have to be preserved when the next crisis strikes? These questions get to the heart of the issue of what are banks supposed to do. There are some common points of agreement on this. Probably top of most people's list would be the payments system, safekeeping of deposits, lending to small- and medium-sized companies, and possibly some forms of personal-sector lending, in particular for housing. There might then be other functions on some people's list, such as funding large infrastructure projects, syndicated lending to large corporate borrowers, IPOs, and mergers and acquisitions. More controversially, some might include activities such as funding pensions and insurance that lie beyond the normal scope of banking.

The purpose of this discussion is not to answer the question of what is banking supposed to do but to note that in the array of policy proposals it has largely been ignored. In particular, if as the ICB or the Volcker Rule attempt to do, one draws a ring round some financial institutions or activities and says that those are more

[38] Allen, F, Carletti, E, and Leonello, A, 'Deposit Insurance and Risk Taking' (2011) 27 *Oxford Review of Economic Policy*.

essential than the remainder, one needs to be pretty clear about what it is at the end of the day that must be protected. One also needs to be very clear about what will happen when failures occur in the remainder of the financial system.

Suppose then that we have identified the commanding heights of the financial system, what then should be the nature of the partnership? The financial crisis has demonstrated that the role of the state is equivalent to that of a provider of catastrophic insurance, namely in normal circumstances the state does little or nothing but in extreme circumstances it protects the commanding heights. The first thing that this implies is that banks should be able to stand on their own feet. They need to have enough capital, liquidity, good management, and ways of dealing with failure to prevent the state from having to intervene in all but the most exceptional circumstances.

This means that those components of the financial system that are protected will have to hold unusually large amounts of capital, liquidity, and demonstrate that they have adequate systems of management in place and ways of organizing restructurings themselves without having to call upon the state to intervene. So, there is some justification for all the regulatory changes and proposals currently on the table regarding micro- and macro-prudential regulation. But where they have erred has been in being too concerned with the micro-conduct of banks, notwithstanding the greater emphasis that has been recently placed on macro-prudential regulation. Where they may well be inadequate is in imposing sufficiently high-capital requirements on the protected parts of the financial system to insure that the state will not have to intervene in all but the most extreme circumstances.

Will this create moral hazard and will the protected banks take undue risks? Moral hazard cannot be entirely eliminated in financial markets but it can be contained by decisive action to replace management and write off investments of banks' shareholders and junior creditors when the state is called upon to intervene and rescue failing banks.

What about the unprotected parts? Will they just wither? The answer is no. They will stand on their own feet like any normally functioning part of an economy and will benefit from not having to endure the higher cost of capital of the protected institutions. And what happens when we enter the next crisis with failures across the board? The private sector will attempt to organize its own rescues through, for example, bail-ins of outstanding debt and when these fail the state should intervene quickly, decisively and effectively in the protected segments by providing not just the traditional lender-of-last-resort facilities but also undertaking restructurings, mergers, and state acquisitions of failing institutions. International coordination will be critical to ensure effective resolution of failing institutions. The partnership will then be clear and the consequences transparent.

A particularly attractive feature of this proposal is that not only does it protect the banking system from collapse in crises but it also encourages it to perform what are regarded as desirable activities in normal times. By balancing the subsidy of the protection against the implicit tax of capital and liquidity requirements, the banking system can be appropriately encouraged to do things that are deemed to be beneficial to the rest of the economy, such as funding small- and medium-sized companies, and providing mortgages for first-time buyers.

The subsidies to banks in fact come not only from rescuing them when they fail but also from the fact that their liabilities (deposits) are part of the payments system and, therefore, borrowed at well below market interest rates. In return for the privileged position that banks enjoy in the payments system as well as from the protection that they enjoy against failure, they should justifiably be expected to perform functions that benefit the wider economy. Establishment of the system advocated here will promote a healthy debate about what economic functions we wish our banks to perform.

In summary, the analysis of the development of equity markets and the failure of banks suggest a common set of policy recommendations. Detailed prescriptive regulation of the conduct of individual institutions should be avoided and can have perverse consequences as was discussed in relation to both equity markets and banks. Instead, regulation of the banking system should be focused on the protection of the system as a whole and on the emergence of appropriate institutional arrangements to promote trust in equity markets.

All this presumes that equity markets and banks are, indeed, essential to the functions that they are presumed to perform. In the last Section, we will question whether even these assumptions are correct.

IV. The Function of Financial Markets

1. Mobile money

A financial revolution is in progress in several developing countries. The revolution is mobile money[39]—the use of mobile phones to make financial transactions, taken to a new level by M-PESA in Kenya with more than 100 schemes worldwide seeking to imitate its success. It has fundamental implications not only for financial inclusion, but also for our understanding of financial systems and regulation in developed economies.

Launched in March 2007 by the telecommunications company, Safaricom, the M-PESA payment and saving service signed up more than 50 per cent of adult Kenyans by the end of 2010. The annual number of domestic payment transactions rose to

[39] This section is based on Mas, I and Mayer, C, Savings as Forward Payments: Innovations on Mobile Money Platforms (2011), SSRN working paper no.1825122 and Klein, M and Mayer, C, Mobile Money and Financial Inclusion: The Regulatory Lessons, World Bank Working Paper WS 5664.

exceed that of Western Union globally. The absolute amounts of transactions are very small reflecting the income level of the users with average savings of around $3.

In Kenya, M-PESA is everywhere. The system allows users to send or withdraw money at over 23,000 shops, compared with about 1,000 bank branches. Changing money at these cash merchants is like buying products at a shop: few lines, opening hours from early till late, and close to places of business or residence. Life is easier and safer, and money is harder to steal or lose.

Transformational as this is for developing and emerging economies in which access to banking was previously restricted to a small proportion of the population, mobile money also has important lessons for banking and regulation everywhere. Indeed, given the cheapness, speed, convenience, and transparency of payments transacted by mobile phones that bypass banks, it may transform payments in developed economies as well if it is not derailed by regulation or vested banking interests.

The real insight it provides comes from the way in which it unbundles banking into its core functions: exchange of money, storing money, transferring, and investing it. The cash merchants are moneychangers. Suppose a worker in Nairobi wants to send money to his wife in a village. The worker goes to a cash merchant and gives the merchant cash. In return, the merchant gives the worker book-entry money (BEM) by instructing M-PESA via a mobile phone to transfer BEM from her account to that of the worker. Exchanging one form of money for another is like exchanging bills for coins. There is no need for prudential regulation any more than there is for machines that exchange coins for notes to be regulated.

M-PESA, provides two functions. It stores money with a custodian and it transfers it. People storing money with M-PESA are rewarded in the same way as if they had stored the money in a safe-deposit box: they get no interest and the nominal value of the money is preserved. The system requires reliability and integrity enforced by normal standards of commercial law and consumer protection but no prudential regulation or capital requirements.

In essence, this is the ultimate form of narrow banking. No fractional banking and no investment of monetary deposits—just pure custodianship. But perfect security and mobility of money come at a price because the predominant form in which most people hold their savings, namely cash deposits, is no longer available for investment. One of the most significant sources of capital, monetary assets that are used for transaction purposes, is removed from the savings net. That is the price of narrow banking and what mobile money demonstrates is that a perfectly safe and efficient monetary system can be created but at the price of raising the cost of capital for those parts of the economy, such as small- and medium-sized enterprises, which traditionally benefit from banking.

As it so happens, in the case of M-PESA the custodians are banks that can employ the monetary deposits in normal banking functions. This reintroduces an element of prudential risk into mobile money but to the benefit of those who are funded by the banks from the monetary deposits. What this demonstrates is that by allocating the cash deposits of mobile money between pure independent custodians and banks, the regulatory authorities can determine an appropriate point on the trade-off between creating a perfectly safe but comparatively unproductive payments system and a useful but riskier one that supports normal banking functions.

The case of mobile money raises questions about whether payments should, in fact, be regarded as a core function of banking. But it also demonstrates the distortions created by excessive regulation. The reason why mobile money first flourished in Kenya is that the authorities took an enlightened view of its regulation. Despite pressure from existing banks to do so, M-PESA was not regulated as a bank and was not subject to the same prudential requirements as banks. Had it been so then it might have been strangled at birth. Elsewhere, where existing banks have exerted more influence on regulation, mobile money has been much slower to develop, for example in India. Mobile money, therefore, illustrates very clearly why the real commanding heights of banking have to be carefully identified, how a failure to do so can lead to inappropriate regulation, and how changing technology will rapidly alter the appropriate relation between the state, regulation, and the banking system.

Turning to equity markets, the cases of China and Korea also raise questions about whether the interpretation that we have placed on the appropriate development of equity markets is correct.

2. China and Korea

Section II.3 noted that the strengthening of investor protection in post-Second World War Japan unexpectedly coincided with the emergence of an insider system of cross-shareholdings between companies and banks. The high growth era of Japan was therefore associated with a system of cross-ownership and insider control within the banking and corporate sector not outside control by individual and institutional investors.

The experience of other high-growth emerging markets is consistent with this. In China, the corporate sector is dominated by state ownership and in Korea by large family holdings, the *chaebols*. Both the state as owner in China and families in Korea played a critical role in the development of these economies. But this economic growth came against the background of mounting evidence of inefficiencies associated with block holdings by banks, families, and the state. In particular, family holdings are linked with the pursuit of private family goals and 'tunnelling' of profits to controlling owners. How did systems with such inherent inefficiencies associated with controlling block holders, nevertheless, sustain such high growth rates?

One answer is that the controlling shareholders pursued excessive growth and overinvestment at the expense of corporate viability. The collapse of the Japanese economy during the 1990s and 2000s is consistent with this over-investment, over-leveraged story. So, too, is the Asian crisis at the end of the 1990s, which was widely attributed in the West to crony capitalism. Nevertheless, these economies have since recovered and continue to display impressive levels of growth.

A second explanation is that there are countervailing benefits associated with controlling shareholders. In particular, in both China and Korea it is widely believed that their presence brings a stability and long-term focus to corporate activities which is missing from Western economies and, in particular, from corporations in the UK and the US with widely dispersed share ownership.

While the state in China and the *chaebols* in Korea are credited with much of their economic success to date, significant concerns are emerging about their continuing stranglehold of corporate activities. In China, the concern is in regard to the bureaucracy and political interference that state ownership brings to what should be commercial decisions. In Korea, there has been much disquiet about the conflict between the interests of the *chaebols* and those of society more generally. This reached a head in the last presidential elections in Korea in which the role of the *chaebols* in Korean society featured prominently as an election issue. But while reform may be needed, neither China nor Korea wish to move to UK- or US-style dispersed-ownership systems. These are felt to be short-term in nature and too focused on profits at the expense of the wider interests of their societies. Instead, the question is whether an alternative long-term owner to the state in China and the families in Korea can in due course be found and who that long-term owner should be.

Equity markets may be important for economic development but dispersed ownership and control by outside shareholders may not. Providing corporations with access to external sources of equity finance from stock markets is not the same as conferring control on those outside investors. The law and finance perspective suggests that the ability of outside investors to exercise control over the corporations in which they invest is a necessary requirement for the provision of external finance. However, the experience of all of Germany, Japan, and the UK in the first half of the twentieth century and that of China, Japan, and Korea in the second half of the century suggests that it is not the case. Ownership was dispersed in the first three countries in the absence of strong investor protection and the last three countries displayed remarkable growth in the absence of external shareholder control. We should, therefore, take care before rushing to policy conclusions about the link between equity markets and the growth of corporations and nations.

V. Conclusions

This Chapter has questioned many of the conventional wisdoms associated with the relation between economic development, financial systems, and the law. It has suggested that strong investor protection has not been a necessary condition for the emergence of dispersed share ownership and was not a sufficient condition in post-war Japan for the emergence of an outsider form of corporate control. Micro-regulation of the governance and conduct of banks can exacerbate not diminish the risks of bank failures. Instead, trust and the emergence of institutions of trust are more important in the development of equity markets and the regulation of banks should be focused on the macro-protection of banking systems rather than individual banks. In return for this protection, there should be a partnership between the state and banks in which banks correspondingly undertake to meet the economic and public needs of countries that other institutions may fail to provide.

Careful consideration should be given to what those needs really are and they are likely to change significantly over time. The emergence of mobile money in several developing economies has demonstrated that payments are not necessarily a core function of banks. Similarly, the expansion of crowdsourcing and peer-to-peer lending might make small- and medium-sized lending less exclusively the remit of banks. The growth of shadow banking has furthermore disaggregated the components of banking into origination, credit evaluation, and asset management.

Finally, the experience of some of the fastest-growing economies in the post-Second World War era has raised questions about the conventional associations of equity markets with economic prosperity. In many cases, the growth has occurred in the presence of shareholding structures and corporate governance arrangements that run exactly counter to what is perceived to be best practice. Simple prescriptions for the regulation of equity markets and banks and for the financial determinants of economic development may not, therefore, stand up to close scrutiny.

Bibliography

Adams, R, 'Governance and the Financial Crisis' (2012) 12 *International Review of Finance*.

Admati, A and Hellwig, M, *The Bankers' New Clothes: What's Wrong with Banking and What to Do About It* (2013).

Allen, F, Carletti, E, and Leonello, A, 'Deposit Insurance and Risk Taking' (2011) 27 *Oxford Review of Economic Policy*.

Beck, T, Demirgüç-Kunt, A, and Levine, R, 'Legal Theories of Financial Development' (2001) 17 *Oxford Review of Economic Policy*.

Beltratti, A and Stulz, R, 'The Credit Crisis around the Globe: Why Did Some Banks Perform Better?' (2012) 105 *Journal of Financial Economics*.

Bolton, P, Freixas, X, and Shapiro, J, 'The Credit Rating Game' (2011) 67 *Journal of Finance*.

Borio, C, 'Towards a Macro-prudential Framework for Financial Supervision and Regulation?' (2003) 49 *CESifo Economic Studies*.

Brunnermeier, M, Crockett, A, Goodhart, C, Persaud, A, and Shin, H, *The Fundamental Principles of Financial Regulation* (2009) 11 Geneva Reports on the World Economy.

Crockett, A, Marrying the Micro- and Macro-prudential Dimensions of Financial Stability (2000), BIS Speeches 21.
Dewatripont, M and Tirole, J, *The Prudential Regulation of Banks* (1994).
Erkens, D, Hung, M, and Matos, P, 'Corporate Governance in the 2007–2008 Financial Crisis: Evidence from Financial Institutions Worldwide' (2012) *Journal of Corporate Finance*.
European Commission, Corporate Governance in Financial Institutions and Remuneration Policies, COM (2010) 284.
European Commission, The EU Corporate Governance Framework, COM (2011) 164.
Ferreira, D, Kirchmaier, T, and Metzger, D, Boards of Banks (2010), ECGI Finance Working Paper No 289/2010.
Financial Reporting Council, The UK Corporate Governance Code (2010).
Franks, J and Mayer, C, 'Bank Control, Takeovers and Corporate Governance in Germany' (1998) 22 *Journal of Banking and Finance*.
Franks, J and Mayer, C, 'Ownership and Control' in Siebert, H (ed.), *Trends in Business Organization: Do Participation and Cooperation Increase Competitiveness?*, (1995) (reprinted in 1997) 9 *Journal of Applied Corporate Finance*.
Franks, J and Mayer, C, 'Ownership and Control of German Corporations' (2001) 14 *Review of Financial Studies*.
Franks, J, Mayer, C, and Miyajima, H, 'The Ownership of Japanese Corporations in the 20th Century' (2014) 27 *Review of Financial Studies*.
Franks, J, Mayer, C, and Rossi, S, 'Spending Less Time with the Family: The Decline of Family Ownership in the UK' in Morck, R (ed.), *A History of Corporate Governance Around the World* (2005).
Franks, J, Mayer, C, and Rossi, S, 'Ownership: Evolution and Regulation' (2009) 22 *Review of Financial Studies*.
Franks, J, Mayer, C, and Wagner, H, 'The Origins of the German Corporation: Finance, Ownership and Control' (2006) 10 *Review of Finance*.
Freixas, X and Mayer, C, 'Banking, Finance and the Role of the State' (2011) 27 *Oxford Review of Economic Policy*.
Freixas, X and Rochet, C, *Microeconomics of Banking* (2nd edn, 2008).
French, K, Baily, M, Campbell, J, Cochrane, J, Diamond, D, Duffie, D, Kashyap, A, Mishkin, F, Rajan, R, Scharfstein, D, Shiller, R, Shin, H, Slaughter, M, Stein, J, and Stulz, R, *The Squam Lake Report: Fixing the Financial System* (2010).
Hanson, S, Kashyap, A, and Stein, J, 'A Macroprudential Approach to Financial Regulation' (2011) 25 *Journal of Economic Perspectives*.
Independent Commission on Banking, Final Report (2011).
Klein, M and Mayer, C, Mobile Money and Financial Inclusion: The Regulatory Lessons, World Bank Working Paper No WS 5664.
Kroszner, R and Rajan, R, 'Is the Glass–Steagall Act Justified? A Study of the U.S. Experience with Universal Banking before 1933' (1994) 84 *American Economic Review*.
La Porta, R, Lopez-de-Silanes, F, and Shleifer, A, 'Corporate Ownership around the World' (1999) 54 *Journal of Finance*.
La Porta, R, Lopez-de-Silanes, F, Shleifer, A, and Vishny, R, 'Investor Protection and Corporate Governance' (2000) 58 *Journal of Financial Economics*.
La Porta, R, Lopez-de-Silanes, F, Shleifer, A, and Vishny, R, 'Law and Finance' (1998) 106 *Journal of Political Economy*.

La Porta, R, Lopez-de-Silanes, F, Shleifer, A, and Vishny, R, 'Legal Determinants of External Finance' (1997) 52 *Journal of Finance*.

La Porta, R, Lopez-de-Silanes, F, Shleifer, A, and Vishny, R, 'The Quality of Government' (1999) 15 *Journal of Law, Economics, and Organization*.

Lavington, F, *The English Capital Market* (1921).

Levine, R, 'Finance and Growth: Theory and Evidence' in Aghion, P and Durlauf, S (eds), *Handbook of Economic Growth* (2005).

Levine, R, 'Financial Development and Economic Growth: View and Agenda' (1997) 35 *Journal of Economic Literature*.

Mas, I and Mayer, C, Savings as Forward Payments: Innovations on Mobile Money Platforms (2011), SSRN Working Paper No 1825122.

Mayer, C and Gordon, J, The Micro, Macro and International Design of Financial Regulation (2012), Columbia Law and Economics Working Paper No 422.

Miles, D, Yang, J, and Marcheggiano, G, 'Optimal Bank Capital' (2012) 123 *Economic Journal*.

Minton, B, Taillard, J, and Williamson, R, 'Financial Expertise of the Board, Risk Taking and Performance: Evidence from Bank Holding Companies' (2014) 49(2) *Journal of Financial and Quantitative Analysis* 351.

Rajan, R and Zingales, L, 'Financial Dependence and Growth' (1998) 88 *American Economic Review*.

Rajan, R and Zingales, L, 'Financial Systems, Industrial Structure and Growth' (2002) 17 *Oxford Review of Economic Policy*.

Schich, S, 'Financial Crisis: Deposit Insurance and Related Financial Safety Net Aspects' (2008) *Financial Market Trends*.

Shin, H, Macroprudential Policies Beyond Basel III (2011), Bank for International Settlement Papers 60.

Thomas, W, *The Provincial Stock Exchanges* (1973).

Walker, D, A Review of Corporate Governance in UK Banks and Other Financial Industry Entities (2009).

Whitehead, C, 'The Volcker Rule and Evolving Financial Markets' (2011) 1 *Harvard Business Law Review*.

CHAPTER 3

FINANCIAL SYSTEMS, CRISES, AND REGULATION

FRANK PARTNOY

I. The Roots of Financial Crises

This Chapter considers, in broad historical perspective and also with respect to the global financial crisis (GFC), why financial systems are crisis-prone and the relationship between financial crises and regulation. It begins with an overview of financial crises generally, and then considers both the historical and potential future role of regulation in financial crises.

Financial crises have been a topic of research and debate for centuries, though the area has become more prominent in recent years due to the GFC and its aftermath.[1] Generally, a financial crisis occurs in the aftermath of a market crash; a sudden and widespread downward movement in financial asset prices. Financial crises typically involve not only sharp declines in the financial markets, but spillover effects into the real economy as well.

Although there have been hundreds of financial crises, and centuries of research about them, scholars still understand very little about crises. Scholars haven't reached much consensus about common problems and conclusions related to the financial crises of the eighteenth century (the French Mississippi bubble and the South Sea bubble), the nineteenth century (the panics and crises of 1825, 1837, 1847, 1857, 1866, 1869, and 1873), the 1929 crash, the Mexican and Asian currency crises in the 1990s, the dot.com bubble, and so on. Economists even continue to debate why prices of Dutch tulip bulbs skyrocketed during February 1637 (when a single Semper Augustus bulb sold for 5,500 guilders, equivalent to more than $25,000 today), and then collapsed to a fraction of their value.[2] The 2007–08 GFC did not generate much consensus either; instead, it created new puzzles.

1. Regulatory overview

Financial market crises are an important target of regulation, for several reasons. First, financial crises lead to allocative inefficiency. The financial system generally allocates resources among savers and borrowers; to the extent prices do not reflect fundamental values and resources are misallocated as parties transact based on incorrect prices. Moreover, to the extent financial asset prices do not reflect fundamental value, investors will be more uncertain about investing in such assets, particularly over the long term. Such uncertainty will hamper investment that

[1] Much of the early debate is covered in Partnoy, F, 'Why Markets Crash and What Law Can Do about It' (2000) 61 *University of Pittsburgh Law Review* 741, 742–7. Portions of this Chapter are based on this article.

[2] Garber, P, 'Tulipmania' (1989) 97 *Journal of Political Economy* 535; Galbraith, JK, *A Short History of Financial Euphoria* (1993) 26–34.

is critical to economic growth. If the financial system is inefficient, the economy will not operate efficiently and economic growth will be lower than it otherwise would have been. Accordingly, to the extent regulation can improve financial stability and reduce the effects of financial crises, it is worth pursuing such policies.[3]

Put another way, financial stability can be thought of as a 'public good', a commodity or service that does not exhibit either 'depletability' (meaning that if an additional user consumes a public good, the benefits of that good are not depleted) or 'excludability' (meaning that it is difficult or impossible to exclude consumers from the benefits of a public good).[4] Financial stability is not depletable because users of financial services who derive benefits from stability do not deprive others of such benefits. Financial stability is not excludable because users of financial services cannot be excluded from its benefits. Accordingly, there is an argument that financial stability, like other public goods, should be provided through regulation.

On the other hand, regulation also can play a role in perpetrating and perpetuating financial crises. Poorly designed regulation can exacerbate market failures and make financial crises more likely and deeper. Some regulatory policies encourage overinvestment or promote moral hazard. Legal rules empower certain informational intermediaries and other gatekeepers in ways that widen informational asymmetry and create dysfunctional incentives. Statutes and regulations can increase agency costs and opacity, and feed individual actors' propensities to make bad decisions.

One of the particularly valuable aspects of this Handbook is to assess various arguments and perspectives about financial markets through the lens of law and regulation. In the aftermath of any individual crisis, scholars tend to point to specific individual causes. For example, one might view the recent GFC variously as being caused by subprime borrowers, credit rating agencies, financial derivatives traders, bank senior executives, and/or a variety of government actors. Because the goal of this Chapter is to describe financial crises in general terms, it will frame the various arguments regarding the causes of financial market crises in a broad, theoretical perspective. John Kenneth Galbraith argued that the 'common denominators' of financial crises do not form much of an economic theory,[5] and perhaps he was right. Nevertheless, the goal of this Chapter will be to attempt to parse how different categories and theories of market and regulatory failure have played a role in financial crises generally.

Although financial asset markets are often cited as examples of nearly perfect competition, even the strongest proponents of the theory of efficient markets

[3] Fisher, S, 'Commentary: Why Is Financial Stability a Goal of Public Policy' in *Maintaining Financial Stability in a Global Economy: A Symposium Sponsored by the Federal Reserve Bank of Kansas City* (1997) 37, 43.

[4] Baumol, W and Blinder, A, *Economics: Principles and Policy* (1985) 543.

[5] Galbraith, n 2 above, 13.

recognize that well-functioning markets require a robust regulatory structure. For example, Ronald Coase notably concluded that in financial markets 'for anything approaching perfect competition to exist, an intricate system of rules and regulations would normally be needed'.[6] In considering the role of regulation in financial crises, it is worth remembering Coase's criticisms of economists' assumptions regarding markets, especially as they relate to law: that economists ignore how law affects market transactions, how law is a necessary prerequisite to well-functioning markets, and how law is a crucial part of exchange transactions in financial instruments.[7] It is with Coase's words in mind that this Chapter turns to the various theories of why financial market crises arise.

2. Cognitive error

The first theory to consider is the most obvious: that financial crises arise because individual market participants are irrational in some way, perhaps because they follow a herd mentality or mob psychology, or because they misperceive risk and reward. According to this cognitive error theory, financial market crises arise in the aftermath of irrational investor mania, and then panic.

The most prominent proponent of this view is the economic historian Charles P Kindleberger,[8] whose work reflects ideas generated earlier by Hyman P Minsky, Irving Fisher, and Charles Mackay.[9] Although the cognitive error school has existed for many decades, behavioural finance research has confirmed its application to financial markets. Central to the cognitive error theory is the notion that panics and crashes are endemic to financial markets because of human nature and investor psychology.

According to the cognitive error theory, markets move through several stages of progressively increasing investor irrationality, which ultimately is corrected during the crisis. First, a 'displacement'[10] creates new opportunities for profit, and therefore new opportunities to reallocate capital. Displacements are difficult to spot when they occur. For example, technological change, such as the invention of railroads or the spread in the use of the Internet for commerce might be a candidate for displacement. Likewise, a displacement might occur because of the outbreak

[6] Coase, R, *The Firm, the Market, and the Law* (1990) 9. [7] ibid, 5, 9–10.

[8] Kindleberger, C, *Manias, Panics, and Crashes: A History of Financial Crises* (1989).

[9] Minsky, H, 'The Financial Instability Hypothesis: Capitalistic Processes and the Behavior of the Economy' in Kindleberger, C and Leffargue, J (eds), *Financial Crises: Theory, History and Policy* (1982) 13–29; Fisher, I, *The Purchasing Power of Money: Its Determination and Relation to Credit, Interest and Crises* (1911); Mackay, C, *Memoirs of Extraordinary Delusions and the Madness of Crowds* (1852).

[10] Kindleberger, n 8 above, 18.

or end of war; a bumper harvest or crop failure; the widespread adoption of inventions such as canals, railroads, and automobiles; or surprising political events.

One candidate for 'displacement' during the recent GFC is the various policy and market changes that encouraged and permitted the repackaging of subprime mortgages into highly rated structured securities. For example, changes in credit rating agency models and methodologies and increased private and public reliance on ratings create opportunities for bankers to profit by underestimating correlation risk and thereby creating new highly rated securities.[11] This was a 'displacement'.

Next, the amount of credit in the economy expands as additional capital is allocated to these new profitable ventures. In many previous crises, the sources of additional credit have been banks, although in the US the capital markets have played a more prominent role in allocating credit in recent decades. In the GFC, the credit expansion came both from banks and large institutional investors.

As with the displacement, it is difficult to assess the normative implications of such credit expansion as it occurs. Is the financing of additional home construction and purchases important to the economy's growth? Or is that new credit foolish, based on investors' misperceptions? These questions are hard to answer in advance.

In the next stage, financial asset prices rise, and these increases create new opportunities for profit, and therefore new opportunities to reallocate capital. Both Minsky and Kindleberger refer to this stage of speculative excess as 'euphoria'. As potential investors observe others generating profits during this period, they, too, want to invest. As Kindleberger noted, '[t]here is nothing so disturbing to one's well-being and judgment as to see a friend get rich'.[12]

At some point the price increases lead to investor euphoria, which may be indistinguishable from wise investor decision-making. As more financial market actors buy into the relevant new ventures, including those who normally would not take on such risks, 'mania' takes hold, and the prices of financial assets increase in a speculative 'bubble'. Again, the terminology is from Minsky and Kindleberger. By its nature, a speculative bubble is based on irrational behaviour and investor cognitive error, although again such phenomena are difficult to identify, except in hindsight.

Finally, at the top of the market, a few savvy investors decide to sell and prices stop increasing. Typically, there is a signal—a bank failure, poor earnings at a key firm, or the publicity surrounding an unusual fraud—which leads speculators to realize the game is over. They rush for the exits and sell, and prices plummet. Panic continues until one or more of three things happens: (i) prices fall so low that some investors begin buying and support the market; (ii) trading is halted; or

[11] Partnoy, F, 'Overdependence on Credit Ratings Was a Primary Cause of the Crisis' in Mitchell, L and Wilmarth, A (eds), *The Panic of 2008: Causes, Consequences, and Implications for Reform* (2010).

[12] Kindleberger, n 8 above, 19.

(iii) a lender of the last resort persuades the market that money will be available to meet the demand for cash from sellers.

The obvious candidate triggering the panic during the GFC was the collapse of Lehman Brothers, although arguably the key signal that led some speculators to short credit default swaps based on subprime mortgages much earlier, in 2007.[13] It is impossible to know whether prices might have fallen low enough in fall 2008 to persuade investors to buy, because regulators were unwilling to allow yields on bank borrowing to rise to market-clearing levels. Instead, regulators began a massive expansion of credit to ensure that funds would be available.

The cognitive error theory allows for differences among crises as to the nature of the displacement, the form of credit expansion, and the type of object of speculation. Subprime mortgages were the issue in the GFC, just as tulip bulbs were the issue in the 1600s, and dot.com companies were the issue in 2000. Although the details of each crisis vary, the cognitive error school argues that there nevertheless persists a certain pattern or structure to crises generally, fuelled by investor irrationality: displacement, credit expansion, mania, panic, and crash.

3. Moral hazard

An alternative school argues that financial crises are precipitated by moral hazard; the taking of excessive risks in the presence of insurance. For example, Robert Shiller has stressed the significance of inefficiencies created by insurance and moral hazard.[14] Likewise, Robert C Merton and Zvi Bodie have discussed the view that financial guarantees cause moral hazard distortions in financial markets.[15] The idea that moral hazard may lead to a financial crisis is not necessarily inconsistent with the cognitive error theory. The primary difference between the theories is that the moral hazard theory explicitly blames financial guarantees for starting the mania phase. In other words, the thrust of the moral hazard theory is that government regulation, rather than private behaviour, is primarily responsible for the dislocations that lead to crisis.

Moral hazard arguments presume that investors believe, correctly or not, that some entity is providing a guarantee against all or some of their loss. It is this guarantee, among other factors, that persuades market participants to overinvest or to assume excessive risk. A financial guarantee might be explicit or implicit. The key

[13] Flannery, M, Houston, J, and Partnoy, F, 'Credit Default Swap Spreads as Viable Substitutes for Credit Ratings' (2010) 158 *University of Pennsylvania Law Review* 2085.

[14] Shiller, R, *Macro Markets: Creating Institutions for Managing Society's Largest Economic Risks* (1993).

[15] Merton, R and Bodie, Z, 'On the Management of Financial Guarantees' (1992) 21 *Financial Management* 87.

is that investors believe that some degree of insurance will be provided in the event of a systemic collapse.

Traces of moral hazard problems have been found in the histories of the most severe financial crises. Guarantees create incentives for market participants to take on imprudent risks, with the expectation that they will receive support in the event of a crash. However, explicit guarantees are rare. The more likely scenario for government guarantees is that they are implicit. For example, before the GFC, supranational organizations such as the International Monetary Fund and the World Bank encouraged the notion that investors or governments likely would receive assistance in times of crisis. The same can be said of the US government, particularly in the aftermath of the Mexican peso crisis. Even if these organizations made no representations regarding any guarantee, investors rationally perceived that regulators would be likely to bail them out in a crisis. According to the moral hazard view, given this belief, such investors would have been willing to take on much larger, and much riskier, positions.

Moral hazard can lead to financial asset prices being artificially high and unsustainable. However, although moral hazard can explain why market participants might take on excessive risk, it does not explain why the correction in asset prices must be sudden, as in a financial crisis. For this explanation, the theory can draw from cognitive error theory and the phenomenon of the 'rush to the exits'.

In addition, proponents of the moral hazard theory face an interesting puzzle. The argument that moral hazard leads to market crises also is an argument against two commonly proposed solutions to the problem of crises: deposit insurance and the lender of the last resort. Paradoxically, financial crises were more common before the existence of these two regulatory remedies. For example, the US faced substantial banking panics nearly every decade before the 1930s, but none from the 1940s until 2008. Is it a coincidence that banking panics stopped at the same time the federal government created federal deposit insurance and the Federal Reserve Bank, the US lender of last resort, and thereby increased the amount of moral hazard? If the moral hazard explanation is correct, shouldn't these safety net programmes have increased the number of panics? Or did the degree of moral hazard build up over time, only to be released in the GFC?

One possible answer is that markets require a certain amount of protection, and therefore must swallow a certain amount of moral hazard, in order to prevent or at least minimize financial crises. Maintaining investor and depositor trust is another important factor. Because the amount of moral hazard is directly related to the information gap between borrowers and lenders, as this information gap has narrowed, due to advances in technology and disintermediation, the quantity of moral hazard created by these safety net programmes might have declined since the 1930s. Indeed, the type of moral hazard at issue in the GFC arguably was of a different kind and degree, not merely to protect depositors or lenders, but also to ring fence liabilities and encourage mergers of insolvent financial institutions.

4. Information asymmetry

Information asymmetry arguments presume that investors are not aware of certain information critical to their investment decisions, and that they sell when they learn of this information. The information gap between investors and issuers is essentially irresolvable and endemic to financial markets. Issuers always have better information than investors about risks and expected returns. Indeed, information asymmetry is a central justification for much financial market regulation.

According to the information asymmetry argument, there is a divergence between financial asset prices and fundamental value because investors lack sufficient information to analyse their investments. To the extent this information gap results in investors undervaluing financial instruments, issuers will close the gap by disclosing positive information to encourage investors to pay more. However, to the extent investors are overvaluing financial instruments, issuers may not have the same incentives to disclose. Rational investors realize that issuers face these incentives and discount the price they are willing to pay for financial instruments to reflect the uncertainty about whether issuers are disclosing all negative information. This 'lemons problem' mitigates some of the negative implications of information asymmetry argument.

As some investors overpay for financial instruments, and market prices diverge from reality, both current investors and issuers have incentives to keep negative information out of the market. New buyers watch prices increasing and decide they, too, must be part of this upward spiral. Insiders at issuers who know about negative information may sell their stock, or even short shares, so that prices reflect information available to issuers, but restrictions on insider trading or short selling prevent such adjustment. In addition, to the extent investors and issuers are not rational, the information asymmetry argument draws from the cognitive error theory. In any event, information gaps lead to investor mania, which ends in panic and ultimately crisis.

The information asymmetry theory has superior explanatory power in the context of day-to-day corporate management decision-making, or even in securities issuance, than in the context of market crashes. Information asymmetry arguments dovetail with the rational bubble school explanations of why markets do not crash, and carry some of the same flaws.

The information asymmetry theory also ignores the fact that issuers may not have good information either. For example, during the period before the GFC some bank managers arguably were as uninformed about their own banks' retention of subprime mortgage and correlation risk as were their counterparties, clients, and shareholders. The assumption of perfect information frequently does not hold, even in modern financial markets, so the fact that investors do not have adequate information does not necessarily mean that issuers do. If neither issuers nor investors have adequate information, information asymmetry becomes less relevant, or at least more subtle. Instead, information uncertainty or unavailability might be the reason investors overpay for financial assets. Nevertheless, information asymmetry is one important theory of why crises arise.

5. Agency costs

Agency costs are central to the study of institutions and markets. Accordingly, and not surprisingly, theories about agency costs are part of explanations of market crises. In general, the agency cost problem is that managers have different objectives from investors. Managers might want to maximize their own income and perquisites or the firm's size, in contrast to investors who want to maximize their own profits.

For example, one explanation of why financial institutions were willing and able to take on substantial subprime and correlation risks during the GFC is that employees were incentivized to take these risks at the expense of their firms' shareholders and other constituents. It is costly, and perhaps impossible, to manage these kinds of complex risks under certain circumstances. Agency costs at least partially explain why prior to the GFC bank employees retained substantial exposure to subprime and correlation risks without disclosing such risks to shareholders.

Agency costs and the problem of the separation of ownership and control within institutions has been a central motivator for corporate and securities regulation. The financial crisis that began with the 1929 crash is perhaps the most prominent example. In direct response to the outcry for regulation arising from the aftermath of the crash, Congress enacted the Securities Act of 1933, which regulates initial distributions of securities, and the Securities Exchange Act of 1934, which among other things regulates post-distribution trading. Similar crisis-then-regulation sequences had occurred during the previous several hundred years, with financial market regulation following as a response to a financial crisis. The Sarbanes–Oxley and Dodd–Frank laws in the US are the most recent examples. In each event, agency costs were a major theoretical justification for new regulation.

6. Market efficiency vs market failure

The above categories of market failures are not uncontroversial. Some scholars deny the premise of the above descriptions, and claim that both these market failures, and the crises they supposedly generate, are often illusory. On its face, this position might appear absurd with respect to certain crises. For example, it seems ludicrous to argue that a one-month decline of 80 per cent in the value of shares in the South Sea Company in 1720, a one-day decline of 22.6 per cent in the Dow Jones

Industrial Average in 1987, or a sudden collapse of the world's largest financial institutions in 2007–08 banks, was in fact a rational response to new information.

Yet, the argument about market efficiency is worth engaging, because it helps to delineate some of the types of financial crises and potentially can inform regulatory decisions. The Efficient Market Hypothesis (EMH) posits that financial assets reflect available information, to varying degrees. If information is not reflected in stock prices, rational investors seeking profits buy and sell these assets until the information is reflected. This mechanism ensures that prices reflect available information.

EMH theories vary in degree, based on the type of information it is assumed will become reflected in prices.[16] EMH proponents argue that financial crises are either responses to new information or low-probability exceptions to the EMH. For example, the 1929 crisis might be characterized as a response to new information about a crisis in global trade coupled with numerous regulatory failures. Likewise, the 1987 US stock market crash, the collapse in tulip bulb prices, and the South Sea bubble bursting all might be said to have been responses to new information.[17]

In each of these cases, there are weaknesses in the empirical argument that market crises were simply a response to the revelation of new information. There is some evidence that banking crises during the 1800s were related to real events in general terms, although it is unclear whether any information about these real events was unavailable to depositors before the panic. Likewise, there is some evidence that crises are natural accompaniments to the business cycle, as when depositors receive information about an economic downturn and withdraw funds. Likewise, the collapse of Lehman Brothers in September 2008 arguably revealed both new information about the exposure of financial institutions to complex risks and the government's unwillingness, or perhaps inability, to rescue every major financial institution.

Yet, information that precipitated each crisis was available to at least some market participants much earlier. Many savvy investors were aware that not only Lehman Brothers, but also other banks, had massive exposure to subprime mortgages and correlation risk a year before Lehman's collapse, and the market for credit default swaps reflected at least some of this investor awareness.[18] In theory, only a small percentage of market participants need access to such information for it to be reflected in market prices.[19] Accordingly, EMH proponents face a difficult

[16] There are weak, semi-strong, and strong forms of the EMH, depending on whether the proponent of the theory believes that past prices, other public information, or non-public information is reflected in current prices; the more information is reflected in prices, the stronger the theory. Fama, E, 'Efficient Capital Markets: II' (1991) 46 *Journal of Finance* 1575, 1600; Gilson, R and Kraakman, R, 'The Mechanisms of Market Efficiency' (1984) 70 *Virginia Law Review* 549, 569–72.

[17] Garber, n 2 above, 552.

[18] Flannery et al., n 13 above.

[19] Romano, R, 'Empowering Investors: A Market Approach to Securities Regulation' (1998) 107 *Yale Law Journal* 2359, 2368 n 21.

question: if the relevant information was available earlier, why did so many investors wait until a particular time to act on the information?

Economists have demonstrated mathematically that even under the assumptions of the EMH, there will be certain large and sudden movements in markets.[20] According to these models, these events will happen with very low probability. Yet, financial crises have occurred with much greater frequency than predicted by these models.

Moreover, the mechanisms through which rational bubbles and crashes appear in mathematical models are similar to the mechanism described by the cognitive error theory: essentially, the models posit that a market has multiple equilibria, one of which occurs when investors come to believe a panic will occur and therefore understand that it is optimal for all investors to withdraw; as all investors withdraw, they precipitate a crisis. A mathematical theory that low-probability large downward price movements occur is essentially the same as a non-mathematical theory that markets crash due to cognitive error.

A perhaps stronger argument by EMH proponents is that financial crises are due to government and regulatory failures more than market failures. Essentially, the argument is that failed government policy or misguided regulation creates market distortions that correct themselves in a sudden fashion. The argument takes various forms. For example, poor macroeconomic and government policies lead to the misallocation of credit, which is primarily responsible for a crisis.[21] Likewise, artificially fixed exchange rates make a rapid devaluation of the domestic currency inevitable at some point. Some writers have argued that government policies to subsidize the US housing market were at the core of the recent crisis, though the support for this argument is empirically weak.[22]

To the extent regulations are known well in advance of a crash, it is difficult to argue that there is some new information that leads investors to sell financial assets all at once. On the other hand, it might be that regulations prevent the market from reaching an equilibrium price, either by creating artificial supply or demand, or by imposing a price floor or ceiling. A government policy of fixing rates can prevent the market from clearing, at least temporarily. Similarly, a government policy subsidizing the purchase of certain financial assets can skew supply or demand, and therefore prices.

Overall, the roots of financial crises are likely a combination of the above theories. In other words, financial crises are partly caused by market failure, and partly caused by regulatory failure.

[20] Diamond, D and Dybvig, P, 'Bank Runs, Deposit Insurance, and Liquidity' (1983) 91 *Journal of Political Economy* 401; Devenow, A and Welch, I, 'Rational Herding in Financial Economics' (1996) 40 *European Economic Review* 603.

[21] Eichengreen, B, *Toward a New International Financial Architecture: A Practical Post-Asia Agenda* (1999) 5–6.

[22] Madrick, J and Partnoy, F, 'Did Fannie Cause the Disaster?' (2011) *New York Review of Books*.

II. Regulation and Financial Crises: Theory

Once researchers have a sense of the roots of financial crises, it should become possible to construct a roadmap for optimal regulation. In the simplest terms, regulation should address the market failures that are central to financial crises. Regulation might not be able to prevent financial crises or even do much to ameliorate the effects of crises. But an understanding of the roots of financial crises should at least illustrate the directions in which regulation should head.

Unfortunately, regulators typically have not followed any such roadmap. Instead of addressing the roots of financial crises, legislators and regulators have addressed symptoms, unrelated issues, politically salient demands, media attention, and the interests of various constituent groups. The result is a mishmash of regulation, some of which is costly and wrongheaded, some of which is good policy but unrelated to financial crises, little of which will likely prevent future crises.

Moreover, much regulation has had the effect of encouraging and exacerbating financial crises. As Erik Gerding has noted, financial regulation can create subsidies for certain players, skew the incentives of some actors to undermine compliance, encourage regulatory arbitrage, promote investor herding, and provide procyclical incentives.[23] More generally, regulation can add to market failures, not only through moral hazard as indicated above, but also by increasing the costs of cognitive error and the magnitude of information asymmetry and agency costs. Regulation can magnify market failure by distorting the market for gatekeeper intermediation and introducing dysfunctional 'regulatory licences', such as the entitlement to be in compliance with regulation simply by obtaining a sufficiently high credit rating.

This Section discusses the potential positive and deleterious aspects of financial regulation and financial crises. It begins with a theoretical discussion of the timing and source of legal rules, and then turns to specific areas and effects of regulation.

1. The timing and source of legal rules

From a theoretical perspective, one useful way to assess regulatory proposals related to financial crises is to analyse both the temporal and legal source variables relevant to a particular rule. In other words, scholars can first assess the when and where of regulation.

[23] Gerding, E, *Law, Bubbles, and Financial Regulation* (2013).

Much modern financial market regulation is focused on ex ante regulation, from capital requirements to investment restrictions to disclosure rules.[24] This emphasis is especially true outside the US, particularly in Asia, where regulators rely less on the private attorney general role of the plaintiffs' bar. In contrast, decades ago, regulators throughout the world, but particularly in the US, took more of an ex post approach. These regulators emphasized adjudication or regulatory assessment after the fact based on general principles rather than specific rules.

The complexity of modern markets has led to the proliferation of ex ante rules, which purport to provide greater certainty to regulators and market participants. In some cases, that certainty is important and welcome. In other cases, it has deleterious consequences. The proliferation of rules raises numerous policy questions, including whether financial markets might be better served by greater regulatory uncertainty. Market participants, then, would be less able to calculate the expected benefits and costs of avoiding regulation based on anticipated probabilities and magnitudes. Moreover, in many prominent cases such certainty is illusory. Even after the rulemaking deadlines under many provisions of the Dodd–Frank Wall Street Reform and Consumer Protection Act of 2010 had passed, there were final rules in place only for a fraction of those items.

Over time, the rights and obligations of financial market participants have moved from ex post adjudication to ex ante specification. Early derivatives were privately negotiated contracts not covered by any specific regulatory regime in which the parties would expect to be able to enforce obligations through contract-related litigation, if at all.[25] Financial institutions, particularly banks and investment banks, negotiated and lobbied for this shift away from ex post adjudication; likewise, in recent years, financial institutions also have explicitly lobbied against, and rejected, both private adjudication and public rulemaking. The most prominent example involved the negotiations that led to the passage of the Commodity Futures Modernization Act of 2000 at the end of the Clinton Administration. Nevertheless, whatever the cause of this shift, whether regulation is specified in advance or after the fact is an important preliminary theoretical question.

2. Trust

One important role of financial regulation is to promote trust. Trust plays a key role in the formation and function of financial markets. The erosion of trust is often a central cause of financial crises, and restoring trust is a key part of the response to crises. Indeed, several prominent economists have argued that '[i]t is possible that

[24] Partnoy, F, 'The Timing and Source of Regulation' (2014) *Seattle University Law Review*.
[25] Swan, E, *Building the Global Market: A 4,000 Year History of Derivatives* (2000).

some broad underlying factor, related to trust, influences the development of all institutions in a country, including laws and capital markets'.[26]

A primary reason for the importance of trust is that financial systems are inherently unstable. Lenders want liquidity, but borrowers want long-term contracts. There is a maturity mismatch inherent in the functioning of a financial market. Lenders cannot both provide long-term contracts and receive liquidity. Borrowers cannot both provide liquidity and receive long-term contracts. For example, in the simplest case banks have illiquid or long-term assets (loans) and liquid liabilities (deposits).

Trust is important to the resolution of this instability. Trust encourages individuals to deposit money with financial institutions. Banks might have a comparative advantage in investing in illiquid, long-term, risky assets, because they are able to differentiate and price credit risks better than other intermediaries. But banks also have a comparative advantage due to the trust that arises from implicit or explicit regulatory support. Deposit insurance, implicit guarantees, and favourable regulatory treatment all give banks an advantage, even if bankers are not particularly good at differentiating and pricing credit risks.

Therefore, one role of financial regulation is to bridge this trust gap by providing an illusion to both lenders and borrowers. To the lenders the financial system gives the illusion of a long-term contract, even though the truth is that lenders may or may not be able to roll over loans for the same maturity they might have specified in an actual long-term contract. To the borrowers the financial system gives the illusion of liquidity, although the truth is that if all lenders sought liquidity simultaneously, as in a bank run, liquidity would not exist.[27] The illusion of a well-functioning financial system is supported by the law of large numbers, the assumption being that, of the large number of lenders, only a few will seek liquidity simultaneously. In short, financial market equilibrium is the result of faith.

For the US in the nineteenth century, this illusion of trust could not be preserved, and financial crises occurred with great regularity. The US experienced a financial crisis roughly every decade through the 1930s. Before 1900, banking panics were common in Europe and the US until central banks were created to eliminate the problem. Since then, an environment of trust has preserved this illusion, buttressed by deposit insurance and the Federal Reserve Bank's pledge to act as a lender of the last resort, and notwithstanding the fact that these institutions create moral hazard. One of the biggest questions that arose during the recent GFC was how much regulatory reaction was required to preserve this long-standing illusion.

However, financial regulation that attempts to encourage trust in a heavy-handed way can be counterproductive. Accordingly, one way that regulation can best

[26] La Porta, R, Lopez-de-Silanes, F, Shleifer, A, and Vishny, R, 'Legal Determinants of External Finance' (1997) 52 *Journal of Finance* 1131, 1150.

[27] Allen, F and Gale, D, 'Optimal Financial Crises' (1998) 53 *Journal of Finance* 1245.

encourage trust is by nurturing the kinds of private relationships that resolve market failures or collective action problems. Regulation can reinforce the spirit of trust necessary for cooperative repeat-play relationships by mimicking rules that might evolve in a world of lower transaction costs through private ordering. Trusting lenders and borrowers are more willing to transact, and increased secondary market liquidity leads to a lower bid-ask spread, which lowers the overall cost of capital and encourages stability. Regulation also can attempt to influence investor expectations in advance to avoid the mania that often predates crises. In any event, trust is an important consideration not often recognized by those considering the role of law in financial markets. The trust paradox is that although financial regulation is less necessary when trust prevails, an important role of financial regulation is to preserve trust.

3. Measurement and specification

Although researchers understand that one traditional role of financial regulation is to help minimize agency costs, they have had difficulties in measuring and specifying how in fact regulations do so. In corporate and securities law, one solution to the problem of conflicts between shareholders and managers is corporate governance. Agency costs arise because managers have different incentives than shareholders. Corporate governance measures are designed to reduce these costs either by aligning managers' incentives with those of shareholders, or by establishing devices to monitor managers. In theory, one can measure the effectiveness of regulation by examining variation in corporate governance.

However, the evidence and methodologies used to understand the role of corporate governance and agency costs are controversial. For example, there are questions about how economists might determine that agency costs and poor enforcement of shareholder rights are correlated with underdeveloped capital markets.[28] Empirical studies typically rely on numerical rankings of various measures, such as the efficiency of the judicial system, the rule of law, the level of corruption, the risk of expropriation, or the risk of repudiation of contracts by the government.

It is difficult, if not impossible, to quantify a country's legal regime on such a scale of, say, one to ten with any hope of accuracy, and such data are not helped by a sophisticated econometric model. Many of the numerical measurements scholars use are based on anecdotal evidence from earlier periods and might not accurately describe the state of agency costs in a particular market. For example, studies of the East Asia crisis of the late 1990s relied on data from the 1980s. At least one

[28] Shleifer, A and Vishny, R, 'A Survey of Corporate Governance' (1997) 52 *Journal of Finance* 737; La Porta, R, Lopez-de-Silanes, F, Shleifer, A, and Vishny, R, 'Law and Finance' (1998) 106 *Journal of Political Economy* 1113, 1124.

often-cited source warns explicitly against attributing any exactitude to numerical rankings: it states that '[s]uch calculations implicitly make a claim for Survey precision that it will not carry'; it notes that the numerical measures are 'little more than a heuristic devise for printing maps or adding up doubtful totals' and that '[a]fter all, the dividing lines between the categories of the Survey are purely arbitrary points at which to cut into continua'; and it states that '[t]he Survey is based on library research, updated by a more or less continuous flow of publications across the author's desk'.[29] One widely cited 1998 study of the efficiency of the judicial system of a country was estimated based on the estimates of the Business International Corporation from 1980 through 1983.[30] The 'law and order' measure from the International Country Risk Guide is determined based on staff members' subjective assessments for each country of both the 'strength and impartiality of the legal system' (law) and 'popular observance of the law' (order), on a scale of one to three.[31]

Moreover, the mathematical specifications of the agency cost models that scholars use to process the above data also are dubious. For example, some studies use a quadratic, concave 'stealing manager' utility function, even though there is no basis for assuming that manager behaviour can be specified by multiplying their amount of stealing by itself.[32] The overall message from these limitations is that scholars should be cautious in relying on agency cost and corporate governance studies.

Nevertheless, there is good reason to believe a basic conclusion of these studies is correct, even if it isn't well supported: poor corporate governance is associated with market crises, and therefore one role of regulation is to improve corporate governance. Certainly, the poor corporate governance explanation fits the state of the financial markets during the 1920s, prior to the Great Crash of 1929. At that time, there was a vast structure of holding companies and investment trusts, and the holding companies controlled large segments of the utility, railroad, and entertainment businesses. Moreover, there was evidence of poor credit allocation decisions due to an inadequate banking system, pressures associated with a large current account deficit and trade-related tensions, and substantial information asymmetry between issuers and investors.[33] In such an environment, regulation can reduce the chance of a financial crisis by improving corporate governance.

Similar conclusions fit the period before the GFC. Corporate governance, particularly at major banks, was weak, and agency costs were high.

[29] Gastil, R, *Freedom in the World: Political Rights and Civil Liberties* (1989) 25–6.

[30] La Porta et al., n 28 above, 1124.

[31] Howell, L, *The Handbook of Country and Political Risk Analysis* (1998) 189, 194.

[32] Johnson, S, Boone, P, Breach, A, and Friedman, E, 'Corporate Governance in the Asian Financial Crisis' (2000) 58 *Journal of Financial Economics* 141, 145.

[33] Galbraith, JK, *The Great Crash: 1929* (1979) 178–82.

Compensation structures incentivized employees to take large risks without bearing substantial downside cost. Disclosure of financial risk was poor. Poor accounting and risk management exacerbated the corporate governance problems during the two decades before the recent crisis.[34] These conclusions are not necessarily controversial, but their scope and magnitude are difficult to measure and specify.

III. Regulation and Financial Crises: Policy

The above theoretical discussion frames the debate about several policy instruments that are available to regulators. At the outset of any policy discussion about financial crises and regulation, it is important to note that there is a view that private ordering in financial markets is the best means of achieving price stability and equilibrium, and that adequate protection against financial crises does not necessarily require regulation. As this argument goes, well-functioning financial markets can offer the best protection at lowest cost, even in the absence of applicable legal rules.

Indeed, in a perfectly competitive market, with zero transactions costs, there would be neither information asymmetry nor agency cost conflicts, and therefore no need for regulation. Accordingly, to the extent financial markets resemble perfect competition, there should be scepticism about whether regulation can improve any policy result. The self-regulatory view is that reputational constraints, the market for corporate control, and rational disclosure incentives are sufficiently robust to make self-regulation superior to government regulation.

However, there are limits on private ordering and no country today relies solely on markets as the guarantor of financial stability. As Ronald Coase noted, markets generally function properly only within a well-defined legal and institutional framework. There is a long-standing debate about whether such a framework must be created by concerted action or whether such institutions will develop spontaneously when the social costs of building them exceed their transactions costs.[35] However, there are limits on private ordering, particularly with respect to governance mechanisms, the first policy area discussed below.

[34] Partnoy, F, *Infectious Greed: How Deceit and Risk Corrupted the Financial Markets* (2003).

[35] North, D, *Growth and Structural Change* (1981); Demsetz, H, 'Toward a Theory of Property Rights' (1967) 57 *American Economic Review* 347.

1. Governance

Third-party intermediaries are not sufficiently constrained by reputational capital. Reputation alone is a poor constraint, because of end-period weaknesses and ambiguity about who within an institution bears any reputational costs. Moreover, inadequate prosecution of senior executives, from both the public and private sector, limits the scope of reputational constraints. In theory, the private attorney general role of plaintiff shareholders and whistleblowers in civil litigation could fill gaps left by the public sector, but those litigants also are subject to serious limits. Large, active shareholders may either lack sufficient incentives to monitor management, or may use their stakes to obtain benefits for themselves only, and not for other shareholders.

In addition, takeovers threats do not play much of a disciplining role in ways that matter to financial crises. Accounting firms are not publicly traded. Credit rating agencies have cemented an oligopoly lock and there has been little merger activity among minor agencies recently. Major banks are now effectively too big to be taken over, and there was little threat of a takeover except during the GFC itself. Accordingly, the threat of takeovers is a weak constraint.

Finally, managers of publicly held intermediary corporations have few incentives independently to disclose negative information. Even managers who decide to disclose information in order to persuade investors to buy a new issue may not want to disclose information in the future, during periods when they are not seeking capital from the public markets. Of course, managers could attempt to bind themselves to making public disclosure continuously, but such binding is costly. In any event, without regulation, the financial market likely would underproduce negative information about financial intermediaries.

Accordingly, governance regulation potentially can fill these gaps. Regulation can impose monitoring and disclosure duties on the board of directors. In theory, these duties will help align the interests of managers and shareholders as the board monitors, and potentially fires, senior managers. However, for a large publicly held firm, the shareholders typically are so dispersed that management may effectively determine the composition of the board. In such instances, it is unlikely that the board will play an effective monitoring role. Of course, a firm with a captive board may lack credibility when it seeks capital from the public markets, but in such cases it is the market and not the legal structure of the board that is doing the monitoring. Consider Citigroup's board before the GFC. There was little effective monitoring of management. Instead, board members were highly compensated and re-elected, even after autumn 2007, when it became clear that monitoring of disclosure and controls was grossly inadequate.

In the aftermath of the 1929 crash, regulators imposed a twin pillar regime of mandatory disclosure and anti-fraud enforcement. Those two pillars were the key architecture features that supported well-functioning markets for decades. Both have been eroded in recent years, as disclosures became boilerplate and anti-fraud prosecution more limited and infrequent. The response to the GFC could have included architecture moves to rebuild those pillars. But instead the Dodd–Frank legislation focused on other priorities and architecture changes in the areas of disclosure and anti-fraud enforcement were minimal. Instead, Dodd–Frank focused on other policy areas, such as living wills and consumer protection, which might improve the functioning of markets in various ways—reducing moral hazard and informational asymmetry—but which would not likely improve the governance of intermediaries. For example, under Dodd–Frank and MiFID II reforms, certain swaps and other derivatives have to be cleared and centrally traded. Although some financial institutions have characterized the centralized clearing rules as a major reform, those institutions already were moving toward centralized clearing and there are vast exceptions to the clearing rules, particularly for non-standardized financial instruments.[36] Another response outside the two-pillar regime is the adoption of so-called 'living wills'. For example, the resolution tools that are a part of the European Union Bank Recovery and Resolution Directive are designed to allow for speedy and relatively low-risk resolution of bank insolvencies. However, they do not address, or prevent, the risk-taking that might lead banks to become insolvent in the first instance, and they do not address the growth, risk, and resolution of non-bank institutions at all.

Two recent examples of governance regulation are worth considering. First is the portion of the Dodd–Frank Act and hundreds of pages of interpretation known as the 'Volcker rule', which attempts to define which categories of bank trading activities are permissible, and which are sufficiently costly from a governance perspective that they should take place only outside of banks. Imagine if, instead of trying to specify what constitutes 'proprietary trading' through an advance rulemaking, Congress instead had adopted a different version of the Volcker rule as just one sentence: 'Banks are not permitted to engage in proprietary trading.' Then, adjudicators would decide later what that sentence means and whether particular conduct fits within the rule's scope. One advantage to this common law-style process is that it would minimize the influence of lobbying and short-term politics. Instead, the development of the meaning of the rule would take place slowly, over the course of years, as both market participants and regulators came to define the details of what it means to engage in 'proprietary trading' as the borders of the rule evolved and were tweaked over time.

As a second example, consider the Delaware Chancery Court decision in the *Citigroup* derivative case. The Court held Citigroup's board to a lax standard of liability for risk-related decisions and monitoring.[37] Future cases will give judges

[36] Houman, H, 'Guilty by Association? Regulating Credit Default Swaps?' (2009) 4 *Entrepreneurial Business Law Journal* 407, 453.

[37] *In re Citigroup Inc. Shareholder Derivative Litigation*, 964 A.2d 106 (Del. Ch. 2009).

an opportunity to determine if the earlier cases were the correct approach, or whether they should follow *Citigroup*. If future courts recognize that financial risk presents a unique question for boards, then the jurisprudence might evolve to hold that boards need to be sufficiently aware of risks and have engaged in adequate risk-management activities in order to satisfy their monitoring duties. Ideally, judges who understand financial risk will reject *Citigroup* and adduce a board's monitoring of financial risk more critically after the fact, thus returning to the Holmesian notion of law as a prediction of what a judge will do.

These two examples illustrate the importance of the theoretical distinction between ex ante and ex post regulatory approaches. With respect to governance, it is difficult to specify the various relevant contingencies in advance. No regulator can imagine how financial institutions might react to a particular specification of what constitutes proprietary trading or a breach of fiduciary duty in financial-risk management. Accordingly, one potentially superior approach to governance is to specify in advance only a broad standard, and then adjudicate the boundaries of that standard later. This was the approach regulators took in the aftermath of the 1929 crisis; it is not the approach regulators have taken in the aftermath of the GFC.

2. Bank capital requirements

One key component of the global financial regulatory architecture of financial institutions is bank capital regulation. Instead of limiting banks with heavy-handed requirements, regulators have essentially partnered with banks to try to ensure that banks have enough capital to support the risks they are taking. Banks engaged in riskier activities are supposed to have more risk-based capital. The primary source of regulatory guidance for such regulation has been the voluntary set of standards suggested by the Basel Committee on Banking Supervision. The idea behind these standards is that they will more accurately reflect market practice.

However, these standards have serious drawbacks. Their heavy reliance on privately provided credit ratings leads to inaccuracies and creates distortions. Credit ratings are less accurate than credit spreads and the standards neither distinguish among issues within a particular rating category nor among issues with different spreads. Credit ratings do not account for numerous risks, as the GFC illustrated. Regulatory reliance on credit ratings, a problematic practice that began during the mid-1970s and has escalated over time, was one of the primary causes of the GFC.[38]

Moreover, banks are able to use derivatives to add risk below the regulatory radar of the Basel Committee terms. Basel-style rules create huge incentives for this type of 'regulatory arbitrage' using derivatives. For example, Basel rules that

[38] Partnoy, F, 'The Siskel and Ebert of Financial Markets?: Two Thumbs Down for the Credit Rating Agencies' (1999) 77 *Washington University Law Quarterly* 619, 626.

rely on short-term measures of balance sheet volatility that do not capture the risks of bank failure. Although such short-term measures of risk may impact the value of a particular bank's stock, because investors use it to generate a discount rate to apply to the institution's projected earnings, these measures are not appropriate for regulatory purposes. Regulators should not care about the volatility of earnings, except to the extent a bank with more volatile earnings also is more likely to fail, a conclusion that does not necessarily follow. If a bank is at risk of failing, it should not assuage regulators that its earnings are relatively constant. Conversely, if a bank is not at risk of failing, it should not be relevant to regulators that its earnings are volatile. Before, during, and after the GFC, Citigroup's balance sheet numbers were stable, not volatile.[39]

Anat Admati and Martin Hellwig have written wisely about proposals for stricter leverage requirements for banks, but regulators have not adopted such proposals.[40] One simple regulatory improvement would be simply to require that bank capital structure be more heavily weighted to equity than debt. Radically reducing leverage would decrease the risk of bank failures, and accordingly would reduce systemic risk. Yet, Admati and Hellwig's proposals have not been adopted, or even seriously considered (Chapter by Alexander in this volume addresses international efforts to regulate bank capital requirements and leverage generally). One factor that influences bank capital requirements is asymmetric lobbying against stricter rules; a class public choice story of concentrated financial interests versus diffuse ones.

3. Capital controls

Related to bank capital requirements are capital controls. Although capital controls generally were not a part of the debate about the GFC, many countries continue to propose or maintain them. Capital controls include restrictions on capital inflows and outflows, currency boards, and circuit breakers for exchanges. Although bank capital requirements have significant potential benefits, these other forms of capital controls are potentially both efficiency reducing and unfair.

First, consider restrictions on capital inflows and outflows. Restrictions on inflows are designed to reduce domestic dependence on foreign capital, and therefore to break the cycle of mania-panic-crash at the mania-panic stage, by deterring foreign investors with so-called 'hot money' from shifting volatile funds into the domestic economy. But inflow restrictions require related domestic financial reform and create incentives for regulatory arbitrage.

[39] Partnoy, F, Off-Balance Sheet Transactions, video presentation at Roosevelt Institution Make Markets Be Markets Conference (2010).

[40] Admati, A and Hellwig, M, *The Bankers' New Clothes: What's Wrong with Banking and What to Do about It* (2013).

Restrictions on outflows are designed to break the cycle at the panic-crash stage, by preventing foreign investors from shifting funds out of the domestic economy. However, when foreign investors seek to exit markets, they are doing so rationally, because they perceive a threat of default or inflationary policy. Because outflow controls are imposed long after foreign investors have decided to invest in a country, they are not particularly effective in preventing excessive risk-taking.

A currency board is an attempt by regulators to commit credibly not to follow inflationary policies. A currency board permits the government to issue local money only to match exactly its gold and hard currency reserves. It makes inflationary policies difficult or impossible, because it would force a contraction in the money supply and an increase in interest rates following capital outflows. The obvious problem with a currency board is ensuring that the board does not exercise influence over the money supply. To the extent market crises arise because investors believe governments will devalue their currencies with the understanding that some supranational organization will come to the rescue, a credible currency board could correct this market failure. However, a currency board cannot affect investors' cognitive error or information deficits, and are therefore limited in their effectiveness.

Circuit breakers are designed to prevent panics associated with investor cognitive error by controlling, or even halting, capital flows following a large temporary decline on an exchange. Circuit breakers are designed to offset selling pressure from traders who use similar models to assess the market, when supply and demand for financial instruments are inelastic and a small price move can cause a crisis.[41]

Circuit breakers pose several regulatory challenges. First, they create incentives for evasion. Securities may be traded on other exchanges or in over-the-counter contracts. They also potentially widen the information gap between investors and market makers. Individual investors typically will not be able to make the last trades before a circuit breaker is imposed, or the first trades after they are lifted. Nor will they be the first to learn about the imposition of the circuit breakers. Rational investors will realize that market makers and insiders will be more likely to profit during a crisis, and this realization will create uncertainty and may increase the cost of capital. Finally, circuit breakers may actually fuel panic: investor cognitive error may increase more during the period in which the circuit breaker is in effect than it would have increased during a period of panic selling.

In sum, there are several regulatory approaches that seek to impose controls on capital flows in times of crisis. Unfortunately, many of these forms of controls create perverse incentives and other inefficiencies, and may worsen, instead of prevent, such crises.

[41] Glauber, R, 'Systemic Problems in the Next Market Crash' (1997) 52 *Journal of Finance* 1184, 1185–7.

4. Lender of the last resort

One traditional solution to the problem of investor panic is for regulators to act as a lender of last resort during financial crises. The obvious problem with this solution is moral hazard: if investors know about the lender of the last resort, they are likely to take on excessive risk.

To reduce moral hazard, the lender of last result can adopt a policy of 'constructive ambiguity', a term used by Gerald Corrigan, former head of the Federal Reserve Bank of New York. Constructive ambiguity means the lender of last resort will have the right to intervene during a crisis, but will not promise to do so. The idea is that uncertainty might optimally balance moral hazard against the costs of investor panic.

In the GFC, central banks played the role of lender of last resort, lending at low rates and buying assets from troubled banks. Regulators were somewhat ambiguous, most notably with Lehman Brothers. Did they save too many institutions or too few? Did they create too much or too little ambiguity by allowing only Lehman to fail?

Ideally, a lender of last resort should lend at an above-market penalty interest rate. However, regulators have not done that. For example, lending to banks during the GFC was at artificially low rates that did not reflect the credit risk of those institutions. The same is true of lending during other crises, including the Asia crisis and the Mexican peso crisis, when lending was subsidized at below-market rates. Note that the success of a lending programme should be based on the relative cost of below-market loans, not on whether those loans are repaid after the crisis.

One alternative version of the lender of last resort role would be to automatically trigger the purchase by regulators of a substantial portfolio of securities in the event of a major short-term market decline. For example, if the S&P 500 index declined more than 20 per cent below the opening price on a given day, regulators would buy contracts at that opening price, acting as an insurer to provide support for the market, with the goal of preventing investor panic and thereby avoiding a full-blown crisis. Regulators might take a similar approach to other assets, promising to buy loans that decline in value by some specified amount during a period of time.[42]

How much moral hazard would such proposals create? Because the purchases would be directed at the market as a whole, no individual company or loan purchaser would know with certainty whether a particular investment would be protected. Instead, any 'bailout' would occur only in the event of a system-wide decline. To the extent this policy affected behaviour, it would encourage investors to buy and hold diversified portfolios of stocks and loans; precisely the strategy recommended by most financial theorists.

[42] Partnoy, F, 'Buy the Loans', *New York Times*, 26 September 2008.

An 'asset purchaser of last resort' policy might be expensive in the event of a substantial market downturn. The central bank could end up owning a large portfolio of stock or loans. However, the GFC suggests that regulators will end up owning such a portfolio in any event. Is it better for taxpayers, who fund the central bank, to pay directly to insure investors in the short term, or pay indirectly to insure in the long term? In other words, would the moral hazard problem be greater or lesser if the central bank transformed the role of lender of last resort into a committed seller of short-term put options?

IV. Conclusion

Historically, research about financial crises has been dominated by financial economists, not legal academics. The primary topics of focus have been financial, not regulatory. The primary message of this Chapter is that scholars should change this focus. Financial crises occur due to a range of market failures, and regulation plays a key role in both mitigating and exacerbating these failures. Research could improve global financial policy by helping both regulators and market participants understand which parts of the regulatory toolkit are likely to work, and what kinds of risk regulation poses. Regulators will not be able to prevent future financial crises, but perhaps, with a better understanding of the theoretical and policy issues, they can help to reduce their incidence and impact.

Bibliography

Admati, A and Hellwig, M, *The Bankers' New Clothes: What's Wrong with Banking and What to Do about It* (2013).
Allen, F and Gale, D, 'Optimal Financial Crises' (1998) 53 *Journal of Finance* 1245.
Baumol, W and Blinder, A, *Economics: Principles and Policy* (1985).
Coase, R, *The Firm, the Market, and the Law* (1990).
Demsetz, H, 'Toward a Theory of Property Rights' (1967) 57 *American Economic Review* 347.
Devenow, A and Welch, I, 'Rational Herding in Financial Economics' (1996) 40 *European Economic Review* 603.
Diamond, D and Dybvig, P, 'Bank Runs, Deposit Insurance, and Liquidity' (1983) 91 *Journal of Political Economy* 401.
Eichengreen, B, *Toward a New International Financial Architecture: A Practical Post-Asia Agenda* (1999).
Fama, E, 'Efficient Capital Markets: II' (1991) 46 *Journal of Finance* 1575.

Fisher, I, *The Purchasing Power of Money: Its Determination and Relation to Credit, Interest and Crises* (1911).
Fisher, S, 'Commentary: Why Is Financial Stability a Goal of Public Policy' in *Maintaining Financial Stability in a Global Economy: A Symposium Sponsored by the Federal Reserve Bank of Kansas City* (1997) 37.
Flannery, M, Houston, J, and Partnoy, F, 'Credit Default Swap Spreads as Viable Substitutes for Credit Ratings' (2010) 158 *University of Pennsylvania Law Review* 2085.
Galbraith, JK, *The Great Crash: 1929* (1979).
Galbraith, JK, *A Short History of Financial Euphoria* (1993).
Garber, P, 'Tulipomania' (1989) 97 *Journal of Political Economy* 535.
Gastil, R, *Freedom in the World: Political Rights and Civil Liberties* (1989).
Gerding, E, *Law, Bubbles, and Financial Regulation* (2013).
Gilson, R and Kraakman, R, 'The Mechanisms of Market Efficiency' (1984) 70 *Virginia Law Review* 549.
Glauber, R, 'Systemic Problems in the Next Market Crash' (1997) 52 *Journal of Finance* 1184.
Houman, H, 'Guilty by Association? Regulating Credit Default Swaps?' (2009) 4 *Entrepreneurial Business Law Journal* 407.
Howell, L, *The Handbook of Country and Political Risk Analysis* (1998).
Johnson, S, Boone, P, Breach, A, and Friedman, E, 'Corporate Governance in the Asian Financial Crisis' (2000) 58 *Journal of Financial Economics* 141.
Kindleberger, C, *Manias, Panics, and Crashes: A History of Financial Crises* (1989).
La Porta, R, Lopez-de-Silanes, F, Shleifer, A, and Vishny, R, 'Law and Finance' (1998) 106 *Journal of Political Economy* 1113.
La Porta, R, Lopez-de-Silanes, F, Shleifer, A, and Vishny, R, 'Legal Determinants of External Finance' (1997) 52 *Journal of Finance* 1131.
Mackay, C, *Memoirs of Extraordinary Delusions and the Madness of Crowds* (1852).
Madrick, J and Partnoy, F, 'Did Fannie Cause the Disaster?' (2011) *New York Review of Books*.
Merton, R and Bodie, Z, 'On the Management of Financial Guarantees' (1992) 21 *Financial Management* 87.
Minsky, H, 'The Financial Instability Hypothesis: Capitalistic Processes and the Behavior of the Economy' in Kindleberger, C and Leffargue, J (eds), *Financial Crises: Theory, History and Policy* (1982) 13.
North, D, *Growth and Structural Change* (1981).
Partnoy, F, 'Buy the Loans', *New York Times*, 26 September 2008.
Partnoy, F, *Infectious Greed: How Deceit and Risk Corrupted the Financial Markets* (2003).
Partnoy, F, 'Overdependence on Credit Ratings Was a Primary Cause of the Crisis' in Mitchell, L and Wilmarth, A (eds), *The Panic of 2008: Causes, Consequences, and Implications for Reform* (2010).
Partnoy, F, 'The Siskel and Ebert of Financial Markets?: Two Thumbs Down for the Credit Rating Agencies' (1999) 77 *Washington University Law Quarterly* 619.
Partnoy, F, 'The Timing and Source of Regulation' (2014) *Seattle University Law Review*.
Partnoy, F, 'Why Markets Crash and What Law Can Do about It' (2000) 61 *University of Pittsburgh Law Review* 741.
Romano, R, 'Empowering Investors: A Market Approach to Securities Regulation (1998) 107 *Yale Law Journal* 2359.

Shiller, R, *Macro Markets: Creating Institutions for Managing Society's Largest Economic Risks* (1993).
Shleifer, A and Vishny, R, 'A Survey of Corporate Governance' (1997) 52 *Journal of Finance* 737.
Swan, E, *Building the Global Market: A 4,000 Year History of Derivatives* (2000).

PART II

THE ORGANIZATION OF FINANCIAL SYSTEM REGULATION

CHAPTER 4

INSTITUTIONAL DESIGN

THE CHOICES FOR NATIONAL SYSTEMS

EILÍS FERRAN

I. The Significance of Institutional Design

After the global financial crisis (GFC), many countries reviewed their institutional structures for financial market regulation and supervision.[1] Changes that took place included the transfer of responsibilities between existing organizations, the amalgamation of stand-alone agencies into other organizations (typically central banks), and the establishment of new bodies, especially in the areas of macro-prudential systemic oversight.[2] In addition, there were also closely related changes to establish or reinforce the institutional apparatus for the resolution of failing institutions. This reaction suggests a link between institutional models and supervisory effectiveness—why, after all, would countries embark upon a costly and disruptive period of institutional upheaval if it were not thought that this would result in a better system? However, other considerations, including political calculations about the impact on public perceptions of different reform options, can also play a significant role in shaping decision-making in periods of heightened public interest in the quality of financial regulation and supervision.[3]

Notwithstanding the political propensity to reach for an institutional fix, there is good reason to regard the organizational structure of financial supervision as a second-order problem rather than a fundamental concern: a good institutional model will not neutralize weak supervisory policies and practices but, on the other hand, dedicated, high-quality supervisory personnel and sensible working practices and arrangements for cooperation can compensate for limitations in the formal

[1] This Chapter emphasizes supervision more than regulation (in its narrow 'rulemaking' sense) because while financial regulators typically have certain rulemaking powers, their role in this sphere is a subordinate one to that of the legislature and, in addition, writing rules is only one part of the spectrum of functions that financial authorities perform.

[2] For example, the current arrangements in France, Germany, and the UK (summarized in tables later in this Chapter) reflect significant institutional changes in financial market supervision that have taken place since 2010. Recent developments in the organization of US financial market supervision, including the establishment of a dedicated consumer protection function, are examined in detail in the Chapter by Pan in this volume. Other countries that have reorganized financial market supervision in the aftermath of the GFC include Belgium, which has moved to a 'twin peaks' model in which the National Bank of Belgium is now in charge of prudential supervision, and Ireland, where there is now a unitary system in the Central Bank in place of two competent entities (the Central Bank and a financial regulator), and consumer education and information functions have been transferred to another entity. South Africa has instigated a financial reform programme that includes the proposed adoption of a twin peaks model in which a prudential regulator and supervisor will be established within the Reserve Bank (the 'Prudential Authority') and the existing Financial Services Board will be transformed into a dedicated market conduct regulator known as the Financial Sector Conduct Authority: Financial Stability Board, Peer Review of South Africa (February 2013).

[3] Ferran, E, 'The Break-up of the Financial Services Authority' (2011) 31 *Oxford Journal of Legal Studies* 455.

institutional arrangements.[4] 'What works'—that is, whether a financial supervisor has been equipped with appropriate powers and with adequate resources to deploy them effectively in the pursuit of sound policies that will promote economic well-being and protect society from harm—is a concern that goes far beyond questions pertaining to the supervisor's institutional set-up.[5] That structures matter, but only to an extent, to economic outcomes and to supervisory efficiency, effectiveness, accountability, and transparency is a proposition that sets the frame of reference for the discussion in this Chapter.

II. Supervisory Models: The Main Options

In broad terms, there are four main supervisory models, which are summarized below.[6]

Functional	Different supervisors are responsible for different lines of business, typically one for each of the three traditional business functions: banking, insurance, and securities market activity. An institution that is licensed to engage in a number of different lines of business will come under the remit of multiple supervisors.
Institutional	The identity of the supervisor is determined by the legal status of the institution—eg bank, insurance company, securities firm. The supervisor is responsible for both prudential (safety and soundness) and conduct of business oversight of the institution. To the extent that the institution's licence permits it to engage in additional lines of business ancillary to its main business, these will also be supervised by the same supervisor even though those activities fall outside the supervisor's specialist expertise.
Integrated (also known as 'single' or 'consolidated')	In its fullest form, one supervisor has fully consolidated responsibility for all institutions and functions. Integrated supervision may be less than full consolidation, such as where banking and insurance supervisory responsibilities are combined in a single authority but there is a separate authority for the securities sector.

(continued)

[4] Pan, EJ, Structural Reform of Financial Regulation (2009), Cardozo Legal Studies Research Paper No 250.

[5] As can be seen from the scope of the leading database on bank regulation and supervision: Barth, JR, Caprio Jr, G, and Levine, R, 'Bank Regulation and Supervision in 180 Countries from 1999 to 2011' (2013) 5 *Journal of Financial Economic Policy* 111.

[6] This taxonomy follows Group of Thirty, *The Structure of Financial Supervision: Approaches and Challenges in a Global Marketplace* (2008). However, terminological practice is not universally

Objectives (also known as 'twin peaks')	Supervisory responsibilities are distributed between (typically) two supervisors, one of which has responsibility primarily for prudential objectives, and the other of which has responsibility primarily for conduct of business objectives. Subsidiary objectives, such as the promotion of competition, may also be present. Responsibility for macro-prudential oversight may be combined with the micro-prudential supervisory role or may be located elsewhere.

These models are over-simplifications of real-world financial supervisory systems, which tend to be the somewhat messy product of an incremental and often accidental process in which institutional 'stickiness' resulting from path dependencies competes with forces militating for change, and ideas for radical overhaul often give way to more pragmatic adaptations. Some actual systems combine elements of more than one model and some can even be hard to place in any of the categories.[7] Specific examples of systems in operation are discussed below and summarized in Tables 4.1–4.5. The language associated with the models itself can be imprecise: for example, 'twin peaks' can denote an integrated arrangement in which there is one authority for banking and insurance and another for capital market actors and activities where each of which has responsibility for both prudential and conduct matters[8] or can describe a 'purer' objectives-based approach in which one authority is responsible for prudential matters across all sectors and the other has comprehensive responsibility for conduct matters.[9] The usefulness of the models is as a starting point or broad approximation.

The fuzziness of real-world supervisory systems is also related to the fact that no model has been proven to be unambiguously superior to all the others: there is no compelling reason to follow one blueprint rather than another when clear cut indicators of the optimal way to assign supervisory responsibilities have not emerged. Furthermore, context matters. What works in a less-developed economy with a relatively unsophisticated financial market is likely to be inadequate for a mature

consistent. Goodhart, C, Hartmann, P, Llewellyn, DT, Rojas-Suarez, L, and Weisbrod, S, *Financial Regulation: Why, How and Where Now?* (1998) 144 identifies three broad approaches (institutional, functional, and objective) but later (151) also introduces the concept of the 'mega regulator', ie integrated or consolidated supervision. Čihák, M and Podpiera, R, Is One Watchdog Better than Three? International Experience with Integrated Financial Sector Supervision (2006), IMF Working Paper WP/06/57 describes objectives (twin peaks) supervision as a form of integrated supervision.

[7] The US system is notoriously hard to categorize. US Treasury Department, *Blueprint for a Modernized Financial Regulatory Structure* (2008), 139 notes that 'The current U.S. regulatory system, while often characterized as functional regulation, could more appropriately be characterized as an institutionally based functional system.'

[8] The French structure (Table 4.3 below) broadly fits with this description.

[9] The UK structure (Table 4.5 below) mostly adheres to this description but it is not a perfect fit because the conduct authority does have responsibility for the prudential oversight of smaller investment firms and other non-bank/insurance company financial market actors.

economy with a large financial sector, and even among developed economies what works for one may be quite unsuitable for another because of country-specific factors, including whether the system of government is federal, confederal, or unitary; whether the economy is bank-based or market-based; prevalent business structures and corporate governance norms; the character of the legal, administrative, and judicial system; historical accidents; and cultural influences. That said, institutional and functional models are coming under strain. The disadvantage of these models is that as the traditional sectoral boundaries have broken down in the face of sophisticated product innovation and the emergence of new activities and organizational structures, this can lead to coverage gaps in supervision that is organized along traditional lines, inconsistent supervisory treatment of functionally equivalent products and services, jurisdictional conflicts between supervisory authorities, and other inefficiencies. Fragmented supervision by specialist authorities can, in addition, result in insufficient attention being given to risks to stability and soundness that might be seen by taking a more holistic view.[10] The move away from functional and institutional models that took place in a number of countries (including Singapore, Norway, Sweden, Denmark, the UK, Germany, Australia, Korea, and Japan) from the 1980s onwards was partly in response to increased consolidation of the financial sectors.[11]

As between the fully integrated or consolidated model and the objectives model, the economies of scale and scope promised[12] by the integrated model made it very popular in the 1990s and 2000s but it has since passed its heyday in terms of exerting influence on policy thinking.[13] Concerns have grown that the model can ask too much of a single authority, that some objectives may be prioritized at the expense of others, and also that it can result in central banks being unwisely side-lined from financial supervision.[14] While one study has found full integration to be associated with higher quality of supervision in insurance and securities and greater consistency of supervision across sectors,[15] the drive for unified supervision

[10] US Treasury Department, n 7 above, 140–1.

[11] Čihák and Podpiera, n 6 above, 3–4.

[12] But not necessarily delivered: Čihák and Podpiera, ibid, finds that integrating supervision does not lead to a substantial reduction in supervisory staff.

[13] Discussing generally the rationale for integrated supervision and its strengths and weaknesses as a model, see Pan, n 4 above; Herring, RJ and Carmassi, J, 'The Structure of Cross-Sector Financial Supervision' (2008) 17 *Financial Markets, Institutions & Instruments* 51; Wymeersch, E, 'The Structure of Financial Supervision in Europe: About Single, Twin Peaks and Multiple Financial Supervisors' (2007) 8 *European Business Organization Law Review* 237; Llewellyn, DT, 'Integrated Agencies and the Role of Central Banks' in Masciandaro, D (ed.), *Handbook of Central Banking and Financial Authorities in Europe* (2006); Masciandaro, D, 'Unification in Financial Sector Supervision: The Trade-off Between Central Bank and Single Authority' (2004) 12 *Journal of Financial Regulation and Compliance* 151; Abrams, RK and Taylor, MW, Issues in the Unification of Financial Sector Supervision (2000), IMF Working Paper WP/00/21; Briault, C, The Rationale for a Single National Financial Services Regulator (1999), FSA Occasional Paper No 2.

[14] US Treasury Department, n 7 above, 141. See also Taylor, MW, 'The Road from "Twin Peaks"—and the Way Back' (2009) 16 *Connecticut Insurance Law Journal* 61.

[15] Čihák and Podpiera, n 6 above.

across sectors has also been found to be negatively associated with economic resilience.[16] The reputation of the fully integrated model was tarnished in particular by the perceived failure of the UK Financial Services Authority (FSA), previously a poster child for the benefits of the model, to mitigate the impact of the GFC. One of the undisputed mistakes made by the UK FSA was to concentrate its efforts and resources on consumer protection concerns at the expense of prudential matters.[17] Michael Taylor, a long-time advocate of the objectives-based model, has suggested that, except in comparatively small countries where the gains from economies of scale may be significant, the fully integrated regulator is unsuitable because it generates large inefficiencies by asking too much of a single organization, and because prudential and conduct of business regulation do not mix.[18] As of 2011, 25 countries were found to have a single authority covering the entire financial sector, of which most were relatively small in terms of both population and GDP.[19]

The objectives-based model is now in the ascendancy in policy circles. One of its main perceived strengths is that it can allow for a clearer focus on different regulatory objectives (though as with every model, there are drawbacks as well including the potential for wasteful inter-agency jurisdictional conflicts and/or duplication of efforts).[20] In 2008, the US Treasury Department identified an objectives-based approach as an optimal long-term structure for the US.[21] It thought that an objectives-based framework should improve regulatory effectiveness by more closely linking the regulatory objectives of market stability regulation, prudential financial regulation, and business conduct regulation to regulatory structure. In its view, the objectives-based framework appeared to have the most potential for targeting regulation to the most relevant types of market failures or institutional structures. Prudential supervision would be focused appropriately and dedicated conduct of business supervision would lead to greater consistency in the treatment of products and activities, minimize disputes among supervisory authorities, and reduce gaps in consumer protection. Others share this positive view: in 2013 the Financial Stability Board commended the South African authorities for instigating reform towards the adoption of a twin peaks model that by concentrating prudential supervisory responsibilities in one agency would, among other things, 'help to improve the oversight of financial conglomerates that dominate the South African financial system'.[22]

The US Treasury Department's strong endorsement of the merits in principle of the objectives model has not translated into bold transitional steps towards

[16] Masciandaro, D, Vega Pansini, R, and Quintyn, M, The Economic Crisis: Did Financial Supervision Matter? (2011), IMF Working Paper WP11/261.

[17] Turner, A, *The Turner Review: A Regulatory Response to the Global Banking Crisis* (2009), discussed in Ferran, n 3 above.

[18] Taylor, n 14 above, 88–9.

[19] Barth et al., n 5 above.

[20] Ferran, n 3 above.

[21] US Treasury Department, n 7 above, 143.

[22] Financial Stability Board, Peer Review of South Africa, 5.

implementation of that approach in the US.[23] The inertia of the US financial supervisory system may be partly related to bureaucratic self-interest among existing agencies in preserving the status quo but the inhibiting effect of the daunting scale of any exercise to effect deep restructuring of such a large and complex set-up must also be factored in.[24] Some other countries have been more dynamic.

III. Examples of Supervisory Models in Use

1. Australia

Australia embraced an objectives-based, twin peaks model in 1998.[25] Elements of the model were significantly overhauled in the aftermath of the high-profile collapse of HIH Insurance in 2001. Certain refinements were introduced after the GFC. However, Australia survived that crisis relatively unscathed and its approach to the institutional design of supervision did not come under the intense negative scrutiny leading to radical reform that was the experience elsewhere. Instead, the Australian approach became a source of inspiration for other countries that were not so lucky.[26] Nevertheless, at the end of 2013, a wide-ranging inquiry into the Australian financial system was instigated to consider the impact of changes to Australia's system since the late 1990s and its future development. The terms of reference for this inquiry covered the role, objectives, funding, and performance of financial regulators, including an international comparison. The context for this inquiry was that Australian banks were thought to suffer from a lack of domestic

[23] On post-crisis changes in the US institutional architecture, see the Chapter by Pan in this volume for detailed analysis. Streamlining was relatively limited in extent: the Office of Thrift Supervision was abolished and, after protracted political debate, the Consumer Financial Protection Bureau was established within the Federal Reserve.

[24] The ability of US financial regulators to resist bold change is susceptible to public choice/regulatory capture explanations: Macey, J, 'Administrative Agency Obsolescence and Interest Group Formation: A Case Study of the SEC at Sixty' (1994) 15 *Cardozo Law Review* 909.

[25] This paragraph draws on Hill, JG, 'Why Did Australia Fare so well in the Financial Crisis?' in Ferran, E, Moloney, N, Hill, J, and Coffee, JC, *The Regulatory Aftermath of the Global Financial Crisis* (2012); Australian Prudential Regulation Authority & Australian Securities and Investments Commission, Memorandum of Understanding (2010); Joe Hockey, Treasurer of the Commonwealth of Australia, Financial System Inquiry, 20 December 2013, <http://jbh.ministers.treasury.gov.au/media-release/037-2013/>.

[26] The practice of referring to Australia as the 'lucky country' goes back to Donald Horne, *The Lucky Country* (1984).

Table 4.1

	Banks	Insurance companies	Investment firms and securities markets conduct	Bank resolution and deposit protection	Macro-prudential supervision/general coordination/ systemic risk oversight
Micro-prudential Supervision	APRA	APRA		APRA, includes FCS administrator role	CFR & RBA
Conduct of Business Supervision	ASIC	ASIC	ASIC		

APRA=Australian Prudential Regulation Authority
ASIC=Australian Securities and Investments Commission
CFR=Council of Financial Regulators (which comprises the RBA (Chair), APRA, ASIC and the Treasury)
FCS=Financial Claims Scheme for depositors and general insurance policyholders
RBA=Reserve Bank of Australia (central bank)
I am grateful to Jennifer Hill for reviewing this summary.

savings and to be heavily dependent on offshore wholesale funding. There were also concerns about competition in banking. The inquiry reported in December 2014 but its extensive recommendations did not include proposals for major change of the regulatory and supervisory architecture.

In outline, the current distribution of responsibilities between the main Australian authorities is as per Table 4.1.

2. Canada

Canada's federal structure has resulted in a quite complex institutional structure for financial market supervision.[27] Bank prudential and conduct supervision are federal matters but in the case of insurance companies responsibilities are shared between federal and provincial authorities. There is no federal securities/capital markets supervisory authority and these matters are the responsibility of the securities commissions of the provinces and territories. Attempts to create a national securities supervisor have been beset by complications including a decision of the Canadian Supreme Court on the constitutional illegality of proposed legislation

[27] This paragraph draws on Financial Stability Board, Peer Review of Canada (2012).

Table 4.2

	Banks	Insurance companies	Investment firms and securities markets conduct	Bank resolution and deposit protection	Macro-prudential supervision/ general coordination/ systemic risk oversight
Micro-prudential Supervision	OSFI	OSFI		CDIC	Various bodies: • Department of Finance • BoC • FISC • SAC • Heads of Agencies Committee • CSA Systemic Risk Committee
Conduct of Business Supervision	FCAC	FCAC Authorities of Provinces/ Territories	Securities Commissions of Provinces/ Territories CSA		
Self-regulation			IIROC MFDA		

BoC=Bank of Canada (central bank)
CDIC=Canada Deposit Insurance Corporation
CSA=Canadian Securities Administrators
FCAC=Financial Consumer Agency of Canada
FISC=Financial Institutions Supervisory Committee
IIROC=Investment Industry Regulatory Organization of Canada
MFDA=Mutual Fund Dealers Association
OSFI=Office of the Superintendent of Financial Institutions
SAC=Senior Advisory Committee
I am grateful to Anita Anand for reviewing this summary.

on the grounds that it fell outside the scope of the federal power that had been relied upon.[28] Work continues on the establishment of such a body and Ontario, British Columbia, Saskatchewan, New Brunswick, and Prince Edward Island have agreed with the federal government to forge ahead on a voluntary basis with a Cooperative Capital Markets Regulatory System. On the other hand, the Canadian system proved to be resilient in the GFC. While certain refinements were effected, the crisis did not trigger a far-reaching overhaul of the Canadian model.

In outline, the current distribution of responsibilities between the main Canadian authorities and other bodies is as per Table 4.2.

[28] *Reference Re Securities Act*, 2011 SCC 66 [2011] 3 SCR 837.

3. France

France strengthened its supervisory framework in the aftermath of the GFC.[29] Existing prudential oversight bodies for banking and insurance that were organized on institutional lines were merged in 2010 into a new prudential authority which is independent but operates under the aegis of the Banque de France. The prudential supervisor's role was extended in 2013 to include resolution powers as well. A board with responsibility for macro-prudential oversight was established in 2010 and reformed in 2013.

In outline, the current distribution of responsibilities between the main French authorities is as per Table 4.3.

As a member of the euro area, the organization of banking supervision in France is affected significantly by the transition to European Banking Union. Primary responsibility for the prudential supervision of the largest French banks is transferred to the European Central Bank (ECB) in accordance with the Single Supervisory Mechanism.

Table 4.3

	Banks	Insurance companies	Investment firms and securities markets conduct	Bank resolution and deposit protection	Macro-prudential supervision/general coordination/ systemic risk oversight
Micro-prudential Supervision	ACPR	ACPR		ACPR FGDR	HCSF
Conduct of Business Supervision	ACPR	ACPR	AMF		

ACPR=L'Autorité de Contrôle Prudentiel et de Résolution
AMF=Autorité des Marchés Financiers
HCSF=Haut Conseil de Stabilité Financière (which gathers together the Ministry of Economy and Finance, the governor of the Banque de France (central bank) (BdF) (also chair of the ACPR), the vice-chair of the ACPR (who represents the insurance sector), the chair of the AMF, the chair of the French accounting standards authority, and three qualified experts appointed by the Presidents of the lower house, of the Senate, and by the Ministry of Economy and Finance)
I am grateful to Pierre-Henri Conac for reviewing this summary.

[29] This draws upon Fernandez-Bollo, E, 'Structural Reform and Supervision of the Banking Sector in France' (2013)(1) *Financial Market Trends*; IMF, France: Financial System Stability Assessment (2012).

4. Germany

In the aftermath of the GFC, Germany made certain changes to the institutional design of financial market supervision but overall its reforms were less radical than in some other European countries.[30] Germany did not dismantle its integrated, single regulator approach, although its version of the model has always been distinctive in the extent to which it accommodates a significant role for the central bank in banking supervision.[31] A new institution with responsibility for resolution was set up[32] and a new body to monitor the overall stability of Germany's financial market was established.[33] In addition, the Bundesbank was given a specific responsibility for the preservation of financial stability.

In outline, the current distribution of responsibilities between the main German authorities is as per Table 4.4.

Germany is also significantly affected by European Banking Union. Primary responsibility for the supervision of the largest German banks is transferred to the ECB.

Table 4.4

	Banks	Insurance companies	Investment firms and securities markets conduct	Bank resolution and deposit protection	Macro-prudential supervision/ general coordination/ systemic risk
Micro-prudential Supervision	BaFin Bundesbank	BaFin		FMSA 6 deposit protection schemes	AFS(FSC)
Conduct of Business Supervision	BaFin	BaFin State (Länder) supervisory authorities	BaFin State (Länder) stock exchange supervisory authorities		

AFS (FSC)=Ausschuss für Finanzstabilität (Financial Stability Committee) (comprised of representatives of the Bundesbank, the Finance Ministry, BaFin and FSMA (non-voting))
BaFin=Bundesanstalt für Finanzdienstleistungsaufsicht (Federal Financial Supervisory Authority)
Bundesbank=central bank
FMSA=Federal Agency for Financial Market Stabilisation (Bundesanstalt für Finanzmarktstabilisierung)
I am grateful to Brigitte Haar for reviewing this summary.

[30] This account draws on FSB Peer Review of Germany (April 2014).

[31] Sanio, J, 'The New Single Regulator in Germany' in Kuppens, T et al. (eds), *Banking Supervision at the Crossroads* (2003).

[32] Pleister, C, 'The Federal Agency for Financial Market Stabilisation in Germany: From Rescuing to Restructuring' (2011)(2) *Financial Market Trends*.

[33] Dombret, A, 'Safeguarding Financial Stability: Framework, Tools and Challenges' Federal Ministry of Finance Monthly Report (December 2012).

5. United Kingdom

Unlike Germany, the UK did conduct a quite fundamental reorganization after the GFC in which responsibility for prudential supervision was restored to the central bank and the fully integrated model was dismantled in favour of an objectives-based, twin peaks approach.[34] Against a background in which strong public disquiet regarding the perceived failure of the established supervisory structure demanded a decisive response, domestic politics played a significant factor in shaping the nature and extent of this exercise. The new prudential authority is an operationally independent subsidiary of the Bank of England. The new conduct authority is an independent body that operates through the same legal vehicle (a company limited by guarantee) as the old single regulator. A subsidiary of the new conduct authority has dedicated responsibility for the oversight of payment systems. In line with international trends, the UK also established a systemic oversight body and a dedicated function (within the Bank of England) for resolution.

In outline, the distribution of responsibilities between the main UK authorities is as per Table 4.5.

Table 4.5

	Banks	Insurance companies	Investment firms and securities markets conduct	Bank resolution and deposit protection	Macro-prudential supervision/general coordination/ systemic risk
Micro-prudential Supervision	PRA	PRA		RD FSCS	FPC
Conduct of Business Supervision	FCA	FCA	FCA		

BoE=Bank of England (central bank)
FCA=Financial Conduct Authority
FPC=Financial Policy Committee (of the BoE) (compromises BoE, Treasury (non-voting), PRA, FCA, and external members)
FSCS=Financial Services Compensation Scheme
PRA=Prudential Regulation Authority (subsidiary of the BoE)
RD=Resolution Directorate (of the BofE)

[34] This paragraph draws on Ferran, n 3 above; Ferran, E, The Reorganisation of Financial Services Supervision in the UK: An Interim Progress Report (2011), University of Cambridge Legal Studies Research Paper No 49.

6. United States

In the US, financial supervision is conducted at both Federal and State level. Many different bodies perform supervisory functions, which contributes to a complex and in certain respects unwieldy overall structure. The economic might of the US and the exceptionally powerful influence that US thinking about financial regulation and supervision has exerted on the rest of the world (influence that, in part, has been possible because of the financial strength behind it) are among the reasons why it is appropriate in this case to dedicate more space to a country-specific discussion. This is provided in the Chapter by Pan in this volume.

IV. The Public Character of Supervision and the Role of Self-Regulation

Responsibility for supervision can be vested in a public body, including a unit within a government department, a central bank, or a separate public authority or agency, or in one or more self-regulatory organizations. The location of supervisory responsibilities within a ministry of finance or other government department can sit rather uneasily with the principle of operational independence from political interference that is stressed by the Basel Committee on Banking Supervision (BCBS),[35] the International Organization of Securities Commissions (IOSCO),[36] and the International Association of Insurance Supervisors (IAIS).[37] Nevertheless, a survey of financial supervisory agencies in International Monetary Fund (IMF) countries by Steven Seelig and Alicia Novoa found that of the supervisors that were units within a government department (which comprised 7 per cent of the 140 respondents from 103 countries), most reported that they were operationally independent on matters of financial sector

[35] BCBS, Core Principles for Effective Banking Supervision (2012), Principle 2.
[36] IOSCO, Objectives and Principles of Securities Regulation (2010), Principle 2.
[37] IAIS, Insurance Core Principles (2011, amended 2012 and 2013), ICP 2.

supervision.[38] A different academic study by Nazire Nergiz Dincer and Barry Eichengreen found that, in 2010, 54.7 per cent of supervisors (whether in central banks or otherwise) were independent according to its criteria.[39] Japan is an example of a major developed economy where the transfer of supervisory functions from a government department to a separate agency was a relatively recent occurrence: it was only in 1998 that financial supervisory power was transferred from the Ministry of Finance to the Financial Supervisory Agency, later reformed into the integrated Financial Services Agency in 2000.

The involvement of central banks in financial supervision and the strengths and weaknesses of this approach compared to supervision by independent agencies dedicated to financial supervision are hotly debated questions. These issues merit a separate Section (see Section V below).

Self-regulation by financial market participants (which may be formalized by way of privately funded self-regulatory organizations (SROs) but may also take looser forms such as guidelines from industry trade associations) is somewhat in retreat nowadays in part because of its associations with discredited 'light touch' approaches.[40] According to Joseph Stiglitz, the very idea that markets can self-regulate is an 'oxymoron'.[41] Yet, self-regulation has both advantages and disadvantages.[42] On the positive side, market participants' proximity to the latest developments and immediate access to cutting-edge expertise gives them informational advantages that make them well placed to develop high-quality standards and guidelines. Participation in the standard-setting process can foster willingness to observe those standards.[43] Self-regulation can promote efficiency and distance supervisory strategies from short-term political influences. For certain purposes market actors may be able to transcend national borders more easily than public authorities who are anchored to their local jurisdictions. In general, market reactions tend to be quicker as well. The deployment of market

[38] Seelig, S and Novoa, A, Governance Practices at Financial Regulatory and Supervisory Agencies (2009), IMF Working Paper WP/09/135. The responding countries accounted for about 91 per cent of global GDP in June 2006.

[39] Nergiz Dincer, N and Eichengreen, B, 'The Architecture and Governance of Financial Supervision: Sources and Implications' (2012) 15 *International Finance* 309, 313–14.

[40] There is no universally fixed definition of 'self-regulation': Boston Consulting Group, *Securities and Exchange Commission: Organizational Study and Reform* (2011) 23.

[41] Stiglitz, JE, *The Stiglitz Report: Reforming the International Monetary and Financial Systems in the Wake of the Global Crisis* (2010).

[42] Ogus, A, 'Rethinking Self-Regulation' (1995) 15 *Oxford Journal of Legal Studies* 97; Black, J, 'Decentring Regulation: Understanding the Role of Regulation and Self-Regulation in a "Post-Regulatory" World' (2001) 54 *Current Legal Problems* 103; Gunningham, N and Rees, J, 'Industry Self-Regulation: An Institutional Perspective' (1997) 19 *Law & Policy* 363; Carson, J, Self Regulation in Securities Markets (2011), World Bank Policy Research Working Papers No 5542; Omarova, ST, 'Rethinking the Future of Self-Regulation in the Financial Industry' (2010) 35 *Brooklyn Journal of International Law* 665.

[43] Boston Consulting Group, n 40 above, 24–5.

resources in monitoring and examination, which internalizes the cost of regulation, can fill gaps that could otherwise open up as a result of overstretched public budgets.

Against self-regulation, the interests of market participants and the public interest in ensuring that financial markets work well for society as a whole do not necessarily coincide. Also, unless self-regulation is underpinned by law in some way, it depends ultimately for its effectiveness on the constraining effects of contractual and market disciplines and, as such, it can lack the firepower needed to constrain misconduct effectively and to incentivize compliance. The resource advantages associated with self-regulation can be imported into state-based regulation via self-funding mechanisms whereby public supervision is funded by levies on the regulated industry. An array of multilateral and bilateral protocols, memoranda of understanding, and other arrangements work around jurisdictional limitations to enable public authorities in different countries to provide powerful and far-reaching assistance to each other. Market actors are not well placed to provide oversight of overall systemic safety.[44] A further potential drawback of unbridled self-regulation is that by keeping in place self-created rules that are barriers to entry for new players, self-regulation can have anti-competitive effects. There are also concerns about private entities' lack of democratic accountability.[45]

An element of new governance analysis identifies a middle path whereby self-regulation can be 'enrolled'[46] within the public system by the formal assignment or delegation of certain responsibilities to private entities that, in turn, are overseen by public agencies.[47] This type of mixed approach, in which self-regulation and public regulation work in a complementary fashion and reinforce each other, is supported by the current IOSCO *Objectives and Principles of Securities Regulation* (Principle 9) as an optional strategy. Its deployment is widespread. An example is provided by US securities regulation in which SROs (in particular, the Financial Industry Regulatory Authority (FINRA), which oversees broker-dealers, and the National Futures Association (NFA), which oversees the derivatives industry) play an important role.[48] The experiences of

[44] Pan, EJ, Understanding Financial Regulation (2011), Cardozo Legal Studies Research Paper No 329.

[45] Boston Consulting Group, n 40 above, 25.

[46] Black, J, 'Enrolling Actors in Regulatory Processes: Examples from UK Financial Services Regulation' [2003] *Public Law* 62.

[47] The term 'new governance' has been described by Christie Ford as 'something of a big tent that captures several discrete but related approaches ... new governance also likely incorporates, or at least bears a strong relationship to, versions of reflexive law, responsive regulation or enforced self-regulation, co-regulation, and management-based regulation': Ford, C, 'New Governance in the Teeth of Human Frailty' [2010] *Wisconsin Law Review* 441, 444–5.

[48] See the Chapter by Payne in this volume.

the Securities and Exchange Commission (SEC) and the Commodity Futures Trading Commission (CFTC) with FINRA and NFA have been said to support the view that SROs usefully augment the efforts of the public authorities and there are proposals to expand the role of SROs by authorizing an SRO with respect to investment advisers.[49]

The US system of reliance on SROs is largely 'a historical product of political compromises and economic expediency'.[50] As such, the detailed features of that arrangement are unique to the US context and are not suitable for export. Nevertheless, the basic idea of combining self-regulation with state regulation is also replicated elsewhere. For example, Table 4.2 indicates the way in which Canadian public regulation also leverages off SROs. Another illustration of the mixed approach that can be found in operation to a greater or lesser extent in many countries is for public authorities to rely on stock exchanges to perform certain regulatory functions, such as establishing rules on eligibility for members and trading activities, conducting front-line market surveillance and inspections, and taking disciplinary actions against members for rule breaches.[51] However, modern market operators' business strategies as for-profit companies in a competitive industry can make it less appropriate to rely on them to discharge extensive quasi-public interest regulatory functions.[52] One area where they have lost out, for example in the EU, is with respect to the oversight of issuer disclosures, including prospectus, which is a responsibility that has now passed from exchanges to public authorities.[53] In the US, many exchanges retain FINRA to perform regulatory services on their behalf.[54]

A World Bank Policy Paper published in 2011 canvassed trends in self-regulation and noted that, in general terms, self-regulation now plays a minor role in Europe and the Middle East, but that it continues to play a strong role in North America, where independent SROs are assuming responsibilities from exchanges, and an expanding role in several Latin American countries. In Asia, reliance on self-regulation has been reduced, but it remains important in most countries. The paper neither endorsed nor rejected the use of self-regulation for emerging markets

[49] SEC Division of Investment Management Staff Study, Enhancing Investment Adviser Examinations (2011), study mandated by section 914 of the Dodd–Frank Wall Street Reform and Consumer Protection Act.

[50] Omarova, n 42 above, 695.

[51] For example, IMF, Singapore Country Report (2013), para 39 (discussing the self-regulatory functions performed by the three Singapore approved exchanges); Boston Consulting Group, n 40 above, 22–3 (discussing the role of US stock exchanges in regulating their members' compliance with securities laws and with the exchanges' own rules).

[52] Carson, n 42 above, 11.

[53] See Moloney, N, *EU Securities and Financial Market Regulation* (2014), ch 2; Ferran, EV and Ho, LC, *Principles of Corporate Finance Law* (2014), ch 13.

[54] Carson, n 42 above, 24–5.

and it did not advocate the adoption of any particular model of self-regulation where an SRO model is used. Nevertheless, it did identify conditions in which self-regulation and SROs can support the achievement of higher standards of regulation, market integrity, and investor protection. It also cautioned that 'If self-regulation is used, important decisions must be made about the scope of SRO responsibilities and powers, as well as the structure, governance, and supervision of SROs. Those subjects are being revisited even in countries with well-established self-regulatory systems.'[55]

V. The Role of the Central Bank in Financial Supervision

There are opposing arguments on the wisdom of locating responsibility for (micro) prudential supervision within central banks but before touching on the pros and cons, it is helpful to record what is not in doubt: when a bank is in trouble, the central bank, as lender of last resort, will be involved regardless of how formal supervisory responsibilities are distributed. The central bank will also always have an interest in overall systemic safety because of the close interrelationship between these issues and the central bank's monetary policy functions and its (usual) responsibilities for the oversight of payment and settlement systems (now including derivatives settlement systems).

No decisive argument has emerged from the economic literature on the interrelationship between central bank and financial outcomes, and empirical evidence on the economic benefits of locating supervision within the central bank or keeping it separate is also mixed.[56] However, a recent study by Nergiz Dincer and

[55] ibid, 16.

[56] The literature on the pros and cons of assigning supervision functions to the central bank is voluminous. It includes: Nergiz Dincer and Eichengreen, n 39 above; Masciandaro, D, 'Back to the Future' (2012) 9 *European Company & Financial Law Review* 112–30; Arnone, M and Gambini, A, 'Architecture of Financial Supervisory Authorities and Banking Supervision' in Masciandaro, D and Quintyn, M (eds), *Designing Financial Supervision Institutions: Independence, Accountability and Governance* (2007); Padoa-Schioppa, T, 'Financial Supervision: Inside or Outside Central Banks' in Kremers, JM et al. (eds), *Financial Supervision in Europe* (2003); Di Noia, C and Di Giorgio, G, 'Should Banking Supervision and Monetary Policy Tasks Be Given to Different Agencies?' (1999) 2 *International Finance* 361; Goodhart, C and Schoenmaker, D, 'Should the Functions of Monetary Policy and Banking Supervision Be Separated?' (1995) 47 *Oxford Economic Papers* 539.

Eichengreen suggests that countries where the supervisor is an independent central bank tend to have more conservatively regulated financial systems, with higher capital ratios but also significantly lower levels of bank credit to the economy on some measures.[57] The authors of the study note that 'the same institutional arrangements likely to confer greater stability (higher capital ratios, lower nonperforming loans) also tend to limit the provision of credit to the economy, other things equal, conceivably translating into less investment for financially constrained firms and lower economic growth'.[58] As of 2011, in 89 countries the central bank was the only bank supervisory authority and in 38 countries the central bank was not a supervisory authority at all.[59] The remaining nine countries that provided information in the survey, a group that included the US, indicated that the central bank was one among multiple supervisors.

A standard argument against assigning micro-prudential supervisory functions to the central bank is that this may give rise to conflicts of interest as between monetary policy and supervisory functions. The example is given of a central bank not wanting to adjust interest rates if doing so might trigger a number of bank failures for which it could be blamed. Such contamination, which could increase moral hazard in supervised banks, must be avoided. Separating the monetary policy and regulatory roles leaves the central bank to determine to monetary policy free from extraneous influences. Another line of argument relates to accountability: the high level of independence that is afforded to central banks in their monetary policy role is not appropriate for supervisory functions, which can involve interference in banking businesses including, in extremis, ordering bank closures (with potential fiscal consequences), and it is better, therefore, to keep these areas of activity clearly separate. Furthermore, the point is made that central banks are not natural candidates for the role of integrated supervisor, at least in economies with sophisticated capital markets whose supervision requires specialist skills that are not usually associated with central bankers. Arguments going the other way include that central banks can be more efficient and effective than integrated supervisors in the area of prudential supervision because of their informational advantages as regards the bank sector and the expected skill set of central bankers.[60] Indeed, not placing prudential supervisory responsibilities with the central bank could impair the efficiency of the process whereby emergency liquidity is provided in a crisis because the central bank may not have immediately to hand all the information it needs on the condition of the struggling banks. It can also be argued that the inevitable involvement of central banks in macro-prudential supervision has implications for the location of responsibility for micro-prudential supervision because

[57] Nergiz Dincer and Eichengreen, n 39 above.

[58] ibid, 312. [59] Barth et al., n 5 above.

[60] Goodhart, C, Schoenmaker, D, and Dasgupta, P, 'The Skill Profile of Central Bankers and Supervisors' (2002) 6 *European Finance Review* 397.

the micro/macro distinction cannot always be clearly maintained.[61] In addition, the independence/accountability argument can be turned around: locating supervision within the central bank may protect it from political interference.

Conflict of interest concerns were a factor in the decision taken in the design of the now much-admired objectives-based Australian financial supervisory architecture to vest responsibility for financial market oversight in an independent authority outside the central bank. However, elsewhere, the existence of conflicts of interest has not proved to be a fatal objection to central bank involvement in supervision. The current position in, for example, France and the UK, where micro-prudential supervision is conducted by a distinct entity within the central bank group, reflects the view that conflicts of interest within an institution can be managed by careful arrangements for the internal separation of functions. The trend in favour of expanding the supervisory role of central banks can be seen to run in tandem with explicit recognition of macro-prudential supervision as a core central bank responsibility.[62] There is also an element of cyclicality about the restoration of central banks to a position of prominence in supervision: having lost ground in the previous decades, central banks were both partially shielded from blame for the GFC and in a position to offer a clear institutional alternative.

VI. Mandate and Powers

Mandates reflect institutional design in the sense that, for example, a fully integrated authority will have objectives that are widely defined to capture the breadth of the responsibilities it is expected to assume, while an authority designed along institutional or functional lines will have much more narrowly focused objectives. As noted earlier in this Chapter, doubts about the wisdom of combining many different objectives within a single mandate have grown and, correspondingly, the appeal of designing institutions along objectives lines, and accordingly with more limited mandates, has increased. Irrespective of the institutional model in use, the mandate

[61] The Chapter by Lastra in this volume examines the question of institutional responsibility for macro-prudential oversight and makes the case for it to be located within central banks.

[62] The term 'macro-prudential' has become prominent relatively recently: Clement, P, 'The Term "Macroprudential": Origins and Evolution' [March 2010] *BIS Quarterly Review* 59. However, in certain respects the new term amounts to putting a label on a responsibility for overall systemic safety that virtually all central banks have implicitly assumed anyway: BIS, Issues in the Governance of Central Banks (2009), 9. See also the Chapter by Lastra in this volume.

must be clear and unambiguous in order to inculcate a strong willingness to take action and fulfil the supervisory role.[63] The need for supervisors to be equipped with the full range of rulemaking, guidance, licensing, monitoring, decision-making, information-gathering, inspection, investigation, and enforcement powers (including powers to cooperate with other authorities both domestic and foreign) that they need to function effectively almost goes without saying. Exactly what range of powers a particular supervisor needs to function effectively will be affected not only by its institutional design and mandate but also by its place within the national administration in general, the role and responsibilities of other administrative and judicial authorities with which it can be expected to interact, and the part played by market disciplines.

VII. Accountability, Governance, and Transparency

Financial supervisors should be operationally independent but they must also be accountable.[64] Getting this balance right is notoriously difficult.[65] Eva Hüpkes, Marc Quintyn, and Michael Taylor attribute the difficulties involved in addressing the 'who guards the guardians?' question not only to the elusive, multifaceted, and complex nature of the concept of accountability, but also to confusion about its relationship with independence; they note that properly designed accountability mechanisms keep an independent supervisory agency 'under control' but do not directly control its policies and practices.[66] Nergiz Dincer and Eichengreen's study underscores the importance of the independence/accountability link: they find that 'supervision by an independent entity, either the central bank or a separate agency of government, is more likely in countries where government agencies have a relatively high level of accountability, consistent with the notion that adequate accountability is a political precondition for regulatory independence'.[67] Accountability legitimizes independence 'thereby buttressing public support for [the supervisor's ...] autonomy and strengthening its public credibility'.[68]

[63] BCBS, n 35 above, Principle 1; IOSCO, n 36 above, Principle 1; IAIS, n 37 above, ICP 1. Viñals, J and Fiechter, J, The Making of Good Supervision: Learning to Say 'No' (2010), IMF Working Paper SPN/10/08, 15–16.

[64] BCBS, n 35 above, Principle 2; IOSCO, n 36 above, Principle A.2; IAIS, n 37 above, ICP 2.

[65] Arnone and Gambini, n 56 above; BIS, n 62 above, ch 7.

[66] Hüpkes, E, Quintyn, M, and Taylor, MW, *Accountability Arrangements for Financial Sector Regulators* (2006), IMF Economic Issue No 39, 2.

[67] Nergiz Dincer and Eichengreen, n 39 above, 323.

[68] BIS, n 62 above, 150.

Inadequate accountability to the general public, through political channels and otherwise, can allow financial supervisors to deviate from their task of guarding finance for the benefit of society as a whole. Thus, for James Barth, Gerard Caprio, and Ross Levine, a crucial factor in the GFC was that weak public oversight of financial regulators and supervisors had allowed those guardians to design and maintain policies that favoured the financial sector in the short term but which were ultimately highly destabilizing.[69] Yet, while it is natural in the aftermath of a crisis to focus on the failure of supervisors to serve the public because they were perhaps too close to influential financial interests, other aspects of accountability are also important, including accountability to the regulated industry itself. Financial firms and individuals working within the industry could be adversely and unfairly affected by inappropriate use of powerful supervisory and enforcement tools and must therefore have a right of challenge. Financial firms also have a strong and legitimate interest in supervisory financial accountability because inefficiencies in the management of costs will be passed through to them in the form of higher fees. Proper accountability to all stakeholders can enhance confidence in supervision and improve its effectiveness.[70]

Accountability arrangements typically include reporting duties, such as annual reports and accounts to the executive and legislative branches of government on performance against the supervisor's statutory mandate (which is, therefore, a key part of the accountability framework[71]), and also ad hoc reports on particular matters.[72] Supervisors may be required specifically to investigate and report on regulatory failure, either on their own initiative[73] or at the behest of the relevant ministry.[74] They may also be subject to investigations or reviews by independent persons in specified circumstances.[75] Procedural requirements (such as requirements to consult interested parties and to conduct cost-benefit analysis prior to adopting new regulatory rules, to provide feedback, and to follow proper processes with respect to enforcement procedures) are also common.[76] So far as direct accountability to industry and consumers is concerned, in addition to public reporting obligations, mechanisms for internal appeals against decisions and rulemaking are well established in legislation,

[69] Barth, JR, Caprio Jr, G, and Levine, R, *Guardians of Finance: Making Regulators Work for Us* (2012).

[70] House of Commons Treasury Committee, *Financial Conduct Authority* (HC 1574, 26th Report of Session 10 January 2012) paras 63–80.

[71] BCBS, n 35 above, Principle 2.3; IOSCO, n 36 above, Principle A.1; IAIS, n 37 above, ICP 2.1.1. Discussing the role of the statutory mandate as a mechanism for fostering accountability: Ferran, E, 'The New Mandate for the Supervision of Financial Services Conduct' (2012) 65 *Current Legal Problems* 411.

[72] Seelig and Novoa, n 38 above, 17–18.

[73] For example, the UK supervisors (the Prudential Regulation Authority and the Financial Conduct Authority) are obliged to conduct such investigations in specified circumstances: Financial Services Act 2012, sections 73–4.

[74] See, eg, UK Financial Services Act 2012, section 77.

[75] ibid, sections 68 and 84.

[76] Seelig and Novoa, n 38 above, 18.

and so too are provisions for full judicial review.[77] These mechanisms are typically supported by duties on supervisors to give reasons for actions taken.[78] However, financial supervisors tend to enjoy statutory immunity from liability in damages for actions taken in good faith.[79] Financial accountability is supported by requirements for external audit, and may be further reinforced by powers for an external auditor to carry out value-for-money reviews.[80] Extra layers of public oversight, such as a public entity charged with responsibility for monitoring supervisory performance,[81] could also be added but as well as the danger in principle of creating an overly cumbersome accountability apparatus, there are also practical considerations about exhausting the pool of appropriately qualified and independent individuals to sit on oversight bodies. The regression has to stop somewhere.

Good internal governance arrangements within the supervisor can support accountability.[82] Moreover, given the stress now placed on the regulatory importance of financial institutions' corporate governance, some would say that it is appropriate for supervisors themselves to lead by example in this regard. Certain similarities between the agency problems within financial supervisors and in commercial firms can make it appropriate to draw upon corporate governance principles in the design of financial supervisory governance, although not all of the issues concerning the relationship between directors and shareholders will have a direct parallel in the supervisory context.[83] The UK Financial Services and Markets Act 2000 obliges the UK financial regulators to 'have regard' to such general accepted principles of good corporate governance as may reasonably be regarded as applicable.[84] The presence of (independent) non-executive directors is one of the key principles of good corporate governance. The study of supervisory governance by Steven Seelig and Alicia Novoa found that about 60 per cent of the agencies surveyed had a combination of part-time and full-time directors.[85]

Clear rules concerning the appointment and dismissal of the members of the supervisor's governing body are considered to be essential.[86] Most countries spell

[77] ibid. [78] ibid, 23.

[79] This is recommended as best practice by international standard-setters: BCBS, n 35 above, Principle 2.9; IAIS, n 37 above, ICP 2.10. For a domestic example see UK Financial Services and Markets Act 2000, sch 1ZA, paras 25 and 33.

[80] See, eg, UK Financial Services Act and Markets Act 2000, sections 1S and 2O (as inserted by the Financial Services Act 2012).

[81] See, eg, the 'sentinel' model advocated by Barth et al., n 69 above.

[82] Quintyn, M, *Governance of Financial Supervisors and its Effects—a Stocktaking Exercise* (2007).

[83] Enriques, L and Hertig, G, 'Improving the Governance of Financial Supervisors' (2011) 12 *European Business Organization Law Review* 357. In its review of the accountability of the Bank of England, the UK Parliamentary Treasury Select Committee found it helpful at various points to compare the arrangements within the Bank to a typical corporate board of directors: House of Commons Treasury Committee, *Accountability of the Bank of England* (HC 874, 21st Report of Session 2010–12).

[84] Financial Services and Markets Act 2000, section 3C. [85] Seelig and Novoa, n 38 above.

[86] BCBS, n 35 above, Principle 2.2; IAIS, n 37 above, ICP 2.2.

out these procedures in legislation.[87] It is usual for the executive branch of government to make key appointments.[88] Confirmation by the legislative branch (eg by a parliamentary committee) may also be required.[89] In some regions, it is not uncommon for government representatives to sit on the board of supervisors but such arrangements require careful organization so as not to compromise supervisory independence.[90] It is important for those in charge to have security of tenure so that they can operate freely and without fear of the threat of arbitrary or politically motivated dismissal.[91] Attention has focused recently on senior supervisory appointments being for a single, non-renewable term in order to reinforce insulation from political control. This model has been implemented, for example, in the UK for the Governor of the Bank of England as part of the package of measures putting the Bank back in charge of prudential supervision.[92]

Supervisory disclosure and transparency can play a significant role in improving supervisory predictability, governance, and accountability.[93] Transparency facilitates direct accountability to the general public and, as such, it can fill gaps in accountability to elected representatives. Greater transparency can boost the public understanding of supervisory policies and practices, thereby enhancing legitimacy. Since it allows for performance to be tracked over time, transparency encourages supervisors to act in a disciplined and consistent way, which can enhance policy effectiveness as well as boosting industry (and general public) confidence in the system. But openness can put supervisors' credibility and reputation on the line, as was demonstrated by the poor reception afforded to the publication of the results of the first stress tests on European banks in 2010, which was led by the Committee of European Banking Supervisors (now the European Banking Authority (EBA)). As the IMF noted: 'Limited information disclosure did little to relieve the intense uncertainty prevalent at that time. The sample of banks included some that quickly proved to pose systemic risks in

[87] Seelig and Novoa, n 38 above, 13.

[88] ibid.

[89] ibid. In the UK, the Parliamentary House of Commons Treasury Committee called for a statutory veto over the appointment of the Governor of the Bank of England. This was resisted by the Government, which argued that the Governor was carrying out executive functions on behalf of the State but in the event ad hoc arrangements were made for the first Governor appointed under the new system (Mark Carney) to appear before the Committee for a pre-appointment hearing. The formal arrangements for the Treasury Committee's oversight of appointments to the top positions in the Financial Conduct Authority also fell short of its demands, but this has not prevented the Committee from assuming a strong oversight role with respect to the Authority's governance: House of Commons Treasury Committee, *Appointment of John Griffith-Jones as Chair-designate of the Financial Conduct Authority* (HC 72, 16th Report of Session 2012–13).

[90] Seelig and Novoa, n 38 above, 13 (more common in Africa, but not found in Europe).

[91] See BCBS, n 35 above, Principle 2.2; IAIS, n 37 above, ICP 2.2.

[92] Bank of England Act 1998, sch 1, para 1 (as amended by the Financial Services Act 2012).

[93] IMF, Code of Good Practices on Transparency in Monetary and Financial Policies (1999).

certain countries.'[94] Lessons were learnt, and the EBA-led 2011 and 2014 exercises were better received.[95]

The use of disclosure and transparency-oriented strategies by financial supervisors is very well established and some aspects, such as the publication of proposed rules for public scrutiny, have been mentioned already. Broadly speaking, financial supervisors make public a wide range of information about their performance in a variety of forms, including annual reports, performance reviews, and feedback statements.[96] The IMF encourages country authorities to participate in a detailed assessment of transparency of monetary and financial policies in the context of their participation in the IMF Financial Sector Assessment Program (FSAP). As of August 2013, 94 countries had completed an assessment of transparency in either monetary policies, financial policies, or both, with 54 country Reports on the Observance of Standards and Codes (ROSCs) having been published on the IMF website (publication is voluntary). The Financial Stability Board's programme of peer reviews, begun in 2010, on the implementation and effectiveness of international financial standards, also performs a valuable transparency-enhancing function.

However, notwithstanding a widespread increase in supervisory transparency, some observers still see room for improvement.[97] Luca Enriques and Gerard Hertig have identified a number of key areas where, they contend, many supervisory agencies could become more transparent (and therefore more subject to market pressure) with no material harm to their effectiveness: the appointment process,[98] business planning, periodic reporting, interactions with lobbies, and, with due qualifications (for example, for emergency situations), decision-making.[99] A recent transparency-enhancing innovation in the UK has been the enactment of a statutory obligation on the conduct regulator to publish records of the meetings of its governing body.[100] This approach mimics the successful practice now adopted by

[94] IMF, European Union: Stress Testing of Banks Technical Note, Financial Sector Assessment Program (2013), 7.

[95] ibid, 8.

[96] Oxera, *Review of Literature on Regulatory Transparency: Update on Recent Developments* (2012).

[97] One recent study of bank supervisors' transparency has found large differences among transparency of supervisors, with the average total score being 9.2 points (out of 15), whereas the minimum is 6.25 points and the maximum 12.75 points, and also a higher level of transparency for supervisors that are not responsible for monetary policy compared with central bank supervisors: Liedorp, FR, Mosch, RHJ, van der Cruijsen, C, and de Haan, J, Transparency of Banking Supervisors (2011), De Nederlandsche Bank Working Paper No 297.

[98] For example, the UK Treasury Committee noted that its pre-appointment hearing with Bank of England Governor-elect Mark Carney provided an opportunity for detailed examination and public scrutiny which, the Committee felt, would assist the Governor in efforts to explain his approach to the public: House of Commons Treasury Committee, *Appointment of Dr Mark Carney as Governor of the Bank of England* (HC 944, 8th Report of Session 2012–13) para 15.

[99] Enriques and Hertig, n 83 above.

[100] Financial Services and Markets Act 2000, sch 1ZA, para 10 (as amended by the Financial Services Act 2012).

an increasing number of central banks (including the Bank of England) to release the minutes of monetary policy meetings.[101] Also recently enacted in the UK are two new regulatory principles on (i) exercising functions as transparently as possible, and (ii) the desirability of publishing information about regulated firms and individuals.[102]

A difference between the monetary policy context and the supervisory domain is that disclosure and transparency-oriented supervisory strategies must be calibrated with special regard to the need to respect the confidentiality of information about individuals or specific financial institutions particularly in circumstances where the information is commercially sensitive or its disclosure could trigger financial instability. The results of bank stress tests provide a pertinent context for the testing of the interface between openness, confidentiality, and stability. The public disclosure of bank stress results is a recent and still controversial innovation as, historically, the outcomes of supervisory examinations usually remained confidential. It has been argued that the disclosure of stress test results on an aggregate basis can be beneficial from a macro-prudential perspective but that the benefits of bank-by-bank disclosure are more debatable for a number of reasons including the risk that banks will develop an incentive to pass the tests rather than engage in prudent behaviour (managing models rather than managing risks), and the potential for panic among banks creditors and counterparties when problems in a particular institution become known (self-fulfilling expectations) or for market participants to relax their own scrutiny of institutions that have received a clean bill of health (moral hazard concerns).[103] The granularity of disclosures about stress-testing methodologies and results varies considerably around the world.[104] The IMF, however, appears to favour publication of as much bank-by-bank detail as possible as not to do so 'could lead to suspicions that the authorities have bad news to hide';[105] it accepts that some matters, such as a bank's business planning, should remain confidential but that 'a possible negative market impact should not in itself be grounds for non-publication, since such market discipline is desirable'.[106]

[101] BIS, n 62 above, 145–9.

[102] Financial Services and Markets Act 2000, section 3B (as amended by the Financial Services Act 2012).

[103] Goldstein, I and Sapra, H, 'Should Banks' Stress Test Results Be Disclosed? An Analysis of the Costs and Benefits' (2014) 8 *Foundations and Trends in Finance* 1. Other papers discussing the costs and benefits of transparency with respect to stress tests include Bernanke, B, Stress Testing Banks: What Have we Learned?, available at <http://www.federalreserve.gov/newsevents/speech/bernanke20130408a.pdf>; Bank of England, A Framework for Stress Testing the UK Banking System (2013), 32–4.

[104] Practice in selected jurisdictions (the EU, Hong Kong, Ireland, Japan, Sweden, the US) is summarized in tabular form in Bank of England, n 103 above, 11.

[105] IMF, European Union: Stress Testing of Banks Technical Note 10.

[106] ibid, 10.

VIII. Costs and Funding

Detailed comparisons of supervisory costs are difficult to draw up because of the myriad different ways in which supervisory responsibilities can be organized, the different mandates given to supervisors, and the wide variations in the nature and size of national financial industries and their importance to local economies.[107] Nevertheless, it is apparent that, even when scaled to account for differences in size of economy and so forth, the amount spent on supervision varies considerably from country to country. According to one estimate, in the mid-2000s annual regulatory costs per billion of GDP ranged from around $500,000 in the US to around $45,000 in Germany; and the US had 133 regulatory staff per million of population while Germany had 16 and France 15.[108] A more recent study by the Financial Stability Board that looks specifically at supervisory resourcing applied by different national authorities to SIFI (systemically important financial institution) supervision has found a wide range: per SIFI, dedicated staffing ranges from a low of 14 people, to a high of more than 100.[109] Differences in the amount spent on supervision can be attributable in part to different preferences as regards supervisory strategies but these preferences are, in turn, shaped by decisions concerning the allocation of resources and are not free-standing. Delegating responsibility for certain supervisory tasks to SROs is one strategy for minimizing the direct financial burden associated with public supervision.[110]

Staff salaries are a significant component of the costs of supervision. The remuneration of supervisory staff may be tied to public sector pay scales or may be set at a higher level to help the supervisor to compete more effectively in attracting and retaining highly qualified staff.[111] However, salary scale imbalances vis-à-vis private sector employers are hard to eliminate. The technical expertise and detailed knowledge and understanding of the system that is acquired by those who work in supervision can make those individuals very attractive prospects for employers in the financial industry and related professions. The 'revolving door' phenomenon and associated risks of regulatory capture therefore present a persistent challenge for financial supervisors.

107 Jackson, HE and Roe, MJ, 'Public and Private Enforcement of Securities Laws: Resource-based Evidence' (2009) 93 *Journal of Financial Economics* 207.

108 Jackson, HE, 'Variation in the Intensity of Financial Regulation: Preliminary Evidence and Potential Implications' (2005) 24 *Yale Journal on Regulation* 253; Jackson and Roe, n 107 above.

109 Financial Stability Board, Intensity and Effectiveness of SIFI Supervision (2010) 5.

110 Pan, n 44 above.

111 OECD, The Financial Crisis: Reform and Exit Strategies (2009), 35 (calling for 'remuneration packages better designed to offer attractive long term career prospects and to retain staff who can realistically regard the financial sector as a viable career alternative as well as tighter restrictions on mobility').

There are two main ways of funding the conduct of supervision: through fees paid by the regulated industry or through an appropriation from public funds (including industry fees collected by the supervisor and then handed over to the general treasury).[112] A fees-based model has the advantage of internalizing costs to the regulated sector. It can also insulate supervisors from political battles over the allocation of public funds. The Financial Stability Board favours the fees-based model because 'it would guarantee a more stable funding source over the cycle; allow for supervisory services to be better priced and adjusted for market developments; and would shield the supervisory agency from being subject to fiscal vacillations'.[113] The US SEC, which as lamented by its then Chair Mary Schapiro 'languishes as one of the few financial regulators still subject to the annual appropriations process' has lobbied for more than 20 years, so far without success, for a switch to a fees-based model.[114] The opposition the SEC has encountered on this matter centres on fears that removing its dependency on the public purse could dilute oversight control. [115] The situation seems unlikely to change: 'After 20 years of trying, the SEC must acknowledge that this solution to its funding problems is unlikely to be achieved.'[116] From a global perspective, the SEC is not an isolated example:

> Many regulators still lack a stable and adequate level of funding, particularly in countries where funding stems from the state budget. In many countries, the impact of inadequate and uncertain funding on the skill level at the regulator is compounded by a requirement that the regulator pay staff at the public employee pay scale, thereby limiting the regulator's ability to recruit qualified personnel and thus its capacity to discharge its functions properly.[117]

A specific issue to be addressed in any funding set-up concerns the destination of the fines that result from disciplinary action taken by the supervisor. For example, until 2012 fines collected by the UK FSA were used to reduce the annual levy on regulated financial institutions. This was changed by the Financial Services Act 2012 (section 109) to require penalties to be paid to HM Treasury after deduction of enforcement costs. In 2012–13, the first year of operation of the new arrangements, the total fine income payable was £342 million, largely due to the fines imposed in respect of LIBOR rigging.[118] The political explanation for this change of approach

[112] Financial Stability Board, Intensity and Effectiveness of SIFI Supervision.

[113] ibid, 5.

[114] Quoted in Johnson, F, 'Senator, Regulators Call for SEC Self-funding in Financial Bill' *Wall Street Journal Online*, 15 April 2010.

[115] Katz, JG, *U.S. Securities and Exchange Commission: A Roadmap for Transformational Reform* (2011) 25–7.

[116] ibid, 27.

[117] Carvajal, A and Elliott, J, Strengths and Weaknesses in Securities Market Regulation: A Global Analysis (2009), IMF Working Paper WP/07/259, para 25.

[118] National Audit Office, The Performance of HM Treasury (2012–13), 12.

to the destination of fines was that it was meant to 'ensure that fines of this nature go to help the taxpaying public, not the financial industry'.[119]

IX. Conclusion

At the end of 2013, Australia launched an inquiry into its financial system with the objective of seeking recommendations that would 'foster an efficient, competitive and flexible financial system, consistent with financial stability, prudence, public confidence and capacity to meet the needs of users'.[120] Australia's aspirations are typical of what countries want of their financial system. This Chapter has examined issues that need to be considered in designing the supervisory institutions that will contribute to the achievement of these goals. There is a broad consensus, as evidenced in international standards, on the responsibilities and powers that financial supervisors need in order to function effectively but this consensus does not extend to institutional design. There is no single 'right' or 'wrong' institutional model for financial supervision. Strong (and weak) financial supervision can come in a variety of packages.

Bibliography

Abrams, RK and Taylor, MW, Issues in the Unification of Financial Sector Supervision (2000), IMF Working Paper WP/00/213.

Arnone, M and Gambini, A, 'Architecture of Financial Supervisory Authorities and Banking Supervision' in Masciandaro, D and Marc Quintyn, M (eds), *Designing Financial Supervision Institutions: Independence, Accountability and Governance* (2007).

Australian Prudential Regulation Authority & Australian Securities and Investments Commission, Memorandum of Understanding (2010).

Bank for International Settlements, Issues in the Governance of Central Banks (2009).

Bank of England, A Framework for Stress Testing the UK Banking System (2013).

Barth, JR, Caprio Jr, G, and Levine, R, 'Bank Regulation and Supervision in 180 Countries from 1999 to 2011' (2013) 5 *Journal of Financial Economic Policy* 111.

[119] George Osborne, Chancellor of the Exchequer, Statement on FSA Investigation into LIBOR, 28 June 2012. Later in 2012, it was announced that charities and support groups would receive £35 million representing the fees levied by the FSA from April 2012: Treanor, J, 'Armed Forces Charities to Get £35m from Fines Levied by City Regulator', *The Guardian Online*, 8 October 2012.

[120] Financial System Inquiry, 20 December 2013.

Barth, JR, Caprio Jr, G, and Levine, R, *Guardians of Finance: Making Regulators Work for Us* (2012).
Basel Committee on Banking Supervision, Core Principles for Effective Banking Supervision (2012).
Bernanke, B, Stress Testing Banks: What Have we Learned? <http://www.federalreserve.gov/newsevents/speech/bernanke20130408a.pdf>.
Black, J, 'Decentring Regulation: Understanding the Role of Regulation and Self-Regulation in a "Post-Regulatory" World' (2001) 54 *Current Legal Problems* 103.
Black, J, 'Enrolling Actors in Regulatory Processes: Examples from UK Financial Services Regulation' [2003] *Public Law* 62.
Boston Consulting Group, Securities and Exchange Commission: Organizational Study and Reform (2011).
Carson, J, Self Regulation in Securities Markets (2011), World Bank Policy Research Working Paper No 5542.
Carvajal, A and Elliott, J, Strengths and Weaknesses in Securities Market Regulation: A Global Analysis (2009), IMF Working Paper WP/07/259.
Čihák, M and Podpiera, R, Is One Watchdog Better than Three? International Experience with Integrated Financial Sector Supervision (2006), IMF Working Paper WP/06/57.
Clement, P, 'The Term "Macroprudential": Origins and Evolution' [March 2010] *BIS Quarterly Review* 59.
Di Noia, C and Di Giorgio, G, 'Should Banking Supervision and Monetary Policy Tasks Be Given to Different Agencies?' (1999) 2 *International Finance* 361.
Dombret, A, Safeguarding Financial Stability: Framework, Tools and Challenges (December 2012), Federal Ministry of Finance Monthly Report.
Enriques, L and Hertig, G, 'Improving the Governance of Financial Supervisors' (2011) 12 *European Business Organization Law Review* 357.
Fernandez-Bollo, É, 'Structural Reform and Supervision of the Banking Sector in France' (2013)(1) *Financial Market Trends*.
Ferran, E, 'The Break-up of the Financial Services Authority' (2011) 31 *Oxford Journal of Legal Studies* 455.
Ferran, E, 'The New Mandate for the Supervision of Financial Services Conduct' (2012) 65 *Current Legal Problems* 411.
Ferran, E, 'The Reorganisation of Financial Services Supervision in the UK: An Interim Progress Report' (2011), University of Cambridge Legal Studies Research Paper 49.
Ferran, E and Ho, LC, *Principles of Corporate Finance Law* (2nd edn, 2014).
Financial Stability Board, Intensity and Effectiveness of SIFI Supervision (2010).
Financial Stability Board, Peer Review of Canada (January 2012).
Financial Stability Board, Peer Review of Germany (April 2014).
Financial Stability Board, Peer Review of South Africa (February 2013).
Ford, C, 'New Governance in the Teeth of Human Frailty' [2010] *Wisconsin Law Review* 441.
Goldstein, I and Sapra, H, 'Should Banks' Stress Test Results Be Disclosed? An Analysis of the Costs and Benefits' (2014) 8 *Foundations and Trends in Finance* 1.
Goodhart C, Hartmann, P, Llewellyn, DT, Liliana Rojas-Suarez, L, and Weisbrod, S, *Financial Regulation: Why, How and Where Now?* (1998).
Goodhart, C and Schoenmaker, D, 'Should the Functions of Monetary Policy and Banking Supervision Be Separated?' (1995) 47 *Oxford Economic Papers* 539.

Goodhart, C, Schoenmaker, D, and Dasgupta, P, 'The Skill Profile of Central Bankers and Supervisors' (2002) 6 *European Finance Review* 397.

Group of Thirty, *The Structure of Financial Supervision: Approaches and Challenges in a Global Marketplace* (2008).

Gunningham, N and Rees, J, 'Industry Self-Regulation: An Institutional Perspective' (1997) 19 *Law & Policy* 363.

Herring, RJ and Carmassi, J, 'The Structure of Cross-Sector Financial Supervision' (2008) 17 *Financial Markets, Institutions & Instruments* 51.

Hill, JG, 'Why Did Australia Fare so well in the Financial Crisis?' in Ferran, E, Moloney, N, Hill JG, and Coffee, JC, *The Regulatory Aftermath of the Global Financial Crisis* (2012).

Hockey, J, Financial System Inquiry (20 December 2013), available at <http://jbh.ministers.treasury.gov.au/media-release/037-2013/>.

Horne, D, *The Lucky Country* (1984).

House of Commons Treasury Committee, *Appointment of Dr Mark Carney as Governor of the Bank of England* (HC 944, 8th Report of Session 2012–13).

House of Commons Treasury Committee, *Appointment of John Griffith-Jones as Chair-designate of the Financial Conduct Authority* (HC 72, 16th Report of Session 2012–13).

House of Commons Treasury Committee, *Financial Conduct Authority* (HC 1574, 26th Report of Session 2010–12).

Hüpkes, E, Quintyn M, and Taylor, MW, Accountability Arrangements for Financial Sector Regulators (2006), IMF Economic Issue No 39.

International Association of Insurance Supervisors, Insurance Core Principles (2010, 2012, 2013).

International Monetary Fund, Code of Good Practices on Transparency in Monetary and Financial Policies (1999).

International Monetary Fund, European Union: Stress Testing of Banks Technical Note (2013).

International Monetary Fund, France: Financial System Stability Assessment (December 2012).

International Monetary Fund, Singapore Country Report (December 2013).

International Organisation of Securities Commissions, Objectives and Principles of Securities Regulation (2010).

Jackson, HE, 'Variation in the Intensity of Financial Regulation: Preliminary Evidence and Potential Implications' (2007) 24 *Yale Journal on Regulation* 253.

Jackson, HE and Roe, MJ, 'Public and Private Enforcement of Securities Laws: Resource-based Evidence' (2009) 93 *Journal of Financial Economics* 207.

Johnson, F, 'Senator, Regulators Call for SEC Self-funding in Financial Bill' *Wall Street Journal Online*, 15 April 2010.

Katz, JG, *U.S. Securities and Exchange Commission: A Roadmap for Transformational Reform* (2011).

Liedorp, FR, Mosch, RHJ, van der Cruijsen, C, and de Haan, J, Transparency of Banking Supervisors (2011), De Nederlandsche Bank Working Paper No 297.

Llewellyn, DT, 'Integrated Agencies and the Role of Central Banks' in Masciandaro, D (ed.), *Handbook of Central Banking and Financial Authorities in Europe* (2006).

Macey, J, 'Administrative Agency Obsolescence and Interest Group Formation: A Case Study of the SEC at Sixty' (1994) 15 *Cardozo Law Review* 909.

Masciandaro, D, 'Back to the Future' (2012) 9 *European Company & Financial Law Review* 112.

Masciandaro, D, 'Unification in Financial Sector Supervision: The Trade-off between Central Bank and Single Authority' (2004) 12 *Journal of Financial Regulation and Compliance* 151.

Masciandaro, D and Quintyn, M (eds), *Designing Financial Supervision Institutions: Independence, Accountability and Governance* (2007).

Masciandaro, D, Vega Pansini, R, and Quintyn, M, The Economic Crisis: Did Financial Supervision Matter? (2011), IMF Working Paper WP11/261.

Moloney, N, *EU Securities and Financial Markets Regulation* (3rd edn, 2014).

National Audit Office, The Performance of HM Treasury 2012–13 (2013).

Nergiz Dincer, N and Eichengreen, B, 'The Architecture and Governance of Financial Supervision: Sources and Implications' (2012) 15 *International Finance* 309.

Ogus, A, 'Rethinking Self-Regulation' (1995) 15 *Oxford Journal of Legal Studies* 97.

Omarova, ST, 'Rethinking the Future of Self-Regulation in the Financial Industry' (2010) 35 *Brooklyn Journal of International Law* 665.

Organisation for Economic Cooperation and Development, The Financial Crisis: Reform and Exit Strategies (2009).

Osborne, G, Statement on FSA Investigation into LIBOR (28 June 2012).

Oxera, Review of Literature on Regulatory Transparency: Update on Recent Developments (2012).

Padoa-Schioppa, T, 'Financial Supervision: Inside or Outside Central Banks' in Kremers, JM et al. (eds), *Financial Supervision in Europe* (2003).

Pan, EJ, Structural Reform of Financial Regulation (2009), Cardozo Legal Studies Research Paper No 250.

Pan, EJ, Understanding Financial Regulation (2011), Cardozo Legal Studies Research Paper No 329.

Pleister, C, 'The Federal Agency for Financial Market Stabilisation in Germany: From Rescuing to Restructuring' (2011)(2) *Financial Market Trends*.

Quintyn, M, *Governance of Financial Supervisors and its Effects—a Stocktaking Exercise* (2007).

Sanio, J, 'The New Single Regulator in Germany' in Kuppens, T et al. (eds), *Banking Supervision at the Crossroads* (2003).

Securities and Exchange Commission Division of Investment Management Staff Study, Enhancing Investment Adviser Examinations (2011).

Seelig, S and Novoa, A, Governance Practices at Financial Regulatory and Supervisory Agencies (2009), IMF Working Paper WP/09/135.

Stiglitz, JE, *The Stiglitz Report: Reforming the International Monetary and Financial Systems in the Wake of the Global Crisis* (2010).

Taylor, MW, 'The Road from "Twin Peaks"—and the Way Back' (2009) 16 *Connecticut Insurance Law Journal* 61.

Treanor, J, 'Armed Forces Charities to Get £35m from Fines Levied by City Regulator', *The Guardian Online*, 8 October 2012.

Turner, A, *The Turner Review: A Regulatory Response to the Global Banking Crisis* (2009).

US Treasury Department, *Blueprint for a Modernized Financial Regulatory Structure* (2008).

Viñals, J and Fiechter, J, The Making of Good Supervision: Learning to Say 'No' (2010), IMF Working Paper SPN/10/08.

Wymeersch, E, 'The Structure of Financial Supervision in Europe: About Single, Twin Peaks and Multiple Financial Supervisors' (2007) 8 *European Business Organization Law Review* 237.

CHAPTER 5

INSTITUTIONAL DESIGN

THE INTERNATIONAL ARCHITECTURE

CHRIS BRUMMER AND
MATT SMALLCOMB

I. Introduction

For more than two decades, dispute resolution has been the 'holy grail' of international financial law. With firms and market participants routinely seeking and selling capital across national boundaries, the rules governing domestic financial markets have become increasingly important—as well as the coherence between and interoperability of national regulatory systems. Where countries diverge with regards to their regulatory practices, standards and expectations, opportunities for regulatory arbitrage, as well as market inefficiencies build up to endanger both the safety and soundness of global financial markets. This has led practitioners and scholars alike to call for an enhanced architecture to grapple with regulatory divergence and to ensure a more coherent supervisory framework for finance.[1]

However, unlike some other prominent areas of international law, such as international trade, international finance remains far from having anything resembling a dispute resolution mechanism. As a result, where regulators and financial authorities disagree as to the optimal approach for regulating markets, there is no forum for settling disputes. Indeed, even where financial authorities fail to implement best practices and consensus-based rules promulgated by international standard-setting bodies, no formal arrangement or process is available for hearing a regulator's complaints, in the open, about a fellow regulator's conduct.

The conspicuous absence of a dispute resolution mechanism has prompted a range of financial authorities to ask why in fact no such device is currently available, especially in light of the global reform efforts underway aimed at enhancing the infrastructure for cross-border finance. This Chapter addresses this issue. By exploring the distinct historical contexts of international trade and finance, this Chapter makes the modest but relatively novel observation that the varying ideological and historical foundations of the two fields, along with the inherently more international orientation of trade regulation as compared to finance, have collectively enabled dispute resolution mechanisms to flourish more easily in trade than in finance.[2] As such, in the absence of a formal mechanism in finance, regulators have had to rely on dispute resolution processes that are not only informal, but which rely on bilateral means of leveraging market access.

[1] For one of the authors' views on this matter, and a specific policy proposal for finance, see Brummer, C, Danger of Divergence: Transatlantic Financial Reform & the G20 Agenda, available at <http://www.atlanticcouncil.org/publications/reports/the-danger-of-divergence-transatlantic-financial-reform-the-g20-agenda>.

[2] Perhaps most relevant in the literature has been Lawrence Baxter's excellent paper, Baxter, L, 'Exploring the WFO Option for Global Banking Regulation' in Boulle, L (ed.), *Globalisation and Governance* (2011) 113, which notes the very different objectives of trade regulation as compared with finance. This Chapter expands this observation and introduces additional historical and institutional factors for a broader theoretical analysis.

II. The Demand for Dispute Resolution in the International Regulatory Architecture

Unlike other areas of international economic law, such as international trade, which are principally organized around binding treaty commitments, international financial law is largely promulgated as a series of best practices, codes of conduct, and standards and principles that can be pitched at high levels of generality in order to achieve consensus among highly diverse parties. Furthermore, even where prescriptive rules or standards are articulated, they are done so with low levels of formal obligation, in order to ensure a modicum of policy flexibility for markets that have very diverse infrastructures. They are not, in other words, memorialized as 'hard law' treaties, but as 'soft law'.

In part because of such flexibility, however, the domestic implementation of international accords can diverge significantly across jurisdictions—and such divergence can generate accusations of unilateralism and disregard for international regulatory processes, on the one hand, to cries of under-regulation on the other. This challenge has become more acute since the 2008 financial crisis when regulators pushed forward a global financial reform package at the G20, which heads of state and financial officials around the world committed to adopt.[3] In areas as diverse as capital regulation for financial institutions, over-the-counter (OTC) derivatives, banker bonuses, and clearance and trading, even advanced financial centres have occasionally differed considerably with regards to how they have operationalized G20 mandates.[4] And these differences have, in turn, led to at times high-profile confrontations between financial authorities, especially between those in the EU and the US, and in the process complicated cross-border cooperation.[5]

As the environment for cooperation has occasionally flailed, demands for greater G20 coordination have been coupled with calls for enhanced capacities for dispute

[3] By way of follow-up to these nonbinding commitments, G20 participants produced progress reports to track Member States' progress towards meeting their summit commitments. For a sampling of the regulatory similarities and divergences that these reports typically show, see G20, Progress Report on the Economic and Financial Actions of the London, Washington, and Pittsburgh G20 Summits (7 November 2009), available at <http://www.g20.utoronto.ca/2009/2009progressreport1107.pdf>; and G20, Meeting of Finance Ministers and Central Bank Governors: Communiqué, Busan, Republic of Korea (5 June 2010), available at <http://www.g20.utoronto.ca/2010/g20finance100605.html>.

[4] See Brummer, C, *Soft Law and the Global Financial System* (2012) 227–9 (discussing the problems of regulatory arbitrage and gaps between and among different countries).

[5] See, eg, Salomon, D, 'Regulators Wrangle on Rules' *Wall Street Journal*, 4 June 2011; Alloway, T, 'Fed Urges Tighter Rules for Foreign Banks' *Financial Times*, 29 November 2012.

resolution in international financial regulation.[6] What exactly such a mechanism means in practice has varied among commentators but, for the most part, scholars envision a formalized system in which countries would be able to bring their grievances about one another's varying regulatory approaches to a neutral independent body.[7] The independent body could then rule on an agency's rulemaking and decide as to whether or not it complied with the best practices promulgated and agreed upon by international standard-setters.

In this way, it is argued, an international dispute mechanism could make several notable contributions to international financial law and global stability more generally. Dispute resolution could reduce ambiguity in the international regulatory system by giving more precise content to regulatory best practices, standards, and principles. Furthermore, by committing to third-party resolution, participants in such a system would be able to more credibly embrace international best practices and expect similar behaviour from their peers. And finally, third-party resolution could settle disagreements between parties with some degree of finality, and in the process prevent or reduce the increasingly public confrontations unsettling international regulatory coordination.

III. The Paradigmatic Model of Dispute Resolution: The WTO's Dispute Settlement Organs

Commentators' calls for greater formalization have not been made in a vacuum. For the most part, they have had a very specific institution in mind—the WTO's Dispute Settlement Mechanism for its Member States. As members of the organization, each signatory to the WTO treaty commits to not only specific tariff-reduction schedules

[6] See, eg, Gadbaw, RM, 'Systemic Regulation of Global Trade and Finance: A Tale of Two Systems' in Cottier, T, Jackson, JH, and Lastra, RM (eds), *International Law in Financial Regulation and Monetary Affairs* (2012) (arguing that the legalistic nature of the international trade regime—embodied by the WTO—enabled trade to fare better than the fragmented international finance regime during the 2008 financial crisis).

[7] By way of example, David Wright—Secretary General of the International Organization of Security Commissions (IOSCO)—stated in late 2013 that international finance would benefit from a body like the WTO with binding adjudicatory powers, lest clashes among national regulators continue to fragment international financial markets. See Jones, H, Markets Need Global Watchdog Group with Power, Officials Say (5 November 2013) *Reuters*, available at <http://www.reuters.com/article/2013/11/05/us-g20-regulation-idUSBRE9A40RN20131105>.

and trade-related commitments, but also to the settlement of disputes by the WTO's dispute resolution organs. Because of the WTO's broad membership and global scope, the WTO dispute resolution system is, not surprisingly, considered the 'central element in providing security and predictability to the multilateral trading system'.[8]

The WTO's dispute resolution process is unique in many ways for its highly developed and effective legal and institutional innovations. Ultimately, the dispute resolution process involves the lodging of a formal complaint, a mandatory 12–15-month mediation-like period, a subsequent appointment of an adjudicatory Panel, and an eventual recommendation to the Dispute Settlement Body (DSB).[9] If one or more of the parties feels aggrieved by the ruling, it may appeal to an Appellate Body by alleging that the Panel made a mistake of law (not one of fact). Compliance with rulings or recommendations from the DSB or the Appellate Body is essentially voluntary, although in cases of prolonged noncompliance the DSB may permit certain limited trade sanctions.

The origins of the WTO and, indeed, of its highly legalistic DSM lay in part in the failed negotiations that sought to establish the International Trade Organization (ITO) in the 1940s. After two debilitating World Wars, the prevailing view among the Allied governments in the early post-war era was that trade liberalization was essential for global stability as well as economic development.[10] By their reasoning,

[8] Understanding on Rules and Procedures Governing the Settlement of Disputes (15 April 1994), Marrakesh Agreement Establishing the World Trade Organization, Annex 2, 1869 U.N.T.S. 401. For a helpful summary of the Dispute Settlement Mechanism (DSM), how it works, and how it differs from the General Agreement on Tariffs and Trade (GATT) system, see generally Bernauer, T, Elsig, M, and Pauwelyn, J, 'Dispute Settlement Mechanism—Analysis and Problems' in Narilikar, A, Daunton, M, and Stern, RM (eds), *The Oxford Handbook on the World Trade Organization* (2012) 485. For a discussion of the Uruguay Round Understanding on Rules and Procedures Governing the Settlement of Disputes (DSU), see WTO, A Summary of the Final Act of the Uruguay Round (2013), available at <http://www.wto.org/english/docs_e/legal_e/ursum_e.htm#Understanding>; see also WTO, Rules of Conduct for the Understanding on Rules and Procedures Governing the Settlement of Disputes (2013), available at <http://www.wto.org/english/tratop_e/dispu_e/rc_e.htm> (setting out various operating rules and guidelines for situations like conflicts of interests and confidentiality).

[9] See WTO, Understanding the WTO: Settling Disputes (2013), available at <http://www.wto.org/english/thewto_e/whatis_e/tif_e/disp1_e.htm>. The Panel's process can be summarized as follows: first, each party presents its case in writing; second, hearings are held at which each party (and interested third parties) can make its case; third, each party can submit rebuttals; fourth, experts may be consulted by the Panel; fifth, the Panel composes an initial, first-draft report, and the parties are allowed two weeks to comment; sixth, the Panel composes and submits an interim report to the parties, for which they have one week to comment; seventh, there is a two-week period of review for consultation between the parties and the Panel; eighth, a final report is issued to the parties and then to the DSB at large (three weeks later); and finally, the DSB (usually) adopts the report, unless there is a consensus against its adoption. See ibid.

[10] See Jackson, JH, *The Jurisprudence of GATT and the WTO: Insights on Treaty Law and Economic Relations* (2000) 418. The idea that trade liberalization was essential for peace was the prevailing view among delegates at the famed Bretton Woods conference in July 1944, where the Allied governments laid the groundwork for the post-war international economic system. The ITO was slated

the absence of a regulatory framework for sustaining international trade had contributed to the conflicts insofar as incessantly higher trade barriers imposed during the first decades of the twentieth century slowed economic growth and aggravated foreign relations between what would ultimately become belligerent countries.[11] A workable trade regime with an effective mechanism for resolving disputes was thus seen as necessary for peace in the post-war era, and on 21 November 1947, 44 countries met in Havana as part of the United Nations Conference on Trade and Employment to explore a new global policy framework.[12]

Under the terms of what would become the Havana Charter, delegates proposed, among other things, the creation of an ITO tasked with issuing trade rules. Whenever a country failed to live up to its obligations, an aggrieved state could seek a bilateral resolution through diplomatic negotiations or a mutually agreed upon arbitration.[13] Then, if (or when) this process failed, the Executive Board of the ITO—an appointed body consisting of delegates from Member States of 'chief economic importance' and 'the broad geographical areas which the Members of the Organization belong'[14]—would investigate the matter and make a binding ruling. Remedies for an aggrieved party included everything from concessions of obligations to an involuntary withdrawal from the ITO.[15]

Despite the fact that 53 countries, including Britain, signed the final act of the Havana conference, prospective participants decided that the ITO Charter would not come into effect unless member governments ratified it—and many countries held back from doing so until it was clear how the US would act.[16] With the ratification question still unresolved in 1946, 23 countries made a then-unnamed parallel agreement that amounted to nearly $10 billion in trade-related concessions.[17] Though more modest in scale, and intended to serve as a temporary precursor to

to be one of the three pillars of the post-war economic order envisioned by this system. See Shell, GR, 'Trade Legalism and International Relations Theory' (1995) 44 *Duke Law Journal* 829, 840. See generally Bederman, DJ, *International Law Frameworks* (2010) 149–50; Rodrik, D, *The Globalization Paradox: Why Global Markets, States, and Democracy Can't Coexist* (2011) 69–76.

[11] See Jackson, n 10 above, 351 ('The framers of [the Bretton Woods] system believed that the disastrous tariff and trade policies of the 1930s had contributed to the outbreak of the Second World War.') (Brackets supplied.)

[12] Many of the delegates expressed support for this Kantian ideal at the conference. See Dillon Jr, TJ, 'The World Trade Organization: A New Legal Order for World Trade?' (1995) 16 *Michigan Journal of International Law* 349, 351.

[13] Final Act Adopted at the Conclusion of the Second Session of the Preparatory Committee of the United Nations Conference on Trade and Development Article 93 (30 October 1947), 55 U.N.T.S. 188 [hereinafter, Havana Charter].

[14] ibid, Article 78. [15] ibid.

[16] See Toye, R, 'The International Trade Organization' in Narilikar, A, Daunton, M, and Stern, RM (eds), *The Oxford Handbook on the World Trade Organization* (2012) 96 (describing the fraught ratification process of the ITO Charter in capitals around the world after the Havana Conference).

[17] Brummer, C, *Minilateralism: How Trade Alliances, Soft Law, and Financial Engineering Are Redefining Economic Statecraft* (2014) 42.

the ITO Charter, the concessions were still unprecedented and impacted nearly one-fifth of global commerce in goods at the time. Two years later in 1948, they would come to be known as the General Agreement on Tariffs and Trade (GATT).[18]

By 1950, the absence of a strong US commitment to the ITO—particularly in the Congress—ultimately proved fatal to the organization.[19] Once it became clear that the ITO was a non-starter, the provisional GATT would become the *de facto* mechanism for conducting multilateral trade negotiations among the world's major trading partners. This was a significant development, of course, for international trade law as the mechanics of the GATT were quite different from those of the proposed ITO. Unlike the ITO Charter, which had called for one-country, one-vote voting and a formal dispute process, the GATT decision-making process was driven by consensus.[20] Dispute resolution under the GATT was a highly inclusive, collaborative effort. Every member's acquiescence was required to solve disputes. Defendant countries would have to agree to the establishment or adoption of panels, as well as the decisions rendered by the panels.[21]

With a membership of relatively like-minded countries, the GATT system evinced, on the one hand, a widely held belief that disparate opinions could be bridged. Over time, however, problems arose that exposed a series of institutional and structural weaknesses, especially as the ranks of GATT swelled in the late 1960s and 1970s from 30 to 77 members.[22] As the organization's membership grew, and became more economically diverse, industrialized countries increasingly complained that developing nations were not required to offer deep tariff 'concessions' during GATT negotiations due to a range of carve outs and exceptions, even while they benefited from others' tariff reductions under the Most Favoured Nation (MFN) rule.[23] Meanwhile, many developing countries viewed the informal nature of GATT dispute resolution with scepticism. Some argued that it allowed Western powers to 'drag their feet' during the dispute resolution process.[24] In

[18] ibid.

[19] See Diebold, W, 'Reflections on the International Trade Organization' (1994) 14 *Northern Illinois University Law Review* 335, 340–6 (arguing in part that the ITO failed because the US business lobby opposed the idea that an international organization could bind its members to certain obligations).

[20] ibid.

[21] See Hudec, R, *Enforcing International Trade Law: The Evolution of the Modern GATT Legal System* (1991) 12.

[22] For a useful overview of the growing pains that GATT experienced during this period, see Srinivasan, TN, 'The Dispute Settlement Mechanism of the WTO: A Brief History and an Evaluation from Economic, Contractarian and Legal Perspectives' (2007) 30 *World Economy* 1033, 1037.

[23] See Rodrik, n 10 above, 73. The MFN rule, which was codified by Article I of the GATT, restricts one country from according another country less favorable terms in an international trade agreement than it has accorded to any other country. See the General Agreement on Tariffs and Trade, Article I (1947); see also Hawking, H, *Commercial Treaties and Agreements* (1951) 61.

[24] Hudec, n 21 above, 54 (arguing that consensus decision making led to delays and failures to implement panel decisions by giving 'defendants the ability to drag their feet at every stage of the process'); see also Shell, n 10 above, 848, citing Trubek, DM, 'Protectionism and Development: Time for a New Dialogue?' (1993) 25 *New York University Journal of International Law & Politics* 345, 364–5

particular, the European Community and Japan were singled out for using the consensus-based system to block the establishment or adoption of panels when complaints were lodged against them, and thus mitigate or avoid the economic and reputational consequences of non-compliance. All the while, powerful states could still railroad weaker ones by bypassing the GATT and relying on their own foreign policy tools—a point increasingly levied as the US, which, frustrated with the lack of progress in obtaining desired outcomes through the GATT, began to threaten unilateral actions under domestic trade laws (namely the Trade Act of 1974).[25] As many critics noted, small and developing countries, by contrast, rarely had the capacity or economic wherewithal to independently resolve a dispute with a larger, developed economy.

In part because of this perceived lack of efficacy, no GATT Member State initiated a complaint through the panel procedures between 1963 and 1969.[26] And although the system was in many ways surprisingly successful given its limitations, complaints continued to build to a crescendo by the time negotiations for the Uruguay Round opened in 1986. Fewer than half of the panels that heard disputes in the 1980s had been able to deliver a final report for judgment, although in terms of absolute numbers the 1980s saw more final reports than in the three previous decades of GATT's existence.[27] And in cases where the parties were able to come to a consensus around a final report delivered by a panel, enforcement was weak.[28] Unilateral, uncoordinated enforcement was, as a result, common.[29]

The WTO dispute resolution system was intended to be a response to these and other challenges.[30] As a matter of basic trade policy, governments around the world were convinced that trade liberalization was necessary for economic growth and development.[31] For leaders in the US and elsewhere, GATT concessions seemed too

(noting that developing countries supported a stronger dispute resolution process within GATT because 'they thought a stronger dispute system would give them additional leverage in negotiating with wealthier states over protectionist laws that limited their ability to export to those states').

[25] For further discussion of US unilateralism during this period—including the adoption of the Trade Act—see Srinivasan, n 22 above, 1038.

[26] No new legal complaints were brought through the GATT panel procedures between 1963 and 1969, with the exception of one minor claim filed in 1969. See Hudec, n 21 above, 11–12.

[27] Parties filed 115 complaints under GATT over the course of the 1980s, and panels that heard disputes delivered decisions in 47 of those cases. This increase in usage likely resulted from the institutionalization of two new GATT procedures during the Tokyo Round in the 1970s. See Srinivasan, n 22 above, 1037–8.

[28] See Hudec, n 21 above, 8–9.

[29] By way of example, 1988 amendments to section 301 of the US Trade Act of 1974 statutorily required retaliatory action by the US prior to the delivery of a GATT final report in some cases. For further discussion of this dynamic, see Schwartz, WF and Sykes, AO, The Economic Structure of Renegotiation and Dispute Resolution in the WTO/GATT System (2002), John M. Olin Law & Economics Working Paper No 143, 2nd series, 26–7.

[30] See Rodrik, n 10 above, 73–6. See also Wolf, M, *Why Globalization Works* (2004) 41; Stiglitz, JE, *Globalization and Its Discontents* (2002) 15–16.

[31] Rodrik, n 10 above, 77.

limited in scope, and deeper inroads needed to be made into services and other areas.[32] And for some, even more importantly, reforms in the dispute resolution system were needed.

Along these lines, a series of new liberalization measures and agreements were introduced, and a new dispute resolution system was launched to heighten members' incentives to comply with their multilateral trade commitments. Together the substantive and institutional reforms would galvanize a new body, the WTO—an unprecedented international organization centred on lowering trade barriers and mediating disputes (and issuing binding decisions) among participating countries. Its members would enjoy an equal vote in decision-making, reduced tariffs and (even more) access to the global markets, but in return would have to accept and abide by the organization's rulings.[33]

The WTO would consequently represent a historic innovation in international economic law—a third-party, multilateral dispute mechanism with teeth. But even today, there are flaws. Perhaps most importantly, the DSU allows governments to impose sanctions only after the dispute resolution process is complete, creating a gap in enforcement where the dispute resolution process is long.[34] Governments are thus prohibited from imposing sanctions to harms that arise before judgments are rendered by dispute resolution panels.[35] Appeals processes, though more expert, can also extend decision-making, and the ability of parties to retaliate can still depend on their own economic size and strength. Still, the WTO does not give parties a blank cheque for unlimited trade violations of infinite duration. Reputational costs are more forthcoming and no longer subject to consensus constraints. And once final rulings are made, compliance is expected, and a largely credible enforcement tool is available even where disagreement among disputants persists. As such, the WTO provides what is by virtually all accounts the most advanced multilateral system of dispute resolution available in international economic law.

[32] For a thoughtful analysis of the efficacy of the WTO's 'one state, one vote' approach, see Ehlermann, C, Decision Making in the World Trade Organization: Is the Consensus Practice of the World Trade Organization Adequate for Making, Revising and Implementing Rules on International Trade? (2005), available at <http://www.wilmerhale.com/pages/publicationsandnewsdetail.aspx?NewsPubId=87647>.

[33] See Rodrik, n 10 above, 79 (citing Esserman, S and Howse, R, 'The WTO on Trial' (January–February 2003) 82 *Foreign Affairs* 130).

[34] Brewster, R, 'The Remedy Gap: Institutional Design, Retaliation, and Trade Law Enforcement' (2011) 80 *George Washington Law Review* 102, 112, 125–30.

[35] As a result, other innovations could possibly enhance even the WTO's effectiveness, including retrospective retaliation mechanisms, and preliminary and more expeditious timing of arbitration panels. ibid, 150–8.

IV. Today's International Financial Regulatory System and its Origins

1. Financial regulation's domestic roots

International financial regulation's roots are very different from those of international trade—and are distinctly domestic. National banking systems have existed for centuries, though their regulation has been at times less than robust, to say the least. Some of the first prudential rules for financial institutions involved the degree to which banks were required to hold gold in case home governments needed to dragoon resources for national defence.[36] Over time, as private banking proliferated, rules would emerge touching on basic licensing requirements, branching, and the private issuance of bank notes. There was also some regulatory experimentation: banks in England in the 1840s, for example, would have to increasingly publish balance-sheet information; and later in the early and mid-nineteenth century, a handful of individual states in the US would not only require basic levels of transparency for incorporated firms (including financial firms), but they would also experiment (albeit temporarily) with local deposit guarantee schemes.[37]

That said, prudential regulations of the kind we are familiar with today, where the public's interest in financial regulation was deeply tied to concerns of systemic and financial stability, arose most prominently in the 1930s, and in the US.[38] In the wake of the 1929 stock market crash and the ensuing Great Depression, legislators moved more deeply into the internal operations of financial institutions to separate banking activities from business activities to reduce the risk of future crises and unwind the concentration of capital building up on Wall Street.[39] Some of the first regulatory bills to pass through Congress in the 1930s included the Banking

[36] See McCollim, G, *Louis XIV's Assault on Privilege, Nicolas Desmaretz and the Tax on Wealth* (2012) 154–5. Indeed, the Bank of England was itself established in 1694 to assist the government in financing war against Louis XIV of France in the Nine Years' War. See ibid. It then eventually developed public functions such as issuing banknotes and overseeing interbank relations. See O'Brien, DP, 'Monetary Base Control and the Bank Charter Act of 1844' (1997) 29 *History of Political Economy* 593, 594–6.

[37] See also Grossman, R, *Unsettled Account* (2010) 139 (noting that England would introduce banking codes requiring minimal capital standards and requirements to publish balance sheets in the 1840s, though ultimately opt for a commercial chartering system in 1857).

[38] Indeed, even in the 1930s, and even in the case of the larger banking systems in Europe like Germany's, regulation routinely focused on the 'war readiness' of a country's financial system vis-à-vis imperial competitors. See Krieghoff, NF, *Banking Regulation in a Federal System: Lessons from American and German Banking History* (2013) 65.

[39] For a legislative history of the US regulatory response to the Great Depression, see Gart, A, *Regulation, Deregulation, Reregulation: The Future of the Banking, Insurance, and Securities Industries* (1994) 31.

Acts of 1933 (commonly referred to as the Glass–Steagall Act) and 1934, which also established bank depository insurance and the FDIC—the first agency tasked with examining and ensuring proper risk management within banks. Along these lines, the rules took the important step of separating investment banking and commercial banking. Similarly, the Securities Acts of 1933 and 1934 were passed, which collectively created the bedrock of US securities regulation and initiated a period of increasing federal oversight over what had been lacklustre self-regulation on and off exchanges.

In his *Public Papers*, President Franklin D Roosevelt wrote that the unifying purpose of these laws, besides fighting the concentration of capital in the hands of the few, was 'letting in the light' to reveal the truth about banks and public companies' business affairs and financial health.[40] But while transparency and stability were top of mind for the president and his New Deal advisors, foreign capital markets and cross-border regulatory arbitrage were not. These early bedrocks of modern financial regulation were created of, by, and for a domestic financial system. Although cross-border bank failures had helped usher in the Great Depression in the late 1920s and early 1930s, international capital flows plummeted thereafter and were subject to stricter government controls throughout the post-war period. Only as capital controls loosened and technology came to connect far-flung markets did the inward-looking tendencies of financial authorities begin to appear frighteningly inadequate.

2. Cross-border banking crisis in 1970s leads to first calls for international financial regulation

International financial regulation would evolve in a belated fashion, and like many other regulatory initiatives, in the wake of high-profile (and international) market failures. In June 1974, the Herstatt Bank of Cologne failed. Up to that point, it was considered to be the 35th largest bank in Germany at the time, and had total assets of DM 2.07 billion.[41] But in September 1973, Herstatt's foreign exchange business suffered losses four times the amount of its capital because of an unanticipated appreciation of the US dollar. When German authorities discovered the loss during a routine audit of the bank, it withdrew Herstatt's banking licence and ordered it into liquidation. This announcement then sent global markets into turmoil because

[40] Roosevelt, FD, *Public Papers* (Vol 1, 1938) 653.

[41] For a brief but informative overview of the Herstatt crisis, see Koleva, G, '"Icon of Systemic Risk" Haunts Industry Decades after Demise' (23 June 2011) *American Banker*, available at <http://www.americanbanker.com/bankthink/bankhaus-herstatt-icon-of-systemic-risk-1039312-1.html>. See Brummer, n 17 above, 99; Singer, DA, *Regulating Capital: Setting Standards for the International Financial System* (2007) 38.

prior to the announcement of Herstatt's closure, several of its counterparties in the US had irrevocably paid Deutschmarks through the German payment system expecting a return payment of US dollars in the future. However, once the German authority's decision was announced, Herstatt's New York correspondent bank (as well as others) suspended Herstatt's account foreclosing any receipt of funds. The mess would end up roiling international markets, and spur calls for greater international coordination.[42]

The Herstatt crisis was a jarring lesson on the potential risks of global banking markets and the value of enhanced coordination. It would also coincide with a similar fiasco in the US—the failure of the Franklin National Bank of New York in May 1974, which was at the time one of the 20 largest in the country.[43] Like Herstatt, its failure would wreak havoc not only in the US, but also on global Eurocurrency markets, exacerbating, in effect, the shock of the Herstatt collapse. Regulators had no choice but to emerge from their previously insulated domestic jurisdictions and acknowledge the need for international regulatory cooperation. By the end of the year, central bank governors of what was then the 'Group of Ten' leading industrialized countries established a committee to address the pressing need for new and better rules for the global banking market.[44] Housed at the Bank for International Settlements in Basel, the Standing Committee on Banking Regulations and Supervisory Practices (now called the Basel Committee on Banking Supervision) took on in the mid-1970s the task of coordinating and harmonizing the prudential regulations of its member governments.

At around the same time, cooperative initiatives were gearing up in other sectors as well. The same forces that drove the internationalization of banking also drove forward the internationalization of securities and derivatives markets. The collapse of the Bretton Woods gold system, along with the attenuation of capital controls and the proliferation of financial and technological innovation, made markets more interconnected than they had ever been before. This development, in turn, spurred a range of institutions to start thinking on a more global scale about how markets were structured. Accountants and auditors created their own cross-border guilds towards the end of the decade to better harmonize rules relating to how financial statements were prepared for investors.[45] Meanwhile, securities regulators from North and South America established the Inter-American Association of Securities Commissions to coordinate the supervision of stock markets and issuers of stocks and bonds, which was then relaunched as the International Organization of Securities Commissions (IOSCO) in 1986.[46]

[42] See Koleva, n 41 above.

[43] See White, E, *The Comptroller and the Transformation of American Banking, 1960–1990* (1992) 27.

[44] See Brummer, n 4 above, 76.

[45] The most influential of these guilds include the International Accounting Standards Board and the International Federation of Accountants.

[46] See Alexander, K, Dhumale, R, and Eatwell, J, *Global Governance of Financial Systems: The International Regulation of Systemic Risk* (2006) 58 (discussing the events which culminated in IOSCO's founding, and giving a brief functional overview of the organization).

Indeed, a range of acronym-laden clubs would pop up in the latter half of the twentieth century—from the Financial Action Task Force (FATF—for money laundering) in 1989, to the International Association of Insurance Supervisors (IAIS—for, not surprisingly, insurance) in 1994—as the pressure to collaborate on shared issues grew. Globalization not only brought markets together, but those who regulated them as well.[47]

But these efforts were for the most part initially less ambitious than they appeared. The primary objective for most regulatory bodies was information-sharing among market supervisors. Authorities sought, above all else, to keep abreast of what their colleagues were doing in their respective jurisdictions, and to identify common points of regulatory interest. And even then, the focus for most collaboration was enforcement cooperation and technical assistance between leading and emerging markets, and not so much joint-policy development.

Thus, even as financial services took on an increasingly cross-border flavour during the late 1980s and early 1990s, financial regulation was still a largely domestic enterprise. Traditional multilateral efforts did little to change this. Many domestic financial regulators that participated in the Uruguay Round of trade negotiations in 1986 made clear that it would be unacceptable to include financial services in the General Agreement on Trade in Services (GATS) without a specific exception for domestic regulation and supervision.[48] Every market was different, the argument went, and needed supervision by national specialists familiar with its constellation of institutions and private firms, and at any rate, the costs of failure of regulation would fall on a country's taxpayers, not the international community.[49]

The significant exception to this trend was the 1988 Basel Accord (Basel I—given its subsequent updates in the following two decades), a product of the Basel Committee.[50] In one of the first concerted forms of international administrative

[47] See Brummer, n 4 above, 60–114.

[48] See Key, SJ, Financial Services in the Uruguay Round and the WTO (1997), Occasional Paper 54, Group of Thirty, 7 (providing a first-hand account of GATS negotiations relating to financial services).

[49] Sydney J Key, a former economist from the Board of Governors of the Federal Reserve Board and a participant in the GATS negotiations, writes that '[w]hen the idea of including financial services in the Uruguay Round was first proposed, financial regulators were concerned about the possibility of a trade agreement interfering with their ability to regulate and supervise financial institutions ... As a result, the GATS contains a so-called prudential carve-out to ensure that the opening of markets that the agreement is intended to achieve will not jeopardize prudential regulation and supervision.' ibid.

[50] See Goodhart, C, *The Basel Committee on Banking Supervision: A History of the Early Years 1974–1997* (2011). For an in-depth analysis of how the various Basel recommendations have been implemented over the years in different jurisdictions, see IMF, Implementation of the Basel Core Principles for Effective Banking Supervision Experience with Assessments and Implications for Future Work (2 September 2008); see also Tarullo, D, 'Administrative Accountability and International Regulatory Networks' (4 November 2008) 14 (unpublished manuscript) (on file with author).

rulemaking, banking regulators sought to create stringent, cross-border capital standards for multinational financial institutions. But it too was ultimately the product of significant wrangling: the US and the UK wanted to raise standards with more risk-based standards for capital, while Japan did not. Thus, after reaching a bilateral accord in 1987, the two countries threatened sanctions if Japan failed to reform. After ceding concessions, rules were 'multilaterized' via the Basel Committee, and as we will see, subject to a variety of subsequent reforms.

3. Fallout from the Asian financial crisis of 1997 triggers unprecedented international regulatory coordination

Perhaps due in part to the difficulty of securing international capital standards, the most significant steps toward broader international standard-making and dispute resolution would wait until 1997 and the outbreak of the Asian financial crisis.[51] As foreign investors poured money into newly opened economies, cavalier domestic banks loaded up on speculative real estate investments without keeping enough cash on hand in the event that their bets went wrong. When bets in Thailand took a bad turn, speculators became concerned with the health of other countries in the region, and Malaysia and Indonesia's currencies cratered, tagged as being guilty by regional association. Lending froze across South East Asia, prompting multibillion-dollar IMF bailouts.[52]

National regulatory agencies, along with international regulatory authorities like IOSCO and the Basel Committee, launched new initiatives to work toward preventing crises of the same sort from happening again in the future. First, a new institution, the Financial Stability Forum, was created in 1999 with the purpose of identifying internationally accepted standards that if adopted by countries could help prevent financial crises.[53] And second, a new programme called the Standards and Codes Initiative was launched to develop and promote high quality rules of the road for international financial activities.[54] The idea was to give what had been low-priority and often ad hoc best practices and regulatory guidance a new prescriptive edge.

[51] For a more detailed overview of the Asian financial crisis, see Radlet, S and Sachs, J, 'The East Asian Financial Crisis: Diagnosis, Remedies, and Prospects' (1998) 1 *Brookings Papers on Economic Activity*, available at <http://www.brookings.edu/~/media/Projects/BPEA/1998%201/1998a_bpea_radelet_sachs_cooper_bosworth.PDF>.

[52] See Stiglitz, n 30 above, 145–8.

[53] Finance Ministers and Central Bank Governors of the G7 initially convened the Financial Stability Forum in 1999. See Tietmeyer, H, *International Cooperation and Coordination in the Area of Financial Market Supervision and Surveillance* (1999) 6.

[54] For an analysis of the efficacy of the Standards and Codes Initiative during its early years, see the IMF and World Bank, The Standards and Codes Initiative—Is it effective? And How Can it Be Improved? (2005), available at <http://www.worldbank.org/ifa/ROSC%20review%202005.pdf>, 8.

To bolster the reforms, the Bretton Woods institutions were brought into the regulatory foray. Up to that point, the role of the IMF and World Bank in matters of financial market regulation was highly limited. At that point, only the IMF was actively involved in market supervision. Article IV of the IMF's Articles of Agreement required that each member collaborate with the Fund and other members via surveillance to assure financial stability (or more precisely, 'orderly exchange arrangements and to promote a stable system of exchange rates').[55]

Under the new reforms, the old Article IV examinations would be broadened to include inspections of members' financial market supervision and oversight. Furthermore, a new Financial Sector Assessment Program (FSAP) was introduced in 1998 to evaluate how the rules operated 'on the ground', in countries at the domestic level.[56] Intended to be more muscular, intrusive, and trenchant, the FSAP would call on experts from the IMF and World Bank to parachute into countries such as Thailand or Korea, to examine for themselves the extent to which national regulators complied with internationally agreed-upon best practices. The results of the inspections would then be shared with the country under examination to help that country's policymakers identify the 'strengths, vulnerabilities, and risks' of their financial systems and design appropriate policy responses.[57]

There was also supposed to be some coercion behind the new system. Most importantly, the codes and standards being assessed under the FSAP were routinely incorporated into IMF and World Bank aid programmes.[58] In theory, this meant that if you wanted a World Bank loan for a power plant, then funding could be tied, however subtly or explicitly, to satisfying some of IOSCO's core principles for sound securities systems. Or if a government needed IMF assistance for a balance-of-payments crisis, it might have to comply with the Basel Committee's best practices or capital standards. In this way, standard-setting bodies became more than just advocates of good principles of government. Their dictates were elevated to sources of real regulatory authority.

But it was still far from a perfect arrangement. One of the most significant problems was that it was a largely voluntary model of global governance. Many countries did not have to subject themselves to FSAP surveillance. Instead, only countries receiving aid from the IMF and World Bank were required to undertake

[55] See Articles of Agreement of the IMF, Article IV (27 December 1945), 60 Stat. 1401, 2 U.N.T.S. 39; see also the IMF, Factsheet: IMF Surveillance (2014) (discussing ways in which the IMF uses Article IV surveillance in practice).

[56] For the IMF's view on why it believed that financial stability assessments under FSAP needed to become a mandatory part of Article IV surveillance, see the IMF, Integrating Stability Assessments under the Financial Sector Assessment Program into Article IV Surveillance (2010), 23–4.

[57] See the IMF, Report of the Managing Director to the International Monetary and Financial Committee on Progress in Strengthening the Architecture of the International Financial System and Reform of the IMF (2000), para 25.

[58] See, eg, the IMF, Financial Sector Assessment Program (FSAP) (2014); see also World Bank, Financial Sector Assessment Program (2014), available at <http://www.worldbank.org/fsap>.

assessments and apply international best practices.[59] The rich world of donor countries largely escaped such annoyances.

Another challenge of the FSAP was that the raw data used for analysis was often self-reported. The idea was, in part, efficiency-oriented, and geared toward getting information quickly from the party with the best access to it—the country whose regulatory system was being evaluated. But for the most part, it was to enhance the collaborative nature of the exercise, and make the process a little less intrusive. The problem, of course, was that the information could be compromised or manipulated.

Even if you could ensure that the information received was reliable, there was no guarantee that the country undertaking an assessment would allow you to pass it on to others. Instead, information gained from the key IMF and World Bank surveillance mechanisms—observance reports, financial sector assessments, and surveys conducted by national regulators—could only be published or disseminated to other authorities at the consent of the assessed country.[60] Having a choice led to an adverse selection problem where countries that performed best would be the most inclined to tell the world about it, and those that did poorly would just quash any disclosure as to the strengths (or weaknesses) of their domestic financial systems.

4. 2008 financial crisis exposes gaps in corpus of international financial law, leads to new system of global coordination among regulators

The 2008 crisis would humble Western policymakers and give new direction to the international surveillance system.[61] When the US housing bubble burst in 2008, global financial institutions reported major losses because of their borrowing against, and exposure to, subprime mortgage-backed securities investments.[62]

[59] As part of World Bank and IMF aid programmes, the two organizations have routinely collaborated to publish FSAP status reports monitoring recipient countries' progress towards implementing IOSCO objectives and principles. For a sampling of recent status reports, see, eg, the IMF and World Bank, Financial Sector Assessment Program: Brazil—IOSCO Objectives and Principles of Securities Regulation (2013); the IMF and World Bank, Financial Sector Assessment Program: Nigeria—IOSCO Objectives and Principles of Securities Regulation (2013).

[60] The IOSCO Multilateral Memorandum of Understanding (MMOU) contains a confidentiality provision which states that any non-public information obtained in the course of any consultation between or among financial regulators shall not be disclosed without the express permission of the concerned financial regulator(s). See IOSCO, Multilateral Memorandum of Understanding Concerning Consultation and Cooperation and the Exchange of Information (2002), 7.

[61] For a more detailed overview of the various causes of the 2008 financial crisis and its effects on international financial regulation, see Brummer, n 4 above, 210–13.

[62] See the Financial Crisis Inquiry Commission, The Financial Crisis Inquiry Report: Final Report of the National Commission on the Causes of the Financial and Economic Crisis in the US (2011), available at <http://www.gpo.gov/fdsys/pkg/GPO-FCIC/pdf/GPO-FCIC.pdf>, 363–5.

The crisis then spread as it became apparent that major banking and financial institutions all over the world held large exposures of 'toxic' assets tied to US real estate.[63] General mistrust among banks about one another's solvency and the robustness of payment systems caused the quasi-disappearance of interbank lending. Huge swaths of the US financial system failed, were bailed out through government-sponsored acquisitions, or were taken over by the government. The affected institutions included commercial banks such as Washington Mutual and Wachovia, investment banks such as Lehman Brothers, and brokerages such as Bear Stearns and Merrill Lynch. Across the globe, too, financial-market turmoil erupted as a result of bailouts required for Germany's Landesbanken, Belgium's Fortis and Dexia banks, the UK's Northern Rock, and many others exposed either directly or indirectly to the US mortgage finance industry.[64]

The crisis highlighted a series of gaps that pervaded not only national regulatory regimes, but also the greater corpus of international financial law. International regulatory forums like the Basel Committee and IOSCO had devoted very little time to thinking about securitization and mortgage-related securities, derivatives, shadow banking, or 'too big to fail' institutions that increasingly dominated the financial systems of advanced industrial countries.[65] Part of the problem was ideological—major industrialized countries viewed many new-fangled financial innovations as mitigating risk instead of enhancing it. Plus, up to that point, major countries had never themselves caused crises, but were instead the first responders when poorer countries found themselves in a financial bind.

As the international regulatory community realized that no one, not even the US, was immune to the dangers of financial meltdowns, a new system for global coordination was devised in 2008 and 2009, along with an ambitious agenda for regulatory reform. In the most significant institutional step, the G20 was named the world's premier economic forum, essentially displacing the G7.[66] Additionally, the Financial Stability Forum (FSF) was renamed the Financial Stability Board (FSB). This Board was elevated to a kind of technocratic counterpart to the G20 to aid in coordinating standard-setting activities of different regulatory agencies and to ensure that complex, interdisciplinary topics did not fall through the cracks of different organizations' mandates.[67]

[63] For an excellent recap of the failure of Countrywide and other US institutions, see Wessel, D, *In Fed we Trust: Ben Bernanke's War on the Great Panic* (2010).

[64] For a timeline chronicling the most sobering milestones of the 2008 crisis, see Kingsley, P, 'Financial Crisis: Timeline' *The Guardian*, 6 August 2012.

[65] Brummer, n 4 above, 220–7.

[66] See White House Office of the Press Secretary, Press Release, Fact Sheet: Creating a 21st Century International Economic Architecture (24 September 2009), available at <http://www.whitehouse.gov/the_press_office/Fact-Sheet-Creating-a-21st-Century-International-Economic-Architecture>.

[67] At the London Summit of the G20 in the immediate aftermath of the 2008 financial crisis, members of the G20 elected to re-establish the FSB 'with a stronger institutional basis and enhanced capacity'. For the text of the new Charter that followed from this charge, see FSB Charter (2009). For

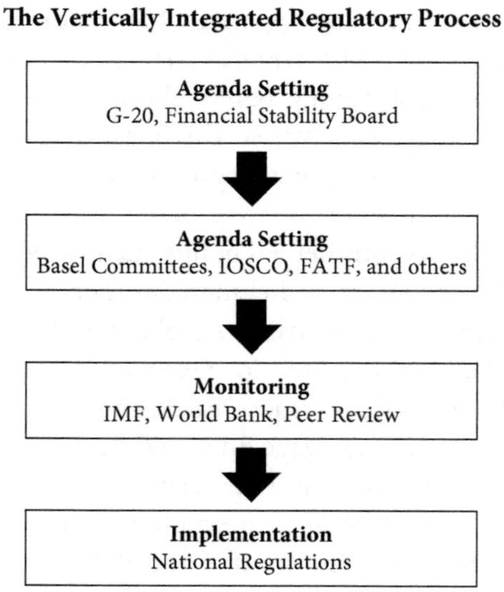

Figure 5.1 The vertically integrated regulatory process

Source: Brummer, *Minilateralism: How Trade Alliances, Soft Law, and Financial Engineering Are Redefining Economic Statecraft* (2014)

Together, the two institutions would more aggressively direct standard-setting processes and work streams, as well as coordinate between what had been rather disparate and disconnected standard-setting bodies. In this way, what was a highly fragmented and somewhat disorganized system was vertically integrated under G20/FSB leadership, and took direction from it (see Figure 5.1). Meanwhile, the Basel Committee, IOSCO, and other forums for accountants, auditors, and insurance regulators, would write new, often more prescriptive rules for the financial industry, and a new 'Basel III' Accord for banks was introduced, along with a slew of other international standards.

Yet, as before, these rules would not be memorialized as treaties, but as informal best practices, observations, reports, and information-sharing exercises between regulators. Even after the crisis, authorities sought to maintain policy flexibility—especially given the potential volatility of market conditions and the weak global economy.

Finally, to support the newly integrated system of rulemaking, surveillance was ramped up. The IMF and the FSB required FSAPs as part of their members' obligations, and would even require to varying degrees publication of their results.[68]

an explanation of how the FSB was designed to address international regulatory coordination issues, see Brummer, C, 'Charter of the Financial Stability Board, Introductory Note' (2012) 51 *International Legal Materials* 828.

[68] International Monetary Fund, Press Release, IMF Expanding Surveillance to Require Mandatory Financial Stability Assessments of Countries with Systemically Important Financial Sectors (27 September, 2010), available at <http://www.imf.org/external/np/sec/pr/2010/pr10357.htm>.

Additionally, in 2009 the FSB launched a series of 'thematic' and 'country' peer reviews to take stock of existing practices in particular policy areas and focus on the progress made by individual FSB members' jurisdictions in implementing FSAP regulatory and supervisory recommendations.[69] Similarly, the Basel Committee, IOSCO, and other standard-setters refined and revamped their own in-house surveillance systems to better track and identify implementation of best practices by their members. Regulatory policies are now routinely put under the microscope and evaluated by the staff of member agencies to determine, often publicly, the degree to which governments have complied with best practices espoused by the group.

V. Comparing the Two Regimes: Factors Mitigating against Formalized Dispute Resolution in International Financial Regulation

The brief historical overview in the previous sections allows for a series of modest observations that provide clues as to the availability of dispute resolution in trade as compared to finance. First, we see that trade regulation, unlike financial regulation, is *an inherently international enterprise*. By definition, it relates to the cross border flow of goods and services, and as such was, quite logically, a preoccupation of UN officials and Bretton Woods representatives hoping to kick-start global growth in late 1940s, and WTO negotiators in the 1980s and 1990s. Because of its international character, the perimeter of domestic oversight is constrained, and relates for the most part to ensuring the compliance of foreign companies (and their home countries) with international treaty commitments and local tariff regimes.

Financial regulation, by contrast, can at least potentially be entirely domestic in nature—and it was for much of the post-war period. Bank regulators policed local institutions to prevent failure, just as securities regulators focused on domestic companies' issuances of stocks and bonds on and off national exchanges. This led to very different diplomatic postures. Because of the essentially international character of trade, trade negotiations have historically been the purview of heads of state and countries' diplomatic corps. Meanwhile, national administrative agencies

[69] See generally FSB Publications—Peer Reviews (2013), available at <http://www.financialstabilityboard.org/list/fsb_publications/tid_141/index.htm>.

have historically managed the process of international regulatory coordination as part and parcel of their domestic mandates—even where in many cases they enjoy no capacity to unilaterally bind their governments.[70]

International trade and financial regulation were also built on very *different ideological foundations.* Trade rests on the idea that governmental intervention in commerce, all else being equal, is 'bad'. As we saw in previous sections, the founders of the modern-day trade regime believed that trade barriers enabled military conflict. Liberalization was thus an antidote to war. This strategic stance then embraced a more purely economic posture in the 1980s, as policy elites concluded that in most cases governmental tariffs per se imposed (unnecessary) costs on consumers insofar as less efficiently made goods came to the market and yet still beat out higher-quality, efficiently made goods.[71] Efforts to beef up the substance and procedural rigour of the GATT system were consequently embraced, culminating in the creation of the WTO in the 1990s.

By contrast, financial regulation operates under the premise that governmental intervention is necessary to protect the safety and soundness of national economies.[72] Most substantive provisions in any country's rulebooks are policy responses to earlier market failures—and the consequences they had for their national economies. Consequently, regulators' focus is largely domestic, even when working abroad. Their mandates are to prevent fraud, bank failures, and the build-up of systemic risks that could undermine their markets—and international coordination is viewed not infrequently as merely a condition precedent for successfully achieving their legislative objectives. The negotiating posture for international coordination is thus quite different from trade, where collaboration is often easier due to the ideological starting point of negotiations—to draw down governmental involvement, as opposed to build it up. All else being equal, local regulators will understand their markets better than foreign counterparts, and must ultimately answer to the

[70] In the US, for example, regulatory agencies cannot individually sign treaties and as a general matter have no authority to bind the US government (though some experts speculate that commitments with legally binding force could theoretically be possible with cooperation from the State Department).

[71] See Milner, H, *Resisting Protectionism: Global Industries and the Politics of International Trade* (1988) (arguing that increased export dependence, multinationality, and intra-company trade created conditions for both states and multinational corporations to prefer free trade beginning in the 1980s). Lawrence Baxter makes similar critical observations and discusses the difficulty of transposing dispute resolution in a regime based on governmental intervention. See Baxter, L, *Exploring the WFO Option for Global Banking Regulation* in Boulle, L (ed.), *Globalisation and Governance* (2011) 113–24.

[72] See, eg, Yellen, JL, Remarks at the National Association of Business Economics 2010 Annual Meeting, Macroprudential Supervision and Monetary Policy in the Post-crisis World (11 October 2010), available at <http://www.palgrave-journals.com/be/journal/v46/n1/full/be201035a.html> ('[w]e need a robust system of regulation and supervision that will recognize and prevent financial excesses before they lead to crisis, while at the same time maintaining an environment conducive to financial innovation').

taxpayers that pay their salaries (and in times of crisis are called to bail out failing banks) where regulation fails. Collaboration is thus often more technical, and more difficult, especially insofar as regulators prize their own authority and approaches over others. There is also always some concern that cooperation could mean dilution of standards where the lower-quality rules of another jurisdiction are adopted.[73]

Finally, the diplomatic infrastructure for dispute resolution in trade has had much *more time to mature* than that of international financial regulation. With a general (albeit limited) consensus built around the preference for the free-trade of goods, the trade infrastructure developed on top of international obligations by the world's post-war free market economies to lower tariffs. In fits and starts, it arose gradually alongside successive rounds of trade liberalization for over half a century, until blossoming into the WTO system we see today.[74]

International financial regulation, by contrast, was never bootstrapped to the GATT or any other multilateral trade regime. It was instead explicitly excluded from formal trade negotiations, and subject to a broad and robust prudential carve out. Indeed, robust international financial regulation has been belated, and took off only after lapses in the developing world undermined Western financial systems in the 1990s—and took its current form where Western failures in supervision likewise undermined the global economy in 2008. Rulemaking has, as a result, been a matter of regulatory 'catch-up', with regulators focusing on shoring up lapses in supervision—not dispute resolution.

With no formal multilateral system at their disposal, financial regulators have operated without the benefit of a treaty infrastructure, much less a wholesale body of prescriptive regulatory commitments. All the while, policy uncertainty has not infrequently been common, especially in times of dramatic reform, with the costs and benefits of adopting any particular regulation unclear. As a result, informal standards have been the modus operandi for coordination.

These institutional dynamics have led to the development of a very different form of dispute resolution in international financial regulation as compared with trade.[75] In trade, we saw highly institutionalized forms of third-party adjudication,

[73] As to how such pressures can play out, see Stafford, P, 'Domestic Pressures Weaken US/EU Consensus' *Financial Times*, 9 January 2011. Trade officials are not immune from these currents of domestic pressure, however, and for some, binding international interventions appear to be more efficacious for trade concerns. For an analysis of this point of view, see Bollyky, T, 'Better Regulation for Freer Trade' (June 2012) *Council on Foreign Relations*, available at <http://www.cfr.org/trade/better-regulation-freer-trade/p28508#>.

[74] See Jackson, JH, 'The General Agreement on Tariffs and Trade in United States Domestic Law' (1967) 66 *Michigan Law Review* 249, 253–7. While it's generally agreed upon that Congress authorized US obligations under GATT, critics charged that it was an unconstitutional delegation of legislative power, or alternatively that GATT is beyond the authority of the Reciprocal Trade Agreements Act as amended in 1945. See Jackson, 255–8.

[75] For a fuller discussion, see Brummer, C and Yadav, Y, *How to Resolve Disputes in International Financial Regulation* (forthcoming).

built in large part on top of existing substantive international obligations and commitments. But in international finance, FSAPs and 'peer review' processes serve as the primary mechanisms for mediating disagreements.[76] Authorities examine rules on the books in foreign jurisdictions, and then compare them to the language and objectives of soft law standards as a means of nudging convergence on policy implementation.

When and if peer review fails, dispute resolution is then operationalized bilaterally where one another's market participants seek to access the other's financial markets as either investors, intermediary banks, or other financial institutions. In short, where a foreign regulator fails to embrace standards or forms of supervision that another regulator finds important, its market participants may have to comply with both their home and host regulations, or face potential sanctions like Japan during Basel I negotiations. On the other hand, if the standards are satisfactory, the foreign regulator's market participants may only have to observe its home-country rules, and can operate relatively freely in the host regulator's markets via 'mutual recognition' or 'substituted compliance' arrangements. In this latter scenario, countries undertake a process of evaluating one another's rules and supervision, and after a process of inspection and potential reform, foreign market participants in the inspected jurisdictions are permitted streamlined or lightly regulated access to a supervisor's market.

The problem, however, is that bilateralism has the tendency of creating tit-for-tat situations that can generate new disputes (or exacerbate existing ones). It is independently exercised by the host state to the foreign market participants. If a host state decides to withhold national treatment, a home state government could likewise retaliate, not for regulatory reasons but for political purposes, and in the process undermine the efficiency and robustness of cross-border financial transactions. Unilateralism of this sort does not necessarily promote the harmonization of global best practices and rules. Instead, this particular system tends to advantage the strong over the weak. Strong regulators with large financial markets are able to avoid compliance, whereas relatively smaller players are forced to comply. Where two strong regulators interact with one another high-profile showdowns can result, undermining confidence in both regulatory systems, as well as their ability to export their regulatory preferences.[77]

[76] For a more detailed discussion of peer review, see Brummer, n 4 above, 166–70.

[77] One such showdown occurred in 2013 when EU Commissioner for Internal Market and Services Michel Barnier publicly announced his opposition to a proposed US rule that would increase the capitalization requirements for foreign banks' US operations. See Barker, A and Braithwaite, T, 'EU Warns US on Bank "Protectionism"' *Financial Times*, 22 April 2013.

VI. Conclusion: The Benefits and Constraints of Trust-Building Diplomacy

Given the limitations of existing modes of dispute resolution, it is unlikely that calls for a formal dispute resolution device for international financial regulation will subside in the near future. However, for the reasons explored in this Chapter, the likelihood of such a device arising is low. Officials will be hesitant to cede their supervisory authority to third-party panels and adjudicators, especially in an era of still considerable policy discensus and uncertainty as to best practices and standards for financial markets.

Another financial crisis could, at least in theory, generate deeper cross-border structural reforms based on even more closely aligned philosophical approaches. It is at least possible, for example, that in the wake of a significant regulatory lapse in a foreign jurisdiction that regulators redouble their efforts to raise global standards for cross-border financial activities. One way of doing this could be a gradual development of cross-border dispute resolution to supplement the implementation process. This scenario is, however, arguably less likely than the alternative response—a retrenchment by regulators and a focus on enhanced territorial supervision. That is, in the wake of or in response to a large-scale financial crisis, regulators could decide to withdraw from cross-border coordination and to 'raise the drawbridge' against under regulated foreign market participants—and interference by foreign regulators.

That said, incremental moves towards greater cooperation have consistently characterized the last half century of international economic law. Certainly, this was the case under the WTO. Under the GATT, there were relatively few irrevocable sovereignty costs that diminished trade policy autonomy insofar as any member could veto the decision of the WTO panel. But over time, countries came to trust the decision-making capacity of the body to greater degree, making way for ever-deeper forms of cooperation. With greater trust, the sovereignty costs of cooperation diminished.

Tools for building trust are also available in finance. Mutual recognition and substituted compliance initiatives among regulators, for example, allow foreign firms to operate locally without registering locally so long as the local regulator deems the firms to be regulated by a foreign authority whose rules and supervisory processes are similar to its own—which is itself a determination made after assessing the foreign regulator's regulations and administrative capacity. This evaluatory process is about more than just reducing duplicative regulatory costs for cross-border activities; it also, when practised well, provides a means for learning about other regimes—and dissecting the advantages and lapses of foreign regulatory approaches. From this learning process, domestic regimes can be potentially improved, both with regard to removing inefficient regulatory burdens and implementing stronger, smarter safeguards and heightened information sharing. Furthermore, it lays the groundwork for shaping common approaches to regulatory challenges, and more effective monitoring of compliance with international best practices.

Ultimately, however, even trust-building exercises will not be enough to quickly make way for a legalized dispute resolution regime of the sort seen in international trade. The bargaining time and tedium required to secure a regime, assuming it was even possible, combined with the still significant uncertainty as to the appropriateness of policy choices and philosophies across jurisdictions, will continue, for the foreseeable future, to overwhelm the benefits of finality and clarity that a formal panel would create. Successful reforms that enhance dispute resolution in international financial regulation will, as a result, likely require new innovations in regulatory statecraft that leverage international financial regulation's existing soft law features in ways that promote the objectives of more formal devices available in other contexts.

Bibliography

Alexander, K, Dhumale, R, and Eatwell, J, *Global Governance of Financial Systems: The International Regulation of Systemic Risk* (2006).

Alloway, T, 'Fed Urges Tighter Rules for Foreign Banks' *Financial Times*, 29 November 2012.

Articles of Agreement of the International Monetary Fund Article IV (27 December 1945), 60 Stat. 1401, 2 U.N.T.S. 39.

Barker, A and Braithwaite, T, 'EU Warns US on Bank "Protectionism"' *Financial Times*, 22 April 2013.

Basel Committee on Banking Supervision, Basel III: A Global Regulatory Framework for More Resilient Banks and Banking Systems (2011).

Baxter, L, 'Exploring the WFO Option for Global Banking Regulation' in Boulle, L (ed.), *Globalisation and Governance* (2011).

Bederman, DJ, *International Law Frameworks* (2010).

Bernauer, T, Elsig, M, and Pauwelyn, J, 'Dispute Settlement Mechanism—Analysis and Problems' in Narilikar, A, Daunton, M, and Stern, RM (eds), *The Oxford Handbook on the World Trade Organization* (2012).

Bollyky, T, 'Better Regulation for Freer Trade' (June 2012), *Council on Foreign Relations*, available at <http://www.cfr.org/trade/better-regulation-freer-trade/p28508#>.

Boyle, A and Harrison, J, 'Judicial Settlement of International Environmental Disputes: Current Problems' (2013) 4 *Journal International Dispute Settlement* 2.

Brewster, R, 'The Remedy Gap: Institutional Design, Retaliation, and Trade Law Enforcement' (2011) 80 *George Washington Law Review* 102.

Brummer, C, 'Charter of the Financial Stability Board, Introductory Note' (2012) 51 *International Legal Materials* 828.

Brummer, C, Danger of Divergence: Transatlantic Financial Reform & the G20 Agenda, available at <http://www.atlanticcouncil.org/publications/reports/the-danger-of-divergence-transatlantic-financial-reform-the-g20-agenda>.

Brummer, C, *Minilateralism: How Trade Alliances, Soft Law, and Financial Engineering Are Redefining Economic Statecraft* (2014).

Brummer, C, 'Post-American Securities Regulation' (2010) 98 *California Law Review* 327.

Brummer, C, *Soft Law and the Global Financial System* (2012).

Crook, JR, 'The International Court of Justice and Human Rights' (2004) 1 *Northwestern Journal of International Human Rights* 1, available at <http://scholarlycommons.law.northwestern.edu/njihr/vol1/iss1/2>.

Diebold, W, 'Reflections on the International Trade Organization' (1994) 14 *Northern Illinois University Law Review* 33.

Dillon Jr, TJ, 'The World Trade Organization: A New Legal Order for World Trade?' (1995) 16 *Michigan Journal of International Law* 349.

Ehlermann, C, Decision Making in the World Trade Organization: Is the Consensus Practice of the World Trade Organization Adequate for Making, Revising and Implementing Rules on International Trade? (2005), available at <http://www.wilmerhale.com/pages/publicationsandnewsdetail.aspx?NewsPubId=87647>.

Esserman, S and Howse, R, 'The WTO on Trial' (January–February 2003) 82 *Foreign Affairs* 130.

Final Act Adopted at the Conclusion of the Second Session of the Preparatory Committee of the United Nations Conference on Trade and Development Article 93 (30 October 1947), 55 U.N.T.S. 188.

Financial Crisis Inquiry Communication, The Financial Crisis Inquiry Report: Final Report of the National Communication on the Causes of the Financial and Economic Crisis in the US (2011), available at <http://www.gpo.gov/fdsys/pkg/GPO-FCIC/pdf/GPO-FCIC.pdf>.

Financial Stability Board Charter (2009).

FSB Publications—Peer Reviews (2013).

Gadbaw, RM, 'Systemic Regulation of Global Trade and Finance: A Tale of Two Systems' in Cottier, T, Jackson, JH, and Lastra, RM (eds), *International Law in Financial Regulation and Monetary Affairs* (2012).

Gart, A, *Regulation, Deregulation, Reregulation: The Future of the Banking, Insurance, and Securities Industries* (1994).

General Agreement on Tariffs and Trade (GATT) (1947).

Goodhart, C, *The Basel Committee on Banking Supervision: A History of the Early Years 1974–1997* (2011).

Hawking, H, *Commercial Treaties and Agreements* (1951).

Helfer, LR and Slaughter, A, 'Why States Create International Tribunals: A Response to Professors Posner and Yoo' (2005) 93 *California Law Review* 899.

Hudec, R, *Enforcing International Trade Law: The Evolution of the Modern GATT Legal System* (1991).

International Monetary Fund, Factsheet: IMF Surveillance (2014).

International Monetary Fund, Financial Sector Assessment Program (FSAP) (2014).

International Monetary Fund, Implementation of the Basel Core Principles for Effective Banking Supervision Experience with Assessments and Implications for Future Work (2 September 2008).

International Monetary Fund, Integrating Stability Assessments under the Financial Sector Assessment Program into Article IV Surveillance (2010).

International Monetary Fund, Press Release, IMF Expanding Surveillance to Require Mandatory Financial Stability Assessments of Countries with Systemically Important Financial Sectors (27 September 2010).

International Monetary Fund, Report of the Managing Director to the International Monetary and Financial Committee on Progress in Strengthening the Architecture of the International Financial System and Reform of the IMF (2000).

International Monetary Fund and World Bank, Financial Sector Assessment Program: Brazil—IOSCO Objectives and Principles of Securities Regulation (2013).

International Monetary Fund and World Bank, Financial Sector Assessment Program: Nigeria—IOSCO Objectives and Principles of Securities Regulation (2013).

International Monetary Fund and World Bank, Implementation of the Basel Core Principles for Effective Banking Supervision: Experiences, Influences, and Perspectives (2002).

International Monetary Fund and World Bank, The Standards and Codes Initiative—Is it Effective? And How Can it Be Improved? (2005), available at <http://www.worldbank.org/ifa/ROSC%20review%202005.pdf>.

International Organization of Securities Commissions, Multilateral Memorandum of Understanding Concerning Consultation and Cooperation and the Exchange of Information (2002).

Jackson, JH, 'The General Agreement on Tariffs and Trade in United States Domestic Law' (1967) 66 *Michigan Law Review* 249.

Jackson, JH, *The Jurisprudence of GATT and the WTO: Insights on Treaty Law and Economic Relations* (2000).

Jones, H, *Markets Need Global Watchdog Group with Power, Officials Say* (5 November 2013) *Reuters*, available at <http://www.reuters.com/article/2013/11/05/us-g20-regulation-idUSBRE9A40RN20131105>.

Keohane, RO, Moravcsik, A, and Slaughter, A, 'Legalized Dispute Resolution: Interstate and Transnational' (2000) 54 *International Organization* 457.

Key, SJ, *Financial Services in the Uruguay Round and the WTO* (1997).

Kingsley, P, 'Financial Crisis: Timeline' *The Guardian*, 6 August 2012.

Koleva, G, '"Icon of Systemic Risk" Haunts Industry Decades after Demise' (23 June 2011) *American Banker*, available at <http://www.americanbanker.com/bankthink/bankhaus-herstatt-icon-of-systemic-risk-1039312-1.html>.

Lavelle, KC, *Money and Banks in the American Political System* (2013).

McCollim, G, *Louis XIV's Assault on Privilege, Nicolas Desmaretz and the Tax on Wealth* (2012).

Milner, H, *Resisting Protectionism: Global Industries and the Politics of International Trade* (1988).

O'Brien, DP, 'Monetary Base Control and the Bank Charter Act of 1844' (1997) 29 *History of Political Economy* 593.

Parra, AR, *The History of ICSID* (2012).

Paulson, C, 'Compliance with Final Judgments of the International Court of Justice Since 1987' (2004) 98 *American Journal of International* Law 434.

Posner, EA and Yoo, JC, 'Judicial Independence in International Tribunals' (2005) 93 *California Law Review* 1.

Pritchard, AC and Thompson, RB, 'Securities Law and the New Deal Justices' (2009) 95 *Virginia Law Review* 841.

Radlet, S and Sachs, J, 'The East Asian Financial Crisis: Diagnosis, Remedies, and Prospects' (1998) 1 *Brookings Papers on Economic Activity*, available at <http://www.brookings.edu/~/media/Projects/BPEA/1998%201/1998a_bpea_radelet_sachs_cooper_bosworth.PDF>.

Rodrik, D, *The Globalization Paradox: Why Global Markets, States, and Democracy Can't Coexist* (2011).

Roosevelt, FD, *Public Papers* (Vol 1, 1938).

Salomon, D, 'Regulators Wrangle on Rules' *Wall Street Journal*, 4 June 2011.

Schwartz, WF and Sykes, AO, The Economic Structure of Renegotiation and Dispute Resolution in the WTO/GATT System (2002), John M. Olin Law & Economics Working Paper No 143, 2nd series, 26–7.

Schwartz, WF and Sykes, AO, 'Toward a Positive Theory of the Most Favored Nation Obligation and its Exceptions in the WTO/GATT System' (1996) 16 *International Review of Law & Economics* 27.

Shearman & Sterling LLP, Basel III Framework: US/EU Comparison (2013), available at <http://www.shearman.com/basel-iii-framework-useu-comparison-09-17-2013/>.

Shell, GR, 'Trade Legalism and International Relations Theory' (1995) 44 *Duke Law Journal* 829.

Singer, DA, *Regulating Capital: Setting Standards for the International Financial System* (2007).

Srinivasan, TN, 'The Dispute Settlement Mechanism of the WTO: A Brief History and an Evaluation from Economic, Contractarian and Legal Perspectives' (2007) 30 *World Economy* 1033.

Stafford, P, 'Domestic Pressures Weaken US/EU Consensus' *Financial Times*, 9 January 2011.

Stiglitz, JE, *Globalization and its Discontents* (2002).

Tarullo, D, 'Administrative Accountability and International Regulatory Networks' (4 November 2008) (unpublished manuscript) (on file with author).

Thompson, RB, 'The SEC after the Financial Meltdown: Social Control over Finance?' (2010) 71 *University of Pittsburgh Law Review* 567.

Tietmeyer, H, *International Cooperation and Coordination in the Area of Financial Market Supervision and Surveillance* (1999).

Toye, R, 'The International Trade Organization' in Narilikar, A, Daunton, M, and Stern, RM (eds), *The Oxford Handbook on the World Trade Organization* (2012).

Trubek, DM, 'Protectionism and Development: Time for a New Dialogue?' (1993) 25 *New York University Journal of International Law & Politics* 345.

Understanding on Rules and Procedures Governing the Settlement of Disputes (15 April 1994), Marrakesh Agreement Establishing the World Trade Organization, Annex 2, 1869 U.N.T.S. 401.

Wessel, D, *In Fed we Trust: Ben Bernanke's War on the Great Panic* (2010).

White, E, *The Comptroller and the Transformation of American Banking, 1960–1990* (1992).

White House Office of the Press Secretary, Press Release, Fact Sheet: Creating a 21st Century International Economic Architecture (24 September 2009), available at <http://www.whitehouse.gov/the_press_office/Fact-Sheet-Creating-a-21st-Century-International-Economic-Architecture>.

Wolf, M, *Why Globalization Works* (2004).

World Bank, Financial Sector Assessment Program (2014), available at <http://www.worldbank.org/fsap>.

World Trade Organization, Rules of Conduct for the Understanding on Rules and Procedures Governing the Settlement of Disputes (2013), available at <http://www.wto.org/english/tratop_e/dispu_e/rc_e.htm>.

World Trade Organization, A Summary of the Final Act of the Uruguay Round (2013), available at <http://www.wto.org/english/docs_e/legal_e/ursum_e.htm# Understanding>.

World Trade Organization, Understanding the WTO: Settling Disputes (2013), available at <http://www.wto.org/english/thewto_e/whatis_e/tif_e/disp1_e.htm>.

Yellen, JL, Remarks at the National Association of Business Economics 2010 Annual Meeting, Macroprudential Supervision and Monetary Policy in the Post-crisis World (11 October 2010), available at <http://www.palgrave-journals.com/be/journal/v46/n1/full/be201035a.html>.

CHAPTER 6

ORGANIZING REGIONAL SYSTEMS

THE EU EXAMPLE*

BRIGITTE HAAR

* This chapter represents the literature as of November 2014.

I. Conceptual Framework

GIVEN its need for multidimensional coordination of financial regulation, the EU example illustrates very well the multiple layers of multilevel governance and their characteristic conceptual difficulties and problems, which regional coordination demands. In order to bring these into focus against the EU background, the overarching Treaty goal to construct an internal market according to Article 3(3) of the Treaty on European Union (TEU) serves as a point of reference, and is the driving force for the related measures laid out in the Treaty on the Functioning of the European Union (TFEU) and to be adopted by the Union, and which shape the internal financial market.[1] Specifically, under Article 26(2) TFEU, the internal market is defined as an area without internal frontiers, calling for the free movement of goods, persons, services, and capital. This broad concept includes an internal market in financial services and markets, which is based on the free movement of services (Article 56 TFEU), the freedom of establishment (Article 49 TFEU), and the free movement of capital (Article 63 TFEU).[2]

It stands to reason that there are various levels at which financial regulation, within the context of integration of Member State markets, faces specific challenges. First of all, there is the obvious need to accommodate cross-border capital flows, and resulting regulatory strategies have to be analysed in this light (discussed in Section II). It is clear that this accommodation of cross-border capital flows in the EU financial market, and the underlying supervisory arrangements in the Member States, are two sides of the same coin and therefore need some orchestration (see Section III). This orchestration raises questions about the relationship between Member State-based supervision at the national, and supranationally based supervision at the EU level. At the same time, different possible types of interaction between these supervisory structures and different levels of supervisory arrangements enter into the picture, such as self-regulation- and competition-based market discipline vs supervisory hierarchies, and multilateral institutional structures vs supervisory colleges, respectively. In the aftermath of the financial crisis of 2007–09, an additional layer of necessary orchestration has emerged: an ever-increasing need for overarching coordination to control systemic risk has become apparent and has led to an enhancement of prudential rules on the way towards a European Banking Union (EBU) (discussed in Section IV). At the same time, the banking and sovereign debt crisis has made clear the remaining

[1] For a brief overview of these cornerstones of market integration see Haar, B, 'European Banking Market' in Basedow, J, Hopt, K, and Zimmermann, R (eds), *Max Planck Encyclopedia of European Private Law* (2012) 545–6.

[2] For the foundation of the internal market in securities and investment services in the Treaty free-movement guarantees see Moloney, N, *EU Securities and Financial Markets Regulation* (3rd edn, 2014) 8–10.

obstacles to financial stability, and to the functioning of financing mechanisms in the eurozone, and more generally to trust in a stable future for the European Monetary Union, all of which have made integration by convergence in a Banking Union an even more important and challenging concern.

II. The Need to Accommodate Cross-Border Capital Flows and Regulatory Strategies

The integration of the EU financial market has been based on the idea of the EU internal market, and initially focused on issuers' interest in satisfying their financing needs cross-border.[3] Therefore, in the banking sector, for example, the First Council Directive on the coordination of banking laws of 1977[4] aimed at harmonizing the rules governing the licensing and supervision of credit institutions which were operating throughout Europe. This coordination-based approach changed fundamentally after the groundbreaking decision of the European Court of Justice in *Cassis de Dijon*[5] to a 'home control' approach. After the European Commission's related subsequent publication of its White Paper on the internal market in 1985, financial regulation was based on the principle of mutual recognition and home control, implying the adequacy of the laws of each of the Member States regarding financial regulation, and requiring them, subject to minimum harmonized standards being adopted at EU level, to restrict free movement only where explicitly permitted in the EC Treaty or where justified by the general good.[6] This mutual recognition approach was extended further, in the banking field, to the grant of a full-fledged European regulatory 'passport' by the Second Council Directive on the coordination of banking laws of 1989.[7] On the basis of this single passport concept,

[3] For a division of the history of EU financial regulation into different phases according to regulatory focus cf Moloney, ibid, 13–19.

[4] First Council Directive 77/780/EEC on the coordination of the laws, regulations and administrative provisions relating to the taking up and pursuit of the business of credit institutions [1977] OJ L 322/30.

[5] Case 120/78 *Rewe-Zentral AG v Bundesmonopolverwaltung für Branntwein* [1979] ECR 649.

[6] European Commission, Completing the Internal Market, White Paper from the Commission to the European Council (COM (1985) 310).

[7] Second Council Directive 89/646/EEC on the coordination of laws, regulations and administrative provisions relating to the taking up and pursuit of the business of credit institutions and amending Directive 77/780/EEC [1989] OJ L 386/1.

a credit institution domiciled in an EU Member State was permitted to do business in any other EU Member State without an additional official authorization from the latter's regulator, so that the authorization from the home state served as a 'passport' to carry on business throughout the EU.

Along with this principle of home country control in the financial services and markets sector, the harmonization of substantive laws of the Member States in the relevant areas was considered a necessary foundation for mutual recognition and the related implicit free-market access by financial actors. Therefore, the Second Banking Directive was supplemented by the Own Funds Directive (Directive 89/299) as well as the Solvency Directive (Directive 1989/647), which for banking operations in the Member States required certain financial resources or a predetermined ratio between assets and off-balance-sheet activities respectively.

The adoption of the collective investment scheme regime by 1985 went even further to regulate market access according to the concept of mutual recognition. The UCITS Directive of 1985 regulated the UCITS (undertakings for collective investment in transferable securities) product with a view to liberalization and free cross-border capital flows.[8] These objectives are firmly linked to the UCITS Directive's reliance on minimum harmonization of investor protection rules and the provision of a regulatory passport; this approach has prevailed in the investment services/asset management sector generally ever since and ultimately led to the extension of these rules by the Alternative Investment Fund Managers Directive to alternative investment fund managers in the aftermath of the financial crisis of 2007–09.[9]

At the same time, the concept of mutual recognition was carried over to the field of issuer disclosure harmonization, in relation to which it was guided by the goal to secure market access for issuers on the basis of harmonized disclosure rules. That is why the original 1980 Listing Particulars Directive imposed certain minimum

[8] Council Directive 85/611/EEC on the coordination of laws, regulations and administrative provisions relating to undertakings for collective investment in transferable securities (UCITS) [1985] OJ L 375/3, as amended by Directive 2001/107/EC [2002] OJ L 41/20, Directive 2001/108/EC [2002] OJ L 41/35 (UCITS III), and as replaced subsequently by Directive 2009/65/EC on the coordination of laws, regulations and administrative provisions relating to undertakings for collective investment in transferable securities [2009] OJ L 32 (UCITS IV). For the 'UCITS V' reform, see the following most important legislative documents: Commission Proposal COM (2012) 350/2; European Parliament, First Reading, 3 July 2013 (T7-0309/2013); Council General Approach, 2 December 2013 (Council Document 17095/13); 2014 UCITS V Directive of 23 July 2014 (which comes into force in 2016) [2014] OJ L 257/186. For the 'UCITS VI' consultation, Product Rules, Liquidity Management, Depositary, Money Market Funds, Long Term Investments launched in July 2012, on UCITS product rules, extraordinary liquidity management tools, depositary passport, money market funds, and long-term investments, see <http://ec.europa.eu/internal_market/consultations/2012/ucits_en.htm>.

[9] Directive 2011/61/EU on Alternative Investment Fund Managers and amending Directives 2003/41/EC and 2009/65/EC and Regulations (EC) No 1060/2009 and (EU) No 1095/2010 [2011] OJ L 174/1.

substantive requirements regarding the information to be disclosed with respect to the issuer of the offered securities and the attributes of the offered securities in the document required on admission to a stock exchange (the listing particulars), and made arrangements to provide for the approval of the listing particulars prior to the listing of the security on an official exchange.[10] On the same premise of mutual recognition, the 1989 Public Offering Directive imposed certain minimum substantive requirements regarding the information to be disclosed in the prospectus to be provided on a public offer of securities with respect to the issuer of the offered securities and the attributes of the offered securities, as well as certain minimum requirements regarding the communication of the prospectus to the competent authorities or national regulators and the distribution of the prospectus.[11]

However, as a precondition for approval, the competent authorities of the Member States could require that the listing particulars or the prospectus be supplemented to include information specific to their respective markets in which the securities were to be listed or offered; eg, the income tax system and the ways in which notices to investors were to be published.[12] Therefore, the scope of the mutual recognition regime for issuers was limited at this stage, but would be further developed by the 2003 Prospectus Directive.[13]

These limitations on mutual recognition came to light even more clearly in the subsequent Investment Services Directive of 1993 (ISD) which was based on the concept of an investment services passport and the related principle of home country supervision of investment services.[14] By contrast with the Listing Particulars Directive and the Public Offering Directive, the ISD was very clearly geared towards investment firms and their activities, but not so much towards investor protection.[15] As the Second Banking Directive had only covered credit institutions where they operated as universal banks—in that the Directive covered investment services activities but only where carried out by a deposit-taking institution—the ISD focused on investment firms.[16]

[10] Directive 80/390/EEC coordinating the requirements for the drawing-up, scrutiny and distribution of the listing particulars to be published for the admission of securities to official stock exchange listing [1980] OJ L66/21 (LPD) Articles 4–23 (repealed by Directive 2001/34/EC on the admission of securities to official stock exchange listing and on information to be published on those securities [2001] OJ L184/1)).

[11] Directive 89/298/EEC coordinating the requirements for the drawing-up, scrutiny and distribution of the prospectus to be published when transferable securities are offered to the public [1989] OJ L124/8 (POD, repealed by Directive 2003/71/EC [2003] OJ L345/64).

[12] LPD, n 10 above, Articles 24a, 24b; POD, n 11 above, Article 21.

[13] Directive 2003/71/EC on the prospectus to be published when securities are offered to the public or admitted to trading (Prospectus Directive) [2003] OJ L 345/64. For details see below.

[14] Directive 93/22/EEC on investment services in the securities field (Investment Services Directive or ISD) [1993] OJ L141/27 (repealed by Directive 2004/39/EC on Markets in Financial Instruments [2004] OJ L 145/1).

[15] Moloney, n 2 above, 329.

[16] Second Council Directive 89/646/EEC, n 7 above, Article 1 No 1 referring to First Council Directive 77/780/EEC on the coordination of the laws, regulations and administrative provisions

Therefore, it included rules addressing the harmonization of authorization conditions and of prudential supervision to secure the foundation for home state control and mutual recognition. But at the same time, the objective of free cross-border provision of services gave rise to national product-oriented rules, the harmonization of which was far from complete. As a result, Member States had considerable leeway to apply the 'general good' exception and thereby to dilute the free provision of services and the related passport principle by applying national product-oriented rules.[17] This is exemplified particularly clearly by Article 11 of the ISD which provided for minimal harmonization of conduct of business principles, leading to widely varying regimes in the Member States.[18] Besides these loopholes for Member State involvement in the field of conduct of business rules created by Article 11, an additional weakening of the market integration mechanism of the ISD was brought about by Articles 17(4) and 18(2). These provisions allowed 'host' country authorities, the authorities of the Member States in which the cross-border activity took place, to impose additional conditions on another Member State's investment firm in the interest of the general good.[19]

In light of the resulting obstacles to market integration under the ISD, the Financial Services Action Plan (FSAP), issued by the European Commission at the turn of the century, marked the beginning of a new period of regulatory policy in the financial sector.[20] With the FSAP, the Commission aimed at the completion of market integration, by adopting 42 measures targeted at retail markets, wholesale markets, prudential rules and supervision, and conditions

relating to the taking up and pursuit of the business of credit institutions [1977] OJ L 322/30. EEC Article 1 (a 'credit institution' means an undertaking whose business is to receive deposits or other repayable funds from the public and to grant credits for its own account...). Since repealed by Directive 2000/12/EC relating to the taking up and pursuit of the business of credit institutions [2000] OJ L 126/1).

[17] With reference to the underlying 'dilemma' between divergent national standards of investor protection and the free circulation of goods and services see Köndgen, J, 'Rules of Conduct: Further Harmonisation?' in Ferrarini, G (ed.), *European Securities Markets: The Investment Services Directive and Beyond* (1998) 115, 129.

[18] Haar, B, 'From Public Law to Private Law: Market Supervision and Contract Law Standards' in Grundmann, S and Atamar, Y (eds), *Financial Services, Financial Crisis and General European Contract Law: Failures and Challenges of Contracting* (2011) 262–3. For an overview of conduct of business rules and their implementation under the ISD see Tison, M, 'Conduct of Business Rules and their Implementation in the EU Member States' in Ferrarini, G, Hopt, K, and Wymeersch, E (eds), *Capital Markets in the Age of the Euro: Cross-Border Transactions, Listed Companies and Regulation* (2002) 65–99. For the wide variation of conduct rules see European Commission, The Application of Conduct of Business Rules under Article 11 of the Investment Services Directive (93/22/EEC) (COM (2000) 722) (see Moloney, n 2 above, 330).

[19] Pointed out as an 'important aspect' by Ferrarini, G, 'Towards a European Law of Investment Services and Institutions' (1994) 31 *Common Market Law Review* 1283, 1297.

[20] European Commission, Financial Services: Building a Framework for Action (1998) (COM (1998) 625) (followed by European Commission, Implementing the Framework for Financial Markets: Action Plan (FSAP) (1999) (COM (1999) 232)).

for an optimal single financial market. With respect to the last objective, the reforms extended to the regulation of alternative trading systems (ATSs), the management of conflicts of interest and the handling and execution of client orders by investment intermediaries, the periodic and continuous disclosures by issuers of listed securities, the prohibition of market manipulation, the production and dissemination of investment recommendations, and the stabilization of new issues and share buy backs. Such an extension of regulation necessarily marked a significant increase in the range and sophistication of EU financial regulation.

How the resulting regulation of markets, such as exchanges, market players, especially investment firms, and market activities, in particular investment services, became intertwined is very well exemplified by the 2004 Markets in Financial Instruments Directive (MiFID I), which replaced the ISD in the aftermath of the FSAP.[21] By comparison with the ISD, MiFID I adopts a broader perspective. As a result, it covers the full range of areas related to investment services, such as organizational requirements for firms and markets, conduct of business requirements for firms, transaction reporting to relevant competent authorities of buy and sell transactions in all financial instruments, and transparency requirements for the trading of shares. The much wider scope of regulation under MiFID I was designed to promote market integration in several respects. For example, by subjecting trading venues in the form of multilateral trading facilities (MTFs) to similar transparency requirements as those which apply to exchanges and, at the same time, exposing exchanges to competition from MTFs, MiFID I facilitates a level playing field between exchanges and other markets.

In particular, MiFID I establishes a framework for the authorization[22], regulation, and supervision[23] of financial exchanges in the EU, which is further amplified under the 'Lamfalussy process' for delegated/administrative rulemaking (discussed in Section III) by detailed 'level 2' rules, adopted as technical implementation measures by the Commission and based on mandates in the pertinent 'level 1' measure, which rules can either take the form of a directive or a regulation, adopted by the Council and Parliament.[24] These level 2 rules formed a suitable basis for a more effective passport regime under MiFID I.[25] Finally, MiFID I governs trade execution by investment firms, providing for a new regime of 'best execution' rules,

[21] Directive 2004/39/EC on Markets in Financial Instruments [2004] OJ L 145/1. For a detailed overview see Casey, J-P and Lannoo, K, *The MiFID Revolution* (2009); Moloney, n 2 above, 331–5, 435–44, 685–94; and, with a focus on investor protection, see Moloney, N, *How to Protect Investors: Lessons from the EC and the UK* (2010) 192–288.

[22] Article 36(1). [23] Articles 37–9.

[24] For further details cf Moloney, n 2 above, 332–3, 859.

[25] For an overview of level 2 measures under MiFID I see Ryan, J, 'An Overview of MiFID' in Skinner, C (ed.), *The Future of investing in Europe's Markets after MiFID* (2007) 13, 15–16.

thus taking another step towards maximum harmonization in a field traditionally regulated by the Member States.[26]

MiFID I also addresses investor protection, deploying a three-pronged strategy to tackle investor protection, in particular by prescribing organizational requirements for the marketplace, by ensuring market integrity by way of transparency rules, and by providing for an EU-wide conduct of business regime.[27]

As far as the regulation of trading is concerned, and with respect to market integration in particular, MiFID I did away with 'concentration' rules, which require the routing of orders to a stock exchange, so that Member States must allow internalization of orders or the execution of orders by firms against their proprietary order books and can no longer restrict the routing of orders to stock exchanges, but must permit execution by MTFs or through the investment firms themselves.[28] This requirement is designed to increase competition in trading.[29] Given the elimination of the concentration rule, and the resulting increase in competition, pre- and post-trade transparency obligations are also imposed under MiFID I and aim to further ensure the effectiveness of EU trading markets.[30] Pre-trade transparency rules accordingly extend to 'systematic internalizers', ie investment firms which on an organized, frequent, and systematic basis, deal on own accounts by executing client orders outside a regulated market or an MTF, requiring them to publish quotes for liquid shares.[31] Post-trade transparency rules apply to all venues and investment firms and govern the obligation to publish data on concluded trades.[32] Furthermore, a transaction-reporting regime requires the reporting of transactions traded on prescribed non-regulated markets and of transactions in over-the-counter (OTC) instruments that are related to instruments traded on prescribed markets.[33]

[26] For details on these rules cf Kirby, A, 'Best Execution' in Skinner, C (ed.), *The Future of Investing in Europe's Markets after MiFID* (2007), 31–63 and Casey and Lannoo, n 21 above, 58–77.

[27] For a concise overview of the objectives of MiFID I see Avgouleas, E, 'A Critical Evaluation of the New EC Financial-Market Regulation: Peaks, Troughs, and the Road Ahead' (2005) 18 *The Transnational Lawyer* 179, 191–7.

[28] MiFID I, Article 22. For a detailed analysis of the internalization of trading orders under MiFID see Ferrarini, G and Recine, F, 'The MiFID and Internalisation' in Ferrarini, G and Wymeersch, E (eds), *Investor Protection in Europe: Corporate Law Making, the MiFID and Beyond* (2006) 235–70.

[29] For the goal of competition in MiFID I see MiFID I, recitals 34, 47, and 48. For further implications of MiFID I with respect to the exchanges and MTFs see Webb, S, 'Exchanges, MTF's, Systematic Internalisers and Data Providers—Winners and Losers in a Post-MiFID World' in Skinner, C (ed.), *The Future of Investing in Europe's Markets after MiFID* (2007) 151–70.

[30] On the significance of price transparency see Casey and Lannoo, n 21 above, 43–4.

[31] For the meaning of 'systemic internalizers' see Article 4i(1)(7), MiFID I; for the pre-trade transparency requirements for MTFs, MiFID I, Article 29; for details on the pre-trade transparency rules see Moloney, n 2 above, 451–4, 480–4.

[32] For post-trade transparency requirements for MTFs see MiFID I, Article 30; for details see Moloney, n 2 above, 484, 487–8.

[33] For the underlying obligation to uphold the integrity of markets, report transactions, and maintain records, see MiFID I, Article 25; for further information see Ryan, n 25 above, 26–7.

Besides trading-transparency rules, MiFID I establishes an extensive conduct of business regime in order to enhance investor protection. This regime addresses, *inter alia*, aspects of client classification, suitability and appropriateness assessments, and questions of 'best execution' and of client order handling.[34] The most important client classification underlying the MiFID I regime is the distinction between retail clients, professional clients, and eligible counterparties, as specified in Annex II of the Directive, that aims to provide investor protection rules suited to the needs of the respective category of investors.[35] Related harmonized client-protection requirements go hand in hand with the classification of investors, and arise from detailed provisions governing the assessment of a client's classification, as laid out in MiFID I, Article 19 and in Article 28 of the related Level 2 Directive.[36] The underlying suitability and appropriateness tests, for example, are part of the 'know your customer' regime which applies under MiFID I. Suitability testing is required for advised services and portfolio management in order to ensure the suitability of the advice or the product with respect to the client's expertise, risk profile, and financial situation.[37] In contrast, the appropriateness assessment applies to non-advised services, requiring an assessment of whether the client has the necessary knowledge and experience in the relevant investment to understand the risks involved.[38] By contrast with the suitability test, the investment firm is not precluded from supplying the service, if it does not receive the necessary information from the client provided it warns the client.[39]

Satisfying the client classification requirements lays the basis for the fulfilment of the standard of best execution under MiFID I, Article 21. The MiFID I best-execution regime is laid down in Article 21 and is part of the wider MiFID I conduct-of-business regime. According to MiFID I, Article 21(1), in order to satisfy this standard, investment firms must follow the goal of value maximization for their clients, but in light of constraints such as the latter's investment objectives.[40] Therefore, best execution is necessarily characterized by a high degree of flexibility because, depending on the client, a variety of factors such as transaction costs, and the speed and likelihood of execution and settlement may enter

[34] MiFID I, Articles 19, 21, 22.

[35] For details see Smith, D and Leggett, S, 'Client Classification' in Skinner, C (ed.), *The Future of Investing in Europe's Markets after MiFID* (2007) 65–73.

[36] Commission Directive 2006/73/EC implementing Directive 2004/39/EC of the European Parliament and the Council as regards organizational requirements and operating conditions for investment firms and defined terms for the purposes of that Directive [2006] OJ L 241/26.

[37] For the requirements of the suitability assessment see MiFID I, Article 19(4); for the criteria in detail cf Commission Directive 2006/73/EC, n 36 above, Article 35, and for an overview of the suitability assessment see Smith and Leggett, n 35 above, 68–9.

[38] For the requirement of the appropriateness assessment see MiFID I, Article 19(5).

[39] MiFID I, Article 19(5), subpara 2; for details on the appropriateness assessment see Casey and Lannoo, n 21 above, 49–53.

[40] See Casey and Lannoo, n 21 above, 41.

into the best-execution assessment.[41] At this point, the underlying suitability and the appropriateness tests play out in favour of investment firms, because compliance with these requirements proves that an order is executed in the manner most favourable for a particular client.[42] This approach, in turn, explains why client classification is a relevant factor to determine best execution.[43] Closely connected with the standard of best execution are the client order handling rules under MiFID I, Article 22, which require investment firms to execute client orders quickly and accurately.[44]

Overall, therefore, the harmonized investor protection regime under MiFID I complements the MiFID I passporting system in order to further cross-border capital flows, thus supporting the internal market. In addition, the regulation of the marketplace, along with the elimination of the aforementioned concentration rule, similarly ensures access for firms to certain trading markets and to clearing and settlement systems.[45] Accordingly, free market access is closely linked to the existence of a level playing field for investment firms across Europe, thanks to the harmonized conduct of business regime under MiFID I. Since host countries cannot impose additional requirements in this respect, investment firms are bound by their home country's regime.[46] The conduct-of-business rules under MiFID I thus ensure a high degree of harmonization, facilitating cross-border activities.[47] In this way, MiFID I led to a substantially higher level of sophistication in EU financial regulation, albeit in order to support home Member State control. As new regulatory challenges have become apparent throughout the recent financial crisis, however, the MiFID I regime is being reformed, as discussed further below.

The FSAP's harmonization and liberalization strategy can be further illustrated by the Prospectus Directive of 2003[48] and by the Market Abuse Directive of 2003[49], which can both be characterized as successful FSAP measures.[50] The Prospectus Directive saw the EU passport concept being deployed for the first time in the issuer disclosure field of regulation, such that a prospectus, once approved in one European Member State could be recognized Europe-wide. This follows from the issuer's obligation to seek approval of the prospectus from the competent authority of the home Member State before its publication (Prospectus Directive, Article 13(1)) and to subsequently file it with this authority (Prospectus Directive, Article

[41] For the factors to be taken into account for the best execution assessment see MiFID, Article 21(1); specifying the flexibility of this approach see Moloney, n 2 above, 519–24.

[42] MiFID I, Article 21(1) and (2); for the related proof requirements see Avgouleas, n 27 above, 195.

[43] Kirby, n 26 above, 42–5.

[44] Ryan, n 25 above, 23.

[45] For these access rules see MiFID I, Articles 33, 34, 42; Casey and Lannoo, n 21 above, 192–3.

[46] MiFID I, Article 31(1), subpara 2, Article 32(1) subpara 2.

[47] Moloney, n 2 above, 333–4.

[48] Prospectus Directive 2003/71/EC, n 13 above.

[49] Directive 2003/6/EC on insider dealing and market manipulation (Market Abuse Directive) [2003] OJ L 96/16.

[50] For the positioning of these directives in the FSAP context see Moloney, n 2 above, 73–5, 125–6, 708–9.

14(1)). Closely connected with the adoption of the home-country principle, the high degree of harmonization of prospectus requirements may justify the classification of the Prospectus Directive as being of a 'maximum harmonization' nature in that it removes all Member State regulatory discretion.[51] Deploying a maximum harmonization approach not only supports mutual recognition but also supports another principal aim of the Prospectus Directive—that of retail investor protection.[52] The Directive's orientation towards retail investors is reflected, in particular, by the issuer's obligation to provide a prospectus summary that must inform the investors about the essential characteristics and risks associated with the issuer, any guarantor, and the securities in brief and non-technical form.[53] Somewhat related to the evolution of the prospectus regime, harmonized disclosure reforms with regard to financial-reporting requirements, and especially under the 2004 Transparency Directive,[54] were also adopted in support of investor confidence, and require accurate and comprehensive ongoing issuer disclosure, thus enhancing market efficiency.[55] Therefore, investor protection and market efficiency can be regarded as two sides of the same coin in the EU's regime for supporting financial market integration.

This close interdependence between market efficiency and investor confidence in the EU's programme for integrating and regulating markets also becomes apparent in the regulatory design of the FSAP's 2003 Market Abuse Directive[56] which seeks to support the efficiency of the price formation process in the EU capital market. In the case of the Market Abuse Directive, this policy willingness to intervene to support market efficiency is shown in the market-driven rationale which drives the insider-dealing regime. According to the European Court of Justice, the Directive takes the extent to which inside information might impact on price movements as a guideline for its materiality.[57] Similarly, the definition of market manipulation under the Market Abuse Directive applies to '... transactions or orders to trade which give, or are likely to give, false or misleading signals as to the supply of, demand for or price of financial instruments, or

[51] See further Moloney, n 2 above, 75; Schammo, P, *EU Prospectus Law* (2011) 70–4; Tison, M, 'Financial Market Integration in the Post FSAP Era—in Search of Overall Conceptual Consistency in the Regulatory Framework' in Ferrarini G and Wymeersch E (eds), *Investor Protection in Europe—Corporate Law Making, the MiFID and Beyond* (2006); and Ferran, E, *Building an EU Securities Market* (2004) 138, 142–4.

[52] Prospectus Directive, n 13 above, recital 19.

[53] ibid, Article 5(2); for details on the concept of prospectus summaries see Schammo, n 51 above, 99–101.

[54] Directive 2004/109/EC on the harmonization of transparency requirements in relation to information about issuers whose securities are admitted to trading on a regulated market (Transparency Directive) [2004] OJ L 390/38.

[55] Transparency Directive, recital 1.

[56] For example, Market Abuse Directive, n 49 above, recitals 2, 12, and 24.

[57] Judgment of the Court of 10 May 2007, Case C-391/04 *Oikonomikon and Amfissas v Georgakis* [2007] ECR I-3741, I-3770–3771. For an overview see Avgouleas, E, *The Mechanics and Regulation of Markets Abuse: A Legal and Economic Analysis* (2005) 75–101, 156–234. With specific reference to the CESR approach, see Moloney, n 2 above, 722–3.

which secure, by a person, or persons acting in collaboration, the price of one or several financial instruments at an abnormal or artificial level', thus requiring a quite direct interference with the price formation process.[58] Further instances of market manipulation under the Directive such as the employment of 'fictitious devices or any other form of deception or contrivance' and 'the dissemination of information through the media . . . , which gives . . . , false or misleading signals as to financial instruments . . .' have the same effect.[59] On the other hand, the regulatory design of the Market Abuse Directive differs from that of the Prospectus Directive because, in addition to the insider prohibition, it also provides for disclosure duties for issuers of listed financial instruments, in order to ensure the publication of any inside information as soon as possible.[60] In light of this latter objective, the Directive goes into more detail, including the duty to keep updated lists of insiders.[61]

Despite these specifications, the regulatory design of the Market Abuse Directive is not maximum harmonization-driven; it can, instead, be characterized as a minimum harmonization measure.[62] This regime, however, is undergoing substantial changes in this respect, as an agreement on a new market abuse regulation, which is designed to tackle insider dealing and market manipulation more intensively, was reached in 2013.[63] The new regime has replaced the existing Market Abuse Directive, and is complemented by the new directive on criminal sanctions for market abuse[64]. In light of its high degree of specification, the new regime can be considered as an important step towards the post-crisis 'single rulebook' as envisioned among others by the European Securities and Markets Authority (ESMA) (discussed in Section III) in its work programme[65]. Harmonization of substantive legal rules aside, however, one has to note that the enforcement of the market abuse regime currently in force is left to the Member States, so that there is some room for divergence. Given the according importance of the enforcement stage to the ultimate success of regulatory harmonization, it comes as no surprise that

[58] Market Abuse Directive, n 49 above, Article 1, no 2 a.

[59] For these definitions of market manipulation see ibid, Article 1, no 2 b and c; for a detailed analysis of the different types of market manipulations see Avgouleas, n 57 above, 103–54.

[60] Market Abuse Directive, n 49 above, Article 6(1); for a detailed comparison see Enriques, L and Gatti, M, 'Is There a Uniform EU Securities Law after the Financial Services Action Plan?' [2008] 14 *Stanford Journal of Law, Business & Finance* 43, 54–63, 71–2.

[61] Market Abuse Directive, n 49 above, Article 6(3).

[62] Enriques and Gatti, n 60 above, 72; Moloney, n 2 above, 712–13; and, highlighting the ambivalence in this area see Gerner-Beuerle, C, 'United in Diversity: Maximum versus Minimum Harmonisation in EU Securities Regulation' (2012) 7 *Capital Markets Law Journal* 317, 328.

[63] Council of the European Union, Interinstitutional File: 2011/0295(COD), Brussels (25 June 2013).

[64] Regulation (EU) No 596/2014 of the European Parliament and of the Council on market abuse (market abuse regulation) and repealing directive 2003/6/EC of the European Parliament and of the Council and Commission Directives 2003/124/EC, 2003/125/EC and 2004/72/EC [2014] OJ L 173/1; Directive 2014/57/EU of the European Parliament and of the Council of 16 April 2014 on criminal sanctions for market abuse (market abuse directive) [2014] OJ L 173/179.

[65] ESMA, 2012 Work Programme 4.

the Market Abuse Directive addresses enforcement strategies across different levels (whether legislative, administrative, or 'soft law' in nature) and accordingly was the first FSAP measure to implement the Lamfalussy model fully. Therefore, it well represents the harmonization strategy of the FSAP, which relied on more detailed regulation without, however, breaking the link to home Member State control.

Whatever its successes, the resulting divergences in implementation at the Member State level made apparent the limits of the FSAP. Despite accelerating the harmonization process, it did not succeed in achieving complete regulatory convergence of national financial regulation. Instead, 'excessive divergence' was found to be one of the driving forces behind the impact of the global financial crisis in the EU by the De Larosière Group.[66] Hence, it seems natural that the EU moved to a 'single rulebook' during the crisis era in order to avoid the tensions between financial stability, financial integration, and national financial policies.

This shift is reflected in the far-reaching crisis-era initiative under the new MiFID II regime (which entered into force in July 2014, will be implemented by the Member States by July 2016, and will be applied from January 2017 onwards) to extend the scope of the existing MiFID I, thus addressing shortcomings that became apparent throughout the financial crisis of 2007–09.[67] In order, for example, to reduce systemic risk, MiFID II aims to extend the scope of MiFID I to more firms and to additional instruments, as well as to electronic trading.[68] To further enhance market integrity, for example, it includes provisions on additional transparency requirements and transaction reports, and on third-country firms seeking to access the EU market.[69] Issues related to investor protection and inducements are also addressed.[70] Finally, a new product-intervention regime is provided for, to be deployed by national regulators in coordination with ESMA. This last point is well suited to highlight another key dimension of EU financial regulation; that is the orchestration of different supervisory arrangements, and the related coordination of Member State-based supervision at the national level and of supranational supervision at the EU-level (as discussed in Section III below).

These recent developments throw light on the fundamental change the harmonization process has undergone throughout its evolution, ever since its inception in the era of the 'approximation of laws' under TFEU Article 114 and with a focus on cross-border capital flows and the better functioning of the internal market. The FSAP at the end of the 1990s was designed to give further impetus to this

[66] The High Level Group on Financial Supervision in the EU, Report (2009), 10–11, 28; for the resulting reconceptualization of the internal market in financial services see Moloney, N, 'EU Financial Market Regulation after the Global Financial Crisis: More Europe or More Risks?' (2010) 47 *Common Market Law Review* 1317, 1324.

[67] Directive 2014/65/EU on markets in financial instruments and amending Directive 2002/92/EC and Directive 2011/61/EU (MiFID II) [2014] OJ 173/349.

[68] MiFID II, Article 17.

[69] MiFID II, Articles 39–43.

[70] MiFID II, Articles 24–30.

harmonization process on the basis of more detailed regulation, but adhered to Member State control with respect to implementation. This imbalance was recognized as a contributing cause of the financial crisis in the EU and resulted in a shift towards a single rulebook that aims at a far-reaching uniformity by means of directives, regulations, implementing acts, standards, guidance, and other similar non-binding instruments.[71]

III. Orchestration of the Underlying Institutional Arrangements

The need for greater coordination of Member-State-based supervision and regulation had become apparent from an early stage in the investment-services area; for example, through the implementation of the '... general presumption in favour of the free provision of services on the basis of home country authorization'[72] under the 1993 ISD. Despite this presumption, as mentioned above (in Section II), ISD, Articles 17(4) and 18(2) offered the possibility to host country authorities to bring to bear rules of conduct to be complied with in the interest of the general good on passporting investment firms.[73] Having received notification from a Member State's investment firm wishing to establish a branch within their territory, host country authorities had the obligation to indicate '... the conditions, including the rules of conduct, with which, in the interest of the general good, the providers of the investment services in question must comply in the host Member State ...'.[74] It goes without saying that only limited harmonization could follow from this approach to rules of conduct. At the same time, however, the market-enhancing effect of the ISD's home control regulatory strategy is quite obvious. By introducing a single licence for investment intermediaries, the ISD reduced market barriers considerably, so that the empirical findings indicating changes towards

[71] Gurlit, E, 'The ECB's Relationship to the EBA' (2014) 25 *Europäische Zeitschrift für Wirtschaftsrecht* 14, 16–17; Moloney, n 66 above, 1326.

[72] European Commission, Communication on the Application of Conduct of Business Rules under Article 11 of the Investment Services Directive (2000) (COM (2000) 722) 14.

[73] ibid; for the regulatory context see Ferrarini, G, 'Contract Standards and the Markets in Financial Instruments Directive. An Assessment of the Lamfalussy Regulatory Architecture' (2005) 1 *European Review of Contract Law* 19, 23–5.

[74] ISD, n 14 above, Article 18(2).

a market-based system in the European financial system were not surprising as the market-enabling dimension of the ISD became apparent.[75]

At the same time, home country control results in Member States' dependence on the quality of each other's regulation and supervision. Therefore, one can expect a relationship between the need for supervisory/regulatory institutional orchestration and the stage of harmonization. Accordingly, it was the implementation of the ambitious FSAP, which sought further market-integration, that called for the further development of the regulatory process in the EU through institutional reform. In particular, the vast number of measures to be adopted under the FSAP required an improved rulemaking process to meet efficiency concerns.[76] Under the subsequently introduced so-called 'Lamfalussy process', based on the 2001 Final Report of the Committee of the Wise Men, the creation of EU financial markets legislation is divided among different EU bodies according to different levels of specification.[77]

The entire procedure is based on the foundation 'level 1' legislation setting out broad framework principles for legislation which are agreed on at the EU level according to established lawmaking procedures.[78] In the interest of a fast legislative procedure, the Lamfalussy Report encouraged greater use of regulations, which are binding and directly applicable in all Member States, as opposed to directives, whose implementation by national authorities could, argued the Report, take up to 18 months.[79] 'Level 2' rules are implementing measures, whose scope has been defined in level 1 acts and which are adopted through 'comitology' procedures (in effect, the rules are adopted by the Commission).[80] Framework principles at level 1 and implementing measures at level 2, of course, easily merge into one another, thus jeopardizing a clear-cut orchestration of rulemaking and supervision, as can become apparent from 'parallel working' on level 1 and level 2 measures, where both forms of measure are negotiated at the same time.[81] But in principle, under the Lamfalussy process, implementing measures were characterized by the delegation of lawmaking functions to the Commission and the related adoption of delegated rules under a modified 'comitology' procedure (which has

[75] Casey and Lannoo, n 21 above, 26.

[76] Committee of Wise Men on the Regulation of European Securities Markets, Final Report (2001) (Lamfalussy Report) 10–12.

[77] ibid, 19–42; cf for a detailed overview Ferran, n 51 above, 61–7.

[78] Lamfalussy Report, n 76 above, 19 and 27; Ferran, n 51 above, 62; and, for an extensive analysis of level 1 legislation and its evolution, see Moloney, n 2 above, 861–5.

[79] Lamfalussy Report, n 76 above, 26.

[80] For a closer analysis of level 2 legislation and its underlying procedure cf Moloney, n 2 above, 865–72 and, with reference to the Market Abuse Directive, Ferran, n 51 above, 81.

[81] For scepticism with regard to the distinction between framework principles at level 1 and level 2 measures see Ferrarini, n 73 above, 28–9. For a criticism of the resulting complexity of the regulatory structure see Moellers, T, 'Sources of Law in European Securities Regulation—Effective Regulation, Soft Law and Legal Taxonomy from Lamfalussy to de Larosière' (2010) 11 *European Business Organization Law Review* 379, 383.

since been modified following the establishment of the European Supervisory Authorities in the wake of the financial crisis). Under the original procedure, and with respect to securities market rulemaking, the Commission, assisted by the then newly-established comitology committee, the political European Securities Committee (ESC), which exercised a primarily oversight-based function but could lead to the Council blocking the delegated measure,[82] and the national regulator-based Committee of European Securities Regulators (CESR), which exercised advisory functions,[83] could adopt delegated/secondary legislation.[84] By 2003, these committees were complemented in the banking and insurance/occupational pensions spheres by the political European Banking Committee (EBC)[85] and European Insurance and Occupational Pensions Committee (EIOPC),[86] and by equivalent advisory committees.

In addition to level 2 rulemaking, under the rulemaking model which followed the 2001 Lamfalussy Report, 'level 3' measures were also adopted in order to support implementation of level 1 and 2 rules at the national level. Level 3 was designed to support enhanced and strengthened cooperation between national regulators and to deliver a consistent and equivalent implementation of level 1 and level 2 legislation at the Member State level.[87] Level 3 was primarily supported by cooperation through CESR and its partner advisory committees, the Committee of European Banking Supervisors (CEBS) and the Committee of European Insurance and Occupational Pensions Supervisors (CEIOPS). At level 3, they issued guidelines for national implementation in order to set best practices, formulated joint interpretative recommendations and standards for matters not covered by EU law, and conducted peer reviews[88], although these advisory committees did not have any rulemaking powers.[89] The four-level regulatory approach adopted under the Lamfalussy Report was completed by level 4, which focused on the enforcement of EU law. According to the Lamfalussy Report, the

[82] Articles 2 b and 5, Council Decision 99/468/EC laying down the procedures for the exercise of implementing powers conferred on the Commission [1999] OJ L184/23. See further Ferran, n 51 above, 77 and Moloney, n 2 above, 869–70.

[83] Lamfalussy Report, n 76 above, 28. For further details on these committees cf Ferran, n 51 above, 77–80. For more details on CESR see Ferran, E, 'Understanding the New Institutional Architecture of EU Financial Market Supervision' in Wymeersch, E, Hopt, K, and Ferrarini, G (eds), *Financial Regulation and Supervision; A Post-Crisis Analysis* (2012) 111, 116–25.

[84] Lamfalussy Report, n 76 above, 28–36; Commission Decision 2001/527/EC establishing the Committee of European Securities Regulators [2001] OJ L191/43 (revised in 2009: Commission Decision 2009/77/EC establishing the committee of European Securities Regulators [2009] OJ L25/23).

[85] Commission Decision 2004/10/EC establishing the European Banking Committee [2004] OJ L003/36. For more details on CEBS see Ferran, n 83 above, 125–9.

[86] Commission Decision 2004/9/EC establishing the European Insurance and Occupational Pensions Committee [2004] OJ L003/34; for more details on CEIOPS cf Ferran, n 83 above, 130.

[87] Lamfalussy Report, n 76 above, 37. [88] ibid.

[89] For a detailed overview of CESR cf Ferran, n 83 above, 116–25.

primary responsibility for this task was to lie with the Commission, which was to be assisted by the Member States, their regulators, the private sector, and the European Parliament.[90] Broadly speaking, and despite the groundbreaking post-crisis institutional reform of the structure of EU financial market supervision (as discussed in Section IV), the newly established European Supervisory Authorities basically operate on the basis of this four-level organizational approach. The increasingly important European Supervisory Authorities are a considerable enhancement, however, of the initial Lamfalussy committees' institutional profile.[91]

While the Lamfalussy model enhanced rulemaking by the EU, difficulties remained. In particular, the centralization and coordination of rulemaking procedures under the Lamfalussy model, on the one hand, and the location of supervision at the Member State level, on the other, suggested a need for further supervisory coordination, and resulted in corresponding proposals in practice and among scholars.[92] The related shortcomings of EU financial regulation and supervision became particularly apparent in the wake of the 2007–09 financial crisis and were expressed in the 2009 de Larosière Report, published by the High Level Group at the request of the European Commission.[93] First and foremost, a major weakness of the regulatory system became apparent in the form of its focus on micro-prudential regulation, and its failure to address macro-prudential risks and to focus on systemic stability.[94] In addition, the de Larosière Group identified problems of competences in supervisory oversight at the Member State level and failures to challenge supervisory practices on a cross-border basis, and a resulting lack of coordination in supervising cross-border groups, so that significant risks created by home supervisors were borne by host countries (summarized in the slogan that is generally attributed to Mervyn King: 'Banks are international in life but national in death').[95] These factors contributed to the risks to the EU internal

90 Lamfalussy Report, n 76 above, 40; Moloney, n 2 above, 864.

91 On the nexus between the Lamfalussy Level 3 Committees and the European Supervisory Authorities see Ferran, n 83 above, 130–8, 144–6.

92 See eg the so-called Himalaya Report of CESR (CESR, Which Supervisory Tools for the EU Securities Markets (2004) (CESR/04-333f)); Centre for European Policy Studies (CEPS), Concrete Steps towards More Integrated Financial Oversight (2008); and, indicating the potential 'mismatch' between rulemaking and supervision, Ferran, n 51 above, 123–4.

93 See High Level Group, n 66 above; for a very brief overview see Di Noia, C and Furlò, M, 'The New Structure of Financial Supervision in Europe: What's Next?' in Wymeersch, E, Hopt, K, and Ferrarini, G (eds), *Financial Regulation and Supervision: A Post-Crisis Analysis* (2012) 172, 174–5; Moloney, N, 'Supervision in the Wake of the Financial Crisis: Achieving Effective "Law in Action"—a Challenge for the EU' in Wymeersch et al., 71, 72, and 78–9; Wymeersch, E, 'The European Financial Supervisory Authorities or ESAs' in Wymeersch et al., 232, 234.

94 De Larosière Report, n 66 above, 11 and 39–40.

95 ibid, 40–1. For details on the lack of cross-border supervision throughout the crisis see Ferrarini, G and Chiodini, F, 'Nationally Fragmented Supervision over Multinational Banks as a Source of Global Systemic Risk: A Critical Analysis of Recent EU Reforms' in Wymeersch, E, Hopt, K, and Ferrarini, G (eds), *Financial Regulation and Supervision: A Post-Crisis Analysis* (2012) 193, 198–202.

financial market resulting from excessive leverage taken on by banks which were not subject to a sufficiently strict and effective prudential oversight.

IV. Two-Tier Financial Oversight to Control Systemic Risk

The financial crisis in the EU accordingly highlighted the need to take account of the macroeconomic implications of regulation, and, in particular, to strengthen the prudential regulation of banks accordingly. At the same time, it became clear that, and aside from the increasingly important need to address macro-prudential stability, micro-prudential supervision also had to be reinforced in order to overcome the shortcomings of the Lamfalussy institutional arrangements discussed in Section III above and to increase their efficiency. Recognizing this need for a two-tier approach, the European Commission came forward with a proposal in 2009 which suggested that micro-prudential supervision be strengthened through a European System of Financial Supervision (ESFS), including the new European Supervisory Authorities (ESAs),[96] and that a European Systemic Risk Board (ESRB), in charge of macro-prudential oversight, be established; this new organizational design was adopted by the Council and European Parliament a year later in 2010.[97]

[96] European Commission, Proposal for a Regulation of the European Parliament and of the Council on Community macroprudential oversight of the financial system and establishing a European Systemic Risk Board (2009) (COM (2009) 499); European Commission, Proposal for a Regulation of the European Parliament and of the Council establishing a European Banking Authority (2009) (COM (2009) 501); European Commission, Proposal for a Regulation of the European Parliament and of the Council establishing a European Insurance and Occupational Pensions Authority (2009) (COM (2009) 502); European Commission, Proposal for a Regulation of the European Parliament and of the Council establishing a European Securities and Markets Authority (2009)(COM (2009) 503); and European Commission, Proposal for a Regulation of the European Parliament and of the Council Amending Directives 1998/26/EC, 2002/87/EC, 2003/6/EC, 2003/41/EC, 2003/71/EC, 2004/39/EC, 2004/109/EC, 2005/60/EC, 2006/48/EC, 2006/49/EC, and 2009/65/EC in respect of the powers of the European Banking Authority, the European Insurance and Occupational Pensions Authority and the European Securities and Markets Authority (2010 Omnibus I Directive) (2009) (COM (2009) 576).

[97] Regulation (EU) No 1092/2010 on European Union macro-prudential oversight of the financial system and establishing a European Systemic Risk Board [2010] OJ L331/1 (ESRB Regulation); Regulation (EU) No 1093/2010 establishing a European Supervisory Authority (European Banking Authority) [2010] OJ L 331/12 (EBA Regulation); Regulation (EU) No 1094/2010 establishing a European Supervisory Authority (European Insurance and Occupational Pensions Authority) [2010] OJ L 331/48 (EIOPA Regulation); Regulation (EU) No 1095/2010 establishing a European Supervisory Authority (European Securities and Markets Authority) [2010] OJ L 331/84 (ESMA Regulation); Directive 2010/78/EU (2010 Omnibus I Directive) [2010] OJ L 331/120.

1. Micro-prudential supervision by the European Supervisory Authorities

In their report, the High Level Group not only highlighted shortcomings in financial supervision in the EU as significant factors fostering the financial crisis, but also pointed to the need for institutional reform to overcome the weaknesses that had been standing in the way of the optimum coordination of rulemaking procedures at EU level, and of supervision at the Member State level, and which had resulted, in particular, in supervisory inefficiencies.[98] These problems are now largely dealt with by the new ESAs, which form part of the ESFS along with the national competent authorities and the ESRB. Each of them is the successor of a level 3 committee—the European Banking Authority (EBA) (the successor of CEBS), ESMA (CESR), and the European Insurance and Occupational Pensions Authority (EIOPA) (CEIOPS).[99] Enjoying legal personality,[100] as well as administrative autonomy, the ESAs must, *inter alia*, improve the functioning of the internal market,[101] support equal conditions of competition,[102] strengthen international supervisory coordination,[103] and ensure appropriate regulation and supervision of the taking of investment and other risk.[104] Furthermore, ESA Regulations, Article 1(5) calls upon the ESAs to be vigilant with respect to the threat of systemic risk.[105] The governance of the ESAs is comprised of a Management Board, which is composed of the ESA Chairperson and six members of the Board of Supervisors, and is responsible for the ongoing functioning of the ESA and its compliance with the ESA Regulations or other applicable rules; a Chairperson and an Executive Director, the latter two being full-time professionals; and a Board of Supervisors (composed of the heads of the national competent authorities (NCAs) and chaired by the Chairperson). In light of the task of the Board of Supervisors to 'give guidance to the work of the Authority' and its status within the ESA as the principal decision-making body, the dominant role of the Board of Supervisors is quite clear.[106]

Even though the ESAs do not adopt rules, they support coordination and convergence and are designed to resolve the potential tension between centralized rulemaking and local supervision. In order to fulfil this task, they have different

[98] Lamfalussy Report, n 76 above, 40–1.

[99] For a detailed account of the institutional background see Ferran, n 83 above, 133–8.

[100] Article 5(1) of the EBA, ESMA, and EIOPA Regulations, n 97 above; in the following the context permitting, these three regulations are referred to collectively as 'ESA Regs'.

[101] ESA Regs, Article (1)(5) (a).

[102] ibid, Article (1)(5)(d).

[103] ibid, Article (1)(5)(c).

[104] ibid, Article (1)(5)(e).

[105] For the objectives of the ESAs as provided for in ESA Regs, Article 1(5) in more detail see Wymeersch n 93 above, 242–5.

[106] ESA Regs, Article 43(1); for a more detailed overview of the governance structure of the ESAs see Wymeersch, n 93 above, 297–311.

instruments at their disposal under the ESA Regulations and the related 2010 Omnibus I Directive.[107]

With respect to supervision, as they have, as noted below, direct supervisory powers to take individual decisions addressed to financial market participants only in some enumerated and exceptional cases (apart from ESMA's direct exclusive supervisory powers related to, for example, credit rating agencies[108]), their coordinating powers might be regarded as limited. They have, for example, coordination functions with respect to NCAs (ESA Regulations, Article 31) as well as within colleges of supervisors (ESA Regulations, Article 21). In addition, they are to support a common supervisory culture (ESA Regulations, Article 29), to engage in peer review that aims to assess the implementation of EU rules (ESA Regulations, Article 30), and to foster coordination and convergence of supervisory practices in the EU.[109] Their direct supervisory powers to intervene directly, specifically enumerated in the ESA Regulations, include the following exceptional cases, subject in each case to conditions:[110] in case of a breach of EU law by an NCA, the ESAs can direct the latter to comply with EU law (and can impose related decisions on market actors);[111] and, in emergency circumstances seriously jeopardizing the functioning of financial markets, the ESAs can require of NCAs the necessary action to respond to the adverse developments (and impose related decisions on market actors).[112] Their power to settle disagreements between NCAs in cross-border situations in a binding mediation (and to impose related decisions on market actors) is a third example of these ESA powers that allow the ESAs to potentially act in a hierarchical manner in relation to national regulators, but which they have not, however, used as yet.[113]

Finally, and in support of rulemaking, the goal of convergence and improvement of national supervision in a functioning internal market, on a level playing field and in a system of undistorted competition, will be furthered by the ESAs because they also have the task of proposing binding regulatory (ESA Regulations, Article 10)

[107] For a detailed enumeration see Wymeersch, E, The Institutional Reforms of the European Financial Supervisory System, an Interim Report (2010), Financial Law Institute, Universiteit Gent Working Paper No 2010-01, 11–16.

[108] Regulation (EU) No 462/2013 amending Regulation (EC) No 1060/2009 on credit rating agencies [2013] OJ L146/1.

[109] For scepticism towards the effectiveness of coordination of national supervisory authorities and peer reviews see Ferrarini, G and Chiarella L, Common Banking Supervision in the Eurozone: Strengths and Weaknesses (2013), ECGI Law Working Paper No 223, 35–6 and Levi, LM, 'The European Banking Authority: Legal Framework, Operations and Challenges Ahead' (2013) 28 *Tulane European and Civil Law Forum* 51, 80–2.

[110] For an overview of the rather 'extensive' powers of ESMA and potential limits arising from the case law of the European Court of Justice see Tridimas, T, 'Financial Supervision and Agency Power: Reflections on ESMA' in Shuibhne, N and Gormley, L (eds), *From Single Market to Economic Union: Essays in Memory of John A. Usher* (2012) 55, 65–76; for an overview see also Di Noia, C and Furlò, M, n 93 above, 180–3.

[111] ESA Regs, n 100 above, Article 17(6).

[112] ibid, Article 18(4).

[113] ibid, Article 19.

and implementing (ESA Regulations, Article 15) 'technical standards', forms of delegated administrative rules which are subsequently adopted by the Commission, and which, by enhancing the Lamfalussy procedure for adopting delegated 'level 2' rules, are targeted towards the establishment of a European single rule book.[114]

Overall, management and coordination in the ESFS deploys different types of orchestration mechanisms. One might go so far as to describe the interplay between the coordination of national supervisors and decision-making in the ESA Board of Supervisors, for example, as a 'hub-and-spoke system'.[115] The Board of Supervisors has the power to adopt all decisions relating to binding legal instruments, thus implementing the ESAs' rulemaking powers.[116] Since it is composed of the heads of the national public authorities competent for the supervision of financial market participants (voting members), in addition to representatives of each of the European Commission, the European Risk Board (ESRB, further explained below) and the other two ESAs as non-voting members, interaction between the rulemaking hub and the implementing spokes on the national supervisory level is secured.[117] But at the same time, there is no denying the fact that the instances where the ESAs can exercise direct supervisory powers to take individual decisions addressed to financial market participants and to national supervisors reveal elements of hierarchy.[118]

2. Macro-prudential supervision by the ESRB

Any classification of the nature of the orchestrating interactions in the ESFS becomes more ambiguous with regard to the ESRB. According to the ESRB Regulation, Article 3(1), 'the ESRB shall be responsible for the macro-prudential oversight of the financial system within the Community ...'. A look at the implementation of this responsibility under the ESRB Regulation Article 3(2) makes clear, however, how closely intertwined macro- and micro-prudential oversight now are in the EU. The decision-making body of the ESRB, its General Board, is comprised of 61 voting and non-voting members reflecting macro- and micro-prudential interests; the former including the governors of the national central banks, the President and the Vice-President of the ECB, a member of the European Commission, and the Chairpersons of the three ESAs (ESRB Regulation, Article 6(1)). But governance difficulties arise. In light of the potential need for effective decision-making

[114] For an overview see Di Noia and Furlò, n 93 above, 178–9. For details on Regulatory Technical Standards (RTS), the related problems of delegation, and the involvement of the Commission cf Levi, n 109 above, 67–73 and Wymeersch, n 93 above, 249–55.

[115] Wymeersch, n 93 above, 235.

[116] ESA Regs, n 100 above, Article 43(2).

[117] For the composition of the Board of Supervisors see ibid, Article 40.

[118] Black, J, 'Restructuring Global and EU Financial Regulation: Character, Capacities, and Learning' in Wymeersch, E, Hopt, K, and Ferrarini, G (eds), *Financial Regulation and Supervision: A Post-Crisis Analysis* (2012) 3, 32.

in a crisis situation, this high number of voting members, possibly dominated by central bankers, may seem inappropriate for the ESRB's mission.[119] This last factor may make the ESRB appear as a coordination mechanism among central bankers, rather than a self-standing organization on its own, particularly as it has been set up by a regulation under Article 114 TFEU as a body without legal personality or autonomous intervention power.[120] This rather weak status is also adversely affected by its lack of legal enforcement powers because, without more, the ESRB's warnings and recommendations (through which it operates) are not legally binding, even though it can bring to bear political pressure on the basis of an 'act or explain' mechanism, when Member States or the respective ESA do not adequately justify their non-compliance with ESRB recommendations (ESRB Regulation, Article 17).[121]

3. Towards a European Banking Union with the Single Supervisory Mechanism

In light of the limits to convergence arising from the competence limitations on the ESAs, and the strictly macro-prudential focus of the ESRB and its 'soft law' status, the Single Supervisory Mechanism (SSM), which is based on a proposal of the European Commission of 2012 and on a regulation adopted in October 2013[122], centralizes specific micro- and macro-prudential supervisory tasks by conferring them on the ECB in relation to credit institutions from Euro Area Member States (and from non-Euro Area Member States that choose to participate). In this way, the participating Member State banking authorities are excluded from exercising their respective supervisory competence. At the same time, however, the designation of the SSM as a 'mechanism' clearly indicates that the newly established framework does not amount to the setting up of a new institution, but confers specific supervisory

[119] House of Lords, European Union Committee, *The EU Financial Supervisory Framework: An Update* (HL Paper 181, 20th Report of Session 2010–12) 25; Ferran, E and Alexander, K, 'Can Soft Law Bodies Be Effective? Soft Systemic Risk Oversight Bodies and the Special Case of the European Systemic Risk Board' (2010) *European Law Review* 751 and Directorate General for Internal Policies, Policy Department A: Economic and Scientific Policies, Economic and Monetary Affairs, Systemic Risk and the ESRB, Briefing Paper (2009) 6.

[120] For more details on the status of the ESRB see Ferran and Alexander, ibid, 23–5. For scepticism with regard to the independence of the ESRB, see Kost de Sevres, N and Sasso, L, 'The New European Financial Markets Legal Framework: A Real Improvement? An Analysis of Financial Law and Governance in European Capital Markets from a Micro- and Macro-economic Perspective' (2011) 7 *Capital Markets Law Journal* 30, 46–7.

[121] On the resulting power of the ESRB see Ferran and Alexander, n 119 above, 30–1.

[122] Council Regulation (EU) No 1024/2013 conferring specific tasks on the European Central Bank concerning policies relating to the prudential supervision of credit institutions [2013] OJ L287/63 (2013 ECB/SSM Regulation).

tasks on the ECB in compliance with the Treaty, and so relies on the ECB for its organizational design.[123]

This reliance on the ECB makes clear that the SSM, as opposed to the ESFS, additionally aims at the governance of monetary policy, instead of exclusively—as has been seen under Section IV.1 with respect to the ESFS—centring on micro-prudential supervision and the coordination involved with regard to implementing measures. This focus is explained by the SSM's specific role in the realization of the EBU and the related leading role for the ECB in the latter's supervisory scheme which provides for close interaction between the ECB and local supervisory authorities; in relying on the ECB, the SSM builds on one of the existing EU entities provided by the EU Treaty instead of establishing a new federal agency. This reliance on the ECB can be traced back to the crisis-era failure of the banking system and the related acknowledgement of the need for a link between the governance of credit and of monetary policy, which became particularly apparent throughout the sovereign debt crisis.[124] The related widespread defaults and resulting business failures underlined the obstacles to financial stability and to the functioning of financing mechanisms in the Euro Area, and, more generally, to trust in the stable future of the European Monetary Union. In addition, during the sovereign debt crisis the 'feedback loop' between banks and sovereigns turned out to be increasingly harmful. Bank rescues resulted in taxpayer-funded bailouts of financial institutions considered too systemic to fail. These bank rescues, in turn, inevitably produced moral hazard problems and distorted the level playing field which EU financial market regulation seeks[125] and put pressure on the Euro Area sovereign debt market and on the viability of the Euro. The avoidance of these problems requires credible backstop mechanisms at the EU level that will do away with the harmful link between banks and sovereigns.[126] That is why a common bank resolution scheme (the Single Resolution Mechanism (SRM) discussed below) is needed in order to spread the risks and costs of bank failure without national biases.[127] At the same time, the SRM (and the SSM) opens up the possibility to recapitalize banks directly, in compliance with state aid rules, without burdening national taxpayers.[128] Such an additional, potential fiscal

[123] According to TFEU, Article 127(6) and Article 25(2) of the Statute of the ESCB/ECB (Protocol [No 4] on the Statute of the European System of Central Banks and of the European Central Bank of 26 October 2012 ([012] OJ C326/230) the jurisdiction of the ECB can be further extended by a legislative act, conferring specific tasks with respect to prudential supervision on the ECB.

[124] Capriglione, F and Semeraro, G, 'Financial Crisis and Sovereign Debt: The European Union between Risks and Opportunities' (2012) 1, Part 1 *Law and Economics Yearly Review* 4, 51–7.

[125] For examples see Ferrarini and Chiodini, n 95 above, 193, 199–201.

[126] Ferrarini and Chiarella, n 109 above, 62–3.

[127] Beck, T, Gros, D, and Schoenmaker, D, 'On the Design of a Single Resolution Mechanism' in European Parliament, Directorate General for Internal Policies (ed.), *Monetary Dialogue* (18 February 2013) 29, 37–8; for the regulation on the Single Resolution Mechanism (SRM) see Regulation (EU) No 806/2014 [2014] OJ L225/1.

[128] European Commission, Communication from the Commission to the European Parliament: A Roadmap towards a Banking Union (2012) (COM (2012) 510), 3 n 5.

backup is provided by the European Stability Mechanism (ESM).[129] The SSM accordingly forms part of the effort to break the link between banks and sovereigns, putting the organization of supervision into the hands of the ECB, an independent institution; the decision-making body of the ESM—the Board of Governors—consists, by contrast, of the finance ministers of the ESM Member States.[130]

In substance, the ECB will be in charge of supervising approximately 120 larger banks under the criteria specified in the 2013 ECB/SSM Regulation (Article 6(4)).[131] Only banks with assets of more than EUR 30 billion or more than 20 per cent of national GDP will be directly supervised by the ECB. In addition, in each participating country, at least the three most significant credit institutions will be subject to direct supervision by the ECB, irrespective of their absolute size. Under these criteria, direct supervision by the ECB will extend to banks accounting for approximately 85 per cent of Euro Area banking assets.[132] According to the 2013 ECB/SSM Regulation (Article 4), the ECB has exclusive competence for the authorization and withdrawal of authorization (and the approval of acquisitions and disposals of major bank shareholdings) of all credit institutions in SSM-participating Member States and, in relation to those credit institutions which come within its direct supervision remit, is, *inter alia*, to act as competent home state authority in the case of credit institutions that want to establish a branch or provide cross-border services in non-Euro Area Member States, and is responsible for ensuring compliance with prudential requirements and supervisory reviews, including stress tests.[133] Despite this seemingly clear-cut division of responsibilities between national authorities and the ECB, the SSM relies on a system of cooperation because, under the 2013 ECB/SSM Regulation (Article 6(6)), local supervisors act as ancillaries to the ECB.[134]

Therefore, to a certain degree, the nexus between banks and sovereigns might be considered to be broken under the SSM.[135] But even though the ECB will be able to exercise overall oversight on the basis of the related 2014 ECB/SSM Framework Regulation,[136] it does not have any disciplinary power except for the power to impose administrative

[129] Wymeersch, E, The Single Supervisory Mechanism or 'SSM', Part One of the Banking Union (2014), National Bank of Belgium Working Paper No 255, 11.

[130] Underlining the independence of the ECB in the context of the SSM, Wymeersch, ibid, 25; for the Board of Governors of the ESM see Article 5(2) para 2 of the Treaty establishing the European Stability Mechanism (ESM) (2012), available at <http://www.european-council.europa.eu/media/582311/05-tesm2.en12.pdf>.

[131] Levi, n 109 above, 97.

[132] Ferrarini and Chiarella, n 109 above, 44.

[133] For an analysis see Ferran, E and Babis, V, 'The European Single Supervisory Mechanism' (2013) 13 *Journal of Corporate Law Studies* 255, 260–6 and Capriglione, F, 'European Banking Union: A Challenge for a More United Europe' (2013) 1 *Law and Economics Yearly Review* 5, 30–2.

[134] For an analysis of the relationship between the ECB and national authorities under the SSM see Ferrarini and Chiarella, n 109 above, 46–9.

[135] For a classification as a 'semi-strong framework' see Ferrarini and Chiarella, n 109 above, 49–61.

[136] Regulation (EU) No 468/2014 establishing the framework for cooperation within the Single Supervisory Mechanism between the European Central Bank and national competent authorities and with national designated authorities (SSM Framework Regulation (ECB/2014/17) [2014] OJ 141/1.

penalties as specifically provided for under the 2013 ECB/SSM Regulation, Article 18, and to pre-empt national supervisors (2013 ECB/SSM Regulation, Article 6 (5)(b)).[137] This makes clear that the completion of Banking Union requires further steps to avoid conflicts of interest between national authorities and the SSM, and to ensure optimal burden sharing and the proper functioning of ECB monetary policy implementation. These outcomes are, in particular, targeted by the recent EU agreements on deposit insurance and crisis management, including resolution, recently reached between the European Parliament and the Member States.[138]

In this context, the recent adoption of the SRM is of particular importance.[139] It is a necessary complement to the SSM to complete Banking Union not only because it may prevent the moral hazard inherent in national bank rescues, but also because it contributes to the greater credibility of the SSM, which would be damaged if it were dependent on national resolution authorities' interventions.[140] The SRM is based on the transfer and mutualization of contributions to the Single Resolution Fund (levied from banks which are subject to supervision by the SSM), so that the link between bank resolution and fiscal resources, potentially vulnerable to abuse, is broken.[141] Since the supervisory board of the SSM will be able to trigger a resolution, the overlap between these two supervisory mechanisms is obvious; national resolution authorities are not, however, left completely aside, being represented on the Single Resolution Board (SRB), the main decision-making body of the SRM and executing SRB resolution plans.[142] As has been shown above, only on the basis of these interconnected measures can corrosive expectations of national bailouts, moral hazard, and excessive risk-taking be eliminated.[143]

In light of this closely knit system of macro-prudential supervision, the question about Banking Union's relationship with the ESFS, and, in particular, the ESRB and the ESAs, necessarily arises. This particularly applies with respect to EBA, given the latter's pan-EU powers and responsibilities for bank supervision. As noted above, EBA has standard-setting powers, ultimately designed to support a single rulebook for the banking sector, and can intervene in case of a

[137] 2013 ECB/SSM Regulation, n 122 above, Article 6(5b).

[138] European Commission, Commissioner Barnier welcomes agreement between the European Parliament and Member States on Deposit Guarantee Scheme (MEMO/13/1176) (17 December 2013), and European Commission Commissioner Barnier welcomes trilogue agreement on the framework for bank recovery and resolution (MEMO/13/1140) (12 December 2013).

[139] See Beck et al., n 127 above.

[140] Véron, N and Wolff, G, Next Steps on the Road to a European Banking Union: The Single Resolution Mechanism in Context, in European Parliament, Directorate General for Internal Policies (ed.), *Monetary Dialogue* (2013) 5, 19–20.

[141] For the establishment of the SRF see European Parliament, Legislative Resolution of 15 April 2014 on the SRM, consideration 11.

[142] SRM Regulation, Articles 43 and 29.

[143] On the need for *ex ante* burden-sharing mechanisms see Ferrarini and Chiarella, n 109 above, 58–9.

breach of EU law by an NCA (see Section IV.1). What is more, in the event of a crisis its power to intervene goes even further, involving contingency planning and stress tests, as well as binding decisions with respect to national authorities.[144] With the establishment of the SSM, the exercise of these powers may be increasingly influenced by the ECB because there will be a non-voting member representing the ECB on EBA's Board of Supervisors and entitled—as opposed to non-voting members of the Board in general—to attend discussions about individual financial institutions.[145] In light of the very different institutional framework, centred on the ECB, of supervision in Banking Union, the widespread fear that the SSM, and the resulting change to EBA governance, could adversely affect EBA's integrating and coordinating functions, and the ensuing political debate about the institutional framework, are hardly surprising.[146] Member States who are not part of the Euro Area are not included in the SSM, but can join it on the basis of a 'close cooperation' regime.[147] As long, however, as non-Euro Area Member States do not see a reason for joining the SSM, the danger of disintegration is apparent.[148] Disintegration risk may be intensified further by the SSM-driven changes to the decision-making procedures of EBA, which aim to accommodate the fears of non-Euro Area Member States mentioned above, and which introduce the requirement of a double majority on certain types of decisions, such as those on regulatory matters. According to these changes approval is required by both a majority of Member States participating in the SSM and a majority of non-participating Member States.[149] The spillover effect of SSM membership and the resulting disproportionate influence of few non-Euro Area countries on EBA decision-making (amounting, in practice, to a potential blocking position by the UK, which is most likely not to join the SSM in the foreseeable future) are quite clear.[150] Therefore, the ultimate goal of

[144] In more detail see amended Regulation (EU) No 1022/2013 amending Regulation (EU) No 1093/2010 establishing a European Supervisory Authority (European Banking Authority) as regards the conferral of specific task on the European Central Bank pursuant to Council Regulation (EU) No 1024/2013 [2013] OJ L287/5; for further discussion on these powers of EBA in emergency situations see Ferrarini and Chiodini, n 95 above, 220–2; Wymeersch, n 93 above, 263–5.

[145] EBA Regulation Article 40(1)(d) and, as amended, Article 40(4a); on the likely effect of this representation see Wymeersch, n 129 above, 69; for more details on the interface between ECB and EBA supervision see Ferran and Babis, n 133 above, 276–8.

[146] House of Lords, European Union Committee, *European Banking Union: Key Issues and Challenges* (7th Report of Session 2012–13) (12 December 2012), § 138.

[147] 2013 ECB/SSM, n 122 above, Article 7; see Wymeersch, n 129 above, 63–4.

[148] Gurlit, n 71 above, 14.

[149] Verhelst, S, 'The Single Supervisory Mechanism: A Sound First Step in Europe's Banking Union?' (2013) *Egmont Paper* 58, 34–5.

[150] ibid, 35; Wymeersch, n 129 above, 70; for criticism see Tröger, T, The Single Supervisory Mechanism—Panacea or Quack Banking Regulation? (2013) 30–2.

a true European Banking Union may be rather ambitious in light of the likely persistence of political bargaining over financial supervision and ensuing compromises on financial supervision.[151] In the end, the SSM may thus also play a disintegrative role for the internal financial market, instead of marking the 'first step towards a Banking Union'.[152]

V. Conclusion

The goal of an internal financial market in the EU has been pursued in different ways according to the different stages of capital market development in the EU. In the beginning, the basic question of how to accommodate cross-border capital flows served as the point of departure for the home country principle and for the ensuing regulatory harmonization strategy. In the second stage, the problem of how to ensure a uniform application of harmonized rules, as a necessary requirement for a truly level playing field, necessarily had to be resolved. That was the background against which the Lamfalussy process, as the essential institutional framework for implementing the FSAP, was designed. In a further step, and following the financial crisis, regulation and supervisory oversight has become more concentrated at EU level, under the new European supervisory architecture (the ESFS), in order to achieve regulatory convergence and to centralize cross-border supervision to the extent deemed appropriate. At the same time, throughout the financial crisis a concern for a different kind of coordination has become apparent, namely the coordination of systemic risk management, on the basis of an overarching macro-prudential oversight in the framework of European Banking Union under the lead of the ECB. The future will tell whether this very ambitious concept is a further step towards the evolution of an integrated market and whether it will satisfy the needs for market integrity and confidence.

[151] For the need for a centralized supervision for a Banking Union, Wymeersch, n 129 above, 6–7; pointing out the threat of political compromise to financial supervision, Ferran and Babis, n 133 above, 255, 282.

[152] With respect to the goal of a Banking Union see consideration 12, 2013 ECB/SSM Regulation, n 122 above; for scepticism see Gurlit, n 71 above, 14, 15.

Bibliography

Avgouleas, E, 'A Critical Evaluation of the New EC Financial-Market Regulation: Peaks, Troughs, and the Road Ahead' (2005) 18 *The Transnational Lawyer* 179.

Avgouleas, E, *The Mechanics and Regulation of Markets Abuse: A Legal and Economic Analysis* (2005).

Beck, T, Gros, D, and Schoenmaker, D, 'On the Design of a Single Resolution Mechanism' in European Parliament, Directorate General for Internal Policies (ed.), *Monetary Dialogue* (18 February 2013) 29.

Black, J, 'Restructuring Global and EU Financial Regulation: Character, Capacities, and Learning' in Wymeersch, E, Hopt, K, and Ferrarini, G (eds), *Financial Regulation and Supervision: A Post-Crisis Analysis* (2012) 3.

Capriglione, F, 'European Banking Union: A Challenge for a More United Europe' (2013) 2, Pt 1 *Law and Economics Yearly Review* 5.

Capriglione, F and Semeraro, G, 'Financial Crisis and Sovereign Debt: The European Union between Risks and Opportunities' (2012) 1, Pt 1 *Law and Economics Yearly Review* 4.

Casey, J-P and Lannoo, K, *The MiFID Revolution* (2009).

Centre for European Policy Studies (CEPS), *Concrete Steps towards More Integrated Financial Oversight* (December 2008).

Chiu, I, *Regulatory Convergence in EU Securities Regulation* (2008).

Di Noia, C and Furlò, M, 'The New Structure of Financial Supervision in Europe: What's Next?' in Wymeersch, E, Hopt, K, and Ferrarini, G (eds), *Financial Regulation and Supervision: A Post-Crisis Analysis* (2012) 172.

Enriques, L and Gutta, M, 'Is There a Uniform EU Securities Law after the Financial Services Action Plan?' (2008) 14 *Stanford Journal of Law, Business & Finance* 43.

Ferran, E, *Building an EU Securities Market* (2004).

Ferran, E, 'Understanding the New Institutional Architecture of EU Financial Market Supervision' in Wymeersch, E, Hopt, K, and Ferrarini, G (eds), *Financial Regulation and Supervision: A Post-Crisis Analysis* (2012) 111.

Ferran, E and Alexander, K, 'Can Soft Law Bodies Be Effective? Soft Systemic Risk Oversight Bodies and the Special Case of the European Systemic Risk Board' (2010) *European Law Review* 751.

Ferran, E and Babis, V, 'The European Single Supervisory Mechanism' (2013) 13 *Journal of Corporate Law Studies* 255.

Ferrarini, G, 'Contract Standards and the Markets in Financial Instruments Directive: An Assessment of the Lamfalussy Regulatory Architecture' (2005) 1 *European Review of Contract Law* 19.

Ferrarini, G, 'Towards a European Law of Investment Services and Institutions' (1994) 31 *Common Market Law Review* 1283.

Ferrarini, G and Chiarella, L, Common Supervision in the Eurozone: Strengths and Weaknesses (2013), ECGI Law Working Paper No 223, available at <http://papers.ssrn.com/sol3/papers.cfm?abstract_id=2309897>.

Ferrarini, G and Chiodini, F, 'Nationally Fragmented Supervision over Multinational Banks as a Source of Global Systemic Risk: A Critical Analysis of Recent EU Reforms' in Wymeersch, E, Hopt, K, and Ferrarini, G (eds), *Financial Regulation and Supervision: A Post-Crisis Analysis* (2012) 193.

Ferrarini, G and Recine, F, 'The MiFID and Internalisation' in Ferrarini, G and Wymeersch, E (eds), *Investor Protection in Europe: Corporate Law Making, the MiFID and Beyond* (2006) 235.

Gerner-Beuerle, C, 'United in Diversity: Maximum versus Minimum Harmonization in EU Securities Regulation' (2012) 7 *Capital Markets Law Journal* 317.

Gurlit, E, 'The ECB's Relationship to the EBA' 25 (2014) *Europäische Zeitschrift für Wirtschaftsrecht* 14.

Haar, B, 'European Banking Market' in Basedow, J, Hopt, K, and Zimmermann, R (eds), *Max Planck Encyclopedia of European Private Law* (Vol 1, 2012) 545.

Haar, B, 'From Public Law to Private Law: Market Supervision and Contract Law Standards' in Grundmann, S and Atamar, Y (eds), *Financial Services, Financial Crisis and General European Contract Law: Failures and Challenges of Contracting* (2011) 259.

Hertig, G and Lee, R, 'Four Predictions on the Future of EU Securities Regulation' (2003) 3 *Journal of Corporate Law Studies* 359.

Kirby, A, 'Best Execution' in Skinner, C (ed.), *The Future of Investing in Europe's Markets after MiFID* (2007) 31.

Köndgen, J, 'Rules of Conduct: Further Harmonisation?' in Ferrarini, G (ed.), *European Securities Markets: The Investment Services Directive and Beyond* (1998) 115.

Kost de Sevres, N and Sasso, L, 'The New European Financial Markets Legal Framework: A Real Improvement? An Analysis of Financial Law and Governance in European Capital Markets from a Micro- and Macro-economic Perspective' (2011) 7 *Capital Markets Law Journal* 30.

Levi, LM, 'The European Banking Authority: Legal Framework, Operations and Challenges Ahead' (2013) 28 *Tulane European and Civil Law Forum* 51.

Moellers, T, 'Sources of Law in European Securities Regulation—Effective Regulation, Soft Law and Legal Taxonomy from Lamfalussy to de Larosière' (2010) 11 *European Business Organization Law Review* 379.

Moloney, N, 'EU Financial Market Regulation after the Global Financial Crisis: More Europe or More Risks?' (2010) 47 *Common Market Law Review* 1317.

Moloney, N, *EU Securities and Financial Markets Regulation* (3rd edn, 2014).

Moloney, N, *How to Protect Investors: Lessons from the EC and the UK* (2010).

Moloney, N, 'The Lamfalussy Legislative Model: A New Era for the EC Securities and Investment Services Regime' (2003) 52 *International and Comparative Law Quarterly* 509.

Moloney, N, 'Supervision in the Wake of the Financial Crisis: Achieving Effective "Law in Action"—a Challenge for the EU' in Wymeersch, E, Hopt, K, and Ferrarini, G (eds), *Financial Regulation and Supervision: A Post-Crisis Analysis* (2012) 71.

Ryan, J, 'An Overview of MiFID' in Skinner, C (ed.), *The Future of Investing in Europe's Markets after MiFID* (2007) 13.

Schammo, P, *EU Prospectus Law* (2011).

Smith, D and Leggett, S, 'Client Classification' in Skinner, C (ed.), *The Future of Investing in Europe's Markets after MiFID* (2007) 65.

Tison, M, 'Conduct of Business Rules and their Implementation in the EU Member States' in Ferrarini, G, Hopt, K, and Wymeersch, E (eds), *Capital Markets in the Age of the Euro: Cross-Border Transactions, Listed Companies and Regulation* (2002) 65.

Tison, M, 'Financial Market Integration in the Post FSAP Era—in Search of Overall Conceptual Consistency in the Regulatory Framework' in Ferrarini, G and Wymeersch, E (eds), *Investor Protection in Europe—Corporate Law Making, the MiFID and Beyond* (2006) 443.

Tridimas, T, 'Financial Supervision and Agency Power: Reflections on ESMA' in Shuibhne, N and Gormley, L (eds), *From Single Market to Economic Union: Essays in Memory of John A. Usher* (2012) 55.

Tröger, T, The Single Supervisory Mechanism—Panacea or Quack Banking Regulation? (2013), SAFE Working Paper Series No 27, available at <http://papers.ssrn.com/sol3/papers.cfm?abstract_id=2311353>.

Verhelst, S, The Single Supervisory Mechanism: A Sound First Step in Europe's Banking Union? (2013), Egmont Paper 58, available at <http://www.egmontinstitute.be/publication_article/the-single-supervisory-mechanism-a-sound-first-step-in-europes-banking- union-2/>.

Véron, N and Wolff, G, Next Steps on the Road to a European Banking Union: The Single Resolution Mechanism in Context, in European Parliament, Directorate General for Internal Policies (ed.), *Monetary Dialogue* (18 February 2013) 5.

Wymeersch, E, 'The European Financial Supervisory Authorities or ESAs' in Wymeersch, E, Hopt, K, and Ferrarini, G (eds), *Financial Regulation and Supervision: A Post-Crisis Analysis* (2012) 232.

Wymeersch, E, The Institutional Reforms of the European Financial Supervisory System, an Interim Report (2010), Financial Law Institute, Universiteit Gent Working Paper No 2010–01, available at <http://papers.ssrn.com/abstract=1541968>.

Wymeersch, E, The Single Supervisory Mechanism or 'SSM', Part One of the Banking Union (1 April 2014), National Bank of Belgium Working Paper No 255, available at <http://papers.ssrn.com/sol3/papers.cfm?abstract_id=2427577>.

Commission Documents

European Commission, Completing the Internal Market, White Paper from the Commission to the European Council, COM (1985) 310 final (1985).

European Commission, Financial Services: Building a Framework for Action, COM (1998) 625 final (1998).

European Commission, Implementing the Framework for Financial Markets: Action Plan, COM (1999) 232 final (1999).

European Commission, Communication on The Application of Conduct of Business Rules under Article 11 of the Investment Services Directive, COM (2000) 722 final (2000).

European Commission, Proposal for a Regulation of the European Parliament and of the Council on Community macroprudential oversight of the financial system and establishing a European Systemic Risk Board, COM (2009) 499 final (2009).

European Commission, Proposal for a Regulation of the European Parliament and of the Council establishing a European Banking Authority, COM (2009) 501 final (2009).

European Commission, Proposal for a Regulation of the European Parliament and of the Council establishing a European Insurance and Occupational Pensions Authority, COM (2009) 502 final (2009).

European Commission, Proposal for a Regulation of the European Parliament and of the Council establishing a European Securities and Markets Authority, COM (2009) 503 final (2009).

European Commission, Proposal for a Regulation of the European Parliament and of the Council Amending Directives 1998/26/EC, 2002/87/EC, 2003/6/EC, 2003/41/EC, 2003/71/EC, 2004/39/EC, 2004/109/EC, 2005/60/EC, 2006/48/EC, 2006/49/EC, and 2009/65/EC in respect of the powers of the European Banking Authority, the European Insurance and Occupational Pensions Authority and the European Securities and Markets Authority, COM (2009) 576 final (2009).

European Commission, Amended Proposal for a Directive of the European Parliament and of the Council on criminal sanctions for insider dealing and market manipulation, COM (2012) 420 final (2012).

European Commission, A Roadmap towards a Banking Union, COM (2012) 510 final (2012).

CHAPTER 7

ORGANIZING REGIONAL SYSTEMS

THE US EXAMPLE

ERIC J PAN*

* The U.S. Securities and Exchange Commission, as a matter of policy, disclaims responsibility for any private publication or statement by any of its employees. The views expressed herein are entirely those of the author and do not reflect the views of the Commission or of the author's colleagues upon the staff of the Commission.

I. Introduction

This Chapter seeks to provide an overview of the structure of the US financial regulatory system in the context of understanding the elements of a theoretically ideal financial regulatory system. It begins by providing a perspective on a regulatory system's key objectives, essential characteristics, most important strategies, and optimal organizational approaches.

In June 2009, President Obama unveiled his administration's White Paper on Financial Regulatory Reform[1] to replace a regulatory system 'crafted in the wake of a 20th century economic crisis … [and] overwhelmed by the speed, scope, and sophistication of a 21st Century global economy'.[2] Several of the ideas laid out in the White Paper later were incorporated in the Dodd–Frank Wall Street Reform and Consumer Protection Act of 2010. In considering the US regulatory system, it is important also to note that the planning of the restructuring of the US regulatory system was contemporaneous of debates about structural regulatory reform in the EU, Canada, and elsewhere. In the UK, policymakers were considering at that time several recommendations to improve the UK financial regulatory system, ranging from the Turner Review submitted by the UK Financial Services Authority in March 2009,[3] to a report presented by the UK Treasury in July 2009,[4] to a White Paper prepared by the Conservative Party also in July 2009.[5] The EU implemented a series of structural reform recommendations set forth by a committee of experts chaired by Jacques de Larosière in February 2009.[6] And in Canada, the Canadian

[1] See generally US Department of the Treasury, Financial Regulatory Reform: A New Foundation: Rebuilding Financial Supervision and Regulation (2009) (hereinafter, US Treasury White Paper).

[2] Press Release, Office of the Press Secretary, Remarks by the President on 21st Century Financial Regulatory Reform (17 June 2009).

[3] United Kingdom Financial Services Authority, The Turner Review: A Regulatory Response to the Global Financial Crisis (2009) (the relationship between the FSA, Bank of England, and HM Treasury is often referred to as the 'tripartite arrangement').

[4] See generally HM Treasury, Reforming Financial Markets (2009).

[5] The Conservative Party, From Crisis to Confidence: Plan for Sound Banking (July 2009), available at <http://www.conservatives.com/News/News_stories/2009/07/~/media/Files/Downloadable%20 Files/PlanforSoundBanking.ashx>.

[6] Press Release, José Manuel Durão Barroso, European Commission Press Point with Jacques de Larosière (25 February 2009) and the de Larosière Group, Report of the High-Level Group on Financial Supervision in the EU (2009). The European Commission endorsed the recommendations of the de Larosière Report in March 2009. See Commission, Communication for the Spring European Council: Driving European Recovery, at 5–7 (COM (2009) 114) (2009). See also: Commission Proposal for a Regulation on Community Macro Prudential Oversight of the Financial System and Establishing a European Systemic Risk Board (COM (2009) 499) (2009); Commission Proposal for a Council Decision Entrusting the European Central Bank with Specific Tasks Concerning the Functioning of the European Systemic Risk Board (COM (2009) 500) (2009); Commission Proposal for a Regulation of the European Parliament and of the Council Establishing a European Banking Authority (COM (2009) 501) (2009); Commission Proposal for a Regulation Establishing a European

federal government was considering an expert panel recommendation to create a single federal securities regulator. Despite this flurry of simultaneous reform activity, the approaches pursued by each jurisdiction were quite different. The proposals reflected different assumptions about the causes of the 2007–09 global financial crisis and uncertainty regarding what should be the objectives of structural reform of financial regulation.

II. Characteristics of a Regulatory System

The design of an optimal regulatory system should begin with an understanding of the objectives of the regulatory system, the ideal characteristics of such a system, the various regulatory strategies that might be applied to achieve those objectives, and, finally, the desired structure of the regulatory system.

1. Regulatory objectives

The first objective of financial regulation is to ensure the safety and soundness of the financial system.[7] Accomplishment of this goal generally consists of three tasks: prudential regulation, business and market conduct regulation, and financial stability protection.[8]

Prudential regulation refers to the range of regulations and regulatory acts applied to certain financial institutions—banks, securities firms, and insurance companies—to ensure that they are financially sound and capable of meeting their market obligations. Regulators have a great interest in the health and operations of these financial institutions as the failure of one or more of these institutions could result in a loss of confidence in the safety and soundness of the financial system, causing a sharp contraction in financial activity, the weakening of other

Insurance and Occupational Pensions Authority (COM (2009) 502) (2009); and Commission Proposal for a Regulation of Establishing a European Securities and Market Authority (COM (2009) 503) (2009).

[7] For a general discussion of the meaning of financial regulation, see Pan, EJ, 'Understanding Financial Regulation' (2012) *Utah Law Review* 1897.

[8] This breakdown of tasks has also been recognized by other commentators. See, eg, Taylor, M, Twin Peaks: A Regulatory Structure for the New Century (1995), Centre for the Study of Financial Innovation Working Paper; Davies, H and Green, D, *Global Financial Regulation* (2008).

financial institutions, and the need for public intervention.[9] Prudential regulation may include, among other things, capital adequacy rules, internal controls, record-keeping requirements, risk assessments, and mandatory professional qualifications for key personnel. Prudential regulation also can refer to the monitoring, inspection, and examination of financial institutions on a continuing basis by the regulator, accompanied by sanctions and prosecution of violations or unsafe practices. The purpose of prudential regulation is to ensure that a financial institution is not assuming risks that could endanger the financial health of the institution and its commitments to investors, depositors, and counterparties. Prudential regulation also provides the regulator with sufficient information to identify potential problems before such problems become serious enough to result in a failure of the institution.

In contrast, business and market conduct regulation, which includes consumer protection regulation, focuses on protecting customers (including investors) who buy financial products or otherwise entrust funds to financial institutions. Business and market conduct regulation provides consumer protection by addressing the unequal position of financial institutions relative to their customers. The most vulnerable customers are retail clients who may lack the sophistication and knowledge necessary to protect themselves from fraud, market abuse, or misleading advice and must rely on financial institutions and the representatives of those financial institutions to protect their interests. Consequently, regulators must address this informational asymmetry by imposing requirements on financial institutions to disclose conflicts of interest, offer appropriate disclosures of risk, provide detailed and understandable information about investments and financial products and services, train their personnel to comprehend the needs of customers and clients in order to provide appropriate advice and assistance, and assume certain fiduciary obligations. Business and market conduct regulation also includes regulations that promote investor protection, including regulations on securities issuers to provide accurate material information on an ongoing basis to investors.

Beyond the regulation of financial institutions and the protection of customers, regulators also must safeguard the overall stability of the financial system. Regulators must sustain the financial infrastructure necessary to keep the financial system operating in a smooth manner. This task includes maintaining the payments system, providing short-term and overnight lending, and managing the money supply. When the failure of a financial institution might cause serious harm to the financial system, the responsibility to ensure financial stability also refers to

[9] See Recent Crisis Reaffirms the Need to Overhaul the US Regulatory System: Testimony before the Senate Committee on Banking, Housing, and Urban Affairs, 111th Congress, GAO-09-1049T (29 September 2009), (testimony of Richard J Hillman, Managing Director Financial Markets and Community Investment), available at <http://www.gao.gov/new.items/d091049t.pdf>.

the need to intervene during times of crisis and to fulfil the role of lender of last resort and liquidity provider.

Financial stability protection is different from other regulatory activities because, frequently, its associated responses require the government to enter the market as a counterparty in financial market transactions. Financial stability regulation is often the responsibility of the central bank, independent of any of its direct regulatory duties.[10] As the bailout of large financial institutions by the US and UK governments have demonstrated, however, financial stability operations that require government intervention as a lender of last resort, a source of liquidity, or a guarantor of financial obligations, are inextricably tied to the protection of customer assets and the soundness of financial institutions, thereby justifying a role for the central bank in the regulatory process.[11]

The other objective of financial regulation is to foster the growth and development of the financial markets. A regulatory system may encourage financial market growth by promoting innovation and permitting the development of new markets for financial services. Regulatory systems are more likely to attract innovation and growth if financial market participants perceive that regulators are responsive to market needs and that applicable regulatory standards are appropriate. In the current global marketplace, an unattractive regulatory environment may lead to regulatory arbitrage—the movement of financial activity to other markets to avoid regulation. Regulatory reform should take into consideration the impact of the structure of the regulatory system on financial market activity.[12]

2. Characteristics of a regulatory system

In order to achieve the objectives described above, a regulatory system should aim to have four basic characteristics: efficiency, accountability, competency, and legitimacy. These four characteristics underpin a regulatory system's effectiveness in meeting its objectives. First, the organization and operation of regulators should seek to provide optimal regulation in an efficient manner. Regulators should design the structure of the regulatory system to avoid redundancy to the extent possible

[10] See, eg, Ferguson Jr, RW, 'Should Financial Stability Be an Explicit Central Bank Objective' in Ugolini, PC et al. (eds), *Challenges to Central Banking from Globalized Financial System* (2003) 208 (noting that one of the fundamental objectives of central banks is to ensure financial stability); and Goodhart, C and Schoenmaker, D, 'Should the Functions of Monetary Policy and Banking Supervision Be Separated?' (1995) 47 *Oxford Economics Papers* 539, 548–9 (discussing the need to give central banks prudential supervisory powers).

[11] See Pan, n 7 above, 19–25.

[12] See Aspinwall, R, 'Conflicting Objectives of Financial Regulation' in *Reforming Money and Finance* (2nd edn, 1997) 179.

where different parts of the regulatory system have overlapping responsibility over a particular financial activity or entity.

Second, policymakers should design the regulatory system to promote accountability. With respect to any regulatory matter, it should be clear which regulator is responsible for addressing the matter. Consequently, a financial institution should know where to direct inquiries or to whom it should raise concerns, and the public and elected officials should hold that regulator responsible for any regulatory problems.

Likewise, the regulatory system needs to promote international accountability. Foreign regulators should know whom to call if there is an issue that requires international coordination. One of the difficulties that plagued the early development of the European financial markets was the lack of an EU regulatory authority that could speak for the EU in matters requiring consultation with the US and other major economic powers.[13] International accountability also means that one regulator should be authorized to represent the country's interests in international forums. The need to identify an agency that is accountable indicates the necessity of consolidating disparate regulatory bodies or at least establishing a hierarchy of regulators.

Third, the regulatory system should be designed to promote competency. It goes without saying that regulators should be competent, but the manner in which the regulatory system is structured can further improve the competency of regulators by ensuring that those regulators with applicable skills and expertise are assigned to certain regulatory tasks. Competency consists of a variety of elements, and among them is expertise.[14] Recruiting and retaining individuals who are knowledgeable about the financial sector and the activities that they are regulating should be a priority of the regulatory system.

Furthermore, the regulatory system should endeavour to assign regulatory responsibility to that part of the regulatory system that is in the best position to collect the necessary information and to respond to issues of regulatory concern. One of the justifications that has been suggested for the delegation of regulatory authority to self-regulatory organizations (SROs) is that financial market participants that make up SROs are in a better position than a government regulator to understand market developments and to identify and resolve potential problems.[15]

Another element of competency is experience. Regulators should work on regulatory problems with which they have experience. This observation is an argument for reorganizing regulators along the lines of regulatory objectives (referred to

[13] See Pan, EJ, 'Harmonization of US–EU Securities Regulation: The Case for a Single European Securities Regulator' (2003) 34 *Law & Policy of International Business* 499, 534–5.

[14] Bratspies, RM, 'Regulatory Trust' (2009) 51 *Arizona Law Review* 575, 608–19.

[15] See Jordan, C and Hughes, P, 'Which Way for Market Institutions: The Fundamental Question of Self-Regulation' (2007) 4 *Berkeley Business Law Journal* 205, 212.

herein as objectives-based regulation), as opposed to merely by financial sector or activity. For example, it may not be desirable to have a regulator with experience in prudential regulation to also oversee business conduct rules. Competency is also a function of culture and experience. Regulatory agencies—like all organizations—develop internal procedures and practices over time that govern how they approach regulatory tasks and apply past lessons to current problems. The US SEC, for example, has a long and distinguished history of being an effective and respected regulator of the US markets.[16] To the extent possible, structural reform of the regulatory system should keep successful existing agencies intact and preserve institutional knowledge and practices.

Fourth, the regulatory system should be legitimate. This Chapter defines legitimacy as the ability of agencies to have their regulations recognized and accepted by market participants. While regulatory agencies may have legitimacy by virtue of their legal authority, regulatory agencies are more effective when market participants view the agencies' actions and decisions as substantively correct, instilling confidence in the competence of the regulators.

Three factors that help a regulatory system earn and retain legitimacy are independence from political interests, accountability to the public, and transparency. The perception that regulators' action is linked to political interests undermines the credibility of regulatory agencies. These perceptions can develop from regulatory actions that favour certain political constituencies or are the result of political trends rather than sound regulatory principles. Commentators have cited one example where political influence may have undermined regulatory legitimacy.[17] Until Japan reformed its regulatory system, the Japanese Ministry of Finance played an unusually active role in regulating Japan's troubled banks. Commentators attributed Japan's slow recovery in the 1990s to the Ministry of Finance's refusal to pressure banks to declare their losses quickly and restructure themselves. Such commentators have suggested that the Ministry of Finance attempted to limit political backlash by helping the banks hide the true extent of their losses. It took several years before investor confidence in the Japanese financial markets returned to normal.

At the same time, however, regulators cannot be entirely independent of political pressure because their legitimacy also stems from their accountability to the public. One concern expressed about the prospect of a single 'super-regulator' in the US is that the US Congress would not be able to control such a powerful agency.[18] This concern resonates with commentators in the US who would have depicted US

[16] See, eg, Seligman, J, *The Transformation of Wall Street* (3rd edn, 2003).

[17] See Davies and Green, n 8 above, 174–6.

[18] See, eg, Hearing on Financial Regulatory Lessons from Abroad before the Senate Committee on Homeland Security and Governmental Affairs, 111th Congress 7 (2009), (testimony of David Green, Former Head of International Policy, UK Financial Services Authority), available at <http://hsgac.senate.gov/public/_files/052109Green.pdf>.

regulatory agencies as having a great deal of day-to-day autonomy from Congress and the President.[19] Such concerns, however, may be mitigated if the legislature and executive retain the power to set the priorities of the regulators, have the power to remove and appoint the heads of regulatory agencies, and are briefed and consulted frequently by the regulatory staff. Regulators, on the other hand, should have the freedom to act without political interference and retain the ability to interpret their statutory objectives in developing relevant rules and regulations.

Finally, regulators should be transparent in how they develop their rules and regulations and conduct enforcement actions. Such transparency can be achieved by holding public meetings, providing notice and comment on new rules and regulations, allowing regulated entities to consult with—and seek guidance from—regulators on an ongoing basis, and disclosing other relevant information about internal deliberations and policy interpretations. It should be noted that central banks are not well known for their transparency, which may raise concerns about their capacity to be financial regulators.[20] Legitimacy, together with efficiency, accountability, and competency, are essential components of a successful financial regulatory system.

3. Regulatory strategies

The most challenging task for regulators is to strike the proper balance between the twin objectives of ensuring the safety and soundness of the financial system, while improving the regulatory environment of the market to provide the conditions for the growth and development of the financial markets. Under-regulation, which can mean either the absence of regulatory action or the under-enforcement of existing regulations, may leave the financial system susceptible to systemic failure, fraud, or loss of confidence by market participants. But over-regulation may prevent financial institutions from doing business in a cost-effective manner and drive financial activity to other, more favourably regulated markets.

In order to find the right balance of regulation, regulators can look to employ certain strategies: regulatory competition, regulatory cooperation, and self-regulation. Regulatory competition is when regulatory regimes are set up as alternatives to one another. Those institutions and persons subject to regulation can move from one regime to another, choosing their preferred regulatory regime. In other words, market participants face a menu of regulatory choices, allowing them to select the

[19] Peters, A, 'Independent Agencies: Government Scourge or Salvation?' (1988) *Duke Law Journal* 286, 286–8.

[20] See Nergiz Dincer, N and Eichengreen, B, Central Bank Transparency: Where, Why, and With What Effects? (2007), National Bureau of Economic Research Working Paper No 13003, available at <http://www.nber.org/papers/w13003.pdf>, 1–2.

set of regulations that best fits their needs. In the context of financial regulation, customers and investors will participate only in those markets which have sufficient regulatory protections. At the same time, financial service providers and corporate issuers will participate only in those markets where the burden of regulatory compliance is considered reasonable.

Regulatory competition addresses the problem of finding the right balance by allowing market participants—investors and customers on the one hand, and financial firms and issuers on the other—the ability to select the regime that best meets their needs. The regime that attracts the largest number of market participants and hosts the greatest level of financial activity is the one that offers the optimal level of regulation. In turn, regulatory competition assumes that regulators will modify and tweak their regulations to become more attractive to both sets of market participants. As a result, regulatory competition empowers the financial markets to identify the most suitable regulatory regime.

One concern frequently raised in connection with regulatory competition is the danger of a 'race to the bottom', where the desire to attract financial service providers and corporate issuers (via deregulation) overwhelms the need to maintain adequate regulatory standards to ensure the safety and soundness of the financial system.[21] The 'race to the bottom' description, however, exaggerates the risk that regulators will abdicate their regulatory responsibility in order to attract new business to their markets. Regulators also have a powerful incentive to impose additional regulation in order to make their markets more attractive to retail and institutional customers and investors.[22]

Regulatory competition may be viewed as an attractive regulatory strategy because it assumes that competitive pressure—pressure on regulators to improve their regulatory systems—will result in the discovery of the optimal regulatory regime. Regulatory competition also may be a superior regulatory strategy if several optimal regulatory regimes exist for market participants with different characteristics. For example, sophisticated institutional investors may elect to invest in markets that have weaker investor protections because they feel more capable of protecting themselves in such a regime, while retail customers and investors may prefer more heavily regulated markets that emphasize stricter disclosure requirements and contain more investor protections.

[21] See, eg, Butler, HN and Macey, JR, 'The Myth of Competition in the Dual Banking System' (1988) 73 *Cornell Law Review* 677, 714–15; Cox, JD, 'Regulatory Duopoly in the US Securities Market' (1999) 99 *Columbia Law Review* 1200, 1229–37.

[22] Jackson, HE, The Selective Incorporation of Foreign Legal Systems to Promote Nepal as an International Financial Services Center (1998), Harvard Law School, John M. Olin Center for Law, Economics, and Business, Discussion Paper No 24, available at <http://ssrn.com/abstract=146600> (noting that the incentives for government to compete include taxes and regulation fees plus various collateral benefits).

One essential ingredient for regulatory competition is a 'passport' system where firms that satisfy the requirements of one regulatory regime are given unfettered access to all other markets.[23] Other countries have attempted to implement similar passport systems, most notably the EU, with limited success.[24] Without a passport system, regulated firms cannot move toward a regime that offers a preferable set of regulatory requirements.

Regulatory competition, however, may not be an appropriate strategy if regulators have reason to believe that market participants do not have complete information or the necessary skill to evaluate the appropriateness of different regulatory regimes, if regulators have insufficient resources or incentives to engage in competition, or if all regulatory regimes must provide minimum regulatory standards regardless of their perceived value to market participants. One alternative regulatory strategy is regulatory cooperation. Regulatory cooperation occurs when regulators from different regimes converge their regulations, resulting in different jurisdictions sharing comparable regulatory standards.[25] Such convergence eliminates the opportunity for market participants to evade these standards by moving to a different regulatory regime.

Regulatory cooperation assumes that the regulators know the appropriate level of regulation for the market and all market participants must abide by the same regulations in every jurisdiction. While there is a risk that the standards set by the regulators may be too high, regulatory cooperation could produce cost savings by eliminating the need for market participants to evaluate the differences between competing regimes and other regulatory costs associated with individual regulatory agencies struggling to stay competitive with one another.

The main challenge associated with regulatory cooperation is the process by which the cooperation takes place. In the case of the EU, the European Commission attempted to impose a common set of regulatory standards on the individual Member States through a series of directives. The initial directives proved unsuccessful as some Member States resisted the European Commission's efforts and refused to implement the directives in a full and consistent manner. More recent efforts by the European Commission to establish a common set of standards have proven more successful through the greater use of European regulation and the

[23] See Improving Securities Regulation in Canada, Provincial-Territorial Securities Initiative, available at <http://www.securitiescanada.org> (stating that Canada has established 'a passport system providing market participants with a single window of access to Canadian capital markets').

[24] Jackson, HE and Pan, EJ, 'Regulatory Competition in International Securities Markets: Evidence from Europe in 1999—Part I' (2001) 56 *Business Lawyer* 653, 662 (describing the passport system used in the EU).

[25] See Schaffer, G, 'Reconciling Trade and Regulatory Goals: The Prospects and Limits of New Approaches to Transatlantic Governance through Mutual Approaches to Transatlantic Governance through Mutual Recognition and Safe Harbor Agreements' (2002) 9 *Columbia Journal of European Law* 29, 70.

issuance of technical standards by the European Supervisory Authorities, such as the European Securities and Markets Authority. The EU experience offers one model for regulatory cooperation at both the national and international levels.

In the case of self-regulation, regulators delegate responsibility for standards setting and rulemaking to representatives of the market. The rationale behind self-regulation is that market participants, by virtue of having better information and knowledge of market events, are in a superior position to determine the appropriate level and scope of regulation. SROs may also be able to respond more quickly, and in a more flexible manner, to market developments. Self-regulation is often considered less expensive (from the perspective of the government) than direct regulation, as the financial industry is charged with paying for its own regulatory apparatus.

A prominent example of self-regulation is the Financial Industry Regulatory Authority (FINRA) in the US. As a self-regulatory organization, FINRA receives its authority from the SEC and funding from its members.[26] When the SEC recognized the first SROs, the then SEC Chairman William O Douglas described the role of the SEC as being like a 'shotgun, so to speak, behind the door'.[27] The SEC would oversee the SROs, but would only intervene if it determined that the SROs were failing to carry out their respective regulatory missions. Over the course of the past 60 years, the SEC has stepped in several times to tighten the regulation of the securities firms and has taken an active role in reviewing the regulatory actions of FINRA (and previously the National Association of Securities Dealers).[28] Nevertheless, the self-regulatory model offers a powerful means to give market participants an influential role in determining the appropriate level and form of regulation.

4. Organization of the regulatory system

The final consideration behind designing the optimal regulatory system is its organization. In thinking about the organization of a regulatory system, three questions

[26] See, eg, FINRA Regulatory Notice 08-07: Regulatory Pricing Proposal 1 (2008), available at <http://www.finra.org/web/groups/industry/@ip/@reg/@notice/documents/notices/p038008.pdf> (noting that FINRA relies on member regulatory fees to fund regulatory programmes).

[27] Seligman, J, 'Cautious Evolution or Perennial Irresolution: Stock Market Self-Regulation during the First Seventy Years of the Securities Exchange Commission' (2004) 59 *Business Lawyer* 1347, 1361 (providing a detailed description of the role of SROs in US securities regulation).

[28] See Dombalagian, OH, 'Demythologizing the Stock Exchange: Reconciling Self-Regulation and the National Market System' (2005) 39 *University of Richmond Law Review* 1069, 1078–89. The need for SEC intervention reveals one of the weaknesses with self-regulation: at times of crisis when the SROs fail to prevent a regulatory failure, the SROs are vulnerable to questions about their legitimacy and accountability. See Dombalagian.

must be answered. First, how should regulatory responsibility be divided among regulators? One possibility is to have regulatory responsibility divided according to each financial sector such that each regulator focuses on a specific type of financial activity. The US offers one example of activity-based regulation, especially in the banking area, where the Office of the Comptroller of the Currency regulates federally chartered banks, state banking authorities regulate state-chartered banks, and the National Credit Union Association supervises credit unions. The advantage of activity-based regulation is that each agency develops a deep expertise in its particular sector, giving it a better understanding of regulated firms' activities and practices.

Another option is to adopt an objectives-based approach. In contrast to the sector-based and activity-based approaches, the objectives-based approach recommends arranging regulators in accordance with the three tasks necessary to ensure the soundness and safety of the financial system. One regulator is responsible for prudential regulation, a second regulator is responsible for business conduct regulation and a third regulator is responsible for financial stability measures. The advantage of the objectives-based approach is that regulators retain a certain degree of specialization (if one assumes that all prudential regulation, business conduct regulation, and financial stability responses are the same regardless of financial sector or activity), while each regulator has a more expansive view of the financial system by virtue of regulating firms that operate across sectors.

The different approaches affect the number of regulatory authorities needed to oversee the regulatory system. The activity-based approach requires more regulatory authorities than the objectives-based approach because the focus of each regulator is narrower. Even in the case of the objectives-based approach, there is a question as to whether regulatory authority should be concentrated in the hands of a single regulator (the single regulator model), two regulators focused respectively on prudential regulation and business (or market) conduct regulation plus a financial stability agency (the twin peaks model), or multiple regulators with one regulator responsible for managing the other regulators (the lead regulator model).

The single regulator model may be attractive because of its simple organizational form. The single regulator does not have to share or coordinate actions with another regulator, eliminating the possibility that issues of concern will fall between the jurisdictional cracks of separate regulators or be the subject of 'turf battles' between agencies. There are economies of scale associated with having a single, large regulator handle all regulatory issues rather than having separate regulators work independently.[29] Proponents of the single regulator model note that the UK's move to a single regulator system in 1998 resulted in cost savings at least in the first four years

[29] See Briault, C, Financial Service Authority, Revisiting the Rationale for a Single National Financial Services Regulator 7 (2002), available at <http://www.fsa.gov.uk/pubs/occpapers/op16.pdf>.

of its existence.[30] A single regulator also is better equipped to oversee more complex financial institutions and financial products, since it has undisputed regulatory authority over all aspects of the financial market. Furthermore, the single regulator model provides ultimate accountability since all queries and concerns automatically fall at its doorstep.

The single regulator model, however, assumes that a single agency can meet all regulatory objectives simultaneously and satisfactorily. This is easier said than done. The single regulator model shifts the decision of setting regulatory priorities and allocating regulatory resources from an external debate (for example, the support of various regulatory agencies through the public budget) to an internal debate wherein the managers of the single regulator decide on regulatory priorities and allocate resources accordingly (often outside of public scrutiny).

Such a shift poses several risks. One risk is that the regulatory authorities may pursue certain objectives at the expense of others, creating areas of under-regulation. Another risk is that the regulatory system may move from being one of many groups of specialists, with intense expertise in their respective areas of regulatory authority, to a single group of generalists. The concern is that sector-specific knowledge and expertise may be lost, undermining the gains in efficiency of having a single regulator oversee all sectors of the market. A third risk is that the lack of clear lines of responsibility within the single regulator model could lead to confusion, especially if the single regulator is attempting to integrate previously independent, and single-minded, regulatory agencies. It is unclear whether a single regulator that is assuming the responsibilities of several former regulatory agencies will be able to organize itself in a more effective manner to eliminate the turf battles and blind spots associated with the older regulatory system.

The twin peaks model also attempts to achieve many of the same benefits as the single regulator model—eliminating regulatory redundancy, reducing overhead, and providing clearer lines of responsibility and authority for regulators.[31] The twin peaks model, however, rejects the premise of the single regulator model—that all regulatory authority can be combined in one body. Instead, the twin peaks model is based on the belief there are differences between the objectives of prudential regulation and those of business conduct regulation—a difference that requires prudential and business conduct regulators to invoke different strategies and approaches. In the case of prudential regulation, the regulator assumes a more cooperative relationship with the financial institution. Its role is to set standards and monitor the maintenance of those standards by the financial institution. To the extent a financial institution fails to meet certain standards or the regulator identifies a possible threat to the soundness of the financial institution, the role of the regulator is to work with the financial institution and find a solution. In

[30] ibid, 16. [31] Taylor, n 8 above, 1.

contrast, a business conduct regulator is in a more adversarial position relative to the financial institution. This regulator is effectively a representative of the customers and investors, using rulemaking powers to impose new requirements on financial institutions, and enforcement powers to discipline and punish financial institutions for business conduct violations.

A concern with giving a single regulator responsibility for both prudential and business conduct regulation is that such a regulator would not apply the appropriate regulatory approach to each task. A single regulator may favour and apply the stronger enforcement approach, suitable more for business conduct regulation than prudential regulation. This stricter regulation establishes an undesirable adversarial relationship in which financial institutions could seek to avoid raising problems with the regulator for fear of prosecution. Such a result, where financial institutions refuse to open themselves up to the regulator, would undermine that regulator's ability to monitor and identify sources of risk to safety and soundness. Alternatively, the regulator could apply the more cooperative approach of prudential regulation to business conduct regulation to the detriment of unwitting customers and investors. The twin peaks model attempts to resolve this conflict by keeping separate prudential and business conduct regulation.

One of the weaknesses of the twin peaks model is the need for coordination between the two agencies. The potential for conflict is greatest when the two agencies representing the respective peaks regulate the same financial firm (consider, for example, the regulation of insurance companies which must satisfy prudential regulatory standards as well as business conduct rules in their dealings with policyholders). As large financial firms continue to expand their activities across the banking, securities, and insurance lines, one would expect the application of both prudential and business conduct regulation to be the norm, and the regulatory actions of one will affect the other.

One can easily imagine how aggressive enforcement of such entities by the business conduct regulator could undermine the safety and soundness of the firm, requiring a response from the prudential regulator. Therefore, some mechanism of coordination must accompany the twin peaks model to resolve the conflict that may arise between the two regulatory halves. It is tempting to assign responsibility for resolving all interagency conflict to elected government officials, but such an approach threatens to politicize the regulatory process.

A third alternative to the single regulator and twin peaks models is the lead regulator model. The model maintains separate regulatory agencies with their lines of authority remaining unchanged. The one change is that a single agency is designated the 'lead regulator' and assumes responsibility for coordinating the regulatory actions of the other agencies. This model is appealing because it builds upon the regulatory experience and expertise of activity-based regulatory systems, while giving the impression that there will be at least one regulator looking at the overall picture.

The lead regulator model, however, raises a number of concerns. First and foremost, which agency should be made the lead regulator? Selecting one agency as the lead assumes that this agency has the expertise and competency to evaluate not only its own regulatory interests but also the interests of the other agencies that are now reporting to it. The model also assumes that the lead agency will not be inherently predisposed to prioritize its regulatory interests above all others. If these assumptions are wrong, then the lead regulator model will likely produce an even greater risk of regulatory failure, as the lead regulator has a greater opportunity to ignore the concerns of its subordinate agencies.

The second concern is that, even if a suitable lead agency is identified, this agency would be unable to manage the other agencies. Just as in the case of the twin peaks model, the lead regulator model will require some mechanism of coordination to resolve conflict, promote the sharing of information between agencies, and enable the lead regulator to direct action from the other agencies as necessary. Such a system would be quite complex.

The exact organization of the regulatory system is less important than the means by which regulatory agencies and internal regulatory divisions are made to work together and act in a coordinated fashion. With respect to each structure, coordination is vital, whether that coordination takes place internally (as in the case of the single regulator model) or externally (as in the case of the twin peaks and lead regulator models).

III. The Structure of the US Financial Regulatory System

1. The regulatory system prior to the Dodd–Frank Act

In the US, multiple federal agencies are involved in financial regulation, with each devoted to regulating specific sectors of the financial system—depository institutions (eg, banks, thrifts, and credit unions), futures, and securities. State agencies often provide additional regulation of the same sectors as well as primary regulation of the insurance sector.

Prior to the Dodd–Frank Act, five different federal agencies shared primary authority for the regulation of US depository institutions. These agencies are the Office of the Comptroller of Currency (OCC), the Federal Reserve, the Federal Deposit Insurance Corporation (FDIC), the Office of Thrift Supervision (OTS), and the National Credit Union Administration (NCUA). Depending on its particular organizational structure, a single depository institution may be eligible for regulation by up to three of these federal agencies as well as a state regulator.

The OCC is an independent office within the US Treasury Department whose function is to charter, regulate, and examine all national banks. The OCC performs regular reviews of national banks to ensure compliance with federal statutes and regulations. If the OCC finds a deficiency, it has broad enforcement powers to levy sanctions on violators.

All national banks chartered by the OCC are also required to be members of the Federal Reserve and are subject to Federal Reserve oversight. In addition, the Federal Reserve regulates state banks that have chosen not to seek an OCC charter but wish to access the Federal Reserve's payment and liquidity facilities. For those state-chartered banks that do elect membership, the Federal Reserve becomes the primary regulator at the federal level. The Federal Reserve is also the national regulatory authority that oversees bank holding companies.

The FDIC administers the Federal Deposit Insurance System. Membership in the FDIC is mandatory for virtually all depository institutions in the US. Banks that are members of the Federal Reserve must also insure themselves through the FDIC. Even those banks which are not affiliated with the Federal Reserve (for example, state banks without an OCC charter and access to the Federal Reserve's payment and liquidity facilities) are often bound to insure themselves through the FDIC. Federal law requires any depository institution that accepts retail deposits, other than credit unions, to carry federal deposit insurance. All depository institutions that the FDIC insures are subject to its regulations. For state-chartered banks that have not joined the Federal Reserve, the FDIC becomes their primary federal regulator.

The OTS was responsible for overseeing federally chartered thrifts. Thrifts, commonly known as savings and loan associations or building and loan associations, are depository institutions focused primarily on providing residential mortgage loans. The OTS chartered all federal thrifts and oversees all aspects of thrift operations using its powers to issue rules and legal interpretations. The Dodd–Frank Act later abolished the OTS, transferring the OTS's former responsibilities to the Federal Reserve, the OCC, and the FDIC. The Federal Reserve acquired regulatory and rulemaking authority over savings and loan holding companies, the OCC acquired supervisory and rulemaking authority over federal savings associations, and the FDIC acquired supervisory and rulemaking authority over state-chartered savings associations.

The NCUA charters and supervises all federal credit unions. It also provides depository insurance for federal credit unions and most state-chartered credit unions through the National Credit Union Share Insurance Fund.

The Federal Financial Institutions Examination Council (FFIEC), which Congress established in 1979, is an interagency coordinating committee seeking to harmonize regulatory policy between the existing depository institution regulators. The

FFIEC includes the OCC, the Federal Reserve, the FDIC, the Consumer Financial Protection Bureau, the NCUA, and the State Liaison Committee, which consists of the Conference of State Bank Supervisors, the American Council of State Savings Supervisors, and the National Association of State Credit Union Supervisors. It is important to note that the FFIEC has no regulatory authority of its own. It can only make recommendations and must rely on its members to effect such recommendations in their respective regulatory areas.

Regulation of futures is split between the Commodity Futures Trading Commission (CFTC), individual derivative and commodity exchanges, and the National Futures Association, which is an SRO. The CFTC was an early adopter of mutual recognition principles, permitting foreign futures exchanges to have direct access to US customers in the US.[32]

The SEC, on the other hand, is the primary regulator of the national securities markets and enforcer of the federal securities laws. Its three-part mission is to: (i) protect investors; (ii) maintain the integrity and stability of securities markets; and (iii) promote efficiency in capital formation. While the SEC engages in a significant amount of rulemaking, it also draws on the work of SROs, which set rules and policies for broker-dealers and trading markets. The SEC and the CFTC share jurisdiction over the regulation of security futures products and swaps.

Unlike the rest of the US financial services industry, state authorities primarily regulate the insurance industry. State insurance regulation falls into two broad categories of regulation. The first area of regulation—solvency or financial regulation—focuses on preventing insurer insolvencies and, in the case of insolvency, mitigating consumer losses. The second area of regulation—consumer protection and market regulation—focuses on unfair marketing practices, including deceptive advertising, unfair policy terms, and unfair treatment of policyholders.

After the October 1987 stock market correction, the President of the US created the President's Working Group on Financial Markets (PWG).[33] The purpose of the PWG was to identify systemic problems in the US financial system and coordinate regulatory responses. The US Treasury Secretary led the PWG comprised of the chairs of the Federal Reserve, the CFTC, and the SEC. The PWG had no independent authority, and its members had only the ability to take action within their respective mandates. As a result, the PWG acted primarily as a forum for discussion of financial policy issues.

[32] See Markham, JW, 'Super Regulator: A Comparative Analysis of Securities and Derivatives Regulation in the United States, the United Kingdom, and Japan' (2003) 28 *Brooklyn Journal of International Law* 319, 341–6 (describing the differences in regulatory philosophies of the SEC and the CFTC).

[33] Executive Order No 12, 631, 53 Fed. Reg. 9421 (18 March 1988).

2. Pre-Dodd–Frank Act calls for regulatory reform

In June 2007, US Treasury Secretary Henry Paulson announced that the US Treasury Department would begin work on a plan to restructure the US financial regulatory system.[34] By the time of Secretary Paulson's announcement, a number of blue ribbon committees and independent studies had voiced concerns that the US regulatory system had become unwieldy, expensive, and inefficient, undermining the competitiveness of US financial markets.[35] These parties had four concerns with the US regulatory system.

First, the parties argued that the US regulatory system was too complex. Too many regulatory agencies at the federal and state levels were regulating the same financial institutions. Securities issuers and financial services firms complained about the high cost of complying with federal and state rules and regulations. An effect of these high costs was that companies, especially those that are small- and medium-sized, had found it difficult to access the capital markets, and financial services firms have had to devote more resources to compliance and litigation departments or exit from certain markets. The lack of coordination between federal and state agencies sometimes has resulted in individual state regulators taking the lead on certain issues which commentators believed could be better handled at the national level or has resulted in substantial regulatory inconsistencies between states.

Second, the lack of coordination between state and federal regulators created a challenging enforcement environment where settling an enforcement action at one level did not prevent other enforcement actions. Third, competition between regulatory agencies to exercise regulatory authority discouraged or hindered the development of new financial products and services. Fourth, the regulatory system did not efficiently regulate the new financial conglomerates with operations around

[34] See Press Release, US Department of the Treasury, Paulson Announces Next Steps to Bolster US Markets' Global Competitiveness (27 June 2007), available at <http://www.ustreas.gov/press/releases/hp476.htm>.

[35] In 2006 and 2007, the Committee on Capital Markets Regulation (supported by US Treasury Secretary Henry Paulson), McKinsey & Co (commissioned by New York City Mayor Michael Bloomberg and the senior US senator from New York, Charles Schumer), and the US Chamber of Commerce each independently prepared reports concluding that there is a decline in US capital markets' competitiveness and that such decline poses a serious threat to the US economy. See, eg, Communication on Capital Markets Regulation, Interim Report (2006) (hereinafter, Interim Report 2006), available at <http://www.capmktsreg.org/pdfs/11.30Committee_Interim_ReportREV2.pdf>; Committee on Capital Markets Regulation, The Competitive Position of the US Public Equity Market (2007) (hereinafter, Competitive Position), available at <http://www.capmktsreg.org/pdfs/The_Competitive_Position_of_the_US_Public_Equity_Market.pdf>; Bloomberg, MR and Schumer, CE, Sustaining New York's and the US' Global Financial Services Leadership (2007), available at <http://www.abanet.org/buslaw/committees/CL116000pub/materials/library/NY_Schumer-Bloomberg_REPORT_FINAL.pdf>; Communication on the Regulation of US Capital Markets in the 21st Century, Report and Recommendations (2007) (hereinafter, US Chamber Report), available at <http://www.uschamber.com/sites/default/files/reports/0703capmarkets_full.pdf>.

the world. The largest US financial institutions, like their foreign counterparts, had active banking, securities, and insurance operations, and faced specialized regulators in each area.

In reaction to these concerns, the US Treasury Department began work on a plan to restructure the US financial regulatory system.

3. US Treasury Blueprint for a Modernized Financial Regulatory Structure

On 31 March 2008, the US Treasury Department released its Blueprint for a Modernized Financial Regulatory Structure (hereinafter, the Blueprint). In the Blueprint, the US Treasury Department proposed consolidating the many federal regulatory agencies into three agencies organized in accordance with the objectives-based approach: one agency focusing on financial stability measures; a second agency focusing on prudential regulation; and a third agency focusing on business conduct regulation.

(a) *Financial stability regulation*

The Blueprint called for the Federal Reserve to take responsibility for financial stability. The Federal Reserve would carry out this role by implementing monetary policy, supplying liquidity to the market when necessary, and exercising formal supervisory powers. The Blueprint sought to broaden the Federal Reserve's authority significantly. It proposed that all financial institutions would be required to file reports with the Federal Reserve allowing the Federal Reserve to have a detailed picture of the entire financial market. In addition, other regulators would be required, upon request, to share any reports that they generate with the Federal Reserve, and the Federal Reserve would have the power to create new reporting requirements as it deemed necessary. Such power would make information sharing between regulators a legal requirement rather than leaving it up to negotiation between regulators on an ad hoc basis or through informal arrangements.

Finally, the Blueprint advocated authorizing the Federal Reserve to put forward any necessary corrective actions to maintain financial stability, including extending the availability of discount window lending to institutions other than depository institutions.

(b) *Prudential regulation*

The Blueprint further recommended creating a Prudential Financial Regulatory Agency (PFRA) to oversee all prudential regulation matters. According to the Blueprint, the PFRA would regulate any financial institution that benefited from any type of explicit government guarantee of their business operations. The PFRA would ensure, among other things, that an institution maintains adequate levels of capital, follows certain investment limits, and has in place suitable risk controls. Otherwise, the existence of the government guarantee without prudential regulation would create a moral hazard, likely causing an erosion in market discipline.

Implicit in the Blueprint's description of the types of institutions that would be subject to PFRA oversight was the notion that previously unregulated institutions may be subject to prudential regulation in the future as the US government expands the scope of its guarantees. Therefore, one of the questions not answered in the Blueprint was how investment banks and other non-bank financial institutions would be regulated. As the US government had been willing to provide limited guarantees in situations like the acquisition of Bear Stearns by JP Morgan Chase, it was reasonable to assume at the time that these financial firms—traditionally outside of the scope of banking supervision—would be subject to new prudential regulatory standards.

(c) *Business conduct regulation*

As a counterpart to the PFRA, the Blueprint proposed consolidating all business conduct regulation under a new Conduct of Business Regulatory Agency (CBRA). The CBRA would monitor the business conduct of all financial institutions, set disclosure and business practice standards, and charter and license financial institutions. A major focus of the CBRA's activities would be on setting appropriate standards for financial institutions entering the market and selling their products and services. In this respect, the CBRA would assume many of the responsibilities currently held by the several depository regulators, state insurance regulators, the SEC, the CFTC, and the Federal Trade Commission.

Recognizing that full implementation of the Blueprint would take several years and require public debate at both the federal and state levels, the US Treasury Department also recommended a series of short-term and intermediate-term actions designed to streamline structural reforms and to address immediate regulatory concerns raised by the current credit crisis. Among the US Treasury Department's recommendations was a proposal to create a national insurance regulator. At present, insurance companies are regulated only at the state level. In presenting the Blueprint, the US Treasury Department expressed the view that there was little coordination of regulatory standards across states and insurance companies found it difficult and costly to provide insurance services in multiple states, hindering the growth of national insurance companies.

In prior years, the need to overcome the myriad of state insurance rules and regulations had become the subject of tension with the EU. The EU expressed dissatisfaction with how several US states impose discriminatory collateral requirements on foreign insurance companies attempting to offer insurance and reinsurance service in the US.[36] In response, the European Commission raised the possibility with the US Treasury Department that US insurance companies be made subject to additional requirements when they conduct business in the EU.[37] This action placed great pressure on the federal government to establish a role in the regulation of insurance companies.

The Blueprint recommended the creation of an 'optional federal charter' for insurance companies. This federal insurance charter programme, which would be administered by a newly created Office of National Insurance based in the US Treasury Department, would allow for the establishment of uniform national standards for licensing and operation of insurance companies. Insurers that obtain a federal insurance charter no longer would be subject to state regulation. Likewise, foreign insurers could apply for a federal charter, offer insurance products in multiple regions of the US, and avoid having to satisfy local state requirements.

The Blueprint anticipated, however, that implementation of a national system for regulating insurance would likely meet strong resistance at the state level. As a compromise, the Blueprint proposed establishing an Office of Insurance Oversight (OIO) within the US Treasury Department with statutory authority to address international regulatory issues and to advise the US Treasury Department on policy issues related to the insurance industry. The OIO also would have the power to ensure that state insurance regulators uniformly implement the international policy goals set by the OIO. Although chartering responsibility would remain largely with the states, the federal government would be able to step in and force state regulators to modify their regulatory requirements as necessary to satisfy federal concerns about the accessibility of the US insurance market to foreign and domestic insurance providers alike.

[36] See, eg, McCreevy, C, European Commissioner for Internal Market and Services, speech to the Insurance Institute of London: The European Commission's Policy Priorities for the Insurance Sector (7 February 2008), available at <http://europa.eu/rapid/pressReleasesAction.do?reference=SPEECH/08/69&format=HTML&aged=0&language=EN>. On collateral requirement McCreevy stated that: 'This may incentivise the United States to reform its rules on collateral. Speaking here at Lloyd's of London, I want to reiterate my view that the collateral requirement, as imposed in the US, is not justified. We have been urging the US to reform these rules but progress has been slow. If real progress is not made soon, this could have a negative impact on US insurers and reinsurers as they will only receive the full benefits under the new EU Solvency II Directive if they are subject to an equivalent solvency regime.'

[37] See, eg, ibid; Sobel, M, US Treasury Deputy Assistant Secretary, Remarks at a Conference of the US Chamber of Commerce: US–EU Regulatory Cooperation, available at <http://www.iasplus.com/usa/0804sobel.pdf>. Sobel noted: 'On Solvency II, Europe is moving to adopt a new regime, perhaps in 2012, which would provide for consolidated supervision of insurance firms at the financial holding company level and a risk-based approach to capital requirements. Solvency II also provides that foreign firms operating in the EU must be supervised on an "equivalent" basis by their home supervisor or face unspecified measures. Large US insurance firms operating in Europe fear the EU will find the US insurance supervisory regime not equivalent and that they in turn will face uncertainties and higher costs in continuing their European operations. This is a matter requiring intensive discussion.'

Finally, expressing the view that the distinction between the securities and futures industries was in the process of disappearing quickly, the Blueprint called for the consolidation of the SEC and the CFTC into a single agency. Pursuant to this goal, the Blueprint anticipated the need to take several steps to harmonize the regulation of securities and futures trading. First, the Blueprint recommended the adoption by the SEC of overarching regulatory principles focused on investor protection, market integrity, and the reduction of systemic risk to unify the regulatory philosophy of the new agency. These principles would be based upon the core principles that serve as the basis of the CFTC's principles-based regulatory approach.[38]

Next, the Blueprint recommended allowing SROs to self-certify their own rules. This proposal would have given greater autonomy to SROs, allowing them to respond quicker to market developments and regulatory actions taken by foreign regulators.

Finally, the proposal called for the creation of a joint CFTC–SEC task force to determine the optimal method for the harmonization of the trading regulations of the securities and futures markets. The Blueprint envisioned eventually merging the SEC and the CFTC into the CBRA.

Public response in the US to the Treasury Blueprint was mixed. State regulators criticized those Blueprint proposals that diminished the role of state authorities in the financial system.[39] Banking associations criticized the Blueprint's plan to consolidate all banking regulation in the hands of a single prudential regulator.[40] They felt that such a regulator would be insensitive to the interests of smaller and more specialized depository institutions, such as thrifts and community banks. Others criticized the Blueprint's unwillingness to recommend tighter supervision of investment banks and hedge funds.

Given such opposition and competing legislative priorities, the outgoing Bush administration never was able to begin implementing the Blueprint. But in light of the events of September 2008, including the failure of AIG, Washington Mutual, Wachovia, and Lehman Brothers, and calls for a $700 billion government bailout fund to purchase troubled assets from US financial institutions, restructuring the US financial regulatory system remained a priority for the new Obama Administration.[41]

[38] The CFTC's core principles are listed in legislation and rules. See 7 USC § 7; 17 C.F.R. Parts 37, 38.

[39] See Labatan, S, 'Doubts Greet Treasury Plan on Regulation' *New York Times*, 1 April 2008, A1.

[40] See, for example, Birnbaum, JH, 'Main Street Regulators Mobilize against Paulson's Overhaul Plan' *Washington Post*, 11 April 2008.

[41] Congress ultimately passed the Emergency Economic Stabilization Act of 2008 in October 2008, authorizing the US Secretary of the Treasury to spend up to $700 billion to purchase distressed assets from, and provide capital support to, financial institutions. See Pub. L. No. 110-343, 122 Stat. 3765.

4. Financial regulatory reform White Paper and the Dodd–Frank Act

In June 2009, within the first six months of President Obama's Administration, the US Treasury Department introduced a White Paper on financial regulatory reform, entitled 'A New Foundation'. Drafted at a time when the US Treasury Department was still managing the effects of the global financial crisis, the White Paper, in contrast to the Blueprint, emphasized financial stability and systemic risk oversight and the supervision of financial conglomerates and systemically important financial institutions. In addition, the White Paper sought to expand the responsibility of existing agencies, including proposing that hedge funds be required to register with the SEC, a new regulatory framework for over-the-counter (OTC) derivatives, stronger capital requirements, and a resolution regime for financial holding companies. The White Paper also made explicit reference to raising international regulatory standards and improving international cooperation, particularly in connection with the newly constituted Financial Stability Board.

In terms of structural reform, the White Paper proposed five significant changes with several of these changes (but not all) ultimately taking effect with the passage of the Dodd–Frank Act the following year. First, the White Paper called for replacing the PWG with a new Financial Stability Oversight Council (FSOC). The FSOC would serve as an interagency coordinating body to facilitate information sharing between regulatory agencies, identify emerging risks, advise the Federal Reserve on the identification of systemically important financial firms, and provide a forum for resolving jurisdictional disputes among regulators. While the PWG was an ad hoc gathering of the US Treasury Secretary and Chairs of the Federal Reserve, the CFTC, and the SEC, the FSOC would be a formal entity. Its membership would include the heads of all of the federal financial regulators (as opposed to the regulatory agencies). The FSOC also would have a separate existence from the regulators with its own permanent, full-time staff, power to collect information from any financial firm, and the ability to refer emerging risks to regulators.

The Dodd–Frank Act did create the FSOC, much along the lines first laid out in the White Paper. A few differences include expanding the membership of the FSOC further to include a state insurance commissioner, a state banking supervisor, and a state securities commissioner, as well as an independent insurance expert appointed by the President. To support the FSOC's mission to identify emerging risks and identify systemically important firms, the Dodd–Frank Act also created the Office of Financial Research (OFR) to support the FSOC through data collection and research.

Second, the White Paper expanded the mandate of the Federal Reserve to supervise and regulate any financial firm—not only banks—deemed to be systemically important. The White Paper noted that the systemic importance of a firm is a combination of size, leverage, and interconnectedness. This expansion of the Federal Reserve's responsibilities, in combination with the identification and monitoring role of the FSOC, promoted the Federal Reserve to be the primary financial stability regulator in the US. The Dodd–Frank Act effected the White Paper's proposal.

Third, the White Paper proposed consolidating the prudential regulation of banks into the hands of a new single federal agency: the National Bank Supervisor. This agency would conduct prudential supervision and regulation of all federally chartered depository institutions and federal branches and agencies of foreign banks. Consequently, the National Bank Supervisor would assume the powers and responsibilities of the OCC, the FDIC, and the OTS, and some of the responsibilities of the Federal Reserve. In addition, the formation of the National Bank Supervisors would be accompanied by the elimination of the federal thrift charter.

This proposal did not survive in the Dodd–Frank Act. The Act retained the structure of multiple prudential regulators that existed prior to 2010. The one change made by the Dodd–Frank Act was to close the OTS and divide up the OTC's responsibilities among the Federal Reserve (which now regulates thrift holding companies and subsidiaries of thrift holding companies), the OCC (which regulates federal thrifts), and the FDIC (which regulates state thrifts).

Fourth, the White Paper proposed the creation of the Office of National Insurance (ONI). The concept of the ONI broadly tracked the OIO proposed by the Blueprint. The ONI would be housed within the US Treasury Department and be responsible for gathering information, developing expertise, negotiating international agreements, and coordinating policy in the insurance sector. The White Paper did not go as far as the Blueprint in calling for the eventual creation of a body (which the Blueprint also called the ONI) to oversee a federal insurance charter. The Dodd–Frank Act did establish the ONI along the same lines proposed in the White Paper.

Finally, the White Paper called for the creation of a new Consumer Financial Protection Agency. The mission of this new agency would be to protect consumers of credit, savings, payment, and other consumer financial products. The agency would have rulemaking, supervisory, and enforcement authority. The creation of such a separate agency could be viewed to be tacit support for the logic behind twin peaks. The White Paper suggested that the presence of several prudential regulators did not provide adequate regulatory attention to consumer protection issues. In line with this proposal, the Dodd–Frank Act established the Consumer Financial Protection Bureau (CFPB).

IV. Conclusion

Overall, structural reform of the US financial regulatory system, as set forth by the Dodd–Frank Act, included some significant additions, but also retained many of the characteristics of the pre-2010 US financial regulatory system. On the one hand, the Dodd–Frank Act clarified how federal regulators would cooperate and exchange information to monitor systemic risk and oversee systemically important firms. To this end, the Federal Reserve Board received new powers, and the Dodd–Frank Act created the FSOC and the OFR. In addition, the formation of the CFPB strengthened regulatory oversight of consumer protection issues. And the Dodd–Frank Act took a small step in giving the federal government a role in insurance regulation.

However, the reforms instituted by the Dodd–Frank Act did not significantly reduce the number of federal agencies, and it retained the activity-based character of the US financial regulatory system. In contrast, the Blueprint's proposal of three large financial regulatory agencies, one focused on financial stability, another on prudential regulation, and a third on business conduct, would have represented a more radical restructuring of the US financial regulatory system, bringing the US closer in line with the structural reforms adopted in Europe, Australia, and Canada.

Bibliography

Aspinwall, R, 'Conflicting Objectives of Financial Regulation' in *Reforming Money and Finance* (2nd edn, 1997) 179.

Butler, N and Macey, J, 'The Myth of Competition in the Dual Banking System' (1988) 73 *Cornell Law Review* 677, 714–15.

Conservative Party, From Crisis to Confidence: Plan for Sound Banking (July 2009), available at <http://www.conservatives.com/News/News_stories/2009/07/~/media/Files/Downloadable%20Files/PlanforSoundBanking.ashx>.

Cox, J, 'Regulatory Duopoly in the US Securities Market' (1999) 99 *Columbia Law Review* 1200, 1229–37.

Davies, H and Green, D, *Global Financial Regulation* (2008).

De Larosière Group, Report of the High-level Group on Financial Supervision in the EU (2009).

Dodd–Frank Wall Street Reform and Consumer Protection Act (2010), Pub. L. No 111–203, 124 Stat. 1376.

Dombalagian, O, 'Demythologizing the Stock Exchange: Reconciling Self-Regulation and the National Market System' (2005) 39 *University Of Richmond Law Review* 1069, 1078–89.

Ferguson Jr, R, 'Should Financial Stability Be an Explicit Central Bank Objective' in Ugolini, PC et al. (eds), *Challenges to Central Banking from Globalized Financial System* (2003) 208.
Financial Services Authority, The Turner Review: A Regulatory Response to the Global Financial Crisis (2009).
Goodhart, C and Schoenmaker, D, 'Should the Functions of Monetary Policy and Banking Supervision Be Separated?' (1995) 47 *Oxford Economics Papers* 539, 548–9.
HM Treasury, Reforming Financial Markets (2009), Cm. 7667.
Jackson, H and Pan, E, 'Regulatory Competition in International Securities Markets: Evidence from Europe in 1999—Part I' (2001) 56 *Business Lawyer* 653, 662.
Markham, J, 'Super Regulator: A Comparative Analysis of Securities and Derivatives Regulation in the United States, the United Kingdom, and Japan' (2003) 28 *Brooklyn Journal of International Law* 319, 341–6.
Pan, E, 'Harmonization of US–EU Securities Regulation: The Case for a Single European Securities Regulator' (2003) 34 *Law & Policy of International Business* 499, 534–5.
Pan, E, 'Understanding Financial Regulation' (2012) *Utah Law Review* 1897.
Peters, A, 'Independent Agencies: Government Scourge or Salvation?' (1988) 1988 *Duke Law Journal* 286, 286–8.
Seligman, S, 'Cautious Evolution or Perennial Irresolution: Stock Market Self-Regulation during the First Seventy Years of the Securities Exchange Commission' (2004) 59 *Business Lawyer* 1347, 1361.
Taylor, M, Twin Peaks: A Regulatory Structure for the New Century (1995), Centre for the Study of Financial Innovation Working Paper.
US Department of the Treasury, Blueprint for a Modernized Financial Regulatory Structure (2008).
US Department of the Treasury, Financial Regulatory Reform: A New Foundation: Rebuilding Financial Supervision and Regulation (2009).

PART III

DELIVERING OUTCOMES AND REGULATORY TECHNIQUES

CHAPTER 8

REGULATORY STYLES AND SUPERVISORY STRATEGIES

JULIA BLACK

I. Introduction

Regulatory regimes move at very different paces, with changes usually prompted by varying combinations of crises, political interests, and ideologies. In the last 30 years, for example, the UK has had four different regimes for regulating financial institutions; each institutional structure radically different from the last. Financial markets have changed almost beyond recognition in that same period. Debates on regulatory strategies have also moved on. In the 1980s, academic and political debate on financial regulation was conducted almost entirely through the lens of economic liberalism: of freeing markets from the 'dead hand of the state' and framed in the polarizing, and ultimately misleading, dichotomies of 'regulation versus deregulation' or 'self-regulation versus government regulation'.

There is now a far more sophisticated debate in the academic and policy literature on the relationship between states and markets, on the range of different regulatory strategies that can be adopted and on how firms respond to regulation.[1] Various terms have become part of the vernacular of regulators to describe different ways of designing and implementing regulatory regimes, including principles-based regulation (PBR), management-based regulation, outcome-focused regulation, risk-based regulation, judgement-based regulation, and 'credible deterrence'. However, these are terms of art which are understood by few outside regulatory circles, and usually only by a handful within them.

This Chapter outlines the developments of some of the key regulatory styles and supervisory strategies which have characterized financial regulation in the UK and, to varying degrees, elsewhere over the last 20–30 years. These are: risk-based regulation, management-based regulation, and principles-based, outcomes focused and judgement-based regulation. Note that throughout, regulation and supervision are used interchangeably to refer to processes of managing risks or behaviour in accordance with a set of norms using a range of strategies including monitoring, suasion, and the imposition of sanctions, and which may be performed by state or non-state bodies alone or in combination. The Chapter traces the development of these approaches in UK financial regulation, then turns to examine their use by regulators in other countries, notably Australia, Canada, Ireland, and New Zealand, and the recent emergence of these approaches at the global level.

[1] For reviews, see Baldwin, R, Cave, M, and Lodge, M (eds), *Oxford Handbook on Regulation* (2012); Baldwin, R, Lodge, M, and Cave, M, *Understanding Regulation* (2012).

II. Tracing the Shifts in Regulatory Approaches in the UK—From the 'Big Bang' to the 'Big Collapse' and its Aftermath

1. 1986–1998: The first experiment—self-regulation with a statutory mandate

In 1984, the UK government, pressed by a number of factors, decided to outlaw fixed commission rates of dealers on the London Stock Exchange, to allow stock brokers and dealers to merge, and to permit their purchase by foreign entities. Known as the 'Big Bang', the move revolutionized the UK financial services industry, changing the character of the City from a 'club' to a competitive, and competed for, market place.[2] The move also created a policy window for the introduction of reforms which had been circulating in a narrow circle of officials and which ultimately were embodied in the Financial Services Act 1986 (FS Act).[3] The Act created a novel institutional structure: self-regulation with a statutory mandate. It provided powers to the executive to confer regulatory powers on a private company (the Securities and Investments Board (SIB)), and also gave the SIB powers to recognize self-regulatory organizations (SROs) as competent to authorize and regulate firms to conduct investment business.[4]

While the institutional architecture for regulation introduced by the FS Act changed twice, radically, over the next 17 years, a number of the core principles and techniques that it introduced for regulating the conduct of investment business are still reflected in UK rules, and indeed have been subsequently reflected in EU requirements through processes of policy diffusion. These include the introduction of customer categorizations and the grading of duties owed to investors dependent on their expertise; duties of suitability imposed on investment advisers when selling to retail investors; the requirement for 'key features' documents for some retail products; the strategies introduced for managing conflicts of interest in multi-function firms, including rules on front running, order execution, and soft commissions; and requirements for best execution.[5]

[2] Moran, M, 'Theories of Regulation and Changes in Regulation: The Case of Financial Markets' (1986) 35 *Political Studies* 185; Plender, J, 'London's Big Bang in International Context' (1986–7) 63(1) *International Affairs* 39; Black, J, *Rules and Regulators* (1997).

[3] Black, n 2 above.

[4] The SIB in turn recognized five self-regulatory organizations. Over the next ten years that number reduced to three through a process of mergers (the Securities and Futures Authority, the Investment Managers Regulatory Organisation, and the Personal Investment Authority).

[5] For the history of each of these sets of provisions see Black, n 2 above. Each has been embodied in the EU Markets in Financial Instruments Directive (Directive 2004/39/EC [2004] OJ 145/1), shortly

The SIB–SRO regime proved a difficult institutional relationship to manage, however, as the FS Act gave few 'system management' powers to the SIB. The SIB pressed for an amendment to the Act to enable it to manage the system, at least to some degree.[6] The solution adopted was ingenious and heavily inspired by the Takeover Code existing at the time. The amendments to the FS Act made by the Companies Act 1992 transformed the way in which the SIB could manage the rules of the SROs in two key ways. It changed the criteria against which the SIB had to evaluate the SROs' rules from a test of whether they provided 'equivalent' investor protection to whether they provided 'adequate' protection, conferring on the SROs greater freedom to formulate their own rules. At the same time, it introduced powers for the SIB to formulate Principles and to designate particular rules which all the SROs would have to incorporate in their rule books, together with the Principles. The result was ten Principles and 40 'Core Rules'. The Principles had two purposes: to guide conduct of regulated firms, and to give shape and substance to the rulebooks of the SROs.[7]

The creation of the Principles and Core Rules marked a watershed in the regulatory style and supervisory strategies of UK financial regulation. For the first time in financial regulation (and possibly elsewhere), rule type was consciously used as an instrument of regulatory strategy.[8] It is important to emphasize that one of the main purposes of the reforms was to manage the relationship between SIB and the SROs. Nonetheless, while this role for the Principles fell away with the change in regulatory structure, the other two roles of principles (guiding conduct and shaping rule books) became important as PBR evolved over the next 20 years.

The SIB still lacked powers to direct the SROs, however, and the difficulties it encountered in managing the redress process for those mis-sold personal pensions illustrated the fundamental weaknesses of the institutional architecture.[9] Combined with the Bank of England's failure to prevent the collapse of Barings Bank in 1996 and the election of a new Labour government in 1997, the demise of the Conservative government's SIB–SRO regime was complete.

to be replaced by the 2014 Markets in Financial Instruments Directive II (Directive 2014/65/EU [2014] OJ L173/349) and Markets in Financial Instruments Regulation (Regulation (EU) No 600/2014 [2014] OJ L173/84). For discussion see Moloney, N, *How to Protect Investors. Lessons from the EC and the UK* (2010); Moloney, N, *EU Securities and Financial Markets Regulation* (3rd edn, 2014).

[6] Black, n 2 above.

[7] ibid; Black, J, '"Which Arrow?" Rule Type and Regulatory Policy' [1995] *Public Law* 94.

[8] Black, 'Which Arrow?' n 7 above.

[9] Black, J and Nobles, R, 'Personal Pension Misselling: The Causes and Lessons of Regulatory Failure' (1998) 61 *Modern Law Review* 789.

2. 1998–2013: The second experiment—integrated regulation

The creation of a single, integrated financial regulator for all financial institutions, including banks, was one of the new Labour government's first announcements on taking power. It was an innovative step at the time: a single, integrated regulator for investor protection, market conduct, and prudential regulation of the entire financial services sector had been tried only in Scandinavia, and there on a much smaller scale.[10] In 1998, the SIB changed its name to the Financial Services Authority (FSA), the SROs sub-contracted their regulatory functions to the FSA for it to perform, and powers for prudential supervision passed to the FSA from the Bank of England under the Banking Act 1997. In 2000, the FSA received its new powers to regulate investment business under the Financial Services and Markets Act (FSMA), taking over the responsibilities of nine previous regulatory bodies and taking on a further role (consumer education) which had previously been the responsibility of no one.

The FSA announced a bold new approach in a clear positioning paper issued in 2000, A New Regulator for a New Millennium (NRNM).[11] In that paper, the FSA set out its interpretation of its powers and objectives, articulating clearly the themes that were to dominate the rhetoric, at least, of its regulatory approach over the next decade, though its success in actually living up to its own aspirations was mixed. These three themes were: a risk-based operational system; a 'tool-based' regulatory approach, distinguishing between the use of tools to manage industry and consumer expectations and to regulate individual institutions; and the responsibilities of senior management. Added to those over the next few years was principles-based regulation. The next section focuses on three of these: risk-based regulation, responsibilities of senior management, and principles-based regulation.

(a) *Risk-based regulation*

The risk-based approach the FSA announced in 2000 has become the hallmark not just of UK regulation but also of regulation in a number of Organization for Economic Cooperation and Development (OECD) jurisdictions, in both financial regulation and other areas.[12] It is an integral element of the OECD Recommendation

[10] Briault, C, The Rationale for a Single National Financial Services Regulator (1999), FSA Occasional Paper Series 2.

[11] FSA, A New Regulator for a New Millennium (2000) (hereafter NRNM).

[12] Hutter, B, The Attractions of Risk-based Regulation: Accounting for the Emergence of Risk Ideas in Regulation (2005), CARR Discussion Paper; Black, J, 'The Emergence of Risk-based Regulation and the New Public Risk Management in the UK' (2005) *Public Law* 512; Rothstein, H, Huber, M, and Gaskell, G, 'A Theory of Risk Colonisation: The Spiralling Regulatory Logics of Societal and Institutional Risk' (2006) 35(1) *Economy and Society* 91; Hutter, B and Lloyd Bostock, S, 'Reforming Regulation of the Medical Profession: The Risks of Risk-based Approaches' (2008) 10(1) *Health, Risk and Society* 69; Gray, J, 'What Next for Risk-based Financial Regulation?' in MacNeil, I and O'Brien, J

on regulatory policies and practices, and mandatory for UK regulators.[13] It has also been adopted by some transnational, non-state regulators.[14]

In its NRNM paper, the FSA launched its intention to develop a risk-based operational system, stating that it would regulate in a way which was 'flexible and proactive', focusing on areas which posed the highest risk to its regulatory objectives, and aiming to anticipate problems rather than simply react to them. It also set out in detail its risk-assessment framework for supervising firms, based on the risks that they posed to the statutory objectives. Firms would be categorized initially on the impact that any failure would have based on their size and scale of business, and then within each category on the basis of the probability of particular risks occurring, based on assessments of their business, controls, and customer relationships. Resources would be directed to firms with high-impact activities.

Notably, the FSA also announced that it was adopting a 'non-zero' failure approach: financial firms could fail, but that would only be a failure on the part of the FSA to achieve its objectives (ie a regulatory failure) if certain criteria were met. These were:

> the extent to which the FSA has taken effective action to avoid risks to consumers by identifying and addressing issues pro-actively; whether, in the event of a collapse of, or lapse in conduct by, a firm, the FSA should have had prior knowledge of the circumstances leading to the event; the impact of the event on consumers and the rest of the industry; the FSA's response to the event, in terms of prompt and effective remedial action; and the overall adequacy of its regulatory arrangements.[15]

It is notable that, in 2013, the Financial Conduct Authority set out its definition of what would constitute a regulatory failure using remarkably similar criteria.[16]

The FSA was not the only regulator experimenting with risk-based regulation in 2000, but it was one of the earliest, although in developing its regime it paid almost no attention to what others were doing either in the UK or elsewhere.[17] Although systematic approaches to risk-based regulation are relatively new, it should be emphasized that prioritization is not: regulators, particularly those with a significant inspection/supervisory mandate, make decisions every day as to how to prioritize their attention and resources, regardless of whether the regulator has formally

(eds), *The Future of Financial Regulation* (2010); Black, J, 'Risk Based Regulation: Choices, Practices and Lessons Learnt', in *Risk and Regulatory Policy: Improving the Governance of Risk* (2010); Black, J and Baldwin, R, 'Really Responsive Risk Based Regulation' (2010) 32(2) *Law and Policy* 181.

[13] OECD, Recommendation on Regulatory Policy (2013); Regulators Compliance Code, Statutory Code of Practice for Regulators (2007).

[14] Marine Stewardship Council, Risk Based Framework for Certification (2009).

[15] NRNM, Appendix 3.

[16] FCA, How the Financial Conduct Authority will report on and investigate regulatory failure (2013).

[17] Black (2005), n 12 above; Black, J, 'The Development of Risk Based Regulation in Financial Services: Just "Modelling Through"?' in Black, J, Lodge, M, and Thatcher, M (eds), *Regulatory Innovation: A Comparative Analysis* (2005).

adopted a 'risk-based' approach. The differences in risk-based systems are that these decisions move 'in' and 'up' the organization from inspectors or supervisors on the front line to senior-management teams and boards; that they are systematic rather than idiosyncratic and ad hoc; and that they are explicit and transparent to all those within the organization and to the firms that they regulate, rather than tacit and buried in the 'nous' of experienced supervisors. So, while prioritization is inevitable, risk-based frameworks can be useful for a regulator in providing a clear, well-articulated set of priorities which the regulator can use to develop regulatory strategy and manage its resources. However, there is an important caveat, which is that in many cases, regulators are not regulating risk, but managing uncertainty. 'Risk-based regulation' is in these contexts a series of 'best guesses' as to what the future will hold and how resilient a firm's operations or the regulatory system as a whole will prove to be should those risks crystallize.

Risk-based regulation is also an inherently complex and potentially self-contradictory strategy. Critically, risk-based regulation entails the management of risk, resources, and reputation.[18] Managing each of these elements is complex in itself. Managing them all successfully simultaneously can be impossible, as they can each pull in different directions. In particular, risk-based means *not* focusing on certain objectives, firms, or activities in preference to those considered higher risk. Furthermore, risks are often contested, leaving resource-allocation decisions open to challenge on the basis of differences in perceptions of risk, and differences in social or political priorities. Also, by their nature, risks can crystallize at unexpected moments—leaving past resource decisions open to challenge on the basis of hindsight. As a result, risk-based regulation is always prey to both social and political differences in prioritization and to events, as the FSA was to discover.

The FSA's risk-based operating system, ARROW, was developed over the course of 2000–05, and revised again in 2006 as ARROW II. As with many risk-based systems, it took some time to bed down within the organization. Risk-based regulation requires a significant cultural shift within organizations, and it is as susceptible to implementation failures as any other strategy. In the case of Northern Rock, the internal audit report found that ARROW II ran parallel to, not integrated with, the supervisory strategy of 'close and continuous' supervision by the bank's 'relationship managers'.[19] ARROW II was simply not followed by the supervisors responsible for the bank, but no one outside of the immediate circle of officials responsible for Northern Rock was aware of this deviation. The power of the relationship manager was too great; that of the internal risk division was too weak, and

[18] Black and Baldwin, n 12 above; Rothstein, H, Irving, P, Walden, T, and Yearsley, R, 'The Risks of Risk-based Regulation: Insights from the Environmental Policy Domain' (2006) 32(8) *Environment International* 1056; Hutter and Lloyd Bostock, n 12 above.

[19] FSA, The Supervision of Northern Rock: A Lessons Learned Review (2008).

senior management were insufficiently engaged to provide an adequate check on how supervisors were performing.[20]

It is the FSA's supervision of RBS which highlights the inherent weaknesses of risk-based regulation most clearly, however. The experience of the FSA shows that although risk-based supervision is meant to focus attention on things that might happen in the future, in practice, regulators have to spend most of their time dealing with things that have happened in the past or are happening right now. Throughout the period from 2000–08, the FSA placed significantly more attention on the regulation of the retail markets than on supervision of the banking and shadow banking system, its attention occupied mainly by the fallout from the failure of an insurance company (Equitable Life), the Treating Customers Fairly initiative, the Retail Distribution Review (both discussed below), and consumer education.[21] The Board review noted, 'This reflected the wide spread of the FSA's responsibilities which … increased the danger that prudential issues would be accorded low priority in periods when economic and financial stability conditions appeared to be benign.'[22]

In addition, the integrated approach which the FSA took to supervision (with one team supervising an institution across all its activities and the whole of the FSA's remit) meant that a significant amount of time was spent on conduct issues rather than prudential issues, as the former were considered more pressing.[23] Partly as a result, supervisors did not gain skills which enabled them to focus on the prudential risks of capital, asset quality, balance sheet composition, and liquidity, [24] reinforcing the bias in their attention to conduct issues.

The low priority given to prudential issues was in accordance with the widespread view at the time that financial innovation had resulted in stabilizing markets, and that the capital rules introduced under the Basel II regime were adequate and appropriate to ensure financial stability. Moreover, the FSA Board was not required to engage with the substantive issues of bank capital adequacy, as the UK's role in this regard was simply to transpose provisions written at the international and EU level.[25] In contrast, significant time was spent by the Board and the FSA on the issue of capital requirements for insurance companies in the wake of the problems arising from the regime the FSA inherited in 2000 and which led in part to the failure of Equitable Life.[26] It is interesting to speculate whether the FSA's approach to the prudential regulation of banks would have been different if the FSA, rather than the Bank of England, had had to deal with the failure of Barings and if there had been such an empty policy space in the area of the prudential regulation of banks as there was for insurance companies at the time.

[20] FSA, The Failure of the Royal Bank of Scotland: Financial Services Authority Board Report (2011) (hereafter, RBS report).

[21] FSA, The Turner Review: A Regulatory Response to the Global Banking Crisis (2009).

[22] RBS report, n 20 above, 263. [23] ibid. [24] ibid, 289. [25] ibid, 263.

[26] ibid, 266.

The FSA also argued strongly that it would not have had the political support to impose tougher regulation on banks in the boom years preceding the crisis,[27] even if they had wanted to. They are probably right. The political economy of risk-based regulation is as fascinating as it is complex. Regulators need a political licence to operate, irrespective of their formal legal powers, and risk-based regulation therefore always operates in a political context. In this case, both the government and the opposition parties had maintained 'a sustained political emphasis' on the need for the FSA to be 'light touch' in its 'approach' in order to maintain London's competitive position.[28] Regulators may be legally and formally independent, but it is a robust regulator indeed that does not take note of such sustained political messages. However, in this instance they accorded with the FSA's view, that prudential regulation of banks was not a significant risk. Minutes of the meetings of the Court of the Bank of England released in January 2015 confirm that this view was shared by the Bank.

The financial crisis clearly disproved that view. In the wake of the report into its supervision of Northern Rock, the FSA introduced significant changes in its approach to the supervision of high-impact firms, particularly banks, changes which intensified after the financial crisis in 2008–09. In the wake of Northern Rock it launched the Supervisory Enhancement Programme (SEP), though this came too late to affect its supervision of Royal Bank of Scotland.[29] The SEP was further intensified in response to the findings of the Turner Review in March 2009,[30] and to international reviews of the role of supervisory failings in the crisis.[31] These reforms were implemented via the Core Prudential Programme launched in the first quarter of 2010.[32] As a result of these reforms, the FSA dramatically increased the scale of resources allocated to the supervision of high-impact firms. RBS moved from being supervised by a team of six people to a team of 23, for example.[33] Far greater focus was placed on firms' business strategy and on the core prudential issues of capital adequacy and liquidity, supported by increased specialist skills[34] and informed by far more detailed reporting of management information to supervisory teams. More detailed attention was given to asset quality, including the use of detailed stress-testing.[35] In addition, the ARROW process was updated to give enhanced guidance to supervisors on assessing a firm's culture to provide greater consistency in assessments, and a more systematic approach was introduced for assessing the quality of the FSA's relationship with firms and the risks that may flow from it.

[27] ibid, 261–2; FSA, Turner Review, n 21 above. [28] RBS report, n 20 above, 261–2.

[29] ibid, 286. [30] FSA, Turner Review, n 21 above.

[31] RBS report, n 20 above, 286. [32] ibid, 29, 286. [33] ibid, 286.

[34] In the FSA's Risk Specialists Division, specialist resource increased from 87 at the end of 2008 to 253 as at end-June 2011: ibid, 288.

[35] ibid, 30.

The FSA's risk-based model thus developed significantly over the 12 years of its operation, prompted by experience and more fundamentally by the massive external shock of the financial crisis. Although 'risk-based' regulation is meant to be forward looking, the FSA's experience demonstrated the challenges regulators face in allocating scarce resources of time, attention, and personnel to high-impact, low-probability risks, that by their nature did not appear to be likely to happen soon, when there were a multitude of things happening right now that demanded the regulator's attention. It also illustrated how risk-based assessments can become process driven and lost in detail. Further, it highlights the relevance of the wider epistemic and cognitive context in which risk assessments are made, and how political pressures can shape the priorities even of a legally independent regulator. But what the FSA's experience did not show was that risk-based approaches should be abandoned. Instead, they have been intensified and, hopefully, improved, as discussed further below. For as noted at the outset, risk-based regulation is a fact of regulatory life—the only choice a regulator has is how to prioritize its attention and resources, not whether it should prioritise them at all.

(b) *Management-based regulation and the responsibilities of senior management*

The second element which defined the FSA's approach from the outset, referenced in the *New Regulator* document but set out in a separate consultation paper, was the explicit emphasis and reliance on senior management responsibility for ensuring the effectiveness of internal governance structures, systems and controls, and the imposition of personal liability on them for their actions.[36] These were encoded in the Approved Persons Regime.[37] A separate set of Principles for Approved Persons was introduced, imposing individual liability on those with 'significant influence functions' (SIFs) to ensure that the business was managed with integrity, due skill and care, and with effective management controls in their areas of responsibility. These were carried over to the new regime and their scope extended, as discussed below.

Reliance on the responsibilities of senior management was a hallmark of the FSA's approach, and in fact has continued into the new regime. The key difference is that while the FSA largely trusted senior management, in the post-crisis era that trust has gone. In relying on senior management to demonstrate that they had

[36] FSA, Approved Persons Regime, CP 26 (1999). Unfortunately the early FSA papers are no longer easily available on the internet but can only be accessed via the National Archives.

[37] Under some of the previous regimes being rolled into the FSA, senior managers had required individual authorizations. The Approved Persons Regime had a far wider scope, however. It was extended out to include those who dealt directly with clients (in the wake of pensions mis-selling), and upwards across the organizations to include matrix management structures, which had escaped under the previous regime.

adequate systems and controls in place, the FSA was adopting a technique well known to the regulatory literature and referred to variously as 'management-based regulation', 'meta-regulation', or 'enforced self-regulation'.[38] Under this strategy, regulators do not prescribe how regulatees should comply, but require them to develop their own systems for compliance and to demonstrate that compliance to the regulator. (In fact, as this author has argued elsewhere, regulators are always reliant on firms' internal systems to ensure compliance: management-based systems simply raise this practical necessity to a conscious regulatory strategy.)[39]

As with all regulatory strategies, management-based regulation has strengths and weaknesses, which can be exacerbated or ameliorated by the way that it is crafted and implemented. It is an important element of health and safety regulation in the UK, where the underlying approach is that the creator of the risk should bear the responsibility for managing it.[40] This approach came to particular prominence in the wake of the Deepwater Horizon oil spill in the US, where the UK and Norwegian regimes were used as strong examples for how those regulatory regimes should be reformed.[41] The technique has the advantages that it enables firms to design systems and processes which are better suited to ensuring compliance within their own organizations than could be done by generic, prescriptive rules, and that it places the onus and responsibility on firms themselves to demonstrate compliance, rather than placing the onus on regulators to demonstrate non-compliance. It has also been advocated as a way of enhancing and giving legitimacy to market or community-based governance, in a re-articulation of a strategy often termed co-regulation.[42]

Any strategy has an Achilles' heel, however. For management-based regulation it is that firms' systems and processes are designed to achieve their own goals, not necessarily those of the regulator. Compliance systems may therefore end up running parallel to the organizations' core operations, rather than being integral to them.[43] As a result, management-based regulation is fundamentally reliant on

[38] See eg Coglianese, C and Lazer, D, 'Management-based Regulation: Prescribing Private Management to Achieve Public Goals' (2003) 37 *Law and Society Review* 691; Braithwaite, J, *Regulatory Capitalism: How it Works, Ideas for Making it Work Better* (2008); Coglianese, C and Mendelson, E 'Meta-Regulation and Self-Regulation' in Baldwin, R, Lodge, M, and Cave, M (eds), *Understanding Regulation* (2012); Gray, J and Hamilton, J, *Implementing Financial Regulation: Theory and Practice* (2006).

[39] Black, J, 'Paradoxes and Failures: "New Governance" Techniques and the Financial Crisis' (75) (6) *Modern Law Review* 1037.

[40] For a recent review of the system, see House of Commons Energy and Climate Change Committee, *UK Deepwater Drilling: Implications of the Gulf of Mexico Oil Spill* (HC 450-I, 2nd Report of Session 2010–11).

[41] National Commission on the BP Deepwater Horizon Oil Spill and Offshore Drilling, Deep Water: The Gulf Oil Industry and the Future of Offshore Drilling (2011) at 69.

[42] Scott, C, 'Reflexive Governance, Regulation and Meta-Regulation: Control or Learning?' in De Schutter, O and Lenoble, J (eds), *Reflexive Governance: Redefining the Public Interest in a Pluralistic World* (2010).

[43] See eg Parker, C and Nielsen, V (eds), *Explaining Compliance: Business Responses to Regulation* (2011).

the simultaneous presence of four elements: firms have to have the appropriate culture and organizational capacity to support the compliance systems which are put in place, and the right incentives to pursue public objectives as well as private profits; and regulators need to possess sufficient skills and industry experience to evaluate firms, and have sufficient courage and political support to challenge them.[44] As the FSA was to find to its and the taxpayers' cost, none of those four conditions pertained. The financial crisis caused an about turn in the FSA's attitude to senior management of financial institutions. The willingness to step back from scrutiny of executive-management decisions, on the basis that financial institutions knew best how to run themselves, disappeared. Almost overnight, the FSA instituted a more intensive and intrusive style of supervision, and was more willing to challenge management judgements and decisions. It also placed a far greater focus on the competence and expertise of top management and non-executive directors involving, for instance, pre-approval interviews for all those occupying SIFs.[45] As discussed below, the regulatory approach has become more prescriptive, scrutiny has intensified, and individual accountability is now the key focus.

(c) *Principles-based regulation*

The third key aspect of the FSA's approach, and for which it became renowned, was PBR. This is one of the more complex, and certainly one of the more controversial, aspects of UK financial regulation in the FSA era. In one sense, the FSA's approach was 'principles-based' from the outset, in that original SIB Principles survived the massive consolidation exercise of merging the rules of nine organizations into a single Handbook. The Principles were re-drafted to fit the FSA's expanded remit and their number increased to 11, but their role in setting the fundamental standards which firms had to uphold remained. The 11 Principles for Business remained in the Financial Conduct Authority (FCA) and Prudential Regulation Authority (PRA) Handbooks on the split in 2013, but the PRA has now adapted them to suit its own remit and re-christened them Fundamental Rules, as part of its gradual revision of the FSA rules applying to firms and areas within its remit.[46]

The FSA emphasized from the outset that the Principles were the 'anchor' for the regime that it had put in place and gave the regulated firms an idea of their responsibilities and the relationship they ought to have with the regulator.[47] In 2005, the FSA reiterated its engagement with PBR. In its Better Regulation Action Plan, noting that its approach to regulation was a 'hybrid of high-level principles and detailed

[44] Black, n 39 above. [45] RBS report, n 20 above, 291.

[46] Available from their websites: <http://www.fca.org.uk>; <http://www.bankofengland.co.uk/pra/Pages/default.aspx>.

[47] Howard Davies, Minutes of Evidence, Treasury Select Committee (13 November 2011), Q166.

rules and guidance', the FSA stated that it aimed to 'change the balance significantly towards a more principles-based approach'.[48]

Much of the Plan focused on the drafting of the Handbook, setting out a range of areas in which the FSA was simplifying, or intending to simplify its rules and make the Handbook more user-friendly. However, it was clear that the redrafting exercise was not an end in itself, but rather aimed at ensuring firms focused on how best to act in order to produce better outcomes for consumers and the industry rather than 'a mechanistic process' of following detailed rules.[49]

The FSA's clearest articulation of its 'principles-based approach' was in its 2007 paper, Principles-Based Regulation—Focusing on the Outcomes that Matter.[50] In that paper, the FSA emphasized that both the rules and its supervisory approach would focus on principles and outcomes, supplemented by clear guidance. Recognizing the significant demands that PBR places on front-line supervisors the FSA assured that it would 'invest in developing the capabilities of our people so that they have the experience, expertise, judgement and communication skills to make principles-based regulation work'.[51] Noting that the continued proliferation of prescriptive rules by its predecessors and in its own Handbook had not failed to prevent misdemeanours by firms, the FSA stated that rather than providing effective regulation, 'detailed rules have become an increasing burden on our own and the industry's resources'.[52] In addition, principles were more 'durable' and able to withstand rapid changes in market structures and practices; were more accessible to senior management; and focused attention on achieving the purpose of the rule rather than simply adhering to the letter.[53] Both the FCA and PRA have maintained this tiered approach to designing their rulebooks, setting out principles or 'fundamental rules' at the outset, and supplementing them with detailed rules and guidance, albeit that detail is increasingly provided by the EU institutions.

While the FSA did start work on pruning the Handbook, it never promised to have a 'bonfire of rules'. Rather, it made it clear that detailed rules were needed, for example, to ensure adequate consumer protection where the impact of a firm's conduct was not visible or only visible after a long period of time, or to ensure comparability of information provided by firms, and to implement EU legislation which is typically highly detailed in its style. PBR was as much a supervisory strategy as a technique for crafting a rule book. It meant focusing on the outcomes to be achieved, and changing the supervisory relationship with and expectations on firms to achieve outcomes rather than mere compliance. Moreover, in contrast to early statements[54] the FSA stated that breach of the Principles was subject to disciplinary action.[55]

[48] FSA, Better Regulation Action Plan (2005). [49] ibid, John Tiner's foreword.

[50] FSA, Principles-based Regulation—Focusing on the Outcomes that Matter (2007).

[51] ibid, 2. [52] ibid, 6. [53] ibid.

[54] Davies, n 47 above.

[55] ibid, 9.

(d) *Principles-based regulation, management-based regulation, and the 'regulatory dividend'*

PBR, or its alter ego, outcomes-focused regulation, is a challenging approach to adopt, however, for both firms and regulators.[56] The FSA found it difficult, in practice, to pull back from detailed assessments of a firm, and the principles-based approach ran in parallel to the risk-based system of supervision. Even the Treating Customers Fairly initiative, discussed below, remained separate from the ARROW assessments until 2009.

But the real reputational blow to PBR came from another source: the financial crisis. Importantly, in a move which linked PBR, management responsibilities, and a potential for 'light touch' regulation, the FSA stated that as part of its PBR approach it would give greater recognition to firms' own management and controls in its supervisory strategy. Citing international and EU developments in capital adequacy for banks and insurance companies in support, it stated: 'well controlled and managed firms that engage positively and openly with us should expect to experience real benefits from our more principles-based approach in the form of a regulatory dividend, for example relatively lower levels of regulatory capital, less frequent risk assessments, greater reliance on firms' senior management or a less intensive risk mitigation programme'.[57] From mid-2006 onwards, the FSA's supervisors assessed firms against criteria relating to their management and controls and whether it had dealt openly with the FSA in order to decide whether, and to what extent, a firm could benefit from a 'regulatory dividend'.[58]

The 'regulatory dividend' was to prove to have significant, and disastrous, consequences. Despite having had a fractious relationship with the FSA for a number of years, the Royal Bank of Scotland was given a regulatory dividend in 2006 and 2007 under its ARROW risk assessments.[59] The FSA Board review team strongly criticized this decision. It declared that cooperation from firms should be a non-negotiable minimum requirement and that the concept of a regulatory dividend was 'flawed' and 'potentially dangerous'.[60] Furthermore, it stated that the

[56] See generally Black, J, Hopper, M, and Band, C, 'Making a Success of Principles Based Regulation' (2006) *Law and Financial Markets Review* 191; Cunningham, L, 'A Prescription to Retire the Rhetoric of Principles Based Systems in Corporate Law, Securities Regulation and Accounting' (2007) 60(5) *Virginia Law Review* 1411; Black, J, 'Forms and Paradoxes of Principles Based Regulation' (2008) 3(4) *Capital Markets Law Journal* 425; Ford, C, 'New Governance, Compliance and Principles-based Securities Regulation' (2008) 45 *American Business Law Journal* 1; Black, J, 'The Rise, Fall and Fate of Principles Based Regulation' in Alexander, K and Moloney, N (eds), *Law Reform and Financial Markets* (2011); Black, n 39 above.

[57] FSA, n 50 above; RBS report, n 20 above, 12; the 'regulatory dividend' had been first announced in the FSA's Better Regulation Action Plan: What we Have Done and What we Are Doing (December 2006). See also the speech by the then FSA CEO, John Tiner, Better Regulation: Objective or Oxymoron? (2006); and the speech by the then FSA Chairman, Principles-based Regulation, What Does it Mean for the Industry? (2006).

[58] RBS report, n 20 above, 257. [59] ibid, 257 and 242. [60] ibid, 242.

FSA's overall approach to assessing whether management skills, effective governance, and appropriate culture were in place 'relied too much on high-level indicators, such as the degree of cooperation by the firm with the FSA supervisors, rather than on detailed enquiry into key potential areas of concern'.[61] Together with the low prioritization given to prudential supervision, discussed above, the result was that insufficient resources were devoted to high-impact banks and, in particular, to their investment banking activities.[62] The regulatory dividend was rapidly abandoned in the autumn of 2008; time will tell if it returns once political and institutional memories of the crisis fade.

(e) *Contrasting experiences: Principles-based regulation and the Treating Customers Fairly initiative*

The FSA's supervisory approach was bifurcated, however, illustrating that in its operation, PBR is in practice a collation of strategies which can be applied with varying degrees of intensity. While on the one hand PBR was linked to the 'regulatory dividend', particularly in prudential supervision, on the other, it also involved a more intensive degree of supervision in the context of the retail markets.

In 2001, the FSA initiated a project which would become central to its regulation of firms' activities in the retail markets: the Treating Customers Fairly (TCF) initiative.[63] The TCF initiative was based on Principle 6, which required firms to 'treat customers fairly'.[64] The FSA determined early on that it would take a conceptual approach to the issue of 'fairness', not a rigid, detailed definition, as it wanted firms to focus on the substantive standards required, not rule-based compliance.[65] In 2003–04, it undertook pilot studies with six of the largest retail firms[66] and, in 2005, it published a report proposing a 'product life-cycle' approach to implementing TCF, requiring firms to ensure that they were treating firms fairly at every stage of the cycle, from product design and marketing through to sale.[67]

TCF was seen by the FSA as the prime example of the operationalization of the principles-based approach. In 2006, the FSA confirmed that the TCF initiative 'is a core part of our move to a more principles-based approach to regulation', believing

[61] ibid. [62] ibid, 27. [63] FSA, Treating Customers Fairly after Point of Sale (2001).

[64] The FSA argued that this was an extension of the earlier requirement to protect the 'reasonable expectations of policy holders': Treasury, Select Committee, Minutes of Evidence (13 November 2001–02), Further Memorandum Submitted by the Financial Services Authority, available at <http://www.publications.parliament.uk/pa/cm200102/cmselect/cmtreasy/317/1111312.htm> (last accessed 6 April 2014).

[65] FSA, Treating Customers Fairly—Progress Report (2002).

[66] FSA Annual Report 2003–04; FSA, Treating Customers Fairly—Progress and Next Steps (2004); FSA, Treating Customers Fairly—Building on Progress (2005); Edwards, J, 'Treating Customers Fairly' (2006) 14(3) *Journal of Financial Regulation and Compliance* 242; Gilad, S, 'Institutionalizing Fairness in Financial Markets: Mission Impossible?' (2011) 5 *Regulation and Governance* 309.

[67] FSA (2004), n 66 above.

that this would 'help to align good business practice in firms and markets with our own statutory objectives'.[68] Rather than introducing more rules to implement the TCF principle, the FSA instead required firms to achieve six outcomes.[69] The outcomes-focused approach to assessing the compliance with the TCF requirements was to provide the basis for the later transition in labels from 'principles-based' to 'outcome-focused' regulation. Furthermore, in addition to monitoring the product cycle, the FSA developed a 'TCF culture framework' to assess the extent to which the firms' culture was contributing to or inhibiting its ability to achieve the TCF outcomes. The FSA continued to monitor compliance with TCF intensively throughout the period to 2008.[70] However, as the crisis unfolded, the FSA's attention and resources switched to prudential supervision, leaving the TCF initiative temporarily beached. [71]

It would be a mistake to think that the FSA relied solely on changing conduct and behaviour to achieve fair outcomes for consumers, however. Firms have proved particularly resilient to regulatory interventions, and retail product mis-selling continued throughout this period. In particular, the widespread mis-selling of personal protection insurance (PPI) suggested that TCF had really not penetrated through to the way firms operated, and more was needed. In 2008, the FSA began work on the 'retail distribution review' (RDR), which came into effect in 2012. Under the RDR, the FSA banned commission-driven selling, required clearer disclosure of whether advisers were offering independent or non-independent advice, and introduced provisions for higher standards of training, competence, and ethics.[72] In addition, the FSA stepped up its enforcement and insistence on compensation for customers, which by mid-2014 totalled £15.1 billion. In order to gain traction, therefore, the TCF initiative has had to be accompanied by an intensive approach to enforcement and litigation, and one of the most radical pieces of

[68] FSA, Treating Customers Fairly—Towards Fair Outcomes for Consumers (2006) 5.

[69] ibid. These were: 'Outcome 1: Consumers can be confident that they are dealing with firms where the fair treatment of customers is central to the corporate culture; Outcome 2: Products and services marketed and sold in the retail market are designed to meet the needs of identified consumer groups and are targeted accordingly; Outcome 3: Consumers are provided with clear information and are kept appropriately informed before, during and after the point of sale; Outcome 4: Where consumers receive advice, the advice is suitable and takes account of their circumstances; Outcome 5: Consumers are provided with products that perform as firms have led them to expect, and the associated service is both of an acceptable standard and as they have been led to expect; Outcome 6: Consumers do not face unreasonable post-sale barriers imposed by firms to change product, switch provider, submit a claim or make a complaint.'

[70] See RBS report, n 20 above, 263–7.

[71] It is notable that TCF received only one mention in the Annual Report 2010–11, although that was to state that Kensington Mortgage Company had been fined £1.225 million for breach of the TCF principle in its mortgage business (which the FSA received powers to regulate in 2009): FSA, Annual Report 2010–11 (2011).

[72] For review of implementation to date, see FCA, TR13/5—Supervising Retail Investment Advice: How Firms Are Implementing the RDR (2013).

structural regulation over the industry the FSA introduced in its lifetime, in effect requiring firms not just to change their practices but also to change their business model and altering the structure of the industry as a whole.

(f) *Summary*

The FSA's development of PBR was thus in many ways schizophrenic. On the one hand, it was coupled with a reliance on high-level assessments of a firm's management and control systems, the assurances given by firms as to their robustness, and the cooperative attitude that they displayed to the regulator. All of this is in line with the 'tit for tat' strategy advocated in the 'responsive regulation' literature.[73] On the other hand, PBR was coupled to a far more intrusive regulatory strategy in the retail sector: the TCF initiative. One of the reasons that this bifurcated approach continued may well have been due to a combination of organizational priorities and operational practices: the TCF initiative had begun as a discrete project and monitoring of TCF was not integrated into the overall risk-based system for supervision, by now ARROW II, until February 2009.[74] It therefore was not subject to the 'regulatory dividend' policy which was applied as part of the ARROW supervisory framework, and by the time that it became integrated the 'regulatory dividend' had been abandoned.

The contrasting ways in which the FSA implemented principles-based regulation meant it lived up to the observations of both its proponents and critics. As noted, PBR is, in practice, a collation of strategies which can be applied with varying degrees of intensity. However, it has become an integral part of the 'blame game' that ensued in the UK and elsewhere after the financial crisis, confounding attempts at an objective discussion. It is not surprising that in the wake of the crisis the label 'principles-based' regulation was replaced with that of 'outcome-focused' regulation. As we will see below, the label 'outcome-focused' has become quite widely adopted by financial supervisors in recent years, though in terms of supervisory practice (rather than rulebook drafting) the distinction between the two is arguably one of form not substance.

It is difficult to overstate the impact the financial crisis had on the internal operations, culture, and attitude of the FSA. The FSA's trust in financial institutions all but disappeared. In a reversal of its previous approach, no further practitioner codes of practice were endorsed. Credible deterrence became the watchword. Scrutiny intensified, the regulatory dividend was dropped, interviews of those moving into SIFs were introduced, and the rhetoric switched to 'be afraid'. Times had changed it.

[73] Ayres, I and Braithwaite, J, *Responsive Regulation: Transcending the Deregulation Debate* (1992).
[74] FSA, Annual Report 2008–09 (2009); FSA, Annual Report 2009–10 (2010), 50.

3. 2010–?: The third experiment—twin peaks

The life cycle of financial regulatory regimes in the UK in the recent past has been intimately linked to changes in governments. By 2010, the FSA was emerging from the financial crisis battered, bruised, with a new legislative mandate,[75] and determined to regain its reputation as an effective regulator. However, it was the creature of a Labour government and reform of financial regulation had been a key element of the Conservative Party's election manifesto. So, on coming to power the new coalition government announced the third radical restructuring of UK financial regulation since 1986.[76] Responsibilities for prudential supervision were moved back to the Bank of England (the political memories of the failure of Barings and the collapse of BCCI under the Bank's supervision having faded to oblivion), and conducted by a subsidiary, the PRA.[77] The FSA was renamed the FCA and left with the rest of its original mandate,[78] but also given a competition objective and responsibility for consumer credit.[79] The Bank was given regulatory responsibilities for clearing houses and payment systems (though subsequently responsibilities for payments systems were given to the FCA).[80] In line with changes in other jurisdictions, the Bank of England became responsible for macro-prudential supervision, exercised through the Financial Policy Committee (FPC). Coordination is facilitated through cross-membership: the chief executive of the PRA is also a deputy governor of the Bank of England; the chief executives of the FCA and PRA sit on each others' boards, and both are members of the FPC.[81]

Every regulatory reform bears the hallmarks of its predecessors, particularly if its predecessors are in existence and able to influence the process of their own reform. Officials at the Bank and the FSA were heavily involved in the negotiation and formulation of the new regime, which is an interesting fact that challenges the traditional 'principal-agent' model used to conceptualize the relationship between executives and regulatory agencies. Furthermore, although the new system only formally took effect on 1 April 2013, in practice the FCA and PRA started operating in shadow form in 2011–12, with the prudential and conduct divisions headed

[75] The Financial Services Act 2010 gave the FSA a financial stability objective and removed the responsibility for consumer education.

[76] HM Treasury (Her Majesty's Treasury), A New Approach to Financial Regulation: Judgement, Focus and Stability (2010): HM Treasury, A New Approach to Financial Regulation: The Blueprint for Reform (2011). See also Ferran, E, 'The Break up of the Financial Services Authority' (2012) 31(3) *Oxford Journal of Legal Studies* 455.

[77] FSMA 2000 as amended by Financial Services Act 2012.

[78] Minus consumer education, which had already moved to a separate body (Money Advice Service) in 2010: Financial Services Act 2010.

[79] FSMA 2000 as amended by Financial Services Act 2012.

[80] Financial Services (Banking Reform) Act 2013; HM Treasury, Opening up UK Payments (2013).

[81] The other members are: the Governor of the Bank (who chairs the FPC), the deputy governors for monetary policy and financial stability, the executive director for financial stability, and three independent members.

up by individuals who went on to become the chief executives of the PRA and FCA respectively on their formal creation in 2013.[82] Both embryonic organizations issued positioning statements setting out their new regulatory approaches in 2012, just as the FSA had done in 2000.[83] The approaches that they adopted in their first year of operation thus had their roots in decisions made while neither formally existed and the FSA was still legally the regulator.

(a) *Risk-based regulation*

Both the FCA and the PRA have retained and sought to enhance their risk-based approaches, which as we have seen had already begun to change in the wake of the crisis. Further, both have stressed that the risk-based approach is not only used in the context of supervision, but also as a strategic framework to determine policy decisions as to whether and how to intervene in the market.[84] Again, this approach has been presaged by the FSA, but the intention is to use market and conduct risk analysis to identify problems earlier.[85]

In the case of the FCA's supervisory framework for firms, the overall structure remains the same: firms are still assessed into one of four risk categories on the basis of the risks they pose to the FCA's objectives, assessed by their impact and probability of the risk occurring. The supervisory framework has been simplified and modified to take into account the FCA's revised mandate. The application of more resources to the highest-impact firms began in 2009 and has continued under the FCA, but the knock-on effect has been that there are far fewer firms who have allocated 'relationship managers'; many more now simply have to contact the call centre if they have any queries.[86] The stated aim is to focus more on continued supervision of the higher-impact firms, rather than the point in time assessments under ARROW, to focus on drivers of issues and behaviour rather than just the issues themselves, to reduce the number of actions that firms are asked to address but to focus instead on a few key areas, and to use section 166 FSMA powers (under which the regulator can commission a third party to undertake an investigation into a firm) far more extensively in the follow-up to supervisory visits to ensure that the appropriate actions have been taken, rather than use FCA resources.[87] Again, the FCA has been helped by new powers which enable it to contract directly with the section 166 investigators, yet still require the firm to pay for them.[88]

[82] Andrew Bailey, executive director at the Bank of England, became director of the supervision unit of the FSA in 2011 and chief executive of the PRA; Martin Wheatley was managing director of the FCA conduct of business unit from 2011 to 2013 and became chief executive of the FCA.

[83] The Bank of England and the FSA, The Prudential Regulation Authority: The PRA's Approach to Banking Supervision (2012); FSA, Journey to the FCA (2012).

[84] FSA, n 83 above. [85] FSA and PRA, n 83 above.

[86] Interview with FSA official, 2013 (notes on file with author).

[87] FSA and PRA, n 83 above; under section 166 FSMA the FSA can appoint third parties to investigate a firm's conduct.

[88] Financial Services Act 2012.

By reducing the number of people dedicated to individual firms, the FCA intends to have more resources available to focus on event-driven work and on sector risk assessments, which can then lead to thematic reviews.[89] Thematic reviews were always intended to be part of the FSA's risk-based approach, and although they did conduct some, it was an area on which the FSA found difficult to focus in the early days of its risk-based framework due to its resource allocation. The FCA has conducted 17 thematic reviews in the period April 2013–April 2014, the majority of which have focused on retail markets.[90] It has not conducted any thematic reviews into the operation of the wholesale markets, though it has had to conduct major event-driven investigations into the manipulation of LIBOR and foreign exchange markets. Thematic reviews are good indications of where the FCA is not looking, however—whether it too will develop blind spots with respect to part of its mandate remains to be seen.

The PRA's 'new approach' document also focused on its new risk-based framework for supervision: the Proactive Intervention Framework (PIF).[91] This differs from ARROW in a number of key respects; notably, the assessment of impact, the risks focused on, and in the supervisory steps that need to be taken. The PRA has five categories of firms, based on their potential to adversely affect financial stability. Potential impact is assessed by the nature of its functions and its significance within the system. Broadly, critical functions are payment, settlement, and clearing; retail banking; corporate banking; intra-financial system borrowing and lending; investment banking; and custody services. The scale of a firm's potential impact depends on its size, complexity, business type, and interconnectedness with the rest of the system.[92]

The changes are partly a function of the additional requirements imposed through the new Basel capital accords and their implementation in the EU,[93] but the lessons from the failure of the light-touch approach to banking supervision had already been learned. Supervision is far more intensive. In addition, the focus is now on the ability to resolve a bank in an orderly way. Whereas the supervisory approach prior to the crisis was to focus on prevention of failure, the post-crisis approach is to focus on both prevention (termed 'resilience') and proximity to failure and resolvability. The PIF sets out the preparations for resolution that need to be put in place

[89] FSA, n 83 above. [90] See <http://www.fca.org.uk>.

[91] PRA, n 83 above. See also: The Strategy for the Bank's Financial Stability Mission 2013/14 (2013); Bank of England, PRA: The PRA's Approach to Banking Supervision (2013); Bank of England, The PRA's Approach to Insurance Supervision (2013); PRA, Statement of Strategy (2014). Note that the PRA's remit also changed under the Financial Services (Banking Reform) Act 2013—it received a secondary competition objective and is required to implement the policy on ring-fencing banks' retail operations from the rest of their business.

[92] Bank of England, PRA: The PRA's Approach to Banking Supervision, n 91 above.

[93] Basel Capital Accords II.5 and III; Capital Requirements Directive IV 2013/36/EU [2013] OJ L176/338.

depending on the supervisors' assessments of these two factors.[94] With respect to smaller firms, however, the focus is primarily on orderly resolution rather than prevention: supervision of those firms, in effect, is to operate on a 'gone concern' basis.[95]

(b) *Senior-management responsibilities—increasing individual accountability*

There has also been a significant shift in the extent to which regulators are prepared to trust senior managers of financial institutions to maintain adequate and appropriate systems and controls, and to foster an appropriate culture within their firms. The decline in trust is the result of two events: the financial crisis and the LIBOR scandal, and subsequently reinforced by the activities of traders in manipulating other parts of the fixed income, currency, and commodity markets.

The financial crisis revealed widespread failings in the governance and senior management of financial institutions worldwide.[96] As noted above, one consequence was that the FSA became far more intrusive in its approach to the appointment of senior managers under the 'approved persons' regime. The regime had been introduced in 2000, but had been used largely as a gateway for people taking up a post initially, rather than as a means of ensuring appropriate behaviour or attributing liability for failure.[97] From 2009–10, the FSA began to interview people who firms were proposing to appoint to SIFs.

However, pinning down individual liability has proved to be extremely difficult. Only one senior director was fined for his conduct in the period leading up to the crisis,[98] and no financial institution was censured at all. The lack of enforcement actions against either firms or individuals significantly damaged the FSA's reputation.[99] It embarked on a campaign of 'credible deterrence' immediately after the crisis, increasing the level of fines and concluding a number of long-standing investigations into insider dealing. Furthermore, in 2013, the FCA began to require individuals personally to attest that required remedial actions had been taken and that controls were fit for purpose, in order to increase their ability to take actions against senior individuals.[100]

[94] PRA, n 91 above.

[95] This approach is also taken to prudential supervision by the FCA: FSA, n 83 above.

[96] FSB, Senior Supervisors Group Report on Risk Management Lessons from the Global Banking Crisis of 2008 (2009); UBS, Shareholder Report on UBS's Write-Downs. Report to Swiss Federal Banking Commission (2008); OECD, Corporate Governance and the Financial Crisis: Key Findings and Main Messages (2009); Walker, D, A Review of Corporate Governance in UK Banks and Other Financial Industry Entities (2009).

[97] Parliamentary Commission on Banking Standards (PCBS), Changing Banking for Good (Vol I, 2013), HL Paper 225-I, HC 175-I, 33.

[98] Peter Cummings of HBOS: FSA Final Notice (12 September 2012).

[99] See, eg, PCBS report, n 97 above.

[100] See, eg, Freshfields Bruckhaus Deringer, The New Regulatory Regime for Senior Bankers in the UK (2014); Adamson, C, A Sustainable Conduct Environment, speech delivered (20 March 2014), available at <http://www.fca.org.uk/news/a-sustainable-conduct-environment>.

The FS Act 2012 modified the requirement for the regulators to take into consideration the responsibilities of senior management, but the most significant changes were introduced in the Financial Services (Banking Reform) Act 2013. Following the recommendations of the Parliamentary Commission on Banking Standards,[101] the 2013 Act introduced a new criminal offence of 'reckless misconduct in the management of a bank' should a bank fail,[102] a 'senior persons' regime for directors and managers of UK banks, and a new 'certification' regime to be run by all financial institutions, which would include individuals such as those submitting prices to indices, who were not caught by the approved persons regime. Senior persons within banks will have to have personal 'statements of responsibilities' and will have to attest that these have been carried out when handing over to their replacements.[103] The new systems will come into force in 2015. The FCA would have preferred to have the approved persons regime abolished and replaced by the senior persons regime for FCA-authorized firms too, but the Treasury refused.[104] Implementation of three different systems (senior persons, approved persons, and certified individuals) may cause some operational problems for dual-authorized firms and, therefore, may require amending in due course. However, the overall message is clear: the trust that regulators, and indeed politicians, placed in senior managers has gone and has been replaced, for the moment at least, with an emphasis on individual responsibility, accountability, and liability.

(c) *The evolution of principles-based regulation in rule design and in operation*

In the aftermath of the financial crisis, Hector Sants, then chief executive of the FSA, announced the official retirement of PBR, stating '[a] principles-based approach does not work for people who have no principles'.[105] PBR relies on trust, and that trust has gone. However, in operational terms, although the rhetoric has shifted from 'principles-based' to 'outcomes-focused' and 'judgement-based' regulation, the overall intention is the same: regulators and firms should focus on ensuring that outcomes are achieved and risks are managed, not just that rules have been complied with. Indeed, the Treasury argued that the failing of the previous regime had been that it was too 'box-ticking' in its approach—suggesting implicitly the FSA had not been principled enough.[106] Whatever the truth of the matter, the first documents issued by the FCA and PRA setting out their respective approaches

[101] PCBS report, n 97 above.

[102] Financial Services (Banking Reform) Act 2013, Part 4.

[103] ibid.

[104] Evidence of Clive Adamson, head of supervision at the FCA to the Treasury Select Committee (7 January 2014).

[105] Sants, H, Delivering Intensive Supervision and Credible Deterrence, speech delivered to the Reuters Newsmakers Event (12 March 2009).

[106] HM Treasury, n 76 above.

stated firmly that they would be 'judgement-based', and this has been echoed in the public statements of both regulators since.[107]

As discussed above, it is notable that the role of 'principles' remains within the PRA and FCA's rule books, though their drafting has changed to reflect the revised remits of the two regulators. The emphasis of the PRA is on judgement-based supervision, but in practice it has to implement quite prescriptive rules emanating from the Basel Capital Accords and EU legislation. The FCA has indicated that while it is still focused on outcomes, it may need to become more prescriptive in how those outcomes should be achieved. For example, with respect to individual liability it has indicated that it will write more detailed rules to supplement the current principles for approved persons.[108]

In a development initiated by the FSA in 2010, the FCA is also adopting a more strategic approach to intervention, shifting its focus from the sales process and cultures to the earlier stages of product development and marketing.[109] 'Product governance' is now the watchword. There is also a greater focus on firms' business models and strategy by both the PRA and the FCA, in order to assess whether these may give rise to stability or conduct risks respectively.[110]

The FCA has also stated it is prepared to become more interventionist. For example, whereas the FSA stated clearly in 2005 that it was not its role to determine firms' pricing policies,[111] in 2013 the FCA stated that it would be focusing on 'value for money' of firms' products, and would consider price intervention in situations where competition was impaired. It would also be prepared to make product intervention rules which could, for example, restrict the use of specified product features or restrict the promotion of particular products 'to some or all consumers'.[112] It was bolstered in this objective by new powers given under the FS Act 2012 to ban products and to bar financial promotions if they are misleading.

PBR always operated in the context of a tiered rule system, of principles, rules, and guidance, but the move to more prescriptive rules is noteworthy. Furthermore, the expanding role of EU legislation over financial services and its post crisis-era ambition to produce a single rulebook for the whole of the EU, fast being realized, is dictating the style and contents of a significant and increasing proportion of the FCA's and PRA's rules, limiting the scope for purposive drafting.

However, one of the central aspects of PBR is that conduct should be in accordance with the principles and purposes of the rules, not the letter. Here, there has been no change; quite the opposite. So, for example, in explaining firms'

[107] FSA, n 83 above; Bank of England, PRA, n 91 above, FCA Business Plan 2014–15 (2014).

[108] The Financial Services (Banking Reform) Act 2013 also empowers regulators to issue rules of conduct for senior persons.

[109] See eg FSA, Retail Product Development and Governance—Structured Product Review (2012).

[110] PRA approach, n 91 above.

[111] FSA, Treating Customers Fairly—Building on Progress (2005).

[112] FSA, Journey to the FCA, n 83 above.

responsibilities under the Unfair Contract Terms legislation, the FCA has emphasized that in addition to the legislative requirements, the Principles for Business require firms to 'treat customers fairly' and ensure that information is 'fair and not misleading'. It has stated that technical compliance with the legislation would therefore not be enough to comply with the Principles: compliance with the purpose, not the letter, is what counts.[113] The PRA has also emphasized that in the context of prudential regulation, technical compliance with rules alone is unlikely to achieve the appropriate outcomes: 'firms should maintain the overriding principle of safety and soundness and act accordingly'.[114]

(d) *Retail-regulation—taking investor behaviour seriously*

It is perhaps a sign of how the cognitive frameworks of financial regulators have begun to shift that the first research paper issued by the FSA was a straightforward, neo-classical economic analysis of market failures, whereas the first research paper issued by the FCA was an analysis of how individuals and markets do not behave in the way assumed by neo-classical economics.[115] The insights of cognitive psychologists have long been a feature of risk regulation in other domains and began to enter the analysis of financial markets through behavioural economics in the late 1980s to early 1990s.[116] Behavioural economics is essentially a counter-point to neo-classical economics, arguing that people, and therefore markets, do not behave in the ways that the standard model of a 'rational actor' assumes. In particular, when making decisions about risks or in situations of uncertainty, their behaviours are affected by a range of cognitive biases.[117]

The implications of cognitive psychologists for financial regulation are potentially significant. The most obvious area of relevance is for how regulators should intervene in the retail markets. Regulators in the UK and elsewhere, notably Australia and Canada, have long realized that disclosure does not have the effects that might be expected on standard economic analysis, but the reason has been attributed mainly to low levels of financial literacy.[118] Financial education campaigns have

[113] FCA, Fair Terms—Key Messages, available at <http://www.fca.org.uk/firms/being-regulated/unfair-contracts/key-messages> (last accessed 22 April 2014).

[114] PRA's approach, n 83 above, 11–12, 17.

[115] Llewellyn, D, The Economic Rationale for Financial Regulation (1999), FSA Occasional Paper 1; FCA, Applying Behavioural Economics at the Financial Conduct Authority (2013), Occasional Paper 1.

[116] See, eg, Shiller, R, *Market Volatility* (1988); Shiller, R, *Irrational Exuberance* (2000); Shiller, R, 'From Efficient Market Theory to Behavioural Finance' (2003) 17(1) *Journal of Economic Perspectives* 83.

[117] Kahneman, D and Tversky, A, 'Prospect Theory: An Analysis of Decision under Risk' (1979) 47 *Econometrica* 263; Kahneman, D, Slovic, P, and Tversky, A, (eds) *Judgement under Uncertainty: Heuristics and Biases* (1982). See further the Chapter by Avgouleas in this volume.

[118] See, eg, FSA, Financial Capability in the UK: Establishing a Baseline (2006); ASIC, National Financial Literacy Strategy (2011); Taskforce on Financial Literacy: Canadians and their Money: Building a Brighter Financial Future (2011).

therefore been undertaken, and the FSA started to 'road test' disclosure documents as early as 2000. Cognitive psychology and behavioural economics suggest that financial literacy is not the only reason that people make poor financial decisions, however, and therefore refining disclosure as a regulatory technique is not enough.[119] For the moment, the FCA's experiments with new approaches informed by behavioural economics have been to alter the drafting of letters to investors informing them of their rights to claim against firms for PPI mis-selling. However, both the FCA initiatives and, in particular, those of the Consumer Financial Protection Bureau in the US, which regulates consumer credit including mortgages,[120] suggest that behavioural economics could have a significant impact on the way that regulators understand market and consumer behaviour and the regulatory strategies they adopt, particularly in the retail markets, in the next few years.

III. Regulatory Approaches in Other Parts of the World

The focus of discussion so far has been on the UK in order to illustrate the development and complexities of some of the key regulatory approaches it has adopted, but the issue of 'how to do' regulation is not a conversation confined to the UK. The remainder of the Chapter outlines how some of the approaches focused on here have fared in other jurisdictions.

1. Risk-based regulation

(a) *The gradual diffusion and mainstreaming of risk-based regulation at the national level*

Policy diffusion is the subject of a significant literature,[121] and risk-based regulation makes an excellent case study. The UK was an early developer of risk-based supervision,

[119] FCA, n 115 above; Avgouleas, E, 'The Global Financial Crisis and the Disclosure Paradigm in Financial Regulation: The Case for Reform' (2009) 6(4) *European Company and Financial Law Review* 440.

[120] CFPB, Strategic Plan FY2013–FY2017 (2013).

[121] See, eg, Meseguer, C, 'Policy Learning, Policy Diffusion, and the Making of a New Order' (2005) 598 *The Annals of the American Academy of Political and Social Science* 167; Braum, D and Gilardi, F, 'Taking "Galton's Problem" Seriously: Towards a Theory of Policy Diffusion' (2006) 18(3) *Journal of Theoretical Politics* 298; True, J and Mintrom, M, 'Transnational Networks and Policy

but it was by no means alone.[122] It had been preceded by the Canadian prudential supervisor (the Office of the Superintendent of Financial Institutions (OSFI)), which in turn had taken inspiration from the CAMELS system used by the Federal Reserve Bank in the US.[123] The UK and US regimes provided the benchmark comparators for the Hong Kong Monetary Authority to develop its risk-based approach from 1998 onwards.[124] The OSFI system, in turn, had a strong influence on the risk-based approach introduced by the Australian prudential regulator, the Australian Prudential Regulation Authority (APRA) in 2002, in the wake of the failure of the HIH insurance company.[125] APRA's 'probability and impact rating system' (PAIRS) and its 'supervisory oversight and response system' (SOARS), in turn, were adopted by the Dutch prudential supervisor, the DNB. The FSA, OSFI, APRA, and DNB approaches have subsequently provided the springboard for the development of risk-based approaches by supervisors in a number of different countries. These include the Central Bank of Ireland's recently introduced PRISM system, which was also influenced by the experience of the FSA in the period leading up to the crisis.[126] The European regulatory bodies have not yet advocated risk-based approaches across all supervisory activities, although the Joint Committee of European Supervisory Authorities has indicated that they may start venturing into these waters, issuing proposals for how supervisors might take a risk-based approach to supervising compliance with anti-money laundering activities.[127] Indeed, the draft fourth Anti Money Laundering Directive and the underlying 2012 standards of the OECD's Financial Action Task Force are excellent examples not only of the risk-based approach being embedded internationally, but also of regulatees being explicitly required to take a risk-based approach to their implementation of the provisions. So, the European Supervisory Authorities are now mandated to adopt risk-based regulation in this area, and we may yet see it rolled out across the common supervisory handbooks currently being developed.

Diffusion: The Case of Gender Mainstreaming' (2001) 45(1) *International Studies Quarterly* 27; Marsh, D and Sharman, J, 'Policy Diffusion and Policy Transfer' (2009) 30(3) *Policy Studies* 269.

[122] Black, n 12 and n 17 above.

[123] CAMELS stands for capital, assets, management capability, earnings, liquidity, and sensitivity to market risk.

[124] HKMA, Hong Kong Banking into the New Millennium—Hong Kong Banking Sector Consultancy Study (1998); HKMA, Supervisory Policy Manual (2014).

[125] Palmer, J, Review of the Role Played by the Australian Prudential Regulation Authority and the Insurance and Superannuation Commission in the Collapse of the HIH Group of Companies (2002); Black, J, 'Managing Risks and Defining the Parameters of Blame' (2006) 28(1) *Law and Policy* 1; Hill, J, 'Why Did Australia Fare so Well in the Global Financial Crisis?' in Ferran, E, Moloney, N, Hill, J, and Coffee, J (eds), *The Regulatory Aftermath of the Global Financial Crisis* (2013).

[126] Central Bank of Ireland, PRISM Explained: How the Central Bank of Ireland Is Implementing Risk Based Supervision (2011); it is probably not accidental that the Deputy Governor and Head of Financial Regulation of the Irish Central Bank from 2010 to 2013, Matthew Elderfield, had previously worked at the FSA.

[127] Joint Committee, Preliminary Report on Anti-money Laundering and Counter Financing of Terrorism Risk Based Supervision (2013), JC-2013-32.

As noted above, risk-based regulation has its strengths and weaknesses. There is no clear correlation between the adoption of a risk-based system of supervision per se, and the presence or absence of regulatory failure before or during the crisis. Although their models have much in common, as practised by the FSA and the Dutch central bank, risk-based regulation failed.[128] In contrast, as practised in Australia and Canada, it was apparently more resilient.[129] Design is clearly important, but how a system is operationalized is clearly more important in determining its effects. Despite its mixed success, risk-based regulation is becoming increasingly adopted by a number of financial regulators, not least under the prompting of the international standard-setting bodies, through processes of policy diffusion and policy learning, often facilitated by the movement of key personnel between regulators on a global basis who act as agents of change.

(b) *Moving to risk-based supervision at the global level*

Risk-based supervision is now seen as the hallmark of good regulation at the global level. The 2009 IOSCO guidance on supervision of market intermediaries recommends to supervisors that they take a 'risk-based approach'.[130] The revised Basel Core Principles for Banking Supervision issued in 2012 require supervisors to adopt effective risk-based systems of supervision, and to intervene early and take timely supervisory actions.[131] The Financial Stability Board (FSB)'s recommendations for the supervision of global systemically important financial institutions (GSIFIs) echoes the call for a risk-based approach.[132]

Risk-based approaches are also being used to assess countries' regulatory systems. The IMF and World Bank assessments introduced in 1999, the Financial Sector Assessment Programs (FSAPs), which include Reports on the Observation of Standards and Codes (ROSCs) issued by the international standard-setting bodies, have become risk-based in both the way they are conducted and the selection of countries which are subject to them. The initial ROSC system required a comprehensive, detailed assessment of all principles. The IMF noted in 2009 that it was becoming

[128] FSA, The Supervision of Northern Rock: A Lessons Learned Review (2008); DNB (De Nederlandsche Bank), Annual Report 2009 (2010), 138–41; DNB, Supervisory Strategy 2010–14 and Themes 2010 (2010), 83–5; DNB, Annual Report 2010 (2011).

[129] However, the extent to which supervisory practices in both Australia and Canada were the reason for their banks' relative resilience, as opposed to other factors such as banks' high deposit base, non-reliance on wholesale funding, strong local lending, and restrictions on the mortgage market, is debatable. For discussion see Hunt, B and Rozhkov, D, *Australian Banks: Selected Issues* (2008); Beltratti, A and Stulz, R, *Why Did Some Banks Perform Better during the Credit Crisis? A Cross-Country Study of the Impact of Governance and Regulation* (2009); Ratnovski, L and Huang, R, *Why Are Canadian Banks More Resilient?* (2009); Hill, n 125 above.

[130] IOSCO, Guidelines to Emerging Market Regulators Regarding Requirements for Minimum Entry and Continuous Risk Based Supervision of Market Intermediaries (2009).

[131] BCBS, Core Principles of Banking Supervision (2012), foreword, para 12.

[132] FSB, Increasing the Intensity and Effectiveness of SIFI Supervision—Progress Report to the G20 Ministers and Governors (2012).

increasingly resource-intensive and, as a result, the IMF was going to have to follow other financial supervisors around the world and become more targeted and risk-based in its approach, at least when updating ROSCs.[133] The BCBS has also issued guidance to the IMF and World Bank that assessments should not cover all core principles, but selected ones based on previous compliance assessments and on an evaluation of relevant risks and vulnerabilities in each country.[134]

The selection of which countries should be evaluated has also been revised significantly in the wake of the crisis. Prior to 2008, the FSAPs were voluntary and not targeted on countries according to a prior risk assessment, but on those which volunteered for assessment—there was little selection by the IMF. Universal voluntary participation proved difficult to manage, hampering the prioritization of scarce FSAP resources.[135] In the immediate wake of the crisis, the G20 agreed that all members should have mandatory FSAPs every five years. However, in 2010, the IMF and World Bank agreed to adopt a risk-based approach and revised the list of countries which would undergo mandatory financial stability assessments to consist only of those countries or regions posing the highest systemic risks to the global financial system based on their size and interconnectedness. In 2013, the IMF revised the methodology for assessing systemic importance again, placing greater focus on interconnectedness, producing an extended list of 29 countries.[136] Inevitably, the increased resources applied to countries posing the highest risks means that there have been few resources left for voluntary FSAPs for non-systemic countries.[137] Whether the IMF will follow other risk-based supervisors and develop alternative strategies for managing their low-risk categories of countries, such as conducting themed FSAPs, remains to be seen.

(c) *Summary*

Risk-based regulation is slowly becoming mainstreamed into regulatory processes around the world, and those who have not yet adopted the approach are being urged to do so through the global standard-setting and monitoring processes. As with any regulatory strategy, risk-based regulation is challenging and prone to both

133 IMF, The Financial Sector Assessment Program after Ten Years: Experience and Reforms for the Next Decade (2009); IMF, Revised Approach to Financial Regulation and Supervision Standards Assessments in FSAP Updates (2009).

134 BCBS Core Principles, Annex 2; see guidance on risk-based DARs and ROSCs: <http://www.imf.org/external/pp/longres.aspx?id=4684>.

135 IMF, Mandatory Financial Stability Assessments under the Financial Sector Assessment Process (2013).

136 IMF, FSAP Fact Sheet (2013); IMF, Mandatory Financial Stability Assessments under the Financial Sector Assessment Process (2013); IMF Executive Board Reviews Mandatory Financial Stability Assessments under the Financial Sector Assessment Program (2014), Press Release No 14/08. The countries are: Australia, Austria, Belgium, Brazil, Canada, China, Denmark, Finland, France, Germany, Hong Kong SAR, India, Ireland, Italy, Japan, Korea, Luxembourg, Mexico, the Netherlands, Norway, Poland, Russia, Singapore, Spain, Sweden, Switzerland, Turkey, the UK, and the US. The countries added since 2010 using the new methodology are Denmark, Finland, Norway, and Poland.

137 ibid.

success or failure, depending on how it is designed and implemented. However, as emphasized above, regulators do not have a choice as to whether or not they have to prioritize their resources, but they do have choices as to how.

2. The fate of principles-based regulation

(a) *Aspiring to outcome-focused and judgement-based regulation at the national and global levels*

As noted above, in the UK the phrase 'principles-based' regulation was rapidly retired in 2008; instead, the terminology is 'outcomes-focused' and 'judgement-based', with a greater emphasis on enforcement. However, both UK regulators emphasize that compliance has to be with the spirit not the letter of the rules. The focus on outcomes rather than technical compliance is shared by a number of regulators around the world, and is emphasized by the global standard-setters as the hallmark of good regulation. Thus, as noted above, the BCBS Core Principles state that risk-based supervision involves 'focusing on outcomes as well as processes, moving beyond passive assessment of compliance with rules'. APRA, OSFI, the PRA, the FCA, the Central Bank of Ireland, and the Hong Kong Monetary Authority all describe their approaches as 'risk-based and outcome-focused'.[138] Indeed, OSFI still describes its approach as 'principles-based'.[139] This language is repeated at the global level. The FSB's progress report on supervision of SIFIs, for example, urges regulators to complement (or move away from) a 'rule-based' approach to one which is more forward-looking and strategic, and to rely on supervisory judgements as to whether or not the right outcomes are being achieved, rather than (solely) assessments as to whether or not rules have been complied with.[140]

However, as the FSB notes, requiring supervisors to use their judgements, to be forward-looking, strategic, and to focus on outcomes is challenging: it requires enhanced supervisory skills, an increased depth of experience, and an increase in resources. Whether governments will be prepared to commit those resources remains to be seen.

(b) *The diffusion of TCF*

In another interesting example of cross-jurisdictional diffusion, the Hong Kong Markets Authority (HKMA) announced in 2013 that it was adopting a 'TCF

[138] Central Bank of Ireland, n 126 above; APRA, The Supervision Blueprint (2011); OSFI, Report on Plans and Priorities 2013–2014 (2013); PRA, n 83 above; FCA, n 82 above.

[139] OSFI, Supervisory Framework—OSFI's Role, available at <http://www.osfi-bsif.gc.ca/Eng/fi-if/rai-eri/sp-ps/Pages/sff.aspx#17> (last accessed 21 April 2014).

[140] FSB, n 132 above.

Charter' to promote a stronger corporate culture among banks of treating their consumers fairly. Basing the initiative on the good practices proposed under the G20 High-Level Principles on Financial Consumer Protection, which (*inter alia*) pick up the FSA's language in providing that 'Treating consumers fairly should be an integral part of the good governance and corporate culture of all financial services providers and authorised agents',[141] the HKMA has worked with the industry to develop the TCF Charter 'as a catalyst for fostering a stronger risk culture towards fair treatment of customers at all levels of banks and at all stages of their relationship with customers'. The Charter is primarily aimed at retail consumers and is designed to complement, not change, current law or regulations or the existing terms and conditions between banks and their customers.[142] It will be interesting to see which other regulators adopt the same focus and terminology with respect to their own retail markets, and the similarities and differences that emerge.

(c) *Principles-based regulation as a global system-management tool*

As noted above, the reasons for the creation of the Principles in the UK regulatory regime were only in part to guide firms' behaviour and act as an aid to interpreting more detailed rules. They were also created in order to manage the regulatory system and the relationship between the SIB and the SROs, and to both constitute and signal the institutional position of the SIB within the system. At the global level, principles play the same system-management role.[143] Principles are being used to manage this complex, polycentric, and multilevel governance system in three notable ways: to establish the institutional position of their issuer, to structure the discretion of other regulators, and to be benchmarks of accountability.

Principles are used to establish their authors' own institutional positions within the regulatory regime and reinforce the scope of their jurisdictions in a contested policy space. It is notable, for example, that the FSB, which is being positioned and is positioning itself as the lead coordinator of global financial regulation, issued two sets of principles within its first 18 months,[144] more than it did in the last ten years in its previous guise as the Financial Stability Council. To date, it has issued five sets of principles and is consulting on a sixth (on effective risk-appetite frameworks).[145] Principles are also used by the other international standard-setting bodies (ISSBs) to regulate other regional or national regulators, not all of whom may be their members, by structuring their discretion. One of the critical aspects of rules or principles is that they can both structure and distribute discretion, conferring

[141] G20 High-level Principles on Financial Consumer Protection (2011), principle 3.

[142] <http://www.hkma.gov.hk/eng/key-information/press-releases/2013/20131028-4.shtml>.

[143] Black, n 56 above.

[144] FSB, Principles for Sound Compensation Practice (2009); FSB, Principles for Cross Border Cooperation and Crisis Management (2009).

[145] Details are available at <https://www.financialstabilityboard.org/list/fsb_publications/tid_177/index.htm>.

space not just between rules/principles, but also within them in which actors can exercise choice. In most areas, the discretion left to national regulators is wide, but in others, notably in the Basel capital accords, the global standards are highly prescriptive, and indeed the BCBS has itself wondered whether they should become less complex.[146] Finally, as we have seen, the principles issued by ISSBs are used as criteria of accountability, acting as benchmarks of performance against which national regulatory regimes are assessed, by both the IMF and World Bank, and increasingly by the ISSBs themselves.

(d) *Summary*

In so far as PBR meant 'light-touch' regulation, it has been abandoned.[147] PBR is more complex than that, however. As we have seen, it has a 'rulebook' dimension and an 'operational' dimension. In its operation, PBR requires a supervisory approach which is essentially the same as the 'outcomes-focused' or 'judgement-based' approaches being advocated at the national level in many countries and at the global level by the ISSBs. The TCF initiative, which the FSA always described as its main example of PBR, has continued, enhanced, and indeed adopted elsewhere, though the continuation of mis-selling shows significant challenges remain in the retail area. And in the design of a rule system used at the global level, PBR is alive and well. However, in one of the many paradoxes of regulation, the proliferation of principles goes hand in hand with the proliferation of increasing quantities of detailed rules, and the extent to which regulators around the world are both desirous and capable of adopting the purposive, outcomes-orientated and judgement-based approach that is an integral part of the new supervisory approaches being urged upon them remains to be seen.[148]

IV. Conclusion

Regulators face a number of challenges. They have to govern at a distance in time and space, managing behaviour, risks, and phenomena which possess almost endless variety and are constantly changing. They are inextricably dependent for their success on the behaviour of individuals and organizations which are autonomous and thus inherently ungovernable. They face problems of seeing and

[146] BCBS, The Regulatory Framework: Balancing Risk Sensitivity, Simplicity and Comparability (2013), Discussion Paper.

[147] See also FSB, n 133 above.

[148] At the international level, see Basel Committee on Banking Supervision, The Regulatory Framework: Balancing Risk Sensitivity, Simplicity and Comparability—Discussion Paper (2013).

knowing what it is they have to govern and have to develop strategies which can be adopted at differing scales, from regulating a few to regulating thousands or hundreds of thousands of organizations which themselves range from small local businesses to huge multinational companies.[149] And regulators have to do all this while organizing themselves and managing their own reputation and legitimacy. It is no wonder that the issue of 'how to do' regulation is thus such a perplexing and preoccupying question for anyone involved. It is also no wonder that there are no easy answers. But as shown by the historical tracing of developments throughout the last 30 years, regulatory approaches are nuanced and often paradoxical strategies which morph over time. Moreover, regulation moves in cycles, affected by a range of factors including economic conditions, lobbying by financial institutions, the epistemic communities of regulatory technocrats, accepted understandings of the nature of markets, democratic demands, and the shifting topographies of political power and interests. Over the last 30 years, however, the overall trend around much of the world has been for increased intensity in regulatory scrutiny over financial markets and financial institutions, particularly in the wake of the crisis. There are also signs of the gradual development of a common language in which to describe and prescribe different types of regulatory approaches. Those approaches are easier to aspire to than they are to implement, however—whether or not regulation succeeds or fails is dependent on a multitude of factors, only some of which are within the regulators' control. There are no easy answers. Amongst the many things they have to do, regulators have to adopt the motto: 'hope for the best, but prepare for the worst'.

Bibliography

Adamson, C, A Sustainable Conduct Environment, speech delivered (20 March 2014), available at <http://www.fca.org.uk/news/a-sustainable-conduct-environment>.

APRA, The Supervision Blueprint (2011).

ASIC, National Financial Literacy Strategy (2011).

Avgouleas, E, 'The Global Financial Crisis and the Disclosure Paradigm in Financial Regulation: The Case for Reform' (2009) 6(4) *European Company and Financial Law Review* 440.

Ayres, I and Braithwaite, J, *Responsive Regulation: Transcending the Deregulation Debate* (1992).

Baldwin, R, Cave, M, and Lodge, M, (eds), *Oxford Handbook on Regulation* (2012).

Baldwin, R, Lodge, M, and Cave, M, *Understanding Regulation* (2012).

Bank of England, PRA: The PRA's Approach to Banking Supervision (2013).

[149] On the problems of scale see Ford, C, 'Prospects for Scalability: Relationships and Uncertainty in Responsive Regulation' (2013) 7(1) *Regulation and Governance* 14.

Bank of England, PRA, The PRA's Approach to Insurance Supervision (2013).
Bank of England, PRA, The Strategy for the Bank's Financial Stability Mission 2013/14 (2013).
Bank of England, PRA, Statement of Strategy (2014).
Bank of England and the FSA, The Prudential Regulation Authority: The PRA's Approach to Banking Supervision (2012).
BCBS, Core Principles of Banking Supervision (2012).
BCBS, Discussion Paper, The Regulatory Framework: Balancing Risk Sensitivity, Simplicity and Comparability (2013).
Beltratti, A and Stulz, R, *Why Did Some Banks Perform Better during the Credit Crisis? A Cross-Country Study of the Impact of Governance and Regulation* (2009).
Black, J, 'The Development of Risk Based Regulation in Financial Services: Just "Modelling Through"?' in Black, J, Lodge, M, and Thatcher, M (eds), *Regulatory Innovation: A Comparative Analysis* (2005).
Black, J, 'The Emergence of Risk-based Regulation and the New Public Risk Management in the UK' (2005) *Public Law* 512.
Black, J, 'Forms and Paradoxes of Principles Based Regulation' (2008) 3(4) *Capital Markets Law Journal* 425.
Black, J, 'Managing Risks and Defining the Parameters of Blame' (2006) 28(1) *Law and Policy* 1.
Black, J, 'Paradoxes and Failures: "New Governance" Techniques and the Financial Crisis' (75)(6) *Modern Law Review* 1037.
Black, J, 'The Rise, Fall and Fate of Principles Based Regulation' in Alexander, K and Moloney, N (eds), *Law Reform and Financial Markets* (2011).
Black, J, 'Risk Based Regulation: Choices, Practices and Lessons Learnt' in *Risk and Regulatory Policy: Improving the Governance of Risk* (2010).
Black, J, *Rules and Regulators* (1997).
Black, J, '"Which Arrow?" Rule Type and Regulatory Policy' [1995] *Public Law* 94.
Black, J and Baldwin, R, 'Really Responsive Risk Based Regulation' (2010) 32(2) *Law and Policy* 181.
Black, J, Hopper, M, and Band, C, 'Making a Success of Principles Based Regulation' (2006) *Law and Financial Markets Review* 1.
Black, J and Nobles, R, 'Personal Pension Misselling: The Causes and Lessons of Regulatory Failure' (1998) 61 *Modern Law Review* 789.
Braithwaite, J, *Regulatory Capitalism: How it Works, Ideas for Making it Work Better* (2008).
Braum, D and Gilardi, F, 'Taking "Galton's Problem" Seriously: Towards a Theory of Policy Diffusion' (2006) 18(3) *Journal of Theoretical Politics* 298.
Briault, C, The Rationale for a Single National Financial Services Regulator (1999), FSA Occasional Paper Series 2.
Central Bank of Ireland, PRISM Explained: How the Central Bank of Ireland Is Implementing Risk Based Supervision (2011).
Coglianese, C and Lazer, D, 'Management-based Regulation: Prescribing Private Management to Achieve Public Goals' (2003) 37 *Law and Society Review* 691.
Coglianese, C and Mendelson, E, 'Meta-regulation and Self-regulation' in Baldwin, R, Cave, M, and Lodge, M (eds), *Oxford Handbook on Regulation* (2012).

Consumer Financial Protection Bureau, Strategic Plan FY2013–FY2017 (2013).
Cunningham, L, 'A Prescription to Retire the Rhetoric of Principles Based Systems in Corporate Law, Securities Regulation and Accounting' (2007) 60(5) *Virginia Law Review* 1411.
DNB (De Nederlandsche Bank), Annual Report 2009 (2010).
DNB, Annual Report 2010 (2011).
DNB, Supervisory Strategy 2010–2014 and Themes 2010 (2010).
Edwards, J, 'Treating Customers Fairly' (2006) 14(3) *Journal of Financial Regulation and Compliance* 242.
FCA, Applying Behavioural Economics at the Financial Conduct Authority (2013), Occasional Paper 1.
FCA, Fair Terms—Key Messages, available at <http://www.fca.org.uk/firms/being-regulated/unfair-contracts/key-messages>.
FCA, Guidance Consultation, Risks to Customers from Financial Incentives (2012).
FCA, How the Financial Conduct Authority Will Report on and Investigate Regulatory Failure (2013).
Ferran, E, 'The Break up of the Financial Services Authority' (2012) 31(3) *Oxford Journal of Legal Studies* 455.
Financial Services Act 2010.
Financial Services Act 2012.
Financial Services (Banking Reform) Act 2013.
Financial Services and Markets Act 2000.
Ford, C, 'New Governance, Compliance and Principles-based Securities Regulation' (2008) 45 *American Business Law Journal* 1.
Ford, C, 'Prospects for Scalability: Relationships and Uncertainty in Responsive Regulation' (2013) 7(1) *Regulation and Governance* 14.
Freshfields Bruckhaus Deringer, The New Regulatory Regime for Senior Bankers in the UK (2014).
FSA, Annual Report 2003–04 (2004).
FSA, Annual Report 2008–09 (2009).
FSA, Annual Report 2009–10 (2010).
FSA, Annual Report 2010–11 (2011).
FSA, Approved Persons Regime, CP 26 (1999).
FSA, Better Regulation Action Plan (2005).
FSA, Better Regulation Action Plan, What we Have Done and What we Are Doing? (2006).
FSA, The Failure of the Royal Bank of Scotland: Financial Services Authority Board Report (2011).
FSA, Financial Capability in the UK: Establishing a Baseline (2006).
FSA, Journey to the FCA (2012).
FSA, A New Regulator for a New Millennium (2000).
FSA, Principles-Based Regulation—Focusing on the Outcomes that Matter (2007).
FSA, Retail Product Development and Governance—Structured Product Review (2012).
FSA, The Supervision of Northern Rock: A Lessons Learned Review (2008).
FSA, Treating Customers Fairly after Point of Sale (2001).
FSA, Treating Customers Fairly—Building on Progress (2005).
FSA, Treating Customers Fairly—Progress and Next Steps (2004).
FSA, Treating Customers Fairly—Progress Report (2002).

FSA, Treating Customers Fairly—Towards Fair Outcomes for Consumers (2006).

FSA, The Turner Review: A Regulatory Response to the Global Banking Crisis (2009).

FSB, Increasing the Intensity and Effectiveness of SIFI Supervision—Progress Report to the G20 Ministers and Governors (2012).

FSB, Principles for Cross Border Cooperation and Crisis Management (2009).

FSB, Principles for Sound Compensation Practice (2009).

FSB, Senior Supervisors Group Report on Risk Management Lessons from the Global Banking Crisis of 2008 (2009).

G20, High-Level Principles on Financial Consumer Protection (2011).

Gilad, S, 'Institutionalizing Fairness in Financial Markets: Mission Impossible?' (2011) 5 *Regulation and Governance* 309.

Gray, J, 'What Next for Risk-based Financial Regulation?' in MacNeil, I and O'Brien, J (eds), *The Future of Financial Regulation* (2010).

Gray, J and Hamilton, J, *Implementing Financial Regulation: Theory and Practice* (2006).

Hill, J, 'Why did Australia Fare so Well in the Global Financial Crisis?' in Ferran, E, Moloney, N, Hill, J, and Coffee, J, *The Regulatory Aftermath of the Global Financial Crisis* (2013).

HM Treasury, A New Approach to Financial Regulation: The Blueprint for Reform (2011).

HM Treasury, A New Approach to Financial Regulation: Judgement, Focus and Stability (2010).

HM Treasury, Opening up UK Payments (2013).

Hong Kong Markets Authority, Hong Kong Banking into the New Millennium—Hong Kong Banking Sector Consultancy Study (1998).

Hong Kong Markets Authority, Supervisory Policy Manual (2014).

House of Commons Energy and Climate Change Committee, *UK Deepwater Drilling: Implications of the Gulf of Mexico Oil Spill* (HC 450-I, 2nd Report of Session 2010–11).

Hunt, B and Rozhkov, D, *Australian Banks: Selected Issues* (2008).

Hutter, B, The Attractions of Risk-based Regulation: Accounting for the Emergence of Risk Ideas in Regulation (2005), CARR Discussion Paper.

Hutter, B and Lloyd Bostock, S, 'Reforming Regulation of the Medical Profession: The Risks of Risk-based Approaches' (2008) 10(1) *Health, Risk and Society* 69.

IMF Executive Board Reviews, Mandatory Financial Stability Assessments under the Financial Sector Assessment Program (2014), Press Release No 14/08.

IMF, The Financial Sector Assessment Program after Ten Years: Experience and Reforms for the Next Decade (2009).

IMF, FSAP Fact Sheet (2013).

IMF, Mandatory Financial Stability Assessments under the Financial Sector Assessment Process (2013).

IMF, Revised Approach to Financial Regulation and Supervision Standards Assessments in FSAP Updates (2009).

IOSCO, Guidelines to Emerging Market Regulators Regarding Requirements for Minimum Entry and Continuous Risk Based Supervision of Market Intermediaries (2009).

Joint Committee, Preliminary Report on Anti-money Laundering and Counter Financing of Terrorism Risk Based Supervision (2013), JC-2013-32.

Kahneman, D, Slovic, P, and Tversky, A (eds), *Judgement under Uncertainty: Heuristics and Biases* (1982).

Kahneman, D and Tversky, A, 'Prospect Theory: An Analysis of Decision under Risk' (1979) 47 *Econometrica* 263.

Llewellyn, D, The Economic Rationale for Financial Regulation (1999), FSA Occasional Paper 1.

Marine Stewardship Council, Risk Based Framework for Certification (2009).

Marsh, D and Sharman, J, 'Policy Diffusion and Policy Transfer' (2009) 30(3) *Policy Studies* 269.

Meseguer, C, 'Policy Learning, Policy Diffusion, and the Making of a New Order' (2005) 598 *The Annals of the American Academy of Political and Social Science* 167.

Moloney, N, *EU Securities and Financial Markets Regulation* (3rd edn, 2014).

Moloney, N, *How to Protect Investors: Lessons from the EC and the UK* (2010).

Moran, M, 'Theories of Regulation and Changes in Regulation: The Case of Financial Markets' (1986) 35 *Political Studies* 185.

National Commission on the BP Deepwater Horizon Oil Spill and Offshore Drilling, Deep Water: The Gulf Oil Industry and the Future of Offshore Drilling (2011).

OECD, Corporate Governance and the Financial Crisis: Key Findings and Main Messages (2009).

OECD, Recommendation on Regulatory Policy (2013); Regulators Compliance Code, Statutory Code of Practice for Regulators (2007).

OSFI, Report on Plans and Priorities 2013–2014 (2013).

OSFI, Supervisory Framework—OSFI's role, available at <http://www.osfi-bsif.gc.ca/Eng/fi-if/rai-eri/sp-ps/Pages/sff.aspx#17>.

Palmer, J, Review of the Role Played by the Australian Prudential Regulation Authority and the Insurance and Superannuation Commission in the Collapse of the HIH Group of Companies (2002).

Parker, C and Nielsen, V (eds), *Explaining Compliance: Business Responses to Regulation* (2011).

Parliamentary Commission on Banking Standards (PCBS), Changing Banking for Good (Vol I, 2013), HL Paper 225-I, HC 175-I.

Plender, J, 'London's Big Bang in International Context' (1986–7) 63(1) *International Affairs* 39.

Ratnovski, L and Huang, R, *Why Are Canadian Banks More Resilient?* (2009).

Rothstein, H, Huber, M, and Gaskell, G, 'A Theory of Risk Colonisation: The Spiralling Regulatory Logics of Societal and Institutional Risk' (2006) 35(1) *Economy and Society* 91.

Rothstein, H, Irving, P, Walden, T, and Yearsley, R, 'The Risks of Risk-based Regulation: Insights from the Environmental Policy Domain' (2006) 32(8) *Environment International* 1056.

Sants, H, Delivering Intensive Supervision and Credible Deterrence, speech presented at Reuters Newsmakers Event (2009).

Scott, C, 'Reflexive Governance, Regulation and Meta-Regulation: Control or Learning?' in De Schutter, O and Lenoble, J (eds), *Reflexive Governance: Redefining the Public Interest in a Pluralistic World* (2010).

Shiller, R, 'From Efficient Market Theory to Behavioural Finance' (2003) 17(1) *Journal of Economic Perspectives* 83.

Shiller, R, *Irrational Exuberance* (2000).

Shiller, R, *Market Volatility* (1988).

Taskforce on Financial Literacy: Canadians and their Money: Building a Brighter Financial Future (2011).

True, J and Mintrom, M, 'Transnational Networks and Policy Diffusion: The Case of Gender Mainstreaming' (2001) 45(1) *International Studies Quarterly* 27.

UBS, Shareholder Report on UBS's Write-Downs. Report to Swiss Federal Banking Commission (2008).

Walker, D, A Review of Corporate Governance in UK Banks and Other Financial Industry Entities (2009).

CHAPTER 9

THE ROLE OF GATEKEEPERS

JENNIFER PAYNE

I. Introduction

This Chapter focuses on the topic of gatekeepers and their regulation, concentrating on developments in the US and the EU. Generally, gatekeepers are regarded as financial intermediaries that operate between issuers and investors, and include auditors, underwriters, lawyers, securities analysts, and credit rating agencies (CRAs).[1] They have a potentially valuable role to play in capital markets as a mechanism for investor protection, as discussed in Section II. However, there have been a number of examples of gatekeeper failure in recent years that have cast doubt on their ability to fulfil this role, starting with a number of high-profile corporate collapses in the early years of this century, such as Enron, Worldcom, and Parmalat,[2] and continuing with concerns about their role arising from the global financial crisis, in particular the role of CRAs in relation to their underestimation of the credit risk of structured credit products.[3] These gatekeeper failures, and the limitations in the gatekeeper model that contributed to them, are discussed in Section III. As a result of these failures, there has been significant attention focused on the need to regulate gatekeepers in recent years. In Section III some of the specific regulatory responses to perceived shortcomings in the ability of financial intermediaries to act as effective gatekeepers are discussed, and in Section IV this regulatory response is analysed more generally. In particular, the question considered is whether the regulatory measures that have been put in place are likely to be effective. Section V briefly concludes.

II. The Role of Gatekeepers

The traditional rationale for financial services and markets regulation is to deal with asymmetric information and other market failures, such as systemic risks, in order to promote market efficiency and efficient resource allocation. One of the predominant mechanisms for dealing with information asymmetry is information disclosure by issuers, both at the stage when securities are first offered to investors, but also via continuing disclosure obligations once a secondary market for the securities has been established.[4] In the securities market, therefore, regulation is predominantly intended to provide investors with protection. This theory

[1] See eg Coffee, J, 'What Caused Enron? A Capsule Social and Economic History of the 1990s' in Clarke, T (ed.), *Theories of Corporate Governance* (2004).

[2] For a discussion of the Enron and Worldcom scandals see Coffee, J, *Gatekeepers: The Professions and Corporate Governance* (2006) esp ch 2, and for a discussion of the Parmalat scandal see Ferrarini, G and Guidici, P, 'Financial Scandals and the Role of Private Enforcement' in Armour, J and McCahery, J (eds), *After Enron: Reforming Corporate Governance and Capital Markets in Europe and the US* (2006).

[3] US Senate Permanent Subcommittee on Investigations (2011), Wall Street and the Financial Crisis: Anatomy of a Financial Collapse, Majority and Minority Staff Report, 6; European Commission, Proposal for a Regulation of the European Parliament and of the Council on Credit Rating Agencies (COM (2008) 704) 1.

[4] For discussion see the Chapter by Enriques and Gilotta in this volume.

of investor protection faces some difficulties, however, that may be mitigated by a group of intermediaries—'gatekeepers'—that can operate between the investor and the issuer.

The term 'gatekeepers' has been used in different ways. It was first employed to mean a group of independent professionals who may be able to prevent issuer wrongdoing by withholding necessary cooperation or consent, thereby controlling access to the capital markets.[5] So, for example, an issuer will generally need to use an investment bank as an underwriter in order to issue securities to the market, and an investment bank can refuse to underwrite an issue if it discovers deficiencies in the issuer's disclosures, thereby denying the issuer access to the capital markets, and providing investors with protection. This need for consent or cooperation can arise because of a legal requirement that the issuer make use of the intermediary's services; for example, it is generally a legislative requirement that issuers obtain an auditor's certification of its financial statements. Alternatively, it may arise because, as a matter of practice, an issuer will not be able to succeed in issuing securities without such assistance. So, for example, an issue of debt securities is unlikely to be successful unless the issuer obtains a decent rating from a CRA, even though there is no legislative requirement for it to do so.

More recently the term 'gatekeeper' has been used in a slightly different sense, to encompass those professionals who can provide investors with protection by providing them with certification or verification services.[6] Often, this will overlap with the role described above, but adopting this second definition brings within the term 'gatekeeper' some intermediaries that would otherwise be excluded. For example, securities analysts do not fit within the first definition, since there is no need for an issuer to make use of a securities analyst before issuing securities to investors, yet it is generally accepted that analysts can operate between issuers and investors in order to provide investors with protection, a key function of a gatekeeper. The first definition also has the potential to encompass a wider group of actors who do not fulfil this function, such as a key supplier of goods or technology to a particular industry without which that industry could not function. The second definition is therefore to be preferred, although, in fact, most of the intermediaries in this Chapter fall within both definitions—analysts being the obvious exception. Understanding this distinction remains useful, however. For instance, it helps to explain the funding differences that are observable among the gatekeepers discussed in this Chapter: issuers tend to be prepared to pay for the services of intermediaries they need, but not for those that they do not.

[5] See Kraakman, R, 'Corporate Liability Strategies and the Costs of Legal Controls' (1984) 93 *Yale Law Journal* 857; Kraakman, R, 'Gatekeepers: The Anatomy of a Third-Party Enforcement Strategy' (1986) 2 *Journal of Law, Economics & Organization* 53.

[6] See eg Coffee, n 2 above, 2.

Adopting this latter understanding of the term 'gatekeeper', intermediaries will be regarded as gatekeepers if they have significant reputational capital that they can pledge in order to verify or certify information produced by an issuer. Issuers have a problem with signalling that their disclosures are credible, since there is clearly an incentive for companies to misinform investors and to inflate the value of the company and its securities if they can. Gatekeepers can solve this problem by assuring investors about the quality of the issuer's signal. This involves the intermediary pledging its reputation, built up over many years, to vouch for the issuer in question. The idea is that investors can trust these intermediaries more than the issuer because they have less of an incentive to deceive investors. Unlike issuers, who might have nothing to lose from a fraud, especially if they expect only to raise money from investors once, and if they have little to fear from ex-post enforcement measures, gatekeepers are 'repeat certifiers'. The intermediary shares none (or very few) of the gains of fraud to which it may be party, and is exposed to a large risk if the fraud is exposed, namely the loss of its reputation into the future, and possibly legal liability. In theory, as long as the gatekeeper has reputational capital at risk the value of which exceeds the expected profit that it will receive from the transaction, it should be faithful to investors and not provide false certification.

So, for example, underwriters (typically investment banks) can perform this certification and verification role for a company issuing securities for the first time. Absent the ability of insiders to communicate credibly their beliefs, or the ability of outsiders to buy inside information, investors will tend to discount the value of the information they receive from the issuer, leading to potential market failure (the 'market for lemons' problem[7]). Using the underwriter as a reputational intermediary can solve this problem. The investment bank represents to the market that it has evaluated the issuer's product in good faith, and that it is prepared to stake its reputation on the value of the security. Effectively, an underwriter can be employed to 'certify' that the issue price is consistent with inside information about the future earnings prospects of the firm.[8]

Similarly, auditors lend their professional reputation to issuers regarding the accuracy and credibility of an issuer's financial statements. Given that auditors are clearly repeat certifiers they should act well in this capacity: rational auditors should never sell their reputation to a particular client by compromising that reputation for an increased reward, since if they do so the lost rents from existing and future clients will far exceed the gain from that single client. By contrast, the role of lawyers as gatekeepers has been slower to develop. Much of a lawyer's work for its client, as advocate, or as 'transaction engineer',[9] is designed to achieve the client's

[7] Akerlof, GA, 'The Market for "Lemons": Quality Uncertainty and the Market Mechanism' (1970) 84 *Quarterly Journal of Economics* 488.

[8] Booth, JR and Smith, RL, 'Capital Raising, Underwriting and the Certification Hypothesis' (1986) *Journal of Financial Economics* 261.

[9] See Coffee, n 2 above, 192.

ends, rather than to uncover wrongdoing. In some circumstances, however, they might be regarded as lending their professional reputations to a transaction, for example where the lawyer vets the disclosure statements being made by the issuer in an initial public offering of shares.[10] This is a more modest role than that which auditors potentially perform. Nevertheless, they can, potentially, be regarded as having some form of gatekeeper role and recent crises have led to the recognition that 'when executives and accountants have been engaged in wrongdoing, there have been some other folks at the scene of the crime—and generally they are lawyers'.[11]

The role of securities analysts as verifiers and certifiers of information about an issuer is reasonably clear. They act as information conduits between the companies they investigate and actual or potential investors in those companies. Specifically, they collect information about issuers, the securities they sell, and the industries in which they operate, along with general market factors. They then evaluate and synthesize the information they obtain and issue a recommendation. At their starkest these might be buy/sell/hold recommendations, but analysts use a variety of terms to describe their recommendations and there is no industry standard in this regard. The role of securities analysts is valuable to investors as they provide an assessment of the company's disclosures, and an analysis of the company's prospects, and as such they fall squarely within the definition of 'gatekeeper' adopted for the purposes of this Chapter. Analysts also have an important role to play in supporting an efficient capital market by turning the information provided by companies into prices.[12]

In contrast to securities analysts, which generally operate in the equity markets, CRAs operate in the bond markets. Their role is somewhat distinct from that of the other intermediaries discussed in this section.[13] CRAs do not verify in the way that an auditor does, nor do they research into the facts in the way an analyst does. They simply suggest the likelihood of default based on assumed facts, via the provision of an investment grade which is linked to a letter (generally from AAA to D). These ratings, based on complex methodologies, are not an assessment of the quality of the investment, but merely an assessment of whether the debt security will perform in accordance with its terms. They provide an opinion on the creditworthiness of a particular issuer

[10] See, generally, Coffee, n 2 above, ch 6.

[11] Senator Corzine, introducing § 307 Sarbanes–Oxley Act to Congress (148 Cong Rec S 6554) (daily edn July 10, 2002).

[12] Gilson, R and Kraakman, R, 'The Mechanisms of Market Efficiency' (1984) 70 *Virginia Law Review* 549.

[13] See, eg, Partnoy, F, How and Why Credit Rating Agencies Are not Like Other Gatekeepers (2006), University of San Diego Legal Studies Research Paper Series No 07-46, available at <http://ssrn.com/abstract=900257>; White, LJ, 'Markets: The Credit Rating Agencies' (2010) *Journal of Economic Perspectives* 211.

or financial instrument, and the likelihood of default. CRAs are nevertheless commonly regarded as gatekeepers, since they can be said to have reputational capital which they lend to an issuer, and ratings do potentially allow investors to assess the relative risk of the issuer or financial instrument that has been rated, thereby reducing information asymmetries. Distilling information about an issuer or its securities into an easily digestible nugget of information can allow issuers to send a credible signal that their securities are of above average quality, and ratings provided by CRAs do have an effect on price.[14] Ratings produced by CRAs are also used for other purposes. In particular, in recent years CRAs have become hard-wired into the regulatory system, so that, for example, ratings are important for institutional investors, as there will generally be restrictions on the debt securities that such investors can hold, by reference to their ratings,[15] and they perform a central role in measuring credit risk for capital adequacy purposes in relation to banks.[16] These developments are significant, indeed some commentators have suggested that this regulatory licence is the core problem regarding the ability of CRAs to act as effective gatekeepers.[17] This regulatory licence certainly complicates the regulation of CRAs, as discussed further in Section III.

Gatekeepers can potentially perform a very valuable role in the capital markets, providing investors with certification or verification services via the reputational capital model. As discussed next, however, there are a number of significant limitations on the ability of gatekeepers to perform this role in practice.

[14] Hand, J, Holthausen, R, and Leftwich, R, 'The Effect of Bond Rating Agency Announcements on Bond and Stock Prices' (1992) 47 *Journal of Finance* 733; Kliger, D and Sarig, O, 'The Information Value of Bond Ratings' (2000) 55 *Journal of Finance* 2879; Dichev, I and Piotroski, J, 'The Long-run Stock Returns Following Bond Ratings Changes' (2001) 56 *Journal of Finance* 173. The effect of ratings changes on price is complex, as the impact of ratings changes is different for firms with low ratings than for firms with high ratings. Note, however, that these studies suggest an asymmetry between downgrades and upgrades: downgrades have a significant negative impact on price, but there is virtually no price change following an upgrade.

[15] See eg Partnoy, F, 'The Siskel and Ebert of Financial Markets? Two Thumbs Down for the Credit-Rating Agencies' (1999) 77 *Washington University Law Quarterly* 619.

[16] See, especially, the Basel Accords, issued by the Basel Committee on Banking Supervision, in particular Basel II (2004) and Basel III (2010) (discussed further in the Chapters by Alexander and Mülbert in this volume). The use of credit ratings in this regard really came to the fore in Basel II and while Basel III seeks to address some of the concerns raised about relying on credit rating in this context, the use of ratings to determine credit risk remains an important part of these rules.

[17] Partnoy, n 15 above, 619, and see also Partnoy, F, Overdependence on Credit Ratings Was a Primary Cause of the Crisis (2009), San Diego Legal Studies Paper No 09-015, available at <http://ssrn.com/abstract=1430653>.

III. The Failure of Gatekeepers

The last decade or so has given rise to a host of examples of gatekeeper failure. The early years of this century saw a string of large-scale and high-profile corporate failures, such as Enron, Worldcom, and Parmalat, where corporate fraud or significant financial irregularity was not spotted or exposed by the companies' various gatekeepers. So, in relation to Enron, for example, the company went from a stock price in excess of $80 in December 2000 to $1 a year later, and when it filed for bankruptcy in December 2001 it was the largest bankruptcy in US history. Between these dates it had been discovered that Enron was a 'house of cards': various Enron executives made use of off balance sheet vehicles and complex financing structures to hide the size of Enron's debt. Yet, these irregularities were not spotted or constrained by Enron's auditors or its lawyers, 16 out of the 17 analysts covering Enron's stock were still publishing buy or strong buy recommendations two months before Enron's bankruptcy even though publicly available information at that time already suggested the stock was overpriced, and until four days before Enron declared bankruptcy in December 2001 its debt was still rated as 'investment grade' by the major CRAs.[18]

The global financial crisis has seen an intensification of concerns regarding gatekeepers. In addition to the general sense that the gatekeepers do not operate a valuable monitoring role, a new issue has arisen, this one focused on CRAs. CRAs are generally felt to perform their role in rating corporate debt relatively well, and they escaped comparatively unscathed from the regulatory changes imposed on gatekeepers in the wake of Enron and similar scandals. The global financial crisis, however, exposed a concern regarding the role of CRAs in developing structured products, such as collateralized debt obligations. The destructive role of opaque complex financial products in the financial crisis has been widely discussed,[19] as has the role of CRAs in developing them.[20] In particular, CRAs developed methodologies for rating these structured products that were highly problematic. Conflicts arose as a result of the fact that by 2006 a significant percentage of CRA revenue depended on structured finance. With these structured products the CRAs were

[18] See generally Coffee, J, 'Understanding Enron: It's about the Gatekeepers, Stupid' (2002) 57 *The Business Lawyer* 1403.

[19] eg Tett, G, *Fool's Gold: How Unrestrained Greed Corrupted a Dream, Shattered Global Markets and Unleashed a Catastrophe* (2009); Stiglitz, J, *Free Fall: America, Free Markets and the Sinking of the World Economy* (2010); Coffee, J, 'Ratings Reform: The Good, the Bad and the Ugly' (2011) *Harvard Business Law Review* 231.

[20] See eg Brunnermeier, MK, 'Deciphering the 2007–08 Liquidity and Credit Crunch' (2009) 23 *Journal of Economic Perspectives* 77; Partnoy, n 17 above; Partnoy, F, 'Historical Perspectives on the Financial Crisis: Ivar Kreugar, the Credit Rating Agencies, and Two Theories about the Function, and Dysfunction, of Markets' (2010) 26 *Yale Journal on Regulation* 431.

said to have acted as 'gate openers' rather than gatekeepers: 'No other gatekeeper has created a dysfunctional multi-trillion dollar market, built on its own errors and limitations.'[21] A further concern regarding CRAs, in the aftermath of the global financial crisis, has revolved around their role in downgrading sovereign debt, and this has also prompted calls for regulatory reform, particularly in Europe.

One question that arises is why these scandals erupted when they did. A great deal has been written to explain how the incentive structures and modes of operation of intermediaries changed in the last years of the twentieth century and the early years of this century, to provide an environment in which gatekeeper failure became increasingly likely.[22] What altered in this period were the stresses and pressures that were placed on the gatekeeper model. It is inherent in the model that it will only work well if the gains received by the gatekeeper are outweighed by the potential loss to its reputation or potential financial loss as a result of litigation. During this period, however, the gains to gatekeepers increased whereas the potential losses were reduced. The resulting failures are not, with hindsight, surprising. Understanding these issues is important, but tackling them is not straightforward, as this Section will also discuss.

These various scandals and crises have demonstrated a number of significant limitations on the way in which gatekeepers operate as an investor protection tool in practice, and have prompted a substantial regulatory response. Of course, the limitations do not operate in the same way for all gatekeepers, and neither has the regulatory response been identical, but the same reputational capital model operates for all gatekeepers, and a number of the common issues and concerns that arise will be discussed here.

1. Conflict of interest

The first limitation on intermediaries operating as effective gatekeepers is the strong possibility of a conflict of interest existing between the intermediary and those that it should be protecting, namely investors. The funding of intermediaries is at the heart of this problem. Intuitively, the greatest investor protection might be thought to arise where the principal–agent relationship is maintained, ie investors select and pay for the intermediary's services. Unfortunately, this model faces severe difficulties. The first is a collective action problem. It is difficult for all investors to get together to negotiate and pay for a gatekeeper's services. If any single

[21] See Partnoy, n 13 above, 2.

[22] See Coffee, n 2 above; Brunnermeier, MK, 'Deciphering the 2007–08 Liquidity and Credit Crunch' (2009) 23 *Journal of Economic Perspectives* 77; Partnoy, n 17 above.

investor decides to act, however, it faces a free-rider problem, in that it will incur all of the effort but reap only a fraction of the reward, so there is no real incentive for a single investor to appoint and pay for a gatekeeper's services. The public goods nature of many such services also causes problems for intermediaries. Take the example of a securities analyst, who cannot effectively prevent the communication of her assessment of an issuer to non-paying investors once she discloses it to the paying investor-client, and therefore she will not be able to capture the full value of her services. Free-riders will be able to acquire the information without compensating the analyst.

As a result of these issues, none of the intermediaries discussed in this Chapter currently operate on an investor-pays (or 'subscriber-pays') model. Instead, other funding models have arisen. Auditors, lawyers, underwriters, and CRAs all operate on an issuer-pays model. This gives rise to an obvious conflict since the gatekeeper is being paid by the person that it is supposed to supervise, so that, as Professor Coffee has described it, the watchdogs are turned into the pets of those that feed them.[23] Where a gatekeeper also provides ancillary services to the issuer, this will intensify the possibility of conflict since it increases the economic bond between the gatekeeper and the issuer, and there has been a well-documented rise in the sale of ancillary services provided by gatekeepers to their clients, particularly by auditors and CRAs.[24]

Securities analysts face a different funding problem: since their services are not strictly necessary for issuers wishing to issue equity securities, there is little incentive for issuers to pay for them. Instead, a number of different kinds of analyst have emerged, according to who employs them. The most common are sell-side analysts, who work for large broker-dealer firms or investment banks. By contrast, buy-side analysts are employed by institutional investors, and engage in private proprietary research for their employers. The remainder of the market comprises a small minority of independent analysts. While buy-side analysts are less vulnerable to conflicts, as they are more closely aligned with their clients, the institutional investors for whom they work, significant conflicts arise for sell-side analysts, and this is where regulatory attention has been focused. Sell-side analysts are generally funded by investment banks, which can then cross-subsidize this role with fees received from other services being offered to the issuer. For example, where investment banks offer underwriting services to issuers, there will generally be a benefit to the issuer if the investment bank's analysts follow the newly issued security in the aftermarket and provide (presumably positive) analyst coverage. So, there will be a pressure on those analysts to provide positive reports.[25] More generally, for

[23] Coffee, n 2 above, 335. [24] ibid; Coffee, n 19 above, 238.

[25] eg Michaely, R and Womack, KL, 'Conflict of Interest and Credibility of Underwriter Analyst Recommendations' (1999) 12 *Review of Financial Studies* 653; Bradley, DJ, Jordan, BD, and Ritter, JR, 'Analyst Behaviour Following IPOs: The Bubble Period Evidence' (2008) 21 *Review of Financial*

sell-side analysts it is clear that they are more likely to generate brokerage commissions for their employer with buy recommendations than sell recommendations, since the audience for buy recommendations is per se larger. These issues tend to mean that there will be a preponderance of optimism and buy recommendations made by sell-side analysts,[26] which tends to lead to an inflation of evaluations regarding securities, and to a problem of herding.[27]

The funding of gatekeepers by a group other than investors separates the principal from the agent and increases the chances that a conflict of interest will arise. A recurring theme in any discussion of gatekeeper regulation is therefore the entrenchment of incentives for intermediaries, and the way in which incentives can distort their role as gatekeepers. This gives rise to challenges for regulators regarding how best to deal with this issue. A number of options are available. Regulators could make use of some or all of the following techniques: (a) disclosure; (b) provisions designed to manage the conflicts that arise; and (c) the imposition of regulatory oversight.

(a) *Disclosure*

Disclosure plays a major role in regulating the capital markets, with most jurisdictions imposing substantial disclosure obligations on issuers.[28] It has a potential role to play in relation to regulating gatekeepers. Disclosure can be used as a regulatory tool in this regard in a number of ways. At its simplest, it might be that gatekeepers are merely required to disclose the fact that they are subject to conflicts, and then it can be left to investors to decide what to do with this information. A slightly more muscular form of disclosure would require gatekeepers to disclose more specific matters, such as the source and amount of their compensation or, in the case of an analyst or CRA, the methodology behind a recommendation.

Regulators have made relatively limited use to date of disclosure as a regulatory tool to manage the conflicts that afflict gatekeepers. Where it is used it tends to involve a mixture of these two different kinds of disclosure, so that gatekeepers are required to disclose the fact and nature of the conflicts to which they are subject, and to provide information about the service they provide, such as the methodologies

Studies 101. Another conflict which can also push analysts in favour of an optimistic recommendation is the need for the analyst to maintain access to the issuer to perform his job.

[26] Research into analysts suggests that a bias towards optimism outranked even overall accuracy in determining career advancement as an analyst (Hong, H and Kubik, J, 'Analysing the Analysts: Career Concerns and Biased Earnings Forecasts' (2003) 58 *Journal of Finance* 313). Empirical research suggests that independent analysts can be no less optimistic: Kowan, A, Groysberg, B, and Healy, P, 'Which Types of Analyst Firms Are More Optimistic?' (2006) *Journal of Accounting and Economics* 119.

[27] See, eg, Welch, I, 'Herding among Security Analysts' (2000) 58 *Journal of Financial Economics* 369.

[28] For discussion see the Chapter by Enriques and Gilotta in this volume.

and key assumptions they have adopted in performing their role.[29] While in theory disclosure of this kind of information can be valuable to investors, in helping them to distinguish the 'good' from the 'bad' gatekeepers, empirical studies have cast doubt on whether these kinds of disclosures do perform this function in practice. Studies regarding CRAs, for example, suggest that these kinds of disclosures do not seem to affect a rating agency's success in the market.[30] Various explanations have been presented for this, including that the disclosures made are insufficiently consistent and standardized to render comparisons by investors possible.[31]

Furthermore, there is a fundamental weakness with the use of this regulatory technique to deal with conflicts of interest. The use of disclosure broadly accepts that these intermediaries are inherently conflicted, and operates to ensure that those relying on the information are aware of this fact. Accepting these conflicts, albeit requiring their disclosure, seems unsatisfactory given the potentially valuable role of gatekeepers discussed above, because these conflicts undermine the role of these intermediaries as gatekeepers and distort the value of the service they provide to investors.[32] Disclosure also shifts the burden onto investors in terms of assessing these conflicts, and then adjusting their own behaviour appropriately. It is not clear, however, that investors are well placed to do so. Research suggests that disclosure is unlikely to work well as a strategy in this context because those to whom the information is disclosed tend to assume that the intermediary will then deal with them fairly, whereas the intermediary, having disclosed, may then feel comfortable about pursuing its own interests aggressively.[33] As a result, the value of disclosure to investors as a regulatory technique in this regard can be questioned. An alternative, and potentially more valuable, form of disclosure is disclosure to regulators, particularly if that disclosure is reasonably standardized, discussed further below.

(b) *Managing the conflicts that arise*

In both the US and the EU, a significant aspect of the regulatory response to the conflict of interest afflicting gatekeepers has been an attempt to ameliorate that conflict by, in effect, imposing prophylactic rules. As a result, rafts of detailed rules have been introduced, aimed predominantly at auditors, CRAs, and sell-side

[29] See in relation to CRAs new rules in the US (Dodd–Frank Wall Street Reform and Consumer Protection Act 2010 ('Dodd–Frank Act'), § 932(a)(8)) and the EU (Regulation (EC) No 1060/2009 on credit rating agencies [2009] OJ L302/1, Article 8, as amended, and fleshed out with by subsequent regulatory technical standards).

[30] Bai, L, 'The Performance Disclosures of Credit Rating Agencies: Are they Effective Reputational Sanctions?' (2010) 7 *NYU Journal of Law and Business* 47, 94.

[31] ibid, 63.

[32] eg Fisch, J and Sale, H, 'Securities Analyst as Agent: Rethinking the Regulation of Analysts' (2003) *Iowa Law Review* 1035.

[33] Cain, DM, Loewenstein, G, and Moore, DA, 'The Dirt on Coming Clean: Perverse Effects of Disclosing Conflicts of Interest' (2005) 34 *The Journal of Legal Studies* 1.

analysts that are designed to reduce the possibility of a conflict arising. These include: (i) requiring the gatekeeper to put in place internal controls in order to identify possible conflicts that may arise and thereby avoid them; (ii) restricting events that might affect the gatekeeper's objectivity, for example by seeking to separate sell-side analysts from the investment banking arm of the business for which they work;[34] and (iii) reducing or excluding gatekeepers from undertaking consultancy or advisory services.[35]

There is a fundamental problem with this focus, however, as it 'faces the regulator with a Sisyphean task. Prohibit one conflict and an alternative one springs up in its place. The regulator's task therefore becomes unending.'[36] The problem arises in this context because the regulators have focused on prohibiting the conflicts that arise rather than tackling the underlying source of the conflict, namely the separation of the principal and agent in these funding models. Little or no attempt is made to tackle the underlying funding model which creates these problems in the first place. A poor substitute is put in place as regards auditors: the issuer-pays model is left intact but the audit committee of the issuer is used in some instances as a mechanism for trying to deal with the potential conflict problem.[37] It is not obvious, however, that the use of audit committees has been a valuable mechanism for enhancing the role of auditors as gatekeepers. In the US, for example, the number of financial statement restatements continued to rise after the introduction of these changes, and deficiencies continued to exist in the internal controls of the major audit firms.[38]

It may seem surprising that the funding model has not been tackled head-on, since it appears to be such an obvious cause of the conflict problem. Once the alternatives are considered, however, the difficulties inherent in any other model become apparent. There are three basic alternatives to the current funding models: (i) a 'subscriber-pays' model whereby investors hire and pay for the gatekeeper's services; (ii) a system by which the payment for the service remains where it is at present (generally with the issuer) but an independent third party, possibly

[34] In the US, for example, investment banking personnel are barred from having influence or control over the compensation of securities analysts, and reviewing any pending analyst report: NASD Rules 2711(b)(1), 2711(d)(1); NYSE Rules 472(b)(1), 472(h)(1).

[35] In relation to auditors for example, the Sarbanes–Oxley Act in the US introduced a list of services that public accounting firms are prohibited from providing to audit clients, such as bookkeeping or accounting services, investment banking services, financial information systems design, and legal services or expert services not related to audit (Sarbanes–Oxley § 201(a) codified at 15 USC § 78j–1).

[36] Coffee, n 2 above, 333.

[37] In the US see Sarbanes–Oxley esp § 202, § 204. In the EU see (in relation to public interest entities) Directive 2006/43/EC statutory audits of annual accounts and consolidated accounts [2006] OJ L157/87, Article 41; Regulation (EU) No 537/2014 on specific requirements regarding statutory audit of public interest entities and repealing Commission Directive 2005/909/EC [2014] OJ L158/9.

[38] Coffee, n 2 above, 165.

a government agency, selects the gatekeeper who will perform the service; and (iii) the gatekeeper service is performed by an independent body, possibly a government agency, either as well as or instead of the usual gatekeeper.

The flaws in a 'subscriber-pays' model are clear. In large part these are due to the public goods nature of many gatekeeper services, and the consequent free-rider issue, discussed above. Indeed, it has been argued that it was this free-rider problem that led the major CRAs in the 1970s to shift to their present issuer-pays model.[39] In addition, investors are likely to resist strongly the requirement that they pay for these services directly. The fact that no 'subscriber-pays' market for gatekeeper services has arisen suggests that such a system will not arise naturally. Some form of incentive is likely to be required to encourage investors to pay for their own ratings. So, for example, investors, specifically institutional investors, may need to be encouraged to source their own credit ratings, perhaps by mandating that such investors could not purchase debt securities until they had done so, although more ambitious models have also been suggested.[40] Furthermore, even if it could be instituted, the subscriber-pays model would not be without its own difficulties; in particular, institutions may have their own conflicts of interest. For example, when institutional investors select and pay for a CRA, it may be in their interests for credit ratings to be high as it increases their choice of investments.[41] Accordingly, shifting from the 'sell' to the 'buy' side of the market may simply swap one set of biases in favour of high ratings in favour of another set of biases in favour of high ratings.[42]

As an alternative to a pure 'subscriber-pays' model, one suggestion is that existing funding arrangements be retained, so that subscribers do not pay for the gatekeeper's services, but that the conflict between investors and gatekeepers be reduced by giving the choice of the gatekeeper to a third party. These models have been suggested, in particular, in relation to analysts[43] and CRAs. For example, as regards CRAs a proposal was put forward in the US for the creation of an independent board to choose which CRA should rate a structured-debt deal.[44] The assumption

[39] For discussion see Gudzowski, M, 'Mortgage Credit Ratings and the Financial Crisis: The Need for a State-run Mortgage Security Credit Rating Agency' (2010) 10 *Columbia Business Law Review* 245, 254–5.

[40] See, eg, Grundfest, J and Hochenberg, EH, Investor Owned and Controlled Rating Agencies: A Summary Introduction, available at <http://ssrn.com/abstract=1494527>.

[41] See Cornaggia, J and Cornaggia, KJ, 'Estimating the Costs of Issuer-Paid Credit Ratings?' (2013) 26 *Review of Financial Studies* 2229.

[42] Coffee, n 2 and n 19 above.

[43] See eg Choi, S and Fisch, J, 'How to Fix Wall Street: A Voucher Financing Proposal for Securities Intermediaries' (2003) 113 *Yale Law Journal* 269; Coffee, n 2 above, 345.

[44] See Dodd–Frank Act 2010, § 939F (the so-called Franken Amendment). This section required the SEC to carry out a study of the feasibility of establishing a system in which a self-regulatory organization assigns rating agencies to determine the credit ratings of structured finance products (the Report was published in December 2012). For discussion, see Manns, J, 'Downgrading Rating Agency Reform' (2013) *George Washington Law Review* 749.

is that taking this decision away from the issuer might reduce the incidence of 'rating shopping' whereby the issuer seeks out the most lenient CRA for this purpose. In this model the selection of the third party will obviously be key. It needs to be a body that will have knowledge and expertise of the gatekeepers in question in order to be able to select a gatekeeper based on objective criteria, such as the gatekeeper's prior record for accuracy. The availability of data to this third party will also be crucial in order to ensure that it has the objective criteria on which to operate. It is questionable, however, whether, given the volume of decisions that would be required, any kind of meaningful decision will, in fact, be possible, or whether the process would become mechanistic, and simply involve a rotation among existing gatekeepers, something that would be a particular concern where a lack of competition exists in the market, such as in relation to CRAs. More problematically, perhaps, such a rotation system would provide gatekeepers with no incentive to compete based on the quality of their services.

Another idea, advocated by some commentators, is to outsource the performance of the gatekeeper function to a government-created and managed body. This idea has only been seriously discussed by commentators in relation to CRAs,[45] although it could be developed for other gatekeepers. The suggestion is that such a body would not be the only provider of ratings, but that investors would be able to compare the ratings provided by the current players in the market with the governmental rating. This idea has had some traction is Europe as a result of US-based CRAs downgrading the sovereign debt of European states. This idea tends to assume, however, that such an institution is likely to issue more accurate and unbiased ratings than existing CRAs, which may not be the case in practice. First, a governmental agency would not be able to pay the same salaries and compensation packages as the private sector and it may therefore only be able to rely on inferior personnel or research, plus it would have the same difficulties as other new entrants into the field in terms of building and developing its methodologies. Second, a government agency would presumably be subject to its own biases and conflicts, and the possibility of regulatory capture. This issue is most obvious in the situation where it is sovereign bonds that are being rated, but biases may also arise in the context of corporate bonds and structured finance.

Moving away from the current funding model for gatekeepers would therefore be difficult, although it seems likely that only by addressing this issue head-on can the difficulties associated with CRAs as gatekeepers really be tackled.[46]

[45] See eg Gudzowski, M, 'Mortgage Credit Ratings and the Financial Crisis: The Need for a State-Run Mortgage Security Credit Rating Agency' (2010) 10 *Columbia Business Law Review* 245.

[46] Coffee, n 2 and n 19 above.

(c) *Regulatory oversight*

Another option for regulators, which can be introduced alongside some or all of the other regulatory mechanisms described above, is to make use of structural reform, ie to enhance the regulatory oversight of gatekeepers. Many gatekeepers began as self-regulating professions. While this self-regulatory model is largely retained for some gatekeepers, such as analysts, for others this is changing. This is illustrated most dramatically in relation to CRAs. In the US, regulation of CRAs was given to the Securities and Exchange Commission (SEC) in 2006,[47] and the Dodd–Frank Act creates a new body, the Office of Credit Ratings at the SEC, to hold rating agencies accountable and to protect investors and businesses.[48] In the EU, the self-regulatory model, based on a Code of Conduct developed by IOSCO (the International Organization of Securities Commissions),[49] has been replaced by a mandatory regime for registering and regulating CRAs, subjecting them to supervision by the European Securities and Markets Authority (ESMA).[50]

Regulatory oversight of gatekeepers can be potentially valuable as a mechanism for increasing investor protection, but whether it fulfils that potential will, of course, depend on the power and remit given to these bodies to manage the conflicts that arise, and how they exercise those powers. One particularly valuable function that public regulators can perform in relation to gatekeepers is to collect accurate and easily understood comparative data on the ratings produced by intermediaries,[51] and to disseminate that information to investors. Regulators can also perform an important role in monitoring and responding to disclosures by intermediaries. For example, CRAs are required to disclose their methodologies, and regulators can potentially provide a meaningful check on CRAs by responding to any deviations from those publicly disclosed methodologies. As discussed, disclosure to investors seems to be a limited tool for ensuring good performance from gatekeepers, but disclosure to regulators, depending on what they then do with those disclosures, could be more effective. In relation to both the US and the EU, their regulatory oversight of CRAs comprises broad and potentially significant powers, including the power of the regulator to require registration, to restrict conflicts of interest, to require disclosure, and to monitor performance.[52] They also have considerable sticks to encourage good performance: both the SEC and ESMA

[47] Credit Rating Agency Reform Act 2006. [48] Dodd–Frank Act, § 932(a)(8).

[49] IOSCO, Code of Conduct Fundamentals for Credit Rating Agencies (2004). The first IOSCO review took place in 2007 resulting in a revised Code in 2008. A further review took place in 2014.

[50] Regulation (EU) No 513/2011 Amending Regulation (EC) No 1060/2009 on Credit Rating Agencies [2011] OJ L145/30.

[51] See Bai, L, 'The Performance Disclosures of Credit Rating Agencies: Are they Effective Reputational Sanctions?' (2010) 7 *NYU Journal of Law and Business* 47.

[52] See Dodd–Frank Act § 932; Regulation (EU) No 513/2011, Article 1(9).

are permitted to impose fines and to suspend or revoke a rating agency's licence.[53] It is still early days, and so it is unclear what use these regulators are going to make of their powers, or how intrusive they will be.

2. The incentive to protect reputation

The value of gatekeepers as a mechanism for investor protection is built on the reputational capital model, set out in Section II. This model relies on there being strong incentives for the intermediary to maintain its reputation, although a credible and significant threat of litigation may also act as an effective incentive for the intermediary. Of course, loss of reputation can have a devastating effect on gatekeepers. Take the example of Enron's auditors, Arthur Anderson. It has been convincingly argued that the downfall of this firm ultimately followed not from its criminal conviction, but because it came to have 'negative' reputational capital.[54] This was an extreme situation, however, and there are reasons to doubt whether loss of reputation in general is a sufficiently strong incentive for gatekeepers to perform their task well. In some instances the erosion in the value of 'reputation' for gatekeepers arises as a result of particular market conditions; for example, it has been suggested that in 'bubble' markets the value of gatekeeper reputation will reduce since investors lose their natural scepticism about issuer disclosures.[55] Other causes of this erosion are more persistent. Two examples of the more persistent kind of effects that can reduce the value of reputation for gatekeepers are discussed here, namely (a) a lack of competition in the market for gatekeepers and (b) the effect of a 'regulatory licence'.

(a) *A lack of competition among gatekeepers*

One issue that can affect a gatekeeper's incentive to maintain its reputation is the amount of competition in the market. In concentrated markets it may not be necessary for the intermediary to maintain an unblemished record, just one that is not significantly worse than its rivals. This issue is particularly obvious in relation to CRAs and auditors. There is almost no competition among CRAs. There are only three major ratings agencies worldwide, and two of them, Moody's and Standard and Poor's, dominate the market. This lack of competition is caused by high barriers to entry (complex methodologies need to be developed by CRAs) but also because regulators have entitled selected ratings agencies to confer *de facto* dispensations on issuers from various regulatory requirements if they receive high

[53] For discussion see Coffee, n 19 above, 246–50 (where it is noted that some importance differences in the powers of the regulators do exist).

[54] Coffee, n 2 above, 4.

[55] ibid, 329–30.

ratings from certain CRAs. In the US, this was achieved via the use of the NRSRO (Nationally Recognized Statistical Rating Organization) licensing system. There is a similar lack of competition in the audit profession. At the current time there are just four main audit firms (the 'Big Four'), which dominate the market.[56] In a market this concentrated, implicit collusion can develop between the firms. This tends to mean that as long as a firm is not spectacularly worse than the other main players then 'investors cannot meaningfully discriminate among shades of grey'.[57] As a result, intermediaries have little incentive to perform better than the other major players in the market. This problem will be exacerbated if it is difficult or unattractive for issuers to switch gatekeepers. It has been suggested, for example, that an issuer will be reluctant to change accounting firms because it is expensive for a new accounting firm to get to know the company, but perhaps more importantly because investors will wonder whether the switch suggests a problem that the first accounting firm had discovered in relation to the issuer's financial statements.[58]

Some attempts have been made to address this issue. In the EU, for example, new provisions require debt issuers to rotate between the CRAs that rate them for certain complex structured financial instruments,[59] and in relation to auditors, some institutions (specifically 'public interest entities') are required to rotate audit firms every ten years.[60] While the market for both CRAs and auditing services remains so concentrated, however, it is difficult to see what requiring firms to rotate around the dominant firms will achieve in terms of investor protection. Consequently, some efforts have been made to tackle these concerns and to encourage new entrants to enter the market. For example, in the US there has been an increase in the numbers of NRSROs, although it is fair to say that this has had little or no impact to date on the dominant position of the three main CRAs. However, competition among gatekeepers is not guaranteed to increase investor protection. Empirical evidence suggests that competition among CRAs may, in fact, reduce investor protection if issuers can then shop for ratings.[61]

(b) *The effect of a 'regulatory licence'*

Another example of a situation whereby the desire to retain a reputation can be reduced arises as a result of the hard-wiring of CRAs into the regulatory system. No other gatekeeper is subject to this particular issue. It has been suggested that CRAs do not so much perform as reputational intermediaries (ie certifying disclosure) but

[56] Coffee, J, 'It's about the Gatekeepers, Stupid' (2002) 57 *Business Lawyer* 1403, 1413–15.

[57] Coffee, n 2 above, 320.

[58] ibid, ch 5.

[59] Regulation (EU) No 462/2013 Amending Regulation (EC) No 1060/2009 on Credit Rating Agencies [2013] OJ L146/1, Article 1(8), inserting new Article 6b.

[60] Regulation (EU) No 537/2014, Article 17.

[61] Bolton, P, Freixas, X, and Shapiro, J, 'The Credit Ratings Game' (2012) 67 *Journal of Finance* 85; Becker, B and Milbourn, T, 'How Did Increased Competition Affect Credit Ratings?' (2011) *Journal of Financial Economics* 493.

rather that they perform a regulatory licence role.[62] The non-informational benefits of a credit rating enable the CRA to confer a 'regulatory licence' on its customers. This might be because a rating enables issuers to escape costly regulatory burdens or prohibitions to which it would otherwise be subject. Alternatively, it might be because the ratings provide a benefit to portfolio managers and institutional investors, because they insulate them from a claim that they breached their fiduciary duty if the investment later turns sour. To the extent that the rating can reduce the cost to the issuer or to the investor, the CRA can sell regulatory licences to help to reduce these costs.[63] As a result, the CRA may be less concerned to preserve its reputation than the reputational capital model would predict. The focus for the CRA may simply be on protecting its ability to issue regulatory licences. Some commentators, perhaps most notably Professor Partnoy, regard this as the primary reason for the failure of CRAs to act as appropriate gatekeepers in recent years,[64] and therefore suggest that the appropriate regulatory response is to remove this licence where possible; for example, by eliminating the need for regulated financial institutions to obtain investment grade ratings before investing. In addition, Professor Partnoy suggests that alternatives to credit ratings, such as credit default swap spreads, should be encouraged as at least a partial substitute for ratings.[65] Given how hard-wired into the system CRAs have become, however, undoing this effect is not straightforward, and regulators have struggled to tackle this issue in a meaningful way. The Dodd–Frank Act, for example, requires that all federal agencies delete references to credit ratings, or requirements for reliance on such ratings, from their regulations, and adopt their own standards of creditworthiness—something which is probably easier said than done.[66] In and of itself this does not seem likely to wean institutional investors, banks, and other market participants off ratings.[67] An alternative approach is to seek to diminish the reliance on ratings by focusing on investors. So, for example, in the EU recent measures seek to reduce the over-reliance on ratings by requiring that financial institutions should not blindly rely only on credit ratings when picking investments, but that they should also make their own assessments.[68] While this is a laudable aim, it is unlikely that such provisions will lead to a significant reduction in investors' reliance on CRAs or impact significantly on the regulatory licence held by ratings agencies. For the foreseeable future, CRAs seem likely to remain part of the financial infrastructure of capital markets.

[62] Coffee, n 2 above, 283; Partnoy, n 15 above.

[63] Partnoy, n 15 above.

[64] Partnoy, n 15 and n 17 above.

[65] Flannery, MJ, Houston, JF, and Partnoy, F, 'Credit Default Swap Spreads as Viable Substitutes for Credit Ratings' (2010) 158 *University of Pennsylvania Law Review* 2085.

[66] Dodd–Frank Act § 939A.

[67] For a discussion of some of the groups that have become dependent on ratings see *Financial Stability Board, Principles for Reducing Reliance on CRA Ratings* (2010).

[68] Regulation (EU) No 462/2013, Article 1(6), inserting new Article 5a.

3. Litigation risk

These problems regarding a reduced desire to preserve reputation can be ameliorated to a certain extent if the intermediary nevertheless faces an effective threat of litigation. Even if it will not suffer from a reputational loss, if the gatekeeper will face financial losses in excess of its expected gains from an involvement in fraud, this can incentivize the intermediary to act as an effective gatekeeper. Since the gatekeeper is an agent of the principal (the issuer), and will therefore receive less profit than the principal itself will make, in theory litigation can operate to more easily deter the gatekeeper than the principal. This mechanism can only succeed, however, if the threat of litigation is credible. It has been suggested that the existence of legal liability for some gatekeepers can operate as a potentially significant tool to ensure their independence.[69] While mechanisms for liability do exist for some gatekeepers to their clients and, more rarely, to third parties, it has been argued that, in general, the litigation risk for gatekeepers declined in the 1990s, particularly in the US.[70] In relation to other gatekeepers, even the possibility of litigation seems effectively absent. This is illustrated most clearly by CRAs.[71] For many years the SEC effectively exempted CRAs from liability under section 11 of the Securities Act 1933, which provides that an 'expert' whose opinion is cited in a registration statement used in connection with a public offering of securities has presumptive liability for any material misstatement that it makes.[72] In addition, in the US the argument has been made that since credit ratings are expressions of opinion they are protected by the First Amendment, although the case law is divided on this question.[73] Recent reforms in both the US[74] and Europe[75] have sought to increase the litigation risk for this gatekeeper in particular.

The use of litigation to increase the investor protection provided by gatekeepers requires some thought. The funding structures, described above, mean that in general investors are not the client and do not pay for the services of the gatekeepers. A separate mechanism needs to be created to provide investors with a means of redress, either directly or via a regulatory body, such as the SEC. An important issue to consider is whether the goal of such redress is deterrence, ie increasing

[69] See, in relation to auditors, Farmer, TA, Rittenberg, LE, and Trompeter, GM, 'An Investigation of the Impact of Economic and Organization Factors on Auditor Independence' (1987) 7(1) *Auditing: A Journal of Practice & Theory* 1.

[70] Coffee, n 56 above, 1403.

[71] Successful litigation against CRAs is rare, but not impossible as two recent Australian cases demonstrate: *Bathurst Regional Council v Local Government Financial Services Pty Ltd (No 5)* [2012] FCA 1200; *ABM AMRO Bank NV v Bathurst Regional Council* [2014] FCAFC 65.

[72] See SEC Rule 436(g): 17 C.F.R. § 230.436(g).

[73] For discussion see Deats, C, 'Talk Isn't that Cheap: Does the First Amendment Protect Credit Rating Agencies' Faulty Methodologies from Regulation?' (2010) 110 *Columbia Law Review* 1818.

[74] Dodd–Frank Act § 933.

[75] Regulation (EU) No 462/2013, Article 1(22), inserting new Article 35a.

the quality of the gatekeepers' certification and verification role, or compensation for investors if that role is inadequately performed, or both. The compensatory approach is more problematic, not least because often it will be impossible for gatekeepers to compensate all, or even most, of their victims.[76] Take the example of the losses caused by errors in the ratings of structured finance products, which ran into billions of dollars. To seek to impose such losses on the CRAs that provided those ratings would bankrupt them, and still many investors would remain uncompensated. This raises a serious difficulty with the use of the litigation threat as a means of regulating gatekeepers. These intermediaries perform an important and valuable role for investors and the market generally, as described in Section II above, and it is understandable that regulators want to ensure that this role is performed to an optimum level. An undue threat of litigation, however, may cause the gatekeepers to react negatively in a way that ultimately harms both the market and investors. One reaction would be to increase the size of their fees, but given the potential scale of the compensation that might be demanded, it is also possible that gatekeepers may react by withdrawing their services. So, for example, one of the reforms put forward in the Dodd–Frank Act,[77] designed to remove an exemption from liability for CRAs under the Securities Act 1933, led to CRAs refusing to allow their ratings to be included in asset-backed bond offering documents, and, as a result, for a brief time the public debt markets froze and offerings were delayed, until the SEC reconsidered the imposition of liability on CRAs in this regard.[78] This demonstrates the need to set the litigation threat at an acceptable level.

A more appropriate and realistic objective for litigation is to focus on deterrence, but even here care is required to ensure that this policy objective is introduced in such a way as to encourage the gatekeeper to perform its task well, and not simply to withdraw its services. A significant litigation threat may also dissuade new entrants from entering the field, and, as discussed, a lack of competition can have a deleterious effect on the likelihood of intermediaries acting as effective investor protection devices. These concerns may operate differently in relation to the various gatekeepers. An error by an auditor in relation to a single company is likely to affect only that one issuer, and investors in it. By contrast, an error by a CRA in developing a particular valuation model might produce inflated ratings in dozens or hundreds of issuers, with the potential losses resulting therefrom being significantly higher. Although the need for deterrence in relation to the CRA might therefore be larger, there is also a correspondingly greater possibility of the CRA withdrawing its services if the threat of liability is too great. Therefore, the threat of litigation, if

[76] For discussion see Coffee, n 19 above, 252–3.

[77] Dodd–Frank Act, § 939G, repealing Rule 436(g) promulgated under the Securities Act of 1933, as amended.

[78] See Coffee, n 19 above, 264–5.

utilized, needs to be implemented carefully. In some instances it may be important to consider safe harbours for the gatekeeper and ceilings on liability.

4. Moral hazard

Finally, it is worth highlighting the potential moral hazard problem that arises as a result of reliance on a gatekeeper's services. The existence of intermediaries may lull other market participants into a false sense of security, causing them to rely on the intermediaries and to seek out less information of their own. Some of the reforms referred to earlier in this Chapter recognize this, and provisions in both the US and the EU, particularly in relation to credit ratings, seek to put the onus back onto investors to carry out their own assessments.[79] This may not be realistic. As Professor Coffee has suggested, '"do-it-yourself" financial analysis of opaque debt instruments is no more feasible for most financial institutions than "do-it-yourself" brain surgery'.[80] Gatekeepers perform a potentially valuable function, and without a meaningful alternative option for investors, simply requiring them to put less reliance on gatekeeper services is unlikely to achieve a great deal.

IV. Comments on the Regulatory Response

So far this century there have been two waves of regulation, the first, post-Enron, that largely focused on auditors and analysts, and the second which responded to the issues and difficulties presented by the global financial crisis and has focused on CRAs, as well as introducing new reforms for other gatekeepers. In particular, the role of CRAs in the financial crisis, through their role in developing structured financial products, and in the aftermath of crisis in relation to their role in downgrading sovereign debt, has kept the regulation of this gatekeeper firmly in the political spotlight in recent years.

It is notable that of the five different gatekeepers discussed in this Chapter, one of them is effectively absent from these regulatory discussions: there appears to be no strong desire to regulate underwriters per se at present. From the investors' point of view, the use of underwriters as gatekeepers appears to be a success, or at least no significant suggestion of failure has emerged. The empirical evidence

[79] See nn 66–8 above and associated text.

[80] Coffee, n 19 above, 233.

suggests that any concerns about the pricing of IPOs and seasoned equity offerings relates to underpricing rather than overpricing.[81] A potential problem can, however, arise where the same investment bank acts as underwriter to an issuer and then its in-house securities analysts provide recommendations in relation to that issuer. To the extent that this conflict exists, the choice seems to have been to tackle it via the regulation of sell-side analysts, ie via the regulation of those analysts attached to investment firms who might be exposed to these conflicts, rather than via the regulation of underwriters.

Of the remaining gatekeepers, the focus of regulatory attention has been on three of them, namely analysts, auditors, and CRAs, with less attention being given to lawyers.[82] This may be because of a comparatively reduced potential for conflict compared with other gatekeepers: the market for legal services is much more competitive and less concentrated than is the market for auditing services or CRAs. There are dozens of large law firms that can be hired by an issuer to provide legal services, in contrast to the Big Four audit firms, and the three main CRAs. In addition, large companies are likely to have their own in-house legal team for many general purposes and may make use of many different law firms for specialist advice in different areas.[83] So, the relationship is likely to be less long term, less intense, and less susceptible to capture. Probably more relevant, however, is the fact that lawyers are not such obvious gatekeepers. First, the fact that lawyers usually operate as advocates or as transaction engineers means that their mindset is generally as facilitators for their clients rather than as representatives of the public, performing some kind of watchdog role. Second, and linked to this, is the fact that lawyers are subject to strict client confidentiality obligations as part of their professional ethics. If lawyers discover some fraud on the part of the client in the process of a due diligence exercise, which the client refuses to disclose, then per se the lawyers' obligation is to keep that discovery confidential and not to disclose it to the public. Although some commentators have argued that the role of lawyers as gatekeepers should be increased,[84] there seems little appetite at the present time for any form of expanded role for lawyers in this regard.

[81] See eg Beatty, RP and Ritter, J, 'Investment Banking, Reputation, and the Underpricing of Initial Public Offerings' (1986) 15 *Journal of Financial Economics* 213; Rock, K, 'Why New Issues Are Underpriced' (1986) 15 *Journal of Financial Economics* 187; Carter, R and Manaster, S, 'Initial Public Offerings and Underwriter Reputation' (1990) 45 *Journal of Finance* 1045.

[82] Where changes have been introduced in this regard they appear to be based on disclosure obligations, eg Sarbanes–Oxley, § 307 and see Securities Act Release No 33-8185 (6 February 2003) (Implementation of Standards of Professional Conduct for Attorneys). Since this obligation does not require reporting outside the client company, there is no breach of client confidentiality.

[83] DeMott, DA, 'The Discrete Roles of General Counsel' (2005) 74 *Fordham Law Review* 955.

[84] Coffee, n 2 above, ch 10; Coffee, J, 'The Attorney as Gatekeeper: An Agenda for the SEC' (2003) 103 *Columbia Law Review* 1293. cf Bainbridge, S and Johnson, C, 'Managerialism, Legal Ethics and Sarbanes Oxley Section 307' (2004) *Michigan State Law Review* 299.

Consequently, only three gatekeepers have come within the regulatory spotlight: analysts, auditors, and CRAs. Even in relation to analysts, the regulatory focus has not been on all analysts, but on only on those analysts where the potential for conflict between the gatekeeper and the investor is perceived to be most acute, namely sell-side analysts. So the focus on gatekeeper regulation in the last decade or so has not been on all gatekeepers, but on a sub-set of them.

An examination of the regulations that have been put in place regarding gatekeepers in this period reveals a number of points. There appears to be general agreement that gatekeepers, particularly auditors, analysts, and CRAs, have failed as investor protection devices and that regulatory intervention is needed to address these failures. There is also general agreement as to why these gatekeepers have failed, namely that their performance has been compromised by serious conflicts of interest, which have been exacerbated in some instances by additional factors such as a lack of competition, a lack of litigation risk, or, in the case of CRAs, the existence of a regulatory licence. The reforms that have been introduced have involved an increased regulatory burden being placed on these gatekeepers. For sell-side analysts, this has predominantly taken the form of prophylactic rules aimed at reducing the level of the conflict that arises, coupled with some disclosure obligations regarding the nature of the conflict that affects them. For CRAs, prophylactic rules again form the core of the regulatory agenda, linked to disclosure obligations, but, in addition, CRAs have been brought within the regulatory remit of public bodies, such as the SEC and ESMA, attempts have been made to increase the litigation risk for CRAs, to increase competition in the CRA market, and to address the regulatory licence issue, albeit weakly. For auditors, prophylactic rules to reduce the conflict form the core of the response in both the EU and the US, and are coupled with rules aimed at dealing with the lack of competition, particularly in the EU, and rules which increase the regulatory oversight of auditors, particularly in the US.

Of course, there have been differences, some significant, in the way that the US and the EU have addressed these issues, not least because the institutional culture and regulatory options in the US and Europe differ. Viewed broadly, however, there has been a relatively consistent approach to regulation of these gatekeepers adopted by US and EU regulators. What is particularly striking is that in both cases there is a noticeable failure to grapple with the fundamental problem head-on, namely the conflict issue caused by the funding models for each gatekeeper and, in the case of CRAs, possibly also the regulatory licence issue. In general, the consequences of the problem are tackled (attempts are made to reduce the conflicts that arise) and some allied issues are addressed, such as the lack of competition in relation to some gatekeepers, but the underlying cause of the conflict (the funding issue) is not. There is little or no meaningful attempt to link investors and gatekeepers through some form of 'subscriber-pays' model, or to put in place an independent third party, possibly a government agency, to either select the gatekeeper or to carry out the gatekeeper function itself on behalf of investors. This is not surprising. For the reasons discussed in Section III above, none of these options are straightforward to implement, and, in any case, it is not always clear that the outcome would be improved since other biases, on the part of institutional investors or government agencies, could be introduced to replace existing biases. Of course, this is not to suggest that efforts cannot or should not be attempted. Similarly, the regulatory licence point, which undoubtedly complicates the issue of CRAs as gatekeepers, has barely been tackled by regulators. Again, this is unsurprising given how hard-wired into the regulatory system CRAs have become. Without these fundamental issues being addressed, however, the validity and overall effectiveness of the regulatory response to these issues of gatekeeper failure discussed in Section III, is undoubtedly reduced.

V. Conclusion

Gatekeepers can perform an important role in the capital markets by lending their reputational capital to issuers in relation to the issuer's disclosures, thereby providing investors with a crucial verification and certification service. There are a number of limitations on the effectiveness of gatekeepers as an investor protection device, however, largely as a result of the conflict of interest arising out of the funding model for gatekeepers, but exacerbated by factors which reduce a gatekeeper's incentive to perform its role well, including a lack of competition in the market, a lack of litigation risk, and, in relation to CRAs, the development of a regulatory licence. Changes in the modes of operation of gatekeepers in the last years of the twentieth century and early years of this century exacerbated these problems and led to a series of high-profile gatekeeper failures. These failures led, in turn, to a focus on reform and regulatory intervention. While the first wave of regulation, following Enron and similar scandals, focused on the regulation of auditors and sell-side analysts, the second wave of regulation, in the wake of the global financial crisis, has had CRAs firmly at its centre. In relation to many of these reforms, it is still too early to determine their precise effect. Dramatic changes, such as the fact that within the EU CRAs are now subject to a single, pan-European regulator in the form of ESMA, have not yet had time to bed in. Despite the raft of measures put in place, however, regulators have largely failed to tackle the core issues that lead to gatekeeper failure, and therefore while many of the measures that have been implemented can be regarded as valuable, the overall effectiveness of the regulatory response can be doubted.

Bibliography

Akerlof, GA, 'The Market for "Lemons": Quality Uncertainty and the Market Mechanism' (1970) 84 *Quarterly Journal of Economics* 488.

Bai, L, 'The Performance Disclosures of Credit Rating Agencies: Are they Effective Reputational Sanctions?' (2010) 7 *NYU Journal of Law and Business* 47.

Bainbridge, S and Johnson, C, 'Managerialism, Legal Ethics and Sarbanes Oxley Section 307' (2004) *Michigan State Law Review* 299.

Beatty, RP and Ritter, J, 'Investment Banking, Reputation, and the Underpricing of Initial Public Offerings' (1986) 15 *Journal of Financial Economics* 213.

Becker, B and Milbourn, T, 'How did Increased Competition Affect Credit Ratings?' (2011) *Journal of Financial Economics* 493.

Bolton, P, Freixas, X, and Shapiro, J, 'The Credit Ratings Game' (2012) 67 *Journal of Finance* 85.

Booth, JR and Smith, RL, 'Capital Raising, Underwriting and the Certification Hypothesis' (1986) *Journal of Financial Economics* 261.

Bradley, DJ, Jordan, BD, and Ritter, JR, 'Analyst Behaviour following IPOs: The Bubble Period Evidence' (2008) 21 *Review of Financial Studies* 101.

Brunnermeier, MK, 'Deciphering the 2007–08 Liquidity and Credit Crunch' (2009) 23 *Journal of Economic Perspectives* 77.

Cain, DM, Loewenstein, G, and Moore, DA, 'The Dirt on Coming Clean: Perverse Effects of Disclosing Conflicts of Interest' (2005) 34 *The Journal of Legal Studies* 1.

Carter, R and Manaster, S, 'Initial Public Offerings and Underwriter Reputation' (1990) 45 *Journal of Finance* 1045.

Choi, S and Fisch, J, 'How to Fix Wall Street: A Voucher Financing Proposal for Securities Intermediaries' (2003) 113 *Yale Law Journal* 269.

Coffee, J, 'The Attorney as Gatekeeper: An Agenda for the SEC' (2003) 103 *Columbia Law Review* 1293.

Coffee, J, *Gatekeepers: The Professions and Corporate Governance* (2006).

Coffee, J, 'It's about the Gatekeepers, Stupid' (2002) 57 *The Business Lawyer* 1403.

Coffee, J, 'Ratings Reform: The Good, the Bad and the Ugly' (2011) *Harvard Business Law Review* 231.

Coffee, J, 'What Caused Enron? A Capsule Social and Economic History of the 1990s' in Clarke, T (ed.), *Theories of Corporate Governance* (2004).

Deats, C, 'Talk Isn't that Cheap: Does the First Amendment Protect Credit Rating Agencies' Faulty Methodologies from Regulation?' (2010) 110 *Columbia Law Review* 1818.

DeMott, DA, 'The Discrete Roles of General Counsel' (2005) 74 *Fordham Law Review* 955.

Dichev, I and Piotroski, J, 'The Long-run Stock Returns following Bond Ratings Changes' (2001) 56 *Journal of Finance* 173.

Farmer, TA, Rittenberg, LE, and Trompeter, GM, 'An Investigation of the Impact of Economic and Organization Factors on Auditor Independence' (1987) 7(1) *Auditing: A Journal of Practice & Theory* 1.

Ferrarini, G and Guidici, P, 'Financial Scandals and the Role of Private Enforcement' in Armour, J and McCahery, J (eds), *After Enron: Reforming Corporate Governance and Capital Markets in Europe and the US* (2006).
Fisch, J and Sale, H, 'Securities Analyst as Agent: Rethinking the Regulation of Analysts' (2003) *Iowa Law Review* 1035.
Flannery, MJ, Houston, JF, and Partnoy, F, 'Credit Default Swap Spreads as Viable Substitutes for Credit Ratings' (2010) 158 *University of Pennsylvania Law Review* 2085.
Gilson, R and Kraakman, R, 'The Mechanisms of Market Efficiency' (1984) 70 *Virginia Law Review* 549.
Grundfest, J and Hochenberg, EH, Investor Owned and Controlled Rating Agencies: A Summary Introduction, available at <http://ssrn.com/abstract=1494527>.
Gudzowski, M, 'Mortgage Credit Ratings and the Financial Crisis: The Need for a State-Run Mortgage Security Credit Rating Agency' (2010) 10 *Columbia Business Law Review* 245.
Hand, J, Holthausen, R, and Leftwich, R, 'The Effect of Bond Rating Agency Announcements on Bond and Stock Prices' (1992) 47 *Journal of Finance* 733.
Hong, H and Kubik, J, 'Analysing the Analysts: Career Concerns and Biased Earnings Forecasts' (2003) 58 *Journal of Finance* 313.
IOSCO, Code of Conduct Fundamentals for Credit Rating Agencies (2004, revised 2008).
Kliger, D and Sarig, O, 'The Information Value of Bond Ratings' (2000) 55 *Journal of Finance* 2879.
Kowan, A, Groysberg, B, and Healy, P, 'Which Types of Analyst Firms Are more Optimistic?' (2006) *Journal of Accounting and Economics* 119.
Kraakman, R, 'Corporate Liability Strategies and the Costs of Legal Controls' (1984) 93 *Yale Law Journal* 857.
Kraakman, R, 'Gatekeepers: The Anatomy of a Third-Party Enforcement Strategy' (1986) 2 *Journal of Law, Economics & Organization* 53.
Michaely, R and Womack, KL, 'Conflict of Interest and Credibility of Underwriter Analyst Recommendations' (1999) 12 *Review of Financial Studies* 653.
Partnoy, F, 'Historical Perspectives on the Financial Crisis: Ivar Kreugar, the Credit Rating Agencies, and Two Theories about the Function, and Dysfunction, of Markets' (2010) 26 *Yale Journal on Regulation* 431.
Partnoy, F, How and Why Credit Rating Agencies Are not Like Other Gatekeepers (2006), University of San Diego Legal Studies Research Paper Series No 07-46, available at <http://ssrn.com/abstract=900257>.
Partnoy, F, Overdependence on Credit Ratings Was a Primary Cause of the Crisis (2009), San Diego Legal Studies Paper No 09-015, available at <http://ssrn.com/abstract=1430653>.
Partnoy, F, 'The Siskel and Ebert of Financial Markets? Two Thumbs Down for the Credit-Rating Agencies' (1999) 77 *Washington University Law Quarterly* 619.
Rock, K, 'Why New Issues Are Underpriced' (1986) 15 *Journal of Financial Economics* 187.
Stiglitz, J, *Free Fall: America, Free Markets and the Sinking of the World Economy* (2010).
Tett, G, *Fool's Gold: How Unrestrained Greed Corrupted a Dream, Shattered Global Markets and Unleashed a Catastrophe* (2009).
US Senate Permanent Subcommittee on Investigations (2011), Wall Street and the Financial Crisis: Anatomy of a Financial Collapse, Majority and Minority Staff Report, 6.
Welch, I, 'Herding among Security Analysts' (2000) 58 *Journal of Financial Economics* 369.

CHAPTER 10

ENFORCEMENT AND SANCTIONING

IAIN MACNEIL

I. Introduction

Enforcement is the process by which a regulatory authority or a person who has suffered harm takes action to punish or remedy a contravention of regulatory rules. It is axiomatic that regulatory rules are capable of enforcement in some way but limited resources generally mean that it is very unlikely that all rules will be enforced or be enforced in the same way. Regulators are generally not mandated to enforce all violations of the rules and can often use their discretion to determine whether to take enforcement action and what type of penalty to impose. Moreover, the pattern and style of enforcement is unlikely to remain stable over time since it is likely to adapt to changes in the entire regulatory system.

The nature and style of enforcement is inevitably linked with regulatory objectives and earlier stages of regulatory engagement (such as rulemaking and supervision), which influence the capacity for enforcement and the manner in which it occurs. In the case of the (now common) financial stability objective, which is pursued through prudential supervision, the focus is on the stability of the financial system as a whole and the capacity for financial distress in a single firm to be transmitted across the entire system. The emphasis on *ex ante* prevention of systemic risk means that *ex post* enforcement action cannot play a major role in prudential supervision because by that time the regulator will have failed to secure the regulatory objective. In those instances there may be no real option to selecting compliance as the only possible enforcement strategy, especially since its focus is preventative and forward-looking rather than remedial and backward-looking as in the case of deterrence. The result is that there is inevitably greater reliance on persuasion than enforcement in prudential supervision. In contrast, *ex post* enforcement action plays a much greater role in the case of conduct regulation because deterrence and restitution are effective means to pursue the objectives of investor and consumer protection.

By comparison with other aspects of financial regulation, enforcement has tended to attract relatively less attention, at least prior to the financial crisis which began in 2007. The initial focus of attention was on the different enforcement styles that were evident in the US and the UK since those two countries share large and sophisticated financial markets but adopt very different approaches to enforcement, with the former giving priority to enforcement and the latter subordinating formal enforcement to supervision and negotiated compliance. The onset of the financial crisis provided further impetus for research into enforcement especially since the absence of enforcement action in the early years of the crisis raised fundamental issues with regard to the capacity of the regulatory system to control misconduct. This perspective led to a widening of the research agenda to encompass issues such as the role of private enforcement in supplementing public enforcement, the degree to which individuals should be held accountable as opposed to their employers and the design of effective sanctions.

This Chapter links these issues with earlier theoretical and empirical research drawn from other regulatory domains. The more specific discussion of enforcement in the context of financial regulation focuses in particular on the regulatory systems in the UK and the US but addresses issues that are relevant for enforcement in any jurisdiction. The Chapter begins by considering the enforcement strategies that may be adopted by the regulator. The key issues here are the extent to which enforcement is appropriate and the manner in which it is linked with the compliance strategies adopted by regulated firms. Consideration is then given to empirical studies of enforcement activity in the UK and the US with a view to determining the impact of different enforcement styles. These studies focus primarily on public enforcement activity by regulators and therefore the following section considers the potential for and the impact of private enforcement. Attention then turns to sanctions. The key questions here relate to who should bear responsibility especially as between individuals and firms and the design of the sanctions regime by reference to the type of sanctions and how they are applied to individual cases. Finally, in recognition of the international nature of many financial markets and firms, the Chapter concludes with an examination of the mechanisms employed by regulators to facilitate enforcement in cases with a cross-border dimension.

II. Enforcement Strategies

1. Options

The range of enforcement strategies available to the regulator can be characterized as extending along a spectrum ranging from deterrence to compliance.[1] In the words of Ayres and Braithwaite: 'The crucial question has become "When to punish; and when to persuade".'[2] The issue is not so much which approach to adopt but when each is likely to be appropriate. A deterrence-based approach to enforcement focuses on certainty and severity of the punishment for contravention and its

[1] For a refinement of the two-dimensional model see Braithwaite, J, Walker, J, and Grabosky, P, 'An Enforcement Taxonomy of Regulatory Agencies' (1987) 9 *Law and Policy* 323, proposing a taxonomy of seven enforcement styles derived from empirical data on enforcement relating to 96 Australian federal, state, and local government agencies involved in business regulation.

[2] Ayres, I and Braithwaite, J, *Responsive Regulation: Transcending the Deregulation Debate* (1992) 21.

potential to deter both the individual transgressor and the wider regulated community. Effective deterrence requires in principle that the expected penalty should exceed the social harm caused by the regulatory contravention[3] but that may be difficult to quantify especially when a regulatory contravention is only one of several causes of the social harm. By way of contrast, a compliance-based approach focuses on the capacity of negotiation and persuasion to promote compliance with regulatory rules.[4]

The selection of deterrence or compliance as a basic strategy can be linked to the characterization of regulated firms and their typical mode of behaviour. According to Kagan and Scholz, there are three generic types of regulated firm: the 'amoral calculator', which bases its approach to compliance on the probability of detection and the severity of the sanction that may be imposed; the 'political citizen', which adopts a responsible approach based on voluntary compliance; and the 'organizationally incompetent', for whom non-compliance is associated with management and organizational structures that do not have the capacity to implement a proper compliance programme.[5] In each case, the appropriate enforcement strategy differs: a deterrence-based approach for the amoral calculator; a compliance-based approach for the political citizen; and an education-based approach for the incompetent organization. But since all regulated persons may display elements of all three characteristics, the real problem is to establish the correct mix in the enforcement strategy.

2. The role of discretion

The level of discretion granted to the regulator with respect to enforcement is a significant factor for the choice of enforcement strategy. Enforcement action is rarely if ever mandated by law and, therefore, the exercise of discretion by regulators with regard to enforcement is a key influence in the operation of regulatory systems. Discretion provides a solution to the uncertainty associated with regulatory rules, permitting them to be applied in a reasonable and contextual manner in an evolving business environment.[6] While some forms of simple prohibition may be capable of mechanistic enforcement, many regulatory rules limit or control conduct in a manner that requires the application of a degree of discretion to the enforcement process.[7] Even when discretion is widely framed, the regulator's enforcement

[3] Becker, G, 'Crime and Punishment: An Economic Approach' (1968) 76 *Journal of Political Economy* 169.

[4] Hutter, B, 'Variations in Regulatory Enforcement Styles' (1989) 11 *Law and Policy* 153.

[5] Kagan, R and Scholz, J, 'The Criminology of the Corporation and Regulatory Enforcement Strategies' in Hawkins, K and Thomas, J (eds), *Enforcing Regulation* (1984).

[6] Scholz, J, 'Voluntary Compliance and Regulatory Enforcement' (1984) 6(4) *Law & Policy* 385.

[7] Hawkins, K and Thomas, J 'The Enforcement Process in Regulatory Bureaucracies' in Hawkins, K and Thomas, J (eds), *Enforcing Regulation* (1984).

strategy is likely to be constrained by regulatory objectives and by generally accepted principles applicable to the exercise of discretion by public authorities.[8]

The priority given by regulators to enforcement as part of the regulatory process is itself an exercise of discretionary power at a strategic level. The Securities and Exchange Commission (SEC) in the US is explicit about the priority given to enforcement: 'First and foremost the SEC is a law enforcement agency.'[9] In the UK, by way of contrast, the Financial Services Authority (FSA) was not, at least prior to the financial crisis, an enforcement-led regulator. Thus, the Director of Enforcement of the FSA remarked in 2008 that 'Ex-ante supervision is an important part of [our] approach reducing the need for ex-post enforcement. The emphasis and resource we give to supervision clearly distinguishes us from the SEC.'[10] Subsequently, the FSA (and now the Financial Conduct Authority (FCA)) moved away from that stance to adopt a strategy that was characterized as 'credible deterrence' and focused more on the role of enforcement.[11]

The regulator's choice of enforcement strategy may be influenced by external factors such as political pressure, interest groups, public prosecution authorities, and courts with overlapping jurisdiction. While the first two are often characterized as influences for rulemaking, they can apply equally to enforcement and regulated firms may themselves participate in the process of shaping the regulator's enforcement strategy.[12] Public prosecution authorities other than the regulator (such as the Department of Justice in the US and the Serious Fraud Office in the UK) may be influential through bringing prosecutions for criminal offences that are linked to regulated activities, while courts may exert pressure through decisions made in the context of private litigation (such as directors' duties in corporate law or fiduciary duties in agency or trust law) indicating that regulatory contraventions may have occurred.

It is also possible for enforcement priorities to be set by reference to issues that extend across the market rather than focusing on individual firms. In the case of the FCA, for example, this type of thematic work is an important dimension of its enforcement activity.[13] Implicit in this approach is the understanding that there

[8] Black, J, Managing Discretion, ALRC Conference Paper (2001), available at <http://www.lse.ac.uk/collections/law/staff%20publications%20full%20text/black/alrc%20managing%20discretion.pdf>; and see the UK Financial Conduct Authority (FCA) Handbook, The Enforcement Guide ('EG') 2, The FCA's approach to enforcement, referring to its regulatory objectives under the Financial Services and Markets Act 2000 (FSMA 2000) as well as transparency, proportionality, and fair treatment of persons who are the subject of enforcement action.

[9] See <http://www.sec.gov/about/whatwedo.shtml>.

[10] Cole, M, 'Enforcing Financial Services Regulation: The UK FSA Perspective', speech by Margaret Cole, Director of Enforcement, FSA, European Policy Forum (4 April 2008).

[11] This change in policy was evident from 2009 onwards.

[12] Scholz, J, 'Deterrence, Cooperation, and the Ecology of Regulatory Enforcement' (1984) 18 *Law and Society Review* 179.

[13] See FCA Handbook, n 8 above, EG 2.7.

may be features of products, distribution channels, remuneration patterns, or market practices which give rise to consumer detriment issues across the board and are less closely linked to the compliance stance of individual firms.

3. Firms' compliance strategies

The enforcement strategy adopted by the regulator is intrinsically linked with the compliance strategy adopted by regulated firms because the most appropriate enforcement strategy is linked with the characterization of regulated firms. Thus, a major focus of research has been to determine how the regulator should adjust regulatory strategy so as to respond appropriately to the compliance stance of individual regulated firms. Implicit in this approach is that the regulator's enforcement strategy should differentiate between firms by taking into account the extent to which they may be willing to engage in voluntary compliance in the absence of the threat of enforcement.

The 'enforcement dilemma' developed by Scholz explained how voluntary cooperation between the regulator and firms may improve compliance.[14] The dilemma focuses on the mutual suspicions that may characterize relationships between the regulator and regulated firms and lead to confrontation even when both sides and society generally would be better off with voluntary compliance and cooperative enforcement. It also recognizes that enforcement choices made by the regulator and regulated firm respectively are contingent: thus, each party's choice influences the other on an ongoing basis. The solution proposed by Scholz is a 'tit for tat' enforcement strategy in which different enforcement options are adopted for 'good' and 'bad' firms (viewed in terms of their compliance strategy). Differentiation of firms is required to set a threshold for voluntary compliance at which the regulator can rely on cooperation and thereby economize on enforcement costs. That process does, however, represent a real challenge and where the regulator has previously not set the voluntary compliance level sufficiently high it may be necessary to send a clear deterrent signal to firms across the board prior to any attempt to refine the enforcement strategy for each firm.

The overall effect of a suitably calibrated 'tit for tat' enforcement strategy is that compliance costs (for the firm) and enforcement costs (for the regulator) are minimized. However, the difficulty in calibrating such a strategy is arguably compounded by the recent emphasis on risk-based regulation which focuses on the risks posed by a firm to the regulatory objectives as a means of setting the intensity of supervision.[15] Since the firm's selection of a compliance strategy is not linked

[14] Scholz, n 6 and n 12 above.

[15] See generally MacNeil, I, 'Risk Control Strategies: An Assessment in the Context of the Credit Crisis' in MacNeil, I and O'Brien, J (eds), *The Future of Financial Regulation* (2010).

with the risks it faces (ie a risky firm can be a 'good' firm in the Scholz enforcement model above) it follows that risk-based regulation does not necessarily provide a reliable guide for the regulator to set its enforcement strategy with respect to that firm. What is required in the enforcement context is an assessment of the risks posed by a firm's compliance strategy in addition to the risks posed by its business model. Another relevant consideration is the frequency of interaction with regulated firms and the visibility of violations.[16] Frequent interactions offer scope for a strategy (such as 'tit for tat') that responds to the degree of cooperation offered by firms whereas less frequent interactions mean that violations are likely to be less visible and therefore a cooperative stance on the part of the regulator is riskier because there may be many other instances that go undetected.

Building on these insights, the 'regulatory pyramid' model proposed by Ayres and Braithwaite has become the most influential model for developing an enforcement strategy which sets an appropriate balance between persuasive and punitive techniques.[17] The pyramid maps both the proportion (which reduces at each successive stage) and severity (which increases at each successive stage) of different types of enforcement action as follows: the first step is persuasion; the second is a warning letter; the third is a civil penalty; the fourth is a criminal penalty; the fifth is licence suspension; and the final stage is licence revocation. The 'regulatory pyramid' was proposed as a general model applicable to all types of business regulation and not specifically as a model for financial regulation but has nevertheless been influential in justifying, especially prior to the 2008 financial crisis, an approach to enforcement based more on persuasion and engagement with regulated firms rather than formal enforcement.[18] However, following the onset of the financial crisis it seems clear that there has been some reversion to a deterrence-based approach as the use of formal enforcement has generally increased, with the FCA in the UK moving to a policy of 'credible deterrence'.

4. Enforcement powers

The capacity of regulators to undertake enforcement is linked with their powers to investigate regulatory contraventions. While the routine provision of information to regulators through the process of supervision may provide some initial information indicating that enforcement action may be desirable, a more detailed examination of the circumstances will normally require the regulator to resort to more

[16] Kagan, A, 'Regulatory Enforcement' in Rosenbloom, D and Schwartz, R (eds), *Handbook of Regulation and Administrative Law* (1994).

[17] Ayres and Braithwaite, n 2 above.

[18] See Black, n 8 above for an adaptation of the regulatory pyramid to the FSMA 2000 system of regulation in the UK.

specific information gathering and investigative powers. In the UK system, for example, the regulators are provided with a wide range of powers which include: requiring regulated firms and connected persons to provide information and documents; requiring individuals under investigation to attend for interview and answer questions; and enabling the regulators to enter premises to gain access to relevant information and records.[19] While the SEC in the US also has a wide range of investigatory powers, International Organization of Securities Commissions (IOSCO) assessments indicate that there are many countries in which the regulator does not have a wide range of investigative powers or where there are not effective penalties for failing to cooperate with regulatory investigations.[20] Bank secrecy laws pose problems across many jurisdictions as do access to phone records and information held by Internet service providers. Even within the EU, there remain significant variations in powers of investigation as between national authorities although, in response, there have been recent moves at EU level to mandate administrative[21] and criminal[22] sanctions so as to require more effective enforcement by the Member States.

Whistleblowing has the potential to improve compliance and enforcement by using information provided by insiders that is not available to the regulatory authorities through the supervisory or enforcement process. The capacity for whistleblowing to contribute to enforcement has been recognized in changes to the legal and regulatory frameworks in the UK and the US in recent years. Two issues have been particularly prominent in these reforms: the protection of whistleblowers from retaliation; and financial incentives. In the UK the focus has been on protecting whistleblowers from retaliation as a result of having disclosed information to an enforcement authority.[23] In particular, whistleblowers are protected from dismissal as a result of making protected disclosures, which include criminal offences and legal obligations such as regulatory rules made under the Financial Services and Markets Act 2000 (FSMA 2000), directors' duties under the Companies Act 2006 or common law fiduciary duties. In the US, the initial focus on anti-retaliation protection for employees contained in the Sarbanes–Oxley Act of 2002 was complemented by financial incentives introduced by the Dodd–Frank Act of 2010.[24] In the case of substantial enforcement penalties levied by the SEC (in excess of one million

[19] See FSMA 2000, sections 165–77 and the FCA Handbook, n 8 above, EG 3 and 4.

[20] Carvajal, A and Elliott, J, The Challenge of Enforcement in Securities Markets: Mission Impossible (2009), IMF Working Paper 09/168.

[21] See eg Article 70 of the 2014 MiFID II Directive (Directive 2014/65/EU [2014] OJ L173/349) listing a range of administrative remedies that must be made available to national competent authorities. MiFID II will replace MiFID (Directive 2004/39/EC [2004] OJ L145/1) as the regulatory framework for EU investment markets in 2017.

[22] See Article 7 of the 2014 Directive on criminal sanctions for market abuse (Directive 2014/57/EU [2014] OJ L173/179).

[23] The relevant provisions are contained in the Public Interest Disclosure Act 1998.

[24] Prior to Dodd–Frank, financial incentives had been limited to penalties imposed for insider trading: see Schonert, N, 'A Fistful of Dollars: Bounty Hunting under the Dodd-Frank Act's Whistleblower Provisions' (2011) 36 *Southern Illinois University Law Journal* 159.

dollars) the awards available to whistleblowers range between 10 and 30 per cent of the total sanctions levied by the SEC.[25] The contrast between the role of financial incentives in the two system is significant and can be linked with the broader role of private enforcement in the US system by comparison with the UK.[26] The EU's recent moves to facilitate whistleblowing in the context of market abuse have left the option to Member States to introduce financial incentives where there is no pre-existing duty to report the breach, the information is new, and leads to the imposition of a financial penalty.[27]

III. Enforcement Policy: Empirical Evidence

1. Measuring enforcement

Empirical studies on enforcement in financial regulation have drawn attention to significant differences in the role and style of enforcement around the world. The first type of study has focused on countries' capacity for enforcement by reference to the legal and regulatory framework for enforcement and sanctions. The second type of study has focused on enforcement activity and, in particular, on measuring enforcement by reference to various metrics, such as the number of enforcement actions, the proportion of a regulator's budget spent on enforcement, and the size of the penalties which are imposed. In both cases, some care is required in interpreting results since the different scope of regulators' responsibilities and the role of enforcement in securing compliance may vary between different countries. For example, as between the UK and the US systems, comparison between the FSA/FCA and the SEC may be useful as a starting point but it must be borne in mind that the responsibilities of the respective regulators vary significantly and that other regulatory and prosecutorial authorities may play a significant role in enforcement in each system.

In the first category, the IMF's 2009 study[28] provided a wide-ranging survey of the implementation of the IOSCO Principles for Securities Regulation relevant for enforcement.[29] A number of interesting conclusions were reached in the study. First,

[25] See <http://www.sec.gov/News/PressRelease/Detail/PressRelease/1370539854258#.Urg1Q_RdXTo> for details of the SEC's largest award to date (USD 14 million).

[26] See further, 'Private enforcement' below.

[27] See Article 32(4) of the 2014 Market Abuse Regulation (Regulation 596/2014 [2014] OJ L173/1).

[28] Carvajal and Elliott, n 20 above.

[29] See <http://www.iosco.org/library/pubdocs/pdf/IOSCOPD154.pdf>: Principles 8 and 9 are of particular relevance for enforcement.

it found a correlation between the income level of a country and the robustness of its legal framework. Second, it observed that the enforcement mandate provided to regulators was often compromised by conflicting regulatory objectives such as the development of securities markets or the promotion of competition. The lack of broad sanctioning powers (such as the ability to impose monetary penalties) or a heavy reliance on criminal penalties without effective cooperation between regulators and prosecuting authorities were also identified as an issue for many countries. Beyond the legal framework, the study reported that the IOSCO assessors found that only about 50 per cent of the countries had developed a credible enforcement programme. The study concluded that lack of resources was at the root of many of the problems identified in the report and, in line with the G20 focus on enforcement as a regulatory priority, urged governments to provide adequate funding and to strengthen their legal and regulatory frameworks.

The first major study in the second category (Jackson 2007) drew attention to variations between countries in the total budgets devoted to financial regulation, as well as to variations in the regulatory budgets devoted to each of the three main financial sectors (banking, securities, and insurance).[30] As regards the total regulatory budgets (based on a variety of measures, such as GDP, population, banking assets, etc.), a significant divergence was noted as between common law countries and civil law counties with the former having average regulatory budgets around four times higher than the latter. That study drew no clear conclusions as to why such a wide variation might exist but speculated that each country might be pursuing an optimal level of financial regulation on the basis that variations in the composition of the financial sector and regulatory objectives might lead to different levels of regulatory intensity.[31] While enforcement was not the main focus of that study, it did note from its limited investigation of enforcement in the US in 2000–02 that sanctions resulting from public enforcement by regulatory agencies accounted for less than half of total sanctions; the remainder being accounted for mainly by (private) class actions.

A later study (Coffee 2007) argued that attention should focus more on the output of the regulatory system (measured by enforcement activity) rather than inputs (measured by regulatory budgets).[32] Focusing on the number of enforcement cases brought by the SEC in the US by comparison with the FSA in the UK and the financial penalties levied by the respective regulators, Coffee argued that the development of robust securities markets could be linked more clearly with enforcement than legal origins. Thus, according to Coffee, the enforcement-led style of the SEC

[30] Jackson, H, 'Variation in the Intensity of Financial Regulation: Preliminary Evidence and Potential Implications' (2007) 24 *Yale Journal on Regulation* 253.

[31] ibid, 286.

[32] Coffee, J, 'Law and the Market: The Impact of Enforcement' (2007) 156(2) *University of Pennsylvania Law Review* 229.

provided better support to the securities market by lowering the cost of capital as evidenced by the valuation premium achieved by foreign companies who 'bonded' to the US system of regulation through foreign listing. As to why the US displayed a greater propensity towards enforcement than the UK, Coffee speculated that it might be because the governance and control rights of shareholders in the US are generally weaker than in the UK and that enforcement might be a substitute for weaker governance.[33]

Prior to the financial crisis, the FSA in the UK had characterized itself as 'non-enforcement led' and that approach was borne out by the findings of Cearns and Ferran who found a clear preference for non-enforcement-led, compliance-promoting strategies in the context of the oversight of financial and corporate governance disclosures.[34] However, the relatively low level of formal enforcement does not tell the whole story since various forms of informal enforcement (such as a private request for remedial action or public censure) may play a more significant role: for example, Armour estimated that while around 3 per cent of listed companies may be subject to some formal type of enforcement action each year, as many as 20 per cent may be subject to some form of informal action.[35] That observation reinforces the view that estimating the effect of diverse forms of regulatory action on regulatory compliance across the system is very complex and, therefore, it cannot logically follow that less formal enforcement action in any one system by comparison with another is necessarily a matter for concern.

It is perhaps surprising that the financial crisis did not lead to a significant rise in public enforcement actions in either the US or the UK since the markets, transactions, and firms most closely associated with the crisis were located in those two countries.[36] That outcome can be rationalized in two ways. One is to conclude that the crisis was not primarily associated with misconduct but, to the extent that it can be attributed to regulatory failure, was mainly linked with lapses in prudential supervision and in particular a lack of focus on systemic risk. The second form of rationalization is to conclude that the enforcement response to the crisis was to focus on deterrence rather than punishment: from that perspective the scale of penalties in successful enforcement actions would be a higher priority than attempting to maximize the number of misconduct cases that were the subject of enforcement. That explanation is consistent with the rise in penalties in the UK in the wake of

[33] ibid, 296.

[34] Cearns, K and Ferran, E, 'Non-enforcement-led Public Oversight of Financial and Corporate Governance Disclosures and of Auditors' (2008) *Journal of Corporate Law Studies* 191.

[35] Armour, J, Enforcement Strategies in UK Corporate Governance: A Roadmap and Empirical Assessment (2008), ECGI Law Working Paper No 106/2008.

[36] See NERA Economic Consulting, SEC Settlement Trends: 2H12 Update (2013); Credit Crisis Litigation Update: It Is Settlement Time (2013); FSA, Enforcement Annual Performance Account 2012/13 (2013).

the financial crisis as well as the overall rise in enforcement settlements in the US (including action by the Department of Justice and private enforcement).[37]

2. Enforcement and outcomes

An alternative line of research has focused on the impact of different regulatory and enforcement approaches on key market variables (outcomes).[38] A study of the impact of the introduction of insider trading laws (mostly in the 1990s) found that the introduction of such laws had no effect on the cost of capital but that their enforcement was associated with a significant fall, implying that investors were willing to accept lower returns and that companies would find it easier to raise capital when enforcement occurred.[39] The FSA's 2007 study of market cleanliness in the UK provided some further support for the significance of enforcement by linking a decline in 'informed price movements' ahead of company announcements to enforcement of the market abuse regime introduced by the FSMA 2000.[40] A 2009 study by CRA International[41] focused on the following market outcomes in five countries[42]: cost of equity; market size and liquidity; listing decisions; and market cleanliness. It focused on the quality of regulation in general rather than specifically on enforcement although it did integrate enforcement data from Coffee (2007) into its assessment. The key conclusion of that study was that the four market outcomes were closely clustered across the five countries, implying that variations in regulatory style (including the intensity of enforcement) tended to balance each other out in the case of developed countries but that comparison with less developed countries showed significant variations in market outcomes.

Despite these efforts, it remains difficult to establish casual links between different approaches to enforcement and the overall quality of the regulatory system. There are two main issues that arise in this context. One is that it is difficult to disaggregate the effects of enforcement from characteristics of the regulatory system as a whole such as the institutional structure and the nature of the rules. A related factor is that it is difficult to decouple the processes of supervision and enforcement and since it may be possible to pre-empt formal enforcement through the

[37] See sources in ibid for aggregate enforcement and settlement data in the UK and US (2008–13).

[38] Following this approach, regulatory enforcement is classified as an input rather than as an output under the approach adopted by Jackson (n 30 above) and Coffee (n 32 above).

[39] Bhattacharya, U and Daouk, H, 'The World Price of Insider Trading' (2002) 57 *Journal of Finance* 75.

[40] Monteiro, M, Zaman, Q, and Leitterstorf, S, Updated Measurement of Market Cleanliness (2007), FSA Occasional Paper Series, 25.

[41] Malcolm, K, Tilden, M, Coope, S, and Xie, C, *Assessing the Effectiveness of Enforcement and Regulation* (2009).

[42] Australia, France, Germany, the UK, and the US.

supervisory process the causal effects of enforcement cannot be isolated. Another issue is that it is generally difficult (for a supervisor and *a fortiori* for an external observer) to observe the operation of firms' compliance strategies and instances of non-compliance within firms with the result that casual links between the regulator's enforcement strategy and the level of compliance across the system are difficult to establish. The level of compliance is a more important indicator for the overall health of a regulatory system than the level of enforcement but the latter is much easier to observe and to quantify. Thus, when comparing different regulatory systems it is never entirely clear whether or to what extent more intense enforcement activity reflects differences in compliance or differences in the regulator's enforcement style.

IV. Public and Private Enforcement

Public enforcement by a regulatory agency is the usual means by which regulatory rules are enforced and the discussion so far has focused on that type of enforcement. The 'public' dimension reflects the fact that enforcement normally takes place in the public domain and is undertaken by a regulator operating under a public law framework for the benefit of society as a whole. The enforcement process may be administrative or criminal and that distinction carries implications for the forum for adjudication, the procedure, and the legal protection that is available for the firm or person against whom the case is brought. Public enforcement may seek restitution or compensation for victims of financial misconduct as well as punishing offenders and in that sense it may well overlap with private enforcement.[43]

Enforcement in the UK system generally takes place within the regulatory body (FCA) subject to safeguards that separate enforcement decisions and personnel from other parts of the regulatory process.[44] Provision is also made for enforcement in the civil and criminal courts through injunctions, restitution orders, and prosecution for a range of criminal offences. In the context of the 'retail' financial market in the UK, the Financial Ombudsman plays an important role in enforcement by exercising its powers to make awards to customers who bring complaints against financial firms. In the US, administrative courts play a more prominent

[43] For example, SEC action in the wake of the financial crisis has recovered almost as much money by way of restitution for harmed investors as has been raised through financial penalties: see <http://www.sec.gov/spotlight/enf-actions-fc.shtml>.

[44] See FCA Handbook, n 8 above, DEPP.

role in SEC enforcement, although it is common for settlement to be reached without the formal process being taken to its conclusion.

Private enforcement is often available as a supplement to or substitute for public enforcement by a regulatory agency.[45] While public enforcement was always an integral part of systems of financial regulation, private enforcement was not recognized until much later and even now remains restricted. Private enforcement in the context of the federal securities laws was first recognized in the US in *J. I Case Co. v Borak*,[46] in which the Supreme Court justified its availability as a necessary supplement to SEC enforcement. In the UK, however, private enforcement is generally available only to private investors,[47] the objective being to ensure that financial markets are not disrupted by opportunistic litigation pursued by professional investors. Another argument made in favour of public over private enforcement is that it provides a better mechanism for setting sanctions because a single public enforcer can take into account the social cost and the probability of detection when deciding punishment.[48] Nevertheless, informal enforcement may still be open to professional investors in the UK in cases where they can exert influence either through the exercise of shareholders' rights or market discipline.[49]

The availability of class actions in the US provides an incentive for private enforcement that is not present in the UK.[50] For private enforcement to work, the expected recovery must exceed the costs and for that reason the class action in the US, which draws investors who have suffered loss into litigation unless they opt out, is closely linked with the prevalence of private enforcement in that country and has been instrumental in boosting private monetary sanctions to a level that over some time frames exceeds public enforcement sanctions.[51] However, private enforcement through class actions remains controversial, since awards paid

[45] See Correia, M and Klausner, M, Are Securities Class Actions Supplemental to SEC Enforcement? An Empirical Analysis (2012), available at <http://recanatibs.tau.ac.il/Eng/_Uploads/dbsAttachedFiles/Correia.pdf>, arguing that class actions do not supplement SEC actions because the targets of such actions diverge from SEC practice.

[46] *J. I Case Co. v Borak* 377 US 426 (1964).

[47] See FSMA 2000, section 138D (formerly section 150).

[48] See Ferrarini, G and Guidici P, 'Financial Scandals and the Role of Private Enforcement: The Parmalat Case' in Armour, J and McCahery, J (eds), *After Enron: Improving Corporate Law and Modernizing Securities Regulation* (2006) 159.

[49] Market discipline may be relevant, eg, in the context of the UK Code of Corporate Governance, which relies heavily on market discipline for enforcement albeit the disclosure obligations associated with the Code form part of the Listing Rules: see FCA Listing Rule 9.8.6(6), which gives effect to the 'comply or explain' principle.

[50] Although US-style 'opt-out' class actions are not available in the UK, so-called 'damages-based awards' are now permissible in England and Wales, under which lawyers are paid a fee which is contingent on success: see the Legal Aid, Sentencing and Punishment of Offenders Act 2012.

[51] See Jackson (n 30 above) and NERA Economic Consulting (n 36 above) for relevant statistics. It is noteworthy that NERA's study of enforcement related to the financial crisis (2007–13) shows that private enforcement accounts for a greater part of total settlements than public enforcement.

by companies to diversified institutional investors can been characterized as an exercise in 'pocket-shifting' in which the profits and losses from different cases offset each other and substantial costs are incurred through transfers to lawyers and other agents.[52] On that view, private enforcement would be more effective if it focused more on culpable directors and officers rather than the corporate entity. A more positive view of private enforcement was provided by La Porta et al. who claimed that 'Public enforcement plays a modest role at best in the development of stock markets.'[53] However, some doubt was cast on that view by later evidence provided by Jackson and Roe showing that there were clear links between public enforcement and deeper securities markets and that informal public enforcement was an important factor in the UK and Japan.[54] Subsequent research in the context of informal oversight of financial and corporate governance disclosures in the UK provided further evidence of the central role played by informal compliance-promoting strategies and the dangers of focusing only on formal enforcement in cross-country comparisons.[55]

Any assessment of the respective roles of public and private enforcement should also take into account that private enforcement of regulatory rules is likely to overlap with the exercise of shareholders' rights in corporate law. This results from the fact that financial regulation and corporate governance may pursue similar objectives (such as risk control) through overlapping techniques such as capital adequacy rules and directors' duties. For example, in the wake of the financial crisis there has been much discussion not only as to whether regulatory rules were breached but also whether directors might face liability for breach of duty for failing properly to control risk.[56] Thus, an overarching view of enforcement in financial regulation must encompass parallel enforcement initiatives which bite on the same set of circumstances. In a wide-ranging study of enforcement patterns across three regulatory authorities in the UK with enforcement powers in corporate law, Armour (2008) found that formal private enforcement was rare but that informal private enforcement by institutional investors (through the exercise of voting rights or the facilitation of takeovers) was a significant factor in addition to informal public enforcement.[57]

[52] Coffee, n 32 above.

[53] La Porta, R, Lopez-de-Silanes, F, and Shleifer, A, 'What Works in Securities Laws?' (2006) 61 *Journal of Finance* 1, 20.

[54] Jackson, H and Roe, M, 'Public and Private Enforcement of Securities Laws: Resource-based Evidence' (2009) 93(2) *Journal of Financial Economics* 207.

[55] Cearns and Ferran, n 34 above.

[56] See, eg, Keay, A, 'Risk, Shareholder Pressure and Short-termism in Financial Institutions. Does Enlightened Shareholder Value Offer a Panacea?' (2011) 5(6) *Law and Financial Markets Review* 435.

[57] Armour, n 35 above.

V. Sanctions

Effective sanctions are central to enforcement. The design of an appropriate sanctions regime requires at least three key issues to be addressed: who is responsible for regulatory contraventions; what type of sanctions should be employed; and what role should informal settlement play within the formal enforcement regime.

1. Responsibility for regulatory contraventions

So far as responsibility for regulatory contraventions is concerned there are, in principle, three models: entity, collective, and individual. While the collective responsibility of the board is stressed in some governance contexts (eg the UK Code of Corporate Governance) it is the entity model of responsibility that dominates in enforcement in the UK system, albeit that provision is also made for individual responsibility. The entity model of responsibility effectively regards the shareholders as beneficiaries of the contravention and is in effect a form of vicarious liability in that the entity may be responsible for its employees irrespective of fault. It arguably fits better with a compliance-based enforcement strategy than the other two options because regulators are better able to track and exercise direct control over organizations than the individuals within them.[58]

However, the problem with entity responsibility is that it does not focus on the moral agent who is responsible for the regulatory contravention. Individual responsibility adopts such an approach and thereby casts the entity as the victim rather than the beneficiary of the contravention, although that characterization may be problematic where the entity has itself benefited as a result of the contravention. The capacity to take action simultaneously against the entity and the individual provides further capacity for the threat of regulatory action to promote compliance since neither the firm nor the individual can be sure of transferring responsibility to the other: in that situation, some degree of 'constructive ambiguity' as to who will be held responsible may act as a useful deterrent even if action is only rarely pursued against individuals.

While individual responsibility does feature in some aspects of the UK regulatory system,[59] it has not featured prominently in enforcement action. This reluctance to pursue individuals is evident in the statutory provision requiring the

[58] Reiss, A, 'Selecting Strategies of Social Control over Organizational Life' in Hawkins, K and Thomas, J (eds), *Enforcing Regulation* (1984).

[59] See generally MacNeil, I, 'The Evolution of Regulatory Enforcement Action in the UK Capital Markets: A Case of "Less Is More"?' (2007) 2(4) *Capital Markets Law Journal* 345, 356. Individual responsibility is the model adopted for directors' duties in corporate law.

regulator to consider whether it is appropriate to take action against an individual as well as a long-established regulatory policy that personal culpability is an essential element of a decision to take enforcement action against an individual.[60] In the US, SEC enforcement action is much more focused on individuals,[61] although private enforcement (in the forms of class actions) generally targets companies. In both systems, non-executive directors appear to be relatively immune to any form of enforcement action, whether civil, administrative, or criminal.[62] However, in response to the perceived failings of the regulatory system and the criminal law to hold directors and senior managers to account for their role in the financial crisis,[63] a criminal offence of negligent management of a bank has been introduced by the UK government.[64] It remains to be seen whether that initiative will result in any greater role for individual responsibility, since acting in accordance with prevailing standards will generally exonerate individuals from liability in negligence even when the prevailing standards may be below what would be regarded by outsiders as prudent standards.[65]

2. The range of sanctions

It has been argued that the range of sanctions must closely match the severity of the contraventions that are enforced.[66] A wider range of sanctions expands the capacity of the regulator to respond effectively to the seriousness of a contravention in a manner that would not be available where a limited range or single sanction (for example, withdrawal of licence) was the only option available. Some systems have followed this approach and provide for a wide range of sanctions. In the UK for example, the range of sanctions available to the regulator includes: financial penalties; public censure; prohibitions on individuals engaging in regulated activity or withdrawal of approval as an 'approved person'; variation and cancellation of permission to engage in regulated activity; injunctions

[60] See FSMA 2000, section 66(1)(b) and the FCA Handbook, n 8 above, EG 2.31.

[61] See <http://www.sec.gov/spotlight/enf-actions-fc.shtml> for relevant statistics related to SEC enforcement actions addressing misconduct that led to or arose from the financial crisis.

[62] Black, B, Cheffins, B, and Klausner, M, 'Outside Director Liability' (2006) 58 *Stanford Law Review* 1055.

[63] See Fisher, J, 'The Global Financial Crisis: The Case for a Stronger Criminal Response' (2013) 7(3) *Law and Financial Markets Review* 159.

[64] See section 36 of the Financial Services (Banking Reform) Act 2013 and the Parliamentary Commission on Banking Standards, *Changing Banking for Good* (2013), HL Paper 27-II, HC 175-II, Vol 2, paras 1182–5.

[65] See FSA, The Failure of the Royal Bank of Scotland, Financial Services Authority Board Report (2011) for an illustration of the problems encountered in taking enforcement action against individuals who have acted in accordance with prevailing standards.

[66] Ayres and Braithwaite, n 2 above.

and restitution orders; and prosecution of criminal offences.[67] Similarly, the SEC in the US has a wide range of sanctions at its disposal in addition to seeking monetary penalties: it can, for example, seek emergency measures such as injunctions or asset freezes, as well as disgorgement of profits made or losses avoided as a result of regulatory contraventions.[68] However, that pattern is not replicated across the world, as demonstrated by IOSCO assessments of regulatory systems which show that the lack of effective sanctions is a common weakness of many systems.[69]

Determining the appropriate role of criminalization in the range of sanctions is not straightforward. Regulatory control is often characterized by moral ambivalence because it relates to conduct that is not per se morally reprehensible but may become so in certain circumstances or when carried to extremes. Criminalization implies a degree of public opprobrium that is not always present in the case of administrative penalties but it is not always conducive to successful enforcement action. Criminalization is a deterrence-based strategy and is an effective response to incidents or acts that are clear-cut and unpredictable but may not work so well in cases where rule-breaking is episodic, repetitive, or continuous.[70] In those instances, a compliance-based approach may be more effective, especially if it is not easy to identify victims or link them with a regulatory contravention. There may also be procedural issues linked to the process of enforcement: in the case of insider dealing, for example, the move towards civil (administrative/regulatory) penalties in the UK in recent years has been driven in part by the difficulty of securing criminal convictions as a result of the higher burden of proof and the protection afforded to the accused in a criminal prosecution. Nevertheless, criminalization has featured prominently in post-crisis regulatory reforms: the UK, for example, has seen the introduction of new criminal offences of making misleading statements to influence the setting of financial benchmarks[71] and negligent mismanagement of a bank.[72]

In some instances, there may be a choice available to the regulator as to whether to pursue a civil/administrative sanction or criminal prosecution. In those cases, it is necessary to make a judgement as to the most appropriate route to choose bearing in mind the seriousness of the misconduct in question and whether the taking of civil or regulatory action might prejudice a subsequent criminal prosecution. While criminal prosecution will not normally be pursued alongside disciplinary measures (eg administrative fines), regulators may well take civil action to seek restitution or injunctions in appropriate cases alongside criminal prosecution.

[67] See generally the FCA Handbook, n 8 above, EG.

[68] See SEC, Agency Financial Report 2012 (2013), available at <http://www.sec.gov/about/secafr2012.shtml>.

[69] Carvajal and Elliott, n 20 above, 20.

[70] Hawkins and Thomas, n 7 above, 14.

[71] See section 91 of the Financial Services Act 2012, introduced in response to the LIBOR scandal.

[72] See n 64 above.

A separate issue from the range and legal character of sanctions is the *level* of sanctions that may be imposed. This is an important issue because in many cases the regulator (or administrative court) imposing a financial penalty has considerable discretion. As a starting point it can be said that the optimal level of sanctions is linked to the enforcement strategy of the regulator. If the policy goal is to achieve the optimal level of deterrence at the lowest cost, then fines should be set at the highest possible level so as to maximize compliance and minimize enforcement costs.[73] However, since deterrence is rarely the only policy objective (following the approach of responsive regulation) that prescription does not offer much in the way of guidance for setting the level of sanctions. Reference to the FCA's guidance on setting financial penalties in the UK illustrates the significance of other policy objectives. The FCA's penalty-setting regime is based on the following principles:

- disgorgement—a firm or individual should not benefit from any breach;
- discipline—a firm or individual should be penalized for wrongdoing; and
- deterrence—any penalty imposed should deter the firm or individual who committed the breach, and others, from committing further or similar breaches.[74]

The recent trend in the UK suggests that the regulator's policy of 'credible deterrence' in the wake of the financial crisis has been given effect in setting financial penalties as the total of financial penalties has risen considerably.[75] In the US, that policy has been evident for much longer and has been clearly demonstrated in the wake of the financial crisis by a step change in the level of settlements reached by global banks with the SEC and the Department of Justice, and with regard to their role in the sub-prime mortgage market.[76]

Another factor relevant for setting the level of penalties is their reputational effect. It has been shown in the case of public-listed firms that the announcement of regulatory sanctions is linked to a fall in the share price of the firm that is much higher than the value of the penalty imposed by the regulator.[77] Moreover, the fall in share price occurs only in cases in which the misconduct involves harm to trading partners, such as mis-selling financial products. When the harm is suffered by third parties (eg in the case of money laundering), there is no share price implication beyond the financial penalty. This carries implications for deterrence, since it implies that lower penalties make be effective in the case of misconduct causing

[73] Becker, G, 'Crime and Punishment: An Economic Approach' (1968) 76 *Journal of Political Economy* 169.

[74] See generally the FCA Handbook, n 8 above, EG.

[75] See FSA, n 36 above, showing that penalties imposed by the regulator rose by almost sixfold in 2012/13.

[76] See NERA Economic Consulting, n 36 above, for an overview of those settlements.

[77] Armour, J, Mayer, C, and Polo A, Regulatory Sanctions and Reputational Damage in Financial Markets (2012), Oxford Legal Studies Research Paper No 62/2010; ECGI Finance Working Paper No 300/2010, available at <http://ssrn.com/abstract=1678028>.

harm to trading partners whereas misconduct causing harm to third parties may require far higher penalties for deterrence to operate effectively. In the case of monetary sanctions against individuals, reputational effects may also be relevant in terms of employability in the context of regulated activity but in the case of other sanctions (eg prohibition or withdrawal of approved person status) the sanction may in any case formally exclude the individual from regulated activity.

3. Settlements and discounts

It is common practice for regulators to settle cases informally rather than by concluding formal enforcement proceedings. The main benefit of settlement is that enforcement action can be concluded more quickly with the result that there are savings in the cost of enforcement, the deterrent effect of enforcement is brought forward and compensation can be provided earlier to investors and consumers. For this reason, settlement plays an important role in the enforcement process in the UK and the US, although that is not always the case in other countries.[78] The UK system provides incentives for firms and individuals to enter into early settlements by providing a discount of up to 30 per cent of a financial penalty (but not any disgorgement element) linked to the stage at which the settlement is reached.[79]

In the wake of the financial crisis, settlement procedures have come under close scrutiny, particularly in the US where concern has been expressed that settlements do not achieve adequate accountability or deterrence when they are made without admission of guilt. The SEC often agrees settlements on a 'neither admit nor deny' basis according to which a defendant is not required to admit to the SEC's allegations of wrongdoing but is not permitted to deny the facts relied on by the SEC. In the case of other federal agencies, settlements may be made on a 'no admit' basis or even on the basis that all the allegations are denied. While all these outcomes in effect provide some protection to the defendant by comparison with the unequivocal guilt associated with successful completion of formal enforcement proceedings, they are typically justified on the basis that settlements would not be feasible if admission of guilt were required because of the implications that admission of guilt would carry for parallel civil proceedings taken by the regulator or investors. Moreover, since settlement provides some protection to the regulator against the possibility of formal proceedings not being successful (especially in a court-based

[78] For the UK see FCA Handbook, n 8 above, EG 5 and FSA, n 36 above; for the US see Testimony on Examining the Settlement Practices of U.S. Financial Regulators, available at <https://www.sec.gov/News/Testimony/Detail/Testimony/1365171489454#.UnEPaXDwbng>; for other countries see Carvajal and Elliott, n 20 above, 21.

[79] See FCA Handbook, n 8 above, DEPP 6.7. There is no comparable discount in the (court-based) process of enforcement in the US, although settlements reached by the SEC outside the formal process may implicitly incorporate such discounts.

enforcement system such as the US), they increase the frequency of sanctioning even if the severity of the sanction is arguably diluted by the absence of admission of guilt.

That aspect of settlements does not arise in the UK system because a settlement is a regulatory decision that is accepted by the firm or individual concerned.[80] Thus, a settlement in the UK context is more properly characterized as part of the formal enforcement process since it subject to the FCA's formal decision-making process, is publicized in the same way as a final decision made without settlement, and is taken into consideration by the regulator in subsequent enforcement decisions with a view to ensuring that enforcement policy is applied consistently.[81]

VI. Internationalization and Cross-Border Enforcement

While financial markets and regulated firms have become global over the past two decades, regulation and enforcement have remained predominantly within the domain of nation states. International regulatory standards such as the Basel Regulatory Capital Framework and the IOSCO Principles of Securities Regulation have been developed but their implementation and enforcement are dependent on adoption into national law. Thus, international financial regulation has been characterized from the perspective of public international law as 'soft law' and stands in contrast to the 'hard law' character of the World Trade Organization (WTO) framework for international trade, which is underpinned by a legally binding treaty and has an adjudication mechanism attached to it.[82] Once implemented into national law, so-called 'soft law' is no different to any other law and the same issues that have already been discussed arise in connection with enforcement. Nevertheless, international firms and transactions pose particular problems for national regulators because there are inherent limitations in the capacity to enforce national laws as a result of their restricted jurisdictional reach. Differences between national law and regulatory systems may also lead to so-called 'regulatory arbitrage' whereby

[80] See FCA Handbook, n 8 above, EG 5.3.

[81] See FCA Handbook, n 8 above, EG 5.22–5.23.

[82] See generally Brummer, C, *Soft Law and the Global Financial System* (2012); Gadbaw, RM, 'Systemic Regulation of Global Trade and Finance: A Tale of Two Systems' in Cottier, T, Jackson, H, and Lastra, R (eds), *International Law in Financial Regulation and Monetary Affairs* (2012). Even within a regional system such as the EU which can generate its own 'hard law', the influence of 'soft law' standards, such as the Basel Accords, is still evident.

firms arrange their business so as to fall under regulatory regimes whose rules or enforcement practices may be more favourable for them.

1. Jurisdiction and extraterritorial enforcement

Globalization and new technology pose major problems for regulatory enforcement because they facilitate internationalization of the financial markets by making it easier for financial firms to conduct business on a remote business without substantial links to the relevant states in which they operate. Thus, activities such as insider dealing, market manipulation, and promotion of fraudulent investment schemes can often just as easily be carried out from outside a state as within. Moreover, internationalization of investment portfolios also means that enforcement issues relating to public offers, disclosure obligations, and advisory duties are more likely to have a cross-border element than was the case in the past.

The jurisdiction of national systems of regulation is usually defined by reference to various types of activity that are carried on within the relevant state.[83] The 'regulatory perimeter' defines activities that require authorization and brings firms conducting those activities under the jurisdiction of the local regulator, although there may be opportunities to engage in business through a licence granted by a firm's home state (as in the case of the EU Single Market) or through specific exemptions granted to foreign firms (such as the 'private placement' regime for issuing securities in the US). Provision may also be made to bring within the regulatory perimeter of state A activities undertaken from that state which are directed at state B. There are also relevant laws and regulations that apply to firms and individuals who are not within the regulatory perimeter, an important example being insider dealing laws; in that case, jurisdiction is normally defined by reference to trading on markets within the state or in securities that are listed in that state. Thus, it has been established in the UK that the FSMA 2000 market abuse regime applies to transactions in securities traded on prescribed markets even if the transaction occurs outside the UK on a market which is not prescribed for the purposes of that regime.[84]

Prior to the decision of the US Supreme Court in the case of *Morrison v National Australia Bank*,[85] the courts in the US applied the twin 'conducts or effects' test to determine whether foreign investors could bring a claim under US securities laws. Those tests focused respectively on whether significant steps were taken in

[83] See, eg, FSMA 2000, section 418, defining when regulated activity is undertaken in the UK.

[84] See the Financial Services and Markets Tribunal decision in *Jabre v FSA*, case 36 (2006), holding that short sales executed from London in the Tokyo market fell within the FSMA 2000 market abuse regime.

[85] 130 S. Ct. 2869 (2010).

the US in pursuit of a fraudulent scheme even if the final transaction took place outside the US and involved only foreign investors; or whether overseas activity had an impact on US investors and securities traded on US securities exchanges. In *Morrison*, the Supreme Court interpreted §10(b) of the Securities Exchange Act of 1934 to exclude extraterritorial effect on the basis that it should be presumed that the Act is concerned primarily with domestic matters unless there is express provision for extraterritorial application. The effect was to exclude so-called 'f-cubed'[86] actions from the jurisdiction of the US courts and to deny a remedy to foreign investors with only a tentative link to the US. *Morrison* does not limit the capacity of US investors to take private enforcement action but it does preclude action by such investors with respect to transactions on foreign exchanges.[87]

2. Cross-border cooperation

The national character and limited territorial jurisdiction of systems of financial regulation poses problems for enforcement in cases with a cross-border dimension. While state A may well legislate that activity conducted from its territory directed at state B falls within the jurisdiction of A, that in itself does not provide a basis for the collection of evidence and other information in state B that may be necessary to bring enforcement proceedings in state A (and vice versa). Thus, cooperation between states may be necessary to facilitate effective enforcement of national laws in the context of international markets.

One solution to the problem of taking enforcement action in the case of misconduct with a cross-border dimension is for regulators to enter into a Memorandum of Understanding (MOU) to facilitate cooperation and exchange of information with regard to supervision and regulatory enforcement. Early forms of MOUs were bilateral and many such MOUs remain in place but a more recent trend has been the creation of multilateral MOUs between members of organizations, such as IOSCO, the International Association of Insurance Supervisors (IAIS), and the European Securities and Markets Authority (ESMA).[88] This approach remains relevant even in the context of the EU despite the creation of EU-level regulatory authorities because enforcement generally remains a matter for national supervisory authorities. However, at the broader international level there remain gaps in

[86] This designation refers to the three foreign characteristics of such claims where (1) foreign investors purchase securities in (2) a foreign corporation (3) traded on a foreign exchange.

[87] See *In re Royal Bank of Scotland Group PLC Sec. Litig.*, 765 F. Supp (2011) at 336, holding that mere listing of securities in the US does not establish jurisdiction for the US courts over transactions occurring on foreign exchanges.

[88] See the IOSCO MOU at <http://www.fktk.lv/texts_files/IOSCO_MMoU.pdf>; the IAIS MOU at <http://www.iaisweb.org/__temp/IAIS_MMoU.pdf>; and the ESMA MOU at <http://www.esma.europa.eu/system/files/05_335.pdf>.

the network of multilateral MOUs as there are many countries which are not signatories who can provide a base for activities and entities that may be more difficult to detect and unravel.

MOUs are not legally binding agreements and they often rely on local legislation to authorize the passing of relevant information to a foreign regulator. The principle of cooperation adopted in MOUs extends only to information and does not involve a foreign regulator in the enforcement process nor does it provide for recognition and enforcement of local administrative fines and other sanctions in a foreign jurisdiction. MOUs generally define the scope of the relevant cooperation and information exchange so as to limit it to the legal responsibilities of the relevant regulators (especially relevant where there is not a single regulator). They normally provide for requests and information provided under MOUs to remain confidential, to be used only for the purposes defined by the MOU, and not to be disclosed to third parties without prior agreement.

VII. Conclusions

Enforcement is a central aspect of any regulatory system but there are wide variations in how it actually operates in any given system. The role of enforcement is a function not only of the formal powers given to the regulator but also of the dynamic interplay of the compliance strategy of regulated firms with the enforcement strategy of the regulator. Empirical studies of enforcement patterns have attempted to measure enforcement levels in different countries and to draw some general conclusions about setting an appropriate level of enforcement.

While these studies provide a useful starting point for considering how any system should calibrate its own enforcement strategy, considerable care is required in taking solutions from one system to another as conditions may vary considerably as regards the role of supervision as a substitute for enforcement, the role of informal enforcement, and the potential for overlapping legal rules (such as directors' duties and fiduciary law) to be enforced. Similarly, the role of private enforcement may be linked with incentives such as class actions in the US, which are often not present in other systems.

An appropriate sanctions regime is a key factor in enforcement. The financial crisis has drawn attention to the potential for individual as opposed to entity responsibility to act as an accountability mechanism as well as a deterrent. It has also acted as a driver for increasing criminalization of regulatory offences so as to harness the reputational sanctions associated with regulatory contraventions. Informal settlements have attracted some criticism for their role in exculpating offenders but can be justified as a means to make efficient use of scarce enforcement resources.

Internationalization of financial markets poses significant problems for enforcement because misconduct may often have a cross-border dimension. This remains a relevant issue even within systems such as the EU which have moved towards harmonized rulebooks because enforcement is primarily a domestic matter. Thus, cooperation between regulators has emerged as an important means to facilitate cross-border enforcement.

BIBLIOGRAPHY

Armour, J, Enforcement Strategies in UK Corporate Governance: A Roadmap and Empirical Assessment (2008), ECGI Law Working Paper No 106/2008.

Armour, J, Mayer, C, and Polo, A, Regulatory Sanctions and Reputational Damage in Financial Markets (2012), Oxford Legal Studies Research Paper No 62/2010; ECGI Finance Working Paper No 300/2010, available at <http://ssrn.com/abstract=1678028>.

Ayres, I and Braithwaite, J, *Responsive Regulation: Transcending the Deregulation Debate* (1992).

Bardach, E and Kagan, R, *Going by the Book: The Problem of Regulatory Unreasonableness* (1982).

Becker, G, 'Crime and Punishment: An Economic Approach' (1968) 76 *Journal of Political Economy* 169.

Bhattacharya, U and Daouk, H, 'The World Price of Insider Trading' (2002) 57 *Journal of Finance* 75.

Bird, H, Chow, D, Lenne, J, and Ramsay, I, ASIC Enforcement Patterns (2004), the University of Melbourne Faculty of Law, Legal Studies Research Paper No 71, available at <http://ssrn.com/abstract=530383>.

Black, B, Cheffins, B, and Klausner, M, 'Outside Director Liability' (2006) 58 *Stanford Law Review* 1055.

Black, J, Managing Discretion, ALRC Conference Paper (2001), available at <http://www.lse.ac.uk/collections/law/staff%20publications%20full%20text/black/alrc%20managing%20discretion.pdf>.

Braithwaite, J, Walker, J, and Grabosky, P, 'An Enforcement Taxonomy of Regulatory Agencies' (1987) 9 *Law and Policy* 323.

Brummer, C, *Soft Law and the Global Financial System* (2012).

Carvajal, A and Elliott, J, The Challenge of Enforcement in Securities Markets: Mission Impossible (2009), IMF Working Paper 09/168.

Cearns, K and Ferran, E, 'Non-Enforcement-led Public Oversight of Financial and Corporate Governance Disclosures and of Auditors' (2008) *Journal of Corporate Law Studies* 191.

Coffee, J, 'Law and the Market: The Impact of Enforcement' (2007) 156(2) *University of Pennsylvania Law Review* 229.

Coffee, J, 'Reforming the Securities Class Action: An Essay on Deterrence and its Implementation' (2006) 106(7) *Columbia Law Review* 1534.

Cole M, Enforcing Financial Services Regulation: The UK FSA Perspective, speech by Margaret Cole, Director of Enforcement, FSA, European Policy Forum (4 April 2008).

Correia, M and Klausner, M, Are Securities Class Actions Supplemental to SEC Enforcement? An Empirical Analysis (2012), available at <http://recanati-bs.tau.ac.il/Eng/_Uploads/dbsAttachedFiles/Correia.pdf>.

Diver, C, 'A Theory of Regulatory Enforcement' (1980) 28 *Public Policy* 257.

Falkner, R, 'FSA Disciplinary Action against Senior Managers' (2012) 9 *Journal of International Banking and Financial Law* 576.

Ferrarini, G and Guidici, P, 'Financial Scandals and the Role of Private Enforcement: The Parmalat Case' in Armour, J and McCahery, J (eds), *After Enron: Improving Corporate Law and Modernizing Securities Regulation* (2006) 159.

Fisher, J, 'The Global Financial Crisis: The Case for a Stronger Criminal Response' (2013) 7(3) *Law and Financial Markets Review* 159.

FSA, Enforcement Annual Performance Account 2012/13 (2013).

FSA, The Failure of the Royal Bank of Scotland, Financial Services Authority Board Report (2011).

Gadbaw, RM, 'Systemic Regulation of Global Trade and Finance: A Tale of Two Systems' in Cottier, T, Jackson, H, and Lastra, R (eds), *International Law in Financial Regulation and Monetary Affairs* (2012).

Gunningham, N, 'Enforcement and Compliance Strategies' in Baldwin, R, Cave, M, and Lodge, M (eds), *The Oxford Handbook of Regulation* (2012).

Hawkins, K and Thomas, J, 'The Enforcement Process in Regulatory Bureaucracies' in Hawkins, K and Thomas, J (eds), *Enforcing Regulation* (1984).

HM Treasury, Consultation Paper, Sanctions for the Directors of Failed Banks (2012).

Hutter, B, 'Variations in Regulatory Enforcement Styles' (1989) 11 *Law and Policy* 153.

Jackson, H, 'Variation in the Intensity of Financial Regulation: Preliminary Evidence and Potential Implications' (2007) 24 *Yale Journal on Regulation* 253.

Jackson, H and Roe, M, 'Public and Private Enforcement of Securities Laws: Resource-based Evidence' (2009) 93(2) *Journal of Financial Economics* 207.

Kagan, R, 'Regulatory Enforcement' in Rosenbloom, D and Schwartz, R (eds), *Handbook of Regulation and Administrative Law* (1994).

Kagan, R and Scholz, J, 'The Criminology of the Corporation and Regulatory Enforcement Strategies' in Hawkins, K and Thomas, J (eds), *Enforcing Regulation* (1984).

Keay, A, The Public Enforcement of Directors' Duties (2013), available at <http://ssrn.com/abstract=2201598>.

Keay, A, 'Risk, Shareholder Pressure and Short-termism in Financial Institutions. Does Enlightened Shareholder Value Offer a Panacea?' (2011) 5(6) *Law and Financial Markets Review* 435.

Kingsford Smith, D, 'A Harder Nut to Crack? Responsive Regulation in the Financial Services Sector' (2011) 44(3) *University of British Columbia Law Review* 695.

La Porta, R, Lopez-de-Silanes, F, and Shleifer, A, 'What Works in Securities Laws?' (2006) 61 *Journal of Finance* 1.

MacNeil, I, 'The Evolution of Regulatory Enforcement Action in the UK Capital Markets: A Case of "Less Is More"?' (2007) 2(4) *Capital Markets Law Journal* 345.

MacNeil, I, 'Risk Control Strategies: An Assessment in the Context of the Credit Crisis' in MacNeil, I and O'Brien, J (eds), *The Future of Financial Regulation* (2010).
Malcolm, K, Tilden, M, Coope, S, and Xie, C, *Assessing the Effectiveness of Enforcement and Regulation* (2009).
May, P and Winter, S, 'Regulatory Enforcement Styles and Compliance' in Parker, C and Lehmann Nielsen, V (eds), *Explaining Compliance, Business Responses to Regulation* (2011).
Monteiro, M, Zaman, Q, and Leitterstorf, S, Updated Measurement of Market Cleanliness (2007), FSA Occasional Paper Series.
NERA Economic Consulting, Credit Crisis Litigation Update: It Is Settlement Time (2013).
NERA Economic Consulting, SEC Settlement Trends: 2H12 Update (2013).
Parliamentary Commission on Banking Standards, *Changing Banking for Good* (2013), HL Paper 27-II, HC 175-II.
Reiss, A, 'Selecting Strategies of Social Control over Organizational Life' in Hawkins, K and Thomas, J (eds), *Enforcing Regulation* (1984).
Scholz, J, 'Deterrence, Cooperation, and the Ecology of Regulatory Enforcement' (1984) 18 *Law and Society Review* 179.
Scholz, J, 'Voluntary Compliance and Regulatory Enforcement' (1984) 6(4) *Law & Policy* 385.
Schonert, N, 'A Fistful of Dollars: Bounty Hunting under the Dodd–Frank Act's Whistleblower Provisions' (2011) 36 *Southern Illinois University Law Journal* 159.
SEC, Agency Financial Report 2012 (2013), available at <http://www.sec.gov/about/secafr2012.shtml>.
Stigler, G, 'The Optimum Enforcement of Laws' (1970) 78 *Journal of Political Economy* 526.
Thomson Reuters Accelus, Global Trends in Enforcement of Financial Services Regulation (2012), available at <http://img.en25.com/Web/ThomsonReutersGRC/SR%20-%20Global%20Trends%20in%20Enforcement%20of%20Financial%20Services%20Regulation.pdf>.

PART IV

FINANCIAL STABILITY

CHAPTER 11

SYSTEMIC RISK AND MACRO-PRUDENTIAL SUPERVISION

ROSA M LASTRA*

* I would like to thank Enmanuel Cedeño-Brea for excellent, comprehensive, and original research assistance; and Charles Goodhart, David Bholat, and Andromachi Georgosouli for helpful comments and suggestions. This chapter draws on chapters 3 and 4 of Lastra, R., *International Financial and Monetary Law* (2nd edn, 2015). Errors or limitations of judgement are mine alone.

THIS Chapter deals with the regulatory and institutional issues associated with the management of systemic risk and the concept of macro-prudential supervision. From a methodological viewpoint, it relies upon a multilevel governance (MLG) approach, considering the domestic, regional, and international dimensions of systemic risk control.

The Chapter commences with a brief introduction outlining why macro-prudential supervision has become so topical. Three additional Sections follow. Section II considers the 'paradigm shift' in the management of systemic risk following the 2007–09 global financial crisis and the drivers behind the changes adopted. Section III addresses the trend towards macro-prudential supervision and considers the definition of macro-prudential policy, comparing its goals and objectives with those of other economic policies. It also presents some of the instruments that are generally included in the macro-prudential policy toolkit. Though some of the instruments are relatively new, some other tools (perhaps with a different name and for a different policy objective) were applied in the past. Indeed, several macro-prudential policy instruments have historical precedence.[1] Section IV discusses some of the institutional challenges for creating arrangements at the international, regional, and domestic levels. It also covers some of the main legal and institutional issues that need to be taken into account in order to develop sound and robust institutional arrangements for macro-prudential supervision across regions and jurisdictions.

I. INTRODUCTION

The 2007–09 global financial crisis challenged many pre-existing conceptions about systemic risk. One of these is the so-called 'composition fallacy',[2] which contends that the safety and soundness of any financial system is the aggregate soundness of all its participating institutions.[3] This fallacy assumed that if individual entities were robust, than the whole system would be resilient. This assumption proved to be misguided. Using an analogy with forest management, the safeguard of the health of the forest requires a different type of strategy than the safeguard of the health of each individual tree. Ecological considerations would also

[1] See generally Bholat, D, Macro-prudential Policy: Historical Precedents and Possible Legal Pitfalls (2013), available at <http://www.lccge.bbk.ac.uk/news/seminar>.

[2] Brunnermeier, M, Crockett, A, Goodhart, C, Persaud, A, and Shin, H, *The Fundamental Principles of Financial Regulation* (2009) 11, Geneva Reports on the World Economy 15.

[3] Osiński, J, Seal, K, and Hoogduin, L, Macroprudential and Micro-prudential Policies: Toward Cohabitation (2013), International Monetary Fund (IMF), Monetary and Capital Markets Department, 6.

warn us against excessive reliance on a 'static' notion of stability; as Andromachi Georgosouli has pointed out,[4] the notion of systemic risk control requires an understanding of resilience as adaptability, thus a dynamic consideration.[5]

Systemic risks pose a threat to financial stability. And, as the crisis evidenced, these types of risks are not confined to the banking system: they can also affect securities and derivatives markets. Such was the case of international insurer, AIG, and investment banks such as Lehman Brothers and Bear Stearns. During the economic meltdown, systemic risks stemmed from non-bank institutions and from financial instruments that traditionally fell outside the regulatory perimeter. Furthermore, systemic risks are not bounded by jurisdictional frontiers; they have a tendency to spread across geographical borders. The dichotomy between global markets and institutions and national law and national policies is particularly acute in the management of systemic risk and in the design of adequate institutional solutions to deal with its negative spillover effects. The financial crisis signified an inflection point towards the adoption of a macro-prudential approach to financial supervision.

II. Systemic Risk in the Aftermath of the Crisis

The onslaught of the financial crisis has triggered a change in the way that financial supervisors tackle systemic risk. The crisis and the ensuing economic downturn were necessary in order to understand the global interconnectedness and

[4] Georgosouli, A, in an unpublished manuscript of 2012 entitled 'Financial Resilience' (cited with the permission of the author) addresses the problem of financial vulnerability shifting away from the financial stability metaphor towards a resilience-oriented scheme of regulation. She defines financial resilience as 'adaptive capacity to change', which 'is measured in terms of one's ability to learn, prepare and, where appropriate, cope and recover from future contingencies'. She concludes: 'Compared to stability-focused regimes, resilience regulation is more consonant to the logic of a capitalist economy. This is because it focuses on the transition of the financial system from one state of being to the next rather than on the system's resistance and its capacity to bounce back to a perceived normality. While financial stability calls for policies that focus on the magnitude and level of contingency of destabilising episodes, financial resilience calls for policies that focus on the socio-structural implications of destabilising episodes irrespective of their magnitude and degree of contingency at a given point in time. Contrary to financial stability-driven systems of regulation, "resilience regulation" gives equal consideration to consumer resilience and systemic resilience and thus it is more likely to lead to more equitable management of financial vulnerability.' Her departure from the 'financial stability-centred view' that currently prevails in the literature provides a fresh approach to the current debate on the subject.

[5] cf Taleb, N, *Antifragile: Things that Gain from Disorder* (2012).

complexity of financial markets, participants, and transactions.[6] The meltdown underscored the fact that systemic risk can have both a national and a transnational impact because of 'the inherent risks posed by large, multinational, interconnected financial institutions'.[7]

Hal Scott defines systemic risk as 'the risk that a national, or the global, financial system will break down'.[8] Systemic risk poses a threat to financial stability. Financial instability can have a knock-on effect on the real economy, sclerotizing growth. There is no consensus on the definition of financial stability.[9] Instead, it is construed as an elusive and evolving concept.[10] However, it is agreed that it 'has become a common concern in the process of globalization as it is so directly linked with economic prosperity and human welfare'.[11]

The absence of a clear-cut definition of financial stability entails that the 'notion of financial stability is often discussed in terms of the concept of systemic risk and its sources'.[12] Systemic risk management—and consequently, macro-prudential supervision—aims to contain the 'build-up of systemic vulnerabilities over time'.[13] The accumulation of such vulnerabilities can provoke a generalized reduction in asset values within a financial system. Crises of this nature can be termed *financial* or *capital* crises—as opposed to the notion of liquidity or *banking* crises.[14] Financial crises imply widespread asset write-downs and write-offs in the balance sheets of financial and non-financial institutions across one or more jurisdictions. These asset devaluations stem from the systemic vulnerabilities that generate financial instability.

The renewed interest in systemic risk that resulted after the financial crisis has underlined the importance of Frank Knight's classic distinction between risk and uncertainty[15] in relation to the informational asymmetries faced by market

[6] Golden, J, 'The Courts, the Financial Crisis and Systemic Risk' (2009) 4 *Capital Markets Law Journal* S141.

[7] Greene, E et al., 'A Closer Look at "Too Big to Fail": National and International Approaches to Addressing the Risks of Large, Interconnected Financial Institutions' (2010) 5(2) *Capital Market Law Journal* 117, 118.

[8] Scott, H, 'Reducing Systemic Risk through the Reform of Capital Regulation' (2010) 13(3) *Journal of International Economic Law* 763.

[9] In the so-called 'Ingves Report', the Bank for International Settlements (BIS) set out to establish a definition of financial stability that would assist in its operational implementation. The report presents at least five different definitions of financial stability found in the recent literature: BIS, Central Bank Governance and Financial Stability (2011) 32.

[10] Lastra, R, *Legal Foundations of International Monetary Stability* (2006) and Lastra, R, *International Financial and Monetary Law* (2nd edn, 2015), ch 4.

[11] Weber, R, 'Multilayered Governance in International Financial Regulation and Supervision' (2010) 13(3) *Journal of International Economic Law* 695.

[12] Galati, G and Moessner, R, Macroprudential Policy—a Literature Review (2013), BIS Working Papers No 337, available at <http://www.bis.org/publ/work337.pdf>, 13.

[13] International Monetary Fund (IMF), Key Aspects of Macroprudential Policy (2013), 7.

[14] Lastra, R and Wood, G, 'The Crisis of 2007–2009: Nature, Causes and Reactions' (2010) 13(3) *Journal of International Economic Law* 534.

[15] Knight, F, *Risk, Uncertainty and Profit* (1921).

participants, regulators, and supervisors.[16] While the notion of 'risk proper' entails a quantity susceptible of measurement, Knightian uncertainty involves unquantifiable risk. Considerations regarding systemic risk should question the measurability of prospect scenarios. In particular, the contemporary definitions of systemic risk might conflate quantifiable contingencies and immeasurable ones.

Moreover, systemic risk has been categorized into two different time-based dimensions. First, the *structural* dimension of systemic risk refers to 'the distribution of risks across the financial sector'.[17] This is a static or snapshot dimension, which considers the aggregate risk in any (set of) financial system(s) at a given point in time. Secondly, there is a *cyclical* dimension that tracks the dynamic changes of systemic risk over time.[18] This cyclical dimension looks at how risk varies over the economic cycle—that is, during booms and slumps, from peak to trough. This distinction is useful for identifying which instruments from the macro-prudential toolkit are fit for each time-dimension of systemic risk.[19]

1. Financial stability as a global public good

The interconnectedness of financial markets has rendered financial stability as a 'national, regional and international goal'.[20] This makes it a global public good[21] that 'does not stop at national borders'.[22] The public good nature of financial stability means that it is a potential source of market failure. Global financial stability combines the two elements of public goods: non-rivalry and non-exclusivity.[23] The non-rivalrous nature of financial stability means that its enjoyment by one jurisdiction will not reduce the amount available to another country. While its non-exclusive characteristic means that jurisdictions that invest heavily to attain it cannot exclude other states from enjoying some of its benefits. Conversely, the

[16] See Avgouleas, E, *Governance of Global Financial Markets: The Law, the Economics and the Politics* (2012) 104.

[17] European Systemic Risk Board (ESRB), Recommendation of the European Systemic Risk Board on Intermediate Objectives and Instruments of Macroprudential Policy (2013), ESRB/2013/1 2013/C170/01.

[18] Elliott, D et al., The History of Cyclical Macroprudential Policy in the United States (2013), Finance and Economics Discussion Series Divisions of Research & Statistics and Monetary Affairs Working Paper No 2013-29.

[19] However, the ESRB considers that 'it is difficult to make a clear-cut distinction between the two dimensions given their close interlinkages', ESRB, n 17 above.

[20] Lastra, R, 'Systemic Risk, SIFIs and Financial Stability' (2011) 6 (2) *Capital Markets Law Journal* 198, 207.

[21] Trachtman, J, 'The International Law of Financial Crisis: Spillovers, Subsidiarity, Fragmentation and Cooperation' (2010) 13(3) *Journal of International Economic Law* 721.

[22] Schoenmaker, D, 'A New Financial Stability Framework for Europe' (2008) 13(3) *The Financial Regulator*.

[23] Miceli, T, *The Economic Approach to Law* (2004) 32.

absence of stability—financial instability—can be symmetrically construed as a global public bad, which also shares the features of lacking rivalry and exclusion.

As with other public goods, public authorities are entrusted with the provision of financial stability. Some countries could have incentives to under-invest in achieving financial stability in order to free-ride on the investments made by other jurisdictions. This can lead to the potential underproduction of financial stability at a cross-border basis.[24]

2. Moral hazard and 'too-big-to' problems

The 'too-big-to' (TBT) set of problems (too-big-to-fail, too-complex-to-fail, too-interconnected-to-fail ...) can be considered as an additional driver behind the latest shift in the supervisory paradigm. These TBT considerations, fuelled by moral hazard and implicit guarantees, posed and continue to pose a significant threat to global financial and economic stability. In addition, many countries harbour institutions that they cannot afford to bail out in the hypothetical case of their failure (too-big-to-save or TBTS).[25] These entities are not only commercial banks. The AIG bailout and the collapse of Lehman Brothers revealed that problems, crises or failures in non-bank institutions could also have systemic dimensions.

These eventualities gave renewed impetus to the challenge of developing a supervisory framework for dealing with the moral hazard posed by Systemically Important Financial Institutions (SIFIs).[26] The G20's Financial Stability Board (FSB) defined SIFIs as 'financial institutions whose distress or disorderly failure, because of their size, complexity and systemic interconnectedness, would cause significant disruption to the wider financial system and economic activity'.[27] SIFIs that pose a threat to global financial stability are referred to as GSIFIs. On November 2011, the FSB issued an initial list of 29 GSIFIs.[28] Moreover, on July 2013, the FSB published

[24] Trachtman, n 21 above.

[25] Countries harboured these institutions both as home and as host states. The distinction between home/host states is relevant for the regulation and supervision of financial institutions and conglomerates. Many financial entities operate on a cross-border basis, while supervision and crisis management largely remain national tasks. Goodhart and Lastra refer to this as the 'cross border problem': cf Goodhart, C and Lastra, R, 'Border Problems' (2010) 13(3) *Journal of International Economic Law* 705. Jay Lawrence Westbrook has also argued that bailing out SIFIs could even be financially troubling for more affluent jurisdictions like the US and the UK: Westbrook, J, 'SIFIs and States' (2013) 49(2) *Texas International Law Journal*.

[26] cf Financial Stability Board (FSB), Reducing the Moral Hazard Posed by Systemically Important Financial Institutions (2010).

[27] cf FSB, Policy Measures to Address Systemically Important Financial Institutions (2011).

[28] ibid, Annex (the irony being that the FSB's designation of certain institutions as SIFIs may create the very problem it is trying to mitigate).

a list of Global Systemically Important Insurers (GSIIs) and the policy measures that will apply to them.[29]

SIFIs and GSIFIs resemble the baobab trees depicted in Antoine de Saint-Exupéry's classic book, *The Little Prince*. In the book's illustration, the baobabs (inspired by the Adansonia genus of trees) are stifling and smothering the planet with the size of their roots and trunks. Like the baobabs, GSIFIs have extended their nexus of activities across the globe, entrenching their roots across many jurisdictions.[30]

The supervisory challenge posed by SIFIs is not exclusive to developed countries. There are many jurisdictions that host GSIFIs. Many other countries have to deal with their own set of SIFIs. This reality prompted the BCBS to issue its Framework for Dealing with Domestic Systemically Important Banks or DSIBs.[31] The FSB also published its report on extending the GSIFI Framework to DSIBs.[32] This underscores the idea that GSIFIs and DSIBs represent two complementary sides of the systemic risk problematic.

III. Macro-Prudential Supervision

1. Definition and evolution

Before the crisis, risk-based supervision was mostly concerned with the safety and soundness of individual institutions (the concept of micro-prudential supervision).[33] After the crisis, the focus has shifted towards the robustness of the whole financial system. For example, the BCBS enhanced the scope of risk-based supervision in its Core Principles for Effective Banking Supervision. The new Core Principles have been widened in order to include

> the need for greater intensity and resources to deal effectively with systemically important banks; the importance of applying a system-wide, macro perspective to the microprudential

[29] FSB, Global Systemically Important Insurers (GSIIs) and the Policy Measures that Will Apply to them (2013).

[30] cf Lastra, R, Inaugural Lecture: The Quest for International Financial Regulation (23 March 2011), Queen Mary University, London, available at <http://www.law.qmul.ac.uk/events/podcasts/lastra2011/>.

[31] Basel Committee on Banking Supervision, A Framework for Dealing with Systemically Important Banks (2012).

[32] FSB, G-SIFI Framework to Domestic Systemically Important Banks: Progress Report to G-20 Ministers and Governor (16 April 2012), available at <http://www.financialstabilityboard.org/publications/r_120420b.pdf>.

[33] See Lastra, R, 'Defining Forward-looking Judgment-based Supervision' (2013) 14(3) *Journal of Banking Regulation* 221.

supervision of banks to assist in identifying, analysing and taking pre-emptive action to address systemic risk; and the increasing focus on effective crisis management, recovery and resolution measures in reducing both the probability and impact of a bank failure.[34]

This system wide perspective is referred to as macro-prudential supervision. The set of measures, tools and processes that financial regulators employ in order to achieve the aforementioned objectives is referred to as 'macro-prudential policy'.

'Macro-prudential' policy has become one of the main features of the post-crisis financial regulatory reform agenda.[35] Although a relatively recent phenomenon, it has already sparked many academic papers, high-level discussions, and policy reports. This progress notwithstanding, macro-prudential policy is still considered to be in its initial phase. Douglas Elliott considers that '(w)e are in the early days of macroprudential policy, akin perhaps to where monetary policy stood in the 1950s'.[36]

The macro-prudential perspective can be a murky concept to grasp, somewhere in between micro-prudential supervision and monetary policy. The contours are not always easy to demarcate. The European Systemic Risk Board (ESRB) states that '(t)he ultimate objective of macro-prudential policy is to contribute to the safeguard of the stability of the financial system as a whole, including by strengthening the resilience of the financial system and decreasing the build-up of systemic risks, thereby ensuring a sustainable contribution of the financial sector to economic growth'.[37] Before the macro-prudential paradigm shift, 'the broader financial system was steered by a combination of monetary policy and microprudential regulation'.[38] With the onslaught of the crisis, the focus has now expanded to take into account the bigger picture: the safety and soundness of the whole financial system as well as the global interconnectedness of systems and infrastructures across borders.

In order to conceptually clarify macro-prudential supervision better, it can be useful to rely on the analogy provided by forest management: 'Macro-prudential supervision is analogous to the oversight of the forest, whereas micro-prudential supervision is analogous to the oversight of individual trees.'[39] This illustration can resonate powerfully when considering that in order to preserve the forest, some individual trees might need to be sacrificed—or overseen with higher concern.

[34] BCBS, Core Principles for Effective Banking Supervision (2012), 2. See also ibid, 8 and 9.

[35] Galati and Moessner, n 12 above.

[36] Elliott, D, 'Macroprudential Policy: Time to Start Experimenting', *The Economist*, 4 June 2013. A similar view has been stated by Haldane, A, Macroprudential Policies—When and How to Use Them (2013), available at <http://www.imf.org/external/np/seminars/eng/2013/macro2/pdf/ah.pdf>.

[37] ESRB, n 17 above, Article 1.

[38] Schoenmaker, D and Wierts, P, Macroprudential Policy: The Need for a Coherent Policy Framework (2011), DSF Policy Paper Series No 13, 2.

[39] Lastra, n 20 above, 198.

Macro-prudential policy looks to provide a backstop for systemic risk containment within the perimeter of individual institutions. It must not be confused with forms of micro-prudential management, like consolidated supervision. In the latter, the focus is on the related entities within a financial group. While macro-prudential supervision is concerned with the relationship between any individual institution (or financial group) and the safety and soundness of the system as a whole.

One of the major challenges of implementing systemic-wide supervision is adequate policy interaction between macro-prudential policy and other economic policies. Additional levels of complexity arise when considering that micro- and macro-prudential supervision are not only limited to the commercial banking sector—but also span across other financial subsectors (insurance, investment banking, shadow banking) on a domestic and transnational level.

2. The macro-prudential policy toolkit

The range of macro-prudential regulation and supervision is broader than the traditional scope of micro-prudential regulation. As a result, the macro-prudential toolkit includes a plethora of instruments. Some of these tools—like transaction taxes and central counterparty (CCP) clearing[40]—are not even '*prudential*' in nature. Others are recognizable. These devices have been borrowed from other areas of economic policy, such as: monetary, fiscal, competition policies, and crisis management.[41] This highlights the fact that even though the macro-prudential perspective is fairly recent, the toolkit drawn so far comprises many familiar instruments from other policy areas.[42]

The macro-prudential policy menu needs to encompass tools for the whole financial system—including areas that fall outside the perimeter of the regulatory radar. The shadow banking sector, market infrastructures, market participants and financial instruments can all pose a significant systemic threat to domestic and transnational financial stability.[43]

[40] Central counterparty (CCP) clearing refers to the interposition of the CCP between counterparties of the original trade thus, the CCP becoming buyer to the seller and seller to the buyer. This process of replacing the original contract with two equal and opposite transactions is referred to as 'novation' where the resulting two transactions are completely independent from each other. See generally Norman, P, *The Risk Controllers: Central Counterparty Clearing in Globalised Financial Markets* (2011).

[41] IMF, n 13 above, 8.

[42] This could add confusion regarding the boundaries of macroprudential policy vis-à-vis other economic policy fields.

[43] The FSB has defined the 'shadow banking system' or 'market-based' financing system as 'credit intermediation involving entities and activities (fully or partially) outside the regular banking system or non-bank credit intermediation in short': FSB, Strengthening Oversight and Regulation of Shadow Banking Policy Framework for Strengthening Oversight and Regulation of Shadow Banking Entities (2013).

The instruments also need to be effective and efficient. The ESRB states that effectiveness refers to how well each instrument mitigates systemic market failures while achieving its policy objective(s),[44] while the efficiency of any macro-prudential tool has been defined as achieving the desired goals and objectives at a minimum cost. However, because macro-prudential supervision is still in its initial implementation phase, the instruments will need adequate testing and calibration.

One of the main challenges in the design of an effective policy is the assessment and calibration of the various instruments in the macro-prudential toolkit. This calibration implies not only using the instruments effectively and efficiently. It also means balancing countervailing tools for different economic policy objectives. Moreover, the regulatory dialectic cycle suggests that financial innovation and 'loophole mining' can create new sources of systemic risk build-up that will have to be addressed.[45]

Downturns in the economic cycle are also likely to stir tensions between macro- and micro-prudential policies. This means that the calibration of macro-prudential tools is contingent to the overall economic cycle. Countercyclical[46] capital buffers are an example of this. This instrument consists of requiring financial institutions to set aside more capital during good times, in order to better withstand potential economic downturns.

3. Macro-prudential tools and objectives

Macro-prudential tools may be divided using the categories of systemic risk referred to earlier in the Chapter, distinguishing between: *cyclical* and *structural* macro-prudential tools.[47] Elliot et al. have argued that in some cases, countries like the US have long been using some of the identified instruments without having labelled them as 'macro-prudential'.[48]

Given the relative short history of macro-prudential supervision as such (even if instruments in the toolkit have been used for decades before) the framework for using it in the pursuit of the financial stability objective is largely experimental, and relies to a large extent on 'work in progress'. Many leading financial regulatory

[44] ESRB, n 17 above.

[45] Kane, E, 'Accelerating Inflation, Technological Innovation, and the Decreasing Effectiveness of Banking Regulation' (1981) 36 (2) *Journal of Finance*. cf Kane, E, The Inevitability of Shadow Banking (2012), available at <http://www.frbatlanta.org/documents/news/conferences/12fmc/12fmc_kane.pdf>.

[46] cf n 49 below.

[47] Schoenmaker and Wierts, n 38 above, 2.

[48] Elliott et al., n 18 above, 3. David Bholat of the Bank of England is conducting a similar type of research in the UK: Bholat, D, Macro-prudential Policy: Historical Precedents and Possible Future Pitfalls, Lecture at Birkbeck, University of London, London, UK (25 October 2013).

trendsetters, like the FSB and the International Monetary Fund (IMF), and domestic and regional macro-prudential supervisors, like the Bank of England (BoE) and the ESRB, have set out to establish an adequate framework for measuring and making macro-prudential policy operational.

A working paper written by IMF staff states that the macro-prudential toolkit must contain three categories of instruments:

(i) instruments constructed to have an impact on the pro-cyclicality[49] of the financial system (for example, countercyclical capital buffers) or on the contribution of a financial institution to systemic risk (for example, Systemically Important Financial Institution surcharges);
(ii) prudential instruments to address a build-up of systemic risk in specific segments of the market (such as loan-to-value ratios) and instruments aimed at constraining general or specific leverage in nonfinancial sectors (such as debt-to-income ratios); and
(iii) tools to address systemic liquidity concerns.[50]

The ESRB has set out a set five intermediate objectives that macro-prudential policy should aim to achieve. These intermediate objectives are:

(i) mitigating and preventing excessive credit growth and leverage;
(ii) mitigating and preventing excessive maturity mismatch and market illiquidity;
(iii) limiting direct and indirect exposure concentrations;
(iv) limiting the systemic impact of misaligned incentives with a view to reducing moral hazard; and
(v) strengthening the resilience of financial infrastructures.[51]

The aforementioned intermediate objectives are seen as transitional steps towards achieving robust financial stability. The ESRB considers that 'identifying intermediate objectives makes macro-prudential policy more operational, transparent and accountable and provides an economic basis for the selection of instruments'.[52]

Table 11.1 summarizes and presents the referred intermediate objectives and includes the matching policy instruments that have been identified by the ESRB—an indicative list comprising different categories—in order to tackle specific market failures that lead to financial instability. The ESRB recommends that instruments should be selected according to their efficiency and effectiveness. However, because

[49] 'Procyclical' tools move together with the economic cycle. This means that they are directly or positively related to economic booms and busts. Conversely, 'countercyclical' tools and policies are negatively or inversely related with the economic cycle. The story of Joseph (present in the Bible and the Quran) serves as a good illustration in order to explain the concept of countercyclicality. As a countercyclical policy, Joseph recommended saving resources during seven years of economic prosperity in Egypt in order to endure the subsequent seven years of scarcity and famine.

[50] Osiński et al., n 3 above, 25.

[51] ESRB, n 17 above.

[52] ibid, para 4.

Table 11.1 Macro-prudential policy intermediate objectives, selected instruments, and market failure

Intermediate Objective	Underlying Market Failure (identified by the ESRB)	Selected Instruments
Mitigate and prevent excessive credit growth and leverage	• Credit crunch externalities: a sudden tightening of the conditions required to obtain a loan, resulting in a reduction of the availability of credit to the non-financial sector. • Endogenous risk-taking: incentives that during a boom generate excessive risk-taking and, in the case of banks, a deterioration of lending standards. Explanations for this include signalling competence, market pressures to boost returns, or strategic interaction between institutions. • Risk illusion: collective underestimation of risk related to short-term memory and the infrequency of financial crises. • Bank runs: the withdrawal of wholesale or retail funding in case of actual or perceived insolvency. • Interconnectedness externalities: contagious consequences of uncertainty about events at an institution or within a market.	• Countercyclical capital buffer • Sectorial capital requirements (including intra-financial system) • Macro-prudential leverage ratio • Loan-to-value requirements (LTV) • Loan-to-income/debt (service)-to-income requirements (LTI)
Mitigate and prevent excessive maturity mismatch and market illiquidity	• Fire sales externalities: arise from the forced sale of assets due to excessive asset and liability mismatches. This may lead to a liquidity spiral whereby falling asset prices induce further sales, deleveraging and spillovers to financial institutions with similar asset classes. • Bank runs. • Market illiquidity: the drying-up of interbank or capital markets resulting from a general loss of confidence or very pessimistic expectations.	• Macro-prudential adjustment to liquidity ratio (eg, liquidity coverage ratio) • Macro-prudential restrictions on funding sources (eg, net stable funding ratio) • Macro-prudential unweighted limit to less stable funding (eg, loan-to-deposit ratio) • Margin and haircut requirements
Limit direct and indirect exposure concentrations	• Interconnectedness externalities. • Fire sales externalities: (here) arise from the forced sale of assets at a dislocated price given the distribution of exposures within the financial system.	• Large exposure restrictions • CCP clearing requirement

Intermediate Objective	Underlying Market Failure (identified by the ESRB)	Selected Instruments
Limit the systemic impact of misaligned incentives with a view to reducing moral hazard	• Moral hazard and 'too big to fail': excessive risk-taking due to expectations of a bailout due to the perceived system relevance of an individual institution.	• SIFI capital surcharges
Strengthen the resilience of financial infrastructures	• Interconnectedness externalities • Fire sales externalities • Risk illusion • Incomplete contracts: compensation structures that provide incentives for risky behaviour.	• Margin and haircut requirements on CCP clearing • Increased disclosure • Structural systemic risk buffer

Source: European Systemic Risk Board (ESRB), Recommendation of the European Systemic Risk Board on Intermediate Objectives and Instruments of Macroprudential Policy (2013), ESRB/2013/1 2013/C170/01

of the incipient implementation of these devices on a systemic-wide scale, there is still limited evidence to evaluate their success or failure.

To sum up, some of the main tools identified with macro-prudential policy and supervision are:

- Countercyclical capital buffers (CCB).
- Sectorial capital requirements. This would include capital requirements for banking, securities intermediation and insurance.
- Macro-prudential leverage ratio. For all entities across sector, not just commercial banks.[53]
- Loan-to-value requirements (LTV). LTV ratios represent the proportion between the value of a secured loan in comparison to the value of an asset used as security for said loan (ie, the value of a mortgage in comparison to the value of the mortgaged asset). LTV ratios aim to reduce the exposure of lenders but they also tackle moral hazard on the borrowers' side, making them hold more 'skin-in-the-game' in order to create a disincentive for defaulting.
- Loan-to-income/debt (service)-to-income requirements (LTI). The LTI ratio measures a borrower's repayment capacity. It compares the borrower's scheduled

[53] Scott remarks on how leading up to the crisis many US investment banks were overleveraged reaching leverage to capital ratios of 30 to 1. Scott, n 8 above, 765.

debt service payments with his/her income. If payments represent a large portion (or exceed) the borrowers income, default might ensue.

- Macro-prudential adjustment to liquidity ratio (eg, liquidity coverage ratio).
- Macro-prudential restrictions on funding sources (eg, net stable funding ratio).
- Macro-prudential unweighted limit to less stable funding (eg, loan-to-deposit ratio).
- Margin and haircut requirements.[54]
- SIFI capital surcharges. This means requiring more stringent capital requirements to SIFIs.
- Margin and haircut requirements on CCP clearing.
- Increased disclosure.
- Structural systemic risk buffer.
- Large exposure restrictions.
- CCP clearing requirements.
- Deposit protection/insurance.

Additional instruments proposed by the IMF, include 'Pigovian' fiscal measures, such as the Financial Stability Contribution (FSC), aimed at providing funds for an effective resolution mechanism, and a Financial Activities Tax (FAT), 'levied on the sum of the profits and remuneration of financial institutions, and paid to general revenue'.[55] In addition, competition policy measures—such as limits against sectorial concentration and merger control—can also be used with macro-prudential objectives. These macro-prudential tools can generate conflicting tensions with the goals traditionally associated with other overlapping economic policies. Consequently, trade-offs can exist between macro-prudential policy and other economic programmes.

The IMF has also identified (in house and externally) two additional sets of tools aimed at addressing the interconnectedness dimension of cross-sectional systemic risk. These sets of tools are (i) network analysis and (ii) price-based measures.[56] By interconnectedness, the IMF staff refer to the 'complex webs of contract relationships across financial institutions'.[57]

Network analysis consists of looking at the nexus of existing multilateral claims (links) between financial institutions (nodes). The main tools for network analysis identified by IMF staff are: (i) centrality analysis; (ii) cluster analysis; and (iii) balance-sheet simulation measures.[58] Centrality analysis looks at the existing

[54] In his comments to this Chapter, Goodhart pointed out that he found the dividing lines rather restrictive in that margin requirements, for example, could be used as an instrument for almost all the intermediate objectives.

[55] IMF, A Fair and Substantial Contribution by the Financial Sector (2010).

[56] Arregui, N et al., Addressing Interconnectedness: Concepts and Prudential Tools (2013), IMF Working Paper WP/13/199, 6.

[57] ibid, 4. [58] ibid.

patterns of linkages between nodes (financial institutions) to understand which of them are crucial to a particular financial system.[59] Cluster analysis compiles nodes that are closer to each other into subsets or 'clusters' with the aim of identifying vulnerable entities and 'gatekeepers' that can spread risk to other institutions. Balance-sheet simulations are hypothetical assessments that assume financial failure in order to test how well institutional balance sheets perform.

On the other hand, price-based measures are defined as 'methodologies developed for the measurement of risk in portfolios of securities [that] have been adapted to the measurement of systemic risk for a "portfolio" of institutions'.[60] One of the main distinctions between network analyses and price-based measures is that while the former tackle 'direct bilateral exposures between institutions', price-based measures can also cover 'indirect spillover channels' across institutions.[61] These tools involve sophisticated quantitative techniques.

Some of the main price-based measures that have been identified in the emerging literature include: CoVaR, distress spillovers, return spillovers, JPoD, and CoPoD.[62] CoVaR is 'the value at risk (VaR) of the financial system conditional on institutions being in distress'.[63] While VaR measures the individual risk of financial institutions, CoVaR aims to study how the risk of one institution affects another.[64] Return spillovers aim to gauge the contribution of one institution to systemic risk. While distress spillovers are an indicator of the systemic contribution of individual institutions, but during distressful times.[65] Moreover, Segoviano and Goodhart have developed a measure for calculating the conditional probabilities of distress (CoPoD) that estimates the probability that one institution experiences financial instability conditional on the distress of another entity. The joint probability of distress (JPoD) can also be calculated for multiple institutions.[66]

[59] See Markose, S, 'Systemic Risk Analytics: A Data Driven Multi-Agent Financial Network (MAFN) Approach' (2013) 14(3) *Journal of Banking Regulation*.

[60] ibid, 7. [61] ibid, 10.

[62] These measures are explained with great detail in Appendix III of Arregui et al., n 56 above, 51–3.

[63] Adrian, T and Brunnermeier, M, CoVaR (2011), Federal Reserve Bank of New York Staff Reports No 348.

[64] ibid.

[65] See Chan-Lau, J, Mitra, S, and Ong, L, 'Identifying Contagion Risk in the International Banking System: An Extreme Value Theory Approach' (2012) *International Journal of Finance and Economics* 17.

[66] See Goodhart, C and Segoviano, M, Banking Stability Measures (2009), IMF Working Paper WP/09/04.

IV. Institutional Arrangements for Macro-Prudential Supervision

The IMF has stated that in order to be effective, macro-prudential policies require a 'strong institutional framework'.[67] Because of the cross-border implications that systemic risks pose to global financial stability, the institutional arrangements need to cover the international, regional and national dimensions. The IMF calls this the *multilateral aspects* of macro-prudential policy.[68] These dimensions justify the need for strong coordination and cooperation in the implementation of macro-prudential policies as well as in cross-border systemic-wide financial supervision and orderly bank resolution schemes for GSIFIs and DSIBs. In turn, the main institutional arrangements that have been originated in the international and domestic perspectives are discussed.

1. The international perspective

In November 2010, the G20 leaders called on the top financial regulatory standard setters to develop the macro-prudential frameworks, requiring that 'these frameworks should take into account national and regional arrangements'.[69] This statement evidences the importance of building sound regional and national institutional and policy structures for macro-prudential supervision. The main forums leading these reforms at the global level are the FSB, the BCBS, and the IMF.

It still might be too early to adequately assess the effectiveness of these forums in paving the way towards systemic-wide supervision. The FSB is the newest—and probably—the least well known of these forums.[70] Its membership includes central banks, finance ministries, and also other international standard-setters and international organizations, such as the IMF, the International Organization of Securities Commissions (IOSCO), and the BCBS.[71] Although its decisions are based on consensus, the limited participation of many emerging economies in its decision-making process could undermine the effectiveness of its scope of influence. This can also give rise to democratic legitimacy concerns. Nonetheless, the

[67] IMF, n 13 above, 27.

[68] ibid, 5.

[69] FSB, IMF, and BIS, Macroprudential Policy Tools and Frameworks: Progress Report to G20 (2011).

[70] See Schembri, L, 'Born of Necessity and Built to Succeed: Why Canada and the World Need the Financial Stability Board', speech by the Deputy Governor of the Bank of Canada (24 September 2013).

[71] The full list is available at <http://www.financialstabilityboard.org/about/fsb_members.htm>.

FSB has led the way in the policy debate of important systemic policy areas, which include SIFIs, GSIIs, shadow banking,[72] TBTF,[73] and information gaps.[74]

The IMF has also become an important player in the macro-prudential trend. The Fund has stated that it 'can play a key role, through its bilateral and multilateral surveillance and in collaboration with standard setters and country authorities, to help ensure the effective use of macroprudential policy for domestic and global stability'.[75] Although its scope has been traditionally focused purely on micro-prudential banking tools, the BCBS has also taken important steps in the transition towards a systemic wide-approach to supervision. As mentioned before, the BCBS has widened the scope of its Core Principles and also developed rules for supervising DSIBs.

2. Regional and domestic perspectives

Many high-level policy reports and academic papers address the key features that should underpin a robust domestic institutional structure for macro-prudential supervision.[76] There is no one-size-fits-all solution when it comes to adopting a macro-prudential institutional arrangement. While some discussions exist regarding which institutions are better fitted to perform macro-prudential oversight, there is some consensus on recommending that every country should build on its existing institutional framework, attending to its own country-specific circumstances.[77] Thus, emerging market economies should implement bespoke institutional frameworks that conform to their existing institutional conditions.

In a joint-policy document, the IMF, the FSB, and the BIS have stated that the main features for robust institutional macro-prudential arrangements should include: (i) a clear legal mandate; (ii) appropriate powers and instruments; (iii) suitable accountability and transparency mechanisms; (iv) composition of the decision-making body; and (v) arrangements for domestic policy coordination.[78] In addition, the IMF has identified at least three models for establishing a robust institutional framework. Table 11.2 provides a summary of these models. The ideal model will depend on the legal and historical features of each country.

The first model assigns macro-prudential oversight to the central bank or monetary authority. The idea is that central bankers should lead in order to better

[72] See FSB, n 43 above.

[73] See FSB, Progress and Next Steps towards Ending 'Too-Big-to-Fail' (2013).

[74] The data gap initiative (DGI) is a 'common data template for global systemically important banks to address key information gaps and to provide the authorities with a strong framework for globally assessing potential systemic risks': FSB and IMF, The Financial Crisis and Information Gaps: Fourth Progress Report on the Implementation of the G-20 Data Gaps Initiative (September 2013).

[75] IMF, n 13 above, 5.

[76] See IMF, n 13 above. cf ESRB, n 17 above.

[77] FSB, IMF, and BIS, n 69 above, 17.

[78] ibid, 15.

coordinate monetary policy and other goals—like price stability—alongside the overarching systemic wide goal of financial stability. The shortcoming from this arrangement is that countervailing policy objectives and instruments could generate frictions. Some studies have pointed out the existence of possible tensions between macro-prudential and monetary policies.[79]

The second model—a variation of the first—suggests an institutional arrangement that assigns macro-prudential policy to a committee within the central bank separate from the committee entrusted with the conduct of monetary policy. This structure can offer the possibility of segregating macro-prudential goals from other policy objectives. This is, for example, the model adopted in the UK with the establishment of the Financial Policy Committee (FPC) within the BoE (separate from the Monetary Policy Committee) by the Financial Services Act 2012. The FPC has been charged with the main objective of 'of identifying, monitoring and taking action to remove or reduce systemic risks with a view to protecting and enhancing the resilience of the UK financial system'.[80]

The IMF, the SFSB, and the BIS state that 'the creation of such committees is most obviously desirable when multiple bodies have a financial stability mandate, or where there is separation between bodies with decision-making and policy implementation powers'.[81] In addition, committees also offer the possibility for collective decision-making and consensus building. Schoenmaker and Wierts point out that 'committees tend to be less effective in timely decision-making'[82] though they still favour committees over decision-making by a single individual.[83]

Charles Goodhart and also Luis Garicano and myself have recommended that the central bank should be in charge of macro-prudential supervision.[84] As regards the specific central banking organizational arrangement, a committee structure provides adequate balancing of its twin mandate (monetary stability and financial stability).

The third model proposes the creation of macro-prudential oversight institutions located outside the central bank though generally with some participation by the central bank. This is, for instance, the model adopted by the Dodd–Frank

[79] See Maddaloni, A and Peydró, J, Monetary Policy, Macroprudential Policy and Banking Stability: Evidence from the Euro Area (2013), European Central Bank Macroprudential Research Network Working Paper Series No 1560, 25. cf Angelini, P et al., Monetary and Macroprudential Policies (2012), European Central Bank Macroprudential Research Network Working Paper Series No 1449, 25.

[80] See <http://www.bankofengland.co.uk/financialstability/pages/fpc/default.aspx>.

[81] FSB, IMF, and BIS, n 66 above, 17.

[82] Schoenmaker and Wierts, n 38 above, 9.

[83] By arguing that 'Committee decision-making tends be more balanced than decision-making by individuals': ibid, 8.

[84] Goodhart, C, The Changing Role of Central Banks (2010), BIS Working Papers No 326, 30; Garicano, L and Lastra, R, 'Towards a New Architecture for Financial Stability: Seven Principles' (2010) 13(3) *Journal of International Economic Law* 612.

Table 11.2 Models for macro-prudential institutional arrangement

Model 1: *Central bank*	Macro-prudential responsibilities are entrusted directly to the Central Bank (with the same governing body in charge of monetary policy and macro-prudential supervision).
Model 2: *Internal body within the central bank*	Macro-prudential responsibilities are assigned to a committee within the Central Bank, which is separate from the committee entrusted with the conduct of monetary policy.
Model 3: *External committee outside of the central bank*	The macro-prudential functions are assigned to an institution outside of the Central Bank, with the participation of the latter and other institutions involved with systemic risk-monitoring.

Source: International Monetary Fund (IMF), Key Aspects of Macroprudential Policy (2013), 30

Act 2010 with the creation of the Financial Stability Oversight Council (FSOC).[85] 'The emergence of councils for financial stability to undertake systemic risk control or macro-prudential supervision is a feature' of on-going financial reforms.[86] The Dodd–Frank Act of 2010 gives the FSOC the power to entrust the Federal Reserve System with responsibility for the regulation of any firm that is deemed to be systemically according to criteria specified in the Act.

In the EU, the ESRB was established, acting on the recommendations of the De Larosière Report, bearing in mind the different jurisdictional domains of the EU (the domain of the ESRB) and the eurozone (for which the European Central Bank (ECB) has jurisdiction)[87] Banking Union is a fundamental change in the institutional design in Europe for the pursuit of financial stability. The conferral of micro-prudential powers and some macro-prudential powers to the ECB through the Single Supervisory Mechanism (SSM) regulation deeply alters the supervisory map in Europe.[88] Banking Union in the EU is a recognition of this need at a regional level. Banking Union is based upon three pillars.

[85] See <http://www.treasury.gov/initiatives/fsoc/about/Pages/default.aspx>. The FSOC is made up of ten voting members and five non-voting members.

[86] Lastra, n 20 above, 198.

[87] High-Level Group on Financial Supervision in the EU, Report on Financial Supervision in the EU (2009) (De Larosière Report).

[88] See Council Regulation (EU) No 1024/2013 conferring specific tasks on the European Central Bank concerning policies relating to the prudential supervision of credit institutions [2013] OJ L287/63; and Regulation (EU) No 1022/2013 amending Regulation (EU) No 1093/2010 establishing a European Supervisory Authority (European Banking Authority) as regards the conferral of specific tasks on the European Central Bank pursuant to Council Regulation (EU) No 1024/2013 [2013] OJ L287/5.

The first pillar is 'single supervision', with the establishment of the SSM. 'Single supervision' in the context of Banking Union means European supervision (conferred upon the ECB) for credit institutions of eurozone Member States and of non-eurozone EU Member States that choose to become part of the SSM.[89] The SSM aims to ensure that the EU's policy relating to prudential supervision is applied in a 'coherent and effective manner' in all Member States concerned[90] and provides the conditionality required in the ESM Treaty for banks to be able to be recapitalized.

The second pillar is 'single resolution', with a Single Resolution Mechanism (SRM)[91]—which should be aligned with the EU Bank Recovery and Resolution Directive (BRRD)[92]—and a Single Resolution Fund. The third pillar is 'common deposit protection'.[93] The jurisdictional area of Banking Union comprises the eurozone Member States and those other Member States that establish close cooperation arrangements.[94,95]

Banking Union is an incomplete edifice, since lender of last resort—'the elephant in the room'—should have been the fourth pillar, and since the arrangements for macro-prudential supervision have become cumbersome, with the ECB, ESRB, and national authorities involved at different levels.

[89] Council Regulation (EU) No 1024/2013 conferring specific tasks on the European Central Bank concerning policies relating to the prudential supervision of credit institutions [2013] OJ L287/63, commonly referred to as SSM Regulation.

[90] ibid, recital 12. See generally Lastra, R, 'Banking Union and Single Market: Conflict or Companionship?' (2013) 36(5) *Fordham International Law Journal*.

[91] Regulation (EU) No 806/2014 of the European parliament and of the Council of 15 July 2014 establishing uniform rules and a uniform procedure for the resolution of credit institutions and certain investment firms in the framework of a Single Resolution Mechanism and a Single Resolution Fund and amending Regulation (EU) No 1093/2010, OJ L 225/1 (30 July 2014) (hereinafter, SRM Regulation).

[92] See Directive 2014/59/EU of the European Parliament and of the Council of 15 May 2014 establishing a framework for the recovery and resolution of credit institutions and investment firms and amending Council Directive 82/891/EEC, and Directives 2001/24/EC, 2002/47/EC, 2004/25/EC, 2005/56/EC, 2007/36/EC, 2011/35/EU, 2012/30/EU, and 2013/36/EU, and Regulations (EU) No 1093/2010 and (EU) No 648/2012, of the European Parliament and of the Council, OJ L 173/190 (12 June 2014) (hereinafter, BRRD).

[93] Although a single deposit guarantee scheme shall not be established for the time being (we will continue to rely upon the existing networks of national deposit guarantee schemes) a new Directive on Deposit Guarantee Schemes repealing Directive 94/19/EC was adopted by the Council and the European Parliament in April 2014. See Directive 2014/49/EU of the European Parliament and of the Council of 16 April 2014 on deposit guarantee schemes, OJ 173/149 (12 June 2014).

[94] For an analysis of the uneasy coexistence between Banking Union and single market see Lastra, R, 'Banking Union and Single Market: Conflict or Companionship?' (2013) 36(2) *Fordham International Law Journal*. See also Ferran, E, European Banking Union and the EU Single Financial Market: More Differentiated Integration, or Disintegration? (2014), University of Cambridge Faculty of Law Research Paper No 29/2014, available at <http://ssrn.com/abstract=2426580>.

[95] The so-called 'SSM framework regulation' was subsequently adopted on 16 April 2014. See Regulation (EU) No 468/2014 of the European Central Bank, establishing the framework for cooperation within the Single Supervisory Mechanism between the European Central Bank and national competent authorities and with national designated authorities [2014] OJ L141/1.

From the point of view of macro-prudential powers—the focus of this Chapter—the assignment of powers to the ECB risks making the ESRB irrelevant.[96]

The transition towards establishing macro-prudential oversight institutions has not been exclusive to the aforementioned leading jurisdictions. Countries like Chile, Mexico, and Brazil have all established financial stability councils.[97] Other notable examples include South Africa, Korea, and New Zealand.[98]

3. Concluding observation: Multilateral macro-prudential coordination

Financial supervision and regulation are in a state of flux, nationally, supranationally, and internationally. Establishing domestic and regional institutional frameworks for macro-prudential policy is an important first step in the pursuit of financial stability. However, in order to be truly effective, these frameworks require that domestic supervisors cooperate and coordinate their policies at an international level.[99] Without adequate cooperation and coordination, the institutional frameworks can become futile, since systemic risk transcends geographic and institutional boundaries. A lack of collaboration could jeopardize the containment of cross-border negative spillovers.

Inter-jurisdictional cooperation and coordination are also necessary for the establishment of orderly resolution mechanisms that support financial stability. Bank resolution regimes are relevant to macro-prudential policy because the failure of an institution can generate financial instability across borders. The two main categories for the SRR (Special Resolution Regime) are the single point of entry (SPE) and the multiple point

[96] Article 5 of the SSM Regulation confers some macro-prudential supervisory powers to the ECB. Thus, in the EU the ESRB shares macro-prudential supervisory responsibilities with national authorities and, following the entry into force of the SSM Regulation, also with the ECB for those Member States that participate in Banking Union (SSM). According to an ECB opinion of 17 December 2014, concerning credit requirements to be adopted by the Estonian National Central Bank: 'The ECB observes that the powers to take macro-prudential measures provided for in Regulation (EU) No 575/2013 and Directive 2013/36/EU are subject to Article 5 of Regulation (EU) No 1024/2013 (hereinafter the "SSM Regulation"), which requires national competent or designated authorities to notify the ECB of their intention to take certain measures. According to Article 5(2) of the SSM Regulation, the ECB may apply more stringent measures aimed at addressing macro-prudential risks. The ECB further notes that, pursuant to Article 9(1) of the SSM Regulation, the ECB may require national competent or designated authorities, by way of instructions, to make use of their macro-prudential powers where the SSM Regulation does not confer such powers on the ECB.' See <https://www.ecb.europa.eu/ecb/legal/pdf/en_con_2014_88_f_sign.pdf>. See also generally chapters 10 and 11 of Lastra, R, *International Financial and Monetary Law* (2nd edn, 2015).

[97] In Chile, the *Consejo de Estabilidad Financiera* was created in October 2011. In turn, Mexico created the *Consejo de Estabilidad del Sistema Financiero (CESF)*. cf Lastra, R and Cedeno-Brea, E, Latin American Financial Reforms (2013), Working Paper presented at the 92nd MOCOMILA—Committee on International Monetary Law of the International Law Association meeting.

[98] IMF, n 13 above, 46.

[99] Greene et al., n 7 above, 129.

of entry (MPE). SPE implies 'applying resolution powers to the top of a group by a single national resolution authority' (a system which suits the bank holding company structure that is ubiquitous in the US), while MPE entails 'applying resolution tools to different parts of the group by two or more resolution authorities acting in a coordinated way' (a system which suits the structure of many cross-border banking establishments in the EU).[100] The role of coordination and cooperation on a multilevel approach is essential. As stated by the IMF in a 2012 Global Financial Stability Report: 'good management by financial institutions with cross-border activities, well-coordinated supervision of cross-border institutions, and transparent methods of dealing with distress are all components of healthy financial globalization'.[101]

Bibliography

Adrian, T and Brunnermeier, M, CoVaR (2011), Federal Reserve Bank of New York Staff Reports No 348.

Agur, I and Sharma, S, Rules, Discretion and Macroprudential Policy (2013), IMF Working Paper WP/13/65.

Angelini, P et al., Monetary and Macroprudential Policies (2012), European Central Bank Macroprudential Research Network Working Paper Series No 1449.

Arregui, N et al., Addressing Interconnectedness: Concepts and Prudential Tools (2013), IMF Working Paper WP/13/199.

Avgouleas, E, *Governance of Global Financial Markets: The Law, the Economics and the Politics* (2012).

Bank for International Settlements (BIS), Central Bank Governance and Financial Stability (2011).

Bank for International Settlements (BIS), Macroprudential Regulation and Policy: Proceedings of a Joint Conference Organized by the BIS and the Bank of Korea (2011), BIS Papers No 60.

Bank of England, Instruments of Macroprudential Policy: A Discussion Paper (2011).

Basel Committee on Banking Supervision, Core Principles for Effective Banking Supervision (2012).

Basel Committee on Banking Supervision, A Framework for Dealing with Systemically Important Banks (2012).

Bholat, D, Macro-prudential Policy: Historical Precedents and Possible Future Pitfalls, Lecture at Birkbeck, University of London, London, UK, (2013).

Brunnermeier, M, Crockett, A, Goodhart, C, Persaud, A, and Shin, H, *The Fundamental Principles of Financial Regulation* (2009) 11 Geneva Reports on the World Economy.

[100] Federal Deposit Insurance Corporation (FDIC) and the Bank of England, Resolving Globally Active, Systemically Important, Financial Institutions: A Joint Paper by the FDIC and the BoE (2012). See also: FSB, Consultative Document on Recovery and Resolution Planning: Making the Key Attributes Requirements Operational (2013).

[101] IMF, Global Financial Stability Report Restoring Confidence and Progressing on Reforms (2012), 112.

Council Regulation (EU) No 1024/2013 conferring specific tasks on the European Central Bank concerning policies relating to the prudential supervision of credit institutions [2013] OJ L287/63.

Elliott, D, 'Macroprudential Policy: Time to Start Experimenting', *The Economist*, 4 June 2013.

Elliott, D et al., The History of Cyclical Macroprudential Policy in the United States (2013), Finance and Economics Discussion Series Divisions of Research & Statistics and Monetary Affairs Working Paper No 2013-29.

European Systemic Risk Board (ESRB), Recommendation of the European Systemic Risk Board on Intermediate Objectives and Instruments of Macroprudential Policy, ESRB/2013/1 2013/C170/01 (2013).

Federal Deposit Insurance Corporation and the Bank of England, Resolving Globally Active, Systemically Important, Financial Institutions: A Joint Paper by the FDIC and the BoE (10 December 2012).

Financial Stability Board (FSB), Reducing the Moral Hazard Posed by Systemically Important Financial Institutions (2010).

FSB, Consultative Document on Recovery and Resolution Planning: Making the Key Attributes Requirements Operational (2013).

FSB, Global Systemically Important Insurers (G-SIIs) and the Policy Measures that Will Apply to them (2013).

FSB, G-SIFI Framework to Domestic Systemically Important Banks: Progress Report to G-20 Ministers and Governors (16 April 2012), available at <http://www.financialstabilityboard.org/publications/r_120420b.pdf>.

FSB, Policy Measures to Address Systemically Important Financial Institutions (2011).

FSB, Progress and Next Steps towards Ending 'Too-Big-to-Fail' (2013).

FSB, Strengthening Oversight and Regulation of Shadow Banking Policy Framework for Strengthening Oversight and Regulation of Shadow Banking Entities (2013).

FSB and IMF, The Financial Crisis and Information Gaps: Fourth Progress Report on the Implementation of the G-20 Data Gaps Initiative (2013).

FSB, IMF, and BIS, Macroprudential Policy Tools and Frameworks: Progress Report to G20 (2011).

Galati, G and Moessner, R, Macroprudential Policy—a Literature Review (2011), BIS Working Papers No 337.

Garicano, L and Lastra, R, 'Towards a New Architecture for Financial Stability: Seven Principles' (2010) 13(3) *Journal of International Economic Law*.

Georgosouli, A, Financial Resilience (2012), unpublished manuscript.

Golden, J, 'The Courts, the Financial Crisis and Systemic Risk' (2009) 4 *Capital Markets Law Journal* S14.

Goodhart, C, The Changing Role of Central Banks (2010), BIS Working Papers No 326.

Goodhart, C, Global Macroeconomic and Financial Supervision: Where Next (2011), National Bureau of Economic Research Working Paper No 17682.

Goodhart, C and Lastra, R, 'Border Problems' (2010) 13(3) *Journal of International Economic Law* 705.

Goodhart, C and Segoviano, M, Banking Stability Measures (2009), IMF Working Paper WP/09/04.

Greene, E et al., 'A Closer Look at "Too Big to Fail": National and International Approaches to Addressing the Risks of Large, Interconnected Financial Institutions' (2010) 5(2) *Capital Market Law Journal* 117.

Haldane, A, Macroprudential Policies—When and How to Use Them (2013), available at <http://www.imf.org/external/np/seminars/eng/2013/macro2/pdf/ah.pdf>.

High-Level Group on Financial Supervision in the EU, Report on Financial Supervision in the EU (De Larosière Report) (2009).

IMF, A Fair and Substantial Contribution by the Financial Sector (2010).

IMF, Global Financial Stability Report Restoring Confidence and Progressing on Reforms (2012).

IMF, Key Aspects of Macroprudential Policy (2013).

Kane, E, 'Accelerating Inflation, Technological Innovation, and the Decreasing Effectiveness of Banking Regulation' (1981) 36(2) *Journal of Finance*.

Kane, E, The Inevitability of Shadow Banking (2012), available at <http://www.frbatlanta.org/documents/news/conferences/12fmc/12fmc_kane.pdf>.

Knight, F, *Risk, Uncertainty and Profit* (1921).

Lastra, R, 'Banking Union and Single Market: Conflict or Companionship?' (2013) 36(5) *Fordham International Law Journal*.

Lastra, R, 'Defining Forward-looking Judgment-based Supervision' (2013) 14(3) *Journal of Banking Regulation* 221.

Lastra, R, *International Financial and Monetary Law* (2nd edn, 2015).

Lastra, R, *Legal Foundations of International Monetary Stability* (2006).

Lastra, R, 'Systemic Risk, SIFIs and Financial Stability' (2011) 6(2) *Capital Markets Law Journal* 198.

Lastra, R and Cedeno-Brea, E, Latin American Financial Reforms (2013), Working Paper presented at the 92nd MOCOMILA—Committee on International Monetary Law of the International Law Association meeting, Lima, Peru.

Lastra, R and Wood, G, 'The Crisis of 2007–2009: Nature, Causes and Reactions' (2010) 13(3) *Journal of International Economic Law*.

Maddaloni, A and Peydró J, Monetary Policy, Macroprudential Policy and Banking Stability: Evidence from the Euro Area (2013), European Central Bank Macroprudential Research Network Working Paper Series No 1560.

Markose, S, 'Systemic Risk Analytics: A Data Driven Multi-Agent Financial Network (MAFN) Approach' (2013) 14(3) *Journal of Banking Regulation*.

Miceli, T, *The Economic Approach to Law* (2004).

Regulation (EU) No 1022/2013 amending Regulation (EU) No 1093/2010 establishing a European Supervisory Authority (European Banking Authority) as Regards the Conferral of Specific Tasks on the European Central Bank Pursuant to Council Regulation (EU) No 1024/2013.

Schembri, L, Born of Necessity and Built to Succeed: Why Canada and the World Need the Financial Stability Board, speech by the Deputy Governor of the Bank of Canada (24 September 2013).

Schoenmaker, D, 'A New Financial Stability Framework for Europe' (2008) 13(3) *The Financial Regulator*.

Schoenmaker, D and Wierts, P, Macroprudential Policy: The Need for a Coherent Policy Framework (2011), DSF Policy Paper Series No 13.

Scott, H, 'Reducing Systemic Risk through the Reform of Capital Regulation' (2010) 13(3) *Journal of International Economic Law* 763.

Taleb, N, *Antifragile: Things that Gain from Disorder* (2012).

Trachtman, J, 'The International Law of Financial Crisis: Spillovers, Subsidiarity, Fragmentation and Cooperation' (2010) 13(3) *Journal of International Economic Law.*

Weber, R, 'Multilayered Governance in International Financial Regulation and Supervision' (2010) 13(3) *Journal of International Economic Law* 695.

Westbrook, J, 'SIFIs and States' (2013) 49(2) *Texas International Law Journal.*

CHAPTER 12

THE ROLE OF CAPITAL IN SUPPORTING BANKING STABILITY

KERN ALEXANDER

I. Introduction

Capital has taken on talismanic significance in banking regulation, as it bolsters confidence in the banking sector and supports the notion that the more shareholders have at risk in a bank, the more prudent they are likely to be in overseeing its management. Financial liberalization in the 1970s and 1980s transformed bank risk management by requiring banks to collect more data on the riskiness of their assets and to build models that estimated the level of capital they should hold to demonstrate their solvency and market performance. Market developments also led regulators in many countries to use risk classifications or weightings as a basis for calculating regulatory capital.[1] Capital became a major focus of bank risk management and also an important objective of banking regulation. The global financial crisis of 2007–08, however, raised important questions about how regulatory capital should be measured and monitored across the banking sector and the overall utility of the risk-based capital regime in supporting financial stability. This Chapter traces the development of the importance of bank capital as a balance-sheet item for risk management and its transformation into the primary measure of banking soundness under the Basel Accord. It discusses how Basel II's introduction of bank risk-measurement techniques for calculating regulatory capital was a major innovation at the time that was viewed as enhancing the competitiveness and performance of the banking industry while achieving banking stability objectives. Basel II, however, underestimated the systemic risks associated with the banking industry's growing reliance on wholesale market funding and proprietary trading and its loose definition of tier one regulatory capital that led to the inability of most European and US banks to withstand the financial crisis in late 2007 and 2008, resulting in massive taxpayer financed government recapitalizations and liquidity support for the banking sector.

The Chapter discusses how Basel III attempts to redesign the role of bank capital in supporting financial stability by linking its definition and measurement not only to the bank's micro-prudential balance-sheet risks, but also to the social costs or externalities that bank risk-taking poses to the broader economy and society. This means that bank capital must be conceptualized and designed according to both the economic optimization objectives of bank risk management and to the broader economic and social objectives of controlling excessive bank risk-taking

[1] Prior to the 1980s, most countries with market-led banking systems used *equity to deposits* or *liabilities to deposits* ratios as measures of bank capital strength. From the early twentieth century until 1983, the United States used *equity to deposit ratios* in the form of a 1 to 10 ratio of equity capital to deposits. These regulatory capital rules were increasingly seen as constraints on the growth and development of the US economy and banking sector. See Golin, J, *The Bank Credit Analysis Handbook—a Guide for Analysts, Bankers and Investors* (2001) 264–5.

and ensuring that the banking system provides a sustainable source of finance for the broader economy. This also involves a direct link between bank capital and bank corporate governance and how this relationship affects broader financial stability and economic sustainability. The Chapter's overall argument is that Basel III represents an extension of the concept of bank capital from merely a balance-sheet item used to enhance the performance and solvency of the bank to a broader notion of 'social' capital that reflects the bank's overall governance and its role and inter-linkages in the banking and financial system and capacity to address and manage macro-prudential risks.

II. What Is Bank Capital and Why Is it Important?

The banking business is distinctive and a source of regulatory concern because unlike most other industries a bank's balance sheet is highly leveraged: its liabilities consist almost wholly of debt with a very low percentage of equity capital.[2] In many cases, the limited liability of bank shareholders and the short-term compensation structure of bankers create an incentive for them to maximize the bank's leverage. As a result, banks are particularly exposed to the possibility of insolvency because their liabilities consist overwhelmingly of debt: most large UK and European banking groups have operated until very recently with less than 3 per cent equity capital as a percentage of their total assets.[3] This means a loss of only 3 per cent on their assets would leave the bank with no equity and insolvent. This is why bank capital regulation has attracted great attention and controversy in the aftermath of the 2007–08 global financial crisis because so many banking institutions—especially the largest banking groups—were undercapitalized and highly leveraged at the time of the crisis and required taxpayer bailouts to avoid a collapse of the banking system.

To understand the role of bank capital, it is necessary first to focus on a bank's balance sheet. One side of the balance sheet describes the bank's assets (for example, loans, investments, cash, buildings, and equipment), while the other side of the balance sheet lists its liabilities, which include mainly debt and capital. Debt liabilities include deposits and other borrowings. Capital includes shareholder equity in the

[2] Heffernan, S, *Modern Banking* (2005) 2. See also Casu, B, Girardone, C, and Molyneux, P, *Introduction to Banking* (2006) 4, 23.

[3] Heffernan, n 2 above, 3–4.

form of paid-in capital (ie, the amount paid for the bank's stock upon issuance) that provides rights to all residual assets including ownership of the bank. Capital also consists of retained earnings, which is the bank's income at the end of the fiscal year (net of expenses) earned during that year, less any dividends paid to shareholders. Capital also consists of preferred stock (or preference shares) that are entitled to specific dividends that may accrue if unpaid, but which afford limited ownership rights, and whose value may be perpetual or have a fixed duration. As discussed below in the regulatory context, preference shares are a less pure or hybrid form of capital that closely resemble debt and do not typically absorb losses for a firm as a going concern. Capital can also be the surplus gain from the sale of shares for more than their par value or stated value. Reserves—such as equity reserves—can also constitute capital when they are set aside from revenues to pay, for example, dividends on preferred shares or to retire preferred shares or senior debt.

Bank capital has four main purposes: to absorb losses against, for example, asset value declines because of non-performance, expected losses arising from inadequate loan loss reserves, and ultimately bank failure; to provide start-up funding for a bank's early operations; to reduce losses to deposit insurance schemes by providing a means to repay the claims of depositors and creditors of a failed bank; and to create incentives for shareholders, directors, and managers to exercise more prudence in overseeing the bank's operations.

A bank's capital serves as a buffer from which any losses are taken, and provides a reserve from which bank depositors and creditors may ultimately be repaid when losses can no longer be absorbed in case of a bank failure. For instance, if a bank has negative income for the year, the capital account is reduced by the amount of the loss. A bank is insolvent if its liabilities exceed its assets. Regulators require a bank's balance sheet to balance, and the difference between the assets and liabilities is the main measure of the bank's net worth and viability. This is why regulators and bank deposit insurers are keenly interested in the amount of a bank's capital buffer. In the event of a bank insolvency and liquidation, the deposit insurer[4] would pay the bank's depositors the amount of the depositors' effective deposit insurance coverage. The bank's assets would be sold and the proceeds used to reimburse the deposit insurer first and then to pay the bank's uninsured creditors, usually leaving shareholders with a worthless investment. If the bank has a severe insolvency problem, its assets may not be enough to reimburse fully the deposit insurer for its payments to insured depositors. A greater equity buffer, however, would give the

[4] In the UK, the deposit insurer is the Financial Services Compensation Scheme, whereas in the US the Federal Deposit Insurance Corporation provides deposit insurance. In other countries, retail depositors are provided insurance or guarantees through different schemes, including industry-financed or government-financed programmes. See Kleftouri, N, 'Rethinking UK and EU Bank Deposit Insurance' (2013) 24(1) *European Business Law Review* 95.

bank the ability to absorb greater losses before it becomes insolvent and the deposit insurer would be less likely to suffer losses as a result of the bank's liquidation. Essentially, bank capital is important at the micro-prudential level of the bank to protect creditors, including depositors. As discussed below, this was an important focus of the Basel II capital agreement which expressly designed bank regulatory capital calculations on the assumption of how best to protect bank creditors.[5]

If a bank's capital is reduced to zero, the bank's assets could in theory be sold to satisfy the claims in full of all the depositors and other liability holders. It is difficult to judge, however, the exact value of a bank's assets, especially during times of market stress when there could be widespread borrower defaults. This is where bank risk management becomes important, especially as it relates to the amount of capital held by the individual banking institution.

III. Bank Capital and Risk Management

Since the 1980s, the calculation of bank regulatory capital has been based primarily on the estimated riskiness of bank assets. This means that the determination of regulatory capital is an important part of bank risk management. The main objective of bank risk management is to measure and manage financial risks for a greater risk-adjusted return on equity for shareholders based on the firm's expected profits minus its expected costs for credit, market, liquidity, and operational risks. Before the financial crisis, average risk-adjusted returns on capital for non-financial companies in developed countries amounted to approximately 9.5 per cent across most industry sectors, while average risk-adjusted returns for large banks and financial institutions averaged in excess of 20 per cent.[6] To achieve such returns, firms must take significant risks, which in the financial sector could potentially threaten financial stability. Financial firms, however, have an incentive to hold economic capital at a level required by the market to optimize their cost of funding. This is intended to protect the creditors of the firm against default, but it does not take into account the limited liability structure of the firm that incentivizes shareholders to pressure

[5] See Basel Committee on Banking Supervision, Basel II Credit Risk Principles (2002), 31.

[6] Admati, A and Hellwig, M, *The Bankers' New Clothes: What's Wrong with Banking and What to Do about It* (2013) 100–09; see also Jackson, P, Beyond Basel II, presentation at Clare College, Cambridge (September 2010); and see *Wall Street Journal* (Europe edition), 29 July 2011, 18 (discussing lower rate of return on equity for banks post-crisis).

management to take on greater leverage to achieve higher risk-adjusted returns but which could potentially put the firm's solvency at risk as well as impose significant social costs on the financial system. Indeed, Alan Greenspan recognized this moral hazard problem for bank shareholders to pressure bank management to take greater risks than what are socially optimal when he stated:

> In August 2007, the risk management structure cracked. All the sophisticated mathematics and computer wizardry essentially rested on one central premise: that the enlightened self-interest of owners and managers of financial institutions would lead them to maintain a sufficient buffer against insolvency by actively monitoring their firms' capital and risk position.[7]

Indeed, the Financial Stability Forum observed in an April 2008 report that the 2007 credit crunch was the result of massive failings in risk management in some of the largest and most sophisticated financial institutions.[8] Executive compensation contributed to excessive risk-taking at banks and other financial firms,[9] while institutional shareholders failed to exercise an effective stewardship role to curb the excessive risk-taking of senior management at leading financial institutions.[10] Risk managers failed to appreciate or understand the externality risks of the structured finance market and, in particular, to understand the extent of the risks of their undercapitalized positions in the mortgage-backed securities market and the over-the-counter (OTC) credit default swap market. This contributed to destructive speculation that fuelled the market bubble and exacerbated the fallout when the markets inevitably collapsed.

1. Balance-sheet management

Any company is sensitive to the size of its balance sheet. Normally, the pricing of its liabilities is a function of the size of its balance sheet. Simply stated, the more assets a company has, the more liabilities are needed to finance these assets. To the extent that these liabilities are debt (as opposed to equity), this introduces more leverage, makes the company look riskier, and hence pushes up the return expectations

[7] Greenspan, A, 'We Need a Better Cushion against Risk' *Financial Times*, 26 March 2009.

[8] Financial Stability Forum, Report of the Financial Stability Forum on Enhancing Market and Institutional Resilience (2008).

[9] Ferrarini, G and Ungureanu, MC, 'Economics, Politics, and the International Principles for Sound Compensation Practices: An Analysis of Executive Pay at European Banks' (2011) 64 *Vanderbilt Law Review* 431.

[10] See Alexander, K, Implementation of Capital Requirements Directive III Remuneration Rules in the UK: Implications, Limitations and Lessons Learned (2012) in Economics and Monetary Affairs, European Parliament, Workshop on Banks' Remuneration Rules (CRD III): Are They Implemented and Do they Work in Practice? (IP/A/ECON/WS/2012-18, PE 464.465). See also Bebchuk, L, Cremers, M, and Peyer, U, The CEO Pay Slice (2010), The Harvard John M. Olin Discussion Paper No 679.

of both debt and equity investors. This ultimately translates into a higher cost of capital.[11]

Bank management is very sensitive to the expectations of their investors and hence constantly monitor the size of the bank's balance sheet. When the decision is taken to reduce assets the number of options available is limited. Outright sale is one option, but where the underlying assets are loans, this is hampered by two factors: first, illiquid loans can be hard to sell. Second, loans sales (normally to other banks) are never popular with the borrower who normally prefers not to see its pool of creditors change. For these two reasons, beginning in the 2000s, banks were drawn to using certain types of structured finance instruments, such as collateralized debt obligations (CDOs), to manage their balance sheets. Illiquid loans can be sold into a CDO more easily than into the secondary loan market. Furthermore, borrowers are more comfortable with their loans being owned by a special purpose vehicle (SPV), which is normally operationally managed by an arranger who is also responsible for transferring the loans from the originator to the SPV as part of the securitization process.

2. Economic capital management

Post-crisis market developments have placed an even greater importance on banks' ability to manage their 'economic capital'—that is, the equity capital needed for banks to support the risks of the expected losses associated with holding assets, while 'regulatory capital' addresses the risks of unexpected losses. Whereas the Basel I Capital Accord used a few categories to classify the riskiness of assets, the economic capital approach uses a model to calculate how risky a portfolio of assets is and how much capital is needed. As discussed below, the intention of Basel II and Basel III is to link regulatory capital to risk ('risk-sensitivity') and hence represents a migration from the Basel I approach of increasing bank capital across the board based on broadly defined risk categories to an economic capital management approach that relies on more precise measures of risk. While this sounds sensible in principle there are substantive definitional issues. Whose risk should the regulator be focused on—the bank's risk or systemic risk? How do we measure risk when we are worried about market failures—using historic prices, market forecasts, or non-market measures?

From an economic capital perspective there are three main contributors to risk: the risk of a particular asset (for example, its issuer may go bankrupt tomorrow), the risk of holding too large an exposure to a particular issuer (100 loans of $1 are less risky than one loan of $100 if the hundred are diversified), and the risk of being

[11] See Adam, A, *Handbook of Asset and Liability Management: From Models to Optimal Return Strategies* (2007).

exposed to an industry sector that is correlated (during a severe oil price downturn all oil companies tend to suffer and, because they are correlated, tend to look like one large exposure). Further, each of these risks change with the length of the holding period. While the first of these risks can be assessed independently, the other two require a portfolio analysis, as the risk of the whole is different from the risk of the parts.

Any transaction that results in the sale of assets that are risky for the institution to hold should have a risk-management benefit. For example, a balance-sheet CDO[12] would generally result in risk reduction. The traditional CDO structure involves the issuance of bonds—'debt obligations'—by an SPV such that the bonds are 'collateralized' by a portfolio of assets owned by the SPV. It is unlikely that the only rationale for a CDO is risk management; it is more likely to offer a combination of benefits. A bank may use a CDO to dispose of risky assets but is normally mindful of the fact that investors may share the same negative sentiment and hence there may be little net commercial advantage from the transfer. A bank may also use a CDO to manage its credit lines—the internal limits placed on the total credit exposure to any one issuer. Often, banks want to do more with a particular client but are constrained by internal limits. Moving the risk (into a CDO or elsewhere) frees up the credit line. The bank's strategy in managing its economic capital is to allocate capital to its most profitable use on a risk-adjusted basis and to optimize its cost of capital by sending a signal to the market that it is solvent.

3. Regulatory capital management

As mentioned above, banks are required to hold regulatory capital that is measured against their risk-based assets. The regulatory capital ratio generally consists of equity capital and subordinated debt divided by the notional value of any risky assets. Banks monitor their risk-based capital ratio very closely and will take steps to manage it. The sale of certain assets is one way of managing it as the notional value of risky assets is reduced. A balance-sheet CDO is a very effective way of managing a bank's risk-based capital as a large number of loans are sold in one transaction. This is often referred to as 'freeing up capital' and is part of the overall process known as 'regulatory capital management'.[13] Since a bank has a finite amount of capital, there

[12] A balance sheet CDO is an important instrument for allowing a bank to manage its regulatory capital position. CDOs are debt instruments that allow investors with differing risk appetites to invest in a broad range of assets that would normally reside on bank balance sheets. The CDO market evolved from the older CBO (bond) and CLO (loan) markets, the name change reflecting the fact that the underlying assets in CDO transactions include a broad range of debt-related products.

[13] See Berger, A, De Young, R, Flannery, M, Lee, D, and Oztekin, O, 'How Do Large Banking Organizations Manage their Capital Ratios' (2008) 34 (2–3) *Journal of Financial Service Research* 123.

is a quantifiable maximum amount of corporate debt that can be taken on. Selling or hedging debt frees up the capital that was allocated and allows it to be used for new lending or other banking business, such as investing in securities.

As discussed below, Basel II was an innovation in the theory and practice of bank capital regulation because it incorporated bank capital management practices into the regulatory capital framework. Under Basel II, the calculation of regulatory capital mainly became based on a process-based framework for assessing financial risk in which the bank supervisor and bank risk officers and management interacted over time to test and improve the bank's risk-measurement and -management processes. The financial crisis of 2007–09 represented a breakdown of the Basel II model-based approach for calculating regulatory capital and measuring financial risks. The model-based approach to measuring risk, which regulators and bank management had accepted and embedded into their bank risk-management practices, failed to estimate the amount of capital and liquidity banks should hold against systemic or macro-prudential risks in the financial system.[14]

IV. International Bank Capital Regulation—the Transition from Basel II to Basel III

The Basel Capital Accord represents the most important international financial regulation agreement. The first Accord (Basel I) was adopted in 1988 with two main objectives: (1) that internationally active banks hold a minimum amount of capital against their risk-based assets; and (2) to promote an international level playing field in bank capital regulation.[15] Although the Basel Capital Accord is not legally binding under international law, it is remarkable that most countries have adopted it and claim to have implemented it. International financial policymakers observed in 2000 that countries and their banks which demonstrate that they have implemented the Accord benefit from a lower cost of capital than countries and banks that have not done so.[16] Some countries implement the Accord faithfully

[14] See Alexander, K, Eatwell, J, Persaud, A, and Reoch, R, Financial Supervision and Crisis Management in the EU (2007), Economics and Monetary Affairs, European Parliament, *Financial Supervision and Crisis Management in the EU* (IP IP/A/ECON/IC/2007-069).

[15] See Norton, J, *Devising International Banking Supervisory Standards* (1995) 18–20.

[16] See Financial Stability Forum, Report of the Follow-up Group on Incentives to Foster Implementation Standards (2000).

and strictly enforce its requirements.[17] However, because the Accord is not mandatory, some countries pick and choose what provisions to comply with, while others impose stricter standards.

Basel I required banks to hold 8 per cent regulatory capital against most of their credit risk assets. The 8 per cent capital requirement consisted mainly of tier one and tier two capital. Tier one capital was primary and most valuable to regulators because it consisted mainly of common equity shares and their equivalent and retained earnings, which could absorb losses for the bank as a going concern. In contrast, tier two capital consisted mainly of subordinated debt and other debt-like instruments, such as preference shares, and convertible instruments. Tier two capital was less loss absorbent than tier one capital because these instruments could only absorb losses at the point of the bank's restructuring or its failure as a going concern. Tier 2 capital was less flexible for regulators because it could not impose losses on the bank as a going concern. This is why Basel I required that tier 2 capital not constitute more than 50 per cent—or 4 per cent of risk-based assets—of the 8 per cent regulatory capital requirement. Tier one capital had to be at least 4 per cent of risk-based assets, and of that 4 per cent at least 50 per cent—or 2 per cent of risk-based assets—had to be *core* tier one capital, consisting of common equity shares and retained earnings. Core tier one capital was most favoured by regulators because it could absorb losses fully for the bank while it was a going concern. It was also flexible because regulators could require banks not to pay dividends from their profits if they did not meet—or would soon breach—minimum capital levels. The rest of tier one capital (non-core) could consist of a broader array of instruments, including preference shares and certain convertible instruments. The core tier one ratio of 2 per cent was therefore the most useful for regulators in enforcing capital standards and if necessary in imposing losses on the bank's shareholders while keeping the bank operating as a going concern.[18]

Basel I was expanded in 1995 to require banks to hold 8 per cent regulatory capital against their trading book risks, but permitted banks to use their own data and value-at-risk (VaR)[19] models to lower their regulatory capital requirements if they could show bank supervisors that their trading book was less risky based on historic

[17] For example, the South African Reserve Bank (South Africa's Bank Regulator) strictly implements and enforces the Basel Accord. See South African Reserve Bank, South Africa's Implementation of Basel II and Basel III, available at <http://www.resbank.co.za/RegulationAndSupervision/BankSupervision/TheBaselCapitalAccord%28Basel%20II%29/Pages/AccordImplementationForum%28AIF%29.aspx> (last accessed 24 July 2014); and South African Reserve Bank, Guidance Note 9/2012 issued in terms of section 6(5) of the Banks Act, 1990—Capital Framework for South Africa Based on the Basel III Framework, available at <http://www.resbank.co.za/Lists/News%20and%20Publications/Attachments/5154/G9%20of%202012.pdf> (last accessed 24 July 2014).

[18] See Golin, n 1 above, 405–11.

[19] See Hull, J, *Risk Management and Financial Institutions* (2012) 183–201, 266, 279, providing a comprehensive discussion of how VaR models are devised and their application to bank risk management.

data and therefore merited a lower capital charge. This model-based approach for determining trading book regulatory capital was the basis on which the banking industry proposed—and regulators later agreed in the Basel II agreement—that regulatory capital for credit risk should also be calculated based on the bank's own data and VaR models with the regulator eventually having to approve the model and the calculations.

Although Basel I achieved its main objective of increasing the level of regulatory capital in the international banking system, it contained many national discretions, loopholes, and incentives for banks to make riskier short-term loans and to transfer less risky assets off their balance sheets.[20] Basel II was proposed in 1999 to address many of these gaps and weaknesses. In doing so, Basel II introduced the 'three pillars' concept—(1) minimum capital; (2) supervisory review; and (3) market discipline—designed to reinforce each other and to create incentives for banks to enhance their risk measurement and management. Basel II's overall objective was to make regulatory capital more sensitive to the micro-prudential risks that banks face and to align regulatory capital with the economic capital that banks were already holding.

Pillar 1 allows banks to calculate their regulatory capital by using statistical models that rely mainly on their own historic default and loss data to estimate their credit, market, and operational risks. Pillar 2 set forth principles of supervisory review that authorize regulators to require banks to comply with broad principles of corporate governance and to adopt an internal capital adequacy assessment process (ICAAP) designed to enhance risk measurement and management. Pillar 3 uses market discipline to require banks to provide more information to the market so shareholders and creditors can monitor bank management more effectively to ensure the bank's soundness and future prospects.

Basel II expanded the use of risk weightings for banks to estimate the riskiness of their assets. A number of parameters determine an asset's risk weighting, including the maturity of the loan, the probability of default, and the bank's loss and exposure given default. Assets with lower risk weightings generally attract lower capital charges, whereas assets with higher risk weightings generally attract higher capital charges. Corporate loans with short-term maturities attract lower risk weightings (lower capital charges), while corporate loans with long-term maturities (seven years or more) attract higher risk weightings (higher capital charges).

When the global credit banking crisis began in late 2007, however, the risk weightings of most European and US banks were shown to be poor indicators of the financial risks to which banks were exposed.[21] Specifically, bank models to estimate their counter-party credit and liquidity risks in the asset-backed

[20] See Goodhart, C, *The Basel Committee on Banking Supervision: A History of the Early Years, 1974–1997* (2011) 351–3.

[21] See discussion in Admati and Hellwig, n 6 above, 170.

securities and derivatives markets underestimated correlations across asset classes. Moreover, the opaqueness of the risk weightings in the credit and trading books made it very difficult, if not impossible, for investors to understand the true risk exposure of a bank. These factors contributed significantly to an undercapitalization of the banking system which weakened its ability to absorb losses in the crisis.

Basel II allowed banks to use their own estimates of credit and market risks to lower their risk weightings for certain asset classes with regulatory approval. This particular approach to calculating regulatory capital—involving the bank estimating its risks and calculating its regulatory capital to be approved by the bank supervisor—was criticized before the crisis as potentially leading to an undercapitalization of the banking sector.[22] If the supervisor approved the bank's model for measuring and managing its risk, the bank might hold a significantly lower level of regulatory capital based on its model calculation. In theory, the Basel II process provided an incentive for banks to improve their risk management by offering them reduced regulatory capital if they could demonstrate that their risk-based models adequately controlled the risks that the bank individually faced against creditors and depositors.[23] However, the risks that Basel II focused on were primarily micro-prudential risks; that is, risks that were largely exogenous—or external—to the bank's balance sheet and not the risks that the bank itself creates for the financial system—so-called endogenous risks—because of its size, interconnectedness, and exposure to liquidity risks.[24] Basel II did not require, therefore, that banks hold adequate capital to cover the social costs—including systemic risks—that banks create.[25]

Although Basel II was not formally adopted in Europe until January 2007 and only applied in the US to the largest US financial holding companies, its flawed model-based approach for measuring and managing risk had become an industry standard for most European and global financial institutions before it was actually adopted into EU law. The model-based approach to measuring risk was already in use by financial institutions in the 1990s to determine their economic capital.[26] The economic capital models of these institutions assumed that volatility was a proxy for risk. This was based on conventional portfolio management theory,[27] and

[22] See Alexander, K, Dhumale, R, and Eatwell, J, *Global Governance of Financial Systems: The International Regulation of Systemic Risk* (2006) 31–3.

[23] See Basel Committee on Banking Supervision, n 5 above, 31.

[24] See Brunnermeier, M, Crockett, A, Goodhart, C, Persaud, A, and Shin, H *The Fundamental Principles of Financial Regulation* (2009) 11 *Geneva Reports on the World Economy* 10–11.

[25] The concept of bank 'social' capital in the regulatory context is developed by Kern Alexander in Alexander, K, Stability and Sustainability in Banking: Should Basel III Address Environmental Risks (2014), Report for the United Nations Environment Programme.

[26] See de Weert, F, *Bank and Insurance Capital Management* (2011) 79.

[27] Indeed, the proliferation of economic capital and other risk-management models over the last 30 years were based on the ideas espoused by Professor Harry Markowitz of the University of Chicago who won a Nobel Prize based on his seminal article in 1952 which articulated the linkages between volatility and risk which became known as modern portfolio theory.

involved the widespread use of volatility-based models, such as VaR. As it turned out in 2007 and 2008 with the onset of the crisis, these standardized VaR models badly underestimated the likelihood of significant falls in asset prices based on external shocks and failed to take into account the likelihood of numerous aftershocks. The use of these volatility-*based* models for determining bank economic capital was the basis for the development of Basel II, and remains the essential basis for measuring risk under Basel III.

Basel II's risk-sensitive market-based approach for calculating regulatory capital had become the banking industry's standard prior to the crisis, but it lacked built-in safeguards against wholesale market liquidity risks and the loss-absorbency of bank capital. At the time of its adoption, Basel II was seen as an important regulatory innovation because it created incentives for banks to improve their risk management and measurement. If the banks could prove to supervisors that they managed their risk effectively based on probability of default and loss given default data, their regulatory capital would drop to a level that more closely approximated the economic capital they were already holding. Unsurprisingly, this model-based approach led to significantly lower levels of regulatory capital for most banks, especially the most systemically important institutions, and contributed greatly to the severity of the global financial crisis—especially for large European banks—when the full-scale of the crisis was felt with the collapse of Lehman Brothers, American International Group (AIG), and several large European banking institutions—the Royal Bank of Scotland, Fortis, Dexia, and ABN AMRO in autumn 2008.[28]

The main problem with Basel II in respect of regulatory capital was that the economic capital models used by banks were accepted by regulators as being valid reference points for the calculation of regulatory capital. The economic capital models under Basel II failed to anticipate macro-prudential risks—eg, drying up of liquidity in the wholesale funding markets—and utilized risk sensitive techniques that could exacerbate systemic risks in the face of extreme events. Moreover, bank supervisors placed little emphasis on the role of 'supervisory review' in Pillar 2 of Basel II which provides discretion to the supervisor to monitor and challenge and if necessary intervene in the management of the bank if it was following weak corporate governance and risk-management practices. Pillar II allows the supervisor to impose additional regulatory capital on the amount of capital that was calculated under Pillar 1. Prior to the crisis it was underutilized as regulators deferred to weak bank governance practices. Essentially, Basel II embodied the failure of financial policymakers and regulators to incorporate systemic risks into the design of regulatory capital and risk management. This would change under Basel III.

[28] See discussion of events leading to these banks collapsing in Darling, A, *Back from the Brink* (2011) 102–14.

V. The Changing Philosophy of Bank Capital Regulation: From Micro-Prudential to Macro-Prudential

Before considering how Basel III expands the breadth and scope of regulatory capital requirements, it is necessary to discuss the underlying theory of prudential regulation that supported Basel II and how that theoretical framework is changing under Basel III. Basel II's micro-prudential approach to regulation and supervision[29] was predominantly concerned with the stability of individual financial institutions and their responses to exogenous risks.[30] However, by focusing on individual institutions, such forms of regulation tend to ignore the impact of financial institutions' risk-taking on the broader financial system. For example, the micro-prudential approach often failed to incorporate into regulatory assessments the impact of a bank's size, degree of leverage, and interconnectedness with the rest of the financial system. Moreover, bank supervisors generally assumed that banks were primarily exposed to exogenous risks; that is, risks that are generated externally to the bank's operations, and that any change, for example, in their credit or market risk exposures would require them to make balance-sheet adjustments (ie, by buying or selling assets) in a more or less similar manner.[31]

Although each bank individually might be adjusting its balance-sheet risk in a prudent manner, the cumulative effect of all banks acting in the same manner would be to increase system-wide risks across the financial sector. This could have the effect of exacerbating a market upturn or downturn. Indeed, the Turner Review (2009),[32] published in the aftermath of the crisis, argued that this sort of regulation mistakenly and fatally relied on an underlying philosophy and an ill-placed faith in market prices and estimations of bank capital as accurate indicators of risk. In seeking to focus their risk assessment at the level of the individual institution, regulators failed to take account of a number of internal amplifying processes

[29] Financial regulation is generally defined as the promulgation and development of rules, standards, and guidelines that govern behaviour in financial markets (ie, the adoption of bank capital rules), whereas financial supervision refers to the discretionary function of monitoring and assessing risks in financial markets, including whether to authorize or de-authorize firms or individuals, or to investigate breaches of regulation and if necessary to bring enforcement actions including imposing sanctions.

[30] See Brunnermeier et al., n 24 above, 31–3.

[31] ibid.

[32] UK Financial Services Authority, The Turner Review: A Regulatory Response to the Global Banking Crisis (2009).

which propagated the effects of one institution's risk-taking to other institutions' balance sheets.

The financial crisis demonstrated weaknesses in the micro-prudential regulatory approach and the need for the supervisor to have broader oversight of risks across the financial system and the capacity to take measures (ie, adjust capital requirements) that support the stability of the financial system as a whole and to take into account the interconnectivity of financial institutions and their effects on the global economy in times of crisis.[33] Macro-prudential regulation consists of three main areas: (1) adjusting the application of regulatory rules to institutions according to developments in the broader economy (ie, counter-cyclical capital requirements);[34] (2) imposing economy-wide controls on the financial sector to limit aggregate risk-taking (ie, capital controls to limit foreign exchange risk or system-wide leverage limits); and (3) prudential requirements for financial infrastructure or firms providing infrastructure services (ie, capital requirements for derivative clearing houses).[35] A growing literature has analysed these different areas of macro-prudential regulation. What is clear in the macro-prudential regulatory literature thus far is the need to strike a balance between macro-prudential regulation and micro-prudential regulation: both are necessary for maintaining financial stability and the conditions for sustainable economic growth.[36]

Despite the enthusiasm for macro-prudential regulation, it is certainly not a panacea, as it does not eliminate credit cycles in an economy. Nor does it address regulatory failure and government subsidies for banks and financial firms which create moral hazard and can induce unsustainable risk-taking. Ultimately, whereas the macro-prudential approach focuses on risks across the financial system as a whole, regulatory and policy measures must be introduced at the level of individual banks. The micro-prudential approach will continue therefore to be important—if not primary—and serve as the foundation for prudential financial regulation. Although it was largely rules-based and backward-looking prior to the crisis, it now will involve regulators asking themselves strategic questions

[33] See EU Commission, Report of the High Level Group on Financial Supervision in the EU, chaired by Jacques De Larosiere (2009). See also ibid, n 25.

[34] Experts have observed that counter-cyclical buffers could be difficult to implement. See Brunnermeier et al., n 24 above, ch 4 (discussing design of counter-cyclical regulation).

[35] Basel Committee on Banking Supervision, Macroprudential Policy Tools and Frameworks, Progress Report to G20 (2011), available at <http://www.bis.org/publ/othp17.htm> (last accessed 5 June 2014).

[36] For instance, Ingves, S, Challenges for the Design and Conduct of Macroprudential Policy, speech at BOK-BIS Conference, Seoul, Korea (January 2011), available at <http://www.riksbank.se/Upload/Dokument_riksbank/Kat_publicerat/Tal/2011/110118e.pdf> (last accessed 13 August 2014), observing that they should reinforce, rather than conflict with, one another, and Brunnermeier et al. argue that the two areas of regulation should interact more. See Brunnermeier et al., n 24 above, 33.

about where risks are being shifted in the system and where capital can be found in the system to limit system-wide losses and how various forms of bank capital can be bailed-in to a bank restructuring.[37] This will be supplemented by macro-prudential supervision, which is largely forward-looking and involves the regulator monitoring risks across the system and markets and forecasting how they might evolve; it requires discretionary authority to take measures that address risks that may not threaten the market today but which may lead to substantial risks in the future.[38]

Despite their different approaches, micro-prudential regulation and supervision *and* macro-prudential regulation and supervision are not mutually exclusive and their tools will overlap considerably. Indeed, by recognizing the links between micro-prudential and macro-prudential regulation, a more coherent and effective framework can be developed for mitigating excessive risk-taking and ensuring that banks hold adequate loss-absorbent capital.

VI. Basel III

The recent amendments to the Basel Capital Accord, known as Basel III,[39] raise important issues regarding whether bank capital regulation has become adequately macro-prudential in its focus and objectives. Although Basel III is largely built on the edifice of Basel II, it attempts to address many of the weaknesses of Basel II that contributed to the crisis. Basel III increases core tier one regulatory capital from 2 per cent to 4.5 per cent, plus a 2.5 per cent capital conservation buffer, and a tighter definition of tier one capital to include only ordinary common shares and retained earnings (excluding other equivalent instruments). It will also impose an additional 2.5 per cent counter-cyclical capital ratio that will be adjusted across the economic cycle.[40] Basel

[37] Prudential Regulation Authority, The Prudential Regulation Authority's Approach to Banking Supervision (2013), 5. See also, Tucker, P, Macro and Microprudential Supervision, speech at British Bankers' Association Annual International Banking Conference, London (29 June 2011), available at <http://www.bankofengland.co.uk/publications/Documents/speeches/2011/speech506.pdf> (last accessed 7 August 2013), 4–5.

[38] As Goodhart has noted, it involves the regulators '[asking] themselves how to protect the system of banks, conditional on another bank, perhaps one of the biggest and most interconnected, having already failed'. See Goodhart, C, Bank Resolution in Comparative Perspective: What Lessons for Europe? (2013), 10, unpublished paper on file with author.

[39] See Basel Committee on Banking Supervision (BCBS), Basel III: A Global Regulatory Framework for More Resilient Banks and Banking Systems (December 2010, revised June 2011). The G20 approved the Basel Committee's revised Capital Accord, known as Basel III, in November 2010.

[40] See Basel Committee on Banking Supervision, Basel III Regulatory Consistency Assessment Program (RCAP) (2013).

Figure 12.1 Basel III's three-pillar framework

Pillar 1	Pillar 2	Pillar 3
Minimum Capital Requirements	Supervisory Review Process	Market Discipline
Additional/Refined Capital Basis - Liquidity Coverage Ratio (LCR) - Net Stable Funding Ratio (NSFR) - OTC Derivatives Charge - Quality and Level of Capital - Leverage Ratio - Capital Conservation Buffers - Counter-cyclical Buffers - Enhanced Loss Absorption Clause (Write-Off or Debt Conversion)	**Supervision (Dialogue)** - Firm-wide Corporate Governance - Managing Risk Concentrations - Alignment of LT Incentives - Sound Compensation Practices - Supervisory Colleges **Capital (ICAAP)** - Firm-wide Risk Management - Valuation Practice, Stress Tests **Supervisory Review Evaluation Process (SREP)** Capital Governance	**Additional/Enhanced Disclosure** - Risk Management Market Credit Operational - Regulatory Capital Components - Detailed Reconciliation of Capital - Regulatory Capital Ratios - Securitization Exposures

III also contains liquidity requirements that include a ratio for stable wholesale funding, liquidity coverage ratios, and an overall leverage ratio. Also, an additional capital charge of up to 2.5 per cent regulatory capital will be required for large and interconnected systemically important financial institutions (SIFIs).

Like Basel II, Basel III remains largely a process-based framework for bank supervisors to interact with bank management and risk officers to assess and measure the risks that individual institutions face. As with Basel II, it consists of three pillars: (1) minimum capital; (2) supervisory review; and (3) market discipline (Figure 12.1). Under Pillar 1, banks are allowed to devise statistical models that rely mainly on their own internal historic default data and risk weights to estimate their credit, market, and operational risks. Based on these risk estimations, the bank calculates the amount of regulatory capital it should hold against these risks.

The financial crisis demonstrated how these models failed to take account of the liquidity risks and counter-party credit risks in the structured finance markets while underestimating correlations across asset classes in the bank's proprietary trading book.[41] Under Pillar 1, regulators will challenge banks more in the construction of their models, while Pillar 2 broadens regulatory authority to require banks to undergo more frequent and demanding stress tests.[42] Enhanced supervisory powers in these areas reflect the Basel Committee's recognition that bank supervisors should be monitoring how banks manage macro-prudential risks.

Under Basel III's Pillar 2 system, states have discretion to impose a range of measures, including additional capital requirements, on individual institutions or groups of institutions in order to address corporate governance weaknesses and unsound risk-management practices. Bank supervisors generally consider their discretion to adjust capital under Pillar 2 to be 'additive' only to the capital calculated under Pillar 1. Therefore, national supervisors should be able to impose higher capital requirements if they believe the bank has inadequate governance and risk-management processes in place. If they determine that the bank has adequate governance structures and risk-management processes, they would require no additional capital. As discussed below, this crucial linkage between the amount of regulatory capital and the quality of the bank's corporate governance will be assessed through Pillar 2's supervisory review evaluation process (SREP). Pillar 3 remains focused on regulatory disclosures by the bank to the market and the use of fair value accounting to value bank assets and trading positions in order to enhance market discipline of the bank risk taking activities.

1. Pillar 1—minimum capital

As mentioned above, Pillar 1 increases the level of core tier one capital from 2 per cent to 4.5 per cent along with an additional capital conservation buffer of 2.5 per cent that takes the tier one requirement up to 7.0 per cent. Pillar 1 also prescribes a tighter definition of tier one capital to include only ordinary common shares and retained earnings, an additional 2.5 per cent counter-cyclical capital ratio; and a leverage ratio of 3 per cent of total assets divided by tier one capital.[43] In addition, it contains new liquidity requirements in the form of a net ratio for stable wholesale funding, and liquidity coverage ratios to ensure that the bank is holding a certain amount of high-quality assets that can be sold quickly to cover short-term liability exposures. Moreover, to address macro-prudential risks posed by large

[41] Moreover, the opaqueness of the risk weightings in the banking book made it very difficult, if not impossible, for investors to understand the true risk exposure of a bank. These factors contributed significantly to an undercapitalization of the banking system which weakened its ability to absorb losses in a crisis.

[42] See BCBS, n 40 above.

[43] See BCBS, n 39 above, 12–15.

and interconnected SIFIs, there is an additional capital charge of between 1 and 2.5 per cent depending on the institution's size and interconnectedness.[44]

As with Basel II, Pillar 1 offers banks three menus—advanced approach, foundation approach, and standardized approach—by which they can measure their risks and calculate regulatory capital. The largest, most sophisticated financial institutions will opt for the advanced approach because it allows them to use their own default and loss data in a statistical model to estimate their unexpected losses and calculate a regulatory capital amount. Large- and medium-sized banks with less data may opt for the foundation approach, which requires the bank to submit probability of default data but the supervisor would supply loss data and calculate the capital requirement. The third menu—the standardized approach—will be used by most small- and medium-sized banks which do not have extensive default and loss data to estimate risk weights and, therefore, will use risk weightings provided by the regulator that are matched to credit rating scores. This less flexible approach requires credit ratings to play the primary role in determining regulatory capital for small- and medium-sized banks.

What is significant about Basel III's Pillar 1 requirements is the importance it places on liquidity requirements, the leverage ratio, and the loss-absorbency of capital. The liquidity coverage ratio would require banks by 2015 to hold a certain ratio of high-quality liquid assets (ie, highly rated government and corporate bonds) that could be sold in a stress scenario to cover a loss of funding for up to one year. The net stable funding ratio would require banks by 2017 to maintain a positive ratio of incoming funds to outgoing funds over a period of time—ordinarily 30 days—and to fund long-term credit exposures with liabilities that have a maturity of not less than one year.[45] Another important feature of the bank capital framework will be the requirement of a leverage ratio of 3 per cent or 33 to 1 (total assets/total common equity).[46] These requirements are generally expected to limit the ability of banks to have excessive reliance on short-term funding that could be withdrawn quickly in a severe market downturn, and when there is a loss of short-term funding (for instance, funding from off balance-sheet entities in the securitization markets), the bank will have at least 20 per cent of its risk-based assets in liquid, high-quality

[44] Higher capital requirements for SIFIs are deemed necessary because banks have an incentive to grow larger in part because by becoming larger they can reduce the relative costs of their funding because investors perceive an implicit guarantee by the state to provide direct or indirect financial support to them during times of market stress. The larger a banking group becomes the lower the costs of its funding relative to its operations. Basel III attempts to address this moral hazard problem by imposing additional capital requirements according to the bank's size, interconnectedness, and global reach.

[45] The goal is to reduce reliance on short-term wholesale market funding for longer-term lending and to rely more on 'stickier' sources of short-term funding (bank deposits) considered to be a more reliable funding source.

[46] Leverage is calculated as the value of assets divided by the value of equity, or in this case, tier 1 capital. The leverage ratio is the inverse of this; ie, the value of equity or tier 1 capital divided by the

assets (ie, AAA-rated government or corporate debt) that can be sold in the market at short notice to offset the loss of funding.

The focus on a significantly higher amount of core tier one equity capital to constitute most of the regulatory capital total and the use of a minimum amount of tier 1 capital in the leverage ratio as a minimum 'backstop' against all assets (risk-based or not) provides a significant departure in the design and purpose of regulatory capital. Under Basel II, banks were free to experiment with their risk measures and to utilize a wider array of financial instruments—ie, common equity shares, participation rights, preference shares and subordinated debt—to constitute most of tier one capital while tier two capital (mainly debt instruments) provided 50 per cent of all regulatory capital. This approach to regulatory capital was deliberately aligned to the economic capital models that banks were already using, whose purpose was to signal bank solvency and performance to the market. By contrast, Basel III now requires banks to hold significantly more core tier 1 and tier 1 capital than what banks were holding in their market-based economic capital models and a cap on leverage. This extra layer of high-quality loss-absorbent capital is designed mainly to address the externality problem or the 'social costs' that bank risk-taking imposes on the financial system and broader economy. By designing regulatory capital to address the social costs of bank risk-taking and related macro-prudential risks, bank regulatory capital has formally taken on a social dimension that addresses broader public policy objectives.[47]

In support of a more effective bank social capital regime, bank regulatory capital will also have a 'counter-cyclical' component that will be measured against points in the economic cycle. Counter-cyclical capital regulation will require banks to hold more capital during good times and allow them to hold less capital than what would normally be required during a downturn in the economic cycle. For example, banks could let their capital levels fall beneath the 9.5 per cent capital requirement (including counter-cyclical buffer) during a recession or financial crisis. This would encourage banks to lend more during an economic or financial downturn. The Basel Committee has introduced a framework for national authorities to consider how to implement counter-cyclical capital buffers[48] and has approved a set of macroeconomic indicators (eg, credit variables) and micro-indicators (ie,

value of assets. So under the Basel III proposals, banks' assets should not exceed 33 times the value of tier 1 capital, or cannot have tier 1 capital that is less than 3 per cent of its assets. See BCBS, n 39 above.

[47] See Alexander, n 24 above, 15–19. This social dimension of bank capital could also address a range of social risks, including environmental risks.

[48] Basel III requires an increased level of tier 1 regulatory capital to 7.0 per cent (including a capital conservation buffer), a tighter definition of tier 1 capital to include only ordinary common shares, an additional 2.5 per cent counter-cyclical capital ratio (yet to be determined for implementation); and liquidity requirements that include a ratio for stable wholesale funding, liquidity coverage ratios, and an overall leverage ratio. Recently, the Basel Committee has agreed on an additional capital charge of up to 2.5 per cent regulatory capital for large and interconnected SIFIs.

bank earnings) to determine how and when counter-cyclical regulatory charges and buffers should be imposed.[49] This will necessarily involve banks using more forward-looking provisions based on expected losses. Moreover, a more effective 'social' capital regime should require not only enhanced quality of tier 1 capital but also more transparency in the way that banks signal to the market the type of capital they are holding. This means that investors should have full information regarding what constitutes all types of bank regulatory. Although not included as regulatory capital, bank loan loss reserves and provisioning for expected losses should be reported to the market. Part of the social function of bank capital should be that it is fully transparent and recognized in the market.

Basel III has attracted substantial criticism from all quarters, including the banking industry which asserts that the increase in tier 1 capital requirements from 2 per cent to 7 per cent (at a minimum) plus a counter-cyclical and SIFI capital surcharge and liquidity requirements are increasing the cost of bank funding, thereby limiting the ability of banks to lend enough to promote an economic recovery.[50] On the other hand, Basel III has been criticized as not raising capital and liquidity requirements enough.[51] These critics argue that despite the stricter capital and liquidity requirements Basel III remains essentially based on a flawed risk-weighting approach to measuring bank risk exposures that relies disproportionately on a micro-prudential assessment of risks, while neglecting broader structural or macro-prudential risks in the financial system. As argued, this fails to address the systemic risks that can arise because of financial innovation and the shifting of risk to financial sectors to which banks are indirectly exposed, such as the risks of banks owning derivatives clearing houses and securities settlement institutions, and their ongoing exposure to derivatives trading and other trading book risks that are serious threats to financial stability.

2. Pillar 2—supervisory review process and bank governance

The supervisory review process, together with Pillar 3 (market discipline), complements Pillar 1 (minimum capital requirements) for ensuring that the bank holds a

[49] See International Monetary Fund, Key Aspects of Macro-prudential Policy (2013), 61, para 141.

[50] Specifically, some criticism has been directed to its treatment of long-term lending, which might reinforce short-termism in bank lending. Also the banks have criticized increased capital and liquidity requirements for off-balance sheet entities that provide non-recourse lending for project finance and other specialized lending projects that support renewable energy sources as unduly limiting lending for green or low-carbon projects. See Hassert, T, presentation at the Basel Infrastructure Conference, Basel (22 May 2014).

[51] See Admati and Hellwig, n 6 above, 222–4.

level of capital and has adequate governance structures in place along with robust risk-management processes and that it communicates its risk exposure to the market to ensure market discipline. Basel III Pillar 2 enhances the supervisory review process by allowing the supervisors to have wide powers of oversight to test the bank's corporate governance structures and its risk-management practices from both a micro-prudential and macro-prudential perspective.[52] Pillar 2 provides for early intervention by supervisors if bank capital does not appear to the supervisor to cover sufficiently the risks inherent in their business activities. Increased capital should not be viewed as the only alternative to addressing a corresponding increase in risks confronting banks. This means that the supervisor has discretion to require the bank to adjust its governance practices and strategic business plans if they prove to be a source of unsustainable risk for the bank itself or—especially in the case of a SIFI—the broader financial system in which it operates. Further, capital should not be regarded as a substitute for fundamentally inadequate governance or risk-management processes.

Pillar 2 introduces the supervisory review evaluation process (SREP) that enhances the bank supervisor's oversight and implementation of the *four key principles* of sound corporate governance and specific guidance relating to risk management and measurement.[53] Principle 1 states that banks should have a process for assessing their overall capital adequacy in relation to their risk profile and a strategy for maintaining their capital levels.[54] Significantly, the bank's board of directors has the responsibility for setting the bank's tolerance for risks and for ensuring that management establishes a process for assessing risks and developing a system relating how its risk level corresponds to the bank's capital level. It also is responsible for monitoring compliance with internal policies.[55] The board is also responsible for establishing '[p]olicies and procedures designed to ensure that the bank identifies, measures, and reports all material risks'.[56]

By the bank establishing adequate systems 'for monitoring and reporting risk exposures'[57] it will allow senior management to '[e]valuate the level and trend of material risks and their effect on capital levels;' as well as '[e]valuate the sensitivity and reasonableness of key assumptions used in the capital assessment measurement system'.[58]

[52] Basel II (as amended) ('Basel III'), Pillar 2, credit risk, Articles 733–5; operational risk, Articles 736–7; market risk, Articles 738–738(v); interest rate risk, Articles 739–40; liquidity risk, Article 741.

[53] It also makes reference to other international principles of bank governance, including the Core Principles for Effective Banking Supervision. See BIS, Core Principles of Banking Supervision (1997).

[54] Basel II (as amended) ('Basel III'), Pillar 2, generally paras 720, 721 (p 204); specifically paras 726–45 (pp 205–9).

[55] ibid. In Pillar 2, Article 730 states: 'The bank's board of directors has responsibility for setting the bank's tolerance for risks. It should also ensure that management establishes a framework for assessing the various risks, develops a system to relate risk to the bank's capital level, and establishes a method for monitoring compliance with internal policies. It is likewise important that the board of directors adopts and supports strong internal controls [...]' (Article 730).

[56] ibid, Article 731. [57] ibid, Article 743. [58] ibid.

With regard to the internal control review, the 'bank should conduct periodic reviews of its risk management process to ensure its integrity, accuracy, and reasonableness' to allow for the '[i]dentification of large exposures'.[59]

Principle 2 provides that supervisors should review and evaluate banks' internal capital adequacy assessments and strategies, as well as their ability to monitor and ensure their compliance with regulatory capital ratios. Supervisors should take appropriate supervisory action if they are not satisfied with the result of this process.[60] The ICAAP was the most common means of implementing the principles.[61] The ICAAP was adopted under Basel II and remains in effect by requiring supervisors to examine a bank's stress-testing results as part of a supervisory review of both the bank's internal capital assessment and its liquidity risk management. In particular, supervisors should consider the results of forward-looking stress testing for assessing the adequacy of capital and liquidity.[62]

Principle 3 provides that supervisors should expect banks to operate above the minimum regulatory capital ratios and should have the ability to require banks to hold capital in excess of the minimum based on an assessment of the bank's governance and risk-management practices.[63] Regulatory capital buffers are to provide for reasonable reassurance that the bank has 'good internal systems and controls, a well-diversified risk profile and a business profile well covered by the Pillar 1 regime [...]'.[64] It is expected that in the normal course of business, 'the type and volume of activities will change, as will the different risk exposures, causing fluctuations in the overall capital ratio'.[65] And principle 4 provides that supervisors should seek to intervene at an early stage to prevent capital from falling below the minimum levels required to support the risk characteristics of a particular bank and should require rapid remedial action if capital is not maintained or restored.[66]

[59] ibid, Article 745.

[60] Paras 746–56 (pp 209–11). Specifically Pillar 2 states (Article 748): 'Supervisors should also review the adequacy of risk measures used in assessing internal capital adequacy and the extent to which these risk measures are also used operationally in setting limits, evaluating business line performance, and evaluating and controlling risks more generally. Supervisors should consider the results of sensitivity analyses and stress tests conducted by the institution and how these results relate to capital plans.'

[61] ibid.

[62] Basel Committee, Peer Review of Supervisory Authorities' Implementation of Stress Testing Principles (2012).

[63] Paras 757–8 (p 211). [64] Para 757.

[65] Para 757 b. The article goes on to state that '[t]here may be risks, either specific [...] or more generally to an economy at large, that are not taken into account in Pillar 1'. Para 757 e.

[66] Paras 759–60 (p 212). The Basel Committee acknowledges that the 'permanent solution to banks' difficulties is not always increased capital' (para 760). Other, specified measures may be necessary, but not effective immediately.

This principle supports the practice of prompt corrective action that allows supervisors to intervene in bank managerial decision-making if problems begin to emerge in the bank's operation and allows the supervisor to take pre-emptive measures if they determine that they are proportionate and necessary (ie, capital raising or restriction of bank distributions).

The SREP provides more exacting standards for bank supervisors to test the risk-management practices of bank risk officers and to incorporate into their stress tests the financial stability risks of hypothetical scenarios involving the bank's exposures to structural or systemic risks. In the case of British banks, the UK Prudential Regulation Authority (PRA) is concerned with the near-term risks to British banks of a growing bubble in UK housing prices. The PRA is also encouraging bank risk officers to run scenario stress testing involving a eurozone sovereign default or eurozone-based bank default. Also, key risk areas of concern include the implications for British banks of a sharp reversal of accommodative monetary policies. These types of stress tests are part of a forward-looking stress-testing approach that is an important element of a bank's internal capital assessment process. Pillar 2 stress testing is essentially concerned with short-term crisis scenarios that could occur in three to five years. In contrast, longer-term risks to the financial sector are generally not subject to stress testing because the availability of data is limited and the assumptions underlying the forecasts lack specificity.

This could be a major weakness in Pillar 2 stress testing because supervisors and bank risk officers are overly concerned with a near term crisis and are not engaged in planning for a longer-term crisis that may occur because of the cumulative build-up of risk across the system and markets. For example, some experts have suggested that the effects of climate change on the economy may lead to the accumulation of high carbon assets in the financial system that might through bank credit exposures lead to banking sector instability. This type of longer-term scenario testing is not presently emphasized in the Pillar 2 framework. Although Pillar 2 provides a flexible framework for bank supervisors to engage with bank risk officers to assess and measure the financial stability risks of macro-prudential risks, its effectiveness in preparing banks for longer-term systemic or macro-prudential risks across the financial system remains to be tested.

In addition, despite the flexibility of approach afforded to the supervisor under the SREP, the UK PRA has had some challenges turning the SREP into an effective supervisory practice. Under the existing Pillar 2 regime there is, in theory, an explicit link between the SREP and PRA's evaluation of risks arising from the oversight, governance, and risk management of the firm. This risk is expressed in the form of a governance scalar, which is applied to firms' Pillar 1 and Pillar 2 capital requirements. It is expressed overall as part of a firm's Individual Capital Guidance (ICG). The Pillar 2 governance scalar policy has been applied differently between supervisory areas. PRA teams worked closely in 2009 to refine the governance scalar policy; however, an agreement could not be reached. Failure to reach a common policy has resulted in inconsistencies between large, small, and international firms.

In contrast, US regulators use the CAMELS[67] approach for assessing bank capital and management adequacy. The US federal banking agencies (the Office of the Comptroller of the Currency (OCC), the Federal Deposit Insurance Corporation (FDIC), and Federal Reserve) all assign examination CAMELS ratings to banks. As part of that process, they evaluate governance and risk management within each of the CAMELS components, but then also assign an overall rating to governance and risk management. These ratings are not tied directly to capital. Instead, they are likely to lead to more intrusive supervision as well as restrictions on business activities and capital distributions. These measures are expected to provide an incentive for firms to improve their governance and risk-management processes.

Additional capital can be imposed under the US Comprehensive Capital Analysis and Review (CCAR). Under this stress-testing regime, the US assesses not only the quality of a bank's capital adequacy assessment process, but also its corporate governance, controls, and risk-measurement and -management practices. The extent to which its ability to determine its risk exposures falls short of expectations can result in the bank being required to hold more capital. It should be emphasized that this assessment is undertaken under the US Pillar 1 framework and so the decision to impose higher capital is based on a narrower set of criteria than the broader set of criteria used by the UK PRA's in its Pillar 2 assessment of a bank's governance and risk management.

The enhanced supervisory oversight of bank corporate governance and risk management, and linking the determination of regulatory capital to sustainable corporate governance and risk-management practices, provides another aspect of how bank capital has taken on a more social dimension, in addition to its earlier role under Basel II in signalling the bank's solvency and performance to the market.

3. Pillar 3—market discipline (enhanced disclosure)

The purpose of Pillar 3—market discipline—is to complement the minimum capital requirements (Pillar 1) and the supervisory review process (Pillar 2). The market discipline approach largely relies on developing a set of disclosure requirements which will allow market participants to assess key pieces of information to investors on the amount and quality of, capital, risk exposures, risk-assessment processes, and hence the overall capital adequacy of the institution. Such disclosure requirements

[67] CAMELS is an acronym used by US bank regulators (especially at the FDIC) to assess the capital adequacy, management practices, and liquidity exposure of US deposit institutions.

have particular relevance for investors and other stakeholders because so much of the risk-measurement process relies on the bank's internal methodologies that give it substantial discretion in determining capital requirements and which are ordinarily only communicated to the bank supervisor.

In principle, banks' disclosures should be consistent with how senior management and the board of directors assess and manage the risks of the bank. Under Pillar 1, banks use specified approaches/methodologies for measuring the various risks they face and the resulting capital requirements. By providing disclosures to the capital markets, it is intended that investors should learn fully of the risks to which banking institutions are exposed. A fuller disclosure regime under Pillar 3 departs from the earlier practice under Basel II of banks making more limited disclosure to the markets about the quality of their capital and riskiness of their assets. Public disclosure to reduce information asymmetries in assessing bank risk-taking is another important regulatory tool to enhance investor and stakeholder understanding of the adequacy and social function of bank capital.

VII. Reforming Basel III along Macro-Prudential Lines

Basel III expands the role for regulatory capital to be concerned not only with micro-prudential balance-sheet risks of individual banks but also with the risks posed by banks to the broader financial system (ie, counter-cyclical capital and liquidity requirements) it also links the application of capital requirements to governance practices in banking institutions and related market developments. Although these are significant enhancements to the bank capital regime, they do not go far enough in certain key areas in addressing macro-prudential financial stability risks. For instance, Basel III continues to allow global banking groups to use risk-weighted internal models to calculate credit, market, and liquidity risks that rely on historic data and risk parameters that are based on individual bank risk exposures and not to systemic risk across the financial system. Although Basel III contains higher core tier 1 and tier 1 capital requirements, liquidity requirements and a leverage ratio, it remains essentially dependent on risk-weighted models that were proven to be unreliable prior to the crisis because of their disproportionate focus on risk management at the level of the individual firm. Rather, international regulatory reforms as set forth by the Financial Stability Board (FSB) are reshaping bank regulation to achieve macro-prudential objectives. This requires not only stricter capital and liquidity requirements for individual institutions, but also monitoring risk exposures across the financial system, including the transfer of credit risk to off balance-sheet entities and the general level of risk across the financial system.[68] Also, SIFIs will be subjected to more intensive prudential regulatory requirements, including higher capital requirements and more scrutiny of their cross-border operations.

In addition, the wide scope of macro-prudential regulation will require a broader definition of prudential supervision to include both *ex ante* supervisory powers, such as licensing, authorization, and compliance with regulatory standards, and *ex post* crisis management measures, such as recovery and resolution plans, deposit insurance, and lender of last resort. Indeed, the objectives of macro-prudential regulation—to monitor and control systemic risks and related risks across the financial system—will require greater regulatory and supervisory intensity that will necessitate increased intervention in the operations of cross-border banking and financial groups and a wider assessment of the risks they pose.[69] The broad area of recovery and resolution will necessarily involve authorities in restructuring and disposing of banking assets and using taxpayer funds to bail out and provide temporary support for ailing financial institutions.[70]

VIII. Conclusion

The Chapter suggests that bank capital risk-measurement and -management practices must be built on a more holistic approach to financial regulation and supervision that links the design of bank regulatory capital to both traditional bank risk-management functions in calculating economic capital *and* to broader social functions that address the impact of bank risk-taking on the economy and society. Basel III makes an important step in achieving this by designing regulatory capital that is more transparent and loss absorbent. Moreover, the counter-cyclical component of bank capital links the determination of bank capital to developments in the broader economy. The SIFI capital surcharge tries to put a price on the size and

[68] For example, the G20/FSB objective of requiring systemically significant financial instruments (ie, OTC derivatives) to be traded on exchanges and centrally cleared with central counterparties is an important regulatory innovation to control systemic risk in wholesale securities markets.

[69] See EU Commission, Report of the High Level Group on Financial Supervision in the EU, chaired by Jacques De Larosiere (2009), 19–23. See also The Turner Review, n 32 above, 27–32.

[70] Indeed, the FSB has stated that '[t]o improve a firm's resolvability, supervisory authorities or resolution authorities should have powers to require, where necessary, the adoption of appropriate measures, such as changes to a firm's business practices, structure or organisation [...] To enable the continued operations of systemically important functions, authorities should evaluate whether to require that these functions be segregated in legally and operationally independent entities that are shielded from group problems.' See FSB, Key Attributes of Effective Resolution Regimes for Financial Institutions (October 2011), Key Attribute 10.5.

interconnectedness of financial institutions and the disproportionate risks they pose to the financial system and society. Basel III builds on Basel II's economic capital optimization approach but expands the concept of regulatory capital to include a social dimension that addresses the broader effect of bank risk-taking on the economy and society. However, Basel III reforms continue to incorporate a disproportionate reliance on risk weightings to determine bank capital, while failing fully to appreciate the broader social impact of an adequately capitalized banking sector. More work needs to be done, therefore, in analysing the social dimension of bank regulatory capital and how it can be regulated to achieve both micro-prudential risk-optimization objectives along with controlling the social costs of bank risk-taking and also providing positive externalities for a more sustainable macro-economy.

Bibliography

Adam, A, *Handbook of Asset and Liability Management: From Models to Optimal Return Strategies* (2007).

Admati, A and Hellwig, A, *The Bankers' New Clothes: What's Wrong with Banking and What to Do about It* (2013).

Alexander, K, Implementation of Capital Requirements Directive III Remuneration Rules in the UK: Implications, Limitations and Lessons Learned (2012), Economics and Monetary Affairs, European Parliament, Workshop on Banks' Remuneration Rules (CRD III): Are they Implemented and Do they Work in Practice? (IP/A/ECON/WS/2012-18, PE 464.465).

Alexander, K, Stability and Sustainability in Banking: Should Basel III Address Environmental Risks (2014), Report for the United Nations Environment Programme.

Alexander, K, Dhumale, R, and Eatwell, J, *Global Governance of Financial System: The International Regulation of Systemic Risk* (2006).

Alexander, K, Eatwell, J, Persaud, A, and Reoch, R, Financial Supervision and Crisis Management in the EU (2007), Economics and Monetary Affairs, European Parliament, Financial Supervision and Crisis Management in the EU (IP IP/A/ECON/IC/2007-069).

Basel Committee, Peer Review of Supervisory Authorities' Implementation of Stress Testing Principles (2012).

Basel Committee on Banking Supervision (BCBS), Basel II Credit Risk Principles (2002).

Basel Committee on Banking Supervision, Basel III: A Global Regulatory Framework for more Resilient Banks and Banking Systems (December 2010, revised June 2011).

Basel Committee on Banking Supervision, Basel III Regulatory Consistency Assessment Program (RCAP) (2013).

Basel Committee on Banking Supervision, Macroprudential Policy Tools and Frameworks, Progress Report to G20 (2011), available at <http://www.bis.org/publ/othp17.htm> (last accessed 5 June 2014).

Bebchuk, L, Cremers, M, and Peyer, U, The CEO Pay Slice (2010), The Harvard John M. Olin Discussion Paper No 679, available at <http://www.law.harvard.edu/programs/corp_gov/papers.shtml>.

Berger, A, De Young, R, Flannery, M, Lee, D, and Oztekin, O, 'How Do Large Banking Organizations Manage their Capital Ratios' (2008) 34 (2–3) *Journal of Financial Service Research* 123.

BIS, Core Principles of Banking Supervision (1997).

Brunnermeier, M, Crockett, A, Goodhart, C, Persaud, A, and Shin, H, *The Fundamental Principles of Financial Regulation* (2009) 11 Geneva Reports on the World Economy 10–11.

Casu, B, Girardone, C, and Molyneux, P, *Introduction to Banking* (2006).

Darling, A, *Back from the Brink* (2011).

EU Commission, Report of the High Level Group on Financial Supervision in the EU, chaired by Jacques De Larosiere (2009).

Ferrarini, G and Ungureanu, M, 'Economics, Politics, and the International Principles for Sound Compensation Practices: An Analysis of Executive Pay at European Banks' (2011) 64 *Vanderbilt Law Review* 431.

Financial Stability Board, Key Attributes of Effective Resolution Regimes for Financial Institutions (October 2011), Key Attribute 10.5.

Financial Stability Forum, Report of the Financial Stability Forum on Enhancing Market and Institutional Resilience (2008).

Financial Stability Forum, Report of the Follow-up Group on Incentives to Foster Implementation Standards (2000).

Golin, J, *The Bank Credit Analysis Handbook—a Guide for Analysts, Bankers and Investors* (2001).

Goodhart, C, *Bank Resolution in Comparative Perspective: What Lessons for Europe?* (2013).

Goodhart, C, *The Basel Committee on Banking Supervision: A History of the Early Years, 1974–1997* (2011).

Greenspan, A, 'We Need a Better Cushion against Risk' *Financial Times*, 26 March 2009.

Hassert, T, presentation at the Basel Infrastructure Conference, Basel (22 May 2014).

Heffernan, S, *Modern Banking* (2005) 2.

Hull, J, *Risk Management and Financial Institutions* (3rd edn, 2012).

Ingves, S, Challenges for the Design and Conduct of Macroprudential Policy, speech at BOK-BIS Conference, Seoul, Korea (January 2011), available at <http://www.riksbank.se/Upload/Dokument_riksbank/Kat_publicerat/Tal/2011/110118e.pdf> (last accessed 13 August 2014).

International Monetary Fund, Key Aspects of Macro-prudential Policy (2013), 61.

Jackson, P, Beyond Basel II, presentation at Clare College, Cambridge (September 2010).

Kleftouri, N, 'Rethinking UK and EU Bank Deposit Insurance' (2013) 24 *European Business Law Review* 1, 95.

Norton, J, *Devising International Banking Supervisory Standards* (1995).

Prudential Regulation Authority, The Prudential Regulation Authority's Approach to Banking Supervision (2013).

South African Reserve Bank, Guidance Note 9/2012 Issued in Terms of Section 6(5) of the Banks Act, 1990—Capital Framework for South Africa Based on the Basel III Framework, available at <http://www.resbank.co.za/Lists/News%20and%20Publications/Attachments/5154/G9%20of%202012.pdf> (last accessed 24 July 2014).

South African Reserve Bank, South Africa's Implementation of Basel II and Basel III, available at <http://www.resbank.co.za/RegulationAndSupervision/BankSupervision/TheBaselCapitalAccord%28Basel%20II%29/Pages/AccordImplementationForum%28AIF%29.aspx> (last accessed 24 July 2014).

Tucker, P, Macro and Microprudential Supervision, speech at British Bankers' Association Annual International Banking Conference, London (29 June 2011), available at <http://www.bankofengland.co.uk/publications/Documents/speeches/2011/speech506.pdf> (last accessed 7 August 2013), 4–5.

UK Financial Services Authority, The Turner Review: A Regulatory Response to the Global Banking Crisis (2009).

Wall Street Journal (Europe edition), 29 July 2011, 18.

de Weert, F, *Bank and Insurance Capital Management* (2011).

CHAPTER 13

MANAGING RISK IN THE FINANCIAL SYSTEM

PETER O MÜLBERT*

* I would like to thank Isabel Schnabel, Günter Franke, and Alexander Schäfer for their most helpful comments and suggestions; Alexander Sajnovits for excellent research assistance; and Annemarie Grimm for excellent editorial assistance. The usual disclaimer applies.

I. Introduction

THE great financial crisis (GFC[1]) of 2007–09 not only dealt a well-nigh fatal blow to the stability of the transatlantic financial system, but also to major elements of received wisdom regarding the functioning and regulation of financial markets. The efficient capital markets hypothesis (ECMH) has taken a severe hit[2] and priorities with respect to financial regulation have changed. As a corollary to financial stability becoming a (macro-)economic policy goal at the 'national, regional and international' level[3] prudential regulation is tasked to adopt a distinct 'macro-prudential' perspective—ie, focusing on the systemic risks to the stability of the financial system as a whole—that complements and even supersedes the traditional micro-prudential perspective that focuses on risks to the soundness of individual financial firms.[4]

[1] GFC usually serves as an acronym for 'the' global financial crisis (eg Mishkin, FS, 'Over the Cliff: From the Subprime to the Global Financial Crisis' (2011) 25(1) *Journal of Economic Perspectives* 49). However, Asian, South American, and African countries were much less affected. See, eg, Davis, K, *Regulatory Reform Post the Global Financial Crisis: An Overview* (2010) 2. For an account of the evolution and the reasons for the GFC see, eg, Gorton, G and Metrick, A, 'Getting Up to Speed on the Financial Crisis: A One-Weekend Reader's Guide' (2012) 50(1) *Journal of Economic Literature* 128 and the papers discussed therein; additionally, see Brunnermeier, MK, 'Deciphering the Liquidity and Credit Crunch 2007–2008' (2009) 23(1) *Journal of Economic Perspectives* 77; Hellwig, MF, 'Systemic Risk in the Financial Sector: An Analysis of the Subprime Mortgage Financial Crisis' (2009) 157 *De Economist* 129.

[2] cf Financial Services Authority (FSA). The Turner Review—a regulatory response to the global banking crises (2009), 39–42 ('Efficient markets can be irrational'). But see Gilson, R and Kraakman, R, Market Efficiency after the Financial Crisis: It's Still a Matter of Information Costs (2014), ECGI Law Working Paper No 242/2014; Davis, n 1 above, 11.

[3] Lastra, R, 'Systemic Risk, SIFIs and Financial Stability' (2011) 6 *Capital Markets Law Journal* 198, 207.

[4] See Section VI.1 with references.

Even before the GFC, though, prudential regulation of financial institutions was not limited to a purely micro-economic perspective. The supervisory authorities' Joint Forum[5] already noted in 2001:

traditionally, the broad objective of supervisors and regulators of the three sectors has been to protect customers, whether these were depositors, investors or policyholders. Over times, ... supervisors have in some cases also been concerned to limit the potential implications of the sudden failure of a financial institution on the financial system and the economy. However, 'the extent to which concerns over "systemic risk" currently do or should play a role in the development of supervisory policies in each sector is not completely clear'.[6]

On the other hand, macro-prudential regulation works to a large extent at the level of individual financial institutions and players in financial markets. As a consequence, the delineation between micro- and macro-prudential regulation tools is sometimes less clear-cut than it seems at first glance. In addition, some tools have a dual function, reducing both risks to the soundness of individual firms and systemic risk to financial stability. Deposit insurance, for instance, is such a dual-purpose mechanism. Conversely, for some tools the objectives of micro-prudential and macro-prudential regulation can come into conflict. For example, asset and funding diversification will make individual firms more resilient but can create additional systemic risk. Conversely, while the rigorous application of the idea of a counter-cyclical capital buffer during a prolonged financial downturn or even a crisis may relieve the pressure to deleverage for some time, it will result in a bank becoming more risky precisely in times when banks need a strong capital base to maintain counterparty and market confidence.

Against that background, the next Section will elaborate on the objectives of micro- and macro-prudential financial regulation (Section II). The following Sections will then present taxonomies of micro-prudential, macro-prudential, and dual-purpose tools of financial regulation (Sections III–V), discussing, in particular, those tools not covered in other Chapters of this volume, ie focusing on tools for managing risk in the (shadow) banking sector while excluding regulatory capital and liquidity requirements (see the Chapter by Alexander in this volume) as well as crisis management and resolution tools (see the Chapter by Armour in this volume). Section VI will discuss some policy aspects followed by some concluding observations (Section VII).

[5] Established in 1996 under the aegis of the Basel Committee on Banking Supervision (BCBS), the International Organization of Securities Commissions (IOSCO), and the International Association of Insurance Supervisors (IAIS). It comprises an equal number of senior bank, insurance, and securities supervisors representing each supervisory constituency.

[6] Joint Forum, Risk Management Practices and Regulatory Capital—Cross-sectoral Comparison (2001) 32; cf Borio, C, 'Towards a Macroprudential Framework for Financial Supervision and Regulation?' (2003) 49(2) *CESifo Economic Studies* 181, 186.

II. Micro- and Macro-Prudential Regulation: Objectives

Prudential regulation of financial institutions will pursue one or both of two objectives:[7] the protection of customers—depositors, investors, and policyholders—and the reduction of systemic risk. (Micro-)prudential regulation to protect customers focuses primarily on the risk of failure of an individual firm. (Macro-)prudential regulation with the objective to reduce systemic risk is concerned with the financial system as a whole.[8]

The Basel Committee on Banking Supervision, though, maintains: 'the primary objective is the soundness of banks and the banking system'.[9] Yet, from an economic and a legal perspective, to shield a firm against failure is only warranted for the purpose of protecting its customers and/or reducing systemic risk, not for the sake of the firm itself.

1. Customer protection

When taking *customer protection* as a starting point—be it for depositors, investors, or policyholders—and focusing on the risks to an individual firm, efficient micro-prudential regulation is informed by a cost-benefit-analysis: the aggregate regulatory costs borne by the firms should be less than the aggregate expected losses customers will suffer from the failure of the firms.

Specifically for the banking sector, when taking the presence of a scheme for depositor protection as given, the traditional micro-economic perspective will be the following: banks finance themselves with insured deposits and, hence, face an incentive to take excessive risks knowing that the losses will be covered by other parties. The goal of prudential regulation is to force banks to internalize losses, thereby protecting the deposit insurance fund and mitigating moral hazard. Hence, in the absence of a contribution that is highly sensitive to a bank's

[7] From the perspective of economic theory, prudential regulation of financial institutions can be justified by market failures because of: (i) negative eternalities; (ii) information asymmetries leading to adverse selection and moral hazard (*ex post* opportunism); and (iii) competitive distortions. For more details see, eg, Joint Forum, Review of the Differentiated Nature and Scope of Financial Regulation—Key Issues and Recommendations (2010), 85–8.

[8] Cecchetti, S, 'The Future of Financial Intermediation and Regulation: An Overview' (1999) 5(8) *Current Issues in Economics and Finance* 1, 3; Borio, n 6 above, 183–5 (lucid juxtaposition of the two perspectives).

[9] Basel Committee on Banking Supervision, Core Principles for Effective Banking Supervision (2012), Core Principle 1.

idiosyncratic risk-taking, the objective of micro-prudential regulation is to lower the probability of the deposit insurer's losses low enough,[10] indeed lowering it to the point that expected losses are lower than the aggregate funding contributions paid by financial institutions.

2. Stabilization of the financial system

The *reduction of systemic risk* as a justification for macro-prudential regulation derives from a macro-economic perspective on financial regulation. Regulation is intended to promote the stability of the financial system which is composed of financial institutions—banks, investment firms, clearing institutions, financial market infrastructures (FMIs—payment systems, central counterparties [CCPs]), collective investment schemes, funds (hedge funds, money market funds, private equity funds, pension funds, real estate funds, etc.), asset managers, insurance companies—and other actors which are linked by markets and infrastructures. Given the four essential functions of the financial system:[11]

- financial intermediation: a way of transferring assets between savers and borrowers;
- risk intermediation: a means of pricing and transferring certain risks;
- liquidity provision: a means of converting assets into cash without undue loss of value; and
- value exchange: a way of making payments, financial stability is often defined as a state in which the financial system, by performing its functions, is capable of facilitating the performance of the real economy.[12] Hence, the objective of macro-prudential regulation is to reduce risk to the financial system when performing its four essential functions.

With a view to financial intermediation, ie the provision of funds, arguably the most fundamental function of financial systems, the objective of macro-prudential regulation can be described more precisely as making sure that, in times of financial crisis, banks will not restore their impaired regulatory capital requirements by selling off risky assets (balance-sheet shrinkage), but will resort to other mechanisms, in particular to strengthening their impaired capital base.[13]

[10] Hanson, SG, Kashyap, AK, and Stein, JC, 'A Macroprudential Approach to Financial Regulation' (2011) 25(1) *Journal of Economic Perspectives* 1, 4.

[11] See Reserve Bank of Australia, Submission to the Financial System Inquiry (2014), 9. It should be noted that the presentation of the core functions of the financial sector differs within literature.

[12] For different definitions of financial stability see Bank of International Settlements, Central Bank Governance and Financial Stability (2011), (so-called Ingves report) 31 *et seq* (box no 1).

[13] See Hanson et al., n 10 above, 5–7. As a caveat, though, the argument implies that risky assets are transferred mostly to other banks and financial firms that are subject to minimal capital

The soundness of individual financial institutions and the efficient and fair functioning of markets are necessary prerequisites for financial stability and require prudential regulation designed with a view to promoting this objective. However, contrary to a long-standing implicit assumption dubbed 'composition fallacy',[14] the financial soundness of all participating individual institutions and markets is not enough to guarantee financial stability. Hence, micro-economic regulatory tools must be complemented by macro-prudential tools which, although often operating at the level of individual firms, aim primarily at avoiding or reducing systemic risk.

III. Micro-Prudential Risk Management: Reducing Risk for Individual Firms

1. Risks for banks and non-bank financial institutions

Financial institutions face risks that differ depending on the type of financial entity and the concrete business model of individual entities. Regarding banks, the Basel Committee on Banking Supervision (BCBS) has identified an extensive but non-exhaustive list of risks comprising, *inter alia*:[15]

- credit risk, including counterparty credit risk: the risk that a borrower will partially default on his obligation to repay the loan or to pay interest;
- liquidity risk: the risk inherent in all maturity transformation processes of being unable to satisfy (short-term) cash flow needs;
- market risk, including interest rate risk and foreign exchange rate risk: the risks of losses from changes in market prices;
- concentration risk: the risk of loss resulting from being overly exposed to a single counterparty or several counterparties belonging to a group, to borrowers/

requirements. A risk-transfer to firms in the non-regulated shadow-banking sector does not impact the other banks' ability to extend credit.

[14] Brunnermeier, M, Crockett, A, Goodhart, C, Persaud, A, and Shin, H, *The Fundamental Principles of Financial Regulation* (2009) 11 Geneva Reports on the World Economy XVI; Osiński, J, Seal, K, and Hoogduin, L, Macroprudential and Microprudential Policies: Towards Cohabitation (2013), IMF Staff Discussion Note 13/05, 5.

[15] See Basel Committee, n 9 above, Principles 17–25.

counterparties in the same geographic region, industry, etc., or to a particular class of assets, etc.;
- country risk, including sovereign risk: the risk of loss caused by events in a foreign country;
- transfer risk: the risk that a borrower will not make debt service payments in a foreign currency because of his inability to obtain the pertinent currency;
- operational risk: the risk of loss resulting from inadequate or failed internal processes, people (fraud) and systems (IT systems) or external events, including legal risk;[16] and
- reputational risk: risk arising from negative perception on the part of other market participants.[17]

Not part of the Basel Committee's list is the senior management of financial institutions. However, recent enhancements to prudential regulation in the EU as well as in the US also focus on management, including directors, senior management, and other risk-takers. In substance, if not in words, senior managers are treated as a separate major risk for the financial institution they are working for.

Other financial institutions, depending on their business, face different sets of risks, including some of the risks listed, but also different ones.[18] The key risks to FMIs, for example are credit, liquidity and operational risks,[19] a breakdown of risks in the insurance sector is to divide them into four categories: (i) business risks; (ii) technical risks relating, eg to actuarial and/or statistical calculations used in estimating liabilities; (iii) investment risks, including credit risk, market risk (including interest rate risk), and liquidity risk; and (iv) non-technical risks, including operational risk (iii).[20]

2. Micro-prudential tools other than capital

(a) *Risk management, governance, and risk culture at firm level*

(1) *Risk management (banks)*

Adequate risk management at firm level is the first line of defence against risk in the financial system. This holds true even for banks that are subject to the detailed

[16] Excluding, strategic and reputational risks, see Basel Committee, n 9 above, 59 n 79.

[17] Basel Committee on Banking Supervision, Enhancement to the Basel II Framework (2009), 19 n 47.

[18] For a very comprehensive list of financial risks see Malz, AM, *Financial Risk Management: Models, History, and Institutions* (2011) Table 1.2.

[19] See Manning, M, Nier, E, and Schanz, J, 'Introduction' in Manning, M, Nier, E, and Schanz, J (eds), *The Economics of Large-value Payments and Settlement: Theory and Policy Issues for Central Banks* (2009) 5–6.

[20] International Association of Insurance Supervisors, Insurance Core Principles, Standards, Guidance and Assessment Methodology (2011/2013), 4 n 4.

Basel-inspired regulatory capital requirements. The *Basel II* framework succinctly states: 'capital should not be regarded as a substitute for addressing fundamentally inadequate control or risk management practices' and recommends considering alternative means for addressing increased risks, 'such as strengthening risk management, applying internal limits, strengthening the level of provisions and reserves, and improving internal controls'.[21] As a consequence, Basel II not only provided for detailed rules regarding how to calculate the risks that are to be supported with regulatory capital, relying heavily on value-at-risk (VaR) models for that purpose, but also introduced internal governance requirements, such as the key principle of board and senior-management supervision (eg concerning the bank's strategic planning process) and the implementation of independent risk management functions, responsible for developing strategies and techniques to identify, assess, monitor, and control (mitigate) operational risks, in particular[22].

A few years later, though, inquiries into the causes of the GFC unanimously concluded that a major cause of the financial crises were deficiencies in risk-management practices and organizational structures at even the largest banks:[23] over-reliance on quantitative risk models and failure to see the 'fat' (tail) risks, misidentification and/or underestimation of specific types of risks (such as liquidity or leverage risks or structured products such as collateralized debt obligations (CDOs), asset-backed securities (ABSs), and others), insensitivity to systemic risks in highly interwoven markets, stress-testing using past events instead of identifying new risks and possible new scenarios, and inappropriate control mechanisms at group level (leading to severe intra-group financial contagion).

The Basel Committee on Banking Supervision responded to these findings by substantial *enhancements* to the Basel II framework with respect to risk management,[24] by dealing more in-depth with the effective risk-management issue in its revised principles for effective corporate governance of banks[25] and its Principles regarding operational risk, in particular[26] and, most recently, by dedicating two

[21] Basel Committee on Banking Supervision, International Convergence of Capital Measurements and Capital Standards, A Revised Framework, Comprehensive Version (2006), 204 n 723.

[22] Basel Committee, n 17 above, eg 149 n 663 (independent risk-management functions), 205 nn 728–30 (board and senior-management supervision).

[23] OECD, Corporate Governance and the Financial Crisis: Key Findings and Main Messages (June 2009), 8 ('Perhaps one of the greatest shocks from the financial crisis has been the widespread failure of risk management'). As to the different failures see, eg, Senior Supervisors Group, Risk Management Lessons from the Global Banking Crisis of 2008 (21 October 2009), 20–8; Nestor Advisors, Banks Boards and the Financial Crisis: A Corporate Governance Study of the 25 Largest European Banks (2009), 46–92; Kirkpatrick, G, 'The Corporate Governance Lessons from the Financial Crisis' (2009)(1) *Financial Market Trends* 6; FSA, Turner Review, n 2 above, 22–4, 44–5; cf Basel Committee, n 17 above, 10–11.

[24] Basel Committee, ibid, 12–20 nn 15–57.

[25] Basel Committee on Banking Supervision, Principles for Enhancing Corporate Governance (2010), Principles 6–8.

[26] Basel Committee on Banking Supervision, Principles for the Sound Management of Operational Risk (2011).

principles of its revised Core Principles for Effective Banking Supervision to risk management.[27] Finally, as regards the risk-specific information technology and data architecture of financial institutions, the Basel Committee adopted its new Principles for effective data aggregation and risk reporting,[28] which have been dubbed the 'Basel Magna Carta of modern data management' but, as new and ambitious IT standards, will present financial institutions with significant implementation challenges.

Legal implementation of these governance enhancements for effective risk management as well as existing supervisory expectations for the three key risk governance functions—board and its committees/risk-management function/compliance function—vary somewhat across countries.[29]

At *EU* level, for example, the so-called Capital Requirements Directive (CRD) IV applying to banks and investment firms,[30] *inter alia*, provides for:

- boards to approve and periodically review the strategies and policies for taking up, managing, monitoring, and mitigating risks, which includes the determination of the institution's risk appetite (Article 76(1));
- risk committees to be established at board level, composed exclusively of non-executive directors (Article 76(3) sub 2); and
- risk management on a consolidated basis (Article 108(2)–(3)) which arguably includes the implementation of group-wide risk control functions to deliver a holistic view of all risks.

Moreover, the risk-management function is strengthened, eg, by promoting its authority, stature, resources, and direct access to board level, also including a more explicit and independent role of chief risk officers (CROs) within the institution (Article 76(5)), and risk governance must include a permanent and effective 'compliance function' designed to manage their specific compliance risks; ie, such pecuniary risks which may arise from violations of or non-compliance with applicable laws, and to implement a 'compliance policy'.

(II) *Corporate governance (banks)*

Good corporate governance mechanisms are important for constraining banks from taking on too much risk. With respect to the role of corporate governance failures in the run-up to the GFC, the EU CRD IV is illustrative of the emergent international consensus: weaknesses in corporate governance 'have contributed to

[27] Basel Committee, n 9 above, Core Principles 15 and 26.

[28] Basel Committee on Banking Supervision, Principles for Effective Risk Data Aggregation and Risk Reporting (2013).

[29] For a comprehensive overview see Financial Stability Board, Thematic Review on Risk Governance (2013).

[30] Council Directive 2013/36/EU on access to the activity of credit institutions and the prudential supervision of credit institutions and investment firms, amending Directive 2002/87/EC and repealing Directives 2006/48/EC and 2006/49/EC (2013) OJ L 176/338.

excessive and imprudent risk-taking in the banking sector which has led to the failure of individual institutions and systemic problems in Member States and globally'.[31] These weaknesses include deficiencies in risk-management governance and remuneration governance, as well as deficiencies in board practices and directors' profiles.

As regards the performance of banks during the GFC, these weaknesses were of varying importance. Corporate governance of risk management was the most important element of governance.[32]

These findings notwithstanding, at both the international and EU/national level, reforms of the corporate governance framework and corporate governance practices have been put into place. The Basel Committee published a revised and renamed version of its recommendations for good corporate governance[33] at banking institutions. The EU CRD IV,[34] in turn, responded to the alleged weaknesses, not only by expanding corporate governance over risk management and compensation, but by introducing a host of additional corporate governance requirements. In particular, larger and more complex institutions must establish a committee structure at board level (risk, compensation, and nomination committees), and separate the roles of CEO and chairman of the board. Moreover, board members and senior management are subject to extensive personal requirements; eg, they

[31] Council Directive 2013/36/EU, n 30 above, recital 55. For similar assessments see, eg, High-Level Expert Group on Reforming the Structure of the EU Banking Sector, Final report (2012), 105 (Liikanen report); The High-Level Group on Financial Supervision in the EU, Report (2009), n 110 (de Larosière report); Financial Services Authority, Effective Corporate Governance (2010), Consultation Paper 10/3, 3 n 1.1, 1.2; Walker, D, A Review of Corporate Governance in UK Banks and Other Financial Industry Entities—Final Recommendations (2009), 9. But see recital 5 of Council Directive 2014/65/EU on markets in financial instruments and amending Directive 2002/92/EC and Directive 2011/61/EU (recast) (2009) OJ L 173/349 (known as MiFID II): there is 'agreement among regulatory bodies at international level' on corporate governance failures being a contributory factor. Indeed, empirical studies, though, arrived at more cautious conclusions than the accepted wisdom among regulators at international level, see Beltratti, A and Stulz, RM, 'The Credit Crisis around the Globe: Why Did Some Banks Perform Better?' (2012) 105 *Journal of Financial Economics* 1; Aebi, V, Sabato, G, and Schmid, M, 'Risk Management, Corporate Governance, and Bank Performance in the Financial Crisis' (2012) 36 *Journal of Banking & Finance* 3213. In particular, several studies found that the presence of institutional shareholders increases the risk of the bank; see Laeven, L and Levine, R, 'Bank Governance, Regulation, and Risk Taking' (2009) 93 *Journal of Financial Economics* 259; Erkens, DH, Hung, M, and Matos, P, 'Corporate Governance in the 2007–2008 Financial Crisis: Evidence from Financial Institutions Worldwide' (2012) 18(2) *Journal of Corporate Finance* 389; Ellul, A and Yerramilli, V, 'Stronger Risk Controls, Lower Risk: Evidence from U.S. Bank Holding Companies' (2013) 68 *The Journal of Finance* 1757. On a related note, some studies found that owner-controlled banks suffered larger losses during the crisis than management-controlled banks, see Gropp, R and Köhler, M, Bank Owner or Bank Managers: Who Is Keen on Risk? Evidence from the Financial Crisis (23 February 2010), European Business School Research Paper No 10-02 (ZEW Discussion Paper No 10-013); Westman, H, The Role of Ownership Structure and Regulatory Environment in Bank Corporate Governance (14 January 2010), Bank of Finland Working Paper.

[32] Aebi et al., n 31 above.

[33] Basel Committee, n 25 above.

[34] Council Directive 2013/36/EU, n 30 above, Article 91(8).

must be 'fit and proper', devote sufficient time to performing their functions, 'act with honesty, integrity and independence of mind to effectively assess and challenge management decisions and to oversee decision-making', and are limited in the number of outside board mandates they may hold.

Many of these requirements represent best practices in corporate governance for firms in general and are thus a matter for shareholders to decide on. It remains to be seen, though, whether extending the perimeter of micro-prudential regulation and supervision to include corporate governance issues even beyond risk management and remuneration will, indeed, contribute towards making banks more resilient.

(III) *Risk culture*

Going beyond risk management and corporate governance risk culture is a comprehensive concept to rein in excessive risk-taking, *inter alia* promoted by the Financial Stability Board (FSB) with a view to systemically important financial institutions (SIFIs), in particular.[35] It comprises the institution's norms, attitudes, and behaviour in relation to risk awareness, risk-taking and risk management. A sound risk culture bolsters effective risk management, promotes sound risk-taking, and ensures that emerging risks in an institution's activities beyond its appetite for risk are dealt with in a timely manner. The foundational elements of a sound risk culture are sound practices for effective risk governance, an effective risk appetite framework with four key elements[36]—framework, statement, risk limits, and clearly defined roles and responsibilities of the board and senior management—and sound compensation practices.

(IV) *Non-bank financial institutions*

Across the board, non-bank financial institutions that fall within the perimeter of micro-prudential regulation and supervision, are subject to more or less extensive micro-prudential risk-management requirements and often also to corporate governance requirements. If there are reasons for extending the regulatory perimeter, the regulator, for the same reasons, will at the very least stipulate some core micro-prudential requirements. In line with this, the Joint Forum notes that the three sets of core principles issued by the Basel Committee,[37] the International Association of Insurance Supervisors,[38] and the International Organization of Securities Commissions (IOSCO),[39] respectively describe criteria, *inter alia*, for

[35] As to the following, see Financial Stability Board. Guidance on Supervisory Interaction with Financial Institutions on Risk Culture (2014), 1–3.

[36] Financial Stability Board, Principles for an Effective Risk Appetite Framework (2013).

[37] Basel Committee, n 9 above.

[38] International Association of Insurance Supervisors, n 20 above.

[39] International Organization of Securities Commissions, Objectives and Principles of Securities Regulation (2010).

risk-management processes and internal controls, albeit varying in accordance with the specific characteristics and attributes of the three sectors.

In the EU specifically, apart from the insurance sector,[40] more or less detailed provisions regarding risk-management and corporate governance issues exist for funds operating as UCITS (undertakings collective investment in transferable securities),[41] managers of alternative (ie, non-UCITS) investment funds,[42] central counterparties,[43] central securities depositories,[44] and regulated markets (exchanges).[45]

(b) *Altering incentives*

(1) *Banks*

From the perspective of depositors and other debtholders, as well as from the financial stability perspective for regulators and supervisors, banks will take on too much risk when acting in the best interest of diversified shareholders. Those owners will favour more risky (volatile) business strategies since they capture higher expected returns, whereas the creditors will bear additional losses, and this limited liability-driven fundamental conflict of interests between shareholders and debtholders is particularly acute for banks.[46] In addition, distorted incentives for directors and senior managers will result in banks taking on even more risk. Apart from misaligned incentive schemes, distortions will result, in particular, from the lower funding costs of large (too-big-to-fail) institutions, which are credited by the market, eg rating agencies, with enjoying implicit government support. Finally, from the regulator/supervisor's financial stability perspective, banks may take on too much systemic risk even when reducing firm-specific risk, eg by diversifying their portfolio of risky assets and/or their funding sources. This results from the fact that, because of (large) banks' interconnectedness due to contractual or indirect

[40] See the Chapter by Everson in this volume.

[41] Council Directive 2009/65/EC on the Coordination of laws, regulations and administrative provisions relating to undertakings for collective investment in transferable securities (UCITS) (2009) OJ L 302/32, Articles 12, 31, 51 (risk).

[42] Council Directive 2011/61/EU on Alternative Investment Fund Managers and amending Directives 2003/41/EC and 2009/65/EC and Regulations (EC) No 1060/2009 and (EU) No 1095/2010 (2011) OJ L 174/1, Articles 15, 18 (risk).

[43] Council Regulation (EU) No 648/2012 on OTC derivatives, central counterparties and trade repositories (2012) OJ L 201/1, Articles 26, 40–9 (risk), 27, 28 (corporate governance); commonly known as EMIR. For more details see the Chapter by Ferrarini and Saguato in this volume.

[44] Council Regulation (EU) No 909/2014 on improving securities settlement in the European Union and on central securities depositories and amending Directives 98/26/EC and 2014/65/EU and Regulation (EU) No 236/2012 (2014) OJ L 257/1, Articles 26 (risk), 27 (corporate governance).

[45] Council Directive 2014/65/EU, n 31 above. Articles 47–8 (risk), 45 (corporate governance).

[46] See, eg Mülbert, PO, Corporate Governance of Banks after the Financial Crisis—Theory, Evidence, Reforms (2010), ECGI Law Working Paper No 130/2010, 19–20, 25–6: International Monetary Fund, Global Financial Stability Report, Risk Taking, Liquidity, and Shadow Banking: Curbing Excess while Promoting Growth, October 2014 (2014), 108–9.

contagion channels, a (large) bank's funding and investment decisions may have a negative external effect on other banks and, hence, increase overall systemic risk. Theoretically, at least the presence of diversified shareholders may act as a check, in particular at highly interconnected firms, offsetting or at least mitigating the preference for excessive risk-taking. This is because these shareholders will suffer also via their portfolio holdings from a shock due to excessive risk-taking that is propagated and amplified within the financial system.[47]

Regarding *senior management* and *directors*, the distorted incentives-issue came to the forefront in the aftermath of the GFC. In many quarters, seriously flawed *compensation* schemes and skewed incentives for board members and senior management were seen as one major contributing factor, or even the single most important cause.[48] Not surprisingly, regulators reacted most swiftly to the financial crisis by providing for micro-prudential requirements regarding compensation.

The *FSB* set 'the tone at the top' by establishing high-level principles of sound compensation practices,[49] which, in turn, were elaborated by the Basel Committee.[50] Numerous regulatory initiatives at the level of the UK, Germany, Switzerland, the US, and the EU,[51] among others, implemented these standards in great(er) detail or went even further. For a cross-country comparison, one way would be to divide

[47] See Gordon, J, 'Corporate Governance and Executive Compensation in Financial Firms: The Case for Convertible Equity-based Pay' (2012) *Columbia Business Law Review* 834, 839–41.

[48] See Council Directive 2010/76/EU amending Directives 2006/48/EC and 2006/49/EC as regards capital requirements for the trading book and for re-securitisations, and the supervisory review of remuneration policies (2010) OJ L 329/3, recitals 1–4; known as Capital Requirements Directive III—CRD III. However, if benchmarked against shareholder interests empirical support for the flawed incentives-thesis, is mixed, at best. Indeed, a succinct summary of the findings of several studies on the effects of remuneration arrived at the following conclusion: 'shareholders gave CEOs the incentives to take on risk, which happened not to pay out in this realisation [ie the GFC]', Mehran, H, Morrison, A, and Shapiro, J, 'Corporate Governance and Banks—What Have we Learned from the Financial Crisis?' in Dewatripont, M and Freixas, X (eds), *The Crisis Aftermath: New Regulatory Paradigms* (2012) 11, 19; similarly Avgouleas, E and Cullen, J, 'Market Discipline and EU Corporate Governance Reform in the Banking Sector: Merits, Fallacies, and Cognitive Boundaries' (2014) 41 *Journal of Law and Society* 28, 46; De Young, R, Peng, EY, and Yan, M, 'Executive Compensation and Business Policy Choices at U.S. Commercial Banks' (2013) 48 *Journal of Financial and Quantitative Analysis* 165, 193 ('bank CEOs respond[ed] in a systematic fashion to wealth incentives'); cf Conyon, MJ, Fernandes, N, Ferreira, MA, Matos, P, and Murphy, KJ, *The Executive Compensation Controversy: A Transatlantic Analysis* (2011) 112. But see de Haan, J and Vlahu, R, Corporate Governance of Banks: A Survey (July 2013), DNB Working Paper No 386, 34–5, for a somewhat different assessment based on a partly different set of studies.

[49] Financial Stability Board, Principles for Sound Compensation Practices (April 2009) (at the time of publication, the FSB still figured as the Financial Stability Forum—FSF); Financial Stability Board, Principles of Sound Compensation Practices—Implementation Standards (September 2009).

[50] Basel Committee on Banking Supervision, Compensation Principles and Standards—Assessment Methodology (2010), 112.

[51] For an overview see Ferrarini, G and Ungureanu, MC, 'Economics, Politics, and the International Principles for Sound Compensation Practices: An Analysis of Executive Pay at European Banks' (2011) 64 *Vanderbilt Law Review* 431, 467–9; more briefly Mülbert, n 46 above, 32–6.

the different components of micro-prudential compensation regulation into the following categories:

(i) field of application; eg, institutions covered (type, size, etc.) and persons covered (board members, top executives, individual risk-takers, others);
(ii) governance structures, eg, remuneration committee at board level/at the top management level;
(iii) substantive rules on remuneration systems; eg, structure, performance assessment for variable compensation, time-horizon for payout of variable compensation, malus components/clawback provisions, limits on fixed bonuses, etc.; and
(iv) transparency and disclosure of compensation packages.

Criticism based in psychological insights as to the effectiveness of regulating compensation[52] notwithstanding, the *EU* went even further when adopting the CRD IV. The Directive not only maintains the very strict detailed rules provided for by the CRD III[53]—arguably 'the world's toughest restrictions on cash bonuses in banks'[54]—but also adds an additional feature known as a bonus cap and requires group-wide compliance with these rules; ie, even for subsidiaries outside the EU. In a nutshell:

- With a view to discouraging risk-taking that exceeds the level of institutions' tolerated risk Article 94(1)(f) requires an appropriate balance between fixed and variable (ie, performance-based) components of executive pay, applying both to senior management and to certain other employees (risk-takers, staff engaged in control functions and highly paid employees (Article 92(2)).
- Assessment of individual performance and calculation of individual remuneration as the regime's key issues are subject to a variety of determinants, Article 94(1). For example, institutions must take into account both financial and non-financial criteria (lit a), set up a multi-year framework to ensure assessment is based on long-term performance (lit b), include adjustments for all types of current or future risks (lit k) and provide for certain deferral arrangements (lit m).
- The 'bonus cap' provided for by Article 94(1)(g) limits the variable component to a maximum ratio of 100 per cent of the fixed component unless Member States permit the institution's shareholders to approve a higher maximum ratio

[52] eg Winter, J, 'The Financial Crisis: Does Good Corporate Governance Matter and How to Achieve it?' in Wymeersch, E, Hopt, KJ, and Ferrarini, G (eds), *Financial Regulation and Supervision* (2012) 368, 382–3 n 12.25–12.26.

[53] Council Directive 2010/76/EU, n 48 above, Annex I 1.

[54] cf Moloney, N, 'EU Financial Market Regulation after the Global Financial Crisis: "More Europe" or More Risks?' (2010) 47(5) *Common Market Law Review* 1317, 1363 (with references in n 275).

provided the overall level of the variable component does not exceed 200 per cent of the fixed component of total remuneration.

- The remuneration committee, existing at larger, more complex institutions and composed solely of non-executive board members has to prepare the board decisions regarding remuneration, Article 95(2), thereby taking into account 'the long-term interests of shareholders, investors and other stakeholders in the institution and the public interest'[55] when preparing decisions on remuneration.

Apart from altering incentives for directors and senior managers via targeted rules limiting the permissible content of compensation schemes, proposals for *other mechanisms* designed to alter incentives did not gain traction.[56] Such mechanisms basically work by incorporating these interests into a bank's corporate objective by mandatory law or, alternatively, by either stipulating a fiduciary duty of directors and officers to depositors, and even to other debtholders or by direct representation of creditors on boards.[57] Ultimately, for these mechanisms to be effective, directors and senior managers must face personal liability for a failure to properly take into account the interests of other constituencies. However, apart from the problem of how to balance the different interests involved, imposing liability on directors and senior managers with a view to promoting financial stability is particularly problematic. First, systemic risk increasing decisions may result in inflicting financial losses on other banks, but not necessarily on the institution taking the risk increasing action. Second, an increase in systemic risk may well result from other banks imitating the business strategy, risk strategy, etc. of a first-mover bank (herding). More generally, liability rules are ill-suited to deal with the fact that, because of (large) banks' interconnectedness due to contractual or indirect contagion channels, a (large) bank's funding and investment decisions may have negative external effects on other banks and, hence, contribute to an overall increase in systemic risk, while not necessarily increasing idiosyncratic risk.

Altering *shareholders'* incentives so that they favour a financial firm taking on less risk reinforces similar changes to the incentives for senior management and the board, but would also work as a stand-alone solution. Abolishing limited liability, at least for certain key decisions taken by shareholders, would realign incentives, but this mechanism faces similar problems with the personal liability of directors and senior managers. Alternatively, restrictions on capital

[55] See below text accompanying n 87 as to the reference to the public interest.

[56] But see Armour, J and Gordon, J, 'Systemic Harms and Shareholder Value' (2014) *Journal of Legal Analysis* 35, 61–76 expanding personal liability for those controlling or monitoring systemically important forms by relaxing the shareholder value norm; Ellis, L, Haldane, A, and Moshirian, F, 'Systemic Risk, Governance and Global Financial Stability' (2014) 45 *Journal of Banking & Finance* 175, 180: extending control rights beyond shareholders to debtholders.

[57] For a brief discussion of these mechanisms see Mülbert, n 46 above, 37–8; Mülbert, PO and Citlau, R, The Uncertain Role of Banks' Corporate Governance in Systemic Risk Regulation (2011), ECGI Law Working Paper No 179/2011, 33–6.

distributions in the form of dividends and share repurchases could partly realign shareholders' incentives with regulatory objectives, eg if a firm may not make a distribution that, added to losses under certain hypothesized stress scenarios, would reduce the firm's regulatory capital below some predefined threshold. Similarly, the bail-in mechanisms could also serve to reshape the incentive structure for shareholders accordingly, if they would face a credible threat of being substantially diluted in a bail-in. Hence, a bail-in must not be limited to a write-down of debt, but must provide for (the possibility of) a mandatory conversion of debt to equity at a point in time when, despite the firm's losses, equity has not yet been fully wiped out, eg when Tier 1 capital is impaired, and at a conversion rate well above the 'fair' conversion ratio (mark-up of 10–25 per cent), ie to the financial detriment of existing shareholders.

(II) *Non-bank financial institutions*

At non-bank financial institutions, incentive distortions are arguably even less of a problem than at banks. Nevertheless, the EU extended micro-prudential compensation regulation in a first step also to cover managers of (non-UCITS) alternative investment funds, and, most recently, even introduced a bank-like most detailed regime for collective investment schemes.[58]

(c) *Strong paternalistic interventions*

Other tools for curbing the riskiness of individual firms that are in use or, at least, under discussion, are of an even stronger paternalistic character.

(I) *Requiring a financial institution to be smart*

A first set of strong paternalistic tools aims at making financial institutions into more sophisticated investors. They should understand the instruments they are investing in, and the risks associated with these products. An example are the investor due diligence requirements for banks and investment firms provided for by the EU Capital Requirements Regulation, requiring these investors to state, *inter alia*, that they have a thorough understanding of all the risk characteristics of a securitization position, including an understanding of the risk characteristics of the exposures underlying the securities position (look-through rule).[59]

[58] Council Directive 2011/61/EU, n 42 above, Article 13 (AIFMs); Council Directive 2009/65/EC, n 41 above, Articles 14a, 14b (as amended by Council Directive 2014/91/EU amending Directive 2009/65/EC on the coordination of laws, regulations and administrative provisions relating to undertakings for collective investment in transferable securities (UCITS) as regards depositary functions, remuneration policies and sanctions (2014) OJ L 275/186).

[59] Article 406 of Council Regulation (EU) No 575/2013 on prudential requirements for credit institutions and investment firms and amending Regulation (EU) No 648/2012 (2013) OJ L 176/1; known as the Capital Requirements Regulation—CRR.

In a similar vein, the regulator limits the freedom of supervised financial institutions to rely on external credit ratings.[60] For example, the CRD IV requires institutions to have internal methodologies for assessing the credit risk of exposures that do 'not rely solely or mechanically on external credit ratings'[61] and an amendment to the Credit Rating Agencies Regulation has extended this approach to financial institutions in general.[62] Although the international drive to reduce the overreliance on ratings is motivated by reducing the financial stability-threatening herding and cliff effects,[63] requiring banks and investment firms to become more sophisticated with respect to the assessment of financial positions they take, this will also mitigate risk at firm level.

(II) *Investment restrictions on banks*

Restrictions regarding the spectrum of instruments banks are allowed to invest in are a rather intrusive tool for mitigating the risk of individual firms. Restrictions on large exposures to individual firms and to groups of connected counterparties have long been known. For example, the Basel Committee on Banking Supervision published pertinent standards in 1991[64] and, very recently, a revised framework to be applied in 2019.[65] The revised framework provides for a general limit to all of a bank's exposure to a single counterparty or group of connected counterparties (including exposures to funds, securitization structures and collective investment undertakings), set at 25 per cent of a bank's Tier 1 capital and designed so that the maximum loss a bank could suffer would not endanger its survival as a going concern. The lower limit set at 15 per cent for exposures between banks that have been designated globally systemically important banks (GSIBs) contributes towards the reduction of system-wide contagion risk and the mitigation of systemic risk.

The bluntest instrument is to constrain the range of financial instruments a bank or another financial institution is allowed to invest in. This idea has gained track in the form of structural regulation, ie ringfencing of retail services (UK: Vickers) or

[60] Initiated by the FSB; see Financial Stability Board, Principles for Reducing Reliance on CRA Ratings (2010); for an international overview of the regulatory initiatives implemented, underway, or still outstanding, see Financial Stability Board, Thematic Review on FSB Principles for Reducing Reliance on CRA Ratings (2014).

[61] Council Directive 2013/36/EU, n 30 above, Article 79(b). Specifically with respect to the use of external ratings in determining the regulatory capital requirements on exposure from securitizations, see Basel Committee on Banking Supervision, Revision to the Securitisation Framework (2014).

[62] See Council Regulation (EU) No 462/2013 amending Regulation (EC) No 1060/2009 on credit rating agencies (2013) OJ L 146/1: amending CRA I (2009) through Article 5a.

[63] Financial Stability Board, Principles for Reducing Reliance on CRA Ratings (2010), 1; see also Basel Committee on Banking Supervision, Basel III: A Global Regulatory Framework for More Resilient Banks and Banking Systems (2011), 4 n 15.

[64] Basel Committee on Banking Supervision, Measuring and Controlling Large Credit Exposures (1991).

[65] Basel Committee on Banking Supervision, Supervisory Framework for Measuring and Controlling Large Exposures (2014). The rules deviate partially from the rules for the control of large exposures provided for in Part Four of Council Regulation (EU) No 575/2013, n 59 above.

structural separation (US: Volcker rule; EU: *Liikanen*).[66] More selective prohibitions are less problematic since restrictions of the investment universe for financial institutions will be less far-reaching and, thus, the structure of portfolios will be less uniform. However, since such prohibitions could only be justified by market failures; ie, if in financial firms, despite all attempts at making them more sophisticated, investors were still to buy products they do not understand, the alternative would be an outright ban on certain products, most notably overly complex structured products.

(III) *Investment restrictions on non-bank financial institutions*

Regarding non-bank financial institutions, micro-prudential investment restrictions are common in the insurance sector[67] and for institutional investors; eg, collective investment schemes and the funds industry.

IV. Macro-Prudential Risk Management: Reducing (Systemic) Risk for the Financial System

1. Systemic risk

A consensus definition of systemic risk has not yet evolved.[68] However, the numerous proposals[69] can be grouped into two categories, depending on whether material harm to the real economy forms part of the definition or not. If one includes the negative impact on the real economy, as most definitions do,[70] and abstracts minor deviations that are very often only linguistic in nature, a reasonable working definition is the risk of 'disruption to financial services caused by a significant impairment of all or parts of the ... financial system that have the potential to have serious negative consequences for the ... [financial] market and the real economy'.[71]

[66] See Section V.2 in more detail.

[67] See the Chapter by Everson in this volume.

[68] Galati, G and Moessner, R, Macroprudential Policy—a Literature Review (December 2010), DNB Working Paper No 267, 12–16.

[69] For a very recent overview see Smaga, P, The Concept of Systemic Risk (2014), SRC Special Paper No 5, 23–4 (Annex 1).

[70] For definitions not including negative effects on the real economy see, eg Scott, HS, 'Reducing Systemic Risk through the Reform of Capital Regulation' (2010) 13(3) *Journal of International Economic Law* 763; Scott, HS, 'The Reduction of Systemic Risk in the United States Financial System' (2010) 33 *Harvard Journal of Law & Public Policy* 671, 673; Mülbert and Citlau, n 57 above, 13–14.

[71] See Council Regulation (EU) No 1092/2010 on European Union macro-prudential oversight of the financial system and establishing a European Systemic Risk Board (2010) OJ L 331/1, recital 27. For very

2. Causes of systemic risks

A generally accepted framework for classifying the different causes of systemic risk has not yet evolved. However, any classification should reflect that in the run-up phase to a systemic shock/event, four steps, at least, can be distinguished:[72]

- (i) an initial shock to one or several financial institutions, often resulting from exogenous developments outside the financial sector, eg recession or natural disaster;
- (ii) transmission of the initial shock to other financial firms; ie, contagion of other interconnected firms, resulting in an amplification of the initial shock;
- (iii) stress caused to other financial firms by the propagated shock; and
- (iv) further amplification because of second-round effects.

The initial shock will rarely be enough to cause a systemic event, but requires amplification within the financial system by transmission to other financial firms and subsequent second-round effects.[73] Systemic risks, then, are those factors that cause an initial shock to evolve into a systemic event. As a corollary, systemic risk is not a binary state of the financial system but a varying quantity, and the contribution of one institution to systemic risk in the financial system at a given point in time. The aspect is captured by analysing systemic risk and designing appropriate risk-reducing macro-prudential policies along two dimensions—cross-sectional/structural: distribution of risk across the financial sector at a given point in time, and at varying times: dynamic changes of systemic risk over time[74]—even though the European Systemic Risk Board (ESRB) considers that 'it is difficult to make a clear-cut distinction between the two dimensions given their close interlinkages'.[75] Moreover, whether an initial exogenous shock results in a systemic event crucially depends on its strength and the number and size of financial institutions affected by it. From this follows that, with respect to the objective of reducing systemic risk, other macro-economic policies, such as monetary, exchange rate and fiscal policies, can also promote financial system stability and, hence, are closely related to macro-prudential policy.[76]

similar definitions see International Monetary Fund, Bank for International Settlements and Financial Stability Board, Guidance to Assess the Systemic Importance of Financial Institutions, Markets and Instruments: Initial Considerations, Report to the G-20 Finance Ministers and Central Bank Governors (October 2009), 5–6; European Central Bank, Special Feature B: The Concept of Systemic Risk (December 2009) *Financial Stability Review* 134; Reserve Bank of Australia, n 11 above, 73.

[72] For a somewhat similar approach see Smaga, n 69 above, 13–15.

[73] For details see Brunnermeier, MK and Oehmke, M, 'Bubbles, Financial Crisis, and Systemic Risk' in Constantinides, GM, Harris, M, and Stulz, RM (eds), *Handbook of the Economics of Finance*, (Vol 2B, 2013) 1221, 1245–70; for a brief overview see Mülbert and Citlau, n 57 above, 15–19.

[74] See, eg Borio, n 6 above, 195–202; Schoenmaker, D and Wierts, P, Macroprudential Policy: The Need for a Coherent Policy Framework (2011), DSF Policy Paper Series Paper No 13, 2.

[75] European Systemic Risk Board (ESRB), Recommendation of the European Systemic Risk Board on Intermediate Objectives and Instruments of Macroprudential Policy, ESRB/2013/1 (2013) OJ C 170/01, 170/7.

[76] Reserve Bank of Australia, n 11 above, 99–100 (cf ibid 52: overview on the explicit use of macro-prudential tools in different countries); International Monetary Fund, Key Aspects of Macroprudential Policy (2013), 9–13 n 19–39.

The process just described implies the following non-exhaustive list of major causes of systemic risk;

- large *size* of banks and other financial institutions (too-big-to-fail institutions—TBTF);[77]
- provision of *non-substitutional* (infrastructure) services; eg, central clearing for derivatives and securities markets (CCPs), operation of high-value payment systems;
- *interconnectedness* of firms in the financial sector based on *contractual* ties such as over-the-counter (OTC) derivatives, short-term interbank funding structures, payment systems such as TARGET and CHIPS (bilateral/direct contagion channels) resulting in domino effects; ie, the losses of an institution will spread to its counterparties, thereby being amplified; and
- correlation of risk-portfolios[78]/funding structures/business models (*interconnectedness* due to *indirect* contagion channels, in particular informational) resulting, *inter alia*, in the common exposure to asset price bubbles, sovereign default, liquidity withdrawal by short-term liquidity providers (money market funds), depositor and counterparty runs in case of information deficiencies in the market about the financial situation of banks with similar exposure profiles or business models and fire sale price[79] declines; ie, the sharp decline in prices of a class of assets resulting from an overleveraged financial institution forced to sell assets on a (illiquid) market where high-valuation buyers are not active; eg, because they are financially constrained.

3. Macro-prudential toolkit

To deal with systemic risk a plethora of mechanisms and tools have been put in place or, at least, proposed, often collectively labelled as a 'macro-economic toolkit'. This nondescript designation reflects, *inter alia*, that shocks that evolve into a systemic event will often come from outside the financial system and that for contagion to occur within the financial system factual channels suffice; ie, decisions and actions by individual institutions have negative external effects on other financial institutions, even in the absence of contractual contagion channels. Moreover, systemic risk is time-varying; ie, both within and outside the financial system the

[77] For a contrary view see Scott, 'The Reduction of Systemic Risk in the United States Financial System', n 70 above, 677: absolute size does not pose systemic risk.

[78] The presence of asset correlation can be difficult to determine, though. During the GFC, asset classes, whose prices were previously uncorrelated, experienced a co-movement of prices that could not be explained by fundamental analysis.

[79] See, eg Shleifer, A and Vishny, R, 'Fire Sales in Finance and Macroeconomics' (2011) 25(1) *Journal of Economic Perspectives* 29.

causes for the occurrence of a systemic shock will build up over time. Accordingly, different categories are used for sub-classifications within the macro-economic toolkit reflecting different aspects of macro-prudential policy.[80]

The Chapter by Lastra in this volume provides a comprehensive list of the main tools identified with macro-prudential policy. Other tools (also) pursuing a macro-prudential objective—even though partly not 'prudential' in nature—include:

- improving the resolvability of financial institutions or, as in the case of systemically important financial institutions at the global (G-SIFIs: G-SIBs, G-SIIs and non-bank non-insurer SIFIs) or domestic (D-SIFIs: D-SIBs and others) level, making them resolvable in the first place;[81]
- taxation of the financial sector, eg in the form of a Financial Transaction Tax (FTT) as a turnover tax on financial transactions, a Financial Activities Tax (FAT) based on profits and remuneration, or a Financial Stability Contribution/bank levy on specific components of the balance sheet of financial institutions;[82]
- bankruptcy and insolvency preferences, eg close-out netting protection;[83]
- prohibition of products that can cause a systemic shock, eg possibly uncovered credit default swaps (CDSs);[84]
- incentivizing banks by imposing restrictions on payouts to owners, by constraining banks' future investment strategy and/or by limiting compensation of directors and senior management to take on additional capital above the regulatory capital requirements[85] and, notwithstanding the debt-overhang disincentive

[80] See, eg European Systemic Risk Board, n 75 above, 170/7–170/8 (classification according to five intermediate objectives); Osiński et al., n 14 above, 25 (three categories); International Monetary Fund, n 76 above, 19–22 n 45–52; and Schoenmaker and Wierts, n 74 above, 2: structural and cyclical tools.

[81] See the Chapter by Armour in this volume.

[82] For a discussion of the different instruments, also with a view to reducing systemic risk, see International Monetary Fund, A Fair and Substantial Contribution by the Financial Sector, Final Report for the G-20 (June 2010), 13–14 and, more generally, the contributions in International Monetary Fund, Claessens, S, Kenn, M, and Pazarbasioglu, C (eds), Financial Sector Taxation: The IMF's Report to the G-20 and Background Material (September 2010); de Mooij, R and Nicodeme, G (eds), *Taxation and Regulation of the Financial Sector* (2014).

[83] Whether these protections are necessary to mitigate systemic risk or, on the contrary, contribute to systemic risk, is controversial, though. See, eg Bolton, P and Oehmke, M, Should Derivatives be Privileged in Bankruptcy (2012), Working Paper (forthcoming in *The Journal of Finance*); Duffie, D and Skeel Jr, DA, 'A Dialogue on the Costs and Benefits of Automatic Stays for Derivatives and Repurchase Agreements' in Scott, KE and Taylor, JB (eds), *Bankruptcy not Bailout—a Special Chapter 14* (2012) Part C, 5; Skeel, DA and Jackson, TH, 'Transaction Consistency and the New Finance in Bankruptcy' (2012) 112 *Columbia Law Review* 152; Roe, MJ, 'The Derivative's Market's Payment Priorities as Financial Crisis Accelerator' (2010) 63 *Stanford Law Review* 539.

[84] See Section VI.2(a) with n 131.

[85] Banks operate with capital ratios that are only marginally higher than the regulatory minimum capital requirement. The effect is more pronounced for large banks, though, since a strong inverse relationship between size and capital ratio exists. Given that, high leverage is sometimes explained

(lenders profit more than shareholders with subordinated claims), to replenish an impaired capital base, eg by using contingent capital, instead of shrinking the balance sheet by selling risky assets;[86] and

- requiring a financial institution's directors and senior management to take into account the negative external effects of their decisions on other financial institutions and, thus, the contribution to increasing systemic risk and reducing financial stability. Arguably, the EU CRD IV,[87] whose goal is to promote financial stability (see recitals 47, 50, and 67), attempts to provide for such a mechanism by stipulating that the remuneration committee of a certain (large) bank, when preparing decisions regarding remuneration, has to take the public interest into account. For such an approach to be operational, though, the regulators need to mandate how to measure the contribution of individual firms to systemic risk and, in addition, to set an upper limit for the permitted systemic risk contribution to systemic risk.

4. Efficient level(s) of systemic risk?

The macro-economic toolkit represents a variety of approaches. Some guidance as to which tools should be used under which circumstances and as to how the tools should be calibrated is provided by the distinction between structural and cyclical tools[88] and the ESRB's classification according to five intermediary objectives with respect to macro-prudential policy.[89] The choice of an appropriate macro-prudential target has even been explicitly listed among the open questions, *inter alia*, because identifying robust predictors of crises has proved difficult.[90]

by strong competition in areas where large banks are most active (Hanson et al., n 10 above, 20). Alternatively, large banks could operate that way since they enjoyed the benefit of implicit state guarantees. In that case, the reduction or even removal of these implicit guarantees should result in large banks increasing their capital ratio, even without regulatory intervention.

[86] See, eg Hanson et al., n 10 above, 10–12. However, even with some regulatory incentivization in place, management and shareholders may still prefer balance shrinkage unless there are not enough assets available for sale to restore the regulatory-encouraged higher capital ratio.

[87] Council Directive 2013/36/EU, n 30 above.

[88] International Monetary Fund, n 76 above, 19–22 n 45–52; Schoenmaker and Wierts, n 74 above, 2.

[89] European Systemic Risk Board, n 75 above, 170/8: mitigation/prevention of excessive credit growth and leverage; mitigation/prevention of excessive maturity mismatch and market illiquidity; limitation of direct and indirect exposure concentrations; limitation of the systemic impact of misaligned incentives with a view to reducing moral hazard; strengthening financial infrastructures' resilience.

[90] Reserve Bank of Australia, n 11 above, 52; cf International Monetary Fund, n 76 above, 23 n 54; Ellis et al., n 56 above, 177–8.

Given the existence of workable and reliable quantitative measures for systemic risk and the contributions of individual firms to systemic risk,[91] a more rigorous approach would be to simulate the effects of different tools on the level of systemic risk and to select the most appropriate tools on that basis.[92] Ultimately, this approach raises the question whether 'efficient' systemic risk or even different levels of efficient systemic risk exist,[93] even though systemic risk is solely concerned with negative outcomes for the economy and, if that were the case, how to determine the efficient amount. To compound the problem even more, the choice among different tools will impact financial institutions and markets differently, allowing for different levels of 'efficient' systemic risk. As a corollary, the path-dependency of financial regulation will have an impact on the level of 'efficient' systemic risk for a given financial system.

V. Micro- and Macro-Prudential Risk-Management Tools: Reducing Risk for a Firm and for the Financial System

1. Disclosure

Transparency regarding risk is a necessary prerequisite for effective risk management by individual firms and for the supervisor to assess the riskiness and risk profile of a firm and the systemic risk in the financial system at a given time. Requiring extensive disclosure is, thus, an important tool in the prudential toolkit, even though the effects are somewhat different with respect to disclosure of firm risk and product risk.

[91] See Bisias, D, Flood, MD, Lo, AW, and Valavanis, S, A Survey of Systemic Risk Analytics (2012), US Department of Treasury, Office of Financial Research Paper No 001 (analysing 31 quantitative measures of systemic risk); for a brief survey see Arnold, B, Borio, C, Ellis, L, and Moshirian, F, 'Systemic Risk, Macroprudential Policy Frameworks, Monitoring Financial Systems and the Evolution of Capital Adequacy' (2012) 16 *Journal of Banking & Finance* 3125, 3126.

[92] But see International Monetary Fund, n 76 above, 23 n 54: the benefit of macro-prudential action for the ultimate objective of preventing or mitigating future crises 'remains difficult to quantify'.

[93] See Acharya, VV, 'A Theory of Systemic Risk and Design of Prudential Bank Regulation' (2009) 5 *Journal of Financial Stability* 224, 225: a central issue is to examine proposals for macro-prudential regulation under a common theoretical framework 'that formalizes the (often) implicit objective of ensuring efficient levels of systemic risk failure'.

Disclosure of *firm risk* will enable other market participants to take an informed decision on whether to enter into a business transaction at all or whether to continue doing business with the bank and, if they do, whether to require collateral, etc. On the flip side, under good economic conditions a high level of transparency will increase the probability of a bank run for individual less healthy banks. As a corollary, systemic risk will be reduced because of a lower level of interconnectedness among banks, because shocks will be less amplified since the least shock-resistant banks are excluded from the contractual network and because better information on banks will reduce the risk of information-induced runs, provided that banks do not have to disclose the structure of their risk portfolio.[94] Given these overall beneficial effects,[95] Pillar 3 of the original Basel II framework[96] introduced extensive disclosure obligations for banks covering quantitative and qualitative aspects of overall capital adequacy and capital allocation, as well as risk exposure and assessment but, as the GFC made clear, still failed to improve market discipline to the extent intended.[97] In recognition of notable weaknesses, the Basel Committee enhanced the framework twice.[98] Recently, it undertook a review of the Pillar 3 disclosure requirements and, with a view to strengthening market discipline, and thereby promoting a safe and sound banking system, presented proposals for tightening disclosure requirements and for promoting greater consistency across banks' disclosures.[99]

Disclosure of *product risk*, eg the risks of structured financial products, is different. Risk management at firm level will benefit; investors will better understand the risk profile of the asset and its portfolio effects on their existing portfolio. The impact on systemic risk, however, will be probably small since banks will rarely have an incentive to refrain from producing the negative externalities on other banks that result from building a correlated risk portfolio.

2. Structural prudential regulation

Structural prudential regulation provides for restrictions on the permissible scope of business activities. Such restrictions may serve the dual objectives of reducing the riskiness of individual firms and systemic risk simultaneously. In order

[94] If, for individual banks, herd behaviour is rational (for a model to this effect see Acharya, n 93 above), disclosure of the detailed composition could well increase systemic risk. Reporting to the supervisor is different, though (see ibid, 248).

[95] For an extended discussion see, Bouvard, M, Chaigneau, P, and de Motta, A, 'Transparency in the Financial System: Rollover Risk and Crises', *The Journal of Finance* (forthcoming).

[96] Basel Committee, n 21 above.

[97] Cf FSA, Turner Review, n 2 above, 45–7.

[98] Basel Committee, n 17 above, 28–34; Basel Committee, Pillar 3 Disclosure Requirements for Remuneration (2011).

[99] Basel Committee on Banking Supervision, Review of the Pillar 3 Disclosure Requirements, Consultative Document (2014).

to be effective with respect to both these goals, restrictions must target high-risk business activities with the effect that financial firms will be markedly smaller or otherwise of lesser systemic importance than without the restriction in place.

The former separation of commercial and investment banking activities in the US, mandated by the Banking Act of 1933 as amended by the Glass–Steagall Act and ultimately abolished by the Gramm–Leach–Bliley Act in 1999, is the best-known and most extensive example of structural prudential regulation. Lessons from the GFC have renewed the interest in that type of regulation and resulted in a number of diverging reform projects in the US, the UK, and the EU, all of which, though, fall short of the stringent Glass–Steagall separation.

(a) *Current structural separation model*

In substance, the current structural separation models can be categorized as follows:

- US (Volcker Rule): ban on banking entities engaging in proprietary trading (ie, short-term speculative risk-taking unrelated to client business, as opposed to market-making, underwriting, hedging) and on their investments in, and on their other relationships with hedge funds and private-equity funds;[100]
- EU proposal (*Liikanen*) with similar regimes in place in Germany and France:[101] complex and largest banks are prohibited from engaging in proprietary trading through dedicated desks and personnel, and from investing in hedge funds; in addition, the supervisor can require the separation of certain potentially risky trading activities, eg market-making, if pursuit of such activities is deemed to compromise financial stability;[102] and
- UK (Vickers): retail core services are to be ring-fenced from investment services into a separate, protected entity, with limited intragroup transactions between the ring-fenced entity and the other members of the group.[103]

The narrowest approach in terms of the scope of activities covered is the Volcker Rule, insofar as client-related activities are not covered.[104] The EU proposal is

[100] Dodd–Frank Act, section 619, 12 USC § 1851 (adding new section 13 to the Bank Holding Company Act (BHCA)). The joint Final Regulation of the five regulatory agencies responsible (Federal Reserve/OCC/FDIC/SEC/CFTC).

[101] See Fernandez-Bollo, É, 'Structural Reform and Supervision of the Banking Sector in France' (2013)(1) *Financial Market Trends* 1.

[102] European Commission, Proposal for a Regulation on Structural Measures Improving the Resilience of EU Credit Institutions (2014) COM(2014)43; based on proposals by the High-level Expert Group, n 31 above, 100–2 (known as the Liikanen Group).

[103] Section 142A–142G FSMA as amended by Chapter 33, Part 1 of the Financial Services (Banking Reform) Act 2013; based on proposals by the Independent Commission on Banking, Final Report—Recommendations (2011), 35–77 n 3.1–3.99 (known as the Vickers report).

[104] cf Scott, 'The Reduction of Systemic Risk in the United States Financial System', n 70 above, 676–7 (doubting the potential to reduce systemic risk).

somewhat broader, since it provides for the possibility that the supervisor can order separation even of market-making; ie, order the bank to end these activities—eg, by selling these activities to an entity that is not part of the banking group. The reasons for these restrictions on financial activities at the level of a banking group are stated by the recitals to the draft EU Regulation as follows: reducing excessive risk-taking, shielding institutions carrying out activities that deserve a public safety net from losses incurred as a result of other activities, refocusing banks on their core relationship-oriented role of serving the real economy, and avoiding bank capital being excessively allocated to trading at the expense of lending to the non-financial economy.[105] All these objectives qualify the proposal as a macro-economic tool. Protection of the individual firm against excessive risk-taking is not given priority; the proposal does not even purport that proprietary trading is a riskier activity than lending, for example.

In contrast, the UK approach mandates ring-fencing of core retail activities from investment services with a view to ensuring that deposit, payment, and overdraft services are continuously available to individuals (consumers) and small businesses, even when the banking group is distressed. Conceptually, the micro-prudential perspective dominates. In particular, banking groups are not required to (re)allocate their capital to core banking activities but in the interest of depositors and consumers only to set their retail activities aside.

(b) *Assessment*

Total structural separation as prescribed in the US, Germany, France, and, with the exception of the UK, possibly even EU-wide, is credited with making banks somewhat smaller and less complex and shielding them from market risk and earnings volatility, as well as from direct and indirect shocks to the prohibited asset classes.[106] On the other hand, banks may pull back from market making and other client-related activities (US) or will even be prohibited from these activities (EU), and will be less diversified and possibly less profitable. Defending or rejecting total separation on the basis of a cost-benefit analysis seems difficult though, since the objective is to reduce systemic risk. Thus, the question may rather be whether alternatives to total structural separation exist that have the same dampening effect on systemic risk, but are less costly for banks and consumers,[107] or that are more effective in reducing systemic risk. If the prohibited activities themselves gave reason for systemic concerns the question would be particularly acute since

[105] European Commission, Proposal, n 102 above, recital 12.

[106] See Gambacorta, L and van Rixtel, A, Structural Bank Regulation Initiatives: Approaches and Implications (2013), BIS Working Papers No 412, 16.

[107] Cf Vinals, J, Pazarbasioglu, C, Surti, J, Narain, A, Erbenova, M, and Chow, J, Creating a Safer Financial System: Will the Volcker, Vickers, and Liikanen Structural Measures Help? (2013), IMF Staff Discussion Note 13/4, 12.

the current approaches focus exclusively on banks and allow for a migration of the prohibited activities to the non-bank sector.

Against this backdrop, the ring-fencing approach— ie, providing for mandatory restrictions on corporate structure—is credited with being superior.[108] It should be noted though, that the goal of the UK model is somewhat less ambitious than the objective of total separation. Basically, the ring-fencing approach deals with the too-important-to-fail dilemma, which, given the current structure of UK banking, is tantamount to the TBTF-dilemma, by mandating group structures that, in the interest of depositors, consumers, and small and medium-sized enterprises (SMEs), allow for easy reorganization of the banking entity that provides core banking services for that group.

3. Deposit insurance

Deposit insurance is a tool for reducing both individual firm risk and systemic risk. Banks, because of their maturity transfer function, are prone to a liquidity risk in the case of a bank run. Deposit insurance reduces that risk by eliminating the rational incentive for depositors to withdraw their deposits if the bank (possibly) faces financial difficulties. At the same time, if the bank does not face idiosyncratic problems but suffers from a problem other banks have as well—or, at least, may have as well—depositors at other banks will also run unless also protected by deposit insurance.

On the other hand, deposit insurance lowers the incentive for depositors to monitor the deposit-taking institution. Managers will respond to that by taking on more risk, eg by pursuing a riskier business strategy, such as operating with a smaller capital ratio. In theory, the effect should be most pronounced for those banks that rely more heavily on deposit-financing, ie mostly smaller banks. However, insofar as very small depositors lack the ability to monitor, as coverage is capped, eg EU-wide at €100,000, and as deposits by other financial institutions are excluded from insurance coverage, the distortions from deposit insurance will be minor. Moreover, the distortive effects will further be mitigated insofar as banks rely on short-term funding by other financial institutions since these institutions have both an incentive to monitor and the ability to run overnight. Finally, if funding by the industry is risk-sensitive—eg if contributions by the firms covered are calibrated to a firm's idiosyncratic risk incurred[109] and its contribution

[108] See Blundell-Wignall, A, Atkinson, P, and Roulet, C, 'Bank Business Models and the Separation Issue' (2014) 2013(2) *Financial Market Trends* 1 (defending the ring-fencing proposal of the OECD Secretariat).

[109] As to this, see Council Directive 2014/49/EU on deposit guarantee schemes (2014) OJ L 173/149, recital 36. For an interesting 'indirect' approach, see Kose, J, Saunders, A, and Senbet, LW, 'A Theory of Bank Regulation and Management Compensation' (2000) 13(1) *Review of Financial Studies*

to systemic risk[110]—this will mitigate the incentive to engage in riskier activities and will make the firm 'internalize' the negative externalities that contribute to systemic risk.

Finally, these effects from deposit insurance are irrespective of whether the guarantee is extended by a government institution or by a private collective scheme organized by the industry. Moreover, they go beyond those of investor-compensation schemes.[111] Their objective is limited to protecting individual investors from financial losses and does not extend to shielding the firm against financial risks from non-compliance with conduct-of-business rules.

4. Mandatory central clearing

Mandatory central counterparty clearing reduces both firm-level and systemic risk, albeit at the cost of hard-wiring into regulation a new class of systemically important financial institutions (CCPs). CCP clearing of securities transactions will reduce counterparty risk since a firm, instead of having multiple counterparties, is left with the CCP as its only counterparty and is, thus, in a much better position to offset claims from the securities transactions entered into with different counterparties. In addition, a market participant facing liquidity problems is somewhat shielded against the risk that his OTC counterparties will run. At the same time, a shock from the failure of a firm (hopefully) stops with the CCP instead of being spread within the financial system through the contract-based interconnectedness of financial firms. Hence, the US as well as the EU, as a lesson from the GFC have introduced regulation with a view to subjecting OTC derivatives to mandatory clearing and settlement[112] as well as mandatory trading on exchanges[113] while the newly created reporting requirements also extend to non-centrally cleared OTC derivatives.[114]

95: in order to incentivize bank owners to put in place optimal management-compensation structures, features of a bank's management-compensations schedule should be explicitly incorporated in the risk-based pricing of deposit insurance.

[110] See Acharya, VV, Santos, JAC, and Yorulmazer, T, 'Systemic Risk and Deposit Insurance Premiums' (2010) 16(1) *Economic Policy Review* 89.

[111] See, eg Council Directive 97/9/EC on investor-compensation schemes (1997) OJ L 84/22.

[112] Council Regulation (EU) No 648/2012, n 43 above, Articles 4–13.

[113] Council Regulation (EU) No 600/2014 on markets in financial instruments and amending Regulation (EU) No 648/2012 (2014) OJ L 173/84, Articles 28–34; known as MiFIR.

[114] For details see the Chapter by Ferrarini and Saguato in this volume.

VI. Micro- and Macro-Prudential Regulation: Policy Issues

1. Hierarchy or coexistence?

In the wake of the GFC, macro-prudential policy has substantially gained in importance with respect to micro-prudential policy, a development sometimes even referred to as a paradigm shift.[115] Increasingly, prudential regulation is tasked with primarily pursuing a macro-economic objective, taking precedence over and above microeconomic regulation of financial firms.[116] Still more cautious positions are to be found, assigning macro-prudential regulation a complementary/supplementary role.[117]

In particular, the latter holds true for the three international standard setting bodies.[118] IOSCO recognizes a set of three objectives of securities regulation: protecting investors, ensuring that markets are fair, efficient, and transparent, reducing systemic risk.[119] The Basel Committee, commenting on the revised version of its Core Principles for Effective Banking Supervision, explicitly states, that the primary objective for banking supervision is the promotion of safety and soundness of banks and the banking system (Core Principle 1), even though the new Core Principles have been widened, *inter alia*, in order to include 'the importance of applying a system-wide, macro perspective to the microprudential supervision of banks to assist in identifying, analysing and taking pre-emptive action to address systemic risk'.[120] Finally, the International Association of Insurance Supervisors, even while admitting that insurance supervisors should address financial and systemic stability concerns,[121] maintains as core principle ICP 1.3: 'The principal objectives of supervision promote the maintenance of a fair, safe and stable insurance sector for the benefit and protection of policyholders.'

These more cautious positions may be informed by some of the following considerations: (i) macro-economic tools mostly operate at the level of individual firms[122] and, hence, it is often difficult to separate micro- and macro-economic objectives;

[115] Arnold et al., n 91 above, 3127.

[116] See, eg, Acharya, n 93 above, 225; Scott, 'The Reduction of Systemic Risk in the United States Financial System', n 70 above, 673.

[117] See, eg, Osiński et al., n 14 above, 5; see the Chapter by Alexander in this volume.

[118] For a different assessment see Joint Forum, n 6 above, 28–9.

[119] International Organization of Securities Commissions, n 39 above, 3.

[120] Basel Committee, n 9 above, 4 n 16 and 2 n 6 (see also 5–6 n 20–1).

[121] International Association of Insurance Supervisors, n 20 above, 4 n 2.

[122] See the Chapter by Alexander in this volume.

(ii) explicit macro-economic policy is still in its early stage[123] even though some of its tools have been around for many years; (iii) as a corollary, appropriate institutional structures for an effective macro-economic policy, including its enforcement, are still under construction or in the testing-phase; and (iv) macro-prudential policy is, at times, difficult to communicate to politicians and the general public, in particular since the gradual building up of systemic risk is accompanied by low market volatility and seemingly strong economic data.[124]

2. Tensions

Micro- and macro-prudential regulation can coexist, overlap, or, at times, conflict with respect to, *inter alia*, the regulatory objectives, the regulatory tools, the risk perimeter, and the institutional perimeter.[125] Prudential tools that operate at the level of individual firms will perform a micro- or a macro-prudential function, or even both, depending on the objective for which they are used. In turn, the micro-economic goal of promoting the soundness of financial firms may conflict with the objective of reducing systemic risk. More generally, traditional micro-economic policy and macro-economic policy will occasionally get into conflict because of their interaction on financial markets, the structure of the network among financial institutions and the behaviour of other financial institutions. In the following, some examples will be provided.

(a) *Easing credit risk transfer (CRT)*

The efficient distribution of risks is among the core functions of the financial system. Hence, the easing of CRT among financial institutions and to investors not only makes it easier for an individual bank to restore its impaired regulatory capital adequacy requirements, but also promotes the efficient allocation of risk. The effect is most pronounced if risks can be reallocated to financial entities not subject to regulatory capital requirements.[126] Otherwise, the banking sector's intermediation function will not be strengthened.

Traditional tools for transferring credit risk are the outright transfer of the loan and, from an economic perspective at least, the taking of an asset as collateral for the loan and taking out an insurance. Securitization can be characterized as an

[123] Ellis et al., n 56 above, 176. See, eg, Osiński et al., n 14 above, 6: analysis and understanding of the concept of systemic risk and the policy instruments necessary to deal with them are still developing.

[124] Cf Arnold et al., n 91 above, 3129: the system looks strongest precisely when it is most fragile ('paradox of financial instability').

[125] See Osiński et al., n 14 above, 7–8.

[126] See, eg, Bank of England and European Central Bank, The Case for a Better Functioning Securitisation Market in the European Union (2014), a Discussion Paper, 8.

advanced version of the first mechanisms, effecting a transfer of the risky assets to investors by way of an special purpose vehicle (SPV) issuing asset-backed securities (ABSs) to investors, eg asset-backed commercial paper (ABCP). Credit derivatives such as credit default swaps (CDSs), around since the 1990s, are akin to collateral and insurance in that credit risk is transferred without also transferring the risky asset.

Before the GFC, for the reasons just mentioned, securitization as an instrument for transferring risk was considered a major advance in financial engineering. The assessment of credit derivatives with a view to financial stability was more guarded[127] though, not the least because they offer a fast and easy way to transfer credit risks at low transaction costs among the contracting parties.

Indeed, as evidenced by the GFC, securitization and other techniques for easing the transfer of credit risks can result in a system-wide 'pollution' with a particular risk enhancing systemic risk because, eg, more financial entities will suffer from a shock. In addition, risk dispersion makes monitoring more difficult. Lack of information on the allocation of risk impairs market discipline and increases the threat of runs by depositors and other counterparties. Finally, supervision will be impaired, in particular if risk is transferred to actors outside the regulatory perimeter. Since these detrimental effects regarding systemic risk and financial stability are negative externalities produced by the acquirers, they occur irrespective of whether the risk is transferred to investors who are less informed or less sophisticated. However, less informed or less sophisticated investors may take on more risk thus producing stronger negative externalities.

In reaction to the notorious role of ABSs involving complex structures and poorly underwritten loans in the GFC, the Basel Committee on Banking Supervision[128] as well as the EU,[129] substantially tightened the (Basel II) requirements for securitizations involving banks and investment firms as originators, sponsors, or investors.

[127] See, eg, Basel Committee on Banking Supervision, the Joint Forum (BCBS, IAS, and IOSCO), Credit Risk Transfer (2005); Duffie, D, Innovations in Credit Risk Transfer: Implications for Financial Stability (2008), BIS Working Paper No 255; but see Wagner, W and Marsh, IW, 'Credit Risk Transfer and Financial Sector Stability' (2006) 2 *Journal of Financial Stability* 173. Cf Nijskens, R and Wagner, W, 'Credit Risk Transfer Activities and Systemic Risk: How Banks Became Less Risky Individually but Posed Greater Risks to the Financial System at the Same Time' (2011) 35 *Journal of Banking & Finance* 1391 (focusing on the effects of CRT activities on transferring banks).

[128] Basel Committee, n 17 above, 4–7; for very recent additional enhancements see Basel Committee, n 61 above. cf the IOSCO recommendations: International Organization of Securities Commissions, Unregulated Financial Markets and Products, Final Report (2009), 18–20 n 58–68; International Organization of Securities Commissions, Global Developments in Securitisation Regulation, Final Report (2012), 48–50 (five recommendations).

[129] See Council Directive 2009/111/EC amending Directives 2006/487/EC, 2006/49/EC and 2007/64/EC as regards banks affiliated to central institutions, certain own funds items, large exposures, supervisory arrangements, and crisis management (2009) OJ L 302/97 (5%-retention, investor due diligence); known as CRD II; Council Directive 2010/76/EU, n 48 above (1250% risk weight). Both Directives have been repealed; securitisations are now governed by Council Regulation (EU) No 575/2013, n 59 above, Articles 406 *et seq*.

The ensuing significant downturn in securitization transactions on the European market recently prompted the Bank of England and the European Central Bank jointly to present reform ideas for a better functioning securitization market with a view to strengthening securitizations, as both a funding tool and risk-transfer tool.[130]

The EU's reaction to credit derivatives in the form of CDSs was even more adverse. Being unofficially credited with having distorted the market for Greek sovereign bonds in 2008 and for the sovereign bonds of other Member States causing higher funding costs,[131] the EU imposed a ban for uncovered sovereign CDSs.[132]

(b) *Requiring highly liquid high-quality assets*

Micro-prudential regulation rarely mandates a specific way to mitigate risk, ie whether to take out insurance or to take assets as collateral etc. The regulation of central counterparties provides a notable exception. Under EU law, eg a CCP is required to take highly liquid assets with minimal credit and market risk as collateral.[133] In addition, the demand for such assets also increased because of the Basel III liquidity requirements framework. As a consequence, a market for lending and borrowing that type of collateral has sprung up between banks, which opens an additional channel for the direct propagation of shocks.[134]

(c) *Requiring/encouraging uniformity*

Generally, every kind of micro-prudential regulation that, in seeking to reduce risk for the individual bank, causes banks to act in a (more) uniform way—either on the funding side or by holding more highly correlated risk portfolios—will increase systemic risk.[135] In particular, the Basel III framework regarding liquidity risk, which

[130] Bank of England and European Central Bank, n 126 above. cf the recommendations regarding, *inter alia*, risk retention and disclosure requirements by the International Organization of Securities Commissions (IOSCO), Global Developments in Securitisation Regulation, Final Report (2012), aimed at ensuring the sound and sustainable development of securitisation markets.

[131] But see Criado, S, Degabriel, L, Lewandowska, M, Lindén, S, and Ritter, P, Report on Sovereign CDS (2010): no conclusive evidence (task force comprising staff from DG COMP, CG ECFIN, and DG MARKT).

[132] See Council Regulation (EU) No 236/2012 on short selling and certain aspects of credit default swaps (2012) OJ L 86/1, Article 14.

[133] Council Regulation (EU) No 648/2012, n 43 above, Article 46.

[134] Because of market size, the development concerns supervisors.

[135] cf Battiston, S, Gatti, DD, Gallegatti, M, Greenwald, B, and Stiglitz, JE, 'Default Cascades: When Does Risk Diversification Increase Stability?' (2012) 8 *Journal of Financial Stability* 138. Note, however, that the impact of a bank's asset diversification on systemic risk depends on whether the bank engages in idiosyncratic diversification or correlated diversification. In the first case, the institution will be more resilient and systemic risk will even decrease whereas in the second case systemic risk will increase (cf Brunnermeier et al., n 14 above, 27). Relatedly, non-linear correlated diversification may not result in increasing systemic risk, see van Oordt, MRC, 'Securitization and the Dark Side of Diversification' (2014) 23(2) *Journal of Financial Intermediation* 214 (discussing tranching of pooled loan portfolios as a tool for non-linear diversification among financial institutions).

requires banks to comply with two new standards for funding liquidity—Liquidity Coverage Ratio (LCR) and Net Stable Funding Ratio (NSFR)[136]—will result in banks holding similar portfolios of high-quality liquid assets, with sovereign bonds forming a substantial proportion. The uniformity effect is exacerbated if regulators, in the interest of promoting sovereign bonds, continue to assign zero risk weight to sovereign bonds. Moreover, micro-prudential regulation targeting large(r) banks without applying the proportionality principle with respect to smaller banks may increase systemic risk if smaller banks are driven out of business by the complexity and high costs of regulation.

For the same reasons, encouraging competition among banks may also increase the correlation of banks' risk portfolio and increase systemic risk if, under these conditions, all banks invest in similar sectors.[137] Hence, the effects from an increase in financial instability must be weighted against the efficiency gains arising from greater competition.[138]

(d) *Stress-testing*

Stress tests are an important forward-looking risk-management tool. Stress tests by individual firms, in order to be meaningful, require that they take macro-economic factors and developments into account. However, stress-testing at the micro-economic level is limited insofar as individual firms are not able to conduct a system-wide stress test which gives a more precise picture of the risks for individual firms, revealing, eg, additional channels of contagion, feedback loops, and second-round effects. Hence, macro-stress tests by the supervisor can result in a different risk assessment of a firm than the micro-oriented self-assesment. For banks, in particular, this creates room for tensions within the supervisory review and evaluation process (SREP) introduced in Pillar 2 of the Basel II framework. As part of that process, the supervisor reviews the adequacy of risk assessment of the institution, including the stress tests conducted.[139] Differences in the stress tests conducted by the institution and the supervisor may well result in (substantial) differences regarding the assessment of the regulatory capital ratio.

[136] See Basel Committee on Banking Supervision, Basel III: International Framework for Liquidity Risk Measurement, Standards and Monitoring (2010): minimum funding requirements for 30 days (LCR) and one year (NSFR), respectively.

[137] But see Anginer, D, Demirgüc-Kunt, A, and Zhu, M, How Does Bank Competition Affect Systemic Stability? (2012), World Bank Policy Working Paper No 5981: greater competition increases risk portfolio diversification (for an overview of the literature on the effects of competition for the resilience of the individual firm, see ibid 3–4).

[138] Acharya, n 93 above, 249.

[139] cf Basel Committee on Banking Supervision, Principles for Sound Stress Testing Practices and Supervision (2009).

3. Including shadow banking within the perimeter of prudential regulation

(a) *Definitions, functions, risks*

Shadow banking has widely come to be understood as 'credit intermediation involving entities and activities (full or partially) outside the regular banking system'[140] or non-bank credit intermediation, in short. Alternative definitions abound, also focusing on both entities and activities[141] or, alternatively, on entities or activities.[142] For example, the International Monetary Fund very recently introduced an 'activity-based' definition: financing of banks and non-bank financial institutions through non-core liabilities regardless of the entity that carries it out.[143]

The shadow-banking system comprises a plethora of different actors, each performing one or more different functions related to shadow-credit intermediation. Defining shadow banking in functional terms as 'vertical slicing' of traditional banks' credit-intermediation process allows the different functions and actors to be arranged along the shadow-credit intermediation chain in sequential order, as follows: (i) loan origination by finance companies; (ii) loan warehousing by conduits; (iii) pooling and structuring of loans into (different tranches of) ABSs by broker-dealers; (iv) ABS warehousing by broker-dealers; (v) pooling and structuring of ABS into (different tranches of) CDOs by broker-dealers; (vi) ABS intermediation by various shadow-bank entities; and (vii) wholesale funding of all these activities and entities by various shadow-bank entities, eg MMFs and other funds.[144]

Explanations for the rise of the shadow-banking system and its spectacular growth before the GFC involve, for example, regulatory arbitrage, often considered to be a main driver,[145] economies of scale and economies of specialization from involving a number of specialized shadow-bank entities,[146] and shadow-credit intermediation as financial innovation in the composition of aggregate money supply.[147]

[140] See, eg, Financial Stability Board, Strengthening Oversight and Regulation of Shadow Banking—an Overview of Policy Recommendations (2013), iv; European Commission, Green Paper Shadow Banking (2012) COM(2012)102, 3.

[141] See, eg, Pozsar, Z, Adrian, T, Ashcraft, AB, and Boesky, H, 'Shadow Banking' (2013) 19(2) *Economic Policy Review* 1, 3.

[142] For an overview see International Monetary Fund, n 46 above, 91.

[143] International Monetary Fund, n 46 above, 66, 91–2.

[144] Pozsar et al., n 141 above, 6–7.

[145] See, eg, Acharya, VV, Schnabl, P, and Suarez, G, 'Securitization without Risk Transfer' (2013) 107 *Journal of Financial Economics* 516; Stanton, R and Wallace, N, CMBS Subordination, Ratings Inflation, and the Crisis of 2007–2009 (2010), National Bureau of Economic Research Working Paper Series No 16206; Schwarcz, SL, 'Regulating Shadow Banking' (2011–12) 31 *Review of Banking & Financial Law* 619, 624.

[146] Adrian, T, Ashcraft, AB, and Cetorelli, N, Shadow Bank Monitoring (2013), FRBNY Staff Reports, Staff Report No 638, 5–6.

[147] Gorton, G and Metrick, A, 'Regulating the Shadow Banking Sector' (Fall 2010) *Brooking Papers on Economic Activity* 261.

Regardless of the reasons for the existence of the shadow-banking system, because of its size, leverage, scalability, complexity, interconnectedness, and close links with the banking system, it is universally credited with being of systemic importance. More specifically, open-ended money market mutual (funds) (MMFs), which are a major source of short-term funding of banks and, more specifically, of securities broker-dealers by way of repurchase agreements (Repos), are themselves subject to the danger of bank-like runs and, hence, are a potential source of strong or even systemic shocks. Moreover, banks are also intertwined with other shadow-banking entities, eg as a prime broker extending collateralized loans to shadow-banking entities or as a provider of guarantees[148] to asset-backed commercial paper conduits. In the case of a run on (short-term) asset-backed commercial papers (ABCPs)—if investors are unwilling to buy (new) roll-over ABCPs, as was the case during the GFC[149]—banks will be hit directly by way of their liquidity-enhancing guarantees, but also indirectly via fire sale externalities, if the conduits have to sell assets at depressed prices, driving down the prices of assets held directly by banks, by other bank-sponsored ABCP conduits, or by MMFs which, in turn, will have to deleverage by reducing their funding of banks through Repos.[150]

(b) *Prudential regulation*

Given these and other risks with the potential of causing a systemic event, one of the main lessons from the GFC resulted in a universal call for (increased) prudential regulation of the shadow-banking sector. The way forward was also clear insofar as shadow banking was the result of regulatory arbitrage: extending the perimeter of prudential regulation in such a manner that regulatory arbitrage is no longer possible or at least very costly for the actors engaging in these activities. With respect to banks operating non-consolidated entities; in particular, extending the perimeter of micro-prudential regulation applying to the bank (also by changes to accounting rules) eliminates the potential for regulatory arbitrage since the micro-prudential capital and liquidity requirements will apply on a consolidated basis.

Apart from rather clear-cut situations of regulatory arbitrage, ie the case of banks operating or sponsoring shadow-banking entities, the how-to-regulate question is more intricate. In a nutshell, the Basel II/III framework is designed for banks as one-stop credit intermediaries, ie for entities that provide the full range of functions in the credit intermediation process all by themselves. In contrast, shadow-banking

[148] Mostly structured as liquidity-enhancing guarantees aimed at minimizing regulatory capital instead of credit guarantees; see Acharya et al., n 145 above.

[149] See Covitz, D, Liang, N, and Suarez, CA, 'The Evolution of a Financial Crisis: Collapse of the Asset-Backed Commercial Paper Market' (2013) 69 *The Journal of Finance* 815; cf Acharya et al., n 145 above.

[150] As to the run on repos in the GFC see more generally Gorton, G and Metrick, A 'Securitized Banking and the Run on Repo' (2012) 104 *Journal of Financial Economics* 425.

entities do not provide all these functions, but only a few or even just one of the services.

Against this backdrop, the FSB, taking a leading role at international level, embarked on formulating policy recommendations for five areas: spillovers between banks and shadow banks; MMFs; non-MMF shadow-banking entities; securitization; and securities lending and repo transactions.[151] Up to now, the FSB delivered in three areas, in particular: with regard to shielding banks against shocks from shadow banks, the Basel Committee published final recommendations (large exposures;[152] banks' investments in equity funds[153]). As regards money market funds, IOSCO developed recommendations to the effect, that MMFs which offer a stable or constant net asset value (NAV) should be converted into floating NAV or should be subject to functionally equivalent prudential requirements on banks that protect against runs.[154] In the area of securitization, IOSCO also issued further policy recommendations.[155] Regarding non-MMFs as well as securities lending and repo transactions, the FSB published high-level principles.[156]

Inroads of EU regulation on shadow-banking entities include the Alternative Investment Fund Managers Directive[157] and the European Market Infrastructure Regulation.[158] As regards money market funds, the Commission presented a proposal[159] which met with strong criticism, though whereas, in the US, the SEC adopted a final regulation along the lines of the IOSCO recommendations.

(c) *Assessment*

Progress in subjecting shadow-banking entities to prudential supervision has been made mostly in the less difficult areas. This holds true for extending micro-prudential regulation of banks that operate or sponsor such entities with a view to avoiding regulatory arbitrage by those banks, but also to the regulation of MMFs already implemented or proposed, at least. Since MMFs are subject to bank-like runs, the regulatory answer is to introduce micro-prudential requirements that are conceptionally similar to capital and liquidity requirements for banks.

[151] Financial Stability Board, n 140 above, 2.

[152] Basel Committee, n 65 above.

[153] Basel Committee on Banking Supervision, Capital Requirements for Banks' Equity Investments in Funds (2013).

[154] International Organization of Securities Commissions, Policy Recommendations for Money Market Funds (2012).

[155] International Organization of Securities Commissions, Global Developments in Securitisation Regulation Final Report (2012).

[156] Financial Stability Board, Strengthening Oversight and Regulation of Shadow Banking—Policy Framework for Strengthening Oversight and Regulation of Shadow Banking Entities (2013); Financial Stability Board, Strengthening Oversight and Regulation of Shadow Banking—Policy Framework for Addressing Shadow Banking Risks in Securities Lending and Repos (2013).

[157] Council Directive 2011/61/EU, n 42 above.

[158] Council Regulation (EU) No 648/2012, n 43 above.

[159] European Commission, Proposal for a Regulation on Money Market Funds (2013) COM(2013)615.

With regard to other shadow-banking entities, the boundary problem, ie determining the appropriate perimeter of micro-prudential regulation, is more difficult. These entities do not perform all of the functions along the credit-intermediation chain and, hence, regulators ultimately have to determine which of these activities need to be subjected to prudential regulation, and for what reasons: micro- or/and macro-prudential ones. On the other hand, the regulator does not face a binary choice in coming up with an appropriate prudential framework for these entities, ie either a Basel II/III-like framework designed for bank-like credit intermedation or no regulation at all. Instead, since these shadow-bank intermediaries perform only some services of the full credit intermediation process, prudential regulation should be tailored to the specific services performed. The regulation of collective investment schemes (mutual funds) and of managers of alternative investment funds by the EU's AIFM Directive, at first glance, seem to be cases in point. Upon closer inspection, though, these pieces of regulation follow the micro-prudential logic, whereas the GFC-informed projects of regulating non-MMFs[160] target their role in initiating and propagating (systemic) shocks.[161] While shadow-banking activities that have a valid economic rationale require specific regulations to reduce any systemic risk that they pose,[162] existing micro-prudential regulation of shadow bank non-MMFs is not necessarily suited to that objective. On the other hand, preserving the shadow-banking system's efficiency should not rank high on the priority list when designing regulation for the purpose of reducing systemic risk.[163]

VII. Concluding Observations

The objectives of traditional micro-economic policy and of macro-economic policy will occasionally come into conflict because of their interaction on financial markets, the structure of the network among financial institutions, and the behaviour of other financial institutions. To resolve these (potential) tensions the regulator may determine whether, in case of conflicts, micro- or macro-prudential

[160] Credit investment funds; exchange-traded funds (ETFs); credit hedge funds, private equity hedge funds, securities broker-dealers; securitization entities; credit insurance providers/financial guarantors; finance companies; trust companies.

[161] See International Monetary Fund, n 46 above, 86: degree of required regulation and oversight depends largely on the degree to which shadow banking contributes to systemic risk.

[162] Claessens, S, Pozsar, Z, Ratnovski, L, and Singh, M, Shadow Banking: Economics and Policy (2012), IMF Staff Discussion Note 12/12, 21.

[163] But see Schwarcz, n 145 above, 640–1.

policy takes precedence.[164] If he refrains from making that choice, he should provide an institutional framework within which a third party—eg, the supervisor or the various authorities tasked with micro- and macro-prudential supervision respectively—will solve the conflict. This begs the question how to organize supervision: as an 'integrated' supervisor or as a tandem of supervisors each charged with a different task but interlinked by the macro-prudential supervisor's unilateral right to issue binding directives to the micro-prudential supervisor?[165] This discussion has just started.[166]

Bibliography

Acharya, VV, 'A Theory of Systemic Risk and Design of Prudential Bank Regulation' (2009) 5 *Journal of Financial Stability* 224.

Acharya, VV, Santos, JAC, and Yorulmazer, T, 'Systemic Risk and Deposit Insurance Premiums' (2010) 16(1) *Economic Policy Review* 89.

Acharya, VV, Schnabl, P, and Suarez, G, 'Securitization without Risk Transfer' (2013) 107 *Journal of Financial Economics* 516.

Adrian, T, Ashcraft, AB, and Cetorelli, N, Shadow Bank Monitoring (2013), FRBNY Staff Reports, Staff Report No 638, available at <http://www.newyorkfed.org/research/staff_reports/sr638.pdf>.

Aebi, V, Sabato, G, and Schmid, M, 'Risk Management, Corporate Governance, and Bank Performance in the Financial Crisis' (2012) 36 *Journal of Banking & Finance* 3213.

Anginer, D, Demirgüc-Kunt, A, and Zhu, M, How does Bank Competition Affect Systemic Stability? (2012), World Bank Policy Working Paper No 5981, available at <http://ssrn.com/abstract=2013865>.

Armour, J and Gordon, J, 'Systemic Harms and Shareholder Value' (2014) 6(1) *Journal of Legal Analysis* 35.

Arnold, B, Borio, C, Ellis, L, and Moshirian, F, 'Systemic Risk, Macroprudential Policy Frameworks, Monitoring Financial Systems and the Evolution of Capital Adequacy' (2012) 16 *Journal of Banking & Finance* 3125.

Avgouleas, E and Cullen, J, 'Market Discipline and EU Corporate Governance Reform in the Banking Sector: Merits, Fallacies, and Cognitive Boundaries' (2014) 41 *Journal of Law and Society* 28.

164 cf Duffie, D, 'Replumbing our Financial System: Uneven Progress' (2013) 9 *International Journal of Central Banking* 251, 252–3: central clearing facilities should be regulated with the objective that it is extremely difficult for them to fail catastrophically; ie, not on the basis of a cost-benefit calculus.

165 According to the so-called Ingves report, such an overlay will not affect the independence of the micro-prudential supervisor (Bank of International Settlements, n 12 above, 56–7). In substance, though that implies a precedence of the macro-economic policy in case of conflicts.

166 See Ingves report, ibid; Osiński et al., n 14 above, 17–21; cf Borio, C, Monetary and Prudential Policies at a Crossroads? New Challenges in the New Century (2006), BIS Working Papers No 216, 19–20; very recently German Council of Economic Experts, More Confidence in Market Processes, Annual Economic Report 2014/2015 (2014), n 368–81.

Bank of England and European Central Bank, The Case for a Better Functioning Securitisation Market in the European Union (2014), A Discussion Paper, available at <https://www.ecb.europa.eu/pub/pdf/other/ecb-boe_case_better_functioning_securitisation_ marketen.pdf>.

Bank of International Settlements, Central Bank Governance and Financial Stability (2011) (Ingves Report).

Basel Committee on Banking Supervision, Basel III: A Global Regulatory Framework for more Resilient Banks and Banking Systems (2011).

Basel Committee on Banking Supervision, Basel III: International Framework for Liquidity Risk Measurement, Standards and Monitoring (2010).

Basel Committee on Banking Supervision, Capital Requirements for Banks' Equity Investments in Funds (2013).

Basel Committee on Banking Supervision, Compensation Principles and Standards—Assessment Methodology (2010).

Basel Committee on Banking Supervision, Core Principles for Effective Banking Supervision (2012).

Basel Committee on Banking Supervision, Enhancement to the Basel II Framework (2009).

Basel Committee on Banking Supervision, Enhancement to the Securitisation Framework (2014).

Basel Committee on Banking Supervision, International Convergence of Capital Measurements and Capital Standards, A Revised Framework, Comprehensive Version (2006).

Basel Committee on Banking Supervision, The Joint Forum (BCBS, IAS, and IOSCO), Credit Risk Transfer (2005).

Basel Committee on Banking Supervision, Measuring and Controlling Large Credit Exposures (1991).

Basel Committee on Banking Supervision, Pillar 3 Disclosure Requirements for Remuneration (2011).

Basel Committee on Banking Supervision, Principles for Effective Risk Data Aggregation and Risk Reporting (2013).

Basel Committee on Banking Supervision, Principles for Enhancing Corporate Governance (2010).

Basel Committee on Banking Supervision, Principles for the Sound Management of Operational Risk (2011).

Basel Committee on Banking Supervision, Principles for Sound Stress Testing Practices and Supervision (2009).

Basel Committee on Banking Supervision, Review of the Pillar 3 Disclosure Requirements, Consultative Document (2014).

Basel Committee on Banking Supervision, Supervisory Framework for Measuring and Controlling Large Exposures (2014).

Battiston, S, Gatti, DD, Gallegatti, M, Greenwald, B, and Stiglitz, JE, 'Default Cascades: When Does Risk Diversification Increase Stability?' (2012) 8 *Journal of Financial Stability* 138.

Beltratti, A and Stulz, RM, 'The Credit Crisis around the Globe: Why Did Some Banks Perform Better?' (2012) 105 *Journal of Financial Economics* 1.

Bisias, D, Flood, MD, Lo, AW, and Valavanis, S, A Survey of Systemic Risk Analytics (2012), US Department of Treasury, Office of Financial Research Paper No 001, available at <http://www.treasury.gov/initiatives/ofr/research/Pages/working-paper-series.aspx>.

Blundell-Wignall, A, Atkinson, P, and Roulet, C, 'Bank Business Models and the Separation Issue' (2014) 2013(2) *Financial Market Trends* 1.

Bolton, P and Oehmke, M, Should Derivatives Be Privileged in Bankruptcy (2012), Working Paper (forthcoming in *The Journal of Finance*), available at <http://ssrn.com/abstract=2023227>.

Borio, C, Monetary and Prudential Policies at a Crossroads? New Challenges in the New Century (2006), BIS Working Papers No 216, available at <http://ssrn.com/abstract=948135>.

Borio, C, 'Towards a Macroprudential Framework for Financial Supervision and Regulation?' (2003) 49(2) *CESifo Economic Studies* 181.

Bouvard, M, Chaigneau, P, and de Motta, A, 'Transparency in the Financial System: Rollover Risk and Crises' *The Journal of Finance* (forthcoming).

Brunnermeier, MK, 'Deciphering the Liquidity and Credit Crunch 2007–2008' (2009) 23(1) *Journal of Economic Perspectives* 77.

Brunnermeier, MK, Crockett, A, Goodhart, C, Persaud, A, and Shin, H, *The Fundamental Principles of Financial Regulation* (2009) 11 Geneva Reports on the World Economy.

Brunnermeier, MK and Oehmke, M, 'Bubbles, Financial Crisis, and Systemic Risk' in Constantinides, GM, Harris, M, and Stulz, RM (eds), *Handbook of the Economics of Finance* (Vol 2B, 2013) 1221.

Cecchetti, S, 'The Future of Financial Intermediation and Regulation: An Overview' (1999) 5(8) *Current Issues in Economics and Finance* 1.

Claessens, S, Pozsar, Z, Ratnovski, L, and Singh, M, Shadow Banking: Economics and Policy (2012), IMF Staff Discussion Note 12/12.

Conyon, MJ, Fernandes, N, Ferreira, MA, Matos, P, and Murphy, KJ, *The Executive Compensation Controversy: A Transatlantic Analysis* (2011).

Council Directive 97/9/EC on investor-compensation schemes (1997) OJ L 84/22.

Council Directive 2009/65/EC on the Coordination of laws, regulations and administrative provisions relating to undertakings for collective investment in transferable securities (UCITS) (2009) OJ L 302/32.

Council Directive 2009/111/EC amending Directives 2006/487/EC, 2006/49/EC and 2007/64/EC as regards banks affiliated to central institutions, certain own funds items, large exposures, supervisory arrangements, and crisis management (2009) OJ L 302/97.

Council Directive 2010/76/EU amending Directives 2006/48/EC and 2006/49/EC as regards capital requirements for the trading book and for re-securitisations, and the supervisory review of remuneration policies (2010) OJ L 329/3.

Council Directive 2011/61/EU on Alternative Investment Fund Managers and amending Directives 2003/41/EC and 2009/65/EC and Regulations (EC) No 1060/2009 and (EU) No 1095/2010 (2011) OJ L 174/1.

Council Directive 2013/36/EU on access to the activity of credit institutions and the prudential supervision of credit institutions and investment firms, amending Directive 2002/87/EC and repealing Directives 2006/48/EC and 2006/49/EC (2013) OJ L 176/338.

Council Directive 2014/49/EU on deposit guarantee schemes (2014) OJ L 173/149.

Council Directive 2014/65/EU on markets in financial instruments and amending Directive 2002/92/EC and Directive 2011/61/EU (2014) OJ L 173/349.

Council Directive 2014/91/EU amending Directive 2009/65/EC on the coordination of laws, regulations and administrative provisions relating to undertakings for collective investment in transferable securities (UCITS) as regards depositary functions, remuneration policies and sanctions (2014) OJ L 275/186.

Council Regulation (EU) No 1092/2010 on European Union macro-prudential oversight of the financial system and establishing a European Systemic Risk Board (2010) OJ L 331/1.

Council Regulation (EU) No 236/2012 on short selling and certain aspects of credit default swaps (2012) OJ L 86/1.

Council Regulation (EU) No 648/2012 on OTC derivatives, central counterparties and trade repositories (2012) OJ L 201/1.

Council Regulation (EU) No 462/2013 amending Regulation (EC) No 1060/2009 on credit rating agencies (2013) OJ L 146/1.

Council Regulation (EU) No 575/2013 on prudential requirements for credit institutions and investment firms and amending Regulation (EU) No 648/2012 (2013) OJ L 176/1.

Council Regulation (EU) No 600/2014 on markets in financial instruments and amending Regulation (EU) No 648/2012 (2014) OJ L 173/84.

Council Regulation (EU) No 909/2014 on improving securities settlement in the European Union and on central securities depositories and amending Directives 98/26/EC and 2014/65/EU and Regulation (EU) No 236/2012 (2014) OJ L 257/1.

Covitz, D, Liang, N, and Suarez, GA, 'The Evolution of a Financial Crisis: Collapse of the Asset-Backed Commercial Paper Market' (2013) 69 *The Journal of Finance* 815.

Criado, S, Degabriel, L, Lewandowska, M, Lindén, S, and Ritter, P, Report on Sovereign CDS (2010): No Conclusive Evidence (task force comprising staff from DG COMP, CG ECFIN, and DG MARKT).

Davis, K, *Regulatory Reform Post the Global Financial Crisis: An Overview* (2010).

de Haan, J and Vlahu, R, Corporate Governance of Banks: A Survey (July 2013), DNB Working Paper No 386, available at <http://ssrn.com/abstract=2297770>.

de Mooij, R and Nicodeme, G (eds), *Taxation and Regulation of the Financial Sector* (2014).

De Young, R, Peng, EY, and Yan, M, 'Executive Compensation and Business Policy Choices at U.S. Commercial Banks' (2013) 48 *Journal of Financial and Quantitative Analysis* 165.

Duffie, D, Innovations in Credit Risk Transfer: Implications for Financial Stability (2008), BIS Working Papers No 255, available at <http://ssrn.com/abstract=1165484>.

Duffie, D, 'Replumbing our Financial System: Uneven Progress' (2013) 9 *International Journal of Central Banking* 251.

Duffie, D and Skeel Jr, DA, 'A Dialogue on the Costs and Benefits of Automatic Stays for Derivatives and Repurchase Agreements' in Scott, KE and Taylor, JB (eds), *Bankruptcy not Bailout—a Special Chapter 14* (2012) Part C, 5.

Ellis, L, Haldane, A, and Moshirian, F, 'Systemic Risk, Governance and Global Financial Stability' (2014) 45 *Journal of Banking & Finance* 175.

Ellul, A and Yerramilli, V, 'Stronger Risk Controls, Lower Risk: Evidence from U.S. Bank Holding Companies' (2013) 68 *The Journal of Finance* 1757.

Erkens, D, Hung, M, and Matos, PP, 'Corporate Governance in the 2007–2008 Financial Crisis: Evidence from Financial Institutions Worldwide' (2012) 18(2) *Journal of Corporate Finance* 389.

European Central Bank, Enhancing the Monitoring of Shadow Banking (February 2013) *Monthly Bulletin* 89.

European Central Bank, 'Special Feature B: The Concept of Systemic Risk' (December 2009) *Financial Stability Review* 134.

European Commission, Green Paper Shadow Banking (2012), COM(2012)102.

European Commission, Proposal for a Regulation on Money Market Funds (2013), COM(2013)615.

European Commission, Proposal for a Regulation on Structural Measures Improving the Resilience of EU Credit Institutions (2014), COM(2014)43.

European Systemic Risk Board (ESRB), Recommendation of the European Systemic Risk Board on Intermediate Objectives and Instruments of Macroprudential Policy (2013), ESRB/2013/1, OJ C 170/01.

Fernandez-Bollo, É, 'Structural Reform and Supervision of the Banking Sector in France' (2013) 2013(1) *Financial Market Trends* 1.

Ferrarini, G and Ungureanu, MC, 'Economics, Politics, and the International Principles for Sound Compensation Practices: An Analysis of Executive Pay at European Banks' (2011) 64 *Vanderbilt Law Review* 431.

Financial Services Authority (FSA), Effective Corporate Governance (2010), Consultation Paper 10/3.

Financial Services Authority (FSA), The Turner Review—a Regulatory Response to the Global Banking Crises (2009).

Financial Stability Board, Guidance on Supervisory Interaction with Financial Institutions on Risk Culture (2014).

Financial Stability Board, Principles for an Effective Risk Appetite Framework (2013).

Financial Stability Board, Principles for Reducing Reliance on CRA Ratings (2010).

Financial Stability Board, Principles for Sound Compensation Practices (April 2009).

Financial Stability Board, Principles of Sound Compensation Practices—Implementation Standards (September 2009).

Financial Stability Board, Strengthening Oversight and Regulation of Shadow Banking—an Overview of Policy Recommendations (2013).

Financial Stability Board, Strengthening Oversight and Regulation of Shadow Banking—Policy Framework for Addressing Shadow Banking Risks in Securities Lending and Repos (2013).

Financial Stability Board, Strengthening Oversight and Regulation of Shadow Banking—Policy Framework for Strengthening Oversight and Regulation of Shadow Banking Entities (2013).

Financial Stability Board, Thematic Review on FSB Principles for Reducing Reliance on CRA Ratings (2014).

Financial Stability Board, Thematic Review on Risk Governance (2013).

Galati, G and Moessner, R, Macroprudential Policy—a Literature Review (December 2010), DNB Working Paper No 267, available at <http://ssrn.com/abstract=1950093>.

Gambacorta, L and van Rixtel, A, Structural Bank Regulation Initiatives: Approaches and Implications (2013), BIS Working Papers No 412, available at <http://www.bis.org/publ/work412.pdf>.

Gilson, R and Kraakman, R, Market Efficiency after the Financial Crisis: It's Still a Matter of Information Costs (2014), ECGI Law Working Paper No 242/2014, available at <http://ssrn.com/abstract=2396608>.

Gordon, J, 'Corporate Governance and Executive Compensation in Financial Firms: The Case for Convertible Equity-based Pay' (2012) *Columbia Business Law Review* 834.

Gorton, G and Metrick, A, 'Getting Up to Speed on the Financial Crisis: A One-Weekend Reader's Guide' (2012) 50(1) *Journal of Economic Literature* 128.

Gorton, G and Metrick, A, 'Regulating the Shadow Banking Sector' (Fall 2010) *Brooking Papers on Economic Activity* 261.

Gorton, G and Metrick, A, 'Securitized Banking and the Run on Repo' (2012) 104 *Journal of Financial Economics* 425.

Gropp, R and Köhler, M, Bank Owners or Bank Managers: Who Is Keen on Risk? Evidence from the Financial Crisis (23 February 2010), European Business School Research Paper No 10-02 (ZEW Discussion Paper No 10-013), available at <http://ssrn.com/abstract=1555663>.

Hanson, SG, Kashyap, AK, and Stein, JC, 'A Macroprudential Approach to Financial Regulation' (2011) 25(1) *Journal of Economic Perspectives* 1.

Hellwig, MF, 'Systemic Risk in the Financial Sector: An Analysis of the Subprime-mortgage Financial Crisis' (2009) 157 *De Economist* 129.

High-Level Expert Group on Reforming the Structure of the EU Banking Sector, Final Report (Liikanen Report) (2012).

The High-Level Group on Financial Supervision in the EU, Report (de Larosière Report) (2009).

Independent Commission on Banking, Final Report—Recommendations (Vickers Report) (2011).

International Association of Insurance Supervisors, Insurance Core Principles, Standards, Guidance and Assessment Methodology (2011/2013).

International Monetary Fund, Bank for International Settlements and Financial Stability Board, Guidance to Assess the Systemic Importance of Financial Institutions, Markets and Instruments: Initial Considerations, Report to the G-20 Finance Ministers and Central Bank Governors (October 2009).

International Monetary Fund, Claessens, S, Keen, M, and Pazarbasioglu, C (eds), Financial Sector Taxation: The IMF's Report to the G-20 and Background Material (September 2010).

International Monetary Fund, A Fair and Substantial Contribution by the Financial Sector, Final Report for the G-20 (June 2010).

International Monetary Fund, Global Financial Stability Report, Risk Taking, Liquidity, and Shadow Banking: Curbing Excess While Promoting Growth (October 2014).

International Monetary Fund, Key Aspects of Macroprudential Policy (2013).

International Organization of Securities Commissions, Global Developments in Securitisation Regulation, Final Report (2012).

International Organization of Securities Commissions, Objectives and Principles of Securities Regulation (2010).

International Organization of Securities Commissions, Policy Recommendations for Money Market Funds (2012).

International Organization of Securities Commissions, Unregulated Financial Markets and Products, Final Report (2009).

Joint Forum, Review of the Differentiated Nature and Scope of Financial Regulation—Key Issues and Recommendations (2010).

Joint Forum, Risk Management Practices and Regulatory Capital—Cross-sectoral Comparison (2001).

Kirkpatrick, G, 'The Corporate Governance Lessons from the Financial Crisis' (2009) (2009)(1) *Financial Market Trends* 1.

Kose, J, Saunders, A, and Senbet, LW, 'A Theory of Bank Regulation and Management Compensation' (2000) 13(1) *Review of Financial Studies* 95.

Laeven, L and Levine, R, 'Bank Governance, Regulation, and Risk Taking' (2009) 93 *Journal of Financial Economics* 259.

Lastra, R, 'Systemic Risk, SIFIs and Financial Stability' (2011) 6 *Capital Markets Law Journal* 198.

Malz, AM, *Financial Risk Management: Models, History, and Institutions* (2011).

Manning, M, Nier, E, and Schanz, J, 'Introduction' in Manning, M, Nier, E, and Schanz, J (eds), *The Economics of Large-value Payments and Settlement: Theory and Policy Issues for Central Banks* (2009) 1.

Mehran, H, Morrison, A, and Shapiro, J, 'Corporate Governance and Banks—What Have we Learned from the Financial Crisis?' in Dewatripont, M and Freixas, X (eds), *The Crisis Aftermath: New Regulatory Paradigms* (2012) 11.

Mishkin, FS, 'Over the Cliff: From the Subprime to the Global Financial Crisis' (2011) 25(1) *Journal of Economic Perspectives* 49.

Moloney, N, 'EU Financial Market Regulation after the Global Financial Crisis: "More Europe" or More Risks?' (2010) 47(5) *Common Market Law Review* 1317.

Mülbert, PO, Corporate Governance of Banks after the Financial Crisis—Theory, Evidence, Reforms (2010), ECGI Law Working Paper No 130/2010, available at <http://ssrn.com/abstract=1448118>.

Mülbert, PO and Citlau, R, The Uncertain Role of Banks' Corporate Governance in Systemic Risk Regulation (2011), ECGI Law Working Paper No 179/2011, available at <http://ssrn.com/abstract=1885866>.

Nestor Advisors, Banks Boards and the Financial Crisis: A Corporate Governance Study of the 25 Largest European Banks (2009).

Nijskens, R and Wagner, W, 'Credit Risk Transfer Activities and Systemic Risk: How Banks Became Less Risky Individually but Posed Greater Risks to the Financial System at the Same Time' (2011) 35 *Journal of Banking & Finance* 1391.

OECD, Corporate Governance and the Financial Crisis: Key Findings and Main Messages (June 2009).

Osiński, J, Seal, K, and Hoogduin, L, Macroprudential and Microprudential Policies: towards Cohabitation (2013), IMF Staff Discussion Note 13/05.

Pozsar, Z, Adrian, T, Ashcraft, AB, and Boesky, H, 'Shadow Banking' (2013) 19(2) *Economic Policy Review* 1.

Reserve Bank of Australia, Submission to the Financial System Inquiry (2014).

Roe, MJ, 'The Derivative's Market's Payment Priorities as Financial Crisis Accelerator' (2010) 63 *Stanford Law Review* 539.

Schoenmaker, D and Wierts, P, Macroprudential Policy: The Need for a Coherent Policy Framework (2011), DSF Policy Paper Series No 13, available at <http://www.dsf.nl/home/research/publications/dsf_policy_papers>.

Schwarcz, SL, 'Regulating Shadow Banking' (2011–12) 31 *Review of Banking & Financial Law* 619.

Schwarcz, SL, 'Systemic Risk' (2008) 97 *Georgetown Law Journal* 193.

Scott, HS, 'Reducing Systemic Risk through the Reform of Capital Regulation' (2010) 13(3) *Journal of International Economic Law* 763.

Scott, HS, 'The Reduction of Systemic Risk in the United States Financial System' (2010) 33 *Harvard Journal of Law & Public Policy* 671.

Senior Supervisors Group, Risk Management Lessons from the Global Banking Crisis of 2008 (21 October 2009).

Shleifer, A and Vishny, R, 'Fire Sales in Finance and Macroeconomics' (2011) 25(1) *Journal of Economic Perspectives* 29.

Skeel, DA and Jackson, TH, 'Transaction Consistency and the New Finance in Bankruptcy' (2012) 112 *Columbia Law Review* 152.

Smaga, P, The Concept of Systemic Risk (2014), SRC Special Paper No 5, available at <http://ssrn.com/abstract=2477928>.

Stanton, R and Wallace, N, CMBS Subordination, Ratings Inflation, and the Crisis of 2007–2009 (2010), National Bureau of Economic Research Working Paper No 16206, available at <http://www.nber.org/papers/w16206.pdf>.

van Oordt, MRC, 'Securitization and the Dark Side of Diversification' (2014) 23(2) *Journal of Financial Intermediation* 214.

Vinals, J, Pazarbasioglu, C, Surti, J, Narain, A, Erbenova, M, and Chow, J, Creating a Safer Financial System: Will the Volcker, Vickers, and Liikanen Structural Measures Help? (2013), IMF Staff Discussion Note 13/4.

Wagner, W and Marsh, IW, 'Credit Risk Transfer and Financial Sector Stability' (2006) 2 *Journal of Financial Stability* 173.

Walker, D, A Review of Corporate Governance in UK Banks and Other Financial Industry Entities—Final Recommendations (2009).

Westman, H, The Role of Ownership Structure and Regulatory Environment in Bank Corporate Governance (14 January 2010), Bank of Finland Working Paper, available at <http://papers.ssrn.com/abstract=1435041>.

Winter, J, 'The Financial Crisis: Does Good Corporate Governance Matter and How to Achieve it?' in Wymeersch, E, Hopt, KJ, and Ferrarini, G (eds), *Financial Regulation and Supervision* (2012) 368.

CHAPTER 14

REGULATING THE INSURANCE SECTOR

MICHELLE EVERSON

I. Overview

Insurance is an ancient business. It made its protean appearance in the eastern Mediterranean among classical traders within the practice whereby loans were advanced on marine cargoes and repaid on successful completion of voyage.

Insurance subsequently acquired its own distinctive features. 'Loss averaging', or the mutualization of risk, first emerged in Rhodes, as pioneering merchants shared out the possible loss of a portion of cargo between all traders with goods on one vessel. Thereafter, the first advance premiums were paid against trading risk within the letters of credit that were characteristic of commerce among early medieval Italian city states.[1] In turn, the economic and social benefits of mutualization, as well as 'futurization',[2] or advance provision for temporal contingencies, were eventually to be recognized far beyond the realm of marine-based trading. First, as the merchants of the Hansa League clubbed together in order to establish mutual funds to guard against fire damage to their businesses; and second, as friendly societies and guilds collected contributions from their members and established joint funds to be disbursed in cases of individual disability.[3] The early modern mercantile effort to guard against fire hazard, together with counterpart socialization of personal welfare risks, was the seed from which contemporary mass insurance business sprang, also establishing an enduring distinction between life and non-life insurance. Crucially, however, it is in the failure of self-help funds and their replacement with commercial insurance providers that we can begin to recognize the enduring tensions that characterize the modern regulatory paradigm within which the sector now operates.

The economic and social purposes of the mutualization of risk are indispensable. The Chicago economist, Frank Knight, famously provided the first modern description of the benefits of futurization, detailing how the entrepreneurial spirit is unleashed, then sustained, where the uncertainties facing an individual business are transformed through mutualization into probabilistic risks, whereby the entrepreneur buys commercial certainty, or secured restitution for potential damage.[4] Futurization is equally relevant in the social sphere. Deploying the contemporary formulations of behavioural economics, the diminishing utility of wealth, together with risk aversion, determines that individuals are not merely willing, but are positively biased towards the immediate purchase of premiums, or the sacrifice of marginal current income, in order to obtain significant future gain in the case of accident or aging.[5] Mutualization, however, is not without its own dangers, above all

[1] See, for a comprehensive history of insurance, Raynes, HE, *A History of British Insurance* (1964), ch 1.

[2] See, for the concept of futurization, including individual and systemic forms, Esposito, D, *The Future of Futures: The Time of Money in Financing and Society* (2013); Esposito, D, 'The Present Use of the Future: Management and Production of Risk on Financial Markets' in Luetge, C and Jauernig, J (eds), *Business Ethics and Risk Management* (2014) 17.

[3] See, for details of their rise and fall, Clarke, M, 'An Introduction to Insurance Contract Law' in Burling, J and Lazarus, K (eds), *Research Handbook on International Insurance Law and Regulation* (2011) 3.

[4] Knight, F, *Risk, Uncertainty and Profit* (1921).

[5] Cohen, LR and Boardman, ME, 'Methodology: Applying Economics to Insurance Law—an Introduction' in Burling, J and Lazarus, K (eds), *Research Handbook on International Insurance Law and Regulation* (2011) 19.

with regard to the creation of sustainable risk pools. As self-help mutuals discovered to their historic cost, informational asymmetries, such as the presence of adverse selection and moral hazard, determine that risk pools can and do unravel where the insured community is dominated by individuals who present a far higher degree of risk than is the mean, or is itself overcome by an overconfident tendency to more rather than less risky behaviour, such that mutual funds are no longer adequate for the purposes of cumulative disbursement. Successful pooling of risk is a technical feat which is wholly dependent upon informational completeness and actuarial exactness. This simple fact proved to be the spur to the professionalization of insurance provision as amateur mutualization failed. At the same time, however, the commercialization of insurance entrenched an enduring regulatory tension between the vital economic and social purposes of insurance and its provision by means of a private market, itself still inherently prone to technical miscarriage.

Insurance is unique. The *sine qua non* of the sector is the management of informational asymmetry. As a consequence, the market, in all of its socio-economic significance, is not simply characterized by potential for market failure, but is instead founded in one; is built upon an information failure that is reason for and integral to its existence. Within this setting—one which also includes multiple interfaces between the market and public, or quasi-public insurance schemes for critical risks that are not suited to, or deemed to be appropriate for actuarial treatment—it is far from surprising that the sector is a focus for regulatory intervention. Instead, the more striking fact is one that, for much of its history, significant segments of the global insurance business, such as the UK market, as well as international reinsurance services were very lightly supervised, if regulated at all. This permissive attitude becomes all the more notable when the capital maximization activities and fiscal importance of the industry are considered. Although approximations of global insurance investment income are elusive,[6] the Association of British Insurers (ABI) has recently noted that the UK insurance industry, the third largest in the world, manages investments amounting to 26 per cent of the UK's total net worth and contributes £10.4 billion in taxes to the UK Government.[7] The insurance sector has always had an additionally vital macro-economic relevance, and especially so, to the extent that—all personalized futurization opportunities apart—its purchase might also be equated with payment of a necessary but unwelcome tax; a fact that might be expected, not only to lead to tightened prudential supervision, but also to draw the attentions of economic policymakers attracted by the utility of sectoral profit.

[6] Although, see International Association of Insurance Supervisors, Global Insurance Market Report (GIMAR) 2010, IAIS, Basel (October 2012), available at <http://www.iaisweb.org/News/Global-Insurance-Market-Report-GIMAR-962> (last accessed March 2014).

[7] Association of British Insurers, UK Insurance Key Facts, AIB, London (September 2012) (continuously updated), available at <https://www.abi.org.uk/Insurance-and-savings/Industry-data/Free-industry-data-downloads/UK-Insurance-Key-Facts-2013>.

Today, the days of regulatory restraint are decisively over. This is particularly true in the UK and EU. At European level, the repeatedly delayed implementation of the Solvency II Directive on the taking up and pursuit of insurance, in 2016,[8] together with the establishment of the European Insurance and Occupational Pensions Authority (EIOPA) in 2010,[9] has not merely advanced the effort to complete the single market for insurance services. Instead, Solvency II and EIOPA establishment have significantly deepened the regulatory framework, as well as introduced a novel and largely unique European supervisory capacity, comprising direct intervention powers at national level, both with regard to consumer protection and within the new European System of Financial Supervision (ESFS) designed to combat systemic risk within EU capital markets.[10] Recent European regulatory vigour has been reproduced at UK level as a part of its EU commitments. It has also been surpassed, however: full-scale UK regulatory reform was initiated by the Financial Services Act of 2012, which transferred the prudential oversight of insurers from the now defunct Financial Services Authority to the Bank of England in the guise of its Prudential Regulation Authority (PRA), as well as afforded the new Financial Conduct Authority (FCA) an unprecedented competence to intervene into the material conduct of insurance business.

The recent wave of intrusion into insurance markets raises many questions, not the least of which are the motivations for enhanced regulation and supervision. To a large degree, heightened sectoral regulation is merely ancillary to the long-standing globalization of financial markets, with European harmonization efforts being reproduced, albeit in a far softer form, as global regulatory coordination now concentrates upon World Trade Organization (WTO) efforts to establish a common definition of 'prudential' supervision within the meaning of the General Agreement on Trade in Services (GATS),[11] as well as upon the related efforts of the International Association of Insurance Supervisors (IAIS) to promote its own 'core principles' of insurance supervision.[12] A worldwide insurance market demands a globally level regulatory playing field. Equally, as the unexpected establishment of EIOPA and its integration within the ESFS demonstrate, the tightened supervisory framework for insurance is also a simple consequence of the financial crisis commencing with the collapse of Lehmann Brothers in 2008,

[8] Directive 2009/138/EC on the taking-up and pursuit of the business of Insurance and Reinsurance [2009] OJ L335/1 (Solvency II).

[9] Regulation (EU) No 1094/2010 establishing a European Supervisory Authority (European Insurance and Occupational Pensions Authority [2010] OJ L331/48.

[10] Comprising Regulation (EU) No 1092/2010 [2010] OJ L331/1 (ESRB Regulation); Regulation No 1096/2010 [2010] OJ L331/162 (ECB/ESRB Regulation); Regulation (EU) No 1095/2010 (ESMA) [2010] OJ L331/84; Regulation (EU) No 1093/2010 (EBA), as well as the EIOPA Regulation.

[11] GATS, Annex on Financial Services (2)(a).

[12] Available at <http://www.iaisweb.org/Supervisory-Material/Insurance-Core-Principles-795> (last accessed March 2014).

and the remedial efforts of regulators worldwide to secure enhanced prudential supervision across capital markets, the resilience of insurance provision during the crisis notwithstanding. Nevertheless, various features of the new regulatory philosophy applied to the sector are particularly striking, and even troubling, especially as regards reinvigorated conflict between the status of the insurance industry as a private market, and enhanced policy expectations with regard to the ability of the industry to satisfy heightened futurization demands within secure capital market operations.

Above all, the choice of the EU to adapt the modified Basel III framework, designed for the regulation of banking services, for the purposes of insurance supervision within its Solvency II legislation, appears highly incongruous, especially in the face of the existence of tailored, albeit less prescriptive, IAIS principles for international insurance regulation, as well as fierce opposition to the Directive on the part of the European market.[13] Although the path for Solvency II adoption was smoothed by financial crisis, preparation for reform predated the global economic collapse, and may be argued to be attributable to a more general European policy goal, famously enunciated in the Lamfalussy review of EU financial service markets, of adapting European insurance markets 'to the pace of global financial market change'.[14] A manifesto for the increased competitiveness of the European sector, the Lamfalussy programme was, nevertheless, marked by the greatest paradox of our age, as market liberalization was portended, not by deregulation, but by its own substantial increase in regulatory standards and supervisory structures, purporting not only to enhance consumer protection, in its competitively new guise as consumer choice, but also to facilitate enhanced market operation.

For all of its cumbersome regulatory nature, Solvency II, together with EIOPA oversight, promises the establishment of a modern EU regulatory environment, informed by sensitively responsive economic and regulatory theory, and dedicated to the perfection rather than dampening of competition, all the while giving its prudential and material assurance that the vital interests of policyholders will be secured, even and especially so, within heightened competition. This regulatory theme of what may be termed 'perfected market competition', similarly finds its echoes at national level, especially in the potentially counterintuitive application by the FCA of the principles of behavioural economics to the material supervision of the UK market (see Section V), and begins to raise the presumption that the enduring tensions between the economic and social purposes of insurance and its provision by means of a private market, are now being recast within a new paradigm,

[13] See, for recent industry comment—one among myriad examples—'Only 6% of Insurance Execs Believe Solvency II Costs are Reasonable', *Post Magazine*, 9 July 2014; for more comprehensive academic comment, see, Quaglia, L, 'The Politics of Insurance Regulation and Supervision Reform in the European Union' (2011) 9 (11) *Comparative European Politics* 100.

[14] Final Report, available at <http://ec.europa.eu/internal_market/securities/docs/lamfalussy/wisemen/final-report-wise-men_en.pdf> (last accessed March 2014).

wherein the vital advantages of futurization must be delegated to vibrant private markets; but *only* to those private markets which are not left to their own devices, but which are carefully constructed and secured in line with abstract economic visions of maximized market utility.

The modern regulatory mission to secure welfare within perfected competition has similarly gained in relevance for private insurance markets as the socio-economic demands made of the industry have increased in line with the retreat from state provision of public welfare, or with the dissolution of once distinct insurance interfaces between, for example, primary public pensions provision and ancillary private arrangements.[15] Where macro-economic, post-welfarist policies are predicated on the intensified futurization potential of big-bang financial markets, including their vital ability to sustain unbroken capital creation, together with the assured tailoring and security of private products for individuals, the imposition upon the industry of evermore arduous supervisory structures is simple reflection of the newly enhanced socio-economic expectations held of it. In this challenging environment of what might, in its turn, be labelled 'socialized private market operation', the vital regulatory question accordingly becomes one of whether this onerously complex paradigm is sustainable: first, in terms of the uniquely integral relationship of the insurance sector with market failure; second, with regard to the multiple global, supranational, and national supervisory regimes that apply to the industry; and third, with an eye to potential mismatches between the regulatory and social expectations held of insurance, at whichever regime level that they arise.

This Chapter investigates this issue. Beginning with an overview of the peculiar nature of insurance and the motivations for its regulation (Section II), it then turns to a history of European insurance integration and, in particular, examines tensions between liberalizing globalization of insurance markets and the traditional regulatory and macro-economic demands made of the insurance sector at national level (Section III). The Chapter then investigates the current regulatory regime as it broadly applies to the insurance sector, both for its substance, and with regard to the plural interlinked sites and structures of global, supranational, and national market supervision (Section IV). The Chapter concludes with a restatement and overview of the enduring tensions between the social and economic purposes of insurance and its provision by means of a private market, paying particular regard to the potentially unsustainable expectations now levelled at the industry (Section V).

[15] See, for retreat, Crouch, C, *The Strange Non-Death of Neo-Liberalism* (2012); see also Esposito, n 2 above.

II. The Insurance Mechanism

The modern insurance policy developed as a private contract. Strikingly, however, as the efforts of one early twentieth-century English judge illustrate, the law has always struggled to describe insurance:

> When you insure a ship or a house you cannot insure that the ship shall not be lost or the house burnt, but what you do insure is that a sum of money shall be paid upon the happening of a certain event. That I think is the first requirement in a contract of insurance. It must be contract whereby for some consideration, usually but not necessarily in periodical payments called premiums, you secure to yourself some benefit, usually but not necessarily the payment of a sum of money, upon the happening of some event. Then the next thing that is necessary is that the event should be one which involves some amount of uncertainty. There must be either uncertainty whether the event will ever happen or not, or if the event is one which must happen at some time there must be uncertainty as to the time at which it will happen. The remaining essential is ... that the insurance must be against something. A contract which would otherwise be a mere wager may become an insurance by reason of the assured having an interest in the subject matter—that is to say, the uncertain event which is necessary to make the contract amount to an insurance must be an event which is *prima facie* adverse to the interest of the insured.[16]

Insurance is not a simple matter of easily separable product process and final product. Instead, the insurance policy is best grasped as signifier for an ongoing operation, or insurance mechanism, made up of five elements. First, the private contractual nature of insurance, whereby individuals experience insurance in a personal form, ostensibly tailored to their own circumstances; second, the economic nature of insurance, wherein futurization is expressed as a financial exercise; third, the subjective nature of a product predicated upon existence of a personalized interest in harm; fourth, the temporal nature of an insurance operation of delayed performance; and finally, the abstract nature of insurance, whereby final performance is similarly subject to uncertainty.

1. Risk and redistribution at the insurance interface

Taken cumulatively, the five elements that make up the insurance mechanism create a seemingly irresistible regulatory impetus, as final performance of the insurance contract is subject to a frustrating myriad of financial and material contingencies. Nevertheless, the abstractly uncertain nature of insurance, or its close relationship with risk, at once creates the peculiar market failure that is integral to its conduct, and also establishes the interface between the private market and

[16] *Prudential Insurance Company v IRC* [1904] 2 KB 658.

public insurance schemes operating in tandem with or beyond the private sector. Insured risk is built on a distributive duality: on the one hand, insurance is 'purchased to offset the risk resulting from perils which expose a person or organization to risk';[17] on the other, insurance is 'a method of managing risk by distributing it among a large number of individuals or enterprises'.[18] The distributive capacity of the private market is, in turn, determined by the actuarial principle, or ability of the sector to manage informational asymmetries.

Returning to economic language, the law of big numbers facilitates the operation whereby individual risk aversion, or the fear of personally catastrophic damage, may be translated into a collectively profitable exercise, as the concomitant law of averages, plus a degree of calculable marginal uncertainty, allow the sector to transform individual uncertainty into insurable certainty. An individual is unable to calculate their own exposure to theft hazard. Insurers, by contrast, can say with near absolute clarity how many instances of theft will occur within a defined group. This market operation is, nonetheless, possible only where the insured pool exhibits a low covariance correlation, or shares a rough mean of exposure to risk, allowing for the establishment of averagely affordable premiums. The disruptive elements of adverse selection, the magnified preference of higher-risk individuals for sacrifice of marginal income to premiums, as well as moral hazard, or unduly risky behaviour, are combatted by the sector in two information-based operations. The first, founded in statistical overview of real-world data, deploys cross-subsidization, or discounted premiums to entice lower-risk individuals into the insured pool. The second builds upon indicative data, compensating for informational deficit on policyholder proclivities by excluding certain behaviours from coverage.[19]

For the market, the operation whereby insurable risks are delineated in line with actuarial mastery of informational asymmetry is a technical, value-neutral operation. Risk mutualization, however, is necessarily closely related to the ethics of redistribution. In this view, actuarial practice partially coincides with libertarian principles of individualized assumption of responsibility for the risks posed by subjective characteristics and personal conduct; albeit, that coincidence is diluted within actuarial approximations. The exact measure of the individualized price to be paid for entrepreneurial spirit is to be found within assumption of an increased insurance burden for business risks. This risk personalization approach, in turn, contrasts starkly with utilitarian or solidaristic insurance principles; the former prepared to accept a greater degree of cross-subsidization between personal risk profiles in pursuit of posited general utility; the latter, dispensing with actuarial accounting in order to establish an egalitarian insurance community, wherein the

[17] Mehr, R, Cammack, E, and Rose, T, *Principles of Insurance* (1985).

[18] Abraham, KS, *Distributing Risk: Insurance, Legal Theory and Public Policy* (1986).

[19] See, for full details, Cohen and Boardman, n 5 above.

redistribution of risk is depersonalized within a welfare community that disregards the subjective characters of its beneficiaries.[20]

In broad socio-economic terms, simultaneous pursuit of contrasting risk visions establishes insurance interfaces, or points of contrast, between the logic of a private market and an impetus for redistribution that cannot be met within normal actuarial operation. For example, just as the low covariance correlation, or similarity of risks, within strictly specified pools for private insurance characterizes and sustains a pure market paradigm, the high covariance correlation, or plurality of risks within universal public health schemes, demands that the latter form of insurance must be financed with at least some degree of participation from general taxation budgets. At the same time, however, insurance interfaces have never been distinct, but are instead porous as public and private schemes impact, the one upon the other, within an interlinked socio-economic environment. As a consequence, the operations of the private market are often subject to interventionist limitations to preserve public provision and support social goals. For example, softer or harder regulatory bans on 'cherry-picking', or the efforts of the private market to entice attractively highly financed, low-risk individuals away from public schemes into their own insurance pools, may be imposed in order to sustain the quasi-actuarial operations of public or semi-public health or pension schemes.[21] Equally, however, the public sphere may also make utilitarian or ethical intervention into market operation; first, encouraging or demanding non-actuarial cross-subsidization, in one exemplary case, in the form of private provision of wide-scale coverage for the high covariance risk of flood damage, financed most commonly by means of imposition of a supplement on all private insurance premiums; and, second, moving beyond a general demand for actuarial good practice, to limit instead the degree to which insurers might ever discriminate against particular conditions or illnesses.[22]

The existence of multiple insurance interfaces may be argued to give credence to the often-repeated sectoral assertion that insurance is distinguished from all other financial services. Although itself value-neutral, the market is, nonetheless, suspended within tensions between libertarian, utilitarian, and solidaristic principles; above all, not simply because utilitarian or ethical goals are betimes required to be integrated into its operations as market externalities, but rather because such interventions may demand reformulation of the primary market operation of actuarial risk pooling and, by the same token, manipulate or discount the informational asymmetries that are integral to the mechanism. Subject to utilitarian policies, as

[20] Abraham, n 18 above.

[21] See, eg, the distorting effects of private insurance market advertising for health insurance on public Medicaid and Medicare schemes in the US: Stone, D, 'The Struggle for the Soul of Health Insurance' (1993) 8(2) *Journal of Health Politics, Policy and Law* 287.

[22] But see, *John Doe and Richard Smith v Mutual of Omaha Insurance Company* 179 f.3d 557 (1999), and the refusal of the US judiciary to proscribe discrimination by life assurers against policyholders who are HIV positive.

well as to socialized and ethical expressions of egalitarian intent, the sector has always or at least since the start of the twentieth century, been prone to socialization demands, or to the requirement that it operate beyond its own market failure.

2. Regulatory modernization

Within this enduring paradigm, contemporary post-welfarism and the retreat of market-disciplined states from tax-based redistribution appear strangely reminiscent, but are also, as we shall see (Section V), a strikingly novel challenge in the established regulatory sphere for insurance. Above all, however, concomitantly heightened socio-economic expectations levelled at the futurization potential of the private market have created a regulatory paradox, whereby less can sometimes mean more, or wherein competition-inducing liberalization is accompanied by its own exponential increase in regulatory and, most cogently, supervisory techniques.

The five contractual, economic, subjective, temporal, and abstract elements of the insurance mechanism give rise to three particular regulatory concerns and forms of supervision, arising at market entry, throughout the conduct of business, as well as on product completion (disbursement). The *material supervision* of insurance corresponds with the concern that the legitimate expectations of the consumer must be met with regard to coverage. Material supervision tackles the contra-punctual informational asymmetry experienced by the insurance consumer in the face of sectoral cooperation and statistical exchange designed to facilitate establishment of sustainable risk pools. Policy terms and conditions

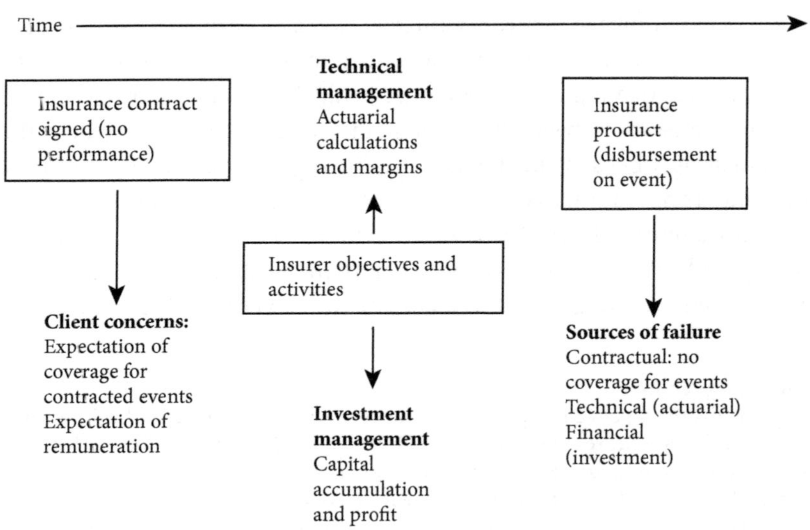

Figure 14.1 The insurance mechanism

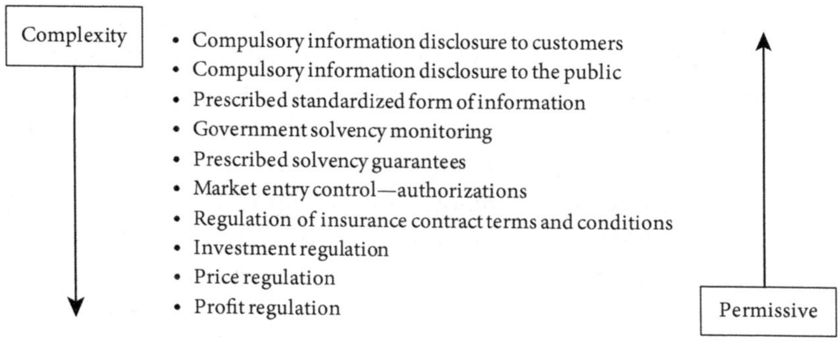

Figure 14.2 The traditional regulatory spectrum

Source: Adapted from Finsinger, J, Hammond, E, and Tapp, J, *Insurance: Competition & Regulation* (1985)

may accordingly be exposed to *ex ante* or *ex post* review, and are also subject to (non-regulatory) application of specialized provisions of contract law.[23] The *technical supervision* of the sector entails oversight of insurance expertise, an operation largely performed at market entry, whereby the qualifications of the insurer are subject to review, but may also extend to sectoral exemption from general application of competition law as regards information sharing and, far more controversially, other elements of competition-dampening cartelization (see Section III). Finally, *prudential supervision* comprises continuous control of investment-based, capital maximization activities.

Writing in the 1980s, the insurance economists, Jörg Finsinger, Elizabeth Hammond, and Julian Tapp,[24] established a progressive typology of supervisory instruments for insurance, ranging from the lowly complex, but highly permissive concept of compulsory information disclosure to the highly complex and restrictive imposition of price and profit regulation. Working against the backdrop of the European Commission's White Paper on the Completion of the European Single Market,[25] and in the context of the existence of significant national regulatory barriers to EU insurance trade, the typology also served to emphasize that the Commission's preferred liberalization strategy of harmonized market entry control and prudential supervision by means of supervised solvency margins, was not a matter of permissive deregulation. Instead, harmonization entailed a

[23] See, eg, within the UK, the application of the Unfair Contract Terms Directive (93/13/EEC [1993] OJ L95/29) to insurance policies. More generally, the law of contract as it applies to insurance policies is a complex topic all of its own, which is not treated in any comprehensive manner within this contribution. See, for details, in particular the failure to harmonize EU contract law as it applies to insurance and consequent efforts to develop model insurance policies, Heiss, H, Clarke, M, and Lakhan, M, 'Europe: Towards a Harmonised European Insurance Contract Law—the PEICL' in Burling, J and Lazarus, K (eds), *Research Handbook on International Insurance Law and Regulation* (2011) 603.

[24] ibid; Finsinger, J, Hammond, E, and Tapp, J *Insurance, Competition & Regulation* (1985).

[25] European Commission, White Paper on Governance COM(2001), 428 (2001).

regulatory strategy of median-complex intervention. In the meantime, however, and in the wake of advances in economic and regulatory theory, 'smart regulation',[26] or competition-sustaining supervision of markets, has evolved its own intricacies. One influential 2006 report accordingly lists the main purposes of insurance supervision as being to monitor solvency, to ensure fair trading, to promote fair access to markets, to promote price stability, as well as, although to a more controversial extent, to support the domestic industry.[27] The shift in rhetorical emphasis beyond traditional perceptions of market failure is palpable, above all within representations of fair trading and access, reflecting new expectations of market utility, or the sector's futurization capacities, particularly with regard to a now dominant understanding of consumer protection that is founded within the provision of individualized consumer price and product choice. Equally, however, the refinement of risk and risk-management theories has also significantly contributed to growing complexity in financial management processes, and especially so in a post-crisis environment.

The increasingly dominant logic of the last 40 years has been one that insurer failure may be averted by means of strict oversight of the sector's liabilities relative to its finances. As a result, solvency requirements have taken centre stage within the global regulatory environment. Seen in this light, the regulatory solvency standards championed by the IAIS may accordingly be viewed as simple quantitative prescriptions for the safe conduct of a still competitive insurance business. Expressed formulaically, the yearly equity calculation of an insurer total,

$$E_{t+1} - E_t = F_t + M_t + K_t - D_{t,}$$

where F are profits (plus miscellaneous capital additions), K is new capital, and D is disbursement. This, in turn, gives rise to a minimum solvency requirement (E*) of,

$$A_t - L_t \geq E^*,$$

where A are assets and L are liabilities.[28] The mathematical elegance of the formula, nevertheless, unravels upon closer examination of the qualitative as well as quantitative nature of the risks faced by the insurer within a competitively regulatory paradigm. Under circumstances of maximized market utility, the sector must manage five broad categories of risk. First, the risks posed to its technical provisions, or income set aside for the purposes of policy disbursement, which are exposed to

[26] See, eg, Commission dedication to 'smart regulation', Smart Regulation in the European Union: Communication from the Commission COM(2010), 543 (2010).

[27] CEPS, The Future of Insurance Regulation and Supervision in the EU: New Developments, New Challenges (Rym Ayadi and Christopher O'Brian, Rapporteurs) (2006).

[28] ibid.

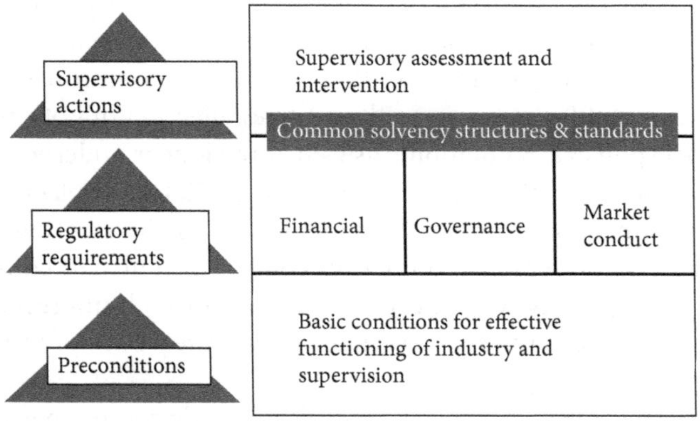

Figure 14.3 IAIS Core Principles

Source: CEPS, The Future of Insurance Regulation and Supervision in the EU: New Developments, New Challenges (Rym Ayadi and Christopher O'Brian, Rapporteurs) (2006)

stochastic catastrophic events, or may be internally mismanaged. Second, potential shortfalls in premium income due to price and demand movements within the market; a risk that once might have been self-managed across the sector within tolerated premium-fixing cartels, but which is now exaggerated under conditions of enhanced competition, creating a new impetus for prudential supervisory intervention at individual insurer level. Third, the existence of counterparty default dangers in re-insurance practice; an ever present peril that has, nevertheless, been greatly magnified where the industry has begun to hedge beyond an established re-insurance market within novel financial instruments such as credit-default swaps. Fourth, the very specific risks arising in relation to the sector's capital maximization activities, in particular, and famously so within the analysis of the causes of financial meltdown, the pro-cyclical bias within Value-at-Risk (VaR) methods of solvency accounting, which can promote over-exposure within a risking market.[29] And finally, operational business risks including the danger of computer systems failure; a potent risk factor for an industry that is wholly dependent upon statistical analysis.

Given the resilience of the sector during financial crisis, the UK PRA is perhaps given too much to teaching its own grandmother to suck eggs when it notes that quantitative 'risk models have been used in understanding and managing insurance risks for many years', but immediately qualifies this statement, urging 'insurers to be prudent in their use of such models given the inherent difficulties with risk measurement', and above all, 'the limitations from the structure and complexity of models, the data used as inputs and key underpinning assumptions'.[30] Nevertheless, the PRA's concomitant management injunction to establish

[29] Black, J, Restructuring Global and EU Financial Regulation: Capacities, Coordination and Learning (2010), LSE Law, Society and Economy Working Papers No 18/2010.

[30] Bank of England, Prudential Regulation Authority, The Prudential Regulation Authority's Approach to Insurance Supervision (2013), para 116.

'independent validation' and 'alternative risk management processes' that both challenge the 'key assumptions supporting the models', as well 'the risks that are not adequately captured by them',[31] together with its self-commitment to the monitoring of this internal function, is an illustrative reflection of both the post-crisis turn to 'really-responsive' regulation,[32] as well as the longer underlying trend, most clearly enunciated within the Second Pillar of Basel III, for the placing of oversight emphasis upon supervision rather than regulation; to the positing of successful pursuit of dual and potentially conflicting goals of heightened competition and increased financial probity within capital markets through unprecedented direct supervisory intervention into the governance structures, both of individual firms and across the market.

The latter-day recognition that risk analysis is not always an objectively quantitative exercise, but may be skewed at the very outset by subjective assumptions—a pertinent example being that a rising market will continue to rise—and, above all, the amplified awareness that some dangers cannot be foreseen,[33] are perhaps only restatements of the seminal distinction long ago made by Frank Knight between risks and uncertainty. That is, between dangers which can be calculated in probabilistic paradigms (risks), and hazards which defy all statistical accounting (uncertainty).[34] Nevertheless, as applied within the post-crisis environment, the current recognition that financial business is conducted in the face of a multitude of interlinked and complex perils, some of which it struggles and fails to comprehend, has not only found expression within the heightened regulatory solvency requirements applied to the financial sector, especially in the form of tougher capital adequacy requirements for banks, but also in the more stringently interventionist supervisory approach to the internal governance of economic solvency requirements, or own risk models and market disclosure. Where the core regulatory principles laid down by the IAILS succinctly note that, to the degree that income and expenditure may be subject to stochastic variation, regulators or insurers may wish to calculate assets and liabilities with prudential margins,[35] supervisory practice within the UK and Europe has taken a far more proactive approach. Above all, the general emphasis placed by the core principles upon good governance and market disclosure is magnified and translated into the UK PRA's mission to work intimately with the industry to ensure that the sector maintains continuous and prudential

[31] Bank of England, n 30 above, para 116.

[32] Baldwin, R and Black, J, 'Really Responsive Risk-Based Regulation' (2010) 32(2) *Law and Policy* 181.

[33] This realization is general to the social sciences and pre-dates the lessons of the financial crisis, above all, where dangers posed by physical processes of, for example, increased reliance on genetically modified organisms is subject to concerns about (non-calculable) uncertainties, such as general environmental damage, see, van Asselt, M and Vos, E, 'Science, Knowledge and Uncertainty in EU Risk Regulation' in Everson, M and Vos, E (eds), *Uncertain Risks Regulated* (2008) 359.

[34] Knight, n 4 above.

[35] Paraphrasing the IAILS, n 12 above.

risk-management processes at all levels of its business and responds pre-emptively to the risks and hazards of constantly changing circumstance within competitive insurance and capital markets.

Contemporary prudential oversight is seemingly advantaged in its responsiveness towards the hazards posed by the competitive forces that a liberalized approach to the regulation of financial service markets has unleashed. Seen in the abstract, and putatively founded within partnership rather than hierarchical direction, the supervisory relationship between overseer and market facilitates competitive operation, also providing an early warning system and means of jointly calibrated response to inherent market uncertainty. Nevertheless, a market-friendly scheme of supervision creates its own intricate complexity in practice. The PRA's injunction to a UK market that 'they should not, however, approach their relationship with the PRA as a negotiation',[36] reveals much that is of concern within such an intimate marriage, above all, its exposure to industry capture;[37] a problem that finds its important counterpart reflection in market-led doubts about the efficiency of such comprehensive supervisory intervention, as well as raises significant issues of institutional design. Post-crisis, these concerns are particularly acute in the wave of reform that has also witnessed the creation of new autonomous authorities to oversee national and supranational implementation of Solvency II (see Section IV). At the same time, they also exist within continuing tensions between the global liberalization of the insurance sector and residual national contexts of macro-economic specificity.

III. Liberalization Tensions: The European Example

In the then words of the European Commission, the Single Market programme applied to the European insurance sector with the aim of ensuring, on the one hand, that '[A]n insurer established in Cologne would note no legal differences were it to pursue business in Bavaria or Scotland' and, on the other, that 'all European citizens should be free to shop where they want for insurance within the Single Market'.[38] Judged against these criteria, the programme

[36] Bank of England, n 30 above, para 47, reiterated in the introduction to the document (p 7).

[37] See Stiglitz, J et al., *The Economic Role of the State* (1989).

[38] Respectively, Sir Leon Brittan, speaking to the Gesamtverband der Deutschen Versicherungswirtschaft (7 March 1990), and the Centre for Insurance Services, University of Leuven (19 March 1990), available as Comm T/22/90.

has failed. Certainly, significant efficiency gains were made within the financial liberalization precipitated by euro adoption, and were, at least up until the post-9/11 slowdown, reflected in waves of mergers and acquisitions, the evolution of *bancassurance*—or the creative integration of the banking, insurance, and financial products that are offered to consumers—as well as in a notable decline in traditional sectoral reliance on fixed-asset securities and a concomitant increase in futurizing risk appetite within capital markets.[39] Nevertheless, these gains, which were also negatively impacted upon during the 2008 crisis, are but a poor measure of market integration, or rather the lack thereof, which finds its most pertinent expression in the extent of cross-border provision of insurance services, especially with regard to mass-market products and market interpenetration. One 1999 study, completed following the 1994 adoption of the Single European Passport for insurance by the third-generation insurance directives,[40] and reaffirmed in 2006,[41] took as its exemplary markers UK and German market segments, only to conclude that, all liberalization apart, there had been zero growth in cross-border trade and 'no influx of new entries from abroad into the highly profitable German market'. More damningly, there was not merely 'no sign as yet of the growth of a single market in insurance products'; instead, 'market analysts do not expect there to be any'; a negative expectation that has been largely satisfied in the intervening period.[42]

The choice made by the 1999 study of German and English regimes to illustrate continuing integration failure is apposite. Not only are they the two most profitable of EU national markets, together making up 30 per cent of its premium income; each were, and to a degree still are, representative of two distinct European approaches to insurance regulation, with Ireland, the Netherlands, France, and portions of the emerging Eastern European market lining up behind the liberal UK approach, and the rest shadowing the far stricter attitude to reserve requirements, investment controls, entry qualifications, and policy conditions traditionally applied within the Federal Republic. Equally, however, and where one of the major expected benefits of global liberalization in general, and European economic integration, in particular, is held to be 'regulatory rationalization', or the separation out of broader economic policy goals from sectoral regulation,[43] the two still discrete market cultures continue to reflect the very specific place of the insurance sector within nationally constructed insurance interfaces and macro-economic policy.

[39] CEPS, n 27 above.

[40] Rees, R, Kessner, E, and Klemperer, P, 'Regulation and Efficiency in European Insurance Markets' (1999) 29 *Economics* 365.

[41] Molle, W, *The Economics of European Integration: Theory, Practice, Policy* (2006).

[42] ibid.

[43] Majone, G, *Regulating Europe* (1996).

1. First-generation integration

Their minimal nature, notwithstanding, the first European efforts to effect minimum harmonization of insurance regulation are notable for their ratcheting up of UK regulatory standards. Council Directive 64/225/EEC had early on realized the simple task of providing for full freedom of establishment and services in the already highly internationalized reinsurance market. By contrast, Directives 73/239/EEC (life) and 79/267/EEC (non-life) achieved only minimum common rules on market access. It proved impossible to settle a shared definition of life assurance business due to extreme divergence in the organization of national markets. Nonetheless, a unified scheme, to be recognized by all host authorities, was established for each line of underwriting by European provisions on market authorizations and solvency standards. No agreement was reached on technical reserves and all other matters of material regulation remained within the competence of home regulators.[44]

For the UK, governed up until 1967 by a minimal freedom with disclosure regime, at which time the Board of Trade introduced a limited scheme of insurance authorization, rationalizing European legislation, transposed in the 1973 Insurance Companies Act, proved opportune, especially following the comprehensive failure of the UK's self-regulatory tradition in the early 1970s. Not only had the market's heavy reliance on competition-dampening cartelization in the matter of motor tariffs been implicated, by virtue of its support for 'incompetent' insurers, in the crash of Vehicle & General Insurance that obliterated 10 per cent of motor market coverage; instead, the sector had also failed to fulfil its traditional role of establishing a rescue fund for London Indemnity & General, one of two life insurers which had damagingly succumbed to the UK's then critical liquidity crisis.[45]

UK regulatory embarrassment, however, was matched by political-economic factors, as adoption of a stricter regime also emerged as a bargaining counter within perennially bad-tempered revisiting of the structure of the insurance interface maintained between an exceptionally vibrant private market and universalized provision of public welfare within the UK. The miraculous escape of the UK insurance industry from the all-pervasive regulating fashions of the early twentieth century—a trend extending even to the US—has been ascribed to the very early assumption by the sector of global dominance and its consequentially

[44] Council Directive 64/225/EEC on freedom of establishment and services for the re-insurance market [1964] OJ L56/878; Council Directive 73/239/EEC on the coordination of the laws, regulations and administrative provisions relating to the take up and pursuit of the business of direct insurance other than life assurance [1973] OJ L228/3; Council Directive 79/267/EEC 1 on the coordination of the laws, regulations and administrative provisions relating to the pursuit of the business of direct life assurance [1979] OJ L63/.

[45] Clayton, G, *British Insurance* (1971).

pivotal position within British balance of trade accounting.[46] Nevertheless, the preparedness of UK policymakers to tolerate a surprising number of insurance failures, all in the service of a competitively vibrant market,[47] was also facilitated by the relatively late evolution of public welfare provision within the UK, itself financed by means of a non-actuarial National Insurance tax. Whereas the origins of restrictive regulation within the Federal Republic can be ascribed to socializing Bismarkian aspiration, or early adoption of quasi-public schemes for health and welfare provision, founded at least in part on statistical accounting, the UK remained free from direct comparison between broadly similar public and private markets. British policymakers were accordingly spared the complex necessity to adjust policy terms and conditions within the private market to preclude cherry-picking from public welfare schemes, as well as to coordinate the mutually supportive operations of public and private sectors; a material supervisory task undertaken in Germany from 1901 onwards by the *Bundesaufsichtsamt für das Versicherungswesen* (BAV).[48]

From the beginning of the twentieth century, the UK industry maintained close ties with government, securing its privileged position through support for public (health and safety) legislative goals and diversion of its considerable financial resource to purchase of government bonds at times of national liquidity crisis.[49] By the same token, however, the sector did not shy away from political confrontation (Figure 14.4), playing the balance of payments joker and appealing directly to elector-policyholders; most notably in the 1949 wake of the socially reforming Beveridge Report, when the then Labour government seized upon its recommendations that, given their congruence, the industry's profitable line in industrial life assurance should be integrated within the public national savings regime: '[T]hey (the insurers) were not investing the shareholders' money, they were investing the people's money which ought to be controlled and invested in the interest of the whole nation.'[50] Successfully fending off this macro-economic mission to switch to an inward investment model, the failure-weakened private market, nonetheless, remained vulnerable to re-emergence of nationalization themes during the political-economic upheavals of the 1970s.[51] In this context, increased regulatory stringency occasioned by UK accession to the then European Economic

[46] ibid; see also, *Post Magazine Almanac* for 1880: The London & Liverpool & Globe alone had US assets totalling $4,402,602 as early as 1785.

[47] Finsinger, J, *Verbraucherschutz auf Versicherungsmärkte* (1988).

[48] Everson, M, 'The Federal Supervisory Authority for Insurance' in Majone, G (ed.), *Regulating Europe* (1996) 202.

[49] See Clayton, n 45 above, 184–91.

[50] John Griffith, Minister of National Insurance, explaining nationalization proposals to the Labour Party Conference, 'The Social Services: State Industrial Assurance', *The Times*, 10 June 1949.

[51] Beale, R, *After the V&G Crash* (1972).

Figure 14.4 Trade above socialization

Source: *Times newspaper*, advertisement placed by the Industrial Life Office (4 October 1949)

Communities was a small price to pay for continuing governmental indulgence with regard to competitively based overseas earning capacity.

2. Judicial activism

The history of the integrative liberalization of European insurance regulation has a special place within European studies. Above all, intransigent German unwillingness to accede to liberalized material supervision in the case of cross-border services bequeathed to Europeanists the first judicial statement of the direct effect of Article 49 Treaty on the Functioning of the European Union (TFEU) in the 1985 *Co-insurance* cases,[52] whereby the then Court of Justice (ECJ) discounted German provisions requiring all persons offering insurance to German consumers to be

[52] *Commission v France, Denmark, Germany & Ireland* [1987] 2 CMLR 69. Note, the Commission were able to make advances in areas of specialist insurance such as co-insurance and motor insurance. The relevant measure here was Directive 78/473/EEC on Community co-insurance.

established within the Republic, and consequently imposed trade liberalization for large-scale risks. The economic rationality of the ECJ, its liberalizing mission to apply its own principles of proportionality to European cross-border business, at least to the degree that notions of consumer protection could no longer be used to justify *ex ante* control of the terms and conditions offered to commercial policyholders, similarly bore fruit in the second-generation insurance directives; albeit, that the distinctions which they established between large- and small-scale risks (non-life insurance), and active and passive policyholders (life insurance) now seem arbitrarily incongruous.[53] Codifying instruments of 'negative' European integration, departing from the traditional effort to harmonize national provisions to detail, instead, the circumstances under which the right to provide services might be exercised, the directives also stipulated that prudential supervision for insurance services would be the sole province of home regulators. They accordingly lifted national bans on 'cumul'—ie, the cumulative provision of cross-border services by an insurer established in a host territory—ended matching assets requirements for such insurers, and restricted the material supervision that might apply to service provision; with the significant caveat that Article 18 of the Non-Life Directive still permitted *ex post* supervision of policy terms and conditions where home regimes were deemed to be insufficient. A matching provision was also provided for by Article 14(5) of the Life Directive which allowed host states to prevent their citizens from entering into commitments abroad where this was felt to be 'contrary to public policy'.

Perhaps more significant, however, was the 1987 case of the *Sachverband der Deutschen Feuerversicher*,[54] whereby the ECJ had its own liberalizing impact upon the residually corporatist organization of insurance regulation within the German Republic. The judgment upheld a European Commission Decision banning a *Sachverband* recommendation for a 30 per cent increase in fire premiums in response to falling market rates, and did so notwithstanding the fact that the fire insurance cartel, whose membership was open to foreign insurers, was subject to German supervisory oversight in the character of the BAV. The core impact of the judgment resided in the observation of the Court that: 'Community Law does not make the implementation of ... [competition policy] ... dependent upon the manner in which the supervision of certain areas of economic activity is organized by national legislation.'[55] With this, the ECJ at last began to unravel the special position of the BAV and insurance regulation within a dichotomous post-war German economy; undermining its status as the one that got away from, or successfully

[53] Second Non-Life Directive, 88/357/EEC [1988] OJ L172/1 (1988); Council Directive 90/619/EEC [1990] OJ L330/50 (1990) on the coordination of laws, regulations and administrative provisions relating to direct life assurance.

[54] Case 45/85 ECR, *Verband der Sachversicherer e.V. v Commission of the European Communities* ECR [1987] 405.

[55] ibid, para 23.

resisted the efforts of Ludwig Erhard's, as both Finance Minister and Chancellor, to include the sector within the liberalized restructuring of the Germany economy.

At one level, the exclusion of the industry from application of Erhard's flagship commitment to anti-trust policies within the German Competition Code (§102 GWB), or his legal expression of the macro-economic policy to be pursued by the competitively reborn Federal Republic, may be ascribed to the market failure that is integral to the insurance mechanism. Cartelization was historically justified as, and deployed in a regulatory exercise to dampen market competition in cases of amplified informational asymmetry. Nevertheless, the continuing intensity of pro-competitive attacks on the BAV, together with its matching ability to resist repeated attempts to end its further practices in restraint of trade, above all in stipulation of a unitary premium calculation mechanism,[56] indicate that conflict also derived from a titanic clash between more fundamental political-economic forces within the Federal Republic; from conflict between a free-market orientation and continuing corporatist faith in interventionist industrial policy. Above all, where the BAV strategically dominated a tight web of industry, consumer, and union interests, such that it was able to ensure that premium levels remained above their costs, stagnant competition within the German marketplace also facilitated the inward investment practices of German insurers; an undoubted contribution to macro-economic steering within the Republic.[57]

The significance of broader political-economic considerations within this constellation is similarly confirmed by the speed with which the Commission acted to diffuse political conflict following ECJ activism, issuing a block exemption from EC competition policy, under which many cartel-like insurance practices continued to be tolerated. Equally, however, proponents of competitive reform within the Republic were able only to distil very limited immediate political capital from the Judgment. The sector became subject to the *Verbotsprinzip*,[58] outlawing cartels within the marketplace, but only to the extent that cooperative industry agreements—including price agreements[59]—were to be registered with the Federal Cartel Office to be subject to review of whether other measures less restrictive of competition were available. 1989 reform of anti-trust law, designed to bring the insurance sector within the pro-competitive regime, was thus arguably compromised at the very outset by continuing governmental emphasis on the role of competition policy in securing 'the best possible care of the population';[60] a generalist precept, facilitative of corporatist steering. As German industrial policy remained captive to an underlying macro-economic dichotomy, the BAV

[56] Maintained until 1980; see, for full details, Finsinger et al., n 24 above.

[57] See, for fuller details, Everson, n 48 above.

[58] Baake, P and Perschau, O 'The Legal and Institutional Regulation of the Law against Measures Restrictive of Competition' in Majone, G (ed.), *Regulating Europe* (1996).

[59] BR, Drucksache 123/89 (p 81).

[60] Wismann (MP), introducing the debate in the Bundestag, BT PiPr, 11/182 (p 14077).

continued to exercise considerable anti-competitive influence,[61] with one very noticeable consequence that subsequent European efforts to restrict industry cooperation to legitimate matters of statistical information exchange—subject always to national-supranational negotiation—have only very recently been fully realized in the revised Block Exemption Regulation 267/2010. Today, only three categories of statistical cooperation, 'necessary for the purpose of calculating risks' are allowed by European competition law: first, the costs of covering specified past risks; second, the compilation of statistical information; and third, joint carrying-out of studies and distribution of results.

3. The Single European Passport

The slow pace of competitive change with regard to final rejection of cartel-based supervision, explains much of the frustration expressed by the economists, Rees, Kessner, and Klemperer, in their 1999 study of the sector. However, in this view, a further measure of disappointment is furnished by the assertion that the third generation of insurance directives, creating the Single European Insurance Passport had likewise failed to capitalize fully on the efficiency gains exhibited by UK, as well as French, sectors in the wave of regulatory reform following 'big bang'.[62] The two framework directives for life and non-life insurance, together with harmonized accounting provisions, designed to provide for one seat authorization of all EU insurance business, represented a notable step in the progressive harmonization of European regulatory provision.[63] The Passport allowed for comprehensive market access, no longer distinguishing between large and small or active and passive risks, and did so on the basis of harmonization of the forms of prudential supervision to be applied by home supervisors, including: minimum benchmark rules for investment of assets for technical provisions; more specific rules for admissibility, diversification, localization, and valuation of assets, including a stipulation that these assets need no longer be held in specified forms, such as state bonds; as well as joint accounting standards, although at this time allowing for use of the measure of historic rather than market value (see Section IV). At the same time, slight advances were also made with regard to material supervision, as the ban on *ex ante* control of policy provisions in cross-border services was reiterated, although *ex post* supervision might be asserted in line with protection of the 'general good'. In addition, further consumer protection measures were pursued in the guise of choice of law provisions

[61] Everson, n 48 above. [62] See Rees et al., n 40 above.

[63] Non Life (now 2002/13/EC [2002] OJ L77/17, Life (now 2002/83/EC [2002] OJ L345/1), together with Accounts (91/674/EEC [1991] OJ L374/7), Insurance Committee (91/675/EEC [1991] OJ L374/32) and Winding Up (2001/17/EC [2001] OJ L110/28).

for insurance contracts and extended cooling-off periods applicable to conclusion of life assurance policies.

However, at a distance of two decades, economic frustration is best understood in terms of EU failure, for all of its harmonizing zeal, prescriptively to pursue the more proactively competitive regulatory strategies then being adopted within liberalizing national regimes. Above all, the application of the 1986 Financial Services Act to the UK insurance sector initiated sea change in the understanding of the place of financial services markets within the competitive life of the nation. Presaged by the 1983 Gower Report and above all its author's curt observation that he was not 'in the business of protecting fools from themselves',[64] the Act began both to maximize futurization potential with regard to capital generation, and applied new futurizing understandings of consumer protection as enhanced consumer choice, encouraging evolution of new financial instruments to be offered to the public, subject only to the proviso that financial intermediaries should offer the consumer 'the best possible advice'.[65]

The 1980s emergence of a now dominant paradigm of market utility necessarily begs the question of whether macro-economic concerns still play their part within financial services regulation, especially in view, for example, of transfer of prudential regulatory functions in Germany away from BAV to the newly established *Bundesaufsichtsamt für das Finanzwesen* (BaFin).[66] An immediate answer, however, must be, yes: born in economic theory, the pursuit of market utility is, nevertheless, expressive of a macro-economic programme, reaching deeper than ever before into the psyche and operation of industry and consumer alike in its restructuring aspirations. At the same time, however, it is clear that insurance interfaces still play their vital, sector-restraining part within an integrated insurance market, especially in view of ECJ refusal to extend the jurisdiction of EU competition law to social insurance schemes, exactly because of the danger of private market cherry-picking.[67] Equally, retarded market interpenetration might be argued to indicate that the cultures of restrictive practice have outlived the political prominence of their masters; a finding also attributable to the pedestrian character of the industry when compared with its banking counterpart. Meanwhile, continuing recognition that insurance regulation may be required to support the domestic industry, might itself extend beyond approval for preservation of critical coverage within the home market to

[64] See, for details, Everson, n 48 above.

[65] Now contained within conduct of business rules administered by the FCA.

[66] However, indications are that corporatist regulatory practices persist within BaFin. See, for details, Keßler, J, Micklitz, H-W, and Reich, N, Darstellung der Arbeitsweise von Finanzaufsichtsbehörden in ausgewählten Ländern und deren Verbraucherorientierung (2009), Working Paper of the German Consumer Federation (Vzbv), available at <http://www.vzbv.de/mediapics/studie_finanzaufsicht_vergleich_eu_zusammenfassung_okt_2009.pdf> (last accessed July 2014).

[67] *Albany International BV v Stichting Bedrijfspensioenfonds Textielindustrie*, Case C-67/96; with joined cases C-115/97, C-116/97, and C-117/97 [1999] ECR I-5751.

include instead residual maintenance of steering capacity over domestic investments; a factor of particular importance beyond developed economies,[68] but perhaps also—to suspicious minds at least—reflected within the protracted nature of negotiations on implementation of Solvency II within Europe.

IV. The Post-Crisis Regime of EU Insurance Supervision

At EU level, the ESFS is not the first supranational endeavour to coordinate financial supervision, following on instead from the competitively oriented Lamfalussy programme. However, lying between Lamfalussy and ESFS adoption, we find not only financial crisis, but also significant change in rhetorical justification for enhanced EU supervisory capacity, as the de Larosière group, convened in response to meltdown, returned to traditional depictions of market failure, concluding that the European system of financial oversight must be reformed: first, to improve an 'inadequate mix' of regulatory and supervisory skills, which had seen too little information gathered and shared 'on the global magnitude of leveraging', and which had concomitantly exhibited a catastrophic failure 'fully [to] understand or evaluate the size of the risks'; and second, to create a coordinated early warning system 'to identify macro-systemic risks of a contagion of correlated horizontal shocks'.[69] Contrasting competition and market failure apprehensions are, nonetheless, far from being mutually exclusive with regard to insurance. Instead, to the degree that long-evinced sectoral campaigning weight has latterly been deployed against proactively liberalizing regulation, including the first pre-crisis drafts of the Solvency II Directive,[70] the financial crisis has provided useful counterweight leverage to policymakers.

Explaining its application to the UK insurance sector of an onerous prudential regulatory burden closely aligned with and in future transposition of competition-inducing Solvency II, the PRA acknowledges industry disquiet, conceding that 'insurers are not systemic in the same way as banks'.[71] Nevertheless, in addition to highlighting the defuturization potential of a sudden withdrawal of general insurance for the populace,

[68] See, eg, the wariness of developed countries within GATS committees dealing with the definition of prudential supervision for WTO purposes, Lang, A and Scott, J, 'The Hidden World of WTO Governance' (2009) 20(3) *European Journal of International Law* 575.

[69] <http://ec.europa.eu/internal_market/finances/docs/de_larosiere_report_en.pdf> (last accessed March 2014).

[70] See n 13 above.

[71] Bank of England, n 30 above, para 15.

the Authority is similarly quick to reiterate the threats which insurance failure, as well as normal business conduct, might pose to banking and financial systems; above all, in view of the growth of group financial services and the role played by insurance guarantees in bank lending (derivatives), as well as with regard to the potential hazards posed to asset prices by (life) insurance investment strategies. In immediate contrast, and the collapse of the American International Group (AIG) apart, history teaches us only that the sector is marked by its exposure to, rather than generation of, systemic risk.[72] Yet, the financial crisis has now done its decisive job, facilitating inclusion of the market within an intrusively permissive regime, modelled on banking supervision standards.

1. Preparing for Solvency II[73]

For the EU's retarded single market project, the greatest advantage of Solvency II tailoring to Basel rather than IAIS standards, lies in its unprecedentedly prescriptive approach; a sharp contrast to the historic vulnerability of benchmark EU coordination provisions to regulatory arbitrage. Solvency II requires Member States to ensure, as its main objective that their supervisory authorities can protect policyholders; as well as, perform a secondary role sustaining the European financial services market. Prudential matters are the sole province of home supervision, and must include verification of solvency and technical provisions 'in accordance with EU standards'.[74] Article 29 lays down the core principles of supervision, including a prospective risk-based approach, ongoing verification of risk management, appropriate on- and off-site inspections, and the proportionate application of Solvency II to the risks posed by an individual business.

In addition to imposing a three-pillar structure of prudential norms, governance requirements, and provisions on disclosure, Solvency II codifies much preceding EU legislation, primarily in the matter of market authorization and conduct of European business (Title I), with additional reiteration of principles of material supervision (Title II). The restated rules on taking up and pursuit of insurance and reinsurance encompass: a single EU authorization for establishment and services; specific forms of business incorporation, with capacity for national variations such as, in the UK, Lloyds; a limitation to insurance activities and strict conditions for simultaneous pursuit of life and non-life business, including separate accounting; as well as restrictions on refusal to authorize for national market reasons. Material supervision is similarly codified, whereby policy term authorization for

[72] See, IAIS, n 12 above.

[73] I am wholly indebted for this Section to the excellent summary of Solvency II given by Robert Purves, see Purves, P, 'Europe: The Architecture and Content of EU Insurance Regulation' in Burling, J and Lazarus, K (eds), *Research Handbook on International Insurance Law and Regulation* (2011) 621.

[74] Article 30(2) (Directive 2009/138/EC).

cross-border services is available only to protect the 'general good', existing rules on choice of laws are confirmed and the information to be given to policyholders is subject to minimum standards.[75]

(a) *Core prudential requirements*

Assets and technical provisions: Solvency II makes its core competition-inducing advance in assets and liabilities accounting. Where Member States were once free to choose historic cost accounting as a launch pad for their regulatory oversight, Solvency II builds instead upon the work of the International Accounting Standards Board (IASB),[76] in order to impose market value accounting. Long criticized for its lack of consistency and transparency, especially where asset purchase price falls below current market value, historic cost accounting for assets, together with amortized value accounting—stable and transparent, but applicable only to redeemable fixed interest securities—is superseded by the far more elegant precept of market value accounting: what would a reasonable party pay for existing assets? Transposed into the EU standard that assets must be valued at the amount for which they could be exchanged between knowledgeable and willing parties in an arm's length transaction, the marketization process also extends to the once subjectively based and, therefore, highly prudential calculation of insurer liabilities, asking instead how much is available to pay claims, such that liabilities must be valued, under equally anonymized conditions, and without adjustment for insurer own-credit-rating, at the amount for which they could be transferred to a buyer.[77]

Translating these precepts into the valuation of technical assets, the Directive mandates that this value must correspond first, to the current amount insurers would have to pay if they were immediately to transfer their obligations to another undertaking (exit value); must secondly, make use of and be consistent with information supplied by financial markets and generally available data on underwriting risks (market consistent valuation); and must finally be calculated in a 'prudent, reliable and objective manner', whereby Article 77(1) also stipulates that technical provisions must be equal to a best estimate plus risk margin, totalling the probability weighted average of future cash flows plus purchaser expectations. Subject to the 'prudent person principle' with regard to their immediate recoverability, no EU localization of assets is required for technical provisions; a measure extending to non-EU insurers deemed to be subject to 'equivalent' prudential supervision.[78]

Solvency requirements: the move to market value italicizes the character of Solvency II as an instrument of regulation in obeisance of market utility. Markets

[75] Title II, Chapter I, section 1, section 3, and section 5 (Directive 2009/138/EC).

[76] See, for details, CEPS, n 27 above.

[77] Article 75 (Directive 2009/138/EC).

[78] Articles 76–86 (Directive 2009/138/EC).

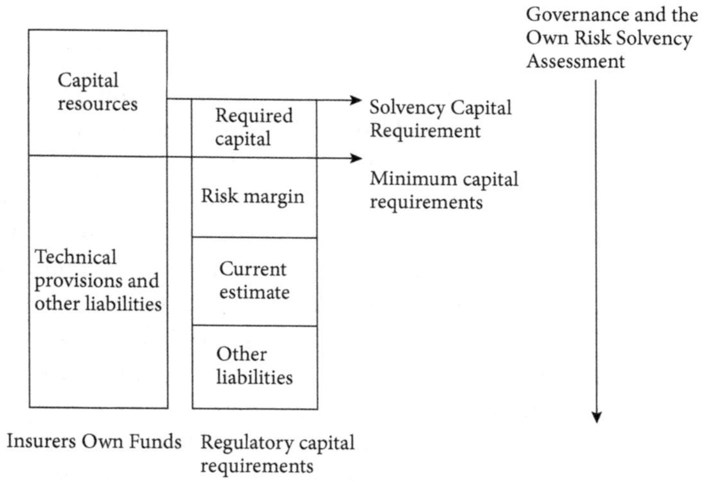

Figure 14.5 Solvency

Source: Modified from CEPS, The Future of Insurance Regulation and Supervision in the EU: New Developments, New Challenges (Rym Ayadi and Christopher O'Brian, Rapporteurs) (2006).

rather than regulators are best placed to assess insurer value. At the same time, however, reiterated emphasis upon accounting prudence also betrays the enduring tension within permissive interventionism; its aim to maximize utility, but also prudentially to master, the subjective risks—or uncertainties—posed by market operation. This theme is continued by Solvency II in the positioning of its capital adequacy rules mid-way between regulatory solvency, or *ex ante* imposition of hierarchical capital adequacy requirements, and a pure economic measure of market-driven solvency; that is, in its core endeavour to prescribe the manner in which an insurer assesses its own solvency relative to market operations. This miraculous conjoining of regulation with competition is performed within VaR methodologies. Where the regulatory capital of the insurer comprises the excess of assets above liabilities, as well as ancillary own funds—or any other funds, such as guarantees, that can be called up to absorb losses—and whereby these funds are classified into tiers for their ability to absorb losses,[79] the Solvency Capital Requirement (SCR), or measure at which the business is held to be normally viable is defined as follows:

In order to promote good risk management and align regulatory capital requirements with industry practices, the SCR should be determined as the economic capital to be held by insurance and reinsurance undertakings in order to ensure that ruin occurs no more often than once in every 200 cases or, alternatively, that those undertakings will still be in a position, with a probability of at least 99.5%, to meet their obligations to policyholders and beneficiaries over the following 12 months. That economic capital should be calculated on

[79] Ancillary funds do not count as Tier One capital, whereby Tier One capital must make up at least one-third of own funds for purposes of solvency calculation.

the basis of the true risk profile of those undertakings, taking account of the impact of possible risk-mitigation techniques, as well as diversification effects (Recital 64).

Member States are required to ensure that undertakings maintain their SCR, calculated annually, according to a standard formula, or to their own approved model; each recalibrated should the risk profile alter and each reflecting real risks, including subjective risks.[80] The standard formula comprises: a basic solvency capital requirement, including, at the least, risk modules for non-life underwriting risk, life underwriting risk, health underwriting risk, market risk, and counterparty default risk; a capital requirement for operational risk, as well as adjustment for the loss absorbing capacity of technical provisions and deferred tax. Own models must satisfy a 'use test' including internal governance structures.[81] In turn, the SCR is underpinned by a Minimum Capital Requirement (MCR), corresponding to a measure of own funds, below which policyholders and beneficiaries would be subject to unacceptable risks should the insurer continue to trade. Not falling below or exceeding 25 per cent or 45 per cent of the SCR, the MCR is to be calculated quarterly, reported in a transparent mode to the supervisor, varies in minimum value for individual insurance classes, and is calculated from a set of technical provisions, written premiums, capital at risk, deferred tax, and operational expenses.

(b) *Governance requirements*

The marvellous resolution of prudential tension between permissive intervention and inherent market uncertainty in quantitative risk models is vitally underscored within a really responsive regulatory paradigm by the emphasis that is placed upon governance; more particularly, good governance, whereby significantly enhanced supervisory capacity is deployed to militate the qualitative failings in market regulation that quantitative analysis alone cannot reach. Solvency II accordingly establishes its own internal governance requirements for the private market in the character of the Own Risk Solvency Assessment (ORSA), further mandating national supervisors to comprehensive and proactive review of the risk-management systems maintained by individual undertakings.[82] Again, shadowing Basel III Pillar Two design, the ORSA requires senior management to conduct internal risk-management exercises ensuring continuous compliance with SCR and MCR requirements, whereby the ORSA includes the specific risk profile of the business, its approved risk tolerance limits, and business strategy. Additionally, the ORSA must be performed in a manner proportionate to the magnitude of risks faced, must be an integral part of business strategy; be reperformed following any alterations in risk circumstances, regularly reported to the home supervisor, and, where appropriate, closely calibrated with internal SCR models.[83]

[80] Articles 100–27 (Directive 2009/138/EC).

[81] Articles 128–31 (Directive 2009/138/EC).

[82] Article 45 (Directive 2009/138/EC).

[83] ibid.

In interventionist counterpoint, Solvency II similarly requires home supervisors to conduct supervisory review, ensuring that firms comply with mandated solvency and reporting requirements—including, importantly, Pillar Three reporting requirements to the market, consumers, and supervisory authorities alike—with adequate respect for the imperative for qualitative assessment. Review accordingly extends far beyond oversight of technical provisions, capital requirements, investment rules, quantity, and quality of own funds, to encompass, in addition, prescribed home oversight, both on paper and in person of internal systems of governance; and includes ORSA approach, ongoing modes of ensuring compliance with risk models, as well as planned and actual response to any change in financial conditions.[84] Finally, capital add-ons may be imposed following supervisory review, where the ORSA departs too greatly from the underlying assumptions of the SCR; or an internal governance model is ineffective in its inability to identify risks.[85]

Measured in terms of the competitive stability of the EU insurance market, the success or failure of Solvency II accordingly resides within the congruence or otherwise of national supervisory cultures. Where, and especially so post-crisis, the core quantitative precepts of the prudential regime are anchored within qualitative supervisory ability to overcome market uncertainty, distinctions between the aims and structure of Member State supervision have the potential both to undermine a coordinated European approach to financial stability, as well as to create its own competitive distortions between market segments subject to regimes of varying supervisory intensity. This latter consideration has caused a degree of concern within the UK-based industry subject to PRA oversight especially with regard to SCR composition.[86] PRA preparations for Solvency II adoption are, at least as regards their dissemination to industry and the public, far in advance of many of their European counterparts. Equally, perhaps reflecting its placement under a more risk adverse umbrella of Central Bank supervision than that experienced, for example, by the autonomous BaFin,[87] the PRA has already given voice to a stringently prudential temperament.

The PRA recognizes that its own 'limited resources mean that it cannot be expected to identify and account for all the risks that insurers may face',[88] and similarly seeks to apply Solvency II proportionately to the market through delineation of four categories of insurer, who are subject to varying degrees of applicable oversight according to their potential for defuturizing failure and generation of systemic risk. The Authority has, nonetheless, signalled its suspicious determination to react vigorously to industry manipulation of internal governance and risk-management structures. Above all, the Authority will object to 'insurers issuing regulatory

[84] Article 36 (Directive 2009/138/EC). [85] Article 37 (Directive 2009/138/EC).

[86] See, eg, 'Guiding Hand', *Post Magazine*, 14 April 2011.

[87] Although, see n 69 above. [88] Bank of England, n 30 above, para 128.

capital instruments that are deliberately structured to meet the letter but not the spirit of [regulatory capital] criteria, notably where their incentive is to minimise issuance cost and promote the attractiveness to investors at the expense of genuine loss-absorbing capacity'.[89] Equipped also with the *ex ante* power to impose disciplinary sanctions on individuals exercising 'significant functions', who knowingly act in contravention of PRA requirements,[90] the Authority's stated intention to make periodic on-site validations of insurer data appears to have bite, not only bark, similarly enhancing apprehension that, with the advent of really responsive regulation, the fragile balance between supervisor as market-facilitating partner and supervisor as permanently distorting shadow within the firm, will always be a tense one.[91]

2. Supervision within the ESFS

These final concerns about the culture of supervision within new regulatory regimes of permissive interventionism are only augmented by parallel reform in response to financial crisis. The establishment of the ESFS is remarkable, not only due to its creation of general tension between the regulatory goals of Lamfalussy and de Larosière, or between a long-standing mission to secure a globally competitive place for the EU financial services market and a latter-day imperative to secure capital market stability; a task made all the more urgent by the systemic re-emergence of global financial meltdown in the related guise of the European sovereign debt crisis.[92] Instead, rapid reform in response to each emergency has created its own stresses within EU institutional structures, above all, with regard to the legality of delegation within the Union following Lisbon Treaty reforms.

The ESFS poses both general and specific challenges to the insurance sector. At global level, the initial establishment of the European Systemic Risk Board (ESRB),[93] in pursuit of macro-prudential control, together with subsequent modification of the workings of the ESFS to accommodate the conferral upon the European Central Bank (ECB) of direct supervision powers over the private banking market through the Single Supervisory Mechanism (SSM),[94] is significant to the exact degree that

[89] Bank of England, n 30 above, para 131.

[90] <http://fshandbook.info/FS/html/PRA/APER>. [91] ibid.

[92] See, for the inherent connection between financial crisis and sovereign debt crisis, Scharpf, F, 'Monetary Union, Fiscal Crisis and the Pre-emption of Democracy' (2011) 9(2) *Zeitschrift für Staats- und Europawissenschaften* 163.

[93] See n 10 above. The ESRB is chaired by the President and Vice President of the ECB and includes governors of national central banks (NCBs), a member of the Commission and the Chairs of the three ESAs. The role of the ESRB is to provide 'macro-prudential' supervision within the ESFS, or to identify and combat 'systemic risks', or hazardous financial activities, which threaten the functioning of the system as a whole.

[94] To be exercised in parallel to the powers of the European Banking Authority (EBA). See Council Regulation (EU) No 1024/2013 [2010] OJ L287/63 conferring specific tasks on the European Central

reform also entails, however obliquely, EU adoption of a structural commitment to 'sound money';[95] or to the reassertion, if not of state, at least of Central Bank steering capacity for futurization, or ECB control over debt and private money-creation. Where ECB intervention within banking supervision, or in the exercise of its influence over ESRB warning powers to combat systemic risk, is directed to limitation of the financial instruments offered on capital markets, its macro-prudential steering capacity becomes one further risk factor, or uncertainty, to be included within insurance risk-management processes, in particular, as regards choice of hedging or investment instruments. The ESFS, however, also poses very specific risks for the sector; in particular, by virtue of its concomitant creation of institutional, as well as efficiency uncertainty within its supervisory realm.

(a) *Institutional uncertainty*

The establishment of EIOPA, the autonomous regulatory authority for insurance, has fundamentally reconfigured the EU sectoral supervision regime. Endowed by its own founding Regulation with triple functions of fostering cooperative competition within the sector, as well as the exercise of prudential oversight over and the combatting of systemic risk within the market, EIOPA replaces the Committee of European Insurance and Occupational Pensions Supervisors (CEIOPS)—a Lamfalussy creation made up of representatives of national regulatory authorities[96]—at the centre of a web of EU and national policymakers and regulators with responsibility for insurance. EIOPA is a creature of crisis: taking the longer view, however, and locating it within a far broader agencification trend,[97] regulatory theory would suggest that the Authority represents increased European supervisory utility. A burgeoning 'fourth branch of government' brings with it all the advantages of autonomous agency operation 'at arm's length' from traditional power:[98] comprehensive integration of expertise within a consequently greatly enhanced policymaking and implementation capacity, and its insulation from politically motivated distortion; as well as, stability in pursuit of regulatory goals, cumulative knowledge-building, and immediate visibility within the regulatory

Bank concerning policies relating to the prudential supervision of credit institutions and Regulation (EU) No 1022/2013 amending Regulation (EU) No 1093/2010 establishing a European Supervisory Authority (European Banking Authority) as regards the conferral of specific tasks on the European Central Bank pursuant to Council Regulation (EU) No 1024/2013 [2013] OJ L287/5.

[95] See, for details, Teubner, G, 'A Constitutional Moment? The Logics of "Hitting the Bottom"' in Kjaer, P, Teubner, G, and Febbrajo, A (eds), *The Financial Crisis in Constitutional Perspective: The Dark Side of Functional Differentiation* (2014) 9.

[96] Decision 2004/9/EC, Establishing a Committee of European Insurance and Occupational Pensions Supervisors.

[97] See, Everson, M, Monda, C, and Vos, E (eds), *European Agencies in between Institutions and Member States* (2014).

[98] Majone, G, Independence v Accountability: European Non-majoritarian Institutions and Democratic Government in Europe (1994), EUI Working Papers (SPS) No 1993/09.

community. This latter factor, for example, has already borne important coordinating fruit, as the new Omnibus II Directive, now only awaiting final Council approval,[99] details the exact circumstances under which EIOPA may mediate in disputes between home and host regulators; a significant advance with regard to the need to overcome perennial home versus host supervisory disputes.[100]

Nevertheless, EIOPA has also emerged within the context of uncertainty on the legitimate place of agencies within the institutional structures of the Union. Together with its partner European Supervisory Authorities (ESAs), the European Banking Authority (EBA), and the European Securities and Markets Authority (ESMA), EIOPA has a dual character as a rulemaking and supervisory authority, and is consequently one of the most powerful agencies ever to emerge at EU level. Charged with 'improving the functioning of the internal market', 'ensuring the integrity, efficiency and orderly functioning' of the sector, combatting 'regulatory arbitrage', championing 'consumer protection' and the strengthening of 'international supervisory coordination',[101] EIOPA supervisory functions are wide-ranging, relating primarily to the cooperative establishment of joint risk-based methodologies for national supervisory authorities through peer review and the issuing of Recommendations and Guidelines.[102] Additionally, however, the agency is afforded one unprecedented domain of rulemaking powers,[103] the power to propose Binding Technical Standards (BTSs), comprising Technical Regulatory Standards (TRSs) for harmonization of EU regulation provisions, and Implementing Technical Standards (ITSs) to be applied at national level. Equally, soft coordination of national supervisory authorities (NSAs) crucially hardens in specific situations: 'breach of Union Law', when EIOPA can make binding EU Recommendations to NSAs or private actors, as well as pursue enforcement proceedings; 'emergency situations', or threats to systemic coherence where EIOPA acts under the umbrella of the ESRB, addressing Decisions to competent national authorities and market institutions; and action in pursuit of 'consumer protection', or to counter innovation threats, where EIOPA may temporarily prohibit detrimental activities.[104]

The crisis-driven granting of rulemaking and intervention powers to ESAs has created its own troublesome institutional dynamic. At ESFS creation, the long-standing ECJ *Meroni* doctrine dating from 1958,[105] was widely thought to preclude full independence of agencies at EU level, which were viewed instead as being

[99] The draft Omnibus II Directive (IP/11/49) (Situation as of July 2014).

[100] Especially with regard to continuing shared competences in material supervision.

[101] Preamble to, and Article 6 EIOPA Regulation, n 9 above.

[102] Article 16 EIOPA Regulation, n 9 above.

[103] Articles 10 and 15 EIOPA Regulation, n 9 above.

[104] Articles 17, 18, and 9 EIOPA Regulation, n 9 above, whereby Article 9 prohibition powers are only activated subject to subsequent legislative grant of competence.

[105] Case (9/56) *Meroni v High Authority* [1957–58] ECR 133.

only ever 'semi-autonomous', independent in fact rather than law, operating under the formal competences of the European Commission. The source of the doctrine was the principle of the balance of powers, which the historic ECJ construed as meaning that executive powers might only be delegated to institutions recognized by European Treaties. As creatures of ad hoc regulatory necessity, agencies had no named place within EU institutional architecture and no formal autonomy. By the same token, the Commission's relations with its own agencies have often been strained; at least to the degree that *de facto* autonomous agency operations threaten to alienate the competences of a Commission held legally accountable for them. Agencies have also been viewed with mistrust by other European institutions, notably the European Parliament, which sees in them a similar executive threat to its prerogatives, as well as Member States, who remain suspicious that agencies might also usurp national competence.[106]

In this febrile constellation, the legal challenge made by the UK Government to emergency intervention powers afforded ESMA was far less surprising than its outcome, whereby the now Court of Justice of the European Union (CJEU) belatedly confirmed direct delegation of EU competence to ESMA; achieving this ESFS-sustaining feat with reference to the inclusion by the Lisbon Treaty of agencies under the institutions against whom European judicial review proceedings might be pursued.[107] However, the *ESMA* case cannot be viewed as a simple legal end to the institutional matter: uncertainty has instead been italicized by the judgment, particularly with respect to the Commission's politically straightened position since the passage of the Lisbon Treaty and consequent potential for mismatch between Commission Implementing Acts to ease transposition of framework directives for European financial services, including Solvency II, and BTS proposed by the ESAs, or emergency actions taken by them. Whereas the TFEU subjects delegation to the Commission of detailed implementing competence for financial services framework directives to temporal constraint in the form of sunset clauses, as well as to standing Parliament and Council recall powers, the sword of Damocles hovers over Brussels heads; meanwhile, EIOPA, with its distanced seat in Frankfurt, and now also operating under the direct protection of the *Meroni* doctrine, maintains its own autonomous competence, not only to propose BTS in elaboration of Solvency II, but also to intervene directly into national markets.

The Commission has moved to mediate the risk that it will be cast as a perpetually rancorous loser in an institutional game of competence accrual, giving reiterated life to the original Lamfalussy construction of legislation and implementation for EU financial services. Amending Solvency II and the EIOPA founding Regulation,

[106] See, Everson, M, A Technology of Expertise: EU Financial Services Agencies (2012), LSE 'Europe in Question' Discussion Paper Series (LEQS) No 49/2012.

[107] In Article 263 TFEU. See Case C-270/12, *United Kingdom v Parliament and Council*, not yet reported, available at <http://curia.europa.eu/juris/>.

the Omnibus II Directive reiterates the existing four-level regime, whereby, at level one, framework directives are elaborated by delegated acts, or Commission Implementing Measures, which are subsequently augmented by means of BTS proposed by EIOPA (level two). The agency then provides guidance to ensure consistent member state implementation and cooperation (level three). Finally, the Commission ensures rigorous enforcement of Community legislation (level four).[108] All clarification, apart, however, Omnibus II reform rests both on the durability of the substantive distinction it makes between Implementing Acts and BTS, as well as of the processes its establishes in cases of conflict between the views and actions of the Commission and EIOPA. In turn, this gives renewed vigour to long-stated concern that, where the purpose of ESA establishment is to promote expert-led market regulation, continuing doubts about the exact extent of their autonomy might create the worst of all possible supervisory worlds, whereby inter-institutional conflict around ESAs stokes regulatory inefficiency within them.[109]

(b) *Efficiency and efficacy concerns*

An interesting peculiarity of general ESA design, which may mediate politically induced inefficiency, is the self-contained nature of expertise assembled within them. Possibly as a consequence of heightened *ex ante* influence afforded to Parliament and Council by the TFEU, ESA establishment has not experienced the unseemly scramble for political representation *inside* the agency more generally witnessed at Union level.[110] Instead, expertise headlines EIOPA in the character of its Board of Supervisors, made up of NSA heads, as well as non-voting representatives from the Commission and the ESRB;[111] the EIOPA Chairperson is similarly to be appointed 'on the basis of merit, skills, knowledge of financial institutions and markets and of experience relevant to financial supervision and regulation'.[112] National interest is also purged with regard to the establishment of duties of ESA independence.[113] Political arbitrage is combatted by simple majority voting in Supervisory and Management Boards: the sole decisional criteria are technocratic in nature and, under theories of expert deliberation,[114] facilitative of the objectivity and epistemic cooperation that might ensure ESA efficiency.

[108] Omnibus Directive, n 99 above.

[109] Moloney, N, 'The European Securities and Markets Authority and Institutional Design for the EU Financial Market—a Tale of Two Competences: Part 1: Rule-making' (2011) 12(1) *European Business Organization Law Review* 41. The major problem is posed by the degree to which the Commission can or cannot reject BTS proposed by EIOPA.

[110] For details of the efforts of the European Parliament to gain parliamentary representation within the management board of the European Food Standards Agency, see Vos, E, 'EU Food Safety Regulation in the Aftermath of the BSE Crisis' (2000) 23 *Journal of Consumer Policy* 227.

[111] Article 40 EIOPA Regulation, n 9 above.

[112] Article 48(2) EIOPA Regulation, n 9 above.

[113] Article 42 EIOA Regulation, n 9 above.

[114] Majone, n 43 above.

Efficiency concerns have, however, also been raised about the expansion of ESA activities to national level supervision and implementation, also by means of ITS. Prevalence of regulatory arbitrage within the less intrusive Lamfalussy system weighed in favour of a hardening of the supranational supervisory competence,[115] which now gives rise to worries about NSA–ESA conflict within hierarchically construed EU financial supervision. Possible discord arises since regulatory standard-setting cannot easily be divorced from supervisory implementation. Instead, the relationship between standards and their ongoing application is a necessarily complex one, not simply because understandings about regulatory aims may differ at each supervisory level, but rather because their successful achievement is necessarily context dependent.[116] Several factors militate in heterarchical rather than hierarchical favour of local implementation flexibility. First, ESAs are relatively inexperienced, parsimoniously financed and currently understaffed.[117] Second, regulatory goals will also necessarily require adaptation in view of Member State institutional specificity. Above all, however, complex Solvency II regulatory methodologies not only require an intense degree of local knowledge in order to overcome informational asymmetries, but also demand regulatory-implementing flexibility to allow for experimentation with regard to rapid financial innovation, as well as for immediate response to systemic shock. Equally, experimental localism may act as a safety-valve within the system, easing contagion potential through a supervisory plurality that guards against the danger that undue centralization will itself facilitate systemic shock.[118]

Efficacy doubts, however, similarly arise with regard to perennial doubts about control over EIOPA operations. Consistent with the general agency design precept that 'no-one controls the agency; yet the agency is under control',[119] the EIOPA Regulation establishes a scheme of plural accountability in order to ensure that the authority is both competent and acts only within its technical mandate. EIOPA is subject to *ex ante* control of its multi-annual work programmes by multiple EU institutions, including the Court of Auditors; ongoing control by means of parliamentary committee hearings; as well as, *ex post* multi-institutional control of budgets and annual reports. In addition, agency Decisions addressed to individual actors may be reviewed by an independent Board of Appeal and by the CJEU.[120] Nonetheless, final doubts about EIOPA

[115] Snowden, P and Lovegrove, S, 'The New European Supervisory Structure' (2011) 83 *Compliance Officer Bulletin* 1.

[116] Moloney, N, 'The European Securities and Markets Authority and Institutional Design for the EU Financial Market—a Tale of Two Competences: Part 2: Rules in Action' (2011) 12(2) *European Business Organization Law Review* 177.

[117] ibid.

[118] Black, n 29 above; Moloney, n 116 above.

[119] Moe, TM, 'Political Institutions: The Neglected Side of the Story' (1990) 6(2) *Journal of Law, Economics and Organization* 213.

[120] Articles 61 and 62 EIOPA Regulation, n 9 above.

accountability remain, particularly with regard to its transparency and responsiveness. In sharp contrast to the US,[121] EU debate is largely devoid of the theme of agency capture. In line with efficiency-based concerns, industry actors are instead regarded as stakeholders within the supervisory process, whose views must be taken seriously in the establishment of sensitive oversight schemes.[122] EIOPA is accordingly mandated to establish stakeholder groups comprising market actors, as well as consumers and academics, and to consult them prior to issuing draft BTS.[123] However, it was exactly this close relationship within financial services, between regulator and regulated, that contributed to financial collapse: above all, the joint application of risk-based models of economic solvency fostered particularly intense relations between regulators and regulated within which the fatal complacency arose that tolerated unsustainable business models as wealth-creating vehicles of innovation. Agency capture potential was instead replaced with the far more subtle, but no less catastrophic danger posed by the creation of a dominant rationality, a shared mode of thinking or 'cognitive failure',[124] which could not recognize, let alone tolerate dissent. To the degree that EIOPA is also a part of the ESRB, it is surely charged with identifying voices, not only of partnership, but also of maverick dissent, and must move beyond its own epistemic community of review, to identify methodological malcontents. In this regard, however, the EU has similarly lagged far behind the US, especially with regard to public accountability through creation of a broad audience for high profile regulatory authorities; a problem only exacerbated by the lack of a European press, the absence of a public sphere of communication, and a tendency to the renationalization of European decision-making within a fragmented, nationally focused media.[125]

In intermediary and prospective conclusion, EIOPA establishment has created a significant new set of supervisory uncertainties within a liberalizing European market. Necessary coordination of national and supranational supervisors presents its own challenges, and perhaps also presages future regulatory complications at global level, especially within the ambit of GATS and WTO efforts to settle a recognized definition for adequately prudential supervision; and particularly so, should EIOPA adopt a disputed competence for itself to conclude international negotiations and agreements[126]—a further challenge to Commission and Member State competences alike.

[121] Stiglitz, n 37 above. See, also, Shapiro, M, *Who Guards the Guardians? Judicial Control of Administration* (1988).

[122] Vos, n 110 above.

[123] Article 37 EIOPA Regulation, n 9 above.

[124] Black, n 29 above.

[125] Everson, n 106 above.

[126] Vos, E, 'European Agencies and the Composite EU Executive' in Everson, M, Monda C, and Vos, E (eds), *European Agencies in-between Institutions and Member States* (2014).

V. Socialized Market Operations

The sense of public ownership over the private market, given voice in the rhetorically nationalizing reminder that insurers 'were investing the people's money',[127] is a long-standing feature of the regulatory realm in which the sector operates. Readily grasped in view of the market's vital socio-economic purpose, made visible within macro-economic steering and manipulation of insurance interfaces, this proprietary impulse has now re-emerged with contemporary futurization expectations; albeit within in a radical new paradigm of market utility. The people's money takes central stage, but does so in a manner undreamt of in the 1940s, forming the investment pool for capital maximization, whereby the competitive market assumes enhanced responsibility for future welfare, not simply in terms of investment return, but also with regard to product personalization. This new constellation, however, creates very particular challenges of its own.

1. Behavioural economics bites back

Liberalizing radicalism does not equate with simple market autonomy, or, in the UK example, historical disdain for intervention. Instead, market utility is accompanied by its own regulatory impetus as abstract economic theory plays a concomitant part in the shaping of the particular concept of consumer welfare that is to be pursued: hence, in a nutshell, the recent emergence of behavioural analysis within the ambit of the material supervision of insurance products. A particularly obdurate barrier—together with divergence in national contract law[128]—to EU insurance liberalization in its compensation for consumer information deficit through regulatory scrutiny of policy terms, material supervision finds its apogee within paternalist supervision models, where the regulator intervenes in order to pre-empt market offers (policy terms), because the consumer, untutored in actuarial intricacy, might choose 'the wrong one'.[129] In sharp contrast, however, where market utility has become the norm, and consumer preference the regulatory lynchpin, both in terms of efficiency-inducing competition between insurers, and with regard to the personalized futurization potential of product innovation, hierarchical market restraint is rejected. Instead, returning to the UK example,

[127] Griffith, n 50 above.

[128] See n 23 above.

[129] August Angerer, BAV President, 'Wettbewerb auf den Versicherungsmärkten aus der Sicht der Versicherungsaufsuchtsbehörde' (1985) 2 *Zeitschrift für die gesamte Versicherungswissenschaft* 221, 224.

permissively interventionist efforts dating from the 1983 Gower Report crystallize around design of mechanisms to steer consumer behaviour.[130]

In this context, behavioural economics emerges as manna from heaven, both in terms of its insights into consumer preference formation, and with regard to its promise to enhance softly effective steering capacity. Now given formal approbation by the UK FCA, core behavioural insights concerning, in particular, present bias and loss aversion among consumers, are seen as a 'means to assess problems in financial markets better' and to 'choose more appropriate remedies', such that the Authority 'will be a more effective regulator as a result'.[131] Above all, and in view of recent mis-selling scandals,[132] identification of peace-of-mind-bias to the purchase of too much insurance, or inappropriate products, is a valuable insight, and is equally usefully combated by behavioural steering mechanisms of 'nudge', or consumer incentivization towards more nuanced understanding of personalized risk-profiling;[133] a similarly expedient tool to discourage consumers away from immediate gratification bias in, say, use of credit cards, towards more constructive futurization opportunities. Yet, vulnerable to the charge that it can just as equally be deployed to adapt people to the purposes of markets, as markets to the preferences of people, behavioural economics similarly raises a renewed spectre of distorting supervisory presence *within* the market; at least to the degree that permissive interventionism may likewise prove destructive in its vaulting ambition.

In the opinion of the FCA, a major 'risk factor' for the industry is the 'structures, processes and management that have been designed into and become embedded in the financial sector, allowing firms to profit from systematic consumer shortcomings'.[134] To the degree that the Authority similarly equates the desire for peace of mind (loss aversion) and consequent cross-subsidization (within risk pools) with 'consumer biases' that must be expunged from the market,[135] the irony that behavioural economics is in large part built on insights garnered by insurers on policyholder behaviour will not be lost on the sector.[136] Certainly, insurers are rarely if ever philanthropic and do misbehave, not least with regard to a further FCA *bête noire*, that of limitation of access to financial products; a failing shockingly apparent in the arbitrary capping by the US market of life assurance policies

[130] Initially in the form of enhanced regulation of insurance intermediaries. Note, the EU also regulates the qualifications if not the conduct of insurance intermediaries (Directive 2002/92/EC [2002] OJ L9/3).

[131] Martin Wheatley, CEO, Financial Conduct Authority, Foreword to Financial Conduct Authority, Applying Behavioural Economics at the Financial Conduct Authority, Occasional Paper No 1 (Kristina Erta, Stefan Hunt, Zanna Iscenko, and Will Brambley), available at <http://www.fca.org.uk/static/documents/occasional-papers/occasional-paper-1.pdf> (last accessed March 2014), at 5.

[132] ibid, 15.

[133] ibid, 9; Sunstein, C and Thaler, R, *Nudge: Improving Decisions about Health, Wealth, and Happiness* (2008).

[134] Financial Conduct Authority, n 131 above, 23.

[135] ibid.

[136] Cohen and Boardman, n 5 above.

concluded by HIV positive policyholders, regardless of the existence of by-now comprehensive actuarial data on progression, or rather non-progression to AIDS, and beyond.[137] In an age of big data, or unparalleled access to statistical information, there is also much room for actuarial refinement. Nevertheless, loss aversion and cross-subsidization are not just market failures, but the market failures upon which the insurance mechanism is built; integral shortcomings to be managed, even manipulated, but never purged, if the market is to remain a market.

2. Risk above uncertainty

Given the FCA's signalled willingness to intervene to correct integral insurance failures, one pertinent question to be posed in the wake of permissive interventionism might accordingly be: what is now left of the market? An elusive sensation that market utility has begun to overwhelm market process only hardens upon reconsideration of the prudential supervision of the sector. Greeting the passage of the 2012 Financial Services Act, the *Guardian* opined that 'financial economics is heading back towards the world as Keynes and Hayek knew it: where economic uncertainty was recognised as such, rather than mathematized and mis-sold as controllable risks'.[138] Equally, to the degree that the PRA has indicated that its supervisory functions will be 'judgement-based',[139] in order to compensate for the brutally exposed failings in abstract economic modelling, market uncertainty has renewed its place within regulatory mentality; reappeared in its hardened suspicion of quantitative risk-modelling.

Yet, tensions inherent to futurization expectations remain. Above all, where the socio-economic purposes of insurance are broadened to compensate for public welfare retreat, and pursued within the deep structures of market utility, the simultaneous quest for contrasting market innovation and prudential oversight locates autonomous supervisory authorities—EIOPA, BaFin, PRA, and FCA—on the front line of the underlying paradox in modern macro-economic market thinking. To be markets, and to supply market utility, markets must fail; yet, the defuturization consequences of market failure are now too great to be borne by markets. Now also the subject of renewed European harmonization efforts in Solvency II (Title V), insurance failure lacks the catastrophic potential of banking failure. Given the temporal nature of the insurance mechanism, the deferred disbursement liabilities of an insolvent undertaking may be resolved during a protracted winding-up period, during which it ceases to incur new business and existing liabilities are

[137] See n 22 above; see also, Stone, D, 'AIDS and the Moral Economy of Insurance' (November 2013), *The American Prospect*, available at <http://prospect.org/article/aids-and-moral-economy-insurance>.

[138] *Guardian*, 'On Knowing Too Much', 10 September 2012, p 26.

[139] Bank of England, n 30 above.

either run-off or transferred within the sector. Nevertheless, at rhetorical level, the spectre of insurance failure, prompts the UK PRA to give voice to this very modern enigma:

> Allowing insurers to fail, so long as failure is orderly ... reflects the view that insurers should be subject to the disciplines of the market. It is important for insurers to be able to fail in an orderly way without public funds being put at risk since apart from being an unwarranted subsidy, the public provision of solvency support to an insurer (or its creditors) can create an expectation of future assistance. This 'moral hazard' in turn increases the risk of future financial instability, as it provides incentives for excessive risk taking and reduces market discipline.[140]

The doctrine of behavioural insight again plays its masterful role. The PRA expects insurers to have a 'risk appetite', but only one which is 'consistent with the PRA's objectives';[141] any other form of hunger is no longer a normally imperfect market process, but rather a moral hazard, a sinful gluttony, preferably to be exorcized in *ex ante* application of the creed of ORSA, at worst to be atoned for in orderly processes of *ex post* market restoration. Within this constellation, uncertainty is just as surely still reduced to risk; something that can be governed. The full extent of the Hayekian truth of a market of spontaneous, unknowable, and unmanageable processes of human exchange relations is still too unpalatable to digest.

3. The regulatory enterprise

A consistent feature of concomitantly amplified socio-economic expectations levelled at private financial markets following state welfare withdrawal, has been political silence about the possible consequences of such public abdication; above all, the inevitability of individual welfare loss due to market failure, but also the difficulties facing the denuded state in the matter of the coordination of competing welfare claims. The gauche character of political debate, however, is also attributable to the belief that the move to autonomous regulation is not an act of deregulation, nor a mandated imposition of *pareto* efficiency, but merely the establishment of a 'regulatory enterprise',[142] within which the sharp divides made between public and private spheres, between efficiency-led regulation and continuing pursuit of social goals necessarily dissolve within a *praxis* of discretionary supervision; a melange or network of radicalized delegation in which all competing regulatory rationales of efficiency and consumer choice, pursuit of legal rights, social solidarity, and consumer protection are still fought out. Equally, the history of the integration of European insurance markets, as well as application to them of

[140] ibid, para 25. [141] ibid, para 108.

[142] Prosser, T, *The Regulatory Enterprise: Government Regulation and Legitimacy* (2010).

post-crisis prudential supervision lends support to this assertion: not least to the degree that retarded integration might still be attributable to more traditional notions of macro-economic steering; but also because authorities, such as EIOPA and the PRA, continue explicitly to struggle to reconcile competing aims of innovation and prudence.

Nevertheless, a regulatory enterprise fractured across a national, supranational, and international environment of financial liberalization necessarily establishes its own measures of instability and uncertainty, especially as regards coordination between competing value claims. An interesting example in this regard, might accordingly be that of the very peculiar equality engendered by the CJEU in the case of *Testes Achats*,[143] proscribing long-standing, gender-based actuarial distinctions in the pricing of motor insurance policies. A further marker of the growth of a distinct European polity, with its own egalitarian intent to intervene into the private market to create a new ethical insurance interface founded in the precept that men should not pay more for insurance than women, the judgment was nevertheless given, not only in apparent disdain for the core insurance operation of personalized apportionment of actuarial risk,[144] but also in blissful ignorance of material supervisory endeavours to preclude efficiency-distorting cross-subsidization from the market. The egalitarian impacts of *Testes Achats* have already been absorbed by the sector, and will surely, on the basis of big data, similarly be reconciled with more libertarian and behaviourally based, utilitarian cross-subsidization concerns in a new set of increasingly-individualized policy exclusions. But what of inevitable and more systemically relevant mismatches between traditional and modern forms of macro-economic steering; between national interfaces of public-private insurance provision and global liberalization processes; between significant industry efficiency gains in new technologies (e-commerce) and magnified costs with regard to increased supervisory intervention;[145] between Central Bank macro-prudential supervision in pursuit of sound money and asset price bubbles created by sudden solvency-driven switches to equity, especially on the part of life assurers; or between advanced economic pursuit of consumer choice and residually paternalistic concern for consumer protection?

Directing his comments at one of the most prominent legal proponents of market utility, Ernst-Joachim Mestäcker, a staunch Hayekian, equates this 'utilitarian' form of mastery within markets with 'ideology in the service of unlimited

[143] Case C-236/09, *Association belges des Consommateurs Test-Achats ASBL v Conseil des ministers* (2011). Not yet reported, available at <http://curia.europa.eu/juris/>.

[144] See, for comprehensive critique, Mabbet, D, A Rights Revolution in Europe? Regulatory and Judicial Approaches to Non-discrimination in Insurance (2011), LSE 'Europe in Question' Discussion Paper Series (LEQS) No 38/2011.

[145] The industry awaits threshold conditions with a degree of trepidation. See, for details, Bank of England, Prudential Regulation Authority, Solvency II: Applying EIOPA's Preparatory Guidelines to PRA-authorised Firms (October 2013), Consultation Paper CP9/13.

government and socialism [sic]'.[146] Mestmäcker might or might not overstate his case with regard to the law and economics movement, and the more extreme positions famously adopted by Richard Posner. However, current European and national preoccupation with perfectly regulated competition perhaps displays a comparable hubris; at least with regard to the ability of any form of supervisory oversight, let alone such a fragmented one, to master such a conflicting set of economic and social goals. To this exact extent, socialization of insurance markets through permissive-interventionism, or miraculously perfected competition, just as surely creates its own set of uncertainties for industry and for consumers alike.

Bibliography

Abraham, S, *Distributing Risk: Insurance, Legal Theory, and Public Policy* (1986).

Angerer, A, 'Wettbewerb auf den Versicherungsmärkten aus der Sicht der Versicher ungsaufsuchtsbehörde' (1985) 2 *Zeitschrift für die gesamte Versicher ungs wissen schaft* 221.

Association of British Insurers, UK Insurance Key Facts AIB, London (September 2012) (continuously updated), available at <https://www.abi.org.uk/Insurance-and-savings/Industry-data/Free-industry-data-downloads/UK-Insurance-Key-Facts-2013>.

Baake, P and Perschau, O, 'The Legal and Institutional Regulation of the Law against Measures Restrictive of Competition' in Majone, G (ed.), *Regulating Europe* (1996).

Baldwin, R and Black, J, 'Really Responsive Risk-based Regulation' (2010) 32(2) *Law and Policy* 181.

Bank of England, Prudential Regulation Authority, The Prudential Regulation Authority's Approach to Insurance Supervision (2013).

Beale, R, *After the V&G Crash* (1972).

Black, J, Restructuring Global and EU Financial Regulation: Capacities, Coordination and Learning (2010), LSE Law Society and Economy Working Papers 18/2010.

CEPS, The Future of Insurance Regulation and Supervision in the EU: New Developments, New Challenges (Rym Ayadi and Christopher O'Brian, Rapporteurs) (2006).

Clarke, M, 'An Introduction to Insurance Contract Law' in Burling, J and Lazarus, K (eds), *Research Handbook on International Insurance Law and Regulation* (2011) 3–18.

Clayton, G, *British Insurance* (1971).

Cohen, LR and Boardman, ME, 'Methodology: Applying Economics to Insurance Law—an Introduction' in Luetge, C and Jauernig, J (eds), *Business Ethics and Risk Management* (2014) 19.

Crouch, C, *The Strange Non-Death of Neo-Liberalism* (2012).

Esposito, D, *The Future of Futures: The Time of Money in Financing and Society* (2013).

Esposito, D, 'The Present Use of the Future: Management and Production of Risk on Financial Markets' in Luetge, C and Jauernig, J (eds), *Business Ethics and Risk Management* (2014).

[146] Mestmäcker, E-J, *A Legal Theory without Law—Posner v Hayek on Economic Analysis of Law* (Beiträge zur Ordnungstheorie und Ordnungspolitik) (2007).

Everson, M, 'The Federal Supervisory Authority for Insurance' in Majone, G (ed.), *Regulating Europe* (1996) 202.
Everson, M, A Technology of Expertise: EU Financial Services Agencies (2012), LSE 'Europe in Question' Discussion Paper Series (LEQS) No 49/2012.
Everson, M, Monda, C, and Vos, E (eds), *European Agencies in-between Institutions and Member States* (2014).
Finsinger, F, Hammond, E, and Tapp, J, *Insurance: Competition & Regulation* (1985).
Finsinger, J, *Verbraucherschitz auf Versicherungsmärkte* (1988).
Heiss, H, Clarke, M, and Lakhan, M, 'Europe: Towards a Harmonised European Insurance Contract Law—the PEICL' in Luetge, C and Jauernig, J (eds), *Business Ethics and Risk Management* (2014) 603.
International Association of Insurance Supervisors, Global Insurance Market Report (GIMAR) 2010, IAILS, Basel (October 2012), available at <http://www.iaisweb.org/News/Global-Insurance-Market-Report-GIMAR-962>.
Keßler, J, Micklitz, H-W, and Reich, N, Darstellung der Arbeitsweise von Finanzaufsichtsbehörden in ausgewählten Ländern und deren Verbraucherorientierung (2009), Working Paper of the German Consumer Federation (Vvzbv), available at <http://www.vzbv.de/mediapics/studie_finanzaufsicht_vergleich_eu_zusammenfassung_okt_2009.pdf>.
Knight, F, *Risk, Uncertainty and Profit* (1921).
Lang, A and Scott, J, 'The Hidden World of WTO Governance' (2009) 20(3) *European Journal of International Law* 575.
Mabbet, D, A Rights Revolution in Europe? Regulatory and Judicial Approaches to Non-discrimination in Insurance (2011), LSE 'Europe in Question' Discussion Paper Series (LEQS) No 38/2011.
Majone, G, Independence v Accountability: European Non-majoritarian Institutions and Democratic Government in Europe (1994), EUI Working Papers SPS 1993/09.
Majone, G, *Regulating Europe* (1996).
Mehr, R, Cammack, E, and Rose, T, *Principles of Insurance* (1985).
Mestmäcker, E-J, *A Legal Theory without Law—Posner v Hayek on Economic Analysis of Law* (Beiträge zur Ordnungstheorie und Ordnungspolitik) (2007).
Moe, TM, 'Political Institutions: The Neglected Side of the Story' (1990) 6(2) *Journal of Law, Economics and Organization* 213.
Molle, W, *The Economics of European Integration: Theory, Practice, Policy* (2006).
Moloney, N, 'The European Securities and Markets Authority and Institutional Design for the EU Financial Market—a Tale of Two Competences: Part 1: Rule-making' (2011) 12(1) *European Business Organization Law Review* 41.
Moloney, N, 'The European Securities and Markets Authority and Institutional Design for the EU Financial Market—a Tale of Two Competences: Part 2: Rules in Action' (2011) 12(2) *European Business Organization Law Review* 177.
Prosser, T, *The Regulatory Enterprise: Government Regulation and Legitimacy* (2010).
Purves, P, 'Europe: The Architecture and Content of EU Insurance Regulation' in Luetge, C and Jauernig, J (eds), *Business Ethics and Risk Management* (2014).
Quaglia, L, 'The Politics of Insurance Regulation and Supervision Reform in the European Union' (2011) 9(11) *Comparative European Politics* 100.
Raynes, HE, *A History of British Insurance* (1964).
Rees, R, Kessner, E, and Klemperer, P, 'Regulation and Efficiency in European Insurance Markets' (1999) 29 *Economics* 365.

Scharpf, F, 'Monetary Union, Fiscal Crisis and the Pre-emption of Democracy' (2011) 9(2) *Zeitschrift für Staats- und Europawissenschaften* 163.

Shapiro, M, *Who Guards the Guardians? Judicial Control of Administration* (1988).

Snowden, P and Lovegrove, S, 'The New European Supervisory Structure' (2011) 83 *Compliance Officer Bulletin* 1.

Stiglitz, J et al., *The Economic Role of the State* (1989).

Stone, D, 'AIDS and the Moral Economy of Insurance' (November 2013), *The American Prospect*, available at <http://prospect.org/article/aids-and-moral-economy-insurance>.

Stone, D, 'The Struggle for the Soul of Health Insurance' (1993) 18(2) *Journal of Health Politics, Policy and Law* 287.

Sunstein, C and Thaler, R, *Nudge: Improving Decisions about Health, Wealth, and Happiness* (2008).

Teubner, G, 'A Constitutional Moment? The Logics of "Hitting the Bottom"' in Kjaer, P, Teubner, G, and Febbrajo, A (eds), *The Financial Crisis in Constitutional Perspective: The Dark Side of Functional Differentiation* (2014) 9.

van Asselt, M and Vos, E, 'Science, Knowledge and Uncertainty in EU Risk Regulation' in Everson, M and Vos, E (eds), *Uncertain Risks Regulated* (2008).

Vos, E, 'EU Food Safety Regulation in the Aftermath of the BSE Crisis' (2000) 23 *Journal of Consumer Policy* 227.

Vos, E, 'European Agencies and the Composite EU executive' in Everson, M, Monda, C, and Vos, E (eds), *European Agencies in-between Institutions and Member States* (2014) 11.

CHAPTER 15

MAKING BANK RESOLUTION CREDIBLE

JOHN ARMOUR*

* Earlier versions of this Chapter benefited from presentations at a BFSLA Conference in Queenstown, a Law and Finance Workshop and Centre for Business Taxation Conference in Oxford, a Commonwealth Central Bank Governors' Meeting in Washington DC, and a seminar at Universidad Autónoma de Madrid. I am grateful for comments on earlier drafts from Luca Enriques, Steven Schwarcz, John Vella, and, especially, the editors of this Handbook.

I. Introduction

THE events of 2007–09 made frighteningly clear the fragility of even the largest financial institutions. Acute difficulties at large financial institutions present governments and regulators with an unenviable dilemma. On the one hand, they are afraid to permit such a firm to enter 'ordinary' insolvency proceedings, lest this transmit financial shock to other, connected, institutions. Such fears were given credence by the Lehman bankruptcy, which very nearly brought about the collapse of the global financial system. Yet, the only alternative at the time was the ad hoc provision of public funds to 'bail out' troubled financial institutions; indeed, it was in trying to avoid such an outcome that the US authorities permitted Lehman to fail. Nevertheless, after the Lehman bankruptcy governments saw themselves as having little alternative but to make such bailouts on a gargantuan scale. In the EU, these commitments peaked at nearly 40 per cent of GDP in 2009;[1] in the US at over 50 per cent in 2008, and in the UK at over 70 per cent in 2009.[2] While most citizens do not understand the complexities of the financial system, every voter can grasp the moral hazard problems and distributional inequity associated with government handouts for the financial sector. One of the most urgent policy questions emerging from the crisis was, therefore, how to improve upon the tools available to resolve the distress of financial institutions. The goal is to ensure that such firms are able to be dealt with in a way that does not wreck the financial system without losses having to be shouldered entirely by the taxpayer.

An insolvency procedure takes time to identify and realize assets of the debtor firm, take account of debts owing and pay creditors in accordance with their priorities. In the case of a failing financial institution, such delay can exacerbate systemic contagion. Consequently, many policymakers and scholars advocated some form of 'special resolution' mechanism for financial firms.[3] The first generation of such procedures, which

[1] European Commission, Executive Summary of the Impact Assessment Accompanying Proposal for a Council Directive on a common system of financial transaction tax and amending Directive 2008/7/EC (2011) (SEC(2011) 1103) 2.

[2] Bank of England, Financial Stability Report (2009), December 2009 No 26, 6.

[3] See, eg, Morrison, ER, 'Is the Bankruptcy Code an Adequate Mechanism for Resolving the Distress of Systemically Important Institutions?' (2010) 82 *Temple Law Review* 449.

generally were based on the Federal Deposit Insurance Corporation (FDIC) receivership regime in the US, involve a waiver of creditors' ordinary property rights in order to complete the process extremely rapidly. 'Good' assets and depositors' claims are transferred to a purchaser literally overnight, and the 'bad' assets that remain in the rump entity are wound down gradually in a way that does not transmit a shock. Resolution regimes of this sort have now been introduced in the UK, Germany, and a number of other countries, and national practices were required to be regularized in accordance with the EU on Bank Recovery and Resolution Directive (BRRD) by 31 December 2014.[4]

Nevertheless, many remain pessimistic about the ability of special resolution mechanisms based on a transfer of assets to scale up to deal with very large, or 'systemically important', financial institutions. There are three basic problems. The first is that it is necessary to find a buyer. For a large bank that is troubled, sheer size will make this a real challenge, especially as competitors may also be suffering liquidity difficulties. The second problem is that some form of external funding will be needed, whether as a sweetener to facilitate a sale or—more likely—to fund continued operations under temporary control of public authorities until a buyer is eventually found. The challenge is to arrange the provision of this funding in such a way that there will be enough of it, but that it will not be a drain on the public purse. The third problem is the international scope of large banking operations. Property laws cannot be waived extraterritorially. Consequently, unless every jurisdiction in which the banking organization operates has signed up to an equivalent resolution procedure and there is general agreement about how the costs of the process are to be shared, there is no guarantee that a coordinated outcome can, in fact, be achieved. A special resolution regime that fails to meet any of these challenges will not be credible, and policymakers will not have escaped the peril of ad hoc bailouts. Consequently, the interference with the rule of law such asset-transfer mechanisms entail is not, in the eyes of some scholars, justified.[5]

A second generation of initiatives has begun to emerge in response to these imperatives. First, there has been a growing realization that resolution can be made more credible by measures taken *ex ante* to make it easier to restructure and/or divide up a complex financial institution should problems emerge. The preparation of tailored 'rescue and resolution plans' is becoming part of the package of enhanced requirements that regulators are imposing on firms. Second, at the EU and G20 level there has been considerable attention paid to the need for international coordination. And third, a new generation of proposals for resolution regimes—popularly dubbed 'bail-in' (as opposed to 'bailout')—focuses on changing the structure of a troubled institution's financial contracts, as opposed to

[4] Directive 2014/59/EU establishing a framework for the recovery and resolution of credit institutions and investment firms [2014] OJ L173/190 (hereafter, the BRRD).

[5] See, eg, Ayotte, K and Skeel Jr, DA, 'Bankruptcy or Bailouts' (2010) 35 *Journal of Corporation Law* 469.

the ownership of its assets. That is, they would effect a reorganization, as opposed to liquidation, of a troubled financial institution. This avoids the need to find a purchaser, and to the extent that the new capital comes from existing creditors, can also avoid the need for public funding. Together, these three initiatives offer the best possibility for credible resolution of a global financial institution: international coordination to identify a 'lead' regulator, which requires the institution to arrange its capital structure such that all contracts are made under the laws of its jurisdiction so as to simplify the execution of a 'bail-in' restructuring.

This Chapter describes these developments and identifies implications. It is structured as follows. Section II examines the rationale for special resolution regimes for financial institutions. Section III then describes and evaluates the implementation of such regimes in the UK, the US, and the EU. Section IV explores how 'second-generation' resolution regimes have responded to the limits of 'first-generation' resolution regimes premised on a sale of assets, and explores more recent initiatives. Section V considers two particular issues; namely, how resolution mechanisms are initiated ('triggered') and funded. Section VI concludes.

II. Why Banks Are Different

1. Bank failure externalities

The case for special provision for troubled financial institutions rests on the existence of negative externalities associated with their failure. That is, the failure of such a firm has a propensity to impose losses on the economy at large that are a multiple of the losses to the firm's investors. For example, the market capitalization of Lehman Bros, Inc. peaked on 29 January 2007 at approximately $60 billion, and the sum of the peak capitalizations of all the 'crisis banks' in the US—those who either failed or required special assistance in order to survive[6]—was approximately $1.2 trillion.[7] These are large sums by any measure; yet, the fallout from the crisis was much larger. Including the various stimulus programmes, the US suffered

[6] The 'crisis banks' were those which failed, merged to avoid failure, or received special emergency assistance. They comprised Citigroup, AIG, Bank of America, Lehman Brothers, Bear Stearns, Merrill Lynch, Goldman Sachs, Morgan Stanley, Wachovia, and Washington Mutual. See Calomiris, CW and Herring, RJ, How to Design a Contingent Convertible Debt Requirement (2011), available at <http://ssrn.com/abstract=1815406>.

[7] See Armour, J and Gordon, JN, 'Systemic Harms and Shareholder Value' (2014) 6 *Journal of Legal Analysis* 35, 43–4.

net fiscal outlays during the 2008–09 financial year of approximately $5 trillion.[8] Despite these efforts, the US economy contracted by 3.5 per cent in the immediately following year 2009, a fall equivalent to a further $9 trillion.[9] These US measures, of course, do not count the costs incurred elsewhere around the world.

The failure of a financial institution can trigger large social losses through a variety of channels. First, there is the possibility of *contagion* within the financial system. Many financial institutions are structurally fragile, because they rely on short-term financing to support long-term investments. For example, the basic business model of a commercial bank involves raising money from depositors (paradigmatically, households) and then lending it to businesses at a higher interest rate. This 'maturity transformation' means that there is a liquidity mismatch: depositors require liquidity, but the money is invested in illiquid loans. If too much liquidity is demanded by depositors, long-term assets must be liquidated in a way that is destructive of value. Of course, banks actively manage this mismatch, but they remain vulnerable to events that trigger a sudden decline in the value of their liquid assets or a sudden increase in demand for liquidity. Commercial banks are not the only type of financial institution that is structurally fragile: for example, investment banks are vulnerable to the sudden withdrawal of short-term financing raised on the repo markets—and the resolution frameworks discussed in this chapter apply also to certain non-bank financial institutions accordingly. However, these regimes are generally referred to, for brevity, as 'bank resolution', which terminology is adopted in this Chapter.

Financial institutions are also typically highly interconnected, meaning that problems at one can easily be transmitted to others. In the most literal sense, this occurs through direct connections between balance sheets, with the liabilities of one institution being assets of others that become devalued on its financial distress. Contagion can also be driven by correlation in investment strategies. Fire-sale liquidation of assets by a distressed institution depresses the value price of the assets and consequently affects other institutions' balance sheets. Contagion could also occur across the liabilities side of firms' balance sheets, where short-term funders (such as depositors) infer from the failure of financial institution A that financial institution B is also likely to face difficulties, consequently provoking a run on B. Such an inference could be drawn if either of the previous two mechanisms of contagion are present—that is, if B holds A's debt, or if B holds assets that A is liquidating. This means that the various mechanisms of contagion can compound each others' effects.

Contagion within the financial sector is particularly harmful because financial institutions collectively perform functions that are of pivotal importance to the 'real' economy. They not only make available credit to business, but also

[8] Schildbach, J, 'Direct Cost of the Financial Crisis', *Deutsche Bank Research*, 14 May 2010, 3–4.

[9] IMF, World Economic Outlook 2011 (2011), 2.

perform valuable screening and monitoring functions in relation to funded business projects.[10]

It is often said that large banks are so systemically important that they are 'too big to [be permitted to] fail'; that is, that the systemic havoc wreaked by their failure would dwarf the costs of any bailout that would be needed to avert the individual institution's failure. The foregoing discussion elucidates that what matters for systemic risk is not the size of a failing institution per se, but (i) the impact the institution's failure would have on other fragile financial institutions; and ultimately more significantly, (ii) the impact the failure of the set of affected institutions would have on the real economy.

2. Bailouts and bankruptcy

When a financial firm is in difficulties, then if its failure would have systemic consequences, the contagion effects described above make it rational for policymakers and regulators to want to step in to avert its failure. The anticipation of such a bailout, however, is likely to have harmful consequences: creditors of institutions that are 'too big to fail' will anticipate such insurance and consequently fail adequately to monitor such firms, with the result that the banks' risk-taking is underpriced.[11] This gives such banks incentives to take excessive risks, and firms that are not too big to fail have incentives to become so.[12] Moreover, *ex post*, it can lead to the weakening of sovereign balance sheets if the distressed firm is sufficiently large relative to national GDP.[13] Thus, before and after crises, policymakers will foreswear such interventions on grounds of moral hazard,[14] but in the midst of a panic, their perspective will inevitably change. Economists refer to this as the problem of 'time inconsistency' on the part of policymakers.

There is reason to believe that such problems of moral hazard may have been a real contributing cause of the crisis. Because of limited liability, shareholders in highly levered firms benefit from investments in risky assets. Risky assets pay higher returns in good states of the world, which the shareholders will enjoy, and the downside losses in bad states of the world will be someone

[10] Bernanke, BS, 'Nonmonetary Effects of the Financial Crisis in the Propagation of the Great Depression' (1983) 73 *American Economic Review* 257.

[11] Stern, GH and Feldman, RJ, *Too Big to Fail: The Hazards of Bank Bailouts* (2004), ch 3.

[12] Baker, D and McArthur, T, 'The Value of the "Too Big to Fail" Big Bank Subsidy', *CEPR Issue Brief* (September 2009) (estimating interest rate spread between large and small banks to have been 0.29 per cent prior to the bailout package in 2008, then widening to 0.78 per cent thereafter).

[13] Acharya, VV, Dreschler, I, and Schnabl, P, A Pyrrhic Victory? Bank Bailouts and Sovereign Credit Risk (2011), NBER Working Paper 17136.

[14] See House of Commons Treasury Committee, *The Run on the Rock: Fifth Report of Session 2007–08* (Vol II, Oral and Written Evidence), Ev 1 (comments of Mervin King, Governor of the Bank of England).

else's problem. Ordinarily, such risk-taking would increase expected costs for creditors, by raising the probability of default. This, in turn, could be expected to increase the firm's cost of credit, making such an investment policy more unattractive to shareholders. But if creditors anticipate a full or partial state guarantee, they will underprice the true cost of credit, and shareholders will have incentives to want to increase both leverage and risk-taking. An event study well before the financial crisis reported that shareholders of financial firms declared by US regulators to be 'too big to fail' enjoyed positive abnormal returns, consistent with the foregoing account.[15] Moreover, an emerging body of empirical literature on the financial crisis finds that the financial firms with governance structures that made them most accountable to shareholders (less CEO autonomy, more independent directors, greater shareholder rights, etc.) were those that took the greatest risks *ex ante* and suffered the greatest losses *ex post*.[16]

Not only does the prospect of bailouts generate perverse incentives *ex ante*, but their operation *ex post* also generates political outcry. Consequently, they were very much a last resort: politicians were only willing to undertake them because they believed the alternatives to be worse. It is worth reflecting on why this was the case.

The only *ex post* alternative to a bailout in many cases was ordinary bankruptcy law. Most nations' bankruptcy laws include 'liquidation' and 'reorganization' procedures, which are, respectively intended to provide for an orderly winding-up and for a restructuring of a firm's debts or sale of its assets. However well they work for ordinary industrial firms, such procedures are unlikely to be appropriate for institutions that pose systemic risks.[17] First, bankruptcy procedures take *time* to complete. A payout is not usually made to creditors until it is determined how much money will be available to do so. Consequently, creditors must bear liquidity risk associated with delay in the proceedings, even if funds are eventually paid. Second, wholesale liquidation of a financial firm's assets can depress the value of these assets generally, harming the balance sheets of any other firm also holding those assets. Third, speculation about where losses will fall during the period before final accounts are prepared can lead to runs by creditors of institutions who are believed to be exposed to the failed bank.

[15] O'Hara, M and Shaw, W, 'Deposit Insurance and Wealth Effects: The Value of Being "Too Big to Fail"' (1998) 45 *Journal of Finance* 1587.

[16] Beltratti, A and Stulz, R, 'The Credit Crisis around the Globe: Why Did Some Banks Perform Better?' (2012) 105 *Journal of Financial Economics* 1; Erkens, DH, Hing, M, and Matos, P, 'Corporate Governance in the 2007–2008 Financial Crisis: Evidence from Financial Institutions Worldwide' (2012) 18 *Journal of Corporate Finance* 389; Ferreira, D, Kershaw, D, Kirchmaier, T, and Schuster, EP, Shareholder Empowerment and Bank Bailouts (2012), LSE Financial Markets Group Discussion Paper 714.

[17] See Bliss, RR, 'Resolving Large Complex Financial Institutions' in Kaufman, GG (ed.), *Market Discipline in Banking: Theory and Evidence* (2003) 3, 10–12.

Given the manifest problems of bailouts, a central goal of policymakers since the crisis has, therefore, been to design resolution mechanisms in a way that mitigates the transmission of contagion more effectively than ordinary bankruptcy, but is less costly than bailouts with discretionary public funds. We now turn to consider the mechanisms that have so far emerged.

III. First-Generation Resolution Mechanisms

For expository purposes, we can consequently divide resolution mechanisms into 'first-generation' and 'second-generation', according to whether their conception pre-dates or post-dates the financial crisis. The first-generation mechanisms take as their model the US FDIC receivership regime, which has been in operation since the 1930s. During and immediately after the financial crisis, this model was rapidly adopted by a number of other countries.

1. The model: FDIC receivership

The US bank receivership regime, administered by the FDIC,[18] was originally introduced as a corollary of the FDIC's bank deposit guarantee scheme. Deposit insurance in the US was originally introduced to protect the welfare of consumer depositors,[19] although many argue it had the serendipitous consequence of mitigating bank runs by reducing depositors' urge to press for payment.[20] It also had the consequence of reducing depositors' incentives to monitor their banks' activities. By giving the FDIC the right to pursue depositors' claims against a troubled bank, the legislative scheme encouraged the insurer to monitor the banks instead. This makes a lot of sense, as the FDIC can overcome the coordination problems depositors would face in monitoring. Consequently, the FDIC's deposit insurance fund has a preferential claim against the assets of any bank in respect of which it makes payouts. Moreover, and importantly for our purposes, the FDIC also has powers to step in as receiver of a failing bank.

[18] Federal Deposit Insurance Act (US) 1950, esp § 11, 12 USC § 1821.

[19] Calomiris, C and White, EN, 'The Origins of Federal Deposit Insurance' in Goldin, CG and Libecap, GD (eds), *The Regulated Economy: A Historical Approach to Political Economy* (1994) 145.

[20] Diamond, D and Dybvig, PH, 'Bank Runs, Deposit Insurance, and Liquidity' (1983) 91 *Journal of Political Economy* 401.

Conceptually, the simplest case is for the FDIC, acting as receiver, to step in and arrange for the liquidation of the assets of a troubled bank.[21] Insured depositors are paid from the FDIC's insurance fund and so suffer no loss. Meanwhile, as the FDIC does not have a need for early liquidity, it can sell the troubled bank's assets at a considered pace so as to avoid fire sale contagion.

However the FDIC if possible prefers a second type of outcome, whereby it arranges for a purchase of the assets *and* assumption of deposits by a transferee bank.[22] Such a purchase and assumption obviates the need for depositors to seek payment from the insurance fund, as their claims become solid once more. After the sale, the FDIC oversees the payment of non-depositor creditors out of the purchase price received.[23] Here, the differences from ordinary bankruptcy are two-fold: the assets are sold more rapidly, and liabilities are transferred as well. An overnight transfer is made possible by the sweeping powers given to the FDIC in a bank receivership, which permit waiver of the ordinary property rights of the bank and its creditors. Where there are doubts about the quality of some of the assets, it becomes necessary to effect partial transfers, whereby the purchaser takes only 'good' assets, leaving 'toxic' assets behind. The rump entity is then subjected to an orderly wind-down over a period of time.

A third possible outcome, known as a 'bridge bank', is a compromise between the first two.[24] This is used if an immediate sale cannot be agreed, but a sale of the troubled bank's business as a whole may be effected at some point in the future. The FDIC transfers the business to a new 'bridge bank', which is owned and operated by the FDIC itself. Depositors who want immediate repayment are paid; the claims of those remaining are guaranteed by the FDIC. In due course, the business is sold to a private sector purchaser—or if none emerges, liquidated.

2. The UK's Special Resolution Regime and EU developments

In the aftermath of the failure of Northern Rock plc in 2007, the UK adopted a range of new provisions for dealing with the distress of financial institutions. At the core of these was the Banking Act 2009, which introduced a Special Resolution Regime (SRR) for banks, modelled quite closely on FDIC receivership.[25] It is worth describing this in some detail as the way in which the SRR is implemented under

[21] See n 18 above, §§ 11(d)(2)(E), (f), (g). [22] ibid, § 11(d)(2)(G).

[23] See Bennett, RL and Unal, H, The Effects of Resolution-Method Choice on Resolution Costs in Bank Failures (2009), FDIC Working Paper.

[24] See n 18 above, § 11(m).

[25] Northern Rock itself was resolved using emergency legislation, the Banking (Special Provisions) Act 2008, upon which the Banking Act 2009 builds.

the UK legislation has subsequently been followed in the EU's new regime for resolution of financial institutions.[26]

At the core of the SRR is a series of mechanisms for waiving ordinary property rights to effect a transfer of the troubled firm (or its assets and liabilities), in return for a payment of compensation. The relevant mechanisms, exercisable through Parliamentary Orders, can effect transfers either of shares in the troubled bank,[27] or of property; that is, some or all of the troubled bank's assets (including those subject to security interests) and liabilities (eg, deposits).[28] In each case, the transfer may be to a private purchaser or to public ownership—in the case of a transfer of property, the latter is effected by transfer to a 'bridge bank'—a new entity owned and operated by the Bank of England on a temporary basis with a view to its subsequently being sold to a private purchaser.

The Banking Act of 2009 invokes sweeping disapplications of ordinary property law so as to bring about transfers by operation of law. Thus, section 34(4) of the Act provides that, '[a property] transfer takes effect despite any restriction arising by virtue of contract or legislation or in any other way'.[29] The powers extend to waiving contractual termination provisions, and to imposing obligations on the transferor entity in relation to the transferee post-transfer. What is more, the legislation also contains a so-called 'Henry VIII' clause, permitting for any other laws (apart from the Act and associated secondary legislation) to be amended as necessary—even retrospectively—so as to give effect to the purposes of the Act.[30]

Pre-transfer owners are granted rights to compensation. The simplest of these are orders for a stipulated payment of money (a 'compensation scheme order') to the troubled bank or its shareholders, in the case of property or share transfers respectively.[31] The value of the compensation is determined by an independent valuer,[32] who must in arriving at a quantum assume no state support for the troubled bank.

[26] This comprises two distinct but overlapping elements: Directive 2014/59/EU, the Bank Recovery and Resolution Directive (BRRD, n 4 above), which harmonizes Member States' regimes, and Regulation 806/2014 establishing a Single Resolution Mechanism for the Banking Union (hereafter, SRM Regulation) [2014] OJ L225/1, which applies only to the eurozone and other member states who choose to opt in.

[27] Banking Act 2009 (UK), sections 14–32. Provisions of this kind were first introduced by the Banking (Special Provisions) Act 2008, sections 3, 5.

[28] Banking Act 2009 (UK), sections 33–48.

[29] While the Act purports to grant extraterritorial effect to such transfers, clearly this may not be recognized by the courts of other jurisdictions as regards assets within their territory. The parties to the transfer as consequently subjected to obligations to take any necessary steps to ensure that the transfer is effective as a matter of foreign law.

[30] See n 28 above, section 75.

[31] ibid, sections 49(2), 50–2. Compensation may be paid either by a private sector recipient of assets, or by the Treasury, or by the FSCS (ibid, section 61). It is to be expected that the transferee will ordinarily be liable to pay the compensation, by way of purchase price.

[32] 'Independent' in the sense that they are not directly appointed by the authorities; rather the Treasury appoints the *person who appoints* the valuer: ibid, section 54(2).

Alternatively, where the assets are transferred either into temporary public ownership, or to a bridge bank, an order may be made giving the transferor an interest in the ultimate consideration obtained from the sale of the assets (a 'resolution fund order'). Where a property transfer is effected, the compensation will be payable to the troubled bank. That entity will then be placed in liquidation to provide for the payment of its creditors in order of priority. If the transfer is only partial—that is, some but not all assets and liabilities are transferred—then unsecured creditors in the remaining entity must receive at least as much as they would have obtained in its liquidation, assuming no financial assistance had been provided to the failing bank by the authorities. Moreover, a so-called 'third party compensation order' must be made in favour of any third party whose property rights were affected by the transfer—for example, secured creditors whose collateral is transferred but whose claims remain against the transferor.[33]

3. Legality of waiver of property rights

The dramatic disruption of property rights entailed by the SRR raises the question whether it can be justified, consistently with constitutional guarantees.[34] Article 1 of the First Protocol to the European Convention on Human Rights, incorporated into English law by the Human Rights Act 1998, provides that no person (legal or natural) shall be 'deprived of his possessions except in the public interest and subject to the conditions provided for by law …'. Many other constitutions contain similar restrictions on governmental takings. A group of former Northern Rock shareholders challenged the compulsory acquisition of their shares by the UK government in February 2008 under the Banking (Special Provisions) Act 2008, emergency legislation which was the partial predecessor of the Banking Act 2009.[35] They argued that the government had violated their Convention rights because they had received inadequate compensation, making the expropriation disproportionate relative to the public benefit it achieved.[36] Specifically, the statutory formula—repeated in the Banking Act 2009—required the shares to be valued on the basis that no government support had been provided. Without liquidity support from the Bank of England, Northern Rock would have had to close and sell its assets on a break-up basis, which the statutory valuer determined would have yielded the shareholders nothing once the firm's creditors and the costs of administration had been paid. However, the firm's assets, valued on a going concern basis,

[33] See n 28 above, sections 49(3), 59–60.

[34] See generally, Hüpkes, E, 'Special Bank Resolution and Shareholders' Rights: Balancing Competing Interests' (2009) 17 *Journal of Financial Regulation and Compliance* 277.

[35] See generally, UKSA Action Group: Northern Rock, available at <http://www.uksa.org.uk/action/northern_rock>.

[36] *SRM Global Master Fund LP v The Commissioners of HM Treasury* [2009] EWCA Civ 788.

were worth more than its liabilities. On this basis, the shareholders argued that it was disproportionate for the government to mandate valuation on a basis that would treat them as worthless. The Court of Appeal rejected the shareholders' argument, pointing out that the intervention by the Treasury had not been for the benefit of the shareholders, but to secure the public interest. Concomitantly, the Treasury was bearing all of the risks associated with the enterprise going forwards, because no private sector buyer was willing to acquire the assets without government guarantees. Consequently, there was no question that the valuation rule was outside the 'margin of appreciation' left to national governments over the determination of the proportionality of particular measures. The shareholders then applied to the European Court of Human Rights (ECtHR), which also decided against them on the basis that in matters of macro-economic policy, governments should be accorded a wide 'margin of appreciation'; especially so in order to combat systemic risk.[37] This is an important precedent because the EU's resolution mechanisms require all Member States to make available to supervisors a very similar set of resolution tools, with the same approach to valuation.[38]

4. Financial collateral and termination provisions

Paradoxically, given that the essence of the Northern Rock shareholders' complaint was that the government asserted excessive powers, a second legal difficulty with the waiver of property rights under the UK regime is that domestic governments lack *sufficient* power to effect a successful outcome. Despite the expansive framing of the powers to waive property rights granted by the Banking Act, domestic legislation is not capable of affecting rights protected by EU law. Under EU law, certain classes of claimant, namely those holding 'financial collateral arrangements', are entitled to protection from the application of insolvency laws or other impediments to the enforcement of their collateral.[39] The protected transactions include those involving a financial institution party whereby cash or securities are transferred by way of security, including under 'repos', and protected mechanisms of enforcement include close-out netting.[40] This permits counterparties to terminate existing positions readily on an event of default, and is intended to serve as a 'firebreak' to contagion following the failure of a financial institution.[41] Unfortunately, such protection poses a major impediment to successful resolution, as automatic termination provisions cannot be caught by the statutory waiver, causing the very

[37] *Grainger v UK*, ECtHR 10 July 2012 (Application No 34940/10).

[38] BRRD, n 4 above, Article 74; SRM Regulation, n 26 above, Article 20.

[39] Directive 2002/47/EC on Financial Collateral Arrangements [2002] OJ L 168/43, as amended by Directive 2009/44/EC [2009] OJ L146/37.

[40] ibid, Articles 2, 4.

[41] ibid, Recital 17.

rapid erosion of the troubled financial firm's goodwill.[42] Consequently, the BRRD modifies the Financial Collateral Directive, to permit a stay of enforcement and close-out netting provisions for up to 48 hours so as to allow resolution to occur.[43]

5. Scope of application

The FDIC's receivership regime originally applied only to deposit-taking institutions, on the basis that these were the only institutions covered by the insurance fund. Lehman Brothers, being a pure investment bank, was therefore not eligible for the receivership regime. The Dodd–Frank Act of 2010 introduced an extended form of the receivership regime, which can be used to resolve non-bank entities designated as systemically risky. This has been done through the establishment of the new Orderly Liquidation Authority (OLA), which is in essence an extension of the FDIC's receivership powers to non-bank financial institutions designated by the new Financial Stability Oversight Council (FSOC) as 'systemically risky' even though not deposit-taking. The OLA contains very similar powers to those available to the FDIC under receivership and is handled by the FDIC.

The rationale for extending the OLA regime to non-bank institutions was that systemic risk is not limited to banks. In particular, non-bank financial institutions such as Lehman can transmit contagion to deposit-taking banks,[44] and thence to the real economy. It may also be the case that the failure of an investment bank directly harms the real economy; harm, in particular, being suffered by their underwriting clients and derivatives counterparties.[45] Despite this, the UK's Banking Act 2009 initially applied the SRR only to deposit-taking institutions. The Financial Services Act 2012 extended its reach to include investment firms, central counterparties, and firms in the same group as a failing bank.[46] Similarly, the EU's resolution mechanisms apply not just to credit institutions, but also to investment firms, financial institution subsidiaries, and holding companies.[47] A recent consultation exercise has explored the extension of similar powers to other systemically important financial institutions, such as central counterparties, central securities depositaries, and systemic insurance companies.[48]

[42] Roe, M, 'The Derivatives Market's Payment Priorities as Financial Crisis Accelerator' (2011) 63 *Stanford Law Review* 539.

[43] BRRD, n 4 above, Articles 70–1 and 118 (inserting new Article 1(6) to Directive 2002/47/EU).

[44] Dumontaux, N and Pop, A, 'Understanding the Market Reaction to Shockwaves: Evidence from the Failure of Lehman Brothers' (2013) 9 *Journal of Financial Stability* 269.

[45] Fernando, CS, May, AD, and Megginson, WM, 'The Value of Investment Banking Relationships: Evidence from the Collapse of Lehman Brothers' (2012) 67 *Journal of Finance* 235.

[46] Financial Services Act 2012 (UK), section 101.

[47] BRRD, n 4 above, Article 1; SRM Regulation, n 26 above, Article 2.

[48] European Commission, Consultation on a Possible Recovery and Resolution Framework for Financial Institutions Other than Banks (5 October 2012).

6. The limits of first-generation resolution mechanisms

The first-generation resolution mechanisms discussed provide a viable mechanism for saving troubled banks. Indeed, more than 4,600 deposit-taking institutions have been through the FDIC's receivership regime in the US since its inception in 1934.[49] However, there are strong reasons for thinking that even these powers are insufficient to deal with the failure of a large complex financial institution, of the type that has been dubbed 'too big to fail'. In short, the mechanisms available do not ensure the *credibility* of the resolution procedures. This means that, should an institution of this variety find itself in financial difficulties, policymakers equipped only with the tools of first-generation resolution mechanisms would not have any viable alternative to a bailout.

Three problems in particular remain. First, despite the sweeping disapplication of ordinary property law rules regarding transfers, it is practically impossible to arrange for the transfer of the assets of a very large complex financial institution over the typical timescale of such procedures—'before the markets open on Monday'. This complexity is particularly acute where, as is likely, the transferee wishes to take some but not all of the troubled institution's assets, which must consequently be partitioned according to their preferred criterion.

Second, most large complex financial institutions operate across borders. This means that for resolution to succeed, there must be coordination between those handling the process in each of the relevant jurisdictions.

Third, the operation of a purchase and assumption transfer requires that a transferee be found with the financial resources to underwrite the liabilities that have been transferred. The bigger—and consequently, more systemic—the firm that has been resolved, the more difficult it will be to find a suitable transferee. For example, Lloyds TSB Group plc acquired the distressed HBOS plc in October 2008. However, the acquisition soon proved to be too much for Lloyds to swallow, itself requiring assistance from the UK government in early 2009.

The nature of these problems forms the impetus for what we may call 'second-generation' resolution mechanisms. These comprise those measures that have been conceived in response to the problems of the financial crisis, as opposed simply to being based on the FDIC receivership regime. We shall now consider them.

[49] In 1934–2013, a total of 4,619 deposit-taking institutions went through FDIC receivership: FDIC, Summary Report of Failures and Assistance Transactions, 1934–2013, available at <http://www2.fdic.gov/hsob/>.

IV. Second-Generation Resolution Mechanisms

1. *Ex ante* planning

A response to the challenge of complexity in resolving large financial institutions has been for supervisors to engage in dialogue with institutions *ex ante* regarding how resolution might successfully be achieved *ex post*. This requires the preparation of detailed resolution *plans*—colloquially known as 'living wills'—setting out how, if an institution fails, its businesses can safely be continued within the framework of resolution. The idea is that, should a resolution process ever be initiated, those conducting it will have a roadmap of the necessary actions for them to carry out in the course of a short period of time.

The Financial Stability Board (FSB) and European policymakers distinguish between 'recovery' and 'resolution' plans.[50] *Recovery plans* are aimed at averting a potential failure of the firm; that is, they encompass strategies for ensuring the continued operation of the firm under circumstances of extreme stress. Such plans are made by financial firms and reviewed by the regulatory authorities. *Resolution plans*, by contrast, are about minimizing the impact of the firm's failure on the rest of the financial system by facilitating the effective resolution by the authorities of a failed firm. These will be made by the authorities, on the basis of information required to be provided by the financial institutions.[51]

The UK provides a representative example of how such plans may be implemented.[52] The Financial Services Act 2010 requires bank supervisors (initially the Financial Services Authority (FSA), now the Prudential Regulation Authority (PRA)) to mandate the production by financial institutions of 'recovery and resolution plans'.[53] The requirement to produce recovery and resolution plans applies not only to deposit-taking institutions but also to investment firms deemed to be systemically significant. Each relevant firm is required to nominate an executive director who will have responsibility for the firm's recovery and resolution plans.

Recovery plans identify objective measures of financial stress, and a range of '*in extremis*' options which the institution can pursue under these circumstances. These can include disposals of sections of the business, raising fresh equity capital, cancelling dividends and variable remuneration, debt-equity swaps, and sale of the

[50] FSB, Effective Resolution of Systemically Important Financial Institutions: Consultative Document (2011), 53; FSA, Recovery and Resolution Plans, Consultation Paper 11/16 (2011), 8–9.

[51] Recovery and Resolution Plans, n 50 above, 29–30.

[52] ibid, n 50.

[53] Financial Services Act 2010 (UK), section 7 (inserting new sections 139B–F into the Financial Services and Markets Act 2000).

firm outright. They also must contain analysis of how the firm would make use of central bank facilities at such a time. Financial institutions required to produce recovery plans are expected to submit them to the authorities for review and also to be reviewed by the firm's board annually.

Resolution plans are made by the authorities, on the basis of extensive information provided by the financial institutions. These include details about group structure, interbank exposures, derivative positions and counterparties, and the like. Most crucially, they are also required to give a complete picture of the economic functions performed by the institution in the UK, so that the authorities can assess which of these may be critical to UK financial stability. The core of the planning then consists of devising ways in which critical economic functions can be separated from non-critical aspects of the business, so as to minimize taxpayer support in any resolution. Firms are also expected to identify and eliminate barriers to resolution inherent in their business structure. For example, they must put in place provisions to ensure continuity of key service providers (eg, IT) and employees, and to have a fund of liquid operational reserves to pay them for a short period post-insolvency.

Similarly, the EU's BRRD provides for all firms to which it applies to be required to draw up recovery plans, and provide their supervisory authorities with such information as is necessary for the preparation of resolution plans.[54] However, national supervisory authorities will have the option to impose only 'simplified' information obligations on institutions the failure of which they do not consider to be systemically important, as determined in accordance with criteria to be set by the European Banking Authority (EBA).[55] In contrast, the Dodd–Frank Act imposes similar requirements only on bank holding companies with total consolidated assets of more than $50 billion, and non-bank financial companies which the FSOC designates as giving rise to systemic risk.[56]

The effective preparation of resolution plans requires supervisors to take a very active role in demanding and scrutinizing information they are given by the firms. The more credible the prospect of resolution, the less likely a financial institution is to obtain a bailout. To the extent that the country in which they are based is able to afford a bailout, complex financial institutions with credible recovery and resolution plans are, therefore, likely to face a higher cost of debt finance than those

[54] BRRD, n 4 above, Articles 5–14. For firms to which the SRM will apply, the European Central Bank (ECB) or national supervisory authorities will submit the information received as regards resolution plans to the SRM Board (SRM Regulation, n 26 above, Article 10(2)). Resolution plans for who will also be responsible in most cases for preparing the resolution plans: SRM Regulation, n 26 above, Article 7.

[55] BRRD, n 4 above, Article 4. EBA is also to develop regulatory technical standards regarding the contents of resolution plans: ibid, Articles 10(9), 12(6).

[56] Dodd–Frank Act (US) §165(d).

which do not.[57] This gives firms in wealth nations every incentive to drag their feet over the production of the necessary information for resolution plans.

Moreover, the successful execution of a resolution plan requires the other problems identified in Section III.6—of international coordination and lack of potential purchasers—also to be resolved. As we shall see, these problems can also be mitigated by appropriate forward-thinking, albeit at a higher level of generality. It is at this level that the FSB has urged supervisory authorities to develop what come to be called 'resolution *strategies*'—frameworks for ensuring that generic problems do not derail a resolution.[58]

2. Multinational coordination of supervision

Significant moves have been made toward the coordination of supervisory authorities as regards both the *ex ante* design of resolution plans and *ex post* execution of resolution. The FSB has encouraged countries to enter into cooperation agreements specific to systemically important financial institutions with multinational operations, specifying how in the event of crisis resolution authority will be allocated and exercised.[59] The appropriate delineation of such agreements of course depends on interaction with supervisory authorities and the nature of any living wills prepared by the organization. An example is the EU's BRRD, which requires Member States to establish group-level resolution colleges, responsible for information-gathering, assessment of resolution plans, and execution of any necessary resolution.[60] Group resolution plans are drawn up and implemented on the basis of consensus between the national authorities responsible for each of the subsidiaries and the group-level resolution authority.[61] In the absence of consensus, national resolution authorities responsible for subsidiaries remain, in principle, free to pursue their own plans. However, EBA is to participate in, and assist in coordinating, these colleges. In particular, it is to act as conciliator if consensus cannot be achieved. This does not guarantee a collective process, but does help increase the chances of success.[62]

Two general strategies may be employed in allocating resolution powers under such agreements. The first is what the US authorities term the 'Single Point of

[57] This assumes that the institution is based in a country which has sufficient sovereign balance-sheet resources to bail the firm out. To the extent that this is not the case, the firm may be expected to *reduce* its cost of credit by preparing credible recovery and resolution plans.

[58] FSB, Effective Resolution, n 50 above; FSB, Recovery and Resolution Planning for Systemically Important Financial Institutions: Guidance on Developing Effective Resolution Strategies (2013).

[59] ibid. [60] BRRD, n 4 above, Article 88. [61] ibid, Articles 13, 92.

[62] In a recent report, the European Court of Auditors concluded that EBA lacked sufficient power to resolve disputes between national supervisory authorities (European Court of Auditors, European Banking Supervision Taking Shape—EBA and its Changing Context, EN2014/05 (2014), 53–5).

Entry' (SPE) approach.[63] The core idea is that only the holding company of a complex financial institution enters the resolution process, and operating companies remain outside receivership. This strategy would greatly reduce the complexity, and increase the chances of success, of a resolution attempt, especially if the firm is multinational. This is because operating companies in diverse jurisdictions would not need to be restructured, and so resolution authorities need only exercise their powers in a single jurisdiction. Moreover, it greatly expedites any exercise of transfer powers: all that need be transferred from the parent company are shares in the operating companies.

For the Single Point of Entry strategy to work, it must be possible for any weaknesses in the balance sheets of operating companies to be addressed through intra-group financing from the parent company. In other words, the group's principal outside financing should be raised at the parent company level. This precondition is satisfied for many large US financial institutions, because of the bank holding company structure utilized as a legacy of the Glass–Steagall separation of commercial and investment banking. However, it could also be utilized elsewhere if supervisors required the group to be structured in this way as part of its resolution planning.[64]

The alternative approach is coming to be known as 'Multiple Point of Entry'.[65] As might be expected, it envisages multiple entities in different jurisdictions going into distinct national resolution procedures, each supervised by a different authority. The likely result is that the group is broken up into constituent parts. This approach would be suitable for organizations for which it is determined that the internal recapitalization necessary for the SPE approach would not work, or for which break-up is deemed appropriate.

Multinational coordination in Europe is likely to be further strengthened by the implementation of two sets of legislation concerning bank resolution. Their respective ambits can be understood as two concentric circles. The outer circle, to which the BRRD applies, comprises all EU Member States. It requires each country to implement common rules regarding the powers available to authorities for bank resolution. In conjunction with the establishment of colleges of supervisors, this will greatly increase the chances of successful common planning.

The inner circle is established by the European Banking Union. This applies to all eurozone countries, and to any non-eurozone EU Member States who elect to opt in. Under the Banking Union, supervisory powers for all banks in relevant

[63] Wigand, JR, Director, FDIC Office of Complex Financial Institutions, Improving Cross Border Resolution to Better Protect Taxpayers and the Economy, remarks to US Senate Subcommittee on National Security and International Trade and Finance (15 May 2013).

[64] Gordon, JN and Ringe, WG, Banking Union Resolution without Deposit Guarantee: A Transatlantic Perspective on What it Would Take (December 2013), Working Paper, Columbia Law School/Copenhagen Business School.

[65] FSB, Recovery and Resolution Planning, n 58 above.

countries were from 4 November 2014 transferred to a new Single Supervisory Mechanism (SSM), for which the European Central Bank (ECB) is the supervisor.[66] The ECB's supervision is direct for 'significant' banks—generally speaking, those having assets exceeding €30 billion, or more than 20 per cent of their home country's GDP—and may be delegated to national supervisory authorities for smaller banks.[67] A new European Single Resolution Mechanism (SRM) will also be established, with effect from the beginning of 2016,[68] which will create a European-level Board and associated institutional architecture for resolution decision-making, along with a single set of rules governing resolution process and powers. The Single Resolution Board (hereafter, the Board) will be responsible for drawing up and overseeing the execution of resolution plans in relation to groups directly supervised by the ECB and other cross-border groups,[69] and the national authorities will execute the relevant resolution powers.[70] The content of the powers to be granted to the SRM track those to be made available to national authorities under the BRRD.[71] In contrast to the operation of the BRRD, however, under which group-level resolution authorities have no power to compel cooperation by national authorities,[72] the Board will have the power to issue general instructions to relevant national resolution authorities, who will be obliged to cooperate.[73]

3. Bail-in tool

The difficulties with effecting a rapid transfer, and even more importantly, of finding a suitable purchaser, have lead European policymakers to advocate a new type of resolution mechanism, which has come to be known simply as 'bail-in'.[74] The nomenclature emerged as a contrast to 'bailouts': the idea is that, rather than the state stepping in to make payments that save creditors from losses, the creditors should be expected to bear the losses themselves. In a sense, this is what any effective resolution mechanism should permit. However, the 'bail-in' powers are very different from the first-generation resolution mechanisms: they are, in effect, expedited *reorganization* procedures, as opposed to liquidation procedures. That

[66] Regulation (EU) No 1024/2013 conferring specific tasks on the European Central Bank concerning policies relating to the prudential supervision credit institutions [2013] OJ L287/63.

[67] ibid, Article 6. The ECB may nevertheless choose to exercise the relevant powers in relation to institutions deemed not to be significant.

[68] SRM Regulation, n 26 above, Regulation 806/2014.

[69] ibid, Articles 7, 8, and 18.

[70] ibid, Article 29. National authorities will also be responsible for drawing up and implementing resolution plans in relation to smaller banking groups: Articles 7 and 9.

[71] ibid, Articles 22–7.

[72] See above, text to notes 60–2.

[73] SRM Regulation, n 26 above, Articles 29–32.

[74] See BRRD, n 4 above, Article 43; SRM Regulation, n 26 above, Article 27; Financial Services (Banking Reform) Act 2013 (UK), section 17 and Schedule 2.

is, they envisage the same corporate entity remaining, but with a restructuring of the terms of its financing.

Just as the first-generation resolution tools seek to expedite the process of liquidating assets by waiving normal property laws, bail-in powers expedite the process of restructuring by waiving shareholders and creditors' ordinary contractual rights. In a normal restructuring, creditors have the right to vote on the terms of any new contracts. Bail-in powers provide for the restructuring of creditors' (and shareholders') rights without their consent *ex post*. The most commonly envisaged such restructuring would be a debt-equity swap, but other possibilities—such as a simple cancellation of equity or debt—also exist.

Just as the asset transfer powers achieve the same outcome as bankruptcy sales, save that interested parties' property rights are waived, a reorganization achieved in this way would waive security holders' property rights. Instead of an entitlement to compensation, however, they would be given new (junior) claims against the troubled firm, in a compulsory debt-equity swap. Broadly speaking, there are two ways in which such a restructuring could be effected:

1. *Contractual trigger* ('contingent capital'): the terms of the relevant debt contracts provide that on the occurrence of a relevant event, the contractual terms will automatically transform.
2. *Regulatory trigger* ('bail-in'): regulators have the power to mandate the transformation of contractual terms, on the occurrence of certain specified events.

The contractual trigger version clearly requires the creditors to consent *ex ante* to subject themselves to the possibility of transformation: in effect, they are buying *contingent capital* claims. While a regulatory trigger may seem non-consensual, provided that the power for such a trigger to be exercised was in existence at the time that the debt was negotiated, creditors can still price in the expected effect of such a power on the value of their claims.[75]

The fact that creditors will price in the expected transformation of their debt has several significant implications. First, the more predictable the circumstances under which restructuring would be triggered, the easier it will be for creditors to price the debt. This will avoid any unnecessary impact on the firm's cost of capital. However, great care must be taken in specifying triggers in order to avoid generating feedback problems. For example, if a conversion is triggered by loss of equity capital as measured by the market price, and is dilutive of shareholders, then the anticipation of conversion will cause the price to drop, which itself will hasten conversion.[76] The possibility of such outcomes has the potential to exacerbate, rather than smooth, instability in periods where financial institutions are stressed.

[75] There are no proposals to impose such a power on pre-existing debt contracts using the measures discussed.

[76] Sundaresan, S and Wang, Z, Design of Contingent Capital with Stock Price Trigger for Conversion (April 2010), Working Paper, Columbia University/FRBNY.

A range of alternative triggers have been proposed in order to minimize the potential for feedback. Some have suggested triggers based on accounting measures—linked, for example, to impairment of regulatory capital, although these may respond too slowly to rapid declines in asset values to be of effective use.[77] A more promising possibility is to condition on a trailing average stock price, damping the effect of sudden swings.[78] Alternatively, pre-emptive rights for existing shareholders can be coupled with convertible debt in a way that also mitigates the problem. For example, if existing shareholders are offered the right to purchase the newly created equity at the conversion price, this removes any incentive for speculative triggering.[79] Yet another suggestion is to make the debt convertible at the option of the issuer (a so-called 'reverse convertible') at any point up to maturity.[80]

The lack of consensus over the desirable properties of pre-specified triggers has lead most regulators to refrain from mandating the use of contractual triggers for recapitalization. On the other hand, there has been general support among policymakers for recapitalization mechanisms based on a regulatory trigger, or 'bail-in', as a desirable part of the resolution toolkit. These do not specify the trigger point in advance; rather they are intended to be used by regulators only *in extremis*, as part of the resolution toolkit. Given that first-generation resolution powers are already available, and that their exercise will result in uncertain losses for creditors, the reasoning is that the addition of a bail-in power will *enhance* certainty, relative to the existing first-generation type resolution powers, by making clearer how losses will lie in a resolution.[81]

Second, it is practically impossible to include very short-term debt in such a compulsory restructuring. To do so could lead to negative feedback loops whereby the prospect of recapitalization becomes a self-fulfilling prophecy. Short-term creditors, fearful of being forced to convert, might either dramatically increase their 'haircuts' or simply refuse to continue to lend.[82] The threat of a bail-in would simply make such lenders refuse to continue to extend credit, forcing the firm into failure at an earlier stage.

Third, firms have an incentive to raise debt finance on terms that would be exempt from restructuring: this would reduce their cost of capital significantly. This could be done by using short-term debt, which, as explained, would need to

[77] Duffie, D, 'A Contractual Approach to Restructuring Financial Institutions' in Schulz G, Scott K, and Taylor J (eds), *Ending Government Bailouts as we Know them* (2010) 109, 114–15.

[78] Calomiris, CW and Herring, RJ, Why and How to Design a Contingent Convertible Debt Requirement (April 2011), Working Paper, Columbia Business School/Wharton School, 25.

[79] Pennacchi, G, Vermaelen, T, and Wolff, CCP, Contingent Capital: The Case for COERCs (March 2011), Working Paper, University of Illinois/INSEAD/Luxembourg School of Finance.

[80] Bolton, P and Samama, F, Contingent Capital and Long Term Investors: A Natural Match? (September 2010), Working Paper, Columbia Business School. On conversion, the issuer foregoes the option to convert at a potentially even more favourable price in the future, and consequently proponents argue this would encourage triggering only in times of severe financial difficulty.

[81] Independent Commission on Banking, Final Report (2011), 103.

[82] See Gorton, G, *Slapped by the Invisible Hand: The Panic of 2007* (2010).

be excluded, or by using debt raised in a jurisdiction which does not recognize the authority of the regulator to effect a transformation of the financial contracts.

These points all have the same implication: for bail-in to work, the firm's debt structure must be designed and monitored carefully by the regulator. That is, the amount of debt subject to bail-in, and the laws under which it is raised, should be subject to continuous scrutiny by the firm's supervisors. This is really just the application of the idea of a 'living will' to restructurings. However, the sorts of issues that are implicated for supervision under it mean that it should be thought of as a conversation running in parallel with the supervision of the firm's capital adequacy requirements. In effect, the bail-in powers create a new form of regulatory capital.

Provided such *ex ante* design and oversight can be achieved, bail-in also offers the possibility of reducing the problems of international coordination relative to first-generation resolution regimes. As no transfer of assets is required, the only need for regulatory coordination is over the triggering of the restructuring. This can be made more straightforward by requiring the firm to raise all the relevant debt in contracts governed by laws of jurisdictions which recognized the authority of the regulator to impose bail-ins.

European countries have lead the way with bail-in powers. The idea is said to have originated with a large Swiss banking group, and modifications to Swiss banking legislation in 2011–13 have made possible the exercise of bail-in powers as a preferred resolution strategy for large complex financial institutions.[83] The EU's BRRD and SRM Regulation contain powers for authorities to impose mandatory restructuring of shareholders' and creditors' claims.[84] They will apply to all credit institutions and investment firms established in the EU (or within the eurozone and other participating countries in the case of the SRM), along with their financial institution subsidiaries and financial holding companies. Very short-term and secured liabilities are excluded from bail-in, as are client money claims and other funds held on trust, covered deposits,[85] the claims of employees, trade creditors, and the tax authorities.[86] Equivalent powers were enacted in the UK ahead of the Directive's implementation, under the Financial Services (Banking Reform) Act 2013.[87]

The EU's resolution regimes require resolution authorities to ensure that relevant firms have sufficient 'bail-inable' debt available.[88] This comprises long-term debt which is not already counted as Tier 1 or 2 capital, which is free from any guarantees or self-funding by the firm and which is not associated with derivative transactions.

[83] FINMA, Resolution of Globally Systemically Important Banks (7 August 2013), available at <http://www.finma.ch/e/finma/publikationen/Documents/pos-sanierung-abwicklung-20130807-e.pdf>, 3–4.

[84] BRRD, n 4 above, Article 43; SRM Regulation, n 26 above, Article 27.

[85] That is, those within the coverage level for deposit guarantee schemes: Directive 2014/49/EU [2014] OJ L173/149, Article 2(1)(5), 6.

[86] BRRD, n 4 above, Article 44; SRM Regulation, n 26 above, Article 27(3).

[87] Section 17 and Schedule 2 (amending Banking Act 2009).

[88] BRRD, n 4 above, Article 45; SRM Regulation, n 26 above, Article 12.

Such liabilities must be governed by the laws of jurisdictions which recognize the decision of a resolution authority to write down the debt. How much debt will be sufficient is a question that is left to be determined by the relevant resolution authorities, in consultation with the relevant supervisor—depending on the size, business model, and propensity for systemic risk of the firm in question. The European Commission reserves the option to harmonize these requirements by submitting a legislative proposal by the end of 2016; for systemic eurozone banks they will be harmonized in any event by the decision-making of the Single Resolution Board.

Paul Tucker, Deputy Governor of the Bank of England, has expressed the provisional view that the appropriate minimum could be set at the firm's Tier 1 capital requirement, plus a margin, minus any surplus equity. This would ensure that there would be sufficient bail-inable debt (plus surplus equity) to ensure that the firm could be recapitalized back to the Tier 1 minimum even if all Tier 1 capital was lost.[89] Moreover, there is a prohibition on any contribution being made from resolution funds—whether national or the eurozone's Single Resolution Fund—unless at least 8 per cent of the outstanding liabilities of the firm have been recapitalized by shareholders and eligible creditors.[90] This effectively places a hard floor on the level of bail-inable claims a financial firm must issue. For UK retail banks subject to the 'ring fence', the UK government proposes to impose a minimum primary loss-absorbency requirement—to include regulatory capital and bail-inable claims—of 17 per cent.[91]

While the use of bail-in has the potential to solve many of the problems identified in relation to 'first-generation' resolution procedures, it in turn raises a new set of issues: the position of creditors holding the bailed-in debt. The sudden recapitalization could itself be a channel for contagion. It is, therefore, imperative that authorities not only supervise the quantum of such debt raised, but also to which parties it is issued. It is inappropriate, for example, to permit banks or systemically relevant financial institutions to hold bail-inable debt in each other. Rather, it is desirable for such debt to be issued primarily to pension funds and insurance companies, which have long-time horizons in their investment portfolios.

We have so far characterized a bail-in as a form of expedited corporate reorganization for a failing bank, which occurs in accordance with a prearranged plan. However, the ability to convert debt into equity could also be used in conjunction with a 'bridge bank' tool. In this variant, assets are transferred to a bridge bank *along with bailed-in claims*. This is, in fact, the preferred approach to resolution announced by the US FDIC.[92]

[89] Tucker, P, Deputy Governor Financial Stability, Bank of England, Resolution and the Future of Finance, speech given at INSOL International World Conference, The Hague (20 May 2013).

[90] BRRD, n 4 above, Article 44(5); SRM Regulation, n 26 above, Article 27(7).

[91] See HM Treasury/BIS, Banking Reform: Draft Secondary Legislation, Cm 8660 (July 2013), 59–66.

[92] See FDIC, 'Resolution of Systemically Important Financial Institutions: The Single Point of Entry Strategy' (2013) 78 *Federal Register* 76614.

The advantage bail-in of the debt claims brings over a straightforward transfer to a bridge bank is that creditors have greater liquidity. The bridge bank tool without bail-in would give creditors shares in whatever proceeds arise from the ultimate sale of the bridge bank assets. This could take years to establish. With bail-in, the creditors' claims are converted to equity at a conversion rate determined by reference to current valuations. The creditors can then sell their shares in the market, which will price them according to expectations about the bank's performance.

Less obvious, however, is what advantage use of a bridge bank brings to straightforward recapitalization of a troubled entity using bail-in. The answer is that this has particular appeal in the US, because of the particular features of the Dodd–Frank Act. Section 214 of this Act prohibits outright the giving of taxpayer assistance to troubled financial institutions. The goal was to prevent taxpayer funds being used to recapitalize troubled firms, and thereby to minimize moral hazard. The way this was implemented in section 214 includes an outright stipulation that all financial companies put into the Dodd–Frank resolution process must be liquidated. This means that US supervisors are not permitted simply to bail in the holding company's creditors; rather the holding company must, in fact, be liquidated. Transfer of its assets to a bridge bank meets this requirement.[93] However, given that all that need be transferred are shares in subsidiaries, this is unlikely to make a significant difference to outcomes.

We have now seen the second-generation resolution mechanisms have the potential to make resolution of large complex financial institutions feasible. In Section V, we explore in more detail two crucial aspects of these schemes: how resolution is initiated ('triggered'), and how any shortfall in funding is met.

V. Triggering and Funding Resolution

1. Triggering resolution

The decision to trigger a resolution process is one for which the stakes are high. Exercise of these powers will expropriate investors, and could result in a significant bill for the public purse. Conversely, failure to exercise them in a timely fashion could result in contagion and the spread of systemic risk and even greater losses for investors and the public purse. These considerations are built into the structuring of legal authority to commence proceedings.

[93] ibid, 76615.

In contrast to ordinary bankruptcy proceedings, resolution proceedings are generally viewed as an administrative, rather than a judicial, process. They operate outside the ordinary framework of the rule of law, in order to permit a more rapid—and, ideally, more expert—decision to be made.[94] The relevant decision to trigger the process is therefore one for specialist agencies. It is desirable for the relevant agency to have both the best available information, and the strongest incentives, to make an appropriate decision. These considerations may to some degree cut against one another. The best available information will be in the hands of the financial institution's regular *supervisor*, who is responsible for monitoring ongoing compliance with capital adequacy requirements and the like. However, there is a concern that this agency may lack strong incentives to take corrective action *ex post*, because to do so may require (or be perceived to require) an admission of its own failure in supervising the institution. To combat the associated problem of regulatory forbearance, it might be thought desirable to place authority for triggering resolution in the hands of a different organization from those responsible for ongoing supervision, namely a *resolution authority*. However, separation of these two functions creates its own problems, especially as the supervisor's role will be crucial in ensuring that feasible recovery and resolution plans are in place, and that adequate bail-inable capital is in place in firms' capital structures. In other words, either the supervisor will be crucial to the credibility of resolution, or the resolution authority must have some ongoing role in the supervision process. This suggests that combined decision-making may well have advantages. These considerations do not point to any obviously superior allocation of decision-making power. In recognition of this, the EU's BRRD leaves the choice to Member States, simply requiring that any conflicts of interest be managed.[95]

The emerging practice appears to be to manage these tensions by involving a combination of authorities in the decision to trigger resolution proceedings: supervisory authorities, resolution authorities, and (where necessary) those controlling any public funds which may be available. For example:

- In the UK, the Banking Act 2009 puts responsibility on the supervisory authority (formerly the FSA, now the PRA) to determine whether a bank is, or is likely to fail to meet its threshold conditions (compliance with regulatory capital requirements etc.).[96] If the PRA so determines, then the decision whether to trigger the

[94] The EU's BRRD gives Member States the option to provide for *ex ante* judicial approval—by an expedited process—of decisions to trigger resolution powers (ibid, Article 85). The SRM Regulation provides for the establishment of a specialist Appeal Panel. See below, text to n 104.

[95] BRRD, n 4 above, Article 3. The text of Article 3(3) states that the supervisory authority may 'exceptionally' be designated as the resolution authority, whereas para (15) of the Preamble states that 'Member States should be free to choose which authorities should be responsible for applying the resolution tools'.

[96] Banking Act 2009 (UK), section 7. The same mechanism is used for the exercise of bail-in powers: Financial Services (Banking Reform) Act 2013 (UK), Sch 2, para 2.

resolution regime is for the resolution authority (Bank of England), in consultation with supervisors and the Treasury.[97] Where public ownership is envisaged, the decision must be made by the Treasury, in consultation with the Bank and the supervisors.[98]

- In the US, entry into the OLA under the Dodd–Frank Act requires that a recommendation be made by supervisors (the Federal Reserve) and the resolution agency (the FDIC),[99] followed by a determination by the Secretary of the Treasury.[100]
- Under the SRM for the eurozone, the process for ECB-systemic banks will be initiated by the supervisor (the ECB) indicating that a bank is failing or is likely to fail.[101] The Single Resolution Board would then, in conjunction with national supervisory authorities, determine whether there is any reasonable prospect of preventing the bank's failure within a reasonable timeframe. If not, and the Board determines resolution is in the public interest, then the Board must adopt a resolution scheme. This would come into effect unless, within 24 hours, either the European Commission or the Council of Ministers (acting by simple majority) opposes or modifies the scheme.

In addition to the need to ensure appropriate information and incentives on the part of the decision-maker, there are also serious concerns about the application of the rule of law to procedures which are likely to operate in an expropriatory fashion at least as regards some investors. To guard against this, the US process gives firms in relation to which the FDIC is to be appointed receiver the option to seek expedited judicial review of the decision. This is a very 'streamlined' judicial review process: a first-instance decision must be received within 24 hours, and the sole criterion on which the decision may be reviewed is whether it was 'arbitrary and capricious'.[102] The EU's BRRD requires Member States to provide for a right to an *ex post* judicial appeal against the exercise of resolution powers,[103] and the SRM Regulation provides for the establishment of a specialist Appeal Panel, from which a further appeal will be available to the Court of Justice of the EU, to hear claims to review the exercise of the Board's powers.[104]

[97] Banking Act 2009 (UK), section 8. [98] ibid, section 9.

[99] Or for broker-dealers, the SEC in consultation with the FDIC, and for insurance companies the Federal Insurance Office in consultation with the FDIC.

[100] Dodd–Frank Act (US), §203.

[101] SRM Regulation, n 26 above, Article 18. In relation to non-systemic banks, the Board may make an assessment of this condition on its own initiative.

[102] Dodd–Frank Act (US), §202.

[103] However, such an appeal shall be subject to a rebuttable presumption that suspension of enforcement of resolution authority decisions shall be against the public interest: BRRD, n 4 above, Article 85.

[104] SRM Regulation, n 26 above, Articles 85–6.

2. Funding resolution

Another extremely challenging set of issues in bank resolution concerns funding. In a transfer process, if the purchaser is unwilling to assume the deposits without some form of guarantee, or if in a recapitalization, there is insufficient bail-inable debt to return the firm to adequately capitalized status, then external funding must be sought. Rather than turn to discretionary taxpayer funds, most resolution mechanisms have built into them a fund which can be used to make good such shortfalls.

A purchaser might be induced to acquire the assets if additional funding could be included to sweeten the deal. For example, JP Morgan was offered an inducement to buy Bear Stearns in the form of a non-recourse loan from the NY Federal Reserve Bank secured by Bear's assets.[105] Alternatively, the distressed firm could be taken into public ownership (as with Northern Rock) or operated by the authorities as a 'bridge bank' for a period until market confidence is restored and then sold for significantly more. However, the interim operations will require funding to support them. The source of such funding is an important controversy in the design of resolution mechanisms. If the money comes from discretionary public expenditure, it becomes a species of bailout, with the associated problems they entail. An alternative is to raise a fund through some sort of levy on other financial institutions.

In the UK, there is a relatively modest role for prefunded assistance. Where, using the SRR, it is sought to get a purchaser to take on deposits—as will usually be the case—then the Financial Services Compensation Scheme (FSCS) is required to guarantee the deposits insofar as it would have been liable to pay out had the bank gone into insolvency.[106] The FSCS provides deposit guarantees and compensation to investors who have actionable claims against insolvent UK financial services firms,[107] and is funded by a levy on regulated financial institutions.

Beyond this, the UK would rely on discretionary public funding to assist in the resolution of a distressed institution—that is, a bailout. The Banking Act 2009 clarified the position as regards accountability over the provision of state financial assistance to support troubled banks and financial institutions. Ordinarily, this is to be done only with the approval of Parliament,[108] but the Treasury has power to pledge public funds—with no limit—even without parliamentary approval where it is satisfied that the need is 'too urgent to permit arrangements to be made for

[105] Orticelli, BJ, 'Crisis Compounded by Constraint: How Regulatory Inadequacies Impaired the Fed's Bailout of Bear Stearns' (2009) 42 *Connecticut Law Review* 647, 662–4.

[106] Banking Act 2009 (UK), section 171 (inserting section 214B of the Financial Services and Markets Act 2000 (UK)).

[107] Kuczynski, A, 'Financial Redress—Complaints, Disputes and Compensation' in Blair, M, Walker, G, and Purves, R (eds), *Financial Services Law* (2nd edn, 2009) 285, 330ff.

[108] HM Treasury, Managing Public Money, para 2.1.1.

the provision of money by Parliament'.[109] The power to provide financial assistance thereby granted may be exercised in favour not only of banks but also any 'financial institution' defined as any institution the Treasury has by order so provided to be classed.[110] The Treasury, therefore, has executive power to bail out any troubled financial firm.

The US Dodd–Frank Act grapples expressly with the problem of resolution funding. A central premise of the legislation is that taxpayers are not to subsidize 'bailouts', and section 214(c) of the Act consequently provides that '[t]axpayers shall bear no losses from the exercise of [the Orderly Liquidation A]uthority'. The Act instead establishes an OLF for the purpose of providing funding to institutions undergoing resolution. However, this is not purely privately funded. Rather, it raises funds in the first instance by FDIC borrowing from the US Treasury.[111] To make good on the undertaking in section 214, safeguards are built in to minimize the OLF's exposure, and it is given recoupment rights from financial institutions.

The first safeguard is that funds provided from OLF to firms in OLA are limited by reference to the asset value of the troubled firm—up to 10 per cent of the total value of the firm's assets, and 90 per cent of the fair value of its assets available for repayment 30 days after the commencement of proceedings.[112] Second, OLF funding enjoys administrative expense priority as regards repayment, meaning that it ranks ahead of all unsecured creditors—and *a fortiori*, shareholders—of the troubled firm in relation to the assets available for repayment. These two safeguards are together intended to ensure that the OLF will be able to get the money it has advanced repaid.

The FDIC is required to seek to repay any OLF borrowings to the Treasury by an assessment on large financial institutions. In the first instance, this is to be imposed on financial institutions who are creditors of a firm undergoing resolution to the extent that they have received repayments in the proceedings—a form of extension of the administrative expense priority enjoyed by the OLF's claims against the firm. To the extent that this is insufficient, the FDIC is to make an assessment on large financial institutions generally, weighted according to its evaluation of their contribution to systemic risk.[113] This is intended to reduce the problems of moral hazard associated with resolution. By placing the responsibility on the shoulders of financial institutions, it generates a degree of potential cross-monitoring, with

[109] Banking Act 2009 (UK), section 228(5). 'Financial assistance' is defined broadly to include 'giving guarantees and indemnities and any other kind of financial assistance (actual or contingent)' (see section 257). In this case, parliamentary accountability is achieved only by means of an *ex post* report and account, although this itself may be delayed or dispensed with if the Treasury thinks it necessary on public interest grounds: sections 228(6)–(7).

[110] ibid, section 230.

[111] The Treasury may then resell the debt: Dodd–Frank Act (US), § 210(n)(5); 12 USC § 5390(n)(5).

[112] ibid, § 210(n)(6); 12 USC § 5390(n)(6).

[113] ibid, § 210(o); 12 USC § 5390(o).

firms having incentives to encourage each other not to place the others at risk. The fact that financial institutions will be paying for any resolution will make them very interested parties in the design of any mechanism, and introduce a natural constraint on the extent to which unnecessary insurance will be paid out.[114]

Despite these safeguards, there is still scope for continued discretionary public support of troubled financial institutions in the US. The FDIC is permitted to operate a troubled firm by way of a bridge bank for up to five years.[115] And while the FDIC is required to make risk-weighted assessments on large financial institutions, it seems likely that the very times when such assessments are most needed—that is, financial crises—are the times when they are least likely to be able to be paid. In light of this, the prohibition on taxpayer losses begins to look little more than hortative.[116]

The EU resolution schemes emphasize an approach that involves prefunded resolution financing. The BRRD obliges Member States to establish domestic resolution funds.[117] For Member States subject to the Banking Union, a new Single Resolution Fund (SRF), controlled by the Board, is to be established.[118] These are to be prefunded, in the sense that firms within the reach of the relevant resolution mechanisms (that is, credit institutions and applicable investment firms) will be obliged to contribute by way of an annual levy until the funds meet a 'target size', determined as a proportion of the liabilities of relevant financial institutions. The proposed initial target is in both cases 1 per cent of the covered deposits of credit institutions in the (relevant) Member States, over a time horizon of ten years for national BRRD funds and eight years for the SRF.[119] To the extent that a resolution must take place where the funds raised are insufficient, both national BRRD funds and the SRF will have the power to raise extraordinary *ex post* contributions, and to borrow against future levies.[120]

The prefunding proposal received strong opposition from the financial industry, who were concerned about the implications for European competitiveness.[121] Excessive contribution requirements might, it was argued, deter financial

[114] See Calomiris, C, How to Fix the Resolution Problem of Large, Complex, Nonbank Financial Institutions, paper presented at Columbia Law School conference on the Global Financial Crisis (March 2010), available at <http://www.law.columbia.edu/null/download?&exclusive=filemgr.download&file_id=154847>.

[115] Dodd–Frank Act (US), § 210(h)(12); 12 USC § 5390(h)(12). While a bridge bank is explicitly not an 'agency' of the US government and its employees are not public employees (§ 210(h)(8); 12 USC § 5390(h)(8)), it is funded by public debt in the first instance (see above, text to nn 111–14) and pays no taxes (§ 210(h)(10); 12 USC § 5390(h)(10)).

[116] See Skeel Jr, DA, *The New Financial Deal: Understanding the Dodd–Frank Act and its (Unintended) Consequences* (2011); Calomiris, CW, An Incentive-Robust Program for Financial Reform (February 2011), Working Paper, Columbia Business School, 25–6.

[117] BRRD, n 4 above, Article 100. [118] SRM Regulation, n 26 above, Article 67.

[119] BRRD, n 4 above, Article 102(1); SRM Regulation, n 26 above, Article 68(1).

[120] BRRD, n 4 above, Article 104; SRM Regulation, n 26 above, Article 71.

[121] See European Commission, Overview of the Results of the Public Consultation on Technical Details of a Possible EU Framework for Bank Resolution and Recovery (5 May 2011), available at <http://ec.europa.eu/internal_market/consultations/docs/2011/crisis_management/consultation_overview_en.pdf>), 17–18.

institutions from operating in the EU, as opposed to the US, if the latter imposes only *ex post* funding. In particular, it is important that any contribution be based on an appropriate risk weighting so as to impart incentives to reduce risk, and not to deter low-risk firms.

An additional funding source for EU bank resolution—both under the BRRD and the SRM—is to require deposit guarantee funds to assist in funding resolution procedures insofar as the funds are spared having to make payments to depositors by the resolution process.[122] Finally, both schemes provide for resolution authorities to be able to contract for backstop funding in the event that the funds otherwise available are insufficient.[123]

VI. Conclusion

This Chapter has considered the problem of the 'resolution' of distressed financial institutions. Many financial institutions differ from ordinary firms in that their failure has the potential to engender systemic risk: contagion in the financial system which ultimately creates losses in the real economy many multiples of the losses to investors in the institution. Consequently, a strong case exists for the application of special procedures to mitigate the transmission of financial shocks. Ad hoc government bailouts create moral hazard for financial firms, encouraging them to take more risks *ex ante*. Conversely, the application of ordinary insolvency law—even with some streamlining—may do too little to stop the spread of contagion.

Consequently, many jurisdictions have introduced, or are designing, 'special resolution' mechanisms for financial institutions. The first generation of such mechanisms were based on the US FDIC receivership regime. They focus on waiving property rights so as to effect a very rapid transfer of complex assets and short-term liabilities to a purchaser who will be able to stand behind those liabilities and thereby ensure stability. Shortfalls are covered by an insurance fund paid which mutualizes losses across the industry. This model works well for small to medium sized domestic banks. However, it is insufficient to provide a credible alternative to bailouts for large, complex financial institutions of the sort which got into difficulty during the financial crisis.

[122] BRRD, n 4 above, Article 109; SRM Regulation, n 26 above, Article 79.
[123] BRRD, n 4 above, Article 105; SRM Regulation, n 26 above, Article 73.

As a result, a series of new measures—which we have termed 'second-generation' resolution mechanisms—have been developed. First, there has been a realization that the level of complexity is such that resolution *ex post* is impossible without careful planning by supervisors *ex ante*. Second, this planning process can be used not only to understand, but also to modify, the structure of complex financial institutions and their regulatory oversight so as to facilitate resolution should it be necessary. Third, the use of 'bail-in' or mandated debt to equity swaps provides a potentially very useful additional resolution tool when used in conjunction with such forward planning and oversight. Fourth, in the context of international financial institutions, coordination and allocation of responsibility among national regulators is an integral part of the planning process.

What policy implications may be drawn from the analysis? First, the central message of this Chapter is that for bank resolution to be credible—that is, to provide a meaningful alternative to discretionary bailouts—it must be thought of as an integral part of the ongoing oversight of financial institutions by regulators, and not as simply a set of mechanisms that are kept for troubled times. Investment in regulatory capacity—recruitment and training to build human capital in the regulatory sector—is, therefore, crucial to ensuring the success of resolution. The FSB's programme of developing guidance as to best practice and dialogue between peer regulators is a welcome initiative that may help in this capacity-building.

Second, in designing resolution mechanisms, some interference with investors' enjoyment of property rights is likely to be justified notwithstanding constitutional safeguards in many countries concerning such enjoyment.

Third, the advent of bail-in as a resolution tool means that care should be taken by domestic regulators to ensure that long term debt issued by foreign (or domestic) banks which may be subject to bail-in is not bought by domestic banks. This could otherwise generate a channel for contagion in the event that the holders of the bail-inable debt are asked to crystallize a loss.

Beyond that, much depends on the nature of a country's banking sector. If a country's banks are primarily domestic institutions of modest size, then resolution can credibly take the form of transfers of assets and insured liabilities to other market participants. In such a milieu, 'first-generation' resolution mechanisms modelled on the FDIC's receivership regime would be perfectly adequate to provide the legal infrastructure to execute the resolution strategy.

However, to the extent that a country's banks form part of a wider international group, resolution will need to rely on the 'second-generation' mechanisms outlined above, if it is to be credible. Consequently, it must be thought about in conjunction with regulators of other countries, and may well vary across institutions. While the lead players may likewise vary, it is likely that a handful of jurisdictions—including the US, the UK, and the eurozone—will drive the agenda in the majority of cases.

BIBLIOGRAPHY

Acharya, VV, Dreschler, I, and Schnabl, P, A Pyrrhic Victory? Bank Bailouts and Sovereign Credit Risk (June 2011), National Bureau of Economic Research Working Paper No 17136.

Armour, J and Gordon, JN, 'Systemic Harms and Shareholder Value' (2014) 6 *Journal of Legal Analysis* 35.

Ayotte, K and Skeel Jr, DA, 'Bankruptcy or Bailouts' (2010) 35 *Journal of Corporation Law* 469.

Baker, D and McArthur, T, 'The Value of the "Too Big to Fail" Big Bank Subsidy' (September 2009), *CEPR Issue Brief*.

Bank of England, *Financial Stability Report* (December 2009) No 26, 6.

Beltratti, A and Stulz, R, 'The Credit Crisis around the Globe: Why Did Some Banks Perform Better?' (2012) 105 *Journal of Financial Economics* 1.

Bennett, RL and Unal, H, The Effects of Resolution-Method Choice on Resolution Costs in Bank Failures (July 2009), FDIC Working Paper.

Bernanke, BS, 'Nonmonetary Effects of the Financial Crisis in the Propagation of the Great Depression' (1983) 73 *American Economic Review* 257.

Bliss, RR, 'Resolving Large Complex Financial Institutions' in Kaufman, GG (ed.), *Market Discipline in Banking: Theory and Evidence* (2003) 3.

Bolton, P and Samama, F, Contingent Capital and Long Term Investors: A Natural Match? (September 2010), Columbia Business School Working Paper.

Calomiris, C, How to Fix the Resolution Problem of Large, Complex, Nonbank Financial Institutions (March 2010), paper presented at Columbia Law School Conference on the Global Financial Crisis, available at <http://www.law.columbia.edu/null/download?&exclusive=filemgr.download&file_id=154847>.

Calomiris, C and White, EN, 'The Origins of Federal Deposit Insurance' in Goldin, CG and Libecap, GD (eds), *The Regulated Economy: A Historical Approach to Political Economy* (1994) 145.

Calomiris, CW, An Incentive-Robust Program for Financial Reform (February 2011), Columbia Business School Working Paper.

Calomiris, CW and Herring, RJ, Why and How to Design a Contingent Convertible Debt Requirement (April 2011), Columbia Business School/Wharton School Working Paper 25.

Diamond, D and Dybvig, PH, 'Bank Runs, Deposit Insurance, and Liquidity' (1983) 91 *Journal of Political Economy* 401.

Duffie, D, 'A Contractual Approach to Restructuring Financial Institutions' in Schulz, G, Scott, K, and Taylor, J (eds), *Ending Government Bailouts as we Know them* (2010) 109, at 114–15.

Dumontaux, N and Pop, A, 'Understanding the Market Reaction to Shockwaves: Evidence from the Failure of Lehman Brothers' (2013) 9 *Journal of Financial Stability* 269.

Erkens, DH, Hing, M, and Matos, P, 'Corporate Governance in the 2007–2008 Financial Crisis: Evidence from Financial Institutions Worldwide' (2012) 18 *Journal of Corporate Finance* 389.

European Commission, Consultation on a Possible Recovery and Resolution Framework for Financial Institutions Other than Banks, Brussels (5 October 2012).

European Commission, Executive Summary of the Impact Assessment Accompanying Proposal for a Council Directive on a common system of financial transaction tax and amending Directive 2008/7/EC (28 September 2011), SEC (2011) 1103 final, Brussels.

European Commission, Overview of the Results of the Public Consultation on Technical Details of a Possible EU Framework for Bank Resolution and Recovery (5 May 2011), available at <http://ec.europa.eu/internal_market/consultations/docs/2011/crisis_management/consultation_overview_en.pdf>.

European Court of Auditors, European Banking Supervision Taking Shape—EBA and its Changing Context (2014), EN2014/05.

FDIC (Federal Deposit Insurance Corporation), 'Resolution of Systemically Important Financial Institutions: The Single Point of Entry Strategy' (2013) 78 *Federal Register* 76614.

Fernando, CS, May, AD, and Megginson, WM, 'The Value of Investment Banking Relationships: Evidence from the Collapse of Lehman Brothers' (2012) 67 *Journal of Finance* 235.

Ferreira, D, Kershaw, D, Kirchmaier, T, and Schuster, EP, Shareholder Empowerment and Bank Bailouts (2012), LSE Financial Markets Group Discussion Paper 714.

FINMA (Swiss Financial Market Supervisory Authority), Resolution of Globally Systemically Important Banks (7 August 2013), available at <http://www.finma.ch/e/finma/publikationen/Documents/pos-sanierung-abwicklung-20130807-e.pdf>.

FSA (Financial Services Authority, UK), Recovery and Resolution Plans (August 2011), Consultation Paper 11/16.

FSB (Financial Stability Board, G20), Effective Resolution of Systemically Important Financial Institutions: Consultative Document (19 July 2011) 53.

FSB (Financial Stability Board, G20), Recovery and Resolution Planning for Systemically Important Financial Institutions: Guidance on Developing Effective Resolution Strategies (16 July 2013).

Gordon, JN and Ringe, WG, Banking Union Resolution without Deposit Guarantee: A Transatlantic Perspective on What it Would Take (December 2013), Columbia Law School/Copenhagen Business School Working Paper.

Gorton, G, *Slapped by the Invisible Hand: The Panic of 2007* (2010).

HM Treasury, *Managing Public Money* (2007).

HM Treasury/BIS, Banking Reform: Draft Secondary Legislation (July 2013), Cm 8660.

House of Commons Treasury Committee, *The Run on the Rock: Fifth Report of Session 2007–08* (Vol II, Oral and Written Evidence).

Hüpkes, E, 'Special Bank Resolution and Shareholders' Rights: Balancing Competing Interests' (2009) 17 *Journal of Financial Regulation and Compliance* 277.

IMF (International Monetary Fund), *World Economic Outlook 2011* (2011).

Independent Commission on Banking (UK), *Final Report* (2011) 103.

Kuczynski, A, 'Financial Redress—Complaints, Disputes and Compensation' in Blair, M, Walker, G, and Purves, R (eds), *Financial Services Law* (2nd edn, 2009) 285.

Morrison, ER, 'Is the Bankruptcy Code an Adequate Mechanism for Resolving the Distress of Systemically Important Institutions?' (2010) 82 *Temple Law Review* 449.

O'Hara, M and Shaw, W, 'Deposit Insurance and Wealth Effects: The Value of Being "Too Big to Fail"' (1998) 45 *Journal of Finance* 1587.

Orticelli, BJ, 'Crisis Compounded by Constraint: How Regulatory Inadequacies Impaired the Fed's Bailout of Bear Stearns' (2009) 42 *Connecticut Law Review* 647.

Pennacchi, G, Vermaelen, T, and Wolff, CCP, Contingent Capital: The Case for COERCs (March 2011), University of Illinois/INSEAD/Luxembourg School of Finance Working Paper.

Roe, M, 'The Derivatives Market's Payment Priorities as Financial Crisis Accelerator' (2011) 63 *Stanford Law Review* 539.

Schildbach, J, 'Direct Cost of the Financial Crisis', *Deutsche Bank Research*, 14 May 2010.

Skeel Jr, DA, *The New Financial Deal: Understanding the Dodd-Frank Act and its (Unintended) Consequences* (2011).

Stern, GH and Feldman, RJ, *Too Big to Fail: The Hazards of Bank Bailouts* (2004), ch 3.

Sundaresan, S and Wang, Z, Design of Contingent Capital with Stock Price Trigger for Conversion (April 2010), Columbia University/FRBNY Working Paper.

Tucker, P, Deputy Governor Financial Stability, Bank of England, Resolution and the Future of Finance, speech given at INSOL International World Conference, The Hague (20 May 2013).

Wigand, JR, Director, FDIC Office of Complex Financial Institutions, 'Improving Cross Border Resolution to Better Protect Taxpayers and the Economy', remarks to US Senate Subcommittee on National Security and International Trade and Finance (15 May 2013).

CHAPTER 16

CROSS-BORDER SUPERVISION OF FINANCIAL INSTITUTIONS

DOUGLAS W ARNER*

* The author gratefully acknowledges the financial support of the Hong Kong Research Grants Council and the Australian Research Council.

I. Introduction

This Chapter discusses regulation and supervision of financial institutions operating across borders. The cross-border supervision of internationally active financial institutions raises a distinct set of institutional and coordination risks to financial stability. As a result of the global and eurozone financial crises, major challenges in this respect have been revealed and increasing efforts are being made at the international level to develop effective approaches.

The Chapter begins with a discussion of questions relating to market access and licensing before turning to questions of supervision, regulation, and resolution. The Chapter concludes with a discussion of the outlook for continued globalization of financial services.

II. Market Access and Licensing

In considering regulation and supervision of financial institutions operating across borders, the initial issue concerns market access.

In the first period of financial globalization from the late 1800s to World War I, access to foreign markets was largely unregulated, as were most activities of financial institutions. Prior to this period, cross-border activities were largely focused on correspondent banking relationships, in which well-known institutions (often referred to as 'merchant banks') tended to deal with one another in the major trade fairs to periodically settle cross-border accounts.[1] Over time, financial institutions active in cross-border business increasingly established representative offices in major commercial and financial centres such as London and Paris in order to facilitate transactions, particularly relating to cross-border payments, trade finance, and foreign exchange business. Probably the most famous example is Rothschilds. In addition, during this period, major British financial institutions increasingly established overseas operations, both in major commercial centres throughout the British Empire as well as major financial centres in Europe and North America. Given the lack of financial services in many parts of the Empire, British institutions not only engaged in wholesale business but also retail business, including deposit-taking. Examples still with us include Barclays and Standard Chartered.

[1] See Martin, F, *Money: The Unauthorized Biography* (2014).

As banks developed in markets outside Europe (such as the US, Canada, and China), these institutions established operations in the major centres of London and Paris in order to support cross-border transactions, with examples including JP Morgan, Royal Bank of Canada, and the Hong Kong and Shanghai Banking Corporation. By this period, an important distinction had developed between the usual approaches to legal structure between common law (ie, British Empire and US) countries and Continental Europe, with the former tending to structure groups on the basis of separate legal entities and the latter more generally using a single institution structure ('universal banking').

At the same time, while regulation and supervision were generally undeveloped, crisis-management systems focusing on the central bank as lender of last resort were well developed in London, with the Bank of England periodically providing liquidity assistance to institutions which faced liquidity crises in the cross-border operations, of which the leading example is Barings in the 1890s.[2] During this period, the lender-of-last-resort arrangement developed in most other significant commercial and financial jurisdictions as well, typically in response to crisis.[3] These systems were to be tested—and largely shown wanting—in the face of the 1929 Crash in the US and the subsequent cross-border contagion and resulting Great Depression of the 1930s.[4]

By the end of World War II, the generally globalized financial markets of the period preceding World War I and the liberal approach to their regulation had come to an end. The story of today's global financial markets is largely that of the reintegration of markets over the second half of the twentieth century; an outcome that most certainly was not the intention of the designers of the international economic architecture at the end of World War II. This reintegration has also been combined with ever-increasing international cooperative efforts in the realm of regulation.

In general, the Bretton Woods and related arrangements were designed to reintegrate trade on the basis of progressive liberalization combined with monetary stability based on fixed exchange rates and current account liberalization to facilitate cross-border trade.[5] Finance was not intended to be reintegrated and thus capital account liberalization does not feature in the remit of the International Monetary Fund (IMF) and the intention for the major institution at the heart of cross-border financial regulation both in the 1930s and today—the Bank for International Settlements (BIS)—was to be wound up. At the same time, major financial institutions and groups had frequently been nationalized or broken up (eg, in the US as

[2] See Bagehot, W, *A Description of the Money Market* (1873); Hadjiemmannuil, C, *Banking Regulation and the Bank of England* (1996).

[3] eg, Federal Reserve.

[4] See Ahamed, L, *Lords of Finance: The Bankers Who Broke the World* (2009).

[5] See Buckley, R and Arner, D, *From Crisis to Crisis: The Global Financial System and Regulatory Failure* (2011).

the result of 1930s financial regulatory developments), leaving only a handful of private financial institutions operating on a cross-border basis (eg, Barclays and Standard Chartered). Nonetheless, both former members of groups (eg, JP Morgan and Morgan Stanley) and state-owned institutions (eg, Bank of China) continued to maintain some limited operations in major foreign jurisdictions, typically in the form of representative offices to facilitate cross-border payments. In addition, particularly US banks began a process of establishing such operations initially to follow their clients' overseas business needs but also those of the US government (eg, Citibank).

Generally speaking, up to the early 1970s, these operations received very little attention—regulatory or otherwise, reflecting the general consensus that international financial activities were very limited in scope and thus risk. This began to change particularly from the 1970s as the process of petrodollar recycling powered the development of the Eurodollar markets; the forerunners of today's global financial markets. The failure of Herstatt Bank in 1974 led to the first major international financial regulatory agreement—the Basel Concordat of 1975—and the establishment of the first international financial regulatory organization, the Basel Committee on Banking Supervision, both of which will be considered further below.[6]

From this time to the late 1980s, market access for foreign financial institutions tended to be limited to those which had been grandfathered (ie, as a result of pre-existing operations, such as those of Barclays and Standard Chartered) or to representative offices in major financial centres, which were seen as necessary to support cross-border trade and payments, as well as lending. The general tendency was to restrict licences to conduct domestic financial services business, thus both protecting the domestic financial system from risks from the involvement of foreign financial institutions as well as protecting domestic institutions from foreign competition and facilitating domestic financial and economic management. Market access was largely restricted to limited licences for representative business only.

The grand exception which emerged from the 1970s to this general approach was to restrict business in local currency and markets but to allow representative offices to engage in wholesale business in foreign currencies. The highest-profile example was that of the UK, in which banks undertaking wholesale international business were largely unregulated as to their international operations; a policy approach which underpinned the massive development of the Eurocurrency markets in the 1970s in London and elsewhere (eg, Singapore) but which culminated in the 1982 developing countries' debt crisis. Like the failure of Herstatt, the 1982 crisis led to a series of international regulatory agreements, including revisions to the Concordat (1983) and the 1988 Basel Capital Accord, as a direct result.

[6] See Norton, J, *Devising International Bank Supervisory Standards* (1995).

By this time, there was now a very clear awareness that international financial markets had become highly developed in the regulatory gaps between domestic financial markets. At the same time, domestic financial markets—particularly in the US and Europe—were beginning to be deregulated and liberalized. This emerges in two strands: the first was a consistent push by the US that lasted until the 2008 global financial crisis of continually pushing for more liberal access for US financial institutions to foreign markets, preferably on the basis of branch structures subject primarily to the home regulatory authority.[7] In this respect, the US consistently, until 2008, sought to promote access for US financial institutions to other markets on the basis of home country regulation. It did not, however, usually extend this approach to financial institutions from other countries seeking access to the US. The second was the decision to move ahead dramatically with financial-services liberalization and integration in Europe, expressed most tangibly in the 'big bang' liberalization in the UK in 1986 but underpinned by a process of pan-EU harmonization to minimum standards, mutual recognition, and finally passporting, under which financial services firms were able to do business anywhere in the EU under largely common regulatory standards and under the supervision of their home regulator (ie, the Member State in which the firm was initially authorized).[8]

The combination of these two strands found its expression in the World Trade Organization (WTO) General Agreement on Trade in Services (GATS)[9] and its constituent provisions addressing financial services by the late 1990s.[10] At the international level, GATS is the most significant 'hard law' framework for financial services, while the EU, of course, is the most significant 'hard law' regional framework for financial services. However, the GATS framework has not been very effective and has largely not progressed in a material sense since its completion at the end of the twentieth century.

The EU framework, however, has progressively developed and, despite some serious questions in the wake of the global and eurozone financial crises, continues to be based upon the passporting premise, albeit now with a regional supervisor for the eurozone (the European Central Bank (ECB)) and essentially common EU regulatory standards.[11] In the aftermath of the global and eurozone crises, though, the EU is now no longer seen as a model for either international or regional financial

[7] See Key, S, *Financial Services in the Uruguay Round and the WTO* (1997).

[8] As discussed further in the Chapter by Haar in this volume. See Walker, G, *International Banking Regulation: Law, Policy and Practice* (2001); Ferran, E, *Building an EU Securities Market* (2005); Moloney, N, *EC Securities Regulation* (2008).

[9] As discussed in the Chapter by Brummer and Smallcomb in this volume.

[10] See Arner, D, *Financial Stability, Economic Growth and the Role of Law* (2007).

[11] See Avgouleas, E and Arner, D, 'The Broken Glass of European Integration: Origins and Remedies of the Eurozone Crisis and Implications for Global Markets' in Lim, C and Mercurio, B (eds), *International Economic Law after the Crisis: A Tale of Fragmented Disciplines* (2014).

services access. The political and economic sacrifices required are simply beyond the present scope of any other context.

Rather, in the aftermath of the global financial crisis, the previous Western consensus in favour of liberalization of market access combined with branch or passport structures is now facing serious questions regarding its future viability. While discussions are continuing regarding potential plurilateral financial-services liberation negotiations under both the WTO and regional agreements (eg, ASEAN/+3 and TTIP), these are now largely focused on separately licensed and regulated subsidiaries in each jurisdiction concerned. This characterization also now largely characterizes access to the US market as well, where access for financial institutions via home supervised branches is effectively no longer an option (though, in fact, it was a limited option even prior to the crisis, reflecting a level of double-standards long common to US treatment of cross-border activities of non-US financial institutions seeking to access the US).[12] While this is particularly evident in the context of banking and particularly retail banking,[13] it is an approach which is increasingly being applied to all financial institutions.

Thus, one could characterize market access for cross-border financial institutions today as an environment where foreign institutions largely remain able to access the majority of foreign markets, but where such access is conditioned upon being regulated and supervised at least for purposes of the activities of the institution within that jurisdiction under the regulatory and supervisory structures of each individual jurisdiction.

III. Supervision of Cross-Border Financial Institutions

If we consider supervision of cross-border financial institutions, a number of models are possible and variations of most of these have been adopted in various contexts.

At one extreme, cross-border operations of financial institutions could be left largely regulated and unsupervised. As noted in the previous Section, this was, in fact, largely the case in the previous period of financial globalization prior to World War I. More recently, this was largely the approach applied to financial

[12] See Taylor, M and Schooner, H, *Global Bank Regulation* (2009).

[13] Bank of England, Consultation Paper CP4/14: Supervising International Banks: The Prudential Regulation Authority's Approach to Branch Supervision (February 2014).

institutions operating in the Eurodollar markets prior to the 1980s. The risks inherent in such approaches can be seen from both the unexpected interconnections linking the 1929 Crash to the Great Depression and the 1980s debt crisis. In the context of the period preceding the global financial crisis, this approach was not too far from an accurate characterization of the regulation and supervision of over-the-counter (OTC) derivatives and shadow banking.[14] One can say that, while periodically implemented, the resulting crises have shown that lack of supervision of cross-border activities can and has resulted in numerous crises. The result has been a series of attempts to address the challenges of regulating and supervising financial institutions operating internationally.

At the other end of the spectrum, perhaps a first best solution would be the establishment of a single international supervisor for cross-border financial institutions. In the wake of the global financial crisis and its resulting lengthy regulatory and supervisory reform agenda, and the subsequent conflicts between individual jurisdictions, this certainly has an increasing appeal from the standpoint of major financial institutions. From the standpoint of the latter, having a single supervisor would address issues of inconsistent (and frequently contradictory) standards across jurisdictions. Particular examples have arisen in respect of conflicts in clearing and settlement requirements for OTC derivatives involving the US and the EU, in which both jurisdictions require clearing with a counterparty registered within the US or the EU respectively, a requirement which is mutually exclusive and results of necessity in institutions doing business across both markets in breaching the rules of one in order to meet the requirements of the other.[15] This would make it possible to build systems across their global operations to address regulatory and supervisory requirements, both reducing costs of compliance as well as increasing effectiveness of compliance and also of supervision. It would also eliminate issues of competition between jurisdictions on the basis of regulation and supervision—eliminating the sorts of regulatory arbitrage that characterized many aspects of global finance prior to the global financial crisis.

Not surprisingly, there have been a variety of proposals for such a system, at least for the largest international financial institutions, ranging from the IMF to the BIS to the WTO to the creation of a new international organization.[16] The political realities of global finance make these ideas largely non-starters at present. Perhaps

[14] On shadow banking see further the Chapter by Avgouleas in this volume. See also Weber, R, Arner, D, Gibson, E, and Baumann, S, 'Addressing Systemic Risk: Financial Regulatory Design' (2014) 49 *Texas International Law Journal* 149.

[15] See Atlantic Council, *The Danger of Divergence: Transatlantic Financial Regulatory Reform and the G20 Agenda* (December 2013).

[16] See Arner, D and Taylor, M, 'The Global Credit Crisis and the Financial Stability Board: Hardening the Soft Law of International Financial Regulation?' (2009) 32 *University of New South Wales Law Journal* 488.

another global financial crisis would be necessary to trigger any significant movement in this direction, but that is by no means a certainty.

However, there is one context in which the single international supervisor has now been implemented: the EU. For credit rating agencies, this is now a correct characterization, with supervision pan-EU by the European Securities and Markets Authority (ESMA). In addition, for the eurozone, the largest banks are now supervised by the ECB, a single regional supervisor, supervising to common EU regulatory standards. Of most significance, the UK has opted out of this arrangement. As noted above in the context of market access, this is an area where the EU experience is at present unlikely to be followed elsewhere, regionally or internationally. It does though show that such a solution is possible, given the necessary context and political will. Whether it will be more successful than previous arrangements is very much yet to be seen. If it proves successful, it is certainly possible that similar approaches could be considered in other contexts, as has been the case with other EU approaches to financial liberalization (particularly those relating to harmonization to common standards, now adopted as the basis of international financial regulatory standards,[17] and mutual recognition, which is often the objective in most financial services access arrangements).

Between the two extremes, the remaining options are framed by the relationship between home and host supervisors, and this has been the focus of the various Basel Concordats and related supervisory guidance, which have responded in turn to the failure of Herstatt, the 1980s debt crisis, and the failures of Banco Ambrosiano in 1982, of BCCI in 1991 and of Barings in 1995, all culminating prior to the global financial crisis in aspects of Basel II and its implementation.[18]

At the global regulator end of the spectrum of home–host relations, one option would be home supervision of all activities of the financial institution regardless of where it was doing business, preferably with access to other jurisdictions on the basis of the branch model so that all operations could be consolidated under a single regulator and providing a clear and comprehensive picture of the activities and risks of the institution. Certainly, this was the preferred model of the US for US institutions at least up to the global financial crisis. In many respects, it continues to be the US's preferred model for its own institutions. Likewise, this is the approach adopted in the EU prior to the eurozone debt crisis. Likewise, it continues for non-eurozone institutions such as those authorized in the UK.

For a financial institution, it provides many of the benefits of a single global supervisor, so long as all (or at least most) of the other jurisdictions in which it operates recognize the home supervisor's standards. Prior to the global financial crisis,

[17] See Brummer, C, *Minilateralism: How Trade Alliances, Soft Law and Financial Engineering Are Redefining International Statecraft* (2014); Avgouleas, E, *Governance of Global Financial Markets: The Law, the Economics, the Politics* (2012).

[18] For a chronological list, see <http://www.bis.org/list/bcbs/tid_24/index.htm>.

this model was also seen as frequently benefiting the host country, which—because of the quality of the US or EU regulatory and supervisory system—did not have to worry about the safety and soundness of the foreign branch but could benefit from access to its services. Prior to the global financial crisis, issues tended to focus on the quality of the home supervisor, with BCCI, in particular, demonstrating that a financial institution could structure itself in such a way as to largely avoid regulation due to the limitations of its chosen home supervisor.[19] Thus, the Concordats and Basel II focused on the relationship between home and host supervisors to make sure that the quality of the home supervisor was sufficient and that the host supervisor had access to sufficient information and powers to protect the interests of its own jurisdiction in the event of problems in a financial institution. The result tended to be a high level of comfort between major supervisors but a high level of suspension of other supervisors, combined with (ex-EU) additional host-country requirements so that host countries could be certain that foreign institutions were no less regulated and supervised than home institutions. This was both a matter of financial stability as well as competitiveness.

In the aftermath of the global and eurozone financial crises, the previous balance between major supervisors (eg the US and the EU) and others has changed, with a loss of trust of the effectiveness of US and EU regulation, and supervision in particular. Likewise, the global financial crisis very directly highlighted the risks of failure of the largest global financial institutions and the very real lack of appropriate arrangements to deal with such failures.

At the other end of the spectrum is the pure host-supervisor approach. At its simplest, this model would involve separate supervision of the activities of each financial institution operating across borders in each jurisdiction in which it operated. From the financial institution's standpoint, this is in all likelihood more expensive and more challenging, in that each jurisdiction will have its own rules and supervisory approach, resulting in the necessity of compliance systems for each jurisdiction and the very real possibility of conflicts between regulations and supervisors in multiple jurisdictions. This was largely the model envisaged at Bretton Woods and the one which has been eroded through international regulatory cooperation, particularly since the 1970s. This would generally not be a branch-access model but rather one in which domestic licences and entities would be required in each jurisdiction according to the specific rules of that jurisdiction.

From the host supervisor's standpoint, this model has some appeal in that foreign institutions are treated exactly the same as domestic institutions (under GATS at least but often the objective in practice would be to limit the activities of foreign institutions in order to protect domestic institutions whenever possible). The greatest weakness of this model is that it lacks systems to share information across

[19] See Kerry, J and Brown, H, The BCCI Affair: Report to the Committee on Foreign Relations, US Senate (1992).

borders so that supervisors in one jurisdiction (whether home or host) have a clear picture of risks elsewhere that could impact upon the safety and soundness of the institution's operations in other markets.

In reality, much of international financial regulation from its advent in the 1970s up to the global financial crisis focused on addressing these problems. In particular, international financial regulation sought (and generally continues to seek) common minimum standards so that financial institutions will operate on a safe and sound basis everywhere (because the minimum standards are prudentially appropriate) and so that financial institutions will be able—to the greatest extent possible—to develop internal systems to meet international standards across their operations thus reducing costs. Such a system should minimize regulatory competition and arbitrage and—when combined with necessary information sharing and enforcement cooperation mechanisms—allow regulators to have a clear picture of the risks of any given financial institution operating on a cross-border basis combined with the powers to take action as necessary (including in conjunction with other regulators—foreign and domestic) to protect financial stability and integrity.

The Basel framework was generally intended to provide the details of exactly this relationship between regulation, home and host supervisors, and financial institutions doing business across borders, carefully seeking to balance between home and host. Likewise, the EU system sought to achieve exactly the same result, albeit through very high common standards culminating in home supervision across the EU through a branch structure.

The global and eurozone financial crises unfortunately exposed the weaknesses in this approach, particularly relating to complexity, interlinkages, and regulatory arbitrage.[20]

In the aftermath of the global and eurozone crises, as discussed above, the eurozone has opted for a common regional regulator for banks while the EU as a whole has opted to retain home supervision but reinforced it with stronger regional regulatory standards (developed through the various de Larosiere authorities which have now been established) in order to eliminate remaining domestic differences.[21] At the international level, as noted above, a single global regulator has not been established. Rather, the approach adopted revolves around regulatory reforms, supervisory colleges, and resolution arrangements.

Supervisory colleges are mechanisms to bring together the main regulators of global systemically important financial institutions (G-SIFIs) for overall supervision. Similar arrangements have also been adopted for regionally systemically important financial institutions (R-SIFIs) in the EU and potentially in other

[20] See Arner, D, 'The Global Credit Crisis of 2008: Causes and Consequences' (2009) 43 *The International Lawyer* 91.

[21] See de Larosiere, J et al., The High-Level Group on Financial Supervision in the EU: Report (February 2009).

regions (eg, Asia-Pacific), and also in some individual jurisdictions for domestically systemically important financial institutions (D-SIFIs). For each G-SIFI, a supervisory college has been established, including signature of a Memorandum of Understanding (MOU) laying out details of roles and relationships.[22] Within that supervisory college, one supervisor will be the lead supervisor (typically the main home supervisor). The supervisory college will meet both as a group and also with senior management of the financial institution every couple of months so that each member has a clear picture of the major activities and risks of the institution, and the institution is able to discuss issues with all its major supervisors at one time. To date, the major focus of the various colleges has been the development and implementation of resolution and recovery plans (RRPs, colloquially known as 'living wills') to provide clear contingency planning for any crisis which may arise.

While certainly a major enhancement of the pre-crisis approach (and one surprising for its absence, in both terms of the periodic meetings of major supervisors and also crisis contingency planning), this arrangement remains untested by a crisis in one of the subject institutions. In addition, combined with the increasing trend towards requirements in each individual jurisdiction for separately capitalized and regulated subsidiaries for all financial institutions—domestic or foreign—there remain real questions about how effective the new supervisory arrangements will be in practice, particularly in the context of crisis resolution.[23] In addition, despite the overall objective of consistency in implementation of international financial regulatory standards, one of the major issues facing financial institutions operating across borders today is conflicts between approaches taken in different jurisdictions, particularly between the US and the EU.[24]

IV. Regulatory Issues and Approaches

Having considered market access and supervisory arrangement, we now turn to international regulatory approaches and standards.

As discussed above, regulation, supervision, and market access considerations intertwine in addressing financial institutions operating across borders. Because of

[22] See Basel Committee on Banking Supervision, Principles for Effective Supervisory Colleges (June 2014); Joint Forum, Report on Supervisory Colleges for Financial Conglomerates (September 2014).

[23] See Arner, D and Norton, J, 'Building a Framework to Address Failure of Complex Global Financial Institutions' (2009) 39 *Hong Kong Law Journal* 95.

[24] See Atlantic Council, The Danger of Divergence: Transatlantic Financial Regulatory Reform and the G20 Agenda (December 2013).

the approach taken to international finance in the aftermath of World War II, there was little need for consideration of such issues. Rather, regulation and supervision were seen to be matters of concern to individual jurisdictions rather than of international concern. However, as finance increasingly became more international over the 1950s and 1960s, risks increased. From a regulatory standpoint, the most common approach in this period was one focused on domestic activities, leaving regulation of international activities either to the foreign regulator or unregulated (as was increasingly the case with the Eurocurrency markets across this period). With the demise of the dollar standard in 1973 and the collapse of Herstatt and Franklin National in 1974, this began to change and finance and central bank officials began to discuss common concerns, particularly through the evolving Groups (G10, Library, G5, and G7) and the BIS, including through the establishment of the Basel Committee (1974, originally as the Committee on Banking Regulations and Supervisory Practices) and others (such as the Eurocurrency Standing Committee (1971), now the Committee on the Global Financial System (since 1999)).

While initial efforts focused on cross-border supervision, the 1980s debt crisis refocused efforts on the establishment of common minimum international regulatory standards, particularly with the 1988 Basel Capital Accord. Initially, the Basel Accord was only for internationally active G10 banks and was designed to both set prudential minimums and a minimum base for regulatory competition, in order to avoid a potential race for the bottom. Thus, Basel I was very much addressed directly to the largest international banks, setting a minimum level for capital as well as establishing a simple system of risk management in the context of the risk weightings and designed to prevent the sorts of problems that had emerged as a result of the 1980s crisis, in which the majority of the largest international banks (mainly US and UK at that point in time) were effectively insolvent. Basel I was designed to set the regulatory approach to take with internationally active banks in an environment of increasing internationalization of finance.

While criticized for its simplicity and for its unintended consequences,[25] Basel I was the first major step in addressing regulation of internationally active banks. While developed in secret by the G10 for their largest banks, in a short space of time it became the main (and most successful) international financial regulatory standard, eventually implemented in more than 100 countries, despite being 'soft law'. Basel I included provisions relating to consolidation of activities for supervisory purposes (to allow for consolidated supervision by both home and host supervisors in order to catch related activities and risks), and also established capital adequacy as the primary regulatory tool for both international and domestic banks.

From the mid-1980s, markets became increasingly international, with both US and European pressure for greater market access to other jurisdictions. Likewise,

[25] See Arner, D, 'The Global Credit Crisis of 2008: Causes and Consequences' (2009) 43 *The International Lawyer* 91.

as markets were both deregulated in terms of activities and reglobalized in the context of access, Basel I suffered from its simplicity and limited scope. Most particularly, it was limited to credit risk—the risk that at the time of its development was seen to dominate in banking. (Other efforts focused on payment risk, particularly the development by central banks of increasingly sophisticated payments systems, eventually culminating in the worldwide standard of real-time gross settlement.) This limitation was exposed very clearly with the failure of Barings in 1995 as a result of unauthorized transactions in Singaporean and Japanese exchange-traded derivatives.[26] This highlighted not only the need to consolidate these sorts of activities particularly for home supervision but also to establish regulatory standards to address these sorts of activities. The result was the 1995/1996 market risk amendment to Basel I.[27]

The market risk amendment added a new category of risk to the Basel framework, namely market risk, and a new approach to its regulation, focused on the internal risk-management models then being developed by sophisticated financial institutions. The approach was largely one which allowed these institutions to develop systems of their own to calculate capital necessary to manage the risks being taken. The view—one which emerged in the 1990s and dominated up to the global financial crisis—was that large sophisticated global financial institutions were far better placed to analyse and manage their risks (market initially but increasing to eventually cover the full spectrum in the context of Basel II) than were regulators. The consensus was that such institutions, in fact, required less regulatory and supervisory attention due to their sophistication and resources and that regulatory attention should instead focus on the less sophisticated institutions (in some ways like Barings) where risks were likely to be less well managed and as a result posed a greater risk to financial stability. This consensus was to be at the heart of the global financial crisis and its replacement (with the opposite view, that the larger and more sophisticated, the greater the risk) has been at the heart of the post-crisis regulatory and supervisory approach.

Basel II was the embodiment of the risk-based approach to supervision as developed in the wake of Barings and the Asian financial crisis of 1997, and as practised prior to the global financial crisis, with leading regulators such as the US Securities and Exchange Commission (SEC) (in the context of large broker-dealers such as Lehman Brothers) and the former UK Financial Services Authority (FSA) (in the context of global financial services operations emanating from London, regardless of home jurisdiction) adopting minimalist approaches to the regulation and

[26] See Bank of England, Report of the Board of Banking Supervision Inquiry into the Circumstances of the Collapse of Barings (July 1995).

[27] See Basel Committee on Banking Supervision, Amendment to the Capital Accord to Incorporate Market Risks (January 1996).

supervision of the largest financial institutions.[28] At its heart, Basel II used the same equation as Basel I, but allowed the same amount of capital (and increasingly less equity as a result of regulatory recognition of a variety of forms of innovative capital) to be spread across a wider range of risks, including not only credit and market but also operational risks within its remit. It was expressly designed for the same purposes as Basel I but was also aimed very much at bringing regulatory, economic, and accounting capital in line with one another, to form a coherent and effective system of risk management. While it comprised (as does Basel III), three pillars of capital, supervisory review, and market discipline, by the time of the global financial crisis, only the first was largely in place.

Going into the global financial crisis, regulators felt that they had developed a perfectly appropriate system to ensure the stability of the global financial system—one in which (in a classic example of regulatory capture) the largest global financial institutions were the closest partners.

In the aftermath of the global financial crisis, as noted above, regulatory focus has shifted to place the largest most complex global institutions in the spotlight: while they may be the most sophisticated, certainly they were not to the extent expected and in any event, it is clear that it is these sorts of institutions that raise the greater risks to domestic, regional, and global financial stability. This is now clear from not only the micro-prudential standpoint of the systemic importance of individual institutions (eg, Citibank, AIG, RBS, UBS, etc.) but also the macro-prudential standpoint arising from their interconnection and interlinkage. At the international level, the Group of 20 (having supplanted the G7 as the leading policymaker in financial regulatory matters) and the Financial Stability Board (the renamed and strengthened Financial Stability Forum, originally established in the aftermath of the Asian financial crisis to set regulatory standards primarily for emerging markets on the basis of US and EU standards) financial regulatory reform agenda focuses very much on regulation of major internationally active institutions (particularly G-SIFIs) and on reform of global markets (eg, OTC derivatives and securitization).

Basel III is thus joined by a new focus on G-SIFIs and resolution arrangements. Basel III itself now extends beyond capital to include new standards for liquidity and leverage; both very much designed to change behaviour of internationally active financial institutions. In respect of capital, it comes with much higher equity requirements (particularly for SIFIs) as well as with higher risk weightings for a broad spectrum of transactions and—very significantly—much less regulatory deference to banks' internal risk-management systems, based instead on regulatory

[28] See US Financial Inquiry Commission, The Financial Crisis Inquiry Report (2011); Financial Services Authority, The Turner Review: A Regulatory Response to the Global Banking Crisis (March 2009).

minimums, and little concern for harmonization of economic, regulatory, and accounting capital.

The result—particularly for G-SIFIs but also all internationally active banks—is a much stricter and more prescriptive regulatory environment, and one which—particularly with the focus in recent years on shadow banking—is seeking to make sure that all parts of the financial system are subject to appropriate regulation, reducing the scope for regulatory arbitrage and hidden risks and interconnections.

Overall, this is probably the correct direction and certainly an appropriate focus in the wake of the most significant international financial crisis since the 1930s. At the same time, it raises very real concerns among financial institutions, in both respect of costs and effectiveness of implementation and risk management.[29] While the cost concerns can perhaps be set to one side (as one must expect higher compliance costs and reduced profitability as necessary results of the regulatory reform package), the question of effectiveness of implementation and risk management, particularly when balanced against the need for the financial sector to play an important role in supporting the real economy, is one that must be considered.

In some areas (eg, OTC derivatives clearing and settlement), there are clear conflicts between regulatory approaches that are unnecessarily making the business of cross-border financial institutions more difficult. Regulators are becoming increasingly attentive to these concerns and it is hoped that solutions will be worked out, as these would benefit all concerned. In others (eg, limitations on activities such as the US Volcker Rule), lack of consensus at the international level means there is now greater divergence between major jurisdictions than has been the case in the past. It is yet to be seen whether these will make a significant difference to stability but so long as extraterritoriality is treated reasonably (as has largely been the case so far), while they have major impact on the structure of financial institution operations, this is manageable for the institutions concerned and may provide opportunities for the development of other markets (eg, in Asia) and institutions (eg, from Asia) that in the long term may be beneficial to the global financial system (or not, depending on whether such structural changes do in fact reduce systemic risk or merely displace it to other at present less regulated portions of the financial system). Ring-fencing—in which traditional core banking activities, particularly deposit-taking and retail business, are legally separated and subject to higher regulatory requirements—as adopted in the UK and likely to be implemented in the EU and possibly Asia, falls into the same category.

In respect of risk displacement, a very real issue is differential treatment between banks, securities firms, and insurance companies, as well as other sorts of firms. This is an area where work is currently underway to develop capital and other

[29] See Arnold, M, 'HSBC Wrestles with Soaring Costs of Managing Compliance' *Financial Times*, 5 August 2014, 13.

regulatory standards across the financial system, thus reducing risks of regulatory arbitrage and producing a more level playing field for institutions engaging in similar sorts of business.[30] This is an area where further attention is necessary from regulators, in order to avoid shifting of risk—one of the key underlying features of the global financial crisis itself.

From the regulatory standpoint, therefore, it can be seen that internationally active financial institutions face a much different environment than prior to the crisis. This is intentional implementation of policy responses to the consensus underlying causes of the global financial crisis and internationally active financial institutions have no choice but to restructure their operations, risk management, and compliance accordingly. At the same time, however, conflicts have emerged between major regulators implementing common approaches in differing and often conflicting manners. This raises concerns not only for financial institutions struggling (in most cases in good faith today, though not necessarily for the first several years following the global financial crisis) to implement these reforms but also for regulators and supervisors concerned with both financial stability and economic growth. Regulatory conflicts certainly raise very real risks of negatively impacting on both objectives and this, therefore, is an area which requires further attention and an effective solution going forward.

One area, however, poses real issues.

V. Crisis Management and Resolution

Prior to the global financial crisis, there was little attention paid to cross-border crisis management in the event of serious difficulties in a G-SIFI and even less to the problem of failure and resolution.[31] Given that the lack of crisis contingency planning and established resolution arrangements for internationally active financial institutions was very much central to the global financial crisis, it is not surprising that this has been a major area of international (G10/FSB), regional (EU) and domestic (eg, US, UK) attention in the aftermath of the crisis.

In relation to contingency planning, there has been considerable progress through the development of RRPs globally, regionally, and domestically, although

[30] See International Organization of Securities Commissions (IOSCO), Consultation Document: A Comparison and Analysis of Prudential Standards in the Securities Sector (March 2014).

[31] See Arner, D and Norton, J, 'Building a Framework to Address Failure of Complex Global Financial Institutions' (2009) 39 *Hong Kong Law Journal* 95.

there are certainly questions regarding their effectiveness.[32] On balance, these efforts are possibly most important in increasing particularly the understanding of supervisors of the operations and structure of major internationally active financial institutions, and of management of their own institutions. Such institutions by the time of the global financial crisis had arguably become too complex to either regulate or manage.[33] In addition, there were clear divergences between actual legal structure and operational structures and systems, resulting in the now well-known idea of financial institutions being global in life but domestic in death. The actual effectiveness of RRPs in the context of a crisis is arguably much more speculative. Nonetheless, given that lack of understanding of the operations of such institutions by both supervisors and management was a major factor in the global financial crisis, these efforts have clear value in this respect. They are also causing financial institution management and supervisors to carefully consider legal structures and operations in order to increase clarity, reduce complexity, and better manage risks. In this respect, one interesting initiative is the development of a global legal entity identifier (LEI) database to provide transparent information on entity structure to regulators, management, and market counterparties.[34]

In respect of resolution arrangements, despite the high level of attention, there has been limited progress at the international level to date.[35] Greater progress has been made in the EU[36] and in individual jurisdictions, most particularly the US and the UK. The overall result is that while there is a much greater understanding of financial institution structure and risks by both supervisors and management, there remain major issues in respect of any actual cross-border failure, which are not subject to easy resolution.[37] In particular, the challenge with resolution is the question of allocation of costs. In the context of the global and eurozone crises, this focused primarily on which government would have to step in to provide support. Clearly, a central objective of post-crisis regulatory reform is ending the risk of government bailouts in future. Unfortunately, despite best intentions, history suggests that in the context of a systemic financial crisis, government involvement will probably still occur. It does, nonetheless, make a great deal of sense to put in place systems which will reduce the likelihood and scale of any future government support. The core issue which arises from the problem of burden sharing focuses

[32] See Avgouleas, E, Goodhart, C, and Schoenmaker, D, 'Bank Resolution Plans as a Catalyst for Action' (2013) 9 *Journal of Financial Stability* 210.

[33] See Herring, R and Carmassi, J, 'The Corporate Structures of International Financial Conglomerates: Complexity and its Implications for Safety and Soundness' in Berger, A, Molyneux, P, and Wilson, J (eds), *The Oxford Handbook of Banking* (2012).

[34] See FSB, A Global Legal Entity Identifier for Financial Markets (June 2012).

[35] See FSB, Progress and Next Steps towards Ending 'Too-Big-to-Fail': Report of the Financial Stability Board to the G-20 (September 2013).

[36] See Binder, J and Singh, D (eds), *The Bank Recovery and Resolution Directive* (2015 forthcoming).

[37] See further the Chapter by Armour in this volume.

on the allocation of the assets of any failed financial institution. In the context of global markets, certain jurisdictions (eg, the US) have an inherent advantage in that there is a significant likelihood of institutional assets being located in the jurisdiction and which are then available to reduce the need for state support and to meet creditors' claims. In the EU, this issue has now largely been addressed but internationally competing insolvency actions in multiple jurisdictions remain a certainty, with the US particularly unwilling to consider potential advance sharing arrangements. While a treaty-based approach (similar to that in the EU) is probably the first best solution, it is unlikely, with the consequent necessity of finding 'soft law' mechanisms. Given that agreements between courts are problematic, perhaps the best approach is one in which authority over failing institutions is retained for as long as possible by the regulator: regulators have much greater flexibility for entering into MOUs and the like, including in the context of RRPs and supervisory college arrangements. Without this, regulators will continue to opt for requirements for separately capitalized subsidiaries as the primary means of market access, thus ensuring regulatory and supervisory authority as well as the availability of assets for creditors.

Thus, while there has been significant progress in respect of regulation and supervision, as well as increased understanding of legal, operational, and risk-management systems, there remain significant issues with respect to any actual failure. The result is that—at least for some time—it is unlikely that another major internationally active financial institution would be allowed to fail. The consequence of this approach is the necessity of stricter regulation and supervision, restricting activities of financial institutions and reducing profitability.

Does this, however, represent a process of deglobalization of finance?

VI. Deglobalization of Finance?

Since the end of World War II, there has been a clear pattern of increasing financial globalization and interconnection. One aspect of this has been the emergence of very large complex financial institutions operating across borders and beyond borders. These were the institutions and markets at the heart of the global financial crisis.

In some ways, it has been surprising that there have been so few discussions regarding the possibility of once again deglobalizing finance, as was done at the end of World War II. Nonetheless, it is clear that a policy of deglobalization has not been chosen at the international level or at the EU level. Rather, the approach has been to continue to seek to support the globalization of finance while building regulatory and supervisory systems to address the risks that arise from major global financial institutions. At the same time, some have suggested that this process of regulatory and supervisory reform is in reality resulting in deglobalization.[38]

If we consider the main trends at the international level and at the regional level with the exception of the EU (namely, continued access to foreign markets via separately capitalized and regulated subsidiaries combined with supervisory colleges and RRPs), this does not appear to be deglobalization of finance. It does make operations of financial institutions more challenging, particularly when differences and/or conflicts arise between individual jurisdictions and it does require careful consideration by both financial-institution management and their regulators and supervisors of legal, operational, and risk-management structures and systems. It does not, however, require financial institutions to cease operating across borders. It does highlight a continuing need for enhancement of international regulatory standards and the development of new mechanisms to address divisions and conflicts as they emerge in order to both support financial stability and enable internationally active financial institutions to develop systems which allow them to manage their compliance operations effectively, while at the same time fulfilling their central function of providing the financing necessary to the functioning of the global economy.

Nonetheless, we are certainly seeing restructuring of the operations of internationally active financial institutions as a result of post-crisis regulatory changes; in particular, higher costs across a range of businesses. The result in many cases is retrenchment—reducing operations which no longer justify the costs of the new regulatory environment, particularly overseas operations. While this does, in fact, result in reduction of cross-border activity, it also arguably better reflects the real risks and the consequent costs of this sort of business.

Bibliography

Ahamed, L, *Lords of Finance: The Bankers Who Broke the World* (2009).

Arner, D, *Financial Stability, Economic Growth and the Role of Law* (2007).

Arner, D, 'The Global Credit Crisis of 2008: Causes and Consequences' (2009) 43 *The International Lawyer* 91.

Arner, D and Norton, J, 'Building a Framework to Address Failure of Complex Global Financial Institutions' (2009) 39 *Hong Kong Law Journal* 95.

[38] See Harper, C and Onaran, Y, 'Global Banking Rules under Siege as Nations Tighten Local Rules' *Bloomberg*, 5 December 2012.

Arner, D and Taylor, M, 'The Global Credit Crisis and the Financial Stability Board: Hardening the Soft Law of International Financial Regulation?' (2009) 32 *University of New South Wales Law Journal* 488.

Arnold, M, 'HSBC Wrestles with Soaring Costs of Managing Compliance' *Financial Times*, 5 August 2014, 13.

Atlantic Council, The Danger of Divergence: Transatlantic Financial Regulatory Reform and the G20 Agenda (December 2013).

Avgouleas, E, *Governance of Global Financial Markets: The Law, the Economics, the Politics* (2012).

Avgouleas, E and Arner, D, 'The Broken Glass of European Integration: Origins and Remedies of the Eurozone Crisis and Implications for Global Markets' in Lim, C and Mercurio, B (eds), *International Economic Law after the Crisis: A Tale of Fragmented Disciplines* (2014).

Avgouleas, E, Goodhart, C, and Schoenmaker, D, 'Bank Resolution Plans as a Catalyst for Action' (2013) 9 *Journal of Financial Stability* 210.

Bagehot, W, *A Description of the Money Market* (1873).

Bank of England, Consultation Paper CP4/14: Supervising International Banks: The Prudential Regulation Authority's Approach to Branch Supervision (February 2014).

Bank of England, Report of the Board of Banking Supervision Inquiry into the Circumstances of the Collapse of Barings (July 1995).

Basel Committee on Banking Supervision, Amendment to the Capital Accord to Incorporate Market Risks (January 1996).

Basel Committee on Banking Supervision, Principles for Effective Supervisory Colleges (June 2014).

Binder, J and Singh, D (eds), *The Bank Recovery and Resolution Directive* (2015 forthcoming).

Brummer, C, *Minilateralism: How Trade Alliances, Soft Law and Financial Engineering Are Redefining International Statecraft* (2014).

Buckley, R and Arner, D, *From Crisis to Crisis: The Global Financial System and Regulatory Failure* (2011).

de Larosiere, J et al., The High-Level Group on Financial Supervision in the EU: Report (February 2009).

Ferran, E, *Building an EU Securities Market* (2005).

Financial Services Authority, The Turner Review: A Regulatory Response to the Global Banking Crisis (March 2009).

Financial Stability Board, A Global Legal Entity Identifier for Financial Markets (June 2012).

Financial Stability Board, Progress and Next Steps Towards Ending 'Too-Big-To-Fail': Report of the Financial Stability Board to the G-20 (September 2013).

Hadjiemmannuil, C, *Banking Regulation and the Bank of England* (1996).

Harper, C and Onaran, Y, 'Global Banking Rules under Siege as Nations Tighten Local Rules' *Bloomberg*, 5 December 2012.

Herring, R and Carmassi, J, 'The Corporate Structures of International Financial Conglomerates: Complexity and its Implications for Safety and Soundness' in Berger, A, Molyneux, P, and Wilson, J (eds), *The Oxford Handbook of Banking* (2012).

International Organization of Securities Commissions (IOSCO), Consultation Document: A Comparison and Analysis of Prudential Standards in the Securities Sector (March 2014).

Joint Forum, Report on Supervisory Colleges for Financial Conglomerates (September 2014).
Kerry, J and Brown, H, The BCCI Affair: Report to the Committee on Foreign Relations, US Senate (1992).
Key, S, *Financial Services in the Uruguay Round and the WTO* (1997).
Martin, F, *Money: The Unauthorized Biography* (2014).
Moloney, N, *EC Securities Regulation* (2008).
Norton, J, *Devising International Bank Supervisory Standards* (1995).
Taylor, M and Schooner, H, *Global Bank Regulation* (2009).
US Financial Inquiry Commission, The Financial Crisis Inquiry Report (2011).
Walker, G, *International Banking Regulation: Law, Policy and Practice* (2001).
Weber, R, Arner, D, Gibson, E, and Baumann, S, 'Addressing Systemic Risk: Financial Regulatory Design' (2014) 49 *Texas International Law Journal* 149.

PART V

MARKET EFFICIENCY, TRANSPARENCY, AND INTEGRITY

CHAPTER 17

DISCLOSURE AND FINANCIAL MARKET REGULATION

LUCA ENRIQUES AND
SERGIO GILOTTA

I. Introduction

Disclosure is a technique of central importance in financial market regulation. Anyone offering securities to the public and/or listing them on a stock exchange has to provide a wealth of information before doing so, and remains subject to disclosure obligations so long as the securities are held by the public or listed. Significant long (and, since after the crisis, short) positions in listed shares have to be disclosed to the public. Anyone launching a takeover bid for a listed company's shares has to provide ample information about himself, his intentions, plans, and so forth. Any financial services contract between a consumer and a bank or investment firm is to be preceded by lengthy disclosures and rules are usually in place to ensure that the client is informed about its ongoing relationship with the financial intermediary.

This Chapter focuses on mandatory disclosure (MD) to the general public as opposed to, on the one hand, the regulation of voluntary disclosure (ie, the general prohibition on false or misleading statements which applies to it) and, on the other, one-on-one disclosure, which is often mandated in the domain of investment and retail-banking services. Our specific focus will be on issuers of securities, but much of our discussion can easily be extended to other forms of MD.

The core function of MD in financial market regulation is to provide economic agents with information to help them make better decisions. Its rationale, in turn, is grounded on the belief that in the absence of MD there would be less information available for such choices than it would be optimal or (which is largely the same) that higher production and dissemination costs would lead to its undersupply.

In the area of financial market regulation, like in others, policymakers tend to make extensive use of disclosure-based techniques. The reasons for this are manifold.[1] First, MD is a cheap regulatory tool, in the sense that extending its scope or content does not usually entail any direct government expenditure.[2] Second, MD is a policy recipe with a high chance of bipartisan support: it offers an answer to the political pressure for 'more regulation', which is especially strong in the aftermath of corporate governance scandals or financial crises,[3] but, on the face of it, stops short of positively prescribing a given behaviour. Relatedly, MD is often the most viable solution, as it encounters less resistance from affected interest groups: these

[1] See Ben-Shahar, O and Schneider, C, 'The Failure of Mandated Disclosure' (2011) 159 *University of Pennsylvania Law Review* 647, 681–4.

[2] ibid, 682. Of course, creating an MD system from scratch entails the costs of setting up an enforcement agency.

[3] From the very outset, a large element of the process of regulatory reform in financial markets has occurred in response to scandals or crises, according to what has been called a 'boom-bust-regulate' pattern: see, eg, Bainbridge, S, 'Dodd–Frank: Quack Federal Corporate Governance Round II' (2011) 95 *Minnesota Law Review* 1779, 1782.

also tend to prefer enhanced disclosure to more invasive solutions aimed at directly constraining behaviour. Finally, MD fits in with two of the most deeply rooted principles of Western societies: namely, the idea of free markets and the autonomy principle.[4]

Nevertheless, MD comes with costs and, like other regulatory techniques, it has inherent limitations that may impair its effectiveness. Policymakers tend to disregard cost considerations and to overestimate the overall efficacy of disclosure-based recipes. In reconsidering the debate over MD in financial markets, this Chapter takes a more balanced view, highlighting why there can be too much of a good thing.

The Chapter is structured as follows: Section II outlines the goals that underlie MD and gives an account of the various rationales for mandatory, as opposed to merely voluntary, disclosure. Section III describes MD's limits and costs. Section IV concludes, addressing some of the challenges policymakers face.

II. Goals and Rationales of MD

This Section discusses the various goals that academics and policymakers associate to disclosure-based regulatory techniques in financial markets. It then addresses the reasons why firms may not be expected to voluntarily disclose optimal amounts of information, and thus the various rationales in support of MD.

1. The goals

Disclosure in financial markets pursues three objectives of core importance: (a) it protects investors and, by thus enhancing their confidence in the market, preserves the well-functioning (if not the very existence) of the (securities) market, thereby supporting its growth; (b) it addresses the agency problems affecting large corporations, thus supporting their ability to serve as a means of organizing, financing and operating today's large entrepreneurial ventures; and (c) it ensures that prices fully reflect all value-relevant information, so as to help financial markets in their fundamental function of efficiently allocating scarce financial resources across the economy.

[4] Ben-Shahar and Schneider, n 1 above, 681.

(a) *Investor protection*

MD is said to serve the purpose of protecting unsophisticated investors who trade in the securities market.[5] The need to protect unsophisticated investors may be based on fairness or efficiency considerations.

The fairness rationale has been almost universally discarded. Today, nobody seriously argues that protecting investors via disclosure is a proper policy just because doing so is … just. Many, instead, and especially policymakers, contend that protecting investors is instrumental to the well-functioning—if not to the very existence—of the market and has thus an efficiency justification. Providing investors with adequate protection increases their confidence in the market.[6] Absent a strong and widespread belief in market integrity, the investing public would withdraw its savings, with disastrous consequences for the entire economic system.

In the same vein, to the extent that ensuring a minimum degree of *perceived* fairness in the securities markets (for example, by banning insider trading and by guaranteeing a minimum level of 'equal access' to information, no matter whether either of these measures per se increases market efficiency) helps retain unsophisticated investors in the market, the fairness rationale converts into an efficiency-grounded justification.[7]

MD protects investors along three main dimensions: first, by providing them with all information reasonably needed to decide on how to invest their savings; ie, about a security's risk and expected returns, the issuing entity, the attached rights, and so forth. Thus, MD helps investors find the kind of investment that best matches their preferences and thus minimizes the risk of incurring in 'wrong'

[5] See generally Seligman, J, 'The Historical Need for a Mandatory Corporate Disclosure System' (1983) 9 *The Journal of Corporation Law* 1. The goal of investor protection dates back to the New Deal and constitutes one of the bedrocks of US securities regulation since its inception: ibid, 51.

[6] ibid, 51–3. The goals of enhanced investor protection and increased public confidence in the financial market underlie all recent EU regulatory efforts in the field of mandatory securities disclosure: see, eg, European Parliament and Council Directive (EC) 2003/6/EC on insider dealing and market manipulation (market abuse) [2003] OJ L96/16 (hereinafter, MAD), Preambles (2), (12), and (24); European Parliament and Council Directive (EC) 2003/71/EC, on the prospectus to be published when securities are offered to the public or admitted to trading and amending Directive 2001/34/EC [2003] OJ L345/64 (hereinafter, Prospectus Directive), Preambles (10), (16), (18), and (19); European Parliament and Council Directive (EC) 2004/109/EC, on the harmonization of transparency requirements in relation to information about issuers whose securities are admitted to trading on a regulated market and amending Directive 2001/34/EC [2004] OJ L390/38 (hereinafter, Transparency Directive), Preamble (1); European Parliament and Council Regulation (EU) 2014/596 on market abuse (market abuse regulation) and repealing Directive 2003/6/EC of the European Parliament and of the Council and Commission Directives 2003/124/EC, 2003/125/EC and 2004/72/EC [2014] OJ L173/1, Preambles (2), (24), (55), and Article 1.

[7] cf Langevoort, D, 'Taming the Animal Spirits of the Stock Markets: A Behavioral Approach to Securities Regulation' (2002) 97 *Northwestern University Law Review* 135, 165–6 (discussing, and then dismissing, a similar rationale for Regulation FD, an SEC regulation enacted in 2000 and prohibiting selective disclosure).

investment decisions, because of insufficient information regarding the securities purchased or sold.

Recent scholarship has cast serious doubts as to the effectiveness of MD in this regard. Problems of bounded rationality and information overload (the incapacity of the individual investor to 'handle' large amounts of information) prevent the unsophisticated investor from really benefiting from MD and may even make matters worse, relative to a situation of less available information (see Section III.2).[8]

Second, MD may protect investors by enabling them not to be 'exploited' by traders having superior information (insiders and professional investors).[9] According to this view, absent MD, unsophisticated investors would systematically lose when trading against such informed counterparties, and would thus soon withdraw their money from the market. MD is said to establish a 'level playing field' between unsophisticated and professional investors (or corporate insiders); ie, to give the former 'equal access' to the same range of information on which the latter base their decisions.[10] This view, usually labelled as 'market egalitarianism', has received strong support in the past and has profoundly influenced the evolution of securities regulation on both sides of the Atlantic (for example, it gave rise to the ban on insider trading in the US and has long shaped much of the SEC policy as regards MD).[11]

Nowadays, academic commentators tend to discard this goal. In an efficient stock market, unsophisticated investors are already protected by market prices, which tend to reflect at any time all relevant information (or at least that portion of relevant information which is publicly available),[12] and thus make sure that they will generally receive a fair price in whatever transaction they engage in.[13] In an efficient market, unsophisticated investors take a free-ride on the efforts of

[8] See eg Paredes, T, 'Blinded by the Light: Information Overload and its Consequences for Securities Regulation' (2003) 81 *Washington University Law Quarterly* 417.

[9] See Easterbrook, F and Fischel, D, 'Mandatory Disclosure and the Protection of Investors' (1984) 70 *Virginia Law Review* 669, 693–5, for a critical view.

[10] See, eg, Chiu, I, 'Examining the Justifications for Mandatory Ongoing Disclosure in Securities Regulation' 26 *The Company Lawyer* 67, 67.

[11] See, eg, *SEC v Texas Gulf Sulphur Co.* 401 F.2d 833 (2d Cir. 1968); see also nn 15–16 below and accompanying text.

[12] According to Eugene Fama's famous tripartition, securities markets can be said to be efficient in weak-form (when current prices reflect the information contained in past prices), semi-strong form (when prices reflect all the information, both present and past, that is publicly available), or strong-form (when they reflect at any time both publicly available and private information). It is worth noting, however, that this distinction was originally aimed at classifying empirical tests of market efficiency. Only later did it evolve as a classification of the different forms in which market efficiency can be intended, and as a scale of the efficiency level of a given market. See Fama, E, 'Efficient Capital Markets: A Review of Theory and Empirical Work' (1970) 25 *Journal of Finance* 383; Gilson, R and Kraakman, R, 'The Mechanisms of Market Efficiency' (1984) 70 *Virginia Law Review* 549, 555–6.

[13] See Easterbrook and Fischel, n 9 above, 694.

sophisticated ones and thus do not need, and would not really benefit from,[14] equal access to information.[15]

And even if such 'equal access' is provided, it would remain largely unused. Gathering and processing all information affecting the value of securities is a complex task requiring specific skills and entails economies of scale and scope, which are unavailable to the retail investor.[16]

Nevertheless, market egalitarianism is still very popular among regulators and courts: in the EU, for instance, it supports the most recent European Court of Justice (ECJ) case law on insider trading[17] and real-time issuer disclosure duties.[18]

Third, MD protects investors in that it discourages fraud, self-dealing, and various other kinds of opportunistic behaviour on the part of managers and controllers.[19] From this standpoint, the goal of investor protection tends to identify with that of improved corporate governance, which is addressed in the next Section.

(b) *Agency cost reduction*

Disclosure plays an important role in corporate governance, as a tool to address agency problems:[20] by decreasing both monitoring[21] and bonding costs,[22] it reduces overall agency costs and thus lowers firms' cost of capital.[23] Its main governance function is to permit *ex post* enforcement of core substantive rules, such as

[14] ibid.

[15] To be sure, assuming that the market is efficient in semi-strong form does not amount to claiming that unsophisticated investors can never 'lose' in whatever transaction they enter into—in fact, they can still be beaten by insiders (a risk they share with the most sophisticated investors)—and, more importantly, does not amount to stating that the market is 'fundamentally' efficient; ie, that its prices reflect real value. For these and other important qualifications about the concept of market efficiency, and a reassessment of the Efficient Market Hypothesis in light of the 2007–09 global financial crisis, see Gilson, R and Kraakman, R, 'Market Efficiency after the Fall: Where Do we Stand after the Financial Crisis?' in Hill, C and McDonnell, B (eds), *Research Handbook on the Economics of Corporate Law* (2012) 456, 457–60; Gilson, R and Kraakman, R, Market Efficiency after the Financial Crisis: It's Still a Matter of Information Costs (2014), available at <http://ssrn.com/abstract=2396608>.

[16] See eg Moloney, N, *EC Securities Regulation* (2nd edn, 2008) 100.

[17] See European Court of Justice, Case C-45/08, *Spector Photo Group NV and Chris Van Raemdonck v Commissie voor het Bank-, Financie- en Assurantiewezen (CBFA).*

[18] See European Court of Justice, Case C-19/11, *Marcus Geltl v Daimler AG* (esp section 33).

[19] Seligman, n 5 above, 51.

[20] See generally Mahoney, P, 'Mandatory Disclosure as a Solution to Agency Problems' (1995) 62 *University of Chicago Law Review* 1047.

[21] ibid, 1051.

[22] See, eg, Rock, E, 'Securities Regulation as a Lobster Trap: A Credible Commitment Theory of Mandatory Disclosure' (2002) 23 *Cardozo Law Review* 675. See also nn 62–3 below and accompanying text.

[23] See generally Kraakman, R, 'Disclosure and Corporate Governance: An Overview Essay' in Ferrarini, G, Hopt, K, and Wymeersch, E (eds), *Reforming Company and Takeover Law in Europe* (2004) 95.

managers' fiduciary duties: absent sufficient information, breaches of those duties would remain largely undetected.[24]

But disclosure rules complement substantive rules of corporate law addressing agency problem issues in many other ways. Let us take self-dealing transactions as an example. A rule requiring, say, shareholder approval of conflicted transactions would be less effective in constraining abusive self-dealing, if companies did not have to provide shareholders with complete information about the proposed transaction terms: MD helps achieve this result.[25] MD plays a similar function, in turn, in many other areas of corporate law, such as board elections, shareholders' say on managerial compensation, proxy fights, approval of fundamental transactions, and so on. In all such cases, disclosure is instrumental to shareholder empowerment.[26]

Disclosure rules also increase managerial consciousness: by forcing managers to continuously collect and organize information, disclosure makes them aware of events and circumstances that they would not perhaps have known—increased knowledge may have a positive effect on managerial performance.[27]

MD's beneficial role in curbing managerial opportunism is indisputable and to a large extent obvious: in a context of marked opacity, where little is known about the firm's operations, managers would obviously find it easier to engage in self-dealing, fraud, and other forms of abuse. On the contrary, with a tight and well-designed system of MD in place any would-be wrongdoer must devise a more ingenious, complex, and costly plan to conceal his actions and escape punishment.[28] All such elements decrease the expected payoff of engaging in fraud, thus making corporate wrongdoing—all else being equal—a less attractive option.

So far, the Chapter has focused on *managerial* opportunism, but disclosure performs the same function with respect to systems where corporate ownership is concentrated and the bulk of agency problems revolves around the relation between controlling shareholders and outside shareholders. In systems of concentrated corporate ownership, disclosure makes it similarly more difficult for controlling shareholders to engage in self-dealing and thus reduces the amount of pecuniary private benefits of control.[29]

[24] See Fox, M, 'Required Disclosure and Corporate Governance' (1999) 62 *Law and Contemporary Problems* 113, 118–20.

[25] ibid, 118–19; Kraakman, n 23 above, 97.

[26] See Fox, n 24 above, 116–18, for a discussion of the role of disclosure in empowering shareholders.

[27] ibid, 123–5. Of course, this point should not be overstated: most of the time, MD rules do not compel managers to actually create any new information, but force them to disclose data they already possess and routinely process for internal managerial purposes.

[28] ibid, 119–20.

[29] See Ferrell, A, 'The Case for Mandatory Disclosure in Securities Regulation around the World' (2007) 2 *Brooklyn Journal of Corporate, Financial & Commercial Law* 81, 88–92, for a comprehensive discussion.

At the same time, however, the effectiveness of disclosure as a technique to prevent fraud and misbehaviour may easily be overstated.

First, as many other legal strategies aimed at controlling managerial or dominant shareholder opportunism, disclosure is inherently imperfect. After all, if a manager decides to breach his fiduciary duties and engage in fraudulent behaviour, he is equally likely to violate disclosure rules, so as to conceal his actions. The 'very bad guys' cannot be expected to be much concerned by MD rules: they would simply violate them, as they violate more substantive rules of conduct, such as the prohibition on unfair self-dealing. The large-scale fraud occurred at Enron—where widespread accounting manipulations and other violations quickly led to the bankruptcy of a seemingly wealthy large company, causing massive losses to both the firm's creditors and shareholders—provides a good illustration of this point: it would be hard to argue that Enron's managers acted within a legal framework in which disclosure duties were scant or unenforced. Enron was required to disclose huge amounts of data, both financial and operational, and its financial statements were audited by (supposed-to-be) independent third parties. Nevertheless, all these barriers proved insufficient to avoid massive fraud.[30]

Second, MD may also have unintended negative consequences. The disclosure of conflicts of interest, for instance, may have perverse effects on the discloser's behaviour, who, after having disclosed his conflicting interest, may consider himself free of any further obligation and thus 'authorized' to pursue his own interest.[31]

A similar point can be made with respect to executive compensation, where enhanced disclosure could have the unintended consequence of increasing average executive pay (the so-called Lake Wobegon effect of compensation disclosure[32]).

[30] For a discussion of the Enron scandal and its implications for US corporate governance see, eg, Gordon, J, 'Governance Failures of the Enron Board and the New Information Order of Sarbanes–Oxley' (2003) 35 *Connecticut Law Review* 1125; Macey, J, 'Efficient Capital Markets, Corporate Disclosure, and Enron' (2004) 89 *Cornell Law Review* 394, discussing Enron's implications for disclosure major theoretical foundations and for the Efficient Capital Market Hypothesis.

[31] cf Cain, D, Loewenstein, G, and Moore, D, 'The Dirt on Coming Clean: Perverse Effects of Disclosing Conflicts of Interest' (2005) 34 *Journal of Legal Studies* 1, esp 6–8 (with reference to conflicts of interest in the domain of professional advice).

[32] Disclosure makes average compensation available to companies' compensation committees' members and CEOs. Even the former will be disinclined to pay the CEO below the industry peers average, because that would signal inferior quality. As an outcome, average executive compensation rises. See eg Davidoff, S and Hill, C, 'Limits of Disclosure' (2013) 36 *Seattle University Law Review* 599, 604, 623–6; Manne, G, 'The Hydraulic Theory of Disclosure Regulation and Other Costs of Disclosure' (2007) 58 *Alabama Law Review* 473, 476–7. Lake Wobegon is a fictional town where all the children are supposed to be above average. See <http://en.wikipedia.org/wiki/Lake_Wobegon>.

(c) *Price accuracy enhancement*

MD may also serve the purpose of increasing market prices accuracy in reflecting relevant information.[33] Increased price accuracy, in turn, enhances liquidity,[34] lowers volatility,[35] decreases firms' cost of capital, and promotes market allocative efficiency,[36] at the benefit of the economic system as a whole.

Increased price accuracy plays a beneficial role also in corporate governance. Efficient stock prices improve the effectiveness of the market for corporate control as a disciplining device:[37] they decrease the costs of identifying underperforming firms to target for hostile acquisition, since efficient prices track more closely real value and thus permit more fine-tuned and univocal inferences, thereby reducing the incidence of 'false negatives'; ie, firms whose negative performance is not reflected in a low market valuation.

Efficient stock prices are also necessary for the proper functioning of incentive compensation. Better functioning incentive compensation, in turn, aligns more closely managers' incentives to those of shareholders and thus reduces agency costs. [38]

The price accuracy enhancement goal of MD is today widely accepted among scholars[39] and represents an increasingly important driver in the evolution of securities regulation.[40] The objective of promoting price accuracy and thereby advancing market efficiency explains many regulatory developments on both sides of the Atlantic: think of the increasing role of 'fair value' in accounting and the increasing weight of forward-looking and 'soft' information relative to backward-looking and hard data.

In 1979, the EU adopted a rule of real-time disclosure which, in its current formulation, requires issuers to immediately disclose all 'price-sensitive' ('material', in US terminology) information.[41] This rule, which represents a bedrock of the

[33] See, eg, Gordon, J and Kornhauser, L, 'Efficient Markets, Costly Information, and Securities Research' (1985) 60 *New York University Law Review* 761; Goshen, Z and Parchomovsky, G, 'On Insider Trading, Markets, and "Negative" Property Rights in Information' (2001) 87 *Virginia Law Review* 1229, 1244–6.

[34] See Kahan, M, 'Securities Laws and the Costs of "Inaccurate" Stock Prices' (1992) 41 *Duke Law Journal* 977, 1017–25; Chiu, n 10 above, 70.

[35] Chiu, n 10 above, 70.

[36] See generally Kahan, n 34 above; Chiu, n 10 above, 70.

[37] See Coffee, J, 'Market Failure and the Economic Case for a Mandatory Disclosure System' (1984) 70 *Virginia Law Review* 717, 742, 747; Fox, n 24 above, 120–1.

[38] See Fox, n 24 above, 121.

[39] See, eg, Goshen, Z and Parchomovsky, G, 'The Essential Role of Securities Regulation' (2006) 55 *Duke Law Journal* 711 (who claim that promoting market efficiency—which, in turn, is determined also by having accurate securities prices—is the goal not only of MD, but of securities regulation as a whole, and that achieving this goal requires protecting and advancing the position of information traders); Kahan, n 34 above, 979 (referring to securities regulation at large). But see Mahoney, n 20 above, 1093–104, for a critical view.

[40] See ibid, 1105–11, where an account of how the price accuracy enhancement goal of MD affected SEC disclosure policy.

[41] See Council Directive (EEC) 79/279/EEC coordinating the conditions for the admission of securities to official stock exchange listing [1979] OJ L066/21, schedule C of the Annex, para 5 (A)

current EU MD system and one of its identifying features,[42] can, at least partly, be explained as an attempt to advance price accuracy.[43]

Although the price accuracy enhancement goal is widely accepted among both academics and policymakers, it raises its own issues. On its face, it justifies the unlimited widening of scope of MD duties: all information that is relevant for assessing firm value becomes a compelling candidate for MD once the goal is price accuracy. No guidance or criterion is available to strike the right balance between the price accuracy goal and countervailing interests such as, most importantly, firms' interest in confidentiality. Rather, the price accuracy goal appears to suggest that the firm's private interest should be unconditionally sacrificed. Because there is something more to confidentiality than individual firms' interests in their own success, this point will be further addressed later.[44]

2. The rationales

Section II.1 gave an account of the various functions that (mandatory) disclosure performs in financial markets and of the many benefits it is thought to bring about. Stating that corporate disclosure is beneficial does not amount, however, to saying that *mandatory* disclosure is necessary or desirable. If information is so valuable for investors, why should market forces not be spontaneously providing it in optimal amounts?[45] This is an issue that has received extensive attention in the

('The company must inform the public as soon as possible of any major new developments in its sphere of activity which are not public knowledge and which may, by virtue of their effect on its assets and liabilities or financial position or on the general course of its business, lead to substantial movements in the prices of its shares'). In 1989, the scope of the rule had been adjusted so as to cover all securities subject to the insider trading prohibition (Council Directive (EEC) 89/592/EEC coordinating regulations on insider dealing [1989] OJ L334/30/EEC, Article 6, para 2). In 2001, the rule was moved, with no modifications, into Article 68 of the European Parliament and Council Directive (EC) 2001/34/EC on the admission of securities to official stock exchange listing and on information to be published on those securities [2001] OJ L184/1, and in 2003 was replaced by MAD's Article 6, according to which 'issuers [must] inform the public as soon as possible of inside [price-sensitive] information which directly concerns the said issuers'. MAD's Article 6 has been replaced, with no significant variations, by Article 17(1) of the Market Abuse Regulation.

[42] US securities regulation, at least as regards the 'law on the books', does not have a rule of real-time disclosure. See, eg, Cox, J, Hillman, R, and Langevoort, D, *Securities Regulation, Cases and Materials* (5th edn, 2006) 621 ('... the information's materiality is a necessary but not a sufficient condition to require its disclosure'), 689. However, the joint operation of the duties to avoid half-truths, to update, and to correct information previously disclosed leads the system very close to the positive establishment of an outright duty of ongoing disclosure. See Cox, J, et al., 690–3; Oesterle, D, 'The Inexorable March toward a Continuous Disclosure Requirement for Publicly Traded Corporations: "Are we There Yet"?' (1998) 20 *Cardozo Law Review* 135.

[43] 'Partly' because the rule has a concurrent anti-insider trading function and, to the extent that it aims to put outsiders and insiders on an equal footing, can be concurrently brought back to market egalitarianism goals.

[44] See Section III.6.

[45] See, eg, Easterbrook and Fischel, n 9 above, 682–5.

literature, ever since the debate on MD has been conducted with an efficiency perspective in mind. The next Sections briefly recall the major results of the debate.

(a) *Information as a public good*

A traditional argument for establishing MD rests upon the public goods-like nature of information. Information is a public good, or at least displays many features of a typical public good: its value is only imperfectly appropriable, given how difficult it is to exclude those who did not pay for it; the use of a given piece of information by someone does not prevent that same piece of information from being used by someone else.

Because of the public goods-like nature of information, private incentives to produce it will be weak and the amount produced less than socially optimal.[46] But, due to collective action problems, investors may also overinvest in information production.[47] Overinvestment occurs as a consequence of the incentives induced by the race to 'beat the market' (ie, to be first in accessing information that is expected to materially change the price of a security),[48] and takes also the form of redundant production; ie, when two or more investors engage in the production of the same piece of information (eg, the firm's earnings for the next reporting quarter).[49] MD eliminates these inefficiencies by centralizing (some say 'collectiviz[ing]'[50]) information production.

The rationale based on the public-good traits of information largely falls short of providing a truly sound justification for MD. Rather, its logic should in itself (ie, assuming no other problems exist with the voluntary production of information) lead to an optimal degree of voluntary disclosure. In fact, if issuer disclosure is a superior means of information production and dissemination, why should it not be spontaneously provided? If investors as a class gain from having disclosure, then firms would gain too in organizing themselves as highly disclosing entities.[51]

(b) *Externalities*

Imperfect appropriability of the value of information affects not only decentralized dynamics of information production (ie, where the individual investor is the

[46] See generally Coffee, n 37 above, who makes this point with reference to securities research. See also Easterbrook and Fischel, n 9 above, 680–2.

[47] See Easterbrook and Fischel, n 9 above, 681–2.

[48] ibid, 682; Franco, J, 'Why Antifraud Prohibitions Are not Enough: The Significance of Opportunism, Candor and Signaling in the Economic Case for Mandatory Securities Disclosure' (2002) 2002 *Columbia Business Law Review* 225, at 349–52.

[49] See Easterbrook and Fischel, n 9 above, 681–2; Coffee, n 37 above, 733–4, with reference to securities research.

[50] eg, Mahoney, n 20 above, 1095, 1111.

[51] See Easterbrook and Fischel, n 9 above, 682–3. See also Bainbridge, S, 'Mandatory Disclosure: A Behavioral Analysis' (2000) 68 *University of Cincinnati Law Review* 1023, 1031.

primary information producer), but also individual firms' decisions on disclosure policies. That is because corporate disclosure entails externalities: therein lies what is perhaps the most well-grounded justification for MD.

Information disclosed by an individual firm is also useful for a better assessment of the value of securities issued by other firms,[52] and thus indirectly benefits other issuers' securities.[53] The closer the similarity with the disclosing firm, the higher the spillover effect, and thus the weaker a firm's incentives to disclose.[54] Disclosing Coca Cola's sales for the second quarter benefits not only Coca Cola investors (both actual and potential ones), who may gauge more precisely the value of Coca Cola shares, but also PepsiCo investors, who, however, do not pay for the benefit they receive. If Coca Cola could obtain a payment from them, it would disclose more.

Further, disclosure may give useful information to a firm's competitors, enhancing their strength and reducing the disclosing firm's competitive advantage.[55] Or it may confer strategic advantages to constituencies, such as suppliers, employees, and customers, that have contrasting interests with those of the firm.[56] The corresponding harm to the disclosing firm is an 'interfirm' cost: the cost borne by the disclosing firm is offset by the benefit that rival firms, customers, and suppliers enjoy.[57] It is thus a private cost, but not a cost to society at large. Because the amount of information voluntarily disclosed is governed by a private cost-benefit trade-off (ie, the individual firm does not internalize the positive externality), private incentives lead to the disclosure of less information than the social optimum.[58]

(c) *Agency problems*

The justifications for MD illustrated so far work even assuming that those who actually provide disclosure—corporate managers—act in order to maximize shareholder welfare. What is missing, according to these views, is neither care nor loyalty on the part of corporate agents, but the right incentives for the issuer itself;

[52] Easterbrook and Fischel, n 9 above, 685–6. [53] ibid, 686. [54] ibid.

[55] The threat posed by disclosure to the firm's competitive position is frequently highlighted in the literature: ibid, 686 ('information (such as that pertaining to new products) may give a competitive advantage to rivals'); Schön, W, 'Corporate Disclosure in a Competitive Environment—the Quest for a European Framework on Mandatory Disclosure' (2006) 6 *Journal of Corporate Law Studies* 259, at 277–9; Guttentag, M, 'An Argument for Imposing Disclosure Requirements on Public Companies' (2004) 32 *Florida State University Law Review* 123, 140; Benston, G, 'The Value of the SEC's Accounting Disclosure Requirements' (1969) 44 *The Accounting Review* 515, 515 (pointing to the costs of revealing information to competitors).

[56] For instance, information about the profitability of a given line of business may help suppliers, customers, and the firm's employees discover managers' reservation price thus enhancing their position when negotiating their contracts with the firm. See Fox, M, 'Retaining Mandatory Securities Disclosure: Why Issuer Choice Is not Investor Empowerment' (1999) 85 *Virginia Law Review* 1335, 1345.

[57] ibid, 1345–6. [58] ibid.

ie, for its shareholders. The agency problem rationale moves from the opposite assumption and justifies mandatory rules on the grounds that managers often do depart from shareholders' interests:[59] they may opportunistically withhold some information valuable to investors.[60]

This justification is most appropriate when related to disclosure of those information items, such as self-dealing transactions and compensation, regarding which managers' self-interest is expected to exert the strongest pressure against disclosure.

But a similar case can be made for 'bad news' as well. The disclosure of negative information has many undesired consequences for managers: it decreases their expected compensation, when it is linked, as it is usual today, to stock performance, and exposes them to an increased risk of being ousted.[61] The worse the news, the greater the harm, and thus the higher the temptation not to disclose.[62]

To be sure, as agency theory suggests, managers and promoters likely have strong incentives to commit *ex ante* to full disclosure.[63] However, to credibly commit to full disclosure for an indefinite period of time may not be feasible by contract. MD rules, and securities regulation more generally, overcome this problem by offering managers and controllers a way to credibly bind themselves to disclosure for an indefinite period of time.[64]

[59] Note that the agency cost rationale for MD may justify it irrespective of the goal one attaches to MD regulation, be it investor protection, price accuracy, or agency costs reduction.

[60] See Fox, n 56 above, 1355–6.

[61] Kraakman, n 23 above, 99–100. See also Kahan, n 34 above, 1028–9.

[62] Kraakman, n 23 above, 100. MD sceptics tend to find this argument unconvincing. Investors have rational expectations and know that managers are eager to disclose good news but prefer to conceal bad news: they would thus infer the bad news from a firm's silence or refusal to disclose. Managers, on their part, have equally rational expectations, so they will anticipate investors' inferences and will disclose both good and bad news, unless the bad news is particularly negative. Investors, in turn, anticipate this reaction too, so if a firm fails to disclose, they will always assume the worst. As an outcome, managers will always choose to disclose, since refusing to do so would always lead to worse consequences than disclosing the bad news, no matter how bad they are (see Easterbrook and Fischel, n 9 above, 677, 683 and Schön, n 55 above, 274–5, for a good description of the mechanics of 'unravelling'). In real-world scenarios, however, a firm's mere act of non-disclosure is not as univocal as it is in theoretical models. It may indicate absence of news, or existence of good news that the firm cannot disclose for competitive reasons (see Easterbrook and Fischel, n 9 above, 677). When investors are unable to make univocal inferences from non-disclosure, the possibility of opportunistic silence reappears and the whole unravelling mechanics breaks down. See Schön, n 55 above, 275; Franco, n 48 above, 272–6; Easterbrook and Fischel, n 9 above, 687–8 (who also stress that there are ways to overcome the problem); and Langevoort, D, 'Information Technology and the Structure of Securities Regulation' (1985) 98 *Harvard Law Review* 747, 785 (pointing to the inadequacy of managerial incentives to disclose bad news).

[63] See generally Jensen, M and Meckling, W, 'Theory of the Firm: Managerial Behavior, Agency Costs, and Ownership Structure' (1976) 3 *Journal of Financial Economics* 305.

[64] See generally Rock, n 22 above; Kraakman, n 23 above, 100.

(d) *The need for a subsidy to informed traders*

Another rationale for the imposition of positive disclosure duties is the need to offer a subsidy to the activity of information gathering and processing by 'informed traders' (professional investors and analysts).[65] Because informed traders are the main contributors to market efficiency, strengthening their position may be justified.[66]

The rationale for subsidizing their activity, in turn, is twofold: (i) information traders can capture only part of the value generated by their activity: in essence, theirs is an information production activity which itself suffers from problems of imperfect appropriability;[67] and (ii) firms cannot be trusted to voluntarily provide information that informed traders need, because of the presence of positive externalities and managerial agency problems.[68] The subsidy rationale, thus, can be largely traced back either to the public good rationale, or to the externality and agency costs ones.

(e) *Standardization*

MD may be needed to ensure standardization in information provided to investors.[69]

Absent MD, even assuming optimal private incentives toward disclosure, each firm would be free to set the timing and format of its own disclosures. The ensuing lack of uniformity would impair data comparability, something which makes information disclosed by each firm inherently less informative and thus less valuable to investors.[70] To the extent that uniformity in disclosure format and comparability of firm-specific information is valuable to investors, it is equally valuable for each issuer. Nevertheless, no individual firm has sufficiently strong incentives to invest in the creation and promotion of a common format for disclosure, given the positive externalities associated with that. In other words, standardization is a public good, from the standpoint of individual firms.

In the absence of MD rules, standardization may thus fail to occur spontaneously and, even if ultimately achieved, the process may nonetheless take a long time. MD can solve this problem and quickly provide a common framework for corporate disclosure.[71]

[65] See Goshen and Parchomovsky, n 39 above, 755–66. [66] See generally ibid.

[67] See Coffee, n 37 above (with reference to the activity of securities research).

[68] See Goshen and Parchomovsky, n 39 above, 758–61.

[69] See Kraakman, n 23 above, 101; Rock, n 22 above, 686; Easterbrook and Fischel, n 9 above, 686–7.

[70] Much of the process of assessing stock value is inherently relational; ie, the value of firm A stock is related to the value of firm B stock, which is related to that of firm C stock, and so on. Homogeneity in the timing, language, and format of information disclosed makes investors' comparisons easier. This, in turn, decreases the costs of information processing and enhances investors' assessments, making prices more informative.

[71] See Kraakman, n 23 above, 101; Easterbrook and Fischel, n 9 above, 686–7.

To be sure, the need for standardization per se provides a rationale only for a very narrow regulatory intervention. It justifies disclosure regulation with regard to modes of disclosure (ie, the regulation would establish 'how' to disclose information to the public). It provides no guidance as to the question of *what* should be disclosed: for this purpose, some other rationale is needed.

3. Concluding remarks

A world without MD would not be completely in the dark: corporate agents would still have incentives to disclose and firms, consequently, would display some degree of transparency.[72] However, the amount and contents of information provided would be likely to be less than socially desirable[73] and tend to shy away from agency cost-sensitive items such as tunnelling and compensation.

Clearly, this is more a starting point than a conclusion. Except perhaps the agency cost rationale, none of the arguments in favour of positive disclosure duties gives precise guidance as to how to address the ensuing—and more challenging—issue of how to design a MD system, and especially of what its contents should be.

III. Some Limits and Drawbacks of MD

Policymakers tend to be biased in favour of MD, for reasons hinted at in Section I. Their deep-rooted intuition is that more information is better than less, or in other words, that the benefits of MD outweigh its costs almost by hypothesis. Taken at face value, the fallacy of this intuition is clear: no firm could create wealth for long, were it bound to give the public full access to its internally generated information. Highlighting the limits and drawbacks of MD is thus helpful to give a better sense of up to what point more disclosure is better than less, or, conversely, what kind of disclosure obligations are bound to raise more problems than they solve.

[72] This is acknowledged even by the strongest MD supporters: see, eg, Fox, n 56 above, 1362: 'In an issuer choice world where we rely on signaling [which amounts to a world of full voluntary disclosure], issuers will have incentives to choose a regime requiring a level of disclosure greater than zero. But, as we have just seen, these incentives will not be great enough to induce issuers to choose a regime requiring a level as high as is socially optimal [...]'.

[73] Franco, n 48 above, 243.

The limited effectiveness of MD may flow from flaws affecting the regulatory and enforcement process, which may lead to ill-designed rules, and from users' limited ability to absorb and correctly process information. The costs of MD stem from varying sources and can be classified as direct or indirect:[74] the direct ones are—among others—the costs of drafting, printing, and mailing the documents, the managerial opportunity costs, and the costs of administering and enforcing the rules. Indirect costs have a more multifaceted and elusive nature. While impossible to quantify, they are in principle higher than direct costs.[75]

1. Policymakers

Regulation is usually advocated as a corrective response to market failure. The existence of a market failure, however, is a necessary but still not a sufficient condition to call for government intervention. It must still be proven (or at least convincingly argued) that regulators will be capable of 'do[ing] it better', which is usually just a matter of presumption.[76]

Policymakers may not necessarily devise good MD systems, on the books and in action. They may deviate from public interest when deciding which rules to set up,[77] whether because they are captured by strong interest groups, or because populism drives their regulatory zeal.

A good example of rules that both cater to issuer insiders' interests and respond to popular hostility against greedy 'speculators' are the EU rules requiring disclosure to the public of any short position higher than 0.5 per cent of a company's shares.[78] The low threshold acts as an indirect curb on short-selling, thereby negatively

[74] See Easterbrook and Fischel, n 9 above, 707–9. There may be, of course, different classifications as well: see, eg, Fox, n 56 above, 1345–6, who distinguishes between 'operational costs' and 'interfirm costs'.

[75] See Easterbrook and Fischel, n 9 above, 708. As a consequence of the difficulties in identifying and measuring MD costs, assessing the overall desirability of disclosure-enhancing reforms is inherently difficult, if not impossible. Recent empirical research on MD fully acknowledges this problem and cautions against the temptation of inferring such desirability from the beneficial effects that frequently result to be associated with these reforms: see, eg, Christensen, H, Hail, L, and Leuz, C, Capital-Market Effects of Securities Regulation: Prior Conditions, Implementation, and Enforcement (2013), ECGI Finance Working Paper No 407/2014 and Chicago Booth Research Paper No 12-04, available at <http://ssrn.com/abstract=1745105> or <http://dx.doi.org/10.2139/ssrn.1745105>, 37–8. For surveys of the empirical literature on disclosure see, eg, Leuz, C and Wysocki, P, Economic Consequences of Financial Reporting and Disclosure Regulation: A Review and Suggestions for Future Research (2008), available at <http://ssrn.com/abstract=1105398> or <http://dx.doi.org/10.2139/ssrn.1105398>; Healy, P and Palepu, K, 'Information Asymmetry, Corporate Disclosure, and the Capital Markets: A Review of the Empirical Disclosure Literature' (2001) 31 *Journal of Accounting and Economics* 405.

[76] See Kraakman, n 23 above, 101.

[77] See Bainbridge, n 51 above, 1058.

[78] See European Parliament and Council Regulation (EU) 236/2012 on short selling and certain aspects of credit default swaps [2012] OJ L86/1, Article 6.

affecting its contribution to market efficiency and its disciplining effect, via share prices, on corporate insiders.[79]

Policymakers may also suffer from cognitive biases, preventing them from making the right choices.[80] The 'hot hand' bias, for instance, may induce regulators to see a pattern (eg, a corporate governance crisis) in a series of facts which are, in fact, casual (a handful of significant reporting irregularities or of unfair self-dealing transactions),[81] leading them to overreaching reactions.

Finally, any MD system's effectiveness crucially depends on the quality of its enforcement institutions: weak, inept, or, even worse, corrupt enforcement agents (including, ultimately, courts) may easily spoil the virtues of any well-designed legislation. In the absence of fair and effective enforcement institutions, MD will hardly matter for investors, who will discount the inability of the disclosure system to ensure compliance. Issuers, however, will incur at least some of the costs of (formally) complying with existing rules, whether because the most blatant violations may still be prosecuted or because selective, bribe-inducing enforcement is possible. Good issuers, in turn, will have to incur the additional costs of credibly signalling, if that is at all possible, their superior quality to the market.

The empirical literature supports the importance of enforcement (and of various other complementary factors) for MD overall effectiveness.[82] For instance, one recent study shows that the beneficial capital market effects following the enactment in the EU of the Market Abuse and the Transparency Directives[83] are more pronounced in countries previously showing high regulatory quality and where stricter implementation and enforcement follows the enactment of the new rules, while they are less pronounced, if not absent at all, in countries with poor regulatory quality and weak enforcement.[84]

Similarly, the adoption of International Financial Reporting Standards (IFRS) is shown to have had beneficial effects only in countries where enforcement is strong and where the institutional environment provides firms with powerful incentives to be transparent.[85]

[79] Short-selling, by allowing traders to sell shares and other financial instruments even when they do not actually own them, permits new negative information to be rapidly and fully reflected into market prices. Thus, prices are put in the condition to more effectively react to managers' poor performance and, as a consequence, the market disciplining effect over managers is enhanced. See Payne, J, 'The Regulation of Short Selling and its Reform in Europe' (2012) 13 *European Business Organization Law Review* 413, 419, 437.

[80] See generally Choi, SJ and Pritchard, AC, 'Behavioral Economics and the SEC' (2003) 56 *Stanford Law Review* 1.

[81] ibid, 25.

[82] See Christensen et al., n 75 above; Daske, H, Hail, L, Leuz, C, and Verdi, R, 'Mandatory IFRS Reporting around the World: Early Evidence on the Economic Consequences' (2008) 46 *Journal of Accounting Research* 1085.

[83] See n 6 above.

[84] Christensen et al., n 75 above, 5–6.

[85] Daske et al., n 82 above, 1089.

2. Users

MD largely relies on the assumption that investors, if provided with all relevant information, will be able to make optimal decisions. Recent scholarship has questioned that assumption. Problems of bounded rationality and information overload[86] would impair individual investors' ability to handle and correctly process information and would systematically keep them from making optimal decisions.

The policy implications of investors' alleged inability to deal with information are seemingly sweeping: if investors are to be regarded as truly unable to make any meaningful use of information, the entire system of MD would be useless and, to the extent that more information leads to even worse decisions, harmful. For such reasons, supporters of this view often suggest that the current system be radically reshaped[87] or scaled back,[88] so as to mitigate information overload and the negative consequences of bounded rationality on individual choices.

Retail investors are clearly those who suffer most from such problems. As a consequence, simplification and reduction in the information provided are policy recipes that appear to be mostly suited for the sale of retail products, such as mutual fund shares.[89] The real challenge there is for policymakers to be able to identify those information items that are strictly necessary and sufficient to let individuals select the right products.[90] Success is far from warranted, given: (i) regulators' incentives (and especially their preference for regulatory strategies that minimize political and liability risk); (ii) the unavoidability of cognitive biases on the part of regulators themselves, consumers, and their financial advisors; and (iii) last but not least, financial industry's pressures.

Yet, information overload and bounded rationality do not impair the foundations of the current system of *issuer* MD. Information made available under existing MD rules is still useful for (and used by) professional investors and analysts: the market in the aggregate is itself capable of absorbing and correctly processing disclosed information.[91]

[86] See generally Paredes, n 8 above.

[87] See, eg, Chen, J and Watson, S, 'Investor Psychology Matters: Is a Prescribed Product Disclosure Statement a Supplement for Healthy Investment Decisions?' (2011) 17 *New Zealand Business Law Quarterly* 412, who give an account of the proposal to substitute prospectuses and other lengthy financial documents with a brief 'product disclosure statement'. The authors, however, warn against the risk of oversimplification that such reform carries.

[88] See generally Paredes, n 8 above, where a cautious invitation to scale back the MD system is advanced.

[89] See Moloney, N, *How to Protect Investors* (2010), ch 5.

[90] For a very positive assessment of EU policymakers' attempt to strike the right balance between information and conciseness in shaping mutual fund products disclosure see ibid, 316–22. For a critical view see Burn, L, 'KISS, but Tell All: Short-Form Disclosure for Retail Investors' (2010) 5(2) *Capital Markets Law Journal* 141, 160–5.

[91] Consequently, retail investors continue to receive (indirect) protection, despite their inability (and perhaps unwillingness) to handle all disclosed information.

3. The fixed costs of disclosure and their effect on small issuers

The efficient level of disclosure is likely to vary from firm to firm,[92] according to idiosyncratic patterns that cannot be perfectly mimicked by regulation. Thus, MD systems will inevitably be both over-inclusive and under-inclusive: for some firms mandated disclosure may be lower than optimal (eg, some useful pieces of information may stay out of MD's scope), while for some others it may be excessive.

An important dimension along which issuers differ from the point of view of disclosure costs is their size. The direct costs of MD are in large part fixed. Therefore, they tend to be more burdensome for smaller listed firms, putting them at a competitive disadvantage vis-à-vis larger ones.[93] Further, the value of confidentiality for small issuers is in principle higher, making disclosure more costly for them than for well-established, large firms.[94]

Regulators are increasingly aware of the need to increase the system's flexibility, so as to take the larger relative weight of disclosure-related costs for small issuers into account. In the EU, the Market Abuse Regulation moves exactly in this direction: issuers trading on 'S[mall and] M[edium-sized] E[nterprise] growth markets' will be subject to a simplified, less burdensome regime as regards ongoing disclosure of price-sensitive information and insiders' lists.[95] In the same vein, the

[92] See Bainbridge, n 51 above, 1057; Fox, n 56 above, 1395 ('Each issuer has a socially efficient level of disclosure …').

[93] See Easterbrook and Fischel, n 9 above, 671; Schön, n 55 above, 288; Leuz and Wysocki, n 75 above, 10; Bushee, B and Leuz, C, 'Economic Consequences of SEC Disclosure Regulation: Evidence from the OTC Bulletin Board' (2005) 39 *Journal of Accounting and Economics* 233 (for indirect empirical evidence); for a comprehensive discussion of disclosure costs for SMEs and of possible solutions to the problem see Ferrarini, G and Ottolia, A, 'Corporate Disclosure as a Transaction Cost: The Case of SMEs' (2013) 9 *European Review of Contract Law* 363.

[94] Small issuers are often non-diversified firms, so their disclosures are in principle more informative (and thus more harmful to their competitive position) than those of large issuers, operating in different business segments and across multiple geographical areas.

[95] See Market Abuse Regulation, Preambles (6), (55), (56) and Articles 17(9), 18(6). See also the European Parliament and Council Directive (EU) 2010/73, on the prospectus to be published when securities are offered to the public or admitted to trading and amending Directive 2001/34/EC [2010] OJ L327/1, Preambles (2), (18), and Article 1, para (7)(b)(ii) (introducing the so-called 'proportionate disclosure regime') and European Parliament and Council Directive (EU) 2013/50/EU, amending Directive 2004/109/EC of the European Parliament and of the Council on the harmonization of transparency requirements in relation to information about issuers whose securities are admitted to trading on a regulated market, Directive 2003/71/EC of the European Parliament and of the Council on the prospectus to be published when securities are offered to the public or admitted to trading and Commission Directive 2007/14/EC laying down detailed rules for the implementation of certain provisions of Directive 2004/109/EC [2013] OJ L294/13, Preambles (2), (3), (4) and Article 1, para (2)(b).

JOBS Act reforms in the US are largely aimed at decreasing the regulatory burdens for smaller issuers seeking external finance.[96]

4. Affecting behaviour

MD is said to have a 'therapeutic' function,[97] when its ultimate goal is to induce desired corporate behaviour. MD may reach this outcome by relying on the negative reputational, or even political, effects of public exposure of a different course of action. In this respect, MD acts as a soft-form substitute of more substantive regulations.

This use of MD as a form of stealth substantive regulation is increasing, especially in the domain of corporate governance, but often has corporate social responsibility purposes, such as the fight against gender or income inequality or the prevention of armed conflicts financing, that have nothing to do with the goals identified in Section II.1.[98]

Stealth substantive regulation via MD may be ineffective and lead to unintended adverse consequences. Increased disclosure of performance-based compensation, for instance, instead of constraining its persistent rise, may induce an alteration in the overall structure of managerial compensation, leading to an increase in its fixed, 'stealth', or on-the-job components.[99] The decrease of the relative weight of performance-based compensation, in turn, may have adverse effects on managers' incentives and thus increase agency costs.[100]

Another example is that of disclosure on internal codes of ethics. The Sarbanes–Oxley Act of 2002 required firms to make extensive disclosure about the adoption of internal codes of ethics and, more importantly, about the waivers that the company may have granted to its top managers.[101] The empirical evidence suggests that the new rules proved ineffective in their purpose of inducing more rigorous adherence to best practices.[102] Indeed, rather than decreasing the number

[96] See Jumpstart our Business Startups Act 2011. It is an open question whether the increase in information asymmetry that the relaxation of the MD system entails (since firms *may* now disclose less value-relevant information to the marketplace) will have the effect of increasing firms' cost of capital or whether they will be able to avoid that via voluntary (ad hoc or industry-standardized) disclosures.

[97] See Bainbridge, n 3 above, 1797–801.

[98] Think of disclosure requirements pertaining to board diversity policies in the EU, the ratio between CEO pay and the average employee's pay in the US, or the rules on conflict minerals on both sides of the Atlantic.

[99] See Bebchuk, L and Fried, J, 'Executive Compensation as an Agency Problem' (2003) 17 *Journal of Economic Perspectives* 71, 79–81 (referring, among other things, to 'pension plans, deferred compensation, post-retirement perks, and consulting contracts').

[100] See Manne, n 32 above, 493–503, for an extensive discussion.

[101] Sarbanes–Oxley Act of 2002, Pub. L. No. 107-204, §406(a)–(b), 116 Stat. 745, 789 (codified at 15 U.S.C. §7264 (2006)).

[102] See generally Rodrigues, U and Stegemoller, M, 'Placebo Ethics: A Study in Securities Disclosure Arbitrage' (2010) 96 *Virginia Law Review* 1; Manne, n 32 above, 487–8.

and scope of waivers granted to top managers, MD induced firms to relax their internal codes.[103]

5. Liability risk

MD increases the risk of litigation, which is not only a source of cost for disclosing firms, but may also negatively interact with firms' voluntary disclosure choices and, ultimately, reduce the overall amount of information disclosed. These negative consequences stem from the risk of liability for affirmative misstatements, which tends to increase as the amount of disclosed information and the frequency of a firm's public announcements increase. Indeed, the larger the amount of information released to the public and the more frequently disclosures have to be made, the higher the probability of issuing an incomplete or misleading statement and the greater the liability risk.

The liability risk associated with MD may reduce the amount of *useful* information provided by firms. For the purpose of minimizing liability risk, issuers may adopt a formalistic approach to MD compliance.[104] They may limit their disclosures to 'boilerplate' information of scarce importance for investors, shying away from more informative, but litigation-prone, disclosures. In the same vein, firms may systematically avoid speaking to the market other than when the law so requires. In this respect, MD tends to crowd out more spontaneous forms of communication between issuers and investors.[105]

Provisions ancillary to MD requirements, such as the prohibition on selective disclosure,[106] can amplify this effect. The ban on selective disclosure restricts communication between firms and the marketplace. The former are no longer allowed to select the audience of their disclosures and are forced to choose between full confidentiality and speaking to the public at large, a setting in which the risk of disclosure-driven litigation is the highest and cannot be minimized *ex ante* via contract. For that reason, a firm will often refrain from disclosing information that it would have been willing to give, however indirectly, the market, had it been able to select a smaller audience.[107]

[103] Manne, n 32 above, 487–8.

[104] See Easterbrook and Fischel, n 9 above, 709 (point out to the problem of fully compliant but obfuscatory disclosures induced by mandatory rules).

[105] See Kitch, E, 'The Theory and Practice of Securities Disclosure' (1995) 61 *Brooklyn Law Review* 763, 770–2, 840–6. But see Franco, n 48 above, 243, 271 (anti-fraud rules chill voluntary disclosure, while MD countervails this problem, by creating an exemption for a firm's affirmative statements issued pursuant to the positive duty).

[106] In the US, see SEC Regulation FD (2000). In the EU, see Market Abuse Regulation, Article 17(8).

[107] See, eg, Langevoort, n 7 above, 164.

Reliance on general standards, instead of more granular, discrete disclosure mandates, may avoid MD's negative effects on issuers' release of useful information: open-ended disclosure duties, such as those mandating prompt disclosure of a firm's material information, increase the liability risk for 'staying silent' in the face of any new significant corporate development, thus offsetting the incentive to forgo disclosure for fears of issuing a statement that may *ex post* be considered as incomplete or deceiving.[108]

However, the use of general standards to counteract MD's chilling effects has a significant drawback: firms become inevitably exposed to a high liability risk irrespective of their disclosure decisions. If, in the face of uncertainty as to the material character of a given piece of information, a firm chooses not to disclose, it exposes itself to the risk of being held liable *ex post* for having breached its disclosure duties. If, for the purpose of avoiding that risk, the firm chooses to disclose, it nonetheless exposes itself to the risk of being held liable for having issued an incomplete or deceiving statement.

The overall cost of a MD system of this kind crucially depends on the intensity of private and public enforcement. In countries where private enforcement is rare and public enforcement less than aggressive, liability risk will be a lesser concern. This may at least in part explain why the EU and the US have different rules on ongoing disclosure of new material information. In the US, where the enforcement of securities regulation is remarkably strong, the enactment of a far-reaching real-time disclosure obligation would have likely raised issuer liability risk to unbearably high levels. That appears not to be the case in Europe, where private enforcement of securities laws is relatively rare and the intensity of public enforcement lower.[109]

6. *Ex ante* effects on value creation

Last, but most importantly, MD may distort firms' investment decisions and induce them to forgo profitable projects.[110] The public release of information about a firm's plans and strategies, when too detailed or premature, enhances competitors'

[108] See n 112 below and accompanying text.

[109] According to varying metrics, private and public enforcement of securities regulation (and corporate law rules aimed at investor protection) is more intense in the US than in major EU jurisdictions: see, eg, Jackson, H and Roe, M, 'Public and Private Enforcement of Securities Laws: Resource-based Evidence' (2009) 93 *Journal of Financial Economics* 207, 214–15; La Porta, R, Lopez-De-Silanes, F, and Shleifer, A, 'What Works in Securities Laws?' (2006) 61 *Journal of Finance* 1, 15–16.

[110] See, Easterbrook and Fischel, n 9 above, 708; Franco, n 48 above, 339. This is, of course, true, *mutatis mutandis*, also of any rule requiring traders or investors who are active in the market for corporate influence or corporate control to reveal their investment strategies by disclosing their long or short positions: see, eg, Enriques, L, Gargantini, M, and Novembre, V, 'Mandatory and Contract-based Shareholding Disclosure' (2010) 15 *Uniform Law Review* 713, 729–32.

free-riding on disclosed information and makes their reaction more effective, thus making the project less profitable in the first place, or no longer profitable at all.[111]

More generally, 'excess' disclosure in the financial market may stifle innovation (or at least that portion of innovation brought about by companies subject to MD): it is well known that innovation needs secrecy—at least when patent protection is ineffective or unavailable, whether because it is too early or because the novel product does not meet the relevant requirements. Disclosure, especially when too detailed, forward-looking and targeted at business information (such as the firm's current R&D), may weaken firms' incentives in the creation of new products, and this represents a straightforward drawback from the point of view of societal welfare.[112]

Public disclosure makes a firm's investment decisions (and their outcomes) more observable by rivals. It thus increases the value of passive strategies based on 'wait and see'.[113] If a free-riding strategy becomes dominant, then competition loses much of its Schumpeterian character,[114] at the expense of growth.[115]

IV. Conclusion

MD systems have a strong tendency to expand over time.[116] This Chapter has provided various reasons why this is the case. One additional reason is MD's reliance on general, open-ended standards, which are expansive by their very nature. Think of the 'materiality' requirement, which contributes to defining the content

[111] See, eg, Easterbrook and Fischel, n 9 above, 708.

[112] See Schön, n 55 above, 287, 294–6; Zingales, L, 'The Future of Securities Regulation' (2009) 47 *Journal of Accounting Research* 391, 394; Gilotta, S, 'Disclosure in Securities Markets and the Firm's Need for Confidentiality: Theoretical Framework and Regulatory Analysis' (2012) 13 *European Business Organization Law Review* 45, 66–9.

[113] Gilotta, n 112 above; Kitch, n 105 above, 856.

[114] Competition is Schumpeterian when it has the traits of 'creative destruction' (high degree of innovation and high degree of turnover across competing firms in the product market): Schumpeter, J, *Capitalism, Socialism, and Democracy* (2013), ch VII.

[115] See Fox, n 56 above, 1346.

[116] See Paredes, n 8 above, 424–5; Schön, n 55 above, 286 (with reference to the EU); Gordon, J, 'The Rise of Independent Directors in the United States, 1950–2005: Of Shareholder Value and Stock Market Prices' (2007) 59 *Stanford Law Review* 1465, 1548–53 (documenting the increase in firms' disclosure in 1950–2005 but underlining that it is due only in part to SEC MD); Ben-Shahar and Schneider, n 1 above, 684 ('disclosure's logic is inherently expansive. Only broad disclosure accommodates the variety of disclosees and circumstances. One can always imagine that disclosing one more datum might help. Because it is hard to anticipate what data will help, safety seems to lie in broad mandates.').

of many MD rules in both the US and the EU: whenever there is uncertainty as to the material character of a given piece of information (and this grey area, given the inherent vagueness of the standard itself, is likely to be wide), firms will be induced to disclose, so as to minimize the risk of being held liable *ex post* by a court which, in hindsight, may easily qualify that piece of information as material.[117]

Yet, another explanation for the expansive tendency of MD systems is that much of the implementation and enforcement of firms' disclosure duties is left to regulatory agencies that naturally lean toward more disclosure rather than less. First, a pro-disclosure stance derives from their investor protection mission: ever since Justice Brandeis's sunlight metaphor, transparency is a synonym for prevention of opportunism and fraud. Second, mandating more disclosure is the chief tool whereby agencies' top officers increase their power and advance their political agenda. Third, it is tempting for policymakers and regulators to use MD as a therapeutic tool to mould corporate agents' behaviour.[118]

Telling when a MD system becomes excessively burdensome is impossible, but unless policymakers exert some self-restraint, the tipping point will eventually be reached (if it has not been already in some jurisdictions). When that is the case, being a listed company becomes unduly costly, and small issuers in particular may be overly discouraged from accessing the public securities markets.[119] This, in turn, may be the source of severe drawbacks. Small, newly established firms are often those providing for the largest part of technological and business innovation. Too strict disclosure rules may inhibit their access to one of the most important sources of external finance, the securities market, making it *ex ante* more difficult to finance their start-up phase[120] and leading to reduced dynamic efficiency at the macro level. As pointed out in Section III.3, regulators seem to have at least partially recognized these risks. Their solution has been to compartmentalize securities markets: disclosure duties for large issuers are untrimmed, while smaller ones are exempted from some of them.

[117] As pointed out in Section III.5, general standards act as a countervailing force to the chilling effect that liability risk for affirmative misstatements has on firms' disclosure decisions. In fact, an open-ended disclosure duty (such as that based on the material character of the information) creates an opposite and equally wide liability risk for 'staying silent' in the face of any new non-trivial development in the firm's affairs, which offsets the tendency to shy away from disclosure generated by liability for affirmative misstatements. As also pointed out, however, this strategy strongly increases disclosure-related liability risk.

[118] See n 93 above and accompanying text.

[119] See Ferrarini and Ottolia, n 93 above, 365 (arguing that recent corporate governance reforms, with their emphasis on enhanced financial disclosure, may have discouraged new SMEs from accessing the public securities markets).

[120] The role of the stock market as a driver for the development of early stage entrepreneurial finance is highlighted in Black, B and Gilson, R, 'Venture Capital and the Structure of Capital Markets: Banks Versus Stock Markets' (1998) 47 *Journal of Financial Economics* 243.

The risk with this polarization is that, as a consequence, policymakers and regulators will hesitate even less before imposing new and broader disclosure duties on large issuers. Further, a polarized system may lead to suboptimal issuers' choices, depending on how the threshold is defined. For instance, if market capitalization is used as a threshold, issuers may switch to the less-regulated market segment by carving out a subsidiary and listing it as a controlled or independent entity: at the margin, the reduction in MD costs may offset the forgone benefits of being a single listed entity.

In parallel to the continuous expansion, in scope and reach, of disclosure duties, the channels through which firms and investors communicate are shrinking. Firms are no longer allowed to selectively convey material information: they are only permitted to speak to the public at large. This sclerotization of the way firms and investors communicate may have the effect of reducing the overall amount of corporate information that is conveyed to the marketplace (see Section III.5).

Sensitive business information that issuers would have disclosed to a restricted audience, possibly under a duty of confidentiality (think of firm's plans and strategies, or its advancements in R&D), may not be disclosed to the public at large (or at least not in the same degree of detail), due to increased competitive concerns.[121]

Similarly, liability concerns may overly discourage firms from disclosing 'soft' information, which in a modern financial market constitutes the most valuable source of insights on a security's value. Soft information is speculative and conjectural (think of management discussion and analysis) rather than factual, qualitative rather than quantitative, forward-looking rather than backward-looking. All these features make it inherently ambiguous in its meaning and thus more prone to misinterpretation by the public—and the courts.

With selective disclosure no longer available, firms may decide to arrest the flow of that kind of information, or to limit it considerably, for fears of deceiving the investing public.[122] If that happens, market efficiency will suffer.

MD rules may well overall benefit both corporate governance and the functioning of securities markets, by providing investors with information that market forces alone would likely not provide. However, stating that MD is desirable amounts to claiming neither that unconditional firm transparency is beneficial nor that imposing *public* disclosure of information is always the best policy. For this reason, policymakers should exert self-restraint when mandating disclosure and pay careful attention to the design of MD contents and modalities.

[121] See, eg, Fischel, D, 'Insider Trading and Investment Analysis: An Economic Analysis of Dirks v. Securities and Exchange Commission' (1984) 13 *Hofstra Law Review* 127, 142; Langevoort, D, 'Investment Analysts and the Law of Insider Trading' (1990) 76 *Virginia Law Review* 1023, 1029; Choi, S, 'Selective Disclosures in the Public Capital Markets' (2002) 35 *University of California Davis Law Review* 533, 541–2.

[122] See, eg, Langevoort, n 121 above, 1029–30.

Bibliography

Ben-Shahar, O and Schneider, C, 'The Failure of Mandated Disclosure' (2011) 159 *University of Pennsylvania Law Review* 647.

Coffee, J, 'Market Failure and the Economic Case for a Mandatory Disclosure System' (1984) 70 *Virginia Law Review* 717.

Easterbrook, F and Fischel, D, 'Mandatory Disclosure and the Protection of Investors' (1984) 70 *Virginia Law Review* 669.

Fox, M, 'Retaining Mandatory Securities Disclosure: Why Issuer Choice Is not Investor Empowerment' (1999) 85 *Virginia Law Review* 1335.

Franco, J, 'Why Antifraud Prohibitions Are not Enough: The Significance of Opportunism, Candor and Signaling in the Economic Case for Mandatory Securities Disclosure' (2002) 2002 *Columbia Business Law Review* 225.

Gilson, R and Kraakman, R, 'The Mechanisms of Market Efficiency' (1984) 70 *Virginia Law Review* 549.

Goshen, Z and Parchomovsky, G, 'The Essential Role of Securities Regulation' (2006) 55 *Duke Law Journal* 711.

Kitch, E, 'The Theory and Practice of Securities Disclosure' (1995) 61 *Brooklyn Law Review* 763.

Leuz, C and Wysocki, P, Economic Consequences of Financial Reporting and Disclosure Regulation: A Review and Suggestions for Future Research (2008), available at <http://ssrn.com/abstract=1105398> or <http://dx.doi.org/10.2139/ssrn.1105398>, 10.

Mahoney, P, 'Mandatory Disclosure as a Solution to Agency Problems' (1995) 62 *University of Chicago Law Review* 1047.

Moloney, N, *EC Securities Regulation* (2nd edn, 2008).

Paredes, T, 'Blinded by the Light: Information Overload and its Consequences for Securities Regulation' (2003) 81 *Washington University Law Quarterly* 417.

Rock, E, 'Securities Regulation as a Lobster Trap: A Credible Commitment Theory of Mandatory Disclosure' (2002) 23 *Cardozo Law Review* 675.

Schön, W, 'Corporate Disclosure in a Competitive Environment—the Quest for a European Framework on Mandatory Disclosure' (2006) 6 *Journal of Corporate Law Studies* 25.

CHAPTER 18

CONDUCT OF BUSINESS REGULATION

ANDREW F TUCH*

* For helpful comments on earlier drafts of this Chapter, I thank Deborah DeMott, Eilís Ferran, Howell Jackson, Arthur Laby, Don Langevoort, Niamh Moloney, Jennifer Payne, and Hillary Sale.

I. Introduction

Conduct of business (COB) regulation governs financial intermediaries' conduct toward their clients; that is, toward the actors—whether individuals or institutions—with whom financial intermediaries transact in providing financial products and services.[1] While the expression 'conduct of business regulation' is not widely employed in some jurisdictions, including the US, it is commonly used by international financial regulatory bodies and by financial regulators in many jurisdictions, including the Member States of the EU.[2] COB regulation governs financial intermediaries acting for or on behalf of their clients, such as in giving advice, exercising discretion, and executing orders. It may also govern intermediaries' arm's-length arrangements with clients—transactions in which intermediaries act as principals, or counterparties, in buying or selling financial products. COB regulation typically applies across the spectrum of financial intermediaries' functional lines of business, including their securities, banking, and insurance activities. It takes various forms, including requirements for registration or licensing; rules governing sales, marketing, and other business practices; and mechanisms of enforcement.[3]

COB regulation serves the objectives of protecting clients (investors) from harm, preserving and enhancing the integrity and orderly operation of financial markets, and otherwise serving the public interest. Because its focus is 'client-facing', it does not encompass 'firm-facing' regulation, such as the imposition of general supervision obligations, record-keeping requirements, or net capital requirements—regulation that nevertheless serves to protect clients.[4] Moreover, because of its focus on conduct, COB regulation does not encompass product regulation except to the extent such rules shape financial intermediaries' conduct toward their clients.

This Chapter considers various functional lines of business, but focuses on securities. As Professor Eddy Wymeersch observed, COB regulation is more symptomatic of securities regulation than of banking and insurance regulation.[5] The latter

[1] In this Chapter, references to 'financial intermediary' encompass both the firm itself and the individuals acting for it. The term 'client' is used to encompass all actors with whom financial intermediaries transact, whether they do so as principal or not, in providing financial products and services.

[2] Sometimes also referred to as 'business conduct' or 'market conduct' regulation, COB regulation is typically contrasted with market stability regulation and safety and soundness regulation. For prominent use of business conduct regulation in the US, see Department of the Treasury, Blueprint for a Modernized Financial Regulatory Structure (2008), 2–5, 14, 19–21, 138, 170–80.

[3] ibid, 171.

[4] The terms 'client-facing' and 'firm-facing' used in this Chapter are adopted from Moloney, N, *How to Protect Investors: Lessons from the EC and the UK* (2010).

[5] Wymeersch, E, 'The Structure of Financial Supervision in Europe: About Single Financial Supervisors, Twin Peaks and Multiple Financial Supervisors' (2007) 8 *European Business Organization Law Review* 237.

areas of financial regulation have been primarily concerned with the solvency of banks and insurance companies, whereas securities regulation has focused on investor protection—an objective served by COB regulation.[6]

The Chapter begins with the regulatory backdrop to COB regulation. It describes the justifications for COB regulation, the modal regulatory strategies used, and the complex frameworks within which COB regulation operates. The Chapter then generally assesses US COB regulation, outlining important market and regulatory developments over the past several decades, and drawing comparisons with corresponding EU and other COB regulation. The Chapter concludes by discussing reforms proposed or adopted in the wake of the global financial crisis of 2007–09.[7]

II. Regulatory Backdrop

1. Coexisting general law obligations

Financial regulation, and COB regulation in particular, is typically considered distinct from the general law, or private law.[8] The sources of financial regulation are legal instruments such as statutes and the rules and regulations of agencies, as well as judicial and other adjudicative opinions interpreting and applying these instruments. In the two jurisdictions with the deepest capital markets[9] and most important financial centres, namely the UK and the US, both COB regulation and the general law apply to regulate the business conduct of financial intermediaries.[10]

[6] See generally Jackson, H, 'Regulation in a Multisectored Financial Services Industry: An Exploratory Essay' (1999) 77 *Washington University Law Quarterly* 319, 348–52.

[7] In view of the complexity of the regulatory regimes considered, this Chapter should be regarded as an introduction to the field.

[8] The term 'general law' is used here to describe laws of general application, including contract law, property law, equity, and tort law. For similar distinctions, see Nelson, P, *Capital Markets Law and Compliance: The Implications of MiFID* (2008) 146, 306 (describing 'general law' in England and Wales); Hudson, A, *The Law of Finance* (2nd edn, 2013) 53–91 (contrasting EU and UK financial regulation with the 'substantive law' or 'private law' of England and Wales); DeMott, D and Laby, A, 'The United States of America' in Busch, D and DeMott, D, *Liability of Asset Managers* (2012) 411, 435–40 (discussing the 'private law' duties of investment advisers); and Baxt, R, Black, A, and Hanrahan, P, *Securities and Financial Services Law* (7th edn, 2008) 529–93 (contrasting Australian financial regulation with 'general law'). The boundaries of general law and financial regulation often blur. Hudson, n 8 above, 66–70.

[9] Cox, J et al., *Securities Regulation: Cases and Materials* (7th edn, 2013) 104.

[10] As to the UK, see Hudson, n 8 above, 53–66. As to the US, see Sitkoff, R, 'The Fiduciary Obligations of Financial Advisers under the Law of Agency' (2014) *Journal of Financial Planning* 42, 42 and SEC, Study on Investment Advisers and Broker-Dealers: As Required by Section 913 of the Dodd–Frank Wall Street Reform and Consumer Protection Act (2011), 45, 51.

The general law serves as an important backdrop against which to consider COB regulatory developments. Under general law, a financial intermediary providing financial products and services may face liability for fraud and for carelessness and disloyalty. Liability for fraud arises where the tort of deceit is committed.[11] Liability for carelessness arises from breach of a duty of care imposed by contract or the tort of negligence.[12] Liability for disloyalty arises from breach of a duty of loyalty, a duty arising where the financial intermediary–client relationship is characterized as fiduciary.[13]

Fiduciary doctrine emanates from the general law. The standard of propriety it imposes is unequalled elsewhere in the general law.[14] Generally speaking, fiduciary duties arise where one party has power or influence over the interests of another who is therefore vulnerable to the former party's exercise of discretion.[15] Some relationships in the financial context are, based on their status, fiduciary relationships. For instance, where a financial intermediary acts as the trustee of a pension fund, a scheme manager, or trustee of a unit trust, it will have fiduciary status.[16] Fiduciary duties may also arise on an ad hoc basis, such as where a financial intermediary provides advice or has discretionary control over a client's assets.[17] Where fiduciary duties arise, they demand 'undivided' or 'single-minded' loyalty, thus limiting the financial intermediary's pursuit of self-interest. Fiduciary duties do so by restraining the intermediary's freedom to act in ways inconsistent, or in conflict, with the interests of its client. In particular, fiduciary doctrine has traditionally required fiduciaries to avoid conflicts of interest, absent the informed consent of the party to whom the duty is owed.[18] In many jurisdictions, however, contracting parties may exclude or disclaim the existence of fiduciary duties.[19]

In the context of financial products and services, the general law alone is inadequate for regulating COB. The general law typically governs conduct in a less

[11] eg, Hudson, n 8 above, 714–30.

[12] Nelson, n 8 above, 306. In some common law jurisdictions, a duty of care may also arise from the fiduciary characterization of a relationship.

[13] *Bristol and West Building Society v Mothew* [1998] ch 1, 18.

[14] ibid, 16–19.

[15] Regarding unifying features of fiduciary relationships, see DeMott, D, 'Beyond Metaphor: An Analysis of Fiduciary Obligation' (1988) 37 *Duke Law Journal* 879, 902.

[16] Hudson, n 8 above, 104.

[17] eg, *Woods v Martins Bank Ltd* [1959] 1 QB 55; *Australian Securities and Investments Commission* (hereinafter, ASIC) *v Citigroup Global Markets Australia Pty Ltd* (No 4) (2007) 160 FCR 35.

[18] As to the position in England and Wales and in Australia, see *Bristol*, n 13 above, 18 and *Breen v Williams* (1996) 186 CLR 71, 113, 137–8. Fiduciary doctrine in the US varies by context, although the duty of loyalty on agents generally conforms to the Anglo-Australian approach of prohibiting conflicts of interest, absent informed consent. Restatement (Third) of Agency, section 8.01; and Sitkoff, n 10 above, 44.

[19] Contractual exclusion would seem permissible in the UK and Australia. Hudson, n 8 above, 112–15; *ASIC v Citigroup Global Markets Australia Pty Ltd* (No 4) (2007) 160 FCR 35. The position is more restrictive in the US. See Restatement (Third) of Agency, section 8.06. The formulation in section 8.06 accords with that recently employed by the Delaware Court of Chancery. See *In re Rural Metro Corp.*, 88 A3d 54, 101 (2014).

granular fashion than does regulation, which may impose specific, prescriptive obligations—an advantage where particular regulatory resolutions are considered desirable. The general law also adapts slowly and unpredictably to changes in market structure and to emerging market practices and technological developments, due to the nature of the judicial process, the generality of the legal concepts involved, and the limitations of judicial expertise. The general law provides no mechanism for public enforcement. It nevertheless applies broadly, thus filling some gaps left by COB regulation.

2. Economic and other justifications

The strategies used in COB regulation find theoretical justification in economics and related disciplines.[20] Standard neoclassical economic analysis asserts the need for regulatory intervention when particular market failures exist.[21] For instance, financial intermediaries with market power, perhaps resulting from high search costs,[22] may set higher prices than competitors. These circumstances would justify mandatory disclosures and direct price regulation.[23] Failures stemming from the 'public good' nature of information may be addressed by disclosure requirements and anti-fraud rules.[24] When a client delegates discretion to a financial intermediary to act on its behalf, (economic) principal-agent theory counsels for mechanisms to help align the intermediary's interests with those of the client and thereby to reduce 'agency costs'.[25] That theoretical framework justifies rules requiring loyalty, such as fiduciary duties.[26] The possibility that a financial intermediary will

[20] For an overview of justifications in the context of retail investors, see Moloney, n 4 above, 45–92. Policymakers often justify regulation on grounds of fairness, eg, Mary Jo White (Chair, SEC), Enhancing our Equity Market Structure, speech at Sandler O'Neil & Partners, LP Global Exchange and Brokerage Conference (5 June 2014), available at <http://www.sec.gov/News/Speech/Detail/Speech/1370542004312#.U6SU8qNLOAI> (last accessed 23 June 2014).

[21] Campbell, J et al., 'Consumer Financial Protection' (2011) 25 *Journal of Economic Perspectives* 91, 92–5.

[22] ibid, 92–3. [23] ibid.

[24] Campbell, J et al., The Regulation of Consumer Financial Products: An Introductory Essay with Four Case Studies (2010), Harvard Kennedy School Faculty Research Working Paper Series No 8, available at <http://dash.harvard.edu/bitstream/handle/1/4450128/Madrian_TheRegulationof.pdf?sequence=1>.

[25] Agency costs arise from the agent's divergence of interests from those of the principal. Jensen, M and Meckling, W, 'Theory of the Firm: Managerial Behavior, Agency Costs and Ownership Structure' (1976) 3 *Journal of Financial Economics* 305, 308–10, 357.

[26] For a more extensive discussion of how (economic) principal-agent theory justifies the imposition of conflict of interest rules, such as duties of loyalty, see Cooter, R and Freedman, B, 'The Fiduciary Relationship: Its Economic Character and Legal Consequences' (1991) 66 *New York University Law Review* 1045; Sitkoff, R, 'The Economic Structure of Fiduciary Law' (2011) 91 *Boston University Law Review* 1041; Tuch, A, 'Conflicted Gatekeepers: The Volcker Rule and Goldman Sachs' (2012) 7 *Virginia Law and Business Review* 365, 378–92.

harm another through its carelessness justifies the imposition of a duty of care.[27] These various justifications have greater force with regard to regulation to protect individual (or retail) investors than that to protect institutional investors, because institutional investors have been considered sophisticated and thus able to 'fend for themselves', such as by contracting with financial intermediaries to protect their financial interests. However, the notion of institutional investors as adequately able to guard their own interests stands on weaker foundations after the financial crisis, when abundant evidence inconsistent with this notion surfaced.[28]

Some strategies used in COB regulation may also be justified by evidence indicating that clients, particularly retail clients, fail to conform to the behavioural assumptions made in neoclassical economics. Investors have biases and cognitive limitations, leading them to make decisions that systematically depart from rationality.[29] Cognitive psychology has demonstrated the tendency of individuals to be overconfident in their judgements, abilities, and prospects; to hold onto opinions 'too tightly and for too long'; to be more disposed towards avoiding a loss than taking a gain; and to anchoring any estimates they form to some initial, possibly arbitrary value.[30] Applying these insights to investor behaviour, behavioural finance has demonstrated seemingly irrational behaviour by investors. A flourishing legal literature has drawn upon insights about the behaviour of investors and cautiously suggested new directions for regulatory intervention.[31]

Importantly, even where regulatory intervention finds theoretical justification, determining the best form of such regulation poses difficult challenges. The fit between economic and other justifications and any resulting regulation is, at best, imprecise.[32] Moreover, the task of crafting desirable COB regulation occurs against the backdrop of the general law. Richard Posner has observed, in general, that any 'market failures' are those of the market and of the rules prescribed by the general law.[33] In

[27] See Shavell, S, *Foundations of Economic Analysis of Law* (2004) 178–81 (referring to firms generally rather than financial intermediaries specifically).

[28] See Langevoort, D, 'Global Securities Regulation after the Financial Crisis' (2010) *Journal of International Economic Law* 799, 809–11; and Langevoort, D, 'The SEC, Retail Investors, and the Institutionalization of the Securities Markets' (2009) 95 *Virginia Law Review* 1025, 1058, 1061–70.

[29] For an overview of the literature in behavioural economics, see Barberis, N and Thaler, R, 'A Survey of Behavioral Finance' in Constantinides, G et al. (eds), *Handbook of the Economics of Finance* (2003) 1054.

[30] ibid, 1065–9. See also Campbell, n 21 above, 94.

[31] Langevoort, D, 'Taming the Animal Spirits of the Stock Markets: A Behavioral Approach to Securities Regulation' (2002) 97 *Northwestern University Law Review* 135; Langevoort, D, 'Selling Hope, Selling Risk: Some Lessons for Law from Behavioral Economics about Stockbrokers and Sophisticated Customers' (1996) 84 *California Law Review* 627; Prentice, R, 'Whither Securities Regulation' (2002) 51 *Duke Law Journal* 1397, 1448–89.

[32] A further difficulty for crafting regulatory strategies stems from the potential behavioural biases of regulators. Choi, S and Pritchard, A, 'Behavioral Economics and the SEC' (2003) 56 *Stanford Law Review* 1, 20–41.

[33] Posner, R, *Economic Analysis of Law* (7th edn, 2007) 389 (referring to common law, rather than general law).

the present context, any failures are those of the market and of the rules prescribed by both the general law and existing COB regulation. Where such failures arise, regulatory reforms must be assessed for their likely effect on people and markets, an exercise often involving expert judgements and contested evidence.[34]

3. Modal regulatory strategies

In regulating COB, major regimes employ a range of regulatory strategies that broadly map onto the general law obligations, but with important differences. The primary strategies are anti-fraud rules and duties of care, loyalty, fair dealing, and best execution—as well as variants of these duties.[35] Other core regulatory strategies include registration or licensing requirements and mechanisms to enforce the duties imposed.

By way of general explanation, anti-fraud rules create a cause of action against parties intentionally engaging in misleading or deceptive conduct.[36] Those rules are often broader than general law fraud rules since they extend beyond intentional affirmative misrepresentations to encompass the failure to disclose material adverse facts.[37] Disclosure requirements promote information production and may differ along a variety of dimensions. Some require highly particularized information about products, services, or intermediaries. Others may be tailored to individual transactions or to the aggregate of transactions in which an intermediary is involved.[38] Duties of best execution concern the execution of trades for clients, including the handling of clients' orders.

Duties of care typically require that the process employed by a financial intermediary in giving advice or making a recommendation be 'suitable'. For instance, the US imposes suitability duties on broker-dealers and investment advisers, as does the EU on investment firms. The concept of 'suitability' draws on certain characteristics of the client involved and the securities or investment strategy under consideration. Most jurisdictions apply somewhat weaker suitability duties for the benefit of institutional clients. In the EU, regulatory strategies regarding suitability are explicitly tailored according to clients' categorization as retail investors, professional investors, or eligible counterparties. Unlike the general law, some jurisdictions also supplement their duties of care with detailed evidential requirements, for instance requiring firms to document their advice to clients.

[34] Breyer, S, *Regulation and its Reform* (1982) 184–8, 191–6.

[35] For a general discussion of the range of regulatory strategies available, see Campbell, n 24 above, 14–19.

[36] However, some anti-fraud provisions do not require scienter, eg, Investment Advisers Act of 1940, section 206(2); and Securities Act of 1933, section 17(a)(2) and (3).

[37] *Hanly v SEC*, 415 F.2d 589, 592 (2d Cir. 1969).

[38] Campbell, n 24 above, 15.

Rules requiring loyalty—that is, rules regulating conflicts of interest—are essential to COB regulation, due in particular to the remuneration-based risks many financial intermediaries face and the organizational structure they employ.[39] But rather than mandate conflict avoidance, COB regulation typically requires financial intermediaries to 'manage' conflicts of interest, especially by disclosing them, except in more egregious situations in which certain conflicts of interest require client consent or are banned. Given the difficulties involved in determining whether a financial intermediary exploits, or acts upon, any conflicting interests it faces, regimes typically leave the task of 'managing' conflicts to firms themselves and provide limited guidance on the meaning of conflict management. Conflict of interest rules in COB regulation thus differ significantly from general law fiduciary duties—but they may not be weaker, since they typically cannot be contractually disclaimed.[40]

Other modal regulatory strategies are registration or licensing requirements and mechanisms of public enforcement. Most COB regimes require financial intermediaries to register with regulatory bodies before they may engage in financial activities with clients, unless an exemption applies. To register, an intermediary must pass certain financial capital and competence tests. Public enforcement ensures that widespread practices may be tackled on a systematic basis by a regulator with access to an array of deterrent mechanisms, among the most powerful of which is the ability to suspend or revoke an intermediary's registration privileges. These modal strategies have no general law counterparts.

4. Complex regulatory frameworks

Many of the frameworks in which COB regulation operates are complex. The US approach involves multiple layers of rules, sources of law, and regulators. The product is a complex and often esoteric amalgam of laws.[41] For example, determining COB regulation for broker-dealers requires resort to federal and state statutes, the rules and regulations of federal and state public regulators, rules and interpretations of self-regulators, and formal and informal pronouncements of regulators.[42] Such regulation coexists with federal and state general law. Enforcement is undertaken by federal and state regulators, by self-regulators, and even by federal and state criminal prosecutors. Multiple private actions may also be under way. The framework may thus give rise to simultaneous, uncoordinated proceedings.[43]

[39] See Sections III.4 and IV.2. [40] eg, Securities Exchange Act of 1934, section 29.

[41] Langevoort, D, 'Brokers as Fiduciaries' (2010) 71 *University of Pittsburgh Law Review* 439, 443 ('Why is this area of the law [concerning broker-dealers] so confusing?').

[42] See Section III. See also DeMott and Laby, n 8 above, 412.

[43] One instance of cooperation among regulators was the 2002 $1.4 billion 'Global Settlement' among various agencies with major financial conglomerates regarding research analysts' skewed

Widely diverging approaches are adopted across securities, futures, insurance, and banking sectors—with different regulators often dedicated to particular pieces of the financial regulatory puzzle.[44]

On top of this, the US regulatory approach reflects piecemeal, incremental reform, rather than coherent, wholesale reinvention. Despite seismic changes introduced in the wake of the global financial crisis by the Dodd–Frank Wall Street Reform and Consumer Protection Act of 2010[45] (hereinafter, the Dodd–Frank Act), the US Depression-era regulatory framework remains largely intact. Reforms have typically responded to high-profile issues of the day. In the securities industry, these have included the receipt of 'soft dollar' benefits by investment advisers, the incorporation of retail brokerage into financial conglomerates, the rise of proprietary trading, and research analyst conflicts of interest.[46] Many such issues reflect competitive pressures that have developed following the end of fixed brokerage commissions in 1975.[47] This piecemeal approach seems likely to continue as regulators grapple with the proliferation of trading venues for securities and the complex order types that these venues offer, as well as the increasing use of algorithmic trading strategies by high-frequency and other trading firms.

The regimes of Member States of the EU, such as the UK, are also complex, stemming in part from the rule harmonization process and the need to accommodate the different legal traditions, regulatory styles, and underlying market practices of the Member States. The EU relies on a complex, often overlapping and occasionally underlapping, patchwork of legal instruments. Numerous directives govern COB regulation.[48] For securities, or investments, the 2004 Markets in Financial Instruments Directive[49] (hereinafter, MiFID I) was implemented by the EU Member States in 2007 to regulate the provision of investment services and activities, including investment advice, portfolio management, and trade execution, in respect of a broad range of financial instruments.[50] While MiFID I will be repealed by the recently agreed 2014 MiFID II/MiFIR regime, which will begin applying in

research reports. SEC Press Release: SEC, NY Attorney General, NASD, NASAA, NYSE and State Regulators Announce Historic Agreement to Reform Investment Practices (20 December 2002).

[44] Department of the Treasury, n 2 above, 25–61; Coffee, J and Sale, H, 'Redesigning the SEC: Does the Treasury Have a Better Idea?' (2009) 95 *Virginia Law Review* 707.

[45] Pub. L. No. 111–203, 124 Stat. 1376 (2010).

[46] See Langevoort, n 41 above, 440 (identifying several high-profile issues). [47] ibid.

[48] As to its overlap with other EU financial services directives, see Linklaters, MiFID II: Key Interactions between MiFID/MiFIR II and Other EU and US Financial Services Legislation (2012) ('[t]hese overlaps result in some cases in conflicting obligations that are impossible to comply with …').

[49] MiFID I includes Directive 2004/39/EC [2004] OJ L 145/1 (hereinafter, MiFID I or MiFID I Level 1) and detailed administrative rules under Directive 2006/73/EC [2006] OJ L 241/26 implementing Directive 2004/39/EC and Commission Regulation (EC) No 1287/2006 [2006] OJ L 241/1 (hereinafter, MiFID I Level 2).

[50] MiFID I regulates investment firms, which are legal persons whose regular business is the provision of investment services to third parties and/or the performance of investment activities on a

2017, the main pillars of COB regulation will remain largely unchanged.[51] The distribution of some insurance-based investment products that fall outside MiFID I is regulated by the Insurance Mediation Directive,[52] and is thus subject to somewhat lighter COB regulation, despite these products' functional equivalence to products falling under MiFID. MiFID I also focuses on duties, and leaves questions of liability for breaches of those duties to be determined at the national level.

Complexities also exist at the national level. The UK implemented MiFID I, as required under EU law, but has relied on Article 3 to 'opt out' with regard to some of its smaller firms.[53] Accordingly, the UK's current COB Sourcebook prescribes rules for both MiFID and non-MiFID firms and business. For non-MiFID firms and business, the UK regulator has had to determine whether to apply MiFID I requirements and definitions. Doing so would harmonize regulation and minimize opportunities for regulatory arbitrage and yet would not be as suited to local conditions as are tailored rules.[54] The UK also has had to decide whether to 'gold-plate' any of the MiFID I requirements—the practice (discouraged by MiFID I) of Member States imposing additional or stricter obligations on local markets and actors beyond the MiFID I requirements.[55] Additionally, the UK must accommodate its 2013 Retail Distribution Review reforms, which banned the payment of certain commissions, into its EU obligations.[56] Despite these challenges, which are replicated to different extents across the Member States, there seems to be increasing consistency among EU Member States, with some Member States applying MiFID I principles to firms and financial instruments outside MiFID I's scope.[57] Of course, in the UK (as in all the Member States), COB regulation also coexists with the general law.[58]

professional basis. MiFID I defines investment services and activities to include investment firms' investment advice, as well as portfolio management and order execution they perform on behalf of clients. Other activities include the reception and transmission of orders, underwriting, and the operation of multilateral trading facilities. MiFID I applies to a broad range of financial instruments, but excludes deposit-based investments and unit-linked insurance investments. See MiFID I Level 1, Article 4 and Annex I.

[51] 2014 MiFID II includes Markets in Financial Instruments Directive 2014/65/EU (hereinafter, 2014 MiFID II) ([2014] OJ L 173/349) and MiFIR includes Markets in Financial Instruments Regulation (EU) No 600/2014 (MiFIR) ([2014] OJ L173/84).

[52] Directive 2002/92/EC [2003] OJ L9/3.

[53] MiFID I includes an optional exemption in Article 3 for firms that do not hold client assets or funds and only advise on and transmit orders for certain financial instruments. This option will be retained under the MiFID II/MiFIR regime, although its availability has been narrowed.

[54] Financial Services Authority, Reforming Conduct of Business Regulation (2006), Consultation Paper 06/19, 12–16.

[55] MiFID I Level 2, Article 4. Conditions apply to Member States that seek to retain or impose COB rules additional to those governed by the Article 4 'gold-plating' ban.

[56] Financial Services Authority, A Review of Retail Distribution (2007), Discussion Paper 07/1.

[57] The UK has taken advantage of Article 3 and imposes its own regulatory regime on Article 3 firms. This regime is 'closely based on MiFID requirements'. Moloney, n 4 above, 24.

[58] See n 8 above.

III. The Distinctive US Experience

This Section describes the distinctive US experience with COB regulation in the field of securities. That experience involves a bifurcated structure adopted in the aftermath of the market collapse of 1929 and Great Depression.[59]

1. A bifurcated regulatory regime

US federal securities law requires financial intermediaries in the business of providing securities-related services,[60] including advice and recommendations, to register with the Securities and Exchange Commission (SEC), unless they are exempt from registration or otherwise not required to register.[61] There are two broad categories of registrant: investment advisers and broker-dealers. Investment advisers are those who, for compensation, are in the business of providing advice, or issuing reports or analyses, regarding securities.[62] They give advice 'for its own sake' and are compensated specifically for that advice,[63] and, importantly, are generally remunerated on the basis of funds under management.[64] They are regulated by the SEC pursuant to the Investment Advisers Act of 1940 (hereinafter, the Advisers Act).[65]

Investment advisers advise both retail and institutional clients. Among their institutional clients are collective investment schemes, or pooled investment vehicles, such as mutual funds, private equity funds, and hedge funds. Where these funds are offered to the public, they are typically regulated by the Investment Company Act of 1940. The advisers to these funds will, nevertheless, be investment advisers and thus subject to the Advisers Act.

In contrast, broker-dealers are those acting as brokers (in the business of 'effecting transactions in securities' for others[66]) or as dealers (in the business of 'buying

[59] For a discussion of market and other conditions leading to reforms, see Loss, L and Seligman, J, *Securities Regulation* (3rd edn, Vol 1, 1998) 166–272.

[60] The term 'securities' is defined in section 2(a)(1) of the Securities Act of 1933 to include notes, stocks, bonds, debentures, investment contracts, and 'any interest or instrument commonly known as a "security"'. Although the definition has produced an unsettled body of law, Cox, n 9 above, 27–8, it is broad, capturing interests in mutual funds, hedge funds, variable insurance products, and exchange traded funds, among other investment vehicles. SEC, n 10 above, 65–6.

[61] In the US, the Commodity Futures Trading Commission has regulatory authority over on-exchange traded futures and over-the-counter (OTC) derivatives (swaps). The relevant self-regulatory organization is the National Futures Association.

[62] Investment Advisers Act of 1940, section 202(a)(11).

[63] *Thomas v Metropolitan Life Insurance Co.*, 631 F.3d 1153, 1166 (2011).

[64] SEC, n 10 above, iii.

[65] The SEC focuses its regulatory attention on investment advisers managing more than $25 million or associated with a mutual fund. That limit was increased to $100 million by the Dodd–Frank Act.

[66] See n 40 above, section 3(a)(4)(A).

and selling securities' on their own behalf[67])—or as both brokers and dealers. Regulated by the Securities Exchange Act of 1934 (hereinafter, the Exchange Act), broker-dealers may give advice or make recommendations about securities (and have done so increasingly in recent decades[68]), but they primarily perform other securities-related functions, including executing client trades and providing generalized or client-specific research. They typically receive transaction-based compensation, such as commissions.[69] Broker-dealers that give advice fall outside the definition of investment adviser provided their investment advice is 'solely incidental to the conduct of [their] business as a broker or dealer' and they receive 'no special compensation' for that advice.[70] Those broker-dealers that must register as investment advisers are dual-registered. Only about 5 per cent of investment advisers are dual-registered, but that number includes nearly all of the largest retail broker-dealers.[71]

Investment advisers and broker-dealers are subject to distinct regulatory regimes. Under the Advisers Act and Exchange Act, respectively, it is generally unlawful for a person to act as an investment adviser or a broker-dealer without being registered with the SEC.[72] In addition, broker-dealers that deal with the public must register with the Financial Industry Regulatory Authority (FINRA),[73] the self-regulatory organization that in 2007 succeeded to the functions of the National Association of Securities Dealers and the regulatory arm of the New York Stock Exchange (NYSE). No industry regulator exists for investment advisers, and separate divisions of the SEC regulate each type of registrant. Accordingly, broker-dealers are subject to both SEC and FINRA regulation and enforcement,[74] while investment advisers face only SEC regulation and enforcement. State registration requirements also apply to both.[75]

Although they are subject to distinct regimes, investment advisers and broker-dealers face broadly similar regulatory strategies in most respects. Both are

67 ibid, section 3(a)(5)(A).

68 Laby, A, 'Reforming the Regulation of Broker-Dealers and Investment Advisers' (2010) 65 *The Business Lawyer* 395, 398.

69 SEC, n 10 above, 7.

70 15 U.S.C. section 80b-2(a)(11)(C).

71 SEC, Staff Study on Enhancing Investment Adviser Examinations as Required by Section 914 of the Dodd–Frank Wall Street Reform and Consumer Protection Act (2011), 37.

72 Investment Advisers Act of 1940, section 203; See n 40 above, section 15(a).

73 SEC, n 10 above, 47. Broker-dealers may also choose to become members of a national securities exchange, such as the NYSE (the rules of which FINRA enforces).

74 FINRA is regarded as 'the best first line defense against unethical or illegal securities practices' by broker-dealers. *First Jersey Securities, Inc. v Bergen*, 605 F.2d 690, 698–9 (3d Cir. 1979). FINRA writes rules and enforces them, and rivals the SEC in terms of its budget and personnel. See Irwin, S et al., 'Self-Regulation of the American Retail Securities Markets—an Oxymoron for What Is Best for Investors?' (2012) 14 *University of Pennsylvania Journal of Business Law* 1055, 1073.

75 But federal law is the primary concern. In 1996, Congress passed the National Securities Markets Improvement Act of 1996 to exempt broker-dealers and investment advisers from states' registration procedures in important contexts. See also n 65 above.

subject to anti-fraud rules.[76] Both owe duties of best execution as well as duties of loyalty, of good faith, and to use particular standards of care.[77] Nevertheless, the rules applicable to each type of registrant differ, although both are subject to section 10(b) and related Rule 10b-5 of the Exchange Act, probably the most formidable anti-fraud provisions in the SEC's regulatory arsenal.[78]

2. Divergent rules of conduct

While the primary difference between the US COB obligations of investment advisers and broker-dealers is often said to be the fiduciary status of the former, rule differences run deeper and are best considered separately with regard to the duties of loyalty and care. Much of the scholarly research has focused on these differences.[79]

Regarding duties of loyalty, investment advisers have the status of fiduciaries, pursuant to the Supreme Court's interpretation in *SEC v Capital Gains Research Bureau, Inc.*[80] of section 206 of the Advisers Act, an anti-fraud provision. According to the Supreme Court, the Advisers Act 'reflects a congressional recognition of the delicate fiduciary nature of an investment advisory relationship, as well as a congressional intent to eliminate, or at least to expose, all conflicts of interest which might incline an investment adviser—consciously or unconsciously—to render advice which was not disinterested'.[81] Broker-dealers, in contrast to investment advisers, do not enjoy the status of fiduciaries, but may be fiduciaries on an ad hoc basis, where the facts and circumstances justify it. Although the exercise of discretion over client assets may well justify fiduciary characterization,[82] judicial decisions are difficult to reconcile and no clear consensus exists as to when broker-dealers owe fiduciary duties.[83]

[76] eg, section 15(c) of the Exchange Act and section 206 of the Advisers Act.

[77] The duty of fair dealing may capture myriad other misconduct, including overcharging, engaging in high-pressure sales techniques, and 'churning'. Broker-dealers' duty of fair dealing derives from anti-fraud provisions of federal securities laws and the so-called shingle theory, under which broker-dealers, by holding themselves out to the public as broker-dealers, make an implied representation that they will deal fairly with their clients. eg, *Charles Hughes & Co. v SEC*, 139 F.2d 434 (2d Cir. 1943), *cert. denied*, 321 U.S. 786 (1944).

[78] Under Rule 10b-5, both investment advisers and broker-dealers are subject to rights of action (both public and private) for material misstatements and omissions made with scienter in connection with the purchase or sale of a security.

[79] eg, Langevoort, n 31 above; Laby, n 68 above; Prentice, n 31 above.

[80] *SEC v Capital Gains Research Bureau, Inc.*, 375 U.S. 180 (1963).

[81] ibid, 191 (internal quotations and citations omitted).

[82] Hazen, T, 'Are Existing Stock Broker Standards Sufficient? Principles, Rules, and Fiduciary Duties' (2010) *Columbia Business Law Review* 710, 737–49; and SEC, n 10 above, 54–5.

[83] Coffee, J and Sale, H, *Securities Regulation: Cases and Materials* (12th edn, 2012) 661; and Cox, n 9 above, 1031.

The duty of care required of broker-dealers is better articulated than that imposed on investment advisers. Broker-dealers are subject to a so-called 'suitability' duty: a duty initially developed some 70 years ago to 'neutralize' the incentives broker-dealers have, by virtue of their remuneration structure, to skew their advice to generate commissions.[84] Today, the main duty stems from FINRA Rule 2111—although a narrower duty also stems from the anti-fraud provisions of the Exchange Act.[85] FINRA also imposes heightened suitability rules for certain activities or products, including variable annuities, penny stocks, day trading, and complex or particularly risky securities.[86] Broker-dealers also owe a 'know-your-customer' duty in their initial dealings with a client,[87] and a duty of fair dealing.

In relevant part, FINRA Rule 2111 requires a broker-dealer to have a 'reasonable basis to believe' that its recommendation is 'suitable' for both some investors (based on having conducted a reasonable investigation) and the particular client involved (based on that client's investment profile).[88] The duty cannot be satisfied by simply disclosing the risk[89] or even by ensuring a client understood the recommendation and decided to follow it,[90] and it cannot be contractually disclaimed.[91] Instead, the issue is whether, based on the information available to the broker-dealer, the recommendation was 'suitable'. There is no requirement to document the process for each client, even though a broker-dealer has a general obligation to evidence compliance with the suitability duty.[92] A broker-dealer may satisfy its reasonable investigation obligation by relying on the client's responses, unless 'red flags' exist regarding the accuracy of the information given to the client or the client's understanding of that information.[93] Since 1996, broker-dealers have owed a suitability duty to their institutional clients, although the duty is more easily satisfied than the one owed to retail clients.[94]

[84] Wrona, J, 'The Best of Both Worlds: A Fact-based Analysis of the Legal Obligations of Investment Advisers and Broker-Dealers and a Framework for Enhanced Investor Protection' (2012) 68 *The Business Lawyer* 1, 20–1.

[85] Unlike the duty deriving from the anti-fraud provisions, the duty deriving from FINRA rules does not require proof of scienter. *In the Matter of the Application of Jack H Stein*, Exchange Act Release No 47335 (10 February 2003).

[86] SEC, n 10 above, 65–6.

[87] FINRA Manual, Rule 2090.

[88] FINRA Manual, Rule 2111. In addition to reasonable basis and customer-specific components (described above), there is also a quantitative component to the suitability duty, which may be violated where excessive trading activity is recommended.

[89] *In the Matter of the Application of Jack H Stein*, n 85 above.

[90] eg, *In the Matter of the Application of Clinton Hugh Holland*, Exchange Act Release No 36621 (21 December 1995), at 10, aff'd, 105 F.3d 665 (9th Cir. 1997).

[91] FINRA Manual, Rule 2111.02.

[92] According to FINRA, the 'extent to which a firm needs to document its suitability analysis depends on an assessment of the customer's investment profile and the complexity of the recommended security …'. See Notice 12–25 (2012) 9.

[93] FINRA Notice 12–25, May 2012, 11.

[94] A broker-dealer satisfies the customer-specific component of its suitability requirement where it has a reasonable basis to believe that the institutional client is capable of evaluating the investment

The 'know your customer' duty requires broker-dealers to document a wide range of customer information at the time of opening an account. Specifically, it requires broker-dealers to use 'reasonable diligence' in opening and maintaining every client account to know the 'essential facts' about their clients.[95]

Investment advisers also owe a duty of care stemming from their fiduciary status as well as a separate suitability duty.[96] The duties of care and suitability incorporate process-based standards of care. In particular, investment advisers' duty of care has been described as comprising an 'affirmative duty of utmost good faith, and full and fair disclosure of all material facts, as well as an affirmative obligation to employ reasonable care to avoid misleading their clients'.[97] The SEC has described the duty as requiring investment advisers to serve their clients' 'best interests'[98] and, more specifically, as requiring 'a reasonable investigation' to ensure recommendations are not based on materially inaccurate or incomplete information.[99] To satisfy the duty of suitability, investment advisers' advice must be the result of a reasonable determination, taking account of the client's financial situation and investment objectives.[100] Neither duty has been well developed by the courts or the SEC.[101]

Broker-dealers owe obligations that may straddle duties of care and loyalty. They must 'observe high standards of commercial honor and just and equitable principles of trade', under FINRA Rule 2010.[102] FINRA may invoke the rule to sanction any conduct, whether or not it is caught by a specific rule or amounts to fraud. That catch-all rule allows FINRA to regulate the 'ethics and morality' of broker-dealers; a role that FINRA's predecessor was regarded as more capable of performing than government.[103] Broker-dealers also owe an obligation of fair dealing. Derived from statutory anti-fraud provisions, the obligation arises from the 'implied representation' that, in hanging out its shingle, a broker-dealer will deal fairly with its customers.[104] Violations of the obligation are typically avoided through disclosure. Commentators

risks and the client affirmatively indicates that it is exercising independent judgement. See FINRA Manual, Rule 2111(b).

[95] Essential facts include those required to, among various objectives, effectively service the client's account and comply with relevant laws. FINRA Manual, Rule 2090.

[96] SEC, n 10 above, 27; Hazen, T, *Treatise on the Law of Securities Regulation* (2014), section 21.4 ('[T]he [SEC] has taken the position that the antifraud provisions of the Investment Advisers Act can be used to enforce a suitability requirement').

[97] *SEC v Capital Gains Research Bureau, Inc.*, 375 U.S. 180, 191–2 (1963) (internal quotations omitted).

[98] eg, Proxy Voting by Investment Advisers, Investment Advisers Act Release No 2106 (2003).

[99] Concept Release on the U.S. Proxy System, Investment Advisers Act Release No 3052 (2010), 119.

[100] SEC, n 10 above, 27–8.

[101] Wrona, n 84 above, 11, 13, and 50–2; and SEC, n 10 above, 123.

[102] FINRA Manual, Rule 2010.

[103] See Seligman, S, *The Transformation of Wall Street* (3rd edn, 2003) 185–6 (quoting William O Douglas, then Chairman of the SEC).

[104] eg, *Charles Hughes & Co. v SEC*, 139 F.2d 434, 436–7 (2d Cir. 1943), *cert. denied*, 321 U.S. 786 (1944).

question the continued viability of this obligation due to the tacit nature of the representation, but the widespread use by broker-dealers of mandatory pre-dispute arbitration clauses in customer agreements has prevented contemporary judicial reconsideration of the obligation.[105] While no explicit counterpart obligations exist for investment advisers, their fiduciary duty may well require equivalent standards of conduct.

3. Similar disclosure practices

Despite their divergent rules of conduct, investment advisers and broker-dealers adopt remarkably similar approaches to conflicts of interest. As explained, investment advisers must either eliminate or disclose material conflicts of interest[106]—and their business interests will usually dictate they take the latter approach. Broker-dealers must also disclose conflicts of interest, such as adverse facts relevant to any recommendations they make, a duty stemming from anti-fraud provisions of the federal securities laws.[107] This disclosure duty for broker-dealers applies even in the absence of any fiduciary relationship[108] and even where their recommendations are suitable.[109] Investment advisers and broker-dealers are also subject to identical requirements to 'establish, maintain and enforce' information barriers.[110]

According to the SEC, the distinction between the regimes for regulating conflicts of interest for broker-dealers and investment advisers boils down to a difference in disclosure practices. With some exceptions,[111] broker-dealers and investment advisers must disclose the conflicts of interest they face—a practice that allows investment advisers to discharge their fiduciary duties and broker-dealers to avoid violating anti-fraud provisions of the Exchange Act. Nevertheless, the extent, form,

[105] See Karmel, R, 'Is the Shingle Theory Dead?' (1995) 52 *Washington and Lee Law Review* 1271, 1284–97.

[106] SEC Release No IA-2333; File No. S7-30-04 Registration under the Advisers Act of Certain Hedge Fund Advisers, citing *SEC v Capital Gains Research Bureau, Inc.*, 375 U.S. 180, 191–4 (1963); SEC, n 10 above, iii.

[107] *In the Matter of Richmark Capital Corp.*, Exchange Act Release No 48758 (7 November 2003) (Commission opinion). Some specific rules also require disclosure of conflicts of interest, eg, Exchange Act Rules 10b-10.

[108] *Leib v Merrill Lynch Pierce Fenner & Smith*, 461 F.Supp. 951, 953 (E.D. Mich. 1978).

[109] SEC, n 10 above, 103.

[110] Investment Advisers Act, section 204A; and n 40 above, section 15(g).

[111] In certain instances, investment advisers are clearly subject to stricter requirements than broker-dealers. First, before trading as principal with a client, an investment adviser must disclose the conflict and obtain its client's consent on a trade-by-trade basis; in contrast, broker-dealers must only disclose the capacity in which they act in the transaction confirmation note. SEC, n 10 above, 119. Second, in recommending proprietary products, investment advisers must disclose the existence of their skewed incentives, whereas broker-dealers need not. *Thomas v Metropolitan Life Insurance Co.*, 631 F.3d 1153 (2011).

and timing of the required disclosures differ between broker-dealers and investment advisers,[112] with investment advisers tending to need to disclose conflicts of interest more often and in greater detail than broker-dealers.[113] Investment advisers largely satisfy their duties of disclosure at the outset of relationships, and annually thereafter, through the use of 'disclosure brochures' (on form ADV).[114] Broker-dealers' disclosures generally need not be written and are typically made during the course of client relationships and on confirmation of transactions.[115] Accordingly, the different fiduciary characterization of investment advisers results in different disclosure practices, not necessarily a stricter standard of loyalty. Given the limitations behavioural finance has shown of the effectiveness of disclosures in sanitizing conflicts of interest,[116] the differences may mean little to investors in practical terms.

4. Remuneration-based risks

Broker-dealers face acute remuneration-based risks. Commission-based remuneration poses a particularly severe risk to the quality of an intermediary's advice. It produces incentives for the intermediary to maximize its commissions and thereby potentially leads to conduct inconsistent with a client's best interests, such as the provision of skewed advice. Accordingly, even though investment advisers and broker-dealers are subject to similar disclosure obligations, broker-dealers (paid by commission) would seem more likely to engage in disloyal conduct—a prediction borne out by the many instances of fraud by rogue broker-dealers.[117] Little in broker-dealer regulation specifically combats these remuneration incentives—and no change is on the horizon.

A further remuneration-based risk concerns third-party payments, or kickbacks, to financial intermediaries advising clients regarding choices from among a range of possible products and services. Professor Howell Jackson refers to this phenomenon as the trilateral dilemma.[118] The dilemma arises because such

[112] ibid, 114. [113] SEC, n 10 above, 106.

[114] But such disclosures may not satisfy investment advisers' disclosure obligations in all cases. SEC, n 10 above, 18 and 23.

[115] ibid, 106. Self-regulatory rules also impose disclosure obligations in particular contexts, eg, FINRA Rule 5121 and NASD Rule 2711.

[116] For evidence suggesting the disclosure of conflicts of interest inadequately protects those to whom the disclosure is made and may even lead to increased bias, see Cain, D et al., 'The Dirt on Coming Clean: Perverse Effects of Disclosing Conflicts of Interest' (2005) 34 *Journal of Legal Studies* 1. However, institutional measures may render disclosure effective in dampening adviser bias. See Church, B and Kuang, X, 'Conflicts of Interest, Disclosure and (Costly) Sanctions: Experimental Evidence' (2009) 38 *Journal of Legal Studies* 505.

[117] Langevoort, n 31 above, 630 (asking why there are 'so many notorious examples of broker cheating').

[118] Jackson, H, 'The Trilateral Dilemma in Financial Regulation' in Lusardi, A (ed.), *Overcoming the Saving Slump: How to Increase the Effectiveness of Financial Education and Saving Programs* (2008) 82.

payments from third parties may skew advisers' advice, producing suboptimal outcomes for clients. However, as Professor Jackson observes, these arrangements may also represent efficient market mechanisms for financing the cost of distributing products and services. The issue has arisen in securities, banking, and insurance contexts, and it includes investment advisers' receipt of 'soft dollar' benefits in return for paying above-market commissions to broker-dealers for executing trades as well as broker-dealers' receipt of payments for directing 'order flows' to securities markets. A vast scholarly literature has resulted.[119] The US regulatory approach has been piecemeal, adopting a broad array of regulatory tools to address the dilemma where it arises. However, the modal response has been the imposition of some sort of fiduciary duty together with disclosure to affected clients.[120]

Section 28(e) of the Exchange Act regulates the receipt by investment advisers of 'soft dollar' benefits. In the absence of a safe harbour, such benefits would violate investment advisers' fiduciary duties. Introduced in 1975, section 28(e) provides a safe harbour permitting investment advisers to pay above-market commissions to receive particular benefits from the broker-dealers to which they direct client orders for execution.[121] The safe harbour applies only if investment advisers determine in good faith that commissions attributable to the benefits are reasonable in relation to those benefits, and they generally disclose those benefits to clients.[122] Though 'soft dollar' benefits represent one instance of the trilateral dilemma, their regulatory treatment reflects the type of piecemeal approach common in US COB regulation.

A further area where remuneration risks may skew advice relates to research analysts, who work for broker-dealer firms. In the wake of scandals following the late 1990s market boom, when research analysts were shown to have skewed their equity research,[123] the SEC, FINRA, and the NYSE implemented rule changes buttressing analyst 'independence'. Among other things, these regulations attempted to insulate research analysts from pressure applied by investment bankers and

[119] eg, Ferrell, A, 'A Proposal for Solving the "Payment for Order Flow" Problem' (2001) 74 *Southern California Law Review* 1027; Jackson, H and Burlingame, L, 'Kickbacks or Compensation: The Case of Yield Spread Premiums' (2007) 12 *Stanford Journal of Law, Business & Finance* 289; Johnsen, D, 'Property Rights to Investment Research: The Agency Costs of Soft Dollar Brokerage' (1994) 11 *Yale Journal on Regulation* 75.

[120] Jackson, n 118 above, 82, 100.

[121] Although expressed to apply to persons who exercise 'investment discretion' over clients' accounts, section 28(e) applies primarily to investment advisers. See SEC, 'Guidance Regarding Client Commission Practices under section 28(e) of the Securities Exchange Act of 1934' (2006), 71 *Federal Register* 41,978–42,051, 41,978 n 3.

[122] See n 40 above, section 28(e).

[123] For a survey of the empirical evidence, see Mehran, H and Stulz, R, 'The Economics of Conflicts of Interest in Financial Institutions' (2007) 85 *Journal of Financial Economics* 267.

required broker-dealer firms to make aggregate disclosures to highlight their incentives to promote trading activity.[124]

5. Regulatory oversight

A recent assessment of the regulatory oversight shows significant differences between broker-dealers and investment advisers.[125] Broker-dealers are subject to more compliance examinations and enforcement actions than investment advisers. According to the study, the number of SEC examinations of investment advisers conducted annually 'decreased 29.8 per cent, from 1,543 examinations in 2004 to 1,083 examinations in 2010'.[126] The fall has been attributed to the growth in the number of investment advisers and their assets under management.[127] The study observed that in 2010 only 9 per cent of investment advisers were examined by the SEC, while over 50 per cent of broker-dealers were examined by FINRA.[128]

IV. International Comparisons

While COB regulation does not benefit from international standard setting, the regulatory strategies employed in important jurisdictions are remarkably similar. Both the EU and Australian regimes require providers of financial services, including advisory and execution services, to be registered.[129] Standards of care, loyalty, and fair dealing must be met,[130] and duties of best execution are also owed.[131] The

[124] SEC, Regulation Analyst Certification; FINRA Manual, Rule 2711; NYSE Rule 472. Transgressions by research analysts led to enforcement action resulting in a 'Global Settlement' involving major financial institutions. See n 43 above.

[125] SEC, Enhancing Investment Adviser Examinations, n 71 above.

[126] ibid, 14.

[127] Walter, E, Statement on Study on Enhancing Investment Adviser Examinations (2011), available at <https://www.sec.gov/news/speech/2011/spch011911ebw.pdf> (last accessed 23 June 2014).

[128] SEC, Enhancing Investment Adviser Examinations, n 71 above, 14, 30–1.

[129] Under MiFID I, firms must be authorized to provide investment services. MiFID I Level 1 Directive, Article 5. For an extensive discussion, see Moloney, N, *EC Securities Regulation* (2nd edn, 2008) 410–23. Australia requires businesses (but not individuals) providing financial services—including those who provide advice about a financial product—to be licensed. Corporations Law (Cth), section 911A.

[130] As to fair dealing, see MiFID I Level 1, Article 19(1) and Corporations Act 2001 (Cth), section 912A(1)(a). Standards of care and loyalty are considered below.

[131] See MiFID I Level 1, Articles 21 and 22, and MiFID I Level 2, Article 48 and ASIC, Market Integrity Rules (Competition in Exchange Markets) (2011).

EU duties of care (and suitability in particular), fair dealing, and best execution are broadly similar to those in the US.[132]

Some important differences nevertheless exist among regimes. For instance, the EU clearly distinguishes among categories of clients and is less willing to regard disclosure as sufficient in managing conflicts of interest. The precise scope of the primary legal instruments varies between jurisdictions.[133] One further difference concerns the extent to which regimes are prepared to undertake major reforms. The US remains tied to the regulatory structure adopted in the mid-1930s and its changes have been incremental and piecemeal. The EU and Australia, in contrast, have undertaken wholesale reforms of COB regulation, perhaps reflecting the less adversarial and contested nature of the politics of financial regulatory reform in these jurisdictions.

1. Standards of conduct

(a) *Client categorization*

MiFID I adopts a threefold categorization of clients, according to their knowledge and experience. It provides them with differing levels of protection, except in the area of conflicts of interest, where all categories receive equal protection. Professional clients are those that meet certain qualitative thresholds regarding their experience, knowledge, and expertise, and that fall into any of a number of enumerated investor classes.[134] For some purposes, professional clients may be eligible counterparties. The residual category is retail clients. Investment firms must inform clients of their categorization and give each the right to request a different categorization. Importantly, eligible counterparties do not receive some protections; in particular, they are not owed duties as to suitability, appropriateness, best execution, order handling, or inducements.[135] Professional clients are owed a somewhat diluted suitability duty. In contrast, US regulation does not categorize clients in the same way, but does prevent some clients from investing in certain securities and relaxes the suitability obligation owed to institutional clients.[136]

[132] The World Bank, Comparing European and US Securities Regulations: MiFID versus Corresponding US Regulations (2010), World Bank Working Paper No 184, 22 (noting the similar duties, but observing that the EU's best execution duty places less emphasis on price than the corresponding US duty).

[133] For instance, MiFID I is both narrower and broader than COB regulation relating to investment advisers and broker-dealers. It is narrower in that it does not apply to advisers to non-discretionary accounts; it is broader in that it applies to financial instruments in addition to securities, such as swaps and futures. See DeMott and Laby, n 8 above, 412–14.

[134] MiFID I Level 1, Annex II.

[135] For discussion, see Moloney, n 129 above, 591–623; and Nelson, n 8 above, 225–53.

[136] See n 138 below and accompanying text.

(b) *Care*

Under MiFID I, the EU imposes a process-based suitability duty on investment firms providing investment advice or portfolio-management services. For retail clients, the duty requires an investment firm to obtain the information 'necessary' for it to have a 'reasonable basis for believing' that its recommendation is suitable. Suitability is defined in terms of the client's investment objectives, risk-bearing ability, and experience and knowledge that would enable it to understand the risks involved.[137] Like the equivalent US rule, the duty requires financial intermediaries to conduct investigations of their clients to establish a 'reasonable basis' for believing that the advice or recommendation is suitable for the client, given the client's characteristics. Neither rule requires that the advice or recommendation (that is, the outcome of that process) in fact be suitable.

MiFID I's suitability duty applies differentially, depending on the category of client involved. The duty set out above applies to retail clients. In the case of professional clients, investment firms may assume that two of the suitability-related factors are satisfied, namely that the clients have the financial capacity to bear the investment risks involved and have the knowledge and experience necessary to understand those risks. In contrast, the US regime dilutes broker-dealers' suitability obligation for 'institutional' clients (a category corresponding to professional clients) where firms have a 'reasonable basis to believe that the institutional [client] is capable of evaluating investment risks independently …'.[138]

MiFID I also imposes a less-protective 'appropriateness' duty for non-advised services, such as execution and transmission services.[139] No equivalent duty applies in the US. The appropriateness duty requires an assessment of the investor's knowledge and experience, but not of her financial situation or objectives. The duty does not apply for sales of 'non-complex' products.

The Australian regime, which came into force in 2013, provides an interesting counterpoint to the EU and US approaches. It imposes a heightened suitability duty, requiring that advice be both in the 'best interests' of a client and 'appropriate' for it.[140] The regime replaced an outcome-based appropriateness duty (which required financial intermediaries to ensure their advice was appropriate for clients) after a 2009 Parliamentary Joint Committee review considered the duty too weak.[141] The duties apply to the giving of personal financial product advice to retail clients. The statute does not define the 'best interests' standard,

[137] MiFID I Level 1, Article 19(4) and MiFID I Level 2, Article 35(1).

[138] FINRA Manual, Rule 2111(b).

[139] MiFID I Level 1, Article 19(5).

[140] Corporations Act 2001 (Cth), sections 961B and 961G. The duties apply to individual advisers, rather than to firms.

[141] Commonwealth of Australia, Parliamentary Joint Committee on Corporations and Financial Services: Inquiry into Financial Products and Services in Australia (2009), 87.

but does prescribe seven 'steps' that, if taken, will allow a 'provider' of advice to satisfy the duty.[142] The statute further requires that it be 'reasonable to conclude' that resulting advice is 'appropriate' to the client.[143] The Australian Securities and Investment Commission will judge 'appropriateness' from the perspective of an advice provider who has complied with the 'best interests' duty.[144] These duties may not be contractually displaced or varied.[145] No equivalent duty applies to protect institutional investors.

(c) *Loyalty*

Although the EU and Australia, like the US, impose 'fiduciary' or 'best interest' duties on advisers, the relevant duties all differ from the conflict-avoidance standard imposed under the general law's fiduciary doctrine.[146] Under MiFID I, the 'fair treatment' obligation in Article 19(1) requires an investment firm to 'act honestly, fairly and professionally in accordance with the best interests of its clients ...'; an obligation the European Commission described as 'reinforced fiduciary duties'.[147] The specific MiFID I conflict of interest provisions emphasize reasonableness and focus more on the intended effect or design of preventative measures than on their practical effectiveness. Article 13(3) of MiFID I requires investment firms to '[take] all reasonable steps', using organizational and other arrangements, 'designed to prevent conflicts of interest ... from adversely affecting the interests of its client'.[148] Despite the reference to 'prevent[ing] conflicts of interest', MiFID I makes clear the obligation is in fact to 'manage' conflicts of interest.[149] Moreover, Article 18(2) suggests that, even where organizational and other arrangements are insufficient to prevent client harm, disclosure—rather than informed client consent—will allow the financial intermediary to proceed.[150] The rules regulating conflicts of interest do not vary according to the category of client.

[142] See n 140 above, section 961B(2). ASIC, Licensing: Financial Product Advisers—Conduct and Disclosure, Regulatory Guide 175 (2013), 67–8. According to ASIC, other steps may also satisfy the best interests duty provided they 'produce at least the same standard of advice for the client' as the safe harbour. See ASIC, 65.

[143] See n 140 above, section 961G.

[144] ASIC, n 142 above, 85–6.

[145] ibid, 85.

[146] See Section II.1.

[147] European Commission, Retail Financial Services Green Paper, 12; Moloney, n 4 above, 213, n 132.

[148] MiFID I Level 1, Article 13(3); MiFID I Level 2, Recital 27.

[149] Article 18(2) refers to the Article 13(3) duty as one to 'manage' conflicts of interest, and firms are required to have in place policies that identify and then 'manage' conflicts of interest. MiFID I Level 2 Directive, Article 22.

[150] In those circumstances, MiFID I Level 1, Article 18(2) requires firm must 'clearly disclose the general nature and/or the sources of the conflicts of interest to the client before undertaking business on its behalf'. See also MiFID I Level 2, Articles 21–3. MiFID I Level 2, Article 22(4) elaborates on the Article 18(2) duty, but falls short of requiring the client's informed consent. See Moloney, n 4 above, 213–14 (suggesting limits on the extent to which disclosure and investor consent can satisfy these duties).

In its implementation of MiFID I, the UK takes an investor-protection view of MiFID I's conflict-management obligation. In its guidance, the Financial Services Authority (FSA) (the Financial Conduct Authority's predecessor) referred to the 'fair treatment' obligation in acknowledging that disclosure may be ineffective to manage some conflicts of interest.[151] Instead, the FSA explained, 'a firm should identify the actual and potential conflicts of interest, and put in place effective arrangements to mitigate those risks'.[152] Additionally, '[i]f a firm cannot manage a conflict, it must carefully consider whether it would be in the best interests of [its] client to go ahead with a transaction or service'.[153] MiFID I's conflict of interest rules fall short of a 'best interest' requirement incorporated into the Article 19(1) 'fair treatment' obligation, and yet are consistent with the US approach of allowing financial intermediaries considerable discretion in determining how to address conflicts of interest.

Australia's conflict of interest regime is noteworthy because it is stricter again than those of the US and the EU. In addition to requiring firms to 'manage' conflicts of interest,[154] the regime introduced a 'conflict priority duty' in its 2013 reforms.[155] The regime also applies beyond securities to banking and insurance activities. The conflicts priority duty requires an advice provider to prioritize the interests of her client where she 'knows, or reasonably ought to know, that the client's interests conflict with [her] own or those of a related party'.[156] Importantly, the duty cannot be discharged or excluded by either client consent or use of a contractual disclaimer.[157]

Generalized comparisons with the US are difficult. Nevertheless, MiFID I imposes a broad-based conflict-'management' obligation, while the US relies more on disclosure and, in some contexts, specific bans.[158] Both regimes fall short

[151] Financial Services Authority, Platforms and More Principles-based Regulation, Feedback Statement 08/01 (2008) 19. The FSA disagreed with the notion that disclosure could cure all conflicts of interest, referring to principle 8 that a firm must 'manage conflicts of interest fairly, both between itself and its clients and between a client and another client'.

[152] ibid, 19. [153] ibid.

[154] See n 140 above, section 912A(1)(aa) (requiring 'adequate arrangements for the management of conflicts of interest'). As to its meaning, see *ASIC v Citigroup Global Markets Australia Pty Ltd* (No 4) (2007) 160 FCR 35 [444]–[445]. cf ASIC, Licensing: Managing Conflicts of Interest, Regulatory Guide 181 (2004) and Tuch, A, 'The Paradox of Financial Services Regulation: Preserving Client Expectations of Loyalty in an Industry Rife with Conflicts of Interest' in Tjio, H (ed.), *The Regulation of Wealth Management* (2008) 53.

[155] See n 140 above, section 961J.

[156] Importantly, the 'conflict priority duty' does not attribute all information in possession of the firm to the adviser in question. According to ASIC, an individual adviser (to whom the duty applies) will be taken to know conflicts of interest disclosed by her firm in its financial services guides, but otherwise will not make inquiries as to the interests of related parties. See ASIC, n 142 above, 91.

[157] ibid.

[158] The World Bank, Comparing European and US Securities Regulations: MiFID versus Corresponding US Regulations (2010), World Bank Working Paper No 184, 21 (describing MiFID I's conflict of interest rules as 'broad and general' and those in the US as 'focused on specific situations').

of requiring financial intermediaries to avoid conflicts of interest in the absence of informed client consent and both give financial intermediaries considerable discretion in addressing conflicts of interest. Australia's regime would seem more client-protective, although its effectiveness is still to be tested.

2. Remuneration-based risks

Like the US, the EU relies on its process-based suitability duty as well as its conflict of interest rules to contain the risks of commission-based compensation. As discussed above, MiFID I's conflict of interest rules rely heavily on disclosure—a strategy that may be poorly suited to protecting trusting retail investors. According to Professor Niamh Moloney, MiFID I 'does not appear to be notably successful in addressing the most acute retail market risks concerning commissions in the sales and advice process'.[159]

The EU more successfully combats the trilateral dilemma, which arises where financial intermediaries receive third-party benefits that may skew the independence of their advice. MiFID I limits investment firms' receipt of inducements in giving advice to or exercising discretion on behalf of clients. MiFID I bans any benefits (including fees, commissions, and non-monetary benefits) in connection with the provision of investment services and activities, namely investment advice, portfolio management, and trade execution for clients.[160] MiFID I permits such benefits provided to or by a third party, provided the benefits are disclosed; are 'designed to enhance the quality of the relevant service to the client'; and do not 'impair' the firm's duty (under Article 19(1)) to act in the client's best interests.[161] The regime thus accepts the potential desirability of third-party benefits, but also imposes broad constraints. The EU once again imposes general rules where the US adopts a piecemeal, context-specific approach.

Australia's recently implemented inducement regime is more strict. It bans financial intermediaries from accepting certain types of remuneration considered to materially sway their ability to give financial product advice to retail clients.[162] The statute prohibits financial services licensees, and their representatives, from accepting 'conflicted remuneration' in providing financial product advice to a retail client.[163] The statute broadly defines 'conflicted remuneration' as any benefit, monetary or non-monetary, the nature or circumstances of which 'could reasonably be

[159] Moloney, n 4 above, 247. According to Professor Moloney, MiFID I relies in part on disclosure to manage commission risks. Moloney, n 4 above, 263.

[160] Level II Directive, Article 26 bans these other inducements by rendering them in violation of the Article 19(1) duty to act honestly, fairly, and professionally in accordance with the best interests of a client.

[161] Level II Directive, Article 26(b). With minor exceptions, the provision bans inducements (as violating the Article 19(1) fair-treatment obligation) unless these conditions are met.

[162] See n 140 above, Div 4 of Part 7.7A.

[163] ibid, sections 963E and 963A.

expected to influence' either the licensee's or the representative's financial product advice or the 'financial product recommended'.[164] It is not evident what changes these reforms have made to market practices and their desirability is also open to question. They implicitly deny the possibility that third-party benefits may improve the quality of a firm's advice or reduce its costs—heavily contested propositions.[165]

3. Enforcement and effectiveness

Generalizations about a regime's intensity of enforcement are difficult to make. Nevertheless, US broker-dealers are more robustly regulated than investment advisers. As between jurisdictions, the US maintains a level of enforcement staff exceeding that of most other countries, even taking account of market size. Private enforcement through the class-action device provides significantly greater deterrent force in the US than elsewhere,[166] although the common use of mandatory arbitration clauses by broker-dealers and investment advisers limits the force of this device. Where litigation does arise, the US pretrial discovery system provides additional deterrence. The deterrent force of COB regulation will vary from country to country within the EU due to differences in enforcement apparatus. The notion that US enforcement was more intensive than UK enforcement, in particular, prevailed in the lead-up to the global financial crisis of 2007–09, with the UK regarded as employing a 'light touch' approach. Nevertheless, since optimal deterrence is so difficult to assess in cross-country comparisons,[167] little would be gained by drawing conclusions.

V. Financial Crisis and Other Recent Developments

While reforms to promote financial stability have been the focus of post-financial crisis regulatory developments, COB regulation has also been tightened. Australia's regime incorporates post-global financial crisis reforms, although the EU and the US have yet to introduce many crisis-inspired reforms. The Dodd–Frank Act tasked regulators with studying various issues and implementing their recommendations. One is the long-standing concern (predating the financial crisis) about the distinct regulatory regimes—and different rules of conduct—for broker-dealers

[164] ibid, section 963A. [165] See nn 118 and 119 above. [166] Cox, n 9 above, 104–5.

[167] Jackson, H, 'Variation in the Intensity of Financial Regulation: Preliminary Evidence and Potential Implications' (2007) 24 *Yale Journal on Regulation* 101.

and investment advisers, based on an increasingly blurred distinction that confuses clients.[168] Tasked with assessing the desirability of imposing a fiduciary duty on broker-dealers when they provide personalized investment advice to retail clients,[169] the staff of the SEC recommended that a 'uniform fiduciary standard' be adopted for both broker-dealers and investment advisers.[170] It seems clear that the duty would lack an implied private right of action. According to the SEC, the proposed duty would oblige investment advisers and broker-dealers to 'eliminate or disclose conflicts of interest'; and further, that 'certain' (unidentified) conflicts would be prohibited.[171] The SEC has yet to implement its recommendation, but one must doubt whether the reforms will have much impact beyond intermediaries' disclosure practices, and little suggests they will combat broker-dealers' commission-based incentives. The Dodd–Frank Act also empowers the SEC to promulgate rules to prohibit or restrict compensation schemes for broker-dealers,[172] but to date nothing suggests the SEC will do so. Similarly, the SEC has indicated no willingness to prohibit or restrict the use of mandatory pre-dispute arbitration clauses by broker-dealers and investment advisers, despite having been granted such power in the Dodd–Frank Act.[173] However, the US COB regime will continue along the path of increasing complexity—the proposed fiduciary standard will 'overlap on top of the existing investment adviser and broker-dealer regimes', adding a further layer of COB regulation.[174]

As a result of another study mandated by the Dodd–Frank Act,[175] the SEC demonstrated the inferior examination and enforcement resources for investment advisers relative to broker-dealers. It predicted that the SEC 'will not have sufficient capacity in the near or long term to conduct effective examinations of registered investment advisers with adequate frequency'.[176] The SEC referred the issue to Congress, suggesting that Congress either levy fees on SEC-registered investment advisers to fund examinations, adopt self-regulatory oversight for investment advisers, or authorize FINRA to examine those investment advisers that are dual-registered as broker-dealers. Congress has yet to act.

Other financial crisis-related COB reforms provide increasing protections for institutional investors. The notion of institutional clients as able to 'fend for themselves' came under attack most dramatically with the SEC enforcement action against Goldman Sachs in 2010 for its sale to sophisticated clients of collateralized debt obligations that were 'designed to fail'. Given the moniker ABACUS 2007-AC1,

[168] As to client confusion, see SEC, n 10 above, 51, 101; and Laby, A, 'Selling Advice and Creating Expectations: Why Brokers Should Be Fiduciaries' (2012) *Washington Law Review* 707, 736–9.

[169] Dodd–Frank Act, section 913.

[170] SEC, n 10 above, 51, 101, and 103.

[171] ibid, vi–vii.

[172] See n 169 above, section 913(g).

[173] ibid, section 921. See also SEC, n 10 above, 44 and 79.

[174] SEC, n 10 above, 109.

[175] SEC, Enhancing Investment Adviser Examinations, n 71 above.

[176] ibid, 3–4.

the transaction led to losses for institutional investors of around $1 billion and produced calls, from Congress and elsewhere, for the imposition of fiduciary duties on broker-dealers, including in their dealings with institutions.[177] The enforcement action gave impetus to Congress' adoption of the Volcker Rule, which bans financial intermediaries with bank affiliates from engaging in a broad range of trading-related activities, including trading on behalf of clients, if doing so would give rise to a 'material conflict of interest'.[178] The implementing regulations provide that a conflict of interest will not be 'material' where an intermediary has disclosed it or used information barriers, unless the intermediary 'knows or should reasonably know that … [nevertheless] the conflict of interest may involve or result in a materially adverse effect on a client, customer, or counterparty'.[179] The Dodd–Frank Act also created two new categories of market participants in derivatives markets—swap dealers and major swap participants—and imposed new COB standards on them, including a 'best interests' duty when advising a state, municipality, pension plan, or endowment.[180]

The 2014 MiFID II/MiFIR regime will retain the central pillars of existing EU COB regulation, but will significantly bolster the regulation of remuneration-based risks. Investment firms will have to inform clients and potential clients 'in good time' whether their advice is 'provided on an independent basis'.[181] Where it is, the firm will be forbidden from accepting fees, commissions, or other benefits from a third party in relation to the service to clients.[182] The regime will thus require clients to pay fees for 'independent' advice and mirror recent reforms in Australia, the UK, and the Netherlands. While likely to significantly diminish the exploitation of remuneration-based conflicts of interest, the prohibition will do nothing for those clients who do not receive independent advice, such as those potentially investing in proprietary products offered by firms. Other provisions in the MiFID II/MiFIR regime will oblige investment firms to ensure they do not remunerate or evaluate staff 'in a way that conflicts with [their duties] to act in the best interests of [their] clients'.[183] Another change will require investment firms that 'manufacture financial instruments for sale to clients' to ensure those instruments are designed to meet the needs of relevant clients[184]—a provision apparently responsive to Goldman's activities in the ABACUS transaction.

The 2014 MiFID II/MiFIR regime will retain the suitability and appropriateness duties, with some additions. When providing investment advice to a retail client,

177 McKinnon, J, 'Lawmakers Target Investment Banks' *Wall Street Journal Online*, 5 May 2010. See also Tuch, n 26 above, 368–70.

178 The Dodd–Frank Act amended the Bank Holding Company Act of 1956 by introducing a new section 13.

179 See 17 CFR 255.7(b)(2)(ii).

180 See n 169 above, Title VII.

181 2014 MiFID II, Article 24(4).

182 ibid, Article 24(7).

183 ibid, Article 24(10).

184 ibid, Article 24(2).

investment firms will have to provide a statement to the client specifying the advice given and how it 'meets the preferences, objectives and other characteristics' of the client.[185] When bundling products and services together, an investment firm will need to apportion the costs of each component, inform clients whether the different components may be bought separately, and even inform clients when bundling creates risks different from those of the component parts.[186] The regime will also provide greater protection for clients trading complex products, by amending the scope of application of the appropriateness duty. While non-complex products will remain outside the rule's reach, structured undertakings for collective investment in transferable securities (UCITS) will now be regarded as complex and thus within the rule's scope.[187] Proposed changes to the client categorization regime, though seemingly minor, include imposing a standard of fair dealing on investment firms in their relationships with eligible counterparties.[188]

Regulators are also responding to pressures arising from fragmented trading markets and new technologies. In the US, trading in exchange-listed equities occurs in multiple trading venues, including 11 exchanges, more than 40 alternative trading systems, and hundreds of broker-dealers.[189] While the competition among venues may lower some trading costs, it also affords broker-dealers more options in executing trades. Because some venues pay broker-dealers for order flow (an instance of the trilateral dilemma) and clients are unable adequately to police broker-dealers' execution decisions, the potential for client harm exists. These risks to client loyalty are exacerbated by technological developments, which include the increasing use of algorithmic trading strategies. The SEC is focusing on these risks and incremental reform to COB regulation can be expected.[190] One proposal involves narrowing the exemptions high-frequency trading firms may rely on to avoid broker-dealer and FINRA registration.[191]

VI. Conclusion

COB regulation in the US is characterized by complexity, piecemeal reform, and a blunt distinction between financial intermediaries that is not adopted in comparable jurisdictions. Unlike other jurisdictions, particularly the EU and Australia,

[185] ibid, Article 25(6). [186] ibid, Article 24(11).

[187] ibid, Article 25(3), (4). [188] ibid, Article 30(1).

[189] White, n 20 above. For a description of the risks to investors arising from changes to market structure and technological developments, see Lewis, M, *Flash Boys* (2014).

[190] White, n 20 above. [191] ibid.

the US has also shown resistance to addressing remuneration-based risks, especially commission risks facing broker-dealers. Still, whether US COB regulation produces weaker deterrence than other regimes is difficult to tell. More detailed cross-jurisdictional analysis would be desirable, particularly regarding liability that arises from breaches of obligations imposed by COB regulation. It is, nevertheless, apparent that US enforcement is robust, at least for broker-dealer interactions with retail clients. While elaborate and often esoteric, the US regime may even be more tailored to subtle differences in financial intermediaries, products, and markets than other regimes. If that were so, however, it would be more the result of good fortune than of careful design.

Bibliography

Bank for International Settlements, The Joint Forum. Client Suitability in the Retail Sale of Financial Products and Services (2008).

Baxt, R, Black, A, and Hanrahan, P, *Securities and Financial Services Law* (7th edn, 2008).

Birdthistle, W and Henderson, T, 'Becoming the Fifth Branch' (2013) 99 *Cornell Law Review* 1.

Black, B, 'Brokers and Advisers—What's in a Name?' (2005) 11 *Fordham Journal of Corporate and Financial Law* 31.

Black, B, 'How to Improve Retail Investor Protection after the Dodd–Frank Wall Street Reform and Consumer Protection Act' (2010) 13 *University of Pennsylvania Journal of Business Law* 101.

Black J, 'Law and Regulation: The Case of Finance' in Braithwaite, J et al. (eds), *Regulating Law* (2004) 33.

Campbell, J, Jackson, H, Madrian, B, and Tufano, P, 'Consumer Financial Protection' (2011) 25 *Journal of Economic Perspectives* 9.

Campbell, J, Jackson, H, Madrian, B, and Tufano, P, The Regulation of Consumer Financial Products: An Introductory Essay with Four Case Studies (2010), Harvard Kennedy School Faculty Research Working Paper Series, available at <http://dash.harvard.edu/bitstream/handle/1/4450128/Madrian_TheRegulationof.pdf?sequence=1>, 7–11.

Carnell, R, Macey, J, and Miller, G, *The Law of Financial Institutions* (5th edn, 2013).

Coffee, J and Sale, H, 'Redesigning the SEC: Does the Treasury Have a Better Idea?' (2009) 95 *Virginia Law Review* 707.

Coffee, J and Sale, H, *Securities Regulation: Cases and Materials* (12th edn, 2012).

Commonwealth of Australia, Parliamentary Joint Committee on Corporations and Financial Services: Inquiry into Financial Products and Services in Australia (2009).

Cox, J, Hillman, R, and Langevoort, D, *Securities Regulation: Cases and Materials* (7th edn, 2013).

DeMott, D, 'Beyond Metaphor: An Analysis of Fiduciary Obligation' (1988) 37 *Duke Law Journal* 879.

DeMott, D and Laby, A, 'The United States of America' in Busch, D and DeMott, D (eds), *Liability of Asset Managers* (2012) 411.

Ferrell, A, 'A Proposal for Solving the "Payment for Order Flow" Problem' (2001) 74 *Southern California Law Review* 1027.

Gadinis, S, 'The SEC and the Financial Industry: Evidence from Enforcement Against Broker-Dealers' (2012) 67 *The Business Lawyer* 679.

Gray, J, 'London Money Markets: Legal and Regulatory Framework' in Blair, M et al. (eds), *Financial Markets and Exchanges Law* (2nd edn, 2012) 243.

Hazen, T, 'Are Existing Stock Broker Standards Sufficient? Principles, Rules, and Fiduciary Duties' (2010) *Columbia Business Law Review* 710.

Hudson, A, *The Law of Finance* (2nd edn, 2013).

Jackson, H, 'Regulation in a Multi-Sectored Financial Services Industry: An Exploratory Essay' (1999) 77 *Washington University Law Quarterly* 319.

Jackson, H, 'The Trilateral Dilemma in Financial Regulation' in Lusardi, AM (ed.), *Improving the Effectiveness of Financial Education and Savings* (2008).

Jackson, H and Burlingame, L, 'Kickbacks or Compensation: The Case of Yield Spread Premiums' (2007) 12 *Stanford Journal of Law, Business & Finance* 289.

Johnsen, D, 'Property Rights to Investment Research: The Agency Costs of Soft Dollar Brokerage' (1994) 11 *Yale Journal on Regulation* 75.

Karmel, R, 'Is the Shingle Theory Dead?' (1995) 52 *Washington and Lee Law Review* 1271.

Kirsch, C, *Investment Adviser Regulation: A Step-by-Step Guide to Compliance and the Law* (3rd edn, 2011).

Laby, A, 'Reforming the Regulation of Broker-Dealers and Investment Advisers' (2010) 65 *The Business Lawyer* 395.

Laby, A, 'SEC v. Capital Gains Research Bureau and the Investment Advisers Act of 1940' (2011) *Boston University Law Review* 1051.

Laby, A, 'Selling Advice and Creating Expectations: Why Brokers Should Be Fiduciaries' (2012) *Washington Law Review* 707.

Langevoort, D, 'Brokers as Fiduciaries' (2010) 71 *University of Pittsburgh Law Review* 439.

Langevoort, D, 'Selling Hope, Selling Risk: Some Lessons for Law from Behavioral Economics about Stockbrokers and Sophisticated Clients' (1996) 84 *California Law Review* 627.

Langevoort, D, 'Taming the Animal Spirits of the Stock Markets: A Behavioral Approach to Securities Regulation' (2002) 97 *Northwestern University Law Review* 135.

MacNeil, I, *An Introduction to the Law on Financial Investment* (2012).

Markham, J, 'Protecting the Institutional Investor—Jungle Predator or Shorn Lamb' (1995) 12 *Yale Journal on Regulation* 345.

Moloney, N, *EC Securities Regulation* (2nd edn, 2008).

Moloney, N, *How to Protect Investors: Lessons from the EC and the UK* (2010).

Nelson, P, *Capital Markets Law and Compliance: The Implications of MiFID* (2008).

Poser, N, 'Liability of Broker-Dealers for Unsuitable Recommendations to Institutional Investors' (2001) *Brigham Young University Law Review* 1493.

Poser, N and Fanto, J, *Broker-Dealer Law and Regulation* (4th edn, 2014).

Prentice, R, 'Whither Securities Regulation' (2002) 51 *Duke Law Journal* 1397.

Schwarcz, D, 'Beyond Disclosure: The Case for Banning Contingent Commissions' (2007) 25 *Yale Law & Policy Review* 289.

SEC, Staff Study on Enhancing Investment Adviser Examinations as Required by Section 914 of the Dodd–Frank Wall Street Reform and Consumer Protection Act (2011).

SEC, Study on Investment Advisers and Broker-Dealers, as Required by Section 913 of the Dodd–Frank Wall Street Reform and Consumer Protection Act (2011).

Smethurst, J, Heukamp, W, Goodliffe, J, and Miller, R et al., 'Conduct of Business Regulation: A Survey of the UK Regime and a Comparison with the US, German and Hong Kong Approach' in Burling, J and Lazarus, K (eds), *Research Handbook on International Insurance Law and Regulation* (2011) 355.

Tuch, A, 'Conflicted Gatekeepers: The Volcker Rule and Goldman Sachs' (2012) 7 *Virginia Law and Business Review* 365.

Tuch, A, 'Financial Conglomerates and Information Barriers' (2014) 39 *Journal of Corporation Law* 563.

Tuch, A, 'The Paradox of Financial Services Regulation: Preserving Client Expectations of Loyalty in an Industry Rife with Conflicts of Interest' in Tjio, H (ed.), *The Regulation of Wealth Management* (2008) 53.

Wrona, J, 'The Best of Both Worlds: A Fact-based Analysis of the Legal Obligations of Investment Advisers and Broker-Dealers and a Framework for Enhanced Investor Protection' (2012) 68 *The Business Lawyer* 1.

CHAPTER 19

REGULATING FINANCIAL MARKET INFRASTRUCTURES

GUIDO FERRARINI AND PAOLO SAGUATO

I. Introduction

The 2007–09 financial crisis led to large-scale reforms to the regulation of securities and derivatives markets.[1] Regulators around the world acknowledged the need for structural reforms to the financial system and to market infrastructures in particular.[2] Due to the global dimension of the crisis and the extent to which financial markets had been revealed to be closely interconnected, national regulators moved the related policy debate to the supranational level. This approach led to the international regulatory guidelines and principles adopted by the G20,[3] which were then developed by the Financial Stability Board (FSB). The new global regulatory framework which has followed has institutionalized financial market infrastructures (FMIs) as key supports for financial stability. The FSB, for example, has highlighted the importance of FMIs to the support of financial stability.

This Chapter focuses on the impact of FMIs and of their regulation on the post-crisis transformation of securities and derivatives markets. It examines, in particular, FMIs' role in the expansion of 'public' securities and derivatives markets, and the progressive shrinkage of 'private' markets (which broadly coincide with the 'unregulated' or 'less regulated' over-the-counter (OTC) markets). The first Section provides an overview of the policy approaches underlying the international crisis-era reforms to FMIs, and focuses on the

[1] From the vast array of analysis from independent think tanks and academics on the causes of the financial crisis and on possible regulatory reforms see, eg, Group of Thirty, Financial Reform: A Framework for Financial Stability (2009); Committee on Capital Markets Regulation, The Global Financial Crisis: A Plan for Regulatory Reform (2009); Acharya, V and Richardson, M, *Restoring Financial Stability: How to Repair a Failed System* (2009); and Squam Lake Working Group on Financial Regulation, Fixing the Financial System (2010).

[2] The public regulatory debate was very active and took place at both an international level (see FSF, Report of the Financial Stability Forum on Enhancing Market and Institutional Resilience (2008) and FSB, Improving Financial Stability, Report of the Financial Stability Board to the G20 Leaders (2009)) and a national level (in the US, eg, US Treasury, The Department of the Treasury Blueprint for a Modernized Financial Regulatory Structure (2008), US Treasury, Financial Regulatory Reform a New Foundation, Rebuilding Financial Supervision and Regulation (2009), and Financial Crisis Inquiry Commission, The Financial Crisis Inquiry Report (2011), and in the EU, eg, The High-Level Group on Financial Supervision in the EU, Report (2009)).

[3] The G20 is the premier forum for international economic cooperation and decision-making. It represents 19 countries (Argentina, Australia, Brazil, Canada, China, France, Germany, India, Indonesia, Italy, Japan, Korea, Mexico, Russia, Saudi Arabia, South Africa, Turkey, the UK, and the US) plus the EU. See for more details <http://www.g20.org>.

dichotomy between the 'systemic risk'[4] and 'transaction costs'[5] approaches to financial markets and FMIs regulation. The following Sections review the current shift from 'private' to 'public' markets internationally, and with respect to the EU and US regimes. Section II analyses the role of trading infrastructures as liquidity providers, in both the securities and derivatives markets. Section III shifts the focus to post-trading infrastructures—central counterparties (CCPs), central securities depositories (CSDs), and trade repositories (TRs)—and their role in supporting financial stability and market transparency. Section IV draws some brief conclusions.

1. Policy approaches to the international post-crisis reforms

The 2007–09 financial crisis, although affecting many sectors of the financial markets, had a severe impact on the derivatives markets, thereby revealing the lack of resilience in the modern financial system and the inadequacy of almost 20 years of deregulatory policies; from the end of the twentieth century, regulators—mostly in the US[6]—for the most part, charged the financial industry with policing private derivatives markets.

The exchange industry, investment intermediaries, and derivatives dealers were the main influences on the self-regulatory mechanisms deployed to police derivatives markets. However, this self-regulation mainly focused on micro-level issues,[7] in order to ensure efficient transactional mechanisms, low entry costs, and high firm profits. Systemic and other macro-level questions were often left aside. As the financial crisis clearly showed, self-regulating entities had poor incentives to address the externalities generated by these private markets on the rest of the economy. As a result, OTC derivatives markets grew exponentially, with limited public regulation and no effective supervision of the systemic risks created by highly interconnected intermediaries. This unstable equilibrium was shattered by the financial crisis, which generated a loss of confidence in the self-regulatory

[4] See Schwarcz, SL, 'Systemic Risk' (2008) 97 *Georgetown Law Journal* 193, 197.

[5] Williamson, OE, 'The Economics of Organization: The Transaction Cost Approach' (1981) 87(3) *The American Journal of Sociology* 548.

[6] See Commodity Futures Modernization Act 2000, 7 USC § 1 (2000); Kloner, D, 'The Commodity Futures Modernization Act of 2000' (2001) 29 *Securities Regulation Law Journal* 286, 293; Stout, LA, 'Derivatives and the Legal Origin of the 2008 Credit Crisis' (2011) 1 *Harvard Business Law Review* 1.

[7] See the activity of the International Swaps and Derivatives Association (ISDA) and the Financial Industry Regulatory Authority (FINRA). On the role of ISDA as a private regulator and private standard-setter body, see Saguato, P, 'Private Regulation in the Credit Default Swaps Market: The Role of ISDA in the New Regulatory Scenario of CDSs' in Cafaggi, F and Miller, GP (eds), *The Governance and Regulation of International Finance* (2013) 32 (focusing on the role played by ISDA in the aftermath of the 2007 crisis, and the dynamics of private and public regulation of financial markets).

framework and cast doubts on the ability of private industry actors and markets to assess systemic and counterparty risks. Public regulators were urged to actively engage in structural reforms, so as to re-establish the conventional hierarchy of public financial market regulation and to provide clear and precise responses to market instability.

The financial crisis did not affect the securities markets directly, although it provoked regulators—mainly in Europe—into re-evaluating the regulatory framework of securities markets. The crisis exposed policymakers to the complexity and opacity of some financial instruments and activities, and this initiated a regulatory debate over the revision of securities market regulation to foster efficiency, transparency, and resilience.

A noteworthy feature of the crisis-era policy discussion on FMIs is its international character, which was demanded by the global dimension of many financial institutions and the cross-border nature of financial transactions. Thus, international consensus was reached among governments and regulators of the leading economies on key guiding principles, which were adopted by the G20, and on more detailed guidelines, which were issued by other international organizations, such as the FSB and the International Organization of Securities Commissions (IOSCO). The role of FMIs as mechanisms for supporting financial stability was a core element of the policy debate on the reform of securities and derivatives markets.

2. 'Systemic risk' vs 'transaction costs'

From a 'public interest' perspective, the crisis-era reforms to FMIs follow two main paths: the micro-level, transaction-costs approach, which focuses on transactions and intermediaries; and the macro-level, systemic-risk approach, which focuses on market structures and other mechanisms to address systemic risk and transparency.

The first approach, which is examined in the second Section of this Chapter, has inspired the reshaping of trading infrastructures. It is directed at the promotion of trade concentration on formal trading venues and at the definition of appropriate levels of trade transparency both pre- and post-trade, and should result in a reduction of transaction costs and enhance the liquidity of securities and derivatives markets. The second approach, which is analysed in the third Section, primarily relates to the derivatives markets, which were the main source of market-based systemic instability in the recent crisis. Regulatory reforms in this segment are focused on reducing the scope and impact of systemic risk through mandatory central clearing for eligible derivatives transactions, and fostering transparency vis-à-vis regulators through mandatory reporting to central TRs.

3. 'Private' vs 'public' markets

This analysis of crisis-era financial reform to FMIs is based on consideration of the role that FMIs currently play in both 'private' and 'public' markets, and also considers how elements of 'publicity' are being injected into 'private' markets.[8]

For the purposes of this discussion, 'private' markets refer to the informal, bilateral, discretionary, and 'dark' trading of financial instruments. The informal character of 'private' markets derives from the absence of specific and formal requirements as to access to the relevant venue (or entity) and the execution of trades. Access depends on the intermediary's discretion, while trading mainly occurs in bilateral relationships, often through customized transactions. Furthermore, 'private' markets are not subject to transparency requirements, so that trades are concluded in an opaque (dark) environment. 'Private' markets are generally associated with the OTC markets and with investments firms and brokers providing trade-execution services directly to their clients.

'Public' markets, on the other hand, are generally represented by either regulated or 'alternative' venues, such as stock exchanges, futures and options exchanges, and more recently multilateral trading facilities (MTFs) and alternative trading systems (ATSs). The public character of these markets resides in their formal, non-discretionary, and multilateral structure. Access to the trading venue is subject to pre-set requirements, which limit the discretion of the venue's operator. In addition, the execution of trades occurs under the rules of the venue, through the matching of multiple parties' orders. 'Public' markets are generally transparent, at least in terms of post-trade transparency.

Mixed organizational models are also emerging—mainly as a result of the crisis-era reforms—and combine, to varying degrees, elements of both private and public markets. As discussed, the reforms have partially 'publicized' some private markets, which have become 'semi-private', as a result; OTC derivatives markets, for instance, are now subject to post-trade transparency requirements. Moreover, all derivative transactions must be reported to a TR, while eligible contracts must be centrally cleared through a CCP. Conversely, some markets have become 'semi-public' as a result of the softening of either pre- or post-trade transparency. For example, some trading venues, despite having a formal organization and multilateral structure, are subject only to post-trade transparency requirements, as is the case with respect to 'dark pools' of liquidity, which are defined by the absence of pre-trade transparency but can be constituted as an ATS, an MTF, an order-crossing system, or even a stock exchange.[9]

[8] See Ferrarini, G and Saguato, P, 'Reforming Securities and Derivatives Trading in the EU: From EMIR to MIFIR' (2013) 13(2) *Journal of Corporate Law Studies* 319.

[9] See IOSCO, Principles for Dark Liquidity. Final Report (2011), 4.

4. The role of FMIs

In the wake of the crisis, FMIs are being subjected to new regulatory requirements designed, on the one hand, to create stability buffers and, on the other, to address the weaknesses which the crisis exposed in private and public markets. FMIs are multilateral systems or networks, which provide trading, clearing, settlement, or reporting services in relation to securities and derivative transactions. They support financial markets by providing essential services, connecting counterparties, reducing transaction costs through economies of scale, managing systemic and counterparty risks, and fostering transparency.[10] An array of new rules now governs FMIs, deriving from the international guidelines set by the G20 and the FSB.[11] This Chapter focuses on their implementation in the two largest financial markets globally; ie, the EU and the US markets. It examines accordingly, with respect to the EU financial market, the European Market Infrastructure Regulation (EMIR),[12] the Market in Financial Instruments Directive and Regulation (MiFID II and MiFIR),[13] and the regulation on improving securities settlement in the EU and on CSDs (CSDR).[14] With respect to the US, it considers the 2010 Dodd–Frank Act,[15] and the role played by the Commodity Futures Trading Commission (CFTC) and Securities and Exchange Commission (SEC) in the regulation and supervision of FMIs. Among the international initiatives, it refers, in particular, to the Principles for Financial Market Infrastructures[16] and the related Disclosure Framework and Assessment Methodology,[17] both issued by the Committee on Payment and Settlement Systems (CPSS) and IOSCO in 2012.

The following two Sections analyse the regulation and role of FMIs in today's fragmented markets, considering first, securities and derivatives trading infrastructures—such as exchanges, MTFs, Organized Trading Facilities (OTFs),

[10] For a global overview of the governance of infrastructure institutions in the financial markets, see Lee, R, *Running the World's Markets—the Governance of Financial Infrastructure* (2011).

[11] See FSB, Improving Financial Regulation—Report of the Financial Stability Board to G20 Leaders (2009).

[12] See Regulation (EU) 648/2012 on OTC derivatives, central counterparties and trade repositories [2012] OJ L201/1 (hereinafter, EMIR).

[13] See Regulation (EU) 600/2014 on markets in financial instruments and amending Regulation (EU) No 648/2012 [2014] OJ L 173/84 (hereinafter, MiFIR); and Directive 2014/65/EU on markets in financial instruments and amending Directive 2002/92/EC and Directive 2011/61/EU [2014] OJ L 173/349 (hereinafter, MiFID II).

[14] See Regulation (EU) No 909/2014 on improving securities settlement in the European Union and on central securities depositories and amending Directives 98/26/EC and 2014/65/EU and Regulation (EU) No 236/2012 [2014] OJ L 257/1 (hereinafter, the CSDR).

[15] See Dodd–Frank Wall Street Reform and Consumer Protection Act, Pub. L. No. 111-203 (2010) (to be codified in many sections of the US Code of Federal Regulations (CFR)) (hereinafter, the 2010 Dodd–Frank Act).

[16] See CPSS-IOSCO, Principles for Financial Market Infrastructures (2012).

[17] See CPSS-IOSCO, Principles for Financial Market Infrastructures: Disclosure Framework and Assessment Methodology (2012).

and Swap Execution Facilities (SEFs)—and second, post-trading infrastructures—such as CCPs, CSDs, and TRs—with a special emphasis on derivatives markets.

II. Market Structure and Trading Infrastructures: Old and New Principles

1. Trading venues: Concept and organization

(a) *Definition of a trading venue*

The concept of a 'trading venue' encompasses various institutions providing a locus—generally an electronic platform—where either securities or derivatives are traded among market participants.[18] Traditionally, only exchanges offered this type of facility, essentially by providing a location for brokers to meet and execute their trades, and by publicizing the related information concerning the prices of executed transactions; ie, providing trade transparency. This saved traders the cost of independently searching for potential counterparties.[19] Another benefit of exchanges has long been the production of information as to the prices of the instruments traded.[20] However, exchanges also perform other activities, such as the listing of securities, the regulation and monitoring of issuers and broker-dealers, and market supervision.[21] Moreover, post-trade services are provided either directly by

[18] See Macey, J and O'Hara, M, 'From Markets to Venues: Securities Regulation in an Evolving World' (2005) 58 *Stanford Law Review* 563; Ferrarini, G and Moloney, N, 'Reshaping Order Execution in the EU and the Role of Interest Groups' (2012) 13 *European Business Organization Law Review* 557, 565–71.

[19] See Fischel, D, 'Organized Exchanges and the Regulation of Dual Class Common Stock' (1987) 54 *University of Chicago Law Review* 119, 121–3 (arguing that there is little fundamental difference between the economic role of a stock exchange and that of an ordinary shopping centre or flea market); Fischel, D and Grossman, S, 'Customer Protection in Futures and Securities Markets' (1984) 4 *Journal of Futures Markets* 273 (making similar statements for futures exchanges); Lee, R, *What Is an Exchange? The Automation, Management, and Regulation of Financial Markets* (1998) 8–33.

[20] See Mulherin, J, Netter, J, and Overdahl, J, 'Prices Are Property: The Organization of Financial Exchanges from a Transaction Cost Perspective' (1991) 34 *Journal of Law and Economics* 591, arguing that a financial exchange is a firm that creates a market in financial instruments; its product is accurate information as reflected in prices.

[21] See Coase, R, *The Firm, the Market and the Law* (1988) 9, arguing that 'exchanges, often used by economists as examples of a perfect market and perfect competition, are markets in which transactions are highly regulated' and suggesting that 'for anything approaching perfect competition to exist, an intricate system of rules and regulations would normally be needed'. For a defence of

exchanges or by institutions linked to them, such as clearing and settlement agents and CCPs, which facilitate the settlement of exchange transactions and make them safer.[22]

With the development of technology, other firms—usually constituted in the form of an investment intermediary—have been enabled to establish organized markets for the trading of securities.[23] Despite competing with exchanges with respect to the provision of liquidity services, these firms do not perform the listing and self-regulation activities which characterize exchanges. The facilities managed by these new entrants are typically termed ATSs in the US[24] and MTFs in Europe. The definition of an MTF under the EU regulatory regime underlines that trading occurs under non-discretionary rules among a plurality of market participants, rather than on a discretionary basis between an intermediary and its individual clients.[25] However, 'bilateral' facilities are also included in the EU definition of a trading venue, in the form of the 'systematic internalizer'; ie, 'an investment firm which, on an organized, frequent and systematic basis, deals on own account by executing client orders outside a regulated market or an MTF'.[26]

exchanges as effective self-regulators, see Mahoney, P, 'The Exchange as Regulator' (1997) 83 *Virginia Law Review* 1453.

[22] Harris, L, *Trading and Exchanges. Market Microstructure for Practitioners* (2003) 35–6.

[23] See Macey, J and O'Hara, M, 'Regulating Exchanges and Alternative Trading Systems: A Law and Economics Perspective' (1999) 28 *Journal of Legal Studies* 17.

[24] SEC, Regulation of Exchanges and Alternative Trading Systems (2000), 17 CFR §§ 202, 240, 242, and 249. The Regulation exempts most alternative trading systems from the definition of 'exchange' and, therefore, the requirement to register as an exchange, if they comply with Regulation ATS. However, any system exercising self-regulatory powers, such as regulating its members' or subscribers' conduct when engaged in activities outside of that trading system, must register as an exchange or be operated by a national securities association. This is because self-regulatory activities in the securities markets must be subject to Commission oversight under § 19 of the 1934 Securities Exchange Act. The SEC allows most alternative trading systems to choose to be regulated either as exchanges or as broker-dealers. The SEC recently adopted a new regulation (Regulation Systems Compliance and Integrity) which aims at strengthening the technology infrastructure of the US securities market; SEC, Regulation Systems Compliance and Integrity (2014), 17 CFR §§ 240, 242, and 249.

[25] Article 4 (1) (15) MiFID I defines an MTF as 'a multilateral system, operated by an investment firm or a market operator, which brings together multiple third-party buying and selling interests in financial instruments—in the system and in accordance with non-discretionary rules—in a way that results in a contract in accordance with the provisions of Title II'. See Directive 2004/39 on markets in financial instruments amending Directives 85/611/EEC and 93/6/EEC and Directive 2000/12/EC and repealing Council Directive 93/22/EEC [2004] OJ L145/1 (hereinafter, MiFID I). See also Commission Directive 2006/73/EC implementing Directive 2004/39/EC as regards organizational requirements and operating conditions for investment firms and defined terms for the purposes of that Directive [2006] OJ L/241/26.

[26] Article 4 (1) (7) MiFID I, n 25 above. For the definition of 'trading venue' as including 'a regulated market, MTF or systematic internalizer acting in its capacity as such' see Article 2 (8) Commission Regulation (EC) 1287/2006 implementing Directive 2004/39/EC as regards record-keeping obligations for investment firms, transaction reporting, market transparency, admission of financial instruments to trading, and defined terms for the purposes of that Directive [2006] OJ L241/1.

(b) *The governance of trading venues*

The governance of trading venues has evolved substantially following technological and competitive developments.[27] First, exchanges, run in the form of either a cooperative or membership association, were generally demutualized, while public exchanges—trading venues open to all interested parties and run by a third entity—were often privatized.[28] The resulting firms became public companies with diffuse shareholders or were merged into or acquired by other exchanges.[29] Second, exchanges mainly focused on the development of electronic platforms and the offer of liquidity services, becoming more similar to their competitors, such as ATSs/MTFs and internalizing firms. They correspondingly became less (or poorly) incentivized to perform self-regulatory activities, to the extent that they generated positive externalities to competing platforms, and powerful conflicts of interest were created between exchanges' regulatory and business activities.[30]

Regulators highlighted these conflicts as problematic and as sufficient to justify regulatory reform.[31] However, they also took the opportunity to expand their regulatory turf and to undertake some of the traditional rulemaking and monitoring functions of exchanges. In 2000, for example, the UK Listing Authority was transferred from the demutualized London Stock Exchange (LSE) to the Financial Services Authority (FSA), now the Financial Conduct Authority (FCA);[32] leaving the Listing Authority to a for-profit firm like the LSE, competing in the international market for trading services, would have raised concerns as to its independence and incentives to efficiently perform the relevant function.

More generally, two types of re-regulation followed the demutualization and privatization of exchanges. First, the governance of trading-venue operators generally has been regulated to reflect the governing policy view that exchanges and other trading venues run by market operators are firms offering transaction

[27] See Cybo-Ottone, A, Di Noia, C, and Murgia, M, 'Recent Developments in the Structure of Securities Markets' (2000) *Brookings-Wharton Papers on Financial Services* 223; Macey, J and O'Hara, M, 'Globalisation, Exchange Governance, and the Future of Exchanges' (1999) *Brookings-Wharton Papers on Financial Services* 1.

[28] On the choice between members' ownership/governance and investors' ownership/governance in this area see Hart, O and Moore, J, 'The Governance of Exchanges: Members' Cooperatives versus Outside Ownership' (1996) 12 *Oxford Review of Economic Policy* 53. See also Ferrarini, G, 'Stock Exchange Governance in the European Union' in Balling, M, Hennessy, E, and O'Brien, R (eds), *Corporate Governance, Financial Markets and Global Convergence* (1998).

[29] See Lee, n 10 above, 169–200.

[30] See Macey and O'Hara, n 18 above, 582, arguing that 'when exchanges engage in self-regulation they generate and enforce rules that directly affect their own commercial interests'.

[31] See IOSCO, Regulatory Issues Arising from Exchange Evolution: Consultation Report (2006), 7, arguing that 'the move by many exchanges to a for-profit business model, together with increased competition in the provision of market services in most markets, raises a number of questions about the appropriate regulatory role of exchanges. These issues run from the compatibility of for-profit operation with public interest objectives to the adequacy and efficiency of regulation.'

[32] See FSA, Review of the Listing Regime (2003).

services to intermediaries and investors in a competitive setting.[33] In both the US and the EU, the various types of trading venues (including ATSs and MTFs) are subject to rules that are increasingly similar across the sector given that these venues perform similar functions.[34] Second, the role of exchanges in the regulation and supervision of listed issuers has been reduced and replaced by public regulation and supervision, which has correspondingly widened its scope of application. This is also the result of the corporate scandals which at the beginning of this century led to extensive reforms of corporate governance and securities regulation, such as the Sarbanes–Oxley Act in the US and similar legislation in Europe.[35]

2. Regulatory responses to market fragmentation

(a) *Fragmentation of markets*

As a result of increased competition between trading venues, securities markets have tended to fragment. Indeed, it is common today for securities to trade in several venues.[36] For instance, shares of blue-chip companies are usually listed in one or more stock exchanges (say the LSE and the New York Stock Exchange (NYSE)), but are often traded also in MTFs (like BATS Chi-X Europe). Similarly, corporate bonds are often listed on a regulated market—regulated markets are trading venues subject to a level of control by a public entity—but also traded on MTFs, internalizing systems, and OTC.[37] This phenomenon has been observed in the EU since the implementation of MiFID I in 2007. Prior to MiFID I, Member States could require all trading in domestically listed stocks to be executed on a national exchange. Several Member States enacted related 'concentration rules' which, however, were abolished by MiFID I.[38] As a result, MTFs can now compete with exchanges, and

[33] See Ferrarini, n 28 above, 139 ff.

[34] See Coffee, JC Jnr and Sale, HA, *Securities Regulation* (12th edn, 2012); Moloney, N, *EU Securities and Financial Markets Regulation* (3rd edn, 2014) 425 ff. For a comparative survey, see IOSCO, Regulatory Issues Raised by Changes in Market Structure: Consultation Report (2013), noting that in most jurisdictions similar rules apply for exchange trading market systems as a 'market place'. However, considerable differences appear to remain as regards OTC trading. For instance, several jurisdictions stated that most of the trading which takes place OTC is not subject to any pre-trade transparency requirement or fair access rule.

[35] See Bainbridge, S, *Corporate Governance after the Financial Crisis* (2012) 3 ff; Belcredi, M and Ferrarini, G (eds), *Boards and Shareholders in Listed Companies* (2013) 3 ff.

[36] See Foucault, T, Pagano, M, and Röell, A, *Market Liquidity* (2013) 236 ff.

[37] See Ferrarini, G, 'Market Transparency and Best Execution: Bond Trading under MiFID' in Tison, M et al. (eds), *Perspectives in Company Law and Financial Regulation: Essays in Honour of Eddy Wymeersch* (2009) 477.

[38] Ferrarini, G, and Recine, F, 'The MiFID and Internalisation' in Ferrarini, G and Wymeersch, E (eds), *Investor Protection in Europe: Corporate Law Making, the MiFID and Beyond* (2006) 235.

new platforms have successfully emerged for the trading of blue-chip stocks, while incumbent exchanges have lost trading activity.[39]

Market fragmentation raises various concerns. First, it may lead to excessive 'price dispersion' (the same security trades at different prices at the same moment in time), which is a form of market inefficiency. Arbitrageurs can exploit the opportunities created by differences in prices, buying in one market and reselling in another at a profit, which makes prices in the two markets converge. However, arbitrage may be costly and arbitrageurs do not always monitor the relevant trades, so that price differences remain in place.[40] Second, market fragmentation raises trading costs for several reasons: (1) 'informed' investors can hide more easily by transacting in different venues, which leads traders to widen spreads for fear of transacting with counterparties possessing superior information; (2) in fragmented markets investors carry search costs in identifying the best price; and (3) in addition, they cannot take advantage of the liquidity externalities of centralized markets.[41]

(b) *International principles*

A recent IOSCO Consultation document analysing changes in market structure and their policy implications argued: 'Securities regulators bear the responsibility for striking an appropriate balance between a market structure that promotes competition among markets, and one that minimizes the potentially adverse effects of fragmentation on market integrity and efficiency, price formation, and best execution of investor orders.'[42] The same document formulates a number of recommendations to promote market liquidity and efficiency, price transparency, and execution quality in a fragmented environment.[43] First, regulators should monitor the impact of fragmentation on market integrity and efficiency across different trading spaces, and seek to ensure that the applicable regulatory requirements are still appropriate. Second, they should ensure that proper arrangements are in place in order to facilitate the consolidation and dissemination of information as close to real time as technically possible and reasonable. Third, regulators should consider the potential impact of fragmentation on the ability of intermediaries to comply with applicable order-handling rules, including best-execution obligations.

[39] See Foucault et al., n 36 above, 237, arguing that as of February 2012 Euronext retained only 60.5 per cent of the trading activity in the CAC40 stocks and the LSE retained only 54.77 per cent of trading activity in the FTSE 100 stocks. See also Ferrarini, G, 'Best Execution and Competition between Trading Venues—MiFID's Likely Impact' (2007) 2 *Capital Markets Law Journal* 404.

[40] See Foucault et al., n 36 above, 238.

[41] See ibid, 238–9, noting that fragmentation also brings benefits, such as competition among trading venues which lowers fees and fosters innovation, while different trading functionalities better serve the interests of investors. See also IOSCO, Transparency and Market Fragmentation Report (2001).

[42] See IOSCO, Regulatory Issues, n 31 above, 17.

[43] See ibid, 18–23.

Fourth, they should regularly monitor the impact of fragmentation on liquidity across trading spaces and ensure that applicable regulatory requirements provide for fair and reasonable access to significant sources of market liquidity on the trading market systems. Fifth, they should monitor for novel forms or variations of market abuse that may arise as a result of technological developments.[44]

3. Current trends in the EU

(a) *The regulation of securities markets*

The application of MiFID I[45] to the EU's equity trading markets in November 2007 heralded a new era for the EU's financial markets.[46] MiFID's securities trading rules were designed to reshape the EU trading market. The abolition of national 'concentration rules', in particular, while contributing to the fragmentation of securities markets (see the preceding paragraph), enhanced competition between trading venues in the EU, harnessing industry innovation and technological advances. MiFID I subsequently went through a review procedure which resulted in the enactment of two pieces of legislation. The first is a Regulation (MiFIR) imposing common rules that apply directly in all EU Member States and which is mainly focused on the mandatory trading of derivatives, disclosure of trade transparency data, and non-discriminatory access to clearing facilities and trading venues. The second is a new Directive (MiFID II), which modifies MiFID mainly with respect to investment services trading rules and internal and external governance requirements for investment firms and trading venues.[47]

In proposing the new texts, the Commission suggested that MiFID I had led to more competition, wider investor choice, a decrease in transaction costs, and deeper integration. It also suggested that the financial crisis experience had 'largely vindicated' MiFID I's design. However, the Commission highlighted four difficulties. The benefits of competition were not flowing efficiently to all market participants and were not always passed on to end users, while market fragmentation had made the trading environment more complex and opaque. MiFID I's classification of trading venues had been outpaced by innovation. The financial crisis had exposed weaknesses in the regulation of non-equity instruments. Finally, rapid innovation and increasing market complexity called for higher levels of investor protection and for a safer, sounder, more transparent and more responsible financial system.

[44] On similar issues, see IOSCO, Technological Challenges to Effective Market Surveillance and Regulatory Tools: Consultation Report (2012), considering the challenges posed by increased speed of trading and difficulties in gathering the increased volume of trading data.

[45] See MiFID I, n 25 above.

[46] See Ferrarini and Moloney, n 18 above.

[47] ibid, 560.

In support of this objective, and at the core of the related MiFID Review, was the concern to extend the EU's regulatory perimeter around trading venues to encompass a wider range of venues, and to apply the same set of rules to this wider set of venues. The regulatory reforms now require firms to trade securities on organized venues, such as regulated markets (RMs) and MTFs. The most radical innovation involving the non-equity assets market—derivatives and bonds—is the introduction of the new OTF regime, which is designed to capture all non-regulated market and MTF trading on organized venues, such as broker-crossing systems and new systems for the trading of clearing-eligible and sufficiently liquid derivatives. The same set of equity transparency rules (pre- and post-trade) will apply to RMs and to operators of MTFs and OTFs.

MiFIR also includes a set of rules on transparency for non-equity instruments, based on the premise that the financial crisis exposed weaknesses in the way information on trading opportunities and prices in financial instruments other than shares is available to market participants. The new rules also introduce a transparency regime in markets for bonds and structured financial products, in order to help the valuation of the same and the efficiency of price discovery.[48]

(b) *The regulation of derivatives markets: EMIR and MiFIR*

Mandatory trading of eligible derivatives on either exchanges or electronic platforms is one of the four pillars of the international OTC derivatives market-reform agenda—the others being standardization, central clearing, and reporting. Whereas the central clearing and trade-reporting reforms primarily aim to reduce systemic risk—by respectively managing financial market exposure and increasing the transparency of OTC derivatives vis-à-vis regulators—exchange trading and trading via electronic platforms primarily aim to increase the efficiency of derivatives markets, while contributing to financial stability.

MiFIR includes an obligation to trade certain derivatives on regulated markets, MTFs, or OTFs, reflecting the agreement reached at the G20 Pittsburgh Summit on 25 September 2009 to move trading on standardized OTC derivatives, which are not intra-group transactions, to exchange or electronic trading venues where appropriate.[49] This agreement provides that a formal regulatory procedure should be defined for mandating trading between financial counterparties and large non-financial counterparties in all derivatives that are clearing-eligible and sufficiently liquid to be traded on a trading venue. The agreement requires the movement of trading on standardized OTC derivatives to either exchanges or electronic platforms where appropriate—a suitable range of eligible venues should be provided, given

[48] See Ferrarini and Saguato, n 8 above, 345 ff.

[49] See the G20, Leaders Statement: The Pittsburgh Summit, available at <http://www.g20.utoronto.ca/2009/2009communique0925.html#system>, para 13.

the lower liquidity of various OTC derivatives.[50] Moving derivatives to trading venues will increase post-trade transparency, given that Article 10 of MiFIR requires market operators and investment firms operating trading venues to make public the price, volume, and time of the transactions executed in respect of derivatives.[51]

4. Current trends in the US: The 2010 Dodd–Frank Act and its implementing regulations

The repatriation of derivative trading on to trading venues is also a feature of the US reforms. Section 732(a)(8) and section 764 of the Dodd–Frank Act require counterparties to execute all swaps, which are subject to the mandatory clearing requirement, on a regulated exchange or on a trading platform. Each trading eligible derivative has to be executed on a registered trading venue, approved by the competent regulator (the CFTC for swaps and the SEC for securities-based swaps), unless no trading venue is able to or has accepted the contract for trading.

More precisely, eligible swaps—ie, non-security-based swaps—must be traded on a 'board of trade'[52] which includes two types of trading venues registered with the CFTC: the Designated Contract Market (DCM)—traditional exchanges trading futures and options—and the newly introduced SEF,[53] which includes smaller electronic swap facilities. Similarly, security-based swaps must be traded on a securities exchange or on the new Security-Based Swap Execution Facility (SBSEF), which broadly covers a regulated multilateral trading system or platform.[54]

SEFs and SBSEFs are also subject to specific regulations and administrative responsibilities. SEFs must ensure the effectiveness of the market by preventing trading abuses, price distortion, and manipulation, by guaranteeing an impartial and fair access to the trading facility by providing and publishing timely data on prices and trading volume, and—from an accountability perspective—by having a stable compliance structure and providing emergency rules for liquidation or transfer of trading positions of defaulting participants.[55]

[50] See MiFIR, n 13 above, recitals 25–8. MiFIR assigns wide regulatory powers to the European Securities and Markets Authority (ESMA)—ESMA is the European financial regulatory institution—which would be asked to develop draft implementing technical standards, ie 'administrative rules', to determine which classes of derivatives (subject to clearing obligations) should be traded on RMs, MTS, OTFs, or third-country trading venues.

[51] See Ferrarini and Saguato, n 8 above, also for a comparison with EMIR's reporting obligations.

[52] See Commodity Exchange Act (CEA), §1a(27), 7 USC §1a(27), which defines 'board of trade' as 'any organized exchange or other trading facility'.

[53] See Dodd–Frank Act, n 15 above, § 733; new §5h CEA, n 52 above.

[54] See Dodd–Frank Act, n 15 above, § 763.

[55] See CFTC, Core Principles and Other Requirements for Swap Execution Facilities; § 17 CFR Part 37 and 38. See SEC, Proposal for Registration and Regulation of Security-based Swap Execution Facilities (2011), available at <http://www.sec.gov/rules/proposed/2011/34-63825.pdf>.

III. Post-Trading Infrastructures: A New International Framework

1. Post-trading infrastructures as stability and transparency providers

(a) *Systemic impact of post-trading infrastructures*

As analysed in Section II, trading infrastructures operate in the bid-and-offer world, matching opposite positions. They contribute to the efficiency of financial market transactions and to the liquidity of markets, by executing orders in an orderly manner and providing pre- and post-trade information. Trading venues act at a transactional level by offering services to buyers and sellers interested in concluding deals. Post-trading infrastructures, conversely, supply clearing, settlement, and reporting services to the trading markets, and perform a systemic function by operating as risk-management and -oversight mechanisms. In a sense, post-trading infrastructures are not only counterparties to financial institutions and investors, but also respond to the public interest as guardians of financial markets: they contribute to financial stability by providing network services and facilitating connections among market participants.

This Section examines three levels of post-trade services—clearing, settlement, and reporting—and the three infrastructures that provide such services: CCPs, CSDs, and TRs. Each post-trading service is aimed at reducing or more generally managing a separate aspect of systemic risk. A CCP interposes between counterparties becoming the 'seller to every buyer and the buyer to every seller'.[56] By netting the opposite positions of its members, a CCP mitigates the overall counterparty credit risk, creates more effective mechanisms to assess potential default risk of its members, and ultimately contributes to the reduction of systemic risk.[57] A CSD traditionally operates in the settlement phase of cash transactions, by holding

[56] CPSS-IOSCO, Recommendations for Central Counterparties (2004), 1.

[57] For a pre-crisis analysis of derivatives clearing houses, see Dale, R, 'Derivatives Clearing Houses: The Regulatory Challenge' in Ferrarini, G (ed.), *European Securities Markets: The Investment Services Directive and Beyond* (1998) 295. The post-crisis academic debate on CCPs addresses, in particular, the effectiveness of CCPs as mitigators of systemic risk. See, among others, Pirrong, C, The Economics of Clearing in Derivatives Markets: Netting, Asymmetric Information, and the Sharing of Default Risk through a Central Counterparty (2009), University of Houston Working Paper, available at <http://ssrn.com/abstract=1340660>; Pirrong, C, 'The Clearinghouse Cure' (2008) *Regulation* 44; Yadav, Y, 'The Problematic Case of Clearinghouses in Complex Markets' (2013) 101 *Georgetown Law Journal* 387; Squire, R, 'Clearinghouses as Liquidity Partitioning' (2014) 99 *Cornell Law Review* 857, available at <http://ssrn.com/abstract=2185064>; Roe, MJ, 'Clearinghouse Overconfidence' (2013) 101 *California Law Review* 1641.

the securities of listed entities—either in certificate form or dematerialized—and managing the transfer of the same from the seller to the buyer; a new and growing function of CSDs relates to the management and transfer of collateral in derivatives trades. In addition, a CSD plays an important role in containing the operational risk of securities markets (CSDs are not active directly in the derivatives market). Finally, TRs, whose role as FMIs has been officially acknowledged by post-crisis regulation, make the relevant market more transparent, providing regulators with information on relevant transactions, and market participants with aggregated data on concluded deals.

(b) *The international regulation of post-trading infrastructures: A global governance perspective*

Systemic counterparty risk and the opacity of derivatives markets were the key triggers of the crisis-era reforms to post-trading. The G20 and the FSB, by requiring all derivatives transactions to be reported to TRs, and all standardized and eligible derivatives to be cleared via CCPs, emphasized the role of the related FMIs as providers of stability and efficiency to the financial system.[58] In particular, policymakers stressed the importance of public regulation in modelling prudential and corporate governance standards for FMIs, given the 'public' nature of their services.

While a broad definition of the role, structure and governance of CCPs and TRs is included in the FSB's key policy document 'Implementing OTC Derivatives Market Reforms',[59] more detailed policy recommendations were jointly drafted by the CPSS and IOSCO in their 'Principles for financial market infrastructures'.[60] These international guidelines apply solely to post-trading infrastructures, and do not cover trading venues.

These documents formulate a number of recommendations aimed at achieving safety and efficiency in the financial markets by containing and reducing systemic risk. In this direction, the CPSS-IOSCO principles recognize the systemic importance of FMIs and the two essential public policy objectives they support: safety and financial stability, and market efficiency. The 26 principles regulators should follow to build the regulatory infrastructure for FMIs can be grouped into four main categories. First, regulators should consider the general organizational structure of the FMI, its legal basis, the governance arrangements (ie, ownership structure, governance policies—composition and responsibilities of the board of directors—internal controls and audit),[61] and the risk-management framework (ie, risk-management policies, procedures, and systems).[62] Second, and addressing in

[58] See FSB, n 11 above. [59] ibid, 1.

[60] See CPSS-IOSCO, n 16 above.

[61] See ibid, 21–35, 101–15. [62] ibid, 88–94.

more detail the risk-management framework, regulators should ensure that FMIs have in place effective credit risk and liquidity risk-management mechanisms (ie, collateral and margin) aimed at mitigating and managing counterparty credit risk, limiting procyclicality in collateral and margin arrangements, and maintaining sufficient liquid resources. Third, regulators should ensure that the FMI establishes default management strategies that guarantee orderly activities of the FMI even in case of participants' default or insolvency (ie, default funds, waterfall plans, segregation, and portability arrangements).[63] Fourth, regulators should impose transparency requirements on FMIs, which ensure that market participants and authorities are informed on both the internal structure, rules and procedures of the FMIs, and market data.[64] The following subsections analyse the crisis-era regulatory reforms in the post-trading area, and both the EU and US reforms—as it is going to emerge—conform with the CPSS-IOSCO principles for FMIs.

2. Current trends in the EU's regulation of post-trading FMIs: EMIR and the Regulation on CSDs

The EU responded to the crisis with a package of regulatory measures aimed at rebuilding confidence in the financial markets and creating a sounder financial system, and which included post-trading reforms. The reforms targeted four main objectives: increasing transparency, managing counterparty credit risk, reducing systemic risk, and fostering operational efficiency. Each of these tasks has been assigned to a specific type of FMI, subject to governance and prudential regulation. The following subsections evaluate the role and governance of CCPs, TRs, and CSDs in the EU context.

(a) *The regulation of CCPs and TRs*

EMIR and its detailed administrative rules, despite being mainly focused on OTC derivatives, are the primary sources for the EU's regulation of CCPs and TRs in general. The vulnerability of the OTC markets to systemic shocks was accordingly the trigger for a wider reshaping of EU FMIs,[65] and at a macro level, TRs and CCPs are now the infrastructure tasked with providing systemic stability and transparency.

[63] ibid, 78–82. [64] ibid, 121–5.

[65] The crisis-era regulatory reforms mainly focused on the OTC derivatives markets because of their role in the financial crisis as accelerators of contagion and as incubators of uncontrolled risk exposures. The pre-crisis market was characterized by self-regulation. The new international guidelines on OTC regulation now provide a common and harmonized framework, based on four pillars:

(1) OTC derivatives standardization;
(2) trading on exchanges and electronic platforms;
(3) central clearing systems; and
(4) mandatory trade reporting.

Clearing activity, due to its unique role in mitigating and reducing counterparty credit risk, is subject to extensive regulation. Title III of EMIR contains the relevant rules. CCPs must be either authorized by the competent authority of the Member State; ie, the relevant national regulator, where they intend to provide clearing services,[66] or recognized—if already existing and operating in a third country—by the EU's new regulator for securities markets, the European Securities and Markets Authority (ESMA).[67] They are, for example, required to have a solid capital base—with a minimum permanent and available capital of 7.5 million euro—which must be always proportionate to the risk deriving from clearing activities.[68] In this regard, ESMA has adopted fixed calculation mechanisms to evaluate capital adequacy with regard to specific forms of risk. In addition, a CCP must always be adequately capitalized against credit risks, counterparty risks, market risks, operational risks, and legal and business risks. Furthermore, it must hold enough financial resources to ensure an effective restructuring procedure, where required, and must be subject to periodic stress-testing, back-testing, and sensitivity analysis, to ensure its financial stability and reliability.[69]

EMIR and its administrative rules also impose many detailed requirements on CCP corporate governance, aimed at increasing transparency, avoiding conflicts of interest, and ensuring accountability.[70] A CCP's ownership structure, for example, must be transparent and every change in qualifying ownership holdings must be reported to ESMA.[71] Strict conflict of interest requirements must be complied with, and sound remuneration policies must be adopted.[72] Due to the

[66] For the authorization process, see EMIR, n 12 above, Articles 14, 17, 18, 19, and 20. The European Association of CCP Clearing Houses (EACH), representing the CCPs operating in Europe, has 20 members, among which CME Clearing Europe (the UK), EuroCCP (the Netherlands, the UK, and Sweden), Eurex Clearing AG (Germany), ICE Clear Europe (the UK), LCH.Clearnet Ltd (the UK), LCH.Clearnet SA (France); data available at <http://www.eachccp.eu/> (last accessed 23 March 2015).

[67] On recognition as a third-country CCP, see EMIR, ibid, Article 25. ESMA had received—as of 23 March 2015—41 applications for recognition as third-country CCP under Article 25 of EMIR. Among the applicants to operate in the EU are: the Chicago Mercantile Exchange (the US), ICE Clear Credit and ICE Clear US (the US), LCH.Clearnet (the US), Hong Kong Securities Clearing Company and OTC Clearing Hong Kong (Hong Kong), Japan Commodity Clearing House, Japan Securities Clearing Corporation and Tokyo Financial Exchange (Japan), Singapore Exchange Derivatives Clearing and the Central Depository (Pte) (Singapore), SIX x-clear (Switzerland); data available at <http://www.esma.europa.eu/system/files/list_of_applicants_tc-ccps.pdf> (last accessed 23 March 2015).

[68] Article 16, EMIR, n 12 above.

[69] See Commission Delegated Regulation (EU) 152/2013 on supplementing Regulation (EU) No 648/2012 of the European Parliament and of the Council with regard to regulatory technical standards on capital requirements for central counterparties [2013] OJ L52/37.

[70] EMIR, n 12 above, Title IV, and Commission Delegated Regulation (EU) 152/2013 on supplementing Regulation (EU) No 648/2012 regard to regulatory technical standards on requirements for central counterparties [2013] OJ L52/41 (hereinafter Del Reg CCP).

[71] EMIR, n 12 above, Articles 30–1; and Del Reg CCP, n 70 above, Article 10.

[72] EMIR, n 12 above, Article 33.

importance of supervising and managing CCPs' risks, each CCP must adopt sound risk-management practices and internal control mechanisms.[73] In addition, a risk committee must operate in every CCP. Within this committee, independent directors sit together with clearing members and client representatives to ensure higher expertise and efficiency. The risk committee is asked to advise the board on any arrangements that may impact the risk management of the CCP.[74]

To ensure the financial stability of CCPs and protect them from the risks of their counterparties' exposures, specific prudential requirements are imposed, which mandate CCPs to call and collect from their members initial and variation margins covering the exposures resulting from market movements and potential defaults.[75] CCPs are also entitled, when necessary, to determine prudent 'haircuts' of the collateral value and consequently to ask for additional guarantees, such as variation margins.[76]

Finally, to ensure the financial robustness of CCPs, CCP members must provide financial resources in the form of capital, default funds, and collateral for cleared transactions, although members' liability is limited with respect to CCPs' obligations. These mechanisms and financial requirements are designed to mutualize the risk of counterparty default among clearing members, thus avoiding the risk of a systemic collapse.[77] The total amount of 'prudential resources' available is designed to enable the CCP to withstand the default of at least two clearing members to which it has the largest exposure.[78] In the event of a clearing member's default, the CCP must follow the so-called 'default waterfall' procedure to cover its exposure. First, the CCP must look to the margins posted by the defaulting member to cover its outstanding positions. Second, if these margins are not sufficient, it must look to the default fund contributions of the defaulting member and, third, at the contributions to the default fund of the non-defaulting members. The CCP can also require non-defaulting clearing members to provide additional funds to ensure the CCP's business continuity. The CCP can never use margins posted by non-defaulting members to cover

[73] Del Reg CCP, n 70 above, Article 4.

[74] EMIR, n 12 above, Article 28.

[75] A 'margin' is the financial guarantee a party provides to its counterparty as a security against losses deriving from an underlying transaction. Collateral generally refers to any property or assets (ie, securities or cash) pledge as a guarantee for an open exposure, or more broadly is the asset used as a margin. Finally, a 'haircut' is the percentage by which the market value of a security or more generally of an asset used as collateral is reduced to reflect the degree of risk—ie, legal risk, market risk, and liquidity risk—underlying it. See Reuters, *Financial Glossary*, available at <http://glossary.reuters.com/index.php?title=Main_Page>.

[76] Del Reg CCP, n 70 above, Articles 17–31.

[77] See Roe, n 57 above, 1676 ff, taking a more sceptical position on the role of risk mutualization mechanisms as effective strategies to reduce systemic risk.

[78] EMIR, n 12 above, Article 43.

losses of another member. Margins are managed in segregated accounts distinct from the CCP's assets.

Moving to TRs, they are data warehouses,[79] which centrally collect and maintain information and records of all derivatives transactions concluded on trading venues or OTC.[80] TRs accordingly provide a 'transparency' service to regulators, by making all data and information reported accessible to ESMA, national supervisory authorities, the European central banks and the European Central Bank (ECB), and the European Systemic Risk Board (ESRB). In addition, TRs periodically publish aggregate data on concluded transactions and make such information available to the public.[81] Despite their crucial role in providing transparency to the market, TRs are subject to lighter regulation than are CCPs, as they pose lower risks to the financial system.

TR regulation is concentrated in three main and related areas: authorization and recognition, governance, and continuity.[82] A TR must be either authorized or recognized by ESMA,[83] provided that the structure of the TR's internal controls and the independence of its governing bodies ensure the independence and effectiveness of its services. In terms of governance, TRs are subject to strict disclosure rules concerning their ownership structure,[84] and are required to have adequate internal control systems, and efficient administrative mechanisms to detect potential conflict of interests related to management and employees. Furthermore, TRs must guarantee the continuity and orderly functioning of their activities and services. TRs are also

[79] EMIR, n 12 above, Article 9 imposes a reporting obligation to a registered TR—within a working day form the conclusion, modification, or termination of a derivative—on all counterparties and CCPs that conclude a derivative contract.

[80] With regard to the content of the TR reports, see Commission Implementing Regulation (EU) 1247/2012 laying down implementing technical standards with regard to the format and frequency of trade reports to trade repositories according to Regulation (EU) No 648/2012 on OTC derivatives, central counterparties and trade repositories [2012] OJ L352/20. For securities markets, by contrast, post-trade transparency is supported by the pre- and/or post-trade transparency requirements imposed by trading venues and governed by MiFID II/MiFIR.

[81] EMIR, n 12 above, Article 81.

[82] See Commission Delegated Regulation (EU) 150/2013 supplementing Regulation (EU) No 648/2012 on OTC derivatives, central counterparties and trade repositories with regard to regulatory technical standards specifying the details of the application for registration as a trade repository [2013] OJ L52/25 (hereinafter, sup Reg TR).

[83] The latest official data from ESMA shows that, as of January 2015, six TRs have been registered with ESMA: DTCC Derivatives Repository Ltd (DDRL) (reporting services for all asset classes), Krajowy Depozyt Papierów Wartosciowych SA (KDPW) (reporting services for all asset classes), Regis-TR SA (reporting services for all asset classes), UnaVista Limited (reporting services for all asset classes), CME Trade Repository Ltd (CME TR) (reporting services for all asset classes), ICE Trade Vault Europe Ltd (ICE TVEL) (reporting services for commodities, credit, equities, interest rates instruments); data available at <http://www.esma.europa.eu/page/Registered-Trade-Repositories> (last accessed 23 March 2015).

[84] A TR, in order to be registered with ESMA, must disclose its ownership structure, by disclosing all holdings equal or higher than 5 per cent of its capital or voting rights or any holding which provides the power to exercise a significant influence on the TR. See sup Reg TR, n 82 above, Article 3.

required to provide ESMA with detailed descriptions of the financial resources available for the performance of their activities and for the management of operational risk.[85] TRs must 'establish, implement, and maintain' a 'business continuity policy' and a 'disaster recovery plan' aimed to ensure the smooth continuity of their services and to ease their resolution in the event of financial distress or failure.[86] The main concerns in regulating TRs, therefore, are transparency and continuity in the processing and publication of the stream of information concerning derivative markets.

(b) *The regulation of CSDs*

The regulation on securities settlement and CSDs (CSDR) completes the framework of post-crisis reforms to FMIs in the EU.[87] Like CCPs, CSDs play an important role in securities transactions and are expanding their business activities to cover the settlement of collateral in the newly reconfigured derivatives markets. CSDs operate in the post-trading phase, enabling either the transfer of securities against cash flows or the transfer of collateral against an open exposure. Settlement and clearing are the crucial post-trading activities directed at supporting the stability and clarity of securities transactions.

The regulation focuses on two issues: the efficiency and safety of settlement mechanisms, and the regulation of CSDs. To provide more efficient and safe settlement, the regulation promotes the dematerialization of securities and requires the harmonization of settlement periods and settlement mechanisms across the EU.[88] With respect to the structure of CSDs, the CSDR provides a common regulatory framework for CSDs, in order to more effectively address the cross-border nature of financial markets and the systemic nature of CSDs. Because of their systemic and essential role in securities markets, and potentially in managing collateral for derivatives trades, CSDs must comply with prudential standards that should ensure the stability and continuity of their activities. Like CCPs and TRs, CSDs are subject to prudential regulation and capital requirements, transparent governance rules, and disclosure obligations for both relevant ownership holdings and with respect to potential conflicts of interests.[89]

3. Current trends in the US: The 2010 Dodd–Frank Act and its implementing regulations

As shown in the previous paragraph, the EU is re-regulating post-trade FMIs in order to attain a higher level of harmonization, reduce the risk of cross-Member-State barriers to market transactions, mitigate systemic risk,

[85] See sup Reg TR, n 82 above, Articles 6, 7, 13.
[86] EMIR, n 12 above, Articles 78–9.
[87] CSDR, n 14 above.
[88] ibid, Articles 5–7.
[89] ibid, Title III.

and ensure the stability of EU financial markets. The US pre-crisis regulation of post-trade FMIs was characterized by industry self-regulation; public regulatory agencies exercised, however, authorization and supervisory powers. The Dodd–Frank Act introduced great changes in this respect, especially with regard to derivatives, pushing the market toward higher levels of transparency and institutionalizing the role of FMIs as stability mechanisms. However, the US approach differs from the EU approach: EMIR (and MiFIR) specifically address the regulation of FMIs, while the Dodd–Frank Act tackles the financial industry in general, focusing on financial institutions and on providing a new architecture for the OTC derivatives markets.

(a) *The regulation of CCPs and CSDs*

In the US, both the CFTC and the SEC are involved in the regulation and supervision of financial markets. This dual organizational structure has conditioned and shaped the Dodd–Frank Act's approach to derivatives markets. The CFTC has been asked to reorganize the 'swap' markets, by setting up a new regime for regulating derivatives CCPs and TRs, but the regime for 'security-based swaps' falls under the authority of the SEC.[90]

CCPs operating in the derivative markets are now subject to strict rules concerning their financial stability, internal and external accountability, and clearing organization transparency.[91] CCPs must be registered as derivatives clearing organizations (DCOs) with the CFTC in order to clear futures and swaps;[92] or as clearing agencies (CAs) with the SEC—if they intend to clear security-based swaps.[93] Non-US CCPs may be considered eligible to operate as clearing organizations in

[90] The 2010 Dodd–Frank Act distinguishes between 'swaps' and 'securities-based swaps', see Dodd–Frank Act, n 15 above, §721(a)(19). For the purpose of this Chapter, the discussion refers to derivatives generally.

[91] Rules for the registration and regulation of derivatives clearing organizations are to be adopted under §725 and §734 of the Dodd–Frank Act, n 15 above. The spirit of the Dodd–Frank creates a market environment where swap users have 'fair and open access' to DCOs and to SEFs and DCMs—see §275(c). The CFTC has implemented this provision, defining the entities that can be considered DCOs and providing the regulatory standard DCOs must comply with. See CFTC, Derivatives Clearing Organization General Provisions and Core Principles 17 CFR §§ 1, 21, 39, and CFTC, Derivatives Clearing Organizations and International Standards § 17 CFR Parts 39, 140, and 190. See SEC.

[92] Currently, there are 14 registered DCOs, among them: ICE Clear Europe Limited, ICE Clear Credit LLC, ICE Clear US, Clearing Corporation, Chicago Mercantile Exchange, LCH.Clearnet LLC, LCH.Clearnet Ltd, LCH.Clearnet SA, and Singapore Exchange Derivatives Clearing Limited; data available at <http://sirt.cftc.gov/sirt/sirt.aspx?Topic=ClearingOrganizations> (last accessed 23 March 2015).

[93] In the US there are three main clearing agencies: the National Securities Clearing Corporation, the Fixed Income Clearing Corporation, and the Options Clearing Corporation; and one primary securities depository, the Depository Trust Company. Data from the SEC website, available at <http://www.sec.gov/divisions/marketreg/mrclearing.shtml> (last accessed 23 March 2015).

the US, without registering with the SEC and the CFTC, if they are subject to comparable comprehensive regulation in their home country.[94]

A second set of CCP rules address internal accountability and corporate governance, and try to mitigate potential conflicts of interests within the CCP and to promote competition in the clearing market.[95] Both DCOs and CAs are subject to ownership limits. The Dodd–Frank Act empowered the CFTC and SEC to adopt limits on the control and voting rights that CCP members may hold in the CCP, to avoid the creation of blocks of controlling shareholders.[96] The CFTC and SEC, for example, gives DCOs and CAs—ie, CCPs—the option to choose between one of two alternative limits on the ownership of voting equity or the exercise of voting power. First, a CCP may require that any individual member does not beneficially own more than 20 per cent of any class of voting equity in the CCP or vote (directly or indirectly) an interest exceeding 20 per cent of voting power of any class of equity interest in the CCP. Further, enumerated entities—such as swap dealers, major swap participants, and big financial institutions (ie, either bank holding companies with $50 billion in consolidated assets or non-bank financial companies supervised by the Board of Governors of the Federal Reserve Systems),[97] regardless of whether they are CCP members, may not collectively beneficially own more than 40 per cent any class of voting equity in a CCP or directly or indirectly vote an interest exceeding 40 per cent of the voting power of any class of equity interest in the CCP. Second, a CCP may require of CCP members and the enumerated entities a 5 per cent individual limit on beneficial ownership of any class of its voting equity or an identical 5 per cent limit on voting power of any class of equity interest in the CCP.[98] The rationale for the ownership requirements is twofold: first, to avoid the risk of concentrated ownership and that of oligopolistic positions being created in the CCP market and thus to foster competition in the clearing market; second, to mitigate potential conflict of interests in the operation of CCPs.

The risk committee plays a crucial role in the oversight of CCPs' risk-management and compliance functions under the new regulatory regime, but the CFTC and the SEC have adopted different approaches. In a CFTC-supervised DCO, the risk-management committee must be composed of at least 35 per cent

[94] As of March 2015, neither the CFTC nor the SEC has adopted any guidance on recognition of non-US CCPs. As a consequence, many EU-based CCPs have registered or have applied for registration with the CFTC.

[95] See Dodd–Frank Act, n 15 above, §765.

[96] See ibid, §726(a).

[97] See ibid, §750. The CFTC and the SEC agreed to adopt the same criteria to fix the limitation on ownership interests for both DCOs and CAs.

[98] See CFTC, Governance Requirements for Derivatives Clearing Organizations, Designated Contract Markets, and Swap Execution Facilities; Additional Requirements Regarding, available at <http://www.cftc.gov/ucm/groups/public/@lrfederalregister/documents/file/2010-31898a.pdf>; see SEC, Ownership Limitations and Governance Requirements for Security-Based Swap Clearing Agencies, Security-based Swap Execution Facilities, and National Securities Exchanges with Respect to Security-based Swaps under Regulation MC, available at <http://www.sec.gov/rules/final/2012/34-68080.pdf>.

independent (ie, 'public') directors—who do not have any material relation with the CCP or its members—and at least 10 per cent customers' representatives must sit in either the risk-management committee or the governing board. A specular composition—with at least 35 per cent independent directors and 10 per cent customer representatives—is required for the board of directors.

On the other hand, in a SEC-supervised CA, two different governance models may be deployed, depending on the ownership structure adopted. If the CA opted for the first-ownership structure (considered above), 35 per cent of the directors must be independent, with no material relations with the CCP and its members, the nominating committee must be composed of a majority of independent directors, and any other committee that has the authority to act on behalf of the board must be composed of at least 35 per cent independent directors. If it opted for the second-ownership structure, the majority of the directors must be independent, the nominating committee must be composed solely of independent directors, and any other committee that has the authority to act on behalf of the board must be composed of a majority of independent directors.

As in the EU regime, margin and capital requirements are the basis for CCP financial stability regulation under the new regime. Initial and variation margin must be collected by CCPs for each cleared transaction in order to guarantee the risk of underlying open exposures, and are the first available resources that a CCP can use in the case of default by a clearing member—margins must be managed by CCPs in segregated accounts and refer to specific clearing members. In addition, capital requirements, including a minimum capital requirement and a mandatory default fund, are designed to provide the CCP with the financial strength needed to deal with the potential defaults of its members or with stressed situations in the financial markets.

With respect to clearing in the securities markets, the SEC, as already noted, is responsible for the oversight of CAs, which must be registered with the Commission as self-regulatory organizations. The SEC distinguishes between two types of CAs: clearing corporations—CCPs in a strict sense, which provide clearing, setting and novation services and which are subject to Dodd–Frank Act regulation; and clearing depositories—CSDs which provide settlement and depositary functions for securities transactions. In the latter case, regulators have left some space for private regulation, empowering CSDs to decide on their internal governance structure.

(b) *The regulation of TRs*

With respect to TRs, the 2010 Dodd–Frank Act requires any swap, whether cleared or not, to be reported to a 'swap data repository', or if no trade repositories are available, to the relevant regulator: either the CFTC or the SEC. Reporting information must include both creation data (the primary economic terms of the transaction: price, amount, volume, parties, duration, and initial margins) and continuation data (any variation to economic terms, including margin variation—in both real time and on a daily basis).[99] TRs, like CCPs, must be authorized by and registered with the relevant authority—the SEC or CFTC—which has extensive powers to regulate their activities.[100] TRs are also required to publicize data on swap transactions and on formal request, to share and disclose this data with domestic and foreign regulators.[101]

IV. Conclusions

FMIs are one of the cornerstones of the crisis-era regulatory reform agenda for financial markets. This Chapter examines the role that trading and post-trading FMIs, and their new regulatory regimes, are playing in the related expansion of 'public' securities and derivatives markets and shrinkage of 'private' markets.

The crisis had a profound impact on the policy/regulatory discussion on FMI regulation, leading to direct public intervention and a restructuring of securities and derivatives markets, and to a withdrawal from self-regulation, particularly in the derivatives segment. The guiding principles for these reforms were set at international level, while implementation of these principles has occurred at national level. The four pillars set by the FSB—standardization, mandatory trading, mandatory clearing, and mandatory reporting—were the common bases for the national regulatory initiatives, which, although sharing the same principles and aiming at the same results, adopted similar, but different solutions. For instance, both EU and US regulation focuses the new derivatives reforms on the role of CCPs: standardized derivatives must be centrally cleared; CCPs must be authorized by the competent regulatory authorities; and CCPs must have sound risk-management practices, they must have a solid capital structure, etc. However, an analysis of the particular norms deployed reveals that there are differences and nuances in the specific reforms adopted. For instance, the EU regime does not provide for any ownership limits on CCP members, while, as described above, both the CFTC

[99] With regard to transparency, the 2010 Dodd–Frank Act contains a modification of §13(d), 13(f), and 13(g) of the Securities Exchange Act of 1934 concerning disclosure rules of relevant holding. More precisely, the Dodd–Frank Act expressly includes within the beneficial ownership reporting requirements the market participant who becomes or is deemed to become a beneficial power of a security upon the conclusion (assuming a long or short position) of a security-based swap under the SEC rules.

[100] The 2010 Dodd–Frank Act does not contain any provisions on the recognition of non-US TRs.

[101] See ibid, §727.

and the SEC have set up stringent limits for CCP members' ownership and voting powers. On the other hand, the approaches adopted towards the structure of the pivotal CCP risk-management committee, despite differing in small details, share the same spirit of having a committee composed both by a third of independent directors and also representatives of customers.

The analysis in this Chapter started with developments in the trading venues FMI segment and moved on to FMIs in the post-trading segment (CCPs, CSDs, and TRs), and showed that regulators are now more deeply involved in FMIs' governance and operation. Regulators have acknowledged the importance of FMIs as systemic mechanisms to ensure stability and to foster efficiency in the financial market. This has resulted in regulatory initiatives, either in the form of recommendations for FMIs or of strict rules, which move in the direction of increasing the systemic scope of FMIs, introducing elements of publicity in to previously private markets, and leading to higher levels of public supervision. The new regulatory regime and the related move towards making FMIs more public in nature reflects the current characterization of FMIs as potential sources of liquidity and as transparency providers to the markets, and as mechanisms to mitigate systemic risk. The crisis-era regulation of FMIs is accordingly moving FMIs from private to public markets by means of constructing intermediate and hybrid forms of semi-public markets within the regulatory system. Regulators, by addressing trading infrastructures and focusing on transactions and intermediaries, have typically intervened at a micro level. They have promoted trade concentration on formal trading venues with an appropriate level of pre- and post-trade transparency with the aim of increasing market efficiency, reducing transaction costs, and enhancing liquidity in the market. But at a macro level, regulators have also reshaped the role played by FMIs by institutionalizing within the regulatory system the role of CCPs, TRs, and CSDs as mechanisms to mitigate systemic risk, foster transparency vis-à-vis regulators, and promote stability.

These market and regulatory trends have a global dimension: the review in this Chapter of the EU and US implementation of international guidelines with respect to FMIs, and the related global market reaction, has revealed that regulators are moving uniformly in setting up the new regulatory framework for FMIs, and that the FMI phenomenon is becoming transnational with respect to regulation and to FMI market participants.

Bibliography

Acharya, V and Richardson, M, *Restoring Financial Stability: How to Repair a Failed System* (2009).

Bainbridge, S, *Corporate Governance after the Financial Crisis* (2012).

Belcredi, M and Ferrarini, G (eds), *Boards and Shareholders in Listed Companies* (2013).

Coase, R, *The Firm, the Market and the Law* (1988).
Coffee Jr, JC and Sale, HA, *Securities Regulation* (12th edn, 2012).
Committee on Capital Markets Regulation, The Global Financial Crisis: A Plan for Regulatory Reform (2009).
CPSS-IOSCO, Principles for Financial Market Infrastructures (2012).
CPSS-IOSCO, Principles for Financial Market Infrastructures: Disclosure Framework and Assessment Methodology (2012).
CPSS-IOSCO, Recommendations for Central Counterparties (2004).
Cybo-Ottone, A, Di Noia, C, and Murgia, M, 'Recent Developments in the Structure of Securities Markets' (2000) *Brookings-Wharton Papers on Financial Services* 223.
Dale, R, 'Derivatives Clearing Houses: The Regulatory Challenge' in Ferrarini, G (ed.), *European Securities Markets: The Investment Services Directive and Beyond* (1998) 295.
Ferrarini, G, 'Best Execution and Competition between Trading Venues—MiFID's Likely Impact' (2007) 2 *Capital Markets Law Journal* 404.
Ferrarini, G, 'Market Transparency and Best Execution: Bond Trading under MiFID' in Tison, M et al. (eds), *Perspectives in Company Law and Financial Regulation: Essays in Honour of Eddy Wymeersch* (2009) 477.
Ferrarini, G, 'Stock Exchange Governance in the European Union' in Balling, M, Hennessy, E, and O'Brien, R (eds), *Corporate Governance, Financial Markets and Global Convergence* (1998).
Ferrarini, G and Moloney, N, 'Reshaping Order Execution in the EU and the Role of Interest Groups' (2012) 13 *European Business Organization Law Review* 557.
Ferrarini, G and Recine, F, 'The MiFID and Internalisation' in Ferrarini, G and Wymeersch, E (eds), *Investor Protection in Europe: Corporate Law Making, the MiFID and Beyond* (2006) 235.
Ferrarini, G and Saguato, P, 'Reforming Securities and Derivatives Trading in the EU: From EMIR to MIFIR' (2013) 13(2) *Journal of Corporate Law Studies* 319.
Financial Crisis Inquiry Commission, The Financial Crisis Inquiry Report (2011).
Financial Services Authority (FSA), Review of the Listing Regime (2003).
Financial Stability Board (FSB), Improving Financial Stability, Report of the Financial Stability Board to the G20 Leaders (2009).
Financial Stability Forum (FSF), Report of the Financial Stability Forum on Enhancing Market and Institutional Resilience (2008).
Fischel, D, 'Organized Exchanges and the Regulation of Dual Class Common Stock' (1987) 54 *University of Chicago Law Review* 119.
Fischel, D and Grossman, S, 'Customer Protection in Futures and Securities Markets' (1984) 4 *Journal of Futures Markets* 273.
Foucault, T, Pagano, M, and Röell, A, *Market Liquidity* (2013).
G20, Leaders Statement: The Pittsburgh Summit.
Group of Thirty, Financial Reform: A Framework for Financial Stability (2009).
Harris, L, *Trading and Exchanges: Market Microstructure for Practitioners* (2003).
Hart, O and Moore, J, 'The Governance of Exchanges: Members' Cooperatives versus Outside Ownership' (1996) 12 *Oxford Review of Economic Policy* 53.
The High-Level Group on Financial Supervision in the EU, Report (2009).
International Organization of Securities Commissions (IOSCO), Transparency and Market Fragmentation Report (2001).
IOSCO, Principles for Dark Liquidity: Final Report (2011).

IOSCO, Regulatory Issues Arising from Exchange Evolution: Consultation Report (2006).

IOSCO, Regulatory Issues Raised by Changes in Market Structure: Consultation Report (2013).

IOSCO, Technological Challenges to Effective Market Surveillance and Regulatory Tools: Consultation Report (2012).

Kloner, D, 'The Commodity Futures Modernization Act of 2000' (2001) 29 *Securities Regulation Law Journal* 286.

Lee, R, *Running the World's Markets—the Governance of Financial Infrastructure* (2011).

Lee, R, *What Is an Exchange? The Automation, Management, and Regulation of Financial Markets* (1998).

Macey, J and O'Hara, M, 'Globalisation, Exchange Governance, and the Future of Exchanges' (1999) *Brookings-Wharton Papers on Financial Services* 1.

Macey, J and O'Hara, M, 'From Markets to Venues: Securities Regulation in an Evolving World' (2005) 58 *Stanford Law Review* 563.

Macey, J and O'Hara, M, 'Regulating Exchanges and Alternative Trading Systems: A Law and Economics Perspective' (1999) 28 *Journal of Legal Studies* 17.

Mahoney, P, 'The Exchange as Regulator' (1997) 83 *Virginia Law Review* 1453.

Moloney, N, *EU Securities and Financial Markets Regulation* (3rd edn, 2014).

Mulherin, J, Netter, J, and Overdahl, J, 'Prices Are Property: The Organization of Financial Exchanges from a Transaction Cost Perspective' (1991) 34 *Journal of Law and Economics* 591.

Pirrong, C, 'The Clearinghouse Cure' (2008) *Regulation* 44.

Pirrong, C, The Economics of Clearing in Derivatives Markets: Netting, Asymmetric Information, and the Sharing of Default Risk through a Central Counterparty (2009), University of Houston, Working Paper, available at <http://ssrn.com/abstract=1340660>.

Roe, MJ, 'Clearinghouse Overconfidence' (2013) 101 *California Law Review* 1641.

Saguato, P, 'Private Regulation in the Credit Default Swaps Market: The Role of ISDA in the New Regulatory Scenario of CDSs' in Cafaggi, F and Miller, GP (eds), *The Governance and Regulation of International Finance* (2013) 32.

Schwarcz, SL, 'Systemic Risk' (2008) 97 *Georgetown Law Journal* 193.

Squam Lake Working Group on Financial Regulation, Fixing the Financial System (2010).

Squire, R, 'Clearinghouses as Liquidity Partitioning' (2013), (forthcoming *Cornell Law Review*), available at <http://ssrn.com/abstract=2185064>.

Stout, LA, 'Derivatives and the Legal Origin of the 2008 Credit Crisis' (2011) 1 *Harvard Business Law Review* 1.

US Treasury, The Department Do the Treasury Blueprint for a Modernized Financial Regulatory Structure (2008).

US Treasury, Financial Regulatory Reform a New Foundation, Rebuilding Financial Supervision and Regulation (2009).

Williamson, OE, 'The Economics of Organization: The Transaction Cost Approach' (1981) 87(3) *The American Journal of Sociology* 548.

Yadav, Y, 'The Problematic Case of Clearinghouses in Complex Markets' (2013) 101 *Georgetown Law Journal* 387.

CHAPTER 20

REGULATING TRADING PRACTICES

ANDREAS MARTIN FLECKNER*

* For many valuable comments and suggestions, the author is indebted to Corinna R Coupette, Andreas Engert, Gen Goto, Alexander Hellgardt, Klaus J Hopt, Howell E Jackson, Christoph Kumpan, Thilo Kuntz, Philipp Aron Leimbach, Martin Mittermeier, Anastasia Sotiropoulou, Holger Spamann, as well as to the Handbook's editors. The usual disclaimers apply.

I. Introduction: Standardization, Self-Regulation, and State Intervention

HIGH-FREQUENCY trading, dark pools, front-running, phantom orders, short selling—the way securities are traded ranks high among today's regulatory challenges. Thanks to a steady stream of news reports, investor complaints, and public investigations, it has become commonplace, in both financial and academic circles, to call for the government to intervene and impose order. The regulation of trading practices, one of the oldest roots of securities law and still a regulatory mystery to many people, is suddenly the talk of the town.

How and why the leading jurisdictions regulate trading practices is best understood by looking back in time.[1] Two key developments mark the beginning of today's regulatory regime: the rise of exchanges and the standardization of trading. Markets with features of an exchange first appeared at the end of the Middle Ages when merchants founded permanent institutions where they could meet, chat, and trade (eg, in Amsterdam or Frankfurt). Other exchanges emerged under mercantilism (for instance, in Berlin and Paris), still others as late as during industrialization (such as the London and the New York Stock Exchange). Over time, those who met at the exchanges began to establish rules, either by tacit custom or explicit enactment, to standardize and thereby facilitate their trading. They decided, *inter alia*, who is given access to the exchange (for example, traders, broker-dealers, market-makers), which items are admitted to trading (such as stocks, bonds, and commodities), how transactions are concluded (bilaterally or through intermediaries, in periodic auctions, or in continuous trading, etc), and what provisions they are subject to (general terms and conditions, usages, customs, *Börsenusancen*). The significance of this standardization process can hardly be overrated. In fact, that *selected individuals deal in negotiable items following specific routines* turned out to be the decisive feature to distinguish exchanges from other markets and fairs.

Due to the identity of those setting the rules and those subject to them, trading on exchanges became one of the first examples of 'self-regulation' in the financial sector. It is true that hardly any exchange has ever enjoyed pure self-regulation because state intervention dates back to the earliest days of trading. Famous examples include a Dutch decree forbidding naked short selling (1610),[2] an English

[1] For historical overviews, see Fleckner, AM and Hopt, KJ, 'Stock Exchange Law: Concept, History, Challenges' (2013) 7 *Virginia Law & Business Review* 513, 523–42 (worldwide) and Fleckner, AM, 'Stock Exchanges at the Crossroads' (2006) 74 *Fordham Law Review* 2541, 2550–9 (US).

[2] Placaet, Tegens het verkoopen ende transporteren der Actien inde Oost-Indische Compagnie (27 February 1610), reprinted in (1658) 1 *Groot Placaet-Boeck* 553–6.

Act restraining stock brokers and dealers (1697),[3] as well as three Prussian orders excluding certain securities from trading (1836, 1840, 1844).[4] But until about a century ago, legislators around the world remained principally silent, and most trading rules arose from self-regulation.[5]

What followed can be described as a global movement away from self-regulation towards state intervention and supervision. The landmark statutes were the German *Börsengesetz* (1896),[6] the US Securities Exchange Act (1934),[7] and the UK Financial Services Act (1986).[8] Originally, most statutory provisions focused on the organization of the exchanges rather than on the process of trading. Over time, however, a hybrid system emerged with more and more government rules that directly police certain trading practices, most recently high-frequency trading and other forms of algorithmic trading. By now, the trend towards state control has long reached the exchange's very heart, the trading process, and those who invented the exchange, the traders. It will therefore be a recurring question throughout the Chapter, in almost all subsections, who is best prepared to address the regulatory problems that arise from trading: the government from afar or the traders on-site. While much has changed since merchants started standardizing trading practices in the Middle Ages, finding the right balance between state intervention and self-regulation has remained the principal challenge.

The rest of the Chapter proceeds as follows. Section II identifies the key rationale for governments to intervene and regulate trading practices: to ensure that prices accurately reflect market supply and demand. Section III critically analyses the

[3] An Act to Restraine the Number and Ill Practice of Brokers and Stock-Jobbers (1697), 8 and 9 *Gul. III*, ch 32.

[4] Verordnung, den Verkehr mit Spanischen und sonstigen, auf jeden Inhaber lautenden Staats- oder Kommunalschuld-Papieren betreffend (19 January 1836) *Gesetz-Sammlung für die Königlichen Preußischen Staaten* (hereinafter, *Gesetz-Sammlung*) 9–11; Verordnung, den Verkehr mit ausländischen Papieren betreffend (13 May 1840) *Gesetz-Sammlung* 123–4; Verordnung, die Eröffnung von Aktienzeichnungen für Eisenbahn-Unternehmungen und den Verkehr mit den dafür ausgegebenen Papieren betreffend (24 May 1844) *Gesetz-Sammlung* 117–18.

[5] For the US, most prominently *Gordon v New York Stock Exchange* (1975) 422 *U.S.* 659, 665 ('The exchanges remained essentially self-regulating and without significant supervision until the adoption of the Securities Exchange Act of 1934'). For the German territories, Fleckner and Hopt, n 1 above, 535–42. In France, a few rules on exchanges appeared as early as 1807, see Articles 71–3 ('des Bourses de commerce') of the Code de Commerce (10–15 September 1807) 164 *Bulletin des lois* 161–284.

[6] Börsengesetz (22 June 1896) *Reichsgesetzblatt* 157–76.

[7] An Act to provide for the regulation of securities exchanges and of over-the-counter markets operating in interstate and foreign commerce and through the mails, to prevent inequitable and unfair practices on such exchanges and markets, and for other purposes (6 June 1934), ch 404, 48 *Stat.* 881–909 (codified as amended at 15 *U.S.C.* §§ 78a–pp) (hereinafter, Securities Exchange Act).

[8] An Act to regulate the carrying on of investment business;... to make new provision with respect to the official listing of securities, offers of unlisted securities, takeover offers and insider dealing; to make provision as to the disclosure of information obtained under enactments relating to fair trading, banking, companies and insurance;... (7 November 1986), 1986 ch 60 (hereinafter, Financial Services Act 1986).

leading jurisdictions' regulatory regimes: their rules, norms, and standards; their regulators, supervisors, and self-regulatory organizations; and their techniques, strategies, and methods. Section IV discusses the implications of the Chapter's central argument—that market-driven price formation should be the key objective in the regulation of trading practices—for three current challenges: algorithmic trading, short selling, and market fragmentation. Section V summarizes the main findings and positions.

II. Rationale: Market-Driven Price Formation as the Key Regulatory Objective

The standard narrative is that securities regulation has three main goals: *market efficiency* (usually associated with low transaction costs, high liquidity, and market integrity), *financial stability* (mitigating systemic risk, the prime regulatory goal in recent years), and *investor protection* (against own mistakes and against others' misconduct, in response to information asymmetries and conflicts of interest).[9] Of these three objectives, it is primarily the first one—market efficiency—that calls for the government to regulate trading practices: to ensure that prices accurately reflect market supply and demand.

1. Market efficiency

Securities exchanges and similar venues play a vital role in society. By establishing marketplaces with standardized trading, exchanges function as intermediaries that help bring together those planning to sell certain items and those hoping to buy them.[10]

[9] A representative summary is provided by the International Organization of Securities Commissions (IOSCO), Objectives and Principles of Securities Regulation (2010), 3 ('protecting investors; ensuring that markets are fair, efficient and transparent; reducing systemic risk'). In scholarship, eg, Coffee, JC and Sale, HA, *Securities Regulation* (12th edn, 2012) 1–9 or Moloney, N, 'Financial Services and Markets' in Baldwin, R, Cave, M, and Lodge, M (eds), *The Oxford Handbook of Regulation* (2010) 437–8.

[10] For brief overviews of the stock exchanges' main functions (such as market organization, regulation, standard-setting, and information distribution, now also generating profits), see Fleckner, n 1 above, 2545–50 and Fleckner and Hopt, n 1 above, 516–17.

The key components of market efficiency—low transaction costs and high liquidity—have never been the prime concern in securities regulation.[11] The reason is that there are strong market mechanisms that put exchanges under a constant pressure to make their trading less costly and more liquid. Competition for orders and listings is the driving factor, and the 'network effect' functions as a powerful catalyst: orders attract more orders because variable costs go down as trading volume increases. Thanks to these and similar mechanisms, exchanges keep on investing in new technologies, expanding their capacity and cutting trading fees. In this respect, there has hardly ever been a need for regulatory intervention.

Instead, the main focus of securities regulators is typically on another factor that makes trading more efficient: market integrity.[12] The underlying idea is that the efficiency of markets will increase when those that frequent them can rest assured that they will not be overcharged or ripped off. For the regulation of trading practices, the key mechanism to achieve that goal is the *price formation process*.[13] Under ideal circumstances, the equilibrium price will accurately reflect market supply and demand, all sell and buy orders will be matched to the extent possible, and price formation will be transparent and fair (equal treatment of traders). If these conditions are met, there is little that the regulation of trading practices can add on top to make markets more efficient.[14]

Why is the price formation process so critical? Because it removes uncertainty and strengthens investor confidence. Whether orders are matched manually by humans on a trading floor in medieval Antwerp, or automatically by an electronic trading system on an off-shore server: no reasonable buyer or seller would place an order if price formation were arbitrary and opaque. Traders do not expect to know the execution price in advance. That would be impossible in most cases. What they do expect, though, is that price formation follows predetermined rules that offer protection from abuse, fraud, and discrimination.

[11] On the rationales for regulating securities trading see, eg, Moloney, N, *EC Securities Regulation* (2nd edn, 2008), 763–6; for exchange law see Fleckner, AM, 'Exchanges' in Basedow, J, Hopt, KJ, and Zimmermann, R (eds), *The Max Planck Encyclopedia of European Private Law* (Vol I, 2012) 659 as well as Fleckner and Hopt, n 1 above, 520–3.

[12] Some observers believe *transparency* is also an end in and of itself; for others it is merely a technique to accomplish the other goals mentioned above.

[13] The vital role of the price formation process seems to have escaped many regulators' and scholars' attention so far (see nn 61 and 62 below; more explicit than others Moloney, n 11 above, 763 and 765). It seems that most observers take the price formation process as a given, set by the laws of nature, while, in fact, it is a design question how prices are found (the 'creativity' of market operators who want to lure high-frequency traders has made this obvious in recent years).

[14] This is not to say that other rules—such as on corporate disclosure or insider dealing—will not help increase market efficiency. The opposite is true. But these provisions influence *if* and *why* orders are placed, not *how* they are matched. To the extent that broker-dealers, investment firms, and other intermediaries route client orders to certain marketplaces, their regulation overlaps with the regulation of trading practices. Figure 20.1 gives an overview of the broader regulatory context.

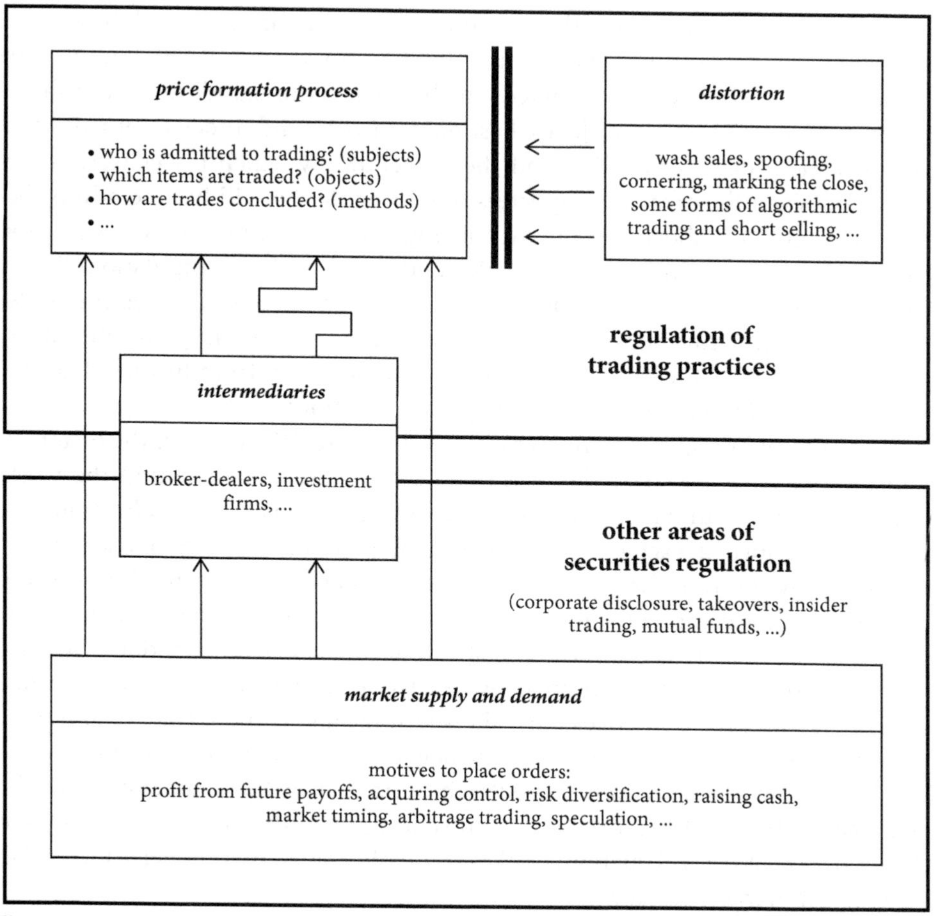

Figure 20.1 The regulation of trading practices and the broader regulatory context

The chief principle that reasonable traders would agree on in advance, besides transparency and fairness, is that the price formation process ought to be *entirely market-driven*. Nothing but supply and demand should dictate prices.[15] The reason for this rationale is that professional traders can expect to be buyers and sellers alike, to be up to date or uninformed, to hold larger or smaller positions, and so on. There is no point in systematically favouring either side.[16]

[15] Market-driven price formation is not to be confused with the question of whether and to what extent market prices reflect the fundamental value of the traded asset, ie, discounted future cash flows (for this question, see the controversy around the Efficient Capital Market Hypothesis).

[16] This, by the way, is a good reason (along with solvency and reliability considerations) to limit market access to professional traders: the more homogenous the traders, the smaller the risks of systematic manipulations. From this perspective, it would also be counterproductive to make market participants disclose whether they trade for their own account or on behalf of a client.

Can individual traders trust the exchanges that price formation will be entirely market-driven, transparent, and fair? There is no clear answer because the exchanges' historical record is mixed. In their efforts to standardize and facilitate trading, exchanges from the earliest days onwards did, indeed, set rules that governed the process of trading and the procedure by which prices were determined. But even the greatest supporters of self-regulation will have to admit that exchanges often fell short of properly policing price formation: there are just too many accounts of artificial price bubbles and direct price manipulations.[17] One possible explanation is the blatant conflict of interest inherent to a regime under which those benefiting most from price distortions are in charge of preventing them: the traders as the exchange owners. So is the lesson from history that governments should intervene and regulate price formation?

Giving the right regulatory answer for today is more difficult than the historical evidence indicates. For over the past two decades, exchanges around the world have undergone a fundamental transformation known as 'demutualization': the traders as the former exchange owners have invited outside investors, and many exchanges have become for-profit entities with publicly traded shares.[18] As a result, some of the classic conflicts of interest have disappeared, and marketplaces now have stronger incentives to scrupulously watch over price formation (to draw orders and thereby increase profits). At least that is the theory.[19] Recent events are less encouraging: exchanges have allowed some algorithmic traders to pursue strategies that are at odds with general principles of securities law or even outright illegal (discussed later). Given the public's outrage over these practices and the exchanges' mixed historical record in preventing price distortions, it seems that self-regulation alone will currently fail to create the public trust in price formation that efficient markets call for.

[17] One of the best books ever written is more than 325 years old and almost 400 pages long, with stories of 'odd' trading practices that could not be more vivid and colourful: de la Vega, I, *Confusion de confusiones* (1688). The author is working on a more detailed account of this fascinating book. Other great works of this genre include [Defoe, D], *An Essay upon Projects* (1697), Mackay, C, *Memoirs of Extraordinary Popular Delusions* (Vol I, 1841) 1–153, and Zola, É, *L'Argent* (1891). There is also plenty of primary evidence, especially as the result of public investigations and court proceedings.

[18] Hart, O and Moore, J, 'The Governance of Exchanges: Members' Cooperatives versus Outside Ownership' (1996) 12(4) *Oxford Review of Economic Policy* 53; Köndgen, J, 'Ownership and Corporate Governance of Stock Exchanges' (1998) 154 *Journal of Institutional and Theoretical Economics* 224; Karmel, RS, 'Turning Seats into Shares: Causes and Implications of Demutualization of Stock and Futures Exchanges' (2002) 53 *Hastings Law Journal* 367; Macey, JR and O'Hara, M, 'From Markets to Venues: Securities Regulation in an Evolving World' (2005) 58 *Stanford Law Review* 563; Fleckner, n 1 above; Oldford, E and Otchere, I, 'Can Commercialization Improve the Performance of Stock Exchanges Even without Corporatization?' (2011) 46 *Financial Review* 67; Fleckner and Hopt, n 1 above, 549–51.

[19] Fleckner, n 1 above, 2590–7 (arguing that there is no legitimate concern that profit-making exchanges will generally under-regulate their markets).

There are a couple of additional motives for governments to intervene and regulate the price formation process. Many jurisdictions use exchange prices as 'reference prices' for accounting and tax purposes, to determine the net asset value of mutual funds, or to price derivatives. This means that price manipulations can have far-reaching consequences. Regulators appointed by the government are more likely to take those externalities into account than local overseers or the parties of the individual transactions. Moreover, while public prosecutors are used to seizing profits from illegal transactions and returning them to the other party, self-regulatory organizations typically lack such powers of disgorgement (and probably cannot adequately contract for them). Last but not least, designing a regulatory regime around the Efficient Capital Market Hypothesis, especially by imposing onerous disclosure obligations, would be a moot point if prices were not primarily market-driven but instead the result of unilateral manipulations.

It follows, then, that governments should step in and shield price formation from deliberate or accidental distortion. The underlying rationale is to strengthen public trust in the price formation process. This is a narrowly defined mandate, not a *carte blanche* for extending state intervention to transactions and trading practices that do not negatively affect price formation.

2. Financial stability

Over the past several years, financial stability has been the chief worry of policymakers around the world. Market infrastructure and trading practices did not escape this trend.[20] Yet, whatever factors caused and fuelled the financial crisis, trading on securities exchanges and similar venues was probably not among them: despite volumes and volatility unseen before, the securities markets performed well and almost without interruptions.[21]

While the financial crisis gives no reason to put financial stability on the agenda of those regulating trading practices, another factor does: the ever-increasing automation of trading. If the infamous 'flash crash' (2010) has taught one lesson, it is that trading practices and market linkages have become so complex that the price

[20] Good examples of the increasing focus on financial stability are Bank for International Settlements (BIS) and IOSCO, Principles for Financial Market Infrastructures (2012) as well as Regulation (EU) No 648/2012 on OTC derivatives, central counterparties and trade repositories [2012] OJ L201/1, as supplemented by various instruments (hereinafter, EMIR). See also IOSCO, Objectives and Principles, n 9 above, 12 ('Regulation should aim to ensure the proper management of large exposures, default risk and market disruption').

[21] US Securities and Exchange Commission (SEC), 'Concept Release on Equity Market Structure, Release No 34-61358' (14 January 2010) 75 *Federal Register* 3594, 3611 ('The Commission notes that, from an operational standpoint, the equity markets performed well during the world-wide financial crisis in the Autumn of 2008 when volume and volatility spiked to record highs').

formation process can get out of control within *seconds*, whereas several *years* of investigation and debate have not sufficed to fully understand what happened.[22]

A novel inspired by the 'flash crash' had to add nothing but a few details to turn a smoothly operating market into a bloodbath—both literally and figuratively.[23] Preventing such a scenario is a valid regulatory objective for governments. But it is a mandate that is quite limited. A few general rules to contain the trading failure and stop it from spreading to other venues will suffice. Local regulators and those on-site will take care of the details (given that avoiding trading interruptions is in almost everyone's interest).

3. Investor protection

As long as price formation is purely market-driven, investor protection does not call for any additional rules on trading practices. For if prices accurately reflect supply and demand, there is hardly anything else investors could be protected from in the process of trading.[24]

In addition, standardized trading is typically restricted to professionals who meet certain requirements of sophistication, reliability, and solvency. Traders who cannot fend for themselves, especially retail investors, are usually denied direct access to the venues under consideration in this Chapter. If they want to place orders, they have to trade through intermediaries, and they will be protected by the rules that govern such investment services.[25]

[22] Schapiro, ML (then SEC Chair), Testimony Concerning the Severe Market Disruption on May 6, 2010 (11 May 2010); Schapiro, ML, Examining the Causes and Lessons of the May 6th Market Plunge (20 May 2010); US Commodity Futures Trading Commission (CFTC) and SEC, Findings Regarding the Market Events of May 6, 2010 (2010); Easley, D, López de Prado, MM, and O'Hara, M, 'The Microstructure of the "Flash Crash"' (2011) 37/2 *The Journal of Portfolio Management* 118; Andersen, TG and Bondarenko, O, 'VPIN and the Flash Crash' (2014) 17 *Journal of Financial Markets* 1.

[23] Harris, R, *The Fear Index* (2011).

[24] Note that Moloney, N, *How to Protect Investors* (2010), an important monograph on investor protection in recent years, *does* feature a section on 'The trading process' (see 345–73). However, most of what Moloney discusses does not *directly* influence the price formation process (such as issuer disclosure (see 363–73) or the duty of 'best execution' (see 355–63)) and is, therefore, outside the scope of the present Chapter (see Figure 20.1).

[25] Another issue is whether retail investors should invest in individual stocks, bonds, and similar financial instruments at all. The reason for such doubts is that retail investors typically lack the funds, the expertise, and the time to properly diversify their portfolios. Most would probably be better off if they limited their investments to mutual funds or—typically with higher yields on efficient markets—to index funds (whose prices are usually not the direct result of a price formation process but instead set by the investment company according to the net asset value). Moloney, n 24 above, esp 350–4 is fully aware of the objections to individual retail investor trading, but a bit more optimistic (along the same lines Moloney, n 9 above, esp 444–5).

III. Analysis: A Multitude of Rules, Regulators, and Techniques

The leading jurisdictions regulate trading practices through a multitude of *rules*, *norms*, and *standards*; they rely on various *regulators*, *supervisors*, and *self-regulatory organizations*; and they resort to a wide range of *techniques*, *strategies*, and *methods*. It would require a monograph to give an overview, let alone a comprehensive study, of the main regulatory regimes. The following subsections will therefore take another path: they will critically analyse some of the regimes' key regulatory features and discuss whether they are sensible, given the rationale for regulating trading practices.

1. Rules, norms, and standards

The bouquet of rules, norms, and standards that affect trading practices could not be more colourful.

International bodies such as the Group of Twenty (G20),[26] the Bank for International Settlements (BIS),[27] the Financial Stability Board (FSB),[28] and the International Organization of Securities Commissions (IOSCO)[29] all frequently publish guidelines, recommendations, and reports that specifically address certain trading practices or indirectly influence their regulation.

[26] Most importantly G20, Leaders' Statement—The Pittsburgh Summit (24 and 25 September 2009) 9 ('All standardized OTC derivative contracts should be traded on exchanges or electronic trading platforms ... and cleared through central counterparties ... '); see also G20, Cannes Summit Final Declaration (4 November 2011), 5 and 7.

[27] BIS, High-Frequency Trading in the Foreign Exchange Market (2011); BIS and IOSCO, Financial Market Infrastructures, n 20 above; BIS and IOSCO, Report on OTC Derivatives Data Reporting and Aggregation Requirements (2012); BIS and IOSCO, Authorities' Access to Trade Repository Data (2013); BIS and IOSCO, Margin Requirements for Non-Centrally Cleared Derivatives (2013).

[28] Following the G20 summit declarations mentioned in n 26 above, eg, FSB, Implementing OTC Derivatives Market Reforms (2010) and FSB, OTC Derivatives Market Reforms—Sixth Progress Report on Implementation (2013) as well as FSB, A Global Legal Entity Identifier for Financial Markets (2012).

[29] Most closely related to the regulation of trading practices in recent years: IOSCO, Regulation of Short Selling (2009); IOSCO, Objectives and Principles, n 9 above; IOSCO, Principles for Direct Electronic Access to Markets (2010); IOSCO, Principles for Dark Liquidity (2011); IOSCO, Regulatory Issues Raised by the Impact of Technological Changes on Market Integrity and Efficiency (2011); IOSCO, Technological Challenges to Effective Market Surveillance (2013); IOSCO, Methodology for Assessing Implementation of the IOSCO Objectives and Principles of Securities Regulation (2011, revised 2013); IOSCO, Regulatory Issues Raised by Changes in Market Structure (2013); IOSCO, Trading Fee Models and their Impact on Trading Behaviour (2013).

For marketplaces in the EU, the most important legal sources are the EU's supranational regulations and directives, such as on markets in financial instruments,[30] on market abuse,[31] on short selling and credit default swaps,[32] or on derivatives, central counterparties, and trade repositories.[33]

The US,[34] the UK,[35] Germany,[36] France,[37] and many other jurisdictions have enacted exchange acts and similar statutes, often supplemented with detailed implementation provisions by the competent supervisory authority (such as the US Securities and Exchange Commission, the UK Financial Conduct Authority, the German *Bundesanstalt für Finanzdienstleistungsaufsicht*, and the French *Autorité des marchés financiers*).[38]

Exchanges and other self-regulatory organizations, for instance broker-dealer associations, have codified their trading provisions in voluminous rule books that are continuously updated.[39] Many exchanges also record the customs, standards, or

[30] Regulation (EU) No 600/2014 on markets in financial instruments ... [2014] OJ L173/84 (hereinafter, MiFIR); Directive 2014/65/EU on markets in financial instruments ... [2014] OJ L173/349 (hereinafter, MiFID II). Still relevant for a transitional period: Directive 2004/39/EC on markets in financial instruments ... [2004] OJ L145/1, as amended and supplemented by various instruments (hereinafter, MiFID I).

[31] Regulation (EU) No 596/2014 on market abuse (market abuse regulation) ... [2014] OJ L173/1; Directive 2014/57/EU on criminal sanctions for market abuse (market abuse directive) [2014] OJ L173/179. Still relevant for a transitional period: Directive 2003/6/EC on insider dealing and market manipulation (market abuse) [2003] OJ L96/16, as supplemented by various instruments.

[32] Regulation (EU) No 236/2012 on short selling and certain aspects of credit default swaps [2012] OJ L86/1, as supplemented by various instruments (hereinafter, EU Short Selling Regulation).

[33] EMIR, n 20 above.

[34] Securities Exchange Act, n 7 above; Commodity Exchange Act (21 September 1922, 15 June 1936), ch 369, 42 *Stat.* 998, ch 545, 49 *Stat.* 1491 (codified as amended at 7 *U.S.C.* §§ 1–27f) (hereinafter, Commodity Exchange Act).

[35] Financial Services and Markets Act 2000 (14 June 2000), 2000 ch 8, as amended, esp Part 18 ('recognised investment exchanges and clearing houses') and Part 18a ('suspension and removal of financial instruments from trading'), replacing the Financial Services Act 1986, n 8 above.

[36] Börsengesetz (16 July 2007) *Bundesgesetzblatt I* 1351–68, as amended; Gesetz über den Wertpapierhandel (Wertpapierhandelsgesetz) (26 July 1994) *Bundesgesetzblatt I* 1749–60, as amended. For the key events in the history of both acts, see Fleckner and Hopt, n 1 above, 542–9.

[37] Code monétaire et financier, Ord. n° 2000-1223 (14 December 2000) 291 *Journal officiel de la République française* (16 December 2000) 20,004, ratified by Article 31 of L. n° 2003-591 (2 July 2003) 152 *Journal officiel de la République française* (3 July 2003) 11,192, as amended, esp Livre IV ('Les marchés') Titre II ('Les plates-formes de négociation').

[38] Most prominently the UK Financial Conduct Authority Handbook (continuously updated), available at <http://fshandbook.info/FS/html/FCA>. Another example is the *Règlement général* of the French *Autorité des marchés financiers* (continuously updated), available at <http://www.amf-france.org/Reglementation/>, also in English. The SEC and the German *Bundesanstalt für Finanzdienstleistungsaufsicht* do not publish any such handbooks. But see, for the US, Title 17 ('Commodity and Securities Exchanges') of the Code of Federal Regulations (hereinafter, C.F.R.).

[39] Such as: NYSE Rules, available at <http://nyserules.nyse.com/>; Rules of the London Stock Exchange—Rule Book, available at <http://www.londonstockexchange.com/>; Börsenordnung für die Frankfurter Wertpapierbörse, available at <http://deutsche-boerse.com/>, also in English; CME Rulebook, available at <http://www.cmegroup.com/rulebook/CME/>. For provisions established

general terms and conditions (*Börsenusancen*) that all contracts entered into at the exchange are subject to.[40]

A closer look would reveal several additional regulatory levels and sources, especially court decisions, administrative rulings, and arbitration awards.[41] But the survey above suffices to show that the current regulation of trading practices could not be further away from a single rule book. This is unfortunate because it gives rise to legal uncertainty. In theory, self-regulatory organizations could mitigate the negative effects of regulatory heterogeneity by incorporating all provisions from higher regulatory levels into their local manuals. The result would be a central reference code for all engaged in trading—comparable to a single rule book, but without its authority.[42] Practice has shown, however, that this approach is not feasible. There are numerous questions for which the various sources provide no or, even worse, conflicting answers. Moreover, changes happen so frequently that it would be impossible to keep track of them in a timely manner, especially if one wanted to include decisions of courts and similar bodies as well.[43]

Another concern is length and complexity. Of the rules, norms, and standards mentioned here, only a few allow exchange members, broker-dealers, and other primary addressees to fully understand the legal regime they are subject to. Most provisions are not even remotely comprehensible. The lame excuse often heard is that the regulation of trading practices has become too complex and too sophisticated to draft rules that an average trader is able to understand. To some degree, this may be true. But the latest generation of regulatory instruments is of a different

by self-regulatory organizations other than exchanges, see most importantly the rules of the US Financial Industry Regulatory Authority, available at <http://www.finra.org/industry/finra-rules>.

[40] The general terms and conditions have only rarely made it into court decisions or into law review articles. One well-known exception were the so-called 'chapter 11 cases' in Germany, ie, unfulfilled trades in shares of US companies that were undergoing restructuring; for more information, see Fleckner, AM, 'Schicksal der Gegenleistungspflicht beim Kauf von Wertpapieren' (2009) 63 *Zeitschrift für Wirtschafts- und Bankrecht* 2064 (based on an expert opinion for a market participant). Another area where investors do care about the general terms and conditions is how they handle 'error trades' or 'mistrades' (see n 67 below and accompanying text).

[41] Landmark court decisions include: Preußisches Oberverwaltungsgericht (Prussian Supreme Administrative Court) (1898) 34 *Entscheidungen des Königlich Preußischen Oberverwaltungsgerichts* 315; *Silver v New York Stock Exchange*, 373 *U.S.* 341 (1963); *Merrill Lynch, Pierce, Fenner & Smith v Ware*, 414 *U.S.* 117 (1973); *Gordon v New York Stock Exchange*, 422 *U.S.* 659 (1975); *Board of Trade of the City of Chicago v Securities and Exchange Commission*, 883 *F.2d* 525 (7th Cir. 1989); *Board of Trade of the City of Chicago v Securities and Exchange Commission*, 923 *F.2d* 1270 (7th Cir. 1991); Court of Justice of the European Union (ECJ), Case C-248/11 (22 March 2012), to be published; ECJ, Case C-270/12 (22 January 2014), to be published.

[42] Market participants are bound by local manuals (through law or contract), but these manuals cannot override rules originating from higher regulatory levels.

[43] Short selling is a good example. Only a few years ago, the SEC was concerned that self-regulatory organizations may 'improperly discourage legal short sales or other types of legitimate trading practices': SEC, 'Fair Administration and Governance of Self-Regulatory Organizations, Release No 34-50699' (18 November 2004) 69 *Federal Register* 71,126, 71,151. Today, the negative effects of short selling dominate the discussion (see below).

'quality': to name just one example, at roughly 350 pages, the two drafts brought forward to replace the EU directive on markets in financial instruments (latest proposals as of 2013)[44] have daunted not only those engaged in trading but also scholars who follow reform developments on the EU level very closely.[45]

Are heterogeneity and verbosity inevitable? Or is there an alternative? One key lesson from history is that all attempts to exhaustively regulate the financial sector are doomed to fail. Policymakers tend to believe that the regulatory regime will be comprehensive when they have closed the loopholes that allowed the last crisis, failing to notice that the markets have moved on and that the next set of regulatory challenges will come up in some other way. It would be better to limit high-level regulation to the core rules, and to leave the fine points to local regulators and to those on-site. This would dramatically reduce the number of regulatory conflicts and bring the local manuals closer to a common reference point or single rule book for all engaged in trading.

2. Regulators, supervisors, and self-regulatory organizations

Too many cooks spoil the broth—the regulation of trading practices with its multitude of regulators, supervisors, and self-regulatory organizations is no exception.

In Germany, for instance, exchange trading is regulated first on-site by the individual exchange and its various bodies, such as its trading surveillance unit (*Handelsüberwachungsstelle*); second on the state level by one of the exchange supervisory authorities (most importantly by the *Hessische Börsenaufsichtsbehörde*, in charge of both the *Frankfurter Wertpapierbörse* and *Eurex Deutschland*); third on the federal level by the Federal Financial Supervisory Authority (*Bundesanstalt für Finanzdienstleistungsaufsicht*); and fourth on the EU level by the European Securities and Markets Authority (ESMA).

A similar multitude of regulators can be observed elsewhere, both in the EU and beyond.[46] Various other bodies with regulatory powers or related competences

[44] Proposal for a Regulation ... on markets in financial instruments ... —General approach (18 June 2013), 2011/0296(COD); Proposal for a Directive ... on markets in financial instruments ... —General approach (18 June 2013), 2011/0298(COD).

[45] Given the paramount influence that these regulatory instruments will have on securities regulation throughout the EU for many years to come, one would expect a plethora of articles discussing them. But it seems that most academics had given up and just waited for the final version (now enacted: MiFIR and MiFID II, both n 30 above). The two main exceptions are Ferrarini, G and Moloney, N, 'Reshaping Order Execution in the EU and the Role of Interest Groups: From MiFID I to MiFID II' (2012) 13 *European Business Organization Law Review* 557, as well as Ferrarini, G and Saguato, P, 'Reforming Securities and Derivatives Trading in the EU: From EMIR to MiFIR' (2013) 13 *Journal of Corporate Law Studies* 319.

[46] Gadinis, S and Jackson, HE, 'Markets as Regulators: A Survey' (2007) 80 *Southern California Law Review* 1239; Lee, R, *Running the World's Markets* (2011), esp 85–116 (ch 3: 'The Allocation of Regulatory Powers over Securities Markets').

could be added (on the local, state, federal, supranational, and international level): legislatures; central banks; governmental agencies to foster competition, protect consumers, or manage public assets; tax authorities; self-regulatory organizations, especially broker-dealer associations such as the US Financial Industry Regulatory Authority; informal working groups across various levels; private standard-setters like the International Swaps and Derivatives Association; or operators of alternative trading facilities. Sometimes all parties involved pull in the same direction, sometimes they go separate ways.[47]

Like the lack of a single rule book, the absence of a single regulator means that there is no one authority that those engaged in trading can ask for guidance when they are in doubt about the rules they are subject to. Instead, they have to approach various authorities with different interests, methods, and philosophies. In theory, any confusion could be avoided by making clear which regulator is responsible for which issue.[48] In practice, however, the allocation of regulatory powers has turned out to be much more complex. Overlapping responsibilities are a common phenomenon.[49] Add cross-border trading and the problems multiply.[50] This is frustrating and costly for those being regulated. But spreading regulatory knowledge over various agencies is also a main contributor to inefficient and ineffective regulation. Continuous communication, consultation, and coordination are essential in order to overcome regulatory fragmentation, but such an exchange of information has practical and legal limits.[51]

Against this background, policymakers would be well-advised to place self-regulation high on their list of regulatory methods.[52] The more they leave to those on-site, the closer the regulation of trading practices will move towards a regime with a single rule book and a single regulator. While concentrating more competencies at higher regulatory levels would have a similar effect, self-regulation comes with a number of additional benefits, such as experience and technical

[47] See, eg, *Gordon v New York Stock Exchange*, 422 *U.S.* 659 (1975), illustrating the interplay between Congress, the SEC, and the courts (Congress was dissatisfied with the SEC and intervened).

[48] IOSCO, Objectives and Principles, n 9 above, 4 ('The responsibilities of the Regulator should be clear and objectively stated'). For details, see Lee, n 46 above, 301–38 (ch 9: 'Who Should Regulate What?').

[49] The US, for instance, has two powerful twin agencies on the federal level, the SEC and the CFTC, whose responsibilities sometimes overlap (see, eg, CFTC and SEC, n 22 above).

[50] For a classic example, see Jackson, HE, Fleckner, AM, and Gurevich, M, 'Foreign Trading Screens in the United States' (2006) 1 *Capital Markets Law Journal* 54; for a current conflict, see Dummett, B, Trichur, R, and Hope, B, 'Canada Is in a Fight to Protect Stock Action' *Wall Street Journal*, 19 November 2014, C1 and C2.

[51] IOSCO, Principles Regarding Cross-Border Supervisory Cooperation (2010); IOSCO, Objectives and Principles, n 9 above, 7 (Principles No 13–15).

[52] Among the more recent evaluations by public bodies, see US General Accounting Office, Securities Markets: Competition and Multiple Regulators Heighten Concerns about Self-Regulation (2002); SEC, Self-Regulatory Organizations, n 43 above; SEC, 'Concept Release Concerning Self-Regulation, Release No 34-50700' (18 November 2004) 69 *Federal Register* 71,256.

expertise, proximity and promptness, acceptance and persuasive power, better resources, detachment from day-to-day politics, and innovation through regulatory competition.[53] The regulation of trading practices is a prime candidate to reap these benefits because there are few areas where the information asymmetry between those on-site and those watching over the markets is greater.[54] That self-regulation has failed many times is of course true. But so have regulators appointed by governments. In fact, there is no empirical data indicating that state regulation has fared any better than self-regulation. Nor are there accounts by historians showing, as critics sometimes claim, that self-regulation in most cases meant *no* regulation. Instead, history reveals a wide spectrum of self-regulatory intensity.

The challenge, then, is to make those on-site use their knowledge and skills to properly regulate the trading process. In general, the chances of regulatory success are good because securities exchanges and similar venues have all the incentives to police their markets, given that many traders and issuers will move on to a competitor if they see a risk of being overcharged or ripped off. In some areas, such as price manipulations by exchange members, conflicts of interest may prevent self-regulation from fulfilling its role—in fact or at least in the eye of the individual trader. Here, the government will have to take a more active role, as explained earlier. But this does not mean that it has to let all benefits of self-regulation pass. The opposite is true: self-regulation can be constructed as a 'statutorily imposed duty'[55] and 'coupled with oversight'[56] by the government,[57] resulting in a hybrid system that, if well designed and sufficiently transparent, combines the benefits of both regulatory concepts. In the famous words of an influential judge and regulator: '[Self-Regulation] is letting the exchanges take the leadership with Government playing a residual role. Government would keep the shotgun, so to speak, behind

[53] On the risks and benefits of self-regulation, see, eg, Miller, SS, 'Self-Regulation of the Securities Markets: A Critical Examination' (1985) 42 *Washington and Lee Law Review* 853; Kahan, M, 'Some Problems with Stock Exchange-based Securities Regulation' (1997) 83 *Virginia Law Review* 1509; Mahoney, P, 'The Exchange as Regulator' (1997) 83 *Virginia Law Review* 1453; Dombalagian, OH, 'Demythologizing the Stock Exchange: Reconciling Self-Regulation and the National Market System' (2005) 39 *University of Richmond Law Review* 1069; Lee, n 46 above, 301–38; Omarova, ST, 'Wall Street as Community of Fate: Toward Financial Industry Self-Regulation' (2011) 159 *University of Pennsylvania Law Review* 411; Birdthistle, WA and Henderson, MT, 'Becoming a Fifth Branch' (2013) 99 *Cornell Law Review* 1.

[54] Who doubts this will get a healthy dose of reality by browsing through Harris, L, *Trading and Exchanges* (2003), the leading treatise. A very readable (and mostly accurate) introduction is the bestseller Lewis, M, *Flash Boys* (2014), covering in great detail topics such as arbitrage trading, co-location, dark pools, flash trading, front-running, kickbacks, maker-taker/taker-maker models, payment for order flow, or the National Best Bid and Offer (NBBO).

[55] *Silver v New York Stock Exchange*, 373 *U.S.* 341, 353 (1963).

[56] *Gordon v New York Stock Exchange*, 422 *U.S.* 659, 667 (1975).

[57] IOSCO, Objectives and Principles, n 9 above, 5 ('such SROs should be subject to the oversight of the Regulator and should observe standards of fairness and confidentiality when exercising powers and delegated responsibilities').

the door, loaded, well oiled, cleaned, ready for use but with the hope it would never have to be used.'[58]

With these and similar safeguards, self-regulation may encompass everything that the regulation of trading practices calls for, such as formulating trading rules, monitoring compliance, and launching enforcement actions. The personal scope of self-regulation can be equally broad and include exchange members, market-makers, and broker-dealers as well as traders and investors with direct access to the marketplace. There are also good reasons to extend self-regulation to affiliates and to the issuers of bonds or stocks. Governments may also choose to rely on exchanges and other self-regulatory organizations to enforce compliance with statutory provisions.[59] In that case, self-regulatory organizations will function as 'front-line regulators'.[60]

Arguing in favour of *self*-regulation should not be confused with proposals for *de*regulation. Quite the contrary, advocating self-regulation is a plea *for* regulation, a plea for a regulatory concept that, on balance, has proven to work well over a long period of time and across many jurisdictions. Its shortcomings are known and manageable.

3. Techniques, strategies, and methods

The regulation of trading practices draws on a vast number of techniques, strategies, and methods. Three common aspects will be analysed here: the level of regulatory detail, the types of regulatory intervention, and surveillance and enforcement.

(a) *Level of regulatory detail*

Should the regulation of trading practices be principles-based or rules-based? This is not an 'either/or' question. Most promising is a combination of both approaches: set the core principles on the international, supranational, or national level, and leave the details to local regulators and to those on-site.

Price formation is a good example. The idea that prices should accurately reflect supply and demand will, if adequately anchored at the top of the regulatory regime, serve as a general guidance on all lower levels and for all parties involved. Legislators[61]

[58] Douglas, WO, *Democracy and Finance* (1940, ed. by Allen, J) 82. Douglas was Chairman of the SEC (1937–9) and Associate Justice of the US Supreme Court (1939–75).

[59] See, eg, Securities Exchange Act, n 7 above, 15 *U.S.C.* § 78f(b)(1) ('enforce compliance by its members and persons associated with its members, with the provisions of this chapter, the rules and regulations thereunder, and the rules of the exchange').

[60] SEC, Self-Regulatory Organizations, n 43 above, 71,128 and 71,129 n 30, as well as in numerous other documents.

[61] The exchange acts and similar statutes could—and should—state much more explicitly that market-driven price formation is the key objective of regulating trading practices (or at least among them). Today, this regulatory goal is typically only implicitly assumed; eg, Securities Exchange Act,

and regulators[62] would therefore be well-advised to designate market-driven price formation as the key objective in the regulation of trading practices (perhaps along with transparency and fairness). It would be unwise, however, to prescribe at higher regulatory levels the details of how to achieve that goal. Trading practices change and evolve more quickly than any political system can react—just compare how long it took to reform the US National Market System or the EU directive on markets in financial instruments, and how quickly market participants adapted to the new regulatory environment (leading, *inter alia*, to an explosion of algorithmic trading and to a sharp increase in market fragmentation, see below). In any case, even if policymakers sped up the adoption of new rules, their regulatory impact would remain dubious because price formation is the prime example of an issue that those involved in trading understand much better than those supervising it: many regulators are not acquainted with basic trading mechanisms (such as the differences between order-driven and quote-driven markets), let alone with the intricacies of today's algorithmic trading.[63] Practical experience has also shown that price formation requires more rules than many people would expect and most regulators from afar could ever come up with.[64]

What happens, for instance, when market participants agree on prices that significantly differ from other prices found around the same time? With the rise of electronic trading, such 'error trades' or 'mistrades' have turned out to be a major regulatory challenge, even long before the 'flash crash' (2010).[65] In Germany, the handling of mistrades belongs to the few trading details that retail investors care about and that, as a consequence, marketplaces use to differentiate their trading systems from the competition.[66] While most disputes are settled behind the scenes, some investors have sued

n 7 above, 15 *U.S.C.* § 78b(2)/(3) (regulation necessary due to the far-reaching implications of the prices that market participants agree upon); Börsengesetz, n 36 above, § 24(2)(1) (exchange prices must be set according to the rules and have to reflect the true market conditions); MiFIR, n 30 above, Recital 17 and Article 5 (volume cap mechanism for private markets to protect the price formation process on exchanges and similar venues), as well as Recital 18 (pre-trade transparency requirements for private markets, for the same reason) and Article 23(1) (no 'trading obligation' for investment firms with regard to transactions that 'do not contribute to the price discovery process').

[62] IOSCO, Objectives and Principles, n 9 above, 12 notes that '[t]he establishment of trading systems including securities exchanges should be subject to regulatory authorization and oversight', but the corresponding principles (No 34–8) do not explain why ('price' is not mentioned once in the entire document, only 'pricing' in the context of collective investment schemes). The much longer document that accompanies the principles frequently refers to 'prices', to 'price discovery', and to the 'price formation process', but does not identify market-driven price formation as the key rationale for regulating trading practices (IOSCO, Methodology, n 29 above).

[63] For an overview of the main trading mechanisms, see Harris, n 54 above, 92–6. Algorithmic trading is discussed below.

[64] See, eg, Deutsche Börse Group, Xetra Release 14.0—Market Model Equities (30 September 2013), a document of 80 pages.

[65] The best international survey is IOSCO, Policies on Error Trades (2005).

[66] Mistrades happen so frequently that the marketplaces nowadays publish mistrade lists on the Internet; most important are <http://www.zertifikate.boerse-frankfurt.de/en/latest-news/

their broker-dealers (or the latter's counterparties), and courts on various levels, including Germany's Federal Court of Justice (*Bundesgerichtshof*), have delivered judgments in mistrade cases.[67] Because rules on error trades must be tailored to the local trading system and its underlying philosophy, policymakers on the international, supranational, or national level should leave this task to local regulators and to those on-site.[68]

Another example is the handling of 'trading halts' or 'trading interruptions': market operators stop trading to allow new information to spread ('discretionary trading interruptions') and to avoid excessive price movements ('automatic trading interruptions' such as 'price limits' or 'circuit breakers').[69] The 'flash crash' and similar incidents suggest that the increase in algorithmic trading may call for a revision of these rules—again a regulatory task that those on-site can accomplish much faster and better than those afield.[70]

(b) *Types of regulatory intervention*

Governments employ various tools to regulate trading practices. Popular types of regulatory intervention are institutionalization, business conduct rules, transparency requirements, trading strategy bans, and taxation.

(1) *Institutionalization*

All major jurisdictions recognize and thereby institutionalize at least two categories of trading venues (with details differing over time and across borders): 'official markets',[71] for which exchanges are the prime example, and 'private markets',[72]

trading-info#tab=mistrades> (Frankfurt Stock Exchange/*Frankfurter Wertpapierbörse*) and <https://www.boerse-stuttgart.de/de/boersenportal/tools-und-services/handelstransparenz/mistradeliste/> (Stuttgart Stock Exchange/*Baden-Württembergische Wertpapierbörse*).

[67] For an analysis of these decisions, see Fleckner, AM, 'Aufhebung nicht marktgerechter Wertpapiergeschäfte (Mistrades)' (2011) 65 *Zeitschrift für Wirtschafts- und Bankrecht* 585.

[68] It does make sense, of course, to compile, compare, and discuss the various rules that marketplaces have come up with (as did IOSCO, Error Trades, n 65 above). But there is no uniform error trade policy that would suit all markets (stressed also on 3, 9, 13–14).

[69] Still a good survey is IOSCO, Report on Trading Halts and Market Closures (2002). In a broader context, see IOSCO, Methodology, n 29 above, 201, 204, 207, 216, 217, 223.

[70] The trend seems to be in the opposite direction; see, eg, SEC, 'Regulation Systems Compliance and Integrity, Release No 34-73639' (19 November 2014) 79 *Federal Register* 72,252 (196 pages, in the SEC's standard format even 743).

[71] The main examples include 'national securities exchanges' (Securities Exchange Act, n 7 above, 15 *U.S.C.* § 78f) and 'designated contract markets' (Commodity Exchange Act, n 34 above, 7 *U.S.C.* § 7) as well as 'Börsen' (Börsengesetz, n 36 above, §§ 2, 4), 'marchés réglementés d'instruments financiers' (Code monétaire et financier, n 37 above, Articles L421-1, L421-4) and 'recognised investment exchanges' (Financial Services and Markets Act 2000, n 35 above, §§ 285, 290), all three 'regulated markets' as defined on the EU level (MiFID I, n 30 above, Article 4(1)(14); MiFIR, n 30 above, Article 2(1)(13), referring to MiFID II, n 30 above, Article 4(1)(21)).

[72] As the term suggests, 'private markets' are typically not officially authorized, registered, or recognized. The seminal regulatory action was SEC, 'Regulation of Exchanges and Alternative Trading Systems, Release No 34-40760' (8 December 1998) 63 *Federal Register* 70,844. It remains to be seen

known, *inter alia*, as alternative trading systems (ATSs) or as over-the-counter (OTC) markets.[73] By dividing the market into separate regulatory segments and imposing distinct rules on different venue types, governments heavily influence where and how orders are executed (see the Chapter by Ferrarini and Saguato in this volume).

While both official and private markets function well as venues that match buyers and sellers, the trading process typically differs. On official markets, order execution is transparent and non-discretionary because governments require price formation to follow predetermined rules (today coded in the automated trading systems).[74] Organizers of private markets, in contrast, typically have discretion with regard to the trading process; there is no need for state intervention, aside from provisions that prevent trading on private markets from distorting price formation on official markets.[75]

Governments and regulators have deepened the separation between official and private markets through various additional measures (eg, through rules that only apply to issuers whose securities are listed on official markets or by using prices found on official markets for tax and accounting purposes). As a result, official markets have become 'reference markets' that set 'reference prices', recognized as such either by law or because market participants believe they accurately reflect supply and demand.

whether 'organised trading facilities' (MiFIR, n 30 above, Article 2(1)(15), referring to MiFID II, n 30 above, Article 4(1)(23)) will turn out to be private or rather hybrid markets.

[73] Ferrarini and Saguato, n 45 above, refer to 'public markets' and 'private markets' (explained on 322–3). The present Chapter favours 'official' over 'public' because 'official' vs 'private' is a binary distinction without any grey areas: a market either is officially authorized, registered, or recognized (most importantly as an 'exchange') or not; whether a market is 'public', in contrast, is a matter of definition. For similar reasons, 'official' is preferred to 'regulated' (all standardized trading in negotiable instruments is to some degree regulated, even on private markets). See generally Fleckner, n 11 above, 658–9 (distinguishing between a formal and a material exchange definition).

[74] Most prominently MiFID I, n 30 above, Recital 6 ('The requirement that the interests be brought together in the system by means of non-discretionary rules set by the system operator means that they are brought together under the system's rules or by means of the system's protocols or internal operating procedures (including procedures embodied in computer software). The term "non-discretionary rules" means that these rules leave the investment firm operating an MTF with no discretion as to how interests may interact'), also Articles 4(1)(14) (definition of 'regulated market'), 4(1)(15) (definition of 'multilateral trading facility (MTF)'), 14(1) (those operating MTFs must 'establish transparent and non-discretionary rules and procedures for fair and orderly trading and establish objective criteria for the efficient execution of orders'), 39(d) (regulated markets must 'have transparent and non-discretionary rules and procedures that provide for fair and orderly trading and establish objective criteria for the efficient execution of orders'); now MiFIR, n 30 above, Recital 7 and MiFID II, n 30 above, Articles 4(1)(21), 4(1)(22), 47(1)(d).

[75] For an example, see MiFIR, n 30 above, Recital 17 as well as Article 5 (regulating private markets in order to protect the price formation process on official markets, see n 61 above). It remains to be seen whether these rules, on balance, go too far in regulating trading practices on private markets.

(II) *Business conduct rules*

Intermediaries are important for the process of trading because they pass on orders of those traders who lack direct market access (such as retail investors).

Governments have imposed many duties on intermediaries, most of which lie outside the scope of the present Chapter (see the Chapter by Tuch in this volume). Some of the business conduct rules for intermediaries, however, govern the allocation of client orders and, therefore, overlap with the regulation of trading practices (recall Figure 20.1). Most rigorous are 'concentration rules' that make it mandatory for intermediaries to route client orders to official markets (a concept that used to be known as *Börsenzwang* in Germany).[76] More complex are today's 'best execution' and 'trade-through' rules.[77] They require intermediaries to send orders to the venue that, based on various criteria, will best serve their clients' interests.[78]

While most of these rules seem to be motivated by investor protection considerations, they can also be understood as a mechanism to make markets more efficient: selecting a venue for client orders creates conflicts of interest and poses the risk that the order allocation will be less than socially optimal (further discussed below in the context of market fragmentation). If governments manage to channel the order flow to the 'right' venues, prices will become more informative and trading more efficient.

(III) *Transparency requirements*

For securities law in general, mandatory disclosure is probably the single most popular form of regulatory intervention (see the Chapter by Enriques and Gilotta in this volume). The regulation of trading practices is no exception: transparency requirements are commonplace.[79]

[76] Introduced through Article 2(12) Zweites Finanzmarktförderungsgesetz (26 July 1994) *Bundesgesetzblatt I* 1749, 1766, codified in Börsengesetz, § 10, later repealed. For new concentration rules with a different scope, see Pittsburgh Summit Declaration, n 26 above, and MiFIR, n 30 above, Articles 23 (trading obligation for investment firms) and 28 (obligation to trade derivatives on certain markets); in scholarship, eg, Hertig, G, 'Mifid and the Return of Concentration Rules' in Grundmann, S et al. (eds), *Festschrift für Klaus J. Hopt* (Vol II, 2010) 1989.

[77] *Newton v Merrill, Lynch, Pierce, Fenner & Smith*, 135 *F.3d* 266 (3rd Cir. 1998); *Newton v Merrill Lynch, Pierce, Fenner & Smith*, 259 *F.3d* 154 (3rd Cir. 2001); 17 *C.F.R.*, n 38 above, § 242.611 ('Order protection rule'); MiFID I, n 30 above, Article 21 ('Obligation to execute orders on terms most favourable to the client'), now MiFID II, n 30 above, Article 27.

[78] Ferrarini, G, 'Best Execution and Competition between Trading Venues—MiFID's Likely Impact' (2007) 2 *Capital Markets Law Journal* 404; Gadinis, S, 'Market Structure for Institutional Investors: Comparing the U.S. and E.U. Regimes' (2008) 3 *Virginia Law & Business Review* 311, esp 340–52; Ferrarini, G, 'Market Transparency and Best Execution: Bond Trading under MiFID' in Tison, M et al. (eds), *Perspectives in Company Law and Financial Regulation* (2009) 477; Hertig, n 76 above, 1990–2; Moloney, n 24 above, 355–63; Coffee and Sale, n 9 above, 662–4.

[79] IOSCO, Objectives and Principles, n 9 above, 12 ('Regulation should promote transparency of trading'). An interesting case study is Boehmer, E, Saar, G, and Yu, L, 'Lifting the Veil: An Analysis of Pre-trade Transparency at the NYSE' (2005) 60 *The Journal of Finance* 783 (showing that

Traders are interested chiefly in two types of information: *pre-trade data* (bid and ask quotes, ie, the highest price at which one market participant is willing to buy, eg, $50.10, and the lowest price for which someone else or the same person is willing to sell, eg, $50.20) and *post-trade data* (execution or transaction data, ie, the object, the volume, the price, the time, etc of trades that have been concluded).

Both types of data are of great importance for price formation and, by extension, for the process of trading.[80] Accordingly, official markets (as defined above) publish pre-trade and post-trade data on a real-time basis.[81] Private markets typically do not—one of their main advantages for those who want to acquire or sell positions without making the public aware of the transaction (often to avoid unfavourable price movements, which is not illegitimate per se). The recent increase in such 'dark trading' has alerted many regulators,[82] and scholars have started evaluating the positive and negative effects of 'dark pools'.[83]

If market-driven price formation was the only regulatory objective, governments would put official markets in a position that would allow them to consider data from as many venues as possible, making their prices accurately reflect the *overall* market supply and demand. In reality, however, policymakers will pursue additional goals (such as fostering competition among marketplaces or honouring legitimate privacy interests), and strike a balance between conflicting

market quality and the informational efficiency of prices may to some extent increase with pre-trade transparency).

[80] IOSCO, Error Trades, n 65 above, 13 ('The availability and integrity of information on bids and offers is a central factor in ensuring price discovery and in strengthening users' confidence that they will be able to trade at fair prices. Similarly, the availability of information in respect to the volumes and prices of completed trades enables market users to take into account the most recent information and to monitor the quality of execution they have obtained').

[81] Examples for *pre-trade* data disclosure obligations: MiFID I, n 30 above, Article 44 ('Pre-trade transparency requirements for regulated markets'); 17 *C.F.R.*, n 38 above, § 242.602 ('Dissemination of quotations in NMS securities'); MiFIR, n 30 above, Articles 3 ('Pre-trade transparency requirements for trading venues in respect of shares, depositary receipts, ETFs, certificates and other similar financial instruments') and 8 ('Pre-trade transparency requirements for trading venues in respect of bonds, structured finance products, emission allowances and derivatives'). Examples for *post-trade* data disclosure obligations: MiFID I, n 30 above, Article 45 ('Post-trade transparency requirements for regulated markets'); 17 *C.F.R.*, n 38 above, § 242.601 ('Dissemination of transaction reports and last sale data with respect to transactions in NMS stocks'); MiFIR, n 30 above, Articles 6 ('Post-trade transparency requirements for trading venues in respect of shares, depositary receipts, ETFs, certificates and other similar financial instruments') and 10 ('Post-trade transparency requirements for trading venues in respect of bonds, structured finance products, emission allowances and derivatives').

[82] SEC, 'Regulation of Non-Public Trading Interest, Release No 34-60997' (13 November 2009) 74 *Federal Register* 61,208; SEC, Equity Market Structure, n 21 above, 3599 and 3612–14; IOSCO, Dark Liquidity, n 29 above; Commission Staff Working Paper, Impact Assessment, SEC(2011) 1226 final (20 October 2011), 10–13, 18, 62, 70, 90–1, 95, 103–5, 122, 131, 160.

[83] Gadinis, n 78 above, 320–2 and *passim*; Hertig, n 76 above, 1992, 1996–7; Ferrarini and Moloney, n 45 above, 562–3, 565–7, 571–81, 583, 588–90; Ferrarini and Saguato, n 45 above, 321, 337–9, 346, 349; Zhu, H, 'Do Dark Pools Harm Price Discovery?' (2014) 27 *Review of Financial Studies* 747.

principles. For the disclosure of trading data, it would be a good compromise to make *post-trade data* publicly available in real-time (as it is already common practice) but disclose dark *pre-trade data* in real-time only to those setting the prices on official markets (ie, today the automated trading system or formerly the floor brokers). The rationale behind this distinction is that post-trade data only indirectly affects price formation, while pre-trade data has an immediate influence on future prices. Keeping pre-trade data private allows dark trading to continue, and secretly including it in the official markets' price formation process will make 'official' prices more informative (and reduce the opportunities to exploit information asymmetries). Under these circumstances, additional restrictions on dark trading would appear unnecessary.[84]

Other transparency mechanisms include requirements to report larger trading positions or to disclose holdings above a certain level.[85] They make it more difficult for traders to systematically distort price formation.

(IV) *Trading strategy bans*

Banning strategies or practices that are believed to disturb trading is probably the most rigorous form of regulatory intervention. It is also one of the oldest techniques, both for the regulation of trading practices and for securities law in general. Important examples include provisions against short selling, against market manipulation, or against 'front-running' (ie, trading ahead of client orders).[86]

Some trading bans help protect price formation from distortion, for instance by stopping patterns that *artificially* inflate prices ('marking the close') or *misleadingly* boost trading volumes ('wash sales'). Other trading bans may have adverse effects on price formation because they hold back orders that, if placed, would make prices more informative. A well-known example is insider trading: if the regulatory aim is to ensure that prices accurately reflect market supply and demand, then banning insider trading is counterproductive.[87] Similar tensions arise from restrictions on algorithmic trading and on short selling (discussed later).

A related regulatory technique that basically stifles certain trading strategies (such as cornering) is to limit the number of shares, bonds, commodities, or derivatives that a given trader may hold at the same time.[88]

[84] But see (volume cap) MiFIR, n 30 above, Recital 17 as well as Article 5 (see nn 61 and 75 above).

[85] For an example in recent years, see SEC, 'Large Trader Reporting, Release No 34-64976' (27 July 2011) 76 *Federal Register* 46,960–47,007.

[86] See generally IOSCO, Objectives and Principles, n 9 above, 12 ('Regulation should be designed to detect and deter manipulation and other unfair trading practices'). Note that banning front-running may also be understood as a business conduct rule.

[87] But there may be other legitimate reasons for outlawing insider trading (such as equal treatment of investors and traders, enforcing fiduciary duties, and encouraging the exchange of information within publicly traded companies).

[88] For a far-reaching reform proposal, see CFTC, 'Position Limits for Derivatives' (7 November 2013) 78 *Federal Register* 75,680.

(v) *Taxation*

Stamp duties and similar taxes on trading are almost as old as the exchanges themselves, but had been abandoned in many places as an outdated regulatory technique. Over the past few years, however, activists, policymakers, regulators, and scholars have rediscovered the idea and put forward various proposals that would charge trading on securities exchanges and elsewhere with a tax ('financial transaction tax').

While some of the earlier proposals for financial transaction taxes had a distinct regulatory impetus (above all reducing fluctuations in currency prices), today the focus is typically on other policy goals (such as increasing tax revenue or 'punishing' the financial sector). The most important exception is high-frequency trading: some people believe that trading at high speeds has negative externalities and that imposing financial transaction taxes will help reduce them. Yet, whether taxing is really a sound regulatory approach, assuming that there are valid reasons for governments to restrict high-frequency trading, is doubtful: traders may respond to financial transaction taxes by increasing leverage—something regulators try to fight elsewhere.

(c) *Surveillance and enforcement*

Some of the rules that regulate trading practices are self-enforcing. For instance, if governments vest securities exchanges with the exclusive power to admit financial instruments to trading, it is technically impossible to use the exchange infrastructure for transactions in instruments that have not been registered with the exchange.[89]

Most other rules call for surveillance and, if market participants fail to comply, for enforcement. Given the multitude of rules and regulators, it is no surprise that the arsenal of enforcement tools is equally diverse. Administrative and criminal sanctions are most important, followed by civil liability regimes that let investors collect damages from non-complying market participants.

What are the most promising enforcement strategies? There is surprisingly little research that could help answer this question. While most people agree that enforcement is of paramount importance, it has failed to draw greater interest so far—in both the regulation of trading practices and other areas of securities law.[90] The few studies hitherto conducted suggest that enforcement intensity varies—both

[89] With the exception of exchanges that collude with traders—a classical problem of who will guard the guards (Iuv. 6.347–8: '*sed quis custodiet ipsos custodes?*'). For an example, see US General Accounting Office, Securities Regulation—Improvements Needed in the Amex Listing Program (November 2001).

[90] As reflected, for instance, by the vagueness of the 'Principles for the Enforcement of Securities Regulation' by IOSCO, Objectives and Principles, n 9 above, 6 (No 10–12).

across[91] and within[92] jurisdictions. But which techniques work best is still an open question.[93]

To further complicate matters, most policymakers and regulators are not entirely free in their choice of enforcement tools. In many jurisdictions, only the legislature can make certain violations a criminal offence, and only courts can impose criminal sanctions. Such restrictions favour rules-based over principles-based regulation.

IV. Implications: Algorithmic Trading, Short Selling, and Market Fragmentation

Policymakers, regulators, and traders currently face a number of regulatory challenges. At the top of many people's agenda are *algorithmic trading*, a rather new phenomenon that has unleashed a storm of criticism; *short selling*, as old as exchange trading and once again under public scrutiny; and *market fragmentation*, an ever-controversial issue that, fuelled by new developments, has now reached a level unseen before. All three issues will be analysed here in light of the Chapter's central argument: that market-driven price formation should be the key objective in the regulation of trading practices.

1. Algorithmic trading

Algorithmic trading (also 'algo' or 'algorithm' trading) is yet another step towards reducing human involvement in trading. Some time ago, automated trading systems started replacing those hectic agents who used to bustle around the trading

[91] Jackson, HE, 'Variation in the Intensity of Financial Regulation: Preliminary Evidence and Potential Implications' (2007) 24 *Yale Journal on Regulation* 253; Coffee, JC, 'Law and the Market: The Impact of Enforcement' (2007) 156 *University of Pennsylvania Law Review* 229; Jackson, HE and Roe, MJ, 'Public and Private Enforcement of Securities Laws: Resource-based Evidence' (2009) 93 *Journal of Financial Economics* 207.

[92] Gadinis, S, 'The SEC and the Financial Industry: Evidence from Enforcement Against Broker-Dealers' (2012) 67 *The Business Lawyer* 679.

[93] For a critical examination, see Hellgardt, A, 'Comparing Apples and Oranges? Public, Private, Tax, and Criminal Law Instruments in Financial Markets Regulation' in Ringe, WG and Huber, PM (eds), *Legal Challenges in the Global Financial Crisis* (2014) 157.

floor, busy to match buy and sell orders. It did not take long before trading floors became a deserted place, maintained merely as scenery for television to commemorate the good old times when the throng of floor brokers formed the heart of the exchange.

While automated trading systems *execute* orders sent to them, algorithmic trading pushes automation one level higher by letting computers *place* orders. The algorithm will decide whether it is a good moment for trading or not, which instruments are most promising to deal in, what quantity will be bought or sold, at which price, and so on. One important advantage of computers over human traders is speed: computers place, change, and cancel orders within fractions of a second. Such 'high-frequency trading' has become so prominent that some observers use 'algorithmic trading' and 'high-frequency trading' interchangeably, notwithstanding the fact that algorithmic trading is not limited to strategies that require prompt execution, while trading fast alone is probably not a trading strategy at all (rather a technique to carry out strategies such as arbitrage trading).

Automated trading systems and algorithmic trading have fundamentally transformed the landscape.[94] Take the New York Stock Exchange as an example. Between 2005 and 2009, its average execution time for small orders decreased from 10.1 to 0.7 seconds, the average daily trading volume rose from 2.1 billion to 5.9 billion shares, the average daily number of trades multiplied from 2.9 million to 22.1 million, and the average trade size fell from 724 to 268 shares (computers tailor orders to current market supply and demand by splitting them).[95] The pace of change was equally dramatic at other venues and in more recent years. While stocks used to be held for many years, some market participants believe that high-frequency trading has reduced the average holding period to a few seconds.[96]

Wherever automated trading systems were about to replace the local floor brokers, various stakeholders and observers voiced concerns. Most vocal were—*honi soit qui mal y pense*—the soon-to-be-redundant floor brokers. But today, few people would argue in favour of bringing back the trading floor and shutting down automated trading systems. Markets with automated trading systems have turned out to be much more efficient, and the regulatory regimes have managed to cope with the challenges that arose from automation. Will the same be true for algorithmic trading? Or is algorithmic trading at odds with fundamental regulatory principles? It is probably too early for an answer because the debate is still in full

[94] A (too) gloomy picture is drawn by Lewis, n 54 above, who believes that US securities trading is 'rigged' in favour of high-frequency traders (see 40, 85, 95, 232, 243, and *passim*).

[95] SEC, Equity Market Structure, n 21 above, 3595–6.

[96] It is difficult to come up with any concrete numbers. But it is highly plausible that the average holding period is down to a few seconds (or even less) on markets that are dominated by high-frequency trading. Note that trading will often be limited to a small fraction of all outstanding shares, with most shares being held by long-term investors who only infrequently trade. From this perspective, the change looks less dramatic.

swing: various regulatory responses to algorithmic trading are on the table,[97] and a vast body of scholarship has emerged weighing its risks and benefits.[98]

Whether price formation is adversely affected by algorithmic trading depends on the strategy that the algorithm follows. Algorithmic trading is not good or bad per se. Some forms of algorithmic trading will distort prices, as do some strategies employed by humans. In other cases, algorithmic trading will make prices more informative. High-frequency trading is the best example: computers can absorb new information much faster and react more quickly than human traders. The sooner prices reflect changes in market supply and demand, the better—prices will be more informative. Under the right circumstances, high-frequency trading will also increase liquidity, reduce volatility, cut spreads between ask and bid quotes, and trim down price differences between venues.

Some of the strategies that algorithmic traders pursue, however, can create risks for the price formation process. To begin with, computers not only *place* orders within fractions of a second but also *cancel* them at the same speed. Perceived liquidity can disappear all of a sudden. What looked like an order to slower market participants may well have been nothing but an attempt to extract information from the order book or to influence the price formation process. Many exchanges have facilitated such strategies by introducing odd order types that traders would not have dreamt of only a few years ago. For instance, 'book-or-cancel' orders will be rejected without entry in the order book if immediate execution is possible—an order type that will upset all those who naïvely believed that orders were placed to get executed rather than placed to *not* get executed.[99] Equally odd is that

[97] SEC, Equity Market Structure, n 21 above, esp 3606–12; BIS, High-Frequency Trading, n 27 above; Commission Staff Working Paper, n 82 above, 11, 25, 29, 37–8, 47, 59, 62, 94–5, 126–9, 152–3, 155, 164, 264; Gesetz zur Vermeidung von Gefahren und Missbräuchen im Hochfrequenzhandel (Hochfrequenzhandelsgesetz) (7 May 2013) *Bundesgesetzblatt I* 1162–6; MiFID II, n 30 above, Recitals 18, 20, 23, 50, 59–68, 113, 157, 159, as well as Articles 2(1)(d)(iii)/(e)/(j)(ii) (exemptions), 4(1)(39)/(40) (definitions), 17 ('Algorithmic trading'), 48 ('Systems resilience, circuit breakers and electronic trading'), 65(1)(h) (organizational requirements for consolidated tape providers), 90(1)(c) (report by the Commission).

[98] Hendershott, T, Jones, CM, and Menkveld, AJ, 'Does Algorithmic Trading Improve Liquidity?' (2011) 66 *Journal of Finance* 1; Hendershott, T and Moulton, PC, 'Automation, Speed, and Stock Market Quality' (2011) 14 *Journal of Financial Markets* 568; Cartea, Á and Penalva, J, 'Where Is the Value in High Frequency Trading?' (2012) 2(3) *Quarterly Journal of Finance* *1; Hautsch, N, *Econometrics of Financial High-Frequency Data* (2012); Ferrarini and Moloney, n 45 above, 560/13, 574–5, 577, 581, 589; Fleckner and Hopt, n 1 above, 556–8; Menkveld, AJ, 'High Frequency Trading and the New Market Makers' (2013) 16 *Journal of Financial Markets* 712; Hagströmer, B and Nordén, L, 'The Diversity of High-frequency Traders' (2013) 16 *Journal of Financial Markets* 741; Brogaard, J, Hendershott, T, and Riordan, R, 'High-Frequency Trading and Price Discovery' (2014) 27 *Review of Financial Studies* 2267.

[99] For the details, see, eg, Deutsche Börse Group, n 64 above, 13. The most prominent order type probe in the US is expected to close with the largest fine ever imposed on a national securities exchange: Patterson, S, 'BATS Faces Big Trading Fine' *Wall Street Journal*, 5 December 2014, C1 and C2.

high-frequency traders were allowed to put their servers on exchange premises to gain a speed advantage over other traders ('co-location').[100] Some even got early access to trade data or news releases.[101]

While such practices threaten to distort price formation and harm less sophisticated traders, nothing of what has been discussed so far calls for an outright ban of algorithmic or high-frequency trading. Nor is there a need for a major overhaul of the regulatory regime. The reason is that most of the practices that critics condemn are outright illegal (for instance, because they violate rules against front-running) or at least in conflict with basic regulatory principles (such as equal treatment of investors or traders); enforcement deficits will not be cured through the creation of duplicate rules. For some other problematic trading practices, only minor amendments to the regulatory regime are necessary (such as transparency rules that restore a level playing field). For still others, no intervention is required because they are in line with overarching regulatory objectives; after all, gains to the detriment of technologically less advanced traders are not illegitimate per se, and they may even increase public welfare by prompting other market participants to invest in technology (up to the point where it becomes a mere arms race).

A more fundamental concern is the aggregated impact that algorithmic trading has on the functioning of the financial markets ('systemic risk'). The infamous 'flash crash' (2010)[102] and a recent novel (2011)[103] nicely illustrate what happens when trading gets out of control.[104] Fortunately, such singular shocks are easy to absorb by adding more layers of redundancy and installing circuit breakers for the few cases in which the system still fails. More concerning is that price formation may get systematically distorted if venues are dominated by a certain trading strategy. This can happen on any market, whether or not computers are involved, but algorithmic trading may make it more likely that one strategy prevails because some strategies are easier to code into an algorithm than others. For instance, if most algorithmic traders run trend-following ('momentum') strategies (buy what soars and sell what falls), this pattern becomes a self-fulfilling prophecy because it pushes prices into the desired direction. However, what critics often 'forget' is that algorithmic traders have to close their position at some point, ie, sell what they have bought or buy what they have sold (discussed in more detail below for short

[100] Frequently discussed in SEC, Equity Market Structure, n 21 above, 3598, 3606, 3608, 3610–11.

[101] See, eg, Patterson, S, 'Traders' Access to Releases Curbed' *Wall Street Journal*, 21 February 2014, C1 and C2; Patterson, S, 'Marketwired Cuts Service to Speedy Traders' *Wall Street Journal*, 20 March 2014, C3; Eaglesham, J and Patterson, S, 'NYSE Settles Charges its Safeguards Fell Short' *Wall Street Journal*, 2 May 2014, C1 and C2; Tracy, R and Patterson, S, 'Fast Traders Get SEC Data Seconds Early' *Wall Street Journal*, 29 October 2014, C1 and C2; Patterson, S, 'SEC to Close Gap in Filings' Release' *Wall Street Journal*, 27–28 December 2014, B1 and B2.

[102] See n 22 for the main studies.

[103] Harris, n 23 above.

[104] This is not to say that the 'flash crash' was caused by algorithmic trading. The point here is that the infamous crash showed what *could* happen in a worst-case scenario.

selling). Closing the position will trigger an opposite price movement—in the case of high-frequency trading often within fractions of a second. Moreover, with fierce competition among high-frequency traders, there may be an inherent limit to many trading strategies because at some point, costs will no longer be outweighed by possible gains (arbitrage trading is the obvious example).

On balance, it seems that the public debate about algorithmic trading so far has given too much weight to the risks and not enough attention to the benefits of automation. At the heart of the debate lies a controversy about market design: what is the optimal level of automation, what is the optimal speed and frequency of trading? Technologically, the answer depends on what is currently feasible. Economically, the determining factor is whether the gains from more automation offset the costs. From the legal standpoint developed in this Chapter, the impact, if any, of increased automation on the price formation process is critical. There are many other market design questions with a similar dimension, such as whether an exchange should have a manual trading floor or an automated trading system, whether trading should be concentrated in a few hours or span the entire day, whether continued trading or periodic auctions are preferable, and so on. Almost all of these questions are typically left to the local regulator or to those on-site. So far, little evidence has emerged that would call for treating algorithmic trading differently.

Again, this is not a plea for deregulation. It is a plea for regulation at lower levels and for self-regulation. Different market operators will come to different answers, depending on the subjects and objects admitted to trading, the preferred market philosophy, the orders the venue hopes to draw, and the broader regulatory environment. Some markets may impose no restrictions on algorithmic trading to attract high-frequency traders. Others may declare an outright ban to lure retail investors. Still others will strike a balance between the two and choose from the various regulatory tools that help police algorithmic trading.[105] A one-size-fits-all approach would obstruct such regulatory tailoring and competition.[106]

[105] Such as registration, admission, and licensing requirements; reporting and disclosure obligations; enhanced supervision and enforcement powers; additional business conduct rules and organizational requirements; revised market abuse rules; cancellation fees and other charges for 'excessive' trading; order-to-trade ratios, minimum quote lives, minimum tick sizes, order and volume limits; random delays and speed bumps; volatility interruptions; exclusion of certain instruments from algorithmic trading; transaction taxes.

[106] Interestingly, the heroes of Lewis's gloomy book (n 54 above) are some individuals who set up a marketplace that is not 'rigged' (to borrow Lewis's term) in favour of certain traders: IEX—the Investors Exchange (portrayed on 151–243 and *passim*); for more recent developments, see Patterson, S, Hope, B, and Demos, T, 'Maverick Trade Venue in Cash Talks' *Wall Street Journal*, 24–25 May 2014, B1 and B2; Hope, B, 'IEX Plan Aims to Drain "Dark Pools"' *Wall Street Journal*, 7 July 2014, C1 and C2; Patterson, S and Strasburg, J, 'IEX Sets Sights on Exchange Status' *Wall Street Journal*, 3 September 2014, C1 and C2. That a new venue was founded to lure traders and investors who are critical of trading practices elsewhere makes it difficult to argue that there is a market failure to which the government should respond, and supports the more cautious approach followed above. For a similar market reaction, see Hope, B, 'NYSE Fees On Some Orders to Be Pared' *Wall Street Journal*,

2. Short selling

All traders hope to buy cheap and sell dear. Most traders buy first, wait for the price to rise, and then sell. A few traders hope to make a profit in reverse order: sell high, wait for the price to drop, and buy low afterwards. Because the latter requires traders to sell items that they are short of at the time of selling, the strategy is known as 'short selling'.[107]

Short selling is as old as exchange trading, and there is nothing special about it except the reverse order of buying and selling. Nevertheless, restrictions on short selling date back to the very first days of trading. A Dutch decree outlawed some forms of short selling as early as four centuries ago.[108] Many similar prohibitions by various governments and regulators followed. The exchanges and those buying from short sellers were not sitting on the sidelines either. They put in place contract penalties for sellers who fail to deliver and established margin requirements to ensure that traders have the necessary funds to cover their losses.[109]

All went well for a long time. Then came the most recent financial crisis, and policymakers feared 'that at a time of considerable financial instability, short selling could aggravate the downward spiral in the prices of shares, notably in financial institutions, in a way which could ultimately threaten their viability and create systemic risks'.[110] The result was a wave of additional restrictions on short selling worldwide, ranging from reporting requirements over market structure modifications to outright bans.[111]

Whether the new rules on short selling are good policy is still a very controversial issue. Most scholars seem to be sceptical.[112] With regard to the price

17 December 2014, C3 and Hope, B and Patterson, S, 'NYSE Plan Would Revamp Trading' *Wall Street Journal*, 18 December 2014, C1 and C2.

107 For the details, see the characteristics developed by IOSCO, Short Selling, n 29 above, 7 and 23, as well as the definition by the EU Short Selling Regulation, n 32 above, Article 2(1)(b).

108 Placaet (27 February 1610), n 2 above.

109 For an example of cases in which non-delivery led to litigation, see Fleckner, n 40 above.

110 EU Short Selling Regulation, n 32 above, Recital 1.

111 Most importantly SEC, '"Naked" Short Selling Antifraud Rule, Release No 34-58774' (14 October 2008) 73 *Federal Register* 61,666; SEC, 'Amendments to Regulation SHO, Release No 34-61595' (26 February 2010) 75 *Federal Register* 11,232; EU Short Selling Regulation, n 32 above. For an international survey, see IOSCO, Short Selling, n 29 above.

112 See, eg, Sirri, ER, 'Regulatory Politics and Short Selling' (2010) 71 *University of Pittsburgh Law Review* 517; Saffi, PAC and Sigurdsson, K, 'Price Efficiency and Short Selling' (2011) 24 *Review of Financial Studies* 821; Juurikkala, O, 'Credit Default Swaps and the EU Short Selling Regulation: A Critical Analysis' (2012) 9 *European Company and Financial Law Review* 307; Payne, J, 'The Regulation of Short Selling and its Reform in Europe' (2012) 13 *European Business Organization Law Review* 413; Boehmer, E and Wu, J, 'Short Selling and the Price Discovery Process' (2013) 26 *Review of Financial Studies* 287; Boehmer, E, Jones, CM, and Zhang, X, 'Shackling Short Sellers: The 2008 Shorting Ban' (2013) 26 *Review of Financial Studies* 1363; Harris, LE, Namvar, E, and Phillips, B, 'Price Inflation and Wealth Transfer during the 2008 SEC Short-Sale Ban' (2013) 11(2) *Journal of Investment Management* 5; Howell, E, 'The European Court of Justice: Selling Us Short?' (2014) 11 *European Company and Financial Law Review* 454.

formation process—the key goal in regulating trading practices—such doubts are warranted. The recent short selling decision of the EU's Court of Justice (2014) nicely reveals why: the Court believed the aim in restricting short selling was 'to prevent an uncontrolled fall in the price of those instruments'.[113] This statement and the regulatory philosophy behind it are at odds with basic principles of price formation. Under ideal circumstances, only one single factor 'controls' the price formation process: the ratio of market supply and demand. All other attempts to influence the price formation process, for instance by excluding certain orders from consideration, are outlawed as market abuse. But banning short selling is exactly that: suppressing *true* orders. As a result, price formation is no longer purely market-driven, and prices become less informative because they fail to accurately reflect supply and demand.[114]

What are the main drivers behind the new short selling restrictions? Critical observers may be tempted to answer that the prime motive is to make short sellers a scapegoat for waning bond and stock prices, to distract voters from the declines' true reasons (such as poor prospects for countries that live beyond their means and for financial institutions that lend them money). But there are also legitimate concerns, such as the fear of market abuse, settlement disruptions, or market inefficiencies.[115]

Most influential seems to be the worry that short selling is to some degree a self-fulfilling prophecy because each new sale will 'aggravate the downward spiral in the prices of shares'.[116] This may be true, but probably only for a limited period of time. What many critics miss is that short sellers, in order to close their position and to realize their profit, have to *buy* one day the instruments that they have short-sold. The infamous Porsche-Volkswagen case nicely illustrates the possible consequences: for a few hours, Volkswagen in 2008 became the world's most valuable company (based on market capitalization) because short sellers had to buy Volkswagen shares at almost any price to avoid contractual penalties ('short

[113] ECJ, Case C-270/12, n 41 above, para 85.

[114] This is even acknowledged by IOSCO, Short Selling, n 29 above, 4 ('short selling plays an important role in the market for a variety of reasons, such as providing more efficient price discovery, mitigating market bubbles, … '), 6 ('potential benefits … such as correcting overpriced stock, facilitating price discovery … '), 11 ('the price-correcting benefit of short selling'), 21 ('major benefit of facilitating a more rapid repricing of over-valued securities … short sellers are often contrarian investors that mitigate steep, temporary price increases'), as well as by the EU Short Selling Regulation, n 32 above, Recital 5 ('under normal market conditions, short selling plays an important role in ensuring the proper functioning of financial markets, in particular in the context of … efficient price formation').

[115] Summarized in IOSCO, Short Selling, n 29 above, 21–2. For a survey of arguments that may support the regulation of short selling, see Payne, n 112 above, 415–18 (for counterarguments see 418–21).

[116] EU Short Selling Regulation, n 32 above, Recital 1. More cautious IOSCO, Short Selling, n 29 above, 4 ('may contribute to disorderly markets') and 5 ('may be problematic in the midst of a loss in market confidence').

squeeze').[117] This risk functions as an inherent limit to short selling, without any state intervention. If it did not, then many other trading strategies would require restrictions as well. Consider buying on credit. Policymakers do not call for more restrictions on credit-financed trading because they understand that there are market forces, such as credit limits and the risk of unfavourable price movements, that will prevent buying on credit from becoming a self-fulfilling prophecy.[118] In addition, there are plenty of provisions that ensure that price formation is purely market driven: disclosure obligations, position limits, market abuse rules, trading halts, circuit breakers, contractual penalties for failure to pay, and so on. Short selling is subject to the same market forces and provisions. There is no reason to go beyond.

3. Market fragmentation

Market fragmentation has reached a level that makes it impossible to regulate trading practices without a quick glance at some market structure issues (the topic of the Chapter by Ferrarini and Saguato in this volume).

Since 1975, when this data was first recorded, the New York Stock Exchange's market share had always been above 75 per cent (for the trading in securities issued by companies primarily listed on the exchange).[119] In January 2005, the New York Stock Exchange's share still stood at 79 per cent.[120] At the end of 2005, however, its market share dropped for the first time below 75 per cent.[121] Only three years later, in mid 2008, it had fallen to roughly 25 per cent.[122] Calling this a 'revolution' in market structure would be an understatement.[123] Since then, shifts in market share have been less dramatic. At the beginning of 2014, the New York Stock Exchange's share in US trading volume amounted to 20.58 per cent, a blink of an eye ahead of BATS

[117] The short squeeze and the events that led to it are described, *inter alia*, in *Elliott Associates v Porsche Automobil Holding*, 759 *F.Supp.2d* 469, 471–3 (2010) as well as in *Viking Global Equities v Porsche Automobil Holding*, 36 *Misc.3d* 1233(A), 2012 *WL* 3640684 1–3 (2012), reversed (on legal grounds) by *Viking Global Equities v Porsche Automobil Holding*, 101 *A.D.3d* 640, 958 *N.Y.S.2d* 35 (2012).

[118] Already observed and aptly summarized by Smith, A, *Lectures on Jurisprudence* (1978 [1766]) 538 ('Persons who game must keep their credit, else no body will deal with them. It is quite the same in stockjobbing. They who do not keep their credit will soon be turned out, and in the language of Change Alley be called lame duck').

[119] Lucchetti, A, 'NYSE's Market Dominance Slips' *Wall Street Journal*, 29 November 2005, C1.

[120] SEC, Equity Market Structure, n 21 above, 3595.

[121] Lucchetti, n 119 above.

[122] NASDAQ Stock Market, NYSE Share Volume in NYSE-Listed Securities (chart), available at <http://media.primezone.com/cache/6948/file/5876.jpg>; McNamara, S, 'Rents and the Floor Brokers' (14 August 2008), *Traders Magazine Online News*, available at <http://www.tradersmagazine.com/news/101848-1.html>. In October 2009, the New York Stock Exchange's market share was approximately 25.1 per cent (SEC, Equity Market Structure, n 21 above, 3595).

[123] For additional data, see SEC, Equity Market Structure, n 21 above, 3595–6 (on execution speed, volume, number of trades, average trade size, all summarized in the text accompanying n 95 above) and 3597–600 (market share of the various trading venues).

Global Markets' 20.54 per cent and Nasdaq OMX Group's 20.01 per cent.[124] The phenomenon is not limited to the US market: the London Stock Exchange's share in UK trading dropped from 96 per cent to below 50 per cent between 2008 and 2011.[125]

What happened that made the traditional exchanges' market share collapse so quickly? Was there a technological revolution? The sudden emergence of new competitors? Did the high-frequency traders cause this? None of the foregoing factors can be totally excluded, but the main answer lies in a completely different field: financial regulation. In 2005, the US Securities and Exchange Commission passed 'Regulation NMS', the highly controversial reform of the 'National Market System' that sets the framework for US securities trading.[126] At roughly the same time, the member states of the EU started implementing the Directive on Markets in Financial Instruments, known as 'MiFID'.[127] On both sides of the Atlantic, policymakers wanted to break the dominance of the traditional exchanges and give way to new start-up marketplaces. That algorithmic trading surged and markets are more fragmented than ever before is, therefore, anything but an unintended consequence. It is the result of a deliberate policy decision.

Market fragmentation affects the process of trading in several ways. In fragmented markets, buy and sell orders will be spread over various venues. If there is no exchange of information, prices will only reflect market supply and demand at each individual venue. As a result, liquidity may take a hit, volatility might rise, and prices may differ from venue to venue and from prices that would have been found if all orders had been executed at the same venue.

Another concern is the allocation of orders. With the same financial instruments traded on different venues, those placing orders have to make a choice. This is fine for those trading on their own account because they will choose the site that best serves their interests. But many orders are placed through intermediaries. If the intermediaries' incentives are not aligned with their clients' interests (due to 'kickbacks' and other forms of 'payment for order-flow'), this may lead to an inefficient allocation of orders (the above-mentioned 'best execution' rules try to prevent such self-dealing but may be difficult to enforce in markets with many similar trading options).[128]

Any regulatory response to market fragmentation will be a trade-off between fostering competition among marketplaces and factoring in as many orders as possible for price formation. That the two key actors, the US (dictating the allocation of orders) and the EU (relying on mandatory disclosure of trading data),

[124] Hope, B, 'NYSE Still No. 1, but Not by Much' *Wall Street Journal*, 12 February 2014, C2.

[125] Fleckner and Hopt, n 1 above, 555.

[126] SEC, 'Regulation NMS, Release No 34-51808' (9 June 2005) 70 *Federal Register* 37,496.

[127] MiFID I, now MiFIR and MiFID II, all n 30 above.

[128] The difficulties for retail investors to monitor order execution are a recurring theme in Moloney, n 24 above, 348, 358, 360, 362, 363. But it is also a challenge for many professional investors and regulators, at least in highly fragmented markets; see, eg, Gadinis, n 78 above, 314, 315, 330–1, 341.

after spirited debates and many compromises, came to 'diametrically opposed approaches',[129] nicely illustrates the wide spectrum of choices that policymakers have.[130] Scholarship on market structure issues is equally diverse.[131]

For price formation and the process of trading, the number of venues seems to be less important than the linkages, if any, that exist between them. The key mechanism is the exchange of pre-trade and post-trade data (discussed earlier as a transparency requirement). If a venue's price formation process considers both orders routed to that market and orders placed on other venues (within the same jurisdiction or beyond), then chances are high that its prices will be close to the prices that would have been found if all orders had been sent to the same place. Under these conditions, the main threat to price formation is not market fragmentation but dark trading. As mentioned earlier, including dark venues' pre-trade data in the price formation process on official markets (without disclosing it to the public) may be a good compromise for all parties involved.

V. Conclusion: Main Findings and Positions

1. The key feature that distinguishes exchanges from other markets and fairs is the standardization of trading. Standardization results in rules that decide who is given access to the exchange, what items are admitted to trading, how transactions are concluded, and so on. Historically, most trading rules arose from self-regulation (Section I).

[129] Gadinis, n 78 above, 313 and 314 (characterizing US rules as 'detailed and interventionist', the EU regime as 'deregulatory and decentralized', both quotes can be found on 313).

[130] More recently Pittsburgh Summit Declaration, n 26 above; SEC, Equity Market Structure, n 21 above; EMIR, n 20 above.

[131] Poser, NS, 'Restructuring the Stock Markets: A Critical Look at the SEC's National Market System' (1981) 56 *New York University Law Review* 883; Calvin, DL, 'The National Market System: A Successful Adventure in Industry Self-Improvement' (1984) 70 *Virginia Law Review* 785; Seligman, J, 'The Future of the National Market System' (1984) 10 *The Journal of Corporation Law* 79; Macey, JR and Haddock, DD, 'Shirking at the SEC: The Failure of the National Market System' (1985) *University of Illinois Law Review* 315; [Note], 'The Perils of Payment for Order Flow' (1994) 107 *Harvard Law Review* 1675; Ferrell, A, 'A Proposal for Solving the "Payment for Order Flow" Problem' (2001) 74 *Southern California Law Review* 1027; Gadinis, n 78 above; Clausen, NJ and Sørensen, KE, 'Reforming the Regulation of Trading Venues in the EU under the Proposed MiFID II—Levelling the Playing Field and Overcoming Market Fragmentation?' (2012) 9 *European Company and Financial Law Review* 275; Fleckner and Hopt, n 1 above, 554–6; Ferrarini and Moloney, n 45 above; Ferrarini and Saguato, n 45 above.

2. Governments should intervene in the regulation of trading practices to ensure that prices set on official markets accurately reflect market supply and demand. The details and most other issues can be left to local regulators and to self-regulatory organizations (Section II).
3. The leading jurisdictions regulate trading practices through a multitude of rules, regulators, and techniques. The current regimes suffer from various flaws. Rules are too long and complex, which gives rise to inconsistencies and contradictions. Regulatory powers are spread over too many agencies, causing regulation to be costly and inefficient. Governments should mitigate these shortcomings by following a principles-based approach at higher regulatory levels and relying on self-regulation to formulate rules for the details (Section III).
4. Algorithmic trading lowers transaction costs, makes markets more efficient, and thereby increases public welfare. High-frequency trading, a popular type of algorithmic trading, helps prices adapt more quickly to changes in market supply and demand. Some algorithmic traders, however, have followed strategies and employed techniques that are at odds with general principles of securities law or even outright illegal. Does this call for a complete overhaul of the regulatory regime? Probably not. If existing rules are properly enforced and, where necessary, slightly amended, the regime already in place will manage to cope with the new trading techniques (Section IV.1).
5. Short selling has been regulated on various levels for over four centuries. Nothing has happened that would require the government to impose additional restrictions (Section IV.2).
6. Market fragmentation is now at a level unseen before. To ensure that prices accurately reflect overall market supply and demand, it is critical that trading venues share their order and transaction data. Dark pools should be required to route their pre-trade data to official markets (without disclosing it to the public) (Section IV.3).
7. From a historical and comparative perspective, many of the recent developments look less dramatic than some observers believe. Governments should focus on the price formation process and ensure that it is purely market-driven. Local regulators and self-regulatory organizations will take care of the rest, just as over the past four centuries. This time is not different.

Bibliography

Boehmer, E and Wu, J, 'Short Selling and the Price Discovery Process' (2013) 26 *Review of Financial Studies* 287.

Brogaard, J, Hendershott, T, and Riordan, R, 'High-Frequency Trading and Price Discovery' (2014) 27 *Review of Financial Studies* 2267.

Coffee, JC and Sale, HA, *Securities Regulation* (12th edn, 2012).

Ferrarini, G and Moloney, N, 'Reshaping Order Execution in the EU and the Role of Interest Groups: From MiFID I to MiFID II' (2012) 13 *European Business Organization Law Review* 557.

Ferrarini, G and Saguato, P, 'Reforming Securities and Derivatives Trading in the EU: From EMIR to MiFIR' (2013) 13 *Journal of Corporate Law Studies* 319.

Fleckner, AM, 'Stock Exchanges at the Crossroads' (2006) 74 *Fordham Law Review* 2541.

Fleckner, AM and Hopt, KJ, 'Stock Exchange Law: Concept, History, Challenges' (2013) 7 *Virginia Law & Business Review* 513.

Gadinis, S, 'Market Structure for Institutional Investors: Comparing the U.S. and E.U. Regimes' (2008) 3 *Virginia Law & Business Review* 311.

Harris, L, *Trading and Exchanges* (2003).

Hertig, G, 'Mifid and the Return of Concentration Rules' in Grundmann, S et al. (eds), *Festschrift für Klaus J. Hopt* (Vol II, 2010) 1989.

Moloney, N, *EC Securities Regulation* (2nd edn, 2008).

Moloney, N, *How to Protect Investors* (2010).

Payne, J, 'The Regulation of Short Selling and its Reform in Europe' (2012) 13 *European Business Organization Law Review* 413.

Zhu, H, 'Do Dark Pools Harm Price Discovery?' (2014) 27 *Review of Financial Studies* 747.

CHAPTER 21

SUPPORTING MARKET INTEGRITY

HARRY McVEA

I. Introduction

Concerns about the integrity of financial markets are as old as financial markets themselves. Practices such as market manipulation, perpetrated through the spreading of false rumours, were widely reported in and around the time of the South Sea Bubble[1]—as, indeed, was the practice of insider dealing.[2] More recently, events surrounding the worst financial crisis since the Wall Street Crash have, if anything, served to intensify interest in and scrutiny of the integrity of financial market activity.[3] Allegations of the opportunistic shorting of stock in the immediate aftermath of the crisis,[4] claims of hedge fund involvement in insider dealing,[5] ongoing concerns about the manipulation of benchmarks,[6] and mounting fears over the use of certain high-frequency trading (HFT) strategies,[7] all underscore the acute sensitivity of both market and public opinion to practices which call into question the integrity of financial market transactions.

At its broadest, this Chapter seeks to chart major shifts—both academic and regulatory—in relation to ongoing debates about the need for measures which seek to protect the integrity of our financial markets. Although the discussion is designed to be global in its reach, the material discussed draws primarily on developments in the EU and US—and to a lesser extent the UK—and focuses on market integrity issues associated with insider dealing and market manipulation (collectively hereinafter, market abuse).

[1] See Dale R, *The First Crash: Lessons from the South Sea Bubble* (2004) 17–19, and sources cited therein.

[2] See, eg, Narron, J and Skeie, D, Crisis Chronicles: The South Sea Bubble of 1720—Repackaging Debt and the Current Reach for Yield (2013), available at <http://libertystreeteconomics.newyorkfed.org/2013/11/crisis-chronicles-the-south-sea-bubble-of-1720repackaging-debt-and-the-current-reach-for-yield.html> (noting the conduct of Sword Blade Bank in events predating the 'bubble').

[3] 'Market integrity' is defined by the International Organization of Securities Commissions (IOSCO), as 'the extent to which a market operates in a manner that is, and is perceived to be, fair and orderly and where effective rules are in place and enforced by regulators so that confidence and participation in the market is fostered': IOSCO, Regulatory Issues Raised by the Impact of Technological Changes on Market Integrity and Efficiency, Final Report of the Technical Committee of IOSCO (2011), 9 (hereinafter, IOSCO, Regulatory Issues (2011)).

[4] See below n 17 and accompanying text.

[5] For a review of the Securities and Exchange Commission (SEC) efforts in the US, see, Thomsen, Hawke, LD, and Calande, P, 'Hedge Funds: An Enforcement Perspective' (2008) 39 *Rutgers Law Journal* 541, 577–93. For similar concerns in the UK pre-crisis, see, Financial Services Authority (FSA), Hedge Funds: A Discussion of Risk and Regulatory Engagement, Discussion Paper 05/04, 53; and, within the EU, see, Narayan N, Hedge Funds: Transparency and Conflict of Interest IP/A/ECON/IC/2007-24 (2004), 30–2.

[6] See generally FSA, *Annual Report* 2012/13.

[7] IOSCO, Addendum to IOSCO Report on Investigating and Prosecuting Market Manipulation (2013), 1. See also, IOSCO, Regulatory Issues (2011), n 3 above, 48.

It is suggested, that the picture which emerges from this survey is as following: first, that the evolving nature of financial markets—in particular, the growing complexity and fragmentation of markets as a result of the proliferation of trading across different venues and developments associated with HFT strategies[8]—has made it more difficult for regulators to monitor for possible cases of market abuse. Furthermore, these developments have not only increased the risk that new variants of market manipulation will emerge, but have afforded opportunities for the use of abusive practices on a scale not previously possible.

Second, although the academic debate with regard to the merits or otherwise of one prominent form of market abuse—insider dealing—remains as alive as ever, there are signs of a shift in the nature of this debate, away from earlier exchanges rooted in clashes between competing theoretical viewpoints, towards one which today focuses on an empirical analysis of the effects of regulation and its enforcement.

Third, from a policy-making/regulatory perspective, there are clear signs of an evolving regulatory landscape characterized by expansionist tendencies. This reflects a shift away from the need to justify why market abuse should be regulated under law, towards an emphasis on identifying where, in the wake of changing market structures and the emergence of new strains of market abuse, the appropriate boundaries of market abuse offences ought to lie. Reform of the EU's market abuse regime offers an ideal vantage point from which to review this shift. What is more, a discussion of the position within the EU—at least from the perspective of the regulation of insider dealing—offers an interesting and important counterpoint to the increasingly anomalous approach adopted in the US.

Finally—and to some extent resonating with EU reforms in relation to enforcement concerns—there is evidence of a global trend towards more active enforcement of market abuse, spearheaded in the main by developments in the US and the UK, most significantly in relation to the use of criminal sanctions as a deterrent for insider dealing.

In presenting and developing these ideas, the structure of the Chapter is as follows. In Section II, the scene is set by identifying the types of conduct/activity which give rise to market integrity concerns, following which the likely incidence of market abuse in modern financial markets is discussed. In Section III, the claimed rationales for prohibitions on market abuse are assessed and, subsequently, new empirical research, which—in the context of insider dealing at any rate—claims to support prohibitions on efficiency grounds, is critiqued. In Section IV, the evolving regulatory landscape is surveyed. Although the focus here is on

[8] HFT is strongly associated with algorithmic trading, in that it is highly quantitative. However, speed of execution and a high daily portfolio turnover and high order to trade ratio (ie, a large number of orders are cancelled in comparison to trades executed) are regarded as key characteristics distinguishing it from other forms of algorithmic trading.

the EU's market abuse regime and recent attempts to remodel its contours, aspects of the EU's evolving regime are contrasted with developments in the US—principally, in relation to the regulation of insider dealing. In Section V, the focus turns to enforcement issues, and, finally, in Section VI, key stands of the discussion are drawn out and conclusions presented.

II. Conduct Which Raises Market Integrity Concerns and the Incidence of Market Abuse

1. Conduct which raises market integrity concerns

Activity which gives rise to market integrity concerns encompasses a wide spectrum of conduct ranging from 'classic' insider dealing (eg, dealing on inside information—as well as encouraging others to deal, or disclosing inside information to others)[9] to various forms of market manipulation. These manipulations themselves cover a wide spread of activities,[10] such as the use of false statements designed to 'move' the market in a particular direction (so-called 'pump and dump' schemes), and the deployment of 'artificial' devices devoid of any 'substantive economic purpose'[11] and designed merely to create a false impression of market activity.[12] Such devices include 'wash trades',[13] 'improper matched orders',[14] 'pools',[15] and 'painting the tape'.[16] The underlying aim of

[9] From a regulatory perspective, this involves trading in the relevant securities in *public* markets.

[10] Commentators often distinguish between transaction-based manipulations (such as transactions involving fictitious devices) and information-based manipulations (such as disseminating false or misleading information). See, eg, Ferrarini, G, 'The European Market Abuse Directive' (2004) 41 *Common Market Law Review* 724.

[11] Donald, D, 'Regulating Market Manipulation through an Understanding of Price Creation' (2011) 6 *National Taiwan University Law Review* 55, 68.

[12] See, *Palmer's Company Law* (Looseleaf) para 11.146; Fischel, D and Ross, D, 'Should the Law Prohibit "Manipulation" in Financial Markets?' (1991) 105 *Harvard Law Review* 503, 504; Financial Conduct Authority (FCA) Handbook, Market Conduct (MAR 1.6.2E); Committee of European Securities Regulators (CESR), Market Abuse Directive: Level 3—first set of CESR guidance and information on the common operation of the Directive (CESR/04-505b) (hereinafter, CESR Guidance).

[13] Where there is no change in the beneficial ownership of the underlying securities other than between the parties acting in concert.

[14] Where matching buy and sell orders are entered into simultaneously by colluding parties.

[15] Where groups of investors trade amongst themselves in order to suggest an active market in the underlying financial instruments.

[16] Where colluding parties entering into a series of transactions shown on a public display facility.

all these schemes is to generate profits or avoid losses by inducing investors to purchase securities which subsequently turn out to have little—or no—marketability or value.

Other manipulations include the misuse of market power by way of 'corners' (which involve, first, building up and, subsequently, manipulating a controlling or dominant market position),[17] or 'abusive squeezes' where a person with significant influence over the supply of a security restricts its liquidity in order to create a price 'spike'.[18]

More recently, in the wake of the financial crisis, regulators saw fit to intervene to prohibit—by way of temporary measures—what was widely viewed as abusive short selling in vulnerable financial institutions. Both the SEC, in the US, and the now-defunct FSA, in the UK, were at the forefront of orchestrating these temporary bans. Broadly, the measures prohibited the active creation or increase of net short positions in the securities of vulnerable financial sector companies and required market disclosure of significant short positions in these securities.[19] Following these interventions, regulators were again forced to take action against leading financial institutions in relation to the manipulation of the London InterBank Offered Rate (LIBOR),[20] and, in recent months, allegations have also surfaced of similar manipulation in relation to the Euro InterBank Offered Rate (EURIBOR).[21]

Unsurprisingly, in the aftermath of the financial crisis, a renewed emphasis on market integrity has also become evident at the global level. In its November 2010 Seoul Communiqué, the G20 leaders tasked the International Organization of Securities Commissions (IOSCO) with developing recommendations to promote market integrity, especially in the context of 'risks posed to the financial system by … technological developments'.[22] According to IOSCO, although traditional forms of market manipulation remain an ongoing feature of financial markets, the evolving nature of these markets—in particular, the increasing range of venues on

[17] See FCA Handbook, n 12 above, MAR 1.6.4E(1).

[18] ibid; CESR Guidance, n 12 above, 12; and Wood, P, *Law and Practice of International Finance* (2008, University edition) paras 24-04–24-12.

[19] See generally, FSA, Short Selling, Discussion Paper 09/1 and Payne, J, 'The Regulation of Short Selling and its Reform in Europe' (2012) 13 *European Business Organization Law Review* 413.

[20] See generally, The Wheatley Review of Libor: Final Report (2012). Notwithstanding the importance of LIBOR, the benchmarks upon which it is based did not fall *directly* within either the EU's or the UK's market abuse regimes. Forthcoming reforms to the EU regime—see Section IV below—will remedy this deficiency. For recent reforms in the UK, see Financial Services Act 2012, section 91 (which makes the manipulation of financial benchmarks a criminal offence). The LIBOR scandal underscores the need for concepts of market abuse which are 'sufficiently flexible to meet the challenges of new technologies for communication and trading'. *Palmer's Company Law*, n 12 above, para 11.146.

[21] JP Morgan, HSBC and Credit Agricole Accused of Euro Rate-fixes (20 May 2014), available at <http://www.bbc.co.uk/news/business-27482358>.

[22] The G20 Seoul Summit Declaration (11–12 November 2010), available at <http://online.wsj.com/public/resources/documents/G20COMMUN1110.pdf>.

which financial products are traded in tandem with the growth of HFT strategies (which are highly quantitative and focus on speed of execution, high daily portfolio turnover, and a high order to trade ratio)—poses significant challenges for regulatory authorities.[23] Abuses which have become a particular focus of attention in the context of HFT strategies include:[24]

- 'momentum ignition'—where a series of orders and trades are initiated in an attempt to set trends and foster rapid price movements;
- 'quote-stuffing'—where markets are flooded with an excessive number of orders which traders place, and then subsequently cancel, to cause uncertainty in the market;
- 'spoofing'—where bids or offers are made with the intention that they will be cancelled in advance of execution;
- 'layering'—where a trader enters several orders (which are subsequently cancelled) with the underlying aim of improving the price of a trade in the opposite direction; and
- 'marking the close' or 'banging the close'—where trading activity takes place either before or during the close of trading with the aim of impacting on settlement prices.

Although such practices are not new, in combination with the proliferation and fragmentation of the markets on which financial instruments are today traded, opportunities for abuse now exist on a scale not previously possible.[25]

2. Estimating the incidence of market abuse

Given the illegal and secretive nature of market abuses, it has proved difficult to ascertain the degree to which market abuse occurs in practice.[26]

With regard to insider dealing, in view of the potential for individual financial gain, the difficulties associated with regulatory detection, and, at least historically, the relatively remote likelihood of sanctions (even where enforcement had followed successful detection), there are clearly strong incentives for individuals to engage in abuse. This is especially so ahead of a proposed takeover bid, where

[23] See n 7 above.

[24] See, eg, IOSCO, Regulatory Issues, n 3 above, 30; and European Securities and Markets Authority (ESMA), Guidelines: Systems and Controls in an Automated Trading Environment for Trading Platforms, Investment Firms and Competent Authorities (ESMA/2012/122) (2012), 16–17 (hereinafter, ESMA Guidelines).

[25] According to IOSCO, HFT more than doubled to as much as 56 per cent of US equity trading in the period from 2005 to 2010. Similarly, in Europe, HFT increased from only 9 per cent of equity trading in 2007 to 38 per cent in 2010: Regulatory Issues (2011), n 3 above, 23.

[26] Though detection rates are not unimportant, the number of people who commit market abuse which goes undetected is simply unknowable.

studies in the UK have routinely revealed abnormally high pre-announcement price movements (APPMs).[27] Similarly, in a recent US study by Beny and Seyhun, pre-takeover announcement spikes in stock prices were found to be 50 per cent higher in 2006–11 than in the pre-2006 period studied.[28] In research cited by the European Commission, involving an analysis of insider trading across ten international markets, it was estimated that insider dealing profits account for between 0.01 and 0.05 per cent of total market turnover.[29] Furthermore, the European Commission estimates that profit gained from insider dealing in the EU's three largest exchanges—Euronext, Deutche Börse, and the LSE Group—expressed as a percentage of market turnover was 0.0356 per cent in the period 2003–09 and 0.0357 per cent in 2009.[30]

In relation to other abusive practices, again reliable indications of the prevalence of abuse are unavailable. According to IOSCO's recent study identifying HFT as a particular area of concern, although no 'clear evidence of the systematic and widespread use of abusive practices by those engaging in HFT' was found, the report nevertheless recognized that 'the submission of large numbers of orders and trades across multiple venues' poses significant challenges for national authorities.[31] Moreover, a growing number of recent cases in both the US and the UK involving manipulative conduct associated with HFT, is suggestive of an emerging problem.[32]

[27] In the UK, see the FSA, 'Market Cleanliness' surveys, regularly referenced in FSA Annual Reports (prior to the establishment of the FCA). The surveys focus only on insider dealing and not other forms of abuse.

[28] Beny, L and Seyhun, N, 'Has Illegal Insider Trading Become More Rampant in the United States? Empirical Evidence from Takeovers' in Bainbridge, S (ed.), *Research Handbook on Insider Trading* (2013) 211, 228.

[29] Capital Markets CRC Limited, Enumerating the Cost of Insider Trading, unpublished (2010) 8, cited in European Commission, Staff Working Paper Impact Assessment (SEC(2011) 1217 f) 16 (hereinafter, Commission, Impact Assessment). See also, Comerton-Forde, C and Putnins, T, The Prevalence and Underpinnings of Closing Price Manipulation (2010), available at <http://ssm.com/abstract-1243042> (suggesting (at 3) that manipulation is a serious issue for exchanges); Khwaja, A and Mian, A, 'Unchecked Intermediaries: Price Manipulation in an Emerging Stock Market' (2005) 78 *Journal of Financial Economics* 203 (suggesting that 'pump and dump' practices by institutional broker-dealers are particularly prevalent in developing countries).

[30] Commission, Impact Assessment, ibid, 200.

[31] IOSCO, Regulatory Issues (2011), n 3 above, 30. Moreover, as IOSCO recognizes, in view of the growth in and relatively low level of scrutiny over over-the-counter (OTC) activity, these markets may 'provide the ideal test markets for the development and refining of manipulative practices': IOSCO, Addendum (2013), n 7 above, 2.

[32] *In re Bunge Global Markets, Inc*, available at <http://www.cftc.gov/ucm/groups/public/@lrenforcementactions/documents/legalpleading/enfbungeorder032211.pdf>; *SEC v Hold Brothers Online*, available at <http://www.sec.gov/litigation/admin/2012/34-67924.pdf>; and *In the Matter of Panther Energy Trading LLC and Michael J Coscia* (CFTC Docket No 13–26) (22 July 2013), available at <http://online.wsj.com/public/resources/documents/pantherorder072213.pdf>; *7722656 Canada Inc & Anor v The Financial Conduct Authority & Ors* [2013] EWCA Civ 1662; FCA Press Release, FCA Fines US based Oil Trader US $903K for Market Manipulation (July 2013) available at <http://www.fca.org.uk/news/fca-fines-us-based-oil-trader>.

According to the European Commission, since the cost of market manipulation is likely to be of the same order of magnitude as insider dealing, it has been suggested that market abuse amounts to a combined cost of 0.0712 per cent of market turnover.[33] Extrapolating this to the European equity market in 2010, the Commission claims that the total value of market abuse (ie, insider dealing and market manipulation) in terms of market turnover, was in the region of EUR 13.3 billion—a figure which the Commission considers to be an underestimate of the total cost of abuse on all EU markets, since it is based only on an assessment of equity markets.[34]

III. A Critical Assessment of the Rationales for Regulating Market Abuse

1. Market manipulation

Although attempts to justify prohibitions on market manipulation—or, at least, certain species of it—have not gone unchallenged,[35] in general legal controls directed at market manipulation have provoked less heated debate than attempts to justify prohibitions on insider dealing.[36] It is widely asserted, for example, that market manipulation amounts to an 'unwarranted' interference in the operation of ordinary market forces of supply and demand which undermines the 'integrity' and efficiency of the market.[37] Not surprisingly defining what amounts to 'unwarranted'

[33] Commission, Impact Assessment, n 29 above, 200 (and studies cited therein).

[34] Interestingly, other studies reveal that irrespective of the real level of market abuse, market players *perceive* market abuse to be a widespread problem. For example, in the CFA's Global Market Sentiment Survey (2014), survey participants identified market fraud (which the survey associated with conduct such as insider dealing) as the second most serious issue facing their *local* markets, and the most serious ethical issue facing *global* markets, available at <http://www.cfainstitute.org/about/research/surveys/Documents/gmss_2014_whitepaper_print.pdf>, 20.

[35] For claims that the law on market manipulation lacks conceptual and definitional clarity see Fischel and Ross, n 12 above. The authors argue that there exists no objective definition of manipulation and that in so far as manipulation is objective it can be dealt with by the law against fraudulent conduct independently of any need to define it in securities law.

[36] In fact, criticism has focused on deficiencies in the formulation of legal rules. See, eg, Donald, n 11 above, 58–60.

[37] See, eg, IOSCO, Investigating and Prosecuting Market Manipulation (2000) (price should be 'set by the unimpeded collective judgment of buyers and sellers'), 8; *North v Marra Developments Ltd* [1982] 56 AJLR 106, NSW CA (noting the importance of markets which reflect 'the

conduct is not without difficulty. It is, of course, widely accepted that deliberately making false statements in order to 'move' the market is objectionable, since fraud infringes notions of perfect, or competitive, markets—and, thus, is said to represent an impediment to market optimality.[38] However, there is a risk that in seeking to prohibit market manipulation, legal rules that are broadly or vaguely framed will impede otherwise legitimate activities which promote price discovery and increase aggregate wealth. Similarly, definitional problems associated with 'artificial' transactions and the 'misuse' of market power, raise the spectre of regulatory over-reach and risk discouraging market innovations—again with adverse effects on wealth creation.

At first glance, characterizing market manipulations as incidents of 'market failure' provides an elegant framework within which to justify regulatory intervention so as to restore market equilibrium. However, on closer inspection, market failure analysis merely serves to camouflage what is ultimately at stake: the determination of which informational advantages are legitimate in the context of market exchanges. As will be explored more fully below in relation to the empirical debate over the merits or otherwise of insider dealing, this is a problem which is not capable of being resolved by way of an appeal to some objective notion of market efficiency.[39]

2. Insider dealing

In contrast to the more muted critiques of regulatory prohibitions on market manipulation, the debate regarding insider dealing has generated a voluminous academic literature,[40] much of it sceptical of the 'narratives' advanced in support of regulation,[41] and some—such as Carlton and Fischel's influential 1983 *Stanford Law Review* article—even suggesting that the desirability of regulating the practice is, ultimately, an 'empirical question'.[42]

Justifications typically articulated to support such controls range from claims that insider dealing jeopardizes the development of fair and orderly markets, and, in so doing, undermines investor confidence;[43] that it is immoral,[44] and contrary to

forces of genuine supply and demand' (*per* Mason J)); and Moloney, N, *EC Securities Regulation* (2nd edn, 2008) 931 and sources cited therein.

38 Clark, R, *Corporate Law* (1986) 151.

39 See ibid, n 72 and accompanying text.

40 Henry Manne's 1966 book, *Insider Trading on the Stock Market* (1966) (hereinafter, *ITSM*), remains, however, the *locus classicus*.

41 Benjamin, J, 'The Narratives of Financial Law' (2010) 30 *Oxford Journal of Legal Studies* 787, 809.

42 Carlton, WD and Fischel, DR, 'The Regulation of Insider Dealing' (1983) 35 *Stanford Law Review* 857, 866, and 873. See also Easterbrook, F, 'Insider Trading, Secret Agents, Evidentiary Privileges, and the Production of Information' [1981] *Supreme Court Review* 309, n 120 ('[a]lthough I think it likely that legal restrictions on [insider] trading are beneficial, the questions ultimately are empirical').

43 Directive 2003/6/EC [2003] OJ L 96/16 (hereinafter, MAD), Recital 2.

44 See Scheppele, KL, '"It's Just Not Right": The Ethics of Insider Trading' (1993) 56 *Law and Contemporary Problems* 123; Allen, A, 'Professor Scheppele's Middle Way: On Minimizing Normativity and Economics in Securities Laws' (1993) 56 *Law and Contemporary Problems* 175;

'good business ethics';[45] that it hurts corporations (and their shareholders),[46] as well as investors generally[47] and market-makers in particular;[48] and that it impairs the allocative efficiency of the financial markets,[49] by distorting managerial incentives with regard to disclosing information,[50] reducing market liquidity,[51] and increasing the cost of capital.[52]

By contrast, those who oppose regulatory controls on insider dealing claim that the rationale, method, and scope of such regulation are misconceived. Specifically, it has been contended that inside information is a property right belonging to the firm, which the firm should be free to allocate as it sees fit;[53] that insider dealing is an effective means of compensating entrepreneurs and managers;[54] that, rather than hindering accurate price formation, insider dealing actually helps to promote it[55]—by providing a less costly means of channelling information about securities into financial markets,[56] and by helping to smooth out undesirable market fluctuations.[57] In doing so, insider dealing is said to help improve the efficiency of markets, both informationally and, by extension, allocatively.[58] What is more, it has also been claimed that neither corporations (or their shareholders),[59] nor investors generally,[60] or market makers in particular,[61] are hurt by the use of inside information; and, finally, it has even been suggested that regulating insider dealing is misconceived, since it cannot be effectively enforced.[62]

Interestingly, there are signs of a shift in the terms of the academic debate surrounding the merits of regulating insider dealing, spurred on, it would seem, by a quest for 'hard facts'. A review of the recent literature reveals that scholars have begun to move away

Schotland, R, 'Unsafe at Any Price: A Reply to Manne, Insider Trading and the Stock Market' (1967) 53 *Virginia Law Review* 1425, 1438–9.

[45] See, eg, Justice, *Report on Insider Trading* (1972) para 3.

[46] See, eg, Haft, RJ, 'The Effect of Insider Trading Rules on the Internal Efficiency of the Large Corporation' (1982) 80 *Michigan Law Review* 1051, 1051–64.

[47] See, eg, Wang, W, 'Trading on Material Non-Public Information on Impersonal Markets: Who Is Harmed and Who Can Sue Whom under SEC Rule 10b-5?' (1981) 54 *Southern California Law Review* 1217, 1234–5.

[48] See Goodhart, CAE, 'The Economics of "Big Bang"' (Summer 1987) *Midland Bank Review* 6, 10.

[49] See generally, Klock, M, 'Mainstream Economics and the Case for Prohibiting Inside Trading' (1994) 10 *Georgia State University Law Review* 297.

[50] See Schotland, n 44 above, 1448–9.

[51] See Klock, n 49 above, 330.

[52] See Mendelson, M, 'Book Review' (1969) 117 *University of Pennsylvania Law Review* 470, 477–8; Brudney, V, 'Insider, Outsiders, and Informational Advantages under Federal Securities Laws' (1979) 93 *Harvard Law Review* 322, 355–6.

[53] See generally, Macey, J, *Insider Trading: Economic, Politics, and Policy* (1991).

[54] See, Carlton and Fischel, n 42 above, 866–72; Macey, n 53 above, 45–7.

[55] See, Carlton and Fischel, n 42 above, 866–8.

[56] ibid, 868.

[57] Manne, H, 'Insider Trading and the Law Professors' (1970) 23 *Vanderbilt Law Review* 547, 574–5.

[58] Manne, n 40 above, 101–2.

[59] See *Schein v Chasen* 313 So 2d 739 (Fla1975).

[60] Cox, JD, 'An Outsider's Perspective of Insider Trading Regulation in Australia' (1990) 12 *Sydney Law Journal* 455, 457–8.

[61] See King, M and Roell, A, 'Insider Trading' (1988) April *Economic Policy* 163, 168 *et seq.*

[62] See Manne, H, 'Insider Trading and Property Rights in New Information' (1985) 4 *Cato Journal* 933, 937.

from earlier exchanges rooted in clashes between competing theoretical viewpoints, towards a newer debate which today focuses on an empirical analysis of the effects of regulation and its enforcement.[63] Although this empirical debate has taken some time to get going,[64] and aspects of it suffer from recognized methodological weaknesses,[65] a body of empirical work has nevertheless begun to emerge that is broadly supportive of legal prohibitions on insider dealing on efficiency grounds.

Thus, for example, studies show that countries in which insider dealing is more prevalent have more volatile stock markets;[66] that the cost of a country's capital decreases significantly after its first insider dealing prosecution,[67] and that analyst following increases after a country's initial enforcement of its insider dealing laws.[68] Studies also suggest that bid-ask spreads widen where market-makers are exposed to better informed traders;[69] and that stock prices reflect more firm specific information in jurisdictions with more stringent insider trading laws.[70] Finally, in Beny's influential 2007 comparative survey, 'Insider Trading Laws and Stock Markets Around the World', the author finds that those countries with 'more stringent insider trading laws are generally associated with more dispersed equity ownership, greater stock price accuracy and greater stock market liquidity.'[71]

In an age where our ability to measure and test claims is better than ever before, an appeal to empiricism to resolve a previously inconclusive academic debate is, unsurprisingly, attractive.[72] Yet, while the reconfiguration of the debate in empirical terms is undoubtedly of interest, such an inquiry is unlikely to shed much light on the important question of what our legal rules ought to be.[73] This is not

[63] To some extent these developments are part of a burgeoning empirical law and finance literature (sparked by the pioneering work of La Porta, R, Lopez-de-Silanes, F, Shleifer, A, and Vishny R—see, eg, 'Legal Determinants of External Finance' (1997) 52 *Journal of Finance* 1131).

[64] Beny, L, 'Insider Trading Laws and Stock Markets around the World: An Empirical Contribution to the Theoretical Law and Economics Debate' (2007) 32 *Journal of Corporation Law* 237, 239.

[65] For a good review of these weaknesses, see Hughes, L, 'Impact of Insider Trading Regulations on Stock Market Efficiency: A Critique of the Law and Economics Debate and a Cross-Country Comparison' (2009) 23(2) *Temple International & Comparative Law Journal* 479.

[66] Du, J and Wei, S, 'Does Insider Trading Raise Market Volatility?' (2004) 114 *Economic Journal* 916, 940.

[67] Bhattacharya, U and Daouk, H, 'The World Price of Insider Trading' (2002) 57 *Journal of Finance* 75, 79.

[68] Bushman, R, Piotroski, J, and Smith, A, 'Insider Trading Restrictions and Analysts' Incentives to Follow Firms' (2005) 60 *Journal of Finance* 35.

[69] Glosten, L and Harris, H, 'Estimating the Components of the Bid/Ask Spread' (1988) 21 *Journal of Financial Economics* 123, 140–1.

[70] Fernandes, N and Ferreira, M, 'Insider Trading Laws and Stock Price Informativeness' (2009) 22 *Review of Financial Studies* 1845, 1880–1.

[71] Beny, n 64 above. However, cf Beny, L, Do Shareholders Value Insider Trading Laws? International Evidence (2006), available at <http://ssrn.com/abstract=296111> (claiming that more stringent insider trading laws are associated with higher corporate valuation in common law countries, but lower corporate valuation in civil law countries).

[72] See Carlton and Fischel, n 42 above, 866.

[73] See, eg, Rachlinski, J, 'Evidence-based Law' (2011) 96 *Cornell Law Review* 901, 918; Woznert, S, 'Evidence-based Law by Jeffrey J Rachlinski' (2011) 96 *Cornell Law Review* 925.

because of a lack of reliable data, problematic though this is; but rather because the 'market tools' used to conduct this empirical analysis—and the conclusions derived from this body of work—rest on a priori assumptions about the nature of markets which are, themselves, not capable of being resolved by empirical analysis.

Thus, for example, standard neoclassical accounts of the operation of the market mechanism stipulate that for markets to deliver optimal societal outcomes, no informational asymmetries should exist—that is to say, conditions must exist which enable each party to make rational decisions based on 'full' or 'perfect' information. Where such conditions do not hold, there is said to exist a market failure which provides a prima facie justification for state intervention to remedy the failure. In relation to informational asymmetries, determining where the exact boundaries of any given market failure lies, tends either to be glossed over, or regarded as self-evident. Yet, to suppose that the debate about whether a particular informational advantage should or should not be used in a given set of market transactions is, in fact, capable of being resolved by the use of studies testing the efficiency or otherwise of that market is misconceived, since the underlying problem can only be addressed by an appeal to non-market values which are themselves beyond the realm of empirical observation. As Justice Allen informs us, although '[e]mpiricism is of great instrumental utility in the law, as a way of informing us how best to achieve some noncontroversial value ... disputes of ultimate value cannot be resolved by empirical investigations'.[74] Carlton and Fischel's claim, noted above, that the 'desirability of regulating insider trading is ultimately an empirical question'[75] is, therefore, misguided, and Beny's enthusiastic appeal for 'more empirical work ... to conclusively resolve the theoretical debate'[76] little more than a chimera.

IV. The Evolving Regulatory Landscape

Notwithstanding the contested nature of the various rationales offered in support of prohibitions on insider dealing (and to a lesser extent market manipulation), there nevertheless exists a widespread global consensus about the need for

[74] Allen, n 44 above, 183, n 22. [75] See n 42 above, 866. [76] Beny, n 71 above, 241.

measures outlawing such conduct.[77] In this respect, developments within the EU offer an excellent vantage point from which to survey the evolving regulatory landscape—both in general terms, and in terms of the EU's regulatory response to recent market integrity concerns. These concerns revolve around abusive short selling in the aftermath of the financial crisis, benchmark manipulation, the growing lack of transparency associated with the fragmentation of markets and trading platforms, and the heightened scope for abusive practices associated with the increasing use of HFT strategies. What is more, the EU regime also provides an interesting and increasingly important counterpoint to the US approach to insider dealing in particular.

1. The EU market abuse regime

Unlike the US regime—the broad contours of which are outlined below—the EU regime on insider dealing rejects any need for a showing of fraud or deception based on a breach of fiduciary duty (or other similar relationship of trust and confidence). Instead, the EU regime—in keeping with a global trend of which it might claim to be an exemplar—is predicated on an underlying policy of regulating market relationships by prohibiting persons from trading on the basis of non-publicly available information.[78] The regime is given legal expression by way of the Market Abuse Directive (MAD)[79]—a key directive in a broader phalanx of measures designed to promote the development of a pan EU capital market—which embodies 'bright line' minimum legislative standards, duly implemented in each EU Member State.

In essence, the EU's market abuse regime, which prohibits both insider dealing and market manipulation (collectively, known as 'market abuse'), is characterized by complex statutory rules which marry technical proscriptions with detailed statutory exemptions,[80] defences, and safe harbours.[81] Accordingly, MAD specifies the key ingredients of each market abuse offence. Thus, in relation to insider dealing, it specifies: the categories of person covered (eg, primary and secondary insiders);[82] the nature of the conduct proscribed (eg, dealing, disclosing, and recommending);[83]

[77] In a study conducted by Bhattacharya and Daouk, as of the end of 1998 of the 103 countries that had stock markets, 87 had laws prohibiting insider dealing: Bhattacharya and Daouk, n 67 above, 75.

[78] The MAD is designed to support the integrity of financial markets by helping to promote public confidence in, and the smooth function of, those markets: Recital 2.

[79] The EU's market abuse regime is currently comprised of: (a) a framework directive called the Market Abuse Directive (MAD) (Directive 2003/6/2003); and (b) three European Commission directives: (i) the Market Manipulation Definitions Directive (Commission Directive 2003/124/2003); (ii) the MAD Implementing Directive (Commission Directive 2003/125/2003); and (iii) the Market Practices and Disclosure Directive (Commission Directive 2004/72/2003); as well as a Commission Regulation called the MAD Implementing Regulation (Commission Regulation 2273/2003).

[80] ibid, Article 7.

[81] ibid, Article 8, on stabilization and buy-backs.

[82] ibid, Articles 2 and 4.

[83] ibid, Articles 2 and 3.

the type of securities caught (eg, equities, debt, derivatives, etc.);[84] the range of public markets to which the prohibition extends ('regulated markets');[85] the nature of the information on which dealing etc. is prohibited ('inside information');[86] and the regime's jurisdictional reach.[87]

The EU's market abuse regime (unlike the position in the US) also embodies a commitment to the continuous disclosure of material information which is designed to promote the timely disclosure of material information, and thus limit the scope for insider dealing *ex ante*. The regime further comprises the use of 'insider lists' (and insider reporting of certain personal transaction), as well as the reporting of suspicious transactions. Although MAD is non-prescriptive with regard to the type of sanctions required, as discussed below, a key feature of forthcoming EU reforms is the introduction of a more uniform and muscular approach to the use of sanctions and, indeed, to enforcement issues generally.

As an ambitious and multifaceted regime with a broad compass, MAD represents a marked improvement on earlier harmonization efforts in the area, and can fairly be regarded as a qualified success. Nevertheless, the regime has also had to face a number of significant challenges. For example, events associated with, and in the aftermath of, the recent financial crisis (namely, abusive short selling and benchmark manipulation), and the growing spectre of abuse associated with the growth of HFT strategies, have sorely tested the credibility of the regime and brought into sharper focus its ability to respond effectively to an ever expanding range of market integrity concerns. Accompanying these recent challenges are more long-standing problems associated with the lack of transparency resulting from the increasing fragmentation of trading venues in the wake of MiFID, and the more general lack of a coordinated pan-European approach to the use of sanctions and enforcement in relation to breaches of the regime.

The EU's response to these challenges has been nuanced and multilayered, involving a combination of: targeted measures, 'soft law' guidelines, and amendments to associated Directives; as well as the outright overhaul of the market abuse regime itself. Thus, in relation to allegations of 'abusive' short selling in the aftermath of the crisis, while it was generally accepted that such conduct would, in principle, amount to market abuse under MAD, it was, nevertheless, felt that more general concerns surrounding short selling were better dealt with by way

[84] These include 'transferrable securities' as widely defined by, Markets in Financial Instruments Directive (MiFID I) Directive 2004/39/EC [2004] OJ 145/1: Article 4(1)(18).

[85] ibid, Article 4(1)(14). Although a trading market may elect not to be a 'regulated market', as a minimum standards directive, Members States may enact laws which go above and beyond the EU minimum—ie, 'gold plate'. The EU regime also extends beyond regulated markets, encompassing trades on other markets where there is a causal connection with the operation of a regulated market.

[86] MAD, n 79 above, Article 1.

[87] ibid, Article 10.

of a targeted measure (the 'Short Selling Regulation') rooted in disclosure and improved market transparency.

In relation to the spectre of abuse associated with the use of certain HFT strategies, the European Securities and Markets Authority (ESMA)—the EU's sectoral regulator responsible for securities markets—has issued 'soft law' guidelines.[88] These guidelines aim to ensure that regulated markets and multilateral trading facilities (MTFs) have in place arrangements which enable them to identify conduct amounting to market abuse in an automated trading environment,[89] and that investment firms which engage in algorithmic trading (with which HFT is strongly associated) have organizational arrangements in place to 'to minimise the risk that their automated trading activity gives rise to market abuse (in particular market manipulation)'.[90] ESMA's soft law guidelines are, in turn, supplemented by amendments to the MiFID I framework by way of a revised MiFID Directive (MiFID II)[91] and a new Regulation (MiFIR)[92] which place a number of restrictions on algorithmic trading, such as specific organizational requirements for firms engaging in algorithmic trading (and, more pertinently, in respect of market making algorithms), as well as measures targeted specifically at HFT participants, including fee structures for excessive order cancellation and minimum tick sizes.[93]

As far as the overhaul and upgrade of MAD itself is concerned, the Commission has chosen two legal mechanisms: a Regulation (the Market Abuse Regulation (MAR)), which is directly applicable in each Member State, designed to reduce regulatory complexity and to promote great legal certainty; and a new Directive (Directive on criminal sanctions for insider dealing and market regulation (CS-MAD)), which requires the creation of criminal offences for serious forms of market abuse.[94] Although recent events associated with concerns about short selling, benchmark manipulation, and the growth of HFT strategies, have added momentum to the reform of MAD, the rationale for the new regime is, in fact, rather more long-standing. For reasons of space, this discussion focuses only on two key areas which, while broad brush, nevertheless offer a sense of the 'general direction of travel' and resonate with at least some of the broader themes touched on earlier—principally the willingness of modern securities regulators to flex their regulatory muscles by expanding the scope of the regimes they regulate, and their increasing willingness to resort to use of criminal sanctions to police those regimes. The two areas focused on in this respect are: (a) efforts to remedy

[88] See n 24 above. [89] ibid, Guideline 5. [90] ibid, Guideline 6.

[91] Directive 2014/65/EU on Markets in Financial Instruments [2014] OJ L173/349.

[92] Regulation (EU) No 600/2014 on Markets in Financial Instruments [2014] OJ L173/84.

[93] The new rules will take effect from January 2017.

[94] Regulation No 596/2014 [2014] OJ L173/1 and Directive 2014/57/EU [2014] OJ L173/179, respectively.

perceived gaps in the scope of the existing EU regime; and (b) efforts to remedy perceived enforcement deficiencies in that regime.

(a) *Remedying perceived gaps in MAD*

Notwithstanding the broad scope of the EU's existing market abuse regime, in the light of both market and regulatory developments a number of gaps in the regime have been identified, which MAR seeks to address. Currently, MAD only prohibits market abuse in relation to financial instruments which are admitted to trading on a regulated market, whereas following the reforms introduced by MiFID, increasingly financial instruments are being traded on MTFs, or on organized trading facilities (OTFs), or on over-the-counter (OTC) markets. Accordingly, MAR seeks to broaden the scope of the EU's regime by including any financial instrument traded on an MTF (or admitted to trading on such a platform, or for which a request for admission to trade on a MTF has been made), or an instrument traded on an OTF, as well as any related financial instruments traded OTC (such as credit default swaps (CDSs)), which can have an effect on the covered underlying market. In this way, MAR is designed to bring the definition of financial instruments used in the context of market abuse into line with that used in MiFID and thus remedy a widely acknowledged mismatch between the two regimes.

MAR also seeks to widen the scope of the existing regime by a series of other reforms, namely:

- extending the definition of inside information for commodity derivatives to encompass all information of a precise nature which is likely to have a significant effect on the price of, and is relevant to, either the related spot commodity contract or the derivative itself (and where this is information which is reasonably expected to be disclosed or required to be disclosed in accordance with relevant legal or regulatory provisions);[95]
- extending the definition of market manipulation to encompass 'cross market manipulations'—for example, transactions in derivatives markets designed to manipulate the price of related spot markets and vice-versa;[96]
- classifying emission allowances as financial instruments and inserting a specific definition of inside information in relation to such instruments;[97]
- expanding the scope of market manipulation to cover activities associated with benchmarks (such as LIBOR and EURIBOR);[98]
- providing an indicative list of practices associated with algorithmic trading and HFT strategies which will be regarded as species of market manipulation;[99]

[95] *FCA Handbook*, n 12 above, Article 7. [96] ibid, Article 12.
[97] ibid, Article 2. [98] ibid. [99] ibid, Article 12, Annex I.

- introducing specific offences of attempted insider dealing and attempted market manipulation;[100] and
- extending the current obligation to report suspicious transactions to the reporting of suspicious unexecuted order and suspicious OTC transactions.[101]

These reforms reveal a commitment by the EU to review and reform the contours of its market abuse regime in the light of developments in market infrastructure.

(b) *Remedying enforcement problems*

As well as seeking to remedy gaps in the MAD regime, the Commission's reforms also aim to remedy acknowledged weaknesses in the way in which the regime is enforced. Under MAD, Member States have adopted a variegated approach to sanctions which has undermined the development of a fully integrated market.[102] The aim of the new reforms, therefore, is to introduce more uniform pan EU enforcement measures which will have greater deterrent effect. These measures combine the introduction of new investigative powers for national regulators (so as to help detect market abuse) with the introduction of a new system of sanctions. These sanctions comprise the use of new administrative penalties (set out in MAR), as well as the use of criminal measures (set out in the CS-MAD) designed to demonstrate a degree of 'social disapproval [which is] qualitatively different' from the use of administrative or compensatory measures.[103]

In relation to administrative sanctions, MAR establishes that the maximum administrative fine should be three times the profits gained or losses avoided in so far as these are ascertainable.[104] For natural and legal persons administrative penalties vary. For the offences of insider dealing and market manipulation, natural persons are subject to a fine of at least €5 million (for legal persons this is at least €15 million (or 15 per cent of the entity's annual turnover)), and, for the remaining offences under MAR, fines ranging between €1 million and €500,000 depending on the exact nature of the offence (for a legal person this ranges between at least €2.5 million (or 2 per cent of total annual turnover) and €1 million). Member States do, however, have a discretion to exceed these limits.

When imposing sanctions, competent authorities are under an obligation to take account of any aggravating factors (such as the gravity of the offence committed), or any mitigating factors (such as an offender's cooperation with an investigation).[105] Where persons commit repeated breaches of the offences of insider dealing and market manipulation, competent authorities may prohibit any such persons from discharging or exercising managerial responsibilities in an investment firm.[106]

[100] ibid, Articles 14 and 15. [101] ibid, Recital 46 and Article 16.

[102] Overall, the picture of Member States' regimes is 'weak and heterogeneous'. Report of the High Level Group on Financial Supervision in the EU (2009) (hereinafter, de Larosière Report) para 84.

[103] CS-MAD, Recital 6. [104] *FCA Handbook*, n 12 above, Article 30.

[105] ibid, Article 31. [106] ibid, Article 30.

In relation to criminal sanctions, since, in accordance with EU law, the approximation of criminal law is only possible by way of a directive, these are dealt with by way of CS-MAD.[107] In short, this requires the creation of criminal offences for serious forms of market abuse. Thus, under CS-MAD, Member States are required to treat serious cases of intentional insider dealing and market manipulation (as well conduct which amounts to inciting or aiding and abetting those offences), and attempted insider dealing and attempted market manipulation, as criminal offences. Legal entities must be rendered subject to sanctions, as well as any individuals directly responsible for the misconduct.[108] Sanctions must be 'effective, proportionate and dissuasive'.[109] For individuals, the maximum sanction is at least four years' imprisonment for market manipulation and insider dealing (and recommending or inducing another person to engage in insider dealing), and two years' for the unlawful disclosure of inside information.[110] For legal persons, sanctions can comprise criminal or non-criminal sanctions.[111] In relation to the latter, these may include fines and sanctions such as: exclusion from entitlement to public benefits or aid; temporary or permanent disqualification from carrying on commercial activities; judicial winding-up; or temporary or permanent closure of establishments which have been used in the commission of the offence.[112] Again, Member States retain a discretion to adopt or maintain more stringent criminal law measures.

In sum, while there is much about the EU's enforcement of its market abuse regime which is likely to remain problematic notwithstanding these reforms, this more muscular approach to enforcement is both timely and welcome—and to a large extent resonates with developments in a number of other jurisdictions, namely the US and the UK.

2. The US approach to insider dealing

The EU approach discussed above—at least in relation to insider dealing—stands in stark contrast to the US's long-standing regulatory approach. In what can be regarded as an increasingly anomalous position, US insider dealing laws remain wedded to what is essentially a 'relationship-based' model emphasizing the

[107] Under the Lisbon Treaty, the UK is not automatically bound by EU legislative proposals in relation to freedom, security, and justice matters. The UK has chosen not to opt into the CS-MAD, albeit that it retains the right to do so.

[108] Legal entities will be liable for a criminal offence if it is committed for their benefit by a person holding a leading position in the firm: Article 7(1) CS-MAD. Moreover, companies may also be criminally liable for offences committed by junior employees for the company's benefit where there has been a corporate failure (eg, where there has been a lack of supervision and control over that person by senior management): Article 7(2).

[109] CS-MAD, Article 6. [110] ibid. [111] ibid, Article 8.

[112] ibid.

protection of fiduciary norms of trust and confidence between parties, the classic example of which is the corporate insider who misappropriates company property (inside information) for personal benefit at the expense of his or her company. Lacking in an overarching legislative definition, the origins of US law on insider dealing instead lie in the development of a somewhat ad hoc corpus of law derived from: (a) section 10(b) of the Securities Exchange Act 1934 (a broad anti-fraud provision rendering it unlawful for any person to employ in connection with the purchase or sale of any security 'any manipulative or deceptive device or contrivance' in contravention of SEC rules); and (b) the now notorious Rule 10b-5 promulgated thereunder.[113]

Accordingly, both SEC administrative rulings and judicial decisions have played a highly significant role in shaping many of the elements of what constitutes insider trading,[114] in a manner 'reminiscent of a common law approach'.[115] Bereft of the more consciously drawn contours of other modern regimes—such as illustrated by the position in the EU—a view has long been expressed that US insider trading jurisprudence is beset by 'considerable ambiguity'[116] and 'undermined by the absence of a definition'.[117] Although at various times during the 1980s Congress considered legislative proposals for a statutory reformulation of the test for 'insider trading', the argument that a statutory definition could 'unintentionally narrow the scope of the law by facilitating schemes to evade the law'[118] has ultimately prevailed.

[113] Rule 10b-5, which was not adopted by the SEC until 1942, states that:

'It shall be unlawful for any person, directly or indirectly, by use of any means or instrumentality of interstate commerce, or of the mails, or of any facility of any national securities exchange,

(1) to employ any device, scheme, or artifice to defraud,
(2) to make any untrue statement of a material fact or omit to state a material fact necessary in order to make the statements made, in the light of the circumstances under which they were made, not misleading, or
(3) to engage in any act, practice, or course of business which operates or would operate as fraud or deceit upon any person, in connection with the purchase or sale of any security.'

[114] For example, the meaning of 'non-public inside information', as well as the degree of *scienter* (*mens rea*) required to generate liability under section 10(b) and Rule 10b-5.

[115] Greene, E and Schmid, O, 'Duty-free Insider Trading?' [2013] *Columbia Business Law Review* 369, 372.

[116] Pitt, H and Shapiro, K, 'The Insider Trading Proscriptions Act of 1987: A Legislative Initiative for a Sorely Needed Clarification of the Law against Insider Trading' (1988) 39 *Alabama Law Review* 415, 417.

[117] Ruiz, L, 'European Community Directive on Insider Dealing: A Model for Effective Enforcement of Prohibitions on Insider Trading in International Securities Markets' (1995) 33 *Columbia Journal of Transnational Law* 217.

[118] Insider Trading and Securities Fraud Act of 1988, HR Rep. No 100–910, 100th Cong, 2d Sess, § 3 (1988). The Insider Trading Sanctions Act of 1983, Hearings before the Subcommittee on Securities of the Senate Committee on Banking, Housing, and Urban Affairs, 98th Cong, 2d Sess 37 (1984) (statement by Fedders J, former SEC Enforcement Division Director).

The absence of a broad statutory definition does, admittedly, afford the US authorities some discretion over how to respond to insider dealing threats, and in many respects US law has proved itself capable of evolving to meet market needs. In the aftermath of the SEC's set-back in *Chiarella*,[119] and, again, not long thereafter in *Dirks*,[120] the general trajectory of US insider dealing law has been undeniably expansionary—achieved in part by way of the Supreme Court's subsequent endorsement of the 'misappropriation theory' in *O'Hagan*,[121] and also by way of detailed SEC rulemaking (often as a means of countering judicial rebuffs).[122] Nevertheless, in being primarily tethered to its 'breach of duty' moorings as the basis for a showing of deceptive conduct under section 10b and Rule 10b-5, the development of US law has, arguably, been hindered by its weak foundations. These foundations have given rise to a jurisprudence which is deficient in terms of its conceptual underpinnings (focusing on an overly narrow 'breach of duty' approach as the basis of deceptive conduct rather than a more broadly based concept involving the regulation of market relationships),[123] under-inclusive in terms of its scope (there have recently been a number of cases where the courts have declined to rule that conduct was in breach of Rule 10b-5),[124] and clumsy and erratic in terms of its ad hoc development (evident by virtue of an element of 'ebb and flow' in legal developments).

More generally, at a time when financial markets are more global and interconnected than ever before, the US approach to the development of its corpus of insider dealing law is increasingly out of step with other major financial centres, particularly in the UK and in continental Europe. Although the EU regime has

[119] 445 US 222 (1980). Here, the Supreme Court held that the duty to 'disclose or abstain'—derived from its earlier ruling in *Texas Gulf Sulphur* 401 F 2d 833 (2d Cir 1968)—was dependent upon whether the defendant owed the issuer of the securities a fiduciary *or other relationship of trust and confidence*. The Supreme Court found that no such relationship existed. Accordingly, since no duty was owed to the issuer, the defendant was free to trade in the issuer's securities on the basis of the material information he possessed.

[120] *Dirks v SEC* 463 US 646 (1983).

[121] *United States v O'Hagan* 521 US 642, 653–4 (1997). The misappropriation theory holds that a person is prohibited from trading on the basis of information which has been misappropriated from its source, irrespective of whether the source of the information is a corporate (or temporary) insider of the issuer in whose securities trading has taken place. Accordingly, while no breach of fiduciary duty by a corporate (or temporary) insider is required to establish liability under the misappropriation theory, a fiduciary or similar duty of trust or confidence to the source of the information must, nevertheless, be established.

[122] For example, the SEC immediately followed its setback in *Chiarella*, with the promulgation of Rule 14e-3, made pursuant to section 14(e) SEA 34 (prohibiting insider dealing in the context of takeovers). The rule applies irrespective of whether the defendant owes or has breached a fiduciary or other duty to the relevant issuer.

[123] See generally, Greene and Schmid, n 115 above.

[124] See, eg, Coffee, J, 'Introduction: Mapping the Future of Insider Trading Law: of Boundaries, Gaps, and Strategies' (2013) *Columbia Business Law Review* 281, 289–96 (discussing recent case law). See also, Bainbridge, S, 'An Overview of Insider Trading Law and Policy: An Introduction to the Insider Trading Research Handbook' in Bainbridge, S (ed.), *Research Handbook on Insider Trading* (2013) 1, 2 (the existing law is characterized by 'a number of problems and curious gaps').

much to learn from the US in terms of the latter's long-standing commitment to active enforcement, it is suggested that the US could learn much from the more comprehensive and systematized 'bright line' approach evident in the EU regime. Indeed, recent efforts to upgrade the EU's market abuse regime, both in terms of its scope and by way of a more muscular approach to enforcement issues—in particular, by way of the endorsement of the use of criminal sanctions for serious market abuses—presages a new era for EU regulation of such conduct. More significantly, forthcoming reforms place the EU in the vanguard of the global charge to tackle market abuse, and, once implemented, mean that the EU regime can fairly lay claim to being the most sophisticated market abuse code in the world.

To some extent, the EU's new approach to the use of criminal sanctions resonates with a global trend towards more intensive enforcement of market abuses and, more especially, the use in some quarters of criminal sanctions to deter insider dealing, as discussed below in Section V.

V. Enforcement Trends

A notable feature of the insider dealing debate over the last 40 years or so has been a disjuncture between the eagerness of countries to enact laws prohibiting insider dealing, and their subsequent unwillingness/inability to enforce those laws. Significantly, evidence is now emerging which suggests that this global picture is slowly beginning to change. According to Clark, from 2009 to the end of March 2010, a number of countries across five continents reported increased levels of insider trading enforcement: Australia, Canada, Italy, China, and Kenya.[125] Furthermore, evidence of significant enforcement developments have also been reported in Hong Kong,[126] Japan,[127] Singapore,[128] France,[129] Germany,[130] and the UK.[131] And in a number of other

[125] See Clark, S, 'Insider Trading and Financial Economics: Where Do we Go from Here?' (2010–11) 16 *Stanford Journal of Law, Business & Finance* 43 and sources cited therein. See also Marriage, M, 'Red Alert over Record Year for Insider Dealing' *Financial Times*, 5 January 2014.

[126] See, Wong, K, 'Former Morgan Stanley Banker Du Jailed for 7 Years' (18 September 2009), *Bloomberg*, available at <http//www.bloomberg.com/apps/news?pid--newsarchive&sid=aZcWlQ2OIrfY>.

[127] Morrison Foerster, available at <http://www.mofo.com/files/Uploads/Images/130116-Insider-Trading-Annual-Review.pdf>.

[128] ibid.

[129] In France, insider dealing fines more than doubled to €19 million in 2013. Marriage, n 125 above.

[130] In 2013, investigations into insider dealing increased from 26 to 42. ibid.

[131] See n 138 below and accompanying text.

jurisdictions, regulators have confirmed that the enforcement of their insider dealing/market abuse laws represents a major priority going forward.[132]

Not surprisingly, the US authorities (primarily, the SEC and the Department of Justice (DoJ)) remain at the forefront of efforts to enforce insider trading laws. According to a recent study by Beny and Seyhun, the authors found that while from 1980 through to the late 1990s, there was a steady, albeit rather modest year-on-year increase in the number of actions brought by the SEC for insider dealing, thereafter there was a 'fundamental turning point' in the Agency's enforcement intensity.[133] Thus, between 1980 and 1990, SEC actions almost doubled (from 20 to 38), and in 2005–10 (following a marked increase from 2000 onwards) they remained relatively steady, at an average of 49 actions per year.[134] The authors also found signs of renewed enforcement intensity in 2010–11, with the SEC reporting 57 insider dealing actions against 124 individuals and entities; an increase of nearly 8 per cent in the number of actions filed by them from the previous fiscal year.[135]

Although Beny and Seyhun adduce only anecdotal evidence to support their claim that there has also been an increase in the number of criminal convictions for insider dealing, they nevertheless show that where convictions have occurred, the severity of punishment has increased.[136] Between 1993 and 1999, fewer than 5 per cent of defendants received custodial sentences of two years or more, whereas between 2000 and 2009 this had increased to more than 25 per cent. Moreover, reflecting the type of renewed SEC enforcement intensity referred to above, in the last two years this has doubled, to around 50 per cent.[137]

To some extent echoing US developments, evidence of a renewed commitment to enforcing insider dealing and wider market abuse laws can also be found in the UK.[138] Here a policy of 'credible deterrence'—pioneered by the now defunct FSA,

[132] See, eg, the Dutch Authority for Financial Markets, the Autoriteit Financiële Markten (AFM), Freshfields Bruckhaus Deringer, European Market Abuse News (Spring 2012); and, in Spain, the Securities Markets Commission (CNMV), Freshfields Bruckhaus Deringer, Global Market Abuse News (Spring 2013).

[133] Beny and Seyhun, n 28 above, 216 (finding that between 1980 and 1990, actions almost doubled (to 38), and that in 2005–10 they remained relatively steady, at an average of 49 actions per year).

[134] The number of SEC investigations into insider dealing has also recently increased in 2013. Marriage, n 125 above.

[135] In 2012, the SEC also settled 118 cases of insider dealing, significantly more than the previous six-year average of 71: Freshfields Bruckhaus Deringer (2013), n 132 above.

[136] Beny and Seyhun, n 28 above, 212 (finding that the probability of serving a prison sentence as well as the length served significantly increased).

[137] Emblematic of US successes on this front is the recent high-profile conviction of Raj Rajaratnam, a former hedge fund manager, who was sentenced to 11 years' imprisonment and fined over $156 million. Furthermore, in March 2013, the SEC announced a record $602 million settlement on insider dealing charges against the hedge fund advisory firm, CR Intrinsic Investors (CR), as well as a $14 million settlement with its affiliate, SAC Capital Advisors.

[138] In the UK the criminal offence of insider dealing is governed by the Criminal Justice act (Part V) 1993, whereas the civil/administrative offence of market abuse is governed by the Financial Services and Markets Act 2000 (FSMA 2000), Part VIII.

and today continued by the newly formed Financial Conduct Authority (FCA)—has been carried out with considerable vigour.[139] As part of this policy, the UK regulator has proved willing to use the full array of enforcement tools at its disposal,[140] including a willingness to bring criminal charges against individuals.[141] Thus, having not commenced its first criminal prosecution for insider dealing until 2008, the FSA had, by July 2013, secured 23 successful convictions.[142] Recent figures confirm that this trend has not abated, with a further seven criminal prosecutions pending. Furthermore, there is evidence to suggest that at the time of its demise, the FSA was both willing and able to investigate and prosecute more complex cases and that an increasing number of defendants were sufficiently cowered to plead guilty to insider dealing charges.[143] To some extent, evidence of the UK's recent focus on the use of criminal sanctions for breaches of its insider dealing laws also resonates with indications of a more muscular approach by the EU in relation to sanctions, as noted above.

A number of factors are likely to underpin this global trend towards more active enforcement of insider dealing laws.[144] First, since markets in which insider dealing is perceived to be rife are likely to be regarded as less attractive centres for cross-border trading, regulators have an incentive to enforcement laws in the hope of attracting more cross-border deals. Second, greater emphasis on enforcement may reflect a market's evolving understanding of conduct which adversely affects market integrity. Thus, a nation's response to enforcing, say, insider dealing violations may, in fact, be emblematic of, and a useful proxy for, the maturity of its financial markets—if not always the quality of its regulatory regime overall. Third, following IOSCO's lead, scope for greater investigative assistance and mutual cooperation among foreign securities authorities is likely to enhance enforcement efforts.[145] Fourth, the use of increasingly sophisticated surveillance techniques

[139] This policy was first introduced in its 2008/2009 Business Plan by Hector Sants (the then CEO of the FSA).

[140] In relation to market abuse under FSMA 2000, Part VIII, these encompass: public censure (section 123(3)); the imposition of a fine (section 123(2)); and, on its own initiative, restitution against an *authorised person* (section 384). The FCA may also apply to the court for: (a) injunctions (section 381(1)); (b) remedial orders (section 381(2)); (c) freezing orders (section 381(3)); and (d) restitutionary and compensatory orders (section 383).

[141] Unlike the SEC in the US, the FCA is vested with authority to prosecute breaches of the CJA (Part V) 1993: FSMA 2000, section 402(1)(a).

[142] <http://www.fca.org.uk/news/firms/four-arrested-in-fca-insider-dealing-investigation>.

[143] Such as the successful conclusion of 'Operation Saturn', involving convictions against an insider dealing ring trading multiple stocks between 2006 and 2008. FSA, Annual Report 2012/13, 39.

[144] See Pitt, H and Hardison, H, 'Games without Frontiers: Trends in the International Response to Insider Trading' (1992) 55 *Law & Contemporary Problems* 199 (explaining a similar albeit less pronounced trend in the late 1980s and early 1990s—at least in relation to the enactment of insider dealing laws).

[145] IOSCO, Multilateral Memorandum of Understanding: Concerning Consultation and Cooperation and the Exchange of Information (2012).

has increased regulators' chances of detecting unusual trading patterns, and thus helped to increase the number of investigations and, subsequently, the number of enforcement actions they are able to bring.[146]

A final and less benign reason for the observed increase in enforcement intensity might reside in the idea that some regulatory authorities regard more vigorous enforcement of conduct such as insider dealing, as a relatively easy and high-profile way of reasserting authority over both their financial markets and the 'actors' they regulate. This is likely to be particularly the case so insofar as regulatory authorities have been the focus of sustained criticism in relation to their performance in the lead up to, and during, the financial crisis. Obvious candidates in this context are the regulatory authorities in both the US and the UK—two jurisdictions which are currently at the forefront of the enforcement charge.

VI. Conclusion

In the aftermath of the global financial crisis there has been renewed interest in, and more intense scrutiny of, activities which raise the spectre of market abuse and, in turn, prompt concerns about market integrity. Such evidence, as exists, suggests that market abuse is a continuing problem in the context of modern financial markets and that it poses acute challenges for regulatory authorities. As both markets and trading strategies continue to evolve, new strains of market abuse have emerged and opportunities for abuse now exist on a scale not previously possible.

Although market manipulation, and especially abusive conduct associated with HFT, is increasingly attracting the gaze of regulators, much academic and regulatory attention continues to focus on insider dealing—a practice long regarded as emblematic of our concerns about market integrity. In the space of only a handful of decades, insider dealing has gone from being a distinctly US preoccupation, to a practice which today attracts global opprobrium. In Europe, which, by virtue of MAD, has been the testing ground for pan-EU measures prohibiting insider dealing and market manipulation—and for the deployment of continuous disclosure measures which seeks to prevent abuse *ex ante*—the regulatory landscape is both complex and evolving. Although long in the shadow of US efforts to promote market integrity, the MAD regime has enabled the EU to emerge as a global player in the fight against market

[146] For example, for developments in the UK, see Sullivan, R, 'FSA Unveils New Market Abuse Detector' *Financial Times*, 7 August 2011 (detailing the introduction of Zen); and in Australia: Drummond, M, 'ASIC Targets Insider Traders with New $44m Surveillance System', *Financial Review*, 24 November 2013 (detailing the introduction of a new surveillance system called 'MAI').

abuse. What is more, reforms which are set to widen the regime's scope, combined with a more muscular approach to the enforcement of it, threaten to catapult the EU's regime to the very forefront of global efforts to 'keep markets clean'.

Ultimately, however, assessing where the right balance is between permitting certain informational advantages and market practices, and outlawing others so as to support and promote market integrity, raises fundamental questions about the nature of those markets, and the conditions necessary for the claimed benefits of market optimality to materialize. Properly understood, financial markets represent socially constructed mechanisms which are designed to harness human energies (and allocate scarce resources) for productive, collectively enriching, purposes. Accordingly, the decision to prohibit insider dealing, and market abuse more generally, turns on a determination of those conditions upon which private investment in the pursuit of private profit on public markets is rendered legitimate. And in order to do this, not only do we need to work out what sort of initiative we wish to encourage/discourage but also, more broadly, what we value as a society. For these reasons, debates about market integrity—and insider dealing in particular—will, irrespective of the search for empirical resolution, forever remain fuzzy, messy, and contestable.[147]

Bibliography

Allen, W, 'Professor Scheppele's Middle Way: On Minimizing Normativity and Economics in Securities Laws' (1993) 56 *Law and Contemporary Problems* 175.

Avgouleas, E, *The Mechanics and Regulation of Market Abuse: A Legal and Economic Analysis* (2005).

Bainbridge, S, 'An Overview of Insider Trading Law and Policy: An Introduction to the Insider Trading Research Handbook' in Bainbridge, S (ed.), *Research Handbook on Insider Trading* (2013) 1.

Benjamin, J, 'The Narratives of Financial Law' (2010) 30 *Oxford Journal of Legal Studies* 787.

Beny, L, 'Do Shareholders Value Insider Trading Laws? International Evidence' (August 2006), available at <http://deepblue.lib.umich.edu/bitstream/handle/2027.42/57217/wp837%20.pdf?sequence=1>.

Beny, L, 'Insider Trading Laws and Stock Markets around the World: An Empirical Contribution to the Theoretical Law and Economics Debate' (2007) 32 *Journal of Corporation Law* 237.

Beny, L and Seyhun, N, 'Has Illegal Insider Trading Become More Rampant in the United States? Empirical Evidence from Takeovers' in Bainbridge, S (ed.), *Research Handbook on Insider Trading* (2013) 211.

Bergmans, B, *Inside Information and Securities Trading: A Legal and Economic Analysis of Liability in the USA and the European Community* (1991).

[147] See, Allen, n 44 above, 176, 182.

Bhattacharya, U and Daouk, H, 'The World Price of Insider Trading' (2002) 57 *Journal of Finance* 75.

Brudney, V, 'Insider, Outsiders, and Informational Advantages under Federal Securities Laws' (1979) 93 *Harvard Law Review* 322.

Bushman, R, Piotroski, J, and Smith, A, 'Insider Trading Restrictions and Analysts' Incentives to Follow Firms' (2005) 60 *Journal of Finance* 35.

Capital Markets CRC Limited, *Enumerating the Cost of Insider Trading* (unpublished, 2010).

Carlton, D and Fischel, D, 'The Regulation of Insider Trading' (1983) 35 *Stanford Law Review* 857.

Clark, R, *Corporate Law* (1986).

Clark, S, 'Insider Trading and Financial Economics: Where Do we Go from Here?' (2010–11) 16 *Stanford Journal of Law, Business & Finance* 43.

Coffee, J, 'Introduction: Mapping the Future of Insider Trading Law: Of Boundaries, Gaps, and Strategies' (2013) *Columbia Business Law Review* 281.

Comerton-Forde, C and Putnins, T, The Prevalence and Underpinnings of Closing Price Manipulation (28 April 2010), available at SSRN: <http://ssm.com/abstract-1243042>.

Committee of European Securities Regulators (CESR), Market Abuse Directive: Level 3—First Set of CESR Guidance and Information on the Common Operation of the Directive (CESR/04–505b) (<http://www.esma.europa.eu/system/files/04_505b.pdf>).

Cox, J, 'An Outsider's Perspective of Insider Trading Regulation in Australia' (1990) 12 *Sydney Law Journal* 455.

CRA, *Assessing the Effectiveness of Enforcement and Regulation* (April 2009).

Dale, R, *The First Crash: Lessons from the South Sea Bubble* (2004).

Donald, D, 'Regulating Market Manipulation through an Understanding of Price Creation' (2011) 6 *National Taiwan University Law Review* 55.

Drummond, M, 'ASIC Targets Insider Traders with New $44m Surveillance System', *Financial Review* (24 November 2013), available at <http://www.afr.com/p/business/sunday/asic_targets_insider_traders_with_UbmmHE8v9cFZaGDfir6QGO>.

Du, J and Wei, S, 'Does Insider Trading Raise Market Volatility?' (2004) 114 *Economic Journal* 916.

Easterbrook, F, 'Insider Trading, Secret Agents, Evidentiary Privileges, and the Production of Information' [1981] *Supreme Court Review* 309.

ESMA, Guidelines: Systems and Controls in an Automated Trading Environment for Trading Platforms, Investment Firms and Competent Authorities (24 February 2012), ESMA/2012/122 (EN), available at <http://www.esma.europa.eu/system/files/esma_2012_122_en.pdf>.

European Commission, Staff Working Paper Impact Assessment (SEC(2011) 1217 final).

Fernandes, N and Ferreira, M, 'Insider Trading Laws and Stock Price Informativeness' (2009) 22 *Review of Financial Studies* 1845.

Ferrarini, G, 'The European Market Abuse Directive' (2004) 41 *Common Market Law Review* 724.

Financial Conduct Authority, FCA Fines US based Oil Trader US $903K for Market manipulation (July 2013).

Financial Services Authority, Annual Report 2012/13.

Financial Services Authority, Hedge Funds: A Discussion of Risk and Regulatory Engagement, Discussion Paper 05/04.

Financial Services Authority, Short Selling, Discussion Paper 09/1.

Fischel, D and Ross, D, 'Should the Law Prohibit "Manipulation" in Financial Markets?' (1991) 105 *Harvard Law Review* 503.

Freshfields Bruckhaus Deringer, *European Market Abuse News* (Spring 2012).

Freshfields Bruckhaus Deringer, *Global Market Abuse News* (Spring 2013).

The G20 Seoul Summit Declaration (11–12 November 2010), available at <http://www.g20.utoronto.ca/2010/g20seoul-doc.pdf>.

Glosten, L and Harris, L, 'Estimating the Components of the Bid/Ask Spread' (1988) 21 *Journal of Financial Economics* 123.

Goodhart, C, 'The Economics of "Big Bang"' (1987) Summer *Midland Bank Review* 6.

Greene, E and Schmid, O, 'Duty-Free Insider Trading?' [2013] *Columbia Business Law Review* 369.

Haft, R, 'The Effect of Insider Trading Rules on the Internal Efficiency of the Large Corporation' (1982) 80 *Michigan Law Review* 1051.

Hughes, L, 'Impact of Insider Trading Regulations on Stock Market Efficiency: A Critique of the Law and Economics Debate and a Cross-Country Comparison' (2009) 23(2) *Temple International & Comparative Law Journal* 479.

IOSCO, Addendum to IOSCO Report on Investigating and Prosecuting Market Manipulation (April 2013) (<http://www.iosco.org/library/pubdocs/pdf/IOSCOPD411.pdf>).

IOSCO, Investigating and Prosecuting Market Manipulation (May 2000).

IOSCO, Multilateral Memorandum of Understanding: Concerning Consultation and Cooperation and the Exchange of Information (<http://www.bcsc.bc.ca/uploadedFiles/IOSCO_MMOU_2012.pdf>).

IOSCO, Regulatory Issues Raised by the Impact of Technological Changes on Market Integrity and Efficiency, Final Report of the Technical Committee of IOSCO (October 2011), available at <http://www.iosco.org/library/pubdocs/pdf/IOSCOPD361.pdf>.

Justice, *Report on Insider Trading* (1972).

Khwaja, A and Mian, A, 'Unchecked Intermediaries: Price Manipulation in an Emerging Stock Market' (2005) 78 *Journal of Financial Economics* 203.

King, M and Roell, A, 'Insider Trading' (1988) April *Economic Policy* 163.

Klock, M, 'Mainstream Economics and the Case for Prohibiting Inside Trading' (1994) 10 *Georgia State University Law Review* 297.

La Porta, R, Lopez-de-Silanes, F, Shleifer, A and Vishny, R, 'Legal Determinants of External Finance' (1997) 52 *Journal of Finance* 1131.

Macey, J, *Insider Trading: Economic, Politics, and Policy* (1991).

Manne, H, 'Insider Trading and Property Rights in New Information' (1985) 4 *Cato Journal* 933.

Manne, H, 'Insider Trading and the Law Professors' (1970) 23 *Vanderbilt Law Review* 547.

Manne, H, *Insider Trading and the Stock Market* (1966).

Marriage, M, 'Red Alert over Record Year for Insider Dealing' *Financial Times*, 5 January 2014.

Mendelson, M, 'Book Review: The Economics Board of Insider Trading Reconsidered' (1969) 117 *University of Pennsylvania Law Review* 470.

Moloney, N, *EC Securities Regulation* (2nd edn, 2008).

Morgan, JP, 'HSBC and Credit Agricole accused of euro rate-fixes' (<http://www.bbc.co.uk/news/business-27482358> (20 May 2014)).

Morrison Foerster, *Insider Trading: Annual Review* (<http://www.mofo.com/files/Uploads/Images/130116-Insider-Trading-Annual-Review.pdf>).

Naik, N, *Hedge Funds: Transparency and Conflict of Interest* IP/A/ECON/IC/2007-24 (<http://www.europarl.europa.eu/RegData/etudes/etudes/join/2007/393519/IPOL-ECON_ET(2007)393519_EN.pdf>).

Narron, J and Skeie, D, 'Crisis Chronicles: The South Sea Bubble of 1720—Repackaging Debt and the Current Reach for Yield' (<http://libertystreeteconomics.newyorkfed.org/2013/11/crisis-chronicles-the-south-sea-bubble-of-1720repackaging-debt-and-the-current-reach-for-yield.html>).

Palmer's Company Law.

Payne, J, 'The Regulation of Short Selling and its Reform in Europe' (2012) 13 *European Business Organization Law Review* 413.

Pitt, H and Hardison, D, 'Games without Frontiers: Trends in the International Response to Insider Trading' (1992) 55 *Law & Contemporary Problems* 199.

Pitt, H and Shapiro, K, 'The Insider Trading Proscriptions Act of 1987: A Legislative Initiative for a Sorely Needed Clarification of the Law against Insider Trading' (1988) 39 *Alabama Law Review* 415.

Rachlinski, J, 'Evidence-Based Law' (2001) 96 *Cornell Law Review* 901.

Report of the High Level Group on Financial Supervision in the EU (the de Larosière Report) (February 2009), available at <http://ec.europa.eu/economy_finance/publications/publication14527_en.pdf>.

Ruiz, L, 'European Community Directive on Insider Dealing: A Model for Effective Enforcement of Prohibitions on Insider Trading in International Securities Markets' (1995) 33 *Columbia Journal of Transnational Law* 217.

Scheppele, K, '"It's Just Not Right": The Ethics of Insider Trading' (1993) 56 *Law and Contemporary Problems* 123.

Schotland, R, 'Unsafe at Any Price: A Reply to Manne, Insider Trading and the Stock Market' (1967) 53 *Virginia Law Review* 1425.

Securities and Exchange Commission, 'SEC Obtains Record $92.8 Million Penalty Against Raj Rajaratnam' (8 November 2011) (<http://www.sec.gov/news/press/2011/2011-233.htm>).

Sullivan, R, 'FSA unveils new market abuse detector' (7 August 2011).

Thomsen, L, Hawke, D, and Calande, P, 'Hedge Funds: An Enforcement Perspective' (2008) 39 *Rutgers Law Journal* 541.

Wang, W, 'Trading on Material Non-Public Information on Impersonal Markets: Who Is Harmed and Who Can Sue Whom under SEC Rule 10b-5?' (1981) 54 *Southern California Law Review* 1217.

The Wheatley Review of Libor: Final Report (September 2012) (<https://www.gov.uk/government/uploads/system/uploads/attachment_data/file/191762/wheatley_review_libor_finalreport_280912.pdf>).

Winslow, D and Anderson, S, 'From "Shoeless" Joe Jackson to Ivan Boesky: A Sporting Response to Law and Economics Criticism of the Regulation of Insider Trading' (1992–93) 81 *Kentucky Law Journal* 295.

Wong, K, 'Former Morgan Stanley Banker Du Jailed for 7 Years' (18 September 2009), *Bloomberg*, available at <http//www.bloomberg.com/apps/news?pid--newsarchive&sid=aZcWlQ2OIrfY>.

Wood, P, *Law and Practice of International Finance* (2008, University Edition).

Woznert, S, 'Evidence-Based Law by Jeffrey J Rachlinski' (2011) 96 *Cornell Law Review* 925.

CHAPTER 22

REGULATING FINANCIAL INNOVATION*

EMILIOS AVGOULEAS

* I am grateful to Charles Goodhart and Jenny Payne for very constructive comments.

I. Fundamental Concepts and Chapter Overview

1. What is financial innovation?

Finance is nothing more than a long chain of innovations leading to development of novel financial products and processes used to improve allocation of capital and risk management. Given the key role that access to capital and ability to handle risk to avoid loss play in fostering economic activity, growth, and promoting social organization, based on economic power, this assertion ought not to be surprising. It is also deeply rooted in history. Human societies have been pushing the boundaries of financial innovation since early antiquity. While there is strong evidence that harvest based derivatives were widely used among ancient Mesopotamians,[1] arguably, the foremost innovation of ancient times was the invention of metallic coins to store value and record debt.[2]

The term financial innovation is mostly a term of art. Yet, on the basis of historical and contemporary analysis an acceptable definition would understand financial innovation to consist of human knowledge breakthroughs and other creative inventions, which lead to the development of:

(a) new financial products that enhance capital allocation such as stocks, bonds, derivatives, and mutual funds;
(b) new organizations and processes that facilitate access to capital, including the establishment of new financial institutions, trading fora, and new forms for extension of credit;
(c) new risk-management techniques utilized to handle risk originating in financial transactions and commercial deals. These in some cases may be indistinguishable from the other two forms of financial innovation, for example, derivatives and securitizations,[3] and in others an essential prerequisite for

[1] See Weber, EJ, Short History of Derivative Security Markets, University of Western Australia, Business School, mimeo (August 2008), available at <http://www.law.uwa.edu.au/__data/assets/pdf_file/0003/94260/08_10_Weber.pdf>. See, in general, Davies, G and Bank, JH, *A History of Money: From Ancient Times to the Present Day* (2002).

[2] See, in general, Kothari, V, *Securitization: The Financial Instrument of the Future* (3rd edn, 2006) ch 1, 2, and 4; Fabozzi, F, Davis, H, and Choudhry, M, *Introduction to Structured Finance* (2006); Avgouleas, E, 'International Credit Markets: Players, Financing techniques, Instruments, and Regulation' in Bidgoli, H (ed.), *The Handbook of Technology Management* (2009) ch 50.

[3] For many the history of modern finance does not start with the Nobel prize-wining works cited below but with Bachelier's legendary doctoral thesis. See Bachelier, L, 'Théorie de la Spéculation'

the development of the other two forms of financial innovations, as is the case with breakthroughs in finance theory.[4] To this effect portfolio theory introduced by the late Harry Markowitz, highlighting the virtues of investment diversification,[5] of the Modigliani–Miller theorem,[6] of the Black–Scholes formula,[7] and of the controversial Capital Asset Pricing Model (CAPM)[8] are behind the overwhelming majority of modern financial product development;

(d) technological innovation utilized to improve product and processes innovation and to advance the frontiers of risk management. It comprises the use of new technology in product design and trading, improved capital allocations, including information dissemination, and in the pricing and distribution of risk. Finally, it encompasses the use of new technology in the context of essential financial infrastructure services, such as payment, clearing and settlement processes.[9]

Illustrative historical examples of financial product innovations and their tight link to process innovation are the invention of tradable government debt in the

(1900) 17 *Annales de l'École Normale Supérieure* 21, trans in Cootner, PH, *The Random Character of the Stock Market Prices* (1964). See also Davis, M and Etheridge, A, *Louis Bachelier's Theory of Speculation: The Origins of Modern Finance* (2006).

[4] Markowitz, HM, 'Portfolio Selection' (1952) 7 *Journal of Finance* 77, which led to Markowitz, H, *Portfolio Selection: Efficient Diversification of Investments* (1959). The path-breaking monograph was based on Markowitz's doctoral dissertation submitted to the University of Chicago. See also Markowitz, 'Foundations of Portfolio Theory' (1991) 46 *Journal of Finance* 469.

[5] Modigliani, F and Miller, MH, *The Cost of Capital, Corporate Finance and the Theory of Investment* (1958) 48 *American Economic Review* 251.

[6] Black, F and Scholes, M, 'The Pricing of Options and Corporate Liabilities' (1973) 81 *Journal of Political Economy* 637. See also Merton, R, 'Theory of Rational Option Pricing' (1973) 4 *Bell Journal of Economics and Management Science* 141. Unsurprisingly, both the theoretical and empirical foundations of Black–Scholes have been strongly criticized. From the contrary literature see Haug, EG and Taleb, NN, 'Option Traders Use (very) Sophisticated Heuristics, Never the Black–Scholes–Merton Formula' (2011) 77 *Journal of Economic Behavior and Organization* 97. On the role of cognitive biases in trading strategies see Avgouleas, E, 'A New Framework for the Global Regulation of Short Sales: Why Prohibition Is Inefficient and Disclosure Insufficient' (2010) 16 *Stanford Journal of Law, Business & Finance* 376.

[7] See Sharpe, WF, 'Capital Asset Prices: A Theory of Market Equilibrium under Conditions of Risk' (1964) 19 *Journal of Finance* 425; Lintner, J, 'The Valuation of Risk Assets and the Selection of Risky Investments in Stock Portfolios and Capital Budgets' (1965) 47 *Review of Economics and Statistics* 13; Traynor, J, 'Towards a Theory of Market Value of Risky Assets', unpublished manuscript (1961). CAPM was regarded as controversial even before the challenge mounted on it by behavioural finance. See also Frankfurter, GM, 'The Rise and Fall of the CAPM Empire: A Review on Emerging Capital Markets' (1995) 4 *Financial Markets, Institutions and Instruments* 104.

[8] See also for essentially similar, albeit differing in their focus, definitions of financial innovation in Delimatsis, P, 'Transparent Financial Innovation in a Post-Crisis Environment' (2013) 1 *Journal of International Economic Law* 159 and Awrey, D, Complexity, Innovation and the Regulation of Modern Financial Markets, Oxford Legal Studies Research Paper No 49/2011.

[9] The first government bond was issued by the Bank of England in 1693 to raise money to finance—no surprises there—a war against ... France. See for a concise overview the Wikipedia entry on government bonds available at <http://en.wikipedia.org/wiki/Government_bond>.

form of bonds,[10] and attendant clustering of trade around coffee houses (eventually evolving into stock exchanges).[11] These were followed by the establishment of the joint stock company[12] and the ensuing flourishing of stock trading, which essentially financed the industrial revolution. Another leading example of financial product and process innovation constitutes the invention of bills of exchange, which played an instrumental role in the expansion of trade from the seventeenth to the twentieth century.[13] A characteristic example of technological innovation is the way that trading in financial instruments and communication of information covering such instruments has been revolutionized over the years.

It is often argued, that financial innovation and technological breakthroughs always go hand in hand. For example, innovative financial processes may refer to adapting trading strategies to the use of technology. This is normally done through so-called algorithmic trading that normally refers to a rapid reaction to market movements to take advantage and, in the process, eliminate trading arbitrage opportunities, based on pre-set computer algorithms, which entail minimal human intervention.[14] This process is an evolution of older automated trading strategies such as portfolio insurance, which was implicated in the 1988 Wall Street crash.[15] The most troublesome aspect of this new form of automated trading is so-called high-frequency trading (HFT).[16]

Yet, while markets' ability to innovate in the realm of capital allocation and risk management is much enhanced by technological breakthroughs, the latter are not a prerequisite of the former.[17] Characteristic examples of technology neutral

[10] See London Stock Exchange—Our History, available at <http://www.londonstockexchange.com/about-the-exchange/company-overview/our-history/our-history.htm>.

[11] In England it became possible to incorporate a joint stock company without prior permission following the enactment of the Joint Stock Companies Act 1844.

[12] See, indicatively, Rodgers, JS, *The Early History of the Law of Bills and Notes: A Study of the Origins of Anglo-American Commercial Law* (1995) ch 2, 5, and 6. For an overview see Ferguson, N, *The Ascent of Money: A Financial History of the World* (2008).

[13] See Recital 59 of Directive 2014/65/EU [2014] OJ L173/349 (MiFID II).

[14] See Avgouleas, E, *The Mechanics and Regulation of Market Abuse—a Legal and Economic Analysis* (2005), ch 2.

[15] From the many descriptions of HFT encountered this seems the most clear: 'HFT covers a range of [trading] activities ... [which use] extraordinarily high-speed order systems, with speeds of less than five milliseconds. HFT often involves the use of algorithms for automated decision-making. HFT strategies usually feature very short time-frames for establishing and liquidating positions, and result in a high daily portfolio turnover. HFT often involves the submission of multiple orders, which are cancelled in milliseconds if not immediately fulfilled. These strategies seek to end the trading day as flat as possible, with the aim of making profit intra-day, rather than inter-day.' PWC, HFT and the Question of Regulation, Brief (2013–14), available at <http://www.pwc.co.uk/financial-services/regulation/other/hft-and-the-question-of-regulation.jhtml?preview=true>.

[16] Of course, that is so if the list of important innovations does not extend to the perennial quest to turn less noble metals into gold, also known as 'alchemy'! But historically proven inability to find the right formula means that such exclusion is accurate...!

[17] See, in general, about the Order, which was essentially the first multinational corporation, Barber, M, *A History of the Order of the Temple* (2012). In an early show of banker's power, and an ominous sign of what was to come centuries later, the Order eventually became too powerful. So, it

risk-management innovations are the ancient financing and cargo risk-sharing arrangements, which proved instrumental for the development of trade in ancient societies. Similarly, technology neutral was the invention of early bank cheques (from which modern-day banknotes have evolved), mainly used as a form of transfer of funds. These were developed at turbulent times by the late medieval 'bankers' (chiefly the knights of the Temple, who also developed the first form of international banking),[18] and then widely used by the Renaissance financiers of Venice and Florence (where the legendary Medici family featured prominently).[19] At the same time, the above instruments are an example of the overlapping properties of the first three forms of financial innovation.

The massive welfare gains brought by earlier financial innovations did not mean that they were not fraught with problems, the most predominant of which was fraud. The South Sea company scandal[20] was not an isolated example. Anglo-American stock market development in the nineteenth century did not just generate a boom in steam-powered manufacturing and railway investment, which meant a drastic cutting down of production and transportation times. It was also marked by a series of large-scale frauds, which gave rise to an instructive body of common law decisions, which make for fascinating reading to this day.[21]

So, financial innovation has not become a Janus-like creature, both a welfare enhancement engine and a cause of major financial catastrophes, just in the last 20–30 years as it is widely assumed. It has always been thus. But in most cases (in the past) general law principles such as liability for prospectus fraud and the 'insurable' interest doctrine[22] were sufficient to deal with abuses, if properly enforced. This assertion is strengthened by the fact that lack of anti-manipulation laws

was eventually accused for blasphemy, witchcraft, and sexual 'offences'. Although the accusations were possibly false, this did not prevent two normally rival powers, the Papacy and the French King Philip IV (known as Philippe Le Bel), who was deeply in debt to the Order, to take radical steps, including a fair amount of 'burning on the stick', to eradicate the Order. ibid.

[18] Hoggson, NF, *Banking through the Ages* (1926); Goldthwaite, RA, *Banks, Places and Entrepreneurs in Renaissance Florence* (1995).

[19] See for the South Sea Bubble and an insightful account of stock market frauds during the 'railway mania': Chancellor, E, *Devil Take the Hindmost, A History of Financial Speculation* (1999).

[20] For analysis of such cases as *Peek v Gurney, New Brunswick and Canada Railway Co v Conybeare; New Brunswick and Canada Railway Co v Muggeridge*, and *Bedford v Bagshaw* in context see Avgouleas, n 14 above, ch 8.

[21] In English law, the concept of 'insurable interest' was fist defined in the Life Assurance Act 1774, which explained that, in the absence of 'insurable interest', taking out an insurance policy is tantamount to a gaming contract, Life Assurance Act 1774, 14 Geo. 3, *c.* 48 (Eng.). The Law Commission has explained that '[a]t its simplest, the doctrine of insurable interest requires that someone taking out insurance gains a benefit from the preservation of the subject matter of the insurance or suffers a disadvantage should it be lost'. See Law Commission and Scottish Law Commission, Insurable Interest (2008), Insurance Contract Law Issues Paper 4, available at <http://www.lawcom.gov.uk/docs/Insurance_Contract_Law_Issues_Paper_4.pdf>.

[22] Avgouleas, E, *Governance of Global Financial Markets: The Law, the Economics, the Politics* (2012), ch 2 and 3.

and lax enforcement of fraud prohibitions were at the heart of most stock market crashes like the South East Bubble and the 1929 crash. Moreover, the smaller size of the financial sector meant that endogenous shocks, namely confidence crises that were not related to general economic upheaval, did not carry an existential threat for the economy.

2. The 'rise' and 'fall' of financial innovation

Contemporary hostility towards financial innovation is not unjustified, on the contrary. In the past 30 years we have borne witness to a marked shift in the goals of financial innovations away from serving the real economy, as most innovations have done until the 1980s, towards uncontrollable rent-seeking[23] aided by ever more self-referential innovations,[24] serving fictitious or artificial economic ends. Namely, financial innovation radically shifted focus from being the servant of economy and society's needs to becoming their master. The reasons for this seismic change in financial innovators' focus and for the radical alteration of their incentives to innovate have been sevenfold[25]:

(a) the advent of open global markets of investible funds led to a multiplication of innovation users and innovation rents;
(b) rapid advancements in telecommunications technology and computing capacity;
(c) the self-referential and easily manipulable mathematical foundations of modern finance theory;
(d) the combination of (b) and (c) above led to the creation of untested and unreliable, yet internally perceived as nearly perfect, new risk management techniques and models, which, in turn, led to:
(e) the creation of a number of exotic, opaque, complex and barely understood high risk–high reward financial products, eg, Collateralized Debt Obligations ((CDOs), essentially amounting to a double securitization process) and their offspring square CDOs;
(f) neo-liberal economic doctrine and deregulation; and
(g) commoditization of economic relationships and risk management leading to a dramatic shift of focus from long-term goals to transactions' speed and

[23] See also Mackenzie, D, *Material Markets: How Economic Agents Are Constructed* (2008).

[24] Derived from a combined reading of the following works: Tett, G, *Fool's Gold: The Inside Story of J.P. Morgan and How Wall St. Greed Corrupted its Bold Dream and Created a Financial Catastrophe* (2009); Avgouleas, n 22 above; and Mackenzie, D, *An Engine, not a Camera: How Financial Models Shape Markets* (2008).

[25] Erturk, I, Froud, J, Johal, S, Leaver, A, and Williams, K, 'The Democratization of Finance? Promises, Outcomes and Conditions' (2007) 14 *Review of International Political Economy* 553.

volume in a drive to maximize commission income and short-term transaction based profit, a process often known as 'financialization'.[26]

The pace of innovation and the level of complexity of contemporary financial innovations eventually became a matter of great regulatory concern, especially following its role in the last global financial crisis (GFC). Perhaps the biggest problem with this new wave of financial innovations was as a result of excessive information asymmetries. A select group of insiders had infinitely better (though still inaccurate or incomplete) view of the products' worth and risks than investors and regulators.[27]

The most stunning innovation of the last two decades is of course the development and expansion of the so-called shadow-banking sector.[28] The shadow-banking system can broadly be described as 'credit intermediation involving entities and activities (fully or partially) outside the regular banking system'.[29] In the author's view the best definition of shadow banking has been given by former Federal Reserve Board chairman Ben Bernanke who described it as follows as comprising[30]:

[A] diverse set of institutions and markets that, collectively, carry out traditional banking functions—but do so outside, or in ways only loosely linked to, the traditional system of regulated depository institutions. Examples of important components of the shadow banking system include securitization vehicles, asset-backed commercial paper (ABCP) conduits, money market mutual funds, markets for repurchase agreements (repos) ...

[26] See Avgouleas, n 22 above, ch 3. This point is also made in a very cognate way in Black, J, Restructuring Global and EU Financial Regulation: Capacities, Coordination and Learning (2010), LSE Law, Society and Economy Working Papers No 18–2010.

[27] The term was, first, used by Paul McCulley, a senior economist in a major fund manager, in 2007. McCulley defined shadow banking as: 'unregulated shadow banks [which] fund themselves with uninsured commercial paper [and] which may or may not be backstopped by liquidity lines from real banks' and which stand in contrast to 'regulated real banks, who fund themselves with insured deposits, backstopped by access to the Fed's discount window'. McCulley, P, 'Teton Reflections' (August/September 2007), *PIMCO Global Central Bank Focus*, available at <http://media.pimco-global.com/pdfs/pdf_sg/GCB%20Focus%20Sept%2007%20SGP-HK.pdf?WT.cg_n=PIMCO-SINGAPORE&WT.ti=GCB Focus Sept 07 SGP-HK.pdf>, 2.

[28] Simplified definition based on FSB, Strengthening Oversight and Regulation of Shadow Banking: An Overview of Policy Recommendations (2013), iv (hereinafter FSB, Strengthening Oversight: An Overview).

[29] See also Pozsar, Z, Adrian, T, Ashcraft, A, and Boesky, H, Shadow Banking (July 2010), Federal Reserve Board of New York Staff Report No 458, 1. This report included the first all-encompassing mapping of the global shadow-banking system and of its main functions. See Adrian and Ashcraft, Shadow Banking: A Review of the Literature (2012), Federal Reserve Bank of New York Staff Report No 580.

[30] Bernanke, B, Some Reflections on the Crisis and the Policy Response, speech to the Russell Sage Foundation and the Century Foundation Conference on 'Rethinking Finance', New York, NY (13 April 2012), available at <http://www.federalreserve.gov/newsevents/speech/bernanke20120413a.htm>.

In principle, the main objective of the shadow-banking system is to facilitate financial intermediation. It can also be used by savers and borrowers, as is the case in China, to bypass interest rate or lending caps. Fundamentally, financial institutions use the shadow-banking system in order to engage in regulatory tax and regulatory arbitrage, which not infrequently means mere avoidance of tax dues, of capital charges, and of regulatory oversight. An indicative list of shadow banking activity and institutions would include:

(a) secured financing based on repo and stock lending agreements (and in turn facilitated by repo-financed dealer firms and securities lenders);
(b) securitization activity centred around: structured investment vehicles (SIVs); asset-backed commercial paper (ABCP) conduits;
(c) hedge funds and other alternative investment vehicles engaged in credit extension;[31] and
(d) money market mutual funds, which compete with banks for short-term savings which they transform into true demand obligations by buying short-term corporate debt and other 'money-like' short maturity claims.

The main function of shadow banks is maturity transformation: they issue short-term liabilities to investors investing in turn the money to long-term assets. But in doing so they lack the central bank liquidity support the regulated sector enjoys at least since the publication of Bagehot's *Lombard Street*.[32] As a result, they are not subject to the thick web of prudential rules that regulate the operation of banks, which enjoy public support (the regulated sector). The run on Money Market Funds, which essentially compete with banks for deposit-like investment products, in September 2008 is rather illustrative. In September 2008 the Reserve Primary Fund, one of the largest money funds, suffered losses on Lehman Brothers debt and could not maintain its $1 per share price, famously 'breaking the buck'. That ignited a run by investors across the money fund industry, cutting off a major source of overnight funding for many corporations.[33] Section III provides an analytical discussion of risks emanating from the shadow-banking sector.

[31] The FSB classifies shadow banking entities as: (i) credit investment funds; (ii) exchange-traded funds (ETFs); (iii) credit hedge funds; (iv) private equity funds; (v) securities broker-dealers; (vi) securitization entities; (vii) credit insurance providers/financial guarantors; (viii) finance companies; and (ix) trust companies. See FSB, Policy Framework for Strengthening Oversight and Regulation of Shadow Banking Entities (2013). Notably, the FSB has suggested an economic function-based (ie, activities-based) perspective for assessing shadow banking activity in non-bank entities rather than one based on form of legal organization.

[32] Bagehot, W, *Lombard Street: A Description of the Money Market* (1873) ch 7. The seminal work on the inherent instability of a system of maturity transformation without a formal safety net is Diamond, DW and Dybvig, PH, 'Bank Runs, Deposit Insurance, and Liquidity' (1983) 91 *Journal of Political Economy* 401.

[33] For facts and a contrary view see Wallison, P, The Fed, not the Reserve Primary Fund, 'Broke the Buck' (28 March 2014), available at <http://www.sec.gov/comments/s7-03-13/s70313-331.pdf>.

3. Chapter overview

Defining from the outset what is understood as financial innovation in the context of this Chapter is expected to prove of great analytical value for the discussion that follows, which is structured into five Sections. Section II offers a concise discussion of the costs, benefits, and risks of financial innovation, given also the recent GFC experiences. It also highlights the most important risks originating in the shadow-banking sector. Section III provides a conceptual overview of contemporary regulatory reforms dealing with financial innovation. This is essentially premised on post-GFC reforms in Europe, the UK, and the US to deal with systemic and financial firm conduct risks associated with innovative financial products and processes. On the basis of analysis preceding it, Section IV provides a concise discussion of the contemporary approaches followed to regulate financial innovation and of their flaws. Section V concludes.

II. Costs and Benefits of Financial Innovation and its Regulation

1. Benefits of financial innovation

In principle, financial innovation is welfare neutral. Yet, most of historical innovations turned into the steam engine of economic and social progress, providing massive boosts to production and commerce, as well as individuals' living standards. This does not mean that innovations such as bond or stock trading were entirely separated from speculation or instances of fraud.[34] But their economic and social utility much exceeded the dis-utilities associated with such innovations, especially in the presence of a robust common law framework to prevent fraud or excessive speculation (gambling).

In this context, whether it is the invention of mutual funds to share risk-investment risk, ATMs, or credit cards simplifying individuals' payments, or stock exchange trading allowing for a transparent view of market prices,[35] the utility of some recent

[34] The notorious manipulation of 'consols' (consolidated BoE bonds) through false rumours in *Rex v De Berenger* (1814) 3 M &S 67 (KB), 105 Eng Rep 536 was followed a year later by an alleged (and strongly disputed by the family) manipulation/front-running, ahead of news of Wellington's victory in Waterloo, by the always better-informed Nathan Rothschild. See Avgouleas, n 14 above, ch 4.

[35] See, in general, Tufano, P, 'Securities Innovations: A Historical and Functional Perspective' (1995) 7 *Journal of Applied Corporate Finance* 90; and Allen, F and Gale, D, *Financial Innovation and Risk Sharing* (1994).

financial innovations is more than obvious. It is less so in other areas, especially with respect to derivatives trading.

In principle, derivatives trading does not only serve as an alternative to trading on cash markets, but also permits investors to manage exposures to risks not easily achieved in any other way. A trader can, for instance, obtain, for a certain fee, protection (insurance) against market[36] or interest rate risk limiting her exposure to the volatility of the market[37] or changing the pattern of payments in a security instrument. Delimatsis, borrowing from Robert Merton,[38] rightly observes that 'as products such as futures, options, swaps and securitized loans become standardized and move from intermediaries to markets, the proliferation of new trading markets in those instruments makes feasible the creation of new custom-designed financial products that improve "market completeness"'. The need to hedge attendant exposures translates into even more transactions increasing volumes and leading the market to high levels of liquidity and a perceived completeness which encourages the introduction to the market of additional products and processes.[39] This creates a virtuous circle of financial innovation. On the other hand, derivatives trading can be so highly leveraged and run into such large amounts as to exacerbate the risk of counterparty default, threaten the solvency of large financial institutions, and ultimately destabilize the financial system. The next paragraph provides a brief description of the massive costs that some financial innovations entail.

2. Rising risks and welfare costs

(a) *Flawed use of financial innovation and the global financial crisis*

A large number of innovations in the past 20 years have appeared entirely divorced from capital allocation and risk management. Even the neutral, in principle, use of technology was turned into a major cause of market instability and even of market abuse. The best example is HFT trading, which has been the source of major controversy in recent years. Its supporters believe that it augments market liquidity, reduces volatility in most circumstances and enhances price discovery. Critics counter that the liquidity provided by HFT is false and can vanish during periods of market stress and while HFT may reduce volatility most of the time, it is also

[36] Stock ownership is perceived as safer investment when 'insured' with put options. For this reason, put options can increase the demand for stock ownership and thus trading volume on cash markets.

[37] eg, through the use of cap/floor options.

[38] Merton, R, 'A Functional Perspective of Financial Intermediation' (1995) 24 *Financial Management* 23, 27.

[39] Delimatsis, n 8 above, 166.

responsible for periodic 'flash crashes'.[40] The SEC–CFTC report on the May 2010 'flash crash' held that, indeed, under stressed market conditions, the automated execution of a large sell order can trigger extreme price movements. This is particularly true when an automated execution algorithm does not take prices into account.[41] Another concern with HFT is that it can be used to manipulate the market employing a number of techniques, including entering into the market a large number of orders ('stuffing') that will later be cancelled.

Investors in innovative financial products such as CDOs experienced serious losses during the GFC. Characteristically, it was not just the buyers/users of these innovations that felt the devastating impact of their hidden risks but also in some cases even their inventors.[42] Worse, financial innovations became a serious source of systemic risk and financial instability,[43] chiefly because they opened up new channels for a very old market 'disease': panic triggered by intense herding. First, markets steadily pursued one-way bets on the continuous rise of asset prices with a speculative purpose regardless of where those bets were placed; ie, the spot or the derivatives markets, rather than hedging risk.[44] Second, financial innovation increased market complexity and opacity, which intensified a panic reaction when the crisis hit, especially after the collapse of Lehman Brothers in September 2008.

Flawed use of financial innovation was nowhere more vividly manifested than when hailed as a catalyst of risk diversification. In specific, structured finance of financial engineering, especially in the guise of securitizations and trading in credit derivatives, was assumed to perfect (especially) credit risk diversification.[45] For example, securitizations not conducted merely for reasons of regulatory

[40] ibid. The first very well-known instance of a HFT triggered crash is the so-called 'May 2010 flash crash' when the Dow Jones Index plummeted over 700 points in a matter of minutes, dropping nearly 1,000 points at its lowest point that day, before recovering to normal levels. The second notorious incident is the so-called *#Twitterflashcrash* which occurred on 23 April 2013. A tweet sent from a hacked Associated Press Twitter account reported explosions in the White House, injuring the President. The Dow Jones immediately plunged 140 points, approximately 1 per cent, but recovered just three minutes later. See PWC, n 15 above.

[41] See Summary Report of the Joint CFTC–SEC Advisory Committee on Emerging Regulatory Issues—Recommendations regarding Regulatory Responses to the Market Events of May 6, 2010, SEC–GFTC (18 September 2011), available at <http://www.cftc.gov/ucm/goups/public/@aboutcftc/documents/file/jacreport_021811.pdf>. The joint SEC–CFTC report strongly favoured as means of regulatory response circuit breakers.

[42] Stephen Partridge-Hicks and Nicholas J Sossidis, the two legendary fund managers whose ingenuity pushed the boundaries of the shadow financial sector and are credited by some as its founders, saw their fortunes crash in 2008. See Unmack, N and Bhaktavatsalam, SV, 'Pioneers of Structured Investments Fight for Survival of Flagship Fund', *New York Times*, 8 April 2008.

[43] Avgouleas, E, 'The Global Financial Crisis, Behavioural Finance and Financial Regulation: In Search of a New Orthodoxy' (2009) 9 *Journal of Corporate Law Studies* 23.

[44] The next few paragraphs draw in part and in a condensed form on analysis of the risks of financial innovation contained in Avgouleas, n 22 above, ch 2 and notes thereto.

[45] See Kothari, V, *Credit Derivatives and Synthetic Securitisation* (2003).

arbitrage, but also involving actual credit risk transfer, are an important way for an issuer to limit concentrated exposures to certain borrowers, loan types, and geographic locations on their balance sheet. Term asset-backed securitization markets are valuable to lenders who can use them to diversify their sources of funding and also to raise long-term, maturity-matched funding to better manage their asset–liability mismatch than they could by solely funding term loans with short-term deposits. Moreover, securitizations allowed lenders to realize economies of scale from over-utilization of their loan origination facilities (eg, branches, call centres), which may not be possible when they retain loans on balance sheet.

At the same time, securitizations are an innovative financing process fraught with inherent and sometimes insurmountable challenges, which may mean that they may work as a risk concentration, instead of the intended, risk diversification mechanism. First, valuing the underlying assets is often hard and credit ratings can prove rather flawed, not just because of the known conflict of interests but also due to intrinsic reasons, as, for example, the fact that the underlying credits may often be impossible to grade due to their diversity or artificiality (for a more comprehensive analysis see the Chapter by Payne in this volume). Also if the originator has retained part of the liquidity risk of securitization vehicles, which tend to rely on short-term debt funding, then the originating bank also becomes vulnerable to any wholesale liquidity runs that securitization vehicles may suffer from time to time.

Moreover, the use of the originate-to-distribute model in securitizations meant the commoditization of risk, especially credit risk, which could then be 'structured'; namely, 'sliced, diced, and re-bundled' in order to be readily sold to capital market investors,[46] in the form of debt securities, or other instruments. But efficient transfer of risk requires that it is transferred in a diversified way, held in reasonable proportions within diversified portfolios, and by institutions able to manage it and absorb losses. In most cases, instruments simply passed between market participants lengthening the chain of financial transactions and the network of economic relationships to a very significant degree not only by multiplying interconnections, but also by increasing the number of market actors that bore a serious amount of systemic risk in their portfolios.[47]

Another characteristic example of the potentially catastrophic consequences of opaque innovations blurring the boundaries between hedging and gambling is trading in credit default swaps (CDSs). First, CDS trading brought together the different parts of the financial system in a very opaque way, strengthening

[46] Haldane, AG, Rethinking the Financial Network, speech (2009), available at <http://www.bankofengland.co.uk/publications/speeches/2009/speech386.pdf>, 8.

[47] ibid.

interconnectedness and making the financial system more fragile. Second,[48] it led to concentration of counterparty risk. CDS trading created a complicated chain of linked exposures, as an institution may hedge one counterparty risk with another CDS, reducing instead of increasing information about the quality of the underlying credit risk. The resulting complexity made impossible the assessment of counterparty risk and identification of weak links in the financial chain and increased uncertainty.[49] The collapse of a major financial institution dealing in those markets could potentially lead to severe domino effects, and—in an extreme scenario—to a complete unwinding of the CDS market. For instance, Lehman Brothers had numerous CDS counterparty exposures relative to its balance sheet and hundreds of counterparties. AIG was in a rather similar position. As both institutions came under stress, the markets panicked worrying less about direct counterparty risk and much more about indirect counterparty risks emanating from elsewhere in the network.

(b) *Financialization and capital allocation efficiency*

Uses of financial innovations are largely products of their times. The surge in innovative financial activity in the past 20 or so years has concurred with the rise in the phenomenon of intense market short-termism with which there is probably a strong causal relationship. Modern finance theory, new technology, and neo-liberal ('the market knows best') doctrine have led to distinct commoditization of economic relationships, including those that used to entail a long-term investment commitment, such as shareholdings and commercial lending. Every form of investment and economic relationship could eventually be made into a tradable asset.

Resulting innovative assets were ostensibly used to hedge the risk of the underlying investment, but in reality their main purpose was speculation. This process of infinite financialization, aided by ample availability of debt to fuel leverage based trading, not only turned markets into fertile grounds for gambling (for example, naked CDS trading), but also shattered financial markets' ability to efficiently allocate capital. The abundant availability of 'rents' for the financial services industry and complex financial innovations meant that the industry became increasingly stronger and more capable to resist and fend off public ordering of financial markets in the 1990s and 2000s, and especially controls on financial innovation.

[48] Hakenes, H and Schnabel, I, 'The Regulation of Credit Derivatives Markets' in Dewatripont, M, Freixas, X, and Portes, R (eds), *Macroeconomic Stability and Financial Regulation: Key Issues for the G20* (2009) 113–27, available as an e-book at<http://www.voxeu.org/reports/G20_ebook.pdf>.

[49] ibid.

3. Shadow banking's 'shadow'

(a) *Overview*

The global estimate for the size of the shadow-banking system in 2012 was 67–8 trillion; an 8–9 per cent year-on-year increase. In broad terms, the aggregate size of the shadow-banking system is around half the size of formal banking system assets.[50] But the shadow-banking sector operates outside the regulatory perimeter and, as said earlier, without a support mechanism against its biggest foe: liquidity runs, a role fulfilled by the Central Bank as a lender of last resort in the formal banking sector.

In accord with many other commentators,[51] the Chapter takes the view that securities lending and repo markets, providing superior bankruptcy rights to other forms of lending,[52] as well as the matter of collateral (re-use) velocity, are clearly the areas of shadow banking most in need of regulatory attention. Repo transactions, of course, can be a good transmitter (lubricant) of monetary policy.[53] But it is often forgotten that these transactions can also facilitate the building of uncontrollable leverage within parts of the shadow-banking system.

Analysts' view that one of the main causes of the last global crisis was a 'run' on the shadow-banking sector and especially on the market for secured finance, which led to a severe liquidity crunch and subsequent panic asset sales (fire-sales),[54] has gained serious traction in the intervening years. Apart from the obvious instability risks that 'liquidity shocks' in the shadow-banking system may cause to the regulated financial sector, due to interconnectedness, the sector may also be the source of a host of other important risks such as intensification of procyclicality, exacerbation of leverage-based bank and financial system instability, and firesales. The next few paragraphs discuss, in turn, each of those risks at greater length.

[50] See Financial Stability Board, Global Shadow Banking Monitoring Report 2013 (2013).

[51] See Perotti, E, The Roots of Shadow Banking, CEPR, Policy Insight 69 (December 2013), available at <http://www.cepr.org/sites/default/files/news/PolicyInsight69.pdf>.

[52] ibid, 5–6. See on this Duffie, D and Skeel, D, A Dialogue on the Costs and Benefits of Automatic Stays for Derivatives and Repurchase Agreements (2012), Rock Center for Corporate Governance Working Paper No 108, Stanford University; Tuckman, B, Amending Safe Harbors to Reduce Systemic Risk in OTC Derivatives Markets, Center for Financial Stability Policy, Symposium speech (23 September 2010), available at <http://www.centerforfinancialstability.org/speeches/BT_symposium_092310.pdf>.

[53] See on the role of collateral in monetary policy transmission Singh, M, Collateral and Monetary Policy Collateral and Monetary Policy (August 2013), IMF Working Paper WP/13/186.

[54] Metrick, A, Regulating the Shadow Banking System (2010), available at <http://ssrn.com/abstract=1676947>. See also Diamond and Dybvig, n 32 above.

(b) *Creation of money-like claims: repo transactions and secured financing*

Invariably, repo transactions involve a collateral provider and a cash lender. The motivation behind a specific repo or securities lending transaction can be either cash or security driven. A cash-driven transaction is one where the collateral provider is seeking to borrow cash, while a security-driven transaction is one where the cash lender is seeking to borrow securities. Clearing banks and custodial agents are strongly involved in the operations of the repo and secured lending markets. Securities dealers are both lenders and borrowers as market makers. Also, they intermediate between financial institutions, which are long in cash, such as money market funds, corporate treasuries, and custodial agents; and institutions, which are short in cash, such as hedge funds and other dealers.

To anyone who has understood the lessons of the GFC about the risks of uncontrollable credit expansion, this quote from Paul Tucker's widely cited 2012 speech on shadow banking should be a cause of major concern:

> [A]nyone holding a securities portfolio can build themselves a shadow bank using the securities lending and repo markets. One simply lends out the securities at call for cash, and then one employs that cash ...[55]

As the FSB has put it: 'the capacity for some non-bank entities and transactions to operate on a large scale in ways that create bank-like risks to financial stability (longer-term credit extension based on short-term funding and leverage)'.[56] These risks may be located at the level of individual players or they may form part of a complex chain of transactions, 'in which leverage and maturity transformation occur in stages, and in ways that create multiple forms of feedback into the regulated banking system'.[57] According to the FSB creation of 'money-like' liabilities can give rise to two kinds of risks[58]:

(a) pure shadow banking risks; and
(b) risks that span both the regulated and the shadow-banking sector.

The main transmission channels of shadow-banking risks to the regulated sector are interconnectedness and asset bubbles induced by uncontrollable credit expansion.

[55] Tucker, P, Shadow Banking: Thoughts for a Possible Policy Agenda, speech given at the European Commission High Level Conference, Brussels (27 April 2012).

[56] FSB, Consultative Document, Strengthening Oversight and Regulation of Shadow Banking: A Policy Framework for Addressing Shadow Banking Risks in Securities Lending and Repos (2012), ii (hereinafter, FSB, Consultative Document, Strengthening Oversight); and FSB, Strengthening Oversight: An Overview, n 28 above, iv.

[57] ibid.

[58] ibid. While the analysis contained in this section is broadly based on a combined reading of the relevant sections of the Financial Stability Board papers on shadow banking, as cited in n 56 above, the categorization of risks and terminology used here reflect the author's understanding of requisite risks and do not strictly follow the FSB's categorization.

(c) *Pure shadow-banking risks*

Using repo to create short-term, money-like liabilities, which facilitate credit growth and maturity/liquidity transformation outside the banking system can pose a risk to financial stability by facilitating regulatory arbitrage. Resulting credit flows aid the build-up of excessive leverage and maturity transformation outside the reach of prudential regulations governing liquidity and capital requirements. This, in turn, gives rise to three important systemic risks: (i) excessive procyclicality; (ii) inadequate valuation practices; and (iii) fire-sales of collateral securities.

Variation of asset values is a cause of procyclicality in any banking system. But a system based on secured financing may be more procyclical because of the direct relationship of funding levels to fluctuating asset values and (via the levels of haircuts) volatility. According to the FSB, the policy goal in this case 'is to restrict, or put a floor on the cost of, secured borrowing against assets subject to pro-cyclical variation in valuations/volatility, to reduce the potential for the excessive leverage to build up and for large swings in system leverage when the financial system is under stress'.[59]

In the aftermath of the default of a counterparty, creditors in the repo financing and securities lending segments are likely to sell collateral securities immediately, because of regulatory restrictions on portfolio holdings, limited operational or risk-management capacity, or a need for liquidity. This may lead to sharp price falls that create mark-to-market losses for all holders of those securities. These losses can, in turn, lead to fresh rounds of firesales by other firms, thereby creating an asset valuation spiral.

Similarly, inaccurate asset valuation practices can exacerbate downside risk and attendant losses. For example, it is likely that the panic in subprime markets and the run on certain big banks with exposures to those markets might have been less severe, if when the prices of sub-prime mortgage-backed securities (MBS) started falling during the early stages of the financial crisis, a number of financial institutions had not failed to mark their positions to true market value (in part due to valuation uncertainty). This had as a result the later revelation of significant losses. Arguably, the decline in MBS prices could have caused a smaller disruption had falling prices been reflected in balance sheets earlier and more gradually through regular marking-to-market.[60] Yet, while the FSB's observation is broadly accurate, this does not mean that adoption of mark-to-market valuation practices is a panacea, as it increases procyclicality.

(d) *Liquidity runs*

As mentioned earlier, a highly leveraged shadow-banking system can be vulnerable to creditor 'runs'. However, whereas banks are subject to a stringent web of prudential regulations and can enjoy lender-of-last-resort liquidity support (in a

[59] FSB, n 56 above, 3.

[60] ibid; FSB, Strengthening Oversight: An Overview, n 28 above.

number of forms, including as collateral market making/discounting facility), the shadow-banking system operates under few if any prudential regulation requirements and no lender-of-last-resort protection. For example, a sudden increase in repo haircuts could create a liquidity shortage for firms that rely heavily on this market for funding. The sudden request to return cash collateral posted against borrowed securities could lead to large losses and firesales if the instruments in which cash collateral has been invested become illiquid.

The FSB intends to propose rules that mitigate the risk of large forced sales of collateral in one market segment acting as a channel of risk transmission beyond that market segment and throughout the broader financial system.[61]

(e) *Procyclicality, exposures to the shadow-banking sector, and interconnectedness*

Securities lending and repo markets allow financial institutions to build direct exposures to each other, which, of course, create a risk of direct contagion. According to the FSB, this can create two potential risks. First, the failure of a large institution could destabilize one or more of its counterparties and possibly the broader markets in which it is active. Second, a financial institution could suffer a liquidity shortage during a period of market stress due to an excessively short maturity profile of its financing. Unrestrained maturity transformation through the shadow-banking system can heighten procyclicality and have an appreciable financial instability impact. As credit supply accelerates, asset prices surge, aided also by herding behaviour and irrational exuberance. What follows in the event of sudden confidence shock is precipitous falls in asset prices and levels of credit with devastating consequences for banking systems and the economy.[62]

III. Regulation of Financial Innovation Post 2008

1. A view of the reforms from the cathedral

Attempts to directly regulate the shadow-banking sector are still in the nascency. There are, however, a host of other reforms, which affect the sector indirectly.

[61] ibid. See also FSB, Strengthening Oversight and Regulation of Shadow Banking—Policy Framework for Addressing Shadow Banking Risks in Securities Lending and Repos (2013).

[62] ibid.

In general, the regulation of financial innovation in the post-2008 era is nearly exclusively based on the Dodd–Frank Act in the US[63] and in Europe on key EU legislation: the new EU Capital Requirements Directive[64] and the Capital Requirements Regulation[65] (together known as CRD IV), the European Markets Infrastructure Regulation (EMIR),[66] MiFID II, and the Market in Financial Instruments Regulation (MiFIR).[67] Most of reform legislation follows the recommendations of G20 leaders' summits and work in its working groups.[68] Therefore, in most of the key jurisdictions—eg, the US and the EU—post-2008 regulation of financial innovation regulation show a certain degree of similarity and may be summarized as follows:

(a) outright prohibition of financial products such as the EU ban on uncovered ('naked') short sales and sovereign CDS trading;[69]
(b) centralization of derivatives trading and clearing and mandatory margin requirements for over-the-counter (OTC) trading;
(c) restrictions on bank involvement in securitizations and shadow banking activity; the best example here is the Volcker Rule restrictions;[70] activities covered by the restrictions of the Volcker Rule (section 619 of the Dodd–Frank Act) include 'proprietary 'investing' and 'sponsoring' a 'covered fund', a term that extends to a variety of shadow-banking vehicles and beyond. A banking entity 'invests' in a 'covered fund' if it acquires or retains any equity, partnership, or other ownership interest in a hedge fund or a private equity fund. A banking entity 'sponsors' a covered fund by: (i) serving as a general partner, managing member, or trustee of the fund; (ii) selecting or controlling (or having employees, officers, or directors, or agents who constitute) a majority of the directors, trustees, or management of the fund; or (iii) sharing with

[63] The Wall Street Reform and Consumer Protection Act, Pub.L. 111–203, H.R. 4173 (commonly referred to as the Dodd–Frank Act).

[64] Directive 2013/36/EU on access to the activity of credit institutions and the prudential supervision of credit institutions and investment firms, amending Directive 2002/87/EC and repealing Directives 2006/48/EC and 2006/49/ ([2013]OJ L 176/338).

[65] Regulation (EU) No 575/2013 on prudential requirements for credit institutions and investment firms and amending Regulation (EU) No 648/2012 ([2013] OJ L 176/1).

[66] Regulation (EU) No 648/2012 on OTC derivatives, central counterparties and trade repositories (EMIR) ([2012] OJ L 201/1).

[67] Regulation (EU) No 600/2014 [2014] OJ L173/84.

[68] eg G20, Leaders' Statement: The Pittsburgh Summit (24–25 September 2009).

[69] Articles 12 and 13 of Regulation (EU) No 236/2012 on short selling and certain aspects of Credit Default Swaps ([2012] OJ L 86/1).

[70] Section 619 of the Dodd–Frank Act, adding a new section 13 to the Bank Holding Company Act of 1956. Its main objective is to check the growth of big banks and curb licensed (commercial) banks' involvement with the riskiest forms of banking, as proprietary trading in derivatives is often perceived to be, and the shadow-banking sector. To insiders is known as the Merkley–Levin provisions on proprietary trading and conflicts of interest, but it is widely referred to as the 'Volcker Rule', due to the fact that this reform started as a proposal by former Federal Reserve Chairman Paul Volcker. Section 619 is narrower in its scope than the initial Volcker proposal.

the fund for corporate, marketing, promotional, or other purposes, the same name or a variation of the same name;

(d) mandatory originator/sponsor investment participation ('retention')[71] in securitizations[72] and comprehensive capital charges for such participations (to also capture risk of off balance-sheet assets) under Basel III and legislation based on it,[73] to realign incentives in the securitization process and redress the flaws of the 'originate-to-distribute' model;

(e) licensing regimes for alternative investment vehicles such as the (excessively) far-reaching EU Alternative Investment Fund Managers Directive (AIFMD);[74]

(f) strict liquidity requirements for money market funds, such as the proposed SEC Rule on Money Market Funds;[75]

(g) new regimes for the governance of financial innovation under a clear regulatory mandate;

(h) new powers given to financial consumer supervisors to ban innovative financial products and services if deemed to harm investor welfare and/or financial stability[76] and establishment of financial consumer authorities, either as independent entities like the US Consumer Financial Protection Bureau[77]

[71] For a discussion of the rationale of risk retention in securitizations see recital 57 of the EU Capital Requirements Regulation 2013.

[72] Under Article 405 (Retained Interest of the Issuer) of the EU Capital Requirements Regulation 2013, the issues must retain material economic interest in the issue that may not be less than 5 per cent and may be measured as: 5 per cent of the nominal value of each of the tranches sold or transferred to the investors.

[73] See Article 82 (securitization risk) of the EU Capital Requirements Directive 2013. The Directive goes as far as to include securitization exposures for the calculation of institution specific countercyclical buffer rates Article 140(4) (c).

[74] Directive 2011/61/EU on Alternative Investment Fund Managers and amending Directives 2003/41/EC and 2009/65/EC and Regulations (EC) No 1060/2009 and (EU) No 1095/2010 ([2010] OJ L 174/1).

[75] The SEC has proposed after a long debate and the marginal rejection of a far-reaching proposal for the licensing of money market funds (MMFs), tabled by its former chairman Mary Schapiro in 2012, a new regime for MMFs mostly targeting their liquidity levels. The SEC has proposed two alternatives for amending rules that govern money market mutual funds under the Investment Company Act of 1940. The two alternatives are designed to address money market funds' susceptibility to heavy redemptions, as was vividly illustrated by the September 2008 panic. The first alternative proposal would require MMFs to transition from the $1 per share principle to a 'floating' net asset value (NAV), turning thus MMFs more similar to other mutual funds. The second alternative proposal would require MMFs to impose a liquidity fee (unless the fund's board determines that it is not in the best interest of the fund) if a fund's liquidity levels fell below a specified threshold and would permit the funds to suspend redemptions temporarily. See SEC, Proposed Rule, Money Market Fund Reform; Amendments to Form PF (June 2013), 17 CFR Parts 210, 230, 239, 270, 274, and 279 Release No 33-9408, IA-3616; IC-30551; File No S7-03-13 RIN 3235-AK61.

[76] eg, Articles 39–43 of 2014 MiFIR.

[77] Title X of the Dodd–Frank Act, known as the Consumer Financial Protection Act of 2010, established the Consumer Financial Protection Bureau (CFPB or Bureau) as an independent agency within the Board of Governors of the Federal Reserve System. The CFPB regulates the offering and provision of consumer financial products and services under federal consumer financial laws. In

established under the Dodd–Frank Act (Title X) or as part of financial regulators' wider remit (for example, in the UK this a role that is now entrusted to the Financial Conduct Authority (FCA));

(i) initiatives to control automated trading, especially HFT,[78] and increase the transparency of all trading venues in the EU, tightening up controls over algorithms via more frequent and robust testing, and circuit breakers to halt excessive trading volatility;

(j) FSB-initiated measures to tackle the procyclical nature of risks and incentives associated with *secured financing contracts such as repos, and securities lending* that may exacerbate funding strains in times of 'runs'. These include improvements in data collection so as to capture more granular information on securities lending and repo exposures between financial institutions, including the composition of the underlying collateral. This would enable authorities to detect concentrations of risk, such as large exposures to particular institutions and heavy dependence on particular collateral asset classes;[79] and

(k) other FSB proposals for the supervision of shadow banking entities, other than MMFs.[80]

In the ensuing paragraphs, the reforms altering the structure and practices of OTC derivatives markets, imposing new governance regimes on innovative products, chiefly to protect consumers—a rationale behind much contemporary reform[81]—and the EU's regulation of automated trading, including HFT, are discussed at some length.

this context, CFPB ensures that the federal consumer financial laws are enforced consistently so that consumers may access markets for financial products, and so that these markets are fair, transparent, and competitive. See 12 U.S.C. § 5511 (Dodd–Frank Act § 1021).

[78] Recital 61 of MiFID II provides the following description of HFT: 'A specific subset of algorithmic trading is high frequency trading where a trading system analyses data or signals from the market at high speed and then sends or updates large numbers of orders within a very short time period in response to that analysis. High frequency trading is typically done by the traders using their own capital to trade and rather than being a strategy in itself is usually the use of sophisticated technology to implement more traditional trading strategies such as market making or arbitrage.' The definition as adopted under MiFID II Article 4(1)(40) is slightly different.

[79] See FSB, Consultative Document: Strengthening Oversight, n 56 above.

[80] The FSB has adopted an economic function-based perspective to the regulation of shadow-banking entities, which allows it to group them on the basis of their underlying economic functions rather than legal names or forms. FSB, n 31 above.

[81] A number of post-2008 consumer protection reforms in the field of financial innovation and calls for financial consumer agencies can be traced to Elizabeth Warren's article 'Unsafe at any Rate' (Summer 2007) 5 *Democracy*, available at <http://www.democracyjournal.org/5/6528.php?page=all>.

2. Centralization of derivatives trading and clearing and margin requirements for OTC trading

To mitigate one of the most important risks attached to trading and settling transactions in innovative financial products (counterparty risk) and remedy a distinct lack of transparency and counterparty exposures in OTC derivatives markets, together the MiFIR and the EMIR introduce central counterparties and trade repositories for OTC derivatives trading. Critically, OTC derivatives trading in the EU (mirroring corresponding provisions in the US Dodd–Frank Act) moves towards centralization and standardization. Thus, Article 28 of the MiFIR provides that certain types of transactions in derivatives between financial counterparties and/or non-financial counterparties, which are not intragroup transactions, are to be conducted on: regulated markets; multilateral trading facilities; organized trading facilities; or third-country trading venues. In the latter case, the Commission must have adopted a decision that the third country provides an equivalent reciprocal recognition of trading venues authorized under MiFID II to admit to trading or trade derivatives declared subject to a trading obligation in that third country.

Under Article 2 of EMIR, OTC derivatives are derivative contracts that are not traded on regulated markets. For such OTC contracts, EMIR provides an obligation to clear the trade ('clearing obligation') with an established central counterparty (CCP) (Articles 4 and 5), which, in turn, will result in a net position sharply reducing counterparty exposures. The characteristics of OTC derivatives that will be subjected to the 'clearing obligation' are, essentially, a regulatory standardization process. Thus, they are being developed by the European Securities and Markets Authority (ESMA) on the basis of whether on the characteristics of the product and volume of transactions CCPs can handle their clearing. For transactions in OTC derivatives that are not subject to a 'clearing obligation', EMIR mandates 'risk mitigation' techniques, including accurate transaction reporting, portfolio reconciliation, market-to-market valuations and corresponding collateral and margin variation, and identification of dispute resolution mechanisms right from the conclusion of the transaction (Article 11). Again, these requirements target mitigation of counterparty risk and legal risks as well as lack of transparency in bilateral derivatives transactions.

3. HFT and dark pools

The key regulatory initiative in this area is the EU Markets in Financial Instruments Directive II (MiFID II), which contains a new licensing and transparency regime for HFT traders and trading venues with lower transparency requirements, normally preferred by wholesale traders, so-called 'dark pools'.

MiFID II provides a number of strict conditions for firms engaging in algorithmic trading,[82] which encompasses HFT.[83] These must be MiFID II-authorized investment firms and subject to regulatory supervision and have systems and risk controls in place to make sure trading systems are resilient and have capacity, and prevent the sending of erroneous orders. Critically, they must also have in place systems and controls (Article 17(1)) to make sure that their trading systems cannot be used in a way that contravenes the proposed Market Abuse Regulation (MAR).

Firms that engage in algorithmic trading should notify their national supervisor, which may require firms to provide details of their algorithmic trading strategies and they must keep adequate records so that this information can be provided to the regulator on request (Article 17(2)). Algorithmic trading firms that engage in market-making should carry out their market-making activities continuously during a specified period of a trading venue's trading hours to provide liquidity on a regular and predictable basis to the trading venues (Article 17(3)). Critically, regulated markets should be able to temporarily halt trading if a significant price movement in a financial instrument occurs over a short period ('circuit breakers'), and should have systems in place to limit the ratio of unexecuted orders.

Moreover, MiFID II establishes a new licensable investment activity for Broker Crossing Networks, a form of OTC trading with much reduced transparency and reporting standards, in the form of a new regulated trading venue: organized trading facilities (OTFs) (Annex I, Section A(9)). This new form of trading venue introduces a clear distinction between OTFs and trading platforms where the operator is allowed to use proprietary capital (unless it trades in illiquid sovereign bonds) to conclude a transaction,[84] which are called systematic internalizers (Article 4(1)(20) and Recital 17, MiFID II). OTFs are subjected to trade transparency requirements and are required to have tailor-made processes and controls rules for the use of algorithmic trading in said venues (Articles 18, 20 MiFID II and Title II, MiFIR). There is, in addition, a prohibition of merging the operation of OTF and systemic internalizer in the same legal entity (Article 20(4)).

[82] MiFID II, Article 4(1)(39) defines as algorithmic trading: '[T]rading in financial instruments where a computer algorithm automatically determines individual parameters of orders such as whether to initiate the order, the timing, price or quantity of the order or how to manage the order after its submission, with limited or no human intervention. This definition does not include any system that is only used for the purpose of routing orders to one or more trading venues or for the confirmation of orders.'

[83] ibid, Article 17.

[84] Article4(1) (23) of MiFID II defines OTFs as: 'multilateral system[s] which [are] not a regulated market or an MTF and in which multiple third-party buying and selling interests in bonds, structured finance products, emission allowances or derivatives are able to interact in the system in a way that results in a contract in accordance with Title II of this Directive'. See also MiFIR Rec. 20.

The combination of OTF-related measures in MiFID II and reporting requirements in its twin the Markets in Financial Instruments Regulation (MiFIR) especially target so-called 'dark pools'.[85] These trading venues took advantage of MiFID trading exemptions and eventually amounted for a large percentage of equities and bonds trading.[86] Yet, 'dark trading' will probably not disappear, as MiFIR gives competent authorities the power to allow relevant firms and trading venues to defer post-trade publication (Article 7(1)) or waive pre-trade requirements (Article 9(1)) for certain traces, subject also to ESMA-issued rules about exempt large-size trades in equities, bonds, and derivatives respectively. So, probably 'dark pools', which tend to be very liquid and favoured by large buy-side investors (eg, pension funds), will probably not disappear, although they will certainly become more transparent.

4. New product intervention and governance regimes for financial products

Article 40(1) of MiFIR provides that: 'ESMA may where it is satisfied on reasonable grounds that the conditions in paragraphs 2 and 3 are fulfilled, temporarily prohibit or restrict in the Union: the marketing, distribution or sale of certain financial instruments or financial instruments with certain features; or a type of financial activity or practice.' Article 41 of the Regulation extends these powers to the European Banking Authority in respect of structured deposits. ESMA shall only take such a radical decision when said financial instruments pose a threat to investor protection or to the orderly functioning and integrity of financial markets or to the stability of the whole or part of the financial system in the EU and regulatory requirements under EU legislation that are applicable to the relevant financial instrument or activity do not address the threat (Article 40(2)). Under Article 40(3), in making a prohibition or restriction decision, ESMA shall take into account the extent to which the action: '(a) does not have a detrimental effect on the efficiency of financial markets or on investors that is disproportionate to the benefits of the action; and (b) does not create a risk of regulatory arbitrage'. Under Article 42 of MiFIR, national competent authorities may take similar action subject to requisite conditions.

[85] Investopedia defines 'dark pools of liquidity' as 'trading volume created by institutional orders that are unavailable to the public. The bulk of dark pool liquidity is represented by block trades facilitated away from the central exchanges... The dark pool gets its name because details of these trades are concealed from the public, clouding the transactions like murky water. Some traders that use a strategy based on liquidity feel that dark pool liquidity should be publicized, in order to make trading more 'fair' for all parties involved.' Available at <http://www.investopedia.com/terms/d/dark_pool_liquidity.asp>.

[86] See Ferrarini, G and Moloney, N, 'Reshaping Order Execution in the EU and the Role of Interest Groups: From MiFID I to MiFID II' (2012) 13 *European Business Organization Law Review* 557.

MiFID II imposes strict suitability requirements for complex investment products (Articles 24, 25) and grants ESMA the power to provide guidelines for the selling of financial products. It also gives similar powers to the European Banking Authority (EBA) as regards structured deposits, which have been included to the ambit of MiFID II. It requires firms that 'manufacture' financial instruments for sale to clients will be required to maintain a product-approval process. Firms must identify the target market for each product and ensure that all relevant risks to that target market are assessed and that the intended distribution strategy is consistent with the identified target market. The target market and performance of products should be subject to periodic review. Firms, which offer or recommend financial instruments but do not manufacture them, must ensure that they understand the features of those products, including the identified target market. Product manufacturers must ensure products meet the needs of their identified target market and must take reasonable steps to ensure that the products are being distributed to that target market.[87]

ESMA has issued, as an interim measure, an opinion on structured financial products offered to retail customers (structured retail products), setting out good practices for firms when manufacturing and distributing these products.[88] ESMA Opinion guidance may be of relevance for other types of financial instruments such as asset-backed securities, or contingent convertible bonds, as well as when financial instruments are being sold to professional clients.[89] These good practices[90] that product providers could put in place to improve their ability to deliver on investor protection in particular focus on:

(a) the complexity of the structured retail products they manufacture and distribute;
(b) the nature and range of investment services and activities undertaken in the course of business; and
(c) the type of investors they target.

ESMA expects national competent authorities to embed these good practices in their supervisory approaches to structured retail product providers.[91]

[87] MiFID II, Article 24(2).

[88] ESMA Opinion 2014/332, Good Practices for Structured Retail Product Governance Arrangements (2014); and ESMA press release 2014/334, 'ESMA Issues Good Practices for Structured Retail Product Governance (27 March 2014).

[89] ibid.

[90] ESMA promulgated good practices cover the following areas: general organization of product governance arrangements; product design; product testing; target market; distributing strategy; value at the date of issuance and transparency of costs; secondary market and redemption; and review process. ibid.

[91] ibid.

IV. Regulating Financial Innovation: What Is Right, What Is Wrong?

The risks of financial innovation that is based on 'perverse' incentives are very real. Not only for the very important reasons mentioned above but also because of the capacity of the industry to 'pervert' finance theory and create infinitely self-referential products whose only purpose is gambling. For example, the aforementioned Black–Scholes formula was, indeed, used to justify the subsequent explosion of quasi-hedging speculation in global derivatives markets. At the same time, the self-referential nature of certain innovations may have been a perversion in the use of the formula itself, taking the findings of the Black–Scholes model to the extreme, since the model was premised to the implicit assumption that a real trading (arbitrage) opportunity exists. The fact that variations of the formula were used to price artificial arbitrage opportunities—for example, writing CDS contracts on CDOs—must have exhausted the principles of dynamic hedging. Not only the intention behind these investment games was pure speculation but also the uncertainty about the price relationship of the two products increased so much, due to the artificiality of the arbitrage opportunity, to render the formula impotent and turned any attempts to 'scientifically' price CDS contracts, in this context, farcical.[92]

But what if creative minds engaged in such 'experiments' at society's expense had a different set of incentives? These inventors were neither particularly sentimental nor did they face serious cognitive restraints? Might it not be that all that these 'wonder-kids' wanted was validation for their views, rewards for their brilliance, and, of course, acceptance.[93]

Financial innovation even in modern times can be a source of great good.[94] Venture capital contribution to economic growth[95] is one great example. Even derided innovations such as securitization can be most useful when it comes to amortizing costs for major development finance projects, or for sharing the risks of low-level funding and investment, especially in the realm of microfinance.[96] Today's

[92] Views of the author but the example was extensively discussed in Lewis, M, *The Big Short: Inside the Doomsday Machine* (2011), esp ch 3–9.

[93] For the motives, behaviours, and attitudes of such inventors see ibid, n 92 above.

[94] Litan, R, In Defense of Much, but not All, Financial Innovation, Brookings Institution (February 2010); Michalopoulos, S, Laeven, L, and Levine, R, Financial Innovation and Economic Growth (September 2009), National Bureau of Economic Research Working Paper No 15356.

[95] Kortum, S and Lerner, J, 'Assessing the Contribution of Venture Capital to Innovation' (2000) 31 *RAND Journal of Economics* 674.

[96] See Avgouleas, E, 'International Financial Regulation, Access to Finance, Systemic Stability, and Development' [2008] *LAW ASIA Journal* 62, April 2009; Schwarcz, S, 'Disintermediating

demographic trends in Western societies, Russia, Japan, and China mean that most people's savings' nest will prove insufficient in the long run. So, savers and pension funds have to increasingly shift from very low yielding investments, such as government bonds, to higher-reward higher-risk assets. In the absence of appropriate products to safely insure the risk of higher-yield investment, it is unlikely that regulators and society will be willing to allow pension funds to assume this high-yield high-return strategy, and rightly so. Therefore, there is plenty of room for innovators to invent products and techniques that can safely facilitate the transformation of today's barely sufficient savings to an acceptable level of pension rewards over a period of time. This is just one of many similar examples of how financial innovation could meet humanity's needs in a number of other sectors, including sustainable development.

The aforementioned contemporary reforms are probably a sound approach to counter the perils of perverse innovation but bans and tight controls may not be the answer to every question. This before we even reach the great paradox of over-regulating the formal banking sector and just engaging into lots of creative but ultimately ineffective thinking when it comes to the unregulated sector. In addition, contemporary reforms make very little distinction between good and bad innovation, as the regulatory response to innovation has been standardization and homogenization. When it comes to countering systemic risk and in order to protect consumers, this is probably an effective and transparent strategy. But, it may also prove 'suffocating'. For example, regulators' move towards complete homogenization of new financial products has alarmed an industry sector as 'unexciting' as building societies.[97] Moreover, no system of market (and human behaviour) ordering is expected to work properly if it is merely based on a system of controls and sanctions.

To this effect it is credibly argued that the best approach is a return to the 'insurable interest' doctrine, which would provide a good way of separating good (hedging) from bad financial innovation (gambling).[98] Article 13 of the EU Short Sales Regulation is an excellent exposition of how the 'insurable interest' test may be revived through the existence of an underlying risk that needs to be hedged without resorting to complex legal and economic interpretations of the test.

Avarice: A Legal Framework for Commercially Sustainable Microfinance' (2011) *University of Illinois Law Review* 1165.

[97] 'The financial services industry has been characterized by greed, ego, appalling conduct and a lack of integrity, but the danger now is that regulation pushes the sector so far down the path of homogeneity that it stifles innovation and hurts customers, Robin Fieth, chief executive at the Building Societies Association has warned.' Holley, E, Regulation is Holding Back Innovation Says Building Society Chief (8 May 2014), *Banking Technology*, available at <http://www.bankingtech.com/219822/regulation-is-holding-back-innovation-says-building-society-chief/>.

[98] Stout, L, 'Derivatives and the Legal Origin of the 2008 Credit Crisis' (2011) 1 *Harvard Business Law Review* 1; Stout, L, 'Why the Law Hates Speculators: Regulation and Private Ordering in the Market for OTC Derivatives' (1999) 48 *Duke Law Journal* 701.

Yet, the 'insurable interest' test cannot be all encompassing. First, having an *ex ante* testing mechanism to control financial innovation, in the same way as medicines are tested, as proposed by Posner and Weyl,[99] may not be feasible. The best way to test how a new product will perform, and what are the real risks attached to it, is a long period of use by the market. Second, the test proposed by Posner and Weyl,[100] and other important thinking about ways to measure the welfare effect versus riskiness effect of financial products,[101] brilliant as it is in its analytical value, it is very complex to be used as a regulatory tool.

It essentially adds yet another layer of complexity on what is already a very complex regulatory system. Regulatory complexity should, in the author's view, be seen as a source of systemic risk in itself. Complex regulations make it very hard for market participants to understand what is prohibited, what is allowed, and what process can be followed to secure best-compliance outcomes. Worse, regulators being, at least, as boundedly rational as market participants and as challenged as the latter by rule complexity (if not more), they will eventually develop compliance heuristics to bypass complexity and simplify monitoring processes.[102] Regulatory groupthink means that the only way to test whether these heuristics are wrong is when disaster erupts.

Furthermore, distinguishing hedging from speculation is easy only in extreme cases and it would be very hard to rely on a 'wagering' versus 'hedging' distinction. In fact, imposing an economic test may prove impossible. Even welfare-enhancing innovations like real estate derivatives based on the Case–Shiller index, which measures real estate prices in US metropolitan areas[103] and was invented to give householders an investment route to diversify their mortgage and house value risks, may also be used for speculation.

Moreover, a possible legal distinction based on actual delivery of the underlying asset would both go contrary to centuries of common law tradition about acknowledgement of contracts for future delivery or it would devastate markets. First, hedging and speculative contracts can be similar in terms of content and legal

[99] Posner, EA and Weyl, EG, 'An FDA for Financial Innovation: Applying the Insurable Interest Doctrine to 21st Century Financial Markets' (2013) 107 *Northwestern University Law Review* 1307.

[100] ibid, 1322–44. Essentially, the Posner and Weyl test provides a first approach on how to measure the potential welfare impact of a new financial product mostly based on the ability of new financial products to reduce overall risk. It draws heavily on Athanasoulis, SG and Shiller, RJ, 'World Income Components: Measuring and Exploiting Risk-Sharing Opportunities' (2001) 91 *American Economic Review* 1031.

[101] eg, Simsek, A, Speculation and Risk Sharing with New Financial Assets (2011), National Bureau of Economic Research Working Paper No 17506; and Brunnermeier, MK et al., 'A Welfare Criterion for Models with Distorted Beliefs' (2014) 119 *Quarterly Journal of Economics* 1753.

[102] See Avgouleas, E, Cognitive Biases and Investor Protection Regulation: An Evolutionary Approach (September 2006), unpublished paper, available at <http://ssrn.com/abstract=1133214>.

[103] For an authoritative description of the indices see Dow Jones Indices, The SP/Case-Shiller Home Price Indices, available at <http://us.spindices.com/index-family/real-estate/sp-case-shiller>.

form.[104] Of course, the mode of performance differs, for example, because it does not involve actual delivery. Imposition of a distinction between actual delivery and cash settlement, a realistic way to distinguish between hedging and speculation, is indeed possible in derivatives markets. But such a distinction would literally extinguish billions of liquidity and information-enhancing transactions in global futures markets and overturn important legal doctrine. Finally, terribly unpopular as it sounds, not all speculation is bad and the best example is covered short sales, which have undisputable virtuous impact on price efficiency.[105]

The link between finance and growth and even more importantly any hopes that finance can aid redistribution has broken, either because it has never been there,[106] or more likely due to financialization. If the latter is the case then fixing financial innovation can be tantamount to fixing finance's allocative (and to an extent distributive) role. This may not be done in the absence of incentives and a comprehensive incentives framework for 'virtuous' financial innovation is exactly what is missing in the regulatory reforms discussed in Section III.4 above. Properly aligned incentives and risk-sharing is what brought about international trade and at a later stage the industrial revolution.[107] Leading commentators even question whether the role of financial markets is exclusively that of a competitive exchange.[108]

Market and technological developments in the past 30 years, discussed in Section I, opened up every conceivable avenue towards industry rent-seeking. This has meant that market self-ordering has failed to 'tame' financial innovation. There is, therefore, an urgent and pressing need to search for an institutional framework based on a system of sanctions (including taxes on speculative deals) and incentives to direct two of the most creative areas of the twenty-first-century economy: finance and technology to the goals of long-term growth and social development. There are three ways to approach the desired recoupling of financial innovation with long-term growth:

(i) ask the market to succeed where it has failed in the past 30 years;
(ii) ban all forms of financial innovation that cannot be reliably proven to promote welfare, more or less the current regulatory attitude; and
(iii) create an institutional framework of regulatory controls and incentives.

[104] See Posner and Weyl, n 99 above, 1347 *et seq*. See also O'Malley, P, 'Moral Uncertainties: Contract Law and Distinctions between Speculation, Gambling, and Insurance' in Erickson, R and Doyle, A (eds), *Risk and Morality* (2003), ch 9, 231–57.

[105] See on the effect of short sales on securities pricing Diamond, DW and Verrecchia, RE, 'Constraints on Short-selling and Asset Price Adjustment to Private Information' (1987) 18 *Journal of Financial Economics* 277; and Bris, A, Goetzmann, WN, and Zhu, N, 'Efficiency and the Bear: Short Sales and Markets around the World' (2007) 62 *Journal of Finance* 1029.

[106] See on this Piketty, T, *Capital in the 21st Century* (2014).

[107] For this argument see Avgouleas, n 22, ch 2 and 9.

[108] Black, J, 'Reconceiving Financial Markets—from the Economic to the Social' (2013) 13 *Journal of Corporate Law Studies* 401.

The reasonable choice must be the third option. Not just for the reasons explained above. Historically proven human propensity to innovate around access to capital and its allocation as well as risk management may not be suppressed regardless of motive. This propensity ought to be harnessed for the common good. Only clear incentives will help. These could include the expectation of profit attached to legally protected exclusive access to new innovations, for a period. Similarly, human attitudes to risk and gambling are hidden in the deepest recess of our psyche whether the cause is greed, addiction, or otherwise. Sanctions more than blanket prohibitions, which, in any case, only address the regulated part of the financial system, might work better. The discussion is not theoretical. For example, a good way to alter incentives to counter the discussed (in Section II) trend of shadow banks to expand short-term lending and uncontrollable credit growth, increasing procyclicality and attendant systemic risks, is by changing bankruptcy rights surrounding repo transactions and the secured financing process in general.[109]

V. Conclusion

The benefits of financial innovation have been accruing to humanity for thousands of years. Yet, the history of financial innovation in the past two decades, for the reasons explained in Sections I and II, is predominantly one of greed, avarice, and rent-seeking. The results were nearly catastrophic for global financial stability and the resulting investor losses very considerable, including a full-blown housing crisis in the US.

Immediately after the collapse of Lehman Brothers and of other financial institutions in the Western world, a gigantic reform effort was set in motion. Contemporary reforms are bulky, complex and far-reaching, targeting market structure, opacity, and complexity and seeking to prevent harmful financial products from entering the market, especially financial consumers' markets. As was made clear in the foregone discussion, the key objective of reform legislation is financial-investor safety and financial stability. In many ways this will probably be achieved in the regulated sector, especially as regards financial consumer protection. Still, ambiguities and worse the fact that contemporary reforms in regulation

[109] On the importance of this reform see Perotti, n 51 above. On the difficulties involved in reforming bankruptcy law in this area Schwarcz, SL and Sharon, O, 'The Bankruptcy-Law Safe Harbor for Derivatives: A Path-Dependence Analysis' (2014) 71 *Washington and Lee Law Review*.

of financial innovation are very complex may undermine the effectiveness of these reforms in the long-run, especially, when enforcement zest has gradually been replaced by regulatory inertia.

On the other hand, the biggest new threats to financial stability come from the unregulated sector. There is no evidence that piling up the prohibitions in the increasingly limited space occupied by the regulated sector in global markets is a panacea. This approach may even suffer from the fallacy of composition: reform regulations which make each targeted part of the financial system safer do not automatically translate to safer financial systems or the extinction of 'malignant' forms of financial innovation.

The standards for the regulation of shadow-banking risks developed by the FSB are, indeed, in the right direction. But it is not known yet how and where they will be implemented. This is an important continuing risk, as loopholes in the geographic reach of the regulatory net in these circumstances can render the entire protective panoply of financial regulation redundant.

It is now clear that capitalism, arguably, the best form of organization of economic activity, favours short-term profit over long-term benefit; a trend that has been exacerbated by financialization. At the same time, we ought to recognize that there is a pressing need for more not less welfare-enhancing innovation. One way to do this is by altering the culture and ethics of the industry. But this is not exclusive nor will it work at all times.

Financial innovators do not necessarily reside in the large organizations whose (sometimes 'rotten') culture regulators tend to target. We need incentives for those whose genius is employed in financial innovation to innovate in a virtuous way. But a comprehensive incentives' framework is starkly missing from current regulatory thinking and from the new framework, especially the one put in place by the Dodd–Frank Act in the US and MiFID II/MiFIR/EMIR etc. in the EU.

Finally, market actors and regulators will remain subject to cognitive and other limitations. As a result, financial innovation's contribution to black swans or fat tails, which are mostly responsible for systemic events of catastrophic magnitude, will remain unnoticed, at least, until it is too late. Therefore, for all of the aforementioned prohibitions, society will remain wary of financial innovation. For the reasons explained above, the contemporary approach of piling up prohibition upon prohibition and at the same time remaining in fear of what financial innovators will come up to next is socially sub-optimal. Therefore, building a framework of convincing incentives and sanctions rather than blanket prohibitions is the next frontier in the regulation of financial innovation, and the area that ought to occupy the most policymakers and financial regulators in the next few years.

BIBLIOGRAPHY

Adrian, T and Ashcraft, A, Shadow Banking: A Review of the Literature (2012), Federal Reserve Bank of New York Staff Report No 580.

Allen, F and Gale, D, *Financial Innovation and Risk Sharing* (1994).

Athanasoulis, SG and Shiller, RJ, 'World Income Components: Measuring and Exploiting Risk-Sharing Opportunities' (2001) 91 *American Economic Review* 1031.

Avgouleas, E, Cognitive Biases and Investor Protection Regulation: An Evolutionary Approach (September 2006), unpublished paper, available at <http://ssrn.com/abstract=1133214>.

Avgouleas, E, 'The Global Financial Crisis, Behavioural Finance and Financial Regulation: In Search of a New Orthodoxy' (2009) 9 *Journal of Corporate Law Studies* 23.

Avgouleas, E, *Governance of Global Financial Markets: The Law, the Economics, the Politics* (2012).

Avgouleas, E, 'International Credit Markets: Players, Financing Techniques, Instruments, and Regulation' in Bidgoli, H (ed.), *The Handbook of Technology Management* (2009), ch 50.

Avgouleas, E, 'International Financial Regulation, Access to Finance, Systemic Stability, and Development' [2008] *LAW ASIA Journal* 62, April 2009.

Avgouleas, E, *The Mechanics and Regulation of Market Abuse—a Legal and Economic Analysis* (2005), ch 2.

Avgouleas, E, 'A New Framework for the Global Regulation of Short Sales: Why Prohibition Is Inefficient and Disclosure Insufficient' (2010) 16 *Stanford Journal of Law, Business & Finance* 376.

Awrey, D, Complexity, Innovation and the Regulation of Modern Financial Markets, Oxford Legal Studies Research Paper No 49/2011.

Bachelier, L, 'Théorie de la Spéculation' (1900) 17 *Annales de l'École Normale Supérieure* 21, trans in Cootner, PH, *The Random Character of the Stock Market Prices* (1964).

Bagehot, W, *Lombard Street: A Description of the Money Market* (1873), ch 7.

Barber, MA, *History of the Order of the Temple* (2012).

Bernanke, B, Some Reflections on the Crisis and the Policy Response, speech to the Russell Sage Foundation and the Century Foundation Conference on 'Rethinking Finance', New York, NY (13 April 2012).

Black, F and Scholes, M, 'The Pricing of Options and Corporate Liabilities' (1973) 81 *Journal of Political Economy* 637.

Black, J, 'Reconceiving Financial Markets—from the Economic to the Social' (2013) 13 *Journal of Corporate Law Studies* 401.

Black, J, Restructuring Global and EU Financial Regulation: Capacities, Coordination and Learning (2010), LSE Law, Society and Economy Working Papers No 18–2010.

Bris, A, Goetzmann, WN, and Zhu, N, 'Efficiency and the Bear: Short Sales and Markets around the World' (2007) 62 *Journal of Finance* 1029.

Brunnermeier, MK et al., 'A Welfare Criterion for Models with Distorted Beliefs' (2014) (119) *Quarterly Journal of Economics* 1753.

Chancellor, E, *Devil Take the Hindmost, A History of Financial Speculation* (1999).

Davies, G and Bank, JH, *A History of Money: From Ancient Times to the Present Day* (2002).

Davis, M and Etheridge, A, *Louis Bachelier's Theory of Speculation: The Origins of Modern Finance* (2006).

Delimatsis, P, 'Transparent Financial Innovation in a Post-Crisis Environment' (2013) 1 *Journal of International Economic Law* 159.

Diamond, DW and Dybvig, PH, 'Bank Runs, Deposit Insurance, and Liquidity' (1983) 91 *Journal of Political Economy* 401.

Diamond, DW and Verrecchia, RE, 'Constraints on Short-selling and Asset Price Adjustment to Private Information' (1987) 18 *Journal of Financial Economics* 277.

Duffie, D and Skeel, D, A Dialogue on the Costs and Benefits of Automatic Stays for Derivatives and Repurchase Agreements (2012), Rock Center for Corporate Governance Working Paper No 108, Stanford University.

Erturk, I, Froud, J, Johal, S, Leaver, A, and Williams, K, 'The Democratization of Finance? Promises, Outcomes and Conditions' (2007) 14 *Review of International Political Economy* 553.

ESMA Opinion 2014/332, Good Practices for Structured Retail Product Governance Arrangements (2014).

Fabozzi, F, Davis, H, and Choudhry, M, *Introduction to Structured Finance* (2006).

Ferguson, N, *The Ascent of Money: A Financial History of the World* (2008).

Ferrarini, G and Moloney, N, 'Reshaping Order Execution in the EU and the Role of Interest Groups: From MiFID I to MiFID II' (2012) 13 *European Business Organization Law Review* 557.

Frankfurter, GM, 'The Rise and Fall of the CAPM Empire: A Review on Emerging Capital Markets' (1995) 4 *Financial Markets, Institutions and Instruments* 104.

FSB, Consultative Document, Strengthening Oversight and Regulation of Shadow Banking: A Policy Framework for Addressing Shadow Banking Risks in Securities Lending and Repos (2012).

FSB, Global Shadow Banking Monitoring Report 2013 (2013).

FSB, Policy Framework for Strengthening Oversight and Regulation of Shadow Banking Entities (2013).

FSB, Strengthening Oversight and Regulation of Shadow Banking—Policy Framework for Addressing Shadow Banking Risks in Securities Lending and Repos (2013).

Goldthwaite, RA, *Banks, Places and Entrepreneurs in Renaissance Florence* (1995).

Hakenes, H and Schnabel, I, 'The Regulation of Credit Derivatives Markets' in Dewatripont, M, Freixas, X, and Portes, R (eds), *Macroeconomic Stability and Financial Regulation: Key Issues for the G20* (2009) 113–27, available as an e-book at <http://www.voxeu.org/reports/G20_ebook.pdf>.

Haldane, AG, Rethinking the Financial Network, speech (2009), available at <http://www.bankofengland.co.uk/publications/speeches/2009/speech386.pdf>.

Haug, EG and Taleb, NN, 'Option Traders Use (very) Sophisticated Heuristics, Never the Black–Scholes–Merton Formula' (2011) 77 *Journal of Economic Behavior and Organization* 97.

Hoggson, NF, *Banking through the Ages* (1926).

Holley, E, Regulation Is Holding Back Innovation Says Building Society Chief (8 May 2014), *Banking Technology*, available at <http://www.bankingtech.com/219822/regulation-is-holding-back-innovation-says-building-society-chief/>.

Kortum, S and Lerner, J, 'Assessing the Contribution of Venture Capital to Innovation' (2000) 31 *RAND Journal of Economics* 674.

Kothari, V, *Credit Derivatives and Synthetic Securitisation* (2003).

Kothari, V, *Securitization: The Financial Instrument of the Future* (3rd edn, 2006).

Law Commission and Scottish Law Commission, Insurable Interest (2008), Insurance Contract Law Issues Paper No 4, available at <http://www.lawcom.gov.uk/docs/Insurance_Contract_Law_Issues_Paper_4.pdf>.

Lewis, M, *The Big Short: Inside the Doomsday Machine* (2011).

Lintner, J, 'The Valuation of Risk Assets and the Selection of Risky Investments in Stock Portfolios and Capital Budgets' (1965) 47 *Review of Economics and Statistics* 13.

Litan, R, In Defense of Much, but not All, Financial Innovation (February 2010), Brookings Institution.

McCulley, P, 'Teton Reflections' (August/September 2007) *PIMCO Global Central Bank Focus*, available at <http://media.pimco-global.com/pdfs/pdf_sg/GCB%20Focus%20Sept%2007%20SGP-HK.pdf?WT.cg_n=PIMCO-SINGAPORE&WT.ti=GCBFocusSept07SGP-HK.pdf>, 2.

Mackenzie, D, *An Engine, not a Camera: How Financial Models Shape Markets* (2008).

Mackenzie, D, *Material Markets: How Economic Agents Are Constructed* (2008).

Markowitz, H, 'Foundations of Portfolio Theory' (1991) 46 *Journal of Finance* 469.

Markowitz, H, *Portfolio Selection: Efficient Diversification of Investments* (1959).

Markowitz, HM, 'Portfolio Selection' (1952) 7 *Journal of Finance* 77.

Merton, R, 'A Functional Perspective of Financial Intermediation' (1995) 24 *Financial Management* 23.

Merton, R, 'Theory of Rational Option Pricing' (1973) 4 *Bell Journal of Economics and Management Science* 141.

Metrick, A, Regulating the Shadow Banking System (2010), available at <http://ssrn.com/abstract=1676947>.

Michalopoulos, S, Laeven, L, and Levine, R, Financial Innovation and Economic Growth (September 2009), National Bureau of Economic Research Working Paper No 15356.

Modigliani, F and Miller, MH, *The Cost of Capital, Corporate Finance and the Theory of Investment* (1958) 48 *American Economic Review* 251.

O'Malley, P, 'Moral Uncertainties: Contract Law and Distinctions between Speculation, Gambling, and Insurance' in Erickson, R and Doyle, A (eds), *Risk and Morality* (2003), ch 9, 231–57.

Perotti, E, The Roots of Shadow Banking, CEPR, Policy Insight 69 (December 2013), available at <http://www.cepr.org/sites/default/files/news/PolicyInsight69.pdf>.

Piketty, T, *Capital in the 21st Century* (2014).

Posner, EA and Weyl, EG, 'An FDA for Financial Innovation: Applying the Insurable Interest Doctrine to 21st Century Financial Markets' (2013) 107 *Northwestern University Law Review* 1307.

Pozsar, Z, Adrian, T, Ashcraft, A, and Boesky, H, Shadow Banking (July 2010), Federal Reserve Board of New York Staff Report No 458, 1.

PWC, HFT and the Question of Regulation, Brief (2013–14), available at <http://www.pwc.co.uk/financial-services/regulation/other/hft-and-the-question-of-regulation.jhtml?preview=true>.

Rodgers, JS, *The Early History of the Law of Bills and Notes: A Study of the Origins of Anglo-American Commercial Law* (1995).

Schwarcz, S, 'Disintermediating Avarice: A Legal Framework for Commercially Sustainable Microfinance' (2011) *University of Illinois Law Review* 1165.

Schwarcz, SL and Sharon, O, 'The Bankruptcy-Law Safe Harbor for Derivatives: A Path-Dependence Analysis' (2014) 71 *Washington and Lee Law Review*.

Sharpe, WF, 'Capital Asset Prices: A Theory of Market Equilibrium under Conditions of Risk' (1964) 19 *Journal of Finance* 425.

Simsek, A, Speculation and Risk Sharing with New Financial Assets (2011), National Bureau of Economic Research Working Paper No 17506.

Singh, M, Collateral and Monetary Policy Collateral and Monetary Policy (August 2013), IMF Working Paper WP/13/186.

Stout, L, 'Derivatives and the Legal Origin of the 2008 Credit Crisis' (2011) 1 *Harvard Business Law Review* 1.

Stout, L, 'Why the Law Hates Speculators: Regulation and Private Ordering in the Market for OTC Derivatives' (1999) 48 *Duke Law Journal* 701.

Summary Report of the Joint CFTC–SEC Advisory Committee on Emerging Regulatory Issues—Recommendations regarding Regulatory Responses to the Market Events of 6 May 2010, SEC–GFTC (18 September 2011).

Tett, G, *Fool's Gold: The Inside Story of J.P. Morgan and How Wall St. Greed Corrupted its Bold Dream and Created a Financial Catastrophe* (2009).

Traynor, J, Towards a Theory of Market Value of Risky Assets (1961), unpublished manuscript.

Tucker, P, Shadow Banking: Thoughts for a Possible Policy Agenda, speech given at the European Commission High Level Conference, Brussels (27 April 2012).

Tuckman, B, Amending Safe Harbors to Reduce Systemic Risk in OTC Derivatives Markets, Center for Financial Stability Policy, Symposium speech (23 September 2010), available at <http://www.centerforfinancialstability.org/speeches/BT_symposium_092310.pdf>.

Tufano, P, 'Securities Innovations: A Historical and Functional Perspective' (1995) 7 *Journal of Applied Corporate Finance* 90.

Unmack, N and Bhaktavatsalam, SV, 'Pioneers of Structured Investments Fight for Survival of Flagship Fund', *New York Times*, 8 April 2008.

Wallison, P, The Fed, not the Reserve Primary Fund, 'Broke the Buck' (28 March 2014), available at <http://www.sec.gov/comments/s7-03-13/s70313-331.pdf>.

Warren, E, 'Unsafe at any Rate' (Summer 2007) 5 *Democracy*, available at <http://www.democracyjournal.org/5/6528.php?page=all>.

Weber, EJ, Short History of Derivative Security Markets, (August 2008), University of Western Australia, Business School, mimeo, available at <http://www.law.uwa.edu.au/__data/assets/pdf_file/0003/94260/08_10_Weber.pdf>.

PART VI

CONSUMER PROTECTION

CHAPTER 23

THE CONSUMER INTEREST AND THE FINANCIAL MARKETS

DIMITY KINGSFORD SMITH AND OLIVIA DIXON

I. Introduction

1. The financial consumer and the retention of investment risk

A paradox lies at the centre of the regulation of the consumer interest in financial markets. It appears when one thinks about the investor as a consumer: for the investor is often conceived as a junior entrepreneur in a sort of joint venture, sharing the risk in which he or she invests and earning a return.[1] The consumer, by contrast, is generally the subject of protection from risk.[2] The paradox is most familiar in the form of the retail shareholder, whom securities law has tried to protect since the 1930s. The paradox is most intense with the pension promise to members of retirement funds. There the risks of investment are amplified by illiquidity, long term, opacity of management and the absence of years to recover, if at retirement it is discovered that the pension promise has not been kept.[3]

Financial consumers seeking services for personal, domestic, and household use, will over their life need a range of financial products. They will need banking to save and transfer cash; credit services, for everyday purchases and at life's turning points. They will require long-term investment services for retirement income. Along the way, consumers will need insurances and, for some, services to move discretionary savings from the savings system to the investment system.

[1] Commonwealth of Australia, Financial System Inquiry: Final Report (1997), 177.

[2] Kingsford Smith, D, 'Financial Services Regulation and the Investor as Consumer' in Howells, G et al. (eds), *The Handbook of Research on International Consumer Law* (2011) 431.

[3] Commonwealth of Australia, n 1 above, 191–2—even in compulsory investments, risk is borne by investors.

By contrast and acknowledging national variations,[4] the consumer interest in goods and services markets is seen as mitigating risk and squarely protective of the interests of the consumer. A consumer of goods usually takes possession, starts to use them and faults are revealed quickly. Often, financial products are long term, complex, and opaque. Generally the financial provider holds much more information and bargaining power than is common with goods and non-financial services.[5] As financial products and services are intangible and their management is with others, a financial consumer must rely on disclosure and the reputation of the provider. It is unusual to be able to tell if something is wrong before it is too late: even regulators with information-gathering powers can be surprised when failures occur.[6]

In terms of retention of risk, some financial products and services lie between ordinary goods and investments. The retail saver, borrower, or insurance policy holder is less exposed than the investor due to prudential regimes, which, while providing systemic stability, also protect the consumer interest:[7] though as the Global Financial Crisis (GFC) demonstrated, even prudential regulation can fail. The financial consumer still takes the risk that the product will not perform, though this is also borne by consumers of physical goods. Even in these relatively basic financial products, there is enough intangibility, complexity, opacity, and time before performance, to distinguish the financial consumer interest from that for goods. By contrast with consumer goods, there are no warranties of performance, only statements about future prospects, and promises that regulated procedures will be followed in managing the investment.

Financial services regulation wrestles with the paradoxical need to regulate to reduce risk (for protection) while at the same time regulating to retain risk (for pursuit of financial returns). Although there has been much translation of ordinary

[4] In Australia there is virtually strict liability for 'misleading and deceptive statements' made to consumers of 'average gullibility': *Fraser v NRMA Holdings Ltd* (1994) 14 ACSR 656; affirmed in part (1995) 15 ACSR 590. In the EU, more robustness of ordinary consumers is required: Moloney, N, *How to Protect Investors* (2010) 92.

[5] Kay, J, *Culture and Prosperity: The Truth about Markets, Why Some Countries Are Rich and Others Remain Poor* (2005), *passim*.

[6] Commonwealth of Australia, Inquiry into Financial Products and Services in Australia (2009), 112–16; House of Commons, Treasury Select Committee, *The Run on the Rock* (Vol 1, 2008), 21–4; Gray, J, 'Financial Regulation Before and After Northern Rock' in Akseli, O and Gray, J (eds), *Financial Regulation in Crisis?* (2011) 72–87; and Securities and Exchange Commission Office of Investigations, Investigation of the SEC's Failure to Uncover Bernard Madoff's Ponzi Scheme (2009), *passim*.

[7] Banks and insurers are prudentially supervised, for capital safety and solvency. Investment regulation concentrates on conduct in actual transactions with investors. Prudential and conduct elements appear in both but prudential elements are intensified with banks and insurers. Australian opinion is firming toward greater prudential regulation for superannuation funds as well: Commonwealth of Australia, Review into the Governance, Efficiency, Structure and Operation of Australia's Superannuation System (2010), Final Report Part I Overview, 15.

consumer protection to financial services,[8] one of the dangers of thinking about the investor in terms of consumer law is that risk retention is overlooked.[9] For example, the baselines of share investment regulation explicitly retain investor risk, but uncertainties remain about how this meshes with consumerism which concentrates on protection for the personal and household needs of the end-user.

2. The 'financial citizen'

The term 'financial citizen' has been coined to capture the fact that virtually everyone must engage with the financial system.[10] This increases as government encourages citizens to deal with financial institutions for welfare services it once provided; for example, retirement income. To be a full citizen of a country with a modern economy, it is necessary to acquire and use financial skills. At least, it is necessary to have a bank account,[11] and in countries like Australia a compulsory superannuation account. This universality heightens the paradox of risk and protection, at the heart of the consumer interest. It also places state policy and regulation at the centre of financialization.

The idea of the financial citizen and the risk retention paradox come together, because restructuring to provide welfare through the markets involves, as Gray and Hamilton describe it, a 'pushing down' of risk to the ordinary individual.[12] Previously, the state, following Marshall's social citizen idea (considered further below), took the risk that consolidated revenue would not be sufficient to fund retirement and welfare needs of its citizens. In the last two decades, these risks have been shifted to the citizen investor, unless that investor is content with schemes like the old-age pension. This shift has been accompanied by narratives of investor entrepreneurship and self-reliance, informed investor choice, investor confidence, and responsibility to become financially literate and resilient to losses. These narratives were particularly evident before the GFC, and in the late 1990s when online

[8] Moloney, n 4 above *passim* for advocacy of the consumer approach to investor protection.

[9] Kingsford Smith, n 2 above, *passim*.

[10] Kingsford Smith, D, 'Regulating Investment Risk: Individuals and the Global Financial Crisis' (2009) 32(2) *University of New South Wales Law Journal* 514. The term seems to have been used first by Gray, J and Hamilton, J, *Implementing Financial Regulation* (2006) (hereafter, Gray and Hamilton) (at 187). Condon and Philipps use a related term 'economic citizen': Condon, M and Philipps, L, 'Transitional Market Governance and Economic Citizenship: New Frontiers of Feminist Theory' (2006) 28 *Thomas Jefferson Law Review* 105, 115. In the consumer credit context see Pearson, G, 'Financial Literacy and the Creation of Financial Citizens' in Kelly-Louw, M, Nehf, J, and Rott, R (eds), *The Future of Consumer Credit Regulation: Creative Approaches to Emerging Problems* (2008) 3. In the superannuation context see Donald, S, 'What's in a Name?' (2011) 33 *Sydney Law Review* 295.

[11] Chowdry, B, 'Can Financial Citizenship Begin at Birth?' (2012) *Stanford Social Innovation Review* 17 argues for the establishment of a bank account at birth for inclusive receipt of entitlements.

[12] Gray and Hamilton, n 10 above, *passim*.

investing was the new financial consumer frontier, and 'day traders' promoted as the epitome of the new retail investor.[13]

Accordingly, this Chapter addresses themes which have emerged from experience of regulating in the financial consumer interest. In Sections II and IV, the ideas of 'financialization' and of the 'financial citizen' are elaborated. What are the conceptions of the 'financial citizen' that have captured the regulatory imagination (even temporarily), and in whose interests have they been pursued? It is argued that post-GFC doubts about the financial model of the market have led to a rethink that recognizes that markets have political, social, and legal dimensions,[14] and that in the retail area these are better examined through the idea of 'financial citizenship'. In Section III, the ordinary individual is considered and whether they have capabilities for financial citizenship: this includes considering research in financial literacy and behavioural finance, which questions how well individuals do at financial decision-making. Finally, in Section V, policy and retail regulation since the GFC is considered and whether it has changed, before concluding.

II. The 'Financial Citizen'

1. 'Financialization', citizenship, and the 'financial citizen'

The 'financial citizen' is an emerging concept whose chief personas are as an investor and consumer of financial products and services for everyday life. The citizen has become 'financialized' because of the insertion of the financial sector into the provision of everyday services, instead of the state.

'Financialization refers to the increasing importance of financial markets, financial motives, financial institutions and financial elites in the operation of the economy and its governing institutions both at the national and the international level.'[15]

The effects of 'financialization' immediate to the financial citizen are that large amounts of capital are invested by individuals, particularly in retirement

[13] Bradley, C, 'Disorderly Conduct: Day Traders and the Ideology of "Fair and Orderly Markets"' (2000) 26(1) *Journal of Corporation Law* 63.

[14] See for the main theoretical alternatives to economic market theories, Black, J, 'Reconceiving Financial Markets—from the Economic to the Social' (2013) 13(2) *Journal of Corporate Law Studies* 401.

[15] Epstein, G, Financialization, Rentier Interests, and Central Bank Policy (2001), manuscript, Department of Economics, University of Massachusetts, Amherst, MA, quoted in Palley, T, Financialisation: What it Is and Why it Matters (2007), The Levy Economics Institute Working Papers, No 525; Palley T, *Financialisation and the Financial Sector* (2013), *passim*; Tomoskovic-Devey, D and

investments, not controlled by government. This increases demand for shares and other investments, and drives up prices. Management and broking fees provide an income boost for the financial sector, increasing its influence. Also, financialization 'creates an investor identity amongst households that then generates favourable political support for policies favoured by large financial interests'[16] in other parts of the economy and society. Financialization also shifts risk from the state to ordinary citizens.

As elaborated in Section IV, the 'financial citizen' is a concept responsive to the process of financialization. It has origins in the 'retail investor' idea; originally the subject of 'investor protection' policies in 1930s US securities exchange legislation. Most evident in the EU,[17] there is a growing distinction between the vision of a fairly robust retail 'investor' and the end-user of 'packaged' investments, mainstream banking, and insurance products, who is characterized more protectively as a 'financial consumer'. In Australia, the compulsion to be a superannuation investor provides a structural legal link between the state, individual, markets, and the expectation that citizens will be self-sufficient in retirement. In many other countries the provision of generous state tax support for retirement savings provides a similar structure for drawing large numbers into the investment markets.[18]

The idea of citizenship is 'characterised by remarkable plasticity' with patterns of relations and expectations changing over time.[19] Theories of citizenship emphasize different civil, economic, identity, and cultural rights at different times, and vary in obligations to participate in politics or in civil society.[20] Indeed, the state itself and its relationship with the citizen have been reimagined frequently.[21] So, in the longer view, it is not surprising that restructuring of the state to move welfare provision from government to households and the financial markets[22] sees a re-envisioned citizenship with a financial component.

This 'financialization' of the personal has led to a 'more holistic approach to retail market policy'[23] and recognition of social, political, and inter-generational implications. As well as the share investor, the consumer interest has been recognized in a wider range of products, even those outside the main financial system,

Lin, K, 'Financialisation: Causes, Income Consequences and Policy Implications' (2013) 18 *North Carolina Banking Institute* 167.

[16] Palley (2007), n 15 above, 24.

[17] Moloney, N, 'The Investor Model Underlying the EU's Investor Protection Regime: Consumers or Investors?' (2012) 13 *European Business Organization Law Review* 169, *passim*.

[18] Australian Treasury, Tax Expenditure Statement 2010/11, ch 3: Tax Expenditures—Retirement Savings, 119ff reports that tax support for private superannuation approaches the cost of age pensions. This support is replicated in other countries with non-compulsory schemes.

[19] Kostakopoulou, D, *The Future Governance of Citizenship* (2008) 2.

[20] ibid, *passim*; Delanty, G, *Citizenship in a Global Age* (2000), *passim*.

[21] Kostakopoulou, n 19 above, 24.

[22] Condon and Philipps, n 10 above.

[23] Moloney, n 4 above, 4.

pay-day lending,[24] and 'alternative investments'.[25] The role of ideas and interests as drivers of financialization has been recognized,[26] in the tax policy that promotes mass markets and in supervisory regulation. Rather than being autonomous and inevitable forces—the 'invisible hand' of popular belief—there is recognition that markets are created and constituted through political processes, social structures, and networks with law as a crucial component.[27] If it ever was, it is no longer accurate to say the state is involved in markets only in the defence of property and enforcement of contracts.

The state is deeply involved in the constitution, regulation, and even the rescue of markets,[28] particularly in their extension to mass markets for individuals. Indeed, mass retail financial markets might not even exist if it were not for the tax support which encourages saving for retirement income. Seen this way, the 'financial citizen' is as much the creation of government policy as he or she is a 'participant' in the machinery of the market.

As an idea which homes in on the engagement of the citizen with the state and the market over questions of material welfare, financial citizenship has precursors. Liberal citizenship has been concerned since Locke with property, contract, and the market.[29] In preserving these rights for the private citizen, market law is the bastion against the state, whose only legitimate role concerning economic relations is to preserve property which the citizen has obtained through their labour.[30] CP Macpherson calls this 'possessive individualism' in its concentration on liberty as a positive freedom of economic relations and concentration on wealth.[31]

A forerunner of a different type is TH Marshall's social citizenship, with an important economic side. Arguing that material deprivation was the enemy of political and civic participation if not equality, Marshall advocated universal provision of health, education, and other resources to counterbalance the

[24] Wilson, T, 'The Inadequacy of the Current Regulatory Response to Payday Lending' (2004) *Australian Business Law Review* 193.

[25] Gray, J, 'Toward a More Resilient Financial System' (2013) 36(2) *Seattle University Law Review* 799.

[26] Williams, T, 'Empowerment of Whom and for What? Financial Literacy Education and the New Regulation of Consumer Financial Services' (2007) 29(2) *Law & Policy* 226; Black, J, 'Reconceiving Financial Markets—from the Economic to the Social' (2013) 13(2) *Journal of Corporate Law Studies* 401; Palley (2007), n 15 above, 24; and Arthur, C, *Financial Literacy Education: Neo-liberalism, the Consumer and the Citizen* (2012), *passim*, for a radical view.

[27] Black, n 26 above, *passim*; Kingsford Smith, D, 'Can There Be a *Fair* Share? Fairness Regulation and Financial Markets' in Sarra, J (ed.), *Explorations of Fairness* (2013), *passim*.

[28] Australian Government Guarantee Scheme for Large Deposits and Wholesale Funding, which also has a tranche for the universal guarantee of deposits up to $250,000 directed to retail depositors; and Gray, n 6 above, describing nationalizations and bailouts in the wake of the GFC.

[29] Delanty, n 20 above, 7–12 and Root, A, *Market Citizenship: Experiments in Democracy and Globalisation* (2007) 19.

[30] Root, n 29 above, 19, 21–2.

[31] Quoted in Delanty, n 20 above, 13–14.

inequalities of initial endowments and the market.[32] This might accurately be called socio-economic citizenship for it gave rights to economic resources in order to allow social and political citizen participation. Rather than having economic rights against the state,[33] the modern-day financial citizen is expected to use financial markets to supply funds for retirement, education, health, or insurances for disability.

2. Limitations of the 'financial citizen' idea

Predictably, there are limits to financial citizenship, and depending on the prevailing image, these have emerged from the supply side (the industry) and at other times from the demand side (financial consumers, usually through consumer organizations). Government and regulators themselves have, national variations aside, generally adhered to a fairly central position that promotes a mix of protection with heavy reliance on disclosure and many statements about the long, slow financial literacy road to 'responsibilization' and resilience of the financial citizen. From these debates and the research discussed in the remaining Sections of this Chapter has emerged a richer picture of the financial citizen and financialization as a goal of welfare policy.

(a) *Financial exclusion and non-citizenship*

A recent survey in Australia concluded that 17.7 per cent of the adult population in Australia were either fully excluded or severely excluded from financial services in 2012;[34] similar figures have been found elsewhere.[35] Hohnen and Hjort[36] argue that the results of a qualitative cross-national study of Nordic countries reveal that the self-responsibility, at the heart of the most individualistic versions of financial citizenship, requires 'a specific set of individual competencies and capacities in order

[32] Kostakopoulou, n 19 above, 27–30; Root, n 29 above, 26–7.

[33] Root, n 29 above, 27 notes that Marshall thought 'citizens should act with a lively sense of responsibility towards the community'.

[34] This figure comprises 1.1 per cent of adults who were fully excluded (they had no financial services products) and 16.6 per cent of adults who were severely excluded (they only had one financial services product): the Centre for Social Impact for National Australia Bank, *Financial Exclusion in Australia* (June 2013).

[35] Kempson, E and Collard, S, Developing a Vision for Financial Inclusion (2012), 1–8 and Raskin, S, Speech on 'Economic and Financial Inclusion in 2011' US Federal Reserve System, available at <http://www.federalreserve.gov/newsevents/speech/raskin20110629a.htm>.

[36] Hohnen, P and Hjort, T, 'Citizens as Consumers: A Discussion of New Emergent Forms of Marginalisation in Nordic Welfare States' (2009) 11(3) *European Journal of Social Security* 271; and Citi Australia and The Australia Institute, Evidence Versus Emotion: How Do we Really Make Financial Decisions? (December 2010), available at <http://www.financialliteracy.gov.au>, focusing on the behaviour of low-income earners and those recently experiencing financial hardship.

to navigate, foresee and plan one's own future'.[37] Promoting financialization of welfare provision contains the danger that individuals may be perceived as financially irresponsible and lacking key attributes as 'citizens'. Berry and Serra go as far as to warn: 'In a financialised society, if we are not financial citizens, then we are not citizens at all.'[38]

As well as being in the interests of fairness[39] and supporting the social and cultural life that full citizenship can bring,[40] there is evidence that financial inclusion brings tangible individual welfare benefits,[41] is related to macro-economic growth,[42] and since the GFC, increased financial stability.[43] While industry argues for self-reliance and engagement with private markets, it also argues when these policies fail that the cause is the lack of financial literacy or capability of those who are not included.[44] The response on the demand side is that exclusion arises from market failure: financial institutions in countries with deep middle classes do not innovate and reduce costs in order to offer services that low-income, remote, and not-for-profit entities need.[45] Reputational concerns about books of low-income customers, limited cross-selling opportunities, and regulation which tends to create standardized business models, make mainstream financial institutions disinclined to serve the financial citizen at the economic margins. Although the long game of rising prosperity and financial literacy should draw in many now excluded, cross-country research suggests that effective improvements in inclusion come through regulation such as the US Community Reinvestment Act and consumer credit legislation.[46]

[37] Hohnen and Hjort, n 36 above (middle-class individuals having the attributes and lower-income individuals less so).

[38] Berry, C and Serra, V, *Financial Citizenship: Rethinking the State's Role in Enabling Individuals to Save* (2012) 4.

[39] Kingsford Smith, n 27 above.

[40] Burkett, I and Drew, B, *Financial Inclusion, Market Failure and New Markets: Possibilities for Community Development Finance Institutions in Australia* (2008).

[41] Allen, F, Demirguc-Kunt, A, Klapper, L, and Peria, M, *The Foundations of Financial Inclusion: Understanding Ownership and Use of Formal Accounts* (2012).

[42] Miharsonarina, A and Kpodar, K, 'Mobile Phones, Financial Inclusion and Growth' (2012) 3(2) *Review of Economics and Institutions*, Article No 4, arguing that financial inclusion and growth support financialization.

[43] Hannig, A and Jansen, S, Financial Inclusion and Financial Stability: Current Policy Issues (2010), ADBI Working Paper 259.

[44] Williams, n 26 above and Cooper, J, Deputy Commissioner ASIC, Speech on 'Helping Retail Investors', SPAA National Conference (2009), demonstrating regulators hold this view too.

[45] Miharsonarina and Kpodar, n 42 above, showing how the introduction of mobile phone banking in Africa (where few have computers) demonstrates that individuals offered suitable services will embrace them.

[46] Marshall, J, 'Financial Institutions in Disadvantaged Areas: A Comparative Analysis of Policies Encouraging Financial Inclusion in Britain and the United States' (2004) 36 *Environment and Planning A* 241; and Wilson, T, 'Consumer Credit Regulation and Rights Based Social Justice: Addressing Financial Exclusion and Meeting the Credit Needs of Low Income Australians' (2012) 35(2) *University of New South Wales Law Journal* 501.

(b) *Mass markets in financial services and the reality of choice*

As demonstrated in Section III, there are persistent and indelible biases and heuristics (shortcuts) in decision-making, which may lead the financial citizen to be much less rational and capable at decision-making than intelligence, education, or financial experience suggest. Some individuals, however, will be sufficiently capable to approximate the capacities classic financial theory attributes to the investor, at least regarding straightforward products, such as bank accounts, credit cards, and general insurance. There is, alas, still a significant obstacle to the exercise of the choice which lies at the heart of the liberal justification for financialization.

The extension of financial services to a mass consumer market has involved the 'industrialization' of retail finance. While personal advice to meet an individual's needs persists,[47] in practice most financial consumers are sold a narrow range of products on non-negotiable standard terms,[48] even when receiving personal advice. In 2011, the Australian Securities and Investments Commission (ASIC) reported that in relation to the top 20 licensees providing financial advice, the vast majority of client funds were held in the top three products in three asset classes: managed investment schemes, platforms, and superannuation. By total funds invested, in platforms with wrap structures 'around 95% of funds are held in the top three products, while around 60% of funds are in the top three retail superannuation products'.[49] This raises questions about the reality of product choice.

There may also be concentration of entities through ownership and control. This vertical integration means that product issuers (manufacturers) are able to introduce their products on a preferential basis through affiliates in the distribution and advising part of the chain. If as in Australia, concentration exists not only in product recommendation and vertical integration but also in market share, then choice is even more limited. In Australia it is thought that approximately 80 per cent of financial advisors are either wholly or substantially owned by or authorized representatives of, institutions or other wealth managers or are part of a bank branch network.[50] This implies mass conflicts of interest especially in remuneration, and sector-wide concerns about the professionalism of advisors towards their clients at the point of recommendation. It is also a salutary reminder that financial capital does not share the collective action problems that the financial citizen has in pursuing political action.

[47] Where personal advice is given and an individual's financial circumstances considered.

[48] Most financial products are sold on a general advice basis considering only the basic purposes of the customer and product features and terms being offered, with product standardization and non-negotiable terms at their zenith.

[49] Australian Securities and Investments Commission (ASIC), Report 251 Review of Financial Advice Industry Practice (2011), 11–13.

[50] Financial System Inquiry, Interim Report (July 2014), 3–72; and Allen et al., n 41 above.

These institutional structures and practices limit the ability of financial citizens to negotiate terms, or to choose more than a generic product or strategy also offered to a mass of other consumers. In reality, the choice enjoyed by financial citizens may be more restricted than the competition and product innovation arguments of the advocates of financialization suggest.

(c) *Absence of institutionalization and financial citizen voice*

The 'plasticity' of financial citizenship is also evident in its changing relationship with capitalism. As Delanty argues in relation to citizenship more generally: 'Democracy of course has been the principal challenge to capitalism in the formation of modernity.'[51] Financialization seeks to untether citizens from Marshallian type state provision and to distance their finances from democratic politics. Instead of choosing their financial future through representative democracy, financial citizens (it is argued) should and do choose through market decisions: Scammell writes that 'the act of consumption is being increasingly suffused with citizenship characteristics and considerations'.[52] Likewise, Rose argues that 'the citizen is to enact his or her democratic obligations as a form of consumption'.[53] Anita Roddick is more direct: 'Business has overtaken politics as the primary shaping force in society, which means consumers are voting every time they flex their spending muscle.'[54]

Not only is the financial citizen's choice argued to be more influential when they are wearing their consumer hat than when they are wearing their voter's hat,[55] but also they are participating in a market that is said to deliver greater benefits through productivity and competition.[56] So, despite the risk retention paradox already described, despite product recommendation and financial sector concentration and conflicts, despite problems of asymmetry of information and bargaining power and regardless of the well-established deficiencies in decision-making recounted in the next Section, is the citizen providing a demotic challenge to financial capitalism simply by the act of consumption? In our opinion, the advocates of the market may be going too far in arguing that financial citizens have this power to change the institutions of financial capitalism and direct their financial futures by consumption alone.

[51] Delanty, n 20 above, 3.

[52] Scammell, M, 'The Internet and Civic Engagement: The Age of the Citizen-Consumer' (2000) 17 *Political Communication* 351.

[53] Rose, N, 'Governing Cities, Governing Citizens' in Isin, EF (ed.), *Democracy, Citizenship and the Global City* (2000) 95–109, 108.

[54] Roddick, quoted in Scammell, n 52 above, 351.

[55] Marshall, TH, 'Citizenship and Social Class' in *Class, Citizenship and Social Development: Essays by T H Marshall* (1964), *passim*; Root n 29 above, 27; and for a more nuanced consideration see Williams, C, 'The Securities and Exchange Commission and Corporate Social Transparency' (1999) 11(6) *Harvard Law Review* 1197, 1284–8.

[56] Palley (2013), n 15 above, 145–64, is critical of this orthodoxy.

While there is little doubt that consumption can give signals about what citizens want, the key weakness in the idea that the financial citizen can shape the institutions of finance through consumption is that there is virtually no political institutionalization of financial citizenship either as consumption or as share ownership. Moloney puts it well: 'retail investors do not yet act as a coherent group in policy making'.[57] There are few avenues for expressing collective political and social values about financialized welfare provision rather than investor's economic valuations. If financial citizens are to move away from pure democratic action (such as the 'Occupy Wall Street' movement) or from individual financial valuation at the other extreme, then they must institutionalize. If, as in Delanty's view 'In its most general sense citizenship is about group membership',[58] then financial citizens need group membership institutions to press questions like 'Where do financial citizens' long-term financial interests lie?'[59] rather than being recruited into markets because of mute signals from their consumption decisions. If as Root suggests citizenship is about taking responsibility,[60] it is difficult to see how the financial citizen can take responsibility if their only power is through anonymous individual transactions.

Where there is collective action it is centred on shareholder and consumer organizations.[61] Spectacular insolvent collapses sometimes result in shareholder[62] or financial consumer action groups,[63] usually to lobby for inquiries, regulatory action, and compensation. However, these rarely evolve into permanent institutions. Even shareholders of the same company, with meeting, speaking, voting, and rights to litigate, have never found it easy to act collectively. Institutional shareholders have enjoyed sporadic successes in changing board membership, but it is really only the agitation of hedge funds and other professional investor activists that have succeeded in obtaining changes of board strategy such as share buy-backs to return cash to shareholders, asset divestitures, and even board positions.[64] Despite their numbers the position of the 'financial citizen' remains one of institutional weakness in all of the political, social, and economic domains by comparison with the supply-side institutions of financial capitalism.

57 Moloney, n 4 above, 18.

58 Delanty, n 20 above, 9.

59 Gray and Hamilton, n 10 above, 224.

60 Root, n 29 above, ix.

61 The Australian Shareholders Association (<http://australianshareholders.com.au>), Choice (<http://www.choice.com.au>), and the Association of Independent Retirees (<http://www.independentretirees.com/>).

62 Northern Rock Shareholders Action Group (<http://www.uksa.org.uk/action/northern_rock>).

63 Maxwell Pensioners Action Group (<http://www.pensionstheft.org/>), the Pension Archive (<http://www.pensionsarchive.org/67/>), and the Storm Investors Consumer Action Group (<http://www.sicag.info/>).

64 SEC Chair Mary Jo White, Remarks at the 10th Annual Transatlantic Corporate Governance Dialogue (3 December 2013), Washington DC; Gilson, RJ and Gordon, JN, 'The Agency Costs of Agency Capitalism: Activist Investors and the Re-evaluation of Governance Rights' (2013) 113 *Columbia Law Review* 863.

The financial citizen idea captures a change in the relationship of the citizen with the state: the 'pushing down' of risk through the financialization of individual and household welfare provision. Financial citizenship shares with liberal citizenship a concentration on individual exercise of economic rights through choice, but in the financial economy not the real economy. It has an uneasy and changing relationship with the state. Uneasy because some versions of financial citizenship regard the proper role of the state as limited, when it is clear that markets are constituted by politico-legal relations and fiscal support for saving is a leading reason for the very existence of mass markets. Changing because, financial citizenship responds to variations in circumstances, ideas, and interests. For example, financial citizenship is shaped by the paradox of the 'investor' whom both law and finance treat as retaining risk, and the financial 'consumer' whom regulation is generally intended to protect. How these two ideas interrelate, and what interests and circumstances will influence their expression in regulation, only time will reveal. In the meantime, financial literacy and the behavioural finance limitations on financial citizenship are now examined.

III. The Capabilities of the 'Financial Citizen' and Financial Decision-Making

Classic finance theories[65] suggest that if the financial citizen is fully informed, he or she will make a rational investment choice; that is, carefully assess the risk and return of all possible investment options to arrive at an investment portfolio that suits his or her level of risk aversion.[66] However, behavioural finance has cast doubt on the efficacy of classic finance theories by focusing on the individual attributes, psychological or otherwise, that shape common financial and investment practices.[67] A large body of evidence now focuses on the limits of disclosure,[68]

[65] Markowitz, H, 'Portfolio Selection' (1952) 7(1) *Journal of Finance* 77; Modigliani, F and Miller, MH, 'The Cost of Capital, Corporation Finance and the Theory of Investment' (1958) 48(3) *American Economic Review* 655; Sharpe, W, 'Capital Asset Prices: A Theory of Market Equilibrium under Conditions of Risk' (1964) 19(3) *Journal of Finance* 425.

[66] See Barber, B and Odean, T, The Behaviour of Individual Investors (2011), available at <http://ssrn.com/abstract=1872211>.

[67] Ritter, J, 'Behavioural Finance' (2003) 11(4) *Pacific-Basin Finance Journal* 429.

[68] Agarwal, S, Driscoll, J, Gabaiz, X, and Laibson, D, The Age of Reason: Financial Decisions over the Life Cycle and Implications for Regulation (2009), Brookings Papers on Economic Activity No 2, 51, 86 and Choi, J, Laibson, D, and Madrian, B, $100 Bills on the Sidewalk: Suboptimal Investment in 401(k) Plans (2008), National Bureau of Economic Research Working Paper No 11554.

suggesting that the financial citizen does not always behave rationally or optimally[69] and may face capability barriers, including financial illiteracy, cognitive heuristics, and behavioural bias that result in sub-optimal financial decision-making.

1. Financial literacy

Although the obscurity of the concept of financial literacy attracts a multitude of definitions, an accepted definition from the OECD defines financial literacy as 'a combination of financial awareness, knowledge, skills, attitude and behaviours necessary to make sound financial decisions and ultimately achieve individual financial wellbeing'.[70] Financial literacy has been globally acknowledged as a key life skill and as an important element of economic and financial stability and development.[71] Classic finance theory regards financial literacy as a form of consumer empowerment,[72] assuming that a well-educated financial citizen will be able to understand investor disclosures that are provided and make informed decisions.[73] Literate, skilled financial citizens are expected to '… search the market effectively, monitor firms attentively, switch providers efficiently, and exercise their consumer power to drive out of the market firms that are dishonest, incompetent, or indifferent to consumers' needs',[74] thereby ensuring market efficiency.[75] Others view financial literacy as a necessary consequence of the push-down from state paternalism to individual 'responsibilization',[76] driven in part by self-responsibility for retirement planning.

In practice, however, financial illiteracy has been identified as a persistent problem by both national and international agencies.[77] Studies generally indicate that financial illiteracy is widespread and that many individuals lack knowledge of even the most basic economic principles.[78] Surveys in OECD

[69] Campbell, J et al., 'Consumer Financial Protection' (2011) 25(1) *Journal of Economic Perspectives* 91; Jolls, C, Sunstein, CR, and Thaler, R, 'A Behavioural Approach to Law and Economics' (1998) 50 *Stanford Law Review* 1470; Howells, G, 'The Potential and Limits of Consumer Empowerment by Information' (2005) 32(3) *Journal of Law and Society* 349.

[70] Atkinson, A and Messy, F-A, Measuring Financial Literacy: Results of the OECD INFE Pilot Study (2012), OECD Working Papers on Finance, Insurance and Private Pensions No 15.

[71] See, eg, G20, G-20 Leaders Declaration, Los Cabos, Mexico (2012) and OECD INFE, OECD/INFE High-Level Principles on National Strategies for Financial Education (2012).

[72] Howells, n 69 above.

[73] Rutledge, SL, Consumer Protection and Financial Literacy: Lessons from Nine Country Studies (2010), World Bank Policy Research Working Papers No 5326, 31.

[74] Williams, T, 'Empowerment of Whom and for What? Financial Literacy Education and the New Regulation of Consumer Financial Services' (2007) 29(2) *Law & Policy* 226, 233.

[75] Georgakopoulos, NL, 'Why Should Disclosure Rules Subsidize Informed Traders?' (1996) 16 *International Review of Law and Economics* 417.

[76] ibid. [77] OECD, Improving Financial Literacy: Analysis of Issues and Policy (2005).

[78] Lusardi, A and Mitchell, OS, 'Baby Boomer Retirement Security: The Roles of Planning, Financial Literacy, and Housing Wealth' (2007) 54(1) *Journal of Monetary Economics* 205; Lusardi, A

countries find that financial literacy is very low among individuals and households irrespective of income and education but especially among groups with lower income and less education.[79] The financial citizen has difficulty answering questions about compound interest, inflation, and risk diversification, and has difficulty in understanding budgeting, saving programmes, and financial information in general.[80] A key finding from such studies is that the financial citizen has difficulty learning from their experiences, and if they do learn, it is a slow process.[81] Similarly, the financial citizen often fails to correct their behaviour to match their experiences and is unaware of their return performances.[82] The GFC, in particular, highlighted vulnerabilities created by financial innovation and the complexity of financial markets. Loan products became too complex for the financial citizen to understand and disclosure was inadequate to identify the risks.[83]

Such low levels of financial literacy have driven financial education strategies at both the national and intergovernmental level in an effort to promote more effective and rational investment decisions. As of June 2013, 47 countries had launched, to various extents, the process to develop a national strategy for financial education[84] with intergovernmental bodies such as the World Bank[85] and the OECD[86] working to coordinate national financial literacy programmes. However, while financial education has been imparted throughout Europe, the US, and elsewhere over the past 30 years,[87] its impact on financial literacy and consumer behaviour is unclear. Clearly, little is understood as to what works, and what does not work, in improving financial behaviour over the long term.[88] Some scholars are sceptical that policy intervention, in the form of financial education, can cure the financial

and Mitchell, OS, 'Planning and Financial Literacy: How Do Women Fare?' (2008) 98(2) *The American Economic Review* 413; Lusardi, A and Mitchell, OS, 'Financial Literacy around the World: An Overview' (2011) 10(4) *Journal of Pension Economics and Finance* 497.

[79] See, eg, Lusardi and Mitchell (2011), n 78 above; Australia and New Zealand Banking Group Limited, Adult Financial Literacy in Australia (2011); Atkinson, A et al., Levels of Financial Capability in the UK: Results of a Baseline Survey for the UK Financial Services Authority (2006).

[80] See FINRA Investor Education Foundation, National Financial Education Study (2012).

[81] Gervais, S and Odean, T, 'Learning to Be Overconfident' (2001) 14 *Review of Financial Studies* 1.

[82] Glaser, M and Weber, M, 'Why Inexperienced Investors Do Not Learn: They Do Not Know Their Past Portfolio Performance' (2007) 4(4) *Finance Research Letters* 203.

[83] Davidoff, S and Hill, C, 'The Limits of Disclosure' (2013) 32(2) *Seattle University Law Review* 599.

[84] OECD INFE, OECD/INFE High-Level Principles on National Strategies for Financial Education (2012) 14.

[85] Xu, L and Zia, B, Financial Literacy around the World: An Overview of the Evidence with Practical Solutions for the Way Forward (2012), The World Bank Policy Research Working Paper No 6107.

[86] OECD INFE, Measuring Financial Literacy: Pilot Results from 14 Countries (2012).

[87] Rutledge, S, Consumer Protection and Financial Literacy: Lessons from Nine Country Studies (2010), The World Bank Policy Research Working Paper No 5326, 33.

[88] See, eg, Cole, S and Kartini Shastry, G, If You Are So Smart, Why Aren't You Rich? The Effects of Education, Financial Literacy, and Cognitive Ability on Financial Market Participation (2012), available at <http://ssrn.com/abstract=1317298>.

citizen's lack of financial capability,[89] while others are more optimistic.[90] However, heterogeneity across financial citizens in investment behaviour suggests that financial education alone cannot cure defects in financial capability.[91] What limits financial capability '... is not information and the knowledge that it takes to process this information, but instead potentially, deep-seated cognitive biases'.[92]

2. Cognitive heuristics

The financial citizen may make financial decisions that deviate from rationality by relying on 'heuristics', that is, rules of thumb, instead of formal techniques.[93] Heuristics are employed as the rationality of the financial citizen is limited by a multitude of factors including the information available, cognitive limitations, and time.[94] These mental shortcuts '... sometimes yield reasonable judgments and sometimes lead to severe and systematic errors'.[95] While convenience and speed necessitate reliance upon a vast array of heuristics,[96] the three fundamental heuristics proposed by Tversky and Kahneman[97] in their seminal research are discussed below.

(a) *Availability*

The availability heuristic implies that the financial citizen will assess the probability of an event by the '... ease with which instances or associations come to mind'.[98]

[89] See Willis, LE, 'Against Financial Literacy Education' (2008) 94 *Iowa Law* Review 197; and UK Financial Services Authority, Evidence of Impact: An Overview of Financial Education Evaluations, Consumer Research Report 68 (2008).

[90] See, eg, Fox, J, Bartholomae, S, and Lee, J, 'Building the Case for Financial Education' (2005) 391 *Journal of Consumer Affairs* 195; Hogarth, JM, 'Financial Literacy and Family & Consumer Sciences' (2002) 941 *Journal of Family and Consumer Sciences* 14; Lyons, A et al., 'Are we Making the Grade? A National Overview of Financial Education and Program Evaluation' (2006) 402 *Journal of Consumer Affairs* 208; Benartzi, S and Thaler, RH, 'Heuristics and Biases in Retirement Savings Behavior' (2007) 21 *Journal of Economic Perspectives* 81.

[91] Campbell, JY, 'Household Finance' (2006) 61 *Journal of Finance* 1553.

[92] Chater, N, Huck, S, and Inderst, R, Consumer Decision-Making in Retail Investment Services: A Behavioural Economics Perspective, Final Report to the European Commission (2010), 40.

[93] ibid.

[94] See Simon, H, 'Theories of Bounded Rationality' in McGuire, CB and Radner, R (eds), *Decision and Organization* (1972) 161 and Schade, C and Koellinger, P, 'Heuristics, Biases and the Behavior of Entrepreneurs' in Minniti, M (ed.), *Entrepreneurship—the Engine of Growth—People* (Vol 1, 2006) 42.

[95] Kahneman, D and Tversky, A, 'Judgment under Uncertainty: Heuristics and Biases' (1973) 185 (4157) *Science* 1124; Shah, AK and Oppenheimer, DM, 'Heuristics Made Easy: An Effort-Reduction Framework' (2008) 134(2) *Psychological Bulletin* 207.

[96] For a survey of the literature, see Hirshleifer, D, 'Investment Psychology and Asset Pricing' (2001) 56 *Journal of Finance* 1533.

[97] Kahneman and Tversky, n 95 above.

[98] ibid.

Recent or dramatic possibilities, such as financial market booms and busts, will be perceived as being more likely to occur than earlier experiences that are more difficult to recall. For example, the dot.com boom of 1999/2000[99] biased financial citizens towards those stocks covered heavily by the media, stocks experiencing high abnormal trading volume, and stocks with extreme one-day returns.[100] Similarly, the GFC resulted in the mass departure of the financial citizen from national financial markets.[101] The availability bias, therefore, leads the financial citizen to make financial decisions by overweighting current or dramatic information as opposed to processing all relevant information.[102]

(b) *Representativeness*

Representativeness refers to the way in which the financial citizen makes subjective probability judgements based on similarity to stereotypes.[103] Advertising,[104] labelling,[105] and particularly past returns[106] have all been found to influence decision-making. For example, a financial citizen subject to the representative bias can be over-optimistic about past winners and over-pessimistic about past losers.[107] At a macro level, it has been argued that this favouritism of past winners and bias away from past losers causes markets to deviate from fair value, with the former becoming overvalued and the latter becoming undervalued.[108] While it is an effective shortcut for making probability assessments, representativeness often leads to substantial errors because it ignores factors that should influence these assessments such as 'the base rate, sample size, and predictability of the target'.[109]

[99] See, eg, Scherbina, A, Asset Price Bubbles: A Selective Survey (2013), IMF Working Paper WP/13/45 and Wheale, PR and Amin, LH, 'Bursting the Dot.com Bubble: A Case Study in Investor Behaviour' (2003) 15(1) *Technology Analysis & Strategic Management* 117.

[100] Barber, B and Odean, T, 'All that Glitters: The Effect of Attention and News on the Buying Behavior of Individual and Institutional Investors' (2008) 21 *Review of Financial Studies* 785.

[101] Kingsford-Smith, D, 'Regulating Investment Risk: Individuals and the Global Financial Crisis' (2009) 32(2) *University of New South Wales Law Journal* 514.

[102] Kahneman and Tversky, n 95 above.

[103] Taffler, RJ, 'The Representativeness Heuristic' in Kent Baker, H and Nofsinger, JR, *Behavioral Finance: Investors, Corporations and Markets* (2010) 259.

[104] Jain, PC and Wu, JS, 'Truth in Mutual Fund Advertising: Evidence on Future Performance and Fund Flows' (2000) 55(2) *Journal of Finance* 937.

[105] Cooper, M, Gulen, H, and Rau, P, 'Changing Names with Style: Mutual Fund Name Changes and their Effects on Fund Flows' (2005) 60 *Journal of Finance* 2825.

[106] See, eg, Barberis, N, Shleifer, A, and Vishny, R, 'A Model of Investor Sentiment' (1998) 49 *Journal of Financial Economics* 1; Bloomfield, R and Hales, J, 'Predicting the Next Step of a Random Walk: Experimental Evidence of Regime-Shifting Beliefs' (2002) 65 *Journal of Financial Economics* 397; Frieder, L, Evidence on Behavioral Biases in Trading Activity (2004), University of California, Los Angeles Working Paper.

[107] Sirri, E and Tufano P, 'Costly Search and Mutual Fund Flows' (1998) 53 *Journal of Finance* 1589.

[108] Shefrin, H, *Beyond Greed and Fear: Understanding Behavioural Finance and the Psychology of Investing* (2007).

[109] Kahneman and Tversky, n 95 above.

(c) *Anchoring and adjustment*

Financial citizens who use the anchoring and adjustment heuristic to make estimates will use an external suggestion or self-generated value as an 'anchor'[110] and adjust this upwards or downwards to account for the information that they have available,[111] although often these adjustments are insufficient.[112] For example, a financial citizen may hold on to an asset for longer than they should by becoming attached to a particular investment believing that it will reach, or return to, a certain price.[113] Labelled the 'disposition effect', experimental and empirical studies have confirmed that the financial citizen has a strong preference for selling stocks that have increased in value since bought relative to stocks that have decreased in value since bought.[114]

3. Behavioural biases

In addition to heuristics, behavioural biases may influence individuals to make choices that are neither rational nor optimal.[115] These biases can affect all types of decision-making, but have particular implications for the financial citizen in relation to investing. Although there are innumerable factors affecting an individual's behaviour, a number of the most influential and debated biases are discussed below.

(a) *Overconfidence*

Psychology documents that the financial citizen will generally exhibit a bias towards being overconfident.[116] Overconfident investors not only under-react

[110] Cervone, D and Peake, PK, 'Anchoring, Efficacy, and Action: The Influence of Judgment Heuristics on Self-Efficacy Judgments and Behavior' (1986) 50 *Journal of Personality and Social Psychology* 492; Chapman, GB and Johnson, EJ, 'The Limits of Anchoring' (1994) 7 *Journal of Behavioral Decision Making* 223.

[111] Kahneman and Tversky, n 95 above; Epley, N and Gilovich, T, 'The Anchoring and Adjustment Heuristic' 17(4) *Psychological Science* 311.

[112] Quattrone, GA et al., Explorations in Anchoring: The Effects of Prior Range, Anchor Extremity and Suggestive Hints (1984), Stanford University Working Paper.

[113] Jacowitz, KE and Kahneman, D, 'Measures of Anchoring in Estimation Tasks' (1995) 21(11) *Personality and Social Psychology Bulletin* 1161.

[114] Shefrin, H and Statman, M, 'The Disposition to Sell Winners too Early and Ride Losers too Long: Theory and Evidence' (1985) 40(3) *The Journal of Finance* 777.

[115] See, eg, Brown, S et al., 'Debt and Financial Expectations: An Individual and Household Level Analysis' (2005) 41(1) *Economic Enquiry* 100; and Weinstein, N, 'Unrealistic Optimism about Future Life Events' (1980) 39(5) *Journal of Personality and Social Psychology* 806.

[116] See, eg, Benos, AV, 'Overconfident Speculators in Call Markets: Trade Patterns and Survival' (1998) 1 *Journal of Financial Markets* 353; Caballe, J and Sakovics, J, 'Speculating Against an Overconfident Market' (2003) 6 *Journal of Financial Markets* 199; Hirshleifer, D and Subrahmanyam, A, 'Investor Psychology and Security Market Under- and Overreactions' (1998) 53 *Journal of Finance* 1893; Gervais, S and Odean, T, 'Learning to Be Overconfident' (2001) 14 *Review of Financial Studies* 1.

to new information, or overweight the value of information, but they also hold unrealistic beliefs as to how high their returns will be.[117] This leads overconfident investors to underestimate risk and trade more in risker securities,[118] particularly if motivated by entertainment[119] or sensation-seeking.[120] Literature suggests that men are more predisposed to overconfidence[121] and overtrading[122] than women, with a negative effect on their returns.[123] Overconfidence may be exacerbated by a further characteristic known as the self-attribution bias,[124] meaning that financial citizens faced with a positive outcome following a decision will view that outcome as a reflection of their ability and skill. However, when faced with a negative outcome, this is attributed to luck or misfortune.[125] This bias interferes with the financial citizen's ability to process negative feedback, which may improve future financial decisions.

(b) *Risk tolerance*

Classic finance theory focuses on the trade-off between risk and return, assuming that a financial citizen seeks the highest return for the level of risk they are willing and able to bear.[126] While risk tolerance is an ambiguous concept, literature supports the proposition that the financial citizen's tolerance for risk is inextricably linked to demographics, including gender, age, marital status, educational level, and income level. Studies have found that higher age decreases risk tolerance whereas higher income increases risk tolerance.[127] Further, single rather than married individuals

[117] Barber, B and Odean, T, 'Trading Is Hazardous to your Wealth: The Common Stock Investment Performance of Individual Investors' (2000) 55(2) *Journal of Finance* 773.

[118] Benos, n 116 above; and Odean, T, 'Volume, Volatility, Price, and Profit When All Traders Are Above Average' (1998) 53 *Journal of Finance* 1887.

[119] Dorn, D and Sengmueller, P, 'Trading as Entertainment?' (2009) 55(4) *Management Science* 591.

[120] Grinblatt, M and Keloharju, M, 'Sensation Seeking, Overconfidence and Trading Activity' (2009) 64(2) *Journal of Finance* 549.

[121] Lundeberg, M, Fox, P, and Puncochar, J, 'Highly Confident but Wrong: Gender Differences and Similarities in Confidence Judgment' (1994) 86(1) *Journal of Educational Psychology* 114; Barber, B and Odean, T, 'Boys Will Be Boys: Gender Overconfidence, and Common Stock Investment' (2001) 116 *Quarterly Journal of Economics* 261.

[122] Barber and Odean, n 121 above; Grinblatt and Keloharju, n 120 above; and Barber and Odean, n 117 above.

[123] See, eg, Fenton-O'Creevy, M et al., 'Trading on Illusions: Unrealistic Perceptions of Control and Trading Performance' (2003) 76(1) *Journal of Occupational and Organizational Psychology* 53; and Shu, P, Chiu, S, Chen, H, and Yeh, Y, 'Does Trading Improve Individual Investor Performance?' (2004) 22(3) *Review of Quantitative Finance and Accounting* 199.

[124] See generally, Pompain, M, *Behavioural Finance and Wealth Management: How to Build Investment Strategies that Account for Investor Bias* (2011).

[125] ibid.

[126] Markowitz, H, 'Portfolio Selection' (1952) 7(1) *Journal of Finance* 77; Sharpe, W, 'Capital Asset Prices: A Theory of Market Equilibrium under Conditions of Risk' (1964) 19(3) *Journal of Finance* 425.

[127] Hira, T, Loibl, C, and Schenk, T, Risk Tolerance and Investor Confidence (2007), Iowa State University; Kannadasan, M, 'Risk Appetite and Attitudes of Retail Investors with Special Reference

tend to be more risk tolerant [128] and men are more risk tolerant than women.[129] Higher levels of attained education are associated with increased risk tolerance[130] and different occupations of financial citizens can be used to differentiate between their levels of financial risk tolerance.[131]

(c) *Social influence*

Social influence and interactions between financial citizens can also affect investment decisions.[132] Naturally, the financial citizen will discuss financial decisions with their family members, neighbours, colleagues, and friends, each of whom exert some level of influence over the decision-making process.[133] Social influence and the media[134] may cause some financial citizens to imitate each other in financial markets, exhibiting 'herding' behaviour[135] with some observers expressing concern that herding exacerbates volatility, destabilizes markets, and increases the fragility of the financial system.[136] Further, technological advancements such as online trading have made the production, retrieval, and distribution of information much easier, faster, and cheaper than ever before,[137] increasing the trading frequency of individual investors.[138]

to Capital Markets' (2006) 41(6) *The Management Accountant* 448; Cohn, RA et al., 'Individual Financial Risk Aversion and Investment Portfolio Composition' (1975) 30 *Journal of Finance* 605.

128 See, eg, Roszkowski, MJ, 'Risk Tolerance in Financial Decisions' in Cordell, DM (ed.), *Readings in Financial Planning* (1998) 281.

129 Yao, R and Hanna, S, 'The Effect of Gender and Marital Status on Financial Risk Tolerance' (2005) 4(1) *Journal of Personal Finance* 66.

130 Grable, J and Lytton, RH, 'Investor Risk Tolerance: Testing the Efficacy of Demographics as Differentiating and Classifying Factors' (1998) 9(1) *Financial Counselling and Planning* 61; Bakeer, HK and Haslem, J, 'The Impact of Investor Socio-economic Characteristics on Risk and Return Preferences' (1974) 2 *Journal of Business Research* 469.

131 Roszkowski, MJ, Snelbecker, GE, and Leimberg, SR, 'Risk-tolerance and Risk Aversion' in Leimberg, SR et al. (eds), *The Tools and Techniques of Financial Planning* (1993) 213.

132 Campbell, DT, 'Social Attitudes and Other Acquired Behavioral Dispositions' in Koch, S (ed.), *Psychology: A Study of Science* (1963) 94.

133 Nosfsinger, JR, 'Social Mood and Financial Economics' (2005) 6(3) *The Journal of Behavioural Finance* 144; Hong, H, Kubik, JD, and Stein, JC, 'Social Interaction and Stock Market Participation' (2004) 59(1) *Journal of Finance* 137; De Marzo, P, Vayanos, D, and Zwiebel, J, 'Persuasion Bias, Social Influence and Uni-Dimensional Opinions' (2003) 118(3) *Quarterly Journal of Economics* 909.

134 Shiller, R, *Irrational Exuberance* (2000) 149–53.

135 Hirshleifer, D and Teoh, SH, 'Herd Behaviour and Cascading in Capital Markets: A Review and Synthesis' (2003) 9 *European Financial Management* 25.

136 See, eg, Morris, S and Shin, H, 'Risk Management with Interdependent Choice' (1999) 15(3) *Oxford Review of Economic Policy* 52; Persaud, A, 'Sending the Herd Off the Cliff Edge: The Disturbing Interaction Between Herding and Market-Sensitive Risk Management Practices' in de Larosière, J (ed.), *Essays on Global Finance* (2000); and Shiller, R, Investor Behavior in the October 1987 Stock Market Crash: Survey Evidence (1987), National Bureau of Economic Research Working Paper No 2446.

137 Johnson, EJ, 'Digitizing Consumer Research' (2001) 28(2) *Journal of Consumer Research* 331.

138 Barber and Odean, n 117 above and Barber, B and Odean, T, 'The Internet and the Investor' (2001) 15 *Journal of Economic Perspectives* 41.

(d) *Framing effects*

Framing refers to alternative wordings of the same objective information that significantly alters decision-making. Thus, different representations of the same scenario can lead to different preferences and decisions, producing preference reversals.[139] Researchers have found that framing decision-problems in a positive light generally results in less-risky choices; with negative framing of problems, riskier choices tend to result.[140] Framing is common in the financial markets where issuers will attempt to steer the financial citizen towards certain products by highlighting their positive features, such as the potential return, and downplay the potential loss that could be suffered.[141]

IV. Regulatory Perceptions and Policies and the 'Financial Citizen'

As already argued, the 'financial citizen' reflects changing ideas about the role of individuals in financial markets. By contrast with older perceptions of the investor, as a subject of investor protection, the contemporary financial citizen, whether investor or consumer, has responsibilities: to exercise informed choice and take responsibility for decisions (particularly losses) in the pursuit of financial self-sufficiency. Since the GFC, there seems to have been a return to a more protective relation between the state and the financial citizen, as explored in this Section.

[139] See, eg, Cox, JC and Grether, DM, 'The Preference Reversal Phenomenon: Response Mode, Markets and Incentives' (1996) 7(3) *Economic Theory* 381; Tversky, A and Thaler, R, 'Anomalies: Preference Reversal' (1990) 4(2) *Journal of Economic Perspectives* 201; Tversky, A and Kahneman, D, 'The Framing of Decisions and the Psychology of Choice' (1981) 211(4481) *Science* 453, 453.

[140] Steul, M, 'Does the Framing of Investment Portfolios Influence Risk-Taking Behavior? Some Experimental Results' (2006) 27(4) *Journal of Economic Psychology* 557; Glaser, M et al., 'Framing Effects in Stock Market Forecasts: The Difference between Asking for Prices and Asking for Returns' (2007) 11(2) *Review of Finance* 325; Diacon, S and Hasseldine, J, 'Framing Effects and Risk Perception: The Effect of Prior Performance Presentation Format on Investment Fund Choice' (2007) 28(1) *Journal of Economic Psychology* 31.

[141] See, eg, Bar-Gill, O and Warren, E, 'Making Credit Safer' (2008) 157(1) *University of Pennsylvania Law Review* 1; and Barr, M, Mullainathan, S, and Shafir, E, Behaviorally Informed Financial Services Regulation (2008), report prepared for the New America Foundation.

1. The 'financial citizen' as protected investor

Most readers will be familiar with the ordinary investor as the beneficiary of regulatory protection from sharpers and conmen: this was the leading idea inspiring the securities and exchange legislation in the US in the 1930s, arguably the first modern regime of securities regulation.[142] In the US at the time, there were two approaches to securities regulation. The first at the heart of the Securities Act 1933 relies on disclosure of detailed financial information to investors.[143] This approach has become the dominant feature of virtually all securities regulation since. It has also become a mainstay of financial consumer regulation. The other, adopted by many US states and persisting until the 1980s, was merit regulation. Rather than relying only on disclosure, merit regimes also gave regulators powers to prohibit securities inappropriate for target investors.[144] Underlying the new securities exchange system in the 1930s was also a link between the welfare of individuals and that of the US economy as a whole:[145] Congress was motivated to pass the new legislation concerned 'that investors were vulnerable in a manipulated marketplace *and* that others suffered when investors disinvested in the market'.[146]

2. The 'financial citizen' as well-informed and confident investor or consumer

Since the 1980s this policy of investor protection has tightened in US case law to an image of the investor as competent, empowered and acting in self protection. Barbara Black argues:

> The Supreme Court tells us that courts should not treat reasonable investors like 'nitwits' and ascribe to them 'child-like simplicity'. ... To the contrary, defendants can indulge in optimistic talk ... since reasonable investors will not be misled by puffery ... Thus courts tell us that reasonable investors 'can do the math' to figure out the financial bottom line ... courts expect reasonable investors to have an awareness of general economic conditions, and to understand the principle of diversification, the time-value of money, the nature of margin accounts and the security industry's compensation structure.[147]

[142] Jennings R et al., *Securities Regulation* (8th edn, 1998) 2; and Hazen, TL, *The Law of Securities Regulation* (1996) 6–8.

[143] Soderquist, LD and Gabaldon, TA, *Securities Regulation* (4th edn, 1999) 2–3; and Hazen, n 142 above, 6.

[144] Soderquist and Gabaldon, n 143 above, 2.

[145] Jennings et al., n 142 above, 2.

[146] Jennings et al., n 142 above, 2–3. This is also a theme of the inaugural address of President Franklin D Roosevelt on 4 March 1933, which directly preceded the passage of the Securities Act 1933. The speech can be found at <http://www.inaugural.senate.gov/swearing-in/address/address-by-franklin-d-roosevelt-1933>.

[147] Black, B, 'Behavioural Economics and Investor Protection: Reasonable Investors and Efficient Markets' (2012–13) 44 *Loyola University Chicago Law Journal* 1493, 1494–5.

As Langevoort and Thompson have written, there has been a long erosion of investor protection in the US which has 'unleashed opportunities for much more aggressive selling efforts'[148] and this seems to be in line with judicial views about investor capacity. This robust image of the investor has been particularly evident in the policy and 'light touch' regulation of online investing[149]—a non-advisory mode of investor directed transactions with particular emphasis on investor empowerment.[150]

In the UK[151] and the EU too, Moloney documents industry-side arguments for the adoption of an image of a 'reasonably well informed, reasonably observant and circumspect consumer', such as already adopted in general EU consumer law.[152] She catalogues the adoption of 'investor confidence' as the policy goal in the early integration of the single retail financial market of the EU.[153] Eventually, this was seen as too high a standard, and 'investor protection' accepted as a more appropriate benchmark, especially given the variable experience of financialization in the EU. Nevertheless, Moloney argues that before the GFC, the identification of the typical retail investor was as a consumer of financial services but a 'consumer' who was empowered and confident.[154] Sometimes, the 'investor' seemed to be subsumed in the 'consumer' description, causing Gray and Hamilton to worry that the distinctively risky nature of investment had been unwittingly and dangerously rolled up into the idea of 'consumer'.[155] Even before the crisis there were serious doubts about the effectiveness of disclosure in retail markets.[156] The UK's Financial Services Authority (now the Financial Conduct Authority) began its programme of six cross-cutting principles to get the industry to 'Treat Customers Fairly'[157] and

[148] Langevoort, D and Thompson R, The Slow Death of Section 5 (2013), available at <http://ssrn.com/abstract=2316858>.

[149] ASIC, Facilitating Online Financial Services Disclosure, RG 221 (2010); ASIC, Electronic Prospectuses, PS 107; and ASIC Interim Policy Statement—Exposure Draft, Internet Discussion Sites, IPS 162 (2000).

[150] Bradley, n 13 above, *passim*; Williamson, K and Kingsford Smith, D, 'Empowered or Vulnerable? The Role of Information for Australian Online Investors' (2010) 34(1) *Canadian Journal of Information and Library Science*; Kingsford Smith, D and Williamson, K, 'How Do Online Investors Seek Information and What Does This Mean for Regulation?' 2004 (2) *The Journal of Information Law and Technology* 12, available at <http://www2.warwick.ac.uk/fac/soc/law/elj/jilt/2004_2/kingsford-smithandwilliamson>.

[151] Gray and Hamilton, n 10 above, 192–4 discuss an earlier change in the objectives of the UK Financial Services Authority (now the Financial Conduct Authority) in respect of which although 'investor protection' is important, it must be 'appropriate', and qualified by competing with other purposes such as 'maintaining market confidence'.

[152] Moloney, n 4 above, 70 note 170 and 90 note 353.

[153] Moloney, n 4 above, 70ff.

[154] Moloney, n 4 above, ch 2, *passim*.

[155] Gray and Hamilton, n 10 above, 183.

[156] Gray and Hamilton, n 10 above, ch 5 for an account of investor understanding of point of sale disclosure.

[157] The Financial Conduct Authority has since adopted the 'Treating Customers Fairly' programme initiated by Financial Services Authority (as Treating Customers Fairly: Towards Fair Outcomes for Consumers (2006)).

its Retail Distribution Review[158] which has banned commissions: both took a more protective approach to financial consumers including investors, an approach continued since the crisis.[159]

In Australia, the adoption of the 'confident investor' and the emphasis on disclosure and choice has been unambiguous. In 1989, one of the objects of the Australian Securities Act[160] provided for the regulator 'to maintain the confidence of investors ... by ensuring adequate protection for such investors'. In 2001, this aim was altered to read only that the regulator should 'promote the confident and informed participation of investors and consumers in the financial system'. Note the inclusion of financial 'consumers' along with investors, something not present before.[161] In the pre-GFC period, in line with the emphasis on investor confidence, heavy reliance was placed on both disclosure and enforcement. Disclosure was to make the financial citizen informed and confident and markets efficient. Enforcement was to free the market from misleading statements and market misconduct such as insider dealing and market manipulation, which could distort decisions and also result in inefficiencies and losses. This emphasis on disclosure and market integrity had its foundations in classical financial theory discussed above, particularly the efficient market hypothesis and the role of information in discovery of securities prices and efficient allocation of capital. However, information efficiency is only approached in the securities of well followed companies, and not in markets for products manufactured by issuers for consumer end-users in which there is no secondary market. Disclosure in retail markets also misses its target, because of financial illiteracy and the biases and heuristics of financial decision-making. We also have abundant evidence that try as they might, regulators everywhere have deep and persistent difficulties with enforcement. As Braithwaite puts it: 'System capacity overload results in a pretence of consistent law enforcement where in practice enforcement is spread around thinly and weakly.'[162] So, relying on enforcement for market integrity has also been a policy with significant shortcomings.

3. The 'financial citizen' since the Global Financial Crisis

In terms of the bi-partisan policies of 'financialization' and financial citizen participation in markets, there has been no change since the GFC. However, the hardship of individual losses and the insights from behavioural finance and literacy

[158] Financial Services Authority, Distribution of Retail Investments: Delivering the RDR—Feedback to Consultation Paper 18/09 and Final Rules (2010); and Financial Services Authority, Retail Distribution Review: Independent and Restricted Advice—Finalised Guidance (2012)

[159] Moloney, n 17 above, 176–7.

[160] Australian Securities Act 1989, section 3(2)(b).

[161] Australian Securities and Investments Act 2001, section 1(2)(b).

[162] Braithwaite, J, *Regulatory Capitalism: How it Works and Ideas for Making it Work Better* (2008) 9.

research about citizen capability has shifted policy language from empowered investors and confident consumers, to 'consumer protection' and in the UK (and dating from the pre-crisis period) to 'treating customers fairly'. Treating customers fairly is based on the assumption that firms too understand consumer illiteracy, biases, and heuristics, and should not 'design and sell products that benefit from consumers not overcoming mistakes, or at times, exacerbating mistakes'.[163] There have been reforms to address structural features of the financial industry such as vertical integration and concentration (by bans on conflicts of interest especially in remuneration), more emphasis on the professionalization and quality of financial advice, and policy on the design of financial products to meet the needs of target groups,[164] in some ways reminiscent of pre-1980s US 'merit regulation'. Some cautious work is also underway to see if the insights of behavioural finance can go beyond diagnosis and prescribe policies for regulatory action.[165]

A good example of both the difficulties of reconciling the retention of risk at the heart of the investor concept with more protective policies, and test of the resolve of post-GFC regulators, can be seen in relation to interests in funds. 'Packaged' financial products involve company securities and often derivatives 'packaged' in a fund: that fund may be a mutual fund, a managed investment scheme, a UCITS,[166] or life insurance linked. 'Structured' products are often even more risky, with investment strategies for the fund dependent on the performance of derivatives. Almost all pension or superannuation funds also hold securities and many hold some derivatives.

If interests in the fund are then sold to retail investors as being suitable for them, they may not realize the risks involved in underlying investments. In all the countries considered in this Chapter, shares are sold under a distinctive prospectus or registration statement regime making them easier to identify. Packaged and structured products and interests in retirement funds in some places are sold under single disclosure and market conduct regimes which also regulate simple financial products with less risk and a clearer consumer tenor. Before the GFC, it was these types of complex products where reliance on disclosure was at its most inadequate: often even advisers did not understand the disclosure well. Worth exploring are proposals to have the issuers of complex products take more responsibility for matching their product to the class of financial citizen to which it is directed. This is a product intervention approach which could address the paradox of having to regulate to both protect investors and allow them to retain risk. It is probably

[163] Financial Conduct Authority, Applying Behavioural Economics at the Financial Conduct Authority (2013) 21; Barr-Gill et al., n 141 above; and Barr et al., n 141 above.

[164] ibid; and ASIC, Complex Products, Report 384 (2014).

[165] Thaler, R and Sunstein C, *Nudge: Improving Decisions about Health, Wealth and Happiness* (2008); Yeung, K, 'Nudge as Fudge' (2012) 75(1) *Modern Law Review* 122; Financial Conduct Authority, n 163 above.

[166] The EU's Undertakings for Collective Investment in Transferable Securities (UCITS) (Directive 2009/65/EU [2009] OJ L302/32).

going too far to say that, in relation to the financial citizen, the legal responsibility of *caveat emptor* has now shifted to *caveat vendor*,[167] but even leading proponents of markets have accepted that the pre-GFC approaches needed to be reconsidered.[168] Section V sets out in more detail how this has been attempted.

V. The 'Financial Citizen' after the Global Financial Crisis

As discussed above, prior to the financial crisis, regulators were largely focused on enhancing market efficiency.[169] However, the GFC refocused regulatory efforts towards addressing systemic vulnerabilities, improving market transparency, and enhancing investor protection. In response to a call by the G20 in February 2011, an OECD-led task force produced the High Level Principles on Financial Consumer Protection, which called on members to 'assess their national frameworks for financial consumer protection in the light of these principles and promote international cooperation to support the strengthening of financial consumer protection in line with, and building upon, the principles'.[170] The regulatory responses being driven at the international level and applied at the national level involve '… a movement away from minimalist regulation and reliance on "light touch supervision" and market discipline, towards a more interventionist approach'.[171]

1. Consumer protection authorities

The GFC highlighted that weaknesses or regulatory gaps with respect to non-bank entities within a financial system can significantly impact consumer protections.[172] A key regulatory response has been to restructure existing, or create new,

[167] Moloney, n 4 above, 92.

[168] Alan Greenspan, then Chair of the US Federal Reserve, in a Congressional hearing on 23 October 2008, admitted that his free-market ideology that markets were self-correcting and shunning regulation was flawed.

[169] For examples in the EU, the Market in Financial Instruments Directive I (MiFID I) (Directive 2004/39/EU [2004] L145/1) and the Undertakings for Collective Investment in Transferable Securities (UCITS) Directive (n 166 above).

[170] OECD, G-20 High Level Principles on Financial Consumer Protection (2011), 4.

[171] Davis, K, *Regulatory Reform Post the Global Financial Crisis: An Overview* (2011) 2.

[172] See Financial Stability Board, Consumer Finance Protection with Particular Focus on Credit (2011).

consumer protection authorities. For example, in the US, the Dodd–Frank Wall Street Reform and Consumer Protection Act 2010 (hereinafter, Dodd–Frank)[173] substantially consolidated core consumer protection functions from seven[174] banking and financial regulators into a new agency, the Consumer Financial Protection Bureau.[175] Additional consumer protections include the creation of an Office of Financial Education, to promote financial literacy and the Office of Investors Advocate (under the Securities and Exchange Commission (SEC)), as well as the establishment of a formal complaint process for consumers. For more detail on this and other developments in the UK and EU covered in this Section, see the Chapter by Moloney in this volume.

2. Product intervention

With product complexity raising doubts as to the effectiveness of disclosure and financial literacy as a means of retail investor protection, certain jurisdictions debated product intervention as a potential solution to fill this regulatory gap. Production intervention can take a number of forms, including controlling marketing and promotions, regulating terms and conditions, and product intervention at the 'manufacturing' stage.[176] Australia decided that 'it is not for the parliament or the government to determine for whom particular investment products are appropriate. This is a decision for individual investors, in consultation with a financial adviser bound by a fiduciary duty to put their clients' interests ahead of their own.'[177]

However, the UK has deemed product intervention to be appropriate in certain circumstances, for certain classes of retail investor, and similar provisions have been implemented in the EU where regulators have been conferred with the power to prohibit or restrict the marketing, distribution, or sale of a particular financial instrument or type of activity.[178]

[173] Dodd–Frank Wall Street Reform and Consumer Protection (hereinafter, Dodd–Frank) Act, Pub. L. No. 111–203, 124 Stat. 1376 (2010).

[174] The Federal Reserve Board; the Office of the Comptroller of the Currency; the Federal Deposit Insurance Corporation; the Office of Thrift Supervision; the National Credit Union Administration; the Federal Trade Commission; and the Department of Housing and Urban Development.

[175] The Bureau's main functions include conducting financial education programmes; collecting, investigating and responding to consumer complaints; and researching and monitoring areas of the financial markets that affect consumers: Dodd–Frank Act, section 1021(b).

[176] Financial Stability Board, Consumer Finance Protection with a Particular Focus on Credit (2011) 15.

[177] Parliamentary Joint Committee on Corporations and Financial Services, Inquiry into Financial Products and Services in Australia (2009), 143. But see recent recommendations in support of product intervention powers in Australia: Commonwealth of Australia Financial System Inquiry Final Report (12 December 2014), ch 4.

[178] See the Chapter by Moloney in this volume for an examination of these developments.

3. Mortgage-lending practices

Literature traces the GFC back to two major factors: irresponsible consumer mortgage-lending practice particularly in the US; and the interrelated securitization of mortgages.[179] Responsible mortgage-lending practices are now being implemented across the US and Europe, with a particular focus on assessing the financial citizen's ability to repay the mortgage loan.[180]

In the US, Dodd–Frank charged the Consumer Financial Protection Bureau with rewriting mortgage-lending rules, including the creation of a new 'ability-to-repay' rule. The rule generally requires lenders to make a reasonable, good-faith determination that a consumer has the ability to repay a mortgage loan before extending the loan.[181] It creates a presumption of compliance for certain qualified mortgages, which may have a debt-to-income ratio limit of no greater than 43 per cent and are subject to various restrictions on loan features perceived as more risky, like interest-only terms, prepayment fees, extended amortization, 'points and fees' in excess of 3 per cent and balloon payments.[182] The purpose is to 'provide a shield against litigation by borrowers who default or mortgage-backed securities holders if loans hit some elevated requirements'.[183]

Similarly, the UK Financial Services Authority[184] released its Mortgage Market Review in 2009, followed by a consultation document in 2010 on responsible lending. In Australia, the National Consumer Credit Protection Act 2009 mandates suitability assessments on the financial citizen's abilities to repay and alignment of the product with the objectives of the consumer. Likewise, in February 2014, the EU adopted a Directive on credit agreements related to residential property.[185] The new regime complements the Consumer Credit Directive adopted in 2008, which aims to provide a high level of consumer protection through standardizing the information that is provided to consumers.[186]

179 Taylor, JB, The Financial Crisis and the Policy Responses: An Empirical Analysis of What Went Wrong (2009), National Bureau of Economic Research Working Paper No 14631; Black, B, 'Protecting the Retail Investor in an Age of Financial Uncertainty' (2009) 34 *University of Dayton Law Review* 5.

180 See also Financial Stability Board, FSB Principles for Sound Residential Mortgage Underwriting Practices (2012).

181 At a minimum, creditors generally must consider eight underwriting factors: (i) current or reasonably expected income or assets; (ii) current employment status; (iii) the monthly payment on the covered transaction; (iv) the monthly payment on any simultaneous loan; (v) the monthly payment for mortgage-related obligations; (vi) current debt obligations, alimony, and child support; (vii) the monthly debt-to-income ratio or residual income; and (viii) credit history. Truth in Lending Act 1968, section 129B, as amended by Dodd–Frank, sections 1411 and 1412.

182 ibid.

183 CFPB, Federal Regulators Provide Guidance on Qualified Mortgage Fair Lending Risks (22 October 2013), Press Release.

184 On 19 December 2012, the Financial Services Act 2012 received royal assent, abolishing the Financial Services Authority with effect from 1 April 2013. Its responsibilities were then split between two new agencies (the Prudential Regulation Authority and the Financial Conduct Authority) and the Bank of England.

185 Mortgage Lending Directive 2014/17/EU [2014] OJ L60/34.

186 Consumer Credit Directive 2008/48/EC [2008] OJ L133/66.

4. Simplified product disclosure

The GFC demonstrated that disclosure is insufficient to overcome information asymmetries and conflicts of interest between the financial citizen, issuers, and financial service agents. Commentators emphasized that the disclosure rationale was undermined by the volume of information[187] and the complexity of the securities being sold, arguing that no one could understand the disclosure.[188] Further, there is scant evidence that increases in disclosure improve decision-making.[189] Regulators have, therefore, turned their focus to the quality of disclosure by simplifying disclosure documents to the financial citizen. In the US, Dodd–Frank empowered the Consumer Finance Protection Bureau to develop standardized consumer information forms for financial products to enhance the consumer's ability to compare competing offers. Similarly, the EU's UCITS funds regime demands the use of a standardized key-investor information document while communicating with consumers,[190] and Australia has introduced a short and standardized product-disclosure statement.[191] Interestingly, although the US SEC proposed a new similar short-form prospectus, a study has found that it had no effect on investor choices.[192]

5. Mitigating conflicts of interest in financial advice

Commission earned by investment advisers from product providers has traditionally contributed to a significant portion of an adviser's income. There is anecdotal evidence that the fee structure of investment products, rather than their suitability, drives their sale to the financial citizen,[193] and that at least some investors are naïve

[187] Ben-Shahar, O and Schneider, C, The Failure of Mandated Disclosure (2010), University of Chicago Law and Economics Olin Working Paper No 516.

[188] See Hu, H, 'Too Complex to Depict? Innovation, "Pure Information," and the SEC Disclosure Paradigm' (2012) 90 *Texas Law Review* 160; Mendales, RE, 'Collateralized Explosive Devices: Why Securities Regulation Failed to Prevent the CDO Meltdown, and How to Fix It' (2009) 5 *University of Illinois Law Review* 1359, 1362; Schwarcz, S, 'Disclosure's Failure in the Subprime Mortgage Crisis' (2008) *Utah Law Review* 1109, 1110; Schwarcz, S, 'Regulating Complexity in Financial Markets' (2009) 87 *Washington University Law Review* 211. This strain also surfaced prior to the financial crisis. See Paredes, T, 'Blinded by the Light: Information Overload and its Consequences for Securities Regulation' (2003) 81 *Washington University Law Quarterly* 417 and Schwarcz, S, 'Rethinking the Disclosure Paradigm in a World of Complexity' (2004) 1 *University of Illinois Law Review* 1.

[189] Agarwal, S et al., 'The Age of Reason: Financial Decisions over the Life Cycle and Implications for Regulation' (2009) 51(2) *Brookings Papers on Economic Activity* 86; and Choi et al., n 68 above.

[190] UCITS Directive (n 166 above), Articles 78–82.

[191] See Corporations Act 2001 (Cth), sections 762A–765A and 1012A–C.

[192] Beshears, J et al., How Does Simplified Disclosure Affect Individual's Mutual Fund Choices? National Bureau of Economic Research Working Paper No 14859 (2008).

[193] Bergstresser, D, Chalmers, J, and Tufano, P, 'Assessing the Costs and Benefits of Brokers in the Mutual Fund Industry' (2009) 22 *Review of Financial Studies* 4129 and Chen, J, Hong, H, and Kubik, J,

about analysts' incentives.[194] In the GFC, retail investors suffered substantial losses through investments made by fund managers acting as their agents, fuelling regulatory intervention and guidance at both the intergovernmental and national level.[195]

In Australia, the Future of Financial Advice reforms introduce a statutory fiduciary duty for financial advisers. Under this reform, advisers have a duty to 'act in the "best interests" of their clients subject to a "reasonable steps" qualification and to place the best interests of their clients ahead of their own when providing personal advice to retail clients'.[196] Similarly, in the US, in a study mandated by Dodd–Frank,[197] the SEC staff recommended rulemaking to impose a uniform fiduciary duty for broker-dealers and investment advisers that offer personalized retail financial advice. In mid-2015 this recommendation remains unimplemented.

However, legislators and regulators in the US have been most active in reining in the aggressive practices of financial services institutions by putting in place explicit rules of conduct. The key focus areas of regulators have been the mortgage origination and credit card issuer practices followed by financial services institutions. The CARD Act, which was passed in 2009, placed numerous restrictions on the charging models employed by credit and debit card issuers.

6. Wholesale and retail investor distinction

Problems with the distinction between a 'wholesale client' and 'retail client' were exposed during the GFC as it became apparent that financial citizens who did not have the necessary experience investing in complex financial products were able to access these on the wholesale market.

A pertinent example is the landmark Australian Federal Court decision in *Wingecarribee Shire Council v Lehman Brothers Australia (in liq)*,[198] a class action involving three representative local councils. This is the first decision globally that examines the conduct of an investment adviser regarding the manufacture and marketing of synthesized collateralized debt obligations (SCDOs). Prior to 2007, Lehman Brothers Australia (now in liquidation) (Lehman Australia) sold SCDOs to various local councils, charities, church groups, and not-for-profits. At the time the SCDOs were sold,

'Outsourcing Mutual Fund Management: Firm Boundaries, Incentives and Performance' (2013) 68(2) *Journal of Finance* 523.

194 Malmendier, U and Shanthikumar, D, 'Are Small Investors Naïve about Incentives?' (2007) 85 *Journal of Financial Economics* 457; and Hong, H, Kubik, JD, and Stein, JC, 'Social Interaction and Stock Market Participation' (2004) 59 *Journal of Finance* 137.

195 See, eg, IOSCO, Good Practices in Relation to Investment Managers Due Diligence When Investing in Structured Finance Instruments (2009).

196 Corporations Act 2001 (Cth), Div 2 of Part 7.7A.

197 Section 913.

198 [2012] FCA 1028. See also *Bathurst Regional Council v Local Government Financial Services Pty Ltd* (No 5) [2012] FCA 1200.

they had a high credit rating and offered high interest rates. The SCDOs lost value during the GFC and, as a consequence, investors incurred substantial losses. A single judge of the Australian Federal Court held that Lehman Australia was liable to compensate the investors for losses incurred as a result of investing in SCDOs. A major question before the Court was: 'How was it that relatively unsophisticated council officers came to invest many millions of ratepayers' funds in these specialised financial instruments?'[199] The Court found that the only way the councils could have come to invest in SCDOs was because Lehman Australia had either recommended and advised them, or used its Investment Managed Portfolio agreement mandate to purchase them. In doing so, the Court found that Lehman Australia 'preyed on [the council officers'] lack of expertise and the trust the councils placed in its expert advice … '.[200] The case sets an important precedent on the treatment of unsophisticated investors and the duties around disclosure of risks in complicated financial products such as SCDOs. It is also the first time that the courts have classified local councils as 'unsophisticated' investors.

The Court's approach is consistent with developments in the EU and US. In the EU, under Annex II of the crisis-era 2014 Markets in Financial Instruments Directive II (MiFID II), municipalities and other local authorities do not qualify as professional investors. Similarly, in the US, the Dodd–Frank Act establishes new duties to particular classes of investors. One such class of investors, referred to in the Act as 'Special Entities', comprises federal agencies, states, state agencies, cities, counties, municipal or political subdivisions of states, employee benefit or governmental plans as defined in ERISA, and endowments.

7. Institutional restructuring

An issue persistently debated post-crisis was the use of taxpayer funds to bail out institutions deemed 'too big to fail'. While many policy solutions were tabled, the UK is legislating to reform the structure of the UK banking system, through the Financial Services (Banking Reform) Act 2013, which received royal assent on 18 December 2013. The Act implements key recommendations of the Independent Commission on Banking,[201] including ring-fencing retail deposits from wholesale banking activities, driven at least in part by the reluctant government bailout of the Royal Bank of Scotland in 2008.[202]

The Independent Commission on Banking's objectives for ring-fencing are threefold. First, to ensure that 'ring-fenced' bodies do not do anything that adversely affects the continuity of core services; this will include ensuring they do not take

[199] ibid, para 14. [200] ibid, para 410.

[201] Independent Commission on Banking, Final Report: Recommendations (2011).

[202] For a history of events leading to the failure of RBS, see, eg, Rayner, G, 'Banking Bailout: The Rise and Fall of RBS', *The Daily Telegraph*, 20 January 2009 and Rt Hon George Osborne MP, speech by the Chancellor of the Exchequer on the Reform of Banking, HM Treasury (4 February 2013), 3.

excessive risks. Second, to ensure that they are protected from external risks, in other words insulated from problems elsewhere in the financial system. Third, to ensure that their failure does not put at risk the continuity of core services—that is to ensure that it is possible to sort out failing banks, without recourse to taxpayer support.[203] Under the proposals, ring-fenced bodies would be required to take deposits from, and provide overdrafts to, financial citizens through separate subsidiaries that could not engage in activities that might expose them to loss, such as trading book activities, purchasing loans or securities, and derivatives trading. Such a restriction on risky investments is intended to preserve the bank's business and assets, and thereby to protect the financial citizen's investment. Perhaps the most important collateral benefit of ring-fencing is that 'there is evidence to suggest that … separation has the potential to change the culture of banks for the better and to make banks simpler and easier to monitor'.[204] However, 'if a bank flouts the [new] rules, the regulator and the Treasury will have the power to break it up altogether—full separation, not just a ring-fence … we will electrify the ring-fence'.[205]

Similarly, while there was no fundamental restructuring of the banking industry in the US to return to the separation between investment and commercial banking activities under the Glass–Steagall Act, the substance of the Volcker Rule is intended to insulate the financial citizen from risky trading activities of banks, and therefore preserve their assets. In relevant part, Dodd–Frank prohibits banks from engaging in proprietary trading[206] or acquiring or retaining any equity, partnership, or other ownership interest in a hedge fund or private equity fund.[207]

VI. Conclusion

In this Chapter, we have argued that the consumer interest in financial markets is shaped by the financialization of welfare provision and best examined through the emerging idea of the 'financial citizen'. This captures a restructured relationship of the citizen with government, also promoted by supply side financial institutions and now accepted by the population at large: individuals will 'financialize'

[203] Department for Business, Innovation and Skills, HM Treasury, Banking Reform: A New Structure for Stability and Growth (2013), para 2.15.

[204] Parliamentary Commission on Banking Standards, First Report (December 2012), section 45, reproduced in Department for Business, Innovation and Skills, HM Treasury, Banking Reform: A New Structure for Stability and Growth (2013), section 2.5.

[205] Rt Hon George Osborne MP, speech by the Chancellor of the Exchequer on the Reform of Banking, HM Treasury (4 February 2013), 4.

[206] Section 1851(a)(1)(A).

[207] Section 1851(a)(1)(B).

the provision of their own personal and household welfare needs, especially retirement income. Governments have combined tax support with law and policy in the constitution and regulation of retail investor and consumer participation in financial markets. In so doing they have 'pushed down' risk, and created a paradox that financial citizens simultaneously retain risk to earn return, while the regulator regulates to protect them. The most market-facing policies of 'financial citizenship' promote a classic finance theory version of the consumer interest, which does not acknowledge the political, social, and moral (especially fairness) aspects of markets and the central role of the state. Criticisms of this version of the 'financial citizen' rightly concentrate on the market failures to which consumers are exposed, the illusion of choice which the market promotes, and the unrealistic expectations placed on the 'rational' consumer, revealed by behavioural research.

Despite the consumer interest being less influential than financial capital, the severity of the social effects of losses has translated into political action. Although still financialized, more consumer-facing versions of the financial citizen idea have prevailed in more protective policy phases (after the two greatest market crashes). The consumer interest has evolved from 'investor protection', to 'investor confidence' and more recently to 'consumer protection' and in some places to 'treating clients fairly'. Through a political and social approach to markets it is possible to see who is included, and who is not. The financial citizenship idea demonstrates contemporary exclusion of those who through the effects of technology, globalization, personal endowments, and life chances outside their control do not share the benefits of financialization.

'Where should financial citizens' long-term financial interests lie?'[208] Now more than two decades into the experience (one might say 'experiment') of financialization, the answer to that question is still not clear. However, some things about the consumer interest in financial markets can be said. There seems no political will to reverse financialization, and for the foreseeable future the financial citizen's long-term interest lies in the financial markets. For the foreseeable future, too, the state will strive to regulate the retention of financial risk by its citizens so they may earn returns, wrestling at the same time to protect them. This regulatory work may become more predictable as citizens become market-minded and financially capable; however, this is also a matter for the long term. Something which can also be said with confidence is that markets will continue to provide innovative products and services on which they hope to make money from the financial citizen. Much of where financial citizens' long-term interests lie, therefore, also depends on how well regulatory approaches adopted since the GFC encourage providers to further the consumer interest as well as their own. Finally, it is not too optimistic to hope that it will be the adaptive quality of citizenship, and the potential of citizenship

[208] Gray and Hamilton, n 10 above.

organizations in galvanizing individuals' social experience of financial markets into politico-regulatory action, that will ultimately answer, 'Where should financial citizens' long-term financial interests lie?'

Bibliography

Agarwal, S et al., 'The Age of Reason: Financial Decisions over the Life Cycle and Implications for Regulation' (2009) 51(2) *Brookings Papers on Economic Activity* 86.

Ajzen, I, *Attitudes, Personality and Behavior* (1988).

Allen, F, Demirguc-Kunt, A, Klapper, L, and Peria, M, *The Foundations of Financial Inclusion: Understanding Ownership and Use of Formal Accounts* (2012).

Atkinson, A et al., Levels of Financial Capability in the UK: Results of a Baseline Survey, Financial Services Authority (2006).

Atkinson, A and Messy, F-A, Measuring Financial Literacy: Results of the OECD INFE Pilot Study (2012), OECD Working Papers on Finance, Insurance and Private Pensions No 15.

Australia and New Zealand Banking Group Limited, Adult Financial Literacy in Australia (2011).

Australia and New Zealand Banking Group Limited, ANZ Survey of Adult Financial Literacy in Australia (2003).

Australian Securities and Investments Commission, Complex Products, Report 384 (2014).

Australian Securities and Investments Commission, Report 251 Review of Financial Advice Industry Practice (2011).

Australian Treasury, Tax Expenditure Statement 2010/11.

Bakeer, HK and Haslem, JA, 'The Impact of Investor Socio-economic Characteristics on Risk and Return Preferences' (1974) 2 *Journal of Business Research* 469.

Barber, B and Odean, T, 'All that Glitters: The Effect of Attention and News on the Buying Behavior of Individual and Institutional Investors' (2008) 21 *Review of Financial Studies* 785.

Barber, B and Odean, T, The Behaviour of Individual Investors (2011), available at <http://ssrn.com/abstract=1872211>.

Barber, B and Odean, T, 'Boys Will Be Boys: Gender Overconfidence, and Common Stock Investment' (2001) 116 *Quarterly Journal of Economics* 261.

Barber, B and Odean, T, 'Trading Is Hazardous to your Wealth: The Common Stock Investment Performance of Individual Investors' (2000) 55(2) *Journal of Finance* 773.

Barberis, N, Shleifer, A, and Vishny, R, 'A Model of Investor Sentiment' (1998) 49 *Journal of Financial Economics* 1.

Bar-Gill, O and Warren, E, 'Making Credit Safer' (2008) 157(1) *University of Pennsylvania Law Review* 1.

Barr, M, Mullainathan, S, and Shafir, E, Behaviorally Informed Financial Services Regulation (2008), report prepared for the New America Foundation.

Ben-Shahar, O and Schneider, C, The Failure of Mandated Disclosure (2010), University of Chicago Law and Economics Olin Working Paper No 516.

Benartzi, S and Thaler, RH, 'Heuristics and Biases in Retirement Savings Behavior' (2007) 21 *Journal of Economic Perspectives* 81.

Benos, AV, 'Overconfident Speculators in Call Markets: Trade Patterns and Survival' (1998) 1 *Journal of Financial Markets* 353.
Bergstresser, D, Chalmers, J, and Tufano, P, 'Assessing the Costs and Benefits of Brokers in the Mutual Fund Industry' 22 *Review of Financial Studies* 4129.
Berry, C and Serra, V, *Financial Citizenship: Rethinking the State's Role in Enabling Individuals to Save* (2012).
Beshears, J et al., How Does Simplified Disclosure Affect Individual's Mutual Fund Choices? (2008) National Bureau of Economic Research Working Paper No 14859.
Black, B, 'Behavioural Economics and Investor Protection: Reasonable Investors and Efficient Markets' (2012–13) 44 *Loyola University Chicago Law Journal* 1493.
Black, B, 'Protecting the Retail Investor in an Age of Financial Uncertainty' (2009) 34 *University of Dayton Law Review* 5.
Black, J, 'Reconceiving Financial Markets—from the Economic to the Social' (2013) 13(2) *Journal of Corporate Law Studies* 401.
Bloomfield, R and Hales, J, 'Predicting the Next Step of a Random Walk: Experimental Evidence of Regime-Shifting Beliefs' (2002) 65 *Journal of Financial Economics* 397.
Bradley, C, 'Disorderly Conduct: Day Traders and the Ideology of "Fair and Orderly Markets"' (2000) 26(1) *Journal of Corporation Law* 63.
Braithwaite, J, *Regulatory Capitalism: How it Works and Ideas for Making it Work Better* (2008).
Brown, S et al., 'Debt and Financial Expectations: An Individual and Household Level Analysis' (2005) 41(1) *Economic Enquiry* 100.
Burkett, I and Drew, B, *Financial Inclusion, Market Failure and New Markets: Possibilities for Community Development Finance Institutions in Australia* (2008).
Caballe, J and Sakovics, J, 'Speculating Against an Overconfident Market' (2003) 6 *Journal of Financial Markets* 199.
Campbell, DT, 'Social Attitudes and Other Acquired Behavioral Dispositions' in Koch, S (ed.), *Psychology: A Study of Science* (1963) 94.
Campbell, J et al., 'Consumer Financial Protection' (2011) 25(1) *Journal of Economic Perspectives* 91.
Campbell, JY, 'Household Finance' (2006) 61 *Journal of Finance* 1553.
Cervone, D and Peake, PK, 'Anchoring, Efficacy, and Action: The Influence of Judgment Heuristics on Self-Efficacy Judgments and Behavior' (1986) 50 *Journal of Personality and Social Psychology* 492.
Chapman, GB and Johnson, EJ, 'The Limits of Anchoring' (1994) 7 *Journal of Behavioral Decision Making* 223.
Chater, N, Huck, S, and Inderst, R, Consumer Decision-Making in Retail Investment Services: A Behavioural Economics Perspective, Final Report to the European Commission/SANCO (2010).
Chen, J, Hong, H, and Kubik, J, 'Outsourcing Mutual Fund Management: Firm Boundaries, Incentives and Performance' (2013) 68(2) *Journal of Finance* 523.
Chowdry, B, 'Can Financial Citizenship Begin at Birth?' (2012) *Stanford Social Innovation Review* 17.
Citi Australia and the Australia Institute, Evidence Versus Emotion: How Do We Really Make Financial Decisions? (December 2010).
Cohn, RA et al., 'Individual Financial Risk Aversion and Investment Portfolio Composition' (1975) 30 *Journal of Finance* 605.

Cole, S and Kartini Shastry, G, If You Are So Smart, Why Aren't You Rich? The Effects of Education, Financial Literacy, and Cognitive Ability on Financial Market Participation (2012), available at <http://ssrn.com/abstract=1317298>.

Commonwealth of Australia, Financial System Inquiry: Final Report (1997).

Commonwealth of Australia, Inquiry into Financial Products and Services in Australia (2009).

Commonwealth of Australia, Review into the Governance, Efficiency, Structure and Operation of Australia's Superannuation System (2010), Final Report Part I Overview.

Condon, M and Philipps, L, 'Transitional Market Governance and Economic Citizenship: New Frontiers of Feminist Theory' (2006) 28 *Thomas Jefferson Law Review* 105.

Cooper, J, Deputy Commissioner ASIC, Helping Retail Investors (2009), speech to the SPAA National Conference.

Cooper, M, Gulen, H, and Rau, P, 'Changing Names with Style: Mutual Fund Name Changes and their Effects on Fund Flows' (2005) 60 *Journal of Finance* 2825.

Cox, JC and Grether, DM, 'The Preference Reversal Phenomenon: Response Mode, Markets and Incentives' (1996) 7(3) *Economic Theory* 381.

Davidoff, S and Hill, C, 'The Limits of Disclosure' (2013) 32(2) *Seattle University Law Review* 599.

Davis, K, *Regulatory Reform Post the Global Financial Crisis: An Overview* (2011).

De Marzo, P, Vayanos, D, and Zwiebel, J, 'Persuasion Bias, Social Influence and Uni-Dimensional Opinions' (2003) 118(3) *Quarterly Journal of Economics* 909.

Delanty, G, *Citizenship in a Global Age* (2000).

Diacon, S and Hasseldine, J, 'Framing Effects and Risk Perception: The Effect of Prior Performance Presentation Format on Investment Fund Choice' (2007) 28(1) *Journal of Economic Psychology* 31.

Donald, S, 'What's in a Name?' (2011) 33 *Sydney Law Review* 295.

Dorn, D and Sengmueller, P, 'Trading as Entertainment?' (2009) 55(4) *Management Science* 591.

Epley, N and Gilovich, T, 'The Anchoring and Adjustment Heuristic' 17(4) *Psychological Science* 311.

Epstein, G, Financialization, Rentier Interests, and Central Bank Policy (2010), manuscript, Department of Economics, University of Massachusetts.

Fenton-O'Creevy, M et al., 'Trading on Illusions: Unrealistic Perceptions of Control and Trading Performance' (2003) 76(1) *Journal of Occupational and Organizational Psychology* 53.

Financial Conduct Authority, Applying Behavioural Economics at the Financial Conduct Authority (April 2013).

Financial Conduct Authority, Policy Statement 13, The FCA's Use of Temporary Product Intervention Rules (2013).

Financial Services Authority, Distribution of Retail Investments: Delivering the RDR—Feedback to CP 18/09 and Final Rules (2010).

Financial Services Authority, Evidence of Impact: An Overview of Financial Education Evaluations, Consumer Research Report 68 (2008).

Financial Services Authority, Retail Distribution Review: Independent and Restricted Advice—Finalised Guidance (2012).

Financial Services Authority, Treating Customers Fairly: Towards Fair Outcomes for Consumers (2006).

FINRA Investor Education Foundation, National Financial Education Study (2012).
Fox, J, Bartholomae, S, and Lee, J, 'Building the Case for Financial Education' (2005) 391 *The Journal of Consumer Affairs* 195.
Frieder, L, Evidence on Behavioral Biases in Trading Activity (2004), University of California, Los Angeles Working Paper.
G20, G20 Leaders Declaration, Los Cabos, Mexico (2012).
Georgakopoulos, NL, 'Why Should Disclosure Rules Subsidize Informed Traders?' (1996) 16 *International Review of Law and Economics* 417.
George, JT and Hwang, C, 'The 52-week High and Momentum Investing' (2004) 59 *Journal of Finance* 2145.
Gilson, RJ and Gordon, JN, 'The Agency Costs of Agency Capitalism: Activist Investors and the Re-evaluation of Governance Rights' (2013) 113 *Columbia Law Review* 863.
Glaser, M et al., 'Framing Effects in Stock Market Forecasts: The Difference Between Asking for Prices and Asking for Returns' (2007) 11(2) *Review of Finance* 325.
Glaser, M and Weber, M, 'Overconfidence and Trading Volume' (2007) 32 *Geneva Risk Insurance Review* 1.
Gray, J, 'Financial Regulation before and after Northern Rock' in Akseli, O, Gray, J, and Campell, D (eds), *Financial Regulation in Crisis?* (2014).
Gray, J, 'Toward a More Resilient Financial System' (2013) 36(2) *Seattle University Law Review* 799.
Gray, J and Hamilton, J, *Implementing Financial Regulation* (2006).
Grinblatt, M and Keloharju, M, 'Sensation Seeking, Overconfidence and Trading Activity' (2009) 64(2) *Journal of Finance* 549.
Grinblatt, M and Keloharju, M, 'What Makes Investors Trade?' (2001) 51 *Journal of Finance* 589.
Hannig, A and Jansen, S, Financial Inclusion and Financial Stability: Current Policy Issues (2010) ADBI Working Paper No 259.
Hazen TL, *The Law of Securities Regulation* (1996).
Hirshleifer, D, 'Investment Psychology and Asset Pricing' (2001) 56 *Journal of Finance* 1533.
Hirshleifer, D and Subrahmanyam, A, 'Investor Psychology and Security Market Under- and Overreactions' (1998) 53 *Journal of Finance* 1893.
Hirshleifer, D and Teoh, SH, 'Herd Behaviour and Cascading in Capital Markets: A Review and Synthesis' (2003) 9 *European Financial Management* 25.
HM Treasury, Department for Business Innovation & Skills, A New Approach to Financial Regulation: Consultation on Reforming the Consumer Credit Regime (2010).
Hogarth, JM, 'Financial Literacy and Family & Consumer Sciences' (2002) 941 *Journal of Family and Consumer Sciences* 14.
Hohnen, P and Hjort, T, 'Citizens as Consumers: A Discussion of New Emergent Forms of Marginalisation in Nordic Welfare States' (2009) 11(3) *European Journal of Social Security* 271.
Hong, H, Kubik, JD, and Stein, JC, 'Social Interaction and Stock Market Participation' (2004) 59(1) *Journal of Finance* 137.
House of Commons, Treasury Select Committee, *The Run on the Rock* (2008).
Howells, G, 'The Potential and Limits of Consumer Empowerment by Information' (2005) 32(3) *Journal of Law and Society* 349.
Hu, H, 'Too Complex to Depict? Innovation, "Pure Information," and the SEC Disclosure Paradigm' (2012) 90 *Texas Law Review* 160.

Jacowitz, KE and Kahneman, D, 'Measures of Anchoring in Estimation Tasks' (1995) 21(11) *Personality and Social Psychology Bulletin* 1161.

Jain, PC and Wu, JS, 'Truth in Mutual Fund Advertising: Evidence on Future Performance and Fund Flows' (2000) 55(2) *Journal of Finance* 937.

Jennings, R et al., *Securities Regulation* (8th edn, 1998).

Jolls, C, Sunstein, CR, and Thaler, R, 'A Behavioural Approach to Law and Economics' (1998) 50 *Stanford Law Review* 1470.

Kahneman, D and Tversky, A, 'Judgment under Uncertainty: Heuristics and Biases' (1973) 185 (4157) *Science* 1124.

Kannadasan, M, 'Risk Appetite and Attitudes of Retail Investors with Special Reference to Capital Market' (2006) 41(6) *The Management Accountant* 448.

Kay, J, *Culture and Prosperity: The Truth about Markets, Why Some Countries Are Rich and Others Remain Poor* (2005).

Kempson, E and Collard, S, *Developing a Vision for Financial Inclusion* (2012).

Kingsford Smith, D, 'Can There Be a *Fair* Share? Fairness Regulation and Financial Markets' in Sarra, J (ed.), *Explorations of Fairness* (2013).

Kingsford Smith, D, 'Financial Services Regulation and the Investor as Consumer' in Howells et al. (eds), *The Handbook of Research on International Consumer Law* (2011) 431.

Kingsford Smith, D, 'Regulating Investment Risk: Individuals and the Global Financial Crisis' (2009) 32(2) *University of New South Wales Law Journal* 514.

Kingsford Smith, D and Williamson, K, 'How Do Online Investors Seek Information and What Does This Mean for Regulation?' 2004 (2) *The Journal of Information Law and Technology* 12, available at <http://www2.warwick.ac.uk/fac/soc/law/elj/jilt/2004_2/kingsford-smithandwilliamson>.

Kostakopoulou, D, *The Future Governance of Citizenship* (2008).

Langevoort, D and Thompson R, IPOS and the Slow Death of Section 5 (2013), available at <http://ssrn.com/abstract=2316858>.

Loewenstein, G, O'Donoghue, T, and Rabin, M, 'Projection Bias in Predicting Future Utility' (2003) 118(4) *Quarterly Journal of Economics* 1209.

Lundeberg, M, Fox, P, and Puncochar, J, 'Highly Confident but Wrong: Gender Differences and Similarities in Confidence Judgment' (1994) 86(1) *Journal of Educational Psychology* 114.

Lusardi, A and Mitchell, OS, 'Baby Boomer Retirement Security: The Roles of Planning, Financial Literacy, and Housing Wealth' (2007) 54(1) *Journal of Monetary Economics* 205.

Lusardi, A and Mitchell, OS, 'Financial Literacy around the World: An Overview' (2011) 10(4) *Journal of Pension Economics and Finance* 497.

Lusardi, A and Mitchell, OS, 'Planning and Financial Literacy: How Do Women Fare?' (2008) 98(2) *The American Economic Review* 413.

Lyons, A et al., 'Are We Making the Grade? A National Overview of Financial Education and Program Evaluation' (2006) 402 *Journal of Consumer Affairs* 208.

Malmendier, U and Shanthikumar, D, 'Are Small Investors Naïve about Incentives?' 85 *Journal of Financial Economics* 457.

Markowitz, H, 'Portfolio Selection' (1952) 7(1) *Journal of Finance* 77.

Marsat, S and Williams, B, Does the Price Influence the Assessment of Fundamental Value? Experimental Evidence (2009), available at <http://ssrn.com/abstract=1938927>.

Marshall, J, 'Financial Institutions in Disadvantaged Areas: A Comparative Analysis of Policies Encouraging Financial Inclusion in Britain and the United States' (2004) 36 *Environment and Planning A* 241.

Mendales, RE, 'Collateralized Explosive Devices: Why Securities Regulation Failed to Prevent the CDO Meltdown, and How to Fix It' (2009) 5 *University of Illinois Law Review* 1359.

Miharsonarina, A and Kpodar, K, 'Mobile Phones, Financial Inclusion and Growth' (2012) 3(2) *Review of Economics and Institutions*.

Modigliani, F and Miller, MH, 'The Cost of Capital, Corporation Finance and the Theory of Investment' (1958) 48(3) *American Economic Review* 655.

Moloney, N, *How to Protect Investors* (2010).

Moloney, N, 'The Investor Model Underlying the EU's Investor Protection Regime: Consumers or Investors?' (2012) 13 *European Business Organization Law Review* 169.

Morris, S and Shin, H, 'Risk Management with Interdependent Choice' (1999) 15(3) *Oxford Review of Economic Policy* 52.

Northcraft, G and Neale, M, 'Experts, Amateurs, and Real Estate: An Anchoring and Adjustment Perspective on Property Pricing Decisions' (1987) 39 *Organizational Behavior and Human Decision Processes* 84.

Nosfsinger, JR, 'Social Mood and Financial Economics' (2005) 6(3) *The Journal of Behavioural Finance* 144.

OECD, G-20 High Level Principles on Financial Consumer Protection (2011).

OECD, Improving Financial Literacy: Analysis of Issues and Policy (2005).

OECD INFE, Measuring Financial Literacy: Pilot Results from 14 Countries (2012).

OECD INFE, OECD/INFE High-Level Principles on National Strategies for Financial Education (2012).

Palley, T, *Financialisation and the Financial Sector* (2013).

Paredes, T, 'Blinded by the Light: Information Overload and its Consequences for Securities Regulation' (2003) 81 *Washington University Law Quarterly* 417.

Parliamentary Joint Committee on Corporations and Financial Services, Inquiry into Financial Products and Services in Australia (2009).

Pearson, G, 'Financial Literacy and the Creation of Financial Citizens' in Kelly-Louw, M, Nehf, J, and Rott, R (eds), *The Future of Consumer Credit Regulation: Creative Approaches to Emerging Problems* (2008).

Persaud, A, 'Sending the Herd off the Cliff Edge: The Disturbing Interaction Between Herding and Market-Sensitive Risk Management Practices' in de Larosière, J, *Essays on Global Finance* (2000).

Pompain, M, *Behavioural Finance and Wealth Management: How to Build Investment Strategies that Account for Investor Bias* (2011).

Quattrone, GA et al., Explorations in Anchoring: The Effects of Prior Range, Anchor Extremity and Suggestive Hints (1984), Stanford University Working Paper.

Raskin, S, Speech on 'Economic and Financial Inclusion in 2011', US Federal Reserve System.

Ritter, J, 'Behavioural Finance' (2003) 11(4) *Pacific-Basin Finance Journal* 429.

Root, A, *Market Citizenship: Experiments in Democracy and Globalisation* (2007).

Roszkowski, MJ, 'Risk Tolerance in Financial Decisions' in Cordell, DM (ed.), *Readings in Financial Planning* (1998).

Roszkowski, MJ, Snelbecker, GE, and Leimberg, SR, 'Risk-tolerance and Risk Aversion' in Leimberg, SR et al. (eds), *The Tools and Techniques of Financial Planning* (1993).

Rutledge, SL, Consumer Protection and Financial Literacy: Lessons from Nine Country Studies (2010), World Bank Policy Research Working Paper No 5326.

Scammell, M, 'The Internet and Civic Engagement: The Age of the Citizen-Consumer' (2000) 17 *Political Communication* 351.

Schade, C and Koellinger, P, 'Heuristics, Biases and the Behavior of Entrepreneurs' in Minniti, M (ed.), *Entrepreneurship—the Engine of Growth—People* (Vol 1, 2006) 42.

Scherbina, A, Asset Price Bubbles: A Selective Survey (2013), IMF Working Paper WP/13/45.

Schwarcz, S, 'Disclosure's Failure in the Subprime Mortgage Crisis' (2008) *Utah Law Review* 1109.

Schwarcz, S, 'Regulating Complexity in Financial Markets' (2009) 87 *Washington University Law Review* 211.

Schwarcz, S, 'Rethinking the Disclosure Paradigm in a World of Complexity' (2004) 1 *University of Illinois Law Review* 1.

Securities and Exchange Commission, Chair Mary Jo White, Remarks at the 10th Annual Transatlantic Corporate Governance Dialogue (3 December 2013), Washington DC.

Securities and Exchange Commission Office of Investigations, Investigation of the SEC's Failure to Uncover Bernard Madoff's Ponzi Scheme (2009).

Shah, AK and Oppenheimer, DM, 'Heuristics Made Easy: An Effort-Reduction Framework' (2008) 134(2) *Psychological Bulletin* 207.

Sharpe, W, 'Capital Asset Prices: A Theory of Market Equilibrium under Conditions of Risk' (1964) 19(3) *Journal of Finance* 425.

Shefrin, H, *Beyond Greed and Fear: Understanding Behavioural Finance and the Psychology of Investing* (2007).

Shefrin, H and Statman, M, 'The Disposition to Sell Winners too Early and Ride Losers too Long: Theory and Evidence' (1985) 40(3) *The Journal of Finance* 777.

Shiller, R, Investor Behavior in the October 1987 Stock Market Crash: Survey Evidence (1987), National Bureau of Economic Research Working Paper No 2446.

Shiller, R, *Irrational Exuberance* (2000).

Shu, P, Chiu, S, Chen, H, and Yeh, Y, 'Does Trading Improve Individual Investor Performance?' (2004) 22(3) *Review of Quantitative Finance and Accounting* 199.

Simon, H, 'Theories of Bounded Rationality' in McGuire, CB and Radner, R (eds), *Decision and Organization* (1972).

Soderquist, LD and Gabaldon, TA, *Securities Regulation* (4th edn, 1999).

Steul, M, 'Does the Framing of Investment Portfolios Influence Risk-Taking Behavior? Some Experimental Results' (2006) 27(4) *Journal of Economic Psychology* 557.

Taffler, RJ, 'The Representativeness Heuristic' in Kent Baker, H and Nofsinger, JR, *Behavioral Finance: Investors, Corporations and Markets* (2010).

Taylor, JB, The Financial Crisis and the Policy Responses: An Empirical Analysis of What Went Wrong (2009), National Bureau of Economic Research Working Paper No 14631.

Thaler, R and Sunstein, C, *Nudge: Improving Decisions about Health, Wealth and Happiness* (2008).

Tomoskovic-Devey, D and Lin, K, 'Financialisation: Causes, Income Consequences and Policy Implications' (2013) 18 *North Carolina Banking Institute* 167.

Tversky, A and Kahneman, D, 'The Framing of Decisions and the Psychology of Choice' (1981) 211(4481) *Science* 453.

Tversky, A and Thaler, R, 'Anomalies: Preference Reversal' (1990) 4(2) *Journal of Economic Perspectives* 201.

Weinstein, N, 'Unrealistic Optimism about Future Life Events' (1980) 39(5) *Journal of Personality and Social Psychology* 806.

Wheale, PR and Amin, LH, 'Bursting the Dot.com Bubble: A Case Study in Investor Behaviour' (2003) 15(1) *Technology Analysis & Strategic Management* 117.

Williams, C, 'The Securities and Exchange Commission and Corporate Social Transparency' (1999) 11(6) *Harvard Law Review* 1197.

Williams, T, 'Empowerment of Whom and for What? Financial Literacy Education and the New Regulation of Consumer Financial Services' (2007) 29(2) *Law & Policy* 226.

Williamson, K and Kingsford Smith, D, 'Empowered or Vulnerable? The Role of Information for Australian Online Investors' (2010) 34(1) *Canadian Journal of Information and Library Science*.

Willis, LE, 'Against Financial Literacy Education' (2008) 94 *Iowa Law Review* 197.

Wilson, T, 'Consumer Credit Regulation and Rights-based Social Justice: Addressing Financial Exclusion and Meeting the Credit Needs of Low Income Australians' (2012) 35(2) *University of New South Wales Law Journal* 501.

Wilson, T, 'The Inadequacy of the Current Regulatory Response to Payday Lending' (2004) *Australian Business Law Review* 193.

Xu, L and Zia, B, Financial Literacy around the World: An Overview of the Evidence with Practical Solutions for the Way Forward (2012), World Bank Policy Research Working Paper No 6107.

Yao, R and Hanna, S, 'The Effect of Gender and Marital Status on Financial Risk Tolerance' (2005) 4(1) *Journal of Personal Finance* 66.

Yeung, K, 'Nudge as Fudge' (2012) 75(1) *Modern Law Review* 122.

CHAPTER 24

REGULATING THE RETAIL MARKETS

NIAMH MOLONEY

I. Introduction

THIS Chapter considers the main features and evolution of the regulatory treatment of retail investors (or individual/household consumers of investment products which are designed to deliver market-based returns and so carry exposure to market risk) and of related policy and scholarship.[1]

The risks faced by this group of financial consumers are distinct to those faced by consumers of financial products more generally (such as credit/banking, mortgage, and insurance products).[2] Consumers of consumer finance products carry, for the most part, less market risk, but the regulatory regime governing such products is increasingly reflecting the particular risks which follow from their ubiquity and the distinct market failures to which the consumer finance market is prone.[3] Access to finance and related exclusion risks are also acute with respect to consumer finance more generally, as discussed in the Chapter by Kingsford Smith and Dixon in this volume. The retail investment markets, by contrast, are smaller although growing, have a more discretionary quality, and the nature of the information asymmetries which drive the market failures in this market are particularly acute given the market risk engaged. Given the importance of household/individual capital to the allocation of resources on an economy-wide basis through market mechanisms, and the increasing need for household/individual provision for welfare needs to be achieved through long-term market savings, the regulatory design choices are also distinct.

Retail market regulatory policy and related retail market scholarship has, at various stages over the last number of decades, been something of a Cinderella when considered in the context of financial regulation and related scholarship more generally. Although the financial crisis, for example, could have been characterized in terms of a 'too many to fail' problem given the extent to which individuals and households were (and are) exposed to the financial markets, the 'too big to fail' characterization has dominated.[4] In many jurisdictions (not all) retail market reforms were not to the fore of the crisis-era reform movement. This subsidiary position reflects the generally fleeting nature of regulatory and governmental attention to, and the typically fluid conceptions of, retail market regulation over time.

Section II considers the different objectives which have shaped retail market regulation, Section III examines the particular challenges which regulatory design poses in the retail markets, Section IV considers foundational governance issues, and Section V considers the three main tools of retail market intervention—disclosure, distribution, and product intervention. Section VI briefly concludes.

[1] It does not address the supervisory and enforcement elements of retail market governance.

[2] See further the Chapter by Kingsford Smith and Dixon in this volume.

[3] For a leading analysis of the need for protection with respect to consumer finance products, given their necessity and ubiquity, see Warren, E, 'Product Safety Regulation as a Model for Financial Services Regulation' (2008) 42 *Journal of Consumer Affairs* 452.

[4] As argued in Zingales, L, 'The Future of Securities Regulation' (2009) 47 *Journal of Accounting Research* 391.

II. Regulating the Retail Markets

1. The origins of retail market regulation

Retail-market-orientated regulation is a relative newcomer among the ever-shifting components of modern financial regulation. Certainly, the US 1933 Securities Act, 1934 Securities Exchange Act, 1940 Investment Advisers Act, and 1940 Investment Company Act—often regarded as the foundations of modern capital market regulation—were originally designed with a strong retail market orientation. The foundational twin pillars of the US regime (the 1933 and 1934 Acts), for example, associated the provision of information on investments with the protection of small investors. But the issuer-disclosure elements, in particular, of the US regime would soon become associated with the support of market efficiency, liquidity, and transparency more generally and to a certain extent would become disassociated from retail market protection, at least in the scholarly debate.[5] In the EU, to take another example, although the harmonized regime governing the EU financial system dates back to the late 1970s and to the initial attempts to regulate the banking market and issuer disclosure, the retail markets would not receive serious regulatory attention at EU level until the 2004 adoption of the Markets in Financial Instruments Directive I (MiFID I).[6]

Although the drivers of financial regulation are many and contested (see further the Chapter by Deakin in this volume), the slow development of retail market regulation can be associated relatively easily with the limited engagement by households with market investments (certainly outside the US) until the closing decades of the twentieth century.[7] In the UK, for example, while the classic tools of capital market regulation (or close substitutes for them)—including issuer disclosure requirements and insider dealing rules—were in place by the mid-twentieth century,[8] it would not be until 2000 and the establishment of the Financial Services Authority (FSA) and its related regulatory infrastructure that a sophisticated and holistic retail market regulatory regime

[5] Famously and influentially in Easterbrook, F and Fischel, D, 'Mandatory Disclosure and the Protection of Investors' (1984) 70 *Virginia Law Review* 1335.

[6] Directive 2004/39/EC [2004] OJ L145/1.

[7] On the development of household investment portfolios internationally see Guido, L, Sapienza, P, and Zingales, L, *Household Portfolios* (2001).

[8] Cheffins, B, 'Does Law Matter? The Separation of Ownership and Control in the United Kingdom' (2001) 30 *Journal of Legal Studies* 459.

began to emerge[9] and to address the risks faced by the growing constituency of household investors.[10]

2. The objectives of retail market regulation

(a) *Protecting investors*

In some respects the objectives and targets of retail market regulation might be regarded as comparatively straightforward. Retail market regulation has certainly not experienced to the same extent the often radical cycles of reform and deregulation, and related perimeter redesigns, that beset financial regulation (and, in particular, wholesale (or professional) market regulation) more generally. It has, for the most part, been on an ever-intensifying regulatory trajectory and been concerned with a (very broadly) stable set of market actors. The wholesale market regulatory pyrotechnics demanded by the financial crisis and arising from the need to engage with, *inter alia*, myriad new technical complexities, complex and elusive objectives relating to market stability and liquidity, a shifting regulatory perimeter, frequently uncharted regulatory territory, and international coordination risks are relatively unknown to retail market design. Similarly, the 'regulatory sine curve', which can be associated with the repeated waves of regulation and deregulation which characterize wholesale financial market regulation and, in particular, the contrasting pre-financial-crisis and crisis-era regulatory periods,[11] is not a feature of the development of retail market regulation. While retail market risks do experience cycles of growth and change, in a number of core respects the challenges and the regulatory landscape are relatively well settled.

Retail market regulation has, from the outset, been concerned with addressing market failures arising from the gaping information asymmetry between retail investors and professional market actors (initially, primarily issuers of securities and, subsequently, extending to suppliers of investment products and investment advisers as

[9] The roots of modern retail market regulation in the UK go further back, however. In particular, the late 1980s saw intense government efforts to address risks in the investment advice sector following a major pension mis-selling scandal, as noted in Section V. See further Black, J and Nobles, R, 'Pension Misselling: The Causes and Lessons of Regulatory Failure' (1998) 61 *Modern Law Review* 789. On the development of household investment in the UK see Ertürk, I, Froud, J, Johal, S, Leaver, A, and Williams, K, 'The Democratization of Finance? Promises, Outcomes and Conditions' (2007) 14 *Review of International Political Economy* 553.

[10] The establishment of the FSA is associated in particular with the failure of the hybrid self-regulatory system set up under the Financial Services Act 1986 to contain mis-selling scandals: Ferran, E, 'Examining the UK Experience in Adopting the UK Single Financial Regulator Model' (2003) 28 *Brooklyn Journal of International Law* 257.

[11] Coffee, J, 'The Political Economy of Dodd-Frank: Why Financial Reform Tends to Be Frustrated and Systemic Risk Perpetuated' (2012) 97 *Cornell Law Review* 1019.

retail investment has become increasingly intermediated[12]) and from the related risks and costs.[13] These risks and costs are exacerbated by the agency relationship which strongly characterizes retail investor engagement with the markets, given the extent to which intermediation of one form or other (such as advised sales or investment in collective investment schemes) characterizes the retail markets.[14] They are also exacerbated by the severe behavioural risks to which retail investors are exposed. As is further discussed in the Chapter by Kingsford Smith and Dixon in this volume, an extensive literature and a rapidly growing empirical data set make clear that retail investors are vulnerable to significant decision-making weaknesses and to biases which damage optimum decision-making. Retail investors are vulnerable to these weaknesses and biases being exploited and, absent exploitation, to making poor investment decisions.

These risks to retail investors are generated through a number of channels. Retail markets vary significantly in structure and features internationally. The US retail investment market, for example, has long been associated with direct household investment in equities (often through personal pension accounts (the 401k)) and collective investment schemes (mutual funds).[15] UK investors tend to focus on packaged products of various types.[16] French investors favour insurance-related investments, while Italian investors have long invested in government bonds.[17] The Australian market is strongly characterized by the mandatory superannuation scheme which requires employees to invest in personal pension accounts.[18] But whatever the market structure and investment profile, intermediation channels of various types typically characterize most retail markets. In particular, retail investors rely heavily on market intermediation in the form of investment product distribution (whether of traditional securities or manufactured products, and through brokerage, advice, or other distribution channels); more advanced forms of intermediation, such as discretionary asset management, tend to be reserved to

[12] For a US perspective see Langevoort, D, 'The SEC, Retail Investors, and the Institutionalization of the Securities Markets' (2009) 95 *Virginia Law Review* 1025 and for an EU perspective see Moloney, N, *How to Protect Investors. Lessons from the EC and UK* (2010) 31–6.

[13] eg Howells, G, 'The Potential and Limits of Consumer Empowerment by Information' (2005) 32 *Journal of Law and Society* 349 and Garten, H, 'The Consumerization of Financial Regulation' (1999) 77 *Washington University Law Quarterly* 287.

[14] eg Choi, S, 'A Framework for the Regulation of Securities Market Intermediaries' (2004) 1 *Berkeley Business Law Journal* 45 and Mahoney, P, 'Manager-Investor Conflicts in Mutual Funds' (2004) 18 *Journal of Economic Perspectives* 161.

[15] eg Zingales, L, *A Capitalism for the People* (2012) and Campbell, J, 'Household Finance' (2006) 61 *Journal of Finance* 1553.

[16] Moloney, n 12 above, 36–7.

[17] On EU investment patterns see further Decision Technology, Chater, N, Huck, S, Inderst, R, and Online Interactive Research, Consumer Decision Making in Retail Investment Services: A Behavioural Economics Perspective (2010).

[18] eg, Australian Financial Planning Association, Financial System Inquiry Submission (31 March 2014).

the most affluent and sophisticated segment of the retail market. But product distribution (including brokerage services provided by the multi-service firm where the firm has multiple relationships with the issuer of securities) is vulnerable to deep conflict of interest risks arising from the limited ability of retail investors to monitor the incidence of commission and similar incentive risks. Exacerbating these risks, investment products can be poorly designed, overly complex, and have a tendency to proliferate, reflecting a failure of market discipline which in turn reflects retail investor decision-making difficulties and incentive risks in the product distribution chain. Retail investors can also face severe difficulties with product and distribution-related disclosures.

The classical regulatory design response to market failures of this type is to correct the foundational information failure by means of disclosure requirements, and thereby to support investors in achieving efficient bargains. But in the retail markets, even allowing for the long tradition of disclosure-related regulation, regulation has long been more interventionist and supportive of the investor decision.[19] Vestiges of the *caveat emptor* principle, which can be strongly associated with the disclosure-based regulation which characterized the early evolution of retail market regulation,[20] can still be found in modern retail market regulation. The EU regime, for example, provides for execution-only trades to be carried out without the support of investment advice albeit that information-related requirements apply.[21] But *caveat emptor*, which was never well entrenched in retail investment regulation,[22] has been in retreat for some time. To return to the EU execution-only example, EU regulation, while supporting execution-only trades, also specifies and limits the nature of the investments which can be purchased through execution-only channels without any form of investment advice. It also, to take a different example, empowers and requires national regulators to prohibit the sale of investment products in defined circumstances.[23] While these examples are EU-specific and from the crisis-era, retail regulation internationally has long sought to address the major market failures which trouble the retail markets through an array of interventionist regulatory tools, including product design rules (initially primarily

[19] For an early discussion see Clark, R, 'The Soundness of Financial Intermediaries' (1976) 86 *Yale Law Journal* 1.

[20] One of the most famous characterizations of which is that by Louis Loss, one of the fathers of modern US securities regulation, who argued that regulation was not designed to take away from the citizen his right to make a fool of himself, but sought to prevent others from making a fool of him: Loss, L and Seligman, J, *Fundamentals of Securities Regulation* (3rd edn, 1998) 177.

[21] Directive 2014/65/EU [2014] OJ L173/349 (Markets in Financial Instruments Directive II (MiFID II)), Article 25.

[22] For an early challenge to *caveat emptor* by one of the fathers of modern UK financial regulation (LCB Gower) see Gower, L, Review of Investor Protection: A Discussion Document (1982) and Gower, L, Review of Investor Protection: Report Part 1 (1984).

[23] Markets in Financial Instruments Regulation (MiFIR) (EU) No 600/2014 [2014] OJ L173/84, Articles 39–43.

in the form of rules addressing the governance and structure of collective investment schemes[24]) and distribution rules (including conduct rules relating to fair treatment, the quality of advice, and conflict of interest management), as well as disclosure requirements. While these tools have long existed in some form, they have become increasingly sophisticated over time and particularly since the closing years of the twentieth century. A related degree of regulatory paternalism has similarly always been a feature of retail market regulation.[25] This has become more marked over time, particularly as the findings of behavioural finance, and the related regulatory commitment to more robust attention to market failures and to the need to shape the retail investor's investment decision, have come to shape regulatory intervention and conceptions of paternalism.[26]

(b) *Empowering investors*

But retail market regulation has experienced at least one cycle of notable change, albeit not of the scale of the crisis-era cycle of change which has transformed wholesale market financial regulation. In the decade or so prior to the financial crisis, and reflecting wider support for more intense 'financialization',[27] retail-market-orientated regulation became strongly associated with the promotion of long-term household saving through the markets and with the related regulatory and policy construction of the independent, empowered, 'financial citizen', engaged with market-based saving.[28] This reflected the imposition (then but also now) of greater responsibility for financial planning and welfare provision on individuals and households, the increasing privatization of welfare, and the seeking by governments of stronger individual financial independence. Market investment had by the closing decade of the twentieth century become increasingly necessary to finance retirement, education, and other social needs, and was becoming more of a mass market, consumer activity and less a speculative, wealth accumulation

[24] For an early example see the US Investment Company Act 1940. As early as 1936, the UK government commissioned an inquiry into the activities of the 'unit trust' (a form of collective investment introduced in the UK in 1931) sector: Fixed Trusts: Report of the Departmental Committee Appointed by the Board of Trade (1936).

[25] Ogus, A, 'Regulatory Paternalism: When Is it Justified' in Hopt, K, Wymeersch, E, Kanda, H, and Baum, H (eds), *Corporate Governance in Context* (2005) 303.

[26] For an early examination of how the findings of behavioural finance can shape regulatory paternalism see Camerer, C, Issacharoff, S, Loewenstein, G, O'Donoghue, T, and Rabin, M, 'Regulation for Conservatives: Behavioral Economics and the Case for "Asymmetric Paternalism"' (2002–03) 151 *University of Pennsylvania Law Review* 1211 and for a recent reassessment see Sunstein, C, *Why Nudge? The Politics of Libertarian Paternalism* (2014).

[27] Associated with the completion of markets and the growth of finance (eg, Deakin, S, 'The Rise of Finance: What Is It, What Might Be Driving It, What Might Stop It?' (2008) 30 *Comparative Labour Law & Policy Journal* 67) and, in particular, with the facilitative international regulatory policy prior to the financial crisis (see, eg, IMF, Global Financial Stability Report (April 2006), ch 1).

[28] See further the Chapter by Kingsford Smith and Dixon in this volume on the nature of the 'financial citizen'.

activity reserved to the few.[29] Households and individuals were accordingly being 'empowered' and 'financialized',[30] in part through regulation, and markets were becoming 'democratized' through large-scale public participation, whether direct or indirect.[31] Retail market regulation came to display 'marketing'[32] and 'responsibilizing' characteristics[33] and to promote the importance of financial independence though long-term market-based savings.[34] It accordingly came to be regarded as seeking to construct capable and informed retail investors who were to be 'enrolled' in the regulatory process,[35] and to monitor the market, exert competitive pressures, and to accept responsibility for their actions.

Key examples from the pre-crisis period of retail market regulation as empowering investors include the emphasis placed by the EU on disclosure and on financial literacy in the period immediately prior to the financial crisis and its liberalization of the investment fund market,[36] the (then) UK FSA's focus on disclosure as a technique for managing commission risks, on marketing communications, on financial literacy, and on consumer empowerment,[37] and the robust approach taken internationally, including in the US, to online trading.[38] This is not to say that the classical tools for protecting retail investors against market failures arising from, in particular, conflicts of interest were not in place. Both the EU (2004 MiFID I) and Australia (under the large-scale reform to the delivery of investment advice adopted under the 2001 Financial Services Reform), for example, imposed firm-facing, conduct of business rules on investment firms, while in the US fiduciary obligations have long been imposed on investment advisers.[39] But in tandem

[29] Zingales, n 4 above.

[30] eg, Kingsford Smith, D, 'Regulating Investment Risk: Individuals and the Global Financial Crisis' (2009) 32 *University of New South Wales Law Journal* 514 and Ireland, P, 'Shareholder Primacy and the Distribution of Wealth' (2005) 68 *Modern Law Review* 49.

[31] eg, Shiller, R, *The Subprime Solution* (2008).

[32] As argued in the work of Donald Langevoort in the context of the US Securities and Exchange Commission (SEC). See, eg, Langevoort, D, 'Managing the Expectations Gap in Investor Protection: The SEC and the Post-Enron Reform Agenda' (2003) 48 *Villanova Law Review* 1139.

[33] See, eg, Pearson, G, 'Reconceiving Regulation: Financial Literacy' (2008) 8 *Macquarie Law Journal* 45 and Williams, T, 'Empowerment of Whom and for What? Financial Literacy Education and the New Regulation of Consumer Financial Services' (2007) 29 *Law & Policy* 226.

[34] For discussion in the context of UK regulatory policy see, eg, Gray, J and Hamilton, J, *Implementing Financial Regulation. Theory and Practice* (2006); in the Australian context see, eg, Ramsay, I, 'Consumer Law, Regulatory Capitalism and New Learning in Regulation' (2006) 28 *Sydney Law Review* 9; in the EU context see, eg, Moloney, n 12 above, 47–60; and in the US context see, eg, Stout, L, 'The Unimportance of Being Efficient: An Economic Analysis of Stock Market Pricing and Securities Regulation' (1998) 87 *Michigan Law Review* 613.

[35] Black, J, 'Decentring Regulation: Understanding the Role of Regulation and Self Regulation in a "Post Regulatory World"' (2001) 54 *Current Legal Problems* 103.

[36] Moloney, n 12 above, generally.

[37] Gray and Hamilton, n 34 above.

[38] Bradley, C, 'Disorderly Conduct and the Ideology of "Fair and Orderly Markets"' (2000) 26 *Journal of Corporation Law* 63.

[39] Laby, A, 'Fiduciary Obligations of Broker-Dealers and Investment Advisers' (2010) 55 *Villanova Law Review* 701 and see the Chapter by Tuch in this volume.

with these protections, a strong empowerment theme began to emerge in retail market design in many major markets.

The prevailing regulatory orthodoxy as to the need to support market engagement by informed and engaged retail investors has, however, been finessed in the wake of the crisis and there is some evidence of a more precautionary approach to the retail markets emerging (Section V). But it seems relatively clear that, even allowing for the destructive consequences of financial system crisis,[40] financial markets allow households to smooth consumption over lifetimes, providing the means to accumulate and de-cumulate assets.[41] Derivative products, for example, carry the promise of allowing households to hedge against future fluctuations in house prices.[42] It seems accordingly that protective and transformative objectives must both be pursued for optimal regulatory design.

But retail market regulatory design can quickly become a hostage to wider political and economic conditions and, in particular, to deregulatory movements which seek to promote easier access to finance more generally. The totemic US disclosure (and related liability) system, for example, has recently been the subject of what has been criticized as a radical deregulatory agenda which has sought to increase the 'private markets' within which offers of securities can be made to investors (including retail investors) subject to a lighter regulatory regime.[43] These reforms, achieved by the 2012 JOBS Act, can be associated with a concern to promote growth although their outcome is deregulation in the retail markets. Similarly, and in contrast with the precautionary approach to retail market regulation pursued elsewhere in the EU's crisis-era agenda (Section V), the EU, in part in support of its post-crisis growth agenda, has adopted a facilitative approach to crowdfunding, which appears to privilege market growth over retail protection and which underscores how the (typically costly) retail market agenda can quickly become secondary to cost concerns.[44]

(c) *Explaining retail market regulation*

Cognate scholarship on retail market regulation has followed a similar trajectory. The retail markets have not always been to the fore in financial regulation

[40] See, eg, Moloney, N, 'Regulating the Retail Markets: Law, Policy, and the Financial Crisis' (2010) 63 *Current Legal Problems* 375.

[41] eg, Dynan, K, Changing Household Financial Opportunities and Economic Security (2009), available via <http://ssrn.com/abstract=1508864>.

[42] As has long been argued by economists Case and Shiller, who have promoted the development of an appropriate and tradable futures contract. eg, Shiller, R, Derivatives Markets for House Prices (2008), Yale Economics Department Working Paper No 46, available at <http://ssrn.com/abstract=1114102> and Case, K and Shiller, R, 'The Efficiency of the Market for Single Family Homes' (1989) 79 *American Economic Review* 125.

[43] Langevoort, D and Thompson, R, 'Publicness in Contemporary Securities Regulation after the JOBS Act' (2013) 101 *Georgetown Law Journal* 337.

[44] eg European Commission, Communication on Long Term Financing of the European Economy (COM (2014) 168) and European Commission, Communication on Unleashing the Potential of Crowdfunding in the EU (COM (2014) 172).

scholarship. With some notable exceptions,[45] the retail markets did not feature strongly as 'law and economics' tools of analysis, and the related application of efficiency theory insights from finance, began to exert a strong influence on financial regulation scholarship from the 1980s.[46] While this form of analysis produced some notable insights relating to the location and incidence of principal/agent risks[47] and to the limitations of market efficiency in the retail markets,[48] it has not generally been productive for retail market analysis. In particular, its basis in a rational actor model, and its concern with wider market efficiency dynamics, has weakened its use as a tool for identifying and addressing risk in key retail market relationships.[49] Similarly, the important insights of the 'law and finance' movement, which came into the ascendant from the late 1990s, were generally concerned with identifying the regulatory drivers of market development generally and not with retail market development and risks.

The empirical heft associated with these forms of analysis is, however, increasingly a feature of retail market scholarship.[50] As retail markets have grown, so too has scholarly interest—from the financial economics perspective as well as the regulatory perspective—in charting the drivers of household market engagement (and in probing the 'limited participation' puzzle),[51] including the effect of trust and of social capital,[52] and the nature of retail investor behaviour.[53] The insights of behavioural finance, which challenge the rational-actor assumption which frames efficiency theory, have proved powerful for retail market analysis, particularly given the explanatory power of behavioural finance with respect to individual investor decisions, and with respect to how regulation can be designed to address

[45] In the US context see Clark, n 19 above, and in the UK, Page, A and Ferguson, R, *Investor Protection* (1992).

[46] Most notably in the form of the application of efficiency theory (see further the Chapter by Deakin in this volume).

[47] eg Mahoney, n 14 above.

[48] eg Jackson, H, 'To What Extent Should Individual Investors Rely on the Mechanisms of Market Efficiency: A Preliminary Investigation of Dispersion in Investor Returns' (2003) 28 *Journal of Corporation Law* 671.

[49] For a critique see Stout, L, 'The Investor Confidence Game' (2002–03) 68 *Brooklyn Law Review* 407.

[50] For a 'call to arms' with respect to the need for empirically informed assessment of the retail markets see Campbell, n 15 above, and for a recent reconsideration of regulatory policy based on empirical insights, see Campbell, J, Jackson, H, Madrian, B, and Tufano, P, 'Consumer Financial Protection' (2011) 25 *Journal of Economic Perspectives* 91.

[51] From the massive literature, predominantly drawn from financial economics scholarship, see, eg, Hong, H, Kubik, J, and Stein, J, 'Social Interaction and Stock-market Participation' (2004) 59 *Journal of Finance* 137.

[52] For a leading example see Sapienza, P, Guiso, L, and Zingales, L, 'Trusting the Stock Markets' (2008) 63 *Journal of Finance* 2557.

[53] An extensive financial economics literature examines the nature of retail investor behaviour. For a leading example in the online trading context see Barber, B and Odean, T, 'Trading Is

and mitigate common biases and decision-making weaknesses and their exploitation by market actors.[54] Important related scholarship includes analyses which seek to construct conceptual models of the retail investor which challenge the rational actor model and related regulatory design choices.[55] Increasing sophistication in regulatory policy and, in particular, the emergence of the 'financial citizen' as a means for achieving government goals has been similarly catalytic. The nature of the 'financial citizen', the extent to which individuals can be 'financialized' and regarded as agents of government withdrawal from welfare provision, and the related implications for regulatory design, have, for example, been extensively probed in an increasingly rich literature.[56]

3. Regulatory strategies

The protective and transformative/empowering objectives of retail market regulation can both be associated, to greater and lesser degrees, with different regulatory strategies. The more traditional protective objective, concerned with preventing malfeasance, can be associated with typical interventionist regulatory strategies, such as process-related controls on distribution and advice, marketing restrictions, and product authorization and governance requirements. The more proactive transformative objective can be associated with empowering strategies, typically disclosure-, choice-, and financial-literacy-based. The main regulatory tools of retail market regulation can accordingly be placed on a spectrum which extends from interventionist supply-side-orientated product design and distribution rules to rules which support private ordering, notably disclosure rules, and which can include also non-regulatory tools, notably investor education strategies. But whatever the objective(s) or combination of objectives pursued, and the blend of regulatory devices and strategies deployed, retail investor regulation poses myriad and often intractable difficulties, as considered in the next Section.

Hazardous to your Wealth: The Common Stock Investment Performance of Individual Investors' (2000) 55 *Journal of Finance* 773.

[54] In the crisis-era context see, eg, Barr, M, Mullainathan, S, and Shafir, E, 'Behaviourally Informed Regulation' in Shafir, E (ed.), *Behavioural Foundations of Policy* (2012) 442. Pre-crisis see, eg, Stout, L, 'The Mechanisms of Market Efficiency: An Introduction to the New Finance' (2003) 28 *Journal of Corporation Law* 635 and Gilson, R and Kraakman, R, 'The Mechanisms of Market Efficiency Twenty Years Later: the Hindsight Bias' (2003) 28 *Journal of Corporation Law* 215.

[55] See, eg, Stout, n 49 above (on the implications of the 'trusting investor' for regulatory design).

[56] See, eg, Kingsford Smith, n 30 above and Gray and Hamilton, n 34 above.

III. The Regulatory Design Challenge

Myriad challenges face the regulator in designing an optimal retail market regime.

The 'retail investor' targeted by intervention has long been an elusive character,[57] although the nature of retail investor behaviour is becoming clearer.[58] But pinning down the retail investor is not entirely a function of empiricism. How the regulator uses empirical data to construct the features of the retail investor either empowered or protected by regulation matters as it tends to determine the intensity of intervention in the investor decision and in the retail markets and the coherence of regulatory policy. An association by the regulatory system of retail investment with discretionary speculation and asset accumulation, capital supply, and accordingly with *caveat emptor* and personal responsibility would, for example, suggest a robust approach to investor capacity. The transformative/empowering approach to regulation in the ascendant pre-crisis has been associated with this type of regulatory construction, and with insufficient account being taken of the need to regard the retail investor as, in effect, 'consuming' investment products which are essential to daily life and of the reality that protection with respect to potential losses and risks is warranted.

Regulation must also be carefully adapted to the reality of retail investor behaviour. But despite a fast-expanding data set, which includes increasingly extensive regulatory efforts,[59] regulators are often grappling in the dark in this area: the determinants of retail investor engagement with the markets, for example, critical variables for any policy which promotes market investment, are not clear.[60] But the crisis-era has given some impetus to empirical efforts. In the EU, the new European Securities and Markets Authority (ESMA) has begun to collect data on EU retail investment trends[61] while in the US the SEC was mandated under the 2010 Dodd–Frank Act to engage in studies on the investment advice/brokerage sector and on investor education.[62]

[57] For an example from the Canadian context see Condon, M, *Making Disclosure: Ideas and Interests in Ontario Securities Regulation* (1998).

[58] eg, recently Fisch, J and Wilkinson-Ryan, T, Why Do Retail Investors Make Costly Mistakes? An Experiment on Mutual Fund Choice (2013), ECGI Law Working Paper No 220/2013, available at <http://ssrn.com/abstract=2086766>.

[59] For a recent example from the EU see Synovate, Consumer Market Study on Advice within the Area of Retail Investment Services—Final Report (2011) (for the European Commission).

[60] For an example from the extensive literature which identifies factors such as peer influence, tax incentives, behavioural factors, household wealth, education, financial literacy, the housing market, and pension provisions see, eg, Guiso, L, Haliassos, M, and Japelli, T, Household Stockholding in Europe: Where Do we Stand and Where Do we Go? (2003), CEPR Discussion Paper No 3694.

[61] eg, ESMA Trends, Risks and Vulnerabilities Report No 1 (2014).

[62] SEC, Study Regarding Financial Literacy among Investors (2012) and SEC, Study on Investment Advisers and Brokers (2011).

Regulation must also adapt nimbly to changing retail market risks. While the retail market does not develop as rapidly as the wholesale market, it is prone to shifts which can place pressure on the regulatory perimeter within which retail market regulation applies. Retail market regulation is generally predicated on the establishment of a perimeter within which 'retail investors' (or more typically, 'non-professional' investors) are subject to the highest level of protection and within which the highest standards apply to intermediation services and the distribution of investments. But this perimeter can become porous under pressure from market innovation. The pre-crisis era, for example, saw some concerns as to the extent to which hedge-fund-like products could be distributed within the retail markets. The EU's investment fund regime, for example, adopted a liberal approach to the portfolio rules governing the major EU investment fund (UCITS) which accommodated the public distribution of hedge-fund-like products, albeit that this placed pressure on core investor protection rules. Similarly, the current development of private funding markets outside the traditional public markets[63] is exerting pressure on long-standing rules governing the sale by issuers of securities, while the related development of online crowdfunding platforms is raising fundamental questions as to the point at which a funding platform takes on the features of a retail market intermediary and so becomes subject to regulation.[64] Incentives risks also change (as they do in the wholesale markets). While incentive risks in distribution have long troubled the retail markets, they can change in character. Over the financial crisis in the EU, for example, evidence emerged of major banks selling proprietary debt-based products in order to repair their balance sheets and of related mis-selling.[65] The risk of mis-selling has increased as banks, under pressure to increase their bail-in-able debt in order to respond to the new resolution requirements which form part of the crisis-era regulatory reform agenda, have incentives to issue debt through their distribution networks.[66]

More generally, retail market regulation is not easy to design or to apply. As discussed in Section V, disclosure is a very limited tool given the behavioural weaknesses to which retail investors are vulnerable. Distribution regulation poses complex problems given the range of issues engaged, from industry structure and incentive issues (particularly with respect to commission payments), to investor access-to-advice difficulties, to the ability and/or willingness of retail investors to

[63] Such as the US SecondMarket, and SharePost and FirstPEX in Europe, which provide liquidity in privately held shares.

[64] eg, Kirby, E and Worner, S, Crowdfunding: An Infant Industry Growing Fast (2014), International Organization of Securities Commissions (IOSCO) Staff Working Paper No SWP 3/2014.

[65] Herbert Smith, A Changing Landscape: Regulatory Developments in the Distribution of Retail Investment Products (2010) and (2012).

[66] See further Section V.3 on how product intervention tools may provide a means for responding nimbly to emerging risks, including those relating to the retail distribution of instruments issued to support firms' resolution plans.

engage with investment advice. Product intervention was, until the financial crisis largely overlooked. Financial literacy strategies are best deployed as very long-term solutions to retail market risks. The regulatory perimeter can be difficult to fix, particularly with respect to the perimeter within which investment products can be distributed to retail investors, and its optimal design can require often fine decisions as to the appropriate level of risk in the retail market, the level of investor responsibility which can be expected, and the extent to which choice can be supported. Regulatory arbitrage risk is typically significant, given the ever-expanding universe of investment products distributed to retail investors. The pressure on regulation is all the greater as the beleaguered retail investor cannot easily support regulation, having limited ability to monitor firms and products and to use disclosures effectively.

Retail market regulators are largely insulated from the discipline and innovation which can be imposed on regulation by the need to respond to global market dynamics. Retail markets are typically local in orientation—the EU's long struggle to promote a cross-border retail market underlines the extent to which the oft-examined home bias shapes retail investment. One notable exception, however, relates to SEC policy pre-crisis when concern to ease US retail investor access to diversified cross-border investments, and increasing levels of cross-border retail investment, were among the policy drivers of the SEC's development of its 'substitute compliance' model for third-country actor access to the US market.[67] For the most part, retail market regulation is typically idiosyncratic and reflects local market structures (such as distribution arrangements) and investment patterns. The EU is unusual in that it applies harmonized retail market regulation across its 28 Member States, notwithstanding the wide divergence of investment patterns and market structures across the EU. But EU-harmonized retail market regulation lags some way behind EU-harmonized wholesale market regulation in terms of sophistication and intensity. The divergence of investment patterns across the EU has also placed considerable pressure on the EU's harmonized regulatory regime for the retail markets. Major EU retail market measures often provide, for example, for local optionality and divergence.[68]

Similarly, the efficiencies and enhancements which can be generated from coordination through international standard-setters such as the Financial Stability Board, the International Organization of Securities Commissions, and the Basel Committee are largely absent in this area as there are few incentives to engage with

[67] Tafara, E and Peterson, R, 'A Blueprint for Cross-Border Access to US Investors: A New International Framework' (2007) 48 *Harvard International Law Journal* 31.

[68] The 2014 MiFID II, eg, prohibits commissions where independent investment advice is provided, but allows Member States to adopt more extensive bans (across proprietary distribution structures, eg): Article 24. This option reflects the limited nature of the MiFID II commission ban which was shaped by the political need to accommodate the concern of some Member States that their proprietary-distribution-based systems be protected.

the retail interest at the international level. Momentum effects arising from the financial crisis have, however, led to a sharpening of the international agenda. The Seoul 2010 G20 meeting led to the crisis-era global agenda somewhat belatedly engaging with the retail interest and to the related November 2011 adoption by the Cannes G20 meeting of the G20/OECD High Level Principles on Consumer Protection.[69] But these Principles operate at a very high level of generality and do not engage directly with the difficult design decisions which regulators seeking to achieve protective and transformative objectives must make, although they have some potential as benchmarks for regulators, including for use in peer-review exercises.

The challenge to the regulator is all the greater as retail market regulation rarely benefits from the reform movements which typically follow crisis and which create space for regulatory risk-taking, innovation, and experimentation. Although the retail investor quickly became a target of the financial-crisis-era reforms in Australia, this reflected the nature of the financial crisis in Australia, which was systemically more limited in scale than in other major economies, but which revealed significant mis-selling and other retail market failures.[70] In the EU, which was gripped by a major systemic crisis and was compelled to engage in a major repair of its financial system and of financial regulation, the retail markets were a latecomer to the reform agenda. To take one example, a major pillar of the crisis-era reform agenda, the Packaged Retail and Insurance-based Investment Products (PRIIPs) Regulation, which addresses product disclosure, was not agreed until April 2014 although initial discussions commenced in 2007. By contrast, most of the major EU crisis-era measures, notwithstanding the radical changes they wrought to regulation and to market structure, were completed in approximately 18 months each. Retail market reforms tend to be incremental and to reflect public reaction to particularly egregious episodes of malfeasance, typically related to mis-selling.

IV. Rulemaking Governance

Ensuring optimal retail governance (regarded in terms of the institutional structures which support rulemaking) is a challenge internationally given the host of complexities engaged, not least among them technical challenges relating to

[69] OECD, G20 High Level Principles on Financial Consumer Protection (2012) and OECD, Draft Effective Approaches to Support the Implementation of the Remaining G20/OECD High Level Principles on Financial Consumer Protection: Informal Consultation (2014).

[70] Hill, J, 'Why Did Australia Fare so Well in the Global Financial Crisis' in Ferran, E, Moloney, N, Hill J, and Coffee, J, *The Regulatory Aftermath of the Global Financial Crisis* (2012) 203, 270–6.

designing outcome-focused rules, a poorly organized and diffuse retail cohort which can struggle to counter industry lobbies, the difficult balances and compromises engaged, including with respect to where the perimeter of public regulation lies, and the ever-present reality of retail market interests being trumped by wider financial stability interests.

The challenges are particularly acute given the well-charted and severe difficulties in supporting retail investor engagement with the rulemaking process, the nature of which is increasingly a concern of retail market scholarship.[71] Direct retail investor engagement with the rulemaking process strengthens accountability and increases the credibility and legitimacy of regulation (which is of acute importance where 'responsibilized' and 'financialized' investors are sought). It may also lead to more empirically informed regulation, reduce capture risks, stiffen what can be a flabby governmental commitment to reform particularly where high industry costs are engaged, and dull the familiar industry clamour against regulation.[72] But retail investors (or the 'panicked mass public'[73]) are ill-informed and poorly organized, particularly when compared with the behemoth industry lobbies, and typically only come to bear on the lawmaking process in times of immense turbulence when their influence can wane very quickly, as the financial crisis period suggests. While the distinction between 'input' legitimacy and 'output' legitimacy, which distinguishes between, for example, legitimacy based on representation and legitimacy based on the achievement of particular goals or outcomes, may provide something of a compromise solution, given the challenges posed by traditional representation,[74] it intensifies the need for optimal institutional design which ensures retail interests are effectively addressed.

One well-established response to the challenges posed by financial governance generally is delegation to an expert agency.[75] In the retail markets, institutional design choices typically arise between consolidated institutional design or (and increasingly commonly) a functionally organized 'twin peaks' model under which prudential (stability-based) regulation and conduct (including investor protection) regulation are separated in distinct agencies.[76] Consolidated institutional design

[71] See, eg, Black, J, Involving Consumers on Securities Regulation: Report for the Taskforce to Modernize Securities Regulation in Canada (2006).

[72] Black, B and Gross, J, 'The Elusive Balance Between Investor Protection and Wealth Creation' (2005) 26 *Pace Law Review* 27.

[73] Braithwaite, J and Drahos, P, *Global Business Regulation* (2000) 122–3 and 159.

[74] eg, Esty, D, 'Good Governance at the Supranational Scale: Globalizing Administrative Law' (2006) 115 *Yale Law Journal* 1490.

[75] See, eg, Everson, M, A Technology of Expertise: EU Financial Services Agencies (2012), LEQS Working Paper No 49/2012 and Barkow, E, 'Insulating Agencies: Avoiding Capture through Institutional Design' (2010) 89 *Texas Law Review* 15.

[76] Leading examples include the UK regime (which includes the Financial Conduct Authority and the Prudential Regulation Authority), the Australian regime (based on the Australian Securities and Investments Commission and the Australian Prudential Regulation Authority), the French model (based on the Autorité des Marchés Financiers (conduct) and the Autorité de Contrôle Prudentiel

benefits from economies of scale, opportunities for supervisory learning, and the ability of the regulator to take a cross-sectoral approach, but it also carries a series of risks, not least among them the risks of rule design becoming a function of static and centralized processes, of groupthink, and of conflicts between different internal divisions. While internal tensions can become particularly acute with respect to supervisory decisions (the prudential division may, for example, seek forbearance where a large mis-selling fine has implications for an institution's capital position), they also impinge on rule design as there may be some institutional incentives to reduce the regulatory burden, including through reliance on 'softer' techniques such as guidance.[77] Retail market interests can also become side-lined when financial stability comes under threat, as is suggested by the consolidated UK FSA's decision to scale back its Treating Customers Fairly (TCF) initiative (see further Section V) in 2008 at a time when stability pressures were acute.

The twin peaks model, by contrast, allows for specialization and the concentrated pursuit of retail market interests. The Australian conduct supervisor, the Australian Securities and Investments Commission (established in 2001), is notable among world regulators for its long focus on mis-selling and the quality of advice, and for its robust and timely crisis-era communications with retail investors on the implications of market turbulence.[78] The roots of the UK Financial Conduct Authority (FCA), established in April 2013, are in the political decision to dismantle the consolidated FSA (established in 2000) given the FSA's perceived regulatory (and supervisory) failures before and over the financial crisis; its establishment does not accordingly reflect a particular attachment to the improvement of retail governance. But it is reasonable to associate the close focus by the FCA in its early years on retail market issues and on related rule design with its more specialist mandate and with its need to strengthen its capacity and authority as a new institution by means of a robust and visible retail agenda.[79] On the other hand, the US SEC, while not directly a 'twin peaks' conduct regulator, specializes in securities markets and has a strong attachment to the retail investor; but it has been repeatedly criticized for not adjusting its reliance on disclosure to reflect retail market realities.[80] Specialist conduct regulators are also unlikely to address the hierarchy of influence difficulties which can arise within consolidated regulators. The UK Prudential Regulation

(prudential)), and the Dutch model (based on the Dutch central bank (prudential) and the Autoriteit Financiële Markten (conduct)).

[77] The potential for prejudicial conflict received some crisis-era scholarly attention in the context of, eg, the impact of the US Consumer Financial Protection Bureau on banking regulation and supervision: eg, Coffee, J and Sale, H, 'Redesigning the SEC—Does the Treasury Have a Better Idea?' (2009) 95 *Virginia Law Review* 707.

[78] See further Moloney, n 40 above.

[79] For its initial statement of intent which is notable for its focus on the retail markets see FSA, Journey to the Financial Conduct Authority (2012).

[80] eg, Langevoort, n 32 above.

Authority, for example, can veto certain FCA decisions in the interests of financial stability. Difficulties can also arise where artificial distinctions are maintained and the opportunity for synergies is lost. The crisis-era establishment of the new US Consumer Financial Protection Bureau in 2011, for example, led to criticism that related consumer financial protection (the new Bureau) and retail investor protection (the SEC and the Commodity Futures Trading Commission) functions were being artificially segregated with a consequent loss of efficiencies.

The EU experience, while in many respects distinct, underlines the difficulties associated with retail governance design, and in particular how stability interests can trump retail interests in many different forms of institutional design. The crisis led to a radical reorganization of EU financial system governance, including the 2011 establishment of ESMA, which is not a traditional regulatory agency. Its function in EU financial market governance (which has (limited) direct supervisory elements and (extensive) supervisory convergence/coordination and quasi-rulemaking elements) is distinct and has been shaped by the particular Treaty, political, and institutional factors which shape EU governance generally.[81] It has, however, a specific retail market mandate and its related powers include the adoption of guidance for EU Member State regulators and for market actors, peer review, market review and analysis, and the adoption of retail market warnings. ESMA has, however, strong incentives to prioritize its parallel financial stability mandate, given the political and institutional dividends which may follow. The current prominence of financial stability, the institutional opportunities which the evolving Banking Union dynamic may create, and the clear pan-EU externalities at stake with respect to financial stability all suggest ESMA is likely to prioritize financial stability over retail market issues. The retail market agenda, closely tied to local Member State markets and associated with intractable problems, may be less attractive. Early evidence, however, suggests some ESMA enthusiasm for the retail markets, despite the gravitational pull of the stability agenda. ESMA's developing 'soft rule-book', for example, includes guidelines on quality of advice issues, it has been quick to issue pan-EU warnings regarding retail market risks, and it has engaged in a number of governance enhancements to strengthen its ability to monitor pan-EU retail market innovation. But the monumental weight of its crisis-era financial stability work programme has generated some concern as to the more limited attention it has given to the retail markets.[82] Overall, however, the early evidence suggests that ESMA has the appetite and the capacity to develop a strong retail agenda, always assuming the financial stability agenda leaves it with sufficient space and

[81] See, eg, Moloney, N, *EU Securities and Financial Markets Regulation* (2014), ch X and XI, and the Chapter by Haar in this volume.

[82] Expressed by consumer respondents in particular to the European Commission's 2013 Consultation on Review of the European System of Financial Supervision (established in 2011 and of which ESMA forms a part).

incentives to do so. More generally, however, effective retail market governance in the EU is ill-served by the current split of retail market issues across the three sector-specific European Supervisory Authorities (ESMA, the European Banking Authority, and the European Insurance and Occupational Pensions Authority) given the cross-sector nature of retail market risk and the prevalence of substitutable products.

The trajectory of reform over the last few decades suggests that while retail market interests do play a part in governance designs and redesigns,[83] radical institutional restructurings are most likely to be a function of wider market turbulence and to reflect the dictates in a given market of optimal stability-orientated governance. Retail market governance may be refreshed and enhanced by such wider governance reforms. But it nonetheless faces distinct risks, notably with respect to its subsidiary position to stability-orientated governance in the typical institutional hierarchy.

V. Regulatory Tools

1. Disclosure

Disclosure regulation has long been associated with retail market regulation,[84] with consumer financial markets described as providing the 'textbook' case of market failure due to information asymmetries.[85] It is not accordingly surprising that disclosure requirements have long been a central feature of retail market regulation. But the design and influence of this form of regulation has changed over time and attests to a reassuring degree of innovation in retail market regulatory design. Originally deployed as a means for addressing information asymmetries, the natural affiliation between disclosure, empowerment, and the construction of the investor as 'informed and empowered', as well as its support of firm and investor autonomy, led to disclosure becoming a key tool of the pre-crisis movement to promote investor engagement. But as data-gathering has become more sophisticated, as the findings of behavioural finance have become more embedded within regulatory design processes, and as the limitations of disclosure have become apparent,

[83] On the myriad factors which shape governance design see the Chapters by Ferran; Brummer and Smallcomb; Haar; and Pan in this volume.

[84] Jackson, H, 'Regulation in a Multi-sectored Financial Services Industry: An Exploration Essay' (1999) 77 *Washington University Law Quarterly* 319.

[85] Campbell et al., n 50 above.

disclosure has moved, at least in some jurisdictions, from enjoying a central position, to taking a less central role and becoming regarded as a backstop support to the investor decision.

Disclosure is a tool of central importance to financial system regulation generally. But while disclosure is widely regarded as having failed over the financial crisis,[86] effective disclosure design for the retail markets has long presented one of the most intractable of regulatory problems. By contrast with most forms of disclosure which tend to be directed towards market efficiency more generally,[87] retail market disclosure, and particularly product disclosure, is an investor-facing tool.[88] But a wealth of evidence underlines the severe difficulties which retail investors face in decoding disclosure and how behavioural dynamics can disable disclosure.[89] The difficulties pervade all elements of retail market disclosure. From product disclosures (where the difficulties relate to, *inter alia*, labelling, cost and risk disclosures, and past performance information) to services-related disclosures (particularly with respect to commission and conflict-of-interest risk) investors struggle with disclosures which can be lengthy, unclear, complex, alarming, insufficiently prioritized, and insufficiently sensitive to risk. Even where strenuous efforts are expended in the attempt to deliver effective disclosure, it does not follow that decision-making will be optimal.[90] Retail market scholarship has accordingly consistently critiqued disclosure as a retail market tool, whether with respect to its many empirically proven failings (particularly with respect to its 'processability', or the extent to which it can be used by investors and achieve the outcomes sought[91]),[92] or with respect to its articulation of a government commitment to empower retail investors who are ill-equipped to support their welfare needs through the markets.[93] Such scholarship has also illuminated the many institutional incentives which can lead to a prejudicial regulatory attachment to disclosure, including incentives to

[86] From the many discussions see Hu, H, 'Too Complex to Depict? Innovation, "Pure Information," and the SEC Disclosure Paradigm' (2012) 90 *Texas Law Review* 160.

[87] Gilson and Kraakmann, n 54 above.

[88] Although an extensive US literature critiques the failure of the US issuer disclosure regime, which supports market efficiency more generally, to address retail investor needs, particularly given the SEC's commitment to issuer disclosure as means of retail market protection. See, eg, Langevoort, D, 'The SEC as Lawmaker: Choices about Investor Protection in the Face of Uncertainty' (2006) 84 *Washington University Law Review* 1591 and Paredes, T, 'Blinded by the Light: Information Overload and its Consequences for Securities Regulation' (2003) 81 *Washington University Law Quarterly* 417.

[89] See, eg, Deaves, R, Dine, C, and Horton W, How Are Investment Decisions Made? Research Study for the Task Force to Modernize Securities Regulation in Canada (2006).

[90] Rachlinski, J, 'The Uncertain Psychological case for Paternalism' (2003) 97 *Northwestern University Law Review* 1165.

[91] eg, Kozup, J and Hogarth, J, 'Financial Literacy, Public Policy and Consumers' Self Protection—More Questions Fewer Answers' (2008) 42 *Journal of Consumer Affairs* 127.

[92] From the extensive US literature see Hu, H, 'The New Portfolio Society, SEC Mutual Fund Disclosure and the Public Corporation Model' (2005) 60 *Business Lawyer* 1303.

[93] eg, from the Australian literature, Ramsay, n 34 above.

promote the markets as safe and fair and, through disclosure design, to minimize the risks of market investment.[94]

Disclosure design for the retail markets has, however, evolved. Short-form disclosures for retail market investment products have led the way in reforming disclosures, with the US, the UK, the Netherlands, and the harmonized EU regimes, for example, all adopting refinements to product-related disclosures in the closing decade of the twentieth century designed to support processability.[95] The EU provides a useful example of how disclosure design and policy can change. Despite the European Commission's long attachment to disclosure, its 2007 Green Paper on Retail Financial Services revealed growing scepticism concerning disclosure, and highlighted concerns that investment product disclosure was too complex, inadequate, difficult to understand, and did not support informed choice.[96] The Commission's related commitment to reviewing the EU retail market disclosure regime, given the risk that the variety and accumulation of information required could impose undue costs on the industry and confuse retail investors, is exemplified by the groundbreaking 2009 Key Investor Information Document (KIID) reform which requires that a highly standardized short-form disclosure document be provided for UCITS mutual funds. The KIID was developed after extensive *ex ante* testing on retail investors and deploys an array of mechanisms to support processability, including a standardized risk indicator, composite cost disclosures, and strict format and presentation rules.

Over the crisis era, and as the EU's approach to the retail markets has become more precautionary, the EU's attention has turned to closer intervention in the retail market, whether with respect to the distribution process or in relation to product intervention. Disclosure remains a key retail market tool, but has increasingly come to be regarded as a support to distribution and product rules given its weaknesses as a direct investor protection tool. It is also becoming increasingly refined. The important 2014 PRIIPs Regulation reforms are designed to apply the KIID model to a wide array of substitutable investment products (and to address thereby regulatory arbitrage risks) and represent something of a 'next generation' in terms of disclosure reform, being more sophisticated with respect to standardization and format than the earlier KIID model.

Disclosure regulation and policy therefore represents something of a microcosm of retail market regulation. Originally a core element of retail market regulation and subsequently becoming tied to the empowerment movement, it has recently

[94] For an example see Zingales, n 4 above.

[95] Respectively, the US 'fund profile' (2007), the UK 'key features document' for packaged products (which has experienced repeated reforms), the Netherlands 'financial information leaflet' (2002), and the EU's simplified UCITS prospectus for UCITS funds (2001).

[96] Commission, Green Paper on Retail Financial Services in the Single Market (2007) (COM (2007) 226).

become of less central importance as regulation has become increasingly interventionist and precautionary. In cognate scholarship, its weaknesses have long been a poster-boy for the inadequacies of retail market regulation and, in particular, of the rational actor and efficiency paradigm. The intensifying efforts to support the processability of disclosure, however, attest to the growing influence of empiricism on retail market regulation and the related potential for mitigation of the risks which retail market design poses.

2. Distribution

Distribution regulation addresses the process through which securities and investment products are distributed to investors through a range of different intermediation channels, including specialist investment advisers, financial institutions selling proprietary products (and their agents), and brokers. Distribution channels which support execution-only transactions and which do not accordingly provide a high level of intermediation are also a feature of retail market distribution. Distribution regulation sits above disclosure in the retail market regulation spectrum and deploys significantly more interventionist techniques. In the UK initially and subsequently in the EU, for example, commission bans have been used to reshape market structure. Given the extent to which retail investors rely on intermediated distribution in some major jurisdictions (including the EU), and the related damage which a widespread loss of confidence in distribution can generate,[97] distribution regulation is also a key means for supporting retail investor engagement with market savings.

Regulation in this area is primarily directed to the principal-agent risks which can be acute in the distribution context. They include fraud, misuse of investor funds, incompetence, and poor advice—the behavioural weaknesses which trouble retail investor decision-making may simply be replaced by adviser weaknesses and not displaced. But remuneration-based conflict-of-interest risk poses the greatest threat to good investor outcomes[98] and is the most significant driver of mis-selling and poor-quality advice internationally.

Remuneration structures have very considerable potential to misalign incentives in the distribution process. The well-documented detriment which can follow includes biased advice, failure to provide debt reduction advice, poor product selection, inappropriate advice to switch products, and ultimately mis-selling. The risks are all the greater given the difficulties retail investors face in identifying

[97] As has repeatedly been highlighted by the UK FSA and its successor, the Financial Conduct Authority.

[98] eg, Krausz, M and Paroush, J, 'Financial Advising in the Presence of Conflicts of Interest' (2002) 54 *Journal of Economics and Business* 55.

conflict-of-interest risk and in assessing relevant disclosures. In addition, retail investors are unlikely to gain experience as investment decisions tend to be irregular, over-reliance on and excessive trust in advisers is common, and the well-documented reluctance of retail investors to pay a fee for advice entrenches remuneration-related risks. Commission and incentive risk in the distribution process is a common problem internationally and has become the subject of strenuous reforms efforts, including (and unusually for retail market regulation) those by international standard-setters.[99]

A range of tools are used to address principal-agent risks in distribution and include conflict-of-interest management rules; suitability/know-your-client rules which seek to ensure that advice is suitable for and targeted to an investor's risk, financial, and capacity profile; disclosure requirements; and specific rules governing remuneration structures. But conflict-of-interest risk has proved to be very difficult to address, and the regulation of distribution has experienced repeated cycles of reform internationally. Based on the EU and Australian experience in particular, the crisis era has led to a significantly more interventionist approach and to a decisive movement away from private ordering (in the form of disclosure-based controls) in this field.

The persistence of large-scale mis-selling in the UK, for example, has led to repeated cycles of reform which ultimately led the FSA to admit in 2007 that more than 20 years of intervention had focused on symptoms and not on root causes.[100] The UK market is comprised of bank-based distribution networks and of independent investment advisers (traditionally, prior to recent reforms, paid by means of commissions from product providers). Early efforts to address the persistent cycles of mis-selling which came to bedevil the UK market from the 1980s included the 1987 'polarization' system designed to 'polarize' the distribution system into tied agents and independent advisers (who advised on a market-wide range of products).[101] Following concerns that this approach was anti-competitive, the 2005 'depolarization' reforms allowed firms to choose from a range of distribution models, including tied, multi-tied, and independent models. Incentive risks (including those arising from commission risks) were managed through disclosure (a major component of the depolarized system which depended on clear disclosure on the nature of the service provided and on remuneration structures), conflict

[99] eg, Basel Committee on Banking Supervision, International Organization of Securities Commissions (IOSCO), and International Association of Insurance Supervisors, Customer Suitability in the Retail Sale of Financial Products and Services (2008) and IOSCO, Suitability Requirements for Complex Financial Products (2013). The 2012 OECD High Level Principles on Financial Consumer Protection highlight that 'the provision of advice should be as objective as possible' (at 6) and that remuneration structures 'should be designed to encourage responsible business conduct, fair treatment of customers and to avoid conflicts of interest' (at 7).

[100] FSA, A Review of Retail Distribution (2007), Discussion Paper 07/1, 5.

[101] See further Black, J, *Rules and Regulators* (1997).

of interest, and suitability rules. The FSA also deployed its related soft-law-based Treating Customers Fairly (TCF) supervisory strategy, which sought to embed the principle that firms treat customers fairly by means of a range of devices including guidance, the imposition of responsibility on senior management, a focus on the capacity of firm systems and controls to support the fair treatment of customers, and specific supervisory strategies.[102] In tandem with this regime, the UK applied the related EU harmonized rule book for investment firms (2004 MiFID I) which imposed fair treatment, disclosure, and suitability rules pan-EU. This regulatory and supervisory matrix did not succeed in preventing large-scale mis-selling scandals, which failure, combined with a related empowerment-driven concern to ensure individuals were equipped to take on more responsibility for welfare provision, led to the major structural reforms heralded by the 2007 Retail Distribution Review reforms[103] which came into force in 2013. These reforms ban commission in the distribution of packaged investment products generally, impose strict labelling requirements as to whether investment advice is 'independent' or 'restricted' given the nature of the product market on which investment advice is based, and introduce new and more stringent qualification rules for investment advisers. Significant market change has followed, including the withdrawal of major banks from the investment advice market, but the extent to which conflict of interest is being removed remains unclear.[104]

Similarly, the US regulatory regime has struggled with the labelling and differential regulatory treatment of 'investment advisers' (who, broadly, provide fee-based advice, are not involved in the management of brokerage/trading accounts, are regarded as fiduciaries, and are subject to stringent fiduciary duties) and 'broker-dealers' (who provide brokerage/trading account management and broking services but only provide advice incidentally, are associated with commission-based remuneration, and are not regarded as fiduciaries). Although both perform very similar functions, the SEC has grappled for some time with the distinction and with the potential for differential regulation of functionally similar distribution services. Following repeated attempts to adopt rules to clarify the status of broker-dealers and the striking down of a remedial 2005 SEC rule, the SEC commissioned the extensive and often critical 2008 Rand Report on the investment advice and brokerage industry.[105] The crisis era saw the advice and brokerage industry come under further scrutiny, with the 2010 Dodd–Frank Act leading

[102] Moloney, n 12 above, 219–24 and Georgosouli, A, 'The FSA's "Treating Customers Fairly" (TCF) Initiative: What Is so Good about it and Why it May not Work' (2011) 38 *Journal of Law and Society* 405. See further the Chapter by Black in this volume.

[103] See FSA, n 100 above.

[104] The distribution market remains under close review by the FCA. eg, FCA, Final Guidance: Risks to Customers from Financial Incentives (2013).

[105] Rand Institute for Civil Justice, Report on Investor and Industry Perspectives on Investment Advisers and Broker-Dealers. Sponsored by the SEC (2008).

to a series of SEC studies into the workings of the US retail investment advice/brokerage market. These were followed by the SEC recommending that reforms be introduced such that a uniform fiduciary standard be applied to broker-dealers and to investment advisers where advice was provided, and by related impact assessment studies over 2013.[106] Whether or not meaningful reform will follow, however, remains to be seen, as discussed in the Chapter by Tuch in this volume.

The Australian regime[107] has similarly been subject to ongoing review and reform. Following the recommendations of the 1997 Wallis Committee,[108] large-scale reform to the delivery of investment advice was adopted in Australia under the Financial Services Reform 2001.[109] The protection of retail investors became a major political priority over the financial crisis, however, following a series of failures in the financial sector and mis-selling scandals. The subsequent 2013 Future of Financial Advice reforms included bans on a range of payments to advisers which were regarded as creating conflict-of-interest risk (including a ban on commissions), new fiduciary duties imposed on advisers, and an enhanced disclosure regime.[110]

In the EU, where the regulatory challenge is acute given the different types of distribution system which operate across different national markets (primarily independent adviser distribution systems and bank-based distribution systems for proprietary products), cycles of reform, culminating in structural reform, have also occurred. The 2004 MiFID I imposed a pan-EU rule book which contained disclosure, conflict-of-interest management, and suitability/know-your-client elements. But it did not address remuneration and commission risks specifically. The incentive risks to which the EU's different distribution channels were exposed were highlighted by the pan-EU mis-selling of structured products prior to the crisis and, as the crisis took root, the mis-selling of proprietary products designed to shore up financial institutions' balance sheets (particularly in Spain) and of complex interest rate hedging products (particularly in the UK). While not on the scale of the UK Retail Distribution Review reforms, significant EU reforms have followed in the shape of a ban on commission payments for independent investment advice and significantly more stringent remuneration rules under the 2014 MiFID II.[111]

These different reforms are all rooted in the particular risks posed by the dominant distribution structures in the relevant market and they have been shaped

[106] SEC Release No 34-69013 and IA-3558.

[107] Distribution reform has also been on the agenda in, eg, Canada: Canadian Securities Administrators, The Standard of Conduct for Advisers and Dealers: Exploring the Appropriateness of Introducing a Statutory Best Interest Duty when Advice Is Provided to Retail Clients (2012), Consultation Paper No 33–403.

[108] Wallis Committee, Final Report on the Financial System Inquiry (1997).

[109] A subsequent series of reforms were adopted in 2005: Australian Treasury, Refinements to Financial Services Regulation. Proposals Paper (2005).

[110] Hill, n 70 above.

[111] MiFID II, n 21 above, Article 24.

by the crisis-era reform movement to different extents. But they share a number of features. They attest to the emergence of a more precautionary and interventionist approach which is some distance from the disclosure controls which characterized early attempts to address distribution risks. The new EU regime, for example, also includes restrictions on the investments which can be sold execution-only (and includes a prohibition on margin services). The reforms also point to the encroachment of public law in an area where fiduciary law has traditionally had some traction given the trust relationship between the investor and adviser,[112] and to related government concern to build investor confidence in distribution channels and an allied reliance on regulation to promote government goals relating to market engagement. The reforms also attest to the risks which retail market regulation can pose and to the difficulties in balancing protective and transformative objectives. The market restructuring which the UK reforms have brought, for example, has been associated with an industry withdrawal from the independent advice market following the commission ban and the emergence accordingly of an 'advice gap',[113] which also reflects the long-established unwillingness of retail investors in the UK (and EU) to pay for advice.

3. Product intervention

Product-related intervention represents (potentially) the most interventionist form of retail market regulation. Its relatively recent evolution attests to the increasingly interventionist approach to regulation being adopted in some major retail markets. Product intervention can extend across a spectrum from *ex ante* product authorization (including product construction/portfolio rules), to oversight of product development processes, to the demarcation of the products which can be distributed in the retail markets (this has been a feature of alternative investment fund regulation in many jurisdictions, including across the EU), to *ex post* product prohibition.

Product intervention in the form of rules addressing the governance and constitution of collective investment schemes (mutual funds) has long been a feature of retail market regulation internationally, although approaches have varied. The EU, for example, imposes detailed (although facilitative) portfolio construction rules on the UCITS collective investment scheme, while the US regime focuses in particular on fund governance. Rules delineating the retail/public product distribution market have also long been a feature of retail market regulation.

112 Notably in the US, but also in the EU. See, eg, Ferrarini, G, 'Contract Standards and the Markets in Financial Instruments Directive' (2005) 1 *European Review of Contract Law* 19.

113 Cass Consulting, The Impact of the Retail Distribution Review on the UK's Markets for Financial Advice: Challenge and Opportunity (2013).

But retail market regulation has been slow to engage with product intervention tools more generally, and in particular with product authorization and prohibition powers. This reflects the significant risks associated with product intervention[114] and which include arbitrage, damage to innovation and investor choice, and moral hazard, given the strong implication of regulatory approval which product authorization, in particular, can generate and the related risk that the product provider takes less care in monitoring the product. The association between product intervention and 'over-regulation' is also considerable.[115]

In the most powerful example of its crisis-era embrace of a more precautionary (and paternalistic) approach to the retail markets, the EU, however, is experimenting with product intervention. The crisis era led to product-related intervention coming to the fore in many EU Member States as an additional tool for addressing retail market risk and in response to persistent mis-selling risks, which risks are often exacerbated by the complex and illiquid structure of some products sold through retail distribution channels.[116] A range of product-related techniques came to be deployed by national regulators, including oversight of the product development process and prohibitions on the marketing of certain products.[117] As is often the case (particularly given the need to avoid competitive distortions and cross-border regulatory costs), a harmonized EU regime has followed. The 2014 MiFIR confers on national regulators a suite of powers to limit or prohibit the distribution or sale of investment products, subject to a range of conditions. Similar powers, designed to activate in emergency conditions and where national regulators have not acted, are conferred on ESMA and the European Banking Authority. The EU has also, under the 2014 MiFID II, imposed a new suite of harmonized rules relating to the product design process, including, in particular, that product design be overseen by senior management and meet the needs of an identified target market.

This recent embrace of product intervention in one of the world's largest retail markets has much to recommend it. Product intervention, and related intervention

[114] Karmel, R, 'Mutual Funds, Pension Funds and Stock Market Volatility—What Regulation by the Securities and Exchange Commission Is Appropriate' (2004–05) 80 *Notre Dame Law Review* 909.

[115] eg, Epstein, R, 'The Neoclassical Economics of Consumer Contracts' (2008) 92 *Minnesota Law Review* 808, and Bar Gill, O, 'The Behavioural Economics of Consumer Contracts' (2008) 92 *Minnesota Law Review* 749.

[116] For a summary of product-related failures across the EU see ESMA, EBA, EIOPA, Joint Position of the ESAs on Manufacturers' Product Oversight & Governance Processes (2013) (JC-2013-77) Annex 1.

[117] eg, in an October 2010 'position' (AMF Position No 2010-05) the French AMF in effect prohibited the marketing of complex structured products to investors; and in 2011, the Belgian regulator (the FSMA) called for the voluntary suspension by the industry of retail distribution of structured products which it deemed to be 'needlessly complex', the Dutch government announced proposals for the Dutch regulator to supervise the development of new financial products, and in the UK a new product intervention regime was adopted, designed to bring a more intrusive approach to retail market regulation (initially set out in FSA, Product Intervention (2011), Discussion Paper No 11/1) and which reflected related changes to primary legislation.

'upstream' in the product distribution process, may provide a means of ensuring better outcomes for those retail investors who do not access advice, and mitigate quality of advice risks for retail investors in an advice relationship. It may also prove a nimble means for addressing emerging incentive risks. The UK FCA in 2014, for example, used its new product intervention powers to restrict the distribution of contingent convertible instruments (CoCos) to retail investors.[118] CoCos absorb firm losses when capital falls below a certain level and so represent an attractive option for firms engaging in resolution planning, but as complex and potentially high-risk investments they pose material risks to retail investors. The FCA's precautionary intervention accordingly illustrates how product intervention tools can be deployed to respond to changes in the incentives which firms may have to engage in distribution practices which may lead to adverse outcomes for retail investors.

But product intervention is a new and untested tool for the EU—as noted in the Chapter by Kingsford Smith and Dixon in this volume, it has been regarded with some scepticism in Australia, otherwise something of a leader in retail market regulatory design. It might be regarded as infusing retail market regulation with an overly paternalistic approach which risks limiting investor autonomy and firm innovation, particularly by means of a more intrusive approach to retail investor risk-taking which may come to sit uneasily with the concern to promote long-term market saving. Making a determination as to whether a product is not suitable for retail distribution, whether through governance/design oversight powers or *ex post* prohibition powers, demands of the regulator that difficult choices, with a strongly paternalistic flavour, and with some risk to the regulator, are made as to the optimum levels of risk and choice in the retail market. It also implies that investor choice and autonomy can be trumped by a regulatory decision (*ex ante* or *ex post*) that certain products should not be distributed to retail investors, and to a more precautionary, consumerist approach to potential detriment. Particular difficulties may arise with governing concepts, particularly the notion of 'complexity' which is being used in the new EU regime as one of the determinants of excessive risk. But prejudicial complexity is difficult to capture through the regulatory system. The UK, for example, has struggled for years with how to use regulatory and market mechanisms to deliver 'simple' investment products which can be price-capped and sold through a simplified advice process.[119] Some degree of complexity in the markets is good for investors and can deliver strong returns.[120]

[118] FCA, Temporary Product Intervention Rules, Restrictions in Relation to the Retail Distribution of Contingent Convertible Instruments, August 2014. At EU-level, ESMA has similarly issued a warning to retail investors on their risks (ESMA/2014/944).

[119] For the most recent iteration see Sergeant Review of Simple Financial Products (2013).

[120] As has been repeatedly highlighted by Robert Shiller: eg, Shiller, R, 'Democratizing and Humanizing Finance' in Kroszner, R and Shiller, R, *Reforming US Financial Markets: Reflections Before and Beyond Dodd-Frank* (2011) 43.

The new EU product intervention regime can be regarded as a significant innovation in retail market regulatory design. There are already strong paternalistic elements in modern retail market regulation, such as the restrictions imposed in many jurisdictions on execution-only product sales and trading, and the demarcation by many jurisdictions of the products which can be distributed in the public markets and the related application of specific disclosure and distribution rules. But product intervention intensifies the level of paternalism in regulatory design. The EU reforms do not, however, represent a radical shift in retail market regulatory design generally. The new product intervention regime might be best regarded as an incremental step in a design trajectory which, for some time, has been towards greater regulatory intervention in the retail markets.

VI. Conclusion

The retail investment market addressed by retail market regulation is somewhat elusive. Its features differ across jurisdictions, reflecting the multiple factors which shape market structure and investor behaviour. But common to retail investment market structures internationally are the multiple market failures which flow from the foundational information asymmetry which strongly characterizes the retail market.

Information asymmetries are common to all segments of the financial system. But the distinctive features of modern retail market regulation stem in particular from the misalignment between the limited capacity of retail investors to process the mandated disclosure which is the classical response to market failure and the governmental imperative to promote stronger market engagement. The nature of the regulatory response to this misalignment has changed over time and has been shaped by shifting governmental and regulatory perceptions of the retail investor, which perceptions sit on a spectrum between vulnerable consumer and empowered and engaged investor. The retail toolbox has accordingly being finessed over time in many jurisdictions: disclosure has increasingly come to be shaped by the empirical realities of investor behaviour; distribution regulation has come to engage with the structural reform necessary to address deep-seated incentive risks; and product intervention is increasingly being deployed as a precautionary tool, given the limited ability of disclosure and distribution requirements, however often finessed, to engage in the heavy lifting required of them.

Retail market regulation can be regarded as distinct in financial regulation generally given the specific regulatory design challenges and risks to which it is prone—among them the very limited extent to which it tends to benefit from the regulatory refreshing which follows crisis and the limited possibilities for international learning—and its need to support strong investor outcomes on a micro basis. Nonetheless, over time and slowly, retail market regulation has come to be more attuned to retail investor behaviour and to how good retail investor outcomes can be delivered. While the reform process tends to be slow and regulatory attention tends to be sporadic, the increasing level of regulatory sophistication, and the likely increasing capacity of retail investors to influence the regulatory process over time, augur well for its future development.

Bibliography

Bar Gill, O, 'The Behavioural Economics of Consumer Contracts' (2008) 92 *Minnesota Law Review* 749.

Barber, B and Odean, T, 'Trading Is Hazardous to your Wealth: The Common Stock Investment Performance of Individual Investors' (2000) 55 *Journal of Finance* 773.

Barr, M, Mullainathan, S, and Shafir, E, 'Behaviourally Informed Regulation' in Shafir, E (ed.), *Behavioural Foundations of Policy* (2012) 442.

Basel Committee on Banking Supervision, International Organization of Securities Commissions, and International Association of Insurance Supervisors, Customer Suitability in the Retail Sale of Financial Products and Services (2008).

Black, B and Gross, J, 'The Elusive Balance between Investor Protection and Wealth Creation' (2005) 26 *Pace Law Review* 27.

Black, J, Involving Consumers on Securities Regulation. Report for the Taskforce to Modernize Securities Regulation in Canada (2006).

Black, J, *Rules and Regulators* (1997).

Black, J and Nobles, R, 'Pension Misselling: The Causes and Lessons of Regulatory Failure' (1998) 61 *Modern Law Review* 789.

Bradley, C, 'Disorderly Conduct and the Ideology of "Fair and Orderly Markets"' (2000) 26 *Journal of Corporation Law* 63.

Camerer, C, Issacharoff, S, Loewenstein, G, O'Donoghue, T, and Rabin, M, 'Regulation for Conservatives: Behavioral Economics and the Case for "Asymmetric Paternalism"' (2002–2003) 151 *University of Pennsylvania Law Review* 1211.

Campbell, J, 'Household Finance' (2006) 61 *Journal of Finance* 1553.

Campbell, J, Jackson, E, Madrian, B, and Tufano, P, 'Consumer Financial Protection' (2011) 25 *Journal of Economic Perspectives*.

Case, K and Shiller, R, 'The Efficiency of the Market for Single Family Homes' (1989) 79 *American Economic Review* 125.

Choi, S, 'A Framework for the Regulation of Securities Market Intermediaries' (2004) 1 *Berkeley Business Law Journal* 45.

Clark, R, 'The Soundness of Financial Intermediaries' (1976) 86 *Yale Law Journal* 1.

Condon, M, *Making Disclosure: Ideas and Interests in Ontario Securities Regulation* (1998).

Deaves, R, Dine, C, and Horton W, How Are Investment Decisions Made? Research Study for the Task Force to Modernize Securities Regulation in Canada (2006).

Decision Technology, Chater, N, Huck, S, Inderst, R, and Online Interactive Research, Consumer Decision Making in Retail Investment Services: A Behavioural Economics Perspective (2010).

Easterbrook, F and Fischel, D, 'Mandatory Disclosure and the Protection of Investors' (1984) 70 *Virginia Law Review* 1335.

Epstein, R, 'The Neoclassical Economics of Consumer Contracts' (2008) 92 *Minnesota Law Review* 808.

Ertürk, I, Froud, J, Johal, S, Leaver, A, and Williams, K, 'The Democratization of Finance? Promises, Outcomes and Conditions' (2007) 14 *Review of International Political Economy* 553.

European Commission, Green Paper on Retail Financial Services in the Single Market (2007) (COM (2007) 226) 16.

Financial Services Authority (FSA), A Review of Retail Distribution (2007), Discussion Paper 07/1.

Fisch, J and Wilkinson-Ryan, T, Why Do Retail Investors Make Costly Mistakes? An Experiment on Mutual Fund Choice (2013), ECGI Law Working Paper No 220/2013, available at <http://ssrn.com/abstract=2086766>.

Garten, H, 'The Consumerization of Financial Regulation' (1999) 77 *Washington University Law Quarterly* 287.

Gilson, R and Kraakman, R, 'The Mechanisms of Market Efficiency Twenty Years Later: The Hindsight Bias' (2003) 28 *Journal of Corporation Law* 215.

Gower, L, Review of Investor Protection. A Discussion Document (1982).

Gower, L, Review of Investor Protection. Report Part 1 (1984).

Gray, J and Hamilton, J, *Implementing Financial Regulation. Theory and Practice* (2006).

Guiso, L, Haliassos, M, and Japelli, T, Household Stockholding in Europe: Where Do we Stand and Where Do we Go? (2003), CEPR Discussion Paper No 3694.

Guiso, L, Sapienza, P, and Zingales, L, *Household Portfolios* (2001).

Hill, J, 'Why Did Australia Fare so Well in the Global Financial Crisis' in Ferran, E, Moloney, N, Hill, J, and Coffee, J, *The Regulatory Aftermath of the Global Financial Crisis* (2012) 203.

Hong, H, Kubik, J, and Stein, J, 'Social Interaction and Stock-market Participation' (2004) 59 *Journal of Finance* 137.

Howells, G, 'The Potential and Limits of Consumer Empowerment by Information' (2005) 32 *Journal of Law and Society* 349.

Hu, H, 'The New Portfolio Society, SEC Mutual Fund Disclosure and the Public Corporation Model' (2005) 60 *Business Lawyer* 1303.

International Organization of Securities Commissions (IOSCO), Suitability Requirements for Complex Financial Products (2013).

Ireland, P, 'Shareholder Primacy and the Distribution of Wealth' (2005) 68 *Modern Law Review* 49.

Jackson, H, 'Regulation in a Multi-sectored Financial Services Industry: An Exploration Essay' (1999) 77 *Washington University Law Quarterly* 319.

Jackson, H, 'To What Extent Should Individual Investors Rely on the Mechanisms of Market Efficiency: A Preliminary Investigation of Dispersion in Investor Returns' (2003) 28 *Journal of Corporation Law* 671.

Karmel, R, 'Mutual Funds, Pension Funds and Stock Market Volatility—What Regulation by the Securities and Exchange Commission Is Appropriate' (2004–05) 80 *Notre Dame Law Review* 909.
Kingsford Smith, D, 'Regulating Investment Risk: Individuals and the Global Financial Crisis' (2009) 32 *University of New South Wales Law Journal* 514.
Kozup, J and Hogarth, J, 'Financial Literacy, Public Policy and Consumers' Self Protection—More Questions Fewer Answers' (2008) 42 *Journal of Consumer Affairs* 127.
Krausz, M and Paroush, J, 'Financial Advising in the Presence of Conflicts of Interest' (2002) 54 *Journal of Economics and Business* 55.
Laby, A, 'Fiduciary Obligations of Broker-Dealers and Investment Advisers' (2010) 55 *Villanova Law Review* 701.
Langevoort, D, 'Managing the Expectations Gap in Investor Protection: The SEC and the Post-Enron Reform Agenda' (2003) 48 *Villanova Law Review* 1139.
Langevoort, D, 'The SEC as Lawmaker: Choices about Investor Protection in the Face of Uncertainty' (2006) 84 *Washington University Law Review* 1591.
Langevoort, D, 'The SEC, Retail Investors, and the Institutionalization of the Securities Markets' (2009) 95 *Virginia Law Review* 1025.
Langevoort, D and Thompson, R, 'Publicness in Contemporary Securities Regulation after the JOBS Act' (2013) 101 *Georgetown Law Journal* 337.
Mahoney, P, 'Manager-Investor Conflicts in Mutual Funds' (2004) 18 *Journal of Economic Perspectives* 161.
Moloney, N, *How to Protect Investors: Lessons from the EC and UK* (2010).
Moloney, N, 'Regulating the Retail Markets: Law, Policy, and the Financial Crisis' (2010) 63 *Current Legal Problems* 375.
Ogus, A, 'Regulatory Paternalism: When Is it Justified' in Hopt, K, Wymeersch, E, Kanda, H, and Baum, H (eds), *Corporate Governance in Context* (2005) 303.
Organization for Economic Cooperation and Development (OECD), High Level Principles on Financial Consumer Protection (2012).
Page, A and Ferguson, R, *Investor Protection* (1992).
Pearson, G, 'Reconceiving Regulation: Financial Literacy' (2008) 8 *Macquarie Law Journal* 45.
Rachlinski, J, 'The Uncertain Psychological Case for Paternalism' (2003) 97 *Northwestern University Law Review* 1165.
Ramsay, I, 'Consumer Law, Regulatory Capitalism and New Learning in Regulation' (2006) 28 *Sydney Law Review* 9.
Rand Institute for Civil Justice, Report on Investor and Industry Perspectives on Investment Advisers and Broker-Dealers (2008), sponsored by the SEC.
Sapienza, P, Guiso, L, and Zingales, L, 'Trusting the Stock Markets' (2008) 63 *Journal of Finance* 2557.
Shiller, R, Derivatives Markets for House Prices (2008), Yale Economics Department Working Paper No 46, available at <http://ssrn.com/abstract=1114102>.
Stout, L, 'The Investor Confidence Game' (2002–03) 68 *Brooklyn Law Review* 407.
Stout, L, 'The Mechanisms of Market Efficiency: An Introduction to the New Finance' (2003) 28 *Journal of Corporation Law* 635.
Stout, L, 'The Unimportance of Being Efficient: An Economic Analysis of Stock Market Pricing and Securities Regulation' (1998) 87 *Michigan Law Review* 613.
Sunstein, C, *Why Nudge? The Politics of Libertarian Paternalism* (2014).

Synovate, Consumer Market Study on Advice within the Area of Retail Investment Services—Final Report (2011).

Warren, E, 'Product Safety Regulation as a Model for Financial Services Regulation' (2008) 42 *Journal of Consumer Affairs* 452.

Williams, T, 'Empowerment of Whom and for What? Financial Literacy Education and the New Regulation of Consumer Financial Services' (2007) 29 *Law & Policy* 226.

Zingales, L, *A Capitalism for the People* (2012).

Zingales, L, 'The Future of Securities Regulation' (2009) 47 *Journal of Accounting Research* 391.

Index